FOURTH EDITION

MEN'S LIVES

Michael S.
Kimmel
State University of New York at Stony Brook

Michael A.
Messner
University of Southern California

ALLYN AND BACON

Boston · London · Toronto · Sydney · Tokyo · Singapore

Editor-in-Chief, Social Sciences: Karen Hanson
Series Editor: Sarah Kelbaugh
Series Editorial Assistant: Jennifer Muroff
Marketing Manager: Karon Bowers
Composition and Prepress Buyer: Linda Cox
Manufacturing Buyer: Suzanne Lareau
Cover Administrator: Linda Knowles
Production Administrator: Deborah Brown
Editorial-Production Service: Susan McNally
Copyeditor: Susanna Brougham
Text Designer: Melinda Grosser
Electronic Composition: Publishers' Design and Production Services, Inc.

Library of Congress Cataloging-in-Publication Data

Men's lives / [compiled by] Michael S. Kimmel, Michael A. Messner. —
    4th ed.
        p.   cm.
    Includes bibliographical references.
    ISBN 0-205-26649-5
    1. Men—United States—Social conditions. 2. Men—United States
—Psychology. 3. Masculinity—United States. 4. Men—United States
—Sexual behavior. I. Kimmel, Michael S. II. Messner, Michael A.
HQ1090.3.M465 1997
305.31—dc21   97-22520
                                                          CIP

Printed in the United States of America
10 9 8 7 6 5 4 3   02 01 00 99 98

for
Amy Aronson
and
Pierrette Hondagneu-Sotelo
for sharing our lives

CONTENTS

PREFACE

Over the past ten years, we have been teaching courses on the male experience, or "men's lives." Our courses have reflected both our own education and recent research by feminist scholars and profeminist men in U.S. society. (By profeminist men, we mean active supporters of women's efforts against male violence and claims for equal opportunity, political participation, sexual autonomy, family reform, and equal education.) Gender, scholars have demonstrated, is a central feature of social life—one of the chief organizing principles around which our lives revolve. Gender shapes our identities and the institutions in which we find ourselves. In the university, women's studies programs and courses about women in traditional disciplines have explored the meaning of gender in women's lives. But what does it mean to be a man in contemporary U.S. society?

This anthology is organized around specific themes that define masculinity and the issues men confront over the course of their lives. In addition, a social-constructionist perspective has been included that examines how men actively construct masculinity within a social and historical context. Related to this construction and integrated in our examination are the variations that exist among men in relation to class, race, and sexuality.

We begin Part One with issues and questions that unravel the "masculine mystique" and reveal various dimensions of men's position in society and their relationships with women and with other men. Parts Two through Nine examine the different issues that emerge for men at different times of their lives and the ways in which their lives change over time. We touch on central moments related to boyhood, adolescence, sports, occupations, marriage, and fatherhood, and explore men's emotional and sexual relationships with women and with other men. The final part, "Men and the Future," explores some of the ways in which men are changing and some possible directions by which they might continue to change.

Although a major component of the traditional, normative definition of masculinity is independence, we are pleased to acknowledge those colleagues and friends whose criticism and support have been a constant help throughout our work on this project. Karen Hanson and Sarah Kelbaugh, our editors at Allyn and Bacon, inherited this project and have embraced it as their own, facilitating our work at every turn. Chris Cardone and Bruce Nichols, our original editors, were supportive from the start and helped get the project going. Many other scholars who work on issues of masculinity, such as

Bob Blauner, Robert Brannon, Harry Brod, Rocco Capraro, Bob Connell, James Harrison, Jeff Hearn, Martin Levine, Joe Pleck, Tony Rotundo, Don Sabo, and Peter Stein, have contributed to a supportive intellectual community in which to work.

We also thank the following reviewers for their helpful comments and suggestions: Margaret Anderson, University of Delaware; Judith Barker, Ithaca College; Nicola Beisel, Northwestern University; Bob Blauner, University of California, Berkeley; Chip Capraro, Hobart and William Smith Colleges; Douglas Gertner, Colorado State University; Christopher Kilmartin, Mary Washington College; Dr. H. Elaine Lindgren, North Dakota State University; Ron Matson, The Wichita State University; Michael Messina-Yauchzy, Syracuse University; Joyce M. Nielsen, University of Colorado at Boulder; Beth Rushing, Kent State University; Don Sabo, D'Youville College; Kathleen Tiemann, University of North Dakota; Diane Villwock, Morehead State University; Tim Wernette, University of Arizona; and Carol S. Wharton, University of Richmond. Colleagues at the State University of New York at Stony Brook and the University of Southern California have also been supportive of this project. We are especially grateful to Diane Barthel, Ruth Schwartz Cowan, John Gagnon, Barry Glassner, Norman Goodman, Nilufer Isvan, Carol Jacklin, and Barrie Thorne. A fellowship from the Lilly Foundation has generously supported Kimmel's work on pedagogical issues of teaching about men and masculinity.

This book is the product of the profeminist men's movement as well—a loose network of men who support a feminist critique of traditional masculinity and women's struggles to enlarge the scope of their personal autonomy and public power. These men are engaged in a variety of efforts to transform masculinity in ways that allow men to live fuller, richer, and healthier lives. The editors of *Changing Men* (with whom we work as Book Review Editor and Sports Editor), the late Mike Biernbaum and Rick Cote, have labored for more than a decade to provide a forum for antisexist men. We acknowledge their efforts with gratitude and respect.

Our families, friends, and colleagues have provided a rare atmosphere that combines intellectual challenge and emotional support. We are grateful to Judith Brisman, Martin Duberman, Eli Zal, Kate Ellis, Frances Goldin, Cathy Greenblat, Pam Hatchfield, Sandi Kimmel, David Levin, Mary Morris and Larry O'Connor, Lillian and Hank Rubin, and Mitchell Tunick. We want especially to acknowledge our fathers and mothers for providing such important models—not of being women or men, but of being adults capable of career competence, emotional warmth, and nurturance (these are not masculine or feminine traits).

Finally, we thank Amy Aronson and Pierrette Hondagneu-Sotelo, to whom we dedicate this edition of the book. We consider ourselves fortunate that they have chosen to share our lives.

M.S.K.
M.A.M.

INTRODUCTION

This is a book about men. But, unlike other books about men, which line countless library shelves, this is a book about men *as men*. It is a book in which men's experiences are not taken for granted as we explore the "real" and significant accomplishments of men, but a book in which those experiences are treated as significant and important in themselves.

Men as "Gendered Beings"

But what does it mean to examine men "as men"? Most courses in a college curriculum are about men, aren't they? But these courses routinely deal with men only in their public roles, so we come to know and understand men as scientists, politicians, military figures, writers, and philosophers. Rarely, if ever, are men understood through the prism of gender.

But listen to some male voices from some of these "ungendered" courses. Take, for example, composer Charles Ives, debunking "sissy" types of music; he said he used traditional tough guy themes and concerns in his drive to build new sounds and structures out of the popular musical idiom (cf. Wilkinson, 1986: 103). Or architect Louis Sullivan, describing his ambition to create "masculine forms": strong, solid, commanding respect. Or novelist Ernest Hemingway, retaliating against literary enemies by portraying them as impotent or homosexual.

Consider also political figures, such as Cardinal Richelieu, the seventeenth-century French First Minister to Louis XIII, who insisted that it was "necessary to have masculine virtue and do everything by reason" (cited in Elliott, 1984: 20). Closer to home, recall President Lyndon Baines Johnson's dismissal of a political adversary: "Oh him. He has to squat to piss!" Or his boast that during the Tet offensive in the Vietnam War, he "didn't just screw Ho Chi Minh. I cut his pecker off!"

Democrats have no monopoly on unexamined gender coloring their political rhetoric. Richard Nixon was "afraid of being acted upon, of being inactive, of being soft, or being thought impotent, of being dependent upon anyone else," according to his biographer, Bruce Mazlish. And don't forget Vice-President George Bush's revealing claim that in his television debate with Democratic challenger Geraldine Ferraro he had "kicked ass." (That few political pundits criticized such unapologetic glee concerning violence against women is again indicative of how invisible gender issues are in our culture.) Indeed, recent political campaigns have revolved, in part, around gender issues, as each candidate attempted to demonstrate that he was not a "wimp" but was a "real man." (Of course, the few successful female politicians face the double task of convincing the electorate that they are not the "weak-willed wimps" that their gender implies in the public mind while at the same time demonstrating that they are "real women.")

These are just a few examples of what we might call gendered speech, language that uses gender terms to make its case. And these are just a few of the thousands of examples one could find in every academic discipline of how men's lives are organized around gender issues, and how gender remains one of the organizing principles of social life. We come to know ourselves and our world through the prism of gender. Only we act as if we didn't know it.

Fortunately, in recent years, the pioneering work of feminist scholars, both in traditional disciplines and in women's studies, and of feminist women in the political arena has made us aware of the centrality of gender in our lives. Gender, these scholars have demonstrated, is a central feature of social life, one of the central organizing principles around which our lives revolve. In the social sciences, gender has now taken its place alongside class and race as the three central mechanisms by which power and resources are distributed in our society, and the three central themes out of which we fashion the meanings of our lives.

We certainly understand how this works for women. Through women's studies courses and also in courses about women in traditional disciplines, students have explored the complexity of women's lives, the hidden history of exemplary women, and the daily experiences of women in the routines of their lives. For women, we know how gender works as one of the formative elements out of which social life is organized.

The Invisibility of Gender: A Sociological Explanation

Too often, though, we treat men as if they had no gender, as if only their public personae were of interest to us as students and scholars, as if their interior experience of gender was of no significance. This became evident when one of us was in a graduate seminar on feminist theory several years ago. A discussion between a white woman and a black woman revolved around the question of whether their similarities as women were greater than their racial differences as black and white. The white woman asserted that the fact that they were both women bonded them, in spite of their racial differences. The black woman disagreed.

"When you wake up in the morning and look in the mirror, what do you see?" she asked.

"I see a woman," replied the white woman.

"That's precisely the issue," replied the black woman. "I see a black woman. For me, race is visible every day, because it is how I am not privileged in this culture. Race is invisible to you, which is why our alliance will always seem somewhat false to me."

Witnessing this exchange, Michael Kimmel was startled. When he looked in the mirror in the morning, he saw, as he put it, "a human being: universally generalizable. The generic person." What had been concealed—that he possessed both race and gender—had become strikingly visible. As a white man, he was able not to think about the ways in which gender and race had affected his experiences.

There is a sociological explanation for this blind spot in our thinking: the mechanisms that afford us privilege are very often invisible to us. What makes us marginal (unempowered, oppressed) are the mechanisms that we understand, because those are the ones that are most painful in daily life. Thus, white people rarely think of themselves as "raced" people, rarely think of race as a central element in their experience. But people of color are marginalized by race, and so the centrality of race is both painfully obvious and urgently needs study. Similarly, middle-class people do not acknowledge the importance of social class as an organizing principle of social life, largely because for them class is an invisible force that makes everyone look pretty much the same. Working-class people, on the other hand, are often painfully aware of the centrality of class in their lives. (Interestingly, upper-class people are often more aware of class dynamics than are middle-class people. In part, this may be the result of the emphasis on status within the upper class, as lineage, breeding, and family honor take center stage. In part, it may also be the result of a peculiar marginalization of the upper class in our society, as in the overwhelming number of television shows and movies that are ostensibly about just plain [i.e., middle-class] folks.)

In this same way, men often think of themselves as genderless, as if gender did not matter in the daily experiences of our lives. Certainly, we can see the biological sex of individuals, but we rarely understand the ways in which *gender*—that complex of social meanings that is attached to biological sex—is enacted in our daily lives. For example, we treat male scientists as if their being men had nothing to do with the organization of their experiments, the logic of scientific inquiry, or the questions posed by science itself. We treat male political figures as if masculinity were not even remotely in their consciousness as they do battle in the political arena.

This book takes a position directly opposed to such genderlessness for men. We believe that men are also "gendered," and that this gendering process, the transformation of biological males into socially interacting men, is a central experience for men. That we are unaware of it only helps to perpetuate the inequalities based on gender in our society.

In this book, we will examine the various ways in which men are gendered. We have gathered together some of the most interesting, engaging, and convincing materials from the past decade that have been written about men. We believe that *Men's Lives* will allow readers to explore the meanings of masculinity in contemporary U.S. culture in a new way.

Earlier Efforts to Study Men

Certainly, researchers have been examining masculinity for a long time. Historically, there have been three general models that have governed social scientific research on men and masculinity. *Biological models* have focused on the ways in which innate biological differences between males and females programmed different social behaviors. *Anthropological models* have examined masculinity cross-culturally, stressing the variations in the behaviors and attributes associated with being a man. And, until recently, *sociological models* have stressed how socialization of boys and girls included accommodation to a "sex role" specific to one's biological sex. Although each of these perspectives helps us to understand the meaning of masculinity and femininity, each is also limited in its ability to fully explain how gender operates in any culture.

Relying on differences in reproductive biology, some scholars have argued that the physiological organization of males and females makes inevitable the differences we observe in psychological temperament and social behaviors. One perspective holds that differences in endocrine functioning are the cause of gender difference, that testosterone predisposes males toward aggression, competition, and violence, whereas estrogen predisposes females toward passivity, tenderness, and exaggerated emotionality. Others insist that these observed behavioral differences derive from the differences between the size or number of sperm and eggs. Since a male can produce 100 million sperm with each ejaculation, whereas a female can produce fewer than 20 eggs capable of producing healthy offspring over the course of her life, these authors suggest that men's "investment" in their offspring is significantly less than women's investment. Other authors arrive at the same conclusion by suggesting that the different size of egg and sperm, and the fact that the egg is the source of the food supply, impels temperamental differences. Reproductive "success" to males means the insemination of as many females as possible; to females, reproductive success means carefully choosing one male to mate with and insisting that he remain present to care for and support their offspring. Still other authors argue that male and female behavior is governed by different halves of the brain; males are ruled by the left hemisphere, which controls rationality and abstract thought, whereas females are governed by the right hemisphere, which controls emotional affect and creativity. (For examples of these works, see Wilson, 1976; Trivers, 1972; Goldberg, 1975; and Goldberg, 1986.)

Observed normative temperamental differences between women and men that are assumed to be of biological origin are easily translated into political prescriptions. In this ideological sleight of hand, what is *normative* (i.e., what is prescribed) is translated into what is *normal*, and the mechanisms of this transformation are the assumed biological imperative. George Gilder, for example, assembles the putative biological differences between women and men into a call for a return to traditional gender roles. Gilder believes that male sexuality is, by nature, wild and lusty, "insistent" and "incessant," careening out of control and threatening anarchic disorder, unless it can be controlled and constrained. This is the task of women. When women refuse to apply the brakes to male sexuality—by asserting their own or by choosing to pursue a life outside the domestic sphere—they abandon their "natural" function for illusory social gains. Sex education, abortion, and birth control are all condemned as facilitating women's escape from biological necessity. Similarly, he argues against women's employment, since the "unemployed man can contribute little to the community and will often disrupt it, but the woman may even do more good without a job than with one" (Gilder, 1986: 86).

The biological argument has been challenged by many scholars on several grounds. The implied causation between two observed sets of differences (biological differences and different behaviors) is misleading, since there is no logical reason to assume that one caused the other, or that the line of causation moves only from the biological to the social. The selection of biological evidence is partial, and generalizations from "lower" animal species to human beings are always suspect. One sociologist asks if these differences are "natural," why their enforcement must be coercive, why males and females have to be forced to assume the rules that they are naturally supposed to play (see Epstein, 1986:8). And one primatologist argues that the evidence adduced to support the current status quo might also lead to precisely the opposite conclusions, that biological differences would impel female promiscuity and male fragility (see Hrdy, 1981). Biological differences between males and females would appear to set some parameters for differences in social behavior, but would not dictate the temperaments of men and women in any one culture. These psychological and social differences would appear to be the result far more of the ways in which cultures interpret, shape, and modify these biological inheritances. We may be born males or females, but we become men and women in a cultural context.

Anthropologists have entered the debate at this point, but with different positions. For example, some anthropologists have suggested that the universality of gender differences comes from specific cultural adaptations to the environment, whereas others describe the cultural variations of gender roles, seeking to demonstrate the fluidity of gender and the primacy of cultural organization. Lionel Tiger and Robin Fox argue that the sexual division of labor is universal because of the different nature of bonding for males and females. "Nature," they argue, "intended mother and child to be together" because she is the source of emotional security and food; thus, cultures have prescribed various behaviors for women that emphasize nurturance and emotional connection (Tiger and Fox, 1984: 304). The bond between men is forged through the necessity of "competitive cooperation" in hunting; men must cooperate with members of their own tribe in the hunt and yet compete for scarce resources with men in other tribes. Such bonds predispose men toward the organization of the modern corporation or governmental bureaucracy.

Such anthropological arguments omit as much as they include, and many scholars have pointed out problems with the model. Why did not intelligence become sex linked, as this model (and the biological model) would imply? Such positions also reveal a marked conservatism: the differences between women and men are the differences that nature or cultural evolution intended, and are therefore not to be tampered with.

Perhaps the best known challenge to this anthropological argument is the work of Margaret Mead. Mead insisted that the variations among cultures in their prescriptions of gender roles required the conclusion that culture was the more decisive cause of these differences. In her classic study, *Sex and Temperament in Three Primitive Societies* (1935), Mead observed such wide variability among gender role prescriptions—and such marked differences from our own—that any universality implied by biological or anthropological models had to be rejected. And although the empirical accuracy of Mead's work has been challenged in its specific arguments, the general theoretical arguments remain convincing.

Psychological theories have also contributed to the discussion of gender roles, as psychologists have specified the specific developmental sequences for both males and females. Earlier theorists observed psychological distancing from the mother as the precondition for independence and autonomy, or suggested a sequence that placed the capacity for abstract reason as the developmental stage beyond relational reasoning. Since it is normative for males to exhibit independence and the capacity for abstract reason, it was argued that males are more successful at negotiating these psychological passages, and implied that women somehow lagged behind men on the ladder of developmental success. (Such arguments may be found in Freud, Erikson, and Kohlberg.)

But these models, too, have been challenged, most recently by sociologist Nancy Chodorow, who argued that women's ability to connect contains a more fundamentally human trait than the male's need to distance, and by psychologist Carol Gilligan, who claimed that women's predisposition toward relational reasoning may contain a more humane strategy of thought than recourse to abstract principles. Regardless of our assessment of these arguments, Chodorow and Gilligan rightly point out that the highly ideological assumptions that make masculinity the normative standard against which the psychological development of *both* males and females was measured would inevitably make femininity problematic and less fully developed. Moreover, Chodorow explicitly insists that these "essential" differences between women and men are socially constructed and thus subject to change.

Finally, sociologists have attempted to synthesize these three perspectives into a systematic explanation of "sex roles." These are the collection of attitudes, attributes, and behaviors that is seen as appropriate for males and appropriate for females. Thus, masculinity is associated with technical mastery, aggression, competitiveness, and cognitive abstraction, whereas femininity is associated with emotional nurturance, connectedness, and passivity. Sex role theory informed a wide variety of prescriptive literature (self-help books) that instructed parents on what to do if they wanted their child to grow up as a healthy boy or girl.

The strongest challenge to all these perspectives, as we have seen, came from feminist scholars, who have specified the ways in which the assumptions about maturity, development, and health all made masculinity the norm against which both genders were measured. In all the social sciences, these feminist scholars have stripped these early studies of their academic facades to reveal the unexamined ideological assumptions contained within them. By the early 1970s, women's studies programs began to articulate a new paradigm for the study of gender, one that assumed nothing about men or women beforehand, and that made no assumptions about which gender was more highly developed. And by the mid-1970s, the first group of texts about men appeared that had been inspired by these pioneering efforts by feminist scholars.

Thinking About Men: The First Generation

In the mid-1970s, the first group of works on men and masculinity appeared that was directly influenced by these feminist critiques of the traditional explanations for gender differences. Some books underscored the costs to men of traditional gender role prescriptions, exploring how some aspects of men's lives and experiences are constrained and underdeveloped by the relentless pressure to exhibit other behaviors associated with masculinity. Books such as Marc Feigen-Fasteau's *The Male Machine* (1974) and Warren Farrell's *The Liberated Man* (1975) discussed the costs to men's health—both physical and psychological—and the quality of relationships with women, other men, and their children of the traditional male sex role.

Several anthologies explored the meanings of masculinity in the United States by adopting a feminist-inspired prism through which to view men and masculinity. For example, Deborah David and Robert Brannon's *The Forty-Nine Percent Majority* (1976) and Joseph Pleck and Jack Sawyer's *Men and Masculinity* (1974) presented panoramic views of men's lives, from within a framework that accepted the feminist critique of traditional gender arrangements. Elizabeth Pleck and Joseph Pleck's *The American Man* (1980) suggested a historical evolution of contemporary themes. These works explored both the "costs" and the privileges of being a man in modern U.S. society.

Perhaps the single most important book to criticize the normative organization of the male sex role was Joseph Pleck's *The Myth of Masculinity* (1981). Pleck carefully deconstructed the constituent elements of the male sex role and reviewed the empirical literature for each component part. After demonstrating that the empirical literature did not support these normative features, Pleck argued that the male sex role model was incapable of describing men's experiences. In its place, he posited a male "sex role strain" model that specified the contemporary sex role as problematic, historically specific, and also an unattainable ideal.

Building on Pleck's work, a critique of the sex role model began to emerge. Sex roles had been cast as the static containers of behaviors and attitudes, and biological males and females were required to fit themselves into these containers, regardless of how ill-fitting these clusters of behaviors and attitudes felt. Such a model was ahistorical and suggested a false cultural universalism, and was therefore ill equipped to help us understand the ways in which sex roles change, and the ways in which individuals modify those roles through the enactments of gender expectations. Most telling, however, was the way in which the sex role model ignored the ways in which definitions of masculinity and femininity were based on, and reproduced, relationships of power. Not only do men as a group exert power over women as a group, but the definitions of masculinity and femininity reproduce those power relations. Power dynamics are an essential element in both the definition and the enactments of gender.

This first generation of research on masculinity was extremely valuable, particularly since it challenged the unexamined ideology that made masculinity the gender norm against which both men and women were measured. The old models of sex roles had reproduced the domination of men over women by insisting on the dominance of masculine traits over feminine traits. These new studies argued against both the definitions of either sex and the social institutions in which those differences were embedded. Shapers of the new model looked at "gender relations" and understood how the definition of either masculinity or femininity was relational, that is, how the definition of one gender depended, in part, on the understanding of the definition of the other.

In the early 1980s, the research on women again surged ahead of the research on men and masculinity. This time, however, the focus was not on the ways in which sex roles reproduce the power relations in society, but rather on the ways in which femininity is experienced differently by women in various social groups. Gradually, the notion of a single femininity—which was based on the white middle-class Victorian notion of female passivity, langorous beauty, and emotional responsiveness—was replaced by an examination of the ways in which women differ in their gender role expectations by race, class, age, sexual orientation, ethnicity, region, and nationality.

The research of men and masculinity is now entering a new stage, in which the variations among men are seen as central to the understanding of men's lives. The unexamined assumption in earlier studies had been that one version of masculinity—white, middle-aged, middle-class, heterosexual—was the sex role into

which all men were struggling to fit in our society. Thus, working-class men, men of color, gay men, and younger and older men were all observed as departing in significant ways from the traditional definitions of masculinity. Therefore, it was easy to see these men as enacting "problematic" or "deviant" versions of masculinity. Such theoretical assertions, however, reproduce precisely the power relationships that keep these men in subordinate positions in our society. Not only does middle-class, middle-aged, heterosexual white masculinity become the standard against which all men are measured, but this definition, itself, is used against those who do not fit as a way to keep them down. The normative definition of masculinity is not the "right" one, but it is the one that is dominant.

The challenge to the hegemonic definition of masculinity came from men whose masculinity was cast as deviant: men of color, gay men, and ethnic men. We understand now that we cannot speak of "masculinity" as a singular term, but must examine *masculinities*: the ways in which different men construct different versions of masculinity. Such a perspective can be seen in several recent works, such as Harry Brod's *The Making of Masculinities* (1987), Michael Kimmel's *Changing Men: New Directions in Research on Men and Masculinity* (1987), and Tim Carrigan, Bob Connell, and John Lee's "Toward a New Sociology of Masculinity" (1985). Bob Connell's *Gender and Power* (1987) and Jeff Hearn's *The Gender of Oppression* (1987) represent the most sophisticated theoretical statements of this perspective. Connell argues that the oppression of women is a chief mechanism that links the various masculinities, and that the marginalization of certain masculinities is an important component of the reproduction of male power over women. This critique of the hegemonic definition of masculinity as a perspective on men's lives is one of the organizing principles of our book, which is the first college-level text in this second generation of work on men and masculinities.

Now that we have reviewed some of the traditional explanations for gender relations and have situated this book within the research on gender in general, and men in particular, let us briefly outline exactly the theoretical perspective we have employed in the book. Not only does our theoretical framework provide the organizing principle of the book as a whole, it also provided some of the criteria for the selection of the articles that are included.

The Social Construction of Masculinities

Men are not born, growing from infants through boyhood to manhood, to follow a predetermined biological imperative encoded in their physical organization. To be a man is to participate in social life as a man, as a gendered being. Men are not born; they are made. And men make themselves, actively constructing their masculinities within a social and historical context.

This book is about how men are made and how men make themselves in contemporary U.S. society. It is about what masculinity means, about how masculinity is organized, and about the social institutions that sustain and elaborate it. It is a book in which we will trace what it means to be a man over the course of men's lives.

Men's Lives revolves around three important themes that are part of a social scientific perspective. First, we have adopted a *social constructionist* perspective. By this we mean that the important fact of men's lives is not that they are biological males, but that they become men. Our sex may be male, but our identity as men is developed through a complex process of interaction with the culture in which we both learn the gender scripts appropriate to our culture and attempt to modify those scripts to make them more palatable. The second axis around which the book is organized follows from our social constructionist perspective. As we have argued, the experience of masculinity is not uniform and universally generalizable to all men in our society. Masculinity differs dramatically in our society, and we have organized the book to illustrate the *variations* among men in the construction of masculinity. Third, we have adopted a *life course* perspective, to chart the construction of these various masculinities in men's lives and to examine pivotal developmental moments or institutional locations during a man's life in which the meanings of masculinity are articulated. Social constructionism, variations among men, and the life course perspective define the organization of this book and the criteria we have used to select the articles included.

The Social Constructionist Model

The social constructionist perspective argues that the meaning of masculinity is neither transhistorical nor culturally universal, but rather varies from culture to culture and within any one culture over time. Thus, males become men in the United States in the late twentieth century in a way that is very different from men in Southeast Asia, or Kenya, or Sri Lanka. The meaning of masculinity varies from culture to culture.

Men's lives also vary within any one culture over time. The experience of masculinity in the contemporary United States is very different from that experience 150 years ago. Who would argue that what it meant to be a "real man" in seventeenth-century France (at least among the upper classes)—high-heeled patent leather shoes, red velvet jackets covering frilly white lace shirts, lots of rouge and white powder makeup, and a taste for the elegant refinement of ornate furniture—bears much resemblance to the meaning of masculinity among a similar class of French men today?

A perspective that emphasizes the social construction of gender is, therefore, both *historical* and *comparative*. It allows us to explore the ways in which the meanings of gender vary from culture to culture, and how they change within any one culture over historical time.

Variations Among Men

Masculinity also varies *within* any one society according to the various types of cultural groups that compose it. Subcultures are organized around other poles, which are the primary way in which people organize themselves and by which resources are distributed. And men's experiences differ from one another in the ways in which social scientists have identified as the chief structural mechanisms along which power and resources are distributed. We cannot speak of masculinity in the United States as if it were a single, easily identifiable commodity. To do so is to risk positing one version of masculinity as normative and making all other masculinities problematic.

In the contemporary United States, masculinity is constructed differently by class culture, by race and ethnicity, and by age. And each of these axes of masculinity modifies the others. Black masculinity differs from white masculinity, yet each of them is also further modified by class and age. A 30-year-old middle-class black man will have some things in common with a 30-year-old middle-class white man that he might not share with a 60-year-old working-class black man, although he will share with him elements of masculinity that are different from the white man of his class and age. The resulting matrix of *masculinities* is complicated by cross-cutting elements; without understanding this, we risk collapsing all masculinities into one hegemonic version.

The challenge to a singular definition of masculinity as the normative definition is the second axis around which the readings in this book revolve.

The Life Course Perspective

The meaning of masculinity is not constant over the course of any man's life, but will change as he grows and matures. The issues confronting a man about proving himself and feeling successful, and the social institutions in which he will attempt to enact his definitions of masculinity will change throughout his life. Thus, we have adopted a *life course perspective* to discuss the ways in which different issues will emerge for men at different times of their lives, and the ways in which men's lives, themselves, change over time. The life course perspective we have employed will examine men's lives at various pivotal moments in their development from young boys to adults. Like a slide show, these points will freeze the action for a short while, to afford us the opportunity to examine in more detail the ways in which different men in our culture experience masculinity at any one time.

The book's organization reflects these three concerns. The first part sets the context through which we shall examine men's lives. Parts Two through Nine follow those lives through their full course, examining central moments experienced by men in the United States today. Specifically, Parts Two and Three touch on boyhood and adolescence, discussing some of the institutions organized to embody and reproduce masculinities in the United States, such as fraternities, the Boy Scouts, and sports groups. Part Four, "Men with Men: Friendships and Fears," describes emotional and physical (but not necessarily sexual) relationships that men develop through their lives. Part Five, "Men and Work," explores the ways in which masculinities are constructed in relation to men's occupations. Part Six, "Men and Health: Body and Mind," deals with heart attacks, stress, AIDS, and other health problems among men. Part Seven, "Men with Women: Intimacy and Power," describes men's emotional and sexual relationships. We deal with heterosexuality and homosexuality, mindful of the ways in which variations are based on specific lines (class, race, ethnicity). Part Eight, "Male Sexualities," studies the normative elements of heterosexuality and probes the controversial political implications of pornography as a source of both straight and gay men's sexual information. Part Nine, "Men in Families," concentrates on masculinities within the family and the role of men as husbands, fathers, and senior citizens. Part Ten, "Men and the Future," examines some of the ways in which men are changing and points to some directions in which men might continue to change.

Our perspective, stressing the social construction of masculinities over the life course, will, we believe, allow a more comprehensive understanding of men's lives in the United States today.

References

Brod, Harry, ed. *The Making of Masculinities*. Boston: Unwin, Hyman, 1987.

Carrigan, Tim, Bob Connell, and John Lee. "Toward a New Sociology of Masculinity" in *Theory and Society*, 1985, 5(14).

Chodorow, Nancy. *The Reproduction of Mothering*. Berkeley: University of California Press, 1978.

Connell, R. W. *Gender and Power*. Stanford, CA: Stanford University Press, 1987.

David, Deborah, and Robert Brannon, eds. *The Forty-Nine Percent Majority*. Reading, MA: Addison-Wesley, 1976.

Elliott, J. H. *Richelieu and Olivares*. New York: Cambridge University Press, 1984.

Epstein, Cynthia Fuchs. "Inevitability of Prejudice" in *Society*, Sept. /Oct., 1986.

Farrell, Warren. *The Liberated Man*. New York: Random House, 1975.

Feigen-Fasteau, Marc. *The Male Machine*. New York: McGraw-Hill, 1974.

Gilligan, Carol. *In a Different Voice*. Cambridge, MA: Harvard University Press, 1982.

Gilder, George. *Men and Marriage*. Gretna, LA: Pelican Publishers, 1986.

Goldberg, Steven. *The Inevitability of Patriarchy*. New York: William Morrow & Co., 1975.

———— "Reaffirming the Obvious" in *Society*, Sept./Oct., 1986.

Hearn, Jeff. *The Gender of Oppression*. New York: St. Martin's Press, 1987.

Hrdy, Sandra Blaffer. *The Woman That Never Evolved*. Cambridge, MA: Harvard University Press, 1981.

Kimmel, Michael S., ed. *Changing Men: New Directions in Research on Men and Masculinity*. Newbury Park, CA: Sage Publications, 1987.

Mead, Margaret. *Sex and Temperament in Three Primitive Societies*. New York: McGraw-Hill, 1935.

Pleck, Elizabeth, and Joseph Pleck, eds. *The American Man*. Englewood Cliffs, NJ: Prentice-Hall, 1980.

Pleck, Joseph. *The Myth of Masculinity*. Cambridge, MA: M.I.T. Press, 1981.

———— and Jack Sawyer, eds. *Men and Masculinity*. Englewood Cliffs, NJ: Prentice-Hall, 1974.

Tiger, Lionel, and Robin Fox. *The Imperial Animal*. New York: Holt, Rinehart & Winston, 1984.

Trivers, Robert. "Parental Investment and Sexual Selection" in *Sexual Selection and the Descent of Man* (B. Campbell, ed.). Chicago: Aldine Publishers, 1972.

Wilkinson, Rupert. *American Tough: The Tough Guy Tradition and American Character*. New York: Harper & Row, 1986.

Wilson, E. O. *Sociobiology: The New Synthesis*. Cambridge, MA: Harvard University Press, 1976.

A quick glance at any magazine rack or television talk-show is enough to make you aware that these days, men are confused. What does it mean to be a "real man"? How are men supposed to behave? What are men supposed to feel? How are men to express their feelings? Who are we supposed to be like: Tootsie or Rambo? Clint Eastwood or Phil Donahue? Rhett Butler or Ashley Wilkes? Dennis Rodman or Bill Clinton?

We are daily bombarded with images and handy rules to help us negotiate our way through a world in which all the rules seem to have suddenly vanished or changed. Some tell us to reassert traditional masculinity against all contemporary challenges. But a strength built only on the weakness of others hardly feels like strength at all. Others tell us

Perspectives on Masculinities

that men are in power, the oppressor. But if men are in power as a group, why do individual men often feel so powerless? Can men change?

These questions will return throughout this book. In this section, several authors begin to examine some of the issues that define the depth of the question about men and masculinity. These articles begin to unravel the "masculine mystique" and suggest various dimensions of men's position in society, their power, their powerlessness, and their confusion. Michael Kaufman takes men's problematic relationship to violence as a core theme in men's experience in society.

But we cannot speak of "masculinity" as some universal category that is experienced in the same ways by each man. "All men are alike," runs a popular wisdom. But are they really? Are gay men's experiences with work, relationships, love, and politics

similar to those of heterosexual men? Do black and Chicano men face the same problems and conflicts in their daily lives that white men face? Do middle-class men have the same political interests as blue-collar men? The answers to these questions, as the articles in this part suggest, are not simple.

Although earlier studies of men and masculinity focused on the apparently universal norms of masculinity, recent work has attempted to demonstrate how different the worlds of various men are. Men are divided along the same lines that divide any other group: race, class, sexual orientation, ethnicity, age, and geographic region. Men's lives vary in crucial ways, and understanding these variations will take us a long way toward understanding men's experiences.

Earlier studies that suggested a single universal norm of masculinity reproduced some of the problems they were trying to solve. To be sure, *all* benefit from the inequality between women and men; for example, think of how rape jokes or male-exclusive sports culture provide contexts for the bonding of men across class, race, and ethnic lines while denying full participation to women. But the single, seemingly universal masculinity obscured ways in which some men hold and maintain power over other men in our society, hiding the fact that all men do not share equally in the fruits of gender inequality.

Here is how sociologist Erving Goffman put it in his important book *Stigma* (New York: Double-day, 1963, p. 128):

> In an important sense there is only one complete un-blushing male in America: a young, married, white, urban, northern, heterosexual Protestant father of college education, fully employed, of good complexion, weight, and height, and a recent record in sports. Every American male tends to look out upon the world from this perspective, this constituting one sense in which one can speak of a common value system in America. Any male who fails to qualify in any one of these ways is likely to view himself—during moments at least—as unworthy, incomplete, and inferior.

As Goffman suggests, middle-class, white, heterosexual masculinity is used as the marker against which other masculinities are measured, and by which standard they may be found wanting. What is *normative* (prescribed) becomes translated into what is *normal*. In this way, heterosexual men maintain their status by the oppression of gay men; middle-aged men can maintain their dominance over older and younger men; upper-class men can exploit working-class men; and white men can enjoy privileges at the expense of men of color.

The articles by Manning Marable and Maxine Baca Zinn challenge popularly held negative stereotypes of black and Chicano males as pathologically "macho." Instead, they suggest that an understanding of ethnic minority men must begin with a critical examination of how institutionalized racism, particularly (but not exclusively) in the economy, shapes and constrains the possibilities, choices, and personal lifestyles of black and Latino men. Calls for "changing masculinities," these articles suggest, must involve an emphasis on *institutional* transformation, to which Marable's argument gives a special political urgency.

Yen Le Espiritu and Harry Brod also explore some of the gendered stereotypes of Asian American masculinity and Jewish masculinity, respectively. Martin P. Levine's article provides a cautionary tale, describing the consequences of oversubscribing to culturally dominant notions of masculinity for gay men in the 1970s and 1980s (in fact, gay men may have been among that definition's most enthusiastic proponents). Finally, Edward H. Thompson, Jr., underscores how older men are often invisible as men in a culture that sees aging as a sign of decline and debility. Taken together, the articles in this section make clear that students of men's lives must pay special attention to the rich diversity of masculinities in our—or any—society.

ARTICLE

Michael Kaufman

The Construction of Masculinity and the Triad of Men's Violence

The all too familiar story: a woman raped, a wife battered, a lover abused. With a sense of immediacy and anger, the women's liberation movement has pushed the many forms of men's violence against women—from the most overt to the most subtle in form—into popular consciousness and public debate. These forms of violence are one aspect of our society's domination by men that, in outcome, if not always in design, reinforce that domination. The act of violence is many things at once. At the same instant it is the individual man acting out relations of sexual power; it is the violence of a society—a hierarchical, authoritarian, sexist, class-divided, militarist, racist, impersonal, crazy society—being focused through an individual man onto an individual woman. In the psyche of the individual man it might be his denial of social powerlessness through an act of aggression. In total these acts of violence are like a ritualized acting out of our social relations of power: the dominant and the weaker, the powerful and the powerless, the ac-

Reprinted from *Beyond Patriarchy: Essays on Pleasure, Power, and Change,* edited by Michael Kaufman. Toronto: Oxford University Press, 1987. Reprinted by permission.

tive and the passive . . . the masculine and the feminine.

For men, listening to the experience of women as the objects of men's violence is to shatter any complacency about the sex-based status quo. The power and anger of women's responses forces us to rethink the things we discovered when we were very young. When I was eleven or twelve years old a friend told me the difference between fucking and raping. It was simple: with rape you tied the woman to a tree. At the time the anatomical details were still a little vague, but in either case it was something "we" supposedly did. This knowledge was just one part of an education, started years before, about the relative power and privileges of men and women. I remember laughing when my friend explained all that to me. Now I shudder. The difference in my responses is partially that, at twelve, it was part of the posturing and pretense that accompanied my passage into adolescence. Now, of course, I have a different vantage point on the issue. It is the vantage point of an adult, but more importantly my view of the world is being reconstructed by the intervention of that majority whose voice has been suppressed: the women.

This relearning of the reality of men's violence against women evokes many deep feelings and memories for men. As memories are recalled and recast, a new connection becomes clear: violence by men against women is only one corner of a triad of men's violence. The other two corners are violence against other men and violence against oneself.

On a psychological level the pervasiveness of violence is the result of what Herbert Marcuse called the "surplus repression" of our sexual and emotional desires.[1] The substitution of violence for desire (more precisely, the transmutation of violence into a form of emotionally gratifying activity) happens unequally in men and women. The construction of masculinity involves the construction of "surplus aggressiveness." The social context of this triad of violence is the institutionalization of violence in the operation of most aspects of social, economic, and political life.

The three corners of the triad reinforce one another. The first corner—violence against women—cannot be confronted successfully without simultaneously challenging the other two corners of the triad. And all this requires a dismantling of the social feeding ground of violence: patriarchal, heterosexist, authoritarian, class societies. These three corners and the societies in which they blossom feed on each other. And together, we surmise, they will fall.

The Social Context

In spite of proclamations from the skewed research of sociobiologists, there is no good evidence that men's violence is the inevitable and natural result of male genes or hormones. To the contrary, anthropology tells us of many early societies with little or no violence against women, against children, or among men. However, given the complexity of the issues concerning the roots of violence, the essential question for us is not whether men are predisposed to violence but what society does with this violence. Why has the linchpin of so many societies been the manifold expression of violence perpetrated disproportionately by men? Why are so many forms of violence sanctioned or even encouraged? Exactly what is the nature of violence? And how are patterns of violence and the quest for domination built up and reinforced?

In other words, the key questions having to do with men's violence are not biological but are related to gender and society—which is why I speak not of "male violence" (a biological category) but rather of "men's violence" (the gender category).

For every apparently individual act of violence there is a social context. This is not to say there are no pathological acts of violence; but even in that case the "language" of the violent act, the way the violence manifests itself, can only be understood within a certain social experience. We are interested here in the manifestations of violence that are accepted as more or less normal, even if reprehensible: fighting, war, rape, assault, psychological abuse, and so forth. What is the context of men's violence in the prevalent social orders of today?

Violence has long been institutionalized as an acceptable means of solving conflicts. But now the vast apparati of policing and war making maintained by countries the world over pose a threat to the future of life itself.

"Civilized" societies have been built and shaped through the decimation, containment, and exploitation of other peoples: extermination of native populations, colonialism, and slavery. Our relationship with the natural environment has often been described with the metaphor of rape. An attitude of conquering nature, of mastering an environment waiting to be exploited for profit, has great consequences when we possess a technology capable of permanently disrupting an ecological balance shaped over hundreds of millions of years.

The daily work life of industrial, class societies is one of violence. Violence poses as economic rationality as some of us are turned into extensions of machines, while others become brains detached from bodies. Our industrial process becomes the modern-day rack of torture where we are stretched out of shape and ripped limb from limb. It is violence that exposes workers to the danger of chemicals, radiation, machinery, speedup, and muscle strain.

The racism, sexism, and heterosexism that have been institutionalized in our societies are socially regulated acts of violence. Our cities, our social structure, our work life, our relation with nature, our history, are more than a backdrop to the prevalence of violence. They are violence; violence in an institutionalized form encoded into physical structures and socioeconomic relations. Much of the sociological analysis of violence in our societies implies simply that violence is learned by witnessing and experiencing social violence: man kicks boy, boy kicks dog.[2] Such experiences of transmitted violence are a reality, as the analysis of wife battering indicates, for many batterers were themselves abused as children. But more essential is that our personalities and sexuality, our needs and fears, our strengths and weaknesses, our selves are created—not simply learned—through our lived reality. The violence of our social order nurtures a psychology of violence, which in turn reinforces the social, economic and political structures of violence. The ever-increasing demands of civilization and the constant building upon inherited structures of violence suggest that the development of civilization has been inseparable from a continuous increase in violence against humans and our natural environment.

It would be easy, yet ultimately not very useful, to slip into a use of the term "violence" as a metaphor for all our society's antagonisms, contradictions, and ills. For now, let us leave aside the social terrain and begin to unravel the nature of so-called individual violence.

The Triad of Men's Violence

The longevity of the oppression of women must be based on something more than conspiracy, something more complicated than biological handicap and more durable than economic exploitation (although in differing degrees all these may feature).

—Juliet Mitchell[3]

It seems impossible to believe that mere greed could hold men to such a steadfastness of purpose.

—Joseph Conrad[4]

The field in which the triad of men's violence is situated is a society, or societies, grounded in structures of domination and control. Although at times this control is symbolized and embodied in the individual father—patriarchy, by definition—it is more important to emphasize that patriarchal structures of authority, domination, and control are diffused throughout social, economic, political, and ideological activities and in our relations to the natural environment. Perhaps more than in any previous time during the long epoch of patriarchy, authority does *not* rest with the father, at least in much of the advanced capitalist and noncapitalist world. This has led more than one author to question the applicability of the term patriarchy.[5] But I think it still remains useful as a broad, descriptive category. In this sense Jessica Benjamin speaks of the current reign of patriarchy without the father. "The form of domination peculiar to this epoch expresses itself not directly as authority but indirectly as the transformation of all relationships and activity into objective, instrumental, depersonalized forms."[6]

The structures of domination and control form not simply the background to the triad of violence, but generate, and in turn are nurtured by, this violence. These structures refer both to our social relations and to our interaction with our natural environment. The relation between these two levels is obviously extremely complex. It appears that violence against nature—that is, the impossible and disastrous drive to dominate and conquer the natural world—is integrally connected with domination among humans. Some of these connections are quite obvious. One thinks of the bulldozing of the planet for profit in capitalist societies, societies characterized by the dominance of one class over others. But the link between the domination of nature and structures of domination of humans go beyond this.

The Individual Reproduction of Male Domination

No man is born a butcher.

—Bertolt Brecht[7]

In a male-dominated society men have a number of privileges. Compared to women we are free to walk the streets at night, we have traditionally escaped domestic labor, and on average we have higher wages, better jobs, and more power. But these advantages in themselves cannot explain the individual reproduction of the relations of male domination, that is, why the individual male from a very early age embraces masculinity. The embracing of masculinity is not only a "socialization" into a certain gender role, as if there is a preformed human being who learns a role that he then plays for the rest of his life. Rather, through his psychological development he embraces and takes into himself a set of gender-based social relations: the person that is created through the process of maturation becomes the personal embodiment of those relations. By the time the child is five or six years old, the basis for lifelong masculinity has already been established.

The basis for the individual's acquisition of gender is that the prolonged period of human childhood results in powerful attachments to parental figures. (Through a very complex process, by the time a boy is five or six he claims for himself the power and activity society associates with masculinity.) He embraces the project of controlling himself and controlling the world. He comes to personify activity. Masculinity is a reaction against passivity and powerlessness, and with it comes a repression of a vast range of human desires and possibilities: those that are associated with femininity.

Masculinity is unconsciously rooted before the age of six, is reinforced as the child develops, and then positively explodes at adolescence, obtaining its definitive shape for the individual. The masculine norm has its own particular nuances and traits dependent on class, nation, race, religion, and ethnicity. And within each group it has its own personal expression. In adolescence the pain and fear involved in repressing "femininity" and passivity start to become evident. For most of us, the response to this inner pain is to reinforce the bulwarks of masculinity. The emotional pain created by obsessive masculinity is stifled by reinforcing masculinity itself.

The Fragility of Masculinity

Masculinity is power. But masculinity is terrifyingly fragile because it does not really exist in the sense we are led to think it exists; that is, as a biological reality—something real that we have inside ourselves. It exists as ideology; it exists as scripted behavior; it exists within "gendered" relationships. But in the end it is just a social institution with a tenuous relationship to that with which it is supposed to be synonymous: our maleness, our biological sex. The young child does not know that sex does not equal gender. For him to be male is to be what he perceives as being masculine. The child is father to the man. Therefore, to be unmasculine is to be desexed—"castrated."

The tension between maleness and masculinity is intense because masculinity requires a suppression of a whole range of human needs, aims, feelings, and forms of expression. Masculinity is one-half of the narrow, surplus-repressive shape of the adult human psyche. Even when we are intellectually aware of the difference between biological maleness and masculinity, the masculine ideal is so embedded within ourselves that it is hard to untangle the person we might want to become (more "fully human," less sexist, less surplus-repressed, and so on) from the person we actually are.

But as children and adolescents (and often as adults), we are not aware of the difference between maleness and masculinity. With the exception of a tiny proportion of the population born as hermaphrodites, there can be no biological struggle to be male. The presence of a penis and testicles is all it takes. Yet boys and men harbor great insecurity about their male credentials. This insecurity exists because maleness is equated with masculinity; but the latter is a figment of our collective, patriarchal, surplus-repressive imaginations.

In a patriarchal society being male is highly valued, and men value their masculinity. But everywhere there are ambivalent feelings. That the initial internalization of masculinity is at the father's knee has lasting significance. Andrew Tolson states that "to the boy, masculinity is both mysterious and attractive (in its promise of a world of work and power), and yet, at the same time, threatening (in its strangeness, and emotional distance). . . . It works both ways; attracts and repels in dynamic contradiction. This simul-taneous distance and attraction is internalized as a permanent emotional tension that the individual must, in some way, strive to overcome."[8]

Although maleness and masculinity are highly valued, men are everywhere unsure of their own masculinity and maleness, whether consciously or not. When men are encouraged to be open, as in men's support and counseling groups, it becomes apparent that there exists, often under the surface, an internal dialogue of doubt about one's male and masculine credentials.

Men's Violence Against Women

In spite of the inferior role which men assign to them, women are the privileged objects of their aggression.

—Simone de Beauvoir[9]

Men's violence against women is the most common form of direct, personalized violence in the lives of most adults. From sexual harassment to rape, from incest to wife battering to the sight of violent pornographic images, few women escape some form of men's aggression.

My purpose here is not to list and evaluate the various forms of violence against women, nor to try to assess what can be classed as violence per se.[10] It is to understand this violence as an expression of the fragility of masculinity combined with men's power. I am interested in its place in the perpetuation of masculinity and male domination.

In the first place, men's violence against women is probably the clearest, most straightforward expression of relative male and female power. That the relative social, economic, and political power can be expressed in this manner is, to a large part, because of differences in physical strength and in a lifelong training (or lack of training) in fighting. But it is also expressed this way because of the active/passive split. Activity as aggression is part of the masculine gender definition. That is not to say this definition always includes rape or battering, but it is one of the possibilities within a definition of activity that is ultimately grounded in the body.

Rape is a good example of the acting out of these relations of power and of the outcome of fragile masculinity in a surplus-repressive society. In the testimonies of rapists one hears over and over again expressions of inferiority, powerlessness, anger. But who can these men feel superior to? Rape is a crime that not only demonstrates physical power, but that does so in the language of male–female sex-gender relations. The testimonies of convicted rapists collected by Douglas Jackson in the late 1970s are chilling and revealing.[11] Hal: "I feel very inferior to others. . . . I felt rotten about myself and by committing rape I took this out on someone I thought was weaker than me, someone I could control." Len: "I feel a lot of what rape is isn't so much sexual desire as a person's feelings about themselves and how that relates to sex. My fear of relating to people turned to sex because . . . it just happens to be the fullest area to let your anger out on, to let your feelings out on."

Sometimes this anger and pain are experienced in relation to women but just as often not. In either case they are addressed to women who, as the Other in a phallocentric society, are objects of mystification to men, the objects to whom men from birth have learned to express and vent their feelings, or simply objects with less social power and weaker muscles. It is the crime against women par excellence because, through it, the full weight of a sexually based differentiation among humans is played out.

Within relationships, forms of men's violence such as rape, battering, and what Meg Luxton calls the "petty tyranny" of male domination in the household[12] must be understood both "in terms of violence directed against women as women and against women as wives."[13] The family provides an arena for the expression of needs and emotions not considered legitimate elsewhere.[14] It is the one of the only places where men feel safe enough to express emotions. As the dams break, the flood pours out on women and children.[15] The family also becomes the place where the violence suffered by individuals in their work lives is discharged. "At work men are powerless, so in their leisure time they want to have a feeling that they control their lives."[16]

While this violence can be discussed in terms of male aggression, it operates within the dualism of activity and passivity, masculinity and femininity. Neither can exist without the other. This is not to blame women for being beaten, nor to excuse men who beat. It is but an indication that the various forms of men's violence against women are a dynamic affirmation of a masculinity that can only exist as distinguished from femininity. It is my argument that masculinity needs constant nurturing and affirmation. This affirmation takes many different forms. The majority of men are not rapists or batterers, although it is probable that the majority of men have used superior physical strength or some sort of physical force or threat of force against a woman at least once as a teenager or an adult. But in those who harbor great personal doubts or strongly negative self-images, or who cannot cope with a daily feeling of powerlessness, violence against women can become a means of trying to affirm their personal power in the language of our sex-gender system. That these forms of violence only reconfirm the negative self-image and the feelings of powerlessness shows the fragility, artificiality, the precariousness of masculinity.

Violence Against Other Men

At a behavioral level, men's violence against other men is visible throughout society. Some forms, such as fighting, the ritualized display violence of teenagers and some groups of adult men, institutionalized rape in prisons, and attacks on gays or racial minorities, are very direct expressions of this violence. In many sports, violence is incorporated into exercise and entertainment. More subtle forms are the verbal putdown or, combined with economic and other factors, the competition in the business, political, or academic world. In its most frightening form, violence has long been an acceptable and even preferred method of addressing differences and conflicts among different groups and states. In the case of war, as in many other manifestations of violence, violence against other men (and civilian women) combines with autonomous economic, ideological, and political factors.

But men's violence against other men is more than the sum of various activities and types of behavior. In this form of violence a number of things are happening at once, in addition to the autonomous factors involved. Sometimes mutual, sometimes one-sided, there is a discharge of aggression and hostility. But at the same time as discharging aggression, these acts of violence and the ever-present potential for men's violence against other men reinforce the reality that relations between men, whether at the individual or state level, are relations of power.[17]

Most men feel the presence of violence in their lives. Some of us had fathers who were domineering, rough, or even brutal. Some of us had fathers who simply were not there enough; most of us had fathers who either consciously or unconsciously were repelled by our need for touch and affection once we had passed a certain age. All of us had experiences of being beaten up or picked on when we were young. We learned to fight, or we learned to run; we learned to pick on others, or we learned how to talk or joke our way out of a confrontation. But either way these early experiences of violence caused an incredible amount of anxiety and required a huge expenditure of energy to resolve.

That anxiety is crystallized in an unspoken fear (particularly among heterosexual men): all other men are my potential humiliators, my enemies, my competitors.

But this mutual hostility is not always expressed. Men have formed elaborate institutions of male bonding and buddying: clubs, gangs, teams, fishing trips, card games, bars, and gyms, not to mention that great fraternity of Man. Certainly, as many feminists have pointed out, straight male clubs are a subculture of male privilege. But they are also havens where men, by common consent, can find safety and security among other men. They are safe houses where our love and affection for other men can be expressed.

Freud suggested that great amounts of passivity are required for the establishment of social relations among men but also that this very passivity arouses a fear of losing one's power. (This fear takes the form, in a phallocentric, male-dominated society, of what Freud called "castration anxiety.") There is a constant tension of activity and passivity. Among their many functions and reasons for existence, male institutions mediate this tension between activity and passivity among men.

My thoughts take me back to grade six and the constant acting out of this drama. There was the challenge to fight and a punch in the stomach that knocked my wind out. There was our customary greeting with a slug in the shoulder. Before school, after school, during class change, at recess, whenever you saw another one of the boys whom you hadn't hit or been with in the past few minutes, you'd punch each other on the shoulder. I remember walking from class to class in terror of meeting Ed Skagle in the hall. Ed, a hefty young football player a grade ahead of me, would leave a big bruise with one of his friendly hellos. And this was the interesting thing about the whole business; most of the time it was friendly and affectionate. Long after the bruises have faded, I remember Ed's smile and the protective way he had of saying hello to me. But we couldn't express this affection without maintaining the active/passive equilibrium. More precisely, within the masculine psychology of surplus aggression, expressions of affection and of the need for other boys had to be balanced by an active assault.

But the traditional definition of masculinity is not only surplus aggression. It is also exclusive heterosexuality, for the maintenance of masculinity requires the repression of homosexuality.[18] Repression of homosexuality is one thing, but how do we explain the intense fear of homosexuality, the homophobia, that pervades so much male interaction? It isn't simply that many men may choose not to have sexual relations with other men; it is rather that they will find this possibility frightening or abhorrent.

Freud showed that the boy's renunciation of the father—and thus men—as an object of sexual love is a renunciation of what are felt to be passive sexual desires. For the boy to deviate from this norm is to experience severe anxiety, for what appears to be at stake is his ability to be active. Erotic attraction to other men is sacrificed because there is no model central to our society of active, erotic love for other males. The emotionally charged physical attachments of childhood with father and friends eventually breed feelings of passivity and danger and are sacrificed. The anxiety caused by the threat of losing power and activity is "the motive power behind the 'normal' boy's social learning of his sex and gender roles." Boys internalize "our culture's definition of 'normal' or 'real' man: the possessor of a penis, therefore loving only females and that actively; the possessor of a penis, therefore 'strong' and 'hard,' not 'soft,' 'weak,' 'yielding,' 'sentimental,' 'effeminate,' 'passive.' To deviate from this definition is not to be a real man. To deviate is to arouse [what Freud called] castration anxiety."[19]

Putting this in different terms, the young boy learns of the sexual hierarchy of society. This learning process is partly conscious and partly unconscious. For a boy, being a girl is a

threat because it raises anxiety by representing a loss of power. Until real power is attained, the young boy courts power in the world of the imagination (with superheroes, guns, magic, and pretending to be grown-up). But the continued pull of passive aims, the attraction to girls and to mother, the fascination with the origin of babies ensure that a tension continues to exist. In this world, the only thing that is as bad as being a girl is being a sissy, that is, being like a girl.[20] Although the boy doesn't consciously equate being a girl or sissy with homosexual genital activity, at the time of puberty these feelings, thoughts, and anxieties are transferred onto homosexuality per se.

For the majority of men, the establishment of the masculine norm and the strong social prohibitions against homosexuality are enough to bury the erotic desire for other men. The repression of our bisexuality is not adequate, however, to keep this desire at bay. Some of the energy is transformed into derivative pleasures—muscle building, male comradeship, hero worship, religious rituals, war, sports—where our enjoyment of being with other men or admiring other men can be expressed. These forms of activity are not enough to neutralize our constitutional bisexuality, our organic fusion of passivity and activity, and our love for our fathers and our friends. The great majority of men, in addition to those men whose sexual preference is clearly homosexual, have, at some time in their childhood, adolescence, or adult life, had sexual or quasi-sexual relations with other males, or have fantasized or dreamed about such relationships. Those who don't (or don't recall that they have), invest a lot of energy in repressing and denying these thoughts and feelings. And to make things worse, all those highly charged male activities in the sportsfield, the meeting room, or the locker room do not dispel eroticized relations with other men. They can only reawaken those feelings. It is, as Freud would have said, the return of the repressed.

Nowhere has this been more stunningly captured than in the wrestling scene in the perhaps mistitled book, *Women in Love*, by D. H. Lawrence. It was late at night. Birkin had just come to Gerald's house after being put off following a marriage proposal. They talked of working, of loving, and fighting, and in the end stripped off their clothes and began to wrestle in front of the burning fire. As they wrestled, "they seemed to drive their white flesh deeper and deeper against each other, as if they would break into a oneness." They entwined, they wrestled, they pressed nearer and nearer. "A tense white knot of flesh [was] gripped in silence." The thin Birkin "seemed to penetrate into Gerald's more solid, more diffuse bulk, to interfuse his body through the body of the other, as if to bring it subtly into subjection, always seizing with some rapid necromantic foreknowledge every motion of the other flesh, converting and counteracting it, playing upon the limbs and trunk of Gerald like some hard wind. . . . Now and again came a sharp gasp of breath, or a sound like a sigh, then the rapid thudding of movement on the thickly-carpeted floor, then the strange sound of flesh escaping under flesh."[21]

The very institutions of male bonding and patriarchal power force men to constantly reexperience their closeness and attraction to other men, that is, the very thing so many men are afraid of. Our very attraction to ourselves, ambivalent as it may be, can only be generalized as an attraction to men in general.

A phobia is one means by which the ego tries to cope with anxiety. Homophobia is a means of trying to cope, not simply with our unsuccessfully repressed, eroticized attraction to other men, but with our whole anxiety over the unsuccessfully repressed passive sexual aims, whether directed toward males or females. Homophobia is not merely an individual phobia, although the strength of homophobia varies from individual to individual. It is a socially constructed phobia that is essential for the imposition and maintenance of masculinity. A key expression of homophobia is the obsessive denial of homosexual attraction; this denial is expressed as violence against other men. Or to put it differently, men's violence against other men is one of the chief means through which patriarchal society simultaneously expresses and discharges the attraction of men to other men.[22]

The specific ways that homophobia and men's violence toward other men are acted out varies from man to man, society to society, and class to class. The great amount of *directly expressed* violence and violent homophobia among some groups of working class youth would be well worth analyzing to give clues to the relation of class and gender.

This corner of the triad of men's violence interacts with and reinforces violence against women. This corner contains part of the logic of surplus aggression. Here we begin to explain the tendency of many men to use force as a means of simultaneously hiding and expressing their feelings. At the same time the fear of other men, in particular the fear of weakness and passivity in relation to other men, helps create our strong dependence on women for meeting our emotional needs and for emotional discharge. In a surplus-repressive patriarchal and class society, large amounts of anxiety and hostility are built up, ready to be discharged. But the fear of one's emotions and the fear of losing control mean that discharge only takes place in a safe situation. For many men that safety is provided by a relationship with a woman where the commitment of one's friend or lover creates the sense of security. What is more, because it is a relationship with a woman, it unconsciously resonates with that first great passive relation of the boy with his mother. But in this situation and in other acts of men's violence against women, there is also the security of interaction with someone who does not represent a psychic threat, who is less socially powerful, probably less physically powerful, and who is herself operating within a pattern of surplus passivity. And finally, given the fragility of masculine identity and the inner tension of what it means to be masculine, the ultimate acknowledgement of one's masculinity is in our power over women. This power can be expressed in many ways. Violence is one of them.

When I speak of a man's violence against himself I am thinking of the very structure of the masculine ego. The formation of an ego on an edifice of what Herbert Marcuse called surplus repression and surplus aggression is the building of a precarious structure of internalized violence. The continual conscious and unconscious blocking and denial of passivity and all the emotions and feelings men associate with passivity—fear, pain, sadness, embarrassment—is a denial of part of what we are. The constant psychological and behavioral vigilance against passivity and its derivatives is a perpetual act of violence against oneself.

The denial and blocking of a whole range of human emotions and capacities are compounded by the blocking of avenues of discharge. The discharge of fear, hurt, and sadness, for example (through crying or trembling), is necessary because these painful emotions linger on even if they are not consciously felt. Men become pressure cookers. The failure to find safe avenues of emotional expression and discharge means that a whole range of emotions are transformed into anger and hostility. Part of the anger is directed at oneself in the form of guilt, self-hate, and various physiological and psychological symptoms. Part is directed at other men. Part of it is directed at women.

By the end of this process, our distance from ourselves is so great that the very symbol of maleness is turned into an object, a thing. Men's preoccupation with genital power and pleasure combines with a desensitization of the penis. As best he can, writes Emmanuel Reynaud, a man gives it "the coldness and the hardness of metal." It becomes his tool, his weapon, his thing. "What he loses in enjoyment he hopes to compensate for in power; but if he gains an undeniable power symbol, what pleasure can he really feel with a weapon between his legs?"[23]

Beyond Men's Violence

Throughout Gabriel García Márquez's *Autumn of the Patriarch*, the ageless dictator stalked his palace, his elephantine feet dragging forever on endless corridors that reeked of corruption. There was no escape from the world of terror, misery, and decay that he himself had created. His tragedy was that he was "condemned forever to live breathing the same air which asphyxiated him."[24] As men, are we similarly condemned; or is there a road of escape from the triad of men's violence and the precarious structures of masculinity that we ourselves recreate at our peril and that of women, children, and the world?

Prescribing a set of behavioral or legal changes to combat men's violence against women is obviously not enough. Even as more and more are convinced there is a problem, this realization does not touch the unconscious structures of masculinity. Any man who is sympathetic to feminism is aware of the painful contradiction between his conscious views and his deeper emotions and feelings.

The analysis in this article suggests that men and women must address each corner of the triad of men's violence and the socioeconomic, psychosexual orders on which they stand. Or to put it more strongly, it is impossible to deal successfully with any one corner of this triad in isolation from the others.

The social context that nurtures men's violence and the relation between socioeconomic transformation and the end of patriarchy have been major themes of socialist feminist thought. This framework, though it is not without controversy and unresolved problems, is one I accept. Patriarchy and systems of authoritarianism and class domination feed on each other. Radical socioeconomic and political change is a requirement for the end of men's violence. But organizing for macrosocial change is not enough to solve the problem of men's violence, not only because the problem is so pressing here and now, but because the continued existence of masculinity and surplus aggressiveness works against the fundamental macrosocial change we desire.

The many manifestations of violence against women have been an important focus of feminists. Women's campaigns and public education against rape, battering, sexual harassment, and more generally for control by women of their bodies are a key to challenging men's violence. Support by men, not only for the struggles waged by women, but in our own workplaces and among our friends is an important part of the struggle. There are many possible avenues for work by men among men. These include: forming counselling groups and support services for battering men (as is now happening in different cities in North America); championing the inclusion of clauses on sexual harassment in collective agreements and in the constitutions or bylaws of our trade unions, associations, schools, and political parties; raising money, campaigning for government funding, and finding other means of support for rape crisis centers and shelters for battered women; speaking out against violent and sexist pornography; building neighborhood campaigns of wife and child abuse; and personally refusing to collude with the sexism of our workmates, colleagues, and friends. The latter is perhaps the most difficult of all and requires patience, humor, and support from other men who are challenging sexism.

But because men's violence against women is inseparable from the other two corners of the triad of men's violence, solutions are very complex and difficult. Ideological changes and an awareness of problems are important but insufficient. While we can envisage changes in our child-rearing arrangements (which in turn would require radical economic changes) lasting solutions have to go far deeper. Only the development of non-surplus-repressive societies

(whatever these might look like) will allow for the greater expression of human needs and, along with attacks on patriarchy per se, will reduce the split between active and passive psychological aims.[25]

The process of achieving these long-term goals contains many elements of economic, social, political, and psychological change, each of which requires a fundamental transformation of society. Such a transformation will not be created by an amalgam of changed individuals; but there *is* a relationship between personal change and our ability to construct organizational, political, and economic alternatives that will be able to mount a successful challenge to the status quo.

One avenue of personal struggle that is being engaged in by an increasing number of men has been the formation of men's support groups. Some groups focus on consciousness raising, but most groups stress the importance of men talking about their feelings, their relations with other men and with women, and any number of problems in their lives. At times these groups have been criticized by some antisexist men as yet another place for men to collude against women. The alternatives put forward are groups whose primary focus is either support for struggles led by women or the organization of direct, antisexist campaigns among men. These activities are very important, but so too is the development of new support structures among men. And these structures must go beyond the traditional form of consciousness raising.

Consciousness raising usually focuses on manifestations of the oppression of women and on the oppressive behavior of men. But as we have seen, masculinity is more than the sum total of oppressive forms of behavior. It is deeply and unconsciously embedded in the structure of our egos and superegos; it is what we have become. An awareness of oppressive behavior is important, but too often it only leads to guilt about being a man. Guilt is a profoundly conservative emotion and as such is not particularly useful for bringing about change. From a position of insecurity and guilt, people do not change or inspire others to change. After all, insecurity about one's male credentials played an important part in the individual acquisition of masculinity and men's violence in the first place.

There is a need to promote the personal strength and security necessary to allow men to make more fundamental personal changes and to confront sexism and heterosexism in our society at large. Support groups usually allow men to talk about our feelings, how we too have been hurt growing up in a surplus-repressive society, and how we, in turn, act at times in an oppressive manner. We begin to see the connections between painful and frustrating experiences in our own lives and related forms of oppressive behavior. As Sheila Rowbotham notes, "the exploration of the internal areas of consciousness is a political necessity for us."[26]

Talking among men is a major step, but it is still operating within the acceptable limits of what men like to think of as rational behavior. Deep barriers and fears remain even when we can begin to recognize them. As well as talking, men need to encourage direct expression of emotions—grief, anger, rage, hurt, love—within these groups and the physical closeness that has been blocked by the repression of passive aims, by social prohibition, and by our own superegos and sense of what is right. This discharge of emotions has many functions and outcomes: like all forms of emotional and physical discharge it lowers the tension within the human system and reduces the likelihood of a spontaneous discharge of emotions through outer- or inner-directed violence.

But the expression of emotions is not an end in itself; in this context it is a means to an end. Stifling the emotions connected with feelings of hurt and pain acts as a sort of glue that allows the original repression to remain. Emotional discharge, in a situation of support and encouragement, helps unglue the ego structures that require us to operate in patterned, phobic,

oppressive, and surplus-aggressive forms. In a sense it loosens up the repressive structures and allows us fresh insight into ourselves and our past. But if this emotional discharge happens in isolation or against an unwitting victim, it only reinforces the feelings of being powerless, out of control, or a person who must obsessively control others. Only in situations that contradict these feelings—that is, with the support, affection, encouragement, and backing of other men who experience similar feelings—does the basis for change exist.[27]

The encouragement of emotional discharge and open dialogue among men also enhances the safety we begin to feel among each other and in turn helps us to tackle obsessive, even if unconscious, fear of other men. This unconscious fear and lack of safety are the experience of most heterosexual men throughout their lives. The pattern for homosexual men differs, but growing up and living in a heterosexist, patriarchal culture implants similar fears, even if one's adult reality is different.

Receiving emotional support and attention from a group of men is a major contradiction to experiences of distance, caution, fear, and neglect from other men. This contradiction is the mechanism that allows further discharge, emotional change, and more safety. Safety among even a small group of our brothers gives us greater safety and strength among men as a whole. This gives us the confidence and sense of personal power to confront sexism and homophobia in all its various manifestations. In a sense, this allows us each to be a model of a strong, powerful man who does not need to operate in an oppressive and violent fashion in relation to women, to other men, or to himself. And that, I hope, will play some small part in the challenge to the oppressive reality of patriarchal, authoritarian, and class societies. It will be changes in our own lives inseparably intertwined with changes in society as a whole that will sever the links in the triad of men's violence.

Notes

My thanks to those who have given me comments on earlier drafts of this paper, in particular my father, Nathan Kaufman, and to Gad Horowitz. As well, I extend my appreciation to the men I have worked with in various counseling situations who have helped me develop insights into the individual acquisition of violence and masculinity.

1. Herbert Marcuse, *Eros and Civilization* (Boston: Beacon Press, 1975; New York: Vintage, 1962): Gad Horowitz, *Repression* (Toronto: University of Toronto Press, 1977).

2. This is the approach, for example, of Suzanne Steinmetz. She says that macrolevel social and economic conditions (such as poverty, unemployment, inadequate housing, and the glorification and acceptance of violence) lead to high crime rates and a tolerance of violence that in turn leads to family aggression. See her *Cycle of Violence* (New York: Praeger, 1977), 30.

3. Juliet Mitchell, *Psychoanalysis and Feminism* (New York: Vintage, 1975), 362.

4. Joseph Conrad, *Lord Jim* (New York: Bantam Books, 1981), 146; first published 1900.

5. See for example Michele Barrett's thought-provoking book *Women's Oppression Today* (London: Verso/New Left Books, 1980), 10–19, 250–1.

6. Jessica Benjamin, "Authority and the Family Revisited: or, A World Without Fathers?" *New German Critique* (Winter 1978), 35.

7. Bertolt Brecht, *Three Penny Novel*, trans. Desmond I. Vesey (Harmondsworth: Penguin, 1965), 282.

8. Andrew Tolson, *The Limits of Masculinity* (London: Tavistock, 1977), 25.

9. Simone de Beauvoir, in the *Nouvel Observateur*, Mar. 1, 1976. Quoted in Diana E. H. Russell and Nicole Van de Ven, eds., *Crimes Against Women* (Millbrae, Calif.: Les Femmes, 1976), xiv.

10. Among the sources on male violence that are useful, even if sometimes problematic, see Leonore E. Walker, *The Battered Woman* (New York: Harper Colophon, 1980); Russell and Van de Ven, *op. cit.*; Judith Lewis Herman, *Father–Daughter Incest* (Cambridge, Mass.: Harvard University Press, 1981);

Suzanne K. Steinmetz, *The Cycle of Violence* (New York: Praeger, 1977); Sylvia Levine and Joseph Koenig, *Why Men Rape* (Toronto: Macmillan, 1980); Susan Brownmiller, *op. cit.*, and Connie Guberman and Margie Wolfe, eds., *No Safe Place* (Toronto: Women's Press, 1985).

11. Levine and Koenig, *op. cit.*, pp. 28, 42, 56, 72.

12. Meg Luxton, *More Than a Labour of Love* (Toronto: Women's Press, 1980), 66.

13. Margaret M. Killoran, "The Sound of Silence Breaking: Toward a Metatheory of Wife Abuse" (M.A. thesis, McMaster University, 1981), 148.

14. Barrett and MacIntosh, *op. cit.*, 23.

15. Of course, household violence is not monopolized by men. In the United States roughly the same number of domestic homicides are committed by each sex. In 1975, 8.0% of homicides were committed by husbands against wives and 7.8% by wives against husbands. These figures, however, do not indicate the chain of violence, that is, the fact that most of these women were reacting to battering by their husbands. (See Steinmetz, *op. cit.*, p. 90.) Similarly, verbal and physical abuse of children appears to be committed by men and women equally. Only in the case of incest is there a near monopoly by men. Estimates vary greatly, but between one-fifth and one-third of all girls experience some sort of sexual contact with an adult male, in most cases with a father, stepfather, other relative, or teacher. (See Herman, *op. cit.*, 12 and *passim*.)

16. Luxton, *op. cit.*, p. 65.

17. This was pointed out by I. F. Stone in a 1972 article on the Vietnam war. At a briefing about the U.S. escalation of bombing in the North, the Pentagon official described U.S. strategy as two boys fighting: "If one boy gets the other in an arm lock, he can probably get his adversary to say 'uncle' if he increases the pressure in sharp, painful jolts and gives every indication of willingness to break the boy's arm" ("Machismo in Washington," reprinted in Pleck and Sawyer, *op. cit.*, 131). Although women are also among the victims of war, I include war in the category of violence against men because I am here referring to the causality of war.

18. This is true both of masculinity as an institution and masculinity for the individual. Gay men keep cer-

tain parts of the self-oppressive masculine norm intact simply because they have grown up and live in a predominantly heterosexual, male-dominated society.

19. Horowitz, *op. cit.*, 99.

20. This formulation was first suggested to me by Charlie Kreiner at a men's counseling workshop in 1982.

21. D. H. Lawrence, *Women in Love* (Harmondsworth: Penguin, 1960), 304–5; first published 1921.

22. See Robin Wood's analysis of the film *Raging Bull*. M. Kaufman, ed. *Beyond Patriarchy*. Toronto: Oxford University Press, 1987.

23. Emmanuel Reynaud, *Holy Virility*, translated by Ros Schwartz (London: Plato Press, 1983), 41–2.

24. Gabriel García Márquez, *Autumn of the Patriarch*, trans. Gregory Rabassa (Harmondsworth: Penguin, 1972), 111; first published 1967.

25. For a discussion on non-surplus-repressive societies, particularly in the sense of being complementary with Marx's notion of communism, see Horowitz, *op. cit.*, particularly chapter 7, and also Marcuse, *op. cit.*, especially chaps. 7, 10, and 11.

26. Rowbotham, *op. cit.*, 36.

27. As is apparent, although I have adopted a Freudian analysis of the unconscious and the mechanisms of repression, these observations on the therapeutic process—especially the importance of a supportive counseling environment, peer-counseling relations, emotional discharge, and the concept of contradiction—are those developed by forms of co-counseling, in particular, reevaluation counseling. But unlike the latter, I do not suppose that any of us can discharge all of our hurt, grief, and anger and uncover an essential self simply because our "self" is created.

2

ARTICLE

Manning Marable

The Black Male: Searching Beyond Stereotypes

What is a Black man? Husband and father. Son and brother. Lover and boyfriend. Uncle and grandfather. Construction worker and share-cropper. Minister and ghetto hustler. Doctor and mine-worker. Auto mechanic and presidential candidate.

What is a Black man in an institutionally racist society, in the social system of modern capitalist America? The essential tragedy of being Black and male is our inability, as men and as people of African descent, to define our-selves without the stereotypes the larger society imposes upon us, and through various institu-tional means perpetuates and permeates within our entire culture. Our relations with our sis-ters, our parents and children, and indeed across the entire spectrum of human relations are im-prisoned by images of the past, false distortions that seldom if ever capture the essence of our being. We cannot come to terms with Black women until we understand the half-hidden stereotypes that have crippled our development and social consciousness. We cannot challenge

Manning Marable, "The Black Male: Searching Beyond Stereotypes," in R. Majors and J. Gordon, eds., *The Ameri-can Black Male* (Chicago: Nelson-Hall, 1993).

racial and sexual inequality, both within the Black community and across the larger Ameri-can society, unless we comprehend the critical difference between the myths about ourselves and the harsh reality of being Black men.

Confrontation with White History

The conflicts between Black and white men in contemporary American culture can be traced directly through history to the earliest days of chattel slavery. White males entering the New World were ill adapted to make the difficult transition from Europe to the American frontier. As recent historical research indicates, the devel-opment of what was to become the United States was accomplished largely, if not primarily, by African slaves, men and women alike. Africans were the first to cultivate wheat on the continent; they showed their illiterate masters how to grow indigo, rice, and cotton; their ex-tensive knowledge of herbs and roots provided colonists with medicines and preservatives for food supplies. It was the Black man, wielding his sturdy axe, who cut down most of the virgin forest across the southern colonies. And in times of war, the white man reluctantly looked to his Black slave to protect him and his property. As early as 1715, during the Yemassee Indian war, Black troops led British regulars in a campaign to exterminate Indian tribes. After another such campaign in 1747, the all-white South Carolina legislature issued a public vote of gratitude to Black men, who "in times of war, behaved themselves with great faithfulness and courage, in repelling the attacks of his Majesty's enemies." During the American Revolution, over two thousand Black men volunteered to join the beleaguered Continental Army of George Washington, a slaveholder. A generation later, two thousand Blacks from New York joined the state militia's segregated units during the War of 1812, and Blacks fought bravely under Andrew Jackson at the Battle of New Orleans. From Crispus Attucks to the 180,000 Blacks who fought in the Union Army during the Civil War, Black men gave their lives to preserve the liberties of their white male masters.

The response of white men to the many sacrifices of their sable counterparts was, in a word, contemptuous. Their point of view of Black males was conditioned by three basic beliefs. Black men were only a step above the animals—possessing awesome physical power but lacking in intellectual ability. As such, their proper role in white society was as laborers, not as the managers of labor. Second, the Black male represented a potential political threat to the entire system of slavery. And third, but by no means last, the Black male symbolized a lusty sexual potency that threatened white women. This uneven mixture of political fears and sexual anxieties was reinforced by the white males' crimes committed against Black women, the routine rape and sexual abuse that all slave societies permit between the oppressed and the oppressor. Another dilemma, seldom discussed publicly, was the historical fact that some white women of social classes were not reluctant to request the sexual favors of their male slaves. These inherent tensions produced a racial model of conduct and social context that survived the colonial period and continued into the twentieth century. The white male–dominated system dictated that the only acceptable social behavior of any Black male was that of subservience—the loyal slave, the proverbial Uncle Tom, the ever-cheerful and infantile Sambo. It was not enough that Black men must cringe before their white masters; they must express open devotion to the system of slavery itself. Politically, the Black male was unfit to play even a minor role in the development of democracy. Supreme Court Chief Justice Roger B. Tawney spoke for his entire class in 1857: "Negroes [are] beings of an inferior order, and altogether unfit to associate with the white race, either by social or political relations; and so far inferior that they have no rights which the white man was bound to respect." Finally, Black males disciplined for various crimes against white supremacy—such as escaping from the plantation, or murdering their masters—were often punished in a sexual manner. On this point, the historical record is clear. In the colonial era, castration of Black males was required by the legislatures of North and South Carolina, Virginia, Pennsylvania, and New Jersey. Black men were castrated simply for striking a white man or for attempting to learn to read and write. In the late nineteenth century, hundreds of Black male victims of lynching were first sexually mutilated before being executed. The impulse to castrate Black males was popularized in white literature and folklore, and even today, instances of such crimes are not entirely unknown in the rural South.

The relations between Black males and white women were infinitely more complex. Generally, the vast majority of white females viewed Black men through the eyes of their fathers and husbands. The Black man was simply a beast of burden, a worker who gave his life to create a more comfortable environment for her and her children. And yet, in truth, he was still a man. Instances of interracial marriage were few, and were prohibited by law even as late as the 1960s. But the fear of sexual union did not prohibit many white females, particularly indentured servants and working-class women, from soliciting favors from Black men. In the 1840s, however, a small group of white middle-class women became actively involved in the campaign to abolish slavery. The founders of modern American feminism—Susan B. Anthony, Elizabeth Cady Stanton, and Lucretia Mott—championed the cause of emancipation and defended Blacks' civil rights. In gratitude for their devotion to Black freedom, the leading Black abolitionist of the period, Frederick Douglass, actively promoted the rights of white women against the white male power structure. In 1848, at the Seneca Falls, New York, women's rights convention, Douglass was the only man, Black or white, to support the extension of voting rights to all women. White women looked to Douglass for leadership in the battle against sexual and racial discrimination. Yet curiously, they were frequently hostile to the continued contributions of Black women to the cause of freedom. When the brilliant orator Sojourner Truth, second only to Douglass as a leading figure in the abolitionist movement, rose to lecture before an 1851 women's convention in Akron, Ohio, white women cried out, "Don't let her speak!" For these white liberals, the destruction of slavery was simply a means to expand democratic rights to white women: the goal was defined in racist terms. Black men like Douglass were useful allies only so far as they promoted white middle-class women's political interests.

The moment of truth came immediately following the Civil War, when Congress passed the Fifteenth Amendment, which gave Black males the right to vote. For Douglass and most Black leaders, both men and women, suffrage was absolutely essential to preserve their new freedoms. While the Fifteenth Amendment excluded females from the electoral franchise, it nevertheless represented a great democratic victory for all oppressed groups.

For most white suffragists, however, it symbolized the political advancement of the Black male over white middle-class women. Quickly their liberal rhetoric gave way to racist diatribes. "So long as the Negro was lowest in the scale of being, we were willing to press his claims," wrote Elizabeth Cady Stanton in 1865. "But now, as the celestial gate to civil rights is slowly moving on its hinges, it becomes a serious question whether we had better stand aside and see 'Sambo' walk into the kingdom first." Most white women reformists concluded that "it is better to be the slave of an educated white man than of a degraded, ignorant black one." They warned whites that giving the vote to the Black male would lead to widespread rape and sexual assaults against white women of the upper classes. Susan B. Anthony vowed, "I will cut off this right arm of mine before I will ever work for or demand the ballot for the Negro and not the [white] woman." In contrast, Black women leaders like Sojourner Truth and Frances E. Watkins Harper understood that the enfranchisement of Black men was an essential step for the democratic rights of all people.

The division between white middle-class feminists and the civil rights movement of Blacks, beginning over a century ago, has continued today in debates over affirmative action and job quotas. White liberal feminists frequently use the rhetoric of racial equality but often find it difficult to support public policies that will advance Black males over their own social group. Even in the 1970s, such liberal women writers as Susan Brownmiller continued to resurrect the myth of the "Black male-as-rapist" and sought to define white women in crudely racist terms. The weight of white history, from white women and men alike, has been an endless series of stereotypes used to frustrate the Black man's images of himself and to blunt his constant quest for freedom.

Confronting the Black Woman

Images of our suffering—as slaves, sharecroppers, industrial workers, and standing in unemployment lines—have been intermingled in our relationship with the Black woman. We have seen her straining under the hot southern sun, chopping cotton row upon row, and nursing our children on the side. We have witnessed her come home, tired and weary after working as a nurse, cook, or maid in white men's houses. We have seen her love of her children, her commitment to the church, her beauty and dignity in the face of political and economic exploitation. And yet, so much is left unsaid. All too often the Black male, in his own silent suffering, fails to communicate his love and deep respect for the mother, sister, grandmother, and wife who gave him the courage and commitment to strive for freedom. The veils of oppression, and the illusions of racial stereotypes, limit our ability to speak the inner truths about ourselves and our relationships to Black women.

The Black man's image of the past is, in most respects, a distortion of social reality. All of us can feel the anguish of our great-grandfathers as they witnessed their wives and daughters being raped by their white masters, or as they wept when their families were sold apart. But do we feel the double bondage of the Black woman, trying desperately to keep her family together and yet at times distrusted by her own Black man? Less than a generation ago, most Black male social scientists argued that the Black family was effectively destroyed by slavery; that the Black man was much less than a husband or father; and that the result was a "Black matriarchy" that crippled the economic, social, and political development of the Black community. Back in 1965, Black scholar C. Eric Lincoln declared that the slavery experience had "stripped the Negro male of his masculinity" and "condemned him to a eunuch-like exis-

tence in a culture that venerates masculine primacy." The rigid rules of Jim Crow applied more to Black men than to their women, according to Lincoln: "Because she was frequently the white man's mistress, the Negro woman occasionally flaunted the rules of segregation. . . . The Negro [male] did not earn rewards for being manly, courageous, or assertive, but for being accommodating—for fulfilling the stereotype of what he has been forced to be." The social by-product of Black demasculinization, concluded Lincoln, was the rise of Black matriarchs, who psychologically castrated their husbands and sons. "The Negro female has had the responsibility of the Negro family for so many generations that she accepts it, or assumes it, as second nature. Many older women have forgotten why the responsibility developed upon the Negro woman in the first place, or why it later became institutionalized," Lincoln argues. "And young Negro women do not think it absurd to reduce the relationship to a matter of money, since many of them probably grew up in families where the only income was earned by the mothers: the fathers may not have been in evidence at all." Other Black sociologists perpetuated these stereotypes, which only served to turn Black women and men against each other instead of focusing their energies and talents in the struggle for freedom.

Today's social science research on Black female–male relations tells us what our common sense should have indicated long ago—that the essence of Black family and community life has been a positive, constructive, and even heroic experience. Andrew Billingsley's *Black Families in White America* illustrates that the Black "extended family" is part of our African heritage that was never eradicated by slavery or segregation. The Black tradition of racial cooperation, the collectivist rather than individualistic ethos, is an outgrowth of the unique African heritage that we still maintain. It is clear that the Black woman was the primary transmitter and repositor of the cultural heritage of our people and played a central role in the socialization and guidance of Black male and female children. But this fact does not by any way justify the myth of a "Black matriarchy." Black women suffered from the economic exploitation and racism Black males experienced—but they also were trapped by institutional sexism and all of the various means of violence that have been used to oppress all women, such as rape, "wife beating," and sterilization. The majority of the Black poor throughout history have been overwhelmingly female; the lowest paid major group within the labor force in America is black women, not men.

In politics, the sense of the Black man's relations with Black women are again distorted by stereotypes. Most of us can cite the achievement of the great Black men who contributed to the freedom of our people: Frederick Douglass, W. E. B. Du Bois, Marcus Garvey, Martin Luther King, Jr., Malcolm X, Paul Robeson, Medgar Evers, A. Philip Randolph. Why then are we often forgetful of Harriet Tubman, the fearless conductor on the Underground Railroad, who spirited over 350 slaves into the North? What of Ida B. Wells, newspaper editor and antilynching activist; Mary Church Terrell, educator, member of the Washington, D.C., Board of Education from 1895 to 1906, and civil rights leader; Mary McLeod Bethune, college president and director of the Division of Negro Affairs for the National Youth Administration; and Fannie Lou Hamer, courageous desegregation leader in the South during the 1960s? In simple truth, the cause of Black freedom has been pursued by Black women and men equally. In Black literature, the eloquent appeals to racial equality penned by Richard Wright, James Baldwin, and Du Bois are paralleled in the works of Zora Neale Hurston, Alice Walker, and Toni Morrison. Martin Luther King, Jr., may have expressed for all of us our collective vision of equality in his "I Have a Dream" speech at the 1963 March on Washington—but it was the solitary act of defiance by the Black woman, Rosa Parks, that initiated the great Montgomery bus boycott in 1955 and gave birth to the modern civil rights movement. The struggle of our foremothers and forefathers transcends the barrier of gender, as Black women have tried to tell their men for generations. Beyond the stereotypes, we find a common heritage of suffering, and a common will to be free.

The Black Man Confronts Himself

The search for reality begins and ends with an assessment of the actual socioeconomic condition of Black males within the general context of the larger society. Beginning in the economic sphere, one finds that the illusion of Black male achievement in the marketplace is undermined by statistical evidence. Of the thousands of small businesses initiated by Black entrepreneurs each year, over 90 percent go bankrupt within thirty-six months. The Black businessman suffers from redlining policies of banks, which keep capital outside his hands. Only one out of two hundred Black businessmen have more than twenty paid employees, and over 80 percent of all Black men who start their own firms must hold a second job, working sixteen hours and more each day to provide greater opportunities for their families and communities. In terms of actual income, the gap between the Black man and the white man has increased in the past decade. According to the Bureau of Labor Statistics, in 1979 only forty-six thousand Black men earned salaries between $35,000 and $50,000 annually. Fourteen thousand Black men (and only two thousand Black women) earned $50,000 to $75,000 that year. And in the highest income level, $75,000 and above, there were four thousand Black males compared to five hundred and forty-eight thousand white males. This racial stratification is even sharper at the lower end of the income scale. Using 1978 poverty statistics, only 11.3

percent of all white males under fourteen years old live in poverty, while the figure for young Black males is 42 percent. Between the ages of fourteen and seventeen, 9.6 percent of white males and 38.6 percent of Black males are poor. In the age group eighteen to twenty-one years, 7.5 percent of white males and 26.1 percent of all Black males are poor. In virtually every oc-cupational category, Black men with identical or superior qualifications earn less than their white male counterparts. Black male furniture workers, for example, earn only 69 percent of white males' average wages; in printing and publishing, 68 percent; in all nonunion jobs, 62 percent.

Advances in high-technology leave Black males particularly vulnerable to even higher un-employment rates over the next decades. Mil-lions of Black men are located either in the "old line" industries such as steel, automobiles, rub-ber, and textiles, or in the public sector—both of which have experienced severe job contractions. In agriculture, to cite one typical instance, the disappearance of Black male workers is striking. As late as forty years ago, two out of every five Black men were either farmers or farm workers. In 1960, roughly 5 percent of all Black men were still employed in agriculture, and another 3 per-cent owned their own farms. By 1983, however, less than 130,000 Black men worked in agricul-ture. From 1959 to 1974, the number of Black-operated cotton farms in the South dropped from 87,074 to 1,569. Black tobacco farmers de-clined in number from 40,670 to barely 7,000 during the same period. About three out of four black men involved in farming today are not self-employed.

From both rural and urban environments, the numbers of jobless Black adult males have soared since the late 1960s. In 1969, for exam-ple, only 2.5 percent of all Black married males with families were unemployed. This percent-age increased to about 10 percent in the mid-1970s, and with the recession of 1982–1984 exceeded 15 percent. The total percentage of all Black families without a single income earner jumped from 10 percent in 1968 to 18.5 percent in 1977—and continued to climb into the 1990s.

These statistics fail to convey the human dimensions of the economic chaos of Black male joblessness. Thousands of jobless men are driven into petty crime annually, just to feed their families; others find temporary solace in drugs or alcohol. The collapse of thousands of black households and the steady proliferation of female-headed, single-parent households is a so-cial consequence of the systematic economic injustice inflicted upon Black males.

Racism also underscores the plight of Black males within the criminal justice system. Every year in this country there are over 2 million ar-rests of Black males. About three hundred thou-sand Black men are currently incarcerated in federal and state prisons or other penal institu-tions. At least half of the Black prisoners are less than thirty years of age, and over one thousand are not even old enough to vote. Most Black male prisoners were unemployed at the time of their arrests; the others averaged less than $8,000 annual incomes during the year before they were jailed. And about 45 percent of the thirteen hun-dred men currently awaiting capital punishment on death row are Afro-Americans. As Lennox S. Hinds, former National Director of the National Conference of Black Lawyers has stated, "Some-one black and poor tried for stealing a few hun-dred dollars has a 90 percent likelihood of being convicted of robbery with a sentence averaging between 94 to 138 months. A white business ex-ecutive who embezzled hundreds of thousands of dollars has only a 20 percent likelihood of con-viction with a sentence averaging about 20 to 48 months." Justice is not "color blind" when Black males are the accused.

What does the economic and social de-struction of Black males mean for the Black community as a whole? Dr. Robert Staples, as-sociate professor of sociology at the University of California–San Francisco, cites some devastating statistics of the current plight of younger Black males:

> Less than twenty percent of all black college graduates in the early 1980s are males. The vast majority of young black men who enter college drop out within two years.
>
> At least one-fourth of all black male teenagers never complete high school.
>
> Since 1960, black males between the ages of 15 to 20 have committed suicide at rates higher than that of the general white population. Suicide is currently the third leading cause of death, after homicides, and accidents, for black males aged 15 to 24.
>
> About half of all black men over age 18 have never been married [or are] separated, divorced, or widowed.
>
> Despite the fact that several million black male youths identify a career in professional athletics as a desirable career, the statistical probability of any black man making it to the pros exceeds 20,000 to one.
>
> One half of all homicides in America today are committed by black men—whose victims are other black men.
>
> The typical black adult male dies almost three years before he can even begin to collect Social Security.

Fred Clark, a staff psychologist for the California Youth Authority, states that the social devastation of an entire generation of Black males has made it extremely difficult for eligible Black women to locate partners. "In Washington, D.C., it is estimated that there is a one to twelve ratio of black [single] males to eligible females," Clark observes. "Some research indicates that the female is better suited for surviving alone than the male. There are more widowed and single black females than males. Males die earlier and more quickly than females when single. Single black welfare mothers seem to live longer than single unemployed black males."

Every socioeconomic and political indicator illustrates that the Black male in America is facing an unprecedented crisis. Despite singular examples of successful males in electoral politics, business, labor unions, and the professions, the overwhelming majority of Black men find it difficult to acquire self-confidence and self-esteem within the chaos of modern economic and social life. The stereotypes imposed by white history and by the lack of knowledge of our own past often convince many younger Black males that their struggle is too overwhelming. Black women have a responsibility to comprehend the forces that destroy the lives of thousands of their brothers, sons, and husbands. But Black men must understand that they, too, must overcome their own inherent and deeply ingrained sexism, recognizing that Black women must be equal partners in the battle to uproot injustice at every level of the society. The strongest ally Black men have in their battle to achieve Black freedom is the Black woman. Together, without illusions and false accusations, without racist and sexist stereotypes, they can achieve far more than they can ever accomplish alone.

References

Billingsley, A. 1968. *Black Families in White America.* Englewood Cliffs, NJ: Prentice-Hall.

Clark, K. 1965. *Dark Ghetto.* New York: Harper and Row.

Davis, A. Y. 1981. *Women, Race and Class.* New York: Random House.

Lincoln, C. E. 1965. "The Absent Father Haunts the Negro Family." *New York Times Magazine,* Nov. 28.

Marable, M. 1983. *How Capitalism Underdeveloped Black America.* Boston: South End Press.

3

ARTICLE

Maxine Baca Zinn

Chicano Men and Masculinity

Only recently have social scientists begun to systematically study the male role. Although men and their behavior had been assiduously studied (Pleck and Brannon, 1978), masculinity as a specific topic had been ignored. The scholar's disregard of male gender in the general population stands in contrast to the preoccupation with masculinity that has long been exhibited in the literature on minority groups. The social science literature on Blacks and Chicanos specifically reveals a long-standing interest in masculinity. A common assumption is that gender roles among Blacks are less dichotomous than among Whites, and more dichotomous among Chicanos. Furthermore, these differences are assumed to be a function of the distinctive historical and cultural heritage of these groups. Gender segregation and stratification, long considered to be a definitive characteristic of Chicanos, is illustrated in Miller's descriptive summary of the literature:

M. Baca Zinn, "Chicano Family Research: Conceptual distortions and alternative directions" appeared in *The Journal of Ethnic Studies* 10:2, pp. 29–44. Reprinted with permission.

Sex roles are rigidly dichotomized with the male conforming to the dominant–aggressive archetype, and the female being the polar opposite—subordinate and passive. The father is the unquestioned patriarch—the family provider, protector and judge. His word is law and demands strict obedience. Presumably, he is perpetually obsessed with the need to prove his manhood, oftentimes through excessive drinking, fighting, and/or extramarital conquests (1979:217).

The social science image of the Chicano male is rooted in three interrelated propositions: (1) That a distinctive cultural heritage has created a rigid cult of masculinity, (2) That the masculinity cult generates distinctive familial and socialization patterns, and (3) That these distinctive patterns ill-equip Chicanos (both males and females) to adapt successfully to the demands of modern society.

The machismo concept constitutes a primary explanatory variable for both family structure and overall subordination. Mirandé critically outlines the reasoning in this interpretation:

The macho male demands complete deference, respect and obedience not only from the wife but from the children as well. In fact, social scientists maintain that this rigid male-dominated family structure has negative consequences for the personality development of Mexican American children. It fails to engender achievement, independence, self-reliance or self-worth—values which are highly esteemed in American society.... The authoritarian Mexican American family constellation then produces dependence and subordination and reinforces a present time orientation which impedes achievement (1977:749).

In spite of the widely held interpretation associated with male dominance among Chicanos, there is a growing body of literature which refutes past images created by social scientists. My purpose is to examine empirical challenges to machismo, to explore theoretical developments in the general literature on gender, and to apply both of these to alternative directions for studying and understanding Chicano men and masculinity. My central theme is that while ethnic status may be associated with differences in masculinity, those differences can be explained by structural variables rather than by references to common cultural heritage.

Theoretical Challenges to Cultural Interpretations: The Universality of Male Dominance

The generalization that culture is a major determinant of gender is widely accepted in the social sciences. In the common portrayal of Chicanos, exaggerated male behavior is assumed to stem from inadequate masculine identity.

The social science literature views machismo as a compensation for feelings of inadequacy and worthlessness. This interpretation is rooted in the application of psychoanalytic concepts to explain both Mexican and Chicano gender roles. The widely accepted interpretation is that machismo is the male attempt to compensate for feelings of internalized inferiority by exaggerated masculinity. "At the same time that machismo is an expression of power, its origin is ironically linked to powerlessness and subordination." The common origins of inferiority and machismo are said to lie in the historical conquest of Mexico by Spain involving the exploitation of Indian women by Spanish men thus producing the hybrid Mexican people having an inferiority complex based on the mentality of a conquered people (Baca Zinn, 1980b:20).

The assumption that male dominance among Chicanos is rooted in their history and embedded in their culture needs to be critically assessed against recent discussions concerning the universality of male dominance. Many anthropologists consider all known societies to be male dominant to a degree (Stockard and Johnson 1980:4). It has been argued that in all known societies male activities are more highly valued than female activities, and that this can be explained in terms of the division of labor between domestic and public spheres of society (Rosaldo, 1973). Women's child-bearing abilities limit their participation in public sphere activities and allow men the freedom to participate in and control the public sphere. Thus in the power relations between the sexes, men have been found to be dominant over women and to control economic resources (Spence 1978:4).

While differing explanations of the cause of male dominance have been advanced, recent literature places emphasis on networks of social relations between men and women and the status structures within which their interactions occur. This emphasis is crucial because it alerts us to the importance of structural variables in understanding sex stratification. Furthermore, it casts doubt on interpretations which treat culture (the systems of shared beliefs and orientations unique to groups) as the cause of male dominance. If male dominance is universal, then it cannot be reduced to the culture of a particular category of people.

Challenges to Machismo

Early challenges to machismo emerged in the protest literature of the 1960s and 1970s and have continued unabated. Challenges are theoretical, empirical, and impressionistic. Montiel, in the first critique of machismo, set the stage for later refutations by charging that psychoanalytic constructs resulted in indiscriminate use of machismo, and that this made findings and interpretations highly suspect (1970). Baca Zinn (1975:25) argued that viewing machismo as a compensation for inferiority (whether its ultimate cause is seen as external or internal to the oppressed), in effect blames Chicanos for their own subordination. Sosa Riddell proposed that the machismo myth is exploited by an oppressive society which encourages a defensive stance on the part of Chicano men (1974). Delgado (1974:6) in similar fashion, wrote that stereotyping acts which have nothing to do with machismo and labeling them as such was a form of societal control.

Recent social science literature on Chicanos has witnessed an ongoing series of empirical challenges to the notion that machismo is the norm in marital relationships (Grebler, Moore, and Guzman, 1970; Hawkes and Taylor, 1975; Ybarra, 1977; Cromwell and Cromwell, 1978; Cromwell and Ruiz, 1979; Baca Zinn, 1980a). The evidence presented in this research suggests that in the realm of marital decision making, egalitarianism is far more prevalent than macho dominance.

Cromwell and Ruiz find that the macho characterization prevalent in the social science literature is "very compatible with the social deficit model of Hispanic life and culture" (1979:355). Their re-analysis of four major studies on marital decision making (Cromwell, Corrales, and Torsellio, 1973; Delchereo, 1969;

Hawkes and Taylor, 1975; and Cromwell and Cromwell, 1978) concludes that "the studies suggest that while wives make the fewest unilateral decisions and husbands make more, joint decisions are by far the most common in these samples . . ." (1979:370).

Other studies also confirm the existence of joint decision making in Chicano families and furthermore they provide insights as to factors associated with joint decision making, most importantly that of wives' employment. For example, Ybarra's survey of 100 married Chicano couples in Fresno, California, found a range of conjugal role patterns with the majority of married Chicano couples sharing decision making. Baca Zinn (1980a) examined the effects of wives' employment outside of the home and level of education through interviews and participation in an urban New Mexico setting. The study revealed differences in marital roles and marital power between families with employed wives and nonemployed wives. "In all families where women were not employed, tasks and decision making were typically sex segregated. However, in families with employed wives, tasks and decision making were shared" (1980a:51).

Studies of the father role in Chicano families also called into question the authoritative unfeeling masculinized male figure (Mejia, 1976; Luzod and Arce, 1979). These studies are broadly supportive of the marital role research which points to a more democratic egalitarian approach to family roles. Luzod and Arce conclude:

> It is not our contention to say that no sex role differences occur within Chicano families, but rather [that they] demonstrate the level of importance which both the father and mother give to respective duties as parents as well as the common hopes and desires they appear to share [more] equally for their progeny than was commonly thought. It therefore appears erroneous to focus only on maternal influences in the Chicano family since Chicano fathers are

seen as being important to the children and moreover may provide significant positive influences on the development of their children (1979:19).

Recent empirical refutations of supermasculinity in Chicano families have provided the basis of discussions of the Chicano male role (Valdez, 1980; Mirandé, 1979, 1981). While these works bring together in clear fashion impressionistic and empirical refutations of machismo, they should be considered critical reviews rather than conceptual refutations. In an important essay entitled, "Machismo: Rucas, Chingasos, y Chingaderas" (1981), Mirandé critically assesses the stereotypic components of machismo, yet he asserts that it also has authentic components having to do with the resistance of oppression. While this is a significant advance, it requires conceptual focus and analysis.

Unanswered Questions, Unresolved Issues, and Unrecognized Problems

The works discussed above provide a refutation of the simplistic, one-dimensional model of Chicano masculinity. As such they constitute important contributions to the literature. My own argument does not contradict the general conclusion that machismo is a stereotype, but attempts to expand it by posing some theoretical considerations.

In their eagerness to dispute machismo and the negative characteristics associated with the trait, critics have tended to neglect the phenomenon of male dominance at societal, institutional, and interpersonal levels. While the cultural stereotype of machismo has been in need of critical analysis, male dominance does exist among Chicanos. Assertions such as the following require careful examination:

There is sufficient evidence to seriously question the traditional male dominant view (Mirandé, 1979:47).

Although male dominance may not typify marital decision making in Chicano families, it should not be assumed that it is nonexistent either in families or in other realms of interaction and organization.

Research by Ybarra (1977) and Baca Zinn (1980) found both egalitarian and male-dominant patterns of interaction in Chicano families. They found these patterns to be associated with distinct social conditions of families, most notably wives' employment. The finding that male dominance can be present in some families but not in others, depending on specific social characteristics of family members, is common in family research.

The important point is that we need to know far more than we do about which social conditions affecting Chicanos are associated with egalitarianism and male dominance at both micro and macro levels of organization. Placing the question within this framework should provide significant insights by enlarging the inquiry beyond that of the culture stereotype of machismo. It is necessary to guard against measuring and evaluating empirical reality against this stereotype. The dangers of using a negative ideal as a normative guide are raised by Eichler (1980). In a provocative work, she raises the possibility that the literature challenging gender stereotypes, while explicitly attempting to overcome past limitations of the gender roles research may operate to reinforce the stereotype. Thus, it could be argued that energy expended in refuting machismo may devote too much attention to the concept, and overlook whole areas of inquiry. We have tended to assume that ethnic groups vary in the demands imposed on men and women. "Ethnic differences in sex roles have been discussed by large numbers of social scientists" (Romer and Cherry, 1980:246). However, these discussions have treated differences as cultural or subcultural in nature. Davidson and Gordon are critical of subcultural explanations of differences in gender roles because they "fail to investigate the larger political and economic situations that affect groups and individuals. They also fail to explain how definition of the roles of women and men, as well as those associated with ethnicity, vary over time and from place to place" (1979:124).

1. What specific social conditions are associated with variation in gender roles among Chicanos?
2. If there are ethnic differences in gender roles, to what extent are these a function of shared beliefs and orientations (culture) and to what extent are they a function of men's and women's place in the network of social relationships (structure)?
3. To what extent are gender roles among Chicanos more segregated and male dominated than among other social groups?
4. How does ethnicity contribute to the subjective meaning of masculinity (and femininity)?

Structural Interpretations of Gender Roles

There is a good deal of theoretical support for the contention that masculine roles and masculine identity may be shaped by a wide range of variables having less to do with culture than with common structural position. Chafetz calls into question the cultural stereotype of machismo by proposing that it is a socioeconomic characteristic:

> . . . more than most other Americans, the various Spanish speaking groups in this country (Mexican American, Puerto Rican, Cuban), . . .

stress dominance, aggressiveness, physical prowess and other stereotypical masculine traits. Indeed the masculine sex role for this group is generally described by reference to the highly stereotyped notion of machismo. In fact, a strong emphasis on masculine aggressiveness and dominance may be characteristic of most groups in the lower ranges of the socioeconomic ladder (1979:54).

Without discounting the possibility that cultural differences in male roles exist, it makes good conceptual sense to explain these differences in terms of sociostructural factors. Davidson and Gordon suggest that the following social conditions affect the development of gender roles in ethnic groups: (1) the position of the group in the stratification system, (2) the existence of an ethnic community, (3) the degree of self identification with the minority group (1979:120). Romer and Cherry more specifically propose that ethnic or subcultural sex role definitions can be viewed as functions of the specific and multiple role demands made on a given subgroup such as skilled or unskilled workers, consumers, etc., and the cultural prism through which these role expectations are viewed (1980:246). Both of these discussions underscore the importance of the societal placement of ethnics in the shaping of gender roles. This line of reasoning should not be confused with "culture of poverty" models which posit distinctive subcultural traits among the lower class. However, it can be argued that class position affects both normative and behavioral dimensions of masculinity.

The assumption that Chicanos are more strongly sex typed in terms of masculine identity is called into question by a recent study. Senour and Warren conducted research to question whether ethnic identity is related to masculine and feminine sex role orientation among Blacks, Anglos, and Chicanos. While significant sex differences were found in all categories, Senour and Warren concluded that Mexican American males did not emerge as super masculine in comparison to Black and Anglo males (1976:2).

There is some support for this interpretation. In roles dealing with masculinity among Black males, Parker and Kleiner (1977) and Staples (1978) find that role performance must be seen in light of the structurally generated inequality in employment, housing, and general social conditions. Staples writes:

> . . . men often define their masculinity in terms of the ability to impregnate women and to reproduce prolifically children who are extensions of themselves, especially sons. For many lower income black males there is an inseparable link between their self image as men and their ability to have sexual relations with women and the subsequent birth of children from those sexual acts. At the root of this virility cult is the lack of role fulfillment available to men of the underclass. The class factor is most evident here, if we note that middle class black males sire fewer children than any other group in this society (1978:178).

What is most enlightening about Staples' discussion of masculinity is that it treats male behavior and male identity not as a subcultural phenomenon, but as a consequence of social structural factors associated with race and class.

A thoughtful discussion of inequality, race, and gender is provided by Lewis (1977). Her analysis enlarges upon Rosaldo's model of the domestic public split as the source of female subordination and male dominance discussed earlier. It has pertinent structural considerations. Lewis acknowledges the notion of a structural opposition between the domestic and public spheres which offers useful insights in understanding differential participation and evaluation of men and women. Nevertheless, she argues that its applicability to racial minority men and women may be questionable since historically Black men (like Black women) have been excluded from participation in public sphere institutions. Lewis asserts:

> What the black experience suggests is that differential participation in the public sphere is a symptom rather than a cause of structural inequality. While inequality is manifested in the exclusion of a group from public life, it is actually generated in the groups' unequal access to power and resources in a hierarchically arranged social order. Relationships of dominance and subordination, therefore, emerge from a basic structural opposition between groups which is reflected in exclusion of the subordinate group from public life (1977:342).

Lewis then argues that among racially oppressed groups, it is important to distinguish between the public life of the dominant and the dominated societies. Using this framework we recognize a range of male participation from token admittance to the public life of the dominant group to its attempts to destroy the public life within a dominated society. She points to the fact that Mexican American men have played strong public roles in their own dominated society, and as Mexican Americans have become more assimilated to the dominating society, sex roles have become less hierarchical. The significant feature of this argument has to do with the way in which attention is brought to shifts in power relationships between the dominant society and racial minorities, and how these shifts effect changes in relationships between the sexes. Lewis' analysis makes it abundantly clear that minority males' exclusion from the public sphere requires further attention.

Chicano Masculinity as a Response to Stratification and Exclusion

There are no works, either theoretical or empirical, specifically devoted to the impact of structural exclusion on male roles and male identity.

However, there are suggestions that the emphasis on masculinity might stem from the fact that alternative roles and identity sources are systematically blocked from men in certain social categories. Lillian Rubin, for example, described the marital role egalitarianism of middle-class professional husbands as opposed to the more traditional authoritarian role of working class husbands in the following manner:

> . . . the professional male is more secure, has more status and prestige than the working class man, factors which enable him to assume a less overtly authoritarian role within the family. There are, after all, other places, other situations where his authority and power are tested and accorded legitimacy. At the same time, the demands of his work role for a satellite wife require that he risk the consequences of a more egalitarian family ideology. In contrast, for the working class men, there are few such rewards in the world outside the home. The family is usually the only place where he can exercise power, demand obedience to his authority. Since his work role makes no demands for wifely participation, he is under fewer and less immediate external pressures to accept the egalitarian ideology (Rubin, 1976:99).

Of course, Rubin is contrasting behaviors of men in different social classes, but the same line of thinking is paralleled in Ramos' speculation that for some Chicanos what has been called "machismo" may be a "way of feeling capable in a world that makes it difficult for Chicanos to demonstrate their capabilities" (Ramos, 1979:61).

We must understand that while maleness is highly valued in our society, it interacts with other categorical distinctions in both manifestation and meaning. As Stoll (1974:124) presents this idea, our society is structured to reward some categories in preference to others (e.g., men over women) but the system is not perfectly rational. First, the rewards are scarce; second, other categories such as race, ethnicity, and

other statuses are included in the formula. Furthermore, the interaction of different categories with masculinity contributes to multiple societal meanings of masculinity, so that "one can never be sure this aspect of one's self will not be called into dispute. One is left having to account for oneself, thus to be on the defensive" (Stoll, 1974:124). It is in light of the societal importance attributed to masculinity that we must assess Stoll's contention that "gender identity is a more profound personal concern for the male in our society than it is for women, because women can take it for granted that they are female" (Stoll, 1974:105). This speculation may have implications for Chicanos as well. Perhaps it will be found that ethnic differences in the salience of gender are not only one of degree but that their relative significance has different meanings. In other words, gender may not be a problematic identifier for women if they can take it for granted, though it may be primary because many still participate in society through their gender roles. On the other hand, men in certain social categories have had more roles and sources of identity open to them. However, this has not been the case for Chicanos or other men of color. Perhaps manhood takes on greater importance for those who do not have access to socially valued roles. Being male is one sure way to acquire status when other roles are systematically denied by the workings of society. This suggests that an emphasis on masculinity is not due to a collective internalized inferiority, rooted in a subcultural orientation. To be "hombre" may be a reflection of both ethnic and gender components and may take on greater significance when other roles and sources of masculine identity are structurally blocked. Chicanos have been excluded from participation in the dominant society's political–economic system. Therefore, they have been denied resources and the accompanying authority accorded men in other social categories. My point that gender may take on a unique and greater significance for men of color is not to justify traditional masculinity, but to point to the need for understanding societal conditions that might contribute to the meaning of gender among different social categories. It may be worthwhile to consider some expressions of masculinity as attempts to gain some measure of control in a society that categorically denies or grants people control over significant realms of their lives.

Turner makes this point about the male posturing of Black men: "Boastful, or meek, these performances are attempts by black men to actualize control in some situation" (Turner, 1977:128). Much the same point is made in discussions of Chicanos. The possibility has been raised that certain aggressive behaviors on the part of Chicano men were "a calculated response to hostility, exclusion, and racial domination," and a "conscious rejection of the dominant society's definition of Mexicans as passive, lazy, and indifferent" (Baca Zinn, 1975:23). Mirandé (1981:35) also treats machismo as an adaptive characteristic, associated with visible and manifest resistance of Chicano men to racial oppression. To view Chicano male behavior in this light is not to disregard possible maladaptive consequences of overcompensatory masculinity, but rather to recast masculinity in terms of responses to structural conditions.

Differences in normative and behavioral dimensions of masculinity would be well worth exploring. Though numerous recent studies have challenged macho male dominance in the realm of family decision making, there is also evidence that patriarchal *ideology* can be manifested even in Chicano families where decision making is not male dominant. Baca Zinn's findings of *both* male dominant and egalitarian families revealed also that the ideology of patriarchy was expressed in all families studied:

> Patriarchal ideology was expressed in statements referring to the father as the "head" of the family, as the "boss," as the one "in charge." Informants continually expressed their beliefs that it "should be so." Findings confirmed that

while male dominance was a cultural ideal, employed wives openly challenged that dominance on a behavioral level (1975:15).

It is possible that such an ideology is somehow associated with family solidarity. This insight is derived from Michel's analysis of family values (cited in Goode, 1963:57). Drawing on cross cultural studies, she reports:

> . . . the concept of the strength or solidarity of the family is viewed as being identical with the father . . . the unity of the family is identified with the prerogatives of the father.

If this is the case, it is reasonable to suggest that the father's authority is strongly upheld because family solidarity is important in a society that excludes and subordinates Chicanos. The tenacity of patriarchy may be more than a holdover from past tradition. It may also represent a contemporary cultural adaptation to the minority condition of structural discrimination.

Conclusion

The assumption that male dominance among Chicanos is exclusively a cultural phenomenon is contradicted by much evidence. While many of the concerns raised in this paper are speculative in nature, they are nevertheless informed by current conceptualization in relevant bodies of literature. They raise the important point that we need further understanding of larger societal conditions in which masculinity is embedded and expressed. This forces us to recognize the disturbing relationship between the stratification axes of race, class, and sex. To the extent that systems of social inequality limit men's access to societally valued resources, they also contribute to sexual stratification. Men in some social categories will continue to draw upon and accentuate their masculinity as a socially valued resource. This in turn poses serious threats to sexual equality. We are compelled to move the study of masculinity beyond narrow confines of subcultural roles, and to make the necessary theoretical and empirical connections between the contingencies of sex and gender and the social order.

References

Baca Zinn, Maxine.

1975 "Political Familism: Toward Sex Role Equality in Chicano Families," *International Journal of Chicano Studies Research* 6:13–26.

1980a "Employment and Education of Mexican American Women: The Interplay of Modernity and Ethnicity in Eight Families." *Harvard Educational Review* 50:47–62.

1980b "Gender and Ethnic Identity Among Chicanos." *Frontiers*: V(2)18–24.

Chafetz, Janet Saltzman.

1974 *Masculine/Feminine or Human*. E. E. Itasca. Ill.: Peacock Publishers, Inc.

Cromwell, Vicky L. and Ronald E. Cromwell.

1978 "Perceived Dominance in Decision-Making and Conflict Resolution Among Anglo, Black and Chicano Couples." *Journal of Marriage and the Family*. 40(Nov.):749–759.

Cromwell, Ronald E. and Rene E. Ruiz.

1979 "The Myth of Macho Dominance in Decision Making Within Mexican and Chicano Families." *Hispanic Journal of Behavioral Sciences*. 1:355–373.

Davidson, Laurie and Laura Kramer Gordon.

1979 *The Sociology of Gender*. Rand McNally College Publishing Co.

Delgado, Abelardo.

1974 "Machismo." *La Luz*. (Dec.):6.

Eichler, Margrit.

1980 *The Double Standard: A Feminist Critique of Feminist Social Science*. St. Martin's Press.

Grebler, Leo, Joan W. Moore and Ralph C. Guzman.

1970 *The Mexican American People: The Nation's Second Largest Minority*. New York: The Free Press.

Hawkes, Glenn R. and Minna Taylor.

1975 "Power Structure in Mexican and Mexican-American Farm Labor Families." *Journal of Marriage and the Family*. 37:807–811.

Hyde, Janet Shibley and B. G. Rosenberg.

1976 Half the Human Experience. *The Psychology of Women*. D. C. Heath and Company.

Lewis, Diane K.

1977 "A Response to Inequality: Black Women, Racism, and Sexism." *SIGNS: Journal of Women in Culture and Society*. 3:339–361.

Luzod, Jimmy A. and Carlos H. Arce.

1979 "An Exploration of the Father Role in the Chicano Family." Paper presented at the National Symposium on the Mexican American Child. Santa Barbara, California.

Mejia, Daniel P.

1976 Cross-Ethnic Father Role: Perceptions of Middle Class Anglo American Parents, Doctoral Dissertation, University of California, Irvine.

Miller, Michael V.

1975 "Variations in Mexican-American Family Life: A Review Synthesis." Paper presented at Rural Sociological Society, San Francisco, California.

Mirandé, Alfredo.

1977 "The Chicano Family: A Reanalysis of Conflicting Views." *Journal of Marriage and the Family*. 39:747–756.

1979 "A Reinterpretation of Male Dominance in the Chicano Family." *Family Coordinator* 28(4): 473–497.

1981 "Machismo: Rucas, Chingasos, y Chingaderas." *De Colores*, Forthcoming.

Montiel, Miguel.

1970 "The Social Science Myth of the Mexican American Family." *El Grito*. 3:56–63.

Parker, Seymour and Robert J. Kleiner.

1977 "Social and Psychological Dimensions of the Family Role Performance of the Negro Male." Pp. 102–117 in Doris Y. Wilkinson and Ronald L. Taylor (editors), *The Black Male in America*. Nelson-Hall.

Pleck, Joseph H. and Robert Brannon.

1978 "Male Roles and the Male Experience: Introduction." *Journal of Social Issues*. 34:1–4.

Ramos, Reyes.

1979 "The Mexican American: Am I Who They Say I Am?" Pp. 49–66 in Arnulfo D. Trejo (editor), *The Chicanos as We See Ourselves*. The University of Arizona Press.

Riddell, Adaljisa Sosa.

1974 "Chicanas and El Movimiento." *Aztlan*. 5(1 and 2):155–165.

Romer, Nancy and Debra Cherry.

1980 "Ethnic and Social Class Differences in Children's Sex-Role Concepts." *Sex Roles*. 6:245–263.

Rosaldo, Michelle and Louise Lamphere.

1974 *Woman, Culture, and Society*. Stanford: Stanford University Press.

Rubin, Lillian.

1976 *Worlds of Pain*. Basic Books.

Senour, Maria Neito and Lynda Warren.

1976 "Sex and Ethnic Differences in Masculinity, Femininity and Anthropology." Paper presented at the meeting of the Western Psychological Association, Los Angeles, California.

Spence, Janet T. and Robert L. Helmreich.

1978 *Masculinity and Femininity: The Psychological Dimensions, Correlates and Antecedents*. University of Austin Press.

Staples, Robert.

1978 "Masculinity and Race: The Dual Dilemma of Black Men." *Journal of Social Issues*. 34:169–183.

Stockard, Jean and Miriam M. Johnson.

1980 *Sex Roles*. Englewood Cliffs, New Jersey: Prentice-Hall

Stoll, Clarice Stasz.

1974 *Male and Female: Socialization, Social Roles, and Social Structure*. William C. Brown Publishers.

Turner, William H.

1977 "Myths and Stereotypes: The African Man in America." Pp. 122–144 in Doris Y. Wilkinson and Ronald L. Taylor (editors), *The Black Male in America*. Nelson-Hall.

Valdez, Ramiro.

1980 "The Mexican American Male: A Brief Review of the Literature." *Newsletter of the Mental Health Research Project*, I.D.R.A. San Antonio: 4–5.

Ybarra-Soriano, Lea.

1977 *Conjugal Role Relationships in the Chicano Family*. Ph.D. diss. University of California at Berkeley.

ARTICLE

Yen Le Espiritu

All Men Are *Not* Created Equal: Asian Men in U.S. History

Today, virtually every major metropolitan market across the United States has at least one Asian American female newscaster. In contrast, there is a nearly total absence of Asian American men in anchor positions (Hamamoto, 1994, p. 245; Fong-Torres, 1995). This gender imbalance in television news broadcasting exemplifies the racialization of Asian American manhood: Historically, they have been depicted as either asexual or hypersexual; today, they are constructed to be less successful, assimilated, attractive, and desirable than their female counterparts (Espiritu, 1996, pp. 95–98). The exclusion of Asian men from Eurocentric notions of the masculine reminds us that not all men benefit—or benefit equally—from a patriarchal system designed to maintain the unequal relationship that exists between men and women. The feminist mandate for gender solidarity tends to ignore power differentials among men, among women, and between white women and men of color. This exclusive focus on gender bars traditional feminists from recognizing the oppression of men of color: the fact that there are men, and not only women, who have been "feminized"

Reprinted by permission of the author.

and the fact that some white middle-class women hold cultural power and class power over certain men of color (Cheung, 1990, pp. 245–246; Wiegman, 1991, p. 311). Presenting race and gender as relationally constructed, King-Kok Cheung (1990) exhorted white scholars to acknowledge that, like female voices, "the voices of many men of color have been historically silenced or dismissed" (p. 246). Along the same line, black feminists have referred to "racial patriarchy"—a concept that calls attention to the white/patriarch master in U.S. history and his dominance over the black male as well as the black female (Gaines, 1990, p. 202).

Throughout their history in the United States, Asian American men, as immigrants and citizens of color, have faced a variety of economic, political, and ideological racism that have assaulted their manhood. During the pre–World War II period, racialized and gendered immigration policies and labor conditions emasculated Asian men, forcing them into womanless communities and into "feminized" jobs that had gone unfilled due to the absence of women. During World War II, the internment of Japanese Americans stripped Issei (first generation) men of their role as the family breadwinner, transferred some of their power and status to the U.S.-born children, and decreased male dominance over women. In the contemporary period, the patriarchal authority of Asian immigrant men, particularly those of the working class, has also been challenged due to the social and economic losses that they suffered in their transition to life in the United States. As detailed below, these three historically specific cases establish that the material existences of Asian American men have historically contradicted the Eurocentric, middle-class constructions of manhood.

Asian Men in Domestic Service

Feminist scholars have argued accurately that domestic service involves a three-way relationship between privileged white men, privileged white women, and poor women of color (Romero, 1992). But women have not been the only domestic workers. During the pre–World War II period, racialized and gendered immigration policies and labor conditions forced Asian men into "feminized" jobs such as domestic service, laundry work, and food preparation.[1] Due to their noncitizen status, the closed labor market, and the shortage of women, Asian immigrant men, first Chinese and later Japanese, substituted to some extent for female labor in the American West. David Katzman (1978) noted the peculiarities of the domestic labor situation in the West in this period: "In 1880, California and Washington were the only states in which a majority of domestic servants were men" (p. 55).

At the turn of the twentieth century, lacking other job alternatives, many Chinese men entered into domestic service in private homes, hotels, and rooming houses (Daniels, 1988, p. 74). Whites rarely objected to Chinese in domestic service. In fact, through the 1900s, the Chinese houseboy was the symbol of upper-class status in San Francisco (Glenn, 1986, p. 106). As

late as 1920, close to 50 percent of the Chinese in the United States were still occupied as domestic servants (Light, 1972, p. 7). Large numbers of Chinese also became laundrymen, not because laundering was a traditional male occupation in China, but because there were very few women of any ethnic origin—and thus few washerwomen—in gold-rush California (Chan, 1991, pp. 33–34). Chinese laundrymen thus provided commercial services that replaced women's unpaid labor in the home. White consumers were prepared to patronize a Chinese laundryman because as such he "occupied a status which was in accordance with the social definition of the place in the economic hierarchy suitable for a member of an 'inferior race'" (cited in Siu, 1987, p. 21). In her autobiographical fiction *China Men*, Maxine Hong Kingston presents her father and his partners as engaged in their laundry business for long periods each day—a business considered so low and debased that, in their songs, they associate it with the washing of menstrual blood (Goellnicht, 1992, p. 198). The existence of the Chinese houseboy and launderer—and their forced "bachelor" status—further bolstered the stereotype of the feminized and asexual or homosexual Asian man. Their feminization, in turn, confirmed their assignment to the state's labor force which performed "women's work."

Japanese men followed Chinese men into domestic service. By the end of the first decade of the twentieth century, the U.S. Immigration Commission estimated that 12,000 to 15,000 Japanese in the western United States earned a living in domestic service (Chan, 1991, pp. 39–40). Many Japanese men considered housework beneath them because in Japan only lower-class women worked as domestic servants (Ichioka, 1988, p. 24). Studies of Issei occupational histories indicate that a domestic job was the first occupation for many of the new arrivals; but unlike Chinese domestic workers, most Issei eventually moved on to agricultural or city trades (Glenn, 1986, p. 108). Filipino and Korean boys and men likewise relied on domestic service for their livelihood (Chan, 1991, p. 40). In his autobiography *East Goes West*, Korean immigrant writer Younghill Kang (1937) related that he worked as a domestic servant for a white family who treated him "like a cat or a dog" (p. 66).

Filipinos, as stewards in the U.S. Navy, also performed domestic duties for white U.S. naval officers. During the ninety-four years of U.S. military presence in the Philippines, U.S. bases served as recruiting stations for the U.S. armed forces, particularly the navy. Soon after the United States acquired the Philippines from Spain in 1898, its navy began actively recruiting Filipinos—but only as stewards and mess attendants. Barred from admissions to other ratings, Filipino enlistees performed the work of domestics, preparing and serving the officers' meals, and caring for the officers' galley, wardroom, and living spaces. Ashore, their duties ranged from ordinary housework to food services at the U.S. Naval Academy hall. Unofficially, Filipino stewards also have been ordered to perform menial chores such as walking the officers' dogs and acting as personal servants for the officers' wives (Espiritu, 1995, p. 16).

As domestic servants, Asian men became subordinates of not only privileged white men but also privileged white women. The following testimony from a Japanese house servant captures this unequal relationship:

> Immediately the ma'am demanded me to scrub the floor. I took one hour to finish. Then I had to wash windows. That was very difficult job for me. Three windows for another hour! . . . The ma'am taught me how to cook. . . . I was sitting on the kitchen chair and thinking what a change of life it was. The ma'am came into the kitchen and was so furious! It was such a hard work for me to wash up all dishes, pans, glasses, etc., after dinner. When I went into the dining room to put all silvers on sideboard, I saw the reflection of myself on the looking glass. In a white coat and apron! I could not control my feelings.

> The tears so freely flowed out from my eyes, and I buried my face with my both arms (quoted in Ichioka, 1988, pp. 25–26).

The experiences of Asian male domestic service workers demonstrate that not all men benefit equally from patriarchy. Depending on their race and class, men experience gender differently. While male domination of women may tie all men together, men share unequally in the fruits of this domination. For Asian American male domestic workers, economic and social discriminations locked them into an unequal relationship with not only privileged white men but also privileged white women (Kim, 1990, p. 74).

The racist and classist devaluation of Asian men had gender implications. The available evidence indicates that immigrant men reasserted their lost patriarchal power in racist America by denigrating a weaker group: Asian women. In *China Men*, Kingston's immigrant father, having been forced into "feminine" subject positions, lapses into silence, breaking the silence only to utter curses against women (Goellnicht, 1992, pp. 200–201). Kingston (1980) traces her father's abuse of Chinese women back to his feeling of emasculation in America: "We knew that it was to feed us you had to endure demons and physical labor" (p. 13). On the other hand, some men brought home the domestic skills they learned on the jobs. Anamaria Labao Cabato relates that her Filipino-born father, who spent twenty-eight years in the navy as a steward, is "one of the best cooks around" (Espiritu, 1995, p. 143). Leo Sicat, a retired U.S. Navy man, similarly reports that "we learned how to cook in the Navy, and we brought it home. The Filipino women are very fortunate because the husband does the cooking. In our household, I do the cooking, and my wife does the washing" (Espiritu, 1995, p. 108). Along the same line, in some instances, the domestic skills which men were forced to learn in their wives' absence were put to use when husbands and wives reunited in the United

States. The history of Asian male domestic workers suggests that the denigration of women is only one response to the stripping of male privilege. The other is to institute a revised domestic division of labor and gender relations in the families.

Changing Gender Relations: The Wartime Internment of Japanese Americans

Immediately after the bombing of Pearl Harbor, the incarceration of Japanese Americans began. On the night of 7 December 1941, working on the principle of guilt by association, the Federal Bureau of Investigation (FBI) began taking into custody persons of Japanese ancestry who had connections to the Japanese government. On 19 February 1942, President Franklin Delano Roosevelt signed Executive Order 9066, arbitrarily suspending civil rights of U.S. citizens by authorizing the "evacuation" of 120,000 persons of Japanese ancestry into concentration camps, of whom approximately fifty percent were women and sixty percent were U.S.-born citizens (Matsumoto, 1989, p. 116).

The camp environment—with its lack of privacy, regimented routines, and new power hierarchy—inflicted serious and lasting wounds on Japanese American family life. In the crammed twenty-by-twenty-five-foot "apartment" units, tensions were high as men, women, and children struggled to recreate family life under very trying conditions. The internment also transformed the balance of power in families: husbands lost some of their power over wives, as did parents over children. Until the internment, the Issei man had been the undisputed authority over his wife and children: he was both the breadwinner and the decision-maker for the entire family. Now "he had no rights, no home, no

control over his own life" (Houston and Houston, 1973, p. 62). Most important, the internment reverted the economic roles—and thus the status and authority—of family members. With their means of livelihood cut off indefinitely, Issei men lost their role as breadwinners. Despondent over the loss of almost everything they had worked so hard to acquire, many Issei men felt useless and frustrated, particularly as their wives and children became less dependent on them. Daisuke Kitagawa (1967) reports that in the Tule Lake relocation center, "the [Issei] men looked as if they had suddenly aged in ten years. They lost the capacity to plan for their own futures, let alone those of their sons and daughters" (p. 91).

Issei men responded to this emasculation in various ways. By the end of three years' internment, formerly enterprising, energetic Issei men had become immobilized with feelings of despair, hopelessness, and insecurity. Charles Kikuchi remembers his father—who "used to be a perfect terror and dictator"—spending all day lying on his cot: "He probably realizes that he no longer controls the family group and rarely exerts himself so that there is little family conflict as far as he is concerned" (Modell, 1973, p. 62). But others, like Jeanne Wakatsuki Houston's father, reasserted their patriarchal power by abusing their wives and children. Stripped of his roles as the protector and provider for his family, Houston's father "kept pursuing oblivion through drink, he kept abusing Mama, and there seemed to be no way out of it for anyone. You couldn't even run" (Houston and Houston, 1973, p. 61). The experiences of the Issei men underscore the intersections of racism and sexism—the fact that men of color live in a society that creates sex-based norms and expectations (i.e., man as breadwinner) which racism operates simultaneously to deny (Crenshaw, 1989, p. 155).

Camp life also widened the distance and deepened the conflict between the Issei and their U.S.-born children. At the root of these tensions were growing cultural rifts between the generations as well as a decline in the power and authority of the Issei fathers. The cultural rifts reflected not only a general process of acculturation, but were accelerated by the degradation of everything Japanese and the simultaneous promotion of Americanization in the camps (Chan, 1991, p. 128; see also Okihiro, 1991, pp. 229–232). The younger Nisei also spent much more time away from their parents' supervision. As a consequence, Issei parents gradually lost their ability to discipline their children, whom they seldom saw during the day. Much to the chagrin of the conservative parents, young men and women began to spend more time with each other unchaperoned—at the sports events, the dances, and other school functions. Freed from some of the parental constraints, the Nisei women socialized more with their peers and also expected to choose their own husbands and to marry for "love"—a departure from the old customs of arranged marriage (Matsumoto, 1989, p. 117). Once this occurred, the prominent role that the father plays in marriage arrangements—and by extension in their children's lives—declined (Okihiro, 1991, p. 231).

Privileging U.S. citizenship and U.S. education, War Relocation Authority (WRA) policies regarding camp life further reverted the power hierarchy between the Japan-born Issei and their U.S.-born children. In the camps, only Nisei were eligible to vote and to hold office in the Community Council; Issei were excluded because of their alien status. Daisuke Kitagawa (1967) records the impact of this policy on parental authority: "In the eyes of young children, their parents were definitely inferior to their grown-up brothers and sisters, who as U.S. citizens could elect and be elected members of the Community Council. For all these reasons many youngsters lost confidence in, and respect for, their parents" (p. 88). Similarly, the WRA salary scales were based on English-speaking ability and on citizenship status. As a result, the Nisei youths and young adults could earn relatively higher wages than their fathers.

This shift in earning abilities eroded the economic basis for parental authority (Matsumoto, 1989, p. 116).

At war's end in August 1945, Japanese Americans had lost much of the economic ground that they had gained in more than a generation. The majority of Issei women and men no longer had their farms, businesses, and financial savings; those who still owned property found their homes dilapidated and vandalized and their personal belongings stolen or destroyed (Broom and Riemer, 1949). The internment also ended Japanese American concentration in agriculture and small businesses. In their absence, other groups had taken over these ethnic niches. This loss further eroded the economic basis of parental authority since Issei men no longer had businesses to hand down to their Nisei sons (Broom and Riemer, 1949, p. 31). Historian Roger Daniels (1988) declared that by the end of World War II, "the generational struggle was over: the day of the Issei had passed" (286). Issei men, now in their sixties, no longer had the vigor to start over from scratch. Forced to find employment quickly after the war, many Issei couples who had owned small businesses before the war returned to the forms of manual labor in which they began a generation ago. Most men found work as janitors, gardeners, kitchen helpers, and handymen; their wives toiled as domestic servants, garment workers, and cannery workers (Yanagisako, 1987, p. 92).

Contemporary Asian America: The Disadvantaged

Relative to earlier historical periods, the economic pattern of contemporary Asian America is considerably more varied, a result of both the postwar restructured economy and the 1965 Immigration Act.[2] The dual goals of the 1965 Immigration Act—to facilitate family reunification and to admit educated workers needed by the U.S. economy—have produced two distinct chains of emigration from Asia: one comprising the relatives of working-class Asians who had immigrated to the United States prior to 1965; the other of highly trained immigrants who entered during the late 1960s and early 1970s (Liu, Ong, and Rosenstein, 1991). Given their dissimilar backgrounds, Asian Americans "can be found throughout the income spectrum of this nation" (Ong, 1994, p. 4). In other words, today's Asian American men both join whites in the well-paid, educated, white collar sector of the workforce *and* join Latino immigrants in lower-paying secondary sector jobs (Ong and Hee, 1994). This economic diversity contradicts the model minority stereotype—the common belief that most Asian American men are college educated and in high-paying professional or technical jobs.

The contemporary Asian American community includes a sizable population with limited education, skills, and English-speaking ability. In 1990, 18 percent of Asian men and 26 percent of Asian women in the United States, age 25 and over, had less than a high school degree. Also, of the 4.1 million Asians 5 years and over, 56 percent did not speak English "very well" and 35 percent were linguistically isolated (U.S. Bureau of the Census, 1993, Table 2). The median income for those with limited English was $20,000 for males and $15,600 for females; for those with less than a high school degree, the figures were $18,000 and $15,000, respectively. Asian American men and women with both limited English-speaking ability and low levels of education fared the worst. For a large portion of this disadvantaged population, even working full-time, full-year brought in less than $10,000 in earnings (Ong and Hee, 1994, p. 45).

The disadvantaged population is largely a product of immigration: Nine tenths are immigrants (Ong and Hee, 1994). The majority enter as relatives of the pre-1956 working-class Asian immigrants. Because immigrants tend to have socioeconomic backgrounds similar to those of their sponsors, most family reunification immigrants represent a continuation of the unskilled and semiskilled Asian labor that emigrated before 1956 (Liu, Ong, and Rosenstein, 1991). Southeast Asian refugees, particularly the second-wave refugees who arrived after 1978, represent another largely disadvantaged group. This is partly so because refugees are less likely to have acquired readily transferable skills and are more likely to have made investments (in training and education) specific to the country of origin (Chiswick, 1979; Montero, 1980). For example, there are significant numbers of Southeast Asian military men with skills for which there is no longer a market in the United States. In 1990, the overall economic status of the Southeast Asian population was characterized by unstable, minimum-wage employment, welfare dependency, and participation in the informal economy (Gold and Kibria, 1993). These economic facts underscore the danger of lumping all Asian Americans together because many Asian men do not share in the relatively favorable socioeconomic outcomes attributed to the "average" Asian American.

Lacking the skills and education to catapult them into the primary sector of the economy, disadvantaged Asian American men and women work in the secondary labor market—the labor-intensive, low-capital service, and small manufacturing sectors. In this labor market, disadvantaged men generally have fewer employment options than women. This is due in part to the decline of male-occupied manufacturing jobs and the concurrent growth of female-intensive industries in the United States, particularly in service, microelectronics, and apparel manufacturing. The garment industry, microelectronics, and canning industries are top employers of immigrant women (Takaki, 1989, p. 427; Mazumdar, 1989, p. 19; Villones, 1989, p. 176; Hossfeld, 1994, pp. 71–72). In a study of Silicon Valley (California's famed high-tech industrial region), Karen Hossfeld (1994) reported that the employers interviewed preferred to hire immigrant women over immigrant men for entry-level, operative jobs (p. 74). The employers' "gender logic" was informed by the patriarchal and racist beliefs that women can afford to work for less, do not mind dead-end jobs, and are more suited physiologically to certain kinds of detailed and routine work. As Linda Lim (1983) observes, it is the "*comparative disadvantage* of women in the wage-labor market that gives them a comparative advantage vis-à-vis men in the occupations and industries where they are concentrated—so-called female ghettoes of employment" (p. 78). A white male production manager and hiring supervisor in a California Silicon Valley assembly shop discusses his formula for hiring:

> Just three things I look for in hiring [entry-level, high-tech manufacturing operatives]: small, foreign, and female. You find those three things and you're pretty much automatically guaranteed the right kind of work force. These little foreign gals are grateful to be hired—very, very grateful—no matter what (Hossfeld, 1994, p. 65).

Refugee women have also been found to be more in demand than men in secretarial, clerical, and interpreter jobs in social service work. In a study of Cambodian refugees in Stockton, California, Shiori Ui (1991) found that social service agency executives preferred to hire Cambodian women over men when both had the same qualifications. One executive explained his preference, "It seems that some ethnic populations relate better to women than men. . . . Another thing is that the pay is so bad" (cited in Ui, 1991, p. 169). As a result, in the Cambodian communities in Stockton, it is often women—and not men—who have greater economic opportunities and who are the primary breadwinners in their families (Ui, 1991, p. 171).

Due to the significant decline in the economic contributions of Asian immigrant men, women's earnings comprise an equal or greater share of the family income. Because the wage each earns is low, only by pooling incomes can a husband and wife earn enough to support a family (Glenn, 1983, p. 42). These shifts in resources have challenged the patriarchal authority of Asian men. Men's loss of status and power—not only in the public but also in the domestic arena—places severe pressure on their sense of well-being. Responding to this pressure, some men accepted the new division of labor in the family (Ui, 1991, pp. 170–173); but many others resorted to spousal abuse and divorce (Luu, 1989, p. 68). A Korean immigrant man describes his frustrations over changing gender roles and expectations:

> In Korea [my wife] used to have breakfast ready for me. . . . She didn't do it any more because she said she was too busy getting ready to go to work. If I complained she talked back at me, telling me to fix my own breakfast. . . . I was very frustrated about her, started fighting and hit her (Yim, 1978, quoted in Mazumdar, 1989, p. 18).

Loss of status and power has similarly led to depression and anxieties in Hmong males. In particular, the women's ability—and the men's inability—to earn money for households "has undermined severely male omnipotence" (Irby and Pon, 1988, p. 112). Male unhappiness and helplessness can be detected in the following joke told at a family picnic, "When we get on the plane to go back to Laos, the first thing we will do is beat up the women!" The joke—which generated laughter by both men and women—drew upon a combination of "the men's unemployability, the sudden economic value placed on women's work, and men's fear of losing power in their families" (Donnelly, 1994, pp. 74–75). As such, it highlights the interconnections of race, class, and gender—the fact that in a racist and classist society, working-class men of color have limited access to economic opportunities and thus limited claim to patriarchal authority.

Conclusion

A central task in feminist scholarship is to expose and dismantle the stereotypes that traditionally have provided ideological justifications for women's subordination. But to conceptualize oppression only in terms of male dominance and female subordination is to obscure the centrality of classism, racism, and other forms of inequality in U.S. society (Stacey and Thorne, 1985, p. 311). The multiplicities of Asian men's lives indicate that ideologies of manhood and womanhood have as much to do with class and race as they have to do with sex. The intersections of race, gender, and class mean that there are also hierarchies among women and among men and that some women hold power over certain groups of men. The task for feminist scholars, then, is to develop paradigms that articulate the complicity among these categories of oppression, that strengthen the alliance between gender and ethnic studies, and that reach out not only to women, but also to men, of color.

Notes

1. One of the most noticeable characteristics of pre–World War II Asian America was a pronounced shortage of women. During this period, U.S. immigration policies barred the entry of most Asian women. America's capitalist economy also wanted Asian male workers but not their families. In most instances, families were seen as a threat to the efficiency and exploitability of the workforce and were actively prohibited.

2. The 1965 Immigration Act ended Asian exclusion and equalized immigration rights for all nationalities. No longer constrained by exclusion laws, Asian immigrants began arriving in much larger numbers than ever before. In the 1980s, Asia was the largest source of U.S. legal immigrants, accounting for 40 percent to 47 percent of the total influx (Min, 1995, p. 12).

References

Broom, Leonard and Ruth Riemer. 1949. *Removal and Return: The Socio-Economic Effects of the War on Japanese Americans.* Berkeley: University of California Press.

Chan, Sucheng. 1991. *Asian Americans: An Interpretive History.* Boston: Twayne.

Cheung, King-Kok. 1990. "The Woman Warrior Versus the Chinaman Pacific: Must a Chinese American Critic Choose Between Feminism and Heroism?" Pp. 234–251 in *Conflicts in Feminism*, edited by Marianne Hirsch and Evelyn Fox Keller. New York and London: Routledge.

Chiswick, Barry. 1979. "The Economic Progress of Immigrants: some apparently universal patterns." In W. Fellner (ED.), *Contemporary Economic Problems.* pp. 357–399. Washington, DC: American Enterprise Institute.

Crenshaw, Kimberlee. 1989. "Demarginalizing the Intersection of Race and Sex: A Black Feminist Critique of Antidiscrimination Doctrine, Feminist Theory and Antiracist Politics." In *University of Chicago Legal Forum: Feminism in the Law: Theory, Practice, and Criticism* (pp. 139–167). Chicago: University of Chicago Press.

Daniels, Roger. 1988. *Asian America: Chinese and Japanese in the United States Since 1850.* Seattle: University of Washington Press.

Donnelly, Nancy D. 1994. *Changing Lives of Refugee Hmong Women.* Seattle: Washington University Press.

Espiritu, Yen Le. 1995. *Filipino American Lives.* Philadelphia: Temple University Press.

Espiritu, Yen Le. 1996. *Asian American Women and Men: Labor, Laws, and Love.* Thousand Oaks, CA: Sage.

Fong-Torres, Ben. 1995. "Why Are There No Male Asian Anchormen on TV?" Pp. 208–211 in *Men's Lives*, 3rd ed., edited by Michael S. Kimmel and Michael A. Messner. Boston: Allyn and Bacon.

Gaines, Jane. 1990. "White Privilege and Looking Relations: Race and Gender in Feminist Film Theory." Pp. 197–214 in _Issues in Feminist Film Criticism_, edited by Patricia Erens. Bloomington: Indiana University Press.

Glenn, Evelyn Nakano. 1983. "Split Household, Small Producer and Dual Wage Earner: An Analysis of Chinese-American Family Strategies." _Journal of Marriage and the Family_, February: 35–46.

Glenn, Evelyn Nakano. 1986. _Issei, Nisei, War Bride: Three Generations of Japanese American Women at Domestic Service_. Philadelphia: Temple University Press.

Goellnicht, Donald C. 1992. "Tang Ao in America: Male Subject Positions in _China Men_." Pp. 191–212 in _Reading the Literatures of Asian America_, edited by Shirley Geok-lin-Lim and Amy Ling. Philadelphia: Temple University Press.

Gold, Steve and Nazli Kibria. 1993. "Vietnamese Refugees and Blocked Mobility." _Asian and pacific migration review_ 2:27–56.

Hamamoto, Darrell. 1994. _Monitored Peril: Asian Americans and the Politics of Representation_. Minneapolis: University of Minnesota Press.

Hossfeld, Karen J. 1994. "Hiring Immigrant Women: Silicon Valley's 'Simple Formula.'" Pp. 65–93 in _Women of Color in U.S. Society_, edited by Maxine Baca Zinn and Bonnie Thornton Dill. Philadelphia: Temple University Press.

Houston, Jeanne Wakatsuki and James D. Houston. 1973. _Farewell to Manzanar_. San Francisco: Houghton Mifflin.

Ichioka, Yuji. 1988. _The Issei: The World of the First Generation Japanese Immigrants, 1885–1924_. New York: The Free Press.

Irby, Charles and Ernest M. Pon. 1988. "Confronting New Mountains: Mental Health Problems Among Male Hmong and Mien Refugees. _Amerasia Journal_ 14: 109–118.

Kang, Younghill. 1937. _East Goes West_. New York: C. Scribner's Sons.

Katzman, David. 1978. "Domestic Service: Women's Work." Pp. 377–391 in _Women Working: Theories and Facts in Perspective_, edited by Ann Stromberg and Shirley Harkess. Palo Alto: Mayfield.

Kim, Elaine. 1990. "'Such Opposite Creatures': Men and Women in Asian American Literature." _Michigan Quarterly Review_, 68–93.

Kingston, Maxine Hong. 1980. _China Men_. New York: Knopf.

Kitagawa, Daisuke. 1967. _Issei and Nisei: The Internment Years_. New York: Seabury Press.

Kitano, Harry H. L. 1991. "The Effects of the Evacuation on the Japanese Americans." Pp. 151–162 in _Japanese Americans: From Relocation to Redress_, edited by Roger Daniels, Sandra C. Taylor, and Harry Kitano. Seattle: University of Washington Press.

Light, Ivan. 1972. _Ethnic Enterprise in America: Business and Welfare Among Chinese, Japanese, and Blacks_. Berkeley and Los Angeles: University of California Press.

Lim, Linda Y. C. 1983. "Capitalism, Imperialism, and Patriarchy: The Dilemma of Third-World Women Workers in Multinational Factories." Pp. 70–91 in _Women, Men, and the International Division of Labor_, edited by June Nash and Maria Patricia Fernandez-Kelly. Albany: State University of New York.

Liu, John, Paul Ong, and Carolyn Rosenstein. 1991. "Dual Chain Migration: Post-1965 Filipino Immigration to the United States." _International Migration Review_ 25 (3): 487–513.

Luu, Van. 1989. "The Hardships of Escape for Vietnamese Women." Pp. 60–72 in _Making Waves: An Anthology of Writings by and about Asian American Women_, edited by Asian Women United of California. Boston: Beacon Press.

Matsumoto, Valerie. 1989. Nisei Women and Resettlement During World War II. Pp. 115–126 in _Making Waves: An Anthology of Writings by and about Asian American Women_, edited by Asian Women United of California. Boston: Beacon Press.

Mazumdar, Sucheta. 1989. "General Introduction: A Woman-Centered Perspective on Asian American History." Pp. 1–22 in _Making Waves: An Anthology by and about Asian American Women_, edited by Asian Women United of California. Boston: Beacon Press.

Min, Pyong Gap. 1995. Korean Americans. Pp. 199–231 in _Asian Americans: Contemporary Trends and Issues_, edited by Pyong Gap Min. Thousand Oaks, CA: Sage.

Modell, John, ed. 1973. *The Kikuchi Diary: Chronicle from an American Concentration Camp*. Urbana: University of Illinois Press.

Montero, Darrell. 1980. *Vietnamese Americans: Patterns of Settlement and Socioeconomic Adaptation in the United States*. Boulder, CO: Westview.

Okihiro, Gary Y. 1991. *Cane Fires: The Anti-Japanese Movement in Hawaii, 1865–1945*. Philadelphia: Temple University Press.

Ong, Paul. 1994. "Asian Pacific Americans and Public Policy." Pp. 1–9 in *The State of Asian Pacific America: Economic Diversity, Issues, & Policies*, edited by Paul Ong. Los Angeles: LEAP Asian Pacific American Public Policy Institute and UCLA Asian American Studies Center.

Ong, Paul and Suzanne Hee. 1994. "Economic Diversity." Pp. 31–56 in *The State of Asian Pacific America: Economic Diversity, Issues, & Policies*, edited by Paul Ong. Los Angeles: LEAP Asian Pacific American Public Policy Institute and UCLA Asian American Studies Center.

Romero, Mary. 1992. *Maid in the U.S.A.* New York: Routledge.

Siu, Paul. 1987. *The Chinese Laundryman: A Study in Social Isolation*. New York: New York University Press.

Stacey, Judith and Barrie Thorne. 1985. "The Missing Feminist Revolution in Sociology." *Social Problems* 32: 301–316.

Takaki, Ronald. 1989. *Strangers from a Different Shore: A History of Asian Americans*. Boston: Little, Brown.

Ui, Shiori. 1991. " 'Unlikely Heroes': The Evolution of Female Leadership in a Cambodian Ethnic Enclave." Pp. 161–177 in *Ethnography Unbound: Power and Resistance in the Modern Metropolis*, edited by Michael Burawoy et al. Berkeley: University of California Press.

U.S. Bureau of the Census. 1993. *We the American Asians*. Washington, DC: U.S. Government Printing Office.

Villones, Rebecca. 1989. "Women in the Silicon Valley." Pp. 172–176 in *Making Waves: An Anthology of Writings by and about Asian American Women*, edited by Asian Women United of California. Boston: Beacon Press.

Wiegman, Robyn. 1991. "Black Bodies/American Commodities: Gender, Race, and the Bourgeois Ideal in Contemporary Film." Pp. 308–328 in *Unspeakable Images: Ethnicity and the American Cinema*, edited by Lester Friedman. Urbana and Chicago: University of Illinois Press.

Yanagisako, Sylvia Junko. 1987. "Mixed Metaphors: Native and Anthropological Models of Gender and Kinship Domains." Pp. 86–118 in *Gender and Kinship: Essays Toward a Unified Analysis*, edited by Jane Fishburne Collier and Sylvia Junko Yanagisako. Stanford: Stanford University Press.

ARTICLE

Harry Brod

Of Mice and Supermen: Images of Jewish Masculinity

This article explores certain cultural images of Jewish men, focusing particularly on the dynamics of power and powerlessness and, closely related to this, of heroism and victimization.[1] As one would expect in any analysis of forms of masculinities, issues of violence and of sexuality will come to play pivotal roles here. The discussion begins with the examination of some well-known images in popular culture, some of them not usually associated with Jewish themes, before it turns to incorporate into the discussion depictions of Jewish men within the Jewish tradition. The first popular culture icon to be discussed is paradigmatically non-Jewish, and one of the questions posed is that of the relationship between representations of the quintessentially non-Jewish and the quintessentially Jewish man.

Heroism and Survival

First consider the fruits of the creative energies of two young Jewish men who lived in Cleveland, Ohio, during the Depression. They enjoyed reading the Sunday comic strips, and

Reprinted from *Gender and Judaism*, edited by T. M. Rudavsky. New York: New York University Press.

decided they would like to try to create a character of their own. Jerry Siegel and Joe Shuster tried to market this character, but found no takers. Finally, somebody decided to accept this character and introduce him in a comic book. The character these two Jews created eventually made his debut on the cover of the first issue of *Action Comics* in June 1938, heralding the first appearance of Superman, who originated the superhero genre.[2] (Prior to that, the heroes were nonsuperpowered figures such as detectives, cops, pirates, etc.)

We don't usually think of Superman, the first and still prototypical superhero, as a Jewish character. Nonetheless, it will be my thesis that we should do so, the counterintuitiveness of such an idea notwithstanding. In fact, much of what I wish to explore is the question of why it goes so much against the grain to imagine Superman as Jewish.

By no means is this the first time such a question has been raised. The cover of the 4 August 1992 issue of the New York *Village Voice* highlights a picture of Superman in his traditional pose leaping into the air, above which, in large red letters, is written "SuperJew!" The cover article's title is "Is Superman Jewish?: The Chosen

Heroes from the *Golem* to Alan Dershowitz" (this being not long after the publication of Dershowitz's book *Chutzpah*). The title as given inside is "Up, Up and Oy Vey!"[3]

Jeff Salamon notes some stereotypically Jewish things about Superman. Kryptonians are superintelligent, and Superman's father Jor-El was a scientist. (I would add that in the Superman canon one never learns what his mother Lara actually did. Her role seems to be to tearfully watch baby Kal-El fly off to Earth in his rocket as the planet Krypton explodes around him). As the sole survivor of his race, he lives in a permanent diaspora. Henry Louis Gates stresses this theme of Superman as an immigrant when he writes of "Superman, the hero from Ellis Island, personified as an (undocumented) alien who had been naturalized by the ultimate American couple, Eben and Sarah Kent."[4]

A striking puzzle arises regarding the relationship between Superman and his alter ego Clark Kent. Perhaps the best way to explain the puzzle is to contrast Superman with another comic book hero, Batman. Batman's secret identity is Bruce Wayne, a real person who predates and grounds the Batman identity, which is a fictional creation. But with Superman, the matter is reversed. Superman is the real person. He really is a being from another planet. Clark Kent is the fiction. There really is no such person, especially in the sense that there is really no such personality as the Clark personality. (He was raised by the Kents, but he left his hometown and went to the big city where nobody knew him, so it is not clear why he needed to maintain this identity when he left Smallville for Metropolis.)[5] Although Bruce Wayne certainly has to maintain fictitious elements of his character and prevaricate in order to preserve his secret identity, he does not create out of whole cloth a persona completely opposite to his real nature, as Clark's personality is to Superman's. The problem, then, is why Superman goes to such great lengths to preserve the Clark persona. And, especially, why does he want Lois Lane to fall in love with Clark

rather than with Superman? Why does he want Lois to fall in love with a lie?

An enlightening answer is given by another cartoonist in the Jewish tradition. In the Introduction to *The Great Comic Book Heroes,* Jules Feiffer writes that this is Superman's joke on the rest of us.[6] Clark is Superman's vision of what other men are really like. We are scared, incompetent, and powerless, particularly around women. Though Feiffer took the joke good-naturedly, a more cynical response would see here the Kryptonian's misanthropy, his misandry embodied in Clark and his misogyny in his wish that Lois be enamored of Clark (much like Oberon takes out his hostility toward Titania by having her fall in love with an ass in Shakespeare's *A Midsummer-Night's Dream*).

At this point recall some of the contemporary villains faced by popular heroes, villains who at first glance appear to be unconnected to Jewish issues, and then relate them to what I have already said. Shortly after the film *Batman Returns* came out, an Op-Ed piece in the *New York Times* called attention to the anti-Semitic stereotypes embedded in the film's villain, the Penguin.[7] He is an evil, ugly, greedy, conspiratorial, smelly, unkempt, ill-mannered, hook-nosed, claw-handed fishmonger out to rule the world and destroy Christmas. Consider this alongside other villainous characters from the *Star Wars* films. I quote from Paul Hoch's *White Hero, Black Beast: Racism, Sexism and the Mask of Masculinity:*

> Two other stereotypical dark beasts appear. The first, the "filthy jawa" is a short, "extraordinarily ugly," "rodent-like" and "shrouded" being who "scurries" about "collecting and selling scrap jabbering in low, guttural croaks and hisses" and giving off offensive odors. Such "vermin" are "disgusting creatures," cringing "hereditary cowards," wandering "migrants" whose "covetous hands" produce nothing but try to pawn off inferior merchandise on the hard-working farmers who are their customers, while these underhand operators "bow and whine with impatient greed." Significantly, "hygiene was unknown among the jawas," for these

"travesties of men had long since degenerated past anything resembling the human race." The jawa is the only race in the entire book whose name is not capitalized throughout. Moreover, the chance of a two consonant name having just the two consonants "j" and "w" of the word Jew in precisely that order is only 21 × 20 (in fact less than one in a million if the extreme infrequency of these particular consonants in English usage is taken into account). The jawa is an anti-Semite's dream! The novel's other dark desert beasts are the Tuscan Raiders, or Sandpeople: "outrageous mahouts" who "pursue a nomadic existence," "vicious desert bandits" who "make sudden raids on local settlers." These "marginally-human" murderers "wrapped themselves mummylike in endless swathings and bandages" and emitted "terrifying grunts of fury and pleasure." In short, the usual stereotype of the marauding Arab. Lest we be in any doubt about these two sets of desert submen who squabble so bitterly among themselves, we are told that some scientists believe "they must be related" and "the jawas are actually the mature form."[8]

We have, then, these two negative images of Jews, and in particular Jewish men, in the culture: the evil, dark image of the Penguin and the jawas, and the also negative, but not evil, Clark Kent–type character. Clark is a sort of quintessential characterization of the Jewish *nebbish*. He's a quasi–intellectual. He's a writer; he wears glasses; he's inept, timid, and cowardly; and he is described as mouselike.

And speaking of mice, one of the reasons I've begun and remained with the theme of comic books is that one of the most extraordinary Jewish books of recent years—indeed one of the most extraordinary books of recent years—is Art Spiegelman's comic book, *Maus,* about Holocaust victims and survivors and their families in the postwar United States.[9] In *Maus,* the Jews of the Holocaust are drawn as mice, the Germans are cats, the Poles are pigs and, when the tale moves to the contemporary scene, non-Jewish Americans are dogs, and American Jews

are drawn with masks of mice on their faces. Spiegelman usually draws himself as a mouse, but occasionally as wearing the mask of a mouse. So his own identity is ambivalent.

I find this a very effective symbolization of the ambivalence of post-Holocaust American Jewish male identity. Spiegelman's self-portrait is particularly striking in that it embraces ambiguity, precisely what most depictions of Jewish men in popular culture avoid, engaging rather in the sort of rigid dichotomous polarization evident in Superman/Clark Kent. On the one hand, Superman is so super that the principal problem his writers have is coming up with a threat to him credible enough to add any suspense to the plot. On the other hand, Clark Kent is such a complete *nebbish* that he's also an unbelievable character. As to the effectiveness of his "disguise," here is an explanation offered by one of the editors of Superman's comic book appearances, E. Nelson Bridwell: "It may surprise the sophisticate of today that she [Lois Lane] took so long to penetrate the simple disguise of a pair of glasses. But in a day when people accepted the chestnut about the girl whose attractions are never noticed until she is seen without her glasses, Superman's camouflage worked."[10] The principle behind the disguise, then, is the old saw that men don't make passes at girls who wear glasses. To the extent that the disguise works, it thus also marks Clark as feminized.

It is precisely the extremism of the polarization between Superman and Clark that makes him such a paradigmatically Jewish American male character. I am here indebted to Paul Breines's *Tough Jews: Political Fantasies and the Moral Dilemma of American Jewry.*[11] Breines argues that the image of the Jewish male as a super-schlemiel is so accepted, even by Jews who want to counter it, that when Jews create a Jewish hero—a tough Jew—he turns out not to have Jewish characteristics at all. Hence, I believe, this Superman created out of the depths of the powerlessness felt by Siegel and Shuster, and hence many other characters cast in the same mold. Herein lies the dilemma: to create a heroic Jewish male image one must abandon the Jewish component and rely on the dominant culture's version of the heroic male. Jewish male heroes must be non-Jewish Jews, to borrow Isaac Deutscher's phrase. This is why it is so impossible to see Superman as a Jewish character. My purpose here is not to explain the circumstances under which Jewish men may have been said to be either mice or Supermen; it is to critique the dichotomized way in which the question is posed, and furthermore to look for alternatives to this inadequate approach to Jewish masculinity.

In *Tough Jews,* Breines discusses Leon Uris's *Exodus,* especially the film version, which defined Jewish heroism for a generation of American non-Jews. Its hero is Ari Ben Canaan, whose name tells us that he is a lion, but also a Canaanite, played in the film by Paul Newman, complete with blue eyes and all. Because the ethos of heroism has changed in recent years, and we now make heroes out of gangsters, instead of Ari Ben Canaan played by Paul Newman we now have Bugsy Siegel played by Warren Beatty; but the principle remains the same. Jews have to out-Gentile the Gentiles in order to make it. The point is made in Breines's book by Arthur Koestler, who was a member of a *Burschenshaft,* a Jewish fraternity, in Vienna in the early part of this century. Koestler writes that the member was

> to demonstrate that "Jews could hold their own in dueling, brawling, drinking and singing just like other people. According to the laws of inferiority and overcompensation," Koestler adds, "they were soon out-Heroding Herod once more"—practicing dueling for hours each day, eventually becoming the "most feared and aggressive swordsmen at the University."[12]

The dichotomization of Jewish masculinity appears again in the following passage from *Tough Jews,* in which Breines quotes from Philip

Roth's *The Counterlife.* A male Jewish "not altogether disillusioned, left-leaning, Zionist intellectual" says the following about American Jews in Israel.[13] Note the counterpoint of a feminized Yiddish culture and language against a masculinized Hebrew and Israeli language and culture, and the need for American Jews to achieve a clear positive Jewish identity through vicarious identification with Jews elsewhere, whether they be Israeli Jews as in this case or the Jews of the Holocaust, as in *Maus:*

> The American Jews get a big thrill from the guns. They see Jews walking around with guns and they think they're in paradise. Reasonable people with a civilized repugnance for violence and blood, they come on tour from America, and they see the guns and they see the beards and they take leave of their senses. The beards to remind them of saintly Yiddish weakness and the guns to reassure them of heroic Hebrew force.[14]

The difficulty of coming to terms with the question of what constitutes heroism and courage in Israel and in the Holocaust emerges again in Lawrence Langer's *New York Times* book review of Tom Segev's *The Seventh Million: The Israelis and the Holocaust,* in which Langer writes:

> Segev offers an illuminating account of how "Holocaust" and "heroism" came to be associated in the public imagination, especially through the naming of the Yad Vashem Holocaust Martyrs' and Heroes Remembrance Authority and the Ghetto Fighters' Museum (and kibbutz). He observes provocatively that because of this association, many surviving victims Holocaust but had not rebelled. The myth of heroism was a heavy burden, at odds with their memories and experiences.[15]

It seems to me that in speaking of the Holocaust, to put the word "merely" in front of the word "survived" is itself a crime against humanity. But according to this book, at least some of the survivors have come to feel this about themselves. The slander of having gone like lambs to the slaughter weighs particularly heavily on Jewish men because of the history of expectations of male heroism. We very much need a more nuanced understanding of the relationship between victimization and heroism, able to overcome the dichotomy between being either a total victim or a total hero. Discussions of the nature of survival in the Holocaust have been distorted by the exaggerated dichotomies between heroism and victimization I have argued to be endemic to discussions of Jewish men.[16]

Sexualities and Their Discontents

Jewish men being seen as powerless, as victims, means they are seen as effeminate in our culture. And effeminacy here signals homosexuality. There are indeed important historical structural parallels between anti-Semitism and the oppression of lesbians and gays in that they share certain essential characteristics. Unlike forms of oppression like racism and sexism, one cannot by and large tell by just looking who is or is not Jewish or lesbian or gay. However, in both anti-Semitism and lesbian and gay oppression there are stereotypes that say you can tell who is who just by appearance and behavior. These two forms of oppression are therefore uniquely suited to terrorize the population as a whole, to have everyone policing themselves lest they appear to be "one of them." Heterosexism has accordingly played the role in the United States in the 1980s that anti-Semitism played in Europe in the 1930s, functioning as pivotal in "law and order" campaigns to intimidate and isolate the population as a whole. The connections between these two phenomena come further into view when one realizes how much of the current wave of Jewish feminism has been Jewish lesbian feminism. In accordance with the Jewish precept of paying one's intellectual debts and honoring one's teachers, we must keep at the forefront of

our consciousness how impoverished Jewish feminism would be without those very important contributions.

The common or analogous marginalization of Jews and other "Others" is also discussed in Michael Kimmel's essay "Judaism, Masculinity, and Feminism," in which Kimmel talks about walking down the streets of New York City in an anti–Vietnam War parade when someone yells from the sidewalk "Drop dead, you commie Jew fag!"[17] Kimmel wonders why that combination of epithets rolls so trippingly off the tongue. What do they have in common? He answers that all three are perceived as being less than real men, as threatening the nation's national and sexual security.

The issue of Jewish men being seen as effeminate within the Jewish tradition is discussed by Lori Lefkovitz in "Coats and Tales: Joseph Stories and Myths of Jewish Masculinity," in which Lefkovitz examines the history of the interpretation of the story of Joseph.[18] The text says little more about Joseph's appearance than that he is beautiful. But at a certain historical moment this becomes an interpretive problem for the rabbis. Perhaps he is too beautiful. Why did he resist the sexual advances of Potiphar's wife anyway? Maybe something's wrong; maybe he is not sufficiently masculine? The story becomes problematic, and various midrashic solutions emerge to try to solve the problem. Some argue that Potiphar's wife was unattractive, whereas others alternatively marvel at Joseph's ability to control his manly lusts. Joseph also partakes of the pattern in which, as Lefkovitz points out,

> It is the younger son, often the child of the more beloved but less fertile wife, the physically smaller, less hirsute, more delicate, more domestic son, the son closer to the mother, a hero of intellect rather than of brawn, who will be chosen by God over his brothers. An awareness of this pattern may have contributed to an image of the Jews as a feminized people ruled by their women.[19]

Feeling themselves under continual threat of feminization, many Jewish men bristle at any suggestions of homosexuality. For example, consider the recent uproar when Labor Party Israeli Knesset member Yael Dayan began speaking of David's love for Jonathan as homosexual in the context of a debate over the rights of gays and lesbians in Israel's military.[20]

The dominant contemporary image of Jewish male heterosexuality in our culture is of sexual incompetence, like Clark Kent or the early Woody Allen. In stark contrast to this contemporary American image Andrea Dworkin's essay "The Sexual Mythology of Anti-Semitism" very usefully reminds us that in Nazi ideology the Jewish male was the rapist, cast in images very similar to the myths of African-American men in the United States.[21] Stereotypes of the sexuality of Jewish men have been much more varied than we often realize.

Circumcision and Rebirth

If there is any quintessential issue of Jewish masculinity, it would have to be circumcision, which raises in a different context many of the issues discussed here. But anyone looking for current discussions of this issue among men in the Jewish community will be met by an almost deafening silence. I have been told more than once that when this subject comes up in rabbinic training, men begin to giggle. The classic theological interpretation of circumcision, of course, treats it as the mark of the covenant. Kabbalistic interpretation regards circumcision as symbolic feminization.[22] Were one to ask most Jews what the significance of circumcision was, one would most likely hear an explanation about the sublimation of sexuality and the suppression of instinct. These accounts look at the effect of circumcision on the male who is circumcised, as

it might seem obvious to do. In contrast, I wish to consider the other male most prominently involved, the father, whom the tradition holds responsible for performing the circumcision.

Various anthropological theories attempt to explain circumcision rituals in many cultures, most of which perform the rite at puberty rather than infancy. The extent to which these theories are applicable to the Jewish case is therefore questionable. Though the theory I wish to apply is in my view better suited to explain circumcision at puberty than infancy, it will nonetheless be useful to follow a certain line of thought.

In tribal cultures, anthropologists tell us, at the stage in life in which he is called upon to have his son circumcised, the father, the patriarch, traditionally faced competition to his authority from two different directions. One is from the tribe. By this point in life, one has established oneself as head of one's own family, presumably with some accumulated wealth. So why, then, would it not be more advantageous to go off and start one's own clan? What keeps one bound to one's tribe of origin? At the birth of a son the tribe has reason to worry that a new competing clan may be inaugurated. The tribe therefore looks for tests by which it might assure itself of the father's loyalty. The father also faces a future potential threat from the son's impending ascension to power. There is now going to be a new male rival, not only for the mother's affections but eventually also for power and authority.

The hypothesis that many anthropologists have come to endorse is that in many cultures circumcision represents the father's making a symbolic sacrifice of the son to the tribe, thereby reassuring the tribe of his loyalty and binding him to the tribe by the sacrifice. Furthermore, it sublimates the father's aggression toward the son. The father might be experiencing impulses to rid himself of this potential rival, to perhaps commit infanticide.

The hostility of fathers toward sons is present in the founding myths of many cultures. In the Greek tradition, and the Freudian tradition that adopts it, prior to the Oedipus complex lies the Laius complex. The story starts because Laius fears his son is going to kill him, so he launches a preemptive strike to get rid of him before he becomes a threat. In the Christian story, the Christian God the Father allows his son Jesus to die on the cross. The Jewish tradition has the Akedah, the story of Abraham and the binding of Isaac. Of those three founding stories, the Jewish case is the only one where the murderous intention is not carried through (Laius did not succeed, but he never changed his intention to kill his son). I would argue that one can link circumcision to the halting of that sacrifice. The symbolic act of cutting replaces Abraham's descending knife.

The halting of Abraham's murderous act is also the birth of the Jewish people, because it reaffirms God's commitment to found a nation, a promise called into question by the possible death of Isaac. This moment is thus a rebirth, specifically a masculine rebirth. The first birth, into the body, was given to Isaac by Sarah. But the rebirth into the covenant, into the spirit rather than the body, is conferred by Abraham. This fits a pattern common in many cultures in which women's birthing powers are appropriated by men, whether by rituals of circumcision or baptism. Men confer the more important life of the soul, whereas women confer merely the life of the body. Sarah's absence from this story is therefore not just an omission in the text. Rather, it is a fundamental part of what the story is about, a story about a male-to-male conferring of life.

This idea of male birth, male creation of life, is very powerful and visible in many cultures. Sometimes the role of women in giving birth is bypassed by a myth of birth coming directly from the land. For example, one of the founding fathers of modern political theory,

Thomas Hobbes, in developing the foundations for his new science of politics instructs his readers "to consider men as if but even now sprung out of the earth, and suddenly, like mushrooms, come to full maturity, without all kind of engagement with each other."[23]

If one were in the grip of this male appropriation of birth, when one arrived in a new land one might come to think that one had a direct relationship to it, unmediated by any other person. So to Europeans arriving on the shores of America, Native Americans were simply invisible. One plants one's flag pole directly in the earth (I choose to retain all the Freudian connotations here) and claims the land as one's own, simply not registering the presence of other people who were there before your arrival. And when Zionists come to Israel to give birth to the new state, the presence of prior inhabitants might also not sufficiently register, were one under the sway of a male vision of giving birth directly from the land, unmediated by any other presence. One cannot then bring under one's purview the people present prior to one's own birth. One lacks the umbilical cord that might connect one back through the generations. I therefore wish to argue that its masculinity has proven to be the Achilles heel of Zionism, its tragic flaw of being unable to adequately recognize the people present on the land before Israel's own birth.

On numerous occasions I have encountered the term "feminist Judaism," by which is meant not simply an egalitarian role for women within Judaism, what some call "Jewish feminism," but rather a Judaism transformed as a whole by the full inclusion of women's perspectives. However, I have never heard a discussion of feminist Zionism and what that might look like. It seems to me that feminist Zionism would not only be egalitarian Zionism, but a Zionism that would have at the center of its vision a consciousness of the needs of other peoples already on the land when modern

Zionism began the work of giving birth to the state of Israel.

Conclusion

I shall close by returning to Superman, now as discussed in Arthur Flannigan-Saint-Aubin's essay "The Male Body and Literary Metaphors for Masculinity," in which he cites an interview with Superman's creators to the effect that they "were never able to imagine the Man of Steel with a penis."[24] His interpretation is that Superman's whole body is phallic, and one can't very well have one penis atop another. He argues further that the Freudian model of masculinity has conceptualized the male genitals as synonymous with the phallus, thereby ignoring the testicles, constituting a massive displacement and denial. Freudians have spoken for generations about castration anxiety as being anxiety about the loss of the phallus. Actual castration, however, involves the testicles, not the penis. This misidentification goes remarkably untreated.

Flannigan-Saint-Aubin sees a model for a desirable masculinity in the new character of Clark Kent. The once familiar characters have undergone major revisions of late in the comic books and even more recently in the ABC television series "Lois & Clark: The New Adventures of Superman." Superman now has his share of existential anxieties—he is a stranger in a strange land, worried about adjusting to terrestrial culture.[25] And Clark is no longer the timid mouse of old. He now has adventures in his own right. Both Superman and Clark are now more complete, integrated personalities. Seeing Clark as a model of masculinity is thus not to adopt a completely passive stance. Rather, this endorses a mode of masculinity designed to overcome the dichotomous polarizations I earlier argued were endemic to portrayals of Jewish men. In his search for a new embodied metaphor to symbolize this new masculinity, Flannigan-Saint-Aubin

comes to envisage testicular as opposed to phallic imagery. As opposed to the phallus, understood as hard, aggressive, and linear, the testicles just sort of "hang loose." They are vulnerable, sensitive, plural rather than singular, and even generative of life, as the source where semen is produced.[26]

Flannigan-Saint-Aubin's image for a more positive masculinity of course refers to men in general, not specifically to Jewish men. I close with a cautionary note about contemporary culture's use of images of Jewish men to embody changes in men along these lines. Some have seen as a sign of progress the presence of a number of positive Jewish male characters on U.S. network television in recent years, including Michael on "thirtysomething," Stuart on "L. A. Law," Joel on "Northern Exposure," and Jerry on "Seinfeld" (who now that he is a comedy writer for a TV show should be seen as a successor to Buddy on the old "Dick Van Dyke Show" whose ambivalent Jewishness is evidenced by his appearance on the "Alan Brady Christmas Show" without comment, while having his Bar Mitzvah in another episode).

The choice of Jewish men to represent such nice, sensitive, "new" men might therefore be seen as an occasion for Jewish pride, especially because they are so identified as Jews, in contrast to what Donna Perlmutter called the "blatant de-Jewification" carried out when such works as Nora Ephron's *Heartburn* and Neil Simon's *Brighton Beach Memoirs* made their transitions to the screen in the eighties.[27] However, I would argue that the choice of Jewish men to embody this type represents a strategy whereby the producers of these shows minimize their risks. Since Jewish men are already seen as feminized by the culture, using them to embody the more "sensitive" traits stereotypically associated with women is therefore both less threatening and more plausible to the audience than if these characters were blond, blue-eyed WASPS. In the same vein a generation ago, the first commercial film released by a major studio to focus on a gay relationship, John Schlesinger's 1971 *Sunday Bloody Sunday,* starred Peter Finch as the bisexual Jewish doctor. While these characterizations certainly do contain positive traits, the common use of Jewish male characters to embody characteristics usually considered "softer" thus presupposes the culture's negative valuation of Jewish men as already feminized, and is thus implicated in this characterization constructed by the culture to be disparaging. Thus, despite what may be initial appearances to the contrary, images of Jewish men continue to incorporate the ambiguities usually present in such images.

Notes

1. I wish to express my thanks to the organizers of the Melton Center's "Gender and Judaism" Conference for inviting me to speak, and thus giving me the opportunity to develop the ideas herein expressed, and to the reviewers of this volume for helping me to refine them. Because I am acutely aware of how it has been women's struggles that have made possible the discussion of gender within Judaism, I greatly appreciate the generosity of spirit shown by devoting a plenary session to the subject of Jewish masculinity.

2. *Action Comics,* No. 1, June 1938, Detective Comics, Inc.

3. *The Village Voice,* 4 August, 1992, 1 & 86.

4. Henry Louis Gates, Jr., "A Big Brother from Another Planet," *New York Times,* 12 September 1993, Section H, 51.

5. The writers and editors of Superman comics were aware of the problem. Among several stories exploring the issue, the cover story of the October 1963 issue of *Action Comics,* No. 305, is "Why Superman Needs a Secret Identity," told as "An Imaginary Story" picturing various catastrophes that would befall Superman and those closest to him were he to lose his secret identity (ed. Mort Weisinger [Sparta, IL: National Periodical Publications], 1–14). The last panel of the story carries an invitation:

"Readers, can you figure out some more reasons why a secret identity is so vital to Superman? We'll print the best letters."

6. Jules Feiffer, ed., *The Great Comic Book Heroes* (New York: Dial Press, 1965), 18–21.

7. *Batman Returns,* Tim Burton, Dir. (Warner Bros., 1992).

8. Paul Hoch, *White Hero, Black Beast: Racism, Sexism, and the Mask of Masculinity* (London: Pluto Press, 1979), 49–50. Hoch is quoting from the novelization of the film.

9. Art Spiegelman, *Maus: A Survivor's Tale,* Vols. 1–2 (New York: Pantheon, 1986, 1991).

10. E. Nelson Bridwell, ed., *Superman: From the Thirties to the Seventies* (New York: Crown, 1971), 13.

11. Paul Breines, *Tough Jews: Political Fantasies and the Moral Dilemma of American Jewry* (New York: Basic Books, 1990).

12. Breines, *Tough Jews,* 141.

13. On the conflict between the "Jewboy" vs. the "nice Jewish boy" in Roth see Barbara Gottfried, "What *Do* Men Want, Dr. Roth?", in *A Mensch among Men: Explorations in Jewish Masculinity,* ed. Harry Brod (Freedom, CA: Crossing Press, 1988), 37–52. In citing this and other essays from a book I edited I do not wish to engage in self-promotion but rather to acknowledge those whose work has influenced my own.

14. Breines, *Tough Jews,* 22.

15. Lawrence L. Langer, "Zion's Response to the Holocaust," *New York Times Book Review,* 18 April 1993, 37.

16. One of the possible sources of a more nuanced understanding of the dialectic of victimization and resistance is recent scholarship on Jewish women's resistance in the Holocaust. I do not wish to assert here that women's actual behavior was necessarily different from men's, but merely that our understanding of the dynamics of survival has greatly benefited from a particularly sophisticated understanding of the dialectic of victimization and heroism provided by feminist scholars working on this subject. See for example Marlene E. Heinemann, *Gender and Destiny: Women Writers and the Holocaust* (New York: Greenwood press, 1986) and Carol Rittner and John

K. Roth, eds., *Different Voices: Women and the Holocaust* (New York: Paragon House, 1993).

17. Michael Kimmel, "Judaism, Masculinity, and Feminism," in Brod, *Mensch,* 153–56.

18. Lori Lefkovitz, "Coats and Tales: Joseph Stories and Myths of Jewish Masculinity," in Brod, *Mensch,* 19–29.

19. Lefkovitz, "Coats and Tails," 20–21. See Arthur Waskow, *Godwrestling* (New York: Schocken, 1978).

20. Michael Parks, "A New View of David Stirs Goliath-Size Roar," *New York Times,* 11 February 1993, Section A2, Cols. 1–2.

21. Andrea Dworkin, "The Sexual Mythology of Anti-Semitism," in Brod, *Mensch,* 118–23.

22. Wolfson, Elliot R. "On Becoming Female: Crossing Gender Boundaries in Kabbalistic Ritual and Myth," paper presented at the Gender and Judaism Conference, Melton Center for Jewish Studies, Ohio State University, Columbus, Ohio, April 26, 1993.

23. Thomas Hobbes, "The Citizen: Philosophical Rudiments Concerning Government and Society," *Man and Citizen: Thomas Hobbes' De Homine and De Cive,* ed. Bernard Gert (Garden City: Doubleday, 1972), 205. Quoted in Christine Di Stefano, "Masculinity as Ideology in Political Theory: Hobbesian Man Considered," *Women's Studies International Forum* 6:6, 1983, 637.

24. Arthur Flannigan-Saint-Aubin, "The Male Body and Literary Metaphors for Masculinity," *Theorizing Masculinities,* eds. Harry Brod and Michael Kaufman (Newbury Park, CA: Sage Publications, 1994), quoting R. Greenberger, J. Byrne, and M. Gold, eds., *The Greatest Superman Stories Ever Told* (New York: D. C. Comics, 1987).

25. The anxiety-ridden comic book superhero was created by Stan Lee (born Stanley Lieber) at Marvel Comics in the 1960s. Spiderman, secretly Peter Parker, was guilt-laden over failing to stop the criminal who then murdered his Uncle Ben, with whom he and his Aunt May lived in Forest Hills (where I grew up) in New York City. Peter's personality was that of a teenage Clark. The role of Jewish men in the comic book industry is a subject worthy of discussion in its own right.

26. Flannigan-Saint-Aubin's approach may perhaps best be understood as an application to men of the sort of approach taken by Luce Irigaray in *This Sex Which Is Not One,* trans. C. Porter (Ithaca: Cornell University Press, 1985).

27. Donna Perlmutter, "Jewishness Goes Back in Closet on the Screen," *Los Angeles Times,* 12 April 1987, Calendar Section, 20–24.

6

ARTICLE

Martin P. Levine

The Life and Death of Gay Clones

> The aims, then, of a sociological approach to homosexuality are to begin to define the factors—both individual and situational—that predispose a homosexual to follow one path as against others; to spell out the contingencies that will shape the career that has been embarked upon; and to trace out the patterns of living in both their pedestrian and their seemingly exotic aspects. Only then will we begin to understand the homosexual. This pursuit must inevitably bring us—though from a particular angle—to those complex matrices wherein most human behavior is fashioned.
> —William Simon and John H. Gagnon,
> "Homosexuality: The Formulation of a Sociological Perspective"

More than two decades ago, William Simon and John Gagnon formulated the first constructionist explanation for the sociocultural organization of gay life. Taking a cue from symbolic interactionist theory, they contextualized the formation of gay life, arguing that "the patterns of adult homosexuality are consequent upon the social structure and values that surround the homosexual after he becomes or conceives of himself as homosexual."[1] In this way, they traced the origin of gay life to the elements of surrounding cultures and social structures.

In other works, Simon and Gagnon stress the role of socialization in the evolution of gay sociocultural patterns.[2] Like most sociologists and anthropologists, they argue that people acquire the cultural values, beliefs, norms, and roles that organize and direct their behavior through socialization into the prevailing sociocultural order. In addition, they feel that patterned regularities in social life occur as a result of individuals shaping their behavior around these sociocultural directives.

According to Simon and Gagnon, gay patterns emerge similarly in societies lacking a separate socialization process for adult homosexuality. They claim that in these cultures men who eventually become gay undergo essentially the same socialization process as other males. That is, they learn the same cultural values, beliefs, norms, and roles as other men. Moreover, they contend that regularities in gay life emerge as gay men shape their behavior within, between, and in reaction to these sociocultural prescriptions.

Subsequent constructionist explanations for gay life narrow the scope of Simon and Gagnon's rather broad formulation. Typically, these accounts appear in sociological studies of homosexuality framed from either a social labeling or a rule perspective.[3] In social labeling studies, stigmatization accounts "for the forms homosexuality" takes, "whether in behavior, identity, or community":

> The single most important factor about homosexuality as it exists in this culture is the perceived hostility of the societal reactions that surround it. From this one critical factor flow many of the features that are distinctive about homosexuality. It renders the business of becoming a homosexual a process that is characterized by problems of access, problems of guilt, and problems of identity. It leads to the emergence of a subculture of homosexuality. It leads to a series of interaction problems involved with concealing the discreditable stigma. And it inhibits the development of stable relationships to a considerable degree.[4]

According to role theory, homosexual roles shape the patterns of gay life.[5] That is, regularities in gay life arise as gay men behaviorally enact the cultural expectations embedded in the homosexual role.

This chapter examines the validity of these three constructionist explanations of gay life for the forms of life associated with the gay clone, a social type that first appeared in the mid-1970s in the "gay ghettos" of America's largest cities.[6] Social scientists use the term "social type" to describe an informal role that is based on collective images of a particular kind of person.[7] The clone role reflected the gay world's image of this kind

of gay man, a doped-up, sexed-out, Marlboro man.

Although the gay world derisively named this social type the clone, largely because of its uniform look and life-style, clones were the leading social type within gay ghettos until the advent of AIDS.[8] At this time, gay media, arts, and pornography promoted clones as the first post-Stonewall form of homosexual life. Clones came to symbolize the liberated gay man.[9]

The material presented here comes from a longitudinal field study conducted from 1977 to 1984 of a clone social world in New York's West Village. The fieldwork included observation and participant observation in such central meeting places within this world as bars, discos, and bathhouses. In addition, extensive participant observation was conducted among three distinct friendship cliques. Furthermore, unidentified interviews were conducted with both key informants and other participants. All three of these techniques have been used to collect follow-up data since the formal fieldwork ceased in 1984.

In what follows, I will show how Simon and Gagnon's constructionist explanation offers the best account for the patterns of clone life in the West Village. To support my argument, I will discuss the social context of the clone social world, the sociocultural organization of the gay social world, and the sociocultural organization of the clone social world. All undocumented words, phrases, and indented quotations in the third section come from my field notes. The words and phrases constitute gay argot and are defined in the notes; they are set off in the text by quotation marks.

The Social Context of the Clone Social World

America underwent profound social changes over the course of the last three decades.[10] During the 1960s and early 1970s, various student, gender, racial, and ethnic liberation movements struggled against the Vietnam War and social oppression. In particular, these movements removed many of the discriminatory sanctions applied against women and racial, ethnic, and sexual minorities and successfully altered the stigmatized cultural roles and identities assigned to these groups.[11] For example, the black movement effectively ended legalized discrimination in housing, employment, and public accommodations and taught African-Americans to be proud of their racial and cultural heritage, which profoundly reduced black people's internalized self-hatred and low self-esteem.[12]

There were also momentous shifts in culturally hegemonic values during the course of these decades.[13] At the end of the 1960s, the burgeoning counterculture spread a libertarian ethos among millions of young, urban, college-educated, and middle-class Americans, which seriously undermined the cultural dominance of the Protestant ethic.[14] In particular, the libertarian ethos deeply undercut the normative influence of the Protestant ethic's values sanctioning sacrifice and self-denial.

By the mid-1970s, the normative decline of the Protestant ethos permitted the rise of another set of values, known as the self-fulfillment ethic, which idealized gratification of all inner needs and desires.[15] The self-fulfillment ethic transformed the counterculture's libertarian ethos into a value set sanctioning unbridled hedonism, materialism, and expressiveness, which subsequently sparked massive consumerism and experimentation with sex and drugs among followers of this ethic.[16]

The altered social climate of the 1980s sharply curtailed the spread of the self-fulfillment ethic.[17] A contraction of disposable income among the middle class and an epidemic of incurable sexually transmitted diseases eroded the economic and physical basis for unrestrained self-gratification. That is, unchecked consumerism and erotic hedonism became impractical in an era of economic deterioration, genital herpes,

hepatitis B, and AIDS. In addition, widespread aspirations for stable relationships further weakened belief in self-fulfillment. More precisely, emergent desires for more permanent relationships and social networks fostered widespread dissatisfaction with the "me-firstism" implicit in the pursuit of unbounded self-gratification.

The waning of the self-fulfillment ethic during the 1980s promoted the growth of alternative value sets that merged values from both the Protestant and the self-fulfillment ethics. Yankelovitch labeled these value sets the ethics of constraint and commitment.[18]

The constraint ethic held that biopsychosocial contingencies sharply restrict gratification of inner needs and desires. It contended that materialistic and hedonistic pursuits had to be weighed against economic, social, and physical limitations. As a result, it sanctioned a form of restrained hedonism in which sensual indulgence was tied to physical well-being and a form of expressive materialism in which materialistic pursuits were linked to autonomy and creativity. In this way, it idealized self-discipline in the quest for restrained hedonism and expressive materialism.

The commitment ethic perceived connectedness as a cultural ideal. Accordingly, it valued attachment to people, avocations, institutions, and communities and approved of self-sacrifice in the service of deeper and more meaningful relationships and sacred or expressive activities.

The ethics of constraint and commitment fostered ready acceptance of sobriety, health maintenance, and erotic limitations among those who endorsed these values.[19] Restrained hedonism prompted millions of urban, educated, middle-class Americans to forsake smoking, alcohol, drugs, and recreational sex for strict regimens of abstinence, exercise, nutritional diets, and relational sex. This in turn provoked widespread participation in twelve-step recovery programs for substance abuse, eating disorders, and "sexual addiction."[20] In addition, expressive materialism created enormous demands among this population for imaginative and self-reliant jobs. Finally, connectedness engendered tremendous commitment within this group to expressive hobbies, historic preservation, and community service.[21] In the sexual realm, it fostered adherence to relational scripts, which sanctioned obligation, fidelity, and romance between sexual partners.[22]

The Sociocultural Organization of the Gay Social World

The social changes of the past three decades profoundly affected the forms of gay life. At the opening of the 1960s, American culture stigmatized homosexuality as a type of gender deviance that required strict social control.[23] That is, gay men were regarded as "failed men," as men who deviated from masculine norms because they were either mentally or morally disordered. In this way, gay men were relegated to cultural roles of "nelly queens," "hopeless neurotics," and "moral degenerates."[24]

The stigmatization of homosexuality fostered harsh social sanctions designed to isolate, treat, correct, or punish gay men. For example, most states criminalized homosexual contact, which exposed gay men to police harassment, imprisonment, and blackmail. Moreover, psychiatry regarded homosexuality as a treatable form of mental illness, which left gay men open to mandatory psychotherapy or psychiatric hospitalization. Finally, family and friends frequently taunted, ostracized, and even violently attacked gay men.

Stigmatization meant that the gay world of the sixties functioned as a deviant subculture.[25] This symbolic world constituted a relatively "impoverished cultural unit."[26] That is, the threat of sanction effectively limited structural and cultural elaboration within this world to covert sets of so-cially isolated, self-hating social networks and gathering places, which were primarily designed to facilitate social and sexual contacts and the management of stigma.[27]

Three techniques for neutralizing stigma largely shaped the patterns of life within this world: passing, minstrelization, and capitulation. Passing accounted for the secrecy that characterized this world and included a set of behaviors that was designed to hide a gay identity and world under a heterosexual facade. Minstrelization explained the patterns of cross-gendering associated with "camp," a behavioral style entailing the adoption of feminine dress, speech, and demeanor. Finally, capitulation accounted for the feelings of guilt, shame, and self-hatred associated with the damaged sense of self that resulted from believing that homosexuality was a form of gender deviance.[28]

Stigma management also engendered significant impediments to erotic expression during this period. The lack of anticipatory socialization for male homosexuality in our culture signified that men who eventually became gay experienced essentially the same erotic socialization as men who grew up to be straight.[29] Socialization agents taught both prehomosexual and preheterosexual youths the dictates of the male sexual script. Consequently, gay men acquired a recreational erotic code that held that sex was objectified, privatized, and phallocentric and an arena for demonstrating manly prowess. Passing and capitulation prevented many gay men from engaging in the recreational sex associated with the male sexual script. The threat that recognition and police raids or entrapment posed to heterosexual passing forced some gay men to shun the opportunities for recreational contacts present in the sexual marketplace of bars, bathhouses, and public restrooms. In addition, the belief that same-sex desires constituted gender deviance blocked others from engaging in recreational sexual contacts.[30]

The gay liberation movement of the sixties fundamentally altered forms of gay life. Many

Gay Lib.
Mvt.

early gay rights activists had participated in either countercultural, antiwar, or civil rights movements and were therefore prepared to advocate libertarian values and the destigmatization of homosexuality. For example, they championed an ethic sanctioning self-expression, especially in regard to experimentation with drugs and sex.[31] In addition, they promoted a construction of same-sex love that stripped homosexuality of its discrediting association with gender deviance. That is, they held that same-sex love was a moral, natural, and healthy form of erotic expression among men who typically conformed to cultural expectations for manly demeanor and appearance.[32] Finally, they actively campaigned to reduce the level of criminal, psychiatric, and social sanction and succeeded in forcing some localities either to repeal sodomy statutes or to cease police harassment of gay men, in compelling the mental health professions to remove same-sex love from the official list of psychological disorders, and in provoking a growing acceptance of gay men in the family, media, and workplace.[33]

The lessening of stigmatization reorganized the patterns of life within gay social worlds located in major urban centers.[34] For example, the reduction of legal and social sanctions removed most constraints against structural and cultural elaboration within these worlds. Accordingly, the range of gay services, traditions, gathering places, and cultural subgroupings widened and deepened: "The dozen largest urban areas of North America now have readily identifiable gay neighborhoods with heavy populations of same-sex couples. Each of these districts features not only openly gay bars and restaurants, but clothiers, bookstores, laundromats, a variety of shops, doctors, lawyers, dentists, and realtors that cater to a gay clientele."[35] In addition, these neighborhoods contained an array of gay sexual, recreational, cultural, religious, political, and professional scenes or subcultures.[36] In these areas, gay men could cruise for anonymous sex, join gay baseball teams, sing in gay choruses, at-

tend gay studies groups, worship in gay churches or synagogues, work for gay Democratic or Republican clubs, see exhibitions of gay art, theater, and cinema, and participate in gay bankers, doctors, or lawyers organizations.

The weakening of sanction and the destigmatized definition of homosexuality also modified the forms of life associated with stigma neutralization. For example, the decline in sanction removed the grounds for heterosexual passing, which provoked many gay men to become openly gay. Moreover, the redefinition of homosexuality as a normal, healthy, masculine form of male sexuality erased the basis for the cross-dressing connected with minstrelization, prompting a wholesale abandonment of camp attire, demeanor, and activities. In addition, this definition of same-sex love eliminated the reason for perceiving homosexuality as gender deviance and fostered a new pride and sense of validity in being both gay and a man. Finally, along with the libertarian ethos, the decrease in sanction and heightened self-esteem eradicated many of the impediments to recreational sexual contacts, which provoked an increase in anonymous erotic activity.[37]

The social changes of the 1970s and 1980s further strengthened these emergent urban gay patterns. During the 1970s, the self-fulfillment ethic sanctioned gratification of inner needs and desires, and many urban gay men became openly gay, materialistic, and hedonistic. Consequently, the forms of urban gay life came to include consumerism, erotic exploration, recreational drug use, and disclosure of sexual orientation.[38]

However, these patterns were forsaken during the early eighties. By then, AIDS, a decline in discretionary income, and yearnings for stable relationships caused unbridled self-gratification to be regarded as unsound behavior. That is, a fatal venereal disease, mounting medical and caregiving expenses, and desires for permanent relationships made recreational sex, consumerism, and drug use appear untenable.[39]

By the mid-1980s, the ethics of constraint and commitment became hegemonic within urban gay worlds. At this time, AIDS, economic deterioration, and longings for secure relationships made urban gay men embrace restrained hedonism, expressive materialism, and connectedness as cultural ideals. For example, the medical dangers associated with sex and poor health maintenance, coupled with a decrease in disposable income, prompted these men to accept values linking gratification of hedonistic and material desires with self-discipline for the purpose of either physical and financial well-being or autonomy and creativity. In addition, health concerns and longings for steady relationships led them to endorse values sanctioning commitment, monogamy, coupling, and celibacy.[40]

The ethics of constraint and commitment provoked new forms of life in urban gay worlds. The ideal of restrained hedonism fostered ready acceptance of temperance, erotic restrictions, and health maintenance among urban gay men. These men increasingly gave up liquor, cigarettes, drugs, and risky sex for rigid regimens of exercise, sleep, diet, and safer sex. Many even entered twelve-step programs to "recover" from substance abuse and "sexual addiction." In addition, expressive materialism drove other gay men to work in fields demanding both creativity and autonomy. Finally, connectedness forced some men to become either caregivers for sick or dying friends and lovers or unpaid volunteers for community-based political or health organizations.[41]

The Sociocultural Organization of the Clone Social World

A unique set of sociocultural patterns distinguished the clone social world in the West Village from other gay cultural entities in New York City. The changes in the forms of life within this world between the 1970s and the 1980s paralleled the outbreak of the AIDS epidemic.

The Pre-AIDS Patterns of the 1970s

Prior to AIDS, the clone social world was structured around a group of socially isolated social networks and gathering places, networks and places segregated from the broader gay as well as the heterosexual world. That is, the participants in these networks and places were mainly clones.

The social networks included "cliques" and "crowds." Cliques functioned as friendship circles and met the men's basic social, emotional, and material needs. In this sense, they were surrogate families. A crowd consisted of a group of cliques that frequented the same meeting spot. For example, the Saint crowd involved the set of cliques that routinely gathered at The Saint disco. In addition, the members of a crowd usually either recognized or knew each other.

The crowds mixed in a round of meeting spots that was known as the "Circuit." The gathering places in the Circuit were mainly locales for social, recreational, or sexual activities. For example, the men dined in Circuit restaurants, worked out in Circuit gyms, cruised in Circuit bars, and had sex in Circuit bathhouses. In addition, the men attended Circuit meeting spots according to a fixed schedule called "Circuit hours." A retail clerk in his mid-twenties explained, "After work, we go to the gym, either the Y or the Bodycenter; then we stop by One Potato or Trilogy for dinner. On Friday nights, we cruise the Eagle and Spike. On Saturday nights, we go dancing at the Saint, and on Sunday nights, we go to the baths."

Three distinctive social patterns characterized the clone social world during this period. First, presentational strategies within this world were typically "butch."[42] For example, these men usually fashioned themselves after such archetypically masculine icons as body builders and blue-collar workers, and commonly wore work boots, flannel shirts, and button-up Levis and had gym bodies, short haircuts, and mustaches or beards.

Moreover, clones dressed in such a way as to highlight male erotic features and availability. For example, these men frequently wore form-fitting T-shirts and Levis that outlined their musculature, genitals, and buttocks. To highlight the penis even further, they often wore no underwear. In addition, they usually wore keys and handkerchiefs that signaled preference for sexual acts and positions: "White vividly describes the effect of eroticized butchness: a strongly marked mouth and swimming soulful eyes (the effect of the mustache); a V shaped torso by metonymy from the open V of the half unbuttoned shirt above the sweaty chest; rounded buttocks squeezed in jeans, swelling out from the cinched-in waist, further emphasized by the charged erotic insignia of colored handkerchiefs and keys; a crotch instantly accessible through the buttons (bottom one already undone) and enlarged by being pressed, along with the scrotum, to one side."[43]

Furthermore, expressive strategies in Circuit gathering places evinced similar themes. For example, the decor and names of many Circuit meeting spots used western, leather, or high-tech motifs. One popular bar conveyed cowboy imagery through such furnishings as wagon wheels, corral posts, and western paintings, and staff uniforms consisted of cowboy hats, shirts, and boots. Other bars expressed this imagery through such names as Badlands or The Eagle.

The spatial design and names of some gathering places also articulated butchness. For example, many bars set aside specific areas for "cruising" and "tricking."[44] Some even showed pornographic films in backrooms. Other places manifested butchness in such names as The Cockring or The International Stud.

Second, erotic patterns within this world included cruising and tricking. Typically, clones cruised Circuit gathering places such as bars, bathhouses, and sex clubs for men who were their "type," that is, their erotic ideal, usually either good looking or "hung," "built," and butch.[45] Generally, clones cruised these men by situating themselves in a position to signal sexual interest and negotiate a time and place for tricking. In most cases, they tricked almost immediately after meeting.

A rough, uninhibited, phallocentric form of sexuality characterized tricking among clones. Tricking frequently involved "deep throating," "hard fucking," and "heavy tit work." For example, fellatio often included vigorously jamming the penis completely down the throat (deep throating), which frequently caused gagging or choking. Anal intercourse usually entailed strenuously ramming the penis entirely up the anus while painfully slapping the buttocks (hard fucking). Nipple stimulation commonly involved robustly sucking, pinching, or biting the nipples to the point of pain (heavy tit work).

Clones often used drugs to overcome pain during rough sex and heighten erotic responsiveness. "Pot," "poppers," and Quaaludes were particularly popular.[46] A thirty-something health professional reported, "I love to do poppers during sex because they cause the muscles in my ass and throat to relax, which allows me to suck dick and get fucked without gagging or feeling any pain."

Most tricks consisted of a single erotic encounter. That is, the men had sex once and never again. For example, a waiter in his twenties in a Circuit restaurant remarked, "I don't know why I give tricks my phone number. No one ever calls. Most of the time you trick with them and they don't even say hello to you the next time you see them."

Third, "partying" constituted the main recreational pattern among clones. These men regularly danced the night away in Circuit discos while "high" on such drugs as MDA, poppers, or cocaine.[47] Typically, the men took drugs at informal clique get-togethers prior to going to the club, usually for the purpose of sensual stimulation for partying. A financial analyst in his early thirties stated, "MDA gives me the energy to dance all night. When I am stoned on MDA I can really get into the music and lights. My legs feel rubbery, like they can move to every beat."

Partying largely occurred on weekend nights in Circuit clubs. On party nights, hundreds of drugged, bare-chested clones jammed the dance floor, where they danced feverishly to throbbing rhythms and dazzling lights while snorting poppers and throwing their arms and clenched fists into the air. The following account incisively depicts partying at the legendary Flamingo:

> As we entered the club at one in the morning (the doors had opened at midnight) I saw a room full of husky men, many of them shirtless, sipping beer or Coke. . . . Everyone in the audience could have put on professional display, since the crowd was extraordinarily muscular. . . . In the inner room people were dancing. . . . The light show was adequate but not obtrusive. . . . the blending of the records . . . the choice of music were superb. . . . Along one wall enthusiasts from the floor had leaped up onto a ledge and were grinding in dervish solitude. The mirror panels were frosted over with condensed sweat. One after another all the remaining shirts were peeled off. A stranger, face impassive, nosed up to us and soon was lending us his hanky soaked in ethyl chloride—a quick transit to the icy heart of a minor moon drifting around Saturn. Just as casually he stumbled off.[48]

The Post-AIDS Patterns of the 1980s

The distinctive sociocultural patterns of the clone social world largely dissolved during the 1980s. The men's previous erotic patterns meant that many clones were infected with HIV. That is, cruising and tricking had spread HIV infection widely among the men.

Many clones either became sick or died from AIDS. In fact, some of the earliest AIDS fatalities in New York City occurred among these men, and more than half the sample of three intensely studied cliques died. The rest were in varying stages of infection and illness. Only a handful tested negative for the HIV antibody.

AIDS-related diseases and fatalities caused clone structural entities either to collapse or to vanish. In most cases, the deaths of members broke cliques. For example, one clique lost six of its eight participants in three years. One survivor, a corporate executive in his late forties, commented, "Almost all the guys from my group have died. The lovers Tom and Jim went first in '82. Then Bob, Chad, and Ted in '83 and '84. Frank died a year later. Only Steve and I are left, but Steve has KS, and my lymph glands are swollen."[49]

In some cases, the burden of continuous sickness, caregiving, and dying split cliques. That is, emotional strains and pressures caused men to abandon the group. A free-lance writer in his thirties explained: "My clique fell apart after Seth, Bill, and Ed died. Al and Brian were afraid that one of us would get sick, so they moved to California. They just could not go through it again. After Seth died, Ben stopped returning our calls. I think he was pissed because he thought Bill, Ed, and I were not there enough for Seth." Moreover, the disintegration of cliques destroyed crowds. That is, the absence of familiar faces and acquaintances dissolved the social ties within crowds. A fashion designer in his late thirties remarked, "When I came here on Sunday evenings in the past, I would know at least half the bar. I could stand here and talk to different friends all night. Now I hardly know anyone, and I don't recognize most of these faces. Most of the old crowd has either died or left town."

Furthermore, the demise of crowds plus official sanctions demolished the Circuit. For example, many clubs, gyms, and restaurants closed for lack of crowd patronage. In this regard, many men believed that lack of crowd clientele shut The Saint. A photographer in his thirties explained: "The Saint's shutdown came as no big surprise. The crowd that went there was dying off. AIDS killed it. I mean how could they keep it open with everyone dying. Each time I went, it was increasingly empty." In addition, local health officials closed bathhouses and sex clubs for being public health hazards.

The remains of the clone social structure blended into the broader gay world. That is, the surviving structural entities were integrated into other gay social worlds. For example, some clone cliques reconstituted themselves as friendship groups in the HIV social world. For example, two surviving members of one clone clique formed a new friendship circle with men from an HIV-positive support group. In addition, a few Circuit bars remained open because they successfully attracted younger gay crowds.

AIDS also altered the meaning of clone erotic, recreational, and presentational patterns. The relation between drug use, inadequate rest, and recreational sex with immunological damage and AIDS caused cruising, tricking, and partying to be perceived as unhealthy and self-destructive, and a widespread decline in these practices resulted. In addition, fear of AIDS erased the reason for eroticized butch imagery.

Several social patterns replaced the previous forms of clone life. First, butch presentational strategies were largely deeroticized. For example, clones still wore manly attire but in such a way as to camouflage musculature, genitals, and buttocks. That is, they wore underwear and looser T-shirts and levis. In addition, clones developed more natural physiques. In this regard, love handles became accepted as indicating health. Furthermore, most gathering places either ceased showing pornographic films or forbid sexual contact in backrooms.

Second, clone erotic patterns switched to safer and relational sex. Typically, clones defined safer sex as protected anal intercourse. In this vein, an actor in his twenties quipped, "The AIDIES [1980s] is the era of latex love." Indeed,

the men routinely shared information about safe and comfortable use of condoms.

However, there was considerable ambiguity about the risk involved in other erotic acts. Almost all the men scoffed at official safer-sex guidelines for kissing and fellatio. Most felt that deep kissing was safe because of the low concentrations of HIV in saliva. They felt similarly about oral sex with no ejaculation or preseminal fluids because there was no exchange of body fluids. Hence, they regularly practiced these behaviors.

In addition, relational sex became normative among clones. That is, sex for most men occurred in the context of sociosexual relationships; they had sex mainly with date, boyfriends, or lovers. In fact, some attended classes on how to date men at an AIDS service organization.

The relational ethos fostered new erotic attitudes. Most men now perceived coupling, monogamy, and celibacy as healthy and socially acceptable. An art dealer who was in his forties stated, "Ten years ago it was déclassé not to have sex. People thought you were weird if you did not trick. Now celibacy is in; people think you are healthy." Conversely, most men devalued routine recreational sex as dated and unhealthy. An educator in his mid-thirties commented while in a bar, "You see the guy over by the wall, the one groping the other guy. He is a real whore. I mean he still cruises the bar for tricks. I've seen him go home with three different people in the last week. You'd think he would know better, with AIDS and all that."

Third, health maintenance and community service became the chief recreational patterns among clones. Typically, the men hoped to boost their immune system through health maintenance. In this way, they felt that strict regimens of rest, diet, and exercise would keep them healthy. Hence, they regularly slept, took vitamins, ate health food, and exercised at health clubs. In addition, many practiced stress reduction and alternative forms of healing, including visualizations, homeopathy, and macrobiotic diets.

Community service chiefly involved caregiving and activism. The men cared for friends with AIDS, who were typically members of their clique. They made them dinner, paid their bills, cleaned their homes, and took them to doctors and hospitals. Moreover, they provided emotional support during the illness, offering love, acceptance, and companionship. At times, they even had power of attorney, with responsibility for making treatment decisions and implementing funeral arrangements. Clones also became unpaid volunteers in political action groups or AIDS service organizations. In particular, many became some of the earliest volunteers at Gay Men's Health Crisis. Others volunteered in more militant direct action groups such as Act-Up.

AIDS made volunteering socially acceptable among clones. Typically, the men devalued volunteering before the epidemic. Many even openly denigrated gay activists as boring. Others saw no need for activism since they did not believe that gay men were oppressed. AIDS forced them to question these assumptions. The government's inadequate response to the AIDS crisis painfully proved that gay men were indeed oppressed. Consequently, many became politicized, and they began to see the importance of volunteering for social and political change.

Conclusion

The material presented in this chapter shows that the best constructionist explanation for the sociocultural organization of clone life in the West Village is Simon and Gagnon's model. According to this model, elements of the surrounding culture and social structure largely shape the forms of life within the gay world. The model incorporates the explanatory factors associated with the other constructionist explanations for clone sociocultural patterns. That is,

this model views homosexual stigma and roles as some of the sociocultural forces molding clone life.

Following Simon and Gagnon, the social context shaped the forms of clone life. That is, AIDS, gay liberation, male gender roles, and the ethics of self-fulfillment, constraint, and commitment molded and remolded sociocultural patterns within the clone social world. For example, gay liberation and the advent of AIDS significantly affected clone social structure. At first, gay liberation's success in lessening legal and social penalization of homosexuality in New York City engendered the formation of socially isolated cliques, crowds, and gathering places. Later, AIDS-related diseases and deaths either dissolved or socially integrated these structural forms into the broader gay world.

In addition, gay liberation, male gender roles, and self-fulfillment values shaped clone social patterns during the 1970s. Gay liberation's redefinition of same-sex love as a manly form of erotic expression provoked masculine identification among clones, which was conveyed through both butch presentational strategies and cruising, tricking, and partying. In particular, butch attire, muscles, and masculine environments vividly articulated the sense that clones were *men*. In a similar vein, the roughness, objectification, anonymity, and phallocentrism associated with cruising and tricking expressed such macho dictates as toughness and recreational sex. Finally, the endurance, impersonality, and risk taking connected with partying conveyed macho ruggedness and activity-centered forms of social interaction. The cultural ideal of self-gratification further encouraged these patterns, sanctioning the sexual and recreational hedonism inherent in cruising, tricking, and partying.

AIDS and the constraint and commitment ethics reformulated these forms in the 1980s. Health concerns encouraged acceptance of values associated with restrained hedonism, which provoked safer sex and health maintenance.

These concerns also prompted endorsement of the ideal of connectedness, which fostered community service and relational sex.

Notes

This chapter is dedicated to the memory of Michael Robert Distler (1950–86). I would like to thank Dr. Kristine Anderson for her help in the preparation of this [article].

1. William Simon and John H. Gagnon, "Homosexuality: The Formulation of a Sociological Perspective," *Journal of Health and Social Behavior* 8 (1967): 179.

2. See, e.g., John Gagnon and William Simon, *Sexual Conduct: The Social Sources of Human Sexuality* (Chicago: Aldine, 1973), chap. 5; William Simon and John H. Gagnon, "The Lesbians: A Preliminary Overview," in *Sexual Deviance,* ed. John H. Gagnon and William Simon (New York: Harper & Row, 1967), pp. 247–82.

3. For social labeling studies of male homosexuality, see Martin S. Weinberg and Colin J. Williams, *Male Homosexuals: Their Problems and Adaptions* (New York: Oxford University Press, 1974); Joseph Harry and William B. DeVall, *The Social Organization of Gay Males* (New York: Praeger, 1978); Laud Humphreys, *Out of the Closets: The Sociology of Homosexual Liberation* (Englewood Cliffs, N.J.: Prentice-Hall, 1972).

4. Carol A. B. Warren, "Homosexuality and Stigma," in *Homosexual Behavior: A Modern Reappraisal,* ed. Judd Marmor (New York: Basic, 1980), p. 139. Kenneth Plummer, *Sexual Stigma: An Interactionist Account* (Boston: Routledge & Kegan Paul, 1975), p. 102.

5. For a discussion of the social role theory of homosexuality, see Mary McIntosh, "The Homosexual Role," *Social Problems* 16 (1968): 182–92.

6. The term "gay ghetto" refers to an urban neighborhood housing a dense concentration of gay institutions and residents. For a discussion of the validity of labeling these areas as ghettos, see Martin P. Levine, "Gay Ghetto," *Journal of Homosexuality* 4 (1979): 363–77.

7. George A. Theodorson and Achilles G. Theodorson, *A Modern Dictionary of Sociology* (New York: Crowell, 1969), p. 444.

8. See Michael Signorile, "Clone Wars," *Outweek,* 28 November 1990, pp. 39–45.

9. See Dennis Altman, *The Homosexualization of America, the Americanization of the Homosexual* (New York: St. Martin's 1982), p. 103; and Randy Alfred, "Clones: A New Definition," *Advocate,* 18 March 1982, pp. 22–23.

10. For an overview of these movements and changes, see Charles A. Reich, *The Greening of America* (New York: Barton, 1970); Daniel Bell, *The Cultural Contradictions of Capitalism* (New York: Basic, 1976); Aldon D. Morris, *Origin of the Civil Rights Movement: Black Communities Organizing for Change* (New York: Free Press, 1984); Jo Freeman, *Politics of Women's Liberation* (New York: Longman, 1975); Edwin M. Schur, *The Awareness Trap: Self-Absorption Instead of Social Change* (New York: McGraw-Hill, 1976); and Daniel Yankelovitch, *New Rules: Searching for Self-Fulfillment in a World Turned Upside Down* (New York: Random House, 1981).

11. See Rhoda Lois Blumberg, *Civil Rights: The 1960 Freedom Struggle* (Boston: Twayne, 1984); and Myra Marx Ferree and Beth B. Hess, *Controversy and Coalition: The New Feminist Movement* (Boston: Twayne, 1985).

12. See Minion K. C. Morrison, *Black Political Mobilization: Leadership, Power, and Mass Behavior* (Albany: State University of New York Press, 1987).

13. See Yankelovitch, *New Rules.*

14. See Reich, *The Greening of America.*

15. See Yankelovitch, *New Rules.*

16. See Schur, *The Awareness Trap.*

17. See Yankelovitch, *New Rules.*

18. See Daniel Yankelovitch, "American Values: Changes and Stability," *Public Opinion* 6 (1984): 2–9.

19. Ibid.

20. Art Levine, "America's Addiction to Addictions," *U.S. News and World Report,* 5 February 1990, pp. 62–63. For a critical treatment of the concept of sexual addiction, see Martin P. Levine and Richard

R. Troiden, "The Myth of Sexual Compulsivity," *Journal of Sex Research* 25 (1988): 47–48.

21. See Yankelovitch, "American Values."

22. See Levine and Troiden, "The Myth of Sexual Compulsivity."

23. I am grateful to Michael S. Kimmel for the concept of homosexuality as gender deviance.

24. For a discussion of the cultural roles for homosexuality, see the introduction to *Gay Men: The Sociology of Male Homosexuality*, ed. Martin P. Levine (New York: Harper & Row, 1979), pp. 1–16.

25. For a review of sanctions, see Humphreys, *Out of the Closets*. For an overview of legal sanctions against gay men during the 1960s, see Edwin M. Schur, *Crimes without Victims: Deviant Behavior and Public Policy: Abortion, Homosexuality, and Drug Addiction* (Englewood Cliffs, N.J.: Prentice-Hall, 1965). For a discussion of psychological conceptualizations and treatment of gay men in the 1960s, see Marcel T. Saghir and Eli Robins, *Male and Female Homosexuality* (Baltimore: Wilkens, 1973); and Ronald Bayer, *Homosexuality and American Psychiatry* (New York: Basic, 1981). For a discussion of social sanctions against gay men, see Weinberg and Williams, *Male Homosexuals*. On deviance, see Howard S. Becker, *Outsiders: Studies in the Sociology of Deviance* (New York: Free Press, 1963).

26. Simon and Gagnon, "Homosexuality," p. 183.

27. See Laud Humphreys, "Exodus and Identity: The Emerging Gay Culture," in Levine, ed., *Gay Men*, pp. 134–47.

28. For a general discussion of stigma management, see Erving Goffman, *Stigma: Notes on the Management of Spoiled Identity* (Englewood Cliffs, N.J.: Prentice-Hall 1963). For an overview of how techniques for neutralizing shaped forms of gay life, see Richard R. Troiden, *Gay and Lesbian Identity: A Sociological Analysis* (Dix Hills, N.Y.: General Hall, 1988), pp. 95–96. For a discussion of the patterns associated with passing, see Carol A. B. Warren, *Identity and Community in the Gay World* (New York: Wiley, 1974). For an overview of homosexual camp, see Esther Newton, *Mother Camp: Female Impersonators in America* (Englewood Cliffs, N.J.: Prentice-Hall, 1972). For a discussion of the effect of stigmatization on gay identity, see Humphreys, *Out of the Closets*, pp. 39–41.

29. See Gagnon and Simon, *Sexual Conduct.*

30. See Warren, *Identity and Community*; and Martin Duberman, "Gay in the Fifties," *Salmagundi* 58–59 (1982): 42–75.

31. See Dennis Altman, *Homosexual: Oppression and Liberation* (New York: Avon, 1971); Barry D. Adam, *The Rise of a Gay and Lesbian Movement* (Boston: Twayne, 1987); John D'Emilio, *Sexual Politics, Sexual Communities: The Making of a Homosexual Minority in the United States, 1940–1970* (Chicago: University of Chicago Press, 1983); Toby Marotta, *The Politics of Homosexuality* (Boston: Houghton Mifflin, 1981).

32. See Peter Fischer, *The Gay Mystique* (New York: Stein & Day, 1972).

33. See Don Teal, *The Gay Militants* (New York: Stein & Day, 1971).

34. See Laud Humphreys and Brian Miller, "Identities in the Emerging Gay Culture," in Marmor, ed., *Homosexual Behavior*, pp. 142–56.

35. Laud Humphreys, "Exodus and Identity," p. 139.

36. For an overview of sociocultural elaboration in urban gay ghettos, see John Alan Lee, "The Gay Connection," *Urban Life* 2 (1979): 175–98.

37. On changes in gay life-styles, see Altman, *The Homosexualization of America*, pp. 1–38. On the abandonment of camp, see Wayne Sage, "Inside the Colossal Closet," in Levine, ed., *Gay Men*, pp. 148–63. For a discussion of gay liberation's redefinition of homosexuality as masculine, see Marotta, *The Politics of Homosexuality*.

38. See Altman, *The Homosexualization of America.*

39. See Dennis Altman, *AIDS in the Mind of America* (Garden City, N.Y.: Anchor/Doubleday, 1986), pp. 82–109; and Andrew Holleran, "The Petrification of Clonestyle," *Christopher Street*, no. 69 (1982): 14–18.

40. John H. Gagnon, "Disease and Desire," *Daedalus* 118, no. 3 (1989): 47–78.

41. See Altman, *AIDS*, pp. 82–109; and Levine and Troiden, "The Myth of Sexual Compulsivity."

42. "Butch" refers to manliness.

43. Edmund White, *States of Desire* (New York: Dutton, 1980), pp. 45–46.

44. "Cruising" refers to the search for sexual partners, and "tricking" denotes anonymous sex.

45. "Hung" signifies having a large penis, and "built" indicates having a muscular body.

46. "Pot" refers to marijuana, "poppers" amyl nitrates. Quaaludes are barbiturates.

47. "Partying" denotes recreational drug use and disco dancing. "High" signifies drunk or stoned. MDA was a hallucinogenic drug with stimulant properties.

48. White, *States of Desire*, pp. 278–79.

49. "KS" refers to Kaposi's Sarcoma.

7

ARTICLE

Edward H. Thompson, Jr.

Older Men as Invisible Men in Contemporary Society

As the 21st century approaches, academic researchers, journalists, professional caregivers, and other opinion makers are beginning to see a shortcoming in our discourse on class, race, and gender. We have ignored age. Marginalization of elders might feel wrong and yet be in perfect accord with ongoing discussions. [This article calls] attention to one group of elders: older men. It is timely, acknowledging that "older men" are a distinct group of men and elders. Their gendered experiences and social lives are different from women their age as well as younger men. It is timely also to look inside the elderly male population to appreciate the diversity among older men when generations are studied separately, class differences become well known, or family status, ethnicity, and race are considered.

. . . Why have elderly men been relatively invisible? Four assessments are offered. Beforehand, Bureau of the Census information is used to develop profiles of the men (and women) within the age band "65 and over." These demographic sketches are constructed to call atten-

tion to the presence of older men in the United States, as well as the diversity among elder males. The sketches provide a necessary window into objective reality. Following this demographic overview, the question of older men's invisibility is addressed systematically in an effort to grasp the problem of such invisibility as one generated in conventional practices of reality and knowledge production. Seeing older men's invisibility as built into the maintenance of core values and the rules of knowledge production helps reveal how social constructions about "old men" and theories addressing the interaction of gender and age pose intriguing research agendas and policy questions.

Daguerreotypes

We are all somewhat aware of the remarkable restructuring of the shape of the age pyramid that has occurred in the United States over the last century. We also are somewhat aware of the remarkable shifts that are forecasted to take place between 2010 and 2025. These are the years when the age cohort of baby boomers will begin their march into the "Third Age" (Laslett, 1987) and their lives as elders. This march of the baby boomers will prove to be both historic for the nation and for older men's lives.

A century ago in 1890, just 4% of the U.S. population was aged 65 and older. The entire elder population numbered approximately 3 million. By 1930, the group has doubled in size to 6.7 million. It more than doubled in size again by 1960, and by the early 1990s nearly doubled once more (Figure 7.1). Currently, there are 32 million men and women age 65 and older. They represent 12% of the nation and include more than 3 million elders over age 85, an age many now identify as "very elderly" rather than the twice stigmatizing tag "old-olds" (U.S. Bureau of the Census, 1993b).

Implicit in these changes and hinted at by the growing size of the nation's elder population is what each individual man experiences: It is much more common for men to at least celebrate their 65th birthday. A long life has become ordinary and predictable. Life expectancy at birth has increased for white males from 48 years in 1900 to 73 years in 1990, and for black males from just 32 years to 66 years (see Table 7.1 for more detail). The proportion of males surviving from birth to age 65 has similarly increased: from 39% to 76% for white males, and from just 19% to 58% for black males (Table 7.2; U.S. Bureau of the Census, 1978, 1993a). The narrowing of the marked racial disparity in men's life expectancy witnessed from the beginning to the end of the century is most often attributed to improved nutrition and the less toxic physical environment in which people work and reside, particularly for African-Americans (McKinlay & McKinlay, 1977). For these very same "health" reasons, the life span for males to be born in the first decade of the 21st century is forecast to be virtually the same for all ethnic and racial groups, and not much greater than found for white males currently (U.S. Bureau of the Census, 1993b). But this prediction for greater equality in life span is debatable. Manton and Soldo (1985) forecast increasing divergence. They observed substantial variation in the timing of death when standard deviations of death rates are examined, rather than the me-

FIGURE 7.1

Number of Elders in the United States, 1870–1990
SOURCE: U.S. Bureau of the Census (1976, 1993a).

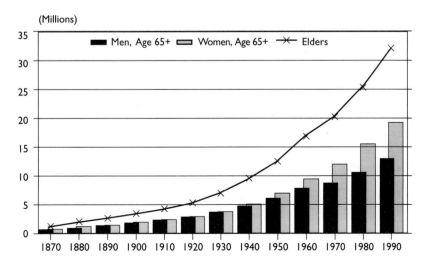

| TABLE 7.1 | Life expectancy at birth (in years) |

	Males		Females	
	White	**Black**	**White**	**Black**
1900	48.2	32.5	51.1	35.0
1929–1931	59.1	47.6	62.7	49.5
1959–1961[a]	67.6	61.5	74.2	66.5
1990	72.6	66.0	79.3	70.3

SOURCE: U.S. Bureau of the Census (1976, 1993a).
[a]Black and other nonwhite "races."

dian number of years of survival, and this variability in mortality has increased over the last two decades.

With many more men routinely living to and beyond age 65, there has been an emerging consciousness of the distinct age groups that exist among elder men (Neugarten, 1975). Formerly, all men aged 65 and older were categorically the same: "old." Distinct elder age groups are now regularly identified (see Table 7.3). The male population aged 65 to 74, for example, is part of what is called the "young elderly."

This group is perhaps the most widely recognized, partly because of these older men's sheer numbers and presence and partly because of the research attention given to their retirements. But as each year passes, this age cohort represents a smaller and smaller proportion of all elder males. In 1990, for instance, the young elderly group, as a percentage of all males aged 65 and older, constituted 62% of older white males and 63% of the elder black males (U.S. Bureau of the Census, 1993a). By comparison, young elders accounted for nearly three of every four elderly

| TABLE 7.2 | Proportion of populations surviving to age 65 (in percentages) |

	Males		Females	
	White	**Black**	**White**	**Black**
1900	39	19	44	22
1929–1931	53	29	61	31
1959–1961[a]	66	51	81	61
1990	76	58	86	75

SOURCE: U.S. Bureau of the Census (1976, 1993a).
[a]Black and other nonwhite "races."

TABLE 7.3	Growth of older male population, 1970–1992 (in thousands)		
	1970	**1992**	**% Increase**
65–69 years old	3,125	4,478	43.3
70–74 years old	2,317	3,643	57.2
75–79 years old	1,562	2,538	62.5
80–84 years old	876	1,446	65.1
85 and over	489	911	86.3
Males, 65+	8,369	13,016	55.5

SOURCE: U.S. Bureau of the Census (1993a, 1993b).

white and black males in 1930. Projections for 2050 indicate that young elders will represent just 47% of elder white males and 52% of elder black males. The key point is that the population of elders is itself aging, with increasing numbers of men in the 85-and-over population. What are the experiences, social worlds, concerns, opportunities, and views of the "over 75"? How do faith experiences change images of self? What opportunities do older men have in their families?

Most striking about the information in Figure 7.1 is the gender difference in mortality over time. Men and women were equally represented in the growing elder population until the 1930s. Then men's morbidity and mortality became measurably distinct from women's. The size of the elder population has since reflected these different mortality rates and, increasingly, the disproportionate number of males to females within the elder population. Today the

minority of elderly are men: 13.0 million versus 19.2 million women (U.S. Bureau of the Census, 1993b). Because of the sex and gender differentials in life expectancy, men are increasingly the minority population as age advances. It is still remarkable for men to reach age 85: The 911,000 men who survived to age 85 in 1992 may well be the fastest-growing cohort, but they represented just 7% of all elderly men (review Table 7.3). By comparison, one in eight elderly women has reached age 85 (U.S. Bureau of the Census, 1993b).

The importance of gender to aging is more visible in Figure 7.2. As presented, the plotted sex ratio of men to women aged 65 and older was balanced at virtually 1:1 until the 1930s. For the next 60 years, however, the sex ratio turned downward and thus a "feminization" of the elder population has been ongoing since the 1930s (Arber & Ginn, 1991; Verbrugge, 1989). By the early 1990s, the nation's elders were rep-

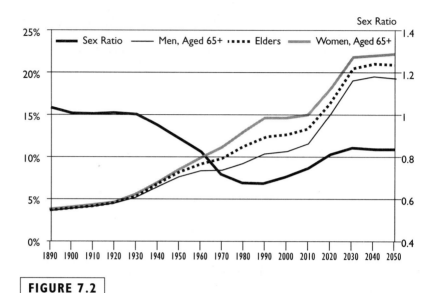

FIGURE 7.2

Proportion of Older Men and Older Women in the United States, 1890–2050
SOURCE: U.S. Bureau of the Census (1976, 1993a, 1993b).

resented by three women for every two men. During this 60-year history, improvements in nutrition, work, and living environments, as well as medical therapies, has multiplied the proportion of elder men from nearly 4% to 10%. However, because gendered morbidity and mortality risk factors paced the deaths differently (Harrison, Chin, & Ficarrotto, 1992; Waldron, 1976; Wingard & Cohn, 1990), the proportion of older women increased at a quicker rate and now approaches 15%.

The often-cited gender gap in longevity, which steadily widened for the last 60 years, may have peaked. Projections for the next 60 years (Figure 7.2) suggest two stunning trends: (a) the sex ratio will tighten considerably, and (b) the proportion of elders will stabilize just above 20% of the nation's population. This means many more men are expected to live to fully experience and extend the normal male life course deep into the Third Age, and, much more so than previously, women will face the life-shortening

risks associated with paid employment. By 2030, it is unlikely that older men could continue to be invisible in the population: They will represent one of every five men in the nation, and among elders there will be, on average, four men per five women. Put differently, older men will account for 20% of all males, twice the shadow they now cast, and this older male population will be the size of today's entire elderly population, a tenacious 32 million. What are the implications for elderly men's (and women's) lives? The forecasts further suggest that women's prior "advantage" in longevity will decrease and within 60 years the numerical ratio of women over men in later life will diminish considerably, particularly for the population under 85.

Although these changes are imminent and will amend the past 60 years' feminization of the elder population, there is no need to wait until the baby boomers march into old age or until elderly men cast off their demographic invisibility before scholars begin to study older men's lives. There are already nearly 13 million men age 65 and older. The minority among elders, and especially the minority among the very elderly, 13 million older men is still a sizable population. It is greater than the number of all undergraduates enrolled full-time in 4-year colleges in 1992 (U.S. Department of Education, 1992), greater than the number of children living in single-parent families in 1980 (Thompson & Gongla, 1983; U.S. Bureau of the Census, 1992), nearly 20 times greater than the number of physicians practicing medicine in 1993 (Roback, Randolph, & Seidman, 1993) and 10 times the number of people incarcerated in correctional institutions in 1990 (U.S. Bureau of the Census, 1993a). Mainstream journals and opinion makers have made us much more familiar with these folks, however smaller their population size.

Reasons for Invisibility

Older men have remained invisible for reasons besides their smaller number. For one, gerontologists have not encouraged the distinction between the concepts of "sex" and "gender." *Gender* is often accepted as if synonymous with *sex,* serving fundamentally as a categorical construct for grouping the aged. Consequently, the literature introduces us to older biological males by virtue of describing a sex difference in aging. However, what surely distinguishes older biological males, as a group, is their cohort-specific, gendered social lives. As much as research has treated all men as if they were genderless (Kimmel & Messner, 1992), fewer researchers have paid attention to the masculinities that older men encounter of those they disclose.

Another reason for older invisibility is that aging and ageism do not affect men and women equally. From a political economy perspective, it is true that older men have a more comfortable, privileged life compared to older women

of the same generation. Consequently, when gender is taken into consideration, elderly women have a much higher profile in gerontological research because the view of aging places women in double jeopardy relative to older men (Sontag, 1972) and because sociological research on "advantaged" groups has traditionally attracted less sustained attention than studies of the disadvantaged (Berger, 1963). In this frame, the pernicious concept of "the aged" is synonymous with a disadvantaged group and thus more synonymous with the providence of older women than older men.

Similarly, the organizations, interest groups, industries, professional societies, and political bodies that make up "the aging enterprise" and serve the elderly in one capacity or another (Estes, 1979, 1993) also furnish ideas about aging and images of elder men. These are elaborately constructed images pressed into public consciousness, and the images the aging enterprise has fabricated are just that—"constructed." To illustrate, for two decades the medical-industrial complex has profited handsomely by medicalizing elderly men's lives more than meeting elderly men's and women's needs. Cardiac catheterization laboratories, fourth- and fifth-generation ventricular pacemakers, arthroscopic surgical technology, and cardiac bypass surgery all derive great profit by "servicing" the elderly male population's health problems and yield much greater profit for the enterprise than would programming to raise the standard of living and health status of all elders. The socially constructed image of elderly men—former breadwinners and national leaders—as "old" and by definition in poor health fuels compassion and, of course, greater profit than the image of most elderly men (and women) as having poor access to health and medical care services. This "compassionate ageism" (Binstock, 1983) is also sexist. It has medicalized elderly men's lives and their perceived well-being, perhaps more than elderly women's. One unintended consequence, for example, of the "compassion" and profiteering is that older men's nonmedical needs become frivolous. The everyday needs of healthy elder males, as well as elder men's need for services other than medical interventions, become remote concerns when compared to the life-and-death emphasis.

In much the same way that gerontologists have inadvertently homogenized elders to make older men genderless, scholars working in the field of gender studies have not paid much notice to men in late life. Older men's masculinities are couched as an invisible part of the dynamics of hegemony or, more simply, ignored. Whether in the research traditions or contemporary theorizing "about men," age is truncated. To illustrate, Daniel Levinson and his colleagues (1978) discuss men's late adulthood in their landmark *The Seasons of a Man's Life* in just seven pages (pages 33–39) and characterize this age in "discontinuous" imagery, as if aging is a negation of masculinity: "A primary developmental task of late adulthood is to find a new balance of involvement with society and with the self. A man in this era is experiencing more fully the process of dying and he should have the possibility of choosing more freely his mode of living" (p. 36). The widely praised second edition of *Men's Lives* that Kimmel and Messner organized for gender scholars has not one article among the 56 that directly probes older men's masculinities. At this point in the development of gender studies, the masculinities of older men have been subordinated to the concerted effort to understand middle-aged and younger men's lives, who are, as Ortega y Gasset (1958) suggest, "the dominant" group. Even when a life course perspective is recognized (e.g., Connell, 1992; Segal, 1990), the theoretical discourse on masculinities has concentrated on social practices of young to middle-aged men and, by default, marginalized the masculinities of elderly men. But, metatheoretically, has the marginalization of older men in the scholarship on gender contributed to the preservation of conventional discourses on

masculinity? Failing to acknowledge elderly men as a distinct group of men may have homogenized not only adulthood but also theory on masculinity.

One can see, with retrospective clarity, how these four initiatives have helped conceal older men's lives. My interest is to examine them collectively in greater detail. The task is to advance the conceptual and theoretical underpinnings for a more long-term discussion of older men as men and as elders.

The Relative Comfort of Older Men's Lives

They are often pictured as poor, standoffish, persnickety, and of ill health. Often they are imagined to be living alone, following singular paths. But as a group, and compared to both older women and younger men, they are more likely to have fewer financial liabilities and more assets, enjoy good health, lead active lives unhindered by disability, and experience few distressing "turning points" or "life events" in this age of the life span.

Although the incomes of elder males, as a group, are lower than younger men's, in a peculiar way "less is more" (Lazer & Shaw, 1987). Older men spend little of their assets. They are more likely to have paid off their home mortgage, and they spend less on the necessities—household operations, food, clothing—as well as discretionary items (Lazer & Shaw, 1987). In fact, older men would seem to be at a quality-of-life advantage, for they may face fewer emotionally wrenching life events than younger males, who cope with the work and family conflicts of two-income households, the downsizing of corporate America, intermittent periods of unemployment, state governments that have gotten out of the education business and children's educational needs, and so on (Chirboga, 1989).

Older men, compared to older women, would also seem to be at a quality-of-life advantage even though they are at a mortality disadvantage; their deaths may come sooner, but later life for older men presents fewer troubles (Kaplan, Anderson, & Wingard, 1991). Consider, for example, older men's living arrangements and marital status. Excluding elders who make up the institutional population, such as those living in nursing homes or other places providing custodial care, elderly men are much more likely than elderly women to live with their spouses. Nearly three quarters of elderly men today are both married and living with their spouses. Barely 1 man in 10 aged 65–74 is a widower, and by the time they are age 75–84, just 2 in 10 are widowed (U.S. Bureau of the Census, 1992). Aging does not oblige many older men to recast their lives and go it alone after the death of a spouse.

By comparison, fewer than 40% of the older women in the nation are both married and living with their spouse. Half of all elder women are widowed, and the vast majority of widows (71%) do not live with others. They, rather than men, follow singular paths. As many as one third of all women aged 65–74 and about one half aged 75 and older lived alone in 1992 (see Figures 7.3

and 7.4 for details). The proportions for older men, by comparison, were 13% and 22%, respectively. The point is not men's earlier deaths. Rather, it is their relatively nonplussed lives, compared to older women of the same age, when living arrangements and marital status are compared. Men are not obliged to bury their spouses and live alone as often as women. It is also because elderly men as a group are more likely to be married and less likely to live alone that they derive several other late-life advantages.

Thus for the vast majority of older men, the company of a spouse affords greater opportunity to enjoy the extension of the life span into the Third Age. Older men rely on their spouses and report greater satisfaction with marriage than do older women (Antonucci & Akiyama, 1987). And as Shumaker and Hill (1991) noted, the protective role of social support is consistently demonstrated for marrieds and white men. For older men, assets—and not just their income and pension—are greater, allowing them greater autonomy. Personal care tasks are maintained by two adults, not just one. Life is experienced in the company of another.

FIGURE 7.3

Marital Status of Older Men, 1992
SOURCE: U.S. Bureau of the Census (1993b).

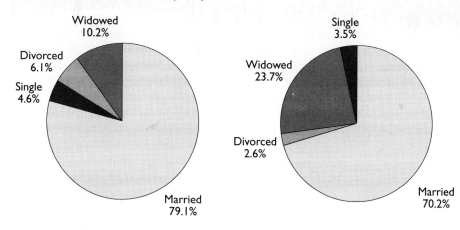

Men, Age 65–74

Widowed
10.2%

Divorced
6.1%

Single
4.6%

Married
79.1%

Men, Age 75+

Single
3.5%

Widowed
23.7%

Divorced
2.6%

Married
70.2%

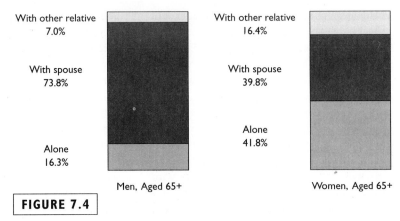

FIGURE 7.4

Living Arrangements of Older Men and Women, 1992
SOURCE: U.S. Bureau of the Census (1993b).

Not surprisingly, the relative advantages to everyday morale and well-being that the community of a spouse affords elderly men does not apply equally to all older men. We need to anticipate and be sensitive to the diversity among elder men. Elderly black men are much less likely to live with a spouse than are white men or men of Hispanic origin. Among the "young elders" aged 65 to 74, the married proportions for each group are 58%, 79%, and 77%, respectively. Add 10 years to compare men aged 75 and older, and the proportions drop roughly 10% to 46%, 70%, and 67%, respectively. This variance in older men's marital status across ethnic and racial lines may be a result of the greater proportion of black men who never marry (U.S. Bureau of the Census, 1992) and the higher levels of marital disruption among blacks. Whatever the reasons, the proportion of elderly men who live alone is higher for blacks (29%) than whites (15%) or men of Hispanic origin (11%).

Socially Constructed Images of Aged Men

Visualize the image. The men hold themselves upright and proud—these middle-aged men whose time of life is shifting from "early" to "middle adulthood" and who are perhaps at a peak in their impact on the world outside the home. They are the "dominant" generation, as Ortega y Gasset defined the age 45–60. They make their ideas and aims the pivotal ones in every sector of society: business, politics, religion, science. But soon they take up wearing bifocals, their skin wrinkles more, their hair turns silvery, they become grandparents, they stoop, and they embrace the season of life that Levinson and his colleagues (1978) call "late adulthood" and, for some, "late, late adulthood."

In the popular culture men in late adulthood no longer occupy center stage. Their generation is no longer the dominant one: It has been displaced by a younger, "Pepsi" generation. Men in late life are classed as "senior" or "old." They become "socially opaque" (Green, 1993). They are presumed to have completed the major part—perhaps all—of their life work. The older man sees himself living in his shadow or death's (Levinson et al., 1978). Writing in *Esquire,* novelist Thomas Morgan (1987, p. 162) describes a memory of his father's 60th birthday: "I do not remember his exact words, only that he seemed to be telling me he was conceding at sixty, perhaps welcoming at sixty that he need not be a part of the future. . . . As it happened, he worked ten more years, but lived, I'm sorry to say, as though it were all an anticlimax."

Television commercials, newspaper presentations, and magazine advertisements fully impart this image, too. No longer in control, wealthy, and urbane, old men are pictured as living neither in the city nor the suburbs but in a small rural town or in the country, near the pasture. Homes are smaller, more plain, without gadgets and machines. Bodies are not virile, rather pleasantly plump. Checked flannel shirts have replaced the dark blue suit. As part of the "grandparent" generation, advertisements will show that the older man's soft lap cat has replaced the younger man's spirited black Labrador retriever. Lemonade is now the drink of choice (Bucholz & Bynum, 1982; Ferraro, 1992; Kaiser & Chandler, 1988; Powell & Williamson, 1985; Swayne & Greco, 1987). Such images seem inflated to the point of parody. Perhaps, as Wernick (1987, p. 283) would maintain, when advertisers and other opinion makers become interested in speaking to and about older men, the more conventional construction of masculinity as a symbolic term will have weakened, and we can then expect a disappearance of what one might call the *metaphorical* old man.

Until then, it seems that the constructed images of older men leave these elders with two strikes against them. First is the prejudice within public (and professional) attitudes regarding "old age" in general (Butler, 1969; Walsh & Connor, 1979). Elders—in particular, elderly men—are thought to suffer significant losses: Their occupational role, their livelihood and community of co-workers, their health and independence, and their masculinity are commonly thought to be displaced by aging. The traditional discourses of masculinity and aging separate adult men into two categories: old and all others. The older man is depicted in a yo-yo fashion, with both positive and negative content (Hummert, 1990). He is portrayed as interactively and psychologically involved in more expressive and caring roles within the family. He is also, by default,

contrasted with an image of the younger, justly preoccupied father and husband whose primary concern is with productive labor and power management. The underlying core values in the discourse extol youth, independence, and economic productiveness and an aversion to aging and anything feminine (Cole, 1986; Fischer, 1978; Green, 1993, p. 53).

By displacing elder men from the mainstream, one result of contemporary cultural coding is the oppression of older men. As Fischer, 1978) observed when he reviewed American cultural documents and chronicled the development of a "cult of youth" from 1770 to 1970, the definition of elder men as oppressors provided a symbol for all other echelons among men to unite against gerontocracy.

The second strike is older men's perceived genderlessness. Ask people to complete the sentence "An old man . . ." and then listen to ungendered ageism and his feminization. Older men are depicted as sedentary, resting on a park bench, passing time, asexual. Images of older men basically portray diminished masculinity (Kite, Deaux, & Miele, 1991; Puglisi & Jackson, 1980–81; Silverman, 1977). To many people, aging is a negation of masculinity, and thus older men become effeminate over time. Given this cultural assumption, older men are used, however unwittingly. The degendered imagery of the older man keeps afloat a masculinity and a discourse that sustains younger men. The conventional discourse describes gender in simply binary terms, wherein aging diminishes men's masculinity and, by default, heightens their femininity over time. Framed this way, images of age-specific and cohort-specific masculinities never rise to a threshold of public consciousness. Rather, the social construction maintains that "old men" are not men at all.

Discourses in the Academy

As the size of elderly female population increased between 1930 and 1990, the importance of gender and aging commanded greater and greater attention among academics and policy makers (Haug, Ford, & Sheafor, 1985; Herzog, Holden, & Seltzer, 1989; Lesnoff-Caravaglia, 1984; Markson, 1985; Matthews, 1979; also see Coyle, 1989). Ironically, as older women's lives and their profound needs gained visibility, older men became more marginal and invisible. In fact, being elderly appears in some quarters to have become synonymous with being female. For example, in *Gender and Later Life,* Arber and Ginn (1991, p. vii) state, "Later life is primarily an experience of women." Their first chapter is powerfully titled "The Feminization of Later Life," because the demographics of aging show that elderly women outnumber elderly men in later life, especially as age advances. The message that is constructed, however, goes beyond making note of a sex differential in longevity. Rather, as women's experience in later life is brought to the foreground, older men's fade from attention. Arber and Ginn's otherwise very fine work makes "later life" as synonymous with women as "gender" has become.

Homogenizing elders—as reflected by mid-century discourses on "the aged" or the new academic discourse on feminization—was once said to be akin to "tabloid thinking" (Binstock, 1983, p. 140). Homogenizing sets the stage to ignore individual differences and to think about "the elderly" only at the collective level as disadvantaged individuals beset by common problems. Kalish (1979) warned that this construction was a form of "new ageism." The new discourse of feminization of the aged goes beyond the devaluation of diversity (Butler, 1969) to thwart discussion of the ways in which the population of older men is itself devalued and the ways in which men's personal experiences of age are challenged by cultural double binds and structurally induced conflicts about masculinities— conflicts such as about their work ethic and their diminished social significance as men, or their relative social opaqueness as individuals versus a collective.

Although the core value behind older men's invisibility is academics' "compassionate ageism" for older women (Binstock, 1983), knowledge production in gerontological studies currently makes for blind spots and a lack of understanding of older men. As Cook (1992, p. 293) warned in an editorial in *The Gerontologist,* "If we want the public and the media to abandon the oversimplifying generalities they often make about age and aging and look instead at the diversity among older people, then gerontologists must stop asking attitudinal and factual questions about 'the elderly' as if they were a homogeneous group."

In the sociologies of the life course and family life, elderly men were not often studied as men but served as the referent point to better understand late-life families, elderly women's lives as caregivers, or younger men. Small wonder then that as much as "wives' sociology" once informed us about family life (Safilios-Rochschild, 1969), there is a "midlife sociology" that has tried to theorize about older men's lives. To illustrate, role-theory sociologies directed attention to the rolelessness of late life. Retired men were envisioned outside the "normal" work spaces, and, by default, they were invading their wives' space—the family home (see literature review in Brubaker, 1990). This early sociological discourse of older men defined their lives as a period of indispensable disengagement from former, power-brokering statuses. Older men were portrayed as obsolete currency in a culture that cherishes power; in disengagement terms, the spotlight was on younger men's welfare. Later discourses of activity theory similarly emphasized the core values of a masculinity that best fits younger employed men's lives. Neither did these theoretical accounts reveal much about older men as a group or about subgroup and individual differences.

Logically, the diversity among young and middle-aged men does not disappear at age 65, 70, or 75, when older men leave the workplace to take up more assiduously their semipublic and private social worlds. Their gendered lives continue. Their relationships with institutions, women, other men, and children press on. Dannefer (1988) pointed out that as men grow older, their accumulated decisions about life course options produce increased differentiation among them. But in what ways? Do age and gender interact to affect older men's thoughts, feelings, behaviors, and relations with others? Do the two interact to affect men as a group?

Aging and Masculinities

Over the last 30 years a body of theoretical literature on men's character in late life (or the postparental years) has emerged to explain the psychological comfort of the individual man as he ages (e.g., Deutscher, 1964; Gutmann, 1987; Livson, 1983; Lowenthal et al., 1975; Vaillant, 1977). By far the greatest common denominator in these accounts is the focus on the individual and his gender orientation. Gender is conceptualized as the "male role" and visualized as the institutionalized practices of men. The common discourse also proposes a single masculinity for each developmental stage that men confront in their life span; thus any diversity in masculinities is age-specific and accounted for by the underlying developmental processes. This theorizing targets the men who "do gender," not the masculinity ideologies (Thompson, Pleck, & Ferrera, 1992) or the structure of gender relations that organize the way men do gender (Connell, 1987; West & Zimmerman, 1987).

Neugarten and Gutmann (1958) and Neugarten, Moore, and Lowe (1965) envision individual aging as a life journey through socially scheduled role entries and exits. Strong age and gender norms structure the march across the life course, and changes in men's (and women's) gender relations are normative for each transition point. However, agreement among theorists ends on this point. When the literature discussing older men is examined, two fundamentally dif-

ferent views have been constructed on the "continuity" of gender across the life span. One viewpoint has proposed a general "discontinuous model" of gender across the life span and a formulation wherein the older man is emasculated by aging. But the common discourse even among these authors breaks up. First, these models offer different assumptions about what determines the changes. Some theorists (such as Gutmann and Huyck—see Chapter 4 in this volume) emphasize an ontogenetic basis for the behavioral, personality, and spiritual changes; others (such as Payne—see Chapter 5 in this volume) attribute distinct life stage differences in men's experiences to structurally induced conflicts and men's accommodations to changes in expectations. Second, discontinuity models present different nuances of discontinuity. Some theorists visualize men experiencing dramatically different gendered worlds in contiguous life stages. In Gutmann's scheme, for example, at the onset of parenthood adult men engage in highly polarized gender relations and exhibit gender-congruent personalities; on exiting this life stage, however, men experience a "nomic rupture" by facing a crossover toward a more feminine world (Sinnott, 1984).

Third, the discontinuity models introduce quite different masculinities for older men. Sinnott (1982, 1984) and Gutmann (1975, 1977, 1987), for instance, theorized a convergence of conventional masculinity and femininity in late life. This pattern of gender convergence in older men's and women's lifestyles and personalities, however, has failed to find much empirical support (McCreary, 1990). Others do not agree with the assertion that either diminished masculinity or increased femininity parallels men's aging; instead they propose that there is greater consistency to masculinities over time (McCrae & Costa, 1982).

The other representation emphasizes the continuity of gender experiences across the life span, particularly as men enter late life. According to the continuity models, becoming an older man might mean adapting to a new masculinity, but one not too different from the previous (Neugarten, 1977; Solomon, 1982). The continuity perspective suggests that men's gendered social worlds do not appreciably change throughout the life course; rather, older men continue to participate in the "institutionalized" practices that significant others expect (Brubaker, 1985; Szinovacz, 1980) and continue to reveal consistency in their self-conceptions.

Within the available literature on aging and masculinities, change in men's character or institutionalized practices is at times thought to be ontogenetic, at other times triggered by the individual man's psychological discomfort with aging. Consistency also is thought to be generated by individual monitoring of psychosocial norms. The discourse is a biographical stage of life and not the masculinities within gender relations or the masculinity ideologies in the culture. Attention is directed to individual experiences with a stage-specific conventional masculinity without deciphering the matrix of masculinities that older men exhibit, the dynamics generated within gender relations, or the kind of masculinity that would be consistent with a (historical) change in the structure of gender relations.

Little has been said about the social conditions under which the different masculinities older men live with are constructed. For example, there is no evidence to suggest that the older men who were familiar with the Depression and who adopted a two-income family model (and thus elected not to be sole breadwinners) practice a different masculinity than sole breadwinners. Could both men participate in the public world of hegemonic masculinity in sports? Are they equally interested? Can they both return home to resume the full caregiving responsibilities of supporting a wife with Alzheimer's?

More work is also needed to address older men's lives in masculine spheres—such as when visiting with friends, whether on the golf course, in a cafeteria, in a veterans' bar, over the back fence (Duneier, 1992; Halle, 1984), or in gen-

der relations. What has emerged to date is an ambiguous image of elderly men in families and society. Are older men in fact marginal and nonessential, perhaps in the way of their wives and younger men? Is their experience one of exclusion? Is it one of rekindling the gerontocracy? The scope of theorizing and research both need to expand from examining only conventions of gender to understanding the ways in which older men's practices support and change gender relations broadly.

The merit of examining ordinary men's lives has become more widely acknowledged (Diamant, 1992; Heller, 1993), but in the investigations of masculinities, older men have not been the men studied. Age distinctions in how adult men embrace manhood, generational differences in masculinity, attention to gender presentations when similarly aged men engage in a common sphere of activity, and the meaning of being a man in the Third Age are largely outside what is understood and need to be brought in theoretically and placed on research agendas.

References

Antonucci, T. C., & Akiyama, H. (1987). An examination of sex differences in social support among older men and women. *Sex Roles, 17,* 737–749.

Arber, S., & Ginn, J. (1991). *Gender and later life: A sociological analysis of resources and constraints.* London: Sage.

Berger, P. L. (1963). *Invitation to sociology: A humanistic perspective.* New York: Anchor.

Binstock, R. H. (1983). The aged as scapegoat. *The Gerontologist, 23,* 136–143.

Brubaker, T. H. (1985). *Later life families.* Beverly Hills, CA: Sage.

Brubaker, T. H. (1990). Families in later life: A burgeoning research area. *Journal of Marriage and the Family, 52,* 959–981.

Buchholz, M., & Bynum, J. E. (1982). Newspaper presentations of America's aged: A content analysis of image and role. *The Gerontologist, 22,* 83–88.

Butler, R. N. (1969). Age-ism: Another form of bigotry. *The Gerontologist, 9,* 243–246.

Chirboga, D. A. (1989). The measurement of stress exposure in later life. In K. S. Markides & C. L. Cooper (Eds.), *Aging, stress and health* (pp. 13–41). New York: John Wiley.

Cole, T. R. (1986). "Putting off the old": Middle class morality, antebellum Protestantism, and the origins of ageism. In D. Van Tassel & P. N. Stearns (Eds.), *Old age in a bureaucratic society* (pp. 49–65). Westport, CT: Greenwood Press.

Connell, R. W. (1987). *Gender and power.* Stanford, CA: Stanford University Press.

Connell, R. W. (1992). A very straight gay: Masculinity, homosexual experience, and the dynamics of gender. *American Sociological Review, 57,* 735–751.

Cook, F. L. (1992). Ageism: Rhetoric and reality. *The Gerontologist, 32,* 292–293.

Coyle, J. M. (1989). *Women and aging: A selected, annotated bibliography.* Westport, CT: Greenwood Press.

Dannefer, D. (1988). Differential gerontology and the stratified life course: Conceptual and methodological issues. In G. L. Maddox & M. P. Lawton (Eds.), *Annual review of gerontology and geriatrics* (Vol. 8, pp. 3–36). New York: Springer.

Deutscher, I. (1964). The quality of postparental life: Definitions of the situation. *Journal of Marriage and the Family, 26,* 52–59.

Diamant, A. (1992, December 14). Academia tackles masculinity: Male studies courses booming on campus. *Boston Globe,* pp. 17, 24.

Duneier, M. (1992). *Slim's table; Race, respectability, and masculinity.* Chicago: University of Chicago Press.

Estes, C. L. (1979). *The aging enterprise.* San Francisco: Jossey-Bass.

Estes, C. L. (1993). The aging enterprise revisited. *The Gerontologist, 33,* 292–298.

Ferraro, K. F. (1992). Cohort changes in images of older adults, 1974–1981. *The Gerontologist, 32,* 296–304.

Fischer, D. H. (1978). *Growing old in America* (Expanded ed.). New York: Oxford University Press.

Green, B. S. (1993). *Gerontology and the construction of older age: A study in discourse analysis.* Hawthorne, NY: Aldine.

Gutmann, D. (1975). Parenthood: A key to the comparative study of the life cycle. In N. Datan & L. Ginsberg (Eds.), *Life-span developmental psychology: Normative life crises* (pp. 167–184). San Diego, CA: Academic Press.

Gutmann, D. (1977). The cross-cultural perspective: Notes toward a comparative psychology of aging. In I. J. Birren & K. W. Schaie (Eds.), *Handbook of the psychology of aging* (pp. 302–321). New York: Van Nostrand Reinhold.

Gutmann, D. (1987). *Reclaimed powers: Toward a new psychology of men and women in late life.* New York: Basic Books.

Halle, D. (1984). *America's working man.* Chicago: University of Chicago Press.

Harrison, J., Chin, J., & Ficarrotto, T. (1992). Warning: Masculinity may be dangerous to your health. In M. Kimmel & M. Messner (Eds.), *Men's lives* (2nd ed., pp. 271–285). New York: Macmillan.

Haug, M., Ford, A. B., & Sheafor, M. (1985). *The physical and mental health of aged women.* New York: Springer.

Heller, S. (1993, February 3). Scholars debunk the Marlboro man: Examining stereotypes of masculinity. *Chronicle of Higher Education,* pp. A9–A11, A15.

Herzog, A. R., Holden, K. C., & Seltzer, M. M. (1989). *Health and economic status of older women.* Amityville, NY: Baywood.

Hummert, M. L. (1990). Multiple stereotypes of elderly and young adults: A comparison of structure and evaluation. *Psychology and Aging, 5,* 182–193.

Kaiser, S. B., & Chandler, J. L. (1988). Audience responses to appearance codes: Old-age imagery in the media. *The Gerontologist, 28,* 692–699.

Kalish, R. A. (1979). The new ageism and the failure models: A polemic. *The Gerontologist, 19,* 398–402.

Kaplan, R. M., Anderson, J. P., & Wingard, D. L. (1991). Gender differences in health-related quality of life. *Health Psychology, 10,* 86–93.

Kimmel, M. S., & Messner, M. A. 91992). *Men's lives* (2nd ed.). New York: Macmillan.

Kite, M. E., Deaux, K., & Miele, M. (1991). Stereotypes of young and old: Does age outweigh gender? *Psychology and Aging, 6,* 19–27.

Laslett, P. (1987). The emergence of the third age. *Aging and Society, 7,* 133–160.

Lazer, W., & Shaw, E. H. (1987). How older Americans spend their money. *American Demographics, 9,* 36–41.

Lesnoff-Caravaglia, G. (1984). *The world of the older woman: Conflicts and resolutions.* New York: Human Sciences Press.

Levinson, D. J., Darrow, C. N., Klein, E. B., Levinson, M. H., & McKee, B. (1978). *The seasons of a man's life.* New York: Knopf.

Livson, F. B. (1983). Gender identity: A life-span view of sex-role development. In R. Weg (Ed.), *Sexuality in the later years* (pp. 105–127). San Diego, CA: Academic Press.

Lowenthal, M. F., Thurnher, M., Chiroboga, D., & Associates. (1975). *Four stages of life: A comparative study of women and men facing transitions.* San Francisco: Jossey-Bass.

Manton, K. G., & Soldo, B. J. (1985). Dynamics of health changes in the oldest old: New perspectives and evidence. *Milbank Memorial Fund Quarterly/Health and Society, 63*(2), 206–285.

Markson, E. W. (1985). *Older women: Issues and prospects.* Lexington, MA: Lexington Books.

Matthews, S. H. (1979). *The social world of old women: Management of self-identity.* Beverly Hills, CA: Sage.

McCrae, R. R., & Costa, P. T. (1982). Aging, the life course, and models of personality. In T. M. Field (Ed.), *Review of human development* (pp. 602–613). New York: Wiley.

McCreary, D. R. (1990). Self-perceptions of life-span gender-role development. *International Journal of Aging and Human Development, 31,* 135–146.

McKinlay, J. B., & McKinlay, S. A. (1977). The questionable contribution of medical measures to the decline of mortality in the United States in the twentieth century. *Milbank Memorial Fund Quarterly/Health and Society, 55,* 405–428.

Morgan, T. B. (1987, May). What does a sixty-year-old man see when he looks in the mirror? *Esquire,* pp. 161–167.

Neugarten, B. L. (1975). The future of the young–old. *The Gerontologist, 15*(1), 4–9.

Neugarten, B. L. (1977). Personality and aging. In J. E. Birren & K. W. Schaie (Eds.), *Handbook of the psychology of aging* (pp. 626–649). New York: Van Nostrand Reinhold.

Neugarten, B. L., & Gutmann, D. (1958). Age-sex role and personality in middle age: A thematic apperception study. *Psychological Monographs, 470,* 1–33.

Neugarten, B. L., Moore, J. W., & Lowe, J. C. (1965). Age norms, age constraints, and adult socialization. *American Journal of Sociology, 70,* 710–717.

Ortega y Gasset, J. (1958). *Man and crisis.* New York: Norton.

Powell, L., & Williamson, J. B. (1985). The mass media and the aged. *Social Policy, 16,* 38–49.

Puglisi, J. T., & Jackson, D. W. (1980–81). Sex role identity and self esteem in adulthood. *International Journal of Aging and Human Development, 12,* 129–138.

Roback, G., Randolph, L., & Seidman, B. (1993). *Physician characteristics and distribution in the United States.* Chicago: American Medical Association.

Safilios-Rochschild, C. (1969). Family sociology or wives' family sociology? A cross-cultural examination of decision-making. *Journal of Marriage and the Family, 31,* 290–301.

Segal, L. (1990). *Slow motion: Changing masculinities, changing men.* New Brunswick, NJ: Rutgers University Press.

Shumaker, S. A., & Hill, D. R. (1991). Gender differences in social support and physical health. *Health Psychology, 10,* 102–111.

Silverman, M. (1977). The old man as woman: Detecting stereotypes of aged men with a femininity scale. *Perceptual and Motor Skills, 44,* 336–338.

Sinnott, J. D. (1982). Correlates of sex roles of older adults. *Journal of Gerontology, 37,* 587–594.

Sinnott, J. D. (1984). Older men, older women: Are their perceived sex roles similar? *Sex Roles, 10,* 847–856.

Solomon, K. (1982). The older man. In K. Solomon & N. B. Levy (Eds.), *Men in transition: Theory and therapy* (pp. 205–240). New York: Plenum.

Sontag, S. (1972). The double standard of aging. *Saturday Review, 55*(39), 29–38.

Swayne, L. E., & Greco, A. J. (1987). The portrayal of older Americans in television commercials. *Journal of Advertising, 16*(1), 47–54.

Szinovacz, M. E. (1980). Female retirement: Effects of spousal roles and marital relationships. *Journal of Family Issues, 1,* 423–440.

Thompson, E. H., & Gongla, P. A. (1983). Single parent families: In the mainstream of American society. In E. D. Macklin & R. H. Rubin (Eds.), *Contemporary families and alternative lifestyles: Handbook on research and theory*. Beverly Hills, CA: Sage.

Thompson, E. H., Pleck, J. H., & Ferrera, D. L. (1992). Men and masculinities: Scales for masculinity ideology and masculinity-related constructs. *Sex Roles, 27,* 573–607.

U.S. Bureau of the Census. (1976). *Historical statistics of the United States: Colonial times to 1970.* Washington, DC: Government Printing Office.

U.S. Bureau of the Census. (1978). *Demographic aspects of aging and the older population in the United States.* Current Population Reports, Series P23, No. 59. Washington, DC: Government Printing Office.

U.S. Bureau of the Census. (1992). *Marital status and living arrangements: March 1992.* Current Population Reports, Series P20, No. 468. Washington, DC: Government Printing Office.

U.S. Bureau of the Census. (1993A). *Statistical abstracts of the United States, 1992.* Washington, DC: Government Printing Office.

U.S. Bureau of the Census. (1993B). *Population projections of the United States, by age, sex, race, and Hispanic origin: 1992 to 2050.* Current Population Reports, Series P25, No. 1092. Washington, DC: Government Printing Office.

U.S. Department of Education. (1992). *Projections of education statistics to 2003.* Washington, DC: Government Printing Office.

Verbrugge, L. M. (1989). Gender, aging and health. In K. S. Markides (Ed.), *Aging and health: Perspectives on gender, race, ethnicity, and class* (pp. 23–78). Newbury Park, CA: Sage.

Vaillant, G. E. (1977). *Adaptation to life.* Boston: Little, Brown.

Waldron, I. (1976). Why do women live longer than men? *Social Science and Medicine, 10,* 349–362.

Walsh, R. P., & Connor, C. L. (1979). Old men and young women: How objectively are their skills assessed? *Journal of Gerontology, 34,* 561–568.

Wernick, A. (1987). From voyeur to narcissist: Imaging men in contemporary advertising. In M. Kaufman (Ed.), *Beyond patriarchy: Essays by men on pleasure, power, and change* (pp. 277–297). Toronto: Oxford University Press.

West, C., & Zimmerman, D. (1987). Doing gender. *Gender and Society, 1,* 125–151.

Wingard, D. L., & Cohn, B. A. (1990). Variations in disease-specific sex-morbidity and mortality ratios: United States vital statistics data and prospective data from the Alameda County study. In M. G. Ory & H. R. Warner (Eds.), *Gender, health, and longevity: Multidisciplinary perspectives* (pp. 25–37). New York: Springer.

"One is not born, but rather becomes, a woman," wrote the French feminist thinker Simone de Beauvoir in her ground-breaking book *The Second Sex* (NY: Vintage, 1958). The same is true for men. And the social processes by which boys become men are complex and important. How does early childhood socialization differ for boys and girls? What specific traits are emphasized for boys that mark their socialization as different? What types of institutional arrangements reinforce those traits? How do the various institutions in which boys find themselves—school, family, and circles of friends—influence their development? What of the special institutions that promote "boy's life" or an adolescent male subculture?

During childhood and adolescence, masculinity becomes a central theme in a boy's life. *New York Times* editor A. M. Rosenthal put the dilemma this way: "So there I was, 13 years old, the smallest boy

PART TWO

Boyhood

in my freshman class at DeWitt Clinton High School, smoking a White Owl cigar. I was not only little, but I did not have longies—long trousers—and was still in knickerbockers. Obviously, I had to do something to project my fierce sense of manhood" (*New York Times*, 26 April 1987). That the assertion of manhood is part of a boy's natural development is suggested by Roger Brown, in his textbook *Social Psychology* (NY: Free Press, 1965, p. 161):

> In the United States, a *real* boy climbs trees, disdains girls, dirties his knees, plays with soldiers, and takes blue for his favorite color. When they go to school, real boys prefer manual training, gym, and arithmetic. In college the boys smoke pipes, drink beer, and major in engineering or physics. The real boy matures into a "man's man" who plays poker, goes hunting, drinks brandy, and dies in the war.

The articles in this section address the question of boys' development, focusing on the institu-

For every boy aged 5 - 12 in the U.S.,
2 G.I. Joe products are sold yearly.

DEMILITARIZE THE PLAYGROUND

tions that shape boys' lives. Barrie Thorne, R. W. Connell, and Ellen Jordan and Angela Cowan describe the gender socialization of schooling, both inside the classroom and on the playground. Michael A. Messner, Geoffrey Canada, and Jeffrey P. Hantover examine the extracurricular socialization that occurs in organized sports, on the streets, or in the Boy Scouts. And Ritch C. Savin-Williams recounts the consequences of early childhood sexual feelings for gay and bisexual boys.

ARTICLE

Barrie Thorne

Girls and Boys Together . . . but Mostly Apart: Gender Arrangements in Elementary School

Throughout the years of elementary school, children's friendships and casual encounters are strongly separated by sex. Sex segregation among children, which starts in preschool and is well established by middle childhood, has been amply documented in studies of children's groups and friendships (e.g., Eder & Hallinan, 1978; Schofield, 1981) and is immediately visible in elementary school settings. When children choose seats in classrooms or the cafeteria, or get into line, they frequently arrange themselves in same-sex clusters. At lunchtime, they talk matter-of-factly about "girls' tables" and "boys' tables." Playgrounds have gendered turfs, with some areas and activities, such as large playing fields and basketball courts, controlled mainly by boys, and others—smaller enclaves like jungle-gym areas and concrete spaces for hopscotch or jumprope—more often controlled by girls. Sex segregation is so common in elementary schools that it is meaningful to speak of separate girls' and boys' worlds.

Reprinted from Willard W. Hartup and Zick Rubin, eds., *Relationships and Development.* Hillsdale, NJ: Lawrence Erlbaum Associates, 1986. Volume sponsored by the Social Science Research Center, Copyright © 1986 by Lawrence Erlbaum Associates, Inc.

Studies of gender and children's social relations have mostly followed this "two worlds" model, separately describing and comparing the subcultures of girls and of boys (e.g., Lever, 1976; Maltz & Borker, 1983). In brief summary: Boys tend to interact in larger, more age-heterogeneous groups (Lever, 1976; Waldrop & Halverson, 1975; Eder & Hallinan, 1978). They engage in more rough and tumble play and physical fighting (Maccoby & Jacklin, 1974). Organized sports are both a central activity and a major metaphor in boys' subcultures; they use the language of "teams" even when not engaged in sports, and they often construct interaction in the form of contests. The shifting hierarchies of boys' groups (Savin-Williams, 1976) are evident in their more frequent use of direct command, insults, and challenges (Goodwin, 1980).

Fewer studies have been done of girls' groups (Foot, Chapman, & Smith, 1980; McRobbie & Garber, 1975), and—perhaps because categories for description and analysis have come more from male than female experience—researchers have had difficulty seeing and analyzing girls' social relations. Recent work has begun to correct this skew. In middle childhood, girls' worlds are less public than those of boys; girls more often interact in private places and in smaller groups or friendship pairs (Eder & Hallinan, 1978; Waldrop & Halverson, 1975). Their play is more cooperative and turn-taking (Lever, 1976). Girls have more intense and exclusive friendships, which take shape around keeping and telling secrets, shifting alliances, and indirect ways of expressing disagreement (Goodwin, 1980; Lever, 1976; Maltz & Borker, 1983). Instead of direct commands, girls more often use directives which merge speaker and hearer, e.g., "let's" or "we gotta" (Goodwin, 1980).

Although much can be learned by comparing the social organization and subcultures of boys' and of girls' groups, the separate worlds approach has eclipsed full, contextual understanding of gender and social relations among children. The separate worlds model essentially involves a search for group sex differences, and shares the limitations of individual sex difference research. Differences tend to be exaggerated and similarities ignored, with little theoretical attention to the integration of similarity and difference (Unger, 1979). Statistical findings of difference are often portrayed as dichotomous, neglecting the considerable individual variation that exists; for example, not all boys fight, and some have intense and exclusive friendships. The sex difference approach tends to abstract gender from its social context, to assume that males and females are qualitatively and permanently different (with differences perhaps unfolding through separate developmental lines). These assumptions mask the possibility that gender arrangements and patterns of similarity and difference may vary by situation, race, social class, region, and subculture.

Sex segregation is far from total, and is a more complex and dynamic process than the portrayal of separate worlds reveals. Erving Goffman (1977) has observed that sex segregation has a "with-then-apart" structure; the sexes segregate periodically, with separate spaces, rituals, and groups, but they also come together and are, in crucial ways, part of the same world. This is certainly true in the social environment of elementary schools. Although girls and boys do interact as boundaried collectivities—an image suggested by the separate worlds approach—there are other occasions when they work or play in relaxed and integrated ways. Gender is less central to the organization and meaning of some situations than others. In short, sex segregation is not static, but is a variable and complicated process.

To gain an understanding of gender which can encompass both the "with" and the "apart" of sex segregation, analysis should start not with the individual, nor with a search for sex differences, but with social relationships. Gender should be conceptualized as a system of relationships rather than as an immutable and dichotomous given. Taking this approach, I have organized my research on gender and children's social relations around questions like the following: How and when does gender enter into group formation? In a given situation, how is gender made more or less salient or infused with particular meanings? By what rituals, processes, and forms of social organization and conflict do "with-then-apart" rhythms get enacted? How are these processes affected by the organization of institutions (e.g., different types of schools, neighborhoods, or summer camps), varied settings (e.g., the constraints and possibilities governing interaction on playgrounds vs. classrooms), and particular encounters?

Methods and Sources of Data

This study is based on two periods of participant observation. In 1976–1977 I observed for 8 months in a largely working-class elementary school in California, a school with 8% Black and 12% Chicana/o students. In 1980 I did fieldwork for 3 months in a Michigan elementary school in similar size (around 400 students), social class, and racial composition. I observed in several classrooms—a kindergarten, a second grade, and a combined fourth–fifth grade—and in school hallways, cafeterias, and playgrounds. I set out to follow the round of the school day as children experience it, recording their interactions with one another, and with adults, in varied settings.

Participant observation involves gaining access to everyday, "naturalistic" settings and taking systematic notes over an extended period of time. Rather than starting with preset categories for recording, or with fixed hypotheses for testing, participant–observers record detail in ways which maximize opportunities for discovery. Through continuous interaction between observation and analysis, "grounded theory" is developed (Glaser & Strauss, 1967).

The distinctive logic and discipline of this mode of inquiry emerges from: (1) theoretical sampling—being relatively systematic in the choice of where and whom to observe in order to maximize knowledge relevant to categories and analysis which are being developed; and (2) comparing all relevant data on a given point in order to modify emerging propositions to take account of discrepant cases (Katz, 1983). Participant observation is a flexible, open-ended, and inductive method, designed to understand behavior within, rather than stripped from, social context. It provides richly detailed information which is anchored in everyday meanings and experience.

Daily Processes of Sex Segregation

Sex segregation should be understood not as a given, but as the result of deliberate activity. The outcome is dramatically visible when there are separate girls' and boys' tables in school lunchrooms, or sex-separated groups on playgrounds.

But in the same lunchroom one can also find tables where girls and boys eat and talk together, and in some playground activities the sexes mix. By what processes do girls and boys separate into gender-defined and relatively boundaried collectivities? And in what contexts, and through what processes, do boys and girls interact in less gender-divided ways?

In the school settings I observed, much segregation happened with no mention of gender. Gender was implicit in the contours of friendship, shared interest, and perceived risk which came into play when children chose companions—in their prior planning, invitations, seeking-of-access, saving-of-places, denials of entry, and allowing or protesting of "cuts" by those who violated the rules for lining up. Sometimes children formed mixed-sex groups for play, eating, talking, working on a classroom project, or moving through space. When adults or children explicitly invoked gender—and this was nearly always in ways which separated girls and boys—boundaries were heightened and mixed-sex interaction became an explicit arena of risk.

In the schools I studied, the physical space and curricula were not formally divided by sex, as they have been in the history of elementary schooling (a history evident in separate entrances to old school buildings, where the words "Boys" and "Girls" are permanently etched in concrete). Nevertheless, gender was a visible marker in the adult-organized school day. In both schools, when the public address system sounded, the principal inevitably opened with: "Boys and girls . . . ," and in addressing clusters of children, teachers and aides regularly used gender terms ("Heads down, girls"; "The girls are ready and the boys aren't"). These forms of address made gender visible and salient, conveying an assumption that the sexes are separate social groups.

Teachers and aides sometimes drew upon gender as a basis for sorting children and organizing activities. Gender is an embodied and visual social category which roughly divides the population in half, and the separation of girls and boys permeates the history and lore of schools and playgrounds. In both schools—although through awareness of Title IX, many teachers had changed this practice—one could see separate girls' and boys' lines moving, like caterpillars, through the school halls. In the 4th–5th grade classroom the teacher frequently pitted girls against boys for spelling and math contests. On the playground in the Michigan school, aides regarded the space close to the building as girls' territory, and the playing fields "out there" as boys' territory. They sometimes shooed children of the other sex away from those spaces, especially boys who ventured near the girls' area and seemed to have teasing in mind.

In organizing their activities, both within and apart from the surveillance of adults, children also explicitly invoked gender. During my fieldwork in the Michigan school, I kept daily records of who sat where in the lunchroom. The amount of sex segregation varied: It was least at the first grade tables and almost total among sixth graders. There was also variation from classroom to classroom within a given age, and from day to day. Actions like the following heightened the gender divide:

> In the lunchroom, when the two second grade tables were filling, a high-status boy walked by the inside table, which had a scattering of both boys and girls, and said loudly, "Oooo, too many girls," as he headed for a seat at the far table. The boys at the inside table picked up their trays and moved, and no other boys sat at the inside table, which the pronouncement had effectively made taboo.

In the end, that day (which was not the case every day), girls and boys ate at separate tables.

Eating and walking are not sex-typed activities, yet in forming groups in lunchrooms and hallways children often separated by sex. Sex segregation assumed added dimensions on the playground, where spaces, equipment, and activities were infused with gender meanings. My inventories of activities and groupings on the playground showed similar patterns in both schools: Boys controlled the large fixed spaces designated for team sports (baseball diamonds, grassy fields used for football or soccer); girls more often played closer to the building, doing tricks on the monkey bars (which, for 6th graders, became an area for sitting and talking) and using cement areas for jumprope, hopscotch, and group games like four-square. (Lever, 1976, provides a good analysis of sex-divided play.) Girls and boys most often played together in kickball, and in group (rather than team) games like four-square, dodgeball, and handball. When children used gender to exclude others from play, they often drew upon beliefs connecting boys to some activities and girls to others:

> A first grade boy avidly watched an all-female game of jump rope. When the girls began to shift positions, he recognized a means of access to the play and he offered, "I'll swing it." A girl responded, "No way, you don't know how to do it, to swing it. You gotta be a girl." He left without protest.

Although children sometimes ignored pronouncements about what each sex could or could not do, I never heard them directly challenge such claims.

When children had explicitly defined an activity or a group as gendered, those who crossed the boundary—especially boys who moved into female-marked space—risked being teased. ("Look! Mike's in the girls' line!" "That's a girl over there," a girl said loudly, pointing to a boy sitting at an otherwise all-female table in the lunchroom.) Children, and occasionally adults, used teasing—especially the tease of "liking" someone of the other sex, or of "being" that sex by virtue of being in their midst—to police gender boundaries. Much of the teasing drew upon heterosexual romantic definitions, making cross-sex interaction risky, and increasing social distance between boys and girls.

Relationships Between the Sexes

Because I have emphasized the "apart" and ignored the occasions of "with," this analysis of sex segregation falsely implies that there is little contact between girls and boys in daily school life. In fact, relationships between girls and boys—which should be studied as fully as, and in connection with, same-sex relationships—are of several kinds:

1. "Borderwork," or forms of cross-sex interaction which are based upon and reaffirm boundaries and asymmetries between girls' and boys' groups;
2. Interactions which are infused with heterosexual meanings;
3. Occasions where individuals cross gender boundaries to participate in the world of the other sex; and
4. Situations where gender is muted in salience, with girls and boys interacting in more relaxed ways.

Borderwork

In elementary school settings boys' and girls' groups are sometimes spatially set apart. Same-sex groups sometimes claim fixed territories such as the basketball court, the bars, or specific lunchroom tables. However, in the crowded, multifocused, and adult-controlled environment of the school, groups form and disperse at a rapid rate and can never stay totally apart. Contact between girls and boys sometimes lessens sex segregation, but gender-defined groups also come together in ways which emphasize their boundaries.

"Borderwork" refers to interaction across, yet based upon and even strengthening gender boundaries. I have drawn this notion from Fredrik Barth's (1969) analysis of social relations which are maintained across ethnic boundaries without diminishing dichotomized ethnic status.[1] His focus is on more macro, ecological arrangements; mine is on face-to-face behavior. But the insight is similar: Groups may interact in ways which strengthen their borders, and the maintenance of ethnic (or gender) groups can best be understood by examining the boundary that defines the group, "not the cultural stuff that it encloses" (Barth, 1969, p. 15). In elementary schools there are several types of borderwork: contests or games where gender-defined teams compete; cross-sex rituals of chasing and pollution; and group invasions. These interactions are asymmetrical, challenging the separate-but-parallel model of "two worlds."

Contests

Boys and girls are sometimes pitted against each other in classroom competitions and playground games. The 4th–5th grade classroom had a boys' side and a girls' side, an arrangement that re-emerged each time the teacher asked children to choose their own desks. Although there was some within-sex shuffling, the result was always a spatial moiety system—boys on the left, girls on the right—with the exception of one girl (the "tomboy" whom I'll describe later), who twice chose a desk with the boys and once with the girls. Drawing upon and reinforcing the children's self-segregation, the teacher often pitted the boys against the girls in spelling and math competitions, events marked by cross-sex antagonism and within-sex solidarity:

> The teacher introduced a math game; she would write addition and subtraction problems on the board, and a member of each team would race to be the first to write the correct answer. She wrote two scorekeeping columns on the board: "Beastly Boys" . . . "Gossipy Girls." The boys yelled out, as several girls laughed, "Noisy girls! Gruesome girls!" The

girls sat in a row on top of their desks; some-times they moved collectively, pushing their hips or whispering "pass it on." The boys stood along the wall, some reclining against desks. When members of either group came back victorious from the front of the room, they would do the "giving five" handslapping ritual with their team members.

On the playground a team of girls occasionally played against a team of boys, usually in kickball or team two-square. Sometimes these games proceeded matter-of-factly, but if gender became the explicit basis of team solidarity, the interaction changed, becoming more antagonistic and unstable:

> Two fifth-grade girls against two fifth-grade boys in a team game of two-square. The game proceeded at an even pace until an argument ensued about whether the ball was out or on the line. Karen, who had hit the ball, became annoyed, flashed her middle finger at the other team, and called to a passing girl to join their side. The boys then called out to other boys, and cheered as several arrived to play. "We got five and you got three!" Jack yelled. The game continued, with the girls yelling, "Bratty boys! Sissy boys!" and the boys making noises—"weee haw" "ha-ha-ha"—as they played.

Chasing

Cross-sex chasing dramatically affirms boundaries between girls and boys. The basic elements of chase and elude, capture and rescue (Sutton-Smith, 1971) are found in various kinds of tag with formal rules, and in informal episodes of chasing which punctuate life on playgrounds. These episodes begin with a provocation (taunts like "You can't get me!" or "Slobber monster!"; bodily pokes or the grabbing of possessions). A provocation may be ignored, or responded to by chasing. Chaser and chased may then alternate roles. In an ethnographic study of chase sequences on a school playground, Christine Finnan (1982) observes that chases vary in number of chasers to chased (e.g., one chasing one,

or five chasing two); form of provocation (a taunt or a poke); outcome (an episode may end when the chased outdistances the chaser, or with a brief touch, being wrestled to the ground, or the recapturing of a hat or a ball); and in use of space (there may or may not be safety zones).

Like Finnan (1982), and Sluckin (1981), who studied a playground in England, I found that chasing has a gendered structure. Boys frequently chase one another, an activity which often ends in wrestling and mock fights. When girls chase girls, they are usually less physically aggressive; they less often, for example, wrestle one another to the ground.

Cross-sex chasing is set apart by special names—"girls chase the boys"; "boys chase the girls"; "the chase"; "chasers"; "chase and kiss"; "kiss chase"; "kissers and chasers"; "kiss or kill"—and by children's animated talk about the activity. The names vary by region and school, but contain both gender and sexual meanings (this form of play is mentioned, but only briefly analyzed, in Finnan, 1981; Sluckin, 1981; Parrott, 1972; and Borman, 1979).

In "boys chase the girls" and "girls chase the boys" (the names most frequently used in both the California and Michigan schools) boys and girls become, by definition, separate teams. Gender terms override individual identities, especially for the other team ("Help, a girl's chasin' me!"; "C'mon Sarah, let's get that boy"; "Tony, help save me from the girls"). Individuals may call for help from, or offer help to, others of their sex. They may also grab someone of their sex and turn them over to the opposing team: "Ryan grabbed Billy from behind, wrestling him to the ground. 'Hey, girls, get 'im,' Ryan called."

Boys more often mix episodes of cross-sex with same-sex chasing. Girls more often have safety zones, places like the girls' restroom or an area by the school wall, where they retreat to rest and talk (sometimes in animated postmortems) before new episodes of cross-sex chasing begin.

Early in the fall in the Michigan school, where chasing was especially prevalent, I watched a second grade boy teach a kinder-garten girl how to chase. He slowly ran backwards, beckoning her to pursue him, as he called, "Help, a girl's after me." In the early grades chasing mixes with fantasy play, e.g., a first-grade boy who played "sea monster," his arms outflung and his voice growling, as he chased a group of girls. By third grade, stylized gestures—exaggerated stalking motions, screams (which only girls do), and karate kicks—accompany scenes of chasing.

Names like "chase and kiss" mark the sexual meanings of cross-sex chasing, a theme I return to later. The threat of kissing—most often girls threatening to kiss boys—is a ritualized form of provocation. Cross-sex chasing among sixth graders involves elaborate patterns of touch and touch avoidance, which adults see as sexual. The principal told the sixth graders in the Michigan school that they were not to play "pom-pom," a complicated chasing game, because it entailed "inappropriate touch."

Rituals of Pollution

Cross-sex chasing is sometimes entwined with rituals of pollution, as in "cooties," where specific individuals or groups are treated as contaminating or carrying "germs." Children have rituals for transferring cooties (usually touching someone else and shouting "You've got cooties!"), for immunization (e.g., writing "CV" for "cootie vaccination" on their arms), and for eliminating cooties (e.g., saying "no gives" or using "cootie catchers" made of folded paper described in Knapp & Knapp, 1976). While girls may give cooties to girls, boys do not generally give cooties to one another (Samuelson, 1980).

In cross-sex play, either girls or boys may be defined as having cooties, which they transfer through chasing and touching. Girls give cooties to boys more often than vice versa. In Michigan, one version of cooties is called "girl stain"; the fourth-graders whom Karkau, 1973, describes, used the phrase "girl touch." "Cootie

queens, "or "cootie girls" (there are no "kings" or "boys") are female pariahs, the ultimate school virtue of gender, but also through some added stigma such as being overweight or poor.[2] That girls are seen as more polluting than boys is a significant asymmetry, which echoes cross-cultural patterns, although in other cultures female pollution is generally connected to menstruation, and not applied to prepubertal girls.

Invasions

Playground invasions are another asymmetric form of borderwork. On a few occasions I saw girls invade and disrupt an all-male game, most memorably a group of tall sixth-grade girls who ran onto the playing field and grabbed a football which was in play. The boys were surprised and frustrated, and, unusual for boys this old, finally tattled to the aide. But in the majority of cases, boys disrupt girls' activities rather than vice versa. Boys grab the ball from girls playing four-square, stick feet into a jumprope and stop an ongoing game, and dash through the area of the bars, where girls are taking turns performing, sending the rings flying. Sometimes boys ask to join a girls' game and then, after a short period of seemingly earnest play, disrupt the game:

> Two second-grade boys begged to "twirl" the jumprope for a group of second-grade girls who had been jumping for some time. The girls agreed, and the boys began to twirl. Soon, without announcement, the boys changed from "seashells, cockle bells" to "hot peppers" (spinning the rope very fast), and tangled the jumper in the rope. The boys ran away laughing.

Boys disrupt girls' play so often that girls have developed almost ritualized responses: They guard their ongoing play, chase boys away, and tattle to the aides. In a playground cycle which enhances sex segregation, aides who try to spot potential trouble before it occurs sometimes shoo boys away from areas where girls are playing. Aides do not anticipate trouble from girls who seek to join groups of boys, with the exception of girls intent on provoking a chase sequence. And indeed, if they seek access to a boys' game, girls usually play with boys in earnest rather than breaking up the game.

A close look at the organization of border-work—or boundaried interactions between the sexes—shows that the worlds of boys and girls may be separate but they are not parallel, nor are they equal. The worlds of girls and boys articulate in several asymmetric ways:

1. On the playground, boys control as much as ten times more space than girls, when one adds up the area of large playing fields and compares it with the much smaller areas where girls predominate. Girls, who play closer to the building, are more often watched over and protected by the adult aides.

2. Boys invade all-female games and scenes of play much more than girls invade boys. This, and boys' greater control of space, correspond with other findings about the organization of gender, and inequality, in our society: compared with men and boys, women and girls take up less space, and their space, and talk, are more often violated and interrupted (Greif, 1982; Henley, 1977; West & Zimmerman, 1983).

3. Although individual boys are occasionally treated as contaminating (e.g., a third grade boy who [to] both boys and girls was "stinky" and "smelled like pee"), girls are more often defined as polluting. This pattern ties to themes that I discuss later: It is more taboo for a boy to play with (as opposed to invade) girls, and girls are more sexually defined than boys.

A look at the boundaries between the separated worlds of girls and boys illuminates within-sex hierarchies of status and control. For example, in the sex-divided seating in the 4th–5th grade classroom, several boys recurringly sat near "female space": their desks were at the gender divide in the classroom, and they were more likely than other boys to sit at a predominantly female table in the lunchroom. These boys—two non-bilingual Chicanos and an overweight "loner" boy who was afraid of sports—were at the bottom of the male hierarchy. Gender is sometimes used as a metaphor for male hierarchies; the inferior status of boys at the bottom is conveyed by calling them "girls":

> Seven boys and one girl were playing basketball. Two younger boys came over and asked to play. While the girl silently stood, fully accepted in the company of players, one of the older boys disparagingly said to the younger boys, "You girls can't play."[3]

In contrast, the girls who more often travel in the boys' world, sitting with groups of boys in the lunchroom or playing basketball, soccer, and baseball with them, are not stigmatized. Some have fairly high status with other girls. The worlds of girls and boys are asymmetrically arranged, and spatial patterns map out interacting forms of inequality.

Heterosexual Meanings

The organization and meanings of gender (the social categories "woman/man," "girl/boy") and of sexuality vary cross-culturally (Ortner & Whitehead, 1981)—and, in our society, across the life course. Harriet Whitehead (1981) observed that in our (Western) gender system, and that of many traditional North American Indian cultures, one's choice of a sexual object, occupation, and one's dress and demeanor are closely associated with gender. However, the "center of gravity" differs in the two gender systems. For Indians, occupational pursuits provide the primary imagery of gender; dress and demeanor are secondary, and sexuality is least important. In our system, at least for adults, the order is re-

versed: heterosexuality is central to our definitions of "man" and "woman" ("masculinity"/
"femininity"), and the relationships that obtain
between them, whereas occupation and dress/
demeanor are secondary.

Whereas erotic orientation and gender are
closely linked in our definitions of adults, we define children as relatively asexual. Activities and
dress/demeanor are more important than sexuality in the cultural meanings of "girl" and "boy."
Children are less heterosexually defined than
adults, and we have nonsexual imagery for relations between girls and boys. However, both
children and adults sometimes use heterosexual
language—"crushes," "like," "goin' with,"
"girlfriends," and "boyfriends"—to define cross-
sex relationships. This language increases through
the years of elementary school; the shift to adolescence consolidates a gender system organized
around the institution of heterosexuality.

In everyday life in the schools, heterosexual
and romantic meanings infuse some ritualized
forms of interaction between groups of boys and
girls (e.g., "chase and kiss") and help maintain sex
segregation; "Jimmy likes Beth" or "Beth likes
Jimmy" is a major form of teasing, which a child
risks in choosing to sit by or walk with someone
of the other sex. The structure of teasing, and
children's sparse vocabulary for relationships between girls and boys, are evident in the following conversation which I had with a group of
third-grade girls in the lunchroom:

> Susan asked me what I was doing, and I said I
> was observing the things children do and play.
> Nicole volunteered, "I like running, boys
> chase all the girls. See Tim over there? Judy
> chases him all around the school. She likes
> him." Judy, sitting across the table, quickly re-
> sponded, "I hate him. I like him for a friend."
> "Tim loves Judy," Nicole said in a loud, sing-
> song voice.

In the younger grades, the culture and lore
of girls contain more heterosexual romantic

themes than that of boys. In Michigan, the first-
grade girls often jumped rope to a rhyme which
began: "Down in the valley where the green
grass grows, there sat Cindy (name of jumper),
as sweet as a rose. She sat, she sat, she sat so
sweet. Along came Jason, and kissed her on the
cheek . . . first comes love, then comes marriage, then along comes Cindy with a baby car-
riage . . ." Before a girl took her turn at
jumping, the chanters asked her "Who do you
want to be your boyfriend?" The jumper always
proffered a name, which was accepted matter-
of-factly. In chasing, a girl's kiss carried greater
threat than a boy's kiss; "girl touch," when defined as contaminating, had sexual connotations. In short, starting at an early age, girls are
more sexually defined than boys.

Through the years of elementary school,
and increasing with age, the idiom of heterosexuality helps maintain the gender divide.
Cross-sex interactions, especially when children
initiate them, are fraught with the risk of being
teased about "liking" someone of the other sex.
I learned of several close cross-sex friendships,
formed and maintained in neighborhoods and
church, which went underground during the
school day.

By the fifth grade a few children began to
affirm, rather than avoid, the charge of having a
girlfriend or a boyfriend; they introduced the
heterosexual courtship rituals of adolescence:

> In the lunchroom in the Michigan school, as
> the tables were forming, a high-status fifth-
> grade boy called out from his seat at the table:
> "I want Trish to sit by me." Trish came over,
> and almost like a king and queen, they sat at
> the gender divide—a row of girls down the
> table on her side, a row of boys on his.

In this situation, which inverted earlier forms, it
was not a loss, but a gain in status to publicly
choose a companion of the other sex. By affirming his choice, the boy became unteasable (note
the familiar asymmetry of heterosexual courtship

rituals: the male initiated). This incident signals a temporal shift in arrangements of sex and gender.

Traveling in the World of the Other Sex

Contests, invasions, chasing, and heterosexually-defined encounters are based upon and reaffirm boundaries between girls and boys. In another type of cross-sex interaction, individuals (or sometimes pairs) cross gender boundaries, seeking acceptance in a group of the other sex. Nearly all the cases I saw of this were tomboys—girls who played organized sports and frequently sat with boys in the cafeteria or classroom. If these girls were skilled at activities central in the boys' world, especially games like soccer, baseball, and basketball, they were pretty much accepted as participants.

Being a tomboy is a matter of degree. Some girls seek access to boys' groups but are excluded; other girls limit their "crossing" to specific sports. Only a few—such as the tomboy I mentioned earlier, who chose a seat with the boys in the sex-divided fourth–fifth grade—participate fully in the boys' world. That particular girl was skilled at the various organized sports which boys played in different seasons of the year. She was also adept at physical fighting and at using the forms of arguing, insult, teasing, naming, and sports-talk of the boys' subculture. She was the only Black child in her classroom, in a school with only 8% Black students; overall that token status, along with unusual athletic and verbal skills, may have contributed to her ability to move back and forth across the gender divide. Her unique position in the children's world was widely recognized in the school. Several times, the teacher said to me, "She thinks she's a boy."

I observed only one boy in the upper grades (a fourth grader) who regularly played with all-female groups, as opposed to "playing at" girls games and seeking to disrupt them. He

frequently played jumprope and took turns with girls doing tricks on the bars, using the small gestures—for example, a helpful push on the heel of a girl who needed momentum to turn her body around the bar—which mark skillful and earnest participation. Although I never saw him play in other than an earnest spirit, the girls often chased him away from their games, and both girls and boys teased him. The fact that girls seek, and have more access to boys' worlds than vice versa, and the fact that girls who travel with the other sex are less stigmatized for it, are obvious asymmetries, tied to the asymmetries previously discussed.

Relaxed Cross-Sex Interactions

Relationships between boys and girls are not always marked by strong boundaries, heterosexual definitions, or by interacting on the terms and turfs of the other sex. On some occasions girls and boys interact in relatively comfortable ways. Gender is not strongly salient nor explicitly invoked, and girls and boys are not organized into boundaries collectively. These "with" occasions have been neglected by those studying gender and children's relationships, who have emphasized either the model of separate worlds (with little attention to their articulation) or heterosexual forms of contact.

Occasions where boys and girls interact without strain, where gender wanes, rather than waxes in importance, frequently have one or more of the following characteristics:

1. The situations are organized around an absorbing task, such as a group art project or creating a radio show, which encourages cooperation and lessens attention to gender. This pattern accords with other studies finding that cooperative activities reduce group antagonism (e.g., Sherif & Sherif, 1953, who studied divisions between boys in a summer camp; and Aronson et al., 1978,

who used cooperative activities to lessen racial divisions in a classroom).

2. Gender is less prominent when children are not responsible for the formation of the group. Mixed-sex play is less frequent in games like football, which require the choosing of teams, and more frequent in games like handball or dodgeball which individuals can join simply by getting into a line or a circle. When adults organize mixed-sex encounters—which they frequently do in the classroom and in physical education periods on the playground—they legitimize cross-sex contact. This removes the risk of being teased for choosing to be with the other sex.

3. There is more extensive and relaxed cross-sex interaction when principles of grouping other than gender are explicitly involved—for example, counting off to form teams for spelling or kickball, dividing lines by hot lunch or cold lunch, or organizing a work group on the basis of interests or reading ability.

4. Girls and boys may interact more readily in less public and crowded settings. Neighborhood play, depending on demography, is more often sex and age integrated than play at school, partly because with fewer numbers, one may have to resort to an array of social categories to find play partners or to constitute a game. And in less crowded environments there are fewer potential witnesses to "make something of it" if girls and boys play together.

Relaxed interactions between girls and boys often depend on adults to set up and legitimize the contact.[4] Perhaps because of this contingency—and the other, distancing patterns which permeate relations between girls and boys—the easeful moments of interaction rarely build to close friendship. Schofield (1981) makes a similar observation about gender and

racial barriers to friendship in a junior high school.

Implications for Development

I have located social relations within an essentially spatial framework, emphasizing the organization of children's play, work, and other activities within specific settings, and in one type of institution, the school. In contrast, frameworks of child development rely upon temporal metaphors, using images of growth and transformation over time. Taken alone, both spatial and temporal frameworks have shortcomings; fitted together, they may be mutually correcting.

Those interested in gender and development have relied upon conceptualizations of "sex role socialization" and "sex differences." Sexuality and gender, I have argued, are more situated and fluid than these individualist and intrinsic models imply. Sex and gender are differently organized and defined across situations, even within the same institution. This situational variation (e.g., in the extent to which an encounter heightens or lessens gender boundaries, or is infused with sexual meanings) shapes and constrains individual behavior. Features which a developmental perspective might attribute to individuals, and understand as relatively internal attributes unfolding over time, may, in fact, be highly dependent on context. For example, children's avoidance of cross-sex friendship may be attributed to individual gender development in middle-childhood. But attention to varied situations may show that this avoidance is contingent on group size, activity, adult behavior, collective meanings, and the risk of being teased.

A focus on social organization and situation draws attention to children's experiences in the present. This helps correct a model like "sex role socialization" which casts the present under the shadow of the future, or presumed "end-points" (Speier, 1976). A situated analysis of arrangements of sex and gender among those of different ages may point to crucial disjunctions in the life course. In the fourth and fifth grades, culturally defined heterosexual rituals ("goin' with") begin to suppress the presence and visibility of other types of interaction between girls and boys, such as nonsexualized and comfortable interaction, and traveling in the world of the other sex. As "boyfriend/girlfriend" definitions spread, the fifth-grade tomboy I described had to work to sustain "buddy" relationships with boys. Adult women who were tomboys often speak of early adolescence as a painful time when they were pushed away from participation in boys' activities. Other adult women speak of the loss of intense, even erotic ties with other girls when they entered puberty and the rituals of dating, that is, when they became absorbed into the institution of heterosexuality (Rich, 1980). When Lever (1976) describes best-friend relationships among fifth-grade girls as preparation for dating, she imposes heterosexual ideologies onto a present which should be understood on its own terms.

As heterosexual encounters assume more importance, they may alter relations in same-sex groups. For example, Schofield (1981) reports that for sixth- and seventh-grade children in a middle school, the popularity of girls with other girls was affected by their popularity with boys, while boys' status with other boys did not depend on their relations with girls. This is an asymmetry familiar from the adult world; men's relationships with one another are defined through varied activities (occupations, sports), while relationships among women—and their public status—are more influenced by their connections to individual men.

A full understanding of gender and social relations should encompass cross-sex as well as within-sex interactions. "Borderwork" helps maintain separate, gender-linked subcultures, which, as those interested in development have begun to suggest, may result in different milieux for learning. Daniel Maltz and Ruth Borker (1983) for example, argue that because of different interactions within girls' and boys' groups, the sexes learn different rules for creating and interpreting friendly conversation, rules which carry into adulthood and help account for miscommunication between men and women. Carol Gilligan (1982) fits research on the different worlds of girls and boys into a theory of sex differences in moral development. Girls develop a style of reasoning, she argues, which is more personal and relational; boys develop a style which is more positional, based on separateness. Eleanor Maccoby (1982), also following the insight that because of sex segregation, girls and boys grow up in different environments, suggests implications for gender differentiated prosocial and antisocial behavior.

This separate worlds approach, as I have illustrated, also has limitations. The occasions when the sexes are together should also be studied, and understood as contexts for experience and learning. For example, asymmetries in cross-sex relationships convey a series of messages: that boys are more entitled to space and to the nonreciprocal right of interrupting or invading the activities of the other sex; that girls are more in need of adult protection, and are lower in status, more defined by sexuality, and may even be polluting. Different types of cross-sex interaction—relaxed, boundaried, sexualized, or taking place on the terms of the other sex—provide different contexts for development.

By mapping the array of relationships between and within the sexes, one adds complexity to the overly static and dichotomous imagery of separate worlds. Individual experiences vary, with implications for development. Some children prefer same-sex groupings; some are more likely to cross the gender boundary and participate in the world of the other sex; some chil-dren (e.g., girls and boys who frequently play "chase and kiss") invoke heterosexual meanings, while others avoid them.

Finally, after charting the terrain of relationships, one can trace their development over time. For example, age variation in the content and form of borderwork, or of cross- and same-sex touch, may be related to differing cognitive, social, emotional, or physical capacities, as well as to age-associated cultural forms. I earlier mentioned temporal shifts in the organization of cross-sex chasing, for mixing with fantasy play in the early grades to more elaborately ritualized and sexualized forms by the sixth grade. There also appear to be temporal changes in same- and cross-sex touch. In kindergarten, girls and boys touch one another more freely than in fourth grade, when children avoid relaxed cross-sex touch and instead use pokes, pushes, and other forms of mock violence, even when the touch clearly couches affection. This touch taboo is obviously related to the risk of seeming to *like* someone of the other sex. In fourth grade, same-sex touch begins to signal sexual meanings among boys, as well as between boys and girls. Younger boys touch one another freely in cuddling (arm around shoulder) as well as mock violence ways. By fourth grade, when homophobic taunts like "fag" become more common among boys, cuddling touch begins to disappear for boys, but less so for girls.

Overall, I am calling for more complexity in our conceptualization of gender and of children's social relationships. Our challenge is to retain the temporal sweep, looking at individual and group lives as they unfold over time, while also attending to social structure and context, and to the full variety of experiences in the present.

Acknowledgment

I would like to thank Jane Atkinson, Nancy Chodorow, Arlene Daniels, Peter Lyman, Zick Rubin, Malcolm Spector, Avril Thorne, and Margery Wolf for comments on an earlier version of this paper. Conversations with Zella Luria enriched this work.

Notes

1. I am grateful to Frederick Erickson for suggesting the relevance of Barth's analysis.

2. Sue Samuelson (1980) reports that in a racially mixed playground in Fresno, California, Mexican-American, but not Anglo children gave cooties. Racial, as well as sexual inequality may be expressed through these forms.

3. This incident was recorded by Margaret Blume, who, for an undergraduate research project in 1982, observed in the California school where I earlier did fieldwork. Her observations and insights enhanced my own, and I would like to thank her for letting me cite this excerpt.

4. Note that in daily school life, depending on the individual and the situation, teachers and aides sometimes lessened, and at other times heightened sex segregation.

References

Aronson, F., et al. (1978). *The jigsaw classroom.* Beverly Hills, CA: Sage.

Barth, F. (Ed.). (1969). *Ethnic groups and boundaries.* Boston: Little, Brown.

Borman, K. M. (1979). Children's interactions in playgrounds. *Theory into Practice, 18,* 251–257.

Eder, D., & Hallinan, M. T. (1978). Sex differences in children's friendships. *American Sociological Review, 43,* 237–250.

Finnan, C. R. (1982). The ethnography of children's spontaneous play. In G. Spindler (Ed.), *Doing the ethnography of schooling* (pp. 358–380). New York: Holt, Rinehart & Winston.

Foot, H. C., Chapman, A. J., & Smith, J. R. (1980). Introduction. *Friendship and social relations in children* (pp. 1–14). New York: Wiley.

Gilligan, C. (1982). *In a different voice: Psychological theory and women's development.* Cambridge, MA: Harvard University Press.

Glaser, B. G., & Strauss, A. L. (1967). *The discovery of grounded theory.* Chicago: Aldine.

Goffman, E. (1977). The arrangement between the sexes. *Theory and Society, 4,* 301–336.

Goodwin, M. H. (1980). Directive-response sequences in girls' and boys' task activities. In S. McConnell-Ginet, R. Borker, & N. Furman (Eds.), *Women and language in literature and society* (pp. 157–173). New York: Praeger.

Grief, E. B. (1980). Sex differences in parent–child conversations. *Women's Studies International Quarterly, 3,* 253–258.

Henley, N. (1977). *Body politics: Power, sex, and nonverbal communication.* Englewood Cliffs, NJ: Prentice-Hall.

Karkau, K. (1973). *Sexism in the fourth grade.* Pittsburgh: KNOW, Inc. (pamphlet).

Katz, J. (1983). A theory of qualitative methodology: The social system of analytic fieldwork. In R. M. Emerson (Ed.), *Contemporary field research* (pp. 127–148). Boston: Little, Brown.

Knapp, M., & Knapp, H. (1976). *One potato, two potato: The secret education of American children.* New York: W. W. Norton.

Lever, J. (1976). Sex differences in the games children play. *Social Problems, 23,* 478–487.

Maccoby, E. (1982). *Social groupings in childhood: Their relationship to prosocial and antisocial behavior in boys and girls.* Paper presented at conference on The Development of Prosocial and Antisocial Behavior. Voss, Norway.

Maccoby, E., & Jacklin, C. (1974). *The psychology of sex differences.* CA: Stanford University Press.

Maltz, D. N., & Borker, R. A. (1983). A cultural approach to male–female miscommunication. In J. J. Gumperz (Ed.), *Language and social identity* (pp. 195–216). New York: Cambridge University Press.

McRobbie, A., & Garber, J. (1975). Girls and subcultures. In S. Hall and T. Jefferson (Eds.), *Resistance through rituals* (pp. 209–223). London: Hutchinson.

Ortner, S. B., & Whitehead, H. (1981). *Sexual meanings.* New York: Cambridge University Press.

Parrott, S. (1972). Games children play: Ethnography of a second-grade recess In J. P. Spradley & D. W. McCurdy (Eds.), *The cultural experience* (pp. 206–219). Chicago: Science Research Associates.

Rich, A. (1980). Compulsory heterosexuality and lesbian existence. *Signs, 5,* 631–660.

Samuelson, S. (1980) The cooties complex. *Western Folklore, 39,* 198–210.

Savin-Williams, R. C. (1976). An ethological study of dominance formation and maintenance in a group of human adolescents. *Child Development, 47,* 972–979.

Schofield, J. W. (1981). Complementary and conflicting identities: Images and interaction in an interracial school. In S. R. Asher & J. M. Gottman (Eds.), *The development of children's friendships* (pp. 53–90). New York: Cambridge University Press.

Sherif, M., & Sherif, C. (1953). *Groups in harmony and tension.* New York: Harper.

ARTICLE

Jeffrey P. Hantover

The Boy Scouts and the Validation of Masculinity

The Boy Scouts of America was formally incorporated in 1910 and by 1916 had received a federal charter, absorbed most of the organizations which had claimed the Scouting name, and was an accepted community institution. The President of the United States was the organization's honorary president, and Scouting courses were offered in major universities. At the end of its first decade, the Boy Scouts was the largest male youth organization in American history with 358,573 scouts and 15,117 scoutmasters.

The Boy Scouts' rapid national acceptance reflected turn-of-the-century concern over the perpetuation and validation of American masculinity. The widespread and unplanned adoption of the Scout program prior to 1916 suggests that Scouting's message, unadorned by organizational sophistication, spoke to major adult concerns, one of which was the future of traditional conceptions of American masculinity.

This paper will argue that the Boy Scouts served the needs of adult men as well as adoles-

Reprinted from *Journal of Social Issues*, Volume 34, Number 1, pages 184–195, 1978.
The author wishes to thank Joseph Pleck and Mayer Zald for their constructive comments.

cent boys. The supporters of the Scout movement, those who gave their time, money, and public approval, believed that changes in work, the family, and adolescent life threatened the development of manliness among boys and its expression among men. They perceived and promoted Scouting as an agent for the perpetuation of manliness among adolescents; the Boy Scouts provided an environment in which boys could become "red blooded" virile men. Less explicitly, Scouting provided men an opportunity to counteract the perceived feminizing forces of their lives and to act according to the traditional masculine script.

The Opportunity to Be a Man: Restriction and Its Consequences

Masculinity is a cultural construct and adult men need the opportunity to perform normatively appropriate male behaviors. Masculinity is not affirmed once and for all by somatic change; physical development is but a means for the performance of culturally ascribed behaviors.

American masculinity is continually affirmed through ongoing action. What acts a man performs and how well he does them truly make a male a man.

However, the availability of opportunities is not constant. Anxiety about the integrity and persistence of the male role can result from a restriction of opportunities experienced by the individual and the groups with which he identifies. Adult experiences produce adult anxieties. Masculine anxiety can arise when adult men know the script and wish to perform according to cultural directions but are denied the opportunity to act: The fault lies in social structuring of opportunities and not in individual capabilities and motivations.

The anxiety men increasingly exhibited about the naturalness and substance of manliness in the period 1880 to World War I flowed from changes in institutional spheres traditionally supportive of masculine definitional affirmation. Feminism as a political movement did raise fears of feminization but, as Filene (1975) suggests, in relation to preexistent anxiety about the meaning of manliness. Changes in the sphere of work, the central institutional anchorage of masculinity, undercut essential elements in the definition of manliness. Men believed they faced diminishing opportunities for masculine validation and that adolescents faced barriers to the very development of masculinity.

Masculine anxiety at the turn of the century was expressed in the accentuation of the physical and assertive side of the male ideal and in the enhanced salience of gender in social life. The enthronement of "muscularity" is evident in leisure activities, literary tastes, and cultural heroes. In the early nineteenth century, running and jumping were not exercises befitting a gentleman (Rudolph, 1962), but now men took to the playing fields, gyms, and wilderness in increasing numbers. Football, baseball, hiking, and camping became popular and were defended for their contribution to the development of traditional masculine character. Popular magazine biogra-

phies of male heroes in the period 1894 to 1913 shifted from an earlier idealization of passive traits such as piety, thrift, and industry to an emphasis on vigor, forcefulness, and mastery (Greene, 1970). Literary masculinization extended beyond mortals like Teddy Roosevelt to Christ who was portrayed as "the supremely manly man": attractive to women, individualistic, athletic, self-controlled, and aggressive when need be—"he was no Prince of Peace-at-any-price" (Conant, 1915, p. 117).

Sex-role distinctions became increasingly salient and rigid. The birth control issue became enmeshed in the debate over women's proper role; diatribes against expanded roles for women accompanied attacks on family limitation. The increased insistence on sexual purity in fiction and real life was a demand for women to accept the traditional attributes of purity, passivity, and domesticity. The emphasis on the chivalric motif in turn-of-the-century youth organizations (Knights of King Arthur, Order of Sir Galahad, Knights of the Holy Grail) can be interpreted as an expression of the desire to preserve male superordination in gender relations.

Perceived Forces of Feminization

Men in the period 1880 to World War I believed that opportunities for the development and expression of masculinity were being limited. They saw forces of feminization in the worlds of adults and adolescents. I will concentrate on changes in the adult opportunity structure. However, the forces of feminization that adolescents were thought to face at home and school should be mentioned, for they contributed to the anxiety of men worried about the present and wary of the future.

For the expanding urban middle class, the professionalization and sanctification of motherhood, the smaller family size, the decline in the number of servants who could serve as buffers between mother and son, and the absence of busy fathers from the home made the mother–son relationship appear threatening to proper masculine socialization. The expansion of the public high school took sons out of the home but did not allay fears of feminization. Female students outnumbered males, the percentage of female staff rose steadily between 1880 and World War I, and the requirements of learning demanded "feminine" passivity and sedentariness. Education would weaken a boy's body and direct his mind along the "psychic lines" of his female instructors. Finally, let me suggest that G. Stanley Hall's concept of adolescence may have generated sex-role anxiety by extending and legitimating dependency as a natural stage in the developmental cycle. A cohort of men who had reached social maturity before the use and public acceptance of adolescence as an age category, who had experienced the rural transition to manhood at an early age, and who had fought as teenagers in the Civil War or knew those who had were confronted with a generation of boys whose major characteristics were dependency and inactivity.

Changes in the nature of work and in the composition of the labor force from 1880 to World War I profoundly affected masculine self-identity. From 1870 to 1910 the number of clerical workers, salespeople, government employees, technicians, and salaried professionals increased from 756 thousand to 5.6 million (Hays, 1957). The dependency, sedentariness, and even security of these middle-class positions clashed with the active mastery, independence, self-reliance, competitiveness, creativity, and risk-taking central to the traditional male ideal (Mills, 1951). In pre–Civil War America, there were opportunities to approach that ideal: It is estimated that over 80% of Americans were farmers or self-employed businessmen (Mills, 1951). They owned the property they worked; they produced tangible goods; and they were

not enmeshed in hierarchical systems of "command and obedience."

Industrialization and bureaucratization reduced opportunities to own one's business, to take risks, exercise independence, compete, and master men and nature. The new expanded middle class depended on others for time, place, and often pace of work. The growth of chain stores crowded out independent proprietors, made small business ventures short lived, and reduced the income of merchants frequently below the level of day laborers (Anderson & Davidson, 1940). Clerical positions were no longer certain stepping stones to ownership; and clerical wages were neither high enough to meet standards of male success nor appreciably greater than those of less prestigious occupations (Filene, 1975; Douglas, 1930).

This changed occupational landscape did not go unnoticed. College graduates were told not to expect a challenging future:

> The world is steadily moving toward the position in which the individual is to contribute faithfully and duly his quota of productive or protective social effort, and to receive in return a modest, certain, not greatly variable stipend. He will adjust his needs and expenses to his income, guard the future by insurance or some analogous method, and find margin of leisure and opportunity sufficient to give large play to individual tastes and preferences. (Shaw, 1907, p. 3)

Interestingly for this paper's thesis, graduates were to seek fulfillment in activities outside work.

The increased entry of women into the labor force raised the specter of feminization as did the changed character of work. In terms of masculine anxiety, the impact was two-fold: the mere fact of women working outside the home in larger numbers and their increased participation in jobs which demanded non-masculine attributes. From 1870 to 1920, there was a substantial increase in the percentage of women aged 16 and over in nonagricultural occupations—from 11.8% to 21.3% (Hill, 1929). Men expressed concern over the entrance of women into a previously exclusive domain of masculine affirmation. (Women's occupations were not enumerated in the federal census until 1860.) Magazine and newspaper cartoons showed women in suits, smoking cigars, and talking business while aproned men were washing dishes, sweeping floors, and feeding babies (Smuts, 1959). Sex-role definition, not simple income, was at stake. Only one-third of employed men in 1910 worked in occupations where women constituted more than 5% of the work force (Hill, 1929). The actual threat posed by working women was more cultural than economic. Women doing what men did disconfirmed the naturalness and facticity of sex-role dichotomization.

Imposed on this general concern was the anxiety of men in white-collar positions. It was into these "nonmasculine" jobs that women entered in large numbers. Women were only 3% of the clerical work force in 1870, but 35% in 1910 (U.S. Department of Commerce, 1870; Hill, 1929). The increase for specific occupations between 1910 and 1920 is even more dramatic, especially for native white women of native parentage: female clerks increased 318%; bookkeepers, accountants, and cashiers, 257%; stenographers and typists, 121%; and sales personnel, 66% (Hill, 1929). It is to be argued that men in these occupations, feminine in character and composition, sought nonoccupational means of masculine validation, one of which was being a scoutmaster.

Scouting and the Construction of Manliness

The Boy Scouts of America responded explicitly to adult sex-role concerns. It provided concerned men the opportunity to support "an or-

ganized effort to make big men of little boys . . . to aid in the development of that master creation, high principled, clean and clear thinking, independent manhood" (Burgess, 1914, p. 12). At the turn of the century, manliness was no longer considered the inevitable product of daily life; urbanization appeared to have removed the conditions for the natural production of manliness. Scouting advertised itself as an environmental surrogate for the farm and frontier:

> The Wilderness is gone, the Buckskin Man is gone, the painted Indian has hit the trail over the Great Divide, the hardships and privations of pioneer life which did so much to develop sterling manhood are now but a legend in history, and we must depend upon the Boy Scout Movement to produce the MEN of the future. (Daniel Carter Beard in Boy Scouts of America, 1914, p. 109)[1]

Scouting's program and structure would counter the forces of feminization and maintain traditional manhood. Following the dictates of Hall's genetic psychology, boys were sexually segregated in a primary group under the leadership of an adult male. The gang instinct, like all adolescent instincts, was not to be repressed but constructively channeled in the service of manhood. By nature boys would form gangs, and the Boy Scouts turned the gang into a Scout patrol. The gang bred virility, did not tolerate sissies, and would make a boy good but not a goody-goody; in short, he would "be a real boy, not too much like his sister" (Puffer, 1912, p. 157; also see Page, 1919).

The rhetoric and content of Scouting spoke to masculine fears of passivity and dependence. Action was the warp and woof of Scouting, as it was the foundation of traditional American masculinity. After-school and summer idleness led to and was itself a moral danger, and scouts were urged to do "anything rather than continue in dependent, and enfeebling, and demoralizing idleness" (Russell, 1914, p. 163). "Spectatoritis" was turning "robust, manly, self-reliant boyhood into a lot of flat-chested cigarette smokers with shaky nerves and doubtful vitality" (Seton, 1910, p. xi). So Scout activities involved all members, and advancement required each boy to compete against himself and nature. Scouting stands apart from most nineteenth-century youth organizations by its level of support for play and its full acceptance of outdoor activities as healthy for boys.

The Scout code, embodied in the Scout Oath, Law, Motto, and requirements for advancement, was a code for conduct, not moral contemplation. It was "the code of red blooded, moral manly men" (Beard, Note 1, p. 9). The action required by the code, not one's uniform or badges, made a boy a scout and differentiated a scout from a non-scout. The British made a promise to act, but the Americans made a more definite commitment to action: they took an oath. More than the British, Americans emphasized that theirs was a "definite code of personal purposes," whose principles would shape the boy's total character and behavior.

The Scout code would produce that ideal man who was master of himself and nature. The American addition to the Scout oath, "To keep myself physically strong, mentally awake, and morally straight," was a condition for such mastery. In pre–Civil War America, "be prepared" meant being prepared to die, having one's moral house in order (Crandall, 1957). The Scout motto meant being prepared to meet and master dangers, from runaway horses to theater fires and factory explosions. In emergencies, it was the scout who "stood firm, quieted those who were panic stricken and unobtrusively and efficiently helped to control the crowds" (Murray, 1937, p. 492). American Scouting added the tenth law: "A Scout is Brave." Bravery meant self-mastery and inner direction, having the courage "to stand up for the right against the coaxing of friends or the jeers or threats of enemies."

The linchpin of the Scout code was the good deed. Boys active in community service reassured males that the younger generation would become manly men. To Scout supporters the movement provided a character building "moral equivalent to war." The phrase was used by William James in 1910 to suggest a kind of Job Corps for gilded youths. They would wash windows, build roads, work on fishing boats, and engage in all types of manual labor. This work would knock the childishness out of the youth of the luxurious classes and would produce the hardiness, discipline, and manliness that previously only war had done (James, 1971). As a result, young men would walk with their heads higher, would be esteemed by women, and be better fathers and teachers of the next generation. Scouts would not accept payment for their good deeds. To take a tip was un-American, un-masculine, and made one a "bit of a boot lick" (Eaton, 1918, p. 38). Adherence to the Scout code would produce traditional manliness in boy's clothing:

> The REAL Boy Scout is not a "sissy." He is not a hothouse plant, like little Lord Fauntleroy. There is nothing "milk and water" about him; he is not afraid of the dark. He does not do bad things because he is afraid of being decent. Instead of being a puny, dull, or bookish lad, who dreams and does nothing, he is full of life, energy, enthusiasm, bubbling over with fun, full of ideas as to what he wants to do and knows how he wants to do it. He has many ideals and many heroes. He is not hitched to his mother's apronstrings. While he adores his mother, and would do anything to save her from suffering or discomfort, he is self-reliant, sturdy and full of vim. (West, 1912, p. 448)

The Scoutmaster and Masculine Validation

Scouting assuaged adult masculine anxiety not only by training boys in the masculine virtues. The movement provided adult men a sphere of masculine validation. Given the character and composition of their occupations and the centrality of occupation to the male sex role, young men in white-collar positions were especially concerned about their masculine identity. They were receptive to an organization which provided adult men the opportunity to be men as traditionally defined.

At the core of the image of the ideal scoutmaster was assertive manliness. Scoutmasters were "manly" patriots with common sense and moral character who sacrificially served America's youth (Boy Scouts of America, 1920). Scouting wanted "REAL, live men—red blooded and right-hearted men—BIG men"; "No Miss Nancy need apply" (Boy Scouts of America, n.d., p. 9). Scoutmasters by the force of their characters, not by their formal positions (as in a bureaucracy), would evoke respect. They were portrayed as men of executive ability who took decisive action over a wide range of problems and were adroit handlers of men and boys. An analysis of the social characteristics and motivation of all the Chicago scoutmasters for whom there are records—original applications—through 1919 (N = 575) raises questions about the veracity of this portrayal (Hantover, 1976).

The first scoutmasters were men of educational, occupational, and ethnic status, but they did not serve solely from a sense of *noblesse oblige* and a disinterested commitment to all boys. They were more concerned about saving middle-class boys from the effeminizing forces of modern society than with "civilizing" the sons of the lower classes. Only four scoutmasters singled out the lower class for special mention; just 8% of the over 700 experiences with youth listed by scoutmasters were with lower-class youth. The typical Chicago scoutmaster was white, under 30, native born, Protestant, college educated, and in a white-collar or professional/semiprofessional occupation. Scoutmasters were more Protestant, better educated, and in higher prestige occupations than the adult male population of Chicago. Many teachers, clergymen, and boys' workers were scoutmasters because Scouting was part of their job, was good training for it, or at least was

congruent with their vocational ideology. If we exclude those men drawn to Scouting by the requirements of their occupations, Scouting disproportionately attracted men who had borne longer the "feminine" environment of the schools and now were in occupations whose sedentariness and dependence did not fit the traditional image of American manliness.

Though the motivational data extracted from the original scoutmaster applications are limited, there does emerge from the number and quality of responses a sense that clerical workers were concerned about the development of masculinity among adolescents and its expression by adults. Clerical workers were more concerned than other occupations unrelated to youth and service about training boys for manhood, filling a boy's time with constructive activities so he would not engage in activities detrimental to the development of manhood, and about the sexual and moral dangers of adolescence.

It is not simply chance, I believe, that clerical workers gave elaborate and individualistic responses which evinced a sense of life's restrictedness and danger. A 26-year-old stenographer, "always having lived in Chicago and working indoors," felt Scouting was a way to get outdoors for himself, not the scouts. A 21-year-old clerk, implying that his career had reached its apogee, praised Scouting for its development of initiative and resourcefulness and admitted that lack of these qualities had handicapped him greatly. A draftsman, only 27, thought "association with the boys will certainly keep one from getting that old and retired feeling." Another young clerk evokes a similar sense of life's restrictedness when he writes that Scouting "affords me an opportunity to exercise control over a set of young men. I learn to realize the value of myself as a force, as a personality."

The masculine anxiety that clerical workers felt may not have been generated by their occupations alone. They brought to the job achievements and attributes which at the turn of the century could have exacerbated that anxiety. Clerical workers had the highest percentage of high school educated scoutmasters of any occupational group. They were subject to the perceived feminine forces of high school without the status compensation of a college education and a professional position. With education controlled, Protestants and native Americans were more likely to be clerical workers. It was the virility and reproductive powers of the native American stock which were being questioned after the Civil War. Women in the better classes (native and Protestant) denied men the opportunity to prove their masculinity through paternity. Albion Small complained, "In some of the best middle-class social strata in the United States a young wife becomes a subject of surprised comment among her acquaintants if she accepts the burdens of maternity! This is a commonplace" (Small, 1915, p. 661). The fecundity and alleged sexuality of the immigrants raised turn-of-the-century fears about the continued dominance of the native Protestant stock. The experiences of key reference groups as well as one's own individual experiences were factors contributing to a sense of endangered masculinity.

Conclusion

Adult sex-role anxiety is rooted in the social structure; and groups of men are differentially affected, depending on their location in the social system and the opportunity structure they face. Critics of men's supposed nature can be dismissed as misguided by medical and religious defenders. But when the opportunity structure underlying masculinity begins to restrict, questioning may arise from the ranks of the men themselves. When taken-for-granted constructs become the objects of examination, anxiety may arise because elements in a cultural system are defended as natural, if not transcendent,

rather than convenient or utilitarian. Under the disconfirming impact of social change, men may at first be more likely to reassert the validity of traditional ends and seek new avenues for their accomplishment than to redefine their ends.

"Men not only define themselves, but they actualize these definitions in real experience—*they live them*" (Berger, Berger & Kellner, 1974, p. 92). Social identities generate the need for self-confirming action. The young men in the scoutmaster ranks were the first generation to face full force the discontinuity between the realities of the modern bureaucratic world and the image of masculine autonomy and mastery and the rhetoric of Horatio Alger. They found in the Boy Scouts of America an institutional sphere for the validation of masculinity previously generated by the flow of daily social life and affirmed in one's work.

Note

1. Beard, D. C. Untitled article submitted to *Youth Companion*. Unpublished manuscript, Daniel Carter Beard Collection, Library of Congress, 1914.

References

Anderson, H. D., & Davidson, P. E. *Occupational trends in the United States*. Stanford: Stanford University Press, 1940.

Berger, P., Berger, B., & Kellner, H. *The homeless mind*. New York: Vintage Press, 1974.

Boy Scouts of America. Fourth annual report. *Scouting*, 1914, 1.

Boy Scouts of America. *Handbook for scoutmasters* (2nd ed.). New York: Boy Scouts of America, 1920.

Boy Scouts of America. *The scoutmaster and his troop*. New York: Boy Scouts of America, no date.

Burgess, T. W. Making men of them. *Good Housekeeping Magazine*, 1914, 59, 3–12.

Conant, R. W. *The virility of Christ*. Chicago: no publisher, 1915.

Crandall, J. C., Jr. *Images and ideals for young Americans: A study of American juvenile literature, 1825–1860*. Unpublished doctoral dissertation, University of Rochester, 1957.

Douglas, P. *Real wages in the United States, 1890–1926*. New York: Houghton Mifflin, 1930.

Eaton, W. P. *Boy Scouts in Glacier Park*. Boston: W. A. Wilde; 1918.

Filene, P. G. *Him, her, self: Sex roles in modern America*. New York: Harcourt Brace Jovanovich, 1975.

Greene, T. P. *America's heroes: The changing models of success in American magazines*. New York: Oxford University Press, 1970.

Hantover, J. P. *Sex role, sexuality, and social status: The early years of the Boy Scouts of America*. Unpublished doctoral dissertation, University of Chicago, 1976.

Hays, S. P. *The response to industrialism: 1885–1914*. Chicago: University of Chicago Press, 1957.

Hill, J. A. *Women in gainful occupations 1870 to 1920* (Census Monograph No. 9, U.S. Bureau of the Census). Washington, D.C.: U.S. Government Printing Office, 1929.

James, W. The moral equivalent of war. In J. K. Roth (Ed.), *The moral equivalent and other essays*. New York: Harper Torchbook, 1971.

Mills, C. W. *White collar*. New York: Oxford University Press, 1951.

Murray, W. D. *The history of the Boy Scouts of America*. New York: Boy Scouts of America, 1937.

Page, J. F. *Socializing for the new order of educational values of the juvenile organization*. Rock Island, Ill.: J. F. Page, 1919.

Puffer, J. A. *The boy and his gang*. Boston: Houghton Mifflin, 1912.

Rudolph, F. *The American college and university*. New York: Knopf, 1962.

Russell, T. H. (Ed.). *Stories of boy life*. No location: Fireside Edition, 1914.

Seton, E. T. *Boy Scouts of America: A handbook of woodcraft, scouting, and life craft*. New York: Doubleday, Page, 1910.

Shaw, A. *The outlook for the average man*. New York: Macmillan, 1907.

Small, A. The bonds of nationality. *American Journal of Sociology*, 1915, *10*, 629–83.

Smuts, R. W. *Women and work in America*. New York: Columbia University Press, 1959.

U.S. Department of Commerce. *Ninth census of the United States, 1870: Population and social statistics* (Vol. I). Washington, D.C.: U.S. Government Printing Office, 1870.

West, J. E. The real boy scout. *Leslie's Weekly*, 1912, 448.

ARTICLE
Michael A. Messner

Boyhood, Organized Sports, and the Construction of Masculinities

The rapid expansion of feminist scholarship in the past two decades has led to fundamental reconceptualizations of the historical and contemporary meanings of organized sport. In the nineteenth and twentieth centuries, modernization and women's continued movement into public life created widespread "fears of social feminization," especially among middle-class men (Hantover, 1978; Kimmel, 1987). One result of these fears was the creation of organized sport as a homosocial sphere in which competition and (often violent) physicality was valued, while "the feminine" was devalued. As a result, organized sport has served to bolster a sagging ideology of male superiority, and has helped to reconstitute masculine hegemony (Bryson, 1987; Hall, 1988; Messner, 1988; Theberge, 1981).

The feminist critique has spawned a number of studies of the ways that women's sport has been marginalized and trivialized in the past (Greendorfer, 1977; Oglesby, 1978; Twin, 1978), in addition to illuminating the continued

Michael A. Messner, *Journal of Contemporary Ethnography*, Vol. 18, No. 4, January 1990, 416–444, copyright © 1990 by Sage Publications, Inc. Reprinted by permission of Sage Publications, Inc.

existence of structural and ideological barriers to gender equality within sport (Birrell, 1987). Only recently, however, have scholars begun to use feminist insights to examine men's experiences in sport (Kidd, 1987; Messner, 1987; Sabo, 1985). This article explores the relationship between the construction of masculine identity and boyhood participation in organized sports.

I view gender identity not as a "thing" that people "have," but rather as a *process of construction* that develops, comes into crisis, and changes as a person interacts with the social world. Through this perspective, it becomes possible to speak of "gendering" identities rather than "masculinity" or "femininity" as relatively fixed identities or statuses.

There is an agency in this construction; people are not passively shaped by their social environment. As recent feminist analyses of the construction of feminine gender identity have pointed out, girls and women are implicated in the construction of their own identities and personalities, both in terms of the ways that they participate in their own subordination and the ways that they resist subordination (Benjamin, 1988; Haug, 1987). Yet this self-construction is not a fully conscious process. There are also deeply woven, unconscious motivations, fears, and anxieties at work here. So, too, in the construction of masculinity. Levinson (1978) has argued that masculine identity is neither fully "formed" by the social context, nor is it "caused" by some internal dynamic put into place during infancy. Instead, it is shaped and constructed through the interaction between the internal and the social. The internal gendering identity may set developmental "tasks," may create thresholds of anxiety and ambivalence, yet it is only through a concrete examination of people's interactions with others within social institutions that we can begin to understand both the similarities and differences in the construction of gender identities.

In this study I explore and interpret the meanings that males themselves attribute to their boyhood participation in organized sport. In what ways do males construct masculine identities within the institution of organized sports? In what ways do class and racial differences mediate this relationship and perhaps lead to the construction of different meanings, and perhaps different masculinities? And what are some of the problems and contradictions within these constructions of masculinity?

Description of Research

Between 1983 and 1985, I conducted interviews with 30 male former athletes. Most of the men I interviewed had played the (U.S.) "major sports"—football, basketball, baseball, track. At the time of the interview, each had been retired from playing organized sports for at least five years. Their ages ranged from 21 to 48, with the median, 33; 14 were black, 14 were white, and two were Hispanic; 15 of the 16 black and Hispanic men had come from poor or working-class families, while the majority (9 of 14) of the white men had come from middle-class or professional

families. All had at some time in their lives based their identities largely on their roles as athletes and could therefore be said to have had "athletic careers." Twelve had played organized sports through high school, 11 through college, and seven had been professional athletes. Though the sample was not randomly selected, an effort was made to see that the sample had a range of difference in terms of race and social class backgrounds, and that there was some variety in terms of age, types of sports played, and levels of success in athletic careers. Without exception, each man contacted agreed to be interviewed.

The tape-recorded interviews were semi-structured and took from one and one-half to six hours, with most taking about three hours. I asked each man to talk about four broad eras in his life: (1) his earliest experiences with sports in boyhood, (2) his athletic career, (3) retirement or disengagement from the athletic career, and (4) life after the athletic career. In each era, I focused the interview on the meanings of "success and failure," and on the boy's/man's relationships with family, with other males, with women, and with his own body.

In collecting what amounted to life histories of these men, my overarching purpose was to use feminist theories of masculine gender identity to explore how masculinity develops and changes as boys and men interact within the socially constructed world of organized sports. In addition to using the data to move toward some generalizations about the relationship between "masculinity and sport," I was also concerned with sorting out some of the variations among boys, based on class and racial inequalities, that led them to relate differently to athletic careers. I divided my sample into two comparison groups. The first group was made up of 10 men from higher-status backgrounds, primarily white, middle-class, and professional families. The second group was made up of 20 men from lower-status backgrounds, primarily minority, poor, and working-class families.

Boyhood and the Promise of Sports

Zane Grey once said, "All boys love baseball. If they don't they're not real boys" (as cited in Kimmel, 1990). This is, of course, an ideological statement; in fact, some boys do *not* love baseball, or any other sports, for that matter. There are millions of males who at an early age are rejected by, become alienated from, or lose interest in organized sports. Yet all boys are, to a greater or lesser extent, judged according to their ability, or lack of ability, in competitive sports (Eitzen, 1975; Sabo, 1985). In this study I focus on those males who did become athletes—males who eventually poured thousands of hours into the development of specific physical skills. It is in boyhood that we can discover the roots of their commitment to athletic careers.

How did organized sports come to play such a central role in these boy's lives? When asked to recall how and why they initially got into playing sports, many of the men interviewed for this study seemed a bit puzzled: after all, playing sports was "just the thing to do." A 42-year-old black man who had played college basketball put it this way:

> It was just what you did. It's kind of like, you went to school, you played athletics, and if you didn't, there was something wrong with you. It was just like brushing your teeth: it's just what you did. It's part of your existence.

Spending one's time playing sports with other boys seemed as natural as the cycle of the seasons: baseball in the spring and summer, football in the fall, basketball in the winter—and then it was time to get out the old baseball glove and begin again. As a black 35-year-old former professional football star said:

> I'd say when I wasn't in school, 95% of the time was spent in the park playing. It was the only thing to do. It just came as natural.

And a black, 34-year-old professional basketball player explained his early experiences in sports:

> My principal and teacher said, "Now if you work at this you might be pretty damned good." So it was more or less a community thing—everybody in the community said, "Boy, if you work hard and keep your nose clean, you gonna be good." Cause it was natural instinct.

"It was natural instinct." "I was a natural." Several athletes used words such as these to explain their early attraction to sports. But certainly there is nothing "natural" about throwing a ball through a hoop, hitting a ball with a bat, or jumping over hurdles. A boy, for instance, may have amazingly dexterous inborn hand–eye coordination, but this does not predispose him to a career of hitting baseballs any more than it predisposes him to a life as a brain surgeon. When one listens closely to what these men said about their early experiences in sports, it becomes clear that their adoption of the self-definition of "natural athlete" was the result of what Connell (1990) has called "a collective practice" that constructs masculinities. The boyhood development of masculine identity and status—truly problematic in a society that offers no official rite of passage into adulthood—results from a process of interaction with people and social institutions. Thus, in discussing early motivations in sports, men commonly talk of the importance of relationships with family members, peers, and the broader community.

Family Influences

Though most of the men in this study spoke of their mothers with love, respect, even reverence, their descriptions of their earliest experiences in sports are stories of an exclusively male world. The existence of older brothers or uncles who served as teachers and athletic role models—as well as sources of competition for attention and status within the family—was very common. An older brother, uncle, or even close friend of the family who was a successful athlete appears to have acted as a sort of standard of achievement against whom to measure oneself. A 34-year-old black man who had been a three-sport star in high school said:

> My uncles—my Uncle Harold went to the Detroit Tigers, played pro ball—all of 'em, everybody played sports, so I wanted to be better than anybody else. I knew that everybody in this town knew them—their names were something. I wanted my name to be just like theirs.

Similarly, a black 41-year-old former professional football player recalled:

> I was the younger of three brothers and everybody played sports, so consequently I was more or less forced into it. 'Cause one brother was always better than the next brother and then I came along and had to show them that I was just as good as them. My oldest brother was an all-city ballplayer, then my other brother comes along he's all-city and all-state, and then I have to come along.

For some, attempting to emulate or surpass the athletic accomplishments of older male family members created pressures that were difficult to deal with. A 33-year-old white man explained that he was a good athlete during boyhood, but the constant awareness that his two older brothers had been better made it difficult for him to feel good about himself, or to have fun in sports:

> I had this sort of reputation that I followed from the playgrounds through grade school, and through high school. I followed these guys who were all-conference and all-state.

Most of these men, however, saw their relationships with their athletic older brothers and uncles in a positive light; it was within these relationships that they gained experience and developed motivations that gave them a competitive "edge" within their same-aged peer group. As a 33-year-old black man describes his earliest athletic experiences:

> My brothers were role models. I wanted to prove—especially to my brothers—that I had heart, you know, that I was a man.

When asked, "What did it mean to you to be 'a man' at that age?" he replied:

> Well, it meant that I didn't want to be a so-called scaredy-cat. You want to hit a guy even though he's bigger than you to show that, you know, you've got this macho image. I remember that at that young an age, that feeling was exciting to me. And that carried over, and as I got older, I got better and I began to look around me and see, well hey! I'm competitive with these guys, even though I'm younger, you know? And then of course all the compliments come—and I began to notice a change, even in my parents—especially in my father—he was proud of that, and that was very important to me. He was extremely important . . . he showed me more affection, now that I think of it.

As this man's words suggest, if men talk of their older brothers and uncles mostly as role models, teachers, and "names" to emulate, their talk of their relationships with their fathers is more deeply layered and complex. Athletic skills and competition for status may often be learned from older brothers, but it is in boys' relationships with fathers that we find many of the keys to the emotional salience of sports in the development of masculine identity.

Relationships with Fathers

The fact that boys' introductions to organized sports are often made by fathers who might otherwise be absent or emotionally distant adds a powerful emotional charge to these early experiences (Osherson, 1986). Although playing organized sports eventually came to feel "natural" for all of the men interviewed in this study, many needed to be "exposed" to sports, or even gently "pushed" by their fathers to become involved in activities like Little League baseball. A white, 33-year-old man explained:

> I still remember it like it was yesterday—Dad and I driving up in his truck, and I had my glove and my hat and all that—and I said, "Dad, I don't want to do it." He says, "What?" I says, "I don't want to do it." I was nervous. That I might fail. And he says, "Don't be silly. Lookit: There's Joey and Petey and all your friends out there." And so Dad says, "You're gonna do it, come on." And in my memory he's never said that about anything else; he just knew I needed a little kick in the pants and I'd do it. And once you're out there and you see all the other kids making errors and stuff, and you know you're better than those guys, you know: Maybe I *do* belong here. As it turned out, Little League was a good experience.

Some who were similarly "pushed" by their fathers were not so successful as the aforementioned man had been in Little League baseball, and thus the experience was not altogether a joyous affair. One 34-year-old white man, for instance, said he "inherited" his interest in sports from his father, who started playing catch with him at the age of four. Once he got into Little League, he felt pressured by his father, one of the coaches, who expected him to be the star of the team:

> I'd go 0-for-four sometimes, strike out three times in a Little League game, and I'd dread the ride home. I'd come home and he'd say, "Go in the bathroom and swing the bat in the mirror for an hour," to get my swing level . . . It didn't help much, though, I'd go out and strike out three or four times again the next game too [laughs ironically].

When asked if he had been concerned with having his father's approval, he responded:

> Failure in his eyes? Yeah, I always thought that he wanted me to get some kind of [athletic] scholarship. I guess I was afraid of him when I

was a kid. He didn't hit that much, but he had a rage about him—he'd rage, and that voice would just rattle you.

Similarly, a 24-year-old black man described his awe of his father's physical power and presence, and his sense of inadequacy in attempting to emulate him:

> My father had a voice that sounded like rolling thunder. Whether it was intentional on his part or not, I don't know, but my father gave me a sense, an image of him being the most powerful being on earth, and that no matter what I ever did I would never come close to him . . . There were definite feelings of physical inadequacy that I couldn't work around.

It is interesting to note how these feelings of physical inadequacy relative to the father lived on as part of this young man's permanent internalized image. He eventually became a "feared" high school football player and broke school records in weight-lifting, yet,

> As I grew older, my mother and friends told me that I had actually grown to be a larger man than my father. Even though in time I required larger clothes than he, which should have been a very concrete indication, neither my brother nor I could ever bring ourselves to say that I was bigger. We simply couldn't conceive of it.

Using sports activities as a means of identifying with and "living up to" the power and status of one's father was not always such a painful and difficult task for the men I interviewed. Most did not describe fathers who "pushed" them to become sports stars. The relationship between their athletic strivings and their identification with their fathers was more subtle. A 48-year-old black man, for instance, explained that he was not pushed into sports by his father, but was aware from an early age of the community status his father had gained through sports. He saw his own athletic accomplishments as a way to connect with and emulate his father:

> I wanted to play baseball because my father had been quite a good baseball player in the

Negro leagues before baseball was integrated, and so he was kind of a model for me. I remember, quite young, going to a baseball game he was in—this was before the war and all—I remember being in the stands with my mother and seeing him on first base, and being aware of the crowd . . . I was aware of people's confidence in him as a serious baseball player. I don't think my father ever said anything to me like "play sports" . . . [But] I knew he would like it if I did well. His admiration was important . . . he mattered.

Similarly, a 24-year-old white man described his father as a somewhat distant "role model" whose approval mattered:

My father was more of an example . . . he definitely was very much in touch with and still had very fond memories of being an athlete and talked about it, bragged about it. . . . But he really didn't do that much to teach me skills, and he didn't always go to every game I played like some parents. But he approved and that was important, you know, That was important to get his approval. I always knew that playing sports was important to him, so I knew implicitly that it was good and there was definitely a value on it.

First experiences in sports might often come through relationships with brothers or older male relatives, and the early emotional salience of sports was often directly related to a boy's relationship with his father. The sense of commitment that these young boys eventually made to the development of athletic careers is best explained as a process of development of masculine gender identity and status in relation to same-sex peers.

Masculine Identity and Early Commitment to Sports

When many of the men in this study said that during childhood they played sports because

"it's just what everybody did," they of course meant that it was just what *boys* did. They were introduced to organized sports by older brothers and fathers, and once involved, found themselves playing within an exclusively male world. Though the separate (and unequal) gendered worlds of boys and girls came to appear as "natural," they were in fact socially constructed. Thorne's observations of children's activities in schools indicated that rather than "naturally" constituting "separate gendered cultures," there is considerable interaction between boys and girls in classrooms and on playgrounds. When adults set up legitimate contact between boys and girls, Thorne observed, this usually results in "relaxed interactions." But when activities in the classroom or on the playground are presented to children as sex-segregated activities and gender is marked by teachers and other adults ("boys line up here, girls over there"), "gender boundaries are heightened, and mixed-sex interaction becomes an explicit arena of risk" (Thorne, 1986; 70). Thus sex-segregated activities such as organized sports as structured by adults, provide the context in which gendered identities and separate "gendered cultures" develop and come to appear natural. For the boys in this study, it became "natural" to equate masculinity with competition, physical strength, and skills. Girls simply did not (could not, it was believed) participate in these activities.

Yet it is not simply the separation of children, by adults, into separate activities that explains why many boys came to feel such a strong connection with sports activities, while so few girls did. As I listened to men recall their earliest experiences in organized sports, I heard them talk of insecurity, loneliness, and especially a need to connect with other people as a primary motivation in their early sports strivings. As a 42-year-old white man stated, "The most important thing was just being out there with the rest of the guys—being friends." Another 32-year-old interviewee was born in Mexico and moved to the United States at a fairly young age. He never knew his father, and his mother died when he was only nine years old. Suddenly he felt rootless, and threw himself into sports. His initial motivations, however, do not appear to be based on a need to compete and win:

> Actually, what I think sports did for me is it brought me into kind of an instant family. By being on a Little League team, or even just playing with all kinds of different kids in the neighborhood, it brought what I really wanted, which was some kind of closeness. It was just being there, and being friends.

Clearly, what these boys needed and craved was that which was most problematic for them: connection and unity with other people. But why do these young males find *organized sports* such an attractive context in which to establish "a kind of closeness" with others? Comparative observations of young boys' and girls' game-playing behaviors yield important insights into this question. Piaget (1965) and Lever (1976) both observed that girls tend to have more "pragmatic" and "flexible" orientations to the rules of games; they are more prone to make exceptions and innovations in the middle of a game in order to make the game more "fair." Boys, on the other hand, tend to have a more firm, even inflexible orientation to the rules of a game; to them, the rules are what protects any fairness. This difference, according to Gilligan (1982), is based on the fact that early developmental experiences have yielded deeply rooted differences between males' and females' developmental tasks, needs, and moral reasoning. Girls, who tend to define themselves primarily through connection with others, experience highly competitive situations (whether in organized sports or in other hierarchical institutions) as threats to relationships, and thus to their identities. For boys, the development of gender identity involves the construction of positional identities, where a sense of self is solidified through separation from others (Chodorow, 1978). Yet feminist psychoanalytic

theory has tended to oversimplify the internal lives of men (Lichterman, 1986). Males do appear to develop positional identities, yet despite their fears of intimacy, they also retain a human need for closeness and unity with others. This ambivalence toward intimate relationships is a major thread running through masculine development throughout the life course. Here we can conceptualize what Craib (1987) calls the "elective affinity" between personality and social structure: For the boy who both seeks and fears attachment with others, the rule-bound structure of organized sports can promise to be a safe place in which to seek nonintimate attachment with others within a context that maintains clear boundaries, distance, and separation.

Competitive Structures and Conditional Self-Worth

Young boys may initially find that sports gives them the opportunity to experience "some kind of closeness" with others, but the structure of sports and athletic careers often undermines the possibility of boys learning to transcend their fears of intimacy, thus becoming able to develop truly close and intimate relationships with others (Kidd, 1990; Messner, 1987). The sports world is extremely hierarchical, and an incredible amount of importance is placed on winning, on "being number one." For instance, a few years ago I observed a basketball camp put on for boys by a professional basketball coach and his staff. The youngest boys, about eight years old (who could barely reach the basket with their shots) played a brief scrimmage. Afterwards, the coaches lined them up in a row in front of the older boys who were sitting in the grandstands. One by one, the coach would stand behind each boy, put his hand on the boy's head (much in the manner of a priestly benediction), and the older boys in the stands would applaud and cheer, louder or softer, depending on how well or poorly the young boy was judged to have performed. The two or three boys who were clearly the exceptional players looked confident that they would receive the praise they were due. Most of the boys, though, had expressions ranging from puzzlement to thinly disguised terror on their faces as they awaited the judgments of the older boys.

This kind of experience teaches boys that it is not "just being out there with the guys—being friends," that ensures the kind of attention and connection that they crave; it is being *better* than the other guys—*beating* them—that is the key to acceptance. Most of the boys in this study did have some early successes in sports, and thus their ambivalent need for connection with others was met, at least for a time. But the institution of sport tends to encourage the development of what Schafer (1975) has called "conditional self-worth" in boys. As boys become aware that acceptance by others is contingent upon being good—a "winner"—narrow definitions of success, based upon performance and winning become increasingly important to them. A 33-year-old black man said that by the time he was in his early teens:

> It was expected of me to do well in all my contests—I mean by my coaches, my peers, and my family. So I in turn expected to do well, and if I didn't do well, then I'd be very disappointed.

The man from Mexico, discussed above, who said that he had sought "some kind of closeness" in his early sports experiences began to notice in his early teens that if he played well, was a *winner*, he would get attention from others:

> It got to the point where I started realizing, noticing that people were always there for me, backing me all the time—sports got to be really fun because I always had some people there backing me. Finally my oldest brother started going to all my games, even though I had never really seen who he was [laughs]—after the game, you know, we never really saw

each other, but he was at all my baseball games, and it seemed like we shared a kind of closeness there, but only in those situations. Off the field, when I wasn't in uniform, he was never around.

By high school, he said, he felt "up against the wall." Sports hadn't delivered what he had hoped it would, but he thought if he just tried harder, won one more championship trophy, he would get the attention he truly craved. Despite his efforts, this attention was not forthcoming. And, sadly, the pressures he had put on himself to excel in sports had taken most of the fun out of playing.

For many of the men in this study, throughout boyhood and into adolescence, this conscious striving for successful achievement became the primary means through which they sought connection with other people (Messner, 1987). But it is important to recognize that young males' internalized ambivalences about intimacy do not fully determine the contours and directions of their lives. Masculinity continues to develop through interaction with the social world—and because boys from different backgrounds are interacting with substantially different familial, educational, and other institutions, these differences will lead them to make different choices and define situations in different ways. Next, I examine the differences in the ways that boys from higher- and lower-status families and communities related to organized sports.

Status Differences and Commitments to Sports

In discussing early attractions to sports, the experiences of boys from higher- and lower-status backgrounds are quite similar. Both groups indicate the importance of fathers and older brothers in introducing them to sports. Both groups speak of the joys of receiving attention and acceptance among family and peers for early successes in sports. Note the similarities, for instance, in the following descriptions of boyhood athletic experiences of two men. First, a man born in a white, middle-class family:

> I loved playing sports so much from a very early age because of early exposure. A lot of the sports came easy at an early age, and because they did, and because you were successful at something, I think that you're inclined to strive for that gratification. It's like, if you're good, you like it, because it's instant gratification. I'm doing something that I'm good at and I'm gonna keep doing it.

Second, a black man from a poor family:

> Fortunately I had some athletic ability, and, quite naturally, once you start doing good in whatever it is—I don't care if it's jacks—you show off what you do. That's your ability, that's your blessing, so you show it off as much as you can.

For boys from both groups, early exposure to sports, the discovery that they had some "ability," shortly followed by some sort of family, peer, and community recognition, all eventually led to the commitment of hundreds and thousands of hours of playing, practicing, and dreaming of future stardom. Despite these similarities, there are also some identifiable differences that begin to explain the tendency of males from lower-status backgrounds to develop higher levels of commitment to sports careers. The most clear-cut difference was that while men from higher-status backgrounds are likely to describe their earliest athletic experiences and motivations almost exclusively in terms of immediate family, men from lower-status backgrounds more commonly describe the importance of a broader community context. For instance, a 46-year-old man who grew up in a "poor working class" black family in a small town in Arkansas explained:

> In that community, at the age of third or fourth grade, if you're a male, they expect you to show some kind of inclination, some kind of skill in football or basketball. It was an expected thing, you know? My mom and my dad, they didn't push at all. It was the general environment.

A 48-year-old man describes sports activities as a survival strategy in his poor black community:

> Sports protected me from having to compete in gang stuff, or having to be good with my fists. If you were an athlete and got into the fist world, that was your business, and that was okay—but you didn't have to if you didn't want to. People would generally defer to you, give you your space away from trouble.

A 35-year-old man who grew up in "a poor black ghetto" described his boyhood relationship to sports similarly:

> Where I came from, either you were one of two things: you were in sports or you were out on the streets being a drug addict, or breaking into places. The guys who were in sports, we had it a little easier, because we were accepted by both groups. . . . So it worked out to my advantage, cause I didn't get into a lot of trouble—some trouble, but not a lot.

The fact that boys in lower-status communities faced these kinds of realities gave salience to their developing athletic identities. In contrast, sports were important to boys from higher-status backgrounds, yet the middle-class environment seemed more secure, less threatening, and offered far more options. By the time most of these boys got into junior high or high school, many had made conscious decisions to shift their attentions away from athletic careers to educational and (nonathletic) career goals. A 32-year-old white college athletic director told me that he had seen his chance to pursue a pro baseball career as "pissing in the wind," and instead, focused on education. Similarly, a 33-year-old white dentist who was a three-sport star in high school, decided not to play sports in college, so he could focus on getting into dental school. As he put it,

> I think I kind of downgraded the stardom thing. I thought it was small potatoes. And sure, that's nice in high school and all that, but on a broad scale, I didn't think it amounted to all that much.

This statement offers an important key to understanding the construction of masculine identity within a middle-class context. The status that this boy got through sports had been *very* important to him, yet he could see that "on a broad scale," this sort of status was "small potatoes." This sort of early recognition is more than a result of the oft-noted middle-class tendency to raise "future-oriented" children (Rubin, 1976; Sennett and Cobb, 1973). Perhaps more important, it is that the *kinds* of future orientations developed by boys from higher-status backgrounds are consistent with the middle-class context. These men's descriptions of their boyhoods reveal that they grew up immersed in a wide range of institutional frameworks, of which organized sports was just one. And—importantly—they could see that the status of adult males around them was clearly linked to their positions within various professions, public institutions, and bureaucratic organizations. It was clear that access to this sort of institutional status came through educational achievement, not athletic prowess. A 32-year-old black man who grew up in a professional-class family recalled that he had idolized Wilt Chamberlain and dreamed of being a pro basketball player, yet his father discouraged his athletic strivings:

> He knew I liked the game. I *loved* the game. But basketball was not recommended; my dad would say, "That's a stereotyped image for black youth. . . . When your basketball is gone and finished, what are you gonna do? One day, you might get injured. What are you gonna look forward to?" He stressed education.

Similarly, a 32-year-old man who was raised in a white, middle-class family, had found in sports a key means of gaining acceptance and connection in his peer group. Yet he was simultaneously developing an image of himself as a "smart student," and becoming aware of a wide range of nonsports life options:

> My mother was constantly telling me how smart I was, how good I was, what a nice person I was, and giving me all sorts of positive strokes, and those positive strokes became a self-motivating kind of thing. I had this image of myself as smart, and I lived up to that image.

It is not that parents of boys in lower-status families did not also encourage their boys to work hard in school. Several reported that their parents "stressed books first, sports second." It's just that the broader social context—education, economy, and community—was more likely to *narrow* lower-status boys' perceptions of real-life options, while boys from higher-status backgrounds faced an expanding world of options. For instance, with a different socioeconomic background, one 35-year-old black man might have become a great musician instead of a star professional football running back. But he did not. When he was a child, he said, he was most interested in music:

> I wanted to be a drummer. But we couldn't afford drums. My dad couldn't go out and buy me a drum set or a guitar even—it was just one of those things; he was just trying to make ends meet.

But he *could* afford, as could so many in his socioeconomic condition, to spend countless hours at the local park, where he was told by the park supervisor

> that I was a natural—not only in gymnastics or baseball—whatever I did, I was a natural. He told me I shouldn't waste this talent, and so I immediately started watching the big guys then.

In retrospect, this man had potential to be a musician or any number of things, but his environment limited his options to sports, and he made the best of it. Even within sports, he, like most boys in the ghetto, was limited:

> We didn't have any tennis courts in the ghetto—we used to have a lot of tennis balls, but no racquets. I wonder today how good I might be in tennis if I had gotten a racquet in my hands at an early age.

It is within this limited structure of opportunity that many lower-status young boys found sports to be *the* place, rather than *a* place, within which to construct masculine identity, status, the relationships. A 36-year-old white man explained that his father left the family when he was very young and his mother faced a very difficult struggle to make ends meet. As his words suggest, the more limited a boy's options, and the more insecure his family situation, the more likely he is to make an early commitment to an athletic career:

> I used to ride my bicycle to Little League practice—if I'd waited for someone to pick me up and take me to the ball park I'd have never played. I'd get to the ball park and all the other kids would have their dad bring them to practice or games. But I'd park my bike to the side and when it was over I'd get on it and go home. Sports was the way for me to move everything to the side—family problems, just all the embarrassments—and think about one thing, and that was sports . . . In the third grade, when the teacher went around the classroom and asked everybody, "What do you want to be when you grow up?," I said, "I want to be a major league baseball player," and everybody laughed their heads off.

This man eventually did enjoy a major league baseball career. Most boys from lower-status backgrounds who make similar early commitments to athletic careers are not so successful. As stated earlier, the career structure of organized sports is highly competitive and hierarchical. In fact, the chances of attaining professional status in sports are approximately 4:100,000 for a white man, 2:100,000 for a black man, and 3:1 million

for a Hispanic man in the United States (Leonard and Reyman, 1988). Nevertheless, the immediate rewards (fun, status, attention), along with the constricted (nonsports) structure of opportunity, attract disproportionately large numbers of boys from lower-status backgrounds to athletic careers as their major means of constructing a masculine identity. These are the boys who later, as young men, had to struggle with "conditional self-worth," and, more often than not, occupational dead ends. Boys from higher-status backgrounds, on the other hand, bolstered their boyhood, adolescent, and early adult status through their athletic accomplishments. Their wider range of experiences and life chances led to an early shift away from sports careers as the major basis of identity (Messner, 1989).

Conclusion

The conception of the masculinity–sports relationship developed here begins to illustrate the idea of an "elective affinity" between social structure and personality. Organized sports is a "gendered institution"—an institution constructed by gender relations. As such, its structure and values (rules, formal organization, sex composition, etc.), reflect dominant conceptions of masculinity and femininity. Organized sports is also a "gendering institution"—an institution that helps to construct the current gender order. Part of this construction of gender is accomplished through the "masculinizing" of male bodies and minds.

Yet boys do not come to their first experiences in organized sports as "blank slates," but arrive with already "gendering" identities due to early developmental experiences and previous socialization. I have suggested here that an important thread running through the development of masculine identity is males' ambivalence toward intimate unity with others. Those boys who experience early athletic successes find in the structure of organized sport an affinity with this masculine ambivalence toward intimacy: The rule-bound, competitive, hierarchical world of sport offers boys an attractive means of establishing an emotionally distant (and thus "safe") connection with others. Yet as boys begin to define themselves as "athletes," they learn that in order to be accepted (to have connection) through sports, they must be winners. And in order to be winners, they must construct relationships with others (and with themselves) that are consistent with the competitive and hierarchical values and structure of the sports world. As a result, they often develop a "conditional self-worth" that leads them to construct more instrumental relationships with themselves and others. This ultimately exacerbates their difficulties in constructing intimate relationships with others. In effect, the interaction between the young male's preexisting internalized ambivalence toward intimacy with the competitive hierarchical institution of sport has resulted in the construction of a masculine personality that is characterized by instrumental rationality, goal-orientation, and difficulties with intimate connection and expression (Messner, 1987).

This theoretical line of inquiry invites us not simply to examine how social institutions "socialize" boys, but also to explore the ways that boys' already-gendering identities interact with social institutions (which, like organized sport, are themselves the product of gender relations). This study has also suggested that it is not some singular "masculinity" that is being constructed through athletic careers. It may be correct, from a psychoanalytic perspective, to suggest that all males bring ambivalences toward intimacy to their interactions with the world, but "the world" is a very different place for males from different racial and socioeconomic backgrounds. Because males have substantially different interactions with the world, based on class, race, and other differences and inequalities, we might expect the construction of masculinity to take on different meanings for boys and men from differing backgrounds (Messner, 1989). Indeed, this study has suggested that boys from higher-status backgrounds face a much broader range of options than do their lower-status counterparts. As a result, athletic careers take on different meanings for these boys. Lower-status boys are likely to see athletic careers as *the* institutional context for the construction of their masculine status and identities, while higher-status males make an early shift away from athletic careers toward other institutions (usually education and non-sports careers). A key line of inquiry for future studies might begin by exploring this irony of sports careers: Despite the fact that "the athlete" is currently an example of an exemplary form of masculinity in public ideology, the vast majority of boys who become most committed to athletic careers are never well-rewarded for their efforts. The fact that class and racial dynamics lead boys from higher-status backgrounds, unlike their lower-status counterparts, to move into non-sports careers illustrates how the construction of different kinds of masculini*ties* is a key component of the overall construction of the gender order.

References

Birrell, S. (1987) "The woman athlete's college experience: knowns and unknowns." *J. of Sport and Social Issues* 11: 82–96.

Benjamin, J. (1988) *The Bonds of Love: Psychoanalysis, Feminism, and the Problem of Domination.* New York: Pantheon.

Bryson, L. (1987) "Sport and the maintenance of masculine hegemony." Women's Studies International *Forum* 10: 349–360.

Chodorow, N. (1978) *The Reproduction of Mothering.* Berkeley: Univ. of California Press.

Connell, R. W. (1987) *Gender and Power.* Stanford, CA: Stanford Univ. Press.

Connell, R. W. (1990) "An iron man: the body and some contradictions of hegemonic masculinity." In M. A. Messner and D. F. Sabo (eds.) *Sport, Men and the Gender Order: Critical Feminist Perspectives.* Champaign, IL: Human Kinetics.

Craib, I. (1987) "Masculinity and male dominance." *Soc. Rev.* 38: 721–743.

Eitzen, D. S. (1975) "Athletics in the status system of male adolescents: a replication of Coleman's *The Adolescent Society.*" *Adolescence* 10: 268–276.

Gilligan, C. (1982) *In a Different Voice: Psychological Theory and Women's Development.* Cambridge, MA: Harvard Univ. Press.

Greendorfer, S. L. (1977) "The role of socializing agents in female sport involvement." *Research Q.* 48: 304–310.

Hall, M. A. (1988) "The discourse on gender and sport: from femininity to feminism." *Sociology of Sport J.* 5: 330–340.

Hantover, J. (1978) "The boy scouts and the validation of masculinity." *J. of Social Issues* 34: 184–195.

Haug, F. (1987) *Female Sexualization.* London: Verso.

Kidd, B. (1987) "Sports and masculinity," pp. 250–265 in M. Kaufman (ed.) *Beyond Patriarchy: Essays by Men on Pleasure, Power, and Change.* Toronto: Oxford Univ. Press.

Kidd, B. (1990) "The men's cultural centre: sports and the dynamic of women's oppression/men's repression," In M. A. Messner and D. F. Sabo (eds.) *Sport, Men and the Gender Order: Critical Feminist Perspectives.* Champaign, IL: Human Kinetics.

Kimmel, M. S. (1987) "Men's responses to feminism at the turn of the century." *Gender and Society* 1: 261–283.

Kimmel, M. S. (1990) "Baseball and the reconstitution of American masculinity: 1880–1920." In M. A. Messner and D. F. Sabo (eds.) *Sport, Men and the Gender Order: Critical Feminist Perspectives.* Champaign, IL: Human Kinetics.

Leonard, W. M. II and J. M. Reyman (1988) "The odds of attaining professional athlete status: refining the computations." *Sociology of Sport J.* 5: 162–169.

Lever, J. (1976) "Sex differences in the games children play." *Social Problems* 23: 478–487.

Levinson, D. J. et al. (1978) *The Seasons of a Man's Life.* New York: Ballantine.

Lichterman, P. (1986) "Chodorow's psychoanalytic sociology: a project half-completed." *California Sociologist* 9: 147–166.

Messner, M. (1987) "The meaning of success: the athletic experience and the development of male identity," pp. 193–210 in H. Brod (ed.) *The Making of Masculinities: The New Men's Studies.* Boston: Allen & Unwin.

Messner, M. (1988) "Sports and male domination: the female athlete as contested ideological terrain." *Sociology of Sport J.* 5: 197–211.

Messner, M. (1989) "Masculinities and athletic careers." *Gender and Society* 3: 71–88.

Oglesby, C. A. (Ed.) (1978) *Women and Sport: From Myth to Reality.* Philadelphia: Lea & Farber.

Osherson, S. (1986) *Finding Our Fathers: How a Man's Life Is Shaped by His Relationship with His Father.* New York: Fawcett Columbine.

Piaget, J. H. (1965) *The Moral Judgment of the Child.* New York: Free Press.

Rubin, L. B. (1976) *Worlds of Pain: Life in the Working Class Family.* New York: Basic Books.

Sabo, D. (1985) "Sport, patriarchy and male identity: new questions about men and sport." *Arena Rev.* 9: 2.

Schafer, W. E. (1975) "Sport and male sex role socialization." *Sport Sociology Bull.* 4: 47–54.

Sennett, R. and J. Cobb (1973) *The Hidden Injuries of Class.* New York: Random House.

Theberge, N. (1981) "A critique of critiques: radical and feminist writings on sport." *Social Forces* 60: 2.

Thorne, B. (1986) "Girls and boys together . . . but mostly apart: gender arrangements in elementary schools," pp. 167–184 in W. W. Hartup and Z. Rubin (eds.) *Relationships and Development.* Hillsdale, NJ: Lawrence Erlbaum.

Twin, S. L. [ed.] (1978) *Out of the Bleachers: Writings on Women and Sport.* Old Westbury, NY: Feminist Press.

11

ARTICLE

Geoffrey Canada

Learning to Fight

On Union Avenue, failure to fight would mean that you would be set upon over and over again. Sometimes for years. Later I would see what the older boys did to Butchie.

Butchie was a "manchild," very big for his age. At thirteen he was the size of a fully grown man. Butchie was a gentle giant. He loved to play with the younger boys and was not particularly athletic. Butchie had one flaw: he would not fight. Everyone picked on him. The older teenagers (fifteen and sixteen) were really hard on him. He was forever being punched in the midsection and chest by the older boys for no reason. (It was against the rules to punch in the face unless it was a "fair fight.")

I don't know what set the older boys off, or why they picked that Saturday morning, but it was decided that Butchie had to be taught a lesson. The older boys felt that Butchie was giving the block a bad reputation. Everyone had to be taught that we didn't tolerate cowards. Suddenly two of them grabbed Butchie. Knowing that something was wrong, that this was not the rough and tumble play we sometimes engaged

From "Learning to Fight" *Fist Stick Knife Gun: A Personal History of Violence in America.* Boston: Beacon, 1995. Adapted by permission of Beacon Press, Boston.

in, Butchie broke away. Six of the older boys took off after him. Butchie zigzagged between the parked cars, trying desperately to make it to his building and the safety of his apartment. One of the boys cut him off and, kicking and yelling, Butchie was snagged.

By the time the other five boys caught up, Butchie was screaming for his mother. We knew that his mother often drank heavily on the weekends and were not surprised when her window did not open and no one came to his aid. One of the rules of the block was that you were not allowed to cry for your mother. Whatever happened you had to "take it like man." A vicious punch to the stomach and a snarled command, "Shut the fuck up," and Butchie became quiet and stopped struggling. The boys marched him up the block, away from his apartment. Butchie, head bowed, hands held behind his back, looked like a captured prisoner.

There are about twelve of us younger boys out that morning playing football in the street. When the action started we stopped playing and prepared to escape to our individual apartment buildings. We didn't know if the older boys were after us, too—they were sometimes unpredictable—and we nervously kept one eye on them and one on a clear avenue of escape. As they marched Butchie down the block it became apparent that we were meant to learn from what was going to Butchie, that they were really doing this for us.

The older boys took Butchie and "stretched" him. This was accomplished by four boys grabbing Butchie, one on each arm, one on each leg. Then they placed him on the trunk of a car (in the early 1960s the cars were all large) and pulled with all their might until Butchie was stretched out over the back of the car. When Butchie was completely, helplessly exposed, two of the boys began to punch him in his stomach and chest. The beating was savage. Butchie's cries for help seemed only to infuriate them more. I couldn't believe that a human body could take that amount of punishment. When they finished with him, Butchie just collapsed in the fetal position and cried. The older boys walked away talking, as if nothing had happened.

To those of us who watched, the lesson was brutal and unmistakable. No matter who you fought, he could never beat you *that* bad. So it was better to fight even if you couldn't win than to end up being "stretched" for being a coward. We all fought, some with more skill and determination than others, but we all fought.

The day my bother John went out to play on the block and had to fight Paul Henry there was plenty of wild swinging and a couple of blows landed, but they did no real damage. When no one got the better of the other after six or seven minutes, the right was broken up. John and Paul Henry were made to shake hands and became best of friends in no time.

John was free. He could go outside without fear. I was still trapped. I needed help figuring out what would happen when I went outside. John was not much help to me about how the block worked. He was proud that he could go out and play while we were still stuck in the house. I mentioned something about going downstairs and having Ma come down to watch

over me and John laughed at me, called me a baby. He had changed, he had accepted the rules—no getting mothers to fight your battles. His only instructions to me were to fight back, don't let the boys your age hit you without hitting back. Within a week I decided I just couldn't take it, and I went downstairs.

The moment I went outside I began to learn about the structure of the block and its codes of conduct. Each excursion taught me more. The first thing I learned was that John, even though he was just a year older than me, was in a different category than I was. John's peers had some status on the block; my peers were considered too young to have any.

At the top of the pecking order were the young adults in their late teens (seventeen, eighteen, and nineteen). They owned the block; they were the strongest and the toughest. Many of them belonged to a gang called the Disciples. Quite a few had been arrested as part of a police crackdown on gangs in the late fifties and early sixties. Several came out of jail during my first few years on Union Avenue. They often spent large amounts of time in other areas of the Bronx, so they were really absentee rulers.

At this time there were some girls involved in gang activities as well; many of the larger male gangs had female counterparts whose members fought and intimidated other girls. On Union Avenue there was a group of older girls who demanded respect, and received it, from even the toughest boys on the block. Some of these girls were skilled fighters, and boys would say "she can fight like a boy" to indicate that a girl had mastered the more sophisticated techniques of fistfighting. Girls on Union Avenue sometimes found themselves facing the same kind of violence as did boys, but this happened less often. All in all there was less pressure on girls to fight for status, although some did; for girls to fight there usually had to be a major triggering incident.

But status was a major issue for boys on the block. The next category in the pecking order was the one we all referred to as the "older boys," fifteen and sixteen years old. They belonged to a group we sometimes called the Young Disciples, and they were the real rulers of Union Avenue. This was the group that set the rules of conduct on the block and enforced law and order. They were the ones who had stretched Butchie.

Next were boys nine, ten, and eleven, just learning the rules. While they were allowed to go into the street and play, most of them were not allowed off the block without their mother's permission. My brother John belonged to this group.

The lowest group was those children who could not leave the sidewalk, children too young to have any status at all. I belonged to this group and I hated it. The sidewalk, while it provided plenty of opportunity to play with other children, seemed to me to be the sidelines. The real action happened in the street.

There were few expectations placed on us in terms of fighting, but we were not exempt. There was very little natural animosity among us. We played punchball, tag, and "red light, green light, one-two-three." It was the older boys who caused the problems. Invariably, when the older boys were sitting on the stoop and one of them had a brother, or cousin amongst us, it would be he who began the prelude to violence.

I'd been outside for more than a week and thought that I had escaped having to fight anyone because all the boys were my friends. But sure enough, Billy started in on me.

"David, can you beat Geoff?"

David looked at me, then back at Billy. "I don't know."

"What! You can't beat Geoff? I thought you was tough. You scared? I know you ain't scared. You betta not be scared."

I didn't like where this conversation was heading. David was my friend and I didn't know Billy, he was just an older boy who lived in my building. David looked at me again and this time his face changed, he looked threatening, he seemed angry.

"I ain't scared of him."

I was lost. Just ten minutes before David and I were playing, having a good time. Now he looked like I was his worst enemy. I became scared, scared of David, scared of Billy, scared of Union Avenue. I looked for help to the other boys sitting casually on the stoop. Their faces scared me more. Most of them barely noticed what was going on, the rest were looking half interested. I was most disheartened by the reaction of my brother John. Almost in a state of panic, I looked to him for help. He looked me directly in the eye, shook his head no, then barely perceptibly pointed his chin toward David as if to say, Quit stalling, you know what you have to do. Then he looked away as if this didn't concern him at all.

The other sidewalk boys were the only ones totally caught up in the drama. They knew that their day would also come, and they were trying to learn what they could about me in case they had to fight me tomorrow, or next week, or whenever.

During the time I was sizing up my situation I made a serious error. I showed on my face what was going on in my head. My fear and my confusion were obvious to anyone paying attention. This, I would later learn, was a rookie mistake and could have deadly consequences on the streets.

Billy saw my panic and called to alert the others. "Look at Geoff, he's scared. He's scared of you, David. Go kick his ass."

It was not lost on me that the questioning part of this drama was over. Billy had given David a direct command. I thought I was saved, however, because Billy had cursed. My rationale was that no big boy could use curses at a little boy. My brother would surely step in now and say, "C'mon, Billy, you can't curse at my little brother. After all, he's only seven." Then he would take me upstairs and tell Ma.

When I looked at John again I saw only that his eyes urged me to act, implored me to act. There would be no rescue coming from him. What was worse, the other older boys had become interested when Billy yelled, "Kick his ass," and were now looking toward David and me. In their eyes this was just a little sport, not a real fight, but a momentary distraction that could prove to be slightly more interesting than talking about the Yankees, or the Giants, or their girlfriends. They smiled at my terror. Their smiles seemed to say, "I remember when I was like that. You'll see, it's not so bad."

Thinking on your feet is critical in the ghetto. There was so much to learn and so much of it was so important. It was my brother's reaction that clued me in. I knew John. He was a vicious tease at times, but he loved me. He would never allow me to be harmed and not help or at least go for help. He was telling me I had to go through this alone. I knew I could run upstairs, but what about tomorrow? Was I willing to become a prisoner in my apartment again? And what about how everyone was smiling at me? How was I ever going to play in the street with them if they thought I was such a baby? So I made the decision not to run but to fight.

I decided to maximize the benefits the situation afforded. I said, not quite with the conviction that I'd hoped for, "I'm not afraid of David. He can't beat me. C'mon. David, you wanna fight?"

There was only one problem—I didn't know how to fight. I hadn't seen Dan taking back John's coat, or John's fight with Paul Henry. But a funny thing happened after I challenged David. When I looked back at him, he didn't look quite so confident. He didn't look like he wanted to fight anymore. This gave me courage.

Billy taunted David, "You gonna let him talk to you like that? Go on, kick his ass."

Then Paul Henry chimed in, "Don't be scared, little Geoff. Go git him."

I was surprised. I didn't expect anyone to support me, especially not Paul Henry. But as I would learn later, most of these fights were viewed as sport by the bystanders. You rooted for the favorite or the underdog. Almost everyone had someone to root for them when they fought.

David put up his balled-up fists and said, "Come one." I didn't know how to fight, but I knew how to pretend fight. So I "put up my dukes" and stood like a boxer. We circled one another.

"Come on."

"No, *you* come on."

Luckily for me, David didn't know how to fight either. The older boys called out encouragement to us, but we didn't really know how to throw a punch. At one point we came close enough to one another for me to grab David, and we began to wrestle. I was good at this, having spent many an hour wrestling with my three brothers.

Wrestling wasn't allowed in a "real" fight, but they let us go at it a few moments before they broke us up. The older boys pronounced the fight a tie and made us shake hands and "be friends." They rubbed our heads and said, "You're all right," and then gave us some pointers on how to really fight. We both basked in the glory of their attention. The other sidewalk boys looked at us with envy. We had passed the first test. We were on our way to becoming respected members of Union Avenue.

David and I became good friends. Since we'd had a tie we didn't have to worry about any other older boys making us fight again. The rule was that if you fought an opponent, and could prove it by having witnesses, you didn't have to fight that person again at the command of the older boys. This was important, because everyone, and I mean everyone, had to prove he could beat other boys his age. Union Avenue, like most other inner-city neighborhoods, had a clear pecking order within the groups as well as between them when it came to violence. The order changed some as boys won or lost fights, but by and large the same boys remained at the top. New boys who came on the block had to be placed in the pecking order. If they had no credentials, no one to vouch for their ability, they had to fight different people on the block until it could be ascertained exactly where they fit in. If you refused to fight, you moved to the bottom of the order. If you fought and lost, your status still remained unclear until you'd won a fight. Then you'd be placed somewhere between the person you lost to and the person you beat.

The pecking order was important because it was used to resolve disputes that arose over games, or girls, or money, and also to maintain order and discipline on the block. Although we were not a gang, there were clear rules of conduct, and if you broke those rules there were clear consequences. The ranking system also prevented violence because it gave a way for boys to back down; if everybody knew you couldn't beat someone and you backed down, it was no big deal most of the time.

My "fight" with David placed me on top of the pecking order for boys on the sidewalk. I managed to get through the rest of the summer without having to fight anyone else. I had learned so much about how Union Avenue functioned that I figured I would soon know all I needed about how to survive on the block.

12

ARTICLE

Ellen Jordan

Angela Cowan

Warrior Narratives in the Kindergarten Classroom: Renegotiating the Social Contract?

The "social contract" becomes part of the lived experience of little boys when they discover that the school forbids the warrior narratives through which they initially define masculinity and imposes a different, public sphere: masculinity of rationality and responsibility. They learn that these narratives are not to be lived but only experienced symbolically through fantasy and sport in the private sphere of desire. Little girls, whose gender-defining fantasies are not repressed by the school, have less lived awareness of the social contract.

Since the beginning of second wave feminism, the separation between the public (masculine) world of politics and the economy and the private (feminine) world of the family and personal life has been seen as highly significant in establishing gender difference and inequality (Eisenstein 1984). Twenty years of feminist research and speculation have refined our understanding of this divide and how it has been

Authors' Note: The research on which this article is based was funded by the Research Management Committee of the University of Newcastle. The observation was conducted at East Maitland Public School and the authors would like to thank the principal, teachers, and children involved for making our observer so welcome.

Reprinted from *Gender & Society*, Vol. 9 No. 6, December 1995 727–743. Reprinted by permission.

developed and reproduced. One particularly striking and influential account is that given by Carole Pateman in her book *The Sexual Contract* (1988).

Pateman's broad argument is that in the modern world, the world since the Enlightenment, a "civil society" has been established. In this civil society, patriarchy has been replaced by a fratriarchy, which is equally male and oppressive of women. Men now rule not as fathers but as brothers, able to compete with one another, but presenting a united front against those outside the group. It is the brothers who control the public world of the state, politics, and the economy. Women have been given token access to this world because the discourses of liberty and universalism made this difficult to refuse, but to take part they must conform to the rules established to suit the brothers.

This public world in which the brothers operate together is conceptualized as separate from the personal and emotional. One is a realm where there is little physicality—everything is done rationally, bureaucratically, according to contracts that the brothers accept as legitimate. Violence in this realm is severely controlled by agents of the state, except that the brothers are sometimes called upon for the supreme sacrifice of dying to preserve freedom. The social contract redefines the brawling and feuding long seen as essential characteristics of masculinity as deviant, even criminal, while the rest of physicality—sexuality, reproduction of the body, daily and intergenerationally—is left in the private sphere. Pateman quotes Robert Unger, "The dichotomy of the public and private life is still another corollary of the separation of understanding and desire. . . . When reasoning, [men] belong to a public world. . . . When desiring, however, men are private beings" (Pateman 1989, 48).

This is now widely accepted as the way men understand and experience their world. On the other hand, almost no attempt has been made to look at how it is that they take these views on board, or why the public/private divide is so much more deeply entrenched in their lived experience than in women's. This article looks at one strand in the complex web of experiences through which this is achieved. A major site where this occurs is the school, one of the institutions particularly characteristic of the civil society that emerged with the Enlightenment (Foucault 1980, 55–7). The school does not deliberately condition boys and not girls into this dichotomy, but it is, we believe, a site where what Giddens (1984, 10–3) has called a cycle of practice introduces little boys to the public/private division.

The article is based on weekly observations in a kindergarten classroom. We examine what happens in the early days of school when the children encounter the expectations of the school with their already established conceptions of gender. The early months of school are a period when a great deal of negotiating between the children's personal agendas and the teacher's expectations has to take place, where a great deal of what Genovese (1972) has described as accommodation and resistance must be involved.

In this article, we focus on a particular contest, which, although never specifically stated, is central to the children's accommodation to school: little boys' determination to explore certain narratives of masculinity with which they are already families—guns, fighting, fast cars—and the teacher's attempts to outlaw their importation into the classroom setting. We argue that what occurs is a contest between two definitions of masculinity: what we have chosen to call "warrior narratives" and the discourses of civil society—rationality, responsibility, and decorum—that are the basis of school discipline.

By "warrior narratives," we mean narratives that assume that violence is legitimate and justified when it occurs within a struggle between good and evil. There is a tradition of such narratives, stretching from Hercules and Beowulf to Superman and Dirty Harry, where the male is depicted as the warrior, the knight-errant, the superhero, the good guy (usually called a "goody" by Australian children), often supported by brothers in arms, and always opposed to some evil figure, such as a monster, a giant, a villain, a criminal, or, very simply, in Australian parlance, a "baddy." There is also a connection, it is now often suggested, between these narratives and the activity that has come to epitomize the physical expression of masculinity in the modern era: sport (Crosset 1990; Duthie 1980, 91–4; Messner 1992, 15). It is as sport that the physicality and desire usually lived out in the private sphere are permitted a ritualized public presence. Even though the violence once characteristic of the warrior has, in civil society and as part of the social contract, become the prerogative of the state, it can still be re-enacted symbolically in countless sporting encounters. The mantle of the warrior is inherited by the sportsman.

The school discipline that seeks to outlaw these narratives is, we would suggest, very much a product of modernity. Bowles and Gintis have argued that "the structure of social relations in education not only inures the student to the discipline of the work place, but develops the types of personal demeanor, modes of self-presentation, self-image, and social-class identifications which are the crucial ingredients of job adequacy" (1976, 131). The school is seeking to introduce the children to the behavior appropriate to the civil society of the modern world.

An accommodation does eventually take place, this article argues, through a recognition of the split between the public and the private. Most boys learn to accept that the way to power and respectability is through acceptance of the conventions of civil society. They also learn that warrior narratives are not a part of this world; they can only be experienced symbolically as fantasy or sport. The outcome, we will suggest, is that little boys learn that these narratives must be left behind in the private world of desire when they participate in the public world of reason.

The Study

The school where this study was conducted serves an old-established suburb in a country town in New South Wales, Australia. The children are predominantly Australian born and English speaking, but come from socioeconomic backgrounds ranging from professional to welfare recipient. We carried out this research in a classroom run by a teacher who is widely acknowledged as one of the finest and most successful kindergarten teachers in our region. She is an admired practitioner of free play, process writing, and creativity. There was no gender de-finition of games in her classroom. Groups composed of both girls and boys had turns at playing in the Doll Corner, in the Construction Area, and on the Car Mat.

The research method used was nonparticipant observation, the classic mode for the sociological study of children in schools (Burgess 1984; Goodenough 1987; Thorne 1986). The group of children described came to school for the first time in February 1993. The observation sessions began within a fortnight of the children entering school and were conducted during "free activity" time, a period lasting for about an hour. At first we observed twice a week, but then settled to a weekly visit, although there were some weeks when it was inconvenient for the teacher to accommodate an observer.

The observation was noninteractive. The observer stationed herself as unobtrusively as possible, usually seated on a kindergarten-sized chair, near one of the play stations. She made pencil notes of events, with particular attention to accurately recording the words spoken by the children, and wrote up detailed narratives from the notes, supplemented by memory, on reaching home. She discouraged attention from the children by rising and leaving the area if she was drawn by them into any interaction.

This project thus employed a methodology that was ethnographic and open-ended. It was nevertheless guided by certain theories, drawn from the work on gender of Jean Anyon, Barrie Thorne, and R. W. Connell, of the nature of social interaction and its part in creating personal identity and in reproducing the structures of a society.

Anyon has adapted the conceptions of accommodation and resistance developed by Genovese (1972) to understanding how women live with gender. Genovese argued that slaves in the American South accommodated to their contradictory situation by using certain of its aspects, for example, exposure to the Christian religion, to validate a sense of self-worth and dignity. Christian beliefs then allowed them to take a critical view of slavery, which in turn legitimated certain forms of resistance (Anyon 1983, 21). Anyon lists a variety of ways in which women accommodate to and resist prescriptions of appropriate feminine behavior, arguing for a significant level of choice and agency (Anyon 1983, 23–6).

Thorne argues that the processes of social life, the form and nature of the interactions, as well as the choices of the actors, should be the object of analysis. She writes, "In this book I begin not with individuals, although they certainly appear in the account, but with *group life*—with social relations, the organization and meanings of social situations, the collective practices through which children ad adults create and recreate gender in their daily interactions" (1993, 4).

These daily interactions, Connell (1987, 139–41) has suggested mesh to form what Giddens (1984, 10–3) has called "cyclical practices." Daily interactions are neither random nor specific to particular locations. They are repeated and re-created in similar settings throughout a society. Similar needs recur, similar discourses are available, and so similar solutions to problems are adopted; thus, actions performed and discourses adopted to achieve particular ends in particular situations have the unintended consequence of producing uniformities of gendered behavior in individuals.

In looking at the patterns of accommodation and resistance that emerge when the warrior narratives that little boys have adapted from television encounter the discipline of the classroom, we believe we have uncovered one of the cyclical practices of modernity that reveal the social contract to these boys.

Warrior Narratives in the Doll Corner

In the first weeks of the children's school experience, the Doll Corner was the area where the most elaborate acting out of warrior narratives

was observed. The Doll Corner in this classroom was a small room with a door with a glass panel opening off the main area. Its furnishings—stove, sink, dolls' cots, and so on—were an attempt at a literal re-creation of a domestic setting, revealing the school's definition of children's play as a preparation for adult life. It was an area where the acting out of "pretend" games was acceptable.

Much of the boys' play in the area was domestic:

> Jimmy and Tyler were jointly ironing a tablecloth. "Look at the sheet is burnt, I've burnt it," declared Tyler, waving the toy iron above his head. "I'm telling Mrs. Sandison," said Jimmy worriedly. "No, I tricked you. It's not really burnt. See," explained Tyler, showing Jimmy the black pattern on the cloth. (February 23, 1993)

> "Where is the baby, the baby boy?" Justin asked, as he helped Harvey and Malcolm settle some restless teddy babies. "Give them some potion." Justin pretended to force feed a teddy, asking "Do you want to drink this potion?" (March 4, 1993)

On the other hand, there were attempts from the beginning by some of the boys and one of the girls to use this area for nondomestic games and, in the case of the boys, for games based on warrior narratives, involving fighting, destruction, goodies, and baddies.

> The play started off quietly, Winston cuddled a teddy bear, then settled it in a bed. Just as Winston tucked in his bear, Mac snatched the teddy out of bed and swung it around his head in circles. "Don't hurt him, give him back," pleaded Winston, trying vainly to retrieve the teddy. The two boys were circling the small table in the center of the room. As he ran, Mac started to karate chop the teddy on the arm, and then threw it on the floor and jumped on it. He then snatched up a plastic knife, "This is a sword. Ted is dead. They all are." He sliced the knife across the teddy's tummy, repeating the action on the bodies of two stuffed dogs. Winston grabbed the two dogs, and with a dog in each hand, staged a dog fight. "They are alive again." (February 10, 1993)

Three boys were busily stuffing teddies into the cupboard through the sink opening. "They're in jail. They can't escape," said Malcolm. "Let's pour water over them." "Don't do that. I'll hurt them," shouted Winston, rushing into the Doll Corner. "Go away, Winston. You're not in our group," said Malcolm. (February 12, 1993)

The boys even imported goodies and baddies into a classic ghost scenario initiated by one of the girls:

"I'm the father," Tyler declared. "I'm the mother," said Alanna. "Let's pretend it's a stormy night and I'm afraid. Let's pretend a ghost has come to steal the dog." Tyler nodded and placed the sheet over his head. Tyler moaned, "ooooOOOOOOOOAHHHH!!!" and moved his outstretched arms toward Alanna. Jamie joined the game and grabbed a sheet from the doll's cradle, "I'm the goody ghost." "So am I," said Tyler. They giggled and wrestled each other to the floor. "No! you're the baddy ghost," said Jamie. Meanwhile, Alanna was making ghostly noises and moving around the boys. "Did you like the game? Let's play it again," she suggested. (February 23, 1993)

In the first two incidents, there was some conflict between the narratives being invoked by Winston and those used by the other boys. For Winston, the stuffed toys were the weak whom he must protect knight-errant style. For the other boys, they could be set up as the baddies whom it was legitimate for the hero to attack. Both were versions of a warrior narrative.

The gender difference in the use of these narratives has been noted by a number of observers (Clark 1989, 250–2; Paley 1984; Thorne 1993, 98–9). Whereas even the most timid, least physically aggressive boys—Winston in this study is typical—are drawn to identifying with the heroes of these narratives, girls show almost no interest in them at this early age. The strong-willed and assertive girls in our study, as in others (Clark 1990, 83–4; Walkerdine 1990, 10–2), sought power by commandeering the role of

mother, teacher, or shopkeeper, while even the highly imaginative Alanna, although she enlivened the more mundane fantasies of the other children with ghosts, old widow women, and magical mirrors, seems not to have been attracted by warrior heroes.[1]

Warrior narratives, it would seem, have a powerful attraction for little boys, which they lack for little girls. Why and how this occurs remains unexplored in early childhood research, perhaps because data for such an explanation are not available to those doing research in institutional settings. Those undertaking ethnographic research in preschools find the warrior narratives already in possession in these sites (Davies 1989, 91–2; Paley 1984, 70–3, 116). In this research, gender difference in the appeal of warrior narratives has to be taken as a given—the data gathered are not suitable for constructing theories of origins; thus, the task of determining an explanation would seem to lie within the province of those investigating and theorizing gender differentiation during infancy, and perhaps, specifically, of those working in the tradition of feminist psychoanalysis pioneered by Dinnerstein (1977) and Chodorow (1978). Nevertheless, even though the cause may remain obscure, there can be little argument that in the English-speaking world for at least the last hundred years—think of Tom Sawyer playing Robin Hood and the pirates and Indians in J. M. Barrie's *Peter Pan*—boys have built these narratives into their conceptions of the masculine.

Accommodation Through *Bricolage*

The school classroom, even one as committed to freedom and self-actualization as this, makes little provision for the enactment of these narratives. The classroom equipment invites children to play house, farm, and shop, to construct cities and roads, and to journey through them with toy cars, but there is no overt invitation to explore warrior narratives.

In the first few weeks of school, the little boys un–self-consciously set about redressing this omission. The method they used was what is known as *bricolage*—the transformation of objects from one use to another for symbolic purposes (Hebdige 1979, 103). The first site was the Doll Corner. Our records for the early weeks contain a number of examples of boys rejecting the usages ascribed to the various Doll Corner objects by the teacher and by the makers of equipment and assigning a different meaning to them. This became evident very early with their use of the toy baby carriages (called "prams" in Australia). For the girls, the baby carriages were just that, but for many of the boys they very quickly became surrogate cars:

> Mac threw a doll into the largest pram in the Doll Corner. He walked the pram out past a group of his friends who were playing "crashes" on the Car Mat. Three of the five boys turned and watched him wheeling the pram toward the classroom door. Mac performed a sharp three-point turn; raced his pram past the Car Mat group, striking one boy on the head with the pram wheel. (February 10, 1993)

> "Brrrrmmmmmm, brrrrrmmmmm," Tyler's revving engine noises grew louder as he rocked the pram back and forth with sharp jerking movements. The engine noise grew quieter as he left the Doll Corner and wheeled the pram around the classroom. He started to run with the pram when the teacher could not observe him. (March 23, 1993)

The boys transformed other objects into masculine appurtenances: knives and tongs became weapons, the dolls' beds became boats, and so on.

> Mac tried to engage Winston in a sword fight using Doll Corner plastic knives. Winston backed away, but Mac persisted. Winston took a knife but continued to back away from Mac. He then put down the knife, and ran away half-

> screaming (semi-seriously, unsure of the situation) for his teacher. (February 10, 1993)

In the literature on youth subcultures, bricolage is seen as a characteristic of modes of resistance. Hebdige writes:

> It is through the distinctive rituals of consumption, through style, that the subculture at once reveals its "secret" identity and communicates its forbidden meanings. It is predominantly the way commodities are *used* in subculture which mark the subculture off from more orthodox cultural formations.... The concept of *bricolage* can be used to explain how subcultural styles are constructed. (1979, 103)

In these early weeks, however, the boys did not appear to be aware that they were doing anything more than establishing an accommodation between their needs and the classroom environment.

This mode of accommodation was rejected by the teacher, however, who practiced a gentle, but steady, discouragement of such bricolage. Even though the objects in this space are not really irons, beds, and cooking pots, she made strong efforts to assert their cultural meaning, instructing the children in the "proper" use of the equipment and attempting to control their behavior by questions like "Would you do that with a tea towel in your house?" "Cats never climb up on the benches in *my* house." It was thus impressed upon the children that warrior narratives were inappropriate in this space.

The children, our observations suggest, accepted her guidance, and we found no importation of warrior narratives into the Doll Corner after the first few weeks. There were a number of elaborate and exciting narratives devised, but they were all to some degree related to the domestic environment. For example, on April 20, Justin and Nigel used one of the baby carriages as a four-wheel drive, packed it with equipment and went off for a camping trip, setting out a picnic with Doll Corner tablecloths, knives, forks, and plates when they arrived. On May 18, Matthew, Malcolm, Nigel, and Jonathan were dogs being fed in the Doll Corner. They then complained of the flies, and Jonathan picked up the toy telephone and said, "Flycatcher! Flycatcher! Come and catch some flies. They are everywhere." On June 1, the following was recorded:

> "We don't want our nappies [diapers] changed," Aaron informed Celia, the mum in the game. "I'm poohing all over your clothes mum," Mac declared, as he grunted and positioned himself over the dress-up box. Celia cast a despairing glance in Mac's direction, and went on dressing a doll. "I am too; poohing all over your clothes mum," said Aaron. "Now mum will have to clean it all up and change my nappy," he informed Mac, giggling. He turned to the dad [Nigel], and said in a baby voice, "Goo-goo; give him [Mac] the feather duster." "No! give him the feather duster; he did the longest one all over the clothes," Mac said to Nigel. (June 1, 1993)

Although exciting and imaginative games continued, the bricolage virtually disappeared from the Doll Corner. The intention of the designer of the Doll Corner equipment was increasingly respected. Food for the camping trip was bought from the shop the teacher had set up and consumed using the Doll Corner equipment. The space invaded by flies was a domestic space, and appropriate means, calling in expert help by telephone, were used to deal with the problem. Chairs and tables were chairs and tables, clothes were clothes and could be fouled by appropriate inhabitants of a domestic space, babies. Only the baby carriages continued to have an ambiguous status, to maintain the ability to be transformed into vehicles of other kinds.

The warrior narratives—sword play, baddies in jail, pirates, and so on—did not vanish from the boys' imaginative world, but, as the later observations show, the site gradually moved from the Doll Corner to the Construction Area

and the Car Mat. By the third week in March (that is, after about six weeks at school), the observer noticed the boys consistently using the construction toys to develop these narratives. The bricolage was now restricted to the more amorphously defined construction materials.

> Tyler was busy constructing an object out of five pieces of plastic straw (clever sticks). "This is a water pistol. Everyone's gonna get wet," he cried as he moved into the Doll Corner pretending to wet people. The game shifted to guns and bullets between Tyler and two other boys. "I've got a bigger gun," Roger said, showing off his square block object. "Mine's more longer. Ehehehehehehehehe, got you," Winston yelled to Roger, brandishing a plastic straw gun. "I'll kill your gun," Mac said, pushing Winston's gun away. "No Mac. You broke it. No," cried Winston. (March 23, 1993)

> Two of the boys picked up swords made out of blue- and red-colored plastic squares they had displayed on the cupboard. "This is my sword," Jamie explained to Tyler. "My jumper [sweater] holds it in. Whichever color is at the bottom, well that's the color it shoots out. Whoever is bad, we shoot with power out of it." "Come on Tyler," he went on. "Get your sword. Let's go get some baddies." (March 30, 1993)

The toy cars on the Car Mat were also pressed into the service of warrior narratives:

> Justin, Brendan, and Jonathan were busy on the Car Mat. The game involved police cars that were chasing baddies who had drunk "too much beers." Justin explained to Jonathan why his car had the word "DOG" written on the front. "These are different police cars, for catching robbers taking money." (March 4, 1993)

> Three boys, Harvey, Maurice, and Marshall, were on the Car Mat. "Here comes the baddies," Harvey shouted, spinning a toy car around the mat. "Crassssshhhhh everywhere." He crashed his car into the other boys' cars and they responded with laughter. "I killed a baddie everyone," said Maurice, crashing his cars into another group of cars. (May 24, 1993)

A new accommodation was being proposed by the boys, a new adaptation of classroom materials to the needs of their warrior narratives.

Classroom Rules and Resistance

Once again the teacher would not accept the accommodation proposed. Warrior narratives provoked what she considered inappropriate public behavior in the miniature civil society of her classroom. Her aim was to create a "free" environment where children could work independently, learn at their own pace, and explore their own interests, but creating such an environment involved its own form of social contract, its own version of the state's appropriation of violence. From the very first day, she began to establish a series of classroom rules that imposed constraints on violent or disruptive activity.

The belief underlying her practice was that firmly established classroom rules make genuine free play possible, rather than restricting the range of play opportunities. Her emphasis on "proper" use of equipment was intended to stop it being damaged and consequently withdrawn from use. She had rules of "no running" and "no shouting" that allowed children to work and play safely on the floor of the classroom, even though other children were using equipment or toys that demanded movement, and ensured that the noise level was low enough for children to talk at length to one another as part of their games.

One of the outcomes of these rules was the virtual outlawing of a whole series of games that groups of children usually want to initiate when they are playing together, games of speed and body contact, of gross motor self-expression and skill. This prohibition affected both girls and boys and was justified by setting up a version of public and private spaces: The classroom was not the proper place for such activities, they "belong" in the playground.[2] The combined

experience of many teachers has shown that it is almost impossible for children to play games involving car crashes and guns without violating these rules; therefore, in this classroom, as in many others (Paley 1984, 71, 116), these games were in effect banned.

These rules were then policed by the children themselves, as the following interchange shows:

> "Eeeeeeheeeeeeeeeeeh!" Tyler leapt about the room. A couple of girls were saying, "Stop it Tyler" but he persisted. Jane warned, "You're not allowed to have guns." Tyler responded saying, "It's not a gun. It's a water pistol, and that's not a gun." "Not allowed to have water pistol guns," Tony reiterated to Tyler. "Yes, it's a water pistol," shouted Tyler. Jane informed the teacher, who responded stating, "NO GUNS, even if they are water pistols." Tyler made a spear out of Clever Sticks, straight after the banning of gun play. (March 23, 1993)

The boys, however, were not prepared to abandon their warrior narratives. Unlike gross motor activities such as wrestling and football, they were not prepared to see them relegated to the playground, but the limitations on their expression and the teacher disapproval they evoked led the boys to explore them surreptitiously; they found ways of introducing them that did not violate rules about running and shouting.

As time passed, the games became less visible. The warrior narratives were not so much acted out as talked through, using the toy cars and the construction materials as a prompt and a basis:

> Tyler was showing his plastic straw construction to Luke. "This is a Samurai Man and this is his hat. A Samurai Man fights in Japan and they fight with the Ninja. The bad guys who use cannons and guns. My Samurai is captain of the Samurai and he is going to kill the sergeant of the bad guys. He is going to sneak up on him with a knife and kill him." (June 1, 1993)
>
> Malcolm and Aaron had built boats with Lego blocks and were explaining the various com-

ponents to Roger. "This ship can go faster," Malcolm explained. "He [a plastic man] is the boss of the ship. Mine is a goody boat. They are not baddies." "Mine's a steam shovel boat. It has wheels," said Aaron. "There it goes in the river and it has to go to a big shed where all the steam shovels are stopping." (June 11, 1993)

It also became apparent that there was something covert about this play. The cars were crashed quietly. The guns were being transformed into water pistols. Swords were concealed under jumpers and only used when the teacher's back was turned. When the constructed objects were displayed to the class, their potential as players in a fighting game was concealed under a more mundane description. For example:

> Prior to the free play, the children were taking turns to explain the Clever Stick and Lego Block constructions they had made the previous afternoon. I listened to Tyler describe his Lego robot to the class: "This is a transformer robot. It can do things and turn into everything." During free play, Tyler played with the same robot explaining its capacities to Winston: "This is a terminator ship. It can kill. It can turn into a robot and the top pops off." (March 23, 1993)

Children even protested to one another that they were not making weapons, "This isn't a gun, it's a lookout." "This isn't a place for bullets, it's for petrol."

The warrior narratives, it would seem, went underground and became part of a "deviant" masculine subculture with the characteristic "secret" identity and hidden meanings (Hebdige 1979, 103). The boys were no longer seeking accommodation but practicing hidden resistance. The classroom, they were learning, was not a place where it was acceptable to explore their gender identity through fantasy.

This, however, was a message that only the boys were receiving. The girls' gender-specific fantasies (Davies 1989, 118–22; Paley 1984, 106–8) of nurturing and self-display—mothers,

nurses, brides, princesses—were accommodated easily within the classroom. They could be played out without contravening the rules of the miniature civil society. Although certain delightful activities—eating, running, hugging, and kissing (Best 1983, 110)—might be excluded from this public sphere, they were not ones by means of which their femininity, and thus their subjectivity, their conception of the self, was defined.

Masculinity, the School Regime, and the Social Contract

We suggest that this conflict between warrior narratives and school rules is likely to form part of the experience of most boys growing up in the industrialized world. The commitment to such narratives was not only nearly 100 percent among the boys we observed, but similar commitment is, as was argued above, common in other sites. On the other hand, the pressure to preserve a decorous classroom is strong in all teachers (with the possible exception of those teaching in "alternative" schools) and has been since the beginnings of compulsory education. Indeed, it is only in classrooms where there is the balance of freedom and constraint we observed that such narratives are likely to surface at all. In more formal situations, they would be defined as deviant and forced underground from the boys' first entry into school.

If this is a widely recurring pattern, the question then arises: Is it of little significance or is it what Giddens (1984, 10–3) would call one of the "cyclical practices" that reproduce the structures of our society? The answer really depends on how little boys "read" the outlawing of their warrior narratives. If they see it as simply one of the broad constraints of school against which they are continually negotiating, then perhaps it has no significance. If, on the other hand, it has in their minds a crucial connection to the definition of gender, to the creation of their own masculine identity, to where they position particular sites and practices on a masculine to feminine continuum, then the ostracism of warrior narratives may mean that they define the school environment as feminine.

There is considerable evidence that some primary school children do in fact make this categorization (Best 1983, 14–5; Brophy 1985, 118; Clark 1990, 36), and we suggest here that the outlawry of the masculine narrative contributes to this. Research by Willis (1977) and Walker (1988) in high schools has revealed a culture of resistance based on definitions of masculinity as *antagonistic* to the demands of the school, which are construed as feminine by the resisters. It might therefore seem plausible to see the underground perpetuation of the warrior narrative as an early expression of this resistance and one that gives some legitimacy to the resisters' claims that the school is feminine.

Is the school regime that outlaws the warrior narratives really feminine? We would argue, rather, that the regime being imposed is based on a male ideal, an outcome of the Enlightenment and compulsory schooling. Michel Foucault has pointed out that the development of this particular regime in schools coincided with the emergence of the prison, the hospital, the army barracks, and the factory (Foucault 1980, 55–7). Although teachers in the first years of school are predominantly female, the regime they impose is perpetuated by male teachers (Brophy 1985, 121), and this preference is endorsed by powerful and influential males in the society at large. The kind of demeanor and self-management that teachers are trying to inculcate in the early school years is the behavior expected in male-dominated public arenas like boardrooms, courtrooms, and union mass meetings.[3]

Connell (1989, 291) and Willis (1977, 76, 84) provide evidence that by adolescence, boys from all classes, particularly if they are ambitious, come to regard acquiescence in the school's de-

mands as compatible with constructing a masculine identity. Connell writes:

> Some working class boys embrace a project of mobility in which they construct a masculinity organized around themes of rationality and responsibility. This is closely connected with the "certification" function of the upper levels of the education system and to a key form of masculinity among professionals. (1989, 291)

Rationality and responsibility are, as Weber argued long ago, the primary characteristics of the modern society theorized by the Enlightenment thinkers as based on a social contract. This prized rationality has been converted in practice into a bureaucratized legal system where "responsible" acceptance by the population of the rules of civil society obviates the need for individuals to use physical violence in gaining their ends or protecting their rights, and where, if such violence is necessary, it is exercised by the state (Weber 1978, 341–54). In civil society, the warrior is obsolete, his activities redefined bureaucratically and performed by the police and the military.

The teacher in whose classroom our observation was conducted demonstrated a strong commitment to rationality and responsibility. For example, she devoted a great deal of time to showing that there was a cause and effect link between the behavior forbidden by her classroom rules and classroom accidents. Each time an accident occurred, she asked the children to determine the cause of the accident, its result, and how it could have been prevented. The implication throughout was that children must take responsibility for the outcomes of their actions.

> Mac accidentally struck a boy, who was lying on the floor, in the head with a pram wheel. He was screaming around with a pram, the victim was playing on the Car Mat and lying down to obtain a bird's eye view of a car crash. Mac rushed past the group and collected Justin on the side of the head. Tears and confusion ensued. The teacher's reaction was to see to

Justin, then stop all play and gain children's attention, speaking first to Mac and Justin plus Justin's group:

T. How did Justin get hurt?
M. [No answer]
T. Mac, what happened?
M. I was wheeling the pram and Justin was in the way.
T. Were you running?
M. I was wheeling the pram.

The teacher now addresses the whole class:

T. Stop working everyone, eyes to me and listen. Someone has just been hurt because someone didn't remember the classroom rules. What are they Harvey?

(Harvey was listening intently and she wanted someone who could answer the question at this point).

H. No running in the classroom.
T. Why?

Other children offer an answer.

Chn. Because someone will get hurt.

T. Yes, and that is what happened. Mac was going too quickly with the pram and Justin was injured. Now how can we stop this happening next time?
Chn. No running in the classroom, only walk. (February 10, 1993)

Malcolm, walking, bumped Winston on the head with a construction toy. The teacher intervened.

T. [To Malcolm and Winston] What happened?
W. Malcolm hit me on the head.
M. But it was an accident. I didn't mean it. I didn't really hurt him.
T. How did it happen?
M. It was an accident.
W. He [Malcolm] hit me.
T. Malcolm, I know you didn't mean to hurt Winston, so how did it happen?
M. I didn't mean it.
T. I know you didn't mean it, Malcolm, but why did Winston get hurt?
Chn. Malcolm was running.

M. No I wasn't.
T. See where everyone was sitting? There is hardly enough room for children to walk. Children working on the floor must remember to leave a walking path so that other children can move safely around the room. Otherwise someone will be hurt, and that's what has happened today. (February 23, 1993)

This public-sphere masculinity of rationality and responsibility, of civil society, of the social contract is not the masculinity that the boys are bringing into the classroom through their warrior narratives. They are using a different, much older version—not the male as responsible citizen, the producer and consumer who keeps the capitalist system going, the breadwinner, and caring father of a family. Their earliest vision of masculinity is the male as warrior, the bonded male who goes out with his mates and meets the dangers of the world, the male who attacks and defeats other males characterized as baddies, the male who turns the natural products of the earth into weapons to carry out these purposes.

We would argue, nevertheless, that those boys who aspire to become one of the brothers who wield power in the public world of civil society ultimately realize that conformity to rationality and responsibility, to the demands of the school, is the price they must pay. They realize that although the girls can expect one day to become the brides and mothers of their pretend games, the boys will never, except perhaps in time of war, be allowed to act out the part of warrior hero in reality.

On the other hand, the school softens the transition for them by endorsing and encouraging the classic modern transformation and domestication of the warrior narrative, sport (Connell 1987, 177; Messner 1992, 10–2). In the school where this observation was conducted, large playground areas are set aside for lunchtime cricket, soccer, and basketball; by the age of seven, most boys are joining in these games. The message is conveyed to them that if they behave like citizens in the classroom, they can become warriors on the sports oval.

Gradually, we would suggest, little boys get the message that resistance is not the only way to live out warrior masculinity. If they accept a public/private division of life, it can be accommodated within the private sphere; thus, it becomes possible for those boys who aspire to respectability, figuring in civil society as one of the brothers, to accept that the school regime and its expectations are masculine and to reject the attempts of the "resisters" to define it (and them) as feminine. They adopt the masculinity of rationality and responsibility as that appropriate to the public sphere, while the earlier, deeply appealing masculinity of the warrior narratives can still be experienced through symbolic reenactment on the sports field.

Conclusion

We are not, of course, suggesting that this is the only way in which the public/private division becomes part of the lived awareness of little boys. We do, however, believe that we have teased out one strand of the manner in which they encounter it. We have suggested that the classroom is a major site where little boys are introduced to the masculinity of rationality and responsibility characteristic of the brothers in civil society; we have been looking at a "cycle of practice" where, in classroom after classroom, generation after generation, the mode of masculinity typified in the warrior narratives is first driven underground and then transferred to the sports field. We are, we would suggest, seeing renegotiated for each generation and in each boy's own life the conception of the "social contract" that is characteristic of the era of modernity, of the Enlightenment, of democracy, and of capitalism. We are watching reenacted the transformation of violence and power as exercised by body over body, to control

through surveillance and rules (Foucault 1977, 9; 1984, 66–7), the move from domination by individual superiors to acquiescence in a public sphere of decorum and rationality (Pateman 1988).

Yet, this is a social *contract*, and there is another side to the bargain. Although they learn that they must give up their warrior narratives of masculinity in the public sphere, where rationality and responsibility hold sway, they also learn that in return they may preserve them in the private realm of desire as fantasy, as bricolage, as a symbolic survival that is appropriate to the spaces of leisure and self-indulgence, the playground, the backyard, the television set, the sports field. Although this is too large an issue to be explored in detail here, there may even be a reenactment in the school setting of what Pateman (1988, 99–115) has defined as the sexual contract, the male right to dominate women in return for accepting the constraints of civil society. Is this, perhaps, established for both boys and girls by means of the endemic misogyny—invasion of girls' space (Thorne 1986, 172; 1993, 63–88), overt expressions of aversion and disgust (D'Arcy 1990, 81; Goodenough 1987, 422), disparaging sexual innuendo (Best 1983, 129; Clark 1990, 38–46; Goodenough, 1987, 433)—noted by so many observers in the classrooms and playgrounds of modernity? Are girls being contained by the boys' actions within a more restricted, ultimately a private, sphere because, in the boys' eyes, they have not earned access to the public sphere by sharing their ordeal of repression, resistance, and ultimate symbolic accommodation of their gender-defining fantasies?

Notes

1. Some ethnographic studies describe a "tomboy" who wants to join in the boys' games (Best 1983, 95–7; Davies 1989, 93, 123; Thorne 1993, 127–9), although in our experience, such girls are rare, rarer even than the boys who play by choice with girls. The

girls' rejection of the warrior narratives does not appear to be simply the result of the fact that the characters are usually men. Bronwyn Davies, when she read the role-reversal story *Rita the Rescuer* to preschoolers, found that many boys identified strongly with Rita ("they flex their muscles to show how strong they are and fall to wrestling each other on the floor to display their strength"), whereas for most girls, Rita remained "other" (Davies 1989, 57–8).

2. This would seem to reverse the usual parallel of outdoor/indoor with public/private. This further suggests that the everyday equation of "public" with "visible" may not be appropriate for the specialized use of the term in sociological discussions of the public/private division. Behavior in the street may be more visible than what goes on in a courtroom, but it is nevertheless acceptable for the street behavior to be, to a greater degree, personal, private, and driven by "desire."

3. There are some groups of men who continue to reject these modes of modernity throughout their lives. Andrew Metcalfe, in his study of an Australian mining community, has identified two broad categories of miner, the "respectable," and the "larrikin" (an Australian slang expression carrying implications of nonconformism, irreverence, and impudence). The first are committed to the procedural decorums of union meetings, sporting and hobby clubs, welfare groups, and so on; the others relate more strongly to the less disciplined masculinity of the pub, the brawl, and the racetrack (Metcalfe, 1988, 73–125). This distinction is very similar to that noted by Paul Willis in England between the "ear'oles" and the "lads" in a working-class secondary school (Willis, 1977). It needs to be noted that this is not a *class* difference and that demographically the groups are identical. What distinguishes them is, as Metcalfe points out, their relative commitment to the respectable modes of accommodation and resistance characteristic of civil society of larrikin modes with a much longer history, perhaps even their acceptance or rejection of the social contract.

References

Anyon, Jean. 1983. Intersections of gender and class: Accommodation and resistance by working-class and affluent females to contradictory sex-role ideologies. In *Gender, class and education*, edited by Stephen Walker and Len Barton. Barcombe, Sussex: Falmer.

Best, Raphaela. 1983. *We've all got scars: What girls and boys learn in elementary school*. Bloomington: Indiana University Press.

Bowles, Samuel, and Herbert Gintis. 1976. *Schooling in capitalist America: Educational reform and the contradictions of economic life*. London: Routledge and Kegan Paul.

Brophy, Jere E. 1985. Interactions of male and female students with male and female teachers. In *Gender influences in classroom interaction*, edited by L. C. Wilkinson and C. B. Marrett. New York: Academic Press.

Burgess, R. G., ed. 1984. *The research process in educational settings: Ten case studies*. Lewes: Falmer.

Chodorow, Nancy. 1978. *The reproduction of mothering: Psychoanalysis and the sociology of gender*. Berkeley: University of California Press.

Clark, Margaret. 1989. Anastasia is a normal developer because she is unique. *Oxford Review of Education* 15:243–55.

———. 1990. *The great divide: Gender in the primary school*. Melbourne: Curriculum Corporation.

Connell, R. W. 1987. *Gender and power: Society, the person and sexual politics*. Sydney: Allen and Unwin.

———. 1989. Cool guys, swots and wimps: The interplay of masculinity and education. *Oxford Review of Education* 15:291–303.

Crosset, Todd. 1990. Masculinity, sexuality, and the development of early modern sport. In *Sport, men and the gender order*, edited by Michael E. Messner and Donald F. Sabo. Champaign, IL: Human Kinetics Books.

D'Arcy, Sue. 1990. Towards a non-sexist primary classroom. In *Dolls and dungarees: Gender issues in the primary school curriculum*, edited by Eva Tutchell. Milton Keynes: Open University Press.

Davies, Bronwyn. 1989. *Frogs and snails and feminist tales: Preschool children and gender*. Sydney: Allen and Unwin.

Dinnerstein, Myra. 1977. *The mermaid and the minotaur: Sexual arrangements and human malaise*. New York: Harper and Row.

Duthie, J. H. 1980. Athletics: The ritual of a technological society? In *Play and culture*, edited by

Helen B. Schwartzman. West Point, NY: Leisure.

Eisenstein, Hester. 1984. *Contemporary feminist thought*. London: Unwin Paperbacks.

Foucault, Michel. 1977. *Discipline and punish: The birth of the prison*. Translated by Alan Sheridan. New York: Pantheon.

————. 1980. Body/power. In *power/knowledge: Selected interviews and other writings 1972–1977*, edited by Colin Gordon. Brighton: Harvester

————. 1984. Truth and power. In *The Foucault reader*, edited by P. Rabinow. New York: Pantheon.

Genovese, Eugene E. 1972. *Roll, Jordan, roll: The world the slaves made*. New York: Pantheon.

Giddens, Anthony. 1984. *The constitution of society: Outline of the theory of structuration*. Berkeley: University of California Press.

Goodenough, Ruth Gallagher. 1987. Small group culture and the emergence of sexist behaviour: A comparative study of four children's groups. In *Interpretive ethnography of education*, edited by G. Spindler and L. Spindler. Hillsdale, NJ: Lawrence Erlbaum.

Hebdige, Dick. 1979. *Subculture: The meaning of style*. London: Methuen.

Messner, Michael E. 1992. *Power at play: Sports and the problem of masculinity*. Boston: Beacon.

Metcalfe, Andrew. 1988. *For freedom and dignity: Historical agency and class structure in the coalfields of NSW*. Sydney: Allen and Unwin.

Paley, Vivian Gussin. 1984. *Boys and girls: Superheroes in the doll corner*. Chicago: University of Chicago Press.

Pateman, Carole. 1988. *The sexual contract*. Oxford: Polity.

————. 1989. The fraternal social contract. In *The disorder of women*. Cambridge: Polity.

Thorne, Barrie. 1986. Girls and boys together . . . but mostly apart: Gender arrangements in elementary schools. In *Relationships and development*, edited by W. W. Hartup and Z. Rubin. Hillsdale, NJ: Lawrence Erlbaum.

————. 1993. *Gender play: Girls and boys in school*. New Brunswick, NJ: Rutgers University Press.

Walker, J. C. 1988. *Louts and legends: Male youth culture in an inner-city school*. Sydney: Allen and Unwin.

Walkerdine, Valerie. 1990. *Schoolgirl fictions*. London: Verso.

Weber, Max. 1978. *Selections in translation*. Edited by W. G. Runciman and translated by Eric Matthews. Cambridge: Cambridge University Press.

Willis, Paul. 1977. *Learning to labour: How working class kids get working class jobs*. Farnborough: Saxon House.

13

ARTICLE

R. W. Connell

Disruptions: Improper Masculinities and Schooling

A couple of decades ago a modest controversy broke out about masculinity and American schooling. The schools, Sexton argued in a widely-read book, were dominated by women and therefore imposed on boys a feminine culture.[1] Red-blooded "boy culture" was marginalized or suppressed, and therefore American males grew to manhood with difficulty in establishing true manliness. This concern was not original with Sexton. As Hantover has shown, the growth of the Boy Scout movement in the United States in the second decade of the century picked up middle-class anxieties about the feminization of boys and offered a kind of masculinizing medicine through Scouting.[2]

This now seems rather comic in the light of the feminist research of the last two decades, which has documented the actual power of men in the education system as in other institutions. The pendulum has swung far in the other direction, with emphasis on the silencing of women's voices in education and in culture more broadly.[3] There can be no honest doubt

Reprinted from *Beyond Silenced Voices: Class, Race, and Gender in United States Schools* by Lois Weis and Michelle Fine by permission of the State University of New York Press.

about the facts of the institutional power of men and the patriarchal character of the public culture.[4]

But this is not to say there are no question to ask about men. To understand a system of power, one ought to look very closely at its beneficiaries. Indeed, I would argue that one of the cultural supports of men's power is the failure to ask questions about masculinity.

The surge of feminist research on education in the 1970s (epitomized in the remarkable 1975 report of the Australian Schools Commission, *Girls, Schools, and Society*) found conventional gender stereotypes spread blanket-like through textbooks, career counseling, teacher expectations, and selection processes. This was theorized as the transmission of an oppressive, restrictive "sex role" to girls, It followed that girls would be advantaged by modifying the sex role or even breaking out of it. This led easily to an educational strategy. A program of redress was required, to expand girls' occupational and intellectual horizons, affirm women's worth, and write women into the curriculum.

Almost all this discussion was about girls and their restrictive "sex role." By implication the boys were getting one too. But here the sex-role approach did not translate smoothly into educational reform. Since men are the privileged sex in current gender arrangements, it is not obvious that boys will be advantaged by teachers' efforts to change their "role." On the contrary, boys may resent and resist the attempt.

A puzzled literature on the "male sex role" in the 1970s scratched pretty hard to find ways by which men are disadvantaged or damaged by their sex role.[5] No convincing educational program ever came of it. Teachers grappling with issues of masculinity for boys are now reaching for new concepts.[6] The expectation now is that anyone working on these questions in schools faces a politicized and emotionally charged situation.

This is very much in accord with the development of research since the 1970s. More intensive research techniques, and more sophisticated theories of gender, have brought out two themes in particular. One is the importance of the institutional structure of education and the institutional practices of gender that children encounter in schools. Hansot and Tyack, in an illuminating historical paper, urge us to "think institutionally" about gender and schooling.[7] Thorne shows how situational is the segregation of the sexes in primary schools.[8] Messner shows how the formal structure of organized sport provides a temporary resolution for developmental problems of masculinity.[9] Kessler et al. point to the ways curricula and school organization separate out different kinds of femininity, and different kinds of masculinity, within the same school.[10] They introduce the idea of the "gender regime" of an institution such as a school, the established order of gender relations within it. A remarkable historical study by Heward of a second-echelon private school in England shows how a gender regime intended to produce a particular pattern of masculinity is produced in response to the class and gender strategies of the families who form the school's clientele.[11]

Close-focus historical work, interview research, and ethnography tend to find complexities and contradictions beneath the gender "stereotypes." Thus Walker's 1987 paper on male youth culture in an inner-city school finds several peer groups positioned very differently in relation to the school's cult of competitive sport: some ethnically based peer groups competing through sport, others rejecting it or being marginalized by it.[12] From such research a concern has emerged about the different versions of masculinity to be found in a given cultural context, and the relations of dominance and subordination among them. This gives a new shape to the issue of the formation of masculinity. It is no longer adequate to see this as the absorption of a sex role. It must be seen as an active process of construction, occurring in a field of power relations that are often tense and contradictory, and often involving negotiation of alternative ways of being masculine.

This paper is an attempt to explore how this process works for certain outsiders. It examines the place of schooling in the lives of two groups of men who are in different ways distanced from the dominant models of masculinity: (a) a group of young unemployed working-class men, recently out of school, growing up in the face of structural unemployment and in the shadow of the prison system; (b) a group of men, mostly some years older and mostly from more affluent backgrounds, who are involved in "green politics," that is, social action on environmental issues.

The first group was contacted mainly through an agency that is responsible for the welfare of unemployed youth and that seeks to place them in training programs. The young men concerned do not consciously reject the hegemonic model of masculinity in their milieu. But where the dominant model of working-class masculinity was built around a wage, a workplace, and the capacity to support a family, these young men *cannot* inhabit such a masculinity; this is ruled out by structural unemployment. They have, in various ways, constructed more fragmented masculinities, some violent and some more passively alienated.[13]

The second group was contacted mainly through organizations in the environmental movement. The men concerned have all been volunteers in "green" campaigns, several of them participating in the famous blockade in the early 1980s that saved the Franklin River from a hydroelectric scheme; some are paid workers in environmental organizations. In the Australian environmental movement there is a strong feminist presence. All these men, accordingly, have had a close encounter with feminism; most, indeed, have been under the necessity of dealing with feminist women on a daily basis. This has put them under strong pressure to adopt a countersexist politics. Several of them have gone on to a conscious attempt at reconstructing masculinity in the light of feminism.[14]

Research on schooling is usually confined to schooling, and thus has difficulty grasping where the school is located in a larger process. This paper is based on life-history interviews with adults that cover family, workplace, sexual relationships, friendships, and politics, in addition to schooling, as settings for the construction of masculinity.

The interviews became the basis of individual case studies, which in turn were grouped for the analysis of collective processes. The interviews were conducted in New South Wales, Australia, in 1985–87; all respondents were English-speaking and mostly of Anglo background.

Rather than following individual narratives, the approach taken in this paper is to identify key moments in the collective process of gender construction, the social dynamic in which masculinities are formed. In such moments the formation of the person, and the history of the educational institution, are simultaneously at issue.

Getting into Trouble

Behind Mal Walton's high school is the bush, and at the edge of the bush are the school toilets. This is where Mal and his friends would gather:

> In high school [my friends] were real hoods† [† indicates an entry in the glossary] too. Like we used to hang down the back . . . we'd sit down there and smoke cigarettes and talk about women, get dirty books out, going through— what do you call it? I can't think of the word. Just the things you do at high school in the first year.

Mal had been placed in the bottom stream, and was evidently regarded by most of his teachers (though not all) as disruptive. The main reason he was in the bottom stream was that he could not read. He was arrested for theft at fifteen, in the year he left school. He has not had a lasting job in the six years since.

Harry the Eel (so called because of his fanatical devotion to the Parramatta football team "the Eels"), now twenty and about to become a father for the second time, used to practice his school smoking in the same fragrant setting:

> I was in a bit of trouble in the last four years of school. I got busted for—what was it? Second Form it was selling porno books. Third Form it was getting drunk at the school fete, and allegedly holding another bloke down and pouring Scotch down his throat—which we didn't do, he was hassling us for a drink. . . . They found him drunk and they said where did you get it? and he mentioned our names and Biff, straight into it. . . . Fourth Form, wasn't much happening in fourth form really, busted in the dunnies† having a smoke?

Eel started an apprenticeship, but his employer went broke and no one else would take over his training. Since then he has been on the dole, with casual jobs from time to time.

Eel hasn't been arrested, but his friend Jack Harley has. Jack is less of a tactician and fought every authority figure from his parents on. He thinks he was labeled a "troublemaker" at school because of an older cousin. He clashed early and often with teachers: "They bring me down, I'll bring them down." He was expelled from at least one school, disrupting his learning—"I never did any good at school." Eventually he assaulted a teacher. The court "took the teacher's word more than they took mine" and gave him a sentence in a juvenile detention center. Here he learned the techniques of burglary and car theft. About three years later he was doing six months in the big people's prison. At twenty-two he is on the dole, looking for a job to support his one-year-old child and his killer bull terrier.

These three young men come from laboring families, in Mal Walton's case from a very poor family. Their experience of school shows the relationship between the working class and education at its most alienating. What they meet in the school is an authority structure: specifically, the state and its powers of coercion. They are compelled to be at school, and once there—as they see it—they are ordered about arbitrarily by the teachers. The school is a relatively soft part of the state, but behind it stands the "hard" machinery of police, courts, and prisons. Push the school too far, and, like Jack Harley, one triggers an intervention by the enforcers.

Up against an authority structure, acts of resistance or defiance mean "getting into trouble." This is one of Jack Harley's commonest phrases and indicates how his actions are constantly defined in relation to institutional power. Fights with other boys, arguments with teachers, theft, poor learning, conflicts with parents, are all essentially the same. One can try to retreat beyond the routine reach of institutional power, as Mal Walton and his friends did in their idyllic moments in the toilet block on the edge of the bush. Yet even there, one will be "in trouble" when the authorities raid the retreat, as they did to Eel.

At the same time trouble has its attractions, and may be courted. Mal Walton, for instance, was caned a lot when he went to a Catholic primary school. So were his friends. In fact, he recalls, they fell into a competition to see who could get caned most. No one would win: "We just had big red hands." Why this competition? "Nothing to do; or probably proving that I was stronger than him or he was stronger than me."

A violent discipline system invites competition in machismo.

More generally, the authority structure of the school becomes the antagonist against which one's masculinity is cut. Jack Harley, in the comment on teachers quotes above, articulated an ethic of revenge that defines a masculine pride common in his milieu. But he lacked the judgment to keep it symbolic. Teachers often put up with verbal aggression as part of their job, but they are hardly likely to stand still when physically attacked. So the courting of trouble calls out an institutional response, which may push an adolescent assertion of masculine pride toward an early-adult criminal career.

"Trouble" is both sexualized and gendered. Getting the "dirty books" out and "talking about women" are as essential a part of the peer group activity as smoking and complaining about teachers. In the mass high school system, sexuality is both omnipresent and illicit. To act or talk sexually becomes a breach or order, a form of "trouble," in itself. But at the same time it is a means of maintaining order—the order of patriarchy—via the subordination of women and the exaltation of one's maleness.

Patrick Vincent, currently on probation for car theft, succinctly explains why he liked being sent to a coeducational high school after being expelled from his boys-only church school: "Excellent, chicks everywhere, good perve."† He boasts that within a week all the girls in his class wanted to climb into his bed. The treatment of young women by these young men is often flatly exploitative.

Knowing Where You Stand

To other boys, the hoods in the toilet may be objects of fear. Danny Taylor recalls his first year in an urban working-class high school. Despite being big for his age, he hated the physical contest:

> When the First Form† joins and all comes together from all different [primary] schools, there's this thing like sorting out who was the best fighter, who is the most toughest and aggressive boy in the form, and all the little mobs* and cliques develop. So it was like this pecking order stuff . . . and I was really frightened of this.

He did not enjoy high school until Form IV (about age sixteen), when "all the bullies left."

This is not peculiar to urban schools. Stewart Hardy, the son of a laboring family in the dry, flat country in the far west of New South Wales, makes the usual contrast between city and country but paints the same kind of picture:

> In the country . . . it was easier for us to get along with each other, although there was the usual dividing: the cool guys hang out together, and the cool girls hang out together, and there was the swots† and the wimps. . . . You knew where you stood, which group you belonged to.

Stewart and Danny joined the wimps and the swots, respectively. Both managed to use the education system to win social promotion (though in both cases limited) out of their class of origin.

The process of demarking masculinities in secondary school has been noticed in ethnographies of working-class schools in Britain and Australia.[15] Willis's vivid picture of the "lads" and the "ear'oles" is justly celebrated. Such demarcation is not confined to working-class schools. A very similar sorting-out has been documented in a ruling-class private school, between the "bloods" (hearty, sporting) and the "Cyrils" (wimpish, academic).[16]

This suggests a typology of masculinities, even a marketplace of masculinities. To "know where you stand," in Stewart Hardy's phrase, seems to mean *choosing* a masculinity, the way one might choose a football team to root for.

It is important to recognize that differing masculinities are being produced in the same school context. But to picture this as a marketplace, a free choice of gender styles, would be misleading. These "choices" are strongly structured by relations of power.

In each of the cases mentioned, the differentiation of masculinities occurs in relation to a school curriculum that organizes knowledge hierarchically and sorts students into an academic hierarchy. By institutionalizing academic failure via competitive grading and streaming, the school forces differentiation on the boys. But masculinity is organized—on the macro scale—around social power. Social power in terms of access to higher education, entry to professions, command of communication, is being delivered by the school system to boys who are academic "successes." The reaction of the "failed" is likely to be a claim to other sources of power, even other definitions of masculinity. Sporting prowess, physical aggression, or sexual conquest may do.

Indeed, the reaction is often so strong that masculinity as such is claimed for the cool guys. Boys who follow an academic path are defined, conversely, as effeminate (the "Cyrils"). When this situation is reached, there is a *contest for hegemony* between rival versions of masculinity. The school, though it has set this contest up, may be highly ambivalent about the outcome. Many school administrations actively seek competitive sporting success as a source of prestige. The first-rate football team, or the school's swimming champions, may attract as much honor and indulgence from the staff as the academic elite.[17]

The differentiation of masculinities, then, is not simply a question of individual difference emerging or individual paths being chosen. It is a collective process, something that happens at the level of the institution and in the organization of peer group relationships.

Indeed, the relationship of any one boy to the differentiation of masculinities may change over time. Stewart hardy remembers being terrified on his arrival at high school (and even before, with "horror tales" about high school circulating in his primary class). He and his friends responded by "clinging to each other for security" in a wimpish huddle in Form 1. But then:

> Once I started getting used to the place and not so afraid of my own shadow, I felt here was my chance to develop a new identity. Now I can be a coolie, I can be tough. So I started to be a bit more belligerent. I started to get in with the gangs a bit, slag off† teachers behind their backs, and tell dirty jokes and stuff like that.

But it didn't last. After a while, as Stewart got older,

> I decided all that stuff was quite boring. It didn't really appeal to me, being a little shit any more, it didn't really suit my personality.

This was not just a matter of Stewart's "personality." His parents and his teachers put on more pressure for academic performance as the School Certificate (Form IV) approached. Indeed, his parents obliged him to stay on at school to Form VI, long after the "gangs" had left.

Over the Hump

The labor market in modern capitalist economies is segmented and stratified in a number of dimensions. Perhaps the most powerful division in it is not any longer the blue-collar/white-collar divide, but the distinction between (a) a broad market for more or less unskilled general labor—whether manual or clerical—and (b) a set of credentialed labor markets for specific trades, semiprofessions, and professions. The public education system, as the main supplier of credentials (certificates, diplomas, degrees), is deeply implicated in this division. When Stewart Hardy's working-class parents ignored his protests and

made him stay on in high school, they were pursuing a family strategy to get him over the hump between these two labor markets and into the world of credentialed labor.

For Stewart it was a rocky path. He resented the pressure, slacked off at school, got involved with a girlfriend, and did "miserably" at the Higher School Certificate (HSC). Soon after that, he ditched the girlfriend and got religion. But after he had been a while in the work force, his parents' pressure bore fruit, and he took himself to a technical college to have a second try at the HSC. This time he did so well that he qualified for university. He is now (aged twenty-four) doing a part-time arts degree and, at the same time, a computer training program organized by his employer, a big bank. He does not see computing as a career, but as a fallback: "If things get tight I can always go back to being a programmer, because there are always jobs for that." He may get into a career through his degree.

Stewart has got the message about qualifications, with a vengeance:

> All the time I wasted before, I could have been at university getting a degree. Seven years out of school and I have absolutely no qualification at all. All I did was bum around and take whatever jobs came up.

The contrast with Mal Walton, Jack Harley, and Patrick Vincent is stark. They are glad of "whatever jobs come up" and expect to be at the mercy of such economic chances as far as they can see into the future. To them it isn't "time wasted," it is life.

Through the mechanism of educational credentials, Stewart hardy has bought into a different construction of masculinity, in which the notion of a long-term career is central. A calculative attitude is taken toward one's own life. A passive and subordinated position in training programs is accepted in order to provide future protection from economic fluctuations. The life course is projected as if up a slope, with periods of achievement distinguished from plateaus of wasted time. The central themes of masculinity here are rationality and responsibility rather than pride and aggressiveness.

Young men from more privileged class backgrounds are likely to take this perspective from the start. Their families' collective practice is likely to be organized around credentials and careers from before they were born. For instance, I come from a family whose men have been in the professions—engineering, the church, medicine, education, law—for several generations. It never occurred to me that I would not go to university in my turn.

In such a milieu the practice of credentialing does not even require active consent, merely the nonoccurrence of a refusal. As Bill Lindeman, son of an administrator and an academic researcher, put it—

> Because I'd had three siblings who'd gone ahead of me, so there was that sort of assumption there, that the opportunity was given to me to not question it, to not go to something else. And I didn't have strong interests: the strongest interest I had was surfing, in the Sixth Form. And there was nothing really to motivate me to go off and do anything else. So I went to Uni.

Here, very visibly, is a life course being constructed collectively and institutionally, through the education system and families' relationships to it. Of course, the young person has to do such things as sit in class and write exam answers: There is a personal practice involved. But to a marked degree it is a passive practice, following an external logic. The person's project is simply to become complicit in the functioning of an institutional system and the privileges it delivers. There is a painful contrast with the personal investments, and cost, involved in the hoods' doomed assaults on the same institutional system. One begins to feel the reason in all that anger.

Dry Sciences

What privileged young men find at the end of the educational conveyor belt is not necessarily to their taste. This becomes very clear in life histories from the environmental activists. Bill Lindeman went to university because there was nothing motivating him to go elsewhere. But after he had been there—and I hope it pleases his teachers—he began to think.

> When I chose science I chose zoology. My sister and my brother had done exactly the same and my other brother was doing physics, so we were all doing science. There was a strong analytical bent there. I chose life science because— that stemmed from my earlier childhood, enjoying natural places. It wasn't till I'd left Uni that I realized I was so bored with ninety-nine point nine percent of it. I just wasn't finding *nature* in laboratories, cutting up rats and dogfish. The vitality and change that you can learn from nature just isn't there. It was dry. I didn't relate it to the living world.

Bill's critique of the abstractness, the unlifelikeness, of biology is a familiar theme in critiques of other disciplines and of academic knowledge in general.[18] Bill's version is informed by his "green' politics. He began to resolve the problem in a research project involving long field trips to the Snowy Mountains, and then became deeply committed to environmental activism. In that context he also became concerned with the remaking of masculinity, though he has not specifically linked this theme back to his academic experience.

There is, nevertheless, a connection. The dry sciences of academic abstraction involve a particular institutionalization of masculinity. Masculinity shapes education, and education forms masculinity. This has become clear from work on the history and philosophy of science. It is not incidental that most of the people constructing Western science over the last four hundred years have been men. The view of the natural world that mainstream science embodies, the language and metaphors of scientific analysis—a discourse of uncovering, penetrating, controlling—have some of their deepest roots in the social relations between men and women. A different kind of knowledge could have been produced, and to some extent is produced, by people whose thinking is shaped by experience of a different location in gender relations. For instance, a science constructed by women might be more likely to use metaphors of wholeness than metaphors of analysis, seek cooperation with nature rather than domination over it.

Some early work in this vein implied that the structure of science reflected masculinity in general, that the attitude of abstraction and domination over nature was based on something intrinsic to being male. This argument would hardly apply to the relation of men to nature in central Australian aboriginal society, where the ethic of humans caring for the land and the land's "ownership" of the people is traditional.[19] Western science is, rather, based on a culturally specific version of masculinity. Indeed, we may see it as a class-specific version. There is a wide gap between technocratic masculinity as embodied in science and the hot, loud, messy masculinity of the "hoods."

Yet the version of masculinity to which Bill Lindeman is pointing is important, even crucially important, in the contemporary world. Winter and Robert some time ago noted the importance of the changing scale and structure of the capitalist economy for the dynamics of masculinity—a theme much ignored by "men's studies" literature since.[20] The dry sciences are connected, on the one hand, to administration, whose importance is obvious in a world of enormous state apparatuses and multinational corporations. On the other hand, they are connected to professionalism, which is a synthesis of knowledge, power, and economic privilege. Professionalism is central both to the application of developing technologies and to the social administration of modern mass populations.

In both respects the sciences are connected to power, and they represent an *institutionalized* version of the claim to power that is central in hegemonic masculinity. But this is not the crude assertion of personal force that is all the power someone like Jack Harley can mobilize. Rather it is the organized, collective power embodied in large institutions like companies, the state, and property markets. This is power that delivers economic and cultural advantage to the relatively small number of people who can operate this machinery. A man who can command this power has no need for riding leathers and engine noise to assert masculinity. His masculinity is asserted and amplified on an immensely greater scale by the society itself.

Reading Feminism

The men in the study who are involved in countersexist politics, or who have adopted some feminist principles, have almost all read feminist books. Indeed, some say this is their main source of feminist ideas, alongside personal relationship with feminist women. In contrast, mass media seem to be the main source of information about feminism (more exactly, misinformation about feminism) among men who have *not* moved toward feminism.

Contemporary feminism is a highly literate political movement. The mobilization of the "second wave" was accompanied by a vast outpouring of writing: new books, new magazines, special issues of old journals, and so on.[21] Students and teachers made up a high proportion of activists. Writers like Simone de Beauvoir, Betty Friedan, and Mary Daly occupy a central place in modern feminism. The conflict of texts is central to the definition of its various factions and currents.[22] To become a feminist does not absolutely require a higher degree in literature, but it is certainly usual that someone consciously becoming feminist will read a lot.

Many people cannot read. This is true absolutely for Mal Walton, whose alienation from school is described above. He was tipped out into the labor market at fifteen unable to read a job advertisement. He is desperately disadvantaged by illiteracy, tries to conceal it from the employment service as well as from employers, and is currently asking his girlfriend to teach him to read. Illiteracy in first-world countries tends to be concentrated among poor and marginalized groups.[23] In a case like Mal's it is easy to see its class driven connection with "getting into trouble," the war on school in which Mal's embattled masculinity was shaped.

More commonly in rich countries like the United States and Australia, young people do learn to read, in the sense that they can decode the letters and spell out the words, but do not put this skill to use for anything much beyond job advertisements and sports results. I think this is true for Eel and for Jack Harley. Patrick Vincent is in between, he can read reasonably well but has difficulty writing. None of these young men ever mention *ideas* they have got from print, only those that come from talk and television.

There is a level of *political literacy* where reading opens up new ideas, poses alternatives to existing reality, explains what forces are at work in the wider world. These young men have not entered this world. They are only likely to if there is a major politicization of the working class and a massive adult education initiative. Since the mass communication system that they are plugged into, commercial television, is totally opposed to radical reform, the strong likelihood is that they never will reach political literacy.

The men who do grapple with the textual politics of feminism are likely to be from privileged class backgrounds; Bill Lindeman's political literacy is an aspect of his easy insertion into higher education. Or they are men who, like Danny Taylor, have used the education system to escape a working-class milieu.

In neither case is the reading likely to be uplifting and enjoyable. The literature they are most likely to encounter, the "public face" of feminism, is—not to put too fine a point on it—hostile to men, and little is included to make distinctions between groups of men.[24] The reader is likely to encounter a lurid picture of men *en bloc* as rapists, batterers, pornographers, child abusers, militarists, exploiters—and women as victims. Titles like *Female Sexual Slavery, Women of Ideas and What Men Have Done to Them, Pornography: Men Possessing Women* set the tone. Young men who read much of this literature and take it seriously seem to have one major reaction: severe feelings of guilt. Barry Ryan sums it up:

> **After university I was at the stage where I could understand academic literature, and I read some pretty heavy stuff, which made me feel terrible about being male for a long time.**

Guilt is an emotion with social effects, but in this case they are likely to be disempowering rather than positive. A young man "feeling terrible about being male" will not easily join with other men in social action. Nor can he feel solidarity (except at some symbolic level) with women. Thus guilt implies that men's personalities must change but undermines the social conditions for changing them, an enterprise that requires substantial interpersonal support.

Nor is there any useful set of texts to turn to. In terms of what is widely available, there is little between popular feminism (which accuses men) and mass media (which ridicule feminism). A small literature of masculinity therapy exists, designed to assuage the guilt feelings of men affected by feminism.[25] This is almost as demobilizing as the guilt itself.

In such a situation, an educational effort in schools and tertiary institutions might bear rich fruit. Courses on sexual politics do exist at both levels. But they are few, especially in schools. Barry Ryan is the only one of the respondents to describe a school course of this kind, in a progressive private school:

The teachers at that free school were the ones who decided to implement that sexism program and we [the students] were involved in it. I remember having to go and make a verbal submission. . . . We got this course together. I remember having all-male groups and the women having all-women groups, and talking about sexism, and that was basically it. We did a lot of discussion about sexism and how we communicated about women. I didn't learn that much in the course itself, it just taught me that it was something that I was going to have to think about. And so from then on I was always thinking about it.

On Barry's account the organizing framework of the course is "sexism," which would imply a focus on attitudes and perhaps a moralization of the issue.

Two respondents described meeting feminist content in tertiary courses, though not as focused as Barry's school course. Both had come back to education after a period in the work force, with a project of personal change in mind. This may explain why they were in courses dealing with such issues. Material on sexual politics is rare in tertiary courses with high proportions of male students.

Reflections

In this paper I have been trying to give some articulation to two "voices" that are at best muted, at worst silenced, in the discourse of patriarchy. The interviews show an aspect of the formation of masculinity that is more conflictual and more contradictory than the older accounts of sex role socialization implied. The school is not necessarily in harmony with other major "agencies" like the family or the workplace. It is not necessarily in harmony with itself. Some masculinities are formed by battering against the school's authority structure, others by smooth insertion into its academic pathways, others again by a tortuous negotiation of possibilities. Teachers' own char-

acters and sexual politics are not brought into focus in these interviews, but they are no less complex than the sexual politics of the pupils.[26]

Educational institutions sometimes explicitly address themes of masculinity, and examples are documented in these interviews. They range from the countersexist course described by Barry Ryan to the organized sports mentioned by many of the respondents. In most of these life stories, sport (Eel is the obvious exception) does not have the significance, either as symbol or as practice, that has been suggested in some other studies of the making of masculinity.[27] It may be that choosing two groups that are in various ways distanced from mainstream versions of masculinity has found life stories in which sport is less important than usual. Or it may be that we need to reconsider the role of sport more generally. It is culturally conspicuous as an arena of masculinity; but mundane institutional processes may be more broadly significant in the shaping of personality as practical being in the world.[28] Only a diminishing minority of men continue to practice team sports after midadolescence.

In the long perspective, I would argue, it is the inexplicit, indirect effects of the way schools work that are crucial. A stark case is the way streaming and "failure" push groups of working-class boys toward alienation, and state authority provides them a perfect foil for the construction of a combative, dominance-focused masculinity. Equally clear is the role of the academic curriculum and its machinery of assessment and selection in institutionalizing a rationalized masculinity in professions and administration.

To put the pint in more familiar language, the "hidden curriculum" in sexual politics is more powerful than the explicit curriculum. This creates a dilemma for people concerned with democratizing gender relations in the schools. What the school acknowledges as its activity in relation to gender, and may therefore be willing to discuss under the heading of "equal opportunity" or "antidiscrimination," is less significant than what it does not acknowledge. A change of awareness, a bringing-effects-to-light, must happen before the full spectrum of the school's influence can even be debated.

The intractable situation in schools has a lot in common with the difficulty of formulating a progressive sexual politics for heterosexual men in other forums. Despite promising beginnings, it has proved difficult to find or create a base for a consistent countersexist practice.[29] The contrast with the political mobilization of gay men in gay liberation, and more recently around AIDS issues, is striking. The structural problem is obvious. Heterosexual men are the dominant group in the gender order of contemporary society; therefore, propping up patriarchy, rather than demolishing it, will advantage them. In a quite basic way, trying to mobilize a countersexist politics is asking heterosexual men to act against their social interests.

Yet if recent research has shown anything, it is that heterosexual masculinity is not homogeneous; it is fissured, divergent, and stressed in many ways. The *possibility* of an educational politics of masculinity exists in these differences and tensions. Can this possibility be turned to practical account?

To the extent that learning depends on "interest," in the psychological sense, the omens are good. There is no lack of interest in questions of sexuality, gender, and sexual politics among boys and young men—as the topics of conversation in Mal Walton's toilet block illustrate. For many it is a matter of absorbing concern.[30]

At present the resources for responding to this interest are deployed in a way that makes them spectacularly difficult to use. Feminist textual politics are inaccessible to most men and require a teeth-gritting effort from the few who make contact. Courses on sexual politics are located mostly in higher education, which most men (like most women) do not reach. They are specifically located in sectors of higher education (such as humanities courses) not entered by most

of the men who do become students. School-level equity programs concerned with gender are mostly targeted on girls, as might be expected given their "equal opportunity" rationale.

The first task, then, is simply to frame programs that stand a chance of reaching large numbers of boys. Given the importance of the academic curriculum and selection process in the shaping of masculinities, it would be self-defeating to rely mainly on "extracurricular" special-purpose programs such as sex education. As Yates has forcefully argued, countersexist action in schools must be concerned with mainstream curriculum and school organization. It is a question of an effort *across the curriculum,* much as language development is now conceived.[31] Thus, a school trying to examine and reflect on masculinity with its pupils will do so in relation to sport, in relation to science, in relation to art and literature, in relation to personal interaction in the peer group and between teachers and pupils, and in relation to the school's own institutional practices such as examining, streaming, and the exercise of authority.

Such an approach is in fact adopted in schools that have had some success in countersexist work in a coeducational situation, such as Hugh Myddleton Junior School in London:

> Monitoring the classroom interactions and the use of social space by boys in the school has led to a firm, if understated, affirmative action policy at the school. For example, the arrival of the new microcomputer equipment led to a decision to prohibit the boys from using it until the girls got a head start. In classrooms traditional girls' activities are validated by granting more space to their discussion and activities. The girls are encouraged to be vocally demonstrative. Boys are encouraged to dance, and a good music-in-the-nursery program has been developed. . . . Changed relations between kids and teachers have been encouraged because Richard [the principal] refuses to be the discipline ogre of the school. . . . A slow deliberate building of gains made over the last ten years

has produced a consensus on sexism that we'd all like to see. It also shows what can be done by a male teacher when he puts effort into the issue seriously.[32]

We are still far from having a well-reasoned overall strategy in gender education within which the countercurrents in masculinity could find a clear voice. Perhaps that is too much to expect at present. But there are some more limited rationales on which teachers can act.

For one thing, the sources of information about sexuality and gender available to boys are often narrow and reactionary. It is an appropriate purpose for schools to introduce their pupils to the *whole* truth about an important area of their lives. That means introducing them to gay sexuality as well as straight, to the range of gender patterns across the world, to issues of rape and domestic violence as well as happy families. To do this requires prioritizing the experiences of those who are usually silenced or marginalized, especially women. This is not likely to be easy to do with many adolescent boys, but it is at least a coherent educational goal and one that may call on motives of curiosity and sympathy to expand horizons.

What this might mean is shown in Lees's splendid study of adolescent girls' experiences of sexuality. Lees argues for making "social education" the basis of sex education:

> Questions relating to the morality of sexual relations, domestic violence and the objectification of girls would be on the agenda. Instead of focusing purely on the mechanics of contraception, reasons for the fact that only a third of sexually active teenagers actually use contraception would be critically examined . . . It is by challenging the terms on which girls participate in social life that boys and girls can be encouraged to see their relationships not in sexist stereotypical ways or as sex objects, but in terms of their human attributes.[33]

It is the inclusion of girls' and women's experiences of sexuality that gives the possibility of challenging sexist and abusive discourse among boys.

The life histories document a good many blocked paths, cases where the development of a patriarchal masculinity follows from a sense of being trapped, or where an attempt at reconstruction peters out in frustration, doubts, or confusion. In my teaching on issues of gender at university level, I have often seen men starting out with good will; then, confronted with the endless facts of gender inequality, and feeling themselves under an increasing fire of blame, turn away because they had no method for dealing with this and saw nothing but more blame and guilt coming down the pipeline.

Developing a sense of agency, a confidence in being able to accomplish something on these issues, is needed. Here cooperative work with feminist women is essential. Educators may get very useful cues from people working on problems about adult masculinity, such as counselors working with battering husbands and unionists taking countersexist action in workplaces.[34] Politics was once defined as "slow boring through hard boards," and no one should expect quick results in this corner of sexual politics. But we now have enough leads, from practice and research, to make the effort worth undertaking.

Glossary for Overseas Readers

Hoods: Toughs, delinquents.

Dunnies: Outdoor toilets, so called from being traditionally painted a dun color.

Perve: The Male Gaze, looking at women as sex objects; or at women's underclothes, a couple having intercourse, etc.

Mob: Group (e.g., a flock of sheep, a peer group of people)—no overtone of Mafia.

Forms I–IV: The six years of high school in the New South Wales system. Form VI leads to the Higher School Certificate at matriculation level.

Most working-class boys leave at Form IV.

Swots: Enthusiastic students, or simply those who "succeed" at academic work.

Slag off: To verbally abuse.

Notes

1. P. Sexton, *The Feminized Male: Classrooms, White Collars, and the Decisions of Manliness* (New York: Random House, 1969).

2. J. P. Hantover, "The Boy Scouts and the Validation of Masculinity," *Journal of Social Issues* 34 (1) (1978): 184–95.

3. A. Rich, *On Lies, Secrets, and Silence* (New York: Norton, 1979).

4. R. W. Connell, *Gender and Power* (Stanford: Stanford University Press, 1987); B. B. Hess and M. M. Ferree, *Analyzing Gender* (Newbury Park, California: Sage, 1987).

5. T. Carrigan, R. W. Connell, and J. Lee, "Toward a New Sociology of Masculinity," *Theory and Society* 14 (5) (1985): 551–604.

6. G. W. Dowsett, *Boys Own* (Sydney: Inner City Education Centre, 1985); C. Thompson, "Education and Masculinity," in A. O. Carelli, ed., *Sex Equity in Education* (Springfield, Illinois: Thomas, 1988), 47–54.

7. E. Hansot and D. Tyack, "Gender in Public Schools: Thinking Institutionally," *Signs* 13 (4) (1988): 741–60.

8. B. Thorne, "Girls and Boys Together . . . but Mostly Apart: Gender Arrangements in Elementary Schools," in *Relationships and Development,* ed. W. W. Hartup and Z. Rubin (Hillsdale, Erlbaum, 1986), 167–84.

9. M. Messner, "Boyhood, Organized Sports, and the Construction of Masculinities," *Journal of Contemporary Ethnography* 18 (4) (1990): 416–44.

10. S. Kessler, D. J. Ashenton, R. W. Connell, and G. W. Dowsett, "Gender Relations in Secondary Schooling," *Sociology of Education* 58 (1) (1985): 34–48.

11. C. Heward, *Making a Man of Him* (London: Routledge, 1988).

12. J. C. Walker, *Louts and Legends* (Sydney: Allen & Unwin, 1988).

13. M. Donaldson, "Labouring Men: Love, Sex and Strife," *Australian and New Zealand Journal of Sociology* 23 (3) (1987): 165–84. R. W. Connell, "Live Fast and Die Young: The Construction of Masculinity among Young Working-Class Men on the Margin of the Labour Market," submitted for publication.

14. R. W. Connell, "Remaking Masculinity in the Context of the Environmental Movement," *Gender and Society,* 4 (4), in press.

15. D. H. Hargreaves, *Social Relations in a Secondary School* (London: Routledge & Kegan Paul, 1967); P. Willis, *Learning to Labour* (Farnborough, England: Saxon House, 1977); J. C. Walker, *Louts and Legends.*

16. R. W. Connell, *Teachers' Work* (Sydney: Allen & Unwin, 1985).

17. R. W. Connell, "An Iron Man: The Body and Some Contradictions of Hegemonic Masculinity," in *Sport, Men, and the Gender Order: Critical Feminist Perspectives,* M. A. Messner and D. F. Sabo, eds. (Champaign, Illinois: Human Kinetics Books, 1990).

18. P. Lafitte, *The Person in Psychology* (London: Routledge & Kegan Paul, 1957); L. Johnson, *Free U.* (Sydney: Free University, 1968); A. Rich, *On Lies, Secrets, and Silence.*

19. K. Maddock, *The Australian Aborigines,* 2d ed. (Ringwood: Australia: Penguin, 1982): 29–36.

20. M. F. Winter and E. R. Robert, "Male Dominance, Late Capitalism, and the Growth of Instrumental Reason," *Berkeley Journal of Sociology* 24 (25) (1980): 249–80.

21. C. Ehrlich, "The Woman Book Industry," *American Journal of Sociology* 78 (1973): 1031–44.

22. H. Eisenstein, *Contemporary Feminist Thought* (London: Unwin Paperbacks, 1984); L. Segal, *Is the Future Female?* (London: Virago, 1987).

23. C. St. J. Hunter and D. Harman, *Adult Illiteracy in the United States* (New York: McGraw-Hill, 1979).

24. L. Segal, *Is the Future Female?*

25. H. Goldberg, *The Inner Male* (New York: Signet, 1987); W. Farrell, *Why Men Are the Way They Are* (New York: Berkeley, 1988).

26. R. W. Connell, *Teachers' Work.*

27. M. Messner, "Boyhood, Organized Sports, and the Construction of Masculinities"; R. W. Connell, "An Iron Man."

28. R. W. Connell, *Gender and Power.*

29. A. Tolson, *The Limits of Masculinity* (London: Tavistock, 1977); J. Snodgrass, *For Men against Sexism* (Albion, CA.: Times Change Press, 1977).

30. D. C. Holland and M. A. Eisenhart, *Educated in Romance* (Chicago: University of Chicago Press, 1990).

31. L. Yates, "The Theory and Practice of Counter-Sexist Education in Schools," *Discourse* 3 (2) (1983): 33–44.

32. G. W. Dowsett, *Boys Own.*

33. S. Lees, *Losing Out: Sexuality and Adolescent Girls* (London: Hutchinson, 1986): 149–50.

34. J. Ptacek, "Why Do Men Batter Their Wives?" in *Feminist Perspectives on Wife Abuse,* ed. K. Yllo and M. Bograd (Newbury Park, California: Sage, 1988), 133–57; D. Adams, "Treatment Models of Men Who Batter: A Profeminist Analysis" in Yllo and Bograd, *Feminist Perspectives on Wife Abuse,* 176–99; S. Gray, "Sharing the Shop Floor," in *Beyond Patriarchy,* ed. M. Kaufman (Toronto: Oxford University Press, 1987).

14

ARTICLE

Ritch C. Savin-Williams

Memories of Childhood and Early Adolescent Sexual Feelings Among Gay and Bisexual Boys: A Narrative Approach

Frequently missing from scientific research on gay, bisexual, and lesbian youths is a sense of the ways in which the events occurring during their childhood and adolescence influence later development. As parents, educators, researchers, and clinicians we seldom ask our children, the students in our classrooms, or the youths in our research protocols or clinics to recall the earliest memories they have of their sexuality. Perhaps we believe that they are without early sexual memories of that it is inappropriate or ill-mannered to pursue such matters. We may want to honor their privacy or may simply be too embarrassed to talk about early childhood sexuality.

As a consequence, relatively little is known regarding several very important issue in pediatric sexology: the existence and content of sexual fantasies, thoughts, and feelings among children and early adolescents; the sexual activities of youths; and the meaning that children and early adolescents ascribe to their sexual desires. Gay and bisexual male youths I interviewed for a forthcoming book provided such information.

Their sexual recollections often originate from first memories of infancy, are exceedingly vivid and saturated with emotionality, and are subsequently interpreted to have had profound significance for the future derivations of their sexual behavior and identity. These youths were permitted to do that which many only dream of— uninhibited self-disclosure.

A gay or bisexual youth may long to reminisce about his early sexual feelings but fear that his personal "story" will have little correspondence with the stories of other men and that he will consequently be ridiculed or rejected. Nevertheless, he may believe that his story has meaning for himself and that the meaning will be clarified by its recall. Because the recounting necessitates sharing with others aspects of an often hidden inner being, telling one's story can be both threatening and self-validating. The latter may be especially true if the youth discovers that others share facets of his unique story and will not reject or think poorly of him because of his early fantasies and sexual activities.

In this [article], the uniqueness that characterizes the developmental history of 44 gay and bisexual youths is portrayed intact through the narration of individual life stories. Similarities

across stories are highlighted, however, to identify broad themes that reveal patterns of childhood and early adolescent memories of sexuality.
The overall goal of the retrospective study that
provided the date for this chapter was to understand developmental issues that are central to the
well-being and resiliency of gay and bisexual
male youths.[1]

The Study

Research Procedures

The youths who agreed to tell their stories
heard about the study through classroom lec-
tures and word of mouth, primarily from those
who had previously volunteered for the study.
After interviewing each youth, I asked for the
name of one or two other individuals who
might be interested in participating.

I interviewed one half of the youths at their
house or apartment and the rest at my office or
a public place of their choosing, such as a café,
park, or car. Tape recorders were too intrusive
for the material requested so I wrote elaborate
notes. The youths understood my method and
were careful to pause in order that I could catch
up when I fell behind. There were many long
pauses and hesitations, which also made it easier to record notes verbatim. The youths' stories
cited in this chapter were derived from my
notes.[2]

I introduced the study by emphasizing the
critical importance of each personal story:

> We all lead unique lives and have unique his-
> tories in terms of how we got to where we
> are today. I am interested in *your* story. In
> some ways your life has probably been like
> many others and in other ways different. If
> there are any questions you do not wish to an-
> swer, that is fine. Just say "pass" and I'll go to
> another question.

The interview consisted of initial questions
regarding age, education, race, religion, community reared in, occupation of parents, and parents'
marital status. The youth rated themselves on
Kinsey's Sexual Orientation Scale and the extent
to which they are open to others about their homosexuality. They reported when they first rec-
ollected having homoerotic attractions, the
number of males and females with whom they
have had sex, their age when puberty began and
how they reacted to it, and the age at which they
first had a wet dream. Questions regarding sexual activities focused on sexual outlets and frequency of orgasms during the junior and senior
high school years, especially in terms of the ways
in which orgasms were achieved: heterosexual
contact, homosexual contact, masturbation, wet
dreams, and bestiality. Circumstances of first orgasm and first infatuation were probed.

Each youth then recounted his personal history of the ways in which he experienced his
sexual identity during childhood and adolescence. This process usually included questions
that focused on thoughts and feelings at particular ages, such as: "At age 12 did you view yourself as gay, bisexual, or straight?" and "If someone
had asked what you were at high school graduation, how would you have answered, both to
the other person and to yourself?" Some youths
remembered exact markers while others recounted that their realization of being gay or bisexual was a gradual process. It became apparent
that the key to eliciting information was to encourage the youths to remember specific events
or times. The details in the stories add both interest to the interview data and credibility to the
stories.

Each youth then recalled his first interpersonal sexual encounter, defined as some variety
of genital contact for one or both partners. After
this memory was elicited, probes included:
"Where did you met?", "Who initiated the interaction?", "Who was this person to you?",
"What happened sexually?", "How did you feel
afterward?", "How did this affect your sense of
being gay?", and "Were there further contacts?"
I then elicited similar information about all in-

dividuals with whom the youth had had sexual activity prior to high school graduation.

There is no guarantee, of course, that the memories recorded in the pages that follow are accurate, but the detail and the commitment to honesty that many of the youths provided is impressive. I generally concluded each interview feeling that the story told was an authentic one and that the specific life history was shared for the first time with another. In only a few cases did the memories appear rehearsed, perhaps the consequence of having shared the story with several others. On many occasions the stories were so emotionally laden that is was difficult to hear them; at times the desire to respond was exceptionally tempting. I frequently added some measure of support, which often elicited further reflections and encouraged in-depth pursuit of the past.

I believe for the most part that the youths felt safe during the interview. All reported afterward that they had enjoyed the experience and several volunteered to be interviewed again if I ever needed them. Their readiness to refer friends to the study further illustrates their feelings of safety and comfort. I felt honored and privileged by their willingness to share some of the most memorable and painful aspects of their lives. In this chapter, I focus on the youths' accounts of early same-sex attractions and feelings.

Characteristics of the Youths

The youths range in age from 17 to 23 years with a mean of almost 21 years. At the time of the interview, three of the youths were seniors in high school. Of the other ten not in college, five graduated from college, four dropped out of college after less than two years, and one never went to college. Twenty-one of the 44 youths were Cornell University students; eight were in other four-year colleges and two in a local community college.

All but four are White, and there is an even split in religious affiliation among "none," Jew-

ish, Protestant, and Catholic. Almost three quarters of the youths grew up in a home in which at least one parent held a high-level professional position, such as lawyer, physician, engineer, or business manager. The vast majority of the mothers worked outside the home, frequently as a schoolteacher, salesperson, or clerical worker. Two thirds of the youths' parents had remained married to each other; one third were divorced or separated. Most of the youths' families lived in small- and medium-sized towns and suburbs.

These youths are not presented as "representative" of the population of gay and bisexual youth. For example, few youths of color or those who are closeted to themselves or to others are included; neither are those of various educational, socioeconomic, and geographical backgrounds adequately sampled. Nonverbally oriented and shy youths probably did not participate in the interview study.

Early Childhood Memories of Same-Sex Attractions
Natural but Wrong

Two thirds of the gay and bisexual youths reported that their same-sex attractions were deeply embodied in their "natural self." By this they implied that their homoerotic attractions were not a matter of choice but were of early, perhaps genetic, origins. Without hesitation they graphically recalled same-sex attractions that emanated from their earliest childhood memories. Early homoerotic attractions visited them without great fanfare, with no clashing of cymbals, and with no abiding shock. They remembered feeling that their attractions to other males had always been present and they frequently identified concrete, distinct memories prior to first grade. Later homoerotic attractions were felt to be contiguous with these feelings.

Same-sex attractions were often first experienced as an obsession of always wanting to be near masculinity. The males who monopolized their attention were occasionally same-age peers, but were more often older teenagers and adults—male teachers, coaches, cousins, or friends of the family.

Mickey, an 18-year-old youth, reported in his interview a lifelong fascination with older males. He grew up in an impoverished small town that included many extended family members and friends. They stopped by his home in the evenings and on weekends to visit his parents and older brothers and sisters.

I can remember wanting the men who visited us to hug me when I was real little, maybe three or four. I've always wanted to touch and be touched by guys, and I was a lot. Guys loved to manhandle me. They would throw me up in the air and I'd touch the ceiling and I'd scream and would love it and would do anything to make it happen more and more. It never was enough and I'd tire them out or I'd go to someone else who would toss me. Sometimes I would be teased for the "little points" [erections] in my pants, but no one, including myself, made much of it.

I guess I was pretty touchable—and I still am based on what guys I know or am with tell me. I didn't understand why because I thought all kids liked it. Others have told me that they liked it too, but somehow I think I liked it more. I craved and adored it and my day would not be a good one unless I had this contact. Only later did I find out why I liked being touched by guys.

At eight I fell in love with Neal, this guy who rode my bus. He was so cool, so big, but I guess he was fourteen or fifteen but he seemed like an adult. He wore these great clothes and was always in fashion and smelled so nice. I always wanted to sit with him or be next to him. But I never could because others always fought to sit next to him. I'd do anything for him and longed just for a look or a nudge. I'd fall down in front of him so he'd help me up or just that he'd no-

tice or respond to me. He quit riding the bus one day and I never knew why but I was sad.

I think I spent my childhood fantasizing about men, not sexually of course, but just being close to them and having them hold me or hug me. I'd feel safe and warm. My dad gave me this and my older brother Mitchell gave me this but all of this was never enough. With the other men I'd feel flushed, almost hot. Maybe those were hot flashes like what women get! Those were good days.

Several youths recognized at the time that these undeniable, lifelong homoerotic attractions were not typical of other boys. Other youths simply assumed, based on the egocentric principle that their thoughts and feelings were shared by others, that all boys must feel as they do but were simply not talking about it. Eventually, however, all youths recognized that these desires were the wrong ones to have and that they should hide their attractions from others. Remarks made by peers, prohibitions taught by parents, and the silence imposed by religious leaders and schoolteachers all contributed to this recognition. Thus, although early same-sex attractions were felt to be instinctive, most of the gay and bisexual youths acknowledged from an early age that their impulses were somehow "wrong," but not necessarily "bad."

As the societal wrongness of their intuitive sexual desires became increasingly apparent, many hoped that their attractions were a phase they would outgrow or that their feelings would eventually make sense in some distant future. View few grasped the possibility that these feelings could have meaning for their sexual identity.

Jeff, a graduate student who grew up in a wealthy suburb of New York City, complete with father, mother, younger sister, and pet dog, exemplified this early developmental awareness.

As a child I knew I was attracted to males. I was caught by my mother looking at nude photographs of men in her magazines and I heard my father say to her that, "He'll grow out of it," and so I thought and hoped I would. But until then I just settled back and enjoyed my keen curiosity to see male bodies.

You see, it did not feel threatening because (a) it felt great, and (b) father said I would grow out of it, and he was always right. So why not enjoy it until it went away?

So when I started fooling around with some of the neighborhood boys I felt different than they did about it. More comfortable than them because although I felt it was wrong I did not feel that it was bad. The wrong was because the sexual feelings, which represented childishness in my mind, had not gone away yet. It was not bad because it felt so natural.

I knew I was attracted to boys but that did not say I had to be gay. I just felt everyone was attracted like I was but just no one talked about it because no one wanted to admit that they were immature. It was a phase that all of us would grow out of. But until then it felt important to keep it a secret, especially from my family because I wanted them to think highly of me because I was the oldest boy and all. But I still sat back and enjoyed it and waited for nature to do its self-correction.

Many youths recalled being punished or verbally threatened by their parents if they continued their sexual activities. These repercussions served as a powerful reason for feeling that same-sex desires and behaviors were wrong, but they did not prevent the youths from recognizing their same-sex attractions at an early age. These desires were not to be shared with others and acting on them was thought to be wrong because if caught, punishment would likely ensue. Balancing desire and fear became a significant dilemma.

A very extroverted child, Randy was the life of his neighborhood in a small city near a large urban center. His family was very socially active and thus Randy was allowed to spend considerable time with his many friends.

I can recall being very interested in sex several years before my friends, around age six or seven. What I wanted most at that point was

to have sex with other boys as frequently as possible and, of course, at that point I was. I considered myself normal and that this behavior that I was doing with Buddy was just a fun thing to do, even though I realized that it was a taboo thing to do. I feared that at some point we might get caught by our parents. We were almost caught several times, but of course we were at it again as soon as we were alone in his basement and he was ready to initiate it; I was always too frightened to tell him I was interested or that I really wanted it.

Before puberty I didn't feel that his behavior made me anything other than what I was. I was aware we needed to keep it a secret, yet one time for a reason I can't remember I told my mom and she handled it very well. She told me, "Don't put it in your rears or hurt yourself." Buddy's mom found out and she just seemed to sort of blow it off as well.

Same-sex attractions for these youths were not foreign but natural, a lifelong intrigue with men's bodies. Eventually, many of the youths recognized that others rarely shared or understood their same-sex desires. They did not consider the meaning that their attractions had, either for the moment or for their future. Only later, with the onset of puberty, were these attractions fully linked with sexuality.

Natural but Different: Gender Nonconformity

Another much smaller group of gay and bisexual youths recognized as well that their same-sex desires were a natural aspect of themselves. Nevertheless, they understood their homoerotic attractions as consistent with their self-perception that they were more similar to girls than boys. They were intrigued and mystified by male bodies; males were enigmatic and unapproachable. They viewed themselves as somehow "different" from their male peers, and this sense of differentness permeated all spheres of their lives. Although they were also drawn to the masculinity of boys and men, they felt more comfortable in the company of girls and women than the other gay and bisexual youths.

Compared to the majority of their male peers, these gay and bisexual youths were at odds in their attitudes, feelings, and behaviors. They felt ill at ease with typical male sports; they especially loathed team sports such as baseball and football. They may have been forced by a father or coach to participate in sports—as a right fielder, a defensive back, or a benchwarmer— and they deeply resented such coercion and their inevitable failure in sports. Stronger preferences were fervently expressed for books, make-believe games, and artistic endeavors. The gay and bisexual youths spent more time during childhood with girls, primarily because the youths had more culturally defined feminine than masculine interests.

Richard, age 19, grew up in a farming area in northern Pennsylvania. His father worked in a nearby grain mill. An only child who maintained a very close relationship with his mother, Richard interpreted his hesitation, and perhaps his inability, to conform to the "masculine jock" image as a consequence of "just being my own self."

> I have always been gay, although I did not know what that meant at the time. But I knew that I always felt queer, out of place in my hometown. I did not play basketball or wrestle, and I was not a farmer nor a slob nor did I shovel cow shit like my classmates. Girl, they would come in smelling like they looked, and you can be sure it was not a number Chanel ever heard of! There was no way that I was going to let this be a part of what I wanted for my life.

> I took part in dance, ballet, singing, and had good manners. I like Broadway musicals, Barbra, Bette, Joan, Liz, Judy, and Greta. I wore stylish clothes and was my own individual self. My teachers appreciated this but not the slobs. Because of this a lot of them said that I was gay, and so I thought I must be, although I did not know what this meant except that it meant I would not be shoveling cow shit!

During recess in grade school, Richard was regularly called "fag" and "sissy." He did not, however, equate these names with having sex with other boys. It simply meant that he was different from the farm boys and was being true to his own self.

> As far back as I can remember, I was always teased about being gay or at least being not very masculine. In first and second grades, I was called a "sissy" and a "fairy" and got pushed around. I became fairly introverted during those years, with only a couple of friends.

> Later, in junior high school, a couple of girls and this other guy who played in the band and me would hang out and laugh at the morons. I knew I was afraid of them, but I did not want to give them the satisfaction of knowing this. I knew I was different, but I did not know what that meant. I was repulsed by these boys, but I also found them fascinating and this split was hard to understand. It just felt like there had to be more to it than just feeling like an outsider.

Another youth, Ben, age 21, remembered what it was like to live on the outside of male childhood. Ben grew up in a more suburban setting than did Richard, but his reactions to being gender nonconforming were nearly identical.

> I had mostly friends who were girls and I can remember playing jump rope, dolls, and hopscotch with them, and I can remember being very interested in hairstyling and practicing on dolls. But my major activity during childhood was drawing, and I was sort of known as "the Artist," even as early as third and fourth grades. Today I can see some very gay themes in my drawings!

> I detested gym and sports, even though I guess I was capable in some of them, like track, but I was just not aggressive enough to excel. I really hated football and thought that it was very crude and brutal.

> Within myself I acknowledged my attractions to males, but I always denied it outwardly. I was ashamed of it, in an intense way. I felt different through all my life, even in kindergarten

when I thought boys were idiots. I liked girls because they were more intelligent and interesting and did things that I thought were more human and refined. They also did the things that I liked doing.

Unfortunately for youths such as Richard and Ben, the consequences of being true to their nature was that other boys viewed them as undesirable playmates and as "weird" because they did not think or act like other boys. Labeled sissy or effeminate, they were rejected by boys and, equally important, they had little desire to fraternize with their male peers. Because other boys did not constitute an enjoyable or safe context for play or socializing, the Richards and Bens turned to girls for activities and consolation. They preferred to dance rather than shovel shit, to sing rather than yell "hike," and to draw rather than bash heads. Thus, childhood and early adolescence were usually portrayed as traumatizing times by these youths if they were subjected to the taunts of their male peers and did not have the support of girls.

Although these gay and bisexual youths may have become isolated and withdrawn from others, the fortunate ones sought and found girls for solace and support. Girls became their saviors, offering sources of emotional sustenance as the male world of childhood became increasingly distasteful. It was to these girls that many gay and bisexual youths subsequently disclosed their sexual affiliations during middle or late adolescence.

Sexless and Masculine

In contrast to the previous two groups of youths, who felt that their same-sex attractions were natural and originated from early childhood, were those relatively few youths I interviewed who claimed that their first memory of homoerotic attractions came after childhood. Sexually explicit childhood feelings, desires, or attractions that they would now label as sexual in nature

were unknown to them. Unsure of how they "became gay," the youths characterized their life before puberty as "sexless," with few memories of sexuality, and as deeply invested in masculine activities, especially sports.

With the onset of physical maturation, thoughts and feelings associated with sexuality were evoked in these gay and bisexual youths. During childhood they chased girls, but this was more of a game that they joined with other boys than a statement about their sexuality or their true sexual interests. There was little indication in their stories that they pursued girls as sex objects.

Jack, a 22-year-old, grew up in western Long Island among wealthy surrounds. His parents owned and operated a real estate firm; his older sister worked as a secretary for the family business. Jack was excused from the family business because of his involvement in sports and his pursuit of well-developed musculature and a tanned body.

I was really into sports. In the summer I played baseball and in the fall I did track, just before the football season started. I wanted to swim, but I had to give that up if I wanted to play football. In the spring was spring track and spring training for baseball. I practiced some sport every day throughout my four years of high school.

I was good but not great, best at track in long-distance running. In football I was a seldom-used receiver and sometimes safety. In baseball I started in left field. I lettered in all three, but only in track was it for all four years.

Maybe I just did not have time, but I was not into sex. I would have to say that I was sexless because I cannot remember any sexual thoughts. I was not interested in girls even though I had several girlfriends. In general I felt left out of what my teammates said they were going through.

When asked during the interview to elaborate on any aspect of his sexuality during childhood, Jack drew a blank. He had many stories of athletic, but not sexual, exploits. After pubertal onset, he discovered his sexuality and expressed wonderment regarding the location of his sexual desires during childhood.

Puberty and Its Effects

Regardless of their activities, feelings, and attractions during childhood, the elusive same-sex attractions of the gay and bisexual youths were demystified with the onset of puberty. The critical instigator may have been the biologically induced increase in sexual libido that arrives with pubertal onset. The youths reported that their sexuality now intruded into every thought, feeling, and behavior; at times this frightened them, and at other times it energized them. The ways in which they responded to the onset of puberty and the accompanying increase in sexual libido were quite diverse.

Although their growing cognizance of same-sex attractions was often electrifying, it could also create immense complications and obstacles for the gay and bisexual youths. In either case, it raised the stakes for their sense of personal identity. The intensity of the sexual feelings that emanated from puberty and the sense of "naughtiness" that some youths reported were often exhilarating. They were the beginning of an intelligibility of previously misunderstood feelings. In this they were a source of great relief. For only a few youths, however, did puberty and its accompanying effects induce clarity regarding the meaning of strongly felt sexual lusts and desires.

Natural but Wrong

For the two thirds of the gay and bisexual youths who recalled feeling same-sex attractions early in life as a natural part of who they are, pubescence usually elicited an awareness of the link between these early attractions and the youths' sexuality. That is, it intensified the sexual component of their feelings and, for the first time, raised the

possibility that this sexuality had long-term repercussions. Although many youths originally expressed hope that the sexual implications would evaporate in time, as puberty progressed they had lingering but persistent doubts that they were similar to other boys in their sexual attractions.

Mickey was fortunate because he had a lesbian aunt who was open about her sexuality. She provided a model for him that gave meaning to his same-sex desire.

> It finally began to creep into my consciousness that I might not be straight. This was in the seventh grade just about the time that I began to masturbate and my erections became a little bit more noticeable. I was proud that I was getting so big that guys didn't want to throw me around but depressed because no one did.
>
> I figured at first that it was a phase, the one I had heard about. But somehow I knew better, and I think this was because I knew what homosexuality was because I have a lesbian aunt, and she, although thought a bit eccentric, is well liked by my family. She was very open about it, although we never talked about her or me. But I knew and I think she came to know about me. I just decided to go on leading my life. I mean, what choice did I really have? If I was, I was, and there was nothing I could do about it.

Randy claimed that "massive confusion" hit him during junior high school. He discovered that several of his older friends were gay and that they had begun to wonder about him. This shocked him into self-analysis; his initial defense was to assume the liberal stance that his sexual attractions depended on the person and not the gender. He was attracted to some girls and to some boys. More important than genitalia were the person's character and personality.

Over time, however, Randy realized that he fantasized about only boys. This was thrilling to him, as long as he did not have to think about it too much. Later he sexually experimented with boys and realized that these experiences were qualitatively more erotic than his sexual experiences with girls had been during the previous two years.

Although puberty could be a freeing time, the accompanying sexual feelings were more often experienced as threatening and frightening. They threatened a childhood homeostasis and frightened their recipients with the meanings and repercussions they carried for the future. Gay and bisexual youths seldom had the experience or language to make sense of that which they were feeling. Their desires were not discussed in school or at home, except in a denigrating fashion. If they were to accept or even articulate their same-sex attractions, they often feared that they would be committing social or emotional suicide.

Natural but Different: Gender Nonconformity

These same fears were often expressed by the small number of youths who reported early same-sex attractions, exhibited gender nonconformity, and experienced a sense of differentness. Although the onset of puberty clarified many aspects of their lives, there was always a cost involved with the growing understanding.

For Sam, a 20-year-old from a small town in upstate New York, adolescence was a difficult period. As the middle child of five, Sam frequently felt isolated, invisible, and unable to share with others that which was most important in his life.

> When I was thirteen I grew hair in places I never did before, and I began to know that all of this meant I was attracted to males, but I dared not say this to anyone, including myself out loud. I knew that no one was interested in what interested me—other guys—and I knew enough to say nothing because no one would listen. I knew it would not be a good situation. But I knew what I liked, and I liked boys.

Another youth expressed similar feelings:

> I felt upset, not cool, not quite right, in angst and confusion. I first centered on certain people who were available as sexual objects, not because I was attracted to them as people. The physical feelings became emotional feelings with emotional situations. And that scared the shit out of me because I did not know what it could mean beyond sex but whatever it was was real. Well, maybe I did know what it was, but I did not have the words for it.

> As I moved into eighth grade, it became more and more clear to me what it was all about, and it was sex, but with a twist, romance.

This realization was seldom positive or uplifting for the gender-nonconforming gay and bisexual youths. Many of them began to realize that their homoerotic sexual feelings, which they knew to be wrong or which were condemned by others, were not disappearing. In addition, most had experienced extensive familial and peer rejection when they were children for these attractions or for their effeminate behavior. As early adolescents, they feared that their long history of failing to conform with social definitions of masculinity would only be prolonged. Sex was one more way in which they would be ostracized and harassed by their peers.

Richard attempted to deny the sexual aspect of his attractions, for personal as well as for interpersonal reasons. Consistent with his childhood pattern, his gender-nonconforming behavior faced an onslaught of ridicule from peers.

> In grade seven, God, I was suddenly bombarded with the reality of being attracted to men's bodies, which really floored me. I felt it had to be normal because the feelings were so intense. Although I now know these were sexual and emotional, at the time I tried not to link it with sexuality, just with being different. I was okay with it in the seventh grade because it was me.

> But I was also ostracized by the farm boys as a faggot because I was effeminate and hung out with the girls. I just did not like homosexuality because I was hit over the head with it. I never asked for it. It was never cool. I never labeled

liking men as gay because it just seemed a part of me. Only later could I consciously link it with sexuality.

Similar to Richard, Ben's response to the growing self-understanding that accompanied puberty was to deny the sexual aspect of his life until a later age: "I didn't talk to anyone about it. I put the feelings in the background. I definitely knew what was going on, but I decided to deny it and that I was going to be that way for the rest of my life."

Sexless and Masculine

The "blank slate" that many of the masculine, sexless youths described as existing prior to pubescence was disrupted with the onset of puberty. At that time, they reported first sexual impulses and homoerotic attractions. Many believed that they did not have control over either the onset or the content of these attractions. Their potential meaning threatened an established equilibrium. The youths' responses were consistent with their past defense against sexuality: suppress, resist, or deny these unwanted feelings.

Awareness for these masculine youths came later and more gradually, often in spurts of recognition. Same-sex desires were clearly present, but there was a profound obstruction that required considerable "data" or a traumatic event to overcome. The defenses were usually effective, at least for the short term. This was true for Jack.

I am not sure I was aware of what homosexuality was about at thirteen. I began to grow and develop and that was good for my athletic performance. My identification just was not in the sexual domain. I did not label myself, other than an "it." I would not have said that I was gay because I did not fit the stereotype of being gay. I was very busy and into a lot of things. Besides sports, I was a social butterfly.

I never looked really inward until college. I did everything in groups. I belonged to several jock groups, and we would go and do things on Fri-

day and Saturday nights. We drank a lot and went out on the town—you know, just drive around. I had a lot of good friends who were girls, but most friendships were actually with other guys. I had "girlfriends" of course, but I felt feeling about them sexually would dirty our relationship.

I can recall vague signs of awareness. Like the time my family went to Fort Lauderdale. I saw all of the guys holding hands and I felt an excitement. I was thirteen or fourteen. Then I saw a Bloomingdale ad for Calvin Klein underwear that I could not take my eyes off of. Then another fleeting moment was when there was this guy, a runner, I fell over.

Gee, I guess I must have been pretty gay, huh? But somehow I blocked the meaning of these things from my mind. And the time when I was sixteen and saw two senior football teammates going at it in the second-floor school bathroom. I had not remembered that for a long time!

Girlfriends were often critical components of the charade, used to protect a youth from self-awareness and to screen him from the accusatory eyes of male peers. Girlfriends were material, not sexual, objects.

Peter, a 17-year-old high school senior, was seldom home while growing up. His parents always encouraged him to "be involved" and Peter readily acceded. This was not difficult because of his penchant for always saying and doing the right thing. Though he was voted "most popular" student during his junior year in high school, there was one part of himself which Peter feared would destroy his popularity. This secret part he felt needed to remain hidden.

I had crushes in early adolescence. One girl and two guys. Before seventh [grade] I had no homosexuality. I wanted to go out with this one girl, but she was hard to get because she was with this other boy and very pretty. I was at the time struggling with being slightly overweight.

By eighth [grade] I began to recognize feelings for male classmates, but I didn't see myself as gay because I liked girls. By ninth [grade] the homosexuality grew stronger. Like, why was I thinking these things?

My first doubt about myself came last year when I was sixteen and I saw on a TV talk show male strippers, models, and dancers. I had feelings toward them I wanted to explore, but I was afraid. I kept it inside. Girlfriends I used as scapegoats, to hide from others—and maybe myself—and to protect me. It was gradual realization. I was seventy-five percent sure I was gay, but I still kept up the hope I wasn't

So, by eleventh [grade] I saw myself as bisexual and I still do, but I lean toward homosexuality.

A growing consciousness of same-sex attractions was particularly difficult for youths who reported feeling sexless during childhood and who actively participated in masculine sports and activities with other boys. Similar to Jack and Peter, most attempted to suppress the onslaught of their homoerotic libido shortly after pubertal onset. Progress toward a gay or bisexual identity was gradual; for some it may become a lifelong process.

Conclusion

The data provided by the 44 gay and bisexual youths support the thesis that although there were common routes to the development of an adult gay or bisexual identity, there was considerable diversity in the particulars. From an early age, the vast majority of the youths believed that they were "different" from other boys their age and that regardless of the source of this feeling, it was a natural aspect of themselves. Same-sex attractions and affections emerged early and were given sexual meaning with the onset of puberty.

Three broad patterns characterized the youths' awareness, interpretation, and affective response to childhood and early adolescent sexual attractions. The most common, shared by two thirds of the youths, consisted of same-sex attractions, which were identified as originating from earliest childhood memories. These attractions felt natural, instinctual, and omnipresent. Many of these youths stated that they "always felt gay." During childhood most recognized that these feelings were not typical of other boys and that it would be wrong to express them because of family and peer prohibitions toward such feelings. Others simply assumed that all boys felt as they did.

These boys were neither particularly masculine nor feminine in their behavior, except for their sexual attractions. They could not understand why other boys were not as preoccupied as they were with homoerotic desires. In this regard, they felt unmasculine but they did not thus construe themselves as feminine.

A second group was composed of gay and bisexual youths who shared this natural, early disposition of same-sex attractions but who were dominated by an overwhelming sense that their differentness could be attributed to their failure to duplicate typical masculine characteristics. In many respects, these youths typified the stereotype that many gay and nongay people have of gay males: cross-gendered in behavior, personality, and interests. The feminized youths detested cultural definitions of masculinity and felt at odds with other boys because they did not share their interests in participating in team sports (especially football and baseball), competition, and aggressive pursuits. Because of their gender nonconformity, they were frequently ostracized by male peers.

To avoid becoming ostracized, they elicited friendships from girls, perhaps because of common interests, including attractions to boys. They were familiar with the arts, creativity, clothing, gentleness, and other features our culture deems feminine. They felt more comfortable and greater camaraderie with girls and their activities than with boys. Few wanted to change either their genitalia or their behavior; they did not view themselves as women in disguise—they were simply repulsed by the "grossness" of masculinity and attracted to the sensitivities of femininity. They were often outcasts in the world of their male peers, an outcome they felt was unfair and unnecessary, but inevitable.

By contrast was the relatively infrequent third pattern, masculinized gay and bisexual youths. By disposition they looked and acted like other boys their age. Their participation in typical masculine pursuits "fooled" peers into believing that they were not gay. The youths were often perceived to be social butterflies, and they actively engaged in male–male competitive sports. Their male friendships were critical to maintain. They wanted to be members of the "male crowd'; they enjoyed being with boys, seeing boys, and smelling boys. They craved the male touch and would do anything to receive it, particularly through participation in sports.

These youths denied that they had sexual feelings or attractions during childhood, perhaps because the direction of their sexual attractions was too threatening to allow into their consciousness. Their pursuit of girlfriends granted them a facade of heterosexuality and a postponement of coming out to self and others. From all appearances each of these youths was "one of the guys" and thus heavily invested in concealing his secret, which, if exposed, would threaten that status.

Similar to the other gay and bisexual boys, homoerotic attractions became too difficult to ignore with the onset of puberty. They tried to shield this information from others because of their overwhelming fear that peers would ostracize them. If teammates discovered the true nature of the youth's sexual desires and lusts, they would be shocked and, according to the interviewee, rejecting. Because of their masculinity, many of these youths masked their homosexuality for many years, appearing to be prototypical, all-American boys. The prize was heterosexual male privilege, such as leadership positions, peer acceptance, popularity, and after-school jobs; the cost, denial of their sexuality, constant fear of losing their masculinity in the eyes of others and

themselves, and a life of lies and unfulfilled potential.

Unknown is the etiology of these patterns and their long-term effects on other aspects of the youths' development, including sexual identity and psychological health. Although several of the youths interviewed experienced same-sex attractions as arising abruptly and "unexpectedly," for the vast majority these feelings emerged as gradual, inevitable, and not particularly surprising. The incorporation of these patterns may be less a matter of choice than an experienced "naturalness" that is derived both from one's biological heritage and from socialization processes that began at an early age. One youth reflected on his emerging sexuality: "It was like being visited by an old friend." There was little indication that these patterns changed during the course of childhood and adolescence among the interviewed youths.

The most pervasive finding was that puberty eroticized these early same-sex affectional attractions, converting them to sexual desires. Puberty brought an acute awareness that same-sex attractions have a sexual component to them. Regardless of their pattern of awareness and interpretation, most of the youths did not immediately embrace their homosexuality and come out to themselves and others with the onset of puberty. Relatively few responded in a positive way to their same-sex desires immediately after pubertal onset. Many youths suppressed from consciousness their homoerotic attractions, allowing them to surface only gradually over an extended period of time. They paid their homoerotic feelings little heed, postponing the consequences for identity until the future. After all, they reasoned, this might be just a phase.

Because few youths believed that they could control their sexual feelings and desires, they ultimately felt that they did not choose their sexual orientation or sexual attractions. Awareness of homoeroticism may have emerged early or late, prior to puberty or thereafter, surfaced gradually or arrived impetuously and instantaneously, felt normal or wrong, or motivated sexual activity or abstinence—yet, it was one aspect of the self that was present without invitation. The development from same-sex attractions to a gay or bisexual identity was simply an unfolding of that which was already present, with puberty playing a crucial role in clarifying that homosensuality had a sexual component. The eventual incorporation of a gay or bisexual identity involved a recognition of that which the homoerotic attractions and sexual behavior meant.

For youths who were consciously aware of their same-sex lust, the sense that this information was not to be shared with others was pervasive. Although homoerotic desires may have felt natural, the youths were told by parents, friends, religious leaders, teachers, and dogma that these attractions were evil and sinful. Many knew that their homosexuality was ill-advised but did not think that it was therefore sick or immoral.

The exploration of these issues is an important endeavor because educators, researchers, and clinicians know little regarding how sexual identity is formed among sexual minorities. For example, it is not known if all patterns are equally healthy or if these patterns are lifelong characteristics. Unquestioned, however, is that from these same-sex attractions emerge first sexual encounters, which can occur during the earliest years of childhood or wait until young adulthood. Similar to initial sexual attractions, they too are interpreted in diverse ways, and these interpretations must be explored.

Notes

1. This [article] is based on data that appear in my manuscript currently in preparation and tentatively titled *Sex and Sexual Identity Among Gay and Bisexual Male Youths.*

2. The stories are usually a very close approximation to that which was reported. I also took the liberty of adding grammatical details and punctuation to aid understanding.

T he old social science orthodoxy about sex-role socialization, from the 1950s until today, held that three institutions—family, church, and school—formed the primary sites of socialization, and the impact of education, family values, and religious training was decisive in shaping people's lives. This view tended to emphasize the centrality of adults in boys' lives. Because adults themselves were constructing the models of socialization, this conclusion seems understandable. But as social scientists began to ask boys and girls about the forces that influenced them, they heard about the increasing importance of peer groups and the media—two arenas where adults had far less reach. In recent years, researchers have begun to explore how homosocial peer groups affect men's lives.

The articles in Part Three focus on masculinities in college, a place where the all-male peer group is

PART THREE

Collegiate Masculinities: Privilege and Peril

especially salient. How does collegiate life organize and reproduce the definitions of masculinity that we learn as young boys? How do specific all-male subcultures develop within these institutions, and what roles do they play? Part Three explores male bonding within collegiate organizations such as fraternities and athletic teams, and within the traditions of an all-male military institution. In recent years these institutions have been increasingly scrutinized and criticized, and some group members have felt besieged and unfairly picked on. Who's right?

Two articles, by Peter Lyman and by A. Ayres Boswell and Joan Z. Spade, focus on fraternities and their role in campus life. They discuss how hegemonic masculinity is reproduced in fraternity life. Why are men in some fraternities more likely to be accused of sexual assault? Todd W. Crosset, Jeffrey R. Benedict, and Mark A. McDonald report

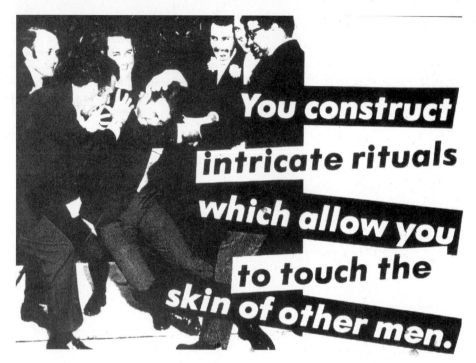

Photo courtesy of Barbara Kruger.

TANK McNAMARA®

by Jeff Millar & Bill Hinds

Tank McNamara © 1989 Millar/Hinds. Distributed by Universal Press Syndicate. Reprinted with permission. All rights reserved.

the results of a survey about the relationship between campus sexual assault and participation in NCAA athletics. Finally, Judi Addelston and Michael Stirratt look at an all-male institution's "last stand" against coeducation and the gender issues that were raised by The Citadel trial.

15

ARTICLE

Peter Lyman

The Fraternal Bond as a Joking Relationship: A Case Study of the Role of Sexist Jokes in Male Group Bonding

One evening during dinner, 45 fraternity men suddenly broke into the dining room of a nearby campus sorority, surrounded the 30 women residents, and forced them to watch while one pledge gave a speech on Freud's theory of penis envy as another demonstrated various techniques of masturbation with a rubber penis. The women sat silently, staring downward at their plates, and listened for about 10 minutes, until a woman law student who was the graduate resident in charge of the house walked in, surveyed the scene and demanded, "Please leave immediately!" As she later described that moment, "There was a mocking roar from the men, 'It's tradition.' I said, 'That's no reason to do something like this, please leave!' And they left. I was surprised. Then the women in the house started to get angry. And the guy who made the penis-envy speech came back and said to us, 'That was funny to me. If that's not funny to you I don't know what kind of sense of humor you have, but I'm sorry.' "

That night the women sat around the stairwell of their house discussing the event, some

From *Changing Men*, edited by Michael Kimmel. Newbury Park, CA: Sage Publications, 1987. Reprinted by permission.

angry and others simply wanting to forget the whole thing. They finally decided to ask the university to require that the men return to discuss the event. When university officials threatened to take action, the men agreed to the meeting. I had served as a faculty resident in student housing for two years and had given several talks in the dorm about humor and gender, and was asked by both the men and the women involved to attend the discussion as a facilitator, and was given permission to take notes and interview the participants later, provided I concealed their identities.

The penis-envy ritual had been considered a successful joke in previous years by both "the guys and the girls," but this year it failed, causing great tension between two groups that historically had enjoyed a friendly joking relationship. In the women's view, the joke had not failed because of its subject; they considered sexual jokes to be a normal part of the erotic joking relationship between men and women. They thought it had failed because of its emotional structure, the mixture of sexuality with aggression and the atmosphere of physical intimidation in the room that signified that the women were the object of a joking relationship between the men. A few women argued that the failed joke exposed the latent domination in men's relation to women, but this view was labeled "feminist" because it endangered the possibility of reconstituting the erotic joking relationship with the men. Although many of the men individually regretted the damage to their relationship with women friends in the group, they argued that the special male bond created by sexist humor is a unique form of intimacy that justified the inconvenience caused the women. In reinterpreting these stories as social constructions of gender, I will focus upon the way the joke form and joking relationships reveal the emotional currents underlying gender in this situation.

The Sociology of Jokes

Although we conventionally think of jokes as a meaningless part of the dramaturgy of everyday life, this convention is part of the way that the social function of jokes is concealed and is necessary if jokes are to "work." It is when jokes fail that the social conflicts that the joke was to reconstruct or "negotiate" are uncovered, and the tensions and emotions that underlie the conventional order of everyday social relations are revealed.

Joking is a special kind of social relationship that suspends the rules of everyday life in order to preserve them. Jokes indirectly express the emotions and tensions that may disrupt everyday life by "negotiating" them (Emerson, 1969, 1970), reconstituting group solidarity by shared aggression and cathartic laughter. The ordinary consequences of forbidden words are suspended by meta-linguistic gestures (tones of voice, facial expressions, catch phrases) that send the message "this is a joke," and emotions that would ordinarily endanger a social relationship can be spoken safely within the micro-world created by the "the joke form" (Bateson, 1955).

Yet jokes are not just stories, they are a theater of domination in everyday life, and the success or failure of a joke marks the boundary within which power and aggression may be used in a relationship. Nearly all jokes have an aggressive content, indeed shared aggression toward an outsider is one of the primary ways by which a group may overcome internal tension and assert its solidarity (Freud, 1960, p. 102). Jokes both require and renew social bonds; thus Radcliffe-Brown pointed out that "joking relationships" between mothers-in-law and their sons-in-law provide a release for tension for people structurally bound to each other but at the same time feeling structural conflict with each other (Radcliffe-Brown, 1959). Joking relationships in medicine, for example, are a medium for the indirect expression of latent emotions or taboo topics that if directly expressed would challenge the physician's authority or disrupt the need to treat life and death situations as ordinary work (see Coser, 1959; Emerson, 1969, 1970).

In each of the studies cited above, the primary focus of the analysis was upon the social function of the joke, not gender, yet in each case the joke either functioned through a joking relationship between men and women, such as in Freud's or Radcliffe-Brown's analysis of mother-in-law jokes, or through the joking relationship between men and women. For example, Coser describes the role of nurses as a safe target of jokes: as a surrogate for the male doctor in patient jokes challenging medical authority; or as a surrogate for the patient in the jokes with which doctors expressed anxiety. Sexist jokes, therefore, should be analyzed not only in general terms of the function of jokes as a means of defending social order, but in specific terms as the mechanism by which the order of gender domination is sustained in everyday life. From this perspective, jokes reveal the way social organizations are gendered, namely, built around the emotional rules of male bonding. In this case study, gender is not only the primary content of men's jokes, but the emotional structures of the male bond is built upon a joking relationship that "negotiates" the tension men feel about their relationship with each other, and with women.

Male bonding in everyday life frequently takes the form of a group joking relationship by which men create a serial kind of intimacy to "negotiate" the latent tension and aggression they feel toward each other. The humor of male bonding relationships generally is sexual and aggressive, and frequently consists of sexist or racist jokes. As Freud (1960, p. 99) observed, the jokes that individual men direct toward women are generally erotic, tend to clever forms (like the double entendre), and have a seductive purpose. The jokes that men tell about women in the presence of other men are sexual and aggressive rather than erotic and use hostile rather than clever verbal forms; and, this paper will argue, have the creation of male group bonding as their purpose. While Freud analyzed jokes in order to reveal the unconscious, in this article, relationships will be analyzed to uncover the emotional dynamics of male friendships.

The failed penis-envy joke reveals two kinds of joking relationships between college men and women. First, the attempted joke was part of an ongoing joking relationship between "the guys and the girls," as they called each other. The guys used the joking relationship to negotiate the tension they felt between sexual interest in the girls and fear of commitment to them. The guys contrasted their sense of independence and play in male friendships to the sense of dependence they felt in their relationships with women, and used hostile joking to negotiate their fear of the "loss of control" implied by intimacy. Second, the failure of the joke uncovered the use of sexist jokes in creating bonds between men; through their own joking relationships (which they called friendship), the guys negotiated the tension between their need for intimacy with other men and

their fear of losing their autonomy as men to the authority of the work world.

The Girls' Story

The women frequently had been the target of fraternity initiation rites in the past, and generally enjoyed this joking relationship with the men, if with a certain ambivalence. "There was a naked Christmas Carol event, they were singing 'We wish you a Merry Christmas,' and 'Bring on the hasty pudding' was the big line they liked to yell out. And we had five or six pledges who had to strip in front of the house and do naked jumping jacks on the lawn, after all the women in the house were lined up on the steps to watch." The women did not think these events were hostile because they had been invited to watch, and the men stood with them watching, suggesting that the pledges, not the women, were the targets of the joke. This made the joke sexual, not sexist, and part of the normal erotic joking relationship between the guys and girls. Still, these jokes were ritual events, not real social relationships; one woman said, "We were just supposed to watch, and the guys were watching us watch. The men set up the stage and the women are brought along to observe. They were the controlling force, then they jump into the car and take off."

At the meeting with the men, two of the women spoke for the group while 11 others sat silently in the center, surrounded by about 30 men. Each tried to explain to the men why the joke had not been funny. The first began, "I'm a feminist, but I'm not going to blame anyone for anything. I just want to talk about my feelings." When she said, "these guys pile in, I mean these huge guys," the men exploded in loud cathartic laughter, and the women joined in, releasing some of the tension of the meeting. She continued, "Your humor was pretty funny as long as it was sexual, but when it went beyond sexual to sexist, then it became painful. You were saying 'I'm better than you.' When you started using sex as a way of proving your superiority it hurt me and made me angry."

The second woman speaker criticized the imposition of the joke form itself, saying that the men's raid had the tone of a symbolic rape. "I admit we knew you were coming over, and we were whispering about it. But it went too far, and I felt afraid to say anything. Why do men always think about women in terms of violating them, in sexual imagery? You have to understand that the combination of a sexual topic with the physical threat of all of you standing around terrified me. I couldn't move. You have to realize that when men combine sexuality and force it's terrifying to women." This woman alluded to having been sexually assaulted in the past, but spoke in a nonthreatening tone that made the men listen silently.

The women spoke about feeling angry about the invasion of their space, about the coercion of being forced to listen to the speeches, and about being used as the object of a joke. But they reported their anger as a psychological fact, a statement about a past feeling, not an accusation. Many began by saying, "I'm not a feminist, but . . . ," to reassure the men that although they felt angry, they were not challenging traditional gender relations. The women were caught in a double-bind; if they spoke angrily to the men they would violate the taboo against the expression of anger by women (Miller, 1976, p. 102). If they said nothing, they would internalize their anger, and traditional feminine culture would encourage them to feel guilty about feeling angry at all (Bernardez, 1978; Lerner, 1980). In part they resolved the issue by accepting the men's construction of the event as a joke, although a failed joke; accepting the joke form absolved the men of responsibility, and transformed a debate about gender into a debate about good and bad jokes.

To be accepted as a joke, a cue must be sent to establish a "frame" [for] the latent hostility of the joke content in a safe context; the men sent such a cue when they stood next to the women during the naked jumping jacks. If the cue "this is a joke" is ambiguous, or is not accepted, the aggressive content of the joke is revealed and generally is responded to with anger or aggression, endangering the relationship. In part the women were pointing out to the men that the cue "this is a joke" had not been given in this case, and the aggressive content of the joke hurt them. If the cue is given properly and accepted, the everyday rules of social order are suspended and the rule "this is fun" is imposed on the expression of hostility.

Verbal aggression mediated by the joke form generally will be [accepted] without later consequences in the everyday world, and will be judged in terms of the formal intention of jokes, shared play marked by laughter in the interest of social order. By complaining to the university, the women had suspended the rules of joke culture, and attempted to renegotiate them by bringing in an observer; even this turned out to be too aggressive, and the women retreated to traditional gender relationships. The men had formally accepted this shift of rules in order to avoid punishment from the university, however their defense of the joke form was tacitly a defense of traditional gender rules that would define male sexist jokes toward women as erotic, not hostile.

In accepting the construction of the event as "just a joke" the women absolved the men of responsibility for their actions by calling them "little boys." One woman said, "It's not wrong, they're just boys playing a prank. They're little boys, they don't know what they're doing. It was unpleasant, but we shouldn't make a big deal out of it." In appealing to the rules of the joke form the men were willing to sacrifice their relationship to the women to protect the rules. In calling the men "little boys" the women were bending the rules trying to preserve the relationship through a patient nurturing role (see Gilligan, 1982, p. 44).

In calling the guys "little boys," the girls had also created a kind of linguistic symmetry between "the boys and the girls." With the exception of the law student, who called the girls "women," the students called the men "guys" and the women "girls." Earlier in the year the law student had started a discussion about this naming practice. The term "women" had sexual connotations that made "the girls" feel vulnerable, and "gals," the parallel to "guys," connoted "older women" to them. While the term "girls" refers to children, it was adopted because it avoided sexual connotations. Thus the women had no term like "the guys," which is a bonding term that refers to a group of friends as equals; the women often used the term "the guys" to refer to themselves in a group. As the men's speeches were to make clear, the term "guys" refers to a bond that is exclusively male, which is founded upon the emotional structure of the joke form, and which justifies it.

The Guys' Story

Aside from the roar of laughter when a woman referred to their intimidating size, the men interrupted the women only once. When a woman began to say that the men obviously intended to intimidate them, the men loudly protested that the women couldn't possibly judge their intentions, that they intended the whole event only as a joke, and the intention of a joke is, by definition, just fun.

At this point the two black men in the fraternity intervened to explain the rules of male joke culture to the women. The black men said that in a sense they understood what the women meant, it is painful being the object of aggressive jokes. In fact, they said, the collective talk of the fraternity at meals and group events was made up of nothing but jokes, including many racist jokes. One said, "I know what you mean. I've had to listen to things in the house that I'd have hit someone for saying if I'd heard them

outside." There was again cathartic laughter among the guys, for the male group bond consisted almost entirely of aggressive words that were barely contained by the responsibility absolving rule of the joke form. A woman responded, "Maybe people should be hit for saying those things, maybe that's the right thing to do." But the black speaker was trying to explain the rules of male joke culture to the women, "if you'd just ignored us, it wouldn't have been any fun." To ignore a joke, even though it makes you feel hurt or angry, is to show strength or coolness, the two primary masculine ideals of the group.

Another man tried to explain the failure of the joke in terms of the difference between the degree of "crudeness" appropriate among the guys and between "guys and girls." He said, "As I was listening at the edge of the room, near the door, and when I looked at the guys I was laughing but when I looked at the girls I was embarrassed. I could see both sides at the same time. It was too crude for your sense of propriety. We have a sense of crudeness you don't have. That's a cultural aspect of the difference between girls and guys."

The other men laughed as he mentioned "how crude we are at the house," and one of the black men added, "you wouldn't believe how crude it gets." Many of the men said privately that while they individually found the jokes about women vulgar, the jokes were justified because they were necessary for the formation of the fraternal bond. These men thought the mistake had been to reveal their crudeness to the women, this was "in bad taste."

In its content, the fraternal bond was almost entirely a joking relationship. In part, the joking was a kind of "signifying" or "dozens," a ritual exchange of insults that functioned to create group solidarity. "If there's one theme that goes on, it's the emphasis on being able to take a lot of ridicule, of shit, and not getting upset about it. Most of the interaction we have is verbally abusing each other, making disgusting references to your mother's sexuality, or the women you were seen with, or your sex organ, the size of your sex organ. And you aren't cool unless you can take it without trying to get back." Being cool is an important male value in other settings as well, such as sports or work; the joke form is a kind of male pedagogy in that, in one guy's words, it teaches "how to keep in control of your emotions."

But the guys themselves would not have described their group as a joking relationship or even as a male bond; they called it friendship. One man said he had found perhaps a dozen guys in the house who were special friends, "guys I could cry in front of." Yet in interviews, no one could recall any of the guys actually crying in front of each other. One said, "I think the guys are very close, they would do nearly anything for each other, drive each other places, give each other money. I think when they have problems about school, their car, or something like that, they can talk to each other. I'm not sure they can talk to each other about problems with women though." The image of crying in front of the other guys was a moving symbol of intimacy to the guys, but in fact crying would be an admission of vulnerability, which would violate the ideals of "strength" and "being cool."

Although the fraternal bond was idealized as a unique kind of intimacy upon which genuine friendship was built, the content of the joking relationship was focused upon women, including much "signifying" talk about mothers. The women interpreted the sexist jokes as a sign of vulnerability. "The thing that struck me the most about our meeting together," one said, "was when the men said they were afraid of trusting women, afraid of being seen as jerks." According to her, this had been the women's main reaction to the meeting by the other women, "How do you tell men that they don't have to be afraid, and what do you do with women who abuse that kind of trust?" One of the men on the boundary of the group remarked that the most hostile misogynist jokes

came from the men with the fewest intimate relationships with women. "I think down deep all these guys would love to have satisfying relationships with women. I think they're scared of failing, of having to break away from the group they've become comfortable with. I think being in a fraternity, having close friendships with men is a replacement for having close relationships with women. It'd be painful for them because they'd probably fail."

Joking mobilized the commitment of the men to the group by policing the individual men's commitments to women and minimized the possibility of dyadic withdrawal from the group (see Slater, 1963). "One of the guys just acquired a girlfriend a few weeks ago. He's someone I don't think has had a woman to be friends with, maybe ever, at least in a long time. Everybody has been ribbing him intensely the last few weeks. It's good natured in tone. Sitting at dinner they've invented a little song they sing to him. People yell questions about his girlfriend, the size of her vagina, does she have big breasts."

Since both the jokes and the descriptions of the parties have strong homoerotic overtones, including the exchange of women as sexual partners, jokes were also targeted at homosexuality, to draw an emotional line between the homosocial male bond and homosexual relationships. Being called "queer," however, did not require a sexual relationship with another man, but only visible signs of vulnerability or nurturing behavior.

Male Bonding as a Joking Relationship

Fraternal bonding is an intimate kind of male group friendship that suspends the ordinary rules and responsibilities of everyday life through joking relationships. To the guys, dyadic friendship with a woman implied "loss of control," namely, responsibility for work and family. In dealing with women, the group separated intimacy from sex, defining the male bond as intimate but not sexual (homosocial), and relationships with women as sexual but not intimate (heterosexual). The intimacy of group friendship was built upon shared spontaneous action, "having fun," rather than the self-disclosure that marks women's friendships (see Rubin, 1983, p. 13). One of the men had been inexpressive as he listened to the discussion, but spoke about fun in a voice filled with emotion, "The penis-envy speech was a hilarious idea, great college fun. That's what I joined the fraternity for, a good time. College is a stage in my life to do crazy and humorous things. In 10 years when I'm in the business world I won't be able to carry on like this [again cathartic laughter from the men]. The initiation was intended to be humorous. We didn't think through how sensitive you women were going to be."

This speech gives the fraternal bond a specific place in the life cycle. The joking relationship is a ritual bond that creates a male group bond in the transition between boyhood and manhood, after the separation from the family, where the authority of mothers limits fun, but before becoming subject to the authority of work. One man later commented on the transitional nature of the male bond, "I think a lot of us are really scared of losing total control over our own lives. Having to sacrifice our individuality. I think we're scared of work in the same way we're scared of women." In this sense individuality is associated with what the guys called "strength," both the emotional strength suggested by being cool, and the physical strength suggested by facing the risks of sports and the paramilitary games they liked to play.

The emotional structure of the joking relationship is built upon the guys' latent anger about the discipline that middle-class male roles imposed upon them, both marriage rules and work rules. The general relationship between organization of men's work and men's domination of women was noted by Max Weber (1958,

pp. 345–346), who described "the vocational specialist" as a man mastered by the rules of organization that create an impersonal kind of dependence, and who therefore seeks to create a feeling of independence through the sexual conquest of women. In each of the epochs of Western history, Weber argues, the subordination of men at work has given rise to a male concept of freedom based upon the violation of women. Although Weber tied dependence upon rules to men's need for sexual conquest through seduction, this may also be a clue to the meaning of sexist jokes and joking relationships among men at work. Sexist jokes may not be simply a matter of recreation or a means of negotiating role stress, they may be a reflection of the emotional foundations of organizational life for men. In everyday work life, sexist jokes may function as a ritual suspension of the rules of responsibility for men, a withdrawal into a microworld in which their anger about dependence upon work and women may be safely expressed.

In analyzing the contradictions and vulnerabilities the guys felt about relationships with women and the responsibilities of work, I will focus upon three dimensions of the joking relationship: (1) the emotional content of the jokes; (2) the erotics of rule breaking created by the rules of the joke form; and (3) the image of strength and "being cool" they pitted against the dependence represented by both women and work.

The Emotional Dynamic of Sexist Jokes

When confronted by the women, the men defended the joke by asserting the formal rule that the purpose of jokes is play, then by justifying the jokes as necessary in order to create a special male bond. The defense that jokes are play defines aggressive behavior as play. This defense was far more persuasive to the men than to the women, since many forms of male bonding play are rule-governed aggression, as in sports and games. The second defense, asserting the relation between sexist jokes and male bonds, points out the social function of sexist jokes among the guys, to control the threat that individual men might form intimate emotional bonds with women and withdraw from the group. Each defense poses a puzzle about the emotional dynamics of male group friendship, for in each case male group friendship seems more like a defense against vulnerability than a positive ideal.

In each defense, intimacy is split from sexuality in order to eroticize the male bond, thereby creating an instrumental sexuality directed at women. The separation of intimacy from sexuality transforms women into "sexual objects," which both justifies aggression at women by suspending their relationships to the men and devalues sexuality itself, creating a disgust at women as the sexual "object" unworthy of intimate attention. What is the origin of this conjunction between the devaluation of sexuality and the appropriation of intimacy for the male bond?

Chodorow (1978, p. 182) argues that the sense of masculine identity is constructed by an early repression of the son's erotic bond with his mother; with this repression the son's capacity for intimacy and commitment is devalued as feminine behavior. Henceforth men feel ambivalent about intimate relationships with women, seeking to replicate the fusion of intimacy and sexuality that they had experienced in their primal relationships to their mothers, but at the same time fearing engulfment by women in heterosexual relationships, like the engulfment of their infant selves by their mothers (Chodorow, 1976). Certainly the content of the group's joke suggests this repression of the attachment to the mother, as well as hostility to her authority in the family. One man reported, "There're an awful lot of jokes about people's mothers. If any topic of conversation dominates the conversation it's 'heard your mother was with Ray [one of the guys] last night.' The guys will say incredibly vulgar things about their mothers, or they'll talk about the anatomy of a guy's girlfriends, or women they'd like to sleep with." While the guys' signifying mother jokes suggest the repression Chodorow describes, the men realized that their view of women made it unlikely that marriage would be a positive experience. One said, "I think a lot of us expect to marry someone pretty enough that other men will think we got a good catch, someone who is at least marginally interesting to chat with, but not someone we'd view as a friend. But at the same time, a woman who will make sufficient demands that we won't be able to have any friends. So we'll be stuck for the rest of our lives without friends."

While the emotional dynamic of men's "heterosexual knots" may well begin in this primordial separation of infant sons from mothers, its structure is replicated in the guys' ambivalence about their fathers, and their anger about the dependence upon rules in the work world. Yet the guys themselves described the fraternal bond as a way of creating "strength" and overcoming dependence, which suggests a positive ideal of male identity. In order to explore the guys' sense of the value of the male bond, their conception of strength and its consequences for the way they related to each other and to women has to be taken seriously.

Strength

Ultimately the guys justified the penis-envy joke because it created a special kind of male intimacy, but while the male group is able to appropriate its members' needs for intimacy and commitment, it is not clear that it is able to satisfy those needs, because strength has been defined as the opposite of intimacy. "Strength" is a value that represents solidarity rather than intimacy, the solidarity of a shared risk in rule-governed aggressive competition; its value is suggested by the cathartic laughter when the first woman speaker said, "These guys poured in, these huge guys."

The eros detached from sexuality is attached to rules, not to male friends; the male bond consists of an erotic toward rules, and yet the penis-envy joke expresses most of all the guys' ambivalence about rules. Like "the lads," the male gangs who roam the English countryside, "getting in trouble" by enforcing social mores in unsocial ways (Peters, 1972), "the guys" break the rules in rule-governed ways. The joke form itself suggests this ambivalence about rules and acts as a kind of pedagogy about the relationship between rules and aggression in male work culture. The joke form expresses emotions and tensions that might endanger the order of the organization, but that must be spoken lest they damage social order. Jokes can create group solidarity only if they allow dangerous things to be said; allow a physical catharsis of tension through laughter; or create the solidarity of an "in group" through shared aggression against an "out group." In each case there is an erotic in joke forms: an erotic of shared aggression, of shared sexual feeling, or an erotic of rule breaking itself.

It has been suggested that male groups experience a high level of excitement and sexual arousal in public acts of rule breaking (Thorne & Luria, 1986). The penis-envy speech is precisely such an act, a breaking of conventional moral rules in the interest of group arousal. In each of the versions of the joking relationship in this group there is such an erotic quality: in the sexual content of the jokes, in the need for women to witness dirty talk or naked pledges, in the eros of aggression of the raid and jokes themselves. The penis-envy speech, a required event for all members of the group, is such a collective violation of the rules, and so is the content of their talk, a collective dirty talking that violates moral rules. The cathartic laughter that greeted the words, "You wouldn't believe what we say at the house," testifies to the emotional charge invested in dirty talk.

Because the intimacy of the guys' bond is built around an erotic of rule breaking, it has the serial structure of shared risk rather than the social structure of shared intimacy. In writing about the shared experience of suffering and danger of men at war, J. Glenn Gray (1959, pp. 89–90) distinguishes two kinds of male bonding, comradeship and friendship. Comradeship is based upon an erotic of shared danger, but is based upon the loss of an individual sense of self to a group identity, while friendship is based upon an individual's intellectual and emotional affinity to another individual. In the eros of friendship one's sense of self is heightened; in the eros of comradeship a sense of self is replaced by a sense of group membership. In this sense the guys were seeking comradeship, not friendship, hence the group constructed its bond through an erotic of shared activities with an element of risk, shared danger, or rule breaking: in sports, in paramilitary games, in wild parties, in joking relations. The guys called the performance of these activities "strength," being willing to take risks as a group and remaining cool.

Thus the behavior that the women defined as aggressive was seen by the men as a contest of strength governed by the rules of the joke form, to which the proper response would have been to remain "cool." To the guys, the masculine virtue of "strength" has a positive side, to discover oneself and to discover a sense of the other person through a contest of strength that is governed by rules. To the guys, "strength" is not the same as power or aggression because it is governed by rules, not anger; it is anger that is "uncool."

"Being Cool"

It is striking that the breaking of rules was not spontaneous, but controlled by the rules of the joke form: that aggressive talk replaces action; that talk is framed by a social form that requires the consent of others; that talk should not be taken seriously. This was the lesson that the black men tried to teach the women in the group session: In the male world, aggression is not defined as violent if it is rule governed rather than anger governed. The fraternal bond was built upon this emotional structure, for the life of the group centered upon the mobilization of aggressive energies in rule-governed activities (in sports, games, jokes, parties), in each arena aggression was highly valued (strength) only when it was rule governed (cool). Getting angry was called "losing control" and the guys thought they were most likely to lose control when they experienced themselves as personally dependent, as in relationships with women and at work.

Rule-governed aggression is a conduct that is very useful to organizations, in that it mobilizes aggressive energies but binds them to order by rules (see Benjamin, 1980, p. 154). The male sense of order is procedural rather than substantive because the male bond is formal (rule governed), rather than personal (based upon intimacy and commitment). Male groups in this sense are shame cultures, not guilt cultures, because the male bond is a group identity that subordinates the individual to the rules, and because social control is imposed through collective judgments about self-control, such as "strength" and "cool." The sense of order within such male groups is based upon the belief that all members are equally dependent upon the rules and that no personal dependence is created within the group. This is not true of the family or of relations with women, both of which are intimate, and, from the guys' point of view, are "out of control" because they are governed by emotion.

The guys face contradictory demands from work culture about the use of aggressive behavior. Aggressive conduct is highly valued in a competitive society when it serves the interests of the organization, but men also face a strong taboo against the expression of anger at work when it is not rule governed. "Competition" imposes certain rules upon aggressive group processes: Aggression must be calculated, not angry; it must be consistent with the power hierarchy of the organization, serving authority

and not challenging it; if expressed, it must be indirect, as in jokes; it must serve the needs of group solidarity, not of individual autonomy. Masculine culture separates anger from aggression when it combines the value "strength" with the value "being cool." While masculine cultures often define the expression of anger as "violent" or "loss of control," anger, properly defined, is speech, not action; angry speech is the way we can defend our sense of integrity and assert our sense of justice. Thus it is anger that challenges the authority of the rules, not aggressive behavior in itself, because anger defends the self, not the organization.

The guys' joking relationship taught them a pedagogy for the controlled use of aggression in the work world, to be able to compete aggressively without feeling angry. The guys recognized the relationship between their male bond and the work world by claiming that "high officials of the university know about the way we act and they understand what we are doing." While this might be taken as evidence that the guys were internalizing their fathers' norms and thus inheriting the mantle of patriarchy, the guys described their fathers as slaves to work and women, not as patriarchs. The guys also asserted themselves against the authority of their fathers by acting out against the authority of rules in the performance of "strength."

The guys clearly benefited from the male authority that gave them the power to impose the penis-envy joke upon the women with essentially no consequences. Men are allowed to direct anger and aggression toward women because social norms governing the expression of anger or humor generally replicate the power order of the group. It is striking, however, that the guys would not accept the notion that men have more power than women do; to them it is not men who rule, but rules that govern men. These men had so internalized the governing of male emotions by rules that their anger itself could emerge only indirectly through rule-governed forms, such as jokes and joking relationships. In these forms their anger could serve only order, not their sense of self or justice.

References

Bateson, G. (1972). A theory of play and fantasy. In *Steps toward an ecology of mind* (pp. 177–193). New York: Ballantine.

Benjamin, J. (1978). Authority and the family revisited, or, A world without fathers. *New German Critique, 4*(3), 13, 35–57.

Benjamin, J. (1980). The bonds of love: Rational violence and erotic domination. *Feminist Studies, 6*(1), 144–174.

Berndardez, T. (1978). Women and anger. *Journal of the American Medical Women's Association, 33*(5), 215–219.

Bly, R. (1982). What men really want: An interview with Keith Thompson. *New Age*, pp. 30–37, 50–5l.

Chodorow, N. (1976). Oedipal asymmetries, heterosexual knots. *Social Problems, 23*, 454–468.

Chodorow, N. (1978). *The reproduction of mothering*. Berkeley: University of California Press.

Coser, R. (1959). Some social functions of laughter: A study of humor in a hospital setting. *Human Relations, 12*, 171–182.

Emerson, J. (1969). Negotiating the serious import of humor. *Sociometry, 32*, 169–181.

Emerson, J. (1970). Behavior in private places. In H. P. Dreitzel (Ed.), *Recent sociology: Vol. 2. Patterns in communicative behavior*. New York: Macmillan.

Freud, S. (1960). *Jokes and their relation to the unconscious*. New York: Norton.

Gilligan, C. (1982). *In a different voice*. Cambridge, MA: Harvard University Press.

Gray, G. J. (1959). *The warriors: Reflections on men in battle*. New York: Harper & Row.

Lerner, H. E. (1980). Internal prohibitions against female anger. *American Journal of Psychoanalysis, 40*, 137–148.

Miller, J. B. (1976). *Toward a new psychology of women*. Boston: Beacon.

Peters, E. L. (1972). Aspects of the control of moral ambiguities. In M. Gluckman (Ed.), *The allocation of responsibility* (pp. 109–162). Manchester: Manchester University Press.

Radcliffe-Brown, A. (1959). *Structure and function in primitive society*. Glencoe, IL: Free Press.

Rubin, L. (1983). *Intimate strangers*. New York: Harper & Row.

Slater, P. (1963). On social regression. *American Sociological Review, 28*, 339–364.

Thorne, B., & Luria, Z. (1986). Sexuality and gender in children's daily worlds. *Social Problems*.

Weber, M. (1958). Religions of the world and their directions. In H. Gerth & C. W. Mills (Eds.), *From Max Weber*. New York: Oxford University Press.

16

ARTICLE

A. Ayres Boswell

Joan Z. Spade

Fraternities and Collegiate Rape Culture: Why Are Some Fraternities More Dangerous Places for Women?

Date rape and acquaintance rape on college campuses are topics of concern to both researchers and college administrators. Some estimate that 60 to 80 percent of rapes are date or acquaintance rape (Koss, Dinero, Seibel, and Cox 1988). Further, 1 out of 4 college women say they were raped or experienced an attempted rape, and 1 out of 12 college men say they forced a woman to have sexual intercourse against her will (Koss, Gidycz, and Wisniewski 1985).

Although considerable attention focuses on the incidence of rape, we know relatively little about the context or the *rape culture* surrounding date and acquaintance rape. Rape culture is a set of values and beliefs that provide an environment conducive to rape (Buchwald, Fletcher, & Roth 1993; Herman 1984). The term applies to a generic culture surrounding and promoting

Author's Note: An earlier version of this article was presented at the annual meeting of the American Sociological Association, August 1993. Special thanks go to Barbara Frankel, Karen Hicks, and Jennifer Volchko for their input into the process and final version and to Judith Gerson, Sue Curry Jansen, Judith Lasker, Patricia Yancey Martin, and Ronnie Steinberg for their careful readings of drafts of this article and for many helpful comments.

From *Gender & Society*, Vol. 10 No. 2, April 1996 133–147. Reprinted by permission of Sage Publications, Inc.

rape, not the specific settings in which rape is likely to occur. We believe that the specific settings also are important in defining relationships between men and women.

Some have argued that fraternities are places where rape is likely to occur on college campuses (Martin and Hummer 1989; O'Sullivan 1993; Sanday 1990) and that the students most likely to accept rape myths and be more sexually aggressive are more likely to live in fraternities and sororities, consume higher doses of alcohol and drugs, and place a higher value on social life at college (Gwartney-Gibbs and Stockard 1989; Kalof and Cargill 1991). Others suggest that sexual aggression is learned in settings such as fraternities and is not part of predispositions or preexisting attitudes (Boeringer, Shehan, and Akers 1991). To prevent further incidences of rape on college campuses, we need to understand what it is about fraternities in particular and college life in general that may contribute to the maintenance of a rape culture on college campuses.

Our approach is to identify the social contexts that link fraternities to campus rape and promote a rape culture. Instead of assuming that all fraternities provide an environment conducive to rape, we compare the interactions of men and women at fraternities identified on campus as being especially *dangerous* places for women, where the likelihood of rape is high, to those seen as *safer* places, where the perceived probability of rape occurring is lower. Prior to collecting data for our study, we found that most women students identified some fraternities as having more sexually aggressive members and a higher probability of rape. These women also considered other fraternities as relatively safe houses, where a women could go and get drunk if she wanted to and feel secure that the fraternity men would not take advantage of her. We compared parties at houses identified as high-risk and low-risk houses as well as at two local bars frequented by college students. Our analysis provides an opportunity to examine situations and contexts that hinder or facilitate positive social relations between undergraduate men and women.

The abusive attitudes toward women that some fraternities perpetuate exist within a general culture where rape is intertwined in traditional gender scripts. Men are viewed as initiators of sex and women as either passive partners or active resisters, preventing men from touching their bodies (LaPlante, McCormick, and Brannigan 1980). Rape culture is based on the assumptions that men are aggressive and dominant whereas women are passive and acquiescent (Buchwald et al. 1993; Herman 1984). What occurs on college campuses is an extension of the portrayal of domination and aggression of men over women that exemplifies the double standard of sexual behavior in U.S. society (Barthel 1988; Kimmel 1993).

Sexually active men are positively reinforced by being referred to as "studs," whereas women who are sexually active or report enjoying sex are derogatorily labeled as "sluts" (Herman 1984; O'Sullivan 1993). These gender scripts are embodied in rape myths and stereotypes such as "She really wanted it; she just said no because she didn't want me to think she was a bad girl" (Burke, Stets, and Pirog-Good 1989; Jenkins and

Dambrot 1987; Lisak and Roth 1988; Malamuth 1986; Muehlenhard and Linton 1987; Peterson and Franzese 1987). Because men's sexuality is seen as more natural, acceptable, and uncontrollable than women's sexuality, many men and women excuse acquaintance rape by affirming that men cannot control their natural urges (Miller and Marshall 1987).

Whereas some researchers explain these attitudes toward sexuality and rape using an individual or a psychological interpretation, we argue that rape has a social basis, one in which both men and women create and recreate masculine and feminine identities and relations. Based on the assumption that rape is part of the social construction of gender, we examine how men and women "do gender" on a college campus (West and Zimmerman 1987). We focus on fraternities because they have been identified as settings that encourage rape (Sanday 1990). By comparing fraternities that are viewed by women as places where there is a high risk of rape to those where women believe there is a low risk of rape as well as two local commercial bars, we seek to identify characteristics that make some social settings more likely places for the occurrence of rape.

Method

We observed social interactions between men and women at a private coeducational school in which a high percentage (49.4 percent) of students affiliate with Greek organizations. The university has an undergraduate population of approximately 4,500 students, just more than one third of whom are women; the students are primarily from upper-middle-class families. The school, which admitted only men until 1971, is highly competitive academically.

We used a variety of data collection approaches: observations of interactions between men and women at fraternity parties and bars, formal interviews, and informal conversations. The first author, a former undergraduate at this school and a graduate student at the time of the study, collected the data. She knew about the social life at the school and had established rapport and trust between herself and undergraduate students as a teaching assistant in a human sexuality course.

The process of identifying high- and low-risk fraternity houses followed Hunter's (1953) reputational approach. In our study, 40 women students identified fraternities that they considered to be high risk, or to have more sexually aggressive members and higher incidence of rape, as well as fraternities that they considered to be safe houses. The women represented all four years of undergraduate college and different living groups (sororities, residence halls, and off-campus housing). Observations focused on the four fraternities named most often by these women as high-risk houses and the four identified as low-risk houses.

Throughout the spring semester, the first author observed at two fraternity parties each weekend at two different houses (fraternities could have parties only on weekends at this campus). She also observed students' interactions in two popular university bars on weeknights to provide a comparison of students' behavior in non-Greek settings. The first local bar at which she observed was popular with seniors and older students; the second bar was popular with first-, second-, and third-year undergraduates because the management did not strictly enforce drinking age laws in this bar.

The observer focused on the social context as well as interaction among participants at each setting. In terms of social context, she observed the following: ratio of men to women, physical setting such as the party decor and theme, use and control of alcohol and level of intoxication, and explicit and implicit norms. She noted interactions between men and women (i.e., physical contract, conversational style, use of jokes) and the relations among men (i.e., their treatment of pledges and other men at fraternity parties). Other than the observer, no one knew the identity of the high- or low-risk fraternities. Although this may have introduced bias into the data collection, students on this campus who read this article before it was submitted for publication commented on how accurately the social scene is described.

In addition, 50 individuals were interviewed including men from the selected fraternities, women who attended those parties, men not affiliated with fraternities, and self-identified rape victims known to the first author. The first author approached men and women by telephone or on campus and asked them to participate in interviews. The interviews included open-ended questions about gender relations on campus, attitudes about date rape, and their own experiences on campus.

To assess whether self-selection was a factor in determining the classification of the fraternity, we compared high-risk houses to low-risk houses on several characteristics. In terms of status on campus, the high- and low-risk houses we studied attracted about the same number of pledges; however, many of the high-risk houses had more members. There was no difference in grade point averages for the two types of houses. In fact, the highest and lowest grade point averages were found in the high-risk category. Although both high- and low-risk fraternities participated in sports, brothers in the low-risk houses tended to play intramural sports whereas brothers in the high-risk houses were more likely to be varsity athletes. The high-risk houses may be more aggressive, as they had a slightly larger number of disciplinary incidents and their reports were more severe, often with physical harm to others and damage to property. Further, in year-end reports, there was more property damage in the high-risk houses. Last, more of the low-risk houses participated in a campus rape-prevention program. In summary, both high- and low-risk fraternities seem to be equally attractive to freshmen men on this campus, and differences between the eight fraternities we studied were not great; however, the high-risk houses had a slightly larger number of reports of aggression and physical destruction in the houses and the low-risk houses were more likely to participate in a rape prevention program.

Results

The Settings

Fraternity Parties   We observed several differences in the quality of the interaction of men and women at parties at high-risk fraternities compared to those at low-risk houses. A typical party at a low-risk house included an equal number of women and men. The social atmosphere was friendly, with considerable interaction between women and men. Men and women danced in groups and in couples, with many of the couples kissing and displaying affection toward each other. Brothers explained that, because many of the men in these houses had girlfriends, it was normal to see couples kissing on the dance floor. Coed groups engaged in conversations at many of these houses, with women and men engaging in friendly exchanges, giving the impression that they knew each other well. Almost no cursing and yelling was observed at parties in low-risk houses; when pushing occurred, the participants apologized. Respect for women extended to the women's bathrooms, which were clean and well supplied.

At high-risk houses, parties typically had skewed gender ratios, sometimes involving more men and other times involving more women. Gender segregation also was evident at these parties, with the men on one side of a room or in the bar drinking while women gathered in another area. Men treated women differently in the high-risk houses. The women's bathrooms in the high-risk houses were filthy, including clogged toilets and vomit in the sinks. When a brother was told of the mess in the bathroom at a high-risk house, he replied, "Good, maybe some of these beer wenches will leave so there will be more beer for us."

Men attending parties at high-risk houses treated women less respectfully, engaging in jokes, conversations, and behaviors that degraded women. Men made a display of assessing women's bodies and rated them with thumbs up or thumbs down for the other men in the sight of the women. One man attending a party at a high-risk fraternity said to another, "Did you know that this week is Women's Awareness Week? I guess that means we get to abuse them more this week." Men behaved more crudely at parties at high-risk houses. At one party, a brother dropped his pants, including his underwear, while dancing in front of several women. Another brother slid across the dance floor completely naked.

The atmosphere at parties in high-risk fraternities was less friendly overall. With the exception of greetings, men and women rarely smiled or laughed and spoke to each other less often than was the case at parties in low-risk houses. The few one-on-one conversations between women and men appeared to be strictly flirtatious (lots of eye contact, touching, and very close talking). It was rare to see a group of men and women together talking. Men were openly hostile, which made the high-risk parties seem almost threatening at times. For example, there was a lot of touching, pushing, profanity, and name calling, some done by women.

Students at parties at the high-risk houses seemed self-conscious and aware of the presence of members of the opposite sex, an awareness that was sexually charged. Dancing early in the evening was usually between women. Close to midnight, the sex ratio began to balance out with the arrival of more men or more women. Couples began to dance together but in a sexual way (close dancing with lots of pelvic thrusts). Men tried to pick up women using lines such as "Want to see my fish tank?" and "Let's go upstairs so that we can talk; I can't hear what you're saying in here."

Although many of the same people who attended high-risk parties also attended low-risk parties, their behavior changed as they moved from setting to setting. Group norms differed across contexts as well. At a party that was held jointly at a low-risk house with a high-risk fraternity, the ambience was that of a party at a high-risk fraternity with heavier drinking, less dancing, and fewer conversations between women and men. The men from both high- and low-risk fraternities were very aggressive; a fight broke out, and there was pushing and shoving on the dance floor and in general.

As others have found, fraternity brothers at high-risk houses on this campus told about routinely discussing their sexual exploits at breakfast the morning after parties and sometimes at house meetings (cf. Martin and Hummer 1989; O'Sullivan 1993; Sanday 1990). During these sessions, the brothers we interviewed said that men bragged about what they did the night before with stories of sexual conquests often told by the same men, usually sophomores. The women involved in these exploits were women they did not know or knew but did not respect, or *faceless victims*. Men usually treated girlfriends with respect and did not talk about them in these storytelling sessions. Men from low-risk houses, however, did not describe similar sessions in their houses.

The Bar Scene   The bar atmosphere and social context differed from those of fraternity parties. The music was not as loud, and both bars had places to sit and have conversations. At all fraternity parties, it was difficult to maintain conversations with loud music playing and no place to sit. The volume of music at parties at high-risk fraternities was even louder than it was at low-risk houses, making it virtually impossible to have conversations. In general, students in the local bars behaved in the same way that students did at parties in low-risk houses with conversations typical, most occurring between men and women.

The first bar, frequented by older students, had live entertainment every night of the week. Some nights were more crowded than others, and the atmosphere was friendly, relaxed, and conducive to conversation. People laughed and smiled and behaved politely toward each other. The ratio of men to women was fairly equal, with students congregating in mostly coed groups. Conversation flowed freely and people listened to each other.

Although the women and men at the first bar also were at parties at low- and high-risk fraternities, their behavior at the bar included none of the blatant sexual or intoxicated behaviors observed at some of these parties. As the evenings wore on, the number of one-on-one conversations between men and women increased and conversations shifted from small talk to topics such as war and AIDS. Conversations did not revolve around picking up another person, and most people left the bar with same-sex friends or in coed groups.

The second bar was less popular with older students. Younger students, often under the legal drinking age, went there to drink, sometimes after leaving campus parties. This bar was much smaller and usually not as crowded as the first bar. The atmosphere was more mellow and relaxed than it was at the fraternity parties. People went there to hang out and talk to each other.

On a couple of occasions, however, the atmosphere at the second bar became similar to that of a party at a high-risk fraternity. As the number of people in the bar increased, they removed chairs and tables, leaving no place to sit and talk. The music also was turned up louder, drowning out conversation. With no place to dance or sit, most people stood around but could not maintain conversations because of the noise and crowds. Interactions between women and men consisted mostly of flirting. Alcohol consumption also was greater than it was on the less crowded nights, and the number of visibly drunk people increased. The more people drank, the more conversation and socializing broke down.

The only differences between this setting and that of a party at a high-risk house were that brothers no longer controlled the territory and bedrooms were not available upstairs.

Gender Relations

Relations between women and men are shaped by the contexts in which they meet and interact. As is the case on other college campuses, *hooking up* has replaced dating on this campus, and fraternities are places where many students hook up. Hooking up is a loosely applied term on college campuses that had different meanings for men and women on this campus.

Most men defined hooking up similarly. One man said it was something that happens

> when you are really drunk and meet up with a woman you sort of know, or possibly don't know at all and don't care about. You go home with her with the intention of getting as much sexual, physical pleasure as she'll give you, which can range anywhere from kissing to intercourse, without any strings attached.

The exception to this rule is when men hook up with women they admire. Men said they are less likely to press for sexual activity with someone they know and like because they want the relationship to continue and be based on respect.

Women's version of hooking up differed. Women said they hook up only with men they cared about and described hooking up as kissing and petting but not sexual intercourse. Many women said that hooking up was disappointing because they wanted longer-term relationships. First-year women students realized quickly that hook-ups were usually one-night stands with no strings attached, but many continued to hook up because they had few opportunities to develop relationships with men on campus. One first-year woman said that "70 percent of hook-ups never talk again and try to avoid one another; 26 percent may actually hear from them or talk to them again, and 4 percent may

actually go on a date, which can lead to a relationship." Another first-year woman said, "It was fun in the beginning. You get a lot of attention and kiss a lot of boys and think this is what college is about, but it gets tiresome fast."

Whereas first-year women get tired of the hook-up scene early on, many men do not become bored with it until their junior or senior year. As one upperclassman said, "The whole game of hooking up became really meaningless and tiresome for me during my second semester of my sophomore year, but most of my friends didn't get bored with it until the following year."

In contrast to hooking up, students also described monogamous relationships with steady partners. Some type of commitment was expected, but most people did not anticipate marriage. The term *seeing each other* was applied when people were sexually involved but free to date other people. This type of relationship involved less commitment than did one of boyfriend/girlfriend but was not considered to be a hook-up.

The general consensus of women and men interviewed on this campus was that the Greek system, called "the hill," set the scene for gender relations. The predominance of Greek membership and subsequent living arrangements segregated men and women. During the week, little interaction occurred between women and men after their first year in college because students in fraternities or sororities live and dine in separate quarters. In addition, many non-Greek upperclass students move off campus into apartments. Therefore, students see each other in classes or in the library, but there is no place where students can just hang out together.

Both men and women said that fraternities dominate campus social life, a situation that everyone felt limited opportunities for meaningful interactions. One senior Greek man said,

> This environment is horrible and so unhealthy for good male and female relationships and interactions to occur. It is so segregated and male dominated. . . . It is our party, with our

rules and our beer. We are allowing these women and other men to come to our party. Men can feel superior in their domain.

Comments from a senior woman reinforced his views: "Men are dominant; they are the kings of the campus. It is their environment that they allow us to enter; therefore, we have to abide by their rules." A junior women described fraternity parties as

> good for meeting acquaintances but almost impossible to really get to know anyone. The environment is so superficial, probably because there are so many social cliques due to the Greek system. Also, the music is too loud and the people are too drunk to attempt to have a real conversation, anyway.

Some students claim that fraternities even control the dating relationships of their members. One senior woman said, "Guys dictate how dating occurs on this campus, whether it's cool, who it's with, how much time can be spent with the girlfriend and with the brothers." Couples either left campus for an evening or hung out separately with their own same-gender friends at fraternity parties, finally getting together with each other at about 2 A.M. Couples rarely went together to fraternity parties. Some men felt that a girlfriend was just a replacement for a hook-up. According to one junior man, "Basically a girlfriend is someone you go to at 2 A.M. after you've hung out with the guys. She is the sexual outlet that the guys can't provide you with."

Some fraternity brothers pressure each other to limit their time with and commitment to their girlfriends. One senior man said, "The hill [fraternities] and girlfriends don't mix." A brother described a constant battle between girlfriends and brothers over who the guy is going out with for the night, with the brothers usually winning. Brothers teased men with girlfriends with remarks such as "whipped" or "where's the ball and chain?" A brother from a high-risk house said that few brothers at his house had girlfriends; some did, but it was uncommon.

One man said that from the minute he was a pledge he knew he would probably never have a girlfriend on this campus because "it was just not the norm in my house. No one has girlfriends; the guys have too much fun with [each other]."

The pressure on men to limit their commitment to girlfriends, however, was not true of all fraternities or of all men on campus. Couples attended low-risk fraternity parties together, and men in the low-risk houses went out on dates more often. A man in one low-risk house said that about 70 percent of the members of his house were involved in relationships with women, including the pledges (who were sophomores).

Treatment of Women

Not all men held negative attitudes toward women that are typical of a rape culture, and not all social contexts promoted the negative treatment of women. When men were asked whether they treated the women on campus with respect, the most common response was "On an individual basis, yes, but when you have a group of men together, no." Men said that, when together in groups with other men, they sensed a pressure to be disrespectful toward women. A first-year man's perception of the treatment of women was that "they are treated with more respect to their faces, but behind closed doors, with a group of men present, respect for women is not an issue." One senior man stated, "In general, college-aged men don't treat women their age with respect because 90 percent of them think of women as merely a means to sex." Women reinforced this perception. A first-year women stated, "Men here are more interested in hooking up and drinking beer than they are in getting to know women as real people." Another woman said, "Men here use and abuse women."

Characteristic of rape culture, a double standard of sexual behavior for men versus women was prevalent on this campus. As one Greek senior man stated, "Women who sleep around as sluts and get bad reputations; men who do are champions and get a pat on the back from their brothers." Women also supported a double standard for sexual behavior by criticizing sexually active women. A first-year woman spoke out against women who are sexually active: "I think some girls here make it difficult for the men to respect women as a whole."

One concrete example of demeaning sexually active women on this campus is the "walk of shame." Fraternity brothers come out on the porches of their houses the night after parties and heckle women walking by. It is assumed that these women spent the night at fraternity houses and that the men they were with did not care enough about them to drive them home. Although sororities now reside in former fraternity houses, this practice continues and sometimes the victims of hecklings are sorority women on their way to study in the library.

A junior man in a high-risk fraternity described another ritual of disrespect toward women called "chatter." When an unknown woman sleeps over at the house, the brothers yell degrading remarks out the window at her as she leaves the next morning such as "Fuck that bitch" and "Who is that slut?" He said that sometimes brothers harass the brothers whose girlfriends stay over instead of heckling those women.

Fraternity men most often mistreated women they did not know personally. Men and women alike reported incidents in which brothers observed other brothers having sex with unknown women or women they knew only casually. A sophomore woman's experience exemplifies this anonymous state: "I don't mind if 10 guys were watching or it was videotaped. That's expected on this campus. It's the fact that he didn't apologize or even offer to drive me home that really upset me." Descriptions of sexual encounters involved the satisfaction of men by nameless women. A brother in

a high-risk fraternity described a similar occurrence:

> A brother of mine was hooking up upstairs with an unattractive woman who had been pursuing him all night. He told some brothers to go outside the window and watch. Well, one thing led to another and they were almost completely naked when the woman noticed the brothers outside. She was then unwilling to go any further, so the brother went outside and yelled at the other brothers and then closed the shades. I don't know if he scored or not, because the woman was pretty upset. But he did win the award for hooking up with the ugliest chick that weekend.

Attitudes Toward Rape

The sexually charged environment of college campuses raises many questions about cultures that facilitate the rape of women. How women and men define their sexual behavior is important legally as well as interpersonally. We asked students how they defined rape and had them compare it to the following legal definition: the perpetration of an act of sexual intercourse with a female against her will and consent, whether her will is overcome by force or fear resulting from the threat of force, or by drugs or intoxicants; or when, because of mental deficiency, she is incapable of exercising rational judgment. (Brownmiller 1975, 368)

When presented with this legal definition, most women interviewed recognized it as well as the complexities involved in applying it. A first-year woman said, "If a girl is drunk and the guy knows it and the girl says, 'Yes, I want to have sex,' and they do, that is still rape because the girl can't make a conscious, rational decision under the influence of alcohol." Some women disagreed. Another first-year woman stated, "I don't think it is fair that the guy gets blamed when both people involved are drunk."

The typical definition men gave for rape was "when a guy jumps out of the bushes and forces himself sexually onto a girl." When asked what date rape was, the most common answer was "when one person has sex with another person who did not consent." Many men said, however, that "date rape is when a woman wakes up the next morning and regrets having sex." Some men said that date rape was too gray an area to define. "Consent is a fine line," said a Greek senior man student. For the most part, the men we spoke with argued that rape did not occur on this campus. One Greek sophomore man said, "I think it is ridiculous that someone here would rape someone." A first-year man stated, "I have a problem with the word rape. It sounds so criminal, and we are not criminals; we are sane people."

Whether aware of the legal definitions of rape, most men resisted the idea that a woman who is intoxicated is unable to consent to sex. A Greek junior man said, "Men should not be responsible for women's drunkenness." One first-year man said, "If that is the legal definition of rape, then it happens all the time on this campus." A senior man said, "I don't care whether alcohol is involved or not; that is not rape. Rapists are people that have something seriously wrong with them." A first-year man even claimed that when women get drunk, they invite sex. He said, "Girls get so drunk here and then come to us. What are we supposed to do? We are only human."

Discussion and Conclusion

These findings describe the physical and normative aspects of one college campus as they relate to attitudes about and relations between men and women. Our findings suggest that an explanation emphasizing rape culture also must focus on those characteristics of the social setting that play a role in defining heterosexual relationships on college campuses (Kalof and Cargill 1991). The degradation of women as

portrayed in rape culture was not found in all fraternities on this campus. Both group norms and individual behavior changed as students went from one place to another. Although individual men are the ones who rape, we found that some settings are more likely places for rape than are others. Our findings suggest that rape cannot be seen only as an isolated act and blamed on individual behavior and proclivities, whether it be alcohol consumption or attitudes. We also must consider characteristics of the settings that promote the behaviors that reinforce a rape culture.

Relations between women and men at parties in low-risk fraternities varied considerably from those in high-risk houses. Peer pressure and situational norms influenced women as well as men. Although many men in high- and low-risk houses shared similar views and attitudes about the Greek system, women on this campus, and date rape, their behaviors at fraternity parties were quite different.

Women who are at highest risk of rape are women whom fraternity brothers did not know. These women are faceless victims, nameless acquaintances—not friends. Men said their responsibility to such persons and the level of guilt they feel later if the hook-ups end in sexual intercourse are much lower if they hook up with women they do not know. In high-risk houses, brothers treated women as subordinates and kept them at a distance. Men in high-risk houses actively discouraged ongoing heterosexual relationships, routinely degraded women, and participated more fully in the hook-up scene; thus, the probability that women would become faceless victims was higher in these houses. The flirtatious nature of the parties indicated that women go to these parties looking for available men, but finding boyfriends or relationships was difficult at parties in high-risk houses. However, in the low-risk houses, where more men had long-term relationships, the women were not strangers and were less likely to become faceless victims.

The social scene on this campus, and on most others, offers women and men few other options to socialize. Although there may be no such thing as a completely safe fraternity party for women, parties at low-risk houses and commercial bars encouraged men and women to get to know each other better and decreased the probability that women would become faceless victims. Although both men and women found the social scene on this campus demeaning, neither demanded different settings for socializing, and attendance at fraternity parties is a common form of entertainment.

These findings suggest that a more conducive environment for conversation can promote more positive interactions between men and women. Simple changes would provide the opportunity for men and women to interact in meaningful ways such as adding places to sit and lowering the volume of music at fraternity parties or having parties in neutral locations, where men are not in control. The typical party room in fraternity houses includes a place to dance but not to sit and talk. The music often is loud, making it difficult, if not impossible, to carry on conversations; however, there were more conversations at the low-risk parties, where there also was more respect shown toward women. Although the number of brothers who had steady girlfriends in the low-risk houses as compared to those in the high-risk houses may explain the differences, we found that commercial bars also provided a context for interaction between men and women. At the bars, students sat and talked and conversations between men and women flowed freely, resulting in deep discussions and fewer hook-ups.

Alcohol consumption was a major focus of social events here and intensified attitudes and orientations of a rape culture. Although pressure to drink was evident at all fraternity parties and at both bars, drinking dominated high-risk fraternity parties, at which nonalcoholic beverages usually were not available and people chugged beers and became visibly drunk. A rape culture is strengthened by rules that permit alcohol only at fraternity parties. Under this system, men control

the parties and dominate the men as well as the women who attend. As college administrators crack down on fraternities and alcohol on campus, however, the same behaviors and norms may transfer to other places such as parties in apartments or private homes where administrators have much less control. At commercial bars, interaction and socialization with others were as important as drinking, with the exception of the nights when the bar frequented by under-class students became crowded. Although one solution is to offer nonalcoholic social activities, such events receive little support on this campus. Either these alternative events lacked the prestige of the fraternity parties or the alcohol was seen as necessary to unwind, or both.

In many ways, the fraternities on this campus determined the settings in which men and women interacted. As others before us have found, pressures for conformity to the norms and values exist at both high-risk and low-risk houses (Kalof and Cargill 1991; Martin and Hummer 1989; Sanday 1990). The desire to be accepted is not unique to this campus or the Greek system (Holland and Eisenhart 1990; Horowitz 1988; Moffat 1989). The degree of conformity required by Greeks may be greater than that required in most social groups, with considerable pressure to adopt and maintain the image of their houses. The fraternity system intensifies the "groupthink syndrome" (Janis 1972) by solidifying the identity of the in-group and creating an us/them atmosphere. Within the fraternity culture, brothers are highly regarded and women are viewed as outsiders. For men in high-risk fraternities, women threatened their brotherhood; therefore, brothers discouraged relationships and harassed those who treated women as equals or with respect. The pressure to be one of the guys and hang out with the guys strengthens a rape culture on college campus by demeaning women and encouraging the segregation of men and women.

Students on this campus were aware of the contexts in which they operated and the choices available to them. They recognized that, in their interactions, they created differences between men and women that are not natural, essential, or biological (West and Zimmerman 1987). Not all men and women accepted the demeaning treatment of women, but they continued to participate in behaviors that supported aspects of a rape culture. Many women participated in the hook-up scene even after they had been humiliated and hurt because they had few other means of initiating contact with men on campus. Men and women alike played out this scene, recognizing its injustices in many cases but being unable to change the course of their behaviors.

Although this research provides some clues to gender relations on college campuses, it raises many questions. Why do men and women participate in activities that support a rape culture when they see its injustices? What would happen if alcohol were not controlled by groups of men who admit that they disrespect women when they get together? What can be done to give men and women on college campuses more opportunities to interact responsibly and get to know each other better? These questions should be studied on other campuses with a focus on the social settings in which the incidence of rape and the attitudes that support a rape culture exist. Fraternities are social contexts that may or may not foster a rape culture.

Our findings indicate that a rape culture exists in some fraternities, especially those we identified as high-risk houses. College administrators are responding to this situation by providing counseling and educational programs that increase awareness of date rape including campaigns such as "No means no." These strategies are important in changing attitudes, values, and behaviors; however, changing individuals is not enough. The structure of campus life and the impact of that structure on gender relations on campus are highly determinative. To eliminate campus rape culture, student leaders and administrators must examine the situa-

tions in which women and men meet and restructure these settings to provide opportunities for respectful interaction. Change may not require abolishing fraternities; rather, it may require promoting settings that facilitate positive gender relations.

References

Barthel, D. 1988. *Putting on appearances: Gender and advertising*. Philadelphia: Temple University Press.

Boeringer, S. B., C. L. Shehan, and R. L. Akers, 1991. Social contexts and social learning in sexual coercion and aggression: Assessing the contribution of fraternity membership. *Family Relations* 40:58–64.

Brownmiller, S. 1975. *Against our will: Men, women and rape*. New York: Simon & Schuster.

Buchwald, E., P. R. Fletcher, and M. Roth, eds. 1993. *Transforming a rape culture*. Minneapolis, MN: Milkweed Editions.

Burke, P., J. E. Stets, and M. A. Pirog-Good. 1989. Gender identity, self-esteem, physical abuse and sexual abuse in dating relationships. In *Violence in dating relationships: Emerging social issues*, edited by M. A. Pirog-Good and J. E. Stets. New York: Praeger.

Gwartney-Gibbs, P., and J. Stockard. 1989. Courtship aggression and mixed-sex peer groups. In *Violence in dating relationships: Emerging social issues*, edited by M. A. Pirog-Good and J. E. Stets. New York: Praeger.

Herman, D. 1984. The rape culture. In *Women: A feminist perspective*, edited by J. Freeman. Mountain View, CA: Mayfield.

Holland, D. C., and M. A. Eisenhart. 1990. *Educated in romance: Women, achievement, and college culture*. Chicago: University of Chicago Press.

Horowitz, H. L. 1988. *Campus life: Undergraduate cultures from the end of the 18th century to the present*. Chicago: University of Chicago Press.

Hunter, F. 1953. *Community power structure*. Chapel Hill: University of North Carolina Press.

Jenkins, M. J., and F. H. Dambrot. 1987. The attribution of date rape: Observer's attitudes and sexual experiences and the dating situation. *Journal of Applied Social Psychology* 17:875–95.

Janis, I. L. 1972. *Victims of groupthink.* Boston: Houghton Mifflin.

Kalof, L., and T. Cargill. 1991. Fraternity and sorority membership and gender dominance attitudes. *Sex Roles* 25:417–23.

Kimmel, M. S. 1993. Clarence, William, Iron Mike, Tailhook, Senator Packwood, Spur Posse, Magic . . . and us. In *Transforming a rape culture,* edited by E. Buchwald, P. R. Fletcher, and M. Roth. Minneapolis, MN: Milkweed Editions.

Koss, M. P., T. E. Dinero, C. A. Seibel, and S. L. Cox. 1988. Stranger and acquaintance rape: Are there differences in the victim's experience? *Psychology of Women Quarterly* 12:1–24.

Koss, M. P., C. A. Gidycz, and N. Wisniewski. 1985. The scope of rape: Incidence and prevalence of sexual aggression and victimization in a national sample of higher education students. *Journal of Consulting and Clinical Psychology* 55:162–70.

LaPlante, M. N., N. McCormick, and G. G. Brannigan. 1980. Living the sexual script: College students' views of influence in sexual encounters. *Journal of Sex Research* 16:338–55.

Lisak, D., and S. Roth. 1988. Motivational factors in nonincarcerated sexually aggressive men. *Journal of Personality and Social Psychology* 55:795–802.

Malamuth, N. 1986. Predictors of naturalistic sexual aggression. *Journal of Personality and Social Psychology* 50:953–62.

Martin, P. Y., and R. Hummer. 1989. Fraternities and rape on campus. *Gender & Society* 3:457–73.

Miller, B., and J. C. Marshall. 1987. Coercive sex on the university campus. *Journal of College Student Personnel* 28:38–47.

Moffat, M. 1989. *Coming of age in New Jersey: College life in American culture.* New Brunswick, NJ: Rutgers University Press.

Muehlenhard, C. L., and M. A. Linton. 1987. Date rape and sexual aggression in dating situations: Incidence and risk factors. *Journal of Counseling Psychology* 34:186–96.

O'Sullivan, C. 1993. Fraternities and the rape culture. In *Transforming a rape culture,* edited by E. Buchwald, P. R. Fletcher, and M. Roth. Minneapolis, MN: Milkweed Editions.

Peterson, S. A., and B. Franzese. 1987. Correlates of college men's sexual abuse of women. *Journal of College Student Personnel* 28:223–28.

Sanday, P. R. 1990. *Fraternity gang rape: Sex, brotherhood, and privilege on campus.* New York: New York University Press.

West, C., and D. Zimmerman. 1987. Doing gender. *Gender & Society* 1:125–51.

17

ARTICLE

Todd W. Crosset

Jeffrey R. Benedict

Mark A. McDonald

Male Student–Athletes Reported for Sexual Assault: A Survey of Campus Police Departments and Judicial Affairs Offices

In recent years, an ongoing public debate has developed regarding the propensity of athletes to commit sexual assault. A succession of publicized rape cases during the 1980s involving high-profile athletes led to increased coverage of sexual assault by sports reporters. During the first half of the 1990s, the unabated number of allegations involving athletes in rape cases (for a summary, see Nelson, 1994) has fed the debate. Some members of the media have suggested that athletes are more prone to commit acts of sexual aggression (Eskanazi, 1990; Hofmann, 1986; Kirshenbaum, 1989; Larimer, 1991; Toufexis, 1990). This claim is disputed by those who believe that athletes are scrutinized more intensely because of their notoriety (Dershowitz, 1994). They contend that thousands of rape cases go unmentioned in news reports each year, yet seldom does a case involving an athlete or any other celebrity go unpublicized. This practice, they argue, creates a distorted perception regarding the proportion of athletes who commit sexual assault and fails to account for the large

number of athletes who do not commit sexually aggressive acts.

Social scientists have offered little to inform this debate. The purpose of this study is to research the association between reported incidents of sexual assault and athletic affiliation in a rigorous fashion.

Introduction

Social Milieu and Sexual Aggression

A number of researchers concerned with sexually aggressive behavior adopt what Malamuth, Sockloskie, Koss, and Tanaka (1991) call an "ecological approach." This approach starts with the recognition that sexually aggressive behavior is a form of violence and not a form of sexuality. It argues that aggression against women results from a complex combination of social and psychological factors, with primary emphasis on sociological factors. Employing multiple regression analysis, Malamuth et al. note that proximate social factors such as peer group environment and masculine hostility toward women have far more influence as predictors of sexual aggression than do distal factors such as violence experienced as

Reprinted from *Journal of Sport & Social Issues*, vol. 19, pages 126–140. Reprinted by permission of Sage Publications, Inc.

a child. Malamuth et al. conclude that future research should focus on the following social factors: (a) factors that contribute to the practice and acceptance of coercion and hostility, (b) factors that promote aggression against targets perceived as weaker or as out groups (e.g., sex segregation), and (c) factors that promote sexism and violence against women (e.g., eroticism of domination).

This approach is supported by the work of anthropologist Peggy Sanday (1981), who found that the frequency of rape varied substantially from one tribal society to another. Cultures that displayed a high level of tolerance for violence, male dominance, and sex segregation had the highest frequency of rape (both individual and gang). These societal characteristics are the basis of what Sanday (1990) calls "rape cultures," which lack the social constraints that discourage sexual aggression or contain social arrangements that encourage sexual aggression. Sanday's findings support the contention that sexual assault is not simply the result of an individual's biological makeup or psychological disposition; rather, it is a behavior that is socially encouraged (Brownmiller, 1975; Russell, 1975; Sanday 1981, 1990).

Athletes and Sexual Assault

Beginning in the late 1970s, academics and social critics began discussing connections between the culture of sport and violence against women (Sabo & Runfola, 1980). In many regards, men's sport resembles a "rape culture." Athletics is highly sex segregated. By design, dominant forms of sport promote hostile attitudes toward rivals and gaining at the expense of another team or person (Kidd, 1990; Messner, 1992; Messner & Sabo, 1994). Male athletic teams often garner high status for physically dominating others (Sabo, 1980). Further, organized competitive sports for men have been described as supporting male dominance and sexist practices (Bryson, 1987; Kidd, 1990; MacKinnon, 1987; Messner, 1992; Whitson, 1990).

Curry (1991), in his study of conversation fragments from a male locker room, found statements that were consistent with what might be found in a "rape culture."

Social scientists have been conducting empirical research on the relationship between athletic participation and sexual assault for a relatively short period of time (Koss & Gaines, 1993). Prior to the early 1990s, there were few attempts to document the connection between athletes and sexual assault.

To date, most academic references to athletes as sexual aggressors involve gang rapes (Ehrhart & Sandler, 1985, as cited by Koss & Gaines, 1993; O'Sullivan, 1991). This literature identifies members of fraternities, followed by members of athletic teams, as the "most likely to engage in group sexual assault" (O'Sullivan, 1991, p. 144).[1] O'Sullivan argues that cohesiveness gained through team membership, sex-segregated housing, and prestige can be factors in facilitating illicit activities. The group dynamics outlined by O'Sullivan confirm those identified by Sanday (1990), who has conducted extensive research on gang rape in college fraternities. Sanday concludes that the group environment binds men emotionally to one another and contributes to their seeing sex relations from a position of power and status.

There is little doubt that men in sex-segregated groups (sports teams, fraternities, military, etc.) are more likely to commit acts of group sexual assault (Ehrhart & Sandler, 1992; O'Sullivan, 1991; Sanday, 1981, 1990). However, there is a lack of scholarly research on athletes as individual perpetrators of simple rape or aggravated rape.

Using multiple regression analysis of data collected through self-reports, Koss and Gaines (1993) attempted to ascertain the influence of athletic affiliation on sexual aggression. They compared the influence of alcohol use, nicotine use, fraternity membership, and athletic affiliation on sexual aggressive behavior on a Division I college campus. Whereas alcohol and nicotine use were strongly associated with the incidence of sexual assault, varsity athletic participation in "revenue-producing sports" was weakly associated with sexually aggressive behavior by men against women at the university.

The study by Koss and Gaines (1993) has limitations. Because they examined only one campus, Koss and Gaines are reluctant to make generalizations applicable to other universities. Further, their comparison population was taken from introductory courses consisting predominantly of first- and second-year students whose average age was 18.9 years. The athletic population was oversampled and selected from all years. The result is a comparison of the group-affiliated student–athlete against "newer" students less likely to have developed strong campus affiliations. In addition, the study used only self-reported data, which carries inherent limitations on validity (Koss & Gaines, 1993). Finally, Koss and Gaines do not distinguish between individual rape and gang rape. Despite these limitations, the research of Koss and Gaines is a groundbreaking step in understanding sexual aggression and college athletes. It is the first rigorous empirical research that identifies athletic affiliation as a predictor (albeit slight) of sexual aggression.

The nature of sexual assault makes it difficult to study. Clinical research in this area is both impractical and unethical. Correlational data can be collected from self-reports or official reports, but both types of data have limitations. Further, we cannot draw conclusions about causality from correlational research. Muehlenhard and Linton (1987) recommend that data from different types of studies converge to provide insight into the problem of sexual assault. Therefore, the design and methodology of this study is to address some of the limitations of the work of Koss and Gaines (1993) and Curry (1991) and determine whether the findings based on official reports of sexual assault are consistent with the findings of previous studies.

The objective of the present study is to examine the relationship between membership on men's varsity sports teams in NCAA Division I universities and officially reported sexual assaults. The study compares the rates of reported sexual assaults for varsity athletes with the rest of the male student population. The data were obtained from records at 30 Division I American universities; 107 cases of sexual assault were examined. The study uses statistical analyses to test the purported relationship between membership on a varsity sports team and officially reported sexual assaults.

Method

In general, there are three locations on a college campus where a victim can officially report sexual assault: campus police, judicial affairs,[2] or a rape crisis/counseling center. Of these, only the first two keep records on the perpetrator. However, at nearly all institutions, neither campus police nor judicial affairs offices indicate whether an alleged perpetrator is a student–athlete. Institutions participating in our study were asked to provide the total number of male students enrolled, student–athletes enrolled, sexual assaults reported, and sexual assaults reported that involved a student–athlete by cross-referencing the names of accused perpetrators with the names on official athletic rosters. The figures were calculated at each institution to protect privacy rights.

We purposely selected Division I institutions and, whenever possible, selected schools with highly ranked popular sports. We assumed that these institutions were most likely to support insulated athletic subworlds and systems of affiliation among athletes that, according to the literature (Curry, 1991; Messner, 1992; Messner & Sabo, 1994; Sabo, 1980), might lead to problematic behavior.

Two Data Sets

We speculated that the initial response to and subsequent adjudication of incidents of sexual assault differed considerably between campus police and judicial affairs officials. Further, we thought that these differences are understood on some level by victims. Campus police officers operate under the same guidelines as do civil police officers. In most cases, a victim would file an official report with campus police only if she desired to file criminal charges and pursue justice through the state court system. By contrast, administrators in judicial affairs are empowered to independently determine the facts in an alleged assault without being subjected to the strict laws of evidence required in a court of law. Although unable to mete out punishment in the same manner as the criminal justice system, institutions are able to provide more immediate recourse to a victim while maintaining her privacy. Through either a student court or a private hearing conducted by a judicial officer or dean, a school can stipulate disciplinary action that ranges from probation to expulsion. A victim who is seeking a timely response, an immediate separation from the perpetrator with respect to housing or class schedules, or adjudication without a criminal trial may be more inclined to report the incident to judicial affairs.

In other words, although both judicial affairs and campus police process official reports of sexual assault, their functions are not identical. Therefore, we have approached the data as two distinct sample sets. Data were collected from 20 campus police departments and 10 judicial affairs offices.

Campus Police Data Set   With regard to campus police departments, our survey group includes institutions from all geographic regions of the United States. We targeted schools with perennial Top 20 basketball or football teams. Schools that landed teams in the men's Top 20

poll for either basketball or football in at least 2 of the 3 years between 1991 and 1993 were mailed surveys. Of the 49 schools targeted, 20 responded—a response rate of 41%. All the reports were usable. The high rate of usability was enhanced by the Campus Security Act (1987), which requires campus police departments to allow public access to information regarding all crime on campus.

Judicial Affairs Data Set   Because judicial affairs offices are not required by the Campus Security Act to reveal information regarding violations of the student codes of conduct, data were much more difficult to obtain than they were from campus police departments. To facilitate a high response rate, we conducted telephone interviews with a judicial affairs representative from institutions in the original sample. Many institutions with Top 20 basketball and football teams were reluctant to participate in this study. Therefore, in addition to 8 Division I institutions with Top 20 athletic programs, we petitioned 8 Division I institutions that did not have perennial Top 20 basketball or football teams. Of these 16 schools that initially agreed to be part of the survey, 12 were able to complete the project (75% response rate) and 10 provided usable data. Judicial affairs offices were asked to provide 3 years of data, covering the academic years from 1991 through 1993. Among the respondents, 2 schools did not have records for 1991 and 1 school did not have data from 1993. Of the 10 schools supplying usable data, 5 were perennial Top 20 football or basketball schools according to our operational definition.

Problems and Solutions

Asking for information regarding sexual assaults on campuses poses a number of problems for the researcher. First, this information is extremely sensitive and potentially damaging to the reputation of an institution. Initially, we assured confidentiality to all potential participants. To overcome further hesitancy on the part of institutions, we garnered the support of two influential people—Jim Ferrier, a member of the International Association of Campus Law Enforcement Administrators, and Carol Bohmer, a legal scholar who has trained judicial affairs officers at institutions around the country. We included their names in the cover letter of our survey. As a result, we were able to gain the cooperation of both police departments and judicial affairs offices at a significant number of schools.

Second, each institution has an obligation to protect the privacy of both the victim and the accused. In keeping with privacy protection laws, the names of individuals accused of sexual assault were neither requested nor revealed. Instead, each participating institution was asked to internally review the names of those students accused of sexual offenses and determine whether they appeared on a varsity team roster at the time of the assault. This required a considerable amount of effort on the part of participating institutions.

Finally, the institutions we surveyed do not adhere to universal definitions for student codes of conduct violations. Rather than asking participating schools to conform to a researcher-created definition of sexual assault, we allowed each institution to maintain its own definition of sexual assault. This procedure ensures that we are reporting data based on codes of conduct violations as described at each institution. The overlap between institutional definitions of sexual assault ensures that all perpetrators reported in this study are accused of either rape, attempted rape, unwanted touching of intimate parts of another person, or the use of threats or intimidation to gain an advantage in nonconsensual sexual contact.

Findings

A summary of the data collected from the two sample sets is listed in Table 17.1.[3]

Male student–athletes comprised 3.8% of the total male student population yet represented 5.5% of the reported sexual assaults to campus police ($n = 38$). For the combined 3 years of the 10 judicial affairs offices, male student–athletes comprised 3.3% of the total male population, yet represented 19% of the perpetrators reported ($n = 69$). A two-tailed t test was conducted on these data to compare the sexual assault perpetrator rate of male student–athletes with that of the rest of the male student population. This test was chosen because we did not hypothesize

| **TABLE 17.1** | Summary of Data Collected from Two Sample Sources |

	Campus Police Questionnaire[a]	**Judicial Affairs Questionnaire (1991–1993)**[b]
Men not on intercollegiate sport teams		
Student population	182,091	252,630
Perpetrators	36	56
Men on intercollegiate sport teams		
Athlete population	6,975	8,739
Perpetrators	2	13

a. Institutions reporting = 20.

b. Institutions reporting = 10; annual reports = 27 (1991 = 8, 1992 = 10, 1993 = 9).

from the outset the direction of the difference between the student–athletes and the rest of the male student population. We tested for significance to the .05 level, or a confidence level of higher than 95%.

Because the judicial affairs data come from different years at the same campuses, we needed to test the appropriateness of combining the 3 years of judicial affairs data. First, the annual data were tested for significance. Then a regression analysis was conducted to determine the appropriateness of combining the 3 years of data for further analysis.[4] Because we found no significant difference between the years, we were able to combine the 3 years to create a larger sample for analysis.

Table 17.2 shows the results of the t test for the campus police questionnaire, each year of the judicial affairs questionnaire, and the combined data from judicial affairs.

Campus Police Questionnaire Results

The t test reveals that, in the reported sexual assaults to campus police, there is no significant difference between male student–athletes and other male students, $t = -0.70$, $p = .490$. That

is, given the current data sample, we cannot state with confidence that collegiate athletes are reported to campus police at a higher rate than are other male students.

Judicial Affairs Questionnaire Results

For the annual data collected from the judicial affairs offices, only in the 1991 academic year are there statistically significant differences between male student–athletes and other male students, $t = -2.45$, $p < .05$, with regard to the rate of being reported for sexual assault. In this year, male student–athletes comprised 2.8% of the total male student population and represented 24% of the perpetrators reported to judicial affairs for sexual assault ($n = 21$).

By contrast, there were no significant differences in sexual assault incident rates between these two groups based on the 1992 data, $t = -1.29$, $p = .229$, or on the 1993 data, $t = -0.57$, $p = .582$. In 1992, student–athletes comprised 3.7% of the total male student population and represented 24% of the perpetrators reported to judicial affairs for sexual assault ($n = 25$). In 1993, student–athletes comprised 3.4% of the population and represented 8.7%

TABLE 17.2 Results of t Test for Campus Police Questionnaire (CPQ) and Judicial Affairs Questionnaire (JAQ)

Survey	Number of Male Nonvarsity Athlete Perpetrators	Men/1,000 Incident Rate	Number of Male Student–Athlete Perpetrators	Men/1,000 Incident Rate	t Statistics
CPQ (1992)	36	0.19	2	0.33	−0.70
JAQ (1991)	16	0.20	5	2.21	−2.45★
JAQ (1992)	19	0.21	6	1.72	−1.29
JAQ (1993)	23	0.25	2	0.67	−0.57
JAQ (1991–1993)	56	0.22	13	1.49	−2.47★

★$p < .05$.

of the perpetrators reported to judicial affairs for sexual assault ($n = 25$).

The t test performed on the combined judicial affairs data (1991–1993) reveals statistically significant differences between male student–athletes and other male students, $t = -2.47$, $p <$ .05. For the combined 3 years, male student–athletes comprised 3.3% of the total male population yet represented 19% of the reported perpetrators ($n = 69$). This result indicates an association between collegiate athletic membership and reports of sexual assault to judicial affairs offices.

Finally, we conducted a comparison of student–athletes involved in the revenue-producing contact sports of football and basketball to all other students–athletes. This comparison was made with the combined judicial affairs data (1991–1993). A two-tailed t test indicated that the difference in incident rates between these groups approached significance but was not quite statistically significant, $t = 1.41$, p = .17. However, it should be noted that, in this sample, male football and basketball players comprised 30% of the student-athlete population, yet are responsible for 67% of the reported sexual assaults.

Limitations

Our data included only those sexual assaults officially reported to either campus police or judicial affairs. Some estimates suggest that 84% of all rapes go unreported (National Victim's Center, 1992). Although the conditions under which women will report sexual assault are not fully understood, we can assume that reports are not random. Any sample based on official reports, therefore, is not a representative sample of sexual assaults that take place on college campuses. The benefit of working with officially reported sexual assaults is the general high reliability of the claims.[5] Further, the small sample size prevents us from using highly sophisticated statistical tests in our data analysis. Therefore, our study does not include an analysis of all the factors associated

with men's sexual aggression toward women; we have no information on the circumstances in which actual cases of sexual aggression occurred. We know only whether the reported perpetrator was a member of an intercollegiate sport team. Given the limitations of the data, we can report only on the statistical relationship between membership on men's intercollegiate sport teams in Division I universities and the incidence of reported sexual assaults at those universities.

Conclusion

Given the nature and scope of this research, conclusions based on the data are necessarily limited. For example, to draw conclusions as to the frequency of sexual assault committed by athletes would be a misapplication of these findings. Further, it needs to be reiterated that it is not clear whether the association between athletic affiliation and sexual assault is causal or the result of behavior only indirectly related to sport.

Nonetheless, this research indicates that male college student–athletes, compared with the rest of the male student population, are responsible for a significantly higher percentage of the sexual assaults reported to judicial affairs offices on the campuses of Division I institutions. Although reports of sexual assault by student–athletes to campus police are not statistically different from those by other male students, athletes are nonetheless slightly overrepresented. When the two data sets are viewed concurrently, athletes appear to be disproportionately involved in incidents of sexual assault on college campuses. Further, these findings lend support to other research that links athletic participation and sexual aggression (Curry, 1991; Koss & Gaines, 1993).

This research makes three significant contributions to this area of study. First, because it relies on official reports, it can be used to counter those who would dismiss the findings based on data from self-reports (Koss & Gaines, 1993). The findings of this study do not contradict those of Koss and Gaines, enhancing the validity of their findings. We can state with increasing confidence that there is some connection between the dynamics of being involved on a men's intercollegiate sports team, particularly in the contact sports of football and basketball in Division I universities, and reported cases of sexual assault at those institutions.

Second, we investigated 30 Division I institutions across the United States, 25 of which support top-ranked teams in either football or basketball. Previous researchers have been reluctant to make broad conclusions on the basis of research drawn from single institutions (Curry, 1991; Koss & Gaines, 1993). Because we sampled a number of institutions, we can assume that our conclusions are generally representative of other large Division I campuses with strong athletic programs.

Finally, this study contributes to a small body of empirical research on an issue that is much discussed yet rarely studied. Popular sports journalism and scholarship alike have attributed one in three sexual assaults committed on college campuses to athletes (Bohmer & Parrot, 1993; Deford, 1993; Eskanazi, 1990; Kane & Disch, 1993; Kirshenbaum, 1989; Melnick, 1992; Nelson, 1991, 1994; Toufexis, 1990). However, after extensive review of the literature, there does not appear to be any empirical evidence to substantiate this claim, which appears consistently in both academic and sport journalism publications.

Claims that one in three campus sexual assaults is committed by a student–athlete have two primary sources: Richard Hofmann (1986) of the *Philadelphia Daily News* and Gerald Eskanazi (1990) of the *New York Times*. In 1986, Hofmann wrote a four-part series on athletes and sexual assault. Hofmann does not contend that his investigation is scientific. He acknowledges that the figures used in his articles were based on an informal poll of university officials. The findings from this poll were then compared to FBI Uniform Crime Reports. Despite the obvious flaws in this type of comparison, both

scholars and journalists have relied on the Hofmann piece to assert that athletes are much more likely to commit sexual assaults.

Askanazi (1990) misrepresented the work of a leading researcher in the area of sexual assault on campus, Mary Koss. He cites a 3-year National Institute of Mental Health study by Koss claiming that, of the cases studied, athletes were involved about a third of the time. Koss did not control for athletic affiliation in this study and disputes the findings Eskanazi attributes to her.[6]

Implications

Clearly, caution must be employed when discussing the implications of our findings. The popular press has overstated the problem in the past, in part by misrepresenting scientific research. At the same time, the findings of this research clearly indicate the existence of a problem. To suggest that all of these cases are simply a result of athletes being targeted because of their high profile status denies reality. The best interest of institutions cannot be served until those working within the institution admit that a problem exists. Athletic departments and coaches have an obvious interest in learning about and addressing the factors that are contributing to athletes being reported for individual acts of sexual assault (and gang rapes) at a higher rate than that of other male students. Reducing the number of sexual attacks committed by athletes on campus will require a significant effort from athletic departments, coaches, and other educational personnel.

Further Research

The lack of rigorous research in this area points to one obvious avenue of study: replication. In addition to replication, we see three broad research needs: exploration of variables associated with sexually aggressive behavior, factors influencing reporting rates, and efficacy of intervention programs.

From the current research, we are unable to explain the association between varsity athletic membership and sexual assault. It is possible that the association we found has little to do with athletic participation but rather is associated with some other behavior only indirectly related to athletics. Despite the association between intercollegiate athletic membership and reported sexual assaults, far stronger associations have been found between sexual assault and alcohol use, nicotine use, and hostile attitudes toward women (Koss & Gaines, 1993). Those who attempt replication, then, will want to test more variables.

Further, there is a need for more studies so that we can learn more about patterns within and between universities and develop explanations for those patterns. For example, although the sample size was small, the data hinted that sexual assault was not endemic to all sports. Contact sports such as football and basketball were overrepresented, raising the possibility that athletes trained to use physical domination on the field are more likely to carry these lessons into their relationships. Even here, reports were not uniform from school to school, suggesting that the social environment of programs may vary significantly and have a substantial impact on the rate of sexual assault.

Conversations between members of the research team and university officials indicated that the prevalence of reported sexual assaults by athletes was dramatic in some instances following changes in coaching staffs. This suggests that coaches may have a significant impact on the team's social milieu and thus on athletes' behavior outside of sport. A qualitative approach to this topic might prove most beneficial.

There is also a need to explore factors influencing rates of reporting. The disparity between the data sets (police and judicial affairs) not only confirms our speculation about the differences between these two reporting sites but also reinforces our earlier cautions about official reports not producing representative samples. This dis-

parity also suggests a new avenue of research: Under what conditions do women report sexual assaults committed by athletes? One possible explanation for the disparity is that women believe that the university will provide swifter recourse while significantly reducing the amount of public humiliation that accompanies a criminal trial. In addition, victims may anticipate an extremely negative response from the broader community if they were to press criminal charges against a Division I athlete. Conversely, women may perceive more severe retribution from other male groups (e.g., fraternity members) with whom they socialize on a regular basis (Martin & Hummer, 1989) than they do from athletes, who are less likely to be a part of their daily lives. Clearly, more research is needed in this area.

Finally, if sexual aggression is a form of behavior that is influenced by social and group cultural factors, subject to control and change, intervention and education may reduce the frequency of sexually aggressive behavior among men, including athletes. Recently, educators have developed sexual assault prevention programs specifically designed to reach athletes (Parrot, 1994). Social researchers must go beyond describing the problem; they must document the relative success of these programs and make recommendations for more effective interventions.

Notes

1. Of the 24 campus gang rapes analyzed by O'Sullivan (1991), 54% were committed by fraternities, 38% by athletes, and 8% by other groups.

2. In general, the term *judicial affairs* refers to a department with jurisdiction over university and college code of conduct violations. Every institution has a method of disciplining students who violate university rules. Although there is not a universal protocol for establishing a judicial affairs office, schools typically have either a dean or judicial affairs director who is responsible for overseeing any alleged violations of the student code of conduct. Most institutions have either a

student court or a body of administrators that hears complaints and determines appropriate sanctions.

3. It should be noted that the original data set included two gang rapes, one of which was committed by a group of student–athletes. Due to the focus of our research, we excluded this data from our sample.

4. The dependent variable for this analysis was the difference between the incident rates for student–athletes and those for other male students. Two dummy variables, coded for year (1991, 1992, 1993), were the independent variables. The regression results showed that neither of the coefficients for the independent variables was statistically significant, $t = 1.44$, $p = .16$; $t = .49$, $p = .63$. Thus the differences between the incident rates were not statistically related to the year of data collection. Therefore, it was determined that combining the 3 years of judicial affairs data for analysis purposes would be appropriate.

5. Although a more representative sample might have been gathered through self-reports, the reliability of this form of data has been the subject of considerable attack in the popular press. Admittedly, there are some limitations inherent with research based on self-reported data. They are nowhere near as pronounced as they appear in the press (see, e.g., Rophie, 1993). The most public attacks have been authored by academics and students who do not have training in statistical research. The willingness of the media to publish these attacks speaks to the level of hostility gender researchers face in these rather reactionary times (Faludi, 1991).

6. Based on a personal conversation with Mary Koss.

References

Bohmer, C., & Parrot, A. (1993). *Sexual assault on campus: The problem and the solution*. Lexington, MA: Lexington.

Brownmiller, S. (1975). *Against our will*. New York: Simon & Schuster.

Bryson, L. (1987). Sport and maintenance of masculine hegemony. *Women's Studies International Forum, 10,* 349–360.

Curry, T. (1991). Fraternal bonding in the locker room: A profeminist analysis of talk about competition and women. *Sociology of Sport Journal, 8,* 119–135.

Deford, F. (1993, March 24). Does team sports culture encourage prospect of rape? *National Public Radio* (Washington, DC).

Dershowitz, A. (1994, August 6). When women cry rape—falsely. *Boston Herald*, p. 13.

Ehrhart, J., & Sandler, D. (1992). *Campus gang rape: Party games?* Washington, DC: Center for Women Policy Studies.

Eskanazi, G. (1990, June 3). The male athlete and sexual assault. *New York Times*, sec. 8, pp. 1, 4.

Faludi, S. (1991). *Backlash: The undeclared war against American women*. New York: Crown.

Hofmann, R. (1986, March 17). Rape and the college athlete. *Philadelphia Daily News*, sec. 9, p. 102.

Kane, M. J., & Disch, L. (1993). Sexual violence and the reproduction of male power in the locker room: The "Lisa Olson incident." *Sociology of Sport Journal, 10,* 4.

Kidd, B. (1990). The men's cultural center: Sports and the dynamic of women's oppression/men's repression. In M. Messner & D. Sabo (Eds.), *Sport, men and the gender order: Critical feminist perspectives*. Champaign, IL: Human Kinetics.

Kirshenbaum, J. (1989, February 27). An American disgrace: A violent and unprecedented lawlessness has arisen among college athletes in all parts of the country. *Sports Illustrated*, p. 16.

Koss, M., & Gaines, J. (1993). The prediction of sexual aggression by alcohol use, athletic participation and fraternity affiliation. *Journal of Interpersonal Violence, 8,* 94–108.

Larimer, T. (1991, December 16). Under pressure to produce winners, some college coaches turn to risky recruits. *The Sporting News*, p. 8.

Malamuth, N., Sockloskie, R., Koss, P., & Tanaka, T. (1991). Characteristics of aggressors against women: Testing a model using a national sample of college students. *Journal of Consulting and Clinical Psychology, 50,* 670–681.

MacKinnon, C. (1987). *Feminism unmodified: Discourses on life and law*. Cambridge, MA: Harvard University Press.

Martin, P., & Hummer, R. (1989). Fraternities and rape on campus. *Gender & Society, 3,* 457–473.

Melnick, M. (1992). Male athletes and sexual assault. *Journal of Physical Education, Recreation, and Dance, 63*(5); pp. 32–35.

Messner, M. (1992). *Power at play: Sports and the problems of masculinity*. Boston: Beacon.

Messner, M., & Sabo, D. (1994). *Sex, violence, and power in sports: Rethinking masculinity*. Freedom, CA: Crossing.

Muehlenhard, C., & Linton, M., (1987). Date rape and sexual aggression in dating situations: Incidence and risk factors. *Journal of Counseling Psychology, 34*, 186–196.

National Victim's Center. (1992, April 23). *Rape in America: Report to the nation*. Arlington, VA: Author.

Nelson, M. B. (1991). *Are we winning yet? How women are changing sports and sports are changing women*. New York: Random House.

Nelson, M. B. (1994). *The stronger women get, the more men love football: Sexism and the American culture of sports*. New York: Harcourt Brace.

O'Sullivan, C. (1991). Acquaintance gang rape on campus. In A. Parrot & L. Bechhofer (Eds.), *Acquaintance rape: The hidden crime* (pp. 120–156). New York: Wiley.

Parrot, A. (1994, January). A rape awareness and prevention model for male athletes. *Journal of American College Health, 42*, 179–184.

Parrot, A., & Bechhofer, L. (1991). *Acquaintance rape: The hidden crime*. New York: Wiley.

Rophie, K. (1993, June 13). Date rape's other victim. *New York Times Magazine*, p. 26.

Russell, D. (1975). *The politics of rape: The victim's perspective*. New York: Stein & Day.

Sabo, D. (1980). Best years of my life? In D. Sabo & R. Runfola (Eds.), *Jock: Sports and male identity* (pp. 74–78). Englewood Cliffs, NJ: Prentice-Hall.

Sabo, D., & Runfola, R. (1980). *Jock: Sports and male identify*. Englewood Cliffs, NJ: Prentice-Hall.

Sanday, P. (1981). The socio-cultural context of rape: A cross-cultural study. *Journal of Social Issues, 37*(4), 5–27.

Sanday, P. (1990). *Fraternity gang rapes: Sex, brotherhood, and privilege on campus*. New York: New York University Press.

Toufexis, A. (1990, August 6). Sex in the sporting life: Do athletic teams unwittingly promote assaults and rapes? *Time*, p. 76.

Whitson, D. (1990). Sport and the social construction of masculinity. In M. Messner & D. Sabo (Eds.), *Sport, men and the gender order: Critical feminist perspectives* (pp. 19–30). Champaign, IL: Human Kinetics.

18

ARTICLE

Judi Addelston
Michael Stirratt

The Last Bastion of Masculinity: Gender Politics at The Citadel

The Citadel, an all-male public college that fought unsuccessfully to continue to exclude women from admission, illustrates the construction and fragility of hegemonic masculinity. This article will use the story of this litigation as a descriptive analysis of hegemonic masculinity. We are not testing an hypothesis; rather, we will use The Citadel as a case study to illuminate the construction of hegemonic masculinity. For more than 150 years, The Citadel has provided education and paramilitary training to male cadets with the aim of turning boys into "whole men." The public status of the institution has recently sparked a legal initiative to force the school to enroll women. Proponents of The Citadel vigorously argued against the admittance of women, arguing that the presence of women would destroy the school's unique masculine character and mission, effectively collapsing both

the walls of the institution and the boundaries of the whole man. The situation facing The Citadel was summarized by the words of a guidance counselor at the school who stated that members of the institution were in an "all-out fight to protect one of the last bastions of true masculinity left in the United States."[1]

This chapter is a qualitative study of an all-male institution currently involved in litigation to desegregate by sex. We will be viewing this institution through the two lenses of gender politics and institutional elitism. Although it is useful to identify these two strands of theory and research in analyzing this case, more often than not, the issues presented are so closely interwoven as to make separating them impossible. However, a detailed understanding of these two issues provides a comprehensive framework with which to view The Citadel. In this sense, we are viewing The Citadel as a "total institution" (Goffman, 1961).

Although writing about The Citadel as if it were an individual is grammatically awkward and ontologically misrepresentative, we will nevertheless portray The Citadel by the public voice it has used during these proceedings, as that is how the institution portrays itself. This

Editor's note: This article was written prior to The Citadel's decision to admit women. In fall, 1997, both The Citadel and VMI admitted their first coeducational classes. It is unclear what effect coeducation will have on this "last bastion of masculinity."

From *Masculinities and Organization*, edited by Cliff Cheng. Newbury Park, Sage Publications, 1996. Reprinted by permission.

voice encompasses the words of administrators, lawyers, public relations staff, cadets, expert witnesses, courtroom testimony, and media accounts. It is the collective opinions of this group of people that we invoke when we talk about The Citadel. We will also present the voices of individuals at The Citadel who do not echo this "party line"; there is a distinct difference between the collective voice and the individual voice at The Citadel.

We will not, however, present the story of Shannon Faulkner. Her fight to become a cadet has been well-documented in other publications (Applebome, 1995; Decker, 1995; Manegold, 1994; Peyser, 1995). Rather, we will use the ideological debates spurred by her court battle to investigate the dialectics of hegemonic masculinity. The possible entrance of a female into the male corp of cadets highlights the difference between sex and gender. Sex is a biological category based on anatomy; gender is the social interpretation of sex (Unger, 1979). Shannon Faulkner embodies The Citadel's anxieties about the conflation of these two concepts. If a *female* were to enter the corps, then becoming a "whole man"—the *performance* of hegemonic masculinity—is called into question. For if a woman can render the same performance as a man—achieve a Citadel degree—then there is little left to The Citadel's claims of the sexual dimorphism necessary to *create* "whole men" (Morgan, 1994).

The Citadel

The Citadel was founded in Charleston, South Carolina, in 1842. The school's defining characteristics are the all-male student population and the intensive program of paramilitary training that structures every aspect of life at the institution. The Citadel's all-male status is prescribed by its mission to mold student cadets into "whole men." The school handbook explains that the school aspires to

develop and graduate "the whole man." The Citadel System is the completeness with which it matures, refines, trains and schools the totality of a young man's character. This finely balanced process is called the "whole man" concept. During four years, cadets will develop academically, physically, militarily and spiritually. (The Citadel, 1992–1993, p. 22)

Although The Citadel was originally founded to benefit "the poor but deserving boys of the state" (The Citadel, 1992, p. 32), the institution's long history in the South has elevated it to an elite status. Many Citadel "families" pass the privilege of attending the school from father to son, building an intergenerational tradition of fraternity surrounding the school.

For proponents of The Citadel, the key to turning boys into men is rigorous training and discipline in an exclusive homosocial environment. A rigid paramilitary hierarchy,[2] termed the Fourth Class System, teaches discipline to male cadets through a demanding code of conduct. In this system, the first-year cadets, called "knobs" due to the appearance of their shaved head, have the lowest status at the school. Knob cadets must conform to special limitations on their behavior, while confronting harassment from upperclassmen and torturous initiation rites. Under the Fourth Class System at The Citadel, cadets gain greater status and privileges as they progress through their 4 years at the school, but they continue to be held to the institution's strict paramilitary rules and regulations.

The Citadel receives about 25% of its funding from South Carolina. The financial support of the state makes The Citadel and a similar school, The Virginia Military Institute, the only all-male, *publicly* funded colleges in the United States. Due to their status as publicly funded institutions that enroll only male students, these schools have been embroiled in litigation aimed at opening their doors to women.[3] In 1992, high school senior Shannon Faulkner was admitted to the school on the basis of her qualifications as detailed in an application that omitted any reference to her gender. On discovering her gender, The Citadel administration revoked her acceptance, and she then sued for access to the school. By order of the Supreme Court, Faulkner was admitted to the corps of cadets in the fall of 1995.[4]

Theories of Hegemonic Masculinity

Theories of hegemonic masculinity will provide a framework for interpreting the situation at The Citadel. Until recently, psychological research has typically conceptualized masculinity as a monolithic set of personality traits and behaviors, such as aggressiveness and inexpressiveness, that are present or absent in varying degrees within the individual (Morawski, 1985; Pleck, 1987). Social constructionist perspectives have produced the understanding that multiple forms of masculinity operate within society (Carrigan, Connell, & Lee, 1987; Connell, 1993). Feminist and postmodern critiques have underscored numerous limitations presented by defining masculinity as a unidimensional, bipolar trait. Such a conception of masculinity isolates the social phenomena of gender within the person and obscures the enactment of gender within social contexts and power relationships (Carrigan et al., 1987; West & Zimmerman, 1991). Recent conceptualizations of masculinities understand men's gender identity as a malleable construction, shaped by interpersonal, situational, and historical forces (Brod, 1987; Connell, 1993, 1995; Kimmel & Messner, 1992).

Hegemonic masculinity, as one prevalent form of masculinity, has supplanted traditional notions of the male sex role (Pleck, 1987). The term *hegemonic* is used to emphasize the dominance of this masculine paradigm within gender order among men. Hegemonic masculinity has

been succinctly defined as "stark homophobia, misogyny, and domestic patriarchy" (Connell, 1993, p. 618). The nuances of hegemonic masculinity include

> the dread of and the flight from women. A culturally idealized form, it is both a personal and a collective project, and is the common sense about breadwinning and manhood. It is exclusive, anxiety-provoking, internally and hierarchically differentiated, brutal and violent. It is pseudo-natural, tough, contradictory, crisis-prone, rich, and socially sustained. Although centrally connected with the institutions of male dominance, not all men practice it, though most benefit from it. (Donaldson, 1993, pp. 645–646)

Two concepts related to hegemonic masculinity are hypermasculinity, defined as "exaggerated, extreme masculine behavior" (Pleck, 1987, p. 31), and protest masculinity, defined as the "instances of extreme sex-typed behavior on the part of some males . . . who are in conflict about or who are insecure about their identities as males" (Broude, 1990, p. 103). Both of these definitions are incorporated within the concept of hegemonic masculinity. By any name, this phenomenon involves behavior considered to be extremely masculine and an assertion of male entitlement.

It is our thesis that, although hegemonic masculinity invokes the power of male privilege, it is also a fragile construction due to its challenging prescriptions and its fundamental opposition to women and gay men. The social sciences and popular culture have often viewed the development of manhood as a treacherous path, fraught with the obstacles of overbearing mothers, absent fathers, feminized schools, homosexual influences, an increasingly bureaucratic workforce, and women's encroachment on traditional male spaces (Ehrenreich, 1983; Hantover, 1978; Herek, 1986; Kimmel, 1987; Pleck, 1987; Segal, 1990; Sexton, 1969). Moreover, hegemonic masculinity is narrowly defined by what it is drawn in opposition to: women, gay men, effeminacy, and so on. Without these borders to police and preserve the context of hegemonic masculinity, the construct begins to unravel. Donaldson (1993), therefore, summarizes the duality of hegemonic masculinity with the statement, "fragile it may be, but it constructs the most dangerous things we live with" (p. 646).

Method

A particularly rich understanding of the situation facing The Citadel emerges from background research that we conducted for the expert testimony of Dr. Michelle Fine. Dr. Fine is a social psychologist at the City University of New York Graduate Center who specializes in research on gender and education. She was asked by the American Civil Liberties Union (ACLU) to be an expert witness for the prosecution. In turn, she asked us, her research assistants, to investigate hegemonic masculinity at The Citadel. Not only was our area of academic research in gender and organizations, but our personal histories combined to afford us unique insights into this paramilitary fraternity—Judi had served in the Israeli army and Mike had been president of his fraternity in college.[5]

The research presented here, solicited by Dr. Fine and the ACLU, includes numerous sources of data that allow for a descriptive analysis of the gender dynamic surrounding The Citadel at this critical moment in its history. These data sources include court depositions and testimony (Faulkner, 1993; Rembert, 1993; Riesman, 1991; Snyder, 1993; Vergnolle, 1993), school documents and publications (The Citadel, 1992, 1992–1993), and media accounts and scholarly works regarding the situation at The Citadel (Applebome, 1995; Faludi, 1994; Mahan & Mahan, 1993; Smothers, 1994). Several days of observation, interviews, and focus groups with cadets, faculty, administrators, and staff during

two site visits to the school in 1993 and 1994 were also provided for Dr. Fine's testimony (Addelston, 1994; Addelston & Stirratt, 1993). The emergent themes from this research are recorded here.

Hegemonic Masculinity at The Citadel

The development and performance of hegemonic masculinity is a vital task for Citadel cadets. As delineated in The Citadel's mission statement, the explicit purpose of the school is to develop the "whole man." For The Citadel, the key ingredient of this process is the homosocial atmosphere, the immersion in an all-male culture. One cadet related a metaphor that Citadel instructors often use to explain the "whole man" philosophy to cadets:

> A whole man is like a table with four sturdy legs. The four legs of the table represent a solid grounding in the academic, military, physical, and spiritual realms, and the table top represents the attainment of the ideals of honor and loyalty. If one leg of the table is not well formed, then the entirety of the table—the whole man—is unsound.

Because the goal of becoming a whole man is held as the paramount aim for cadets at The Citadel, the elements of a whole man can be examined to illuminate the performance of masculinity at The Citadel. The following analysis will focus on the academic, military, and physical components of the "whole man."

Academically, many cadets stated that they attend The Citadel to experience the discipline of its academic program and to improve their grades. The school aims to promote study habits among cadets by reserving several hours of "study periods" each day during which cadets are required to do homework. Many cadets felt that this programming and the austere environment at The Citadel helped them with their studies. Several cadets explained that their high school grades had suffered through involvement with partying, girlfriends, or alcohol and drug use, and that they have been able to reform their study habits at The Citadel. A sophomore cadet offered himself as evidence, stating, "Look, in high school I had a 2.3 GPA, but now I've got a solid 3.2."

The academic rigors of The Citadel are often undermined on several fronts, however. Although the cadets cited academics at The Citadel as one of its strengths, the school is ranked fourth out of five categories of academic competitiveness by *Barron's Profiles of American Colleges* (Barron's Educational Series, 1992), earning the category "Less Competitive." Colleges in this category "admit students with averages below C who rank in the top 65% of the graduating class" and "usually admit 85% or more of their applicants" (p. 254). A female psychology professor confessed that the strenuous paramilitary training and hazing at the school meant that "invariably, there are two or three students who sleep through every class." One senior cadet explained that he believed the study periods were instituted to compensate for this problem, "so that we don't get overwhelmed with the military training." He also explained that cadets vary in the seriousness with which they use these hours; he preferred to spend them in the library, studying and talking with his girlfriend.[6]

The academic realm aids in the production of hegemonic masculinity through the social dynamics of the all-male classroom. Many cadets state that the absence of women in the classroom keeps them focused on their studies instead of interaction with women. One faculty member echoed this point, testifying that the "introduction [of] females in the classroom [would] distract the cadets because they are lusty" (Rembert, 1993, p. 87). The all-male classroom also shapes the relationship between students and faculty. A junior cadet, asked to explain who his favorite professors were, cited a male English teacher who, the cadet explained, was

> just cool . . . like, the first day of class, he will give this big speech about literature, and then he'll sit at his desk and say, "this semester, we're going to study the finer texts," and then he'll hold up a *Penthouse* that he has under his desk.

The cadet went on to say that his act inevitably produced a strong outburst of laughter among the student cadets. In this incident, the male faculty member used the homosocial context of the classroom to bond with the students through the pornographic ostracism of women. This "academic" exercise helps to establish women as the denigrated out-group.

Militarily, Citadel cadets hone their performance of hegemonic masculinity through the demands of the school's hierarchical Fourth Class System. This process begins on the first day when each cadet receives a short military haircut and the official uniform of The Citadel to be worn at all times. The cadets are organized into squads and receive military training to obey orders and act as a cohesive unit. Under the Fourth Class System, each cadet is subject to the authority of older upperclassmen and a specific code of conduct, and cadets gain status and privileges as they advance through the system. First-year knobs have the lowest status at the school and must conform to numerous restrictions placed on their conduct. Knobs are required to walk in the gutters and streets of the campus and never on the sidewalks or lawns, and during meals they are allowed to eat only after they have served the upperclassmen and have received permission to commence eating. Rooms in the barracks have no locks on the doors, allowing upper-class cadets to burst into knob rooms for inspections at any hour. The grueling nature of this system is reflected in the fact that approximately 15% of each knob class drops out of the school within the first month, and that the school publishes a handbook for parents to help them and their sons understand and adjust to the process (The Citadel, 1992).

The performance of hegemonic masculinity lies at the core of The Citadel's paramilitary training. Many cadets were aware of the rigorous demands of the Fourth Class System before they enrolled in The Citadel and cited this training as a reason they chose the school. A cadet in his junior year saw the paramilitary training as a test of his manhood, explaining, "I figured that if I could make it at The Citadel, I could make it anywhere." One Citadel administrator commented on his belief that the Fourth Class System had a transformative effect on cadets, stating that "lots of boys [who come here] are nerds and this place turns them around." The paramilitary structure of the institution not only provides cadets with a test of their masculinity, but it also unites them within a fraternal bond. One Citadel graduate explained, "I personally think the greatest experience I had at The Citadel was the experience I had learning how to become a team with my fellow classmates." Finally, the paramilitary training at The Citadel provides a context for cadets to display their masculinity before others. Every Friday afternoon, the cadets participate in a drill exercise and march before spectators who are usually composed of girlfriends, families, and school alumni. Taking the field in full-dress uniforms, rifles in hand, these cadets work to demonstrate their military precision and masculine prowess to themselves and to others.[7]

Physically, cadets at The Citadel prove their masculinity by engaging in sports, intensive training, and punishing hazing practices. Citadel athletes are pushed to great lengths to succeed in their sporting activities. The irony of being on a sports team at The Citadel is that athletes are expected to win every game (and often hazed if they do not). Also, they are not highly regarded by their peers, because they get out of many of the military exercises, replacing them with athletic practice (cf. Drescher, 1992).

Citadel cadets also endure a series of physically punishing institutionalized rituals and incidents of informal hazing. Near the end of the school year, knob cadets traditionally engage in the "stair-rushing ceremony." In this ritual, members of the knob class must successfully mount a flight of stairs in the barracks that is obstructed by senior class members. During a site visit to the school, this "ceremony" left one knob cadet hospitalized with a leg injury, and a senior cadet explained that several cadets invariably wind up in the infirmary after this ceremony. Another cadet described the birthday ceremony where a cadet's birthday is celebrated by stripping him of his clothes and tying him naked to a chair in the middle of the foyer of the barracks. One graduate explained the following:

> On one's birthday at The Citadel, if you are unlucky enough to have your birthday fall between September and June while you were in school, your classmates come and get you and they take all your clothes off. They take the black kind of dye that goes around the edges of your shoes and they paint your testicles. (Snyder, 1993, p. 34)

These types of rituals and hazing practices create a sense among the cadets that they have shared intimate experiences and have surmounted difficult tasks designed to test their masculinity. Snyder goes on to narrate the importance of this fraternal bond:

> I think everybody who ever meets a group or whoever has contact with The Citadel, will tell you it's a special group. That they cannot believe that there is no [other] fraternity that has that closeness. . . . It's kind of like a brotherhood, or a fraternity of men that will stand by one another, that will fight for one another, that will do everything they can to help each other. (pp. 69, 71)

As in the homosocial bonding within fraternities, this creates a sense of in-group solidarity and superiority (Sanday, 1990).

Interpretations of Masculine Fortifications at The Citadel

As a "bastion of masculinity," certain objects at The Citadel act as "fortifications" that perpetuate masculine practices at the school and demark these practices from the outside world. These objects—the barracks, the uniforms, and The Ring—illustrate the meaning and practice of manhood at The Citadel. In each of these fortifications, we see the construction of The Citadel as a fragile institution, sheltering rites of manhood from the contaminating presence of women.

The confines of the barracks cloak a number of unofficial ceremonies at The Citadel that are predicated on nudity and hazing, such as the birthday ceremony.[8] Hazing, although forbidden, is practiced in the barracks away from the purview of the school's administrators. One such hazing practice is stringing up a cadet nude and threatening him with a sword near his testicles (Drescher, 1992). The barracks shelter these hazing rites that are designed to test the cadet's (hegemonic) masculinity and unofficially help to create the "whole man."

In the push to build the "whole man," the uniform is another essential ingredient necessary in ironing out difference and patching together manly solidarity. As Morgan (1994) states, "The uniform absorbs individualities into a generalized and timeless masculinity while also connoting a control of emotion and a subordination to a higher rationality" (p. 166). The homogenizing purpose behind the uniforms is most clear in the school's rhetoric around race that one administrator summarized by referencing the gray cadet uniforms: "I don't see black and white, just gray." However, one wonders how successful the uniform is at achieving such ends given the number of racist incidents of the school over the years.[9] Nonetheless, the uniforms intend to strip the cadets of their individual identities and foster a sense of solidarity and in-group equality.

The Ring is another material embodiment of masculinity at The Citadel. The goal for each Citadel cadet is to graduate from the school and receive "The Ring," a symbol for the completion of the school's demanding military regimen and the attainment of manhood. The attainment of The Ring is so important to some cadets that they initially tie it to their hand to ensure that it is not lost or stolen. The masculine symbolism of The Ring is evidenced by the unwillingness of cadets to have women touch or try on The Ring. When a female interviewer asked one cadet to show her his Ring, he adamantly stated that "you can't try it on though—that would bring bad luck." The Ring signifies attainment of manhood and membership in the exclusive fraternity of The Citadel. As such, one cadet mentioned a time when he was "nearly knocking over tables and chairs" in a restaurant to reach another man who was wearing The Ring. When the uniform comes off, and masculinity can no longer be contained by the gray, The Ring becomes the symbol of masculinity. In many ways, The Ring may be seen in the same light as a wedding ring; The Ring binds the cadet to The Citadel and all it embodies until death.

"Skirts," "Fags," and the Rhetoric of Difference

In providing an institutional context for the performance of hegemonic masculinity and the development of a male social identity, the all-male structure of The Citadel isolates women and gay men as critical out-groups that unite

Citadel men into a collective masculine entity. Paramilitary trainers and peers constantly hold cadets to standards of hegemonic masculinity and chastise them through comparisons to women and gay men. One Citadel alumnus testified that at The Citadel, you could either be a

> "whole man" [or] a fag, a women. Those are your choices. Get the ring or be a woman and that is the way it is presented to you every day. You spend your entire career . . . connoting women with negativism. When you screw up, you are a woman. I came out of The Citadel thinking that I was automatically fundamentally more superior than half of the human race. Every time I did anything wrong at The Citadel, someone made the point of telling me I was, with expletives, a woman, you're weak, why don't you go to a woman's school, you belong in a woman's school. What is the matter, are you having your period? Why can't you do the push ups? Are you a woman? Why don't we go get a skirt for you? (Vergnolle, 1993, pp. 80–84)

To explain this virulent misogyny, Riesman (1991) has testified that "boy's schools [are] permeated with boys values, and boys gain self-esteem and self-confidence by depreciation of girls and women" (p. 103). In this way, the construction of the "whole man" at The Citadel is predicated on denigrating women and gay men as out-groups.

The cadets speak very clearly and vehemently about their desire and need to exclude women from The Citadel. Many cadets said they passed over other coed schools and specifically came to The Citadel to avoid women's influence in their lives. In one focus group, all the cadets strongly agreed with the comment of one cadet who said that women in the classroom would "contaminate" the learning environment, because the male cadets would no longer feel able to speak or act freely in the classroom. The unity that the all-male environment provides them would be adversely affected by women who would contaminate their vehicle to becoming "whole men." For many

cadets, the solution is to close the school and "just kill The Citadel" before admitting women; it would no longer be The Citadel if women were there. They see The Citadel as a haven, a place where the very structure and essence of the school protects them from outside forces that they see as obstacles on the road to manhood. Women embody those dangers through ideologies of oppositional difference; only in a woman-free space can they unite to truly become men (cf. Deaux, 1985).

To justify the exclusion of women from the corps of cadets, The Citadel relies on a rhetoric of gender differences (Fine & Addelston, 1996). These arguments outline differences between women and men physically, psychologically, and socially. In addition, they heighten concerns about male privilege and practical concerns regarding the admittance of women. One aspect of this discourse focuses on physical differences between men and women. Many of the cadets view women as physically weaker than themselves and, therefore, unable to meet the rigorous paramilitary style of The Citadel especially during the demanding "knob year." During a focus group, one cadet offered the example of a march where he had to carry an M-60, a heavy machine gun. He felt that a woman would not be able to carry this gun and, that if women were on that march, he and the other men would have to take extra duties to accommodate the women. The cadets felt that the paramilitary tasks and the physical hazing met by the cadets would need to be diluted for the women, and this, they claimed, would lower the standards at The Citadel and create resentment among the male cadets. In another example, all cadets have their heads shaved on entering The Citadel. Most cadets we spoke with said that they would want the women to shave their heads too, but they worried that this would not be required of the women, creating a difference that they found upsetting. The cadets claim the presence of "weak" women would depress them because of the supposed special treatment the women would require in the corps.

The second element of the gender difference rhetoric is psychological. Many cadets detailed the extreme physical and psychological stress induced by the grueling knob year and confessed their doubts that women could successfully complete such an emotionally demanding year. Two faculty members at The Citadel echoed this position by (mis)appropriating psychological research in a report justifying the exclusion of women from the school (Mahan & Mahan, 1993). They claim that the psychological research of Gilligan (1982) and Deaux (1985) demonstrates that women and men learn, interact, develop, and behave differently. This is cause for maintaining a woman-free environment for the cadets so they may develop "in freedom . . . away from the mother-dominant home . . . and safe from female reaction" (p. 3).

In arguing for the exclusion of women, The Citadel also underscores gender differences within the realm of social interaction. Many cadets felt that, if women were present, "good manners" would require them to pay greater attention to their personal appearance and demeanor. This relates to arguments that maintain that women in the classroom would be distracting, because women would divert the men from their scholarship by causing the cadets to think about sex. In this perspective, the construal of women shifts from that of a weak vessel unable to endure the rigors of The Citadel to a powerful threat of temptation to the cadets. However, women still remain delicate social entities in other ways. If women were admitted, the cadets also feel that they would no longer be able to use vulgar language because "ladies" are not supposed to hear such words. When a female interviewer asked several cadets to state the "bad" words that they used, they refused to speak them, claiming propriety. Ironically, women are thus construed to be at once weak and powerful agents that threaten The Citadel.

The Citadel further justifies the exclusion of women from the school through an assertion of male entitlement and privilege. Many cadets emphasize that they deliberately chose to attend The Citadel over other coed schools, because they wanted to immerse themselves in its all-male culture and participate in the attendant benefits of its fraternity. One cadet said that rather than enrolling in less expensive coed schools, he "paid good money" to experience The Citadel's all-male program. Many of the cadets further felt that admitting women to The Citadel would prompt a "lowering of standards" in the form of a weakened Fourth Class System and relaxed physical demands within the paramilitary training. Both in focus groups and individually, cadets claim that West Point and Annapolis had to lower their standards after women were admitted to these institutions, causing the schools to lose their respected, privileged status (Yoder, 1989).

Finally, The Citadel denies women access to the school due to practical concerns about the costs of integrating women into the corps of cadets. These arguments are based on the premise that women would require a separate barracks and new uniforms, and that there is no money to invest in these enterprises. If women were to be admitted, the school's preliminary plan would be to house them in the infirmary. Many people also feel that The Ring, as a potent symbol of the attainment of manhood, would need to be redesigned if women were admitted. Not only would smaller sizes be needed, but a new model should be designed to represent the fundamental change in the school. Concerns for The Ring and what it represents are so strong that one graduating cadet said that "if women come here, I'm not gonna wear my Ring."

Another key ingredient in making the "whole man" is the homosociality of The Citadel; homosociality defined by "social preferences for members of one's own gender but does not necessarily imply erotic attraction" (Britton, 1990, p. 423). There is much evidence of homophobia on campus; for example, when we asked the editor of the school newspaper about homosexuality on campus, he quickly replied it did not exist. Yet after a brief pause, he acknowledged that "about every three years, they catch two guys fooling around and throw them out." Citadel alumnus Vergnolle (1993) tells that one way to humiliate another cadet is to call him a "fag." The threat of being labeled a homosexual was used "jokingly" in one class we observed; the (male) professor chastised a cadet who was talking to a fellow student by saying, "Stop talking to your boyfriend."

Britton (1990) demonstrates that homophobia is an essential ingredient in the maintenance of patriarchal organizations and is even more virulent in same-sex institutions because "homophobia helps maintain the boundary between social and sexual interaction in a sex-segregated society" (p. 424). More pointedly.

> violations of prevailing norms threaten the collectivity. Homophobia's identity maintenance function [is the] fear of being labeled deviant [that] unites members. Men homosocial in outlook prefer other men's company and work to maintain all-male institutions. The relationship to homophobia lies in maintaining the boundary between social and sexual interaction in a homosocially stratified society. (p. 425)

Shilts (1993) also documents how homophobia is used as a tool to create a cohesive in-group in the armed forces. The Citadel is thus able to use homophobia as a tool to promote the homosocial bonding it requires to create the "whole man."

Collective and Individual Voices

"Just Say No . . . To Women At The Citadel!"

—Bumper sticker on a cadet's car

"Death Before Dikes" (sic)

—Bumper sticker on a cadet's car

"Save the Males!"

—Button worn by cadets at Citadel trial

The justifications for the exclusion of women described above permeate the collective voice of The Citadel cadets. In talking with groups in the classrooms, mess hall, or barracks, the cadets did not deviate from this "party line" while they were speaking in front of one another. Indeed, during a classroom focus group or at a mess hall lunch table, the cadets would often not only agree with one another, but they would even collectively advance an argument or describe a situation by building off of one another's sentences, creating a single coherent narrative from the voices of several individuals. The cadets' collective voice sheds insight into their notions of masculinity as they describe their attraction to The Citadel and the problems they have regarding the admission of women.

However, the collective voice of the young men use when speaking in group situations often fractures within individual narratives. The contrast that may exist between collective and individual voices was illustrated by the case of one cadet. This cadet, when speaking before a group of his peers in a classroom focus group, was adamant about keeping women out of The Citadel, because he felt women would adversely affect his classroom studies. However, when we spoke with his professor after the group session, we found out that this cadet was taking classes at the (coed) College of Charleston and had privately told his professor how much he enjoyed having women in the classroom as there was more diversity and a wider range of opinions and ideas.[10]

Not every cadet feels that change at The Citadel is bad. Several of the seniors we spoke with alone feel that it is fine for women to be at The Citadel, but they are very glad to be leaving before that happens. They are happy that they were able to go through The Citadel the way it is now; they feel they benefited from their experiences, and feel sorry for the men in future classes because they will have to deal with the school as coed. Most of the African American and Hispanic cadets with whom we spoke agreed that if women want to come to The Citadel and are able to meet the physical requirements and survive the Fourth Class system, then they should be allowed to do so. They feel that no one should be excluded based on a social category but that anyone who can do the required work should be allowed to participate. One black cadet, who has publicly expressed his support for women entering The Citadel, used analogies of race to illustrate this point. He stated that when black cadets entered The Citadel, standards were kept the same but were altered slightly to accommodate the needs of the black cadets. He used the example of shaving. All cadets must be clean shaven at all times, yet this would create skin rashes for black cadets, who are thus allowed to shave every other day. And, he said, "The walls of The Citadel did not fall."

Almost all of the cadets we spoke with one-on-one said that although they are not happy about women coming to The Citadel, they see it as an inevitable event. Several cadets gave possible solutions to housing women cadets in this context. Some suggested that another barracks could be built, and one cadet said that they could use the existing barracks and alternate single-sex floors. This indicates that some cadets are thinking (albeit individually) of *how* and not *whether* women will be housed at The Citadel.

Another discrepancy between the collective and individual voice was heard in discussing academics. In group situations, especially in the classrooms, cadets claimed that the rigors of The Citadel helped them improve their academic standing. However, an alternative story was heard in talking individually with the cadets. Many cadets told us privately that their grades had slipped during the knob year due to the ordeal of paramilitary training. They stated that they did not have sufficient time or energy to put into their schoolwork, as the Fourth Class System took up most of their time. Several cadets said they would often fall asleep in class due to the fatigue of hazing and training. In addition, some seniors we spoke with said that their grades

suffered in their last year due to excessive drinking and partying on weekends.

Many cadets said privately that if women are able to perform the physical tasks of The Citadel, they should be admitted. They could see women being admitted but were very clear that they did not want to see women get special treatment. The key for these cadets was that the system stay the same. The cadets did not want to see The Citadel's system of discipline and rigor changed.

We see, then, a tension between the official ideology of the organization and individual voices. Morgan (1994) claims this tension arises because of the conflicts in ideology between a military institution that focuses on a group identity and a liberal democracy that focuses on the rights of the individual. As The Citadel is a paramilitary organization, we can see that "there seems to be a possibility and indeed the requirement for the elaboration of a range of masculinities rather than a single hegemonic masculinity. Such a range is obviously not without bounds and some masculinities are more hegemonic than others. However, the military cannot be seen as straightforwardly a site for the construction of a single embodied masculinity" (p. 174).

Women at The Citadel

Despite all the claims The Citadel makes that women would be a distraction to the cadets and that the cadets need a male-only environment, there are women everywhere on The Citadel campus, both physically and symbolically. First, about 15% of the faculty are women.[11] The second category of women are on the staff: the secretaries, who are predominantly white, and the kitchen staff, who are black. The third category of women are the cadet's girlfriends. Although women are not allowed in the barracks, when the cadets are free to leave the campus, there are many young women hanging out outside the gates of each barrack. The fourth category of women are the night students and all the women who have access to the sports facilities and the library. We spoke with several women night students and they were uniform in their conviction that The Citadel should be coed, because they pay taxes that support the school. The fifth category of women, the mothers, are symbolically present as icons for the cadets to respect, yet distance from. The final category of women must also be imported. They are the icons of contempt used to insult and denigrate a cadet when he does not measure up to par.

Although women are present at The Citadel in many ways, the only category they are not present in is that of equal status peers. Research on the effects of equal status contact shows that it is an integral part of a comprehensive program to ameliorate prejudice (Katz & Taylor, 1988). The deleterious effects of lack of equal status contact between the male cadets and women is stated by a Citadel graduate: "[After graduation] I did not at the time know how to function around females who were my equals or superiors" (Vergnolle, 1993, p. 79). Another Citadel alumnus, who had joined the Army after graduation and was currently enrolled in the night program, told us that "these boys are in for a big shock when they join the real military because they will be operating with women as equals and superiors." This point is best narrated by a faculty member, also a Citadel graduate, who explained that "it's my belief that if the women are treated equally with the men, if regrettably they must attend The Citadel, *then it will cause the men to respect the women because there's not a double standard*" [italics added] (Rembert, 1993, p. 12). The importing of women as icons of contempt serves to police the borders of masculinity The Citadel strives to infuse into the cadets. These disdainful images of women remind the cadets to what depths they can fall if they do not measure up to The Citadel's standards of the "whole man." Deaux (1985) reports that these sex divisions serve to create opposi-

tional categories; all that is "woman" is, therefore, "not man." This reinforces cadets' beliefs of differences between the sexes to maintain exclusionary practices and also serves to enhance in-group solidarity and boost self-esteem (Tajfel & Turner, 1979).

Conclusion

Each school has its own distinct "hidden curriculum" that is successfully absorbed by its students. The "hidden curriculum" within each school is the covert message that the school endorses and "teaches" to the students (Anyon, 1979). It is through this "hidden curriculum" that the fragility of hegemonic masculinity is best illustrated. Explicitly barring women from the corps, examples of *Penthouse* as great literature, being called a "skirt" or a "fag" in derision, and viewing women as contaminating agents are all examples of the "hidden curriculum." By giving the cadets women's backs to stand on, the cadets are psychologically elevated; by sacrificing the women to maintain their social order, the cadets reap social and economic benefits; denigration of homosexuals is used to bolster in-group cohesion. Ideological arguments for sameness and difference serve to camouflage possibilities for transformation and perpetuate institutional discriminatory practices. By making explicit what is illicit in hegemonic masculinity—power, hierarchy, and the denigration of out-groups—one is able to peel away the layers that hide the "hidden curriculum" of the institution. As a "total institution" (Goffman, 1961), The Citadel presents itself to the cadets as an all-encompassing monolith that holds total power over their lives. The uniform and hazing practices also serve to deindividuate the cadets and facilitate the degradation of the Self that The Citadel fosters to (re)build the "whole man" in its image.

Thus, the hidden curriculum at this total institution underscores how sex differences are used to justify exclusion, and how these differences illuminate the fragility of hegemonic masculinity. It is our thesis that hegemonic masculinity is inherently fragile, because it is built on the exclusion of the Other. Once members of the out-group become members of the in-group, what is left to bolster the "whole man?" The Citadel's mission is to create "whole men," a task they see as necessitating the exclusion of women and gay men; boys cannot become men unless they are in a (hetero) male-only environment and use women as a denigrated out-group to bolster their self-esteem as men. The subtext and "hidden curriculum" of the mission of The Citadel is that women and gay men are a bad influence on boys and must be kept out to promote boys' journey into manhood. If women and gay men, as out-groups, were to become part of the in-group, part of the corps, they would no longer be metaphorically available for the cadets to use as the denigrated Other. This construction of hegemonic masculinity is inherently fragile because its boundaries are precariously balanced on the exclusion of relevant out-groups. Should gay men and women penetrate this fortress of hegemonic masculinity, The Citadel believes its fortifications surrounding the "whole man" would collapse, and the institution would crumble.[12]

The Citadel's hidden curriculum has held men as distinct from and superior to women for more than 150 years. As The Citadel prepares for the landmark integration of women into its corps of cadets, the school will not only have to refine its mission, but the men of The Citadel will also need to redefine their version of masculinity. The presence of women as equal status peers will interrupt the homosociality of the organization and disable these men from propping their distinctive social identity on the crutch of an excluded and denigrated female out-group. Faulkner (1993, p. 19) herself has offered what is perhaps the best ideological suggestion for a gender integrated new Citadel, proposing that

"it wouldn't be a brotherhood anymore, it would be a family."

Notes

1. The speaker of this quote is in essence stating that The Citadel is the last bastion of *hegemonic* masculinity.

2. Although The Citadel employs a paramilitary style, it is not formally connected to any of the branches of the Armed Services of America. Cadets wear uniforms and engage in the rudimentaries of a military-style basic training. ROTC exists on the campus, but only about 30% of the students enroll in it; the Fourth Class System and the paramilitary style of The Citadel are not connected to the ROTC program—rather—they *are* the essence of The Citadel

3. The military service academies, such as West Point, opened their doors to women in 1976 (Yoder, 1989). It is ironic, then, that although The Citadel claims to emulate the military service academies, they are steadfast in their refusal to integrate by sex.

4. Shannon Faulkner dropped out of The Citadel after 1 week. She stated that the 2-year-long battle had taken its toll on her emotional health and she had become physically ill during the first week in the corps. Her experience is not unlike that of the first African American children to attend white schools in Kansas; Shannon Faulkner was escorted at all times by Federal Marshals and had surveillance cameras placed outsider her room. Apparently, the strength of hegemonic masculinity at The Citadel was powerful enough to push her out but not before she (an individual women) terrorized an entire institution. Her legacy lies in all the women who are currently applying to The Citadel, about 200 in the last year, and with a female high school senior the courts have allowed to take Faulkner's place in the litigation.

5. Although we entered The Citadel with great trepidation and fears of being seen as "the enemy," we found an administration and a student body that was very willing to talk to us and present "their" side of the lawsuit. Both on and off the campus, cadets were eager to share with us their thoughts and feelings. We found a uniform story presented, regardless of whether Judi or Mike was asking questions. However, due to the sensitive nature of the legal proceedings, we were prohibited from taking names or identifying characteristics of respondents, including recording interviews and conversations, during our site visits to the school.

6. Although The Citadel is an all-male college, there are women everywhere on campus. The only place women are not allowed is in the barracks.

7. Each cadet is issued an M-14, with the firing pin removed. This illustrates what former Citadel president Vice-Admiral Stockdale called "playing soldier" (Drescher, 1993, p. 76). Faludi (1994) likens the impotence of the guns and other military hardware on the campus to "the over-all effect of a theme park for post–Cold War kids" (p. 64).

8. One cadet told us of the Senior Wool Burn that takes place at midnight on the quad. The seniors, just before they graduate, go to quad wearing their winter wool uniforms, which are hated because they itch. They build a bonfire, strip, and throw their uniforms on the fire while dancing naked around it.

9. There have been several racist incidents over the years. The yearbooks from 1977 and 1982 portray cadets dressed as Klansmen (members of a white supremacy group) and in one photograph show the lynching of a black cadet. In 1987, a black student was awakened during the night by several other cadets in white hoods who left a burning paper cross in his room. Although he brought charges against them, they were not expelled but reprimanded, and he left the school a few days later. In 1992, a black cadet woke up to a noose dangling above his bed, allegedly placed there by white cadets after he refused to sing "Dixie" for them the previous day. One black cadet told us that he had problems during his first year of "a racial nature." He began lifting weights and transferred to a different company to escape his tormentors, employing an individual means of redress in the face of institutional denials of race problems.

10. The benefits of coeducational classrooms is an opinion shared by the majority of the faculty at The Citadel. In a survey of the faculty conducted in 1992 by the Faculty Council, 71% responded "yes" to the question "do you favor the admission of women to The Citadel Corps of Cadets." When asked to choose between making The Citadel a private college, establishing a separate military college for women in South Carolina, or admitting women to the corps of cadets, 80% of the faculty chose admitting women to the corps.

11. One woman professor we spoke with said that the cadets often call her a "feminazi," which she attributes to an effort to ridicule her and reduce her power over the cadets.

12. This construction of hegemonic masculinity is fragile not only because it may be breached by men's equal status contact with women but because "the traditional male role is a self-denying and stoic–heroic combination of characteristics that takes its toll on men's physical and emotional health" (Levant, 1990). The fragility of men's health has been documented through multiple paradigms of psychological stressors (Eisler & Skidmore, 1987; O'Neil, Helms, Gable, David, & Wrightsman, 1986) and physical ailments (Doyle, 1995; Levant, 1995; Messner & Sabo, 1990).

References

Addelston, J. (1994). [Field notes.]

Addelston, J., & Stirratt, M. J. (1993). [Field notes.]

Anyon, J. (1978). Ideology and United States history textbooks. *Harvard Educational Review, 49,* 361–385.

Applebome, P. (1995, April 14). Appeals court opens way for female cadet at The Citadel. *New York Times,* p. 10.

Barron's Educational Series. (1992). *Barron's profiles of American colleges.* Hauppauge, NY: Author.

Britton, D. (1990). Homophobia and homosociality: An analysis of boundary maintenance. *The Sociological Quarterly, 31,* 423–439.

Brod, H. (Ed.). (1987). *The making of masculinities: The new men's studies.* New York: Routledge.

Broude, G. (1990). Protest masculinity: A further look at the causes and the concept. *Ethos, 18,* 103–122.

Carrigan, T., Connell, B., & Lee, J. (1985). Toward a new sociology of masculinity. *Theory and Society, 5,* 551–604.

Connell, R. W. (1993). The big picture: Masculinities in recent world history. *Theory and Society, 22,* 597–623.

Connell, R. W. (1995). *Masculinities.* Los Angeles: University of California Press.

Deaux, K. (1985). Sex and gender. *Annual Review of Psychology, 36*, 49–81.

Decker, T. (1995, August 13). She's a cadet. *New York Newsday*, p. A7.

Donaldson, M. (1993). What is hegemonic masculinity? *Theory and Society, 22*, 643–657.

Doyle, J. (1995). *The male experience*, Madison, WI: Brown & Benchmark.

Drescher, H. (1992). What is The Citadel? *Sports Illustrated, 77*, 71–79.

Ehrenreich, B. (1983). *The hearts of men: American dreams and the flight from commitment*. New York: Anchor.

Eisler, R., & Skidmore, J. (1987). Masculine gender role stress: Scale development and component factors in the appraisal of stressful situations. *Behavior Modification, 11*, 123–136.

Faludi, S. (1994). The naked Citadel. *The New Yorker, 70*, 62–81.

Faulkner, S. (1993). Deposition in *Johnson v. Jones*, U.S. District Court: Charleston Division.

Fine, M., & Addelston, J. (1996). On sameness and difference. In S. Wilkenson (Ed.), *Feminist Social Psychology II*. London: Sage.

Gilligan, C. (1982). *In a different voice*. Cambridge, MA: Harvard University Press.

Goffman, E. (1961). *Asylums: Essays on the social situation of mental patients and other inmates*. Garden City, NY: Anchor.

Hantover, J. (1978). The Boy Scouts and the validation of masculinity. *Journal of Social Issues, 34*, 184–195.

Herek, G. (1986). On heterosexual masculinity. *American Behavioral Scientist, 29*, 563–577.

Katz, P., & Taylor, D. (Eds.). (1988). *Eliminating racism: Profiles in controversy*. New York: Plenum.

Kimmel, M. (1987). The contemporary "crisis" of masculinity in historical perspective. In H. Brod (Ed.), *The making of masculinities: The new men's studies*. New York: Routledge.

Kimmel, M., & Messner, M. (Eds.). (1992). *Men's lives*. New York: Macmillan.

Levant, R. (1990). Psychological services designed for men: A psychoeducational approach. *Psychotherapy, 27*, 309–315.

Levant, R. (1995). *Masculinity reconstructed*. New York: E. P. Dutton.

Mahan, A., & Mahan, T. (1993). *The Citadel: The case for single gender education*. Unpublished manuscript submitted on behalf of the defendants in *Johnson v. Jones*. U.S. District Court: Charleston Division.

Manegold, C. (1994, September 11). The Citadel's lone wolf: Shannon Faulkner. *New York Times Magazine*, pp. 56–60.

Messner, M., & Sabo, D. (Eds.). (1990). *Sport, men, and the gender order*. Champaign, IL: Human Kinetics Books.

Morawski, J. (1985). The measurement of masculinity and femininity: Engendering categorical realities. In A. Stewart & M. B. Lykes (Eds.), *Gender and personality: Current perspectives of theory and research* (pp. 108–135). Durham: Duke University Press.

Morawski, J. (1990). Toward the unimagined: Feminism and epistemology in psychology. In R. Hare-Mustin & J. Marecek (Eds.), *Making a difference: Psychology and the construction of gender*. (pp. 150–183). New Haven, CT: Yale University Press.

Morgan, D. (1994). Theater of war: Combat, the military and masculinities. In H. Brod & M. Kaufman (Eds.), *Theorizing masculinities* (pp. 165–182). Thousand Oaks, CA: Sage.

O'Neil, J., Helms, B., Gable, R., David, L., & Wrightsman, L. (1986). Gender-role conflict scale: College men's fear of femininity. *Sex Roles, 14*, 335–350.

Peyser, M. (1995, August 28). Sounding retreat. *Newsweek*, pp. 38–40.

Pleck, J. (1987). The theory of male sex-role identity: Its rise and fall, 1936 to the present. In H. Brod (Ed.), *The making of masculinities: The new men's studies*. New York: Routledge.

Rembert, N. (1993). Deposition in *Johnson v. Jones*. U.S. District Court: Charleston Division.

Riesman, D. (1991). Deposition in *United States of America v. Commonwealth of Virginia et al*. U.S. District Court: Roanoke Division.

Sanday, P. R. (1990). *Fraternity gang rape: Sex, brotherhood, and privilege on campus*. New York: New York University Press.

Segal, L. (1990). *Slow motion: Changing masculinities, changing men*. New Brunswick, NJ: Rutgers University Press.

Sexton, P. (1969). *The feminized male*. New York: Random House.

Shilts, R. (1993). *Conduct unbecoming: Lesbians and gays in the U.S. military*. New York: St. Martin's.

Smothers, R. (1994, July 23). Citadel is ordered to admit a woman to its cadet corp. *New York Times*, p. 6.

Snyder, W. (1993). Deposition in *United States of America v. Jones*. U.S. District Court: Charleston Division.

Tajfel, H., & Turner, J. (1979). An integrative theory of intergroup conflict. In W. G. Austin & S. Worchel (Eds.), *Social psychology of intergroup relations* (pp. 33–47). Monterey, CA: Brooks/Cole.

The Citadel. (1992). *Parents guide*. Charleston, SC: Author.

The Citadel. (1992–1993). *The guidon*. Charleston, SC: Author.

Unger, R. (1979). Toward a redefinition of sex and gender. *American Psychologist, 34*, 1085–1094.

West, C., & Zimmerman, D. (1991). Doing gender. In J. Lorber & S. Farrell (Eds.), *The social construction of gender* (pp. 13–37). Newbury Park, CA: Sage.

Vergnolle, R. (1993). Deposition in *Johnson v. Jones*. U.S. District Court: Charleston Division.

Yoder, J. (1989). Women at West Point: Lessons for token women in male-dominated occupations. In J. Freeman (Ed.), *Women: A feminist perspective* (3rd ed.). Palo Alto, CA: Mayfield.

What is the nature of men's relationships with other men? Do most men have close, intimate male friends, or do they simply bond together around shared activities and interests? How do competition, homophobia, and violence enter into men's relationships with each other?

Traditionally, in literature and in popular mythology, the Truly Great Friendships are those among men. In the late 1960s and early 1970s, the concept of civilization being a "fraternity of men" was criticized by feminists, who saw women as isolated and excluded from public life. In the mid-1970s, though, the men's liberation literature began to focus on the *quality* of men's relationships, and found them wanting. Men, we discovered, have "acquaintances," "activities buddies," but rarely true friends with

PART FOUR

Men with Men: Friendships and Fears

whom they can intimately share their inner lives. Lillian Rubin and others argued that it is not that men do not want or need closeness with other men, it is just that they are so very threatened by the actuality of intimacy. Thus, when men organize their time together around work, watching a game, or playing cards, the structure of the activity mediates their time together, thus maintaining a "safe" level of emotional distance.

But why do men need emotional distance from each other? And what are the costs of maintaining emotionally shallow relationships with other men? What kinds of pressures does this place on women to be the primary "emotion workers" in men's lives? Typically, when asked who his best friend is, a man will name a woman, often his wife. (Few women, by the way, will name their husband—most will name another woman.) Men rarely feel comfortable with intimate self-disclosure with other men, as Karen Walker describes in her article. Certainly, an overemphasis on competition among males, from a very early age, is one factor that places a damper on intimate self-disclosure among men. Why would a man give away information that would make him vulnerable among his competitors in a game, education, or the workplace?

Another important barrier to male–male intimacy, as the article by Gregory K. Lehne points out, is homophobia. The fear of homosexuality—or of being thought to be homosexual by others—places severe limitations on the emotional, verbal, and physical interactions among men. Homophobia, as Gregory M. Herek suggests in his article, can have some very negative consequences.

Yet men do make friends, and often the friendships among men whose masculinity stands in opposition to the hegemonic norm can create friendships that are exemplary. Peter M. Nardi discusses the contemporary political importance of friendships among gay men, and Martin Simmons illustrates the ways that confronting racism together becomes a central element in cementing black men's friendships.

19

ARTICLE

Karen Walker

"I'm Not Friends the Way She's Friends": Ideological and Behavioral Constructions of Masculinity in Men's Friendships

Contemporary ideologies about men's friendships suggest that men's capacity for intimacy is sharply restricted. In this view, men have trouble expressing their feelings with friends. Whether due to the development of the masculine psyche or cultural prescriptions, men are viewed as highly competitive with friends. Because of their competition, they are unlikely to talk about intimate matters such as feelings and relationships. The literature on gender differences in friendship suggests that the ideologies reflect actual behavior. Researchers have found that men limit verbal self-disclosure with friends, especially when compared to women (Aukett, Ritchie, & Mill, 1988; Caldwell & Peplau, 1982; Reid & Fine, 1992; Rubin, 1985; Sherrod, 1987; Swain, 1989). Men share activities with friends (Rubin, 1985; Swain, 1987). On the other hand, there are also suggestions that the degree of self-disclosure among men may be underestimated (Hacker, 1981; Rawlins, 1992; Wright, 1982), particularly among men from particular groups (Franklin, 1992). My research on friendship shows that men and women share the stereotypes about gender differences in friendship, but

Reprinted from *Masculinities* 2 (2) 1994, pages 38–55. Reprinted with permission.

in specific friendships, men discuss their relationships and report relying on men friends for emotional support and intimacy (Walker, 1994). In addition, many activities of friendship—seeing friends for dinner, sharing ritual events, and visiting—are things both men and women do. Barry Wellman (1992) argues that there has been a widespread "domestication" of male friendship, with men seeing friends in their home in much the same way women do.

In much of the literature on gender differences in friendship, ideology has been mistaken for behavior. In part, researchers seem to have made this mistake because they have asked general, instead of specific, questions about friendship.[1] As a result, they have elicited good representations of what respondents *believe* their behavior is—beliefs that are shaped by the respondents' own ideologies. What they have sometimes failed to elicit is information about specific friendships in which variations from the ideologies may be substantial. Because researchers report what respondents tell them, it is easy to understand why researchers make this mistake. What becomes more difficult to understand is how the confusion between the ideology of friendship and friendship behavior comes to be constructed in everyday life. Why do men maintain their belief that men are less open than women in the face of considerable evidence that they do discuss their feelings with their friends? This is even more crucial because the stereotype of intimate friendship that men believe characterizes women's friendship is currently highly valued. Feminist scholars and writers have successfully revalued women's intimate relationships to the detriment of earlier ideals that privileged male bonding. While not all respondents in this study positively evaluated the stereotype of women's openness with friends, many did, as evidenced by one professional man who said,

> I mean, we [men] talk about sports and politics sometimes, any kind of safe [topic], if you will. Not that any [every] kind of interaction needs to be intimate or this and that, but it's much different when you talk to women. Women catch on. I remember once seeing Robert Bly, and he said something that is really so in my experience, that women get to the heart of things and that they get there so quickly that it makes you, uh, it can put men into a rage because women are able to articulate these kinds of things that men can't.

Given the belief that being intimate and "getting to the heart of things" is good, and given the evidence that men are more intimate in practice than the ideology suggests, *why don't men challenge the ideology?*

There seem to be several answers to this question. First, when men do not conform to the masculine ideals about how they should act with their friends, they are occasionally censured. In the practice of masculine friendship, the positive evaluation of feminine intimacy disappears. Because of their friends' reactions, men come to see their behavior as anomalous and bad, and they do not reevaluate the extent to which the ideology of masculine friendship accurately reflects behavior.

Second, social class influences men's capacities for conforming to gender ideologies. Professional men are somewhat more likely than working-class men to conform to gendered norms with respect to intimate behavior (Franklin, 1992; Walker, 1994). Also, professional men's social class makes them—with other middle-class men—the primary groups on which cultural stereotypes are based. Literature written specifically about men's friendships often relies on research of middle-class men, particularly college-aged men (Caldwell and Peplau, 1982; Rawlins, 1992; Reid and Fine, 1992; Rubin, 1985; Swain, 1989). Very recently, some researchers have noted that men who are other than middle-class or white may have different types of friendships from the ideology (Franklin, 1992; Hansen, 1992), but the knowledge of the existence of other forms of masculine friendship among working-class African American and white men has not influenced the ideology of friendship.

Third, there *are* gender differences in behavior, and these differences reinforce stereotypes about gendered forms of friendship, even if the differences differ substantively from the substance of the ideology. For instance, male respondents in this study used the telephone somewhat differently from the ways women used it. Through their use of the telephone men constructed their masculinity, and in so doing they reinforced their notions that men are not open. As I will show, men claimed they called their friends for explicitly instrumental reasons—to make plans, get specific information, and so on—but not to find out how friends were, which they connected to women's telephone use. These practices generally supported the idea that women were better at maintaining friendships and talking to friends about feelings even though men's telephone conversations often included talk about personal matters. But a desire to talk to friends about personal matters was rarely the motive for phone calls.

In this article I examine the ways gender ideology about friendships is maintained through four behaviors and men's interpretations of those behaviors: telephone use, jokes, the use of public space, and how men talk about women. It is only when we understand how men behaviorally construct gender within friendship that we can begin to understand how men use these behavioral constructions to support ideological constructions of masculine friendship practices.

Method of Study

This paper relies on research from a study of men's and women's same-gender and cross-gender friendships. I interviewed 9 working-class and 10 professional men (as well 18 working-class and 15 middle-class women). Within each class I individually interviewed some men who were friends with other respondents in the study. Interviewing friends allowed me to gather information on group interaction that would have been unavailable had I interviewed isolated individuals. In addition, I was able to explore issues that were most salient to groups of friends. Finally, by interviewing friends I could examine the extent to which friends agree on what their interactions were like. This was particularly important when there was a discrepancy between behavior and ideology: Some men did not report on behavior that contradicted the masculine ideology of friendship either because they were unwilling to disclose that their behavior did not match the cultural ideal or because such behavior was somewhat meaningless to them, and they forgot it.

Respondents ranged in age from 27 to 48. Class location was determined by both life style and individuals' work. Thus, working-class respondents tended to have high school educations or less, although one self-employed carpenter had a 4-year degree in accounting. Working-class men were in construction and some service occupations. Most working-class men lived in densely populated urban neighborhoods in row houses or twins in Philadelphia. Professional respondents had graduate degrees, and they worked as academics, administrators, lawyers, and therapists. Professionals lived in the suburbs of Philadelphia or in urban apartments.

Interviews were semistructured, and respondents answered both global questions about their friendship patterns as well as questions about activities and topics of conversations in which they engaged with each friend they named. The use of in-depth interviews that included both global and specific questions allowed me to gather data indicating the frequent discrepancies between cultural ideologies of masculine friendships and actual behaviors. In addition, in-depth interviews allowed me to compare working-class and professional respondents' experiences.

Recently, Christine Williams and Joel Heikes (1993) have observed that male nurses shaped responses to interview questions in ways that took into account the gender of the interviewer. In this study, my status as a woman interviewer appeared to have both positive and negative implications for data collection. On the one hand, being a woman made it more likely that men admitted behavior that contradicted gender ideology. Sociologists studying gender and friendship have consistently argued that men do not engage in self-disclosure with other men (Caldwell & Peplau, 1982; Reid & Fine, 1992). Other research shows that men are likely to be more self-disclosing with women than with men (O'Meara, 1989; Rubin, 1985). While my research shows that men engaged in self-disclosure more frequently with friends than the literature suggests, they did so with men they considered close friends. Frequently close friends were people they knew for a long time or people with whom they spent much time. Wright (1982) notes that long-time men friends engage in self-disclosure. I suspected that certain kinds of disclosures that men made during the interviews might have been more difficult to make to an unknown man instead of to me, an unknown woman.

On the other hand, respondents suggested that they more heavily edited their responses to questions about how they discussed women with their men friends than they did other questions. They frequently sprinkled their responses with comments recognizing my gender, "You don't have a gun in there, do you? (laugh)" or "I don't mean to be sexist here." I suspected that responses were much more benign than they would have been if I were a man. Thus, when I discuss men's talk about women below I believe that my data underestimate the extent to which men's talk about women constructs gender tensions.

Behavioral Construction of Masculinity

In recent years sociologists of gender have come to emphasize the active construction of gender. Gender is seen as an ongoing activity fundamental to all aspects of social life rather than a static category in which we place men or women (Connell, 1987; Leidner, 1991; West & Zimmerman, 1987). One advantage of a social constructionist perspective is that it allows researchers to explore both the ideological as well as the behavioral construction of gender. Gender is constructed *ideologically* when men and women believe that certain qualities, such as intimacy, characterize one gender rather than another. The way men and women interpret life and its meaning for them is deeply influenced by their ideological beliefs. Gender is constructed *behaviorally* in the activities men and women do and the way they do them.

Sometimes ideology and behavior match— such as when men talk about gender differences in telephone use and report behavior that differs from women's behavior. Sometimes ideology and behavior do not match. When there is a mismatch, the interesting problem of how ideology is sustained when behavior contradicts it

emerges. I argue that, in the specific case of friendship, specific behaviors supported men's gendered ideologies. Men discounted or ignored altogether evidence that discredited a distinctly masculine model of friendship. This occurred because gender is a category culturally defined by multiple qualities. When men included themselves in the masculine gender category based on some behavior, they tended unreflectively to accept as given the cultural boundaries of the entire category *even if other of their behaviors contradicted those boundaries.*

Among respondents there were several ways masculinity was constructed in the activities of friendship. First, where men met, particularly working-class men, became a mark of masculinity. Second, the way men used the telephone distinguished masculine from feminine behavior. Third, men used jokes in particular ways to establish masculinity and also to manage tensions between actual behavior and gender ideologies. Finally, men friends talked about women in ways that emphasized the differences and tensions between men and women.

There are class differences in the behaviors that form particular patterns of masculinity. Differential financial constraints, the social expectations of particular kinds of work, and lifestyle differences played roles in shaping particular forms of masculinity. The use of jokes was somewhat more elaborated among working-class men than among professional men, but reports of jokes and joking behavior emerged in both groups. Professional men talked about wives and the strains of work and family differently from working-class men; as I will discuss, this resulted from different work experiences.

Besides class differences, which I will address throughout the article, there were individual differences. All men did not engage in all the behaviors that I argue contribute to the construction of masculinity. One professional man said that while he talked "about what specific women are like," he did not talk about women in general and men who talked about what women are generally like "would not be my friends." Other men did not report the use of jokes and joking behavior in their friendships. Sociology frequently avoids discussion about individuals who do not participate in the behaviors that the sociologist argues shows the existence of meaningful social patterns. Unfortunately, doing so often reifies behavioral differences. This is a particular problem in the discussion of gender because there is currently (and happily for the existence of a lively, informed debate) a very close link between the results of social research on gender and broad social and political debates about men's and women's differences.

I wish, therefore, to give the reader a general indication of the individual variability in the gendered behaviors in which men engaged. In all the behaviors discussed below at least half, and frequently more, of the men participated in the behaviors whereas few women did. There were, however, individual exceptions to these behaviors, and those exceptions point to a flexibility in gendered behavior that, while not as expansive as many would wish, is broader than we frequently recognize. Current social theory about gender emphasizes the agentic nature of the construction of gender. It is a practice in which men and women have a considerable range of actions from which to choose. At given historical points, certain actions may be dictated more than others, and therefore individual men and women may frequently act in ways that conform to current ideology. But even when cultural ideology demands close adherence to particular practices, the practical nature of gender means that some individuals will not conform. Further, the multiplicity of practices that create gender enables individuals to maintain their positions within gender categories without much difficulty.

Men's Use of Public Space

The use of public space for informal and apparently unplanned socializing is much more common among men than among women, and it marks the gender boundaries between men and women. The frequent use of public space by working-class men for informal socializing emerges in ethnographies of men's groups (Anderson, 1976; Kornblum, 1974; Liebow, 1967; Whyte, 1981). Working-class men in this study met in public spaces such as local bars and playgrounds. There they talked about work and family, and they made informal connections with other men. Sometimes they picked up side work, sometimes they hung out. At the time of our interview, one working-class man said that he spent some of his time at a local bar selling advertisements in a book to raise money for a large retirement dinner for a long-time coach of a community football team. He also spent time there drinking and talking to friends.

Working-class men also met in semipublic spaces such as gyms or clubs. While membership in these spaces was frequently restricted, the spaces themselves functioned in similar ways to public spaces. Men met regularly and informally in public and semipublic spaces one or more times a week. Unlike women who made definite plans to meet friends occasionally in bars, the men assumed because of past practice that on particular nights of the week they would meet friends.

Wellman (1992) suggests that the use of public space for male socializing is diminishing, and men's friendships are becoming domesticated as their friendships move into the home and hence more like women's. This phenomenon of domestication was evident among professional respondents, most of whom reported socializing infrequently in public spaces. But it was not evident among the working-class respondents in this study. All but one of the working-class respondents had been brought up in the same communities in which they lived when I interviewed them. Among these men there were long-time, continuous patterns of public socializing. While Wellman's point is important, the domestication of male friendship seems to be influenced by circumstances in men's lives and is probably occurring unevenly. Further, barring significant structural changes in working-class men's formal and informal work lives, the domestication of male friendships is unlikely to be complete.

Men's Telephone Use

Discussions of men's telephone use as a construction of gender make the most sense when contrasted with women's telephone use. Many men noted that their wives used the telephone very differently from them. A few, primarily working-class men, stated that they disliked talking on the telephone, and they used it only for instrumental reasons (e.g., to make appointments or get specific information). Other men, both professional and working class, said their wives called friends just to see how they were doing and then talked for a long time, whereas men did not do so. Thus men ideologically constructed gender through their understandings of telephone practices. In addition, both men and women constructed gender behaviorally through using the telephone in different ways.

Telephone use differed slightly by class and work experiences, but even accounting for the effects of class and work, there were substantial gender differences. Men frequently reported that the purpose of their most recent telephone calls with friends was instrumental: lawyers discussed cases, men discussed upcoming social plans, and some working-class men made plans to do side work together. Because of this instrumental motive for telephone calls to friends, many professional men reported that their frequent telephone contact was from their offices during working hours. Men rarely reported that they called friends just to say "hi" and find out how they were. One professional man, Mike,[2] reported differences between his wife and himself in being friends,

I'm not friends the way she's friends. *How are you friends differently?* I don't work on them. I

don't pick the phone up and call people and say, "How are you?"

While Mike reported that, in fact, he did call one friend to find out how he was doing at least once a year, most telephone contact was initiated when friends made plans to visit from out of town or he had business matters to discuss with friends. One result of this behavior was tremendous attrition in his friendship network over time. Mike was a gregarious man who reported many past and current friends, but he tended to lose touch with past friends once business reasons for keeping in touching with them diminished, even those who continued to live in Philadelphia. He only reported talking to two friends six or more times a year on the telephone. One of those friends was a man with whom he had professional ties, and they called one another when they did business. The other friend, Gene, was one of the few men who called friends for social conversations. The fairly frequent calls between Gene and Mike may have been initiated by Gene.

Gil, a working-class man, usually spoke to friends on the phone to arrange meetings. Although he kept in touch with two friends largely through telephone use (he worked two jobs during the week and one of his friends worked on weekends—theirs was a telephone friendship), he said,

> I don't talk to them a long time because I'm not a phone person. I'd rather see them in person because I don't like holding the phone and talking because you really can't think of things to say too often on the phone, but when you're in person you can think of more things, cause I like prefer sitting and talk to a person face-to-face . . . I'll talk to people 10, 15 minutes sometimes, but I prefer not to if I can. But some you just can't get off the phone, no matter what you do. And you're like, "Uh, great, well, I'll talk to you a little bit later." And they go into another story. You know [my friend] Cindy will do that, Cindy is great for that. Now Joanne [my wife] can talk on the phone for two

to three hours ... And then the person she's with is not too far away so she could just walk over and talk, you know.

Peter, a young working-class man, reported that he "avoided the phone as much as possible." He did not call friends to chat, and he only used the telephone for social chats with one friend, a woman:

> I'm not a phone person, but yeah, I do [talk to a specific friend] because she talks on the phone, she likes the phone so ... She'll talk and I'll yes and no (laughs).

Peter did not do side jobs with other men, thus his reasons for using the telephone were sharply limited. Peter and Gil both reported that their telephone preferences were different from those of women they knew. Their general comment "I'm not a phone person" was a representation of their identity, and it was substantiated by their behavior that differs from women's behavior. Typically, working-class men spoke on the telephone once or twice a week to those with whom they did side jobs. One man who ran a bookmaking business with a friend reported that they spoke several times a day about business. Men spoke much less frequently than that to friends for other reasons.

Although most men reported calling friends for instrumental reasons, many men reported that their telephone conversations were not limited to the reason for the call. During telephone calls men discussed their families or their work after they finished with their business. During telephone calls made to discuss social plans several men discussed infertility problems with their wives. Another complained to a friend about his marital problems during a phone call initiated to plan side work. One man called a friend to make plans for a birthday dinner for the caller's wife. During the conversation he told his friend how many feelings the interview I had with him had stirred up (the friend had referred me to him). These conversations, then, had several functions for men's friendships. The telephone was pri-

marily considered a tool for business or to make social plans, but it was also used as means of communicating important personal information. Most men, however, deemphasized the telephone's function in the communication of personal information.

About one fourth of the men reported that they did call friends simply to find out how they were. Most of the time these men reported calling out-of-town friends with whom they lacked other regular means of contact, and most of the time their calls were infrequent—one to three times a year. In one exception, a professional man regularly called friends to see how they were (and sometimes became irritated and upset when the friends did not reciprocate by initiating some percentage of the telephone calls). He talked with one local friend once a week for no other reason than to keep in touch, but this pattern was unique. The friend he called had limited mobility, and the men rarely saw one another. The telephone was a primary vehicle for their friendship. In this instance, the two men's calls differed little from some women's calls.

There was tremendous variation in telephone use among men, but the variation does not erase the differences across genders. While only one quarter of the men in this study reported that they ever called friends to visit over the telephone and three quarters called for instrumental reasons, over four-fifths of the women reported that they called friends to visit. Also, men's reported frequency of telephoning friends was consistently lower than women's. Whereas two-thirds of all women reported that they spoke with at least one friend three or more times a week, less than one quarter of the men did so.

The finding that men use the telephone less than women and that women use it for social visiting has been noted by others (Fischer, 1992; Rakow, 1991). Fischer (1992) argues,

> research shows that, discounting their fewer opportunities for social contact, women are

more socially adept and intimate than men, for whatever reasons—psychological constitution, social structure, childhood experiences or cultural norms. The telephone therefore fits the typical female style of personal interaction more closely than it does the typical male style (p. 235).

Fischer's comments may hold a clue about how ideologies of gender are maintained despite the evidence of intimate behaviors among men. Men and women both see the telephone as something women use more than men, and they see it as a way women are intimate. Men's telephone practices provided evidence to respondents that men are incapable of intimacy whereas women are very intimate with friends. Although women used the telephone more often for intimate conversation than men, men used opportunities at work and in public hangouts to talk intimately (one respondent reported that when they got together in the bar "we're worse than a bunch of girls when it comes to that [talking about their spouses]!"). Although telephone patterns are a poor measure of intimacy in friendship, men used them as such. Several men commented on hearing their wives call friends and talk about personal information. Doing so substantiated their impressions of women's friendships. Also, because the men focused on the reasons for their calls rather than on the contents of telephone calls, telephone use acted to provide confirmation that stereotypes about friendship are true.

Men's Jokes

Men's use of jokes is another way in which men construct their masculinity. In his ethnography, *America's Working Man*, David Halle (1984) points to several functions jokes serve among men: they reaffirm values of friendship and generosity, they ritually affirm heterosexuality among men whose social circumstances create a level of physical and emotional intimacy culturally regarded as unmasculine, and they mediate

disputes. These functions were evident in the way working-class men talked about jokes and humor in their friendships. They were less evident among the professional men, for reasons suggested by Halle.

Men friends, particularly working-class men, used harsh teasing as a form of social control to reinforce certain behaviors. One working-class man said that he and his friends were the worst "ball breakers" in the world. If a man did not show up at the bar or at some social event then my respondent said they heard about it from all their friends. Among these men the friendship group was highly valued, but also, like many contemporary friendships, somewhat fragile. Work and family responsibilities that kept men away from the friendship group might put a friend at risk of being teased.

Other men said that the failure to reciprocate favors, such as help with household projects, might be a basis for teasing friends. This was a particularly important way of defusing tension as well as reaffirming values of friendship for working-class men. They frequently depended on friends to help them attain higher standards of living: friends provided craft services whose prices are high in the formal market and thus many working-class people's material lives were somewhat improved through the help of friends. Failure to reciprocate had implications not only for friendship but also for family income. Jokes about a friend's failure to reciprocate became a public statement about his failure to conform to recognized norms, and they were a way for someone to handle his anger at his friend.

Another way jokes constructed masculinity was to highlight an activity that was outside the purview of men's activities that they nonetheless did. For instance, Greg and Chris were friends from law school who saw each other seven or eight times a year. One of those times was a yearly shopping trip to buy Christmas presents. Men generally claimed they did not shop—those who did usually said they went to hardware stores when they were doing a project with a friend. The shopping trip Greg and Chris went on was a traditional joke between them both. It began in law school when Greg asked Chris to go with him to buy a negligee for Greg's girlfriend. When they got to the store Chris ran away and Greg was left feeling terribly embarrassed. Ever since, they went shopping once a year, but both men downplayed the shopping aspect of the trips and highlighted the socializing. They said they did not accomplish very much on their trips. They also said they used the time to buy gag gifts for people instead of serious gifts. Turning the shopping spree into a joke subverted the meaning of shopping as something women do, and the trip became a ritual reaffirmation of masculinity.

Jokes were sometimes used as pseudoinstrumental reasons to call friends on the phone when men lacked instrumental reasons; they thus maintained the masculinity of men's telephone practices. Men called each other and told one another jokes and then moved into more personal topics. Gene, for instance, befriended Al's lover, Ken, before Al died of AIDS. During Al's illness Gene was an important source of support for both men, and he continued to keep in touch with Ken after Al's death. They talked regularly on the telephone, but most of the conversations initiated by Ken began with jokes. After Ken and Gene had exchanged jokes the two men moved on to other topics, including their feelings for Al.

Finally, men used jokes to exaggerate gender differences and denigrate women. Gene considered himself sympathetic to women's issues. He said that he and his friends

> will tell in a joking way, tell jokes that are hostile towards feminism or hostile towards women. It's like there's two levels of it. One is, we think the joke is funny in and of itself or we think the joke is funny because it's so outrageously different from what's politically correct. You know, so we kind of laugh about it, and then we'll laugh that we even had the gall to tell it.

Not all men mentioned the importance of humor to friendship, the existence of jokes among friends, or the tendency to tease friends, but about half the respondents indicated that jokes and teasing were part of their friendship. Also, jokes and joking behavior were not limited solely to men. A few women also told jokes and engage in joking behavior with their friends, but men emphasized the behavior as part of their friendships, whereas women did not. Also, women reported using jokes in a much more restricted way than men. For men, jokes are an elaborated code with multiple meanings and functions.

Men Talk About Women

Finally, men constructed masculinity through their behavior with men friends through their talk about what women are like. While not every man reported that he engaged in discussions about women with his friends, most men did. Comments about women emphasized men's and women's differences. Men, for instance, discussed how their wives had higher housekeeping standards than they, their wives' greater control over child rearing, and their greater propensity to spend money impulsively; they also discussed women's needs for relationships. These comments helped men interpret their relationships with their wives and served to reassure men that their experiences were not unusual.

> We would talk about like how long it would take them to get dressed . . . my wife took exceptionally long to get dressed, four or five hours in the bathroom. Um, but I mean, I don't think I talk a whole lot about women, when I did I guess I generalized and that kind of stuff, like how a wife expects a husband to kind of do everything for her. (Working-class man)

> What we talked about was the differences, differences we have with our wives in terms of raising kids. . . . And how sometimes we feel, rightly or wrongly, we both agreed that we didn't have quite as much control over the

situation or say in the situation as we might have liked . . . That's something that a lot of my friends who have younger kids, I've had that discussion with. I've talked to them about it in terms of something that I think mothers, in particular, have a different input into their child's lives than do fathers. (Professional man)

Through these sorts of discussions with men friends—some brief and jocular, some more sustained and serious—men defined who women are, and who they were, in contrast, as men. These discussions with friends frequently reinforced stereotypes about women and men.

Women were spendthrifts:

One individual may call me up and say, "Geez, my wife just went out and bought these rugs. I need that like a hole in the head. You know, this is great, I have these oriental rugs now, you know, I'm only going to spill coffee on it." (Professional man)

Women attempted to control men's free time:

[We might talk about] how much we're getting yelled at or in trouble or whatever, you know what I mean, for not doin' stuff around the house, or workin' over somebody else's house too much or staying out at the bars too late. (Working-class man)

Women were manipulative:

Sometimes they seem, they don't know what they want, or what they want is something different than what they tell you they want. You know, tough to figure out, [we say] that they can be manipulative . . . Conniving. (Professional man)

Men evaluated women's behaviors and desires through such talk. They reported that such talk was a way of getting feedback on their marital experiences. Talking with friends frequently relieved the tensions men felt in their cross-gender relationships, and it did so without requiring men to change their behaviors vis-à-vis women. Men rarely reported that they accommodated themselves to their wives because their friends

suggested that they should: in an unusual case, one working-class man said his friend told him that women needed to be told, "I love you," all the time, and he thought his friend had been helpful in mitigating some strains in his marriage through their talk.

More frequently, men's jokes and comments about women—about their demands for more housekeeping help, their ways with money, and their desires to have men home more often—served to delegitimize women's demands. Men talked about women as unreasonable; as one man above said, "everybody needs time away." This tendency to delegitimize wives' demands was more apparent among working-class men than among the professional men. Professionals reported that their jobs, not unreasonable wives, prevented them from greater involvement in child care, and they sometimes talked with friends about this as an inevitable part of professional life. The effect, however, was similar because talk among both professional and working-class men friends supported the status quo. Instead of becoming a problem to be solved, professional men and their friends determined that professional life unfortunately, but inevitably, caused men to limit their family involvement. (One man who consistently seemed to play with the boundaries of masculinity had tried to solve the problem through scheduling his work flexibly along the lines that a friend had suggested. He reported that he still did not have enough time for his family.)

These four behaviors: using public spaces for friendship socializing, men's telephone practices, joking, and talking about women in particular ways are some ways that men construct masculinity in their friendships. There are many others. Discussions of sports, for instance, are one obvious other way men construct their masculinity, and such discussions were common among respondents. Like women's telephone use and ease with intimacy, men's talk about sports has become part of our cultural ideology about gendered friendships. Not all respondents, however, participated in such talk, and of those who did, some did not enjoy such talk but engaged in it because it was expected.

Cultural Ideology of Men and Friendship

When I began this article I asked not only how men construct masculinity through their behaviors but also why there was a discrepancy between the cultural ideology of men's friendship's, which maintains that men do not share intimate thoughts and feelings with one another, and reports of specific behaviors that show that they do. It is in part by recognizing that the construction of gender is an ongoing activity that incorporates many disparate behaviors that this question becomes answerable. While one behavior in an interaction may violate the norms of gender ideology, other behaviors are simultaneously conforming to other ideologies of masculinity. When men reflect back on their behavior they emphasize those aspects of their behavior that give truth to their self-images as men. The other behavior may be reported, but, in this study, it did not discredit men's gender ideologies.

Second, as I noted earlier, masculinity is frequently reified, and behavior that does not conform does not affect the overall picture of masculinity. Men belong in the gender category to which they were assigned at birth, and their past in that category reassures them that they belong there. Occasionally respondents recognized that men do things that contradict gender ideology. One man told me about a friend of his who "does thoughtful things for other men." When I asked what he did, and he said:

> Uh, remembers their birthdays. Will buy them gifts. Uh, and does it in a way that's real, I think, really, uh, I don't know, it's not uh, it's not uh, feminine in the sense of, feminine, maybe in the perjorative sense . . . I mean, I remember that John, uh, John's nurturing I saw, not that I was

> a recipient of it so much although I was in his company a lot and got to see him. Uh, I thought, boy, this guy's a, this guy's a real man, this guy. This guy's all right, you know.

Though my respondent identified his friend's behavior as different, almost feminine, he made sure to tell me that the man is a "real man." This seemed problematic for him, his language became particularly awkward, full of partial sentences. But in the end, the fact that his friend was a man and that my respondent liked and respected him enabled him to conclude, "this guy's a real man."

At other times, recognition that behavior contradicts gender ideology elicits censure instead of acceptance. When men censure one another for such behavior, they reinforce the idea that such behavior is anomalous and should not be expressed. For instance, Gene, who consciously worked at intimacy with his friends, told me about sitting and drinking with a friend of his one night when Gene was depressed. His friend asked him how things were going and Gene told him he was depressed because he was feeling financial pressures. Gene felt "house poor" and upset with himself for buying a house that would cause him to feel such pressures when he had determined that he would not do such a thing. His friend's response was, "Oh, that's the last time I ask you how you're feeling." On an earlier occasion Gene called his gay friend in California on the telephone crying because he had just broken off with a woman he had been dating. His friend comforted him at the time, but later he said, "I didn't know you had it in you [to express yourself like that]." Gene believed that men had greater difficulties with self-disclosure than women, and these events acted as support for his beliefs instead of counterexamples. In both cases friends had let him know his self-disclosing behavior was either intolerable or unusual. His gay friend seemed to admire Gene's ability to call him up in tears by giving him a back-handed compliment, but this was a man who had rejected many norms of heterosexuality, and who saw Gene as participating in hegemonic masculinity (Connell, 1987) and teased him for it. Gene's interpretation of these events coincided with his friends: he was behaving in ways men normally did not.

In another case, Anna, a woman respondent, told me about her husband Tom's experience with his best friend. Anna had been diagnosed with a serious chronic illness that had profound consequences for her lifestyle, and Tom was depressed about it. One night he went out with two friends, Jim, Tom's best friend, and another man who was unhappy about his recent divorce. According to Anna, Jim commented that he wished he did not know either Tom or the other man at the time because they were both so depressed. From this, Anna said she and Tom concluded that men did not express their feelings and were not as intimate with one another as women were.

These sorts of events reinforce men's notions that men are emotionally distant. Self-disclosure and attempts to express one's feelings are seen as anomalous, even if desirable—desirable because the contemporary evaluation on friendship as defined primarily by feminists is that women have better friendships than men. Women, by the way, also reported occasions when their friends were unsympathetic to their expressions of distress. The conclusions women and men drew about their unsympathetic friendship differed, however. Women concluded that particular friends lacked sympathy. Unlike men, they did not think their expressive behavior was inappropriate or unusual.

Conclusion

I have conceptualized gender as an ongoing social creation rather than a role individuals learn or a personality type they develop that causes differences in behavior. Individuals construct gender on an ideological and a behavioral level.

On a behavioral level, many social acts contribute to the overall construction of masculinity. Men do not talk on the phone unless they have something specific they wish to find out or arrange. Men friends joke around together. Men hang out in bars. Men also talk about women and their wives in ways that distinguish women from men and define gender tensions and men's solutions to them. Some of these behaviors have become part of the cultural ideology of men's friendships. Respondents, for instance, talked generally about differences between men's and women's telephone use. Some also said that women stayed home with their friends whereas men went out. But the relationship between behavior and ideology is not so direct and simple that behaviors in which most men participate become part of the cultural ideology. To the extent that talking about women, for instance, is perceived as sharing personal information, then talking about women is something men do not recognize as characteristic of their friendships.

Because so many actions construct masculinity and gender is a practice over which individuals have some control, the failure to conform to the cultural ideology of masculine friendship does not necessarily threaten either the cultural ideology or the individual's position in the masculine gender category. This becomes particularly important in understanding why the many men who share personal information with friends continue to believe that men are inexpressive and find intimacy difficult. I have found that the exchange of intimate information is something most respondents, men and women, engaged in, but most people also did it with selected friends. Furthermore, talking about personal matters or sharing feelings frequently constituted a small portion of all friendship interactions. Thus, for men whose identities included a notion that they, as men, were not open with friends, the times when they were open were insignificant. There were many other activities of friendship that men preferred to emphasize.

It is useful to expand the debate over gender differences in friendship to include behaviors other than intimacy that has dominated the recent literature on gender and friendship (Allan, 1989; Miller, 1983; Rawlins, 1992; Rubin, 1985; Sherrod, 1987; Swain, 1987). The narrowness of the debate has limited our understandings of why men's friendships have been meaningful and important to them. Working-class men's reliance on friends for services and material support becomes invisible. The importance of joking behavior as a communicative style and its functions in maintaining stable relationships for both working-class and professional men disappear. Finally, the narrow debate over intimacy obscures some implications of how men talk to one another about women for gender relations and inequality.

A version of this article was presented at the 1993 annual meetings of the American Sociological Association in Miami. The author gratefully acknowledges the comments of Robin Leidner and Vicki Smith.

Notes

1. Some researchers have made this mistake as part of a more general positive evaluation of women. Some of this literature is explicitly feminist and draws on literature which emphasizes and dichotomizes gender differences.

2. All names of the respondents have been changed.

References

Allan, G. (1989). *Friendship: Developing a sociological perspective.* Boulder, CO: Westview.

Anderson, E. (1976). *A place on the corner.* Chicago: University of Chicago Press.

Aukett, R., Ritchie, J., & Mill, K. (1988). Gender differences in friendship patterns. *Sex Roles, 19,* 57–66.

Caldwell, M. A., & Peplau, L. A. (1982). Sex differences in same-sex friendships. *Sex Roles, 8,* 721–732.

Connell, R. W. (1987). *Gender and power.* Stanford, CA: Stanford University Press.

Fischer, C. (1992). *America calling: A social history of the telephone to 1940.* Berkeley: University of California Press.

Franklin, C. W. II (1992). Friendship among Black men. In P. Nardi (Ed.), *Men's friendships* (pp. 201–214). Newbury Park, CA: Sage.

Hacker, H. M. (1981). Blabbermouths and clams: Sex differences in self-disclosure in same-sex and cross-sex friendship dyads. *Psychology of Women Quarterly, 5,* 385–401.

Halle, D. (1984). *America's working man: Work, home, and politics among blue-collar property owners.* Chicago: University of Chicago Press.

Hansen, K. V. (1992). Our eyes behold each other: masculinity and intimate friendship in antebellum New England. In P. Nardi (Ed.), *Men's friendships* (pp. 35–58). Newbury Park, CA: Sage.

Kornblum, W. (1974). *Blue collar community.* Chicago: University of Chicago Press.

Leidner, R. (1991). Serving hamburgers and selling insurance: Gender, work, and identity in interactive service jobs. *Gender & Society, 5,* 154–177.

Liebow, E. (1967). *Tally's corner: A study of Negro streetcorner men.* Boston: Little, Brown.

Miller, M. (1983). *Men and friendship.* Boston: Houghton Mifflin.

O'Meara, J. D. (1989). Cross-sex friendship: Four basic challenges of an ignored relationship. *Sex Roles, 21,* 525–543.

Rakow, L. F. (1991). *Gender on the line: Women, the telephone, and community life.* Urbana, IL: University of Illinois Press.

Rawlins, W. (1992). *Friendship matters: Communication, dialectics, and the life course.* New York: Aldine de Gruyter.

Reid, H. M., & Fine, G. A. (1992). Self-disclosure in men's friendships. In P. Nardi (Ed.), *Men's friendships* (pp. 132–152). Newbury Park, CA: Sage.

Rubin, L. (1985). *Just friends: The role of friendship in our lives.* New York: Harper & Row.

Sherrod, D. (1987). The bonds of men: Problems and possibilities in close male relationships. In H. Brod (Ed.), *The making of masculinities* (pp. 213–239). Boston: Allen and Unwin.

Swain, S. (1989). Covert intimacy: Closeness in men's friendships. In B. Risman & P. Schwartz

(Eds.), *Gender and intimate relationships*, (pp. 71–86). Belmont, CA: Wadsworth.

Walker, K. (1994). Men, women and friendship: what they say; what they do. *Gender & Society*, 8, 246–265.

Wellman, B. (1992). Men in networks: Private communities, domestic friendships. In P. Nardi (Ed.), *Men's friendships* (pp. 74–114). New bury Park, CA: Sage.

West, C., & Zimmerman, D. (1987). Doing gender. *Gender & Society*, 1, 125–151.

Whyte, W. F. (1981). *Street corner society: The social structure of an Italian slum* (3rd ed.). Chicago: The University of Chicago Press.

Williams, C. L., & Heikes, E. J. (1993). The importance of researcher's gender in the in-depth interview: Evidence from two case studies of male nurses. *Gender & Society*, 7, 280–291.

Wright, P. (1982). Men's friendships, women's friendships and the alleged inferiority of the latter. *Sex Roles*, 8, 1–20.

20

ARTICLE

Gregory K. Lehne

Homophobia Among Men: Supporting and Defining the Male Role

Homophobia is the irrational fear or intolerance of homosexuality. Although both men and women can be homophobic, homophobia is most often associated with the fear of male homosexuality. Homophobia is not currently classified as a "mental illness" (neither is homosexuality), although psychiatrists such as Dr. George Weinberg (1972) have stated, "I would never consider a patient healthy unless he had overcome his prejudice against homosexuality." Homophobia is the threat implicit in "*What are you, a fag?*" If male homosexuality were no more threatening than being left-handed, for example, homophobia would not exist. In many ways, and in all but extreme cases, homophobia is a socially determined prejudice much like sexism or racism, rather than a medically recognized phobia.

Homophobia, as I will show, does not exist in most cases as an isolated trait or prejudice; it is characteristic of individuals who are generally rigid and sexist. Homophobia, with its associated dynamic of fear of being labeled a homosexual, is an underlying *motivation* in maintaining the

male sex role. I believe that it must be eliminated for fundamental changes to occur in male and female roles. To support this thesis, I will discuss first whether homophobia reflects an accurate perception and understanding of homosexuality or whether it is an irrational fear. Then I will examine the social aspects of homophobia and personal characteristics of people who are highly homophobic. Finally, I will explore the social functions of homophobia in maintaining the male sex role, and its effects on society and the individual.

Is Homophobia Irrational?

Homophobia is irrational because it generally embodies misconceptions and false stereotypes of male homosexuality. These belief systems, or prejudices, are rationalizations supporting homophobia, not causes of homophobia. Levitt and Klassen's 1973 Kinsey Institute study of 3,000 American adults found the following beliefs about homosexuality to be widespread: homosexuals are afraid of the opposite sex (56% of the sample believed this), homosexuals act like the opposite sex (69%), only certain occupations are appropriate for homosexuals, homosexuals molest children (71%), and homosexuality was unnatural.

First, let us consider the mistaken belief that homosexual men do not like women. Since relations with women (especially sexual) are considered one of the proving grounds of masculinity, homosexual men who do not treat women as sex objects are regarded as suspect and unmanly in our male-oriented culture. Research does not support the belief, however, that homosexual males are afraid of women. About 20% of men who consider themselves homosexuals have been married, or currently are married; about half of these gay men are fathers (Bell and Weinberg, 1978). Around 75% of homosexual males have engaged in heterosexual kissing and necking, and about 50% have participated in heterosexual intercourse in their youth, with a frequency and success rate highly similar to that of heterosexual males (Saghir and Robins, 1973). About 50% of the homosexual men in this comprehensive study reported to have at some time established a relationship with a woman, lasting more than one year and including sexual relations.

Although homosexual males were not adequately satisfied with their heterosexual experiences, they generally did not have negative reactions toward women or heterosexual activities. In studies measuring the change in the penis [in response] to various stimuli, it was found that homosexual men gave neutral (not negative) responses to pictures of female nudes (McConaghy, 1967; Freund, Langevin, Gibiri, and Zajac, 1973), pictures of mature vulva or breasts (Freund, Langevin, and Zajac, 1974), or auditory or written descriptions of heterosexual intercourse (Freund, Langevin, Chamberlayne, Deosoran, and Zajac, 1974). Heterosexual men, in comparison, were turned on by the pictures of female nudes, but revealed their homophobia through decreased penile volume in response to

pictures of male nudes, or male homosexual activities (McConaghy, 1967; Turnbull and Brown, 1977). Thus, the evidence shows that homosexual males have no particular aversion to women or heterosexual intercourse, although heterosexual males often do have aversions to male nudes and homosexual activity.

Another popular stereotype is that homosexual men are similar to women, in appearance and/or psychological functioning. For example, Tavris (1977) reports that 70% of the *Psychology Today* readership believes that "homosexual men are not fully masculine." Studies reported by Freedman (1971) as well as Saghir and Robins (1973) suggest that only about 15% of male homosexuals appear effeminate. Effeminacy itself is highly stigmatized in the homosexual subculture. Weinberg and Williams (1974) estimate that not more than 20% of male homosexuals are suspected of being gay by the people they come in contact with, although Levitt and Klassen (1973) report that 37% of the American public believes that "it is easy to tell homosexuals by how they look."

Appearances aside, some studies indicate that homosexual men are psychologically sex typed similar to heterosexual men (e.g., Heilbrun and Thompson, 1977), whereas others find they are more androgynous or sex-role undifferentiated than heterosexuals (Spence and Helmreich, 1978). Homosexual men have not been found to be similar to women in their psychological functioning. Androgynous sex-role behavior, expressing a wider variety of interests and sensitivity than stereotypic male or female roles, is believed by many to represent a better level of psychological adjustment than more rigid sex-role-defined personalities (for example, see Kaplan and Bean, 1976). Several studies report that the psychological adjustment of homosexuals who have accepted their sexual orientation is superior in many cases to most heterosexual males in terms of openness and self-disclosure, self-actualization, lack of neurotic tendencies, and happiness or exuberance (Bell and Weinberg, 1978; Freedman, 1975; Weinberg and Williams, 1974).

Levitt and Klassen (1973) found that many people (the percentages given in parentheses below) stereotyped some professions as appropriate for homosexuals and others as inappropriate. For example, the "unmasculine" careers of artist (83%), beautician (70%), florist (86%), and musician (84%) were believed appropriate for homosexual men. But the "masculine" careers of medical doctors (66%), government officials (66%), judges (76%), teachers (76%), and ministers (75%) were considered inappropriate for homosexuals.

Gallup in 1977 found a decrease since 1970 in public opinion seeking to deny homosexuals the right to be doctors (44%), teachers (65%), or ministers (54%). Notice that the professions that people would close to homosexuals are those characteristic bastions of either male power or social influence. In the real world of work, however, there is no evidence that homosexual men tend to avoid characteristically "masculine" or professional occupations. Ironically it may be true that heterosexual men avoid certain stereotyped "homosexual" occupations, resulting in a higher proportion of homosexuals in those fields.

Many studies of homosexual males have found that they tend to be disproportionately concentrated in higher status occupations, especially those requiring professional training (Saghir and Robins, 1973; Weinberg and Williams, 1974). A study in Germany suggests that homosexual males tend to be more upwardly mobile than comparable heterosexuals (Dannecker and Reiche, 1974). This carefully conducted study of a large group of homosexuals found that the social class of the families of homosexual men was representative of the general population, whereas the social status of the homosexual men themselves was higher than would be predicted from their family backgrounds, even when the mobility trends of the entire population were taken into account. This suggests that in spite of the prejudice that homosexuals encounter in work,

they are still highly successful in fields outside the low-status occupations that the general public seems to feel are appropriate for homosexuals.

Although the belief that homosexuals often molest children is widespread, I have been unable to locate any scientific research supporting it. A pedophile, an adult who seeks sex with young children, generally does not have sexual relationships with other adults and thus could not appropriately be considered either heterosexual or homosexual. Many of these individuals have sex with children of either gender. Pedophilia is a rare disturbance. Heterosexual rape, involving adolescents or adults, is much more common than homosexual rape, according to court records and sexual experience surveys. The fear that homosexuals molest children (or rape adolescents) is grossly exaggerated, and ultimately is based on the confusion of pedophilia with homosexuality.

There is evidence supporting the effectiveness of gay people in positively dealing with children. Gay parents tend to provide a psychologically healthy environment for their own children, who are actually no more predisposed than the children of heterosexuals to become homosexuals themselves, or to exhibit signs of psychological disturbance (Bell, 1973; Kirkpatrick, Roy, and Smith, 1976). Dorothy Riddle (1978) has done a sensitive analysis of the positive ways in which gay people relate to children, and their effectiveness as role models fostering healthy psychological development in children. Public fears of the negative effects of gay people on children tend to be totally unfounded.

A final misconception relevant to homophobia is the idea that homosexuality is "unnatural." Evidence reviewed by Ford and Beach (1951) indicates that homosexual activities occur in the majority of species of animals. Some porpoises form lifelong, monogamous, homosexual relationships. Homosexual relations are common, and are important in establishing dominance, among monkeys and various canines.

Lorenz (1974) has discussed homosexual coupling among geese and other birds, concluding that it is often very adaptive.

Homosexual activities are as common or "natural" in human society as in the animal world. In 49 of the 77 societies for which we have adequate anthropological data, homosexual activities are socially sanctioned; in some situations they are virtually compulsory (Churchill, 1967). In most of Europe and many other parts of the world, homosexual relations are legal. The "unnatural" rationalization supporting homophobia receives further disconfirmation from the experiences of the 37% of the American male population who Kinsey, Pomeroy, and Martin (1948) reported had homosexual experiences to orgasm after adolescence.

Robert Brannon characterizes contemporary scientific thinking about the "naturalness" of homosexuality in this way:

> Every human society in the world today, from vast industrial nations to the smallest and simplest tribes in remote parts of the world, has some degree of homosexuality. Every society in the history of the Earth for which we have records, going back to the beginnings of recorded history, had some degree of homosexuality.
>
> Some of these societies accepted homosexuality readily while others severely condemned it, but *all* human societies have been aware of it because homosexuality has always existed wherever human beings have existed.
>
> The closest scientific analogy to homosexuality is probably the phenomenon of left-handedness, the origins and causes of which also remain unknown to science. Like homosexuality, left-handedness exists for a minority of people in every human society on record. There is no more objective reason to consider homosexuality unnatural than there is to consider left-handedness unnatural.

These facts about homosexuality suggest an interesting dilemma. Even if the stereotypes about homosexuality were accurate (I have tried to show that they are not), then why should homosexuality be threatening to males who presumably do not fit these stereotypes? If these stereotypes are not valid, then how and why are the rationalizations of homophobia maintained?

Since sexual orientation, unlike race or sex, is rarely known for certain in everyday interactions, it is relatively easy to maintain false stereotypes of the invisible minority of homosexuals. Men who appear to exhibit parts of the stereotypes are labeled homosexual, and the rest are presumed to be heterosexual. Thus, as long as most homosexuals conceal their sexual preference, homophobia is easily maintained, because heterosexuals are rarely aware of homosexuals who do not reflect their stereotypes of homosexuality.

Since stereotypes of homosexuals are not characteristic of most homosexuals, it is clear that these stereotypes are not learned from direct experiences with homosexuals. Homophobia is socially learned and transmitted. It precedes and encourages the development of stereotypes of homosexuals, in a world in which most homosexuals are not known. The presence of homophobia even among some homosexuals, whose experiences disconfirm stereotypes of homosexuality, suggests that homophobia must be derived from other sources. For homophobia to exist as a threat, it is necessary that the associated stereotypes of homosexuality be false; otherwise the taunt, "*What are you, a fag?*," would be so patently untrue that it would not be threatening.

Homophobia and Social Beliefs

Although there is no rational basis for the negative stereotypes of homosexuals, and thus homophobia, nevertheless homophobia is widespread. It is characteristic of entire societies as well as individuals. The bases for homophobic social attitudes are generally related to (1) religious beliefs that homosexuality is morally wrong, (2) scientific theories of homosexuality as an illness or deviance, and (3) social beliefs that homosexuality is damaging to society.

Religious prohibitions have sometimes been considered to be the source of homophobia (Symonds, 1896; Churchill, 1967; Weinberg, 1972; Weinberg and Williams, 1974). The United States, as a result of its Puritan heritage, is generally considered one of the most homophobic (and erotophobic) cultures in the world. Although some researchers (such as Irwin and Thompson, 1977) have shown a strong relationship between church attendance, religious beliefs, and antihomosexual attitudes, religion seems unlikely to be a causal factor in homophobia for most Americans.

Science seems to have replaced religion as a source of justification of homophobia for many people. However, there is no scientific evidence that homosexuality is a mental illness. In 1973 the American Psychiatric Association removed the classification of homosexuality from its official list of mental illnesses. The belief among many psychiatrists that homosexuality is a mental illness, in spite of the lack of scientific evidence, is probably a result of their uncritical acceptance of common stereotypes of homosexuals (see Fort, Steiner, and Conrad, 1971; Davidson and Wilson, 1973), and the important fact that they frequently overgeneralize from homosexuals who were possibly mentally ill, and sought treatment, to the entire homosexual population. Nevertheless, the psychologically untenable conceptualization of homosexuality per se as a mental illness, which can be "cured," is still believed by 62% of the American adult population, according to Levitt and Klassen (1973).

Certain psychological theories, such as Freud's, posit that although homosexuality is not an illness, it is nevertheless also not "normal." Freud viewed it as a form of arrested psychosexual development, related to aspects of the parent/child relationship. Psychoanalysts such as Bieber (Bieber *et al.*, 1962) have selectively analyzed cases of homosexuals from their clinical practice that they interpret as supporting Freud's theory. Bieber's conclusions have not been supported in other studies sampling a cross section of homosexuals (Saghir and Robins, 1973).

Freud further believed that homophobia, and also paranoia, is related to "latent homosexuality," which he thought to be present in nearly everyone, since he conceived of people being born ambisexual and later developing heterosexuality. Freud's belief in latent homosexuality has received general acceptance in our culture, both among heterosexuals and homosexuals. Latency, by definition, implies the existence of no behavioral evidence. Therefore if it is possible for anyone to be a latent homosexual, in spite of the absence of sexual activity, it becomes extremely difficult for a person to prove beyond a doubt that he is not a homosexual. Thus, the concept of latent homosexuality contributes in a major way to homophobia, for it allows the possibility that anyone might be a secret homosexual even though the person does not exhibit any of the stereotypes, or behaviors, of homosexuals.

Sociological studies of homosexuality provide another popular scientific justification of homophobia, as they tend to label homosexuality as deviant since it is practiced by only a small proportion of society. However, the term *deviant* has taken on moral connotations not in keeping with its scientific meaning of "not majority." (See Scarpitti and McFarlane, 1975, for further discussion of this point.) When Simmons (1965) asked a cross section of Americans to list the people who they considered deviant, the most common response was homosexuals (49%). The equation of deviance with bad or immoral, although it may be indicative of popular thinking, is not inherent in sound sociological research.

Another possible source of homophobia is the belief that homosexuality is damaging to society. An Opinion Research Center poll in 1966 showed that more than 67% of the people contacted viewed homosexuality as "detrimental to society." The Harris Survey has been asking large cross sections of American households whether they feel homosexuals (and other groups) do more harm than good for the country. In 1965 homosexuals were placed third (behind Communists and atheists), with 82% of the males and 58% of the females thinking they were primarily a danger to the country. In 1973 about 50% of the respondents still felt that homosexuals did more harm than good. Levitt and Klassen (1973) similarly found that 49% of their sample agreed that "homosexuality is a social corruption which can cause the downfall of a civilization." These studies do not make it clear, however, why homosexuality is perceived as a social menace, especially by men. Legislatures in 24 states have decriminalized sexual activities commonly engaged in by consenting homosexual adults, as recommended in the model penal code of the American Bar Association. Homosexuality is also legal in most other countries, including Canada, England, Germany, and France. Thus, there is not general official support or evidence, either here or abroad, for the misconception that homosexuality is damaging to society.

Two arguments have been frequently advanced against legalization of homosexuality, in states considering legal reform. Groups such as firemen and policemen have argued that if homosexuality is legalized, homosexuals will "sexually corrupt" their fellow workers. (This is also a belief of 38% of Americans, according to Levitt and Klassen, 1973.) In reality, homosexual men have little interest in sexual relationships with unwilling heterosexual colleagues.

The most influential argument advanced against decriminalizing homosexuality is that it would allow homosexuals to "convert" or to molest children. We have discussed the distinction between pedophiles and homosexuals and the mistaken stereotype that homosexuals molest children. The children's issue is a red herring because in no state has legalization of sex

acts between adults and children ever been proposed. Homosexuals are not seduced or converted into homosexuality. In a study by Lehne (1978) only 4% of the male homosexuals reported that they were somewhat seduced into their first homosexual act, and in not one case was force involved. By comparison, Sorensen (1973) reports that the first sexual experience of 6% of adolescent girls was heterosexual rape. Lehne's study also found that most of the homosexual men reported that they were aware of their sexual orientation (because of their sexual fantasies) about four to five years before their first homosexual experience. The notion that homosexuals, legally or illegally, will seduce, rape, or convert others into homosexuality is not supported by any substantial data. There seems to be no reason to believe that homosexuals act any less morally than most Americans of different sexual orientations, or that they in fact pose a threat to society.

Homophobia and the Individual

Although homophobia is still widespread in American society, it is increasingly a fear of only a minority of people. Studies of homophobia in individuals suggest that it is not an isolated prejudice or fear; it is consistently related to traditional attitudes about sex roles and other social phenomena. This supports the conceptualization that homophobia functions as a motivation or threat in defining and maintaining the male role.

In an early study of homophobic attitudes, Smith (1971) found that college students who held negative attitudes toward homosexuals were significantly more status conscious, more authoritarian, and more sexually inflexible than individuals scoring low on homophobia. Later research refined Smith's methodology and analysis to show that homophobia is most closely related to traditional sex-role beliefs, and to general lack of support for equality between the sexes (see Morin and Garfinkle, 1978).

MacDonald (MacDonald, 1974, 1976; MacDonald, Huggins, Young, and Swanson, 1973; MacDonald and Games, 1974) developed effective scales of Attitudes toward Homosexuality and a Sex Role Survey. In research with several different adult populations, he demonstrated clear relationships between negative attitudes toward homosexuality and support for the double standard in sex-role behavior and conservative standards of sexual morality. Through the analysis of the semantic differential, he showed that homosexual males are devalued and viewed as less powerful due to their association with femininity, whereas lesbians are seen to be more powerful than heterosexual women because they are believed to be more masculine. Similar analyses were also reported by Storms (1978) and Shively, Rudolph, and DeCecco (1978). The public confusion between sexual orientation and sex role contributes to the devaluation of homosexuals, since they are believed to violate sex-role norms.

MacDonald's findings have been confirmed by numerous other researchers. Weinberger and Millham (1979) concluded that "homophobia is associated with valuing traditional gender distinctions," whereas Minnigerode (1976) found that nonfeminist and conservative sex attitudes were closely related to homophobia. These and other researchers found that people reacted more negatively to same-sex homosexuals, and in particular men were more negative toward male homosexuals than they were toward lesbians, and men overall were more negative in their homophobic attitudes than were women (Nutt and Sedlacek, 1974; Steffensmeier and Steffensmeier, 1974; Turnbull and Brown, 1977). Some researchers, including MacDonald, did not find such clear sex differences; Morin and Garfinkle (1978) have reviewed these studies and related the lack of findings of sex differences to the different methodologies that were used.

A constellation of traditional or sex-negative beliefs was found to be characteristic of homophobic individuals in several other studies. Morin and Wallace (1975, 1976) found that belief in a traditional family ideology was a slightly better predictor of homophobia than traditional beliefs about women; traditional religious beliefs and general sexual rigidity were also related. Negative beliefs about premarital and extramarital affairs were closely associated with homophobia in Nyberg and Alston's (1976–77) analysis of a representative sample of the American population. With a similar sample, Irwin and Thompson (1977) found traditional sex-role standards to be closely related to homophobia. Individuals with nontraditional sex-role behavior were less likely to hold negative attitudes toward homosexuality (Montgomery and Burgoon, 1977), whereas personal anxiety and guilt about sexual impulses were also characteristic of homophobic individuals (Berry and Marks, 1969; Millham, San Miguel, and Kellogg, 1976).

The general picture that emerges from this research is that individuals who are not comfortable with changes in sex roles and sexual behavior are most likely to be homophobic. Cross-cultural research has confirmed the relationship between high levels of sex-role stereotyping and antihomosexual attitudes among West Indians, Brazilians, and Canadians (Dunbar, Brown, and Amoroso, 1973a; Dunbar, Brown, and Vourinen, 1973b; Brown and Amoroso, 1975). Research with homosexuals has also shown that although they are not generally as homophobic as heterosexuals, those holding negative attitudes toward homosexuality are also likely to have traditional beliefs of sex-role stereotyping. Those homosexuals with positive attitudes and self-concepts are more likely to support equality between the sexes and have positive views on feminism (May, 1974; Lumby, 1976; McDonald and Moore, 1978; Glenn, 1978). Thus, homophobia seems to be a dynamic in maintaining traditional sex-role distinctions, rather than an isolated belief or attitude.

The negative influence of homophobic attitudes on social behavior has been demonstrated in several clever research studies. Morin, Taylor, and Kielman (1975) showed that in an interview situation, men and women sit farther away from an interviewer wearing a "Gay and Proud" button than they do from the same nonidentified interviewer; this effect is strongest for men, who sit three times as far away from a male homosexual than a lesbian. On a task arranging stick figures, Wolfgang and Wolfgang (1971) found that homosexuals were placed farther away than were marijuana users, drug addicts, and the obese, and past homosexuals were viewed as even less desirable and less trustworthy than present homosexuals. Subjects, particularly men, in another experiment were found to be significantly less willing to personally interact with homosexuals than heterosexuals (Millham and Weinberger, 1977). San Miguel and Millham (1976) found that people with homophobic attitudes were significantly more aggressive toward homosexuals than heterosexuals, even when they lost money in a cooperation experiment as a result of their aggression. They were highly aggressive regardless of whether their interaction with the individual prior to labeling as a homosexual was positive, and they were most aggressive toward homosexuals perceived as otherwise similar to themselves. Clearly homophobia is not only reflected in attitudes, but influences social behavior, and thus can have a potent influence in maintaining conformity to conventional sex-role behavior.

The process of homosexual labeling also has strong influences on behavior. Men labeled as homosexuals were perceived as more feminine, emotional, submissive, unconventional, and weaker than when the same men were not labeled (Weissbach and Zagon, 1975). Karr (1978) found also that the male who identified another man as a homosexual was perceived as more masculine, sociable, and desirable, and

that highly homophobic individuals would sit farther away from the labeled homosexual. Karr effectively demonstrates that one's status as a man can be improved in social situations merely by the act of labeling someone else as gay. Another study found that men who were (incorrectly) labeled as a homosexual became increasingly more stereotypically masculine in their behavior (Farina, 1972); thus, the stigmatization of homosexuals can be a powerful molder of social behavior and conformity to traditional sex roles.

This growing body of research clearly supports the conceptualization that homophobia among individuals is closely related to traditional beliefs about sex roles, rather than individual prejudices against homosexuals. Furthermore, it demonstrates that these homophobic attitudes devalue in thought and action anyone who deviates from traditional sex-role stereotypes, and that this devaluation is reflected in social behavior. Homophobia reduces the willingness of others to interact with a suspected or labeled homosexual, and it may support direct aggression against the labeled deviant. Clearly homophobia is a powerful motivation for maintaining traditional sex-role behavior. MacDonald's assertions (1974, 1976) that sex-role issues are crucial for gay liberation, and that people seeking changes in traditional sex roles must be prepared to also challenge homophobia, are strongly supported by these data.

Homophobia and the Male Role

The male role is predominantly maintained by men themselves. Men devalue homosexuality, then use this norm of homophobia to control other men in their male roles. Since any male could potentially (latently) be a homosexual, and since there are certain social sanctions that can be directed against homosexuals, the fear of being labeled a homosexual can be used to ensure that males maintain appropriate male behavior. Homophobia is only incidentally directed against actual homosexuals—its more common use is against the heterosexual male. This explains why homophobia is closely related to beliefs about sex-role rigidity, but not to personal experience with homosexuals or to any realistic assessment of homosexuality itself. Homophobia is a threat used by societies and individuals to enforce social conformity in the male role, and maintain social control. The taunt "*What are you, a fag?*" is used in many ways to encourage certain types of male behavior and to define the limits of "acceptable" masculinity.

Since homosexuals in general constitute an invisible minority that is indistinguishable from the 49% male majority in most ways except for sexual preference, any male can be accused of being a homosexual, or "latent" homosexual. Homosexuality, therefore, can be "the crime of those to whom no crime could be imputed." There is ample historical evidence for this use of homophobia from Roman times to the present. For example, even homosexual fantasies were made illegal in Germany in 1935, and Hitler sent more than 220,000 "homosexuals" to concentration camps (Lauritsen and Thorstad, 1974). It is probable that many of these men actually were not homosexuals. But since there was no satisfactory way for individuals to prove that they were not homosexuals (and for this offense in Germany, accusation was equivalent to conviction), imputed homosexuality was the easiest way to deal with undesirable individuals. Homosexuality was likewise an accusation during the American McCarthy hearings in the 1950s when evidence of Communism was lacking. The strong association of homophobia with authoritarianism means that the potential for this exploitation of homophobia is very real during times of stress and strong-arm governments. This is no accident, but is in fact an explanation for the maintenance of homophobia. When homosexuality is stigmatized, homophobia exists as a device of social control, directed specifically against men to maintain male behavior appropriate to the social situation.

Homophobia may also be used to enforce social stereotypes of appropriate sex-role behavior for women. In general men define and enforce women's roles, and men who do not participate in this process may be suspected of being homosexuals. The direct use of homophobia to maintain female roles is necessary only in extreme cases, since male power is pervasive. But it is sometimes alleged that women who do not defer to men, or who do not marry, or who advocate changes in women's roles, are lesbians. There are, of course, other factors besides homophobia that maintain sex roles in society. I am arguing not that the elimination of homophobia will bring about a change in sex roles, but that homophobia must be eliminated before a change in sex roles can be brought about.

The Personal Pain of Homophobia

The pain that *heterosexual* males bear as a consequence of homophobia is so chronic and pervasive that they probably do not notice that they are in pain, or the possible source of their discomfort. Homophobia is especially damaging to their personal relationships. Homophobia encourages men to compete. Since competition is not a drive easily turned on and off at will, there is probably a tendency for homophobic men to compete with others in their personal lives as well as at work. Only certain types of relationships are possible between competitors. Love and close friendship are difficult to maintain in a competitive environment because to expose your weaknesses and admit your problems is to be less than a man, and gives your competitor an advantage.

When men realize the intensity of their bonds with other men, homosexuality can be very threatening, and might lead to a limiting of otherwise fulfilling relationships. On the basis of a suggestion from Lester Kirkendall, I've asked men to describe their relationships with their best male friends. Many offer descriptions that are so filled with positive emotion and satisfaction that you might think they were talking about their spouses (and some will admit that they value their close male friendships more than their relationship with their wife, "although they're really different, not the same at all"). However, if I suggest that it sounds as if they are describing a person whom they love, these men become flustered. They hem and haw, and finally say, "Well, I don't think I would like to call it love, we're just best friends. I can relate to him in ways I can't with anyone else. But, I mean, we're not homosexuals or anything like that." Homosexual love, like heterosexual love, does not imply participation in sex, although many people associate love with sex. The social stigma of homosexual love denies these close relationships the validity of love in our society. This potential loss of love is a pain of homophobia that many men suffer because it delimits their relationships with other men.

Because men are unwilling to admit the presence of love in their male friendships, these relationships may be limited or kept in careful check. If male love is recognized, these men may be threatened because they may mistakenly believe this indicates they are homosexuals. Male friendships offer an excellent opportunity to explore ways in which individuals can relate as equals, the type of relationship that is increasingly demanded by liberated women. Most men have learned to relate to some other men as equals, but because they deny themselves the validity of these relationships they respond to equality with women out of fear, or frustration that they don't know how to deal with this "new" type of relationship. Loving male relationships are part of the experiences of many men that are rarely thought about or discussed because of homophobia. As a consequence, many men are unable to transfer what they have

learned in these male relationships to their relationships with women. They may also deny to themselves the real importance of their relationships with other men. Male love is so pervasive that it is virtually invisible.

Homophobia also circumscribes and limits areas of male interest. Homophobic men do not participate in sissy, womanly, "homosexual" activities or interests. Maintenance of the male sex role as a result of homophobia is as limiting for men as female sex roles are for women. An appreciation of many aspects of life, although felt by most men at different times in their lives, cannot be genuinely and openly enjoyed by men who must defend their masculinity through compulsively male-stereotyped pursuits. Fear of being thought a homosexual thus keeps some men from pursuing areas of interest, or occupations, considered more appropriate for women or homosexuals.

The open expression of emotion and affection by men is limited by homophobia. Only athletes and women are allowed to touch and hug each other in our culture; athletes are allowed this only because presumably their masculinity is beyond doubt. But in growing up to become men in our culture, we learned that such contact with men was no longer permissible, that only homosexuals enjoy touching other men, or that touching is only a prelude to sex. In a similar way men learn to curb many of their emotions. They learn not to react emotionally to situations in which, although they may feel the emotion, it would be unmasculine to express it. Once men have learned not to express some of their emotions, they may find it difficult to react any other way, and may even stop feeling these emotions. Men are openly allowed to express anger and hostility, but not sensitivity and sympathy. The expression of more tender emotions among men is thought to be characteristic only of homosexuals.

Is a society without homophobia a fairytale, or will it become a reality? Only when men begin to make a serious attempt to deal with their prejudice against homosexuality can we look forward to living in a world that is not stratified by rigid sex-role distinctions.

References

Alston, J. P. "Attitudes toward extramarital and homosexual relations." *Journal of the Scientific Study of Religion*, 1974, *13*, 479–481.

Bell, A. P. "Homosexualities: Their range and character," In J. K. Cole & R. Dienstbier (Eds.), *Nebraska Symposium on Motivation*, Vol. 21. Lincoln: University of Nebraska Press, 1973.

Bell, A. P., & M. Weinberg. *Homosexualities: A Study of Human Diversity*. New York: Simon & Schuster, 1978.

Berry, D. F., & F. Marks. "Antihomosexual prejudice as a function of attitudes toward own sexuality." *Proceedings of the 77th Annual Convention of the American Psychological Association*, 1969, *4*, 573–574.

Bieber, I., et al. *Homosexuality: A Psychoanalytic Study of Male Homosexuals*. New York: Basic Books, 1962.

Brown, M., & D. Amoroso. "Attitudes toward homosexuality among West Indian male and female college students." *Journal of Social Psychology*, 1975, *97*, 163–168.

Churchill, W. *Homosexual Behavior Among Males: A Cross-Cultural and Cross Species Investigation*. Englewood Cliffs, N.J.: Prentice-Hall, 1967.

Dannecker, M., & R. Reiche. *Der gewoehnliche Homosexuelle*. Frankfurt am Main, Germany: S. Fischer, 1974.

Davidson, G., & T. Wilson. "Attitudes of behavior therapists toward homosexuality." *Behavior Therapy*. 1973, *4*(5), 686–696.

Dunbar, J., M. Brown, & D. Amoroso, "Some correlates of attitudes toward homosexuality." *Journal of Social Psychology*, 1973, *89*, 271–279. (a)

Dunbar, J., M. Brown, & S. Vourinen. "Attitudes toward homosexuality among Brazilian and Canadian college students." *Journal of Social Psychology*, 1973, *90*, 173–183. (b)

Farina, A. "Stigmas potent behavior molders." *Behavior Today*, 1972, *2*, 25.

Ford, C., & F. Beach. *Patterns of Sexual Behavior*, New York: Harper & Row, 1951.

Fort, J., C. Steiner, & F. Conrad. "Attitudes of mental health professionals toward homosexuality and its treatment." *Psychological Reports*, 1971, *29*, 347–350.

Freedman, M. *Homosexuality and Psychological Functioning*. Belmont, Ca.: Brooks/Cole, 1971.

Freedman, M. "Homosexuals may be healthier than straights." *Psychology Today*, 1975, *1*(10), 28–32.

Freund, K., R. Langevin, R. Chamberlayne, A. Deosoran, & Y. Zajac. "The phobic theory of male homosexuality." *Archives of General Psychiatry*, 1974, *31*, 495–499.

Freund, K., R. Langevin, S. Gibiri, & Y. Zajac. "Heterosexual aversion in homosexual males." *British Journal of Psychiatry*, 1973, *122*, 163–169.

Freund, K., R. Langevin, & Y. Zajac. "Heterosexual aversion in homosexual males: A second experiment." *British Journal of Psychiatry*, 1974, *125*, 177–180.

Gallup, G. "Gallup poll on gay rights: Approval with reservations." *San Francisco Chronicle*, July 18, 1977, 1, 18.

Gallup, G. "Gallup poll on the attitudes homosexuals face today." *San Francisco Chronicle*, July 20, 1977, 4.

Glenn, G. L. "Attitudes toward homosexuality and sex roles among homosexual men." Unpublished M. A. Thesis: Antioch University/Maryland, 1978.

Heilbrun, A. B., & N. L. Thompson. "Sex-role identity and male and female homosexuality." *Sex Roles*, 1977, *3*, 65–79.

Irwin, P., & N. L. Thompson. "Acceptance of the rights of homosexuals: A social profile." *Journal of Homosexuality*, 1977, *3*, 107–121.

Kaplan, A. G., & J. P. Bean (Eds.). *Beyond Sex Role Stereotypes: Readings toward a Psychology of Androgyny*. Boston: Little, Brown, 1976.

Karr, R. "Homosexual labeling and the male role." *Journal of Social Issues*, 1978, *34*(3), 73–84.

Kinsey, A., W. Pomeroy, & C. Martin. *Sexual Behavior in the Human Male*. Philadelphia: Saunders, 1948.

Kirkpatrick, M., R. Roy, & K. Smith. "A new look at lesbian mothers." *Human Behavior*, August 1976, 60–61.

Langevin, R., A. Stanford, & R. Block. "The effect of relaxation instructions on erotic arousal in homosexual and heterosexual males." *Behavior Therapy*, 1975, *6*, 453–458.

Lauritsen, J., & D. Thorstad. *The Early Homosexual Rights Movement* (1864–1935). New York: Times Change Press, 1974.

Lehne, G. "Gay male fantasies and realities." *Journal of Social Issues*, 1978, *34*(3), 28–37.

Levitt, E., & A. Klassen. "Public attitudes toward sexual behavior: The latest investigation of the Institute for Sex Research." Paper presented at the annual convention of the American Orthopsychiatric Association, 1973.

Levitt, E., & A. Klassen. "Public attitudes toward homosexuality: Part of the 1970 National Survey by the Institute for Sex Research." *Journal of Homosexuality*, 1974, *1*, 29–43.

Lorenz, K. Interviewed by R. Evans in *Psychology Today*, November 1974, 82–93.

Lumby, M. E. "Homophobia: The quest for a valid scale." *Journal of Homosexuality*, 1976, *2*, 39–47.

MacDonald, A. "The importance of sex role to gay liberation." *Homosexual Counselling Journal*, 1974, *1*, 169–180.

MacDonald, A. "Homophobia: Its roots and meanings." *Homosexual Counselling Journal*, 1976, *3*, 23–33.

MacDonald, A., & R. Games. "Some characteristics of those who hold positive and negative attitudes toward homosexuals." *Journal of Homosexuality*, 1974, *1*, 9–27.

MacDonald, A., J. Huggins, S. Young, & R. Swanson. "Attitudes toward homosexuality: Preservation of sex morality or the double standard?" *Journal of Counselling and Clinical Psychology*, 1973, *40*, 161. Extended report available from the author (1972).

May, E. P. "Counselors', psychologists', and homosexuals' philosophies of human nature and attitudes toward homosexual behavior." *Homosexual Counselling Journal*, 1974, *1*, 3–25.

McConaghy, N. "Penile volume changes to moving pictures of male and female nudes in heterosexual and homosexual males." *Behavior Research and Therapy*, 1967, *5*, 43–48.

McDonald, G., & R. Moore. "Sex-role self-concepts of homosexual men and their attitudes toward both women and male homosexuality." *Journal of Homosexuality*, 1978, *4*, 3–14.

Millham, J., C. San Miguel, & R. Kellogg. "A factor analytic conceptualization of attitudes toward male and female homosexuals." *Journal of Homosexuality*, 1976, *2*, 3–10.

Millham, J., & L. Weinberger. "Sexual preference, sex role appropriateness and restriction of social access." *Journal of Homosexuality*, 1972, *2*, 343–357.

Minnigerode, F. "Attitudes toward homosexuality: Feminist attitudes and social conservation." *Sex Roles*, 1976, *2*, 347–352.

Montgomery, C., & M. Burgoon. "An experimental study of the interactive effects of sex and androgyny on attitude change." *Communication Monographs*, 1977, *44*, 130–135.

Morin, S., & E. Garfinkle. "Male homophobia." *Journal of Social Issues*, 1978, *34*, 29–47.

Morin, S., K. Taylor, & S. Kielman. "Gay is beautiful at a distance." Paper presented at the meeting of the American Psychological Association, Chicago, August 1975.

Morin, S., & S. Wallace. "Religiosity, sexism, and attitudes toward homosexuality." Paper presented at the meeting of the California State Psychological Association, March 1975.

Morin, S., & S. Wallace. "Traditional values, sex-role stereotyping, and attitudes toward homosexuality." Paper presented at the meeting of the Western Psychological Association, Los Angeles, April 1976.

Nutt, R., & W. Sedlacek. "Freshman sexual attitudes and behaviors." *Journal of College Student Personnel*, 1974, *15*, 346–351.

Nyberg, K., & J. Alston. "Analysis of public attitudes toward homosexual behavior." *Journal of Homosexuality*, 1976–77, *2*, 99–107.

Riddle, D. "Relating to children: Gays as role models." *Journal of Social Issues*, 1978, *34*, 38–58.

Rooney, E., & D. Gibbons. "Social reactions to crimes without victims." *Social Problems*, 1966, *13*, 400–410.

Saghir, M., & E. Robins. *Male and Female Homosexuality: A Comprehensive Investigation*. Baltimore: Williams & Wilkins, 1973.

San Miguel, C., & J. Millham. "The role of cognitive and situational variables in aggression toward homosexuals." *Journal of Homosexuality*, 1976, *2*, 11–27.

Scarpitti, F., & P. McFarlane (Eds.). *Deviance: Action, Reaction, Interaction.* Reading, Mass.: Addison-Wesley, 1975.

Shively, M., J. Rudolph, & J. DeCecco. "The identification of the social sex-role stereotypes." *Journal of Homosexuality*, 1978, *3*, 225–234.

Simmons, J. "Public stereotypes of deviants." *Social Problems*, 1965, *13*, 223–232.

Smith, K. "Homophobia: A tentative personality profile." *Psychological Reports*, 1971, *29*, 1091–1094.

Sorensen, R. *Adolescent Sexuality in Contemporary America.* New York: World, 1973.

Spence, J., & R. Helmreich. *Masculinity & Femininity.* Austin, Tx.: University of Texas Press, 1978.

Steffensmeier, D., & R. Steffensmeier. "Sex differences in reactions to homosexuals: Research continuities and further developments." *The Journal of Sex Research*, 1974, *10*, 52–67.

Storms, M. "Attitudes toward homosexuality and femininity in men." *Journal of Homosexuality*, 1978, *3*, 257–263.

Symonds, J. *A Problem in Modern Ethics*, London: 1896.

Tavris, C. "Men and women report their views on masculinity." *Psychology Today*, January, 1977, 35.

Turnbull, D., & M. Brown. "Attitudes toward homosexuality and male and female reactions to homosexual slides." *Canadian Journal of Behavioural Science*, 1977, *9*, 68–80.

Weinberg, G. *Society and the Healthy Homosexual.* New York: Doubleday, 1972.

Weinberg, M., & C. Williams. *Male Homosexuals.* New York: Oxford University Press, 1974.

Weinberger, L., & J. Millham. "Attitudinal homophobia and support of traditional sex roles." *Journal of Homosexuality*, 1979, *4*, 237–246.

Weissbach, T., & G. Zagon. "The effect of deviant group membership upon impressions of personality." *Journal of Social Psychology*, 1975, *95*, 263–266.

Wolfgang, A., & J. Wolfgang. "Exploration of attitudes via physical interpersonal distance toward the obese, drug users, homosexuals, police and other marginal figures." *Journal of Clinical Psychology*, 1971, *27*, 510–512.

21

ARTICLE

Peter M. Nardi

The Politics of Gay Men's Friendships

Towards the end of Wendy Wasserstein's Pulitzer Prize–winning play, *The Heidi Chronicles*, a gay character, Peter Patrone, explains to Heidi why he has been so upset over all the funerals he has attended recently: "A person has so many close friends. And in our lives, our friends are our families" (Wasserstein, 1990: 238). In his collection of stories, *Buddies*, Ethan Mordden (1986: 175) observes: "What unites us, all of us, surely, is brotherhood, a sense that our friendships are historic, designed to hold Stonewall together. . . . It is friendship that sustained us, supported out survival." These statements succinctly summarize an important dimension about gay men's friendships: Not only are friends a form of family for gay men and lesbians, but gay friendships are also a powerful political force.

Mordden's notion of "friends is survival" has a political dimension that becomes all the more salient in contemporary society where the political, legal, religious, economic, and health concerns of gay people are routinely threatened by the social order. In part, gay friendship can be seen as a political statement, since at the core of the concept of friendship is the idea of "being

Reprinted by permission of the author.

oneself" in a cultural context that may not approve of that self. For many people, the need to belong with others in dissent and out of the mainstream is central to the maintenance of self and identity (Rubin, 1986). The friendships formed by a shared marginal identity, thus, take on powerful political dimensions as they organize around a stigmatized status to confront the dominant culture in solidarity. Jerome (1984: 698) believes that friendships have such economic and political implications, since friendship is best defined as "the cement which binds together people with interests to conserve."

Suttles (1970: 116) argues that

> The very basic assumption friends must make about one another is that each is going beyond a mere presentation of self in compliance with "social dictates." Inevitably, this makes friendship a somewhat deviant relationship because the surest test of personal disclosure is a violation of the rules of public propriety.

Friendship, according to Suttles (1970), has its own internal order, albeit maintained by the cultural images and situational elements that structure the definitions of friendship. In friendship, people can depart from the routine and

display a portion of the self not affected by social control. That is, friendships allow people to
go beyond the basic structures of their cultural
institutions into an involuntary and uncontrollable exposure of self—to deviate from public
propriety (Suttles, 1970).

Little (1989) similarly argues that friendship is an escape from the rules and pieties of social life. It's about identity: who one is rather
than one's roles and statuses. And the idealism
of friendship "lies in its detachment from these
[roles and statuses], its creative and spiritual
transcendence, its fundamental skepticism as a
platform from which to survey the givens of
society and culture" (Little, 1989: 145). For gay
men, these descriptions illustrate the political
meaning friendship can have in their lives and
their society.

The political dimension of friendship is
summed up best by Little (1989; 154–155):

> the larger formations of social life—kinship, the
> law, the economy—must be different where
> there is, in addition to solidarity and dutiful
> role-performance, a willingness and capacity for
> friendship's surprising one-to-one relations,
> and this difference may be enough to transform
> social and political life. . . . Perhaps, finally, it is
> true that progress in democracy depends on a
> new generation that will increasingly locate it-
> self in identity-shaping, social, yet personally lib-
> erating, friendships.

The traditional, nuclear family has been the
dominant model for political relations and has
structured much of the legal and social norms of
our culture. People have often been judged by
their family ties and history. But as the family
becomes transformed into other arrangements,
so do the political and social institutions of society. For example, the emerging concept of
"domestic partnerships" has affected a variety of
organizations, including insurance companies,
city governments, private industry, and religious institutions (Task Force on Family Diversity Final Report, 1988).

For many gay people, the "friends as family" model is a political statement, going beyond the practicality of developing a surrogate
family in times of needed social support. It is
also a way of refocusing the economic and political agenda to include nontraditional family
structures composed of both romantic and non-
romantic nonkin relationships.

In part, this has happened by framing the
discussions in terms of gender roles. The
women's movement and the emerging men's
movement have highlighted the negative political implications of defining gender roles according to traditional cultural norms or limiting them
to biological realities. The gay movement, in
turn, has often been one source for redefining
traditional gender roles and sexuality. So, for example, when gay men exhibit more disclosing
and emotional interactions with other men, it
demonstrates the limitations of male gender roles
typically enacted among many heterosexual male
friends. By calling attention to the impact of homophobia on heterosexual men's lives, gay
men's friendships illustrate the potentiality for
expressive intimacy among all men.

Thus, the assumptions that biology and/or
socialization have inevitably constrained men
from having the kinds of relationships and inti-
macies women often typically have can be called
into question. This questioning of the dominant
construction of gender roles is in itself a sociopolitical act with major implications on the legal,
religious, and economic order.

White (1983:16) also sees how gay people's
lives can lead to new modes of behavior in the
society at large:

> In the case of gays, our childlessness, our mini-
> mal responsibilities, the fact that our unions are
> not consecrated, even our very retreat into gay
> ghettos for protection and freedom: all of these
> objective conditions have fostered a style in
> which we may be exploring, even in spite of
> our conscious intentions, things as they will
> someday be for the heterosexual majority. In
> that world (as in the gay world already), love

will be built on esteem rather than passion or convention, sex will be more playful or fantastic or artistic than marital—and friendship will be elevated into the supreme consolation for this continuing tragedy, human existence.

If, as White and others have argued, gay culture in the post-Stonewall, sexual liberation years of the 1970s was characterized by a continuous fluidity between what constituted a friend, a sexual partner, and a lover, then we need to acknowledge the AIDS decade of the 1980s as a source for restructuring of gay culture and the reorganization of sexuality and friendship. If indeed gay people (and men in particular) have focused attention on developing monogamous sexual partnerships, what then becomes the role of sexuality in the initiation and development of casual or close friendships? Clearly, gay culture is not a static phenomenon, unaffected by the larger social order. Certainly, as the moral order in the AIDS years encourages the re-establishment of more traditional relationships, the implications for the ways sexuality and friendships are organized similarly change.

Friends become more important as primary sources of social and emotional support when illness strikes; friendship becomes institutionally organized as "brunch buddies" dating services or "AIDS buddies" assistance groups; and self-help groups emerge centering on how to make and keep new friends without having "compulsive sex." While AIDS may have transformed some of the meanings and role of friendships in gay men's lives from the politicalization of sexuality and friendship during the post-Stonewall 1970s, the newer meanings of gay friendships, in turn, may be having some effect on the culture's definitions of friendships.

Interestingly, the mythical images of friendships were historically more male-dominated: bravery, loyalty, duty, and heroism (see Sapadin, 1988). This explained why women were typically assumed incapable of having true friendships. But today, the images of true friendship are often expressed in terms of women's traits: intimacy, trust, caring, and nurturing, thereby excluding the more traditional men from true friendship. However, gay men appear to be at the forefront of establishing the possibility of men overcoming their male socialization stereotypes and restructuring their friendships in terms of the more contemporary (i.e., "female") attributes of emotional intimacy.

To do this at a wider cultural level involves major sociopolitical shifts in how men's roles are structured and organized. Friendships between men in terms of intimacy and emotional support inevitably introduce questions about homosexuality. As Rubin (1985: 103) found in her interviews with men: "The association of friendship with homosexuality is so common among men." For women, there is a much longer history of close connections with other women, so that the separation of the emotional from the erotic is more easily made.

Lehne (1989) has argued that homophobia has limited the discussion of loving male relationships and has led to the denial by men of the real importance of their friendships with other men. In addition, "the open expression of emotion and affection by men is limited by homophobia. . . . The expression of more tender emotions among men is thought to be characteristic only of homosexuals" (Lehne, 1989: 426). So men are raised in a culture with a mixed message: strive for healthy, emotionally intimate friendships, but if you appear too intimate with another man you might be negatively labelled homosexual.

This certainly wasn't always the case. As a good illustration of the social construction of masculinity, friendship, and sexuality, one need only look to the changing definitions and concepts surrounding same-sex friendship during the nineteenth century (see Rotundo, 1989; Smith-Rosenberg, 1975). Romantic friendships could be erotic but not sexual, since sex was linked to reproduction. Because reproduction was not possible between two women or two men, the close relationship was not interpreted as being a sexual one:

> Until the 1880s, most romantic friendships were thought to be devoid of sexual content. Thus a woman or man could write of affectionate desire for a loved one of the same gender without causing an eyebrow to be raised (D'Emilio and Freedman, 988: 121).

However, as same-sex relationships became medicalized and stigmatized in the late 19th century, "the labels 'congenital inversion' and 'perversion' were applied not only to male sexual acts, but to sexual or romantic unions between women, as well as those between men" (D'Emilio and Freedman, 1988: 122). Thus, the twentieth century is an anomaly in its promotion of female equality, the encouragement of male–female friendships, and its suspicion of intense emotional friendships between men (Richards, 1987). Yet, in Ancient Greece and the medieval days of chivalry, comradeship, virtue, patriotism, and heroism were all associated with close male friendship. Manly love, as it was often called, was a central part of the definition of manliness (Richards, 1987).

It is through the contemporary gay, women's, and men's movements that these twentieth century constructions of gender are being questioned. And at the core is the association of close male friendships with negative images of homosexuality. Thus, how gay men structure their emotional lives and friendships can affect the social and emotional lives of all men and women. This is the political power and potential of gay friendships.

References

D'Emilio, John and Freedman, Estelle. (1988). *Intimate Matters: A History of Sexuality in America*. New York: Harper & Row.

Jerome, Dorothy. (1984). Good company: The sociological implications of friendship. *Sociological Review*, 32(4), 696–718.

Lehne, Gregory K. (1989 [1980]). Homophobia among men: Supporting and defining the male role. In M. Kimmel and M. Messner (Eds.), *Men's Lives* (pp. 416–429). New York: Macmillan.

Little, Graham. (1989). Freud, friendship, and politics. In R. Porter and S. Tomaselli (Eds.), *The Dialectics of Friendship* (pp. 143–158). London: Routledge.

Mordden, Ethan. (1986). *Buddies*. New York: St. Martin's Press.

Richards, Jeffrey. (1987). "Passing the love of women": Manly love and Victorian society. In J. A. Mangan and J. Walvin (Eds.), *Manliness and Morality: Middle-Class Masculinity in Britain and America (1800–1940)* (pp. 92–122). Manchester, England: Manchester University Press.

Rotundo, Anthony. (1989). Romantic friendships: Male intimacy and middle-class youth in the northern United States, 1800–1900. *Journal of Social History*, 23(1), 1–25.

Rubin, Lillian. (1985). *Just Friends: The Role of Friendship in Our Lives*. New York: Harper & Row.

Sapadin, Linda. (1988). Friendship and gender: Perspectives of professional men and women. *Journal of Social and Personal Relationships*, 5(4), 387–403.

Smith-Rosenberg, Carroll. (1975). The female world of love and ritual: Relations between women in nineteenth-century America. *Signs*, 1(1): 1–29.

Suttles, Gerald. (1970). Friendship as a social institution. In G. McCall, M. McCall, N. Denzin, G. Suttles, and S. Kurth, *Social Relationships* (pp. 95–135). Chicago: Aldine.

Task Force on Family Diversity. (1988). *Strengthening Families: A Model for Community Action*. City of Los Angeles.

Wasserstein, Wendy. (1990). *The Heidi Chronicles*. San Diego: Harcourt, Brace, Jovanovich.

White, Edmund. (1983). Paradise found: Gay men have discovered that there is friendship after sex. *Mother Jones*, June, 10–16.

22

ARTICLE

Gregory M. Herek

Psychological Heterosexism and Anti-Gay Violence: The Social Psychology of Bigotry and Bashing

Roughly two thirds of Americans[1] condemn homosexuality or homosexual behavior as morally wrong or a sin; this pattern has not changed significantly since the late 1970s.[2] According to Gallup polls (Colasanto, 1989), only a plurality of Americans felt in 1989 that homosexual relations between consenting adults should be legal (47% versus 36% who say they should not be legal). Many heterosexual Americans also reject gay people at the personal level. In 1987 a Roper poll found that 25% of the respondents to a national survey would strongly object to working around people who are homosexual, and another 27% would prefer not to do so; only 45% "wouldn't mind." In a 1985 *Los Angeles Times* poll, 35% of the respondents reported that they felt discomfort around either gay men (6%) or lesbians (11%) or both (18%); 50% reported that they did *not* feel *un*comfortable around gay people.

Despite this evidence for widespread condemnation and avoidance of lesbians and gay men, other data indicate that heterosexual Americans are increasingly reluctant to condone discrimination on the basis of sexual orientation (e.g., Colasanto, 1989; Schneider & Lewis, 1984; see Rayside & Bowler, 1988, for evidence of a similar trend in Canada). Roper surveys found that the proportion of Americans agreeing that "homosexuals should be guaranteed equal treatment under the law in jobs and housing" rose from 60% in 1977 to 66% in 1985, while the proportion supporting legalized discrimination declined from 28% to 22%. Similarly, the proportion of American adults surveyed by the Gallup organization who say that homosexual men and women should have equal rights in terms of job opportunities increased from 56% in 1977 to 59% in 1982 and to 71% in 1989; the proportion opposing such rights declined from 33% to 28% to 18%, respectively (Colasanto, 1989).

Respondents sometimes show more willingness to discriminate when asked about specific occupations, but a steady trend toward supporting gay rights still is evident. In Gallup polls (Colasanto, 1989), the proportion stating that gay people should be hired as doctors increased from 44% in 1977 to 56% in 1989; similar increases were observed for hiring them as salespersons (from 68% to 79%), members of the armed forces (51% to 60%), clergy (36% to 44%), and elementary schoolteachers (27% to 42%). For all of these occupations, the long-term trend appears to be toward increased public opposition to discrimination on the basis of sexual orientation.

Cultural and Psychological Heterosexism

I define *heterosexism* as an ideological system that denies, denigrates, and stigmatizes any non-heterosexual form of behavior, identity, relationship, or community. Cultural heterosexism, like institutional racism and sexism, is manifested in societal customs and institutions. Through cultural heterosexism, homosexuality is rendered invisible and, when it becomes visible, is condemned by society. The poll data cited above make it clear that, although cultural heterosexism is pervasive in society, Americans display considerable variability in their individual attitudes toward lesbians and gay men. This observation reveals the inadequacy of an analysis of heterosexism that is restricted to its cultural manifestations.

In this article, I discuss *psychological heterosexism*—the manifestation of heterosexism in individuals' attitudes[3] and actions—and its role in violence against lesbians and gay men. In particular, I consider how psychological and situational factors affect the attitudes and behaviors of heterosexual individuals. The article is based on the assumptions that (a) psychological heterosexism and anti-gay violence are often functional for the person who manifests them; (b) the principal function served by these attitudes and actions differs for each person, depending upon her or his psychological needs; and (c) the translation of individual needs into anti-gay attitudes and behaviors involves a complex interaction of deep-seated personality characteristics, salient aspects of the immediate situation, and cultural definitions of sexuality and gender. In short; no single explanation of psychological heterosexism applies to all people.[4]

In the next section of the article, I discuss heterosexism as an attitude or prejudice and consider how it can serve different psychological functions for different people. Following that, I apply a similar analysis to overt acts of anti-gay behavior.

The Psychological Functions of Heterosexism

Why do some heterosexuals feel strongly hostile toward gay people while others are tolerant or accepting in their attitudes? In my own empirical research (Herek, 1984, 1987), I have tried to answer this question by using a perspective that earlier researchers applied to Whites' attitudes toward Blacks and Americans' attitudes toward Russians (e.g., McClintock, 1958; Smith, Bruner, & White, 1956.) This perspective is called the *functional approach* to attitudes. Its central assumption is that people hold and express particular attitudes because they get some sort of psychological benefit from doing so. In other words, attitudes and opinions serve psychological functions for the person who holds them. According to the functional approach, two people can have very different motivations for expressing what appears to be the same attitude. Or they can express opposing opinions for essentially the same reason. Further, an individual's attitudes are more likely to change when they stop being functional or actually become dysfunctional.

Using this perspective, I analyzed essays about homosexuality written by 205 heterosexual college students (Herek, 1987) and found three principal psychological functions underlying the students' attitudes. I labeled the first of these the *experiential* function.[5] Attitudes serving an experiential function assisted the students in making sense of their previous interactions with gay people. Those who had experienced pleasant interactions with a gay man or lesbian generalized from that experience and accepted gay people in general. For example, one woman wrote:

> [I have generally positive attitudes because] I have come to know some of these people and find them no different from any other people. This has not always been the case. In junior high and high school I didn't condemn so to speak but I held strong opinions against them. This was an attitude formed without any knowledge of homosexuality or homosexuals. When I first came to [college] I still had some of the same attitudes. Little did I know that the guy in the next room was gay. We became good friends and did things together all the time. Eventually he told me and it was then that I realized that homosexuals only differ in sexual preference.

Others reported negative attitudes resulting from their unpleasant experiences with gay men or lesbians. Another woman wrote:

> Personally, I don't like most male homosexuals. I once worked under one and worked with some and they were everything homosexuals are stereotyped to be—someone once said "male homosexuals have all the bad qualities of women" (shrewishness, pettiness, etc.)—and unfortunately for the men I worked with this statement applied.

Whether favorable or unfavorable, experiential attitudes help an individual to make sense of past experiences and fit them into a larger worldview, one that is organized primarily in terms of her or his own self-interest.

Because only about 30% of American adults know an openly gay person,[6] most heterosexuals' attitudes are not based on actual experiences with gay people. The attitudes of some of the remaining 70% probably serve an *anticipatory* function. Like the experiential function, the anticipatory function helps an individual to understand the world and to develop strategies for maximizing rewards and minimizing negative experiences.

Unlike the experiential function, however, the anticipatory function is not based on past experiences with lesbians and gay men. Rather, it is based on the anticipation of future interactions with them.

For most of the 70% of Americans who do not personally know lesbians or gay men, however, homosexuality and gay people are primarily symbols. Whereas attitudes toward people with whom one has direct experience function primarily to organize and make sense of those experiences, attitudes toward symbols serve a different kind of function. Such attitudes help people to increase their self-esteem by expressing important aspects of themselves—by declaring (to themselves and to others) what sort of people they are. Affirming who one *is* often is accomplished by distancing oneself from or even attacking people who represent the sort of person one is *not* (or does not want to be).

Many respondents in my study wrote essays that appeared to serve this type of function. Some essays, for example, manifested what I call a *social identity* function:[7]

> I have generally positive attitudes toward homosexuals because I don't think sexual preferences are a basis of judgment of someone's character or personality. Sexual preferences are a personal matter, and as long as a homosexual doesn't offend anyone or force his temptations on someone who is unwilling, there is no reason to condemn him/her. Homosexual tendencies aren't a deficit in someone's upbringing. I have these attitudes because of my own upbringing to be open-minded and non-stereotypical or non-judgmental.

An example of negative social identity attitudes:

> [I have generally negative attitudes because] in the Bible it clearly states that homosexuality is a *sin*. I believe that no one can be a Christian if he/she is a homosexual. I believe the Bible is correct, and I follow its beliefs word for word. I am a Christian.

The opinions expressed in these essays appeared to help the authors to increase their feelings of self-esteem in two ways. Consequently, I divided the social identity function into two interrelated components. The first of these is the *value-expressive* function. Attitudes serving a value-expressive function enable people to affirm their belief in and adherence to important values that are closely related to their self-concepts. In one of the latter essays printed above, for example, the author expressed her personal philosophy of "live and let live." For her, being gay represented a personal issue; her values dictated that people should not be condemned for what they do in their personal lives so long as they do not force themselves on unwilling others. Expressing her views about gay people allowed her to express her personal values about individual liberties, which were fundamental to her perception of herself as an open-minded person.

Although the last essay above conveyed a considerably different message, it also manifested a value-expressive function. Through it, the writer expressed her need to perceive herself in terms of her religious faith. In her view, opposing homosexuality was an integral part of being a good Christian, which was of central importance to feeling good about herself. It was not homosexuality per se that was important; homosexuality was a symbol for all that is immoral and contrary to her religious views. If her religion were to define left-handedness as it now defines homosexuality, she would probably express comparable hostility toward left-handed people.

The second component of the social identity function is *social expression*. With this function, expressing an attitude strengthens one's sense of belonging to a particular group and helps an individual to gain acceptance, approval, or love from other people whom she or he considers important (e.g., peers, family, neighbors). When social-expressive attitudes are hostile, gay people are perceived as the epitome of outsiders; denigrating them solidifies one's own status as an insider, one who belongs to the group.

When social-expressive attitudes are positive, lesbians and gay men are regarded favorably by one's group or are members of that group. In either case, the approval that is won through expressing these attitudes increases the individual's own self-esteem, which is of central importance to her or him. Sometimes social support for attitudes is experienced directly, as when others tell us that they agree with our opinions or approve of our actions, that they accept us and like us. At other times, the support is indirect or imagined, as when we experience satisfaction because we feel that others would approve of us if they knew what we were saying or doing. The writers in these two essays most likely experienced both kinds of reinforcement for their attitudes. Their friends and family probably directly supported one's open-mindedness and the other's religiosity. At the same time, expressing their views probably helped them to feel kinship with larger social groupings (namely, open-minded people and good Christians).

I observed one other attitude function that also treats lesbians and gay men as symbols: the *ego-defensive* function. Defensive attitudes lower a person's anxiety resulting from her or his unconscious psychological conflicts, such as those surrounding sexuality or gender. This function is summarized in the notion that heterosexuals who express anti-gay prejudice do so out of fear that they themselves are latent homosexuals. This explanation for anti-gay prejudice has become widespread in recent years. Although it is used more often than is appropriate, it does fit some people for whom lesbians or gay men symbolize unacceptable parts of themselves (e.g., "effeminacy" for some men, "masculinity" for some women). Expressing anti-gay hostility represents an unconscious strategy through which they can avoid an internal conflict by externalizing it—projecting it onto a suitable symbol apart from themselves. By rejecting (or even attacking) gay people, the defensive individual can deny that unacceptable aspect of him- or herself while also symbolically attacking it. Defensive attitudes are often expressed in strong feelings of disgust toward homosexuality or in perceptions of danger from gay people of one's own gender. For example, one woman wrote:

> [I have generally negative attitudes] because I feel homosexuality is not a normal lifestyle. I do, however, feel more comfortable with a male homosexual than with a lesbian. Male homosexuals may have a different lifestyle but they are not physically dangerous to me as a woman, and I feel casual friendships between myself and male homosexuals are less tense. Lesbianism, however, is disgusting to me.

Another essay with defensive themes hinted strongly at some of the author's struggles with his own sexuality. Denying that anyone is truly homosexual, he expressed the unrealistic belief that society encourages young people to become gay:

> I don't believe such tendencies come about because of a person's true feelings. Our society keeps telling everyone that it's okay to be a les or fag, and that there's nothing wrong with it. Many guys and girls who have never had sexual relations with the opposite sex think they're "different" right away and they turn gay because everyone says it's okay anyway. I don't think anyone should hold the passive view that "if they don't bother me, let them be" because they are ruining this country's morals in a very disguised fashion. I feel people with these tendencies aren't that abnormal—they've just been taken in by society's view that it's okay. Let's give these people help so they can enjoy life to its fullest like everyone else.

The value-expressive, social-expressive, and ego-defensive functions share a common characteristic: With all of them, anti-gay prejudice helps people to define who they are by directing hostility toward gay people as a symbol of what they are not. With the value-expressive function, a heterosexual's attitudes help to define the world according to principles of good and evil,

right and wrong; by opposing the embodiment of evil (gay people), the individual affirms her or his own morality and virtue. With the social-expressive function, one's attitudes help to designate who is in the in-group and who is in the out-group; by denigrating outsiders (lesbians and gay men), the individual affirms her or his own status as an insider. With the defensive function, attitudes toward gay people help to affirm and "own" the good or acceptable parts of the self while denying the bad or unacceptable parts. Unacceptable feelings (such as homoerotic desires, "feminine" tendencies for men, or "masculine" tendencies for women) are projected onto gay people, who are then disliked. In this way, individuals can symbolically (and often unconsciously) prove to themselves that those unacceptable feelings are not their own.

Here then is a nexus between psychological and cultural heterosexism: *Psychological heterosexism can serve these functions only when an individual's psychological needs converge with the culture's ideology.* Anti-gay prejudice can be value expressive only when an individual's self-concept is closely tied to values that also have become socially defined as antithetical to homosexuality. It can be social expressive only insofar as an individual strongly needs to be accepted by members of a social group that rejects gay people or homosexuality. It can be defensive only when lesbians and gay men are culturally defined in a way that links them to an individual's own psychological conflicts.

The functions discussed here are summarized in Table 22.1, from which it can be seen that the benefits received from attitudes toward lesbians and gay men are contingent upon either of two principal sources. One source is gay people themselves. With attitudes serving an experiential function, lesbians and gay men have been the source of pleasant or unpleasant experiences in the past. Holding and expressing attitudes consistent with that earlier experience allows an individual to exert some control over

TABLE 22.1	The Psychological Functions of Heterosexism	
Name of Function	**Description**	**Benefit to Individual**
Evaluative functions		
Experiential	Generalizes from past experiences with specific lesbians or gay men to create a coherent image of gay people in relation to one's own interests.	Makes sense of past experiences and uses them to guide behavior.
Anticipatory	Anticipates benefits or punishments expected to be received directly from lesbians or gay men.	In absence of direct experience with gay men or lesbians, plans future behavior so as to maximize rewards and minimize punishments.
Expressive functions		
Social identity:		
Value-expressive	Lesbians or gay men symbolize an important value conflict.	Increases self-esteem by affirming individual's view of self as a person who adheres to particular values.
Social-expressive	Lesbians or gay men symbolize the in-group or out-group.	Increases self-esteem by winning approval of others whose opinion is valued; increases sense of group solidarity.
Defensive:	Lesbians or gay men symbolize unacceptable part of the self.	Reduces anxiety associated with a psychological conflict by denying and externalizing the unacceptable aspect of self and then attacking it.

Note: With the evaluative functions, benefit is contingent upon direct experiences with lesbians and gay men. With the expressive functions, benefit is contingent upon the consequences of expressing the attitude.

future experiences, either by avoiding what has been unpleasant or by seeking out what has been pleasant. With the anticipatory function, the individual has not had direct interactions with lesbians or gay men in the past but expects to have them in the future and expects gay people to be the source of either benefit or detriment; the attitude helps the individual to prepare for those anticipated interactions. Because these attitudes involve an evaluation or appraisal of gay men and lesbians as a group in terms of whether they have been or will be a source of reward or punishment, I refer to them as the *evaluative* attitude functions (Herek, 1986b).[8]

With the social identity (value-expressive and social-expressive) and defensive functions, in contrast, the source of benefit is not contingent upon the actions or characteristics of lesbians and gay men but upon what happens when the individual expresses her or his attitudes. Lesbians and gay men serve as symbols of personal values, group membership, or unconscious conflicts. They are a means to an end: Expressing a particular attitude toward them helps the individual to affirm her or his self-concept in terms of important values, to feel accepted by significant others, or to reduce anxieties. Consequently, I refer to them as the *expressive* functions.

Distinguishing between the evaluative and expressive functions is useful because it suggests different strategies for reducing prejudice. Prejudice that serves one of the evaluative functions can best be reduced through direct experiences with lesbians and gay men. Prejudice that serves an expressive function can be reduced through addressing the individual's identity needs, affiliation needs, or unconscious conflicts. Some implications of this distinction for reducing psychological heterosexism are discussed more fully in the final section of this chapter.

The Psychological Functions of Anti-Gay Violence

In the discussion so far, psychological heterosexism has been examined as an attitude—that is, something "in the heads" of individuals. But what about behaviors such as actively discriminating against gay people or physically attacking them? When a teenage boy participates in a gang attack against a gay man on the street, for example, do his actions serve psychological functions for him in the same way that heterosexist attitudes do? In this section, I consider how the functional approach can be applied to hate crimes against lesbians and gay men.

Violence Serving Evaluative Functions

Some anti-gay crimes may serve an experiential function by enabling the attacker to make sense of his or her past negative interactions with a particular lesbian or gay man. Although discussions of anti-gay violence usually focus on the victim's status as a representative of the lesbian or gay male community, it should be recognized that gay people are not immune from attacks based on personal dislike or vengeance. They can be targeted by an individual with whom they have previously had an argument or disagreement unrelated to their sexual orientation. Or a perpetrator may have had a negative experience with someone who is gay and then attacked another gay person (e.g., a friend of the first individual) as a proxy. From the viewpoint of the victim, the attack may well be experienced as a hate crime regardless of the assailant's actual motives. But from the perpetrator's perspective, the attack was directed at a specific individual rather than all gay women and men.

Other violent attacks against gay people may be based on an anticipatory function. For example, the perpetrator perceives gay people to be vulnerable and unlikely to resist and consequently targets them for robbery (Harry, 1982). The assailant's primary motivation in this case is the desire for personal gain with minimal risk (*actuarial* crimes). The victim and the larger community are likely to experience this as a hate crime, especially if anti-gay epithets are uttered by the assailant. But the perpetrator might well have been responding more to situational cues than to personal prejudice—for example, an unexpected opportunity to rob an easy target.

Violence Serving an Expressive Function

Value-Expressive Violence Value-expressive violence provides a way for perpetrators to express important values that are the basis for their self-concepts. The value-expressive motivation was illustrated in an interview conducted by journalist Michael Collins with members of a Los Angeles gang called the Blue Boys. At one point in Collins's interview, the gang's leader justified their actions in value-expressive terms. Characterizing homosexuality as a serious societal problem, he stated that the gang members would not "sit back and watch the poisoning of America." He further portrayed the group members as upholding important values when he compared their violent assaults on gay men to "the work of Batman or some other masked avenger." His comments are consistent with the rhetoric of hate groups such as the Ku Klux Klan, which regularly appeal to moral authority (see Segrest & Zeskind, 1989). Value-based justifications for anti-gay violence often derive from societal norms surrounding the institution of gender. Although disengaged from the conventional moral order, perpetrators may develop rationalizations that designate gay people as worthy of punishment and that allow attackers to see themselves as "rendering gender justice and reaffirming the natural order of gender-appropriate behavior."

Social-Expressive Violence Membership in a social group often is a central component of one's identity. By clearly differentiating and then attacking an out-group, anti-gay violence can help in-group members to feel more positive about their group and, consequently, about themselves as well. For example, Weissman interviewed several young men who had thrown eggs and oranges at gay men at a gay bar in Greenwich Village. They generally described the incident as a practical joke, but it appears also to have strengthened their sense of group solidarity. The informal leader explained, "Peer pressure has a lot to do with it. Sometimes you're forced into doing something to prove yourself to others." Another group member described his feelings after the incident: "Relief. A kind of high. There was also a strong, close feeling that we were all in something together."

Social-expressive motivations also were apparent among the Blue Boys. They had a clearly formed in-group, signified by their "uniform" of blue baseball jackets, their blue bats, and their framed "Statement of Principles," which they claimed to have signed in blood. Additionally, the Blue Boys' leader also seemed to seek recognition and acceptance from a larger audience; he

fantasized that people who read about the group's exploits would cheer them on, much the way that baseball fans cheer a home run.

Perpetrators of anti-gay sexual assaults also may be motivated by needs to maintain status and affiliation with their peers. From a series of interviews with perpetrators of male–male rapes, for example, Groth and Burgess (1980, p. 808) concluded, "Some offenders feel pressured to participate in gang rape to maintain status and membership with their peers. . . . [A]cceptance and recognition by one's peers becomes a dynamic in group rape, and mutual participation in the assault serves to strengthen and confirm the social bond among the assailants."

Ego-Defensive Violence Anti-gay assaults can provide a means for young males to affirm their heterosexuality or masculinity by attacking someone who symbolizes an unacceptable aspect of their own personalities (e.g., homoerotic feelings or tendencies toward effeminacy). This process may be partly conscious, as evidenced in comments by the Blue Boys. Their leader repeatedly affirmed that they were "*real* men" who were "out there fucking chicks every night" and explained that they "chose the blue baseball bats because it's the color of the boy. The man is one gender. He is not female. It is male. There is no confusion. Blue is the color of men, and that's the color that men use to defeat the anti-male, which is the queer."

The Blue Boys appeared to use their anti-gay beatings as a way of establishing their own manhood. Their brutal assaults on men whom they perceived as the antithesis of masculinity may have been an attempt to deny any trace of femininity in themselves.

The ego-defensive motivations of anti-gay attacks probably often are hidden from the perpetrators themselves. A dramatic example can be found in the brutal murder of Robert Hillsborough by a gang of young men in San Francisco in the summer of 1977 (Shilts, 1982). One of the men convicted of the murder, 19-year-old John Cordova, stabbed Hillsborough 15 times while shouting "Faggot, faggot." What makes this story a possible example of defensive attitudes is the interesting fact that Cordova was sexually attracted to men but he could not admit it to himself. He had an occasional sexual relationship with a male construction contractor, who said that Cordova often initiated sexual encounters but "never wanted to act like he knew what he was doin' " during them (Shilts, 1982, p. 168). Cordova would always wake up as if he were in a daze, insisting he had no idea what had happened the night before. When he stabbed Hillsborough over and over, Cordova may have been unconsciously attacking and striking out at his own homosexual desires.

Ego-defensive motives also can underlie sexual assaults in which the perpetrator apparently wished to punish the victim as a way of dealing with his own unresolved and conflictual sexual interests. Groth and Burgess (1980, p. 808) quoted an assailant who had assaulted a young hustler after having sex with him:

> After I came, I dragged him out of the car and punched him out and called him a punk. I told him I was going to kill him. Then I threw his clothes out of the car and took off. I was angry at him. I don't know why. At what I was doing, I guess, is what I was really angry at.

Groth and Burgess (1980) speculated that assailants in male–male rape who are conflicted about their own homosexual attraction may see the victim as a temptation and may subsequently use rape in an attempt to punish him for arousing them.

Violence with Multiple Motivations

In many anti-gay assaults, the perpetrators act from several motives simultaneously. Multiple motivations seem especially likely in street assaults by young male perpetrators. Such assailants are at an age when establishing their adult identity, including their manhood, is of considerable

importance (Erikson, 1963). Many of them strongly embrace what the culture has defined as "masculine" characteristics, while rejecting "feminine" characteristics (Horwitz & White, 1987). Identity formation is both a personal and a social process; it must be done for oneself, for one's peers, and for the larger society. Consequently, gay men and lesbians may serve simultaneously as multiple symbols for young male gangs. They may represent (a) unacceptable feelings or tendencies experienced privately by each gang member (for example, deviations from heterosexuality or culturally prescribed gender roles), (b) the out-group, and (c) what society has defined as evil. At the same time, such attacks may be based in part on past experiences with gay people. The perpetrator, for example, may have had an unpleasant interaction with an individual who incidentally was gay and may seek vengeance by attacking a proxy for that individual. Consequently, gang attacks may simultaneously serve experiential, ego-defensive, social-expressive, and value-expressive functions for the perpetrators.

Other perpetrators also are likely to have multiple motives for their anti-gay attacks. Police officers, for example, work to uphold societal values in an institution where the sense of the in-group is strong and where masculinity traditionally has been revered (Niederhoffer, 1967). Some have interacted with gay people only when arresting them. Especially for young policemen, who may still be solidifying their adult identities, anti-gay violence may serve psychological functions quite similar to those previously discussed for street gangs. Similarly, parents who assault their lesbian daughters or gay sons may have multiple motivations: They may be trying to banish unacceptable feelings from a child whom they consider to be an extension of their own identity (an ego-defensive function), while fulfilling their culturally defined parental role of imparting society's values to their children (a value-expressive function) and while seeking to protect the integrity of their family from what they perceive as outside, perhaps alien influences (a social-expressive function). The assault also may result in part from the parent's feelings of anger and frustration that have built up toward the child during a long series of unpleasant interactions (an experiential function).

Situational Influences on Anti-Gay Violence

From the examples in this section, it should be clear that the primary cause of anti-gay violence is not always the attacker's own personal prejudice against lesbians and gay men. Although anti-gay (or, for that matter, progay) actions may reflect an individual's deeply felt attitudes and beliefs, this is not always the case. A heterosexual person's behaviors toward lesbians and gay men may be more a product of immediate circumstances than of her or his strong dislikes (or likes) for lesbians and gay men. In this sense, I agree with Ehrlich's observation that the term *hate crime* can be misleading if it implies that the attacker's motivation always is intense personal hatred for the victim's group. Acts of anti-gay violence need not always be driven primarily by psychological heterosexism (although it is likely to be present to some extent in all anti-gay hate crimes). Instead, such crimes can serve a variety of social and psychological functions for those who commit them. Rather than acting from their own bigotry, for example, some perpetrators of violence against lesbians and gay men may be responding primarily to peer pressure or other situational factors. This was illustrated in the comments of a young man interviewed by Weissman: "We were trying to be tough to each other. It was like a game of chicken—someone dared you to do something and there was just no backing down."

This observation points to another reason for distinguishing between psychological and cultural heterosexism. Whereas psychological heterosexism may not always be the principal reason for an anti-gay attack (e.g., a gang might

well have selected another type of "outsider" as a suitable victim), the importance of cultural heterosexism cannot be underestimated. For it is cultural heterosexism that defines gay people as suitable targets that can be "used" for meeting a variety of psychological needs. And anti-gay attacks, regardless of the perpetrator's motivation, reinforce cultural heterosexism. Thus, when a teenage gang member attacks a gay man on the street, it is a hate crime *not* because hate necessarily was the attacker's primary motive (it may or may not have been) but because the attack expresses cultural hostility, condemnation, and disgust toward gay people and because it has the effect of terrorizing the individual victim as well as the entire lesbian and gay community. The attack in effect punishes the gay person for daring to be visible.

In summary, although cultural heterosexism is the principal determinant of anti-gay hate crimes as a cultural phenomenon, additional factors must be considered to explain why a particular person commits a specific act of anti-gay violence. Among these are the individual's past experiences with the victim (if any), her or his psychological needs and personality characteristics, and the demands created by the immediate situation (e.g., peer pressures).

Strategies for Change

The functional approach is important not only because it explains the motivations for individuals' attitudes and actions but also because it suggests a strategy for combating anti-gay prejudice and violence, namely, by making them dysfunctional. This involves determining what psychological functions are served by a person's feelings or behaviors and then intervening in either of two ways: preventing the individual's anti-gay attitudes or actions from fulfilling that psychological need or helping her or him to meet the same need in another, less destructive way.

Consider, for example, someone whose anti-gay attitudes result from a value-expressive need to perceive herself as a religious person. Attempts to reduce her prejudice by eliminating the role played by religious values in her self-concept is not likely to succeed. It might be possible, however, to disentangle her condemnation of gay people from her moral beliefs so that she can continue to express her religious values but without attacking lesbians and gay men. This might be accomplished by presenting her with alternative, noncondemnatory theological perspectives on homosexuality by religious leaders whom she respects. She also might be influenced by juxtaposing her religious values against equally important but contradictory values. If she places a high value on patriotism, for example, she might be influenced by arguments that appeal to justice and liberty. A third source of change might be her realization that a person whom she loves (e.g., a close friend or relative) is gay. This might create a conflict between her moral condemnation of homosexuality as a symbol and her feelings for the flesh-and-blood individual whom she has always considered to be a good person and whom she now knows to be gay (see Herek, 1984, 1986b, 1987, 1991, for further discussion).

This approach requires that institutions and society, as well as individuals, be targeted for change. Individual anti-gay attitudes and actions will become dysfunctional when they are no longer supported by religious and political institutions, when they are not reinforced by social norms, and when they are not integral to society's images of sexuality and gender. Even more broadly, anti-gay prejudice and violence will become much less functional when the majority of heterosexual Americans stop perceiving homosexuality in symbolic terms and instead associate it with their close friends and loved ones who are lesbian or gay.

Coming out to heterosexuals is perhaps the most powerful strategy that lesbians and gay men have for overcoming psychological heterosexism and anti-gay violence. Empirical research with other minority groups has shown that intergroup contact often reduces prejudice in the majority group when the contact meets several conditions: When it makes shared goals salient, when intergroup cooperation is encouraged, when the contact is ongoing and intimate rather than brief and superficial, when representatives of the groups are of equal status, and when they share important values (Allport, 1954; Amir, 1976). These conditions occur most often when lesbians and gay men disclose their sexual orientation to their relatives, friends, neighbors, and coworkers. When heterosexuals learn that someone about whom they care is gay, formerly functional prejudice can quickly become dysfunctional. The untruth in stereotypes becomes obvious, social norms are perceived to have changed, and traditional moral values concerning sexuality are juxtaposed against the values of caring for a loved one. Thus having a friend, coworker, or family member who is openly gay can eventually change a prejudiced person's perception of homosexuality from an emotionally charged, value-laden symbolic construct to a mere demographic characteristic, like hair color or political party affiliation.

Coming out, however, is difficult and possibly dangerous. It requires making public an aspect of oneself that society perceives as more appropriately kept private. It can mean being defined exclusively in terms of sexuality by strangers, friends, and family. It also can mean being newly perceived as possessing some sort of disability or handicap, an inability to be what one should be as man or woman. In the worst situations, it can mean being completely rejected or even physically attacked by those to whom one has come out. Many gay people remain in the closet because they fear these negative interpersonal consequences as well as discrimination and stigmatization. Additionally, continually having to overcome invisibility is itself a frustrating experience; allowing others to assume that one is heterosexual often is the path of least resistance.

The challenge, therefore, is for all people who abhor heterosexism to do whatever they can to remove these barriers, to create a social climate in which coming out is safer and easier. This requires a comprehensive approach in which we all confront heterosexism in both its cultural and its psychological manifestations. As a first step, we must confront hate crimes against lesbians and gay men and other minority groups; we must clearly establish that these crimes are unacceptable and punish the perpetrators. We also must work to change the individual attitudes that give rise to such attacks and that tolerate them. And we must change the institutions that perpetuate prejudice by keeping lesbians and gay men invisible and punishing them when they come out.

Our culture already has witnessed the beginnings of a transformation as more and more lesbians and gay men have come out to those around them and as they have challenged heterosexism in its many forms—both psychological and cultural. Prejudice and violence work to prevent this transformation; they threaten to set back the clock by making gay people invisible once again. It is up to each of us to confront prejudice, to challenge violence, and to fight invisibility.

Notes

1. Following popular usage, the word *American* is used in this chapter to describe residents of the United States of America.

2. For example, see polls by ABC (August, 1987), the *Los Angeles Times* (August, 1987), Roper (September, 1985), Yankelovich (March, 1978), and Gallup (November, 1978). When not otherwise indicated, the national survey data described in this chapter were obtained through the Roper Center, University of Connecticut at Storrs. I am grateful to Professor Bliss Siman of Baruch College, City University of New York, for her assistance in securing these data.

3. In this chapter, the term *attitude* is used to refer to an individual's evaluative stance toward a particular group of persons or objects. Such an evaluation might be described with terms such as *good–bad, like–dislike,* or *favorable–unfavorable.* The term *opinion* is used interchangeably with *attitude.* An attitude or opinion can be expressed privately (to oneself) or publicly (through speaking, writing, or some other observable behavior).

4. In this chapter, I purposely avoid the term *homophobia,* which has often been used to describe such attitudes (Herek, 1984; Smith, 1971; Weinberg, 1972). Any single word is necessarily limited in its ability to characterize a phenomenon that encompasses issues of morality, legality, discrimination, civil liberties, violence, and personal discomfort. *Homophobia* is particularly ill-suited to this purpose, however, for three reasons. First, it is linguistically awkward; its literal meaning is something like "fear of sameness." Second, anti-gay prejudice is not truly a phobia; it is not necessarily based on fear; nor is it inevitably irrational or dysfunctional for individuals who manifest it (Fyfe, 1983; Herek, 1986a; Nungesser, 1983; Shields & Harriman, 1984). Third, using homophobia can easily mislead us into thinking of anti-gay prejudice in exclusively individual terms, as a form of mental illness rather than as a pattern of thought and behavior that can actually be adaptive in a prejudiced society.

5. In my earlier papers (Herek, 1986b, 1987), I used the term *experiential-schematic.* This somewhat cumbersome term has been shortened for the current chapter.

6. For example, 29% of the respondents to a 1986 *Newsweek*/Gallup poll indicated they knew a gay person. In a 1983 *Los Angeles Times* poll, the figure was 30%.

7. In my earlier papers (Herek, 1986b, 1987), I used the term *social expressive.* For greater clarity, I have substituted the term *social identity* in this chapter.

8. The term *instrumental* also might be used to describe these functions, in that they are based on the attitude object's instrumental value to the person holding the attitude. All attitudes can be considered instrumental, however, to the extent that they provide some sort of psychological benefit to the holder. I think that understanding this dual usage of *instrumental* helps to resolve Ehrlich's disagreement with Harry over whether violence is instrumental or symbolic. Harry uses the term in the more specific sense of benefits derived directly from the victim (e.g., valuables obtained through robbery); his usage matches the evaluative functions described here. Ehrlich's use of *instrumental* refers to the actor's need for some general benefit from the violence; this usage includes both evaluative and expressive violence and matches the more general concept of *function* as used in this chapter.

References

Allport, G. (1954). *The nature of prejudice*. New York: Addison-Wesley.

Amir, Y. (1976). The role of intergroup contact in change of prejudice and intergroup relations. In P. Katz (Ed.), *Towards the elimination of racism* (pp. 245–308). New York: Pergamon.

Colasanto, D. (1989, October 25). Gay rights support has grown since 1982, Gallup poll finds. *San Francisco Chronicle*, p. A21.

Erikson, E. H. (1963). *Childhood and society* (2nd ed.). New York: Norton.

Fyfe, B. (1983). "Homophobia" or homosexual bias reconsidered. *Archives of Sexual Behavior, 12*, 549–554.

Groth, A. N., & Burgess, A. W. (1980). Male rape: Offenders and victims. *American Journal of Psychiatry, 137*(7), 806–810.

Harry, J. (1982). Derivative deviance: The cases of extortion, fag-bashing, and shakedown of gay men. *Criminology, 19*, 251–261.

Herek, G. M. (1984). "Beyond homophobia": A social psychological perspective on attitudes toward lesbians and gay men. *Journal of Homosexuality, 10*(1/2), 1–21.

Herek, G. M. (1986a). The social psychology of homophobia: Toward a practical theory. *NYU Review of Law & Social Change, 14*(4), 923–934.

Herek, G. M. (1986b). The instrumentality of attitudes: Toward a neofunctional theory. *Journal of Social Issues, 42*(2), 99–114.

Herek, G. M. (1987). Can functions be measured? A new perspective on the functional approach to attitudes. *Social Psychology Quarterly, 50*, 285–303.

Herek, G. M. (1991). Stigma, prejudice, and violence against lesbians and gay men. In J. Gonsiorek & J. Weinrich (Eds.), *Homosexuality: Research implications for public policy* (pp. 60–80). Newbury Park, CA: Sage.

Horwitz, A. V., & White, H. R. (1987). Gender role orientations and styles of pathology among adolescents. *Journal of Health and Social Behavior, 28*, 158–170.

McClintock, C. (1958). Personality syndromes and attitude change. *Journal of Personality, 26*, 479–492.

Niederhoffer, A. (1967). *Behind the shield: The police in urban society*. Garden City, NY: Doubleday.

Nungesser, L. G. (1983). *Homosexual acts, actors, and identities*. New York: Praeger.

Rayside, D., & Bowler, S. (1988). Public opinion and gay rights. *Canadian Review of Sociology and Anthropology, 25*, 649–660.

Schneider, W., & Lewis, I. A. (1984, February). The straight story on homosexuality and gay rights. *Public Opinion*, pp. 16–20, 59–60.

Segrest, M., & Zeskind, L. (1989). *Quarantines and death: The Far Right's homophobic agenda*. (Available from the Center for Democratic Renewal, P.O. Box 50469, Atlanta, GA 30302)

Shields, S. A., & Harriman, R. E. (1984). Fear of male homosexuality: Cardiac responses of low and high homonegative males. *Journal of Homosexuality, 10*(1/2), 53–67.

Shilts, R. (1982). *The mayor of Castro Street: The life and times of Harvey Milk*. New York: St. Martin's.

Smith, K. T. (1971). Homophobia: A tentative personality profile. *Psychological Reports, 29*, 1091–1094.

Smith, M. B., Bruner, J. S., & White, R. W. (1956). *Opinions and personality*. New York: John Wiley.

Weinberg, G. (1972). *Society and the healthy homosexual*. New York: St. Martin's.

23

ARTICLE

Martin Simmons

The Truth About Male Friendships

If a dude buys me a drink, drops the winning two points through the hoop or comes stepping out with a fine woman, I might say, "My man! Slap me five!" Twenty or 30 minutes later, I might lay another "my man" on someone else. It's not that the term "my man" used in these contexts doesn't mean anything. It's just that it doesn't mean anything much. It's transitory, and has more to do with the style and stance that Black men adopt with each other during brief encounters than with the real substance of their relationships.

But when I say "My *main* man," I'm talking about my stone ace boon coon. My running cut buddy. My partner. Number One. Him and me against the world. And that's different. It is not temporary or transitory. It's been long-term, and frankly, I hope it will be forever. Or at least until one of us is dropped into a hole in the ground.

For Black men in this society, the world is a hostile, dangerous place—a jungle. It is uncompromising territory where a man is either the hunter or the hunted; he either seizes the power or loses it; he either rises to the never-ending

tests of his manhood or falls a victim. Since Black men's relationship to power and sense of manhood has always been challenged in this land, we must always be on the move, always wary, always careful, always thinking and always on guard. We must walk that fine line between paranoia and prudence. It helps if we have a main man to walk it with. In fact, I think it's critical.

Without that main partner who helps you keep sight of the line, you can easily fall prey to the hunter. Without that main man to walk with, relate to, bounce thoughts off, you can easily lose sight of the real meaning of power and manhood. To walk alone means that it is always necessary to present a "front," an image, a projection of bravado that ensures protection.

Every Black man knows such bravado is sometimes a must. In public he knows he is supposed to be a bad dude. He is expected to brag and strut and lie. To do otherwise is to be considered less than a man. But in his private moments, those honest times when he faces only himself, he is—regardless of his true strength—likely to be haunted by insecurities, fears, doubts and an overwhelming sense of powerlessness. He can lie to the world, but never to the image in the mirror.

Reprinted from *Essence*, November 1981: 134, 137, 139–140.

Of course, most men travel through life in some sort of partnership with women. It is relatively easy for a man to find a woman to whom he can relate. It seems to me, though, that if he is a thinking man, he knows the areas of his psyche that he can and cannot allow a woman access to. He can rarely let her know that he can or wants to be violent, that he is sometimes so angry with a world that would cheat him of his manhood that he often wants to kill or explode, because he knows that her response would be maternal and protective. She would want him to suppress those feelings lest they bring him harm. Furthermore, if they've been to bed a couple of times, he knows that he has a claim on her feelings, and he knows the things that she could be sympathetic to. He can therefore let her see that he is gentle, tender or sometimes even afraid.

But just let him go bopping down to the corner talking about how gentle or tender he is. Or let him try to tell the guys over a beer that he doesn't control his woman, that he doesn't sock it to her because he can't or doesn't want to. He'd be laughed out of the bar, and branded a punk, a chump, a fool—maybe even a faggot. In front of the boys, he'd better have made it with every woman he has ever said he wanted. He'd better be rough, tough, don't take no stuff. Out in the jungle, he'd better be a lion.

It's hard. It ain't funny. The image of the rootin'-tootin', six-shootin' Black man willing to fight and die because someone stepped in front of him in the supermarket line, thereby challenging his manhood, takes a lot of energy to keep up. At some point he *must* relax—totally, completely and absolutely.

So a man is lucky to find another man in whose presence he does not have to brag and strut and lie. Extremely lucky to find a cut buddy, an ace, a main man to fall back on. I've been that lucky. I have a main man.

Any man who has roamed the jungle alone—and I have—knows that the slightest hill can be as steep and slippery as Mt. Everest in January. But I also know that a good friend is another set of hands to help you make the climb. My ace not only has his own pick and climbing boots but has an extra set for me. He's got my back, and if necessary, I can get a lift on his shoulders. If I slip, I know he'll grab me. If I fall, he'll catch me. All he expects is that I do the same for him.

This is not to say that women don't often give such support to men. But I know the truth is that whatever the relationship a man has with a woman, rarely will he tell her everything, or be too weak in her presence, because he knows that she, like everyone else, ultimately expects him to be a lion. Besides, other men expect a man to exercise control over a woman, and to reveal weakness to her means relinquishing a measure of control. Most important, however, a man knows that women do not have to move through the jungle in quite the same way he does. Though as Black people we are up against the same forces, those forces strike men and women in entirely different ways—with entirely different results.

Black men do not become cut buddies unless they have in common a basic and instinctive understanding of each other's psychological and emotional needs, as well as the forces they must confront, and share a willingness to meet those needs and forces. This instinctive understanding is built on shared experiences, which is why so many main-man partnerships go back to grade school or high school or the military. Although my partner and I spent our youths in widely separated places and environments, we are both struggling artists, we both know that it is the loneliest business in the world.

More important, my partner and I know the common forces that we as Black men are up against as we move to forge our definitions of what it means to be men. We know that no one—not friends, not family, not the wife who may want you to get a nine to five and a steady income—no one, except your main man, believes in your worth as a writer until it is demonstrated by some commercial standard of success; your name on a book jacket, your byline appearing 40 times.

Try to build a dream or realize a vision and the world won't buy in until the elevator reaches the fifth floor. But your main man buys in at the basement. He believes in you because he knows you. He believes in you because to believe in you is to believe in himself and the power of every Black man to make his dream come true, his own way in the world.

Since meeting seven years ago, my main man and I have faced crises together, fought battles side by side and back to back, cruised the jungle as twin panthers each looking out for predators who would endanger us.

For a Black man in particular, to roam the jungle alone—without the backup of a main man—is to be without perspective or protection. It means being afraid, and feeling that you are the only one who knows fear. It means thinking that no one else thinks like you do, and wondering if you should trust your own thoughts. It means not knowing that other men are sometimes gentle, sometimes weak, sometimes crazy—just as you sometimes are. It means you have no positive way to measure manhood or maleness, so what gets played out in behavior are false and often negative definitions of maleness: brutality, cold-bloodedness, hardheartedness. In short, being a "bad dude," being the kind of man you think you're supposed to be, which, in a very real way, can mean being insane.

But with a main man, an ace, you have not only another set of hands but another set of eyes—eyes that see you and accept you as you are and reflect what he is, too. My main man came of age at about the same time I did. We see the same world, which means we can reinforce each other's position in it. We share the same attitude toward life in all important respects. We walk in the same direction and we

walk side by side. We understand each other, advise each other and keep each other on track. Together we are more than when we are apart, because our strengths are complementary and our weaknesses compensatory.

I can confide in my ace, share secrets and real feelings and never fear that he'll think I'm a fool, or a clown or a coward—or anything less than a man. As I said before, I know I'm lucky because so much of what being a man is supposed to mean has to do with being a "strong, silent type" who keeps his emotions in check and his feelings locked away. Deep emotional friendships among men are not usually encouraged. I know, too, that truly trusting relationships between any two people are not common because trust, faith and honesty with another person have somehow become equated with weakness.

As for me, I know that having this running buddy has made me stronger. I respect the brother, I trust the brother. I love the brother. He is my other ear, eye and mind. His opinions matter as much to me as my own. They take on equal weight, they get equal consideration. In this jungle of a world, he halves my burdens and doubles my joys.

Unfortunately, there are women who feel threatened by the relationship my partner and I have. Though they may have girlfriends, they somehow don't grasp the need for men to run together or hang together. The fact is, men need the company of each other as much as women need the company of other women or men need the company of women. Men need to shoot the breeze, talk shit, chase women and run the jungle together. More to the point, Black men need to reaffirm their worth in this place that is constantly denying that worth—and such affirmation can only come from other Black men.

When I tell my partner that during a job interview, the white boy sitting behind the desk said that my resume would threaten most of the white males already in the company and that therefore he wouldn't hire me, I know that my main man understood the insidiousness of that in a way that my woman never could. What Black men ultimately understand with each other is that we "are all in this together." Women provide sympathy. Most men, I think, neither need nor want sympathy from other men. What they need and get in good male relationships is *empathy*. Black men's thoughts and conversations are colored by the fact that society treats them always as political entities. Black men who come together, therefore, have a "you and me against the world" attitude. It seems to me that women are more insular and home-centered, and their concerns tend to be for those things they label "security" and "stability." Their attitude when they are with their men is "you and me. I fixed you a hot meal. Don't worry about the world tonight."

A woman who truly loved me and had my interests at heart would understand that her view of the world and the world's view of her are unlike those of the man in her life. She would realize that in many ways there can be no empathetic understanding between us. She would, therefore, not try to come between me and my main man. She would understand the differences between my relationship with her and with my partner, and recognize that both are equally important and equally necessary. And, if she could be honest with herself, she would know that both are limited: neither she nor he can be my whole world.

My cut buddy, although he will give me a blunt and honest opinion of the woman I'm dealing with, would not attempt to come between her and me because he knows she fulfills needs he can't. He knows that what I seek, what he seeks and what most men seek from women is the fulfillment of relatively mundane, though

absolutely critical, needs: sex, physical warmth and touching, love, care for their health, home and children.

I think that men who cannot or have not established deep friendships with other men— men who have no main man or say that their best friends are their wives or their women— are men without strong psychological support, without another worldly male view, without a truly empathetic understanding of the social and political forces at work in the jungle, so they are often too paranoid, prudent or alone to challenge the world.

"Him and me against the world" may sound like a serious phrase for a serious world, but it's not always so heavy. There are times when I'm hanging with my ace and the world is lightweight. We can talk and laugh and joke and run a smooth, sweet double-game on any and everybody. Fortunately, we are as different physically as we are alike spiritually. This physical difference means that women who are attracted or attractive to me are seldom attracted or attractive to him and vice versa. Therefore, we never have to fight over women.

Which is not to say that we don't compete. Like most men, we are both very competitive— and we both play to win. We just confine our competition to the game board or to those situations in which competition will benefit both of us by sharpening and honing our skills, our perspective and our ability to do battle with the world at large.

When we do compete, the winner gloats and crows and laughs in the loser's face. God knows, we're both poor winners. But we aren't poor losers because, win or lose against each other, I know in the final go-down that I can count on him. My main man. My running partner. My ace. Me and him against the world.

I n what ways is work tied to male identity? Do men gain a sense of fulfillment from their work, or do they view it as necessary drudgery? How might the organization of workplaces play on, reinforce, or sometimes threaten the types of masculinity that males have already learned as youngsters? How does the experience of work (or of not having work) differ for men of different social classes, ethnicities, and sexual preference groups? And how do recent structural changes in society impact upon the masculinity–work relationship? The articles in this section address these issues and more.

The rise of urban industrial capitalism saw the creation of separate "public" and "domestic" spheres of social life. As women were increasingly relegated to working in the home, men were increasingly absent from the home, and the male "breadwinner

FIVE

PART

Men and Work

role" was born. The sexual division of labor, this gendered split between home and workplace, has led to a variety of problems and conflicts for women and for men. Women's continued movement into the paid labor force, higher levels of unemployment, and the rise of a more service-oriented economy have led to dramatic shifts in the quality and the quantity of men's experiences in their work.

Articles by Christine L. Williams and Jennifer Pierce explore the experience of work for men— the former by examining the ways in which men who do "women's work" are also involved in gender restoration, and the latter by exploring the gender confirmation of the work of corporate lawyers. Manual Peña and Timothy Nonn explore the gendered meanings of work at the other side of the economic pyramid, among Mexican workers and among the homeless and unemployed, respectively.

Music, 1985, oil on canvas, 70 × 60. Copyright © 1985 by Greg Drasler.

The work world has also become an arena of the battle of the sexes, as the aftermath of the Clarence Thomas confirmation hearings made clear. The article by Patti A. Giuffe and Christine L. Williams examines the ways in which sexual harassment concerns raise important issues in interactions between men and women of different races and sexual orientations at all work sites.

24

ARTICLE

Manuel Peña

Class, Gender, and Machismo: The "Treacherous-Woman" Folklore of Mexican Male Workers

> Interpretation proper . . . always presupposes, if not a conception of the unconscious itself, then at least some mechanism of mystification or repression in terms of which it would make sense to seek a latent meaning behind a manifest one, or to rewrite the surface categories of a text in the stronger language of a more fundamental interpretive code. (Jameson 1981, 60)

The twentieth-century Mexican *canción-ranchera*[1] is noted for the prevalence of one theme—*la mujer traicionera* (the treacherous woman)[2] and other complementary stereotypes. Stereotypical, also, is the eternal lament of these songs, which is accompanied by the ever-present *copa de vino*—the wine glass—to help the forlorn lover drown his despair. If we were to interpret the ranchera at face value, we might conclude that Mexican women are a treacherous and debased lot and that Mexican men are emotional weaklings who readily succumb to alcoholism to obliterate their sorrows. Neither of these conclusions would be correct. If anything, the traditional Mexican woman is faithful to a fault, although the second

Reprinted from *Gender & Society*, Vol. 5 No. 1, March 1991: 30–46 © 1991 Sociologists for Women in Society.

assumption, the Mexican's strong attraction to alcohol, may stand closer scrutiny.

What, then, are we to make of the theme of the treacherous woman and similar debased-female stereotypes, such as that of the perverted wench? These are prevalent not only in the canción ranchera but also in a kind of folklore that forms the subject of this article—the folklore of machismo (Paredes 1966). The article explores the theme of the treacherous woman in the folklore of machismo and its relationship to Mexican working-class male ideology. It proposes that, in addition to legitimizing the oppression of women, the folklore symbolically conflates class and gender, shifting the point of conflict from the former, which is shrouded in mystification, to the latter, which is more susceptible to conscious ideological manipulation.

The interpretation offered here differs from previous analyses of Mexican machismo. Paredes (1966), for example, attributed much of the symbolism of the folklore of machismo to Mexican middle-class men and their reaction to the overbearing presence of the Americans and their sense of cultural superiority. Paz (1961), Ramos (1962), and other scholars have analyzed Mexican machismo generally as the psychohistorical product of a traumatic Spanish conquest. I agree with Paredes that machismo is a universal phenomenon and not the result of conquest trauma; however, I do not think it is primarily an expression of Mexican middle-class men's resentment toward Americans. In fact, as Ramos (1962) and others have observed, the style of discourse in which macho folklore best flourishes—vulgar language, sadistic insults, the utter degradation of women—is more characteristic of working-class men than their middle-class counterparts.

This article argues that the folkloric theme of the treacherous woman is a key element in the ideology of machismo and that both are intimately tied to Mexican working-class, male culture. This ideology derives its power not from the psychohistorical effects of a conquest trauma, as Ramos and others have proposed, but from the specific conditions that have historically shaped Mexican culture—extreme economic exploitation and its attendant deprivation and alienation. The article uses a historical–materialist theory to link class, gender, and culture and thereby reveals the connection among folklore, the ideology of machismo, and the oppressed economic condition of the Mexican male worker.

On Method

The data for the article were collected during fieldwork I conducted between 1986 and 1988 among Mexican immigrant men who worked for a large agribusiness firm near Fresno, California. The firm, which I shall call S&J Growers, employed about 450 men and women during the peak summer season—harvesting, packing, and shipping a variety of fruits and nuts. All the women (a total of about 50), as well as a handful of men, were employed in the packing shed. The remainder of the men worked in the fields and orchards. The vast majority of the workers were undocumented at the time I began the fieldwork. However, most of them

became eligible for amnesty under the provisions of the U.S. Immigration Reform and Control Act of 1986, and by 1988 many of the men and women at S&J Growers had been granted amnesty.

I conducted the research exclusively among the men who worked in the orchards. Most of that research was carried out during the summers of 1986 and 1987, when I logged more than 400 hours picking fruit alongside the men who collaborated with me in this study. They knew the *patrón* had given me permission to collect "stories and jokes" from them, which made it easier for me to intervene in their work routine. During my first days in the field, I would walk up to a group of workers, introduce myself, and begin picking fruit next to them. I would then engage them in casual conversation to get acquainted. Later, as I became more familiar to the men and they more open with me, I started bringing a portable cassette recorder to the field. With microphones discreetly concealed in my shirt pocket, I taped a number of conversations, as well as over 100 assorted jokes, riddles, and rhymes, known collectively as *charritas* to the workers.

Among the charritas collected is the subcategory with which this article is concerned—*charritas coloradas* (red jokes)—which form the core of the folklore of machismo and whose unvarying message is "sadism toward women and symbolic threats of sodomy toward other males" (Paredes 1966, 121). I should point out that the workers were at first reluctant to share these often-risqué charritas with me. In due time, however, this type of humor surged to the forefront, and once the workers convinced themselves that I was especially interested in charritas coloradas, these became the dominant genre performed.

The methods I employed in my research—participation and observation—were keyed to the performance context of the charritas as a generator of meaning and interpretation. The charritas cannot be properly analyzed outside that context. Any given context, however, is inevitably altered by the ethnographer's biases. As advocates of reflexive anthropology have often reminded us, ethnography is not the science of cultural analysis but the art of writing "partial truths" (Clifford 1986, 7). Thus, although the limitations inherent in the fieldwork enterprise do not, by any means, invalidate our interpretations, they do commit us to one-sided accounts, since it is impossible for the ethnographer to know and portray a whole way of life (Clifford 1986, 7–8). This interpretive ethnography is no exception.

Charritas and Treacherous Women

As Paredes correctly noted (1966), the woman is singled out for a special, if ignominious, role in the folklore of machismo. Typically, in the charrita colorada she may be reduced to a state of absolute sexual passivity, an unwitting object for the sadistic amusement of the macho.[3] Or, as is more common in the canción ranchera, she may be portrayed as a heartless wench who betrays her lover without the slightest sense of remorse.[4] In either case, the folkloric portrayal stands in stark contrast to the normative expectations of the idealized Mexican woman—the mother described by Díaz-Guerrero (1975, 3) as the source of boundless love and "absolute self-sacrifice."

The charritas analyzed in the following pages illustrate both portrayals. The immediate context in which they were performed is important, because all of them were embedded in discourse with clear implications for gender relations as conceived by these male workers. For example, during a conversation with four men, aged 18 to 25, regarding the differences between Mexican and Mexican-American women, a number of points were raised with respect to gender roles and the relationship that should obtain between men and women. In the context

of this relationship, the man proclaimed the superiority of the Mexican woman over her Mexican-American counterpart, whom they considered lazy, footloose, unfaithful, and generally insubordinate to men's authority. One of the workers complained that Mexican-American women, or Chicanas, were *muy libertinas*—"too unrestrained or licentious":[5]

> I don't want the same thing to happen to me as it did to a neighbor, who married a woman from here, and not even with blows could he control her, to keep her from running around like a harlot.

Another worker summed up the tenor of the discussion with the following assessment:

> Over there [in Mexico] one has command over them, and scolds them and all that. But not here; if she feels that things don't suit her, she gets out and leaves.

At length, the conversation took on a lighter vein, and it was then that one of the men made the offensive but tongue-in-cheek observation that, "*las chicanas son más putas que las gallinas* [Chicanas are worse whores than hens]." Taking my cue from this folkloric statement, I asked for some charritas about women. The two that follow were particularly keyed to the conversation of the moment. The first one articulates the theme of the treacherous woman, who, out of sheer perversity, picks up and walks out on her man to go and enjoy the "fast life":

> A man was left by his wife—she liked the fast life [*le gustaba el pedo*]. And the man lost himself in drinking. He would get drunk, and he would get like this, sitting down, with his slobber [*baba*] coming out of his mouth. And he was sitting on a chair like this [the performer mimics a drunk man], with slobber all the way down. And somebody said to him, "Señor, ¡la baba, la baba!" "Sí," he answered, "sí lavaba—y planchaba y todo, pero se me fué, ¡la hija de la chingada!"

The humor in this charrita lies in its word play, of course. When the man is alerted to the slobber drooling from his mouth (*¡la baba, la baba!*), he interprets what he hears as a question related to his wife's competence as a homemaker: *¿lavaba, lavaba?*—"Did she wash [clothes]?" To which he replies, "Yes, she washed—and she ironed and everything, but she left me, the bitch."

As soon as the laughter and other gratuitous remarks elicited by this charrita died down, another worker volunteered the following one, in which the woman is depicted as a debased, sex-driven pervert who in the end gets more than she has bargained for. The repeated references to her as a *vieja* (here, a whorelike figure) underscore her depraved, perverse character:

> There was this woman who liked the thing, you know, who liked for men to stick the thing in her. And then she came to a field like this [gesturing toward the field around us], where there was a lot of *raza* [Mexican men]. She says, "I've come for one who is really big, who can fill me up," she says. No, well, they all started to show up. "Let's see here, Carlos [the author of the first charrita], you who have such a big one." No, they all showed up, and she sized them all, and the vieja would say, "No, I want a bigger one." And they all came, one after another. And she says, "No, bigger." "No," they say, "bring Gollo." So Gollo arrives and he was really big. So he starts to get down on her, until he left her so worn out she couldn't even get up, the vieja. He was so big, he left her all hurt—but he won the bet. So she starts walking, all hurt, she couldn't even walk, when a robber comes out with a knife and says, *"El dinero, o la degollo."* *"¡No, no,"* she cries, *"la de Gollo ya no, la de Gollo ya no!"*

In this charrita, again, the humor revolves around a linguistic misinterpretation: *El dinero o la degollo* translates into "the money or I'll decapitate you [*la degollo*]." However, the woman, still reeling from Gollo's sexual assault, confuses *la degollo* for the identically sounding but even more terrifying *la de Gollo*—Gollo's "it," that is, his penis. The robber's threat is thus heard as,

"The money, or you get Gollo's penis [again]." In the end, besides debasing the woman, the charrita redeems macho pride, which is embodied in the symbol of male prowess, Gollo's enormous penis (cf. Paredes 1966, 121; Paz 1961, 82; Ramos 1962, 59–60). The men were obviously aware of all these implications, and their cheers and raucous laughter left no doubt that they enjoyed seeing their side triumph in this small skirmish between men and women.

Charritas often bolster common beliefs about gender relations. For example, I was engaged in conversation with three workers, one in his late teens, the other two in their 30s. Again, at my initiative the conversation turned to relations between men and women, especially in Chicano versus Mexican marriages:

MP: Are you telling me that the woman from here is more difficult to get along with than the woman from over there?

J: I believe so. The woman from over there will follow you wherever you want. The one from here, if she doesn't want to, she won't go. She stays here. You marry a young one from here and two, three years later you're single. You come here, they go out dancing. "Your wife, where is she?" She goes here, she goes there.

B: You know what advantage the women have here? The women from here, the ones who are alone who have been left [by their husbands] are supported by welfare. And over there they are not. That's why they [women in Mexico] don't leave you.

At this point, the conversation switched to the men's explanations as to why Chicanos do not come out to the fields to work, but moments later one of the men engaged in the conversation remembered that a fellow working nearby had made up a charrita especially for me. He called him over and had him recite it for all present. It was a rhyme:

At the top of that mountain
I have a carton of beer;
open your legs Teresa,
'cause I'm coming at you headlong.

While this charrita does not depict the woman as treacherous or debased, it does reduce her to a pliant, submissive creature whose function, at least implicitly, is to satisfy the sexual whims of her man. Coming as it did moments after a serious discussion about women, it reinforced the general tone of the conversation from the men's point of view: It is a man's inalienable right to exercise control over a woman, to possess her sexually when he wishes—in effect, to render her defenseless and penetrate her at will. The men appreciated the performer's inventiveness and his artistic handling of the topic and rewarded him with claps and cheers of approval.

Several more charritas followed on the heels of this one, as the men around us began to warm up to the session. One, offered by el Jarocho, a man well known even among these hardened workers as a real "macho," was particularly clever and subtle:

Pussy [*culito*], when you were mine
you sounded like a [tight] wooden rattle.
Now that you're no longer mine
you sound like a cow's ass [*culote*]

Lusty cheers of approbation followed el Jarocho's performance, as the men evidently identified with the rhyme's message, which in the original Spanish accentuates the woman's transformation from virgin to wornout hag by a subtle linguistic shift—the diminutive *culito* replaced by the augmentative *culote*. The cause of the change is ambiguous: It is either the result of the man's formidable penis or her fickle and dissolute life. Given the scornful tone of the rhyme, the latter seems the more correct interpretation. Heightening the effect is the extreme vulgarity of the rhyme, which dehumanizes the woman by reducing her to the level of an animal.

Their treatment of women aside, and the enjoyment the men derived from them, charrita colorada performances often led to exchanges of sadistic insults that at times resulted in half-serious, half-playful duels—particularly among the younger men. On the surface, these insults, mock fights, and macho humor could be interpreted as expressions of sexual deviance, interpersonal hostility, or even the psychocultural inferiority that Ramos (1962) and others have attributed to Mexican men. More fundamentally, however, they signify an unconscious betrayal of the profound social conflict and resentment that existed in the lives of the joke tellers. In short, they were symbolic manifestations of a complex social reality enmeshed in the interplay of class, gender, and culture.

Pelados, Machismo and Psychohistory: A Critical Reassessment

Working-class men like those I have been describing here, as well as the culture of machismo associated with them, have hardly gone unnoticed in previous Mexican (and American) scholarship. Samuel Ramos, the respected Mexican philosopher, was an early and influential critic, being principally responsible for developing a portrait of Mexican man and culture that has long resisted challenge. That portrait needs to be reassessed, in light of this and other recent research (Colombres 1982).

In a highly influential book, *El perfil del hombre y la cultura en Mexico* (1934; English version, *Profile of Man and Culture in Mexico*, published in 1962), Ramos dealt at length with the culture of machismo and the "best model for its study"—the *pelado* of proletarian origins (Ramos 1962, 58). *El perfil* drew a stark portrait of the pelado—the penniless, dissolute, glib-tongued character immortalized by the comic Cantinflas.

More than that, for Ramos the pelado was the purest incarnation of the Mexican "national character"—a resentful, distrusting misanthrope with a constant need to vent his deep-seated feelings of hostility and inferiority on enemies seen and unseen. Ramos excoriated this perennial child of Mexico's extreme social-class disparity, castigating him for his warped machismo and crude life-style. In short, for Ramos the pelado is nothing more than "a form of human rubbish from the great city . . . a being without substance" (1962, 61–62).

From a sociological perspective, male proletarian workers like those at S&J Growers are no different from Ramos's pelado. Indeed, the popular perception of the modern proletarian man, which derives in great part from Ramos's analysis, does not differ significantly from the latter's original characterization of the pelado. The mass media portrays the modern male proletarian as Ramos did his predecessor—a culturally crude and violent macho. Yet the present research suggests a more complex picture of this quintessential Mexican than Ramos or the media have perceived. For instance, in everyday life most of the men at S&J Growers, at least, were not nearly as violent as Ramos's pelados—those "explosive beings with whom relationship is dangerous" (1962, 59). Nor, for that matter, were they as callous toward women as the folklore of machismo would suggest, if taken at face value.

In fact, the men who delighted in the performance of charritas and other types of macho humor also evinced the other side of machismo—the typically Mexican sense of *respeto* that idealizes women. Like Mexican men everywhere, these workers bestowed an inordinate share of courtesy, protectiveness, and even reverence upon their mothers, sisters, wives, and "significant others," as long as their male supremacy was not challenged (cf. Díaz-Guerrero 1975, 1–15, 89–111; Mirandé 1988). In particular, the older married men who had families in

Mexico expressed their concerns about making enough money to send back home, being away from their growing children for long periods, and burdening their wives with added domestic responsibilities while they were absent.

Yet their code of machismo impelled the men toward cultural behavior that can only be termed destructive. They drank and celebrated with abandon, often with disastrous results, such as bloody fights and vehicular accidents. Almost invariably, alcohol intensified their feelings of machismo and the crudities associated with it—vulgarity, sadistic behavior, blind anger—all those cultural negatives that Ramos originally attributed to the pelado. And, like the pelado, these agricultural workers arrogated to themselves a special kind of virility, "creating thereby the illusion that personal valor is the Mexican's particular characteristic" (Ramos 1962, 63).

According to Ramos, the liabilities associated with the culture of machismo are deeply rooted in Mexican psychohistory, which spawned a collective inferiority complex that coalesced early on in the personality of the proletarian pelado. For this critic of Mexican culture, all the manifestations of the Mexican man's inferiority—his distrust, aggressiveness, resentment, timidity, deception, crude language, and all the rest of the Mexican's imputed cultural ills—can be traced to the original rape of the Indian mother by the Spanish conquistador.

Ramos's psychohistorical theory continues to inform more recent but no less pessimistic analyses of the Mexican man (Echanove Trujillo 1973; Goldwert 1983; Paz 1961). In focusing on conquest and colonization as the ultimate causes of cultural disharmony, these analyses ignore the intricate relationship among class, gender, and culture and the possible role these may play in the development of Mexican machismo. Instead, to psychohistorically minded analysts, the Mexican man's pent-up anger, gross language, and distrust must be "psychic transformations . . . instinctive tricks devised to protect the ego from itself" (Ramos 1962, 66), that is, from facing up to the fact that the Mexican has a deeply rooted inferiority complex.

The men I worked with did at times display the pent-up anger, the distrust, and all the behavior of the pelado that so vexed Ramos. Like the pelado, they displayed their "black resentment" toward "every quarter that has been hostile to them" (Ramos 1962, 59). Sometimes free-floating, this resentment surfaced in acts of aggression such as drunken fights; sometimes it was directed at convenient targets such as the Mexican American, whom they criticized incessantly. Occasionally, I saw this anger aimed directly at those whom the workers felt were exploiting them, from abusive foremen to the *patrones* who exercised arbitrary power over them. Resentment toward the latter was the most seething, yet suppressed. I saw it flash momentarily in the defiant faces of young men summarily dismissed for not conforming to the management's strict grooming requirements— no beards, long sideburns, or hair below the shirt collar. The men also spoke angrily of comrades being paid less than the newly legislated minimum wage. Yet, as one man bitterly complained, "We are a bunch of chickens; we don't know how to unite and protest against injustice."

Resentment thus flowed like a powerful undercurrent in the stream of these undocumented workers' culture. It was expressed as well in sublimated ways—the real "psychic transformations" out of which the folklore of machismo is spun. An interpretive question arises: To what extent are cultural expressions like the folklore of machismo symbolic alibis for sources of frustration rooted in other spheres of these workers' lives? I am not pointing here to inferiority complexes born of the rape of ancestral mothers by Spanish conquistadors (to borrow Paredes's colorful phrase), but to the daily adversities thrown up against the workers by an economic system that condemns them to perpetual struggle, impoverishment, and alienation.

If the folklore of machismo is not the product of psychohistory but a reflection of fundamental economic structures, why the psychic transformation? Why, in other words, should the folklore be so obsessed with the degradation of women, when the source of resentment is class exploitation? This leads us to the heart of the interpretive challenge. Are we, after all, dealing here with a latter-day version of Ramos's pelado, who is not only the essence of the Mexican national character, but "a most vile category of social fauna" (Ramos 1962, 58)? I would assert otherwise. In their daily struggle these men are, as a group, not lacking in responsibility, initiative, compassion—in short, the full range of human qualities that Ramos found so wanting in the pelado.

Treacherous Women and the Displacement of Class Conflict

In alluding to the charritas as a form of symbolic alibi, I had in mind a form of communication that ideologically displaces a given type of social relationship (in this case, a class relationship) while transposing it from its concrete actualization in a "realized signifying system" (Williams 1981, 207). Such a signifying system is intrinsic to the economic system that produces it, in that it serves at the level of discourse to "realize," mediate, or be an alibi for the set of social relations circumscribed by that order.

Examples of signifying systems include currency, literature, art, and even shelter, which assumes a powerful signifying function the more it reflects the social status of its owner (Williams 1981). In fact, any object, when "disengaged from its mere actuality and used to impose meaning upon experience" (Geertz 1973, 45) can serve this signifying function. However, the process of signification is not uncomplicated:

Between the world of social relations and its cultural articulation lies a jungle of ambiguities, metaphysical subtleties, and even subterfuge, which can exert a powerful, distorting effect on communication and set the stage for the development of ideology, as Marx defined the term.

As an expression of working-class culture, the folklore of machismo can be considered a realized signifying system (while keeping in mind its potential for ideological displacement). As a signifier, or, what Jameson (1981) might term an *ideologeme*, it points to, but simultaneously displaces, a class relationship and its attendant conflict. At the same time, it introduces a third element, the gender relationship, which acts as a mediator between signifier (the folklore) and signified (the class relationship). Additionally, as a signifier for class conflict, the folklore of machismo should be considered one component in a broader, though inchoate, communicative strategy, whose function is the "defense of patterns of belief and value" (Geertz 1973, 231)— that is, the defense of men's basic sense of social solidarity in the face of life's adversities. In sum, like other everyday expressions—their opinions about Mexican Americans, for example—the male workers' folklore is part of a larger ideology that ultimately coincides with their subordinate class position and its orientation toward life.

Gender enters the analysis through the beliefs that these men hold about the family and the subordinate status that women should occupy. These beliefs verify what Kelly wrote about the working-class family:

> The family in modern society has served as the domain for the production and training of the working class. . . . And it has served to compensate the worker whose means of subsistence were *alienated from him but who could have private property in his wife.* (1984, 15; emphasis added)

> To men oppressed by the organization of labor and maldistribution of social wealth and power in society after society, the dual order of patriarchal society provides in many . . . instances the satisfaction of dominion over women. (1984, 61)

In the modern world of capitalist, male-dominant economic systems and the ideologies that sustain them, the subordinate sectors of society have at least three options in responding to their subordination, depending on the sociohistorical moment. They may, as one alternative, propagate ideas that openly challenge, at least in part, the ideology of the dominant groups (Deckard 1979; Gramsci 1971; Swingewood 1977). They may, as a second alternative, adopt beliefs and values that are in large part a surrender to the hegemony of the ruling classes—a phenomenon particularly evident in advanced capitalist nations (Habermas 1970; Marcuse 1964). Or, as is the case with the workers being discussed here, the men of a subordinate class may invent cultural strategies that, through a crucial process of ideological displacement, *shift the point of conflict* from the public domain of class relations between men to the private domain of domestic relations between men and women. This shift is critical to an interpretation of the folklore of machismo.

First, we may suggest that the obedience and servitude Mexican working-class men expect of their women is an integral part of the principle of compensation, understood in both its economic and psychocultural sense. However, in neither sense is this compensation adequate, as it does not resolve the problem of economic deprivation based on class inequality. Worse, the male workers cannot consciously challenge this state of affairs, for they are not equipped, culturally or politically, to recognize the structural basis of that inequality. They cannot even identify the conflict zone that marks the boundary between the two competing, inherently antagonistic classes in capitalist society, for it is no longer the locus of conflict (Habermas 1970, 109).

Indeed, the ideological system that governs life in postcapitalist society has successfully banished from all consciousness the notion of "domination . . . exercised in such a manner that one class subject confronts another as an identifiable group . . . [However] this does not mean that class antagonisms have been abolished but that they have become *latent*" (Habermas 1970, 109, emphasis in original). The conflict zone has thus been displaced; the regnant bourgeois ideology of "classless inequality" has shifted the point of contestation from the class boundary, where it belongs, to the "underprivileged regions of life"—to the oppressed class itself. The members of the oppressed class reformulate class distinctions and antagonisms, giving them new shape in subtraditions that may not directly address class inequality, but are nonetheless consonant with their experiences and orientations. It is in this realm of social life that ideologically mediated signifying systems work themselves out.

In the case under discussion, the persistent class inequality that Mexican working-class men face, immune as it is from cultural penetration, deflects the political unconscious (Jameson 1981) toward a more overt, less mystified (though no less ideological) source of conflict and inequality—the relationship between men and women. Fully cognizant of his supremacy in the latter relationship, the working-class man wrings every bit of compensation out of his advantage, which he enhances by symbolically conflating two distinct relationships—class and gender. The folklore of machismo plays a critical role in this conflation. Through the process of ideological displacement, the folklore shifts attention from its latent text, a class relationship that it signifies but cannot articulate, and focuses that attention on its manifest text, a gender relationship that it articulates but does not signify.

It is thus in the realm of gender relations that class conflict is reformulated and given new cultural purpose—the total subjugation of women. In consequence, oppressive yet tolerated cultural practices thrive: physical and psychological violence against women—in the form of beatings and the denial of personal autonomy—as well as symbolic violence, in the form of degrading but richly elaborated cultural expression like the folklore of machismo and its treacherous-woman stereotype.

Conclusion: The Limits of an Ideology

It may be a bleak commentary on gender relations, but the folklore and other expressed attitudes of the workers at S&J Growers would seem to indicate that Mexican working-class men are a perfect empirical case of Kelly's compensation principle. As noted, they have a most sexist orientation toward gender relations and view the woman as simply part of man's dominion, to be completely subjected to his will. To the workers this relationship is a perfectly natural development and a just form of "compensation" for their sacrifice. Countless times the men reiterated their belief in the justification for such an arrangement. As one man put it, "The woman should be subject to the man—the man to work and the woman to the house chores." Another worker summed up the general attitude with this statement: "The man has a right to his 'slips' [*resvaladitas*], the woman is supposed to bear it."

On the face of it, these statements would seem to be nothing more than crude rationalizations for a system of inequality based not on class, but on gender, since the advantages that men gain from sexism—as a sui generis phenomenon—cut across class lines. More important, the recognition that male sexism is an integral component in gender relations enables us to address a charge made by critics of the approach advocated here—that the folklore of machismo cannot be a signifier for class conflict, since it is not unique to working-class men. That its performance is not uncommon among the men of the dominant classes is true enough, but have these men nothing to gain from perpetuating the myth of the treacherous woman? By contrast, as I have tried to show, for working-class men the obsession with machismo goes beyond gender domination and, in fact, links up ideologically with the problem of class inequality.

The men themselves were at least dimly aware of the complexities and contradictions inherent in their culture of machismo. For instance, when asked why the charrita colorada was so popular among his peers, an older informant replied, "We carry on like this to make light of things for a moment, to forget the problems of life for a moment—the toil, the struggle." Another worker, politically more sophisticated than his peers, observed, "This is pure bullshit; the problems of life are not solved by this [charritas and macho humor generally]." Addressing his companions' sense of male supremacy and its sexist humor, a man (one of the few married to a Chicana) stated his opinion succinctly: "I believe one does it all for the sake of machismo—as if we have to prove that we are men."

Other similar statements, generally voicing the workers' acute awareness of their economic insecurity *and* their need to "prove that we are men," indicate that they are not oblivious to the forces that keep them in a state of poverty. Such statements also point toward an awareness, however diffuse, that the precariousness of their economic status, along with the frustration this status generates, is a major factor contributing to the men's vociferous defense of their privileged male roles on the one hand, and their gross insensitivity to the needs and rights of women on the other. Their embattled position—their desire to control women and their fear of losing that control—is plainly evident in their disapproval of changes they perceive among Mexican-American women, whom they consider muy libertinas.

The workers' negative attitude toward the Chicana is interwoven into the theme of the treacherous woman. While the latter exists for the most part as a fictitious element in the folklore of machismo (after all, *real* Mexican women are *not* that way), for these men it acquires a measure of verisimilitude when projected onto the Mexican-American woman. In short, the Chicana not only serves as a handy scapegoat for the workers' worst fears, but her perceived insubordination provides a convenient prop on which to hang the ideology of machismo. Given their sexist attitude, it is not surprising that the men at S&J Growers were especially critical of Mexican-American men for letting their "natural" authority over women erode by giving in to their demand for equality. Most important, they feared that these changes were being exported to Mexico and that soon women there would also "want to be like men."

Caught in a bind between the sexist, patriarchal culture they espouse, the discontent and powerlessness they feel as a result of their subordinate economic status (with its constant threat to their masculine pride), and the inexorable shift in gender relations that a changing capitalist society promotes, the workers at S&J Growers have responded with a familiar defense. They have succumbed to the displaced compensation that the ideology of machismo provides, no matter how self-defeating. In serious, reflective conversation the workers attempted, at least, to rationalize this machismo and its open acceptance of the subordination of women. They argued that the man works long hours, he protects his family from hardship, he therefore deserves the woman's unswerving devotion and maybe a *parranda* (binge) with his fellows once a week. In the folklore of machismo's distorted message, however, rational explanations vanished. Instead, the rhetorical power of the folkloric performance morally and sexually degraded women, thereby validating what these workers felt was their last birthright as sovereign *mejicanos*—their supreme machismo.

An exaggerated sense of machismo links undocumented male workers to the pelado and other notorious figures in Mexican history (e.g., the nineteenth-century *léparo*). But still another, grimmer experience cements the link among these proletarian outcasts—extreme exploitation, at both the economic and the cultural level. Serrón expressed this truth bluntly: "[Economic] exploitation is a fact of Mexican life—a sad, disfiguring, warped, and tragic fact of life in everyday Mexico" (1980, 197). And, as in other capitalist countries, in Mexico economic exploitation works hand in hand with cultural exploitation. Through the latter, the classes that control economic life also control the tenor of public discourse, creating a formidable brake against any counterdiscourse that might raise the consciousness of the dispossessed masses vis-à-vis the class dynamics that maintain them in subordination (Vellinga 1979).

Possessing neither the class consciousness nor the political means to end their exploitation, the Mexican male workers of the late twentieth century do not seem to have developed much in the way of cultures that contest the established order. They have yielded instead to the sexist ideology of machismo, which also serves the interests of the ruling classes by imposing cultural limits on a working-class consciousness that might develop solidarity between women and men. The range of this working-class consciousness reduced, these male proletarians translate their economic subordination into symbolic expression that voices their class resentment in terms that are culturally rewarding, if politically displaced. It is in this context that folkloric images of heartless, deceitful women who drive men to the depths of alcoholic despair play out their grim, mythic role.

Notes

1. The canción ranchera derives from a type of folksong known until the 1930s as a *canción típica mexicana*. Since the 1930s, it has been commercially manufactured primarily for the consumption of the working class. The theme of the treacherous woman appears in countless canciones dating as far back as the nineteenth century. However, it did not become dominant until the advent of the canción ranchera proper.

2. The Spanish word *traicionera* has multiple connotations, which are difficult to translate precisely. In popular usage, as a referent for a woman who has been unfaithful to her lover, traicionera may be closer to the English words *perfidious, unfaithful,* or *betraying.* Nonetheless, despite the imprecision, *treacherous* glosses a wider range of meanings than the other words, and so that is the term used in this article.

3. Compare Paz (1961) on the *chingón*: "The *chingón* is the macho, the male; he rips open the *chingada*, the female, who is pure passivity, defenseless against the exterior world" (p. 77).

4. The following stanzas are from *La mancornadora,* an old canción of unknown origin, and *La traicionera,* composed by the apotheosis of the ranchera genre, the late, idolized composer, José Alfredo Jiménez.

La mancornadora

Ando ausente del bién que adoré,
apasionado por una mujer;
solo tomando disipi mis penas
con las copas llenas para divagar.

. . . .

Y si tú fueras legal con mi amor,
tú gozarías de mi protección;
pero en el mundo tú fuiste traidora,
la mancornadora de mi corazón.

The Ensnaring Woman

I'm away from the love I adore,
impassioned over a woman;
only drinking can I dispel my sorrows
with filled glasses to distract me.

. . . .

And if you were sincere with my love,
you would enjoy my protection;
but in the world you were a betrayer,
the one who ensnared my heart.

La traicionera

Nunca creí que esa ingrata
me fuera tan traicionera;
'qué la traición que me hiciste
no se queda como quiera;
recuerda que me juraste
una pasión verdadera.

The Betraying Woman

I never believed that cruel woman
would turn out so treacherous;
for the treachery you did to me
will not remain just like that;
remember you solemnly promised me
a sincere passion.

5. All quotations are my translations from the Spanish.

References

Clifford, James. 1986. Introduction: Partial truths. In *Writing culture: The poetics and politics of ethnography*, edited by James Clifford and George E. Marcus. Berkeley: University of California Press.

Colombres, Adolfo, ed. 1982. *La cultura popular*. Mexico, D. F.: Premia Editora.

Deckard, Barbara Sinclair. 1979. *The women's movement: Political, socioeconomic, and psychological issues*. New York: Harper & Row.

Díaz-Guerrero, Rogelio R. 1975. *The psychology of the Mexican: Culture and personality*. Austin: University of Texas Press.

Echanove Trujillo, Carlos. 1973. *Sociología mexicana*. Mexica, DF: Editorial Porrua.

Geertz, Clifford. 1973. *The interpretation of cultures*. New York: Basic Books.

Goldwert, Marvin. 1983. *Machismo and conquest: The case of Mexico*. Lanham, MD: University Press of America.

Gramsci, Antonio. 1971. *Selections from the prison notebooks*, translated by Q. Hoare and G. N. Smith. New York: International Publishers.

Habermas, Jürgen. 1970. *Toward a rational society: Student protest, science, and politics*. Boston: Beacon.

Jameson, Fredric. 1981. *The political unconscious: Narrative as a socially symbolic act*. Ithaca, NY: Cornell University Press.

Kelly, Joan. 1984. *Women, history, and theory*. Chicago: University of Chicago Press.

Marcuse, Herbert. 1964. *One-dimensional man*. Boston: Beacon.

Mirandé, Alfredo. 1986. Qué gacho es ser macho: It's a drag to be a macho man. *Aztlan: A Journal of Chicano Studies* 17:63–89.

Paredes, Américo. 1966. The Anglo-American in Mexican folklore. In *New voices in American studies*, edited by Ray B. Browne and Donald H. Wenkelman. Lafayette, IN: Purdue University Press.

Paz, Octavio. 1961. *The labyrinth of solitude*. New York: Grove.

Ramos, Samuel. 1934. *El perfil del hombre y la cultura en México* (Profile of man and culture in Mexico). Mexico, D. F.: Imprenta Mundial.

———. 1962. *Profile of man and culture in Mexico*. Austin: University of Texas Press.

Serrón, Luis A. 1980. *Scarcity, exploitation, and poverty: Malthus and Marx in Mexico*. Norman: University of Oklahoma Press.

Swingewood, Alan. 1977. *The myth of mass culture*. London: Macmillan.

Vellinga, Menno. 1979. *Economic development and the dynamics of class: Industrialization, power and control in Monterrey, Mexico*. Assen, The Netherlands: Van Gorcum.

Williams, Raymond, 1981. *The sociology of culture*. New York: Schocken Books.

25

ARTICLE

Christine L. Williams

The Glass Escalator: Hidden Advantages for Men in the "Female" Professions

The sex segregation of the U.S. labor force is one of the most perplexing and tenacious problems in our society. Even though the proportion of men and women in the labor force is approaching parity (particularly for younger cohorts of workers) (U.S. Department of Labor 1991:18), men and women are still generally confined to predominantly single-sex occupations. Forty percent of men or women would have to change major occupational categories to achieve equal representation of men and women in all jobs (Reskin and Roos 1990:6), but even this figure underestimates the true degree of sex segregation. It is extremely rare to find specific jobs where equal numbers of men and women are engaged in the same activities in the same industries (Bielby and Baron 1984).

This research was funded in part by a faculty grant from the University of Texas at Austin. I also acknowledge the support of the sociology departments of the University of California, Berkeley; Harvard University; and Arizona State University. I would like to thank Judy Auerbach, Martin Button, Robert Nye, Teresa Sullivan, Debra Umberson, Mary Waters, and the reviewers at *Social Problems* for their comments on earlier versions of this paper. © 1992 by the Society for the Study of Social Problems. Reprinted from *Social Problems*, Vol. 39, No. 3, August 1992, pp. 253–267 by permission.

Most studies of sex segregation in the work force have focused on women's experiences in male-dominated occupations. Both researchers and advocates for social change have focused on the barriers faced by women who try to integrate predominantly male fields. Few have looked at the "flip-side" of occupational sex segregation: the exclusion of men from predominantly female occupations (exceptions include Schreiber 1979; Williams 1989; Zimmer 1988). But the fact is that men are less likely to enter female sex-typed occupations than women are to enter male-dominated jobs (Jacobs 1989). Reskin and Roos, for example, were able to identify 33 occupations in which female representation increased by more than nine percentage points between 1970 and 1980, but only three occupations in which the proportion of men increased as radically (1990:20–21).

In this paper, I examine men's underrepresentation in four predominantly female occupations—nursing, librarianship, elementary school teaching, and social work. Throughout the twentieth century, these occupations have been identified with "women's work"—even though prior to the Civil War, men were more likely to be employed in these areas. These four occupations, often called the female "semi-pro-fessions" (Hodson and Sullivan 1990), today range from 5.5 percent male (in nursing) to 32 percent male (in social work). (See Table 25.1.) These percentages have not changed substan-tially in decades. In fact, as Table 25.1 indicates, two of these professions—librarianship and so-cial work—have experienced declines in the proportions of men since 1975. Nursing is the only one of the four experiencing noticeable changes in sex composition, with the proportion of men increasing 80 percent between 1975 and 1990. Even so, men continue to be a tiny mi-nority of all nurses.

Although there are many possible reasons for the continuing preponderance of women in these fields, the focus of this paper is discrimina-tion. Researchers examining the integration of women into "male fields" have identified dis-crimination as a major barrier to women (Jacobs 1989; Reskin 1988; Reskin and Hartmann 1986). This discrimination has taken the form of laws or institutionalized rules prohibiting the hir-ing or promotion of women into certain job spe-cialties. Discrimination can also be "informal," as when women encounter sexual harassment, sab-

otage, or other forms of hostility from their male co-workers resulting in a poisoned work envi-ronment (Reskin and Hartmann 1986). Women in nontraditional occupations also report feeling stigmatized by clients when their work puts them in contact with the public. In particular, women in engineering and blue-collar occupations en-counter gender-based stereotypes about their competence which undermine their work per-formance (Epstein 1988; Martin 1980). Each of these forms of discrimination—legal, informal, and cultural—contributes to women's underrep-resentation in predominantly male occupations.

The assumption in much of this literature is that any member of a token group in a work setting will probably experience similar dis-criminatory treatment. Kanter (1977), who is best known for articulating this perspective in her theory of tokenism, argues that when any group represents less than 15 percent of an or-ganization, its members will be subject to pre-dictable forms of discrimination. Likewise, Jacobs argues that "in some ways, men in female-dominated occupations experience the same difficulties that women in male-dominated oc-cupations face" (1989:167), and Reskin con-tends that any dominant group in an occupation will use their power to maintain a privileged po-sition (1988:62).

However, the few studies that have consid-ered men's experience in gender atypical oc-cupations suggest that men may not face discrimination or prejudice when they integrate predominantly female occupations. Zimmer (1988) and Martin (1988) both contend that the effects of sexism can outweigh the effects of to-kenism when men enter nontraditional occupa-tions. This study is the first to systematically explore this question using data from four oc-cupations. I examine the barriers to men's entry into these professions; the support men receive from their supervisors, colleagues and clients; and the reactions they encounter from the pub-lic (those outside their professions).

TABLE 25.1 Percent male in selected occu-pations, selected years			
Profession	1990	1980	1975
Nurses	5.5	3.5	3.0
Elementary teachers	14.8	16.3	14.6
Librarians	16.7	14.8	18.9
Social workers	31.8	35.0	39.2

Source: U.S. Department of Labor. Bureau of Labor Statistics. *Employment and Earnings* 38:1 (January 1991), Table 22 (Employed civilians by detailed occupation), 185; 28:1 (January 1981), Table 23 (Employed persons by detailed occupation), 180; 22:7 (January 1976), Table 2 (Employed persons by detailed occupation), 11.

Methods

I conducted in-depth interviews with 76 men and 23 women in four occupations from 1985–1991. Interviews were conducted in four metropolitan areas: San Francisco/Oakland, California; Austin, Texas; Boston, Massachusetts; and Phoenix, Arizona. These four areas were selected because they show considerable variation in the proportions of men in the four professions. For example, Austin has one of the highest percentages of men in nursing (7.7 percent), whereas Phoenix's percentage is one of the lowest (2.7 percent) (U.S. Bureau of the Census 1980). The sample was generated using "snowballing" techniques. Women were included in the sample to gauge their feelings and responses to men who enter "their" professions.

Like the people employed in these professions generally, those in my sample were predominantly white (90 percent).[1] Their ages ranged from 20 to 66 and the average age was 38. The interview questionnaire consisted of several open-ended questions on four broad topics: motivation to enter the profession; experiences in training; career progression; and general views about men's status and prospects within these occupations. I conducted all the interviews, which generally lasted between one and two hours. Interviews took place in restaurants, my home or office, or the respondent's home or office. Interviews were tape-recorded and transcribed for the analysis.

Data analysis followed the coding techniques described by Strauss (1987). Each transcript was read several times and analyzed into emergent conceptual categories. Likewise, Strauss' principle of theoretical sampling was used. Individual respondents were purposively selected to capture the array of men's experiences in these occupations. Thus, I interviewed practitioners in every specialty, oversampling those employed in the *most* gender atypical areas (e.g., male kindergarten teachers). I also selected respondents from throughout their occupational hierarchies—from students to administrators to retirees. Although the data do not permit within-group comparisons, I am reasonably certain that the sample does capture a wide range of experiences common to men in these female-dominated professions. However, like all findings based on qualitative data, it is uncertain whether the findings generalize to the larger population of men in nontraditional occupations.

In this paper, I review individuals' responses to questions about discrimination in hiring practices, on-the-job rapport with supervisors and co-workers, and prejudice from clients and others outside their profession.

Discrimination in Hiring

Contrary to the experience of many women in the male-dominated professions, many of the men and women I spoke to indicated that there is a *preference* for hiring men in these four occupations. A Texas librarian at a junior high school said that his school district "would hire a male over a female."

I: Why do you think that is?

R: Because there are so few, and the . . . ones that they do have, the library directors seem to really . . . think they're doing great jobs. I don't know, maybe they just feel they're being progressive or something, [but] I have had a real sense that they really appreciate having a male, particularly at the junior high. . . . As I said, when seven of us lost our jobs from the high schools and were redistributed, there were only four positions at junior high, and I got one of them. Three of the librarians, some who had been here longer than I had with the school district, were put down in elementary school as librarians. And I definitely think that being male made a difference in my being moved to the junior high rather than an elementary school.

Many of the men perceived their token status as males in predominantly female occupations as an *advantage* in hiring and promotions. I asked an Arizona teacher whether his specialty (elementary special education) was an unusual area for men compared to other areas within education. He said,

> Much more so. I am extremely marketable in special education. That's not why I got into the field. But I am extremely marketable because I am a man.

In several cases, the more female-dominated the specialty, the greater the apparent preference for men. For example, when asked if he encountered any problem getting a job in pediatrics, a Massachusetts nurse said,

> No, no, none.... I've heard this from managers and supervisory-type people with men in pediatrics: "It's nice to have a man because it's such a female-dominated profession."

However, there were some exceptions to this preference for men in the most female-dominated specialties. In some cases, formal policies actually barred men from certain jobs. This was the case in some rural Texas school districts, which refused to hire men in the youngest grades (K–3). Some nurses also reported being excluded from positions in obstetrics and gynecology wards, a policy encountered more frequently in private Catholic hospitals.

But often the pressures keeping men out of certain specialties were more subtle than this. Some men described being "tracked" into practice areas within their professions which were considered more legitimate for men. For example, one Texas man described how he was pushed into administration and planning in social work, even though "I'm not interested in writing policy; I'm much more interested in research and clinical stuff." A nurse who is interested in pursuing graduate study in family and child health in Boston said he was dissuaded from entering the program specialty in favor of a concentration in "adult nursing." A kindergarten teacher described the difficulty of finding a job in his specialty after graduation: "I was recruited immediately to start getting into a track to become an administrator. And it was men who recruited me. It was men that ran the system at that time, especially in Los Angeles."

This tracking may bar men from the most female-identified specialties within these professions. But men are effectively being "kicked upstairs" in the process. Those specialties considered more legitimate practice areas for men also tend to be the most prestigious, better paying ones. A distinguished kindergarten teacher, who had been voted city-wide "Teacher of the Year," told me that even though people were pleased to see him in the classroom, "there's been some encouragement to think about administration, and there's been some encouragement to think about teaching at the university level or something like that, or supervisory-type position." That is, despite his aptitude and interest in staying in the classroom, he felt pushed in the direction of administration.

The effect of this "tracking" is the opposite of that experienced by women in male-dominated occupations. Researchers have reported that many women encounter a "glass ceiling" in their efforts to scale organizational and professional hierarchies. That is, they are constrained by invisible barriers to promotion in their careers, caused mainly by sexist attitudes of men in the highest positions (Freeman 1990).[2] In contrast to the "glass ceiling," many of the men I interviewed seem to encounter a "glass escalator." Often, despite their intentions, they face invisible pressures to move up in their professions. As if on a moving escalator, they must work to stay in place.

A public librarian specializing in children's collections (a heavily female-dominated concentration) described an encounter with this "escalator" in his very first job out of library school. In his first six-months' evaluation, his supervisors commended him for his good work in storytelling and related activities, but they criticized him for "not shooting high enough."

> Seriously. That's literally what they were telling me. They assumed that because I was a male—and they told me this—and that I was being hired right out of graduate school, that somehow I wasn't doing the kind of management-oriented work that they thought I should be doing. And as a result, really they had a lot of bad marks, as it were, against me on my evaluation. And I said I couldn't believe this!

Throughout his ten-year career, he has had to struggle to remain in children's collections.

The glass escalator does not operate at all levels. In particular, men in academia reported some gender-based discrimination in the highest positions due to their universities' commitment to affirmative action. Two nursing professors reported that they felt their own chances of promotion to deanships were nil because their universities viewed the position of nursing dean as a guaranteed female appointment in an otherwise heavily male-dominated administration. One California social work professor reported his university canceled its search for a dean because no minority male or female candidates had been placed on their short list. It was rumored that other schools on campus were permitted to go forward with their searches—even though they also failed to put forward names of minority candidates—because the higher administration perceived it to be "easier" to fulfill affirmative action goals in the social work school. The interviews provide greater evidence of the "glass escalator" at work in the lower levels of these professions.

Of course, men's motivations also play a role in their advancement to higher professional positions. I do not mean to suggest that the men I talked to all resented the informal tracking they experienced. For many men, leaving the most female-identified areas of their professions helped them resolve internal conflicts involving their masculinity. One man left his job as a school social worker to work in a methadone drug treatment program not because he was encouraged to leave by his colleagues, but because "I think there was some macho shit there, to tell you the truth, because I remember feeling a little uncomfortable there . . . ; it didn't feel right to me." Another social worker, employed in the mental health services department of a large urban area in California, reflected on his move into administration:

> The more I think about it, through our discussion, I'm sure that's a large part of why I wound up in administration. It's okay for a man to do the administration. In fact, I don't know if I fully answered a question that you asked a little while ago about how did being male contribute to my advancing in the field. I was saying it wasn't because I got any special favoritism as a man, but . . . I think . . . because I'm a man, I felt a need to get into this kind of position. I may have worked harder toward it, may have competed harder for it, than most women would do, even women who think about doing administrative work.

Elsewhere I have speculated on the origins of men's tendency to define masculinity through single-sex work environments (Williams 1989). Clearly, personal ambition does play a role in accounting for men's movement into more "male-defined" arenas within these professions. But these occupations also structure opportunities for males independent of their individual desires or motives.

The interviews suggest that men's underrepresentation in these professions cannot be attributed to discrimination in hiring or promotions. Many of the men indicated that they received preferential treatment because they were men. Although men mentioned gender discrimination in the hiring process, for the most part they were channeled into the more "masculine" specialties within these professions, which ironically meant being "tracked" into better paying and more prestigious specialties.

Supervisors and Colleagues: The Working Environment

Researchers claim that subtle forms of work place discrimination push women out of male-dominated occupations (Jacobs 1989; Reskin and Hartmann 1986). In particular, women report feeling excluded from informal leadership and decision-making networks, and they sense hostility from their male co-workers, which makes them feel uncomfortable and unwanted (Carothers and Crull 1984). Respondents in this study were asked about their relationships with supervisors and female colleagues to ascertain whether men also experienced "poisoned" work environments when entering gender atypical occupations.

A major difference in the experience of men and women in nontraditional occupations is that men in these situations are far more likely to be supervised by a member of their own sex. In each of the four professions I studied, men are overrepresented in administrative and managerial capacities, or, as in the case of nursing, their positions in the organizational hierarchy are governed by men (Grimm and Sterm 1974; Phenix 1987; Schmuck 1987; Williams 1989; York, Henley and Gamble 1987). Thus, unlike women who enter "male fields," the men in these professions often work under the direct supervision of other men.

Many of the men interviewed reported that they had good rapport with their male supervisors. Even in professional school, some men reported extremely close relationships with their male professors. For example, a Texas librarian described an unusually intimate association with two male professors in graduate school:

I can remember a lot of times in the classroom there would be discussions about a particular topic or issue, and the conversation would spill over into their office hours, after the class was over. And even though there were . . . a couple of the other women that had been in on the discussion, they weren't there. And I don't know if that was preferential or not . . . it certainly carried over into personal life as well. Not just at the school and that sort of thing. I mean, we would get together for dinner . . .

These professors explicitly encouraged him because he was male:

I: Did they ever offer you explicit words of encouragement about being in the profession by virtue of the fact that you were male? . . .

R: Definitely. On several occasions. Yeah. Both of these guys, for sure, including the Dean who was male also. And it's an interesting point that you bring up because it was, oftentimes, kind of in a sign, you know. It wasn't in the classroom, and it wasn't in front of the group, or if we were in the student lounge or something like that. It was . . . if it was just myself or maybe another one of the guys, you know, and just talking in the office. It's like . . . you know, kind of an opening-up and saying, "You know, you are really lucky that you're in the profession because you'll really go to the top real quick, and you'll be able to make real definite improvements and changes. And you'll have a real influence," and all this sort of thing. I mean, really, I can remember several times.

Other men reported similar closeness with their professors. A Texas psychotherapist recalled his relationships with his male professors in social work school:

I made it a point to make a golfing buddy with one of the guys that was in administration. He and I played golf a lot. He was the guy who kind of ran the research training, the research part of the master's program. Then there was a sociologist who ran the other part of the research program. He and I developed a good friendship.

This close mentoring by male professors contrasts with the reported experience of women in nontraditional occupations. Others have noted a lack of solidarity among women in nontraditional occupations. Writing about military academies, for example, Yoder describes the failure of token women to mentor succeeding generations of female cadets. She argues that women attempt to play down their gender difference from men because it is the source of scorn and derision.

> Because women felt unaccepted by their male colleagues, one of the last things they wanted to do was to emphasize their gender. Some women thought that, if they kept company with other women, this would highlight their gender and would further isolate them from male cadets. These women desperately wanted to be accepted as cadets, not as *women* cadets. Therefore, they did everything from not wearing skirts as an option with their uniforms to avoiding being a part of a group of women. (Yoder 1989:532)

Men in nontraditional occupations face a different scenario—their gender is construed as a *positive* difference. Therefore, they have an incentive to bond together and emphasize their distinctiveness from the female majority.

Close, personal ties with male supervisors were also described by men once they were established in their professional careers. It was not uncommon in education, for example, for the male principal to informally socialize with the male staff, as a Texas special education teacher describes:

> Occasionally I've had a principal who would regard me as "the other man on the campus" and "it's us against them," you know? I mean, nothing really that extreme, except that some male principals feel like there's nobody there to talk to except the other man. So I've been in that position.

These personal ties can have important consequences for men's careers. For example, one California nurse, whose performance was judged marginal by his nursing supervisors, was transferred to the emergency room staff (a prestigious promotion) due to his personal friendship with the physician in charge. A Massachusetts teacher acknowledged that his principal's personal interest in him landed him his current job.

> **I:** You had mentioned that your principal had sort of spotted you at your previous job and had wanted to bring you here [to this school]. Do you think that has anything to do with the fact that you're a man, aside from your skills as a teacher?
>
> **R:** Yes, I would say in that particular case, that was part of it. . . . We have certain things in common, certain interests that really lined up.
>
> **I:** Vis-à-vis teaching?
>
> **R:** Well, more extraneous things—running specifically, and music. And we just seemed to get along real well right off the bat. It is just kind of a guy thing; we just liked each other . . .

Interviewees did not report many instances of male supervisors discriminating against them, or refusing to accept them because they were male. Indeed, these men were much more likely to report that their male bosses discriminated against the *females* in their professions. When asked if he thought physicians treated male and female nurses differently, a Texas nurse said:

> I think yeah, some of them do. I think the women seem like they have a lot more trouble with the physicians treating them in a derogatory manner. Or, if not derogatory, then in a very paternalistic way than the men [are treated]. Usually if a physician is mad at a male nurse, he just kind of yells at him. Kind of like an employee. And if they're mad at a female nurse, rather than treat them on an equal basis, in terms of just letting their anger out at

them as an employee, they're more paternalistic or there's some sexual harassment component to it.

A Texas teacher perceived a similar situation where he worked:

I've never felt unjustly treated by a principal because I'm a male. The principals that I've seen that I felt are doing things that are kind of arbitrary or not well thought out are doing it to everybody. In fact, they're probably doing it to the females worse than they are to me.

Openly gay men may encounter less favorable treatment at the hands of their supervisors. For example, a nurse in Texas stated that one of the physicians he worked with preferred to staff the operating room with male nurses exclusively—as long as they weren't gay. Stigma associated with homosexuality leads some men to enhance, or even exaggerate their "masculine" qualities, and may be another factor pushing men into more "acceptable" specialties for men.

Not all men who work in these occupations are supervised by men. Many of the men interviewed who had female bosses also reported high levels of acceptance—although levels of intimacy with women seemed lower than with other men. In some cases, however, men reported feeling shut-out from decision making when the higher administration was constituted entirely by women. I asked an Arizona librarian whether men in the library profession were discriminated against in hiring because of their sex:

Professionally speaking, people go to considerable lengths to keep that kind of thing out of their [hiring] deliberations. Personally, is another matter. It's pretty common around here to talk about the "old girl network." This is one of the few libraries that I've had any intimate knowledge of which is actually controlled by women. . . . Most of the department heads and upper level administrators are women. And there's an "old girl network" that works just like the "old boy network," except that the important conferences take place in the women's

room rather than on the golf course. But the political mechanism is the same, the exclusion of the other sex from decision making is the same. The reasons are the same. It's somewhat discouraging . . .

Although I did not interview many supervisors, I did include 23 women in my sample to ascertain their perspectives about the presence of men in their professions. All of the women I interviewed claimed to be supportive of their male colleagues, but some conveyed ambivalence. For example, a social work professor said she would like to see more men enter the social work profession, particularly in the clinical specialty (where they are underrepresented). Indeed, she favored affirmative action hiring guidelines for men in the profession. Yet, she resented the fact that her department hired "another white male" during a recent search. I questioned her about this ambivalence:

I: I find it very interesting that, on the one hand, you sort of perceive this preference and perhaps even sexism with regard to how men are evaluated and how they achieve higher positions within the profession, yet, on the other hand, you would be encouraging of more men to enter the field. Is that contradictory to you, or . . . ?

R: Yeah, it's contradictory.

It appears that women are generally eager to see men enter "their" occupations. Indeed, several men noted that their female colleagues had facilitated their careers in various ways (including mentorship in college). However, at the same time, women often resent the apparent ease with which men advance within these professions, sensing that men at the higher levels receive preferential treatment which closes off advancement opportunities for women.

But this ambivalence does not seem to translate into the "poisoned" work environment described by many women who work in male-dominated occupations. Among the male interviewees, there were no accounts of sexual harassment. However, women do treat their male colleagues differently on occasion. It is not uncommon in nursing, for example, for men to be called upon to help catheterize male patients, or to lift especially heavy patients. Some librarians also said that women asked them to lift and move heavy boxes of books because they were men. Teachers sometimes confront differential treatment as well, as described by this Texas teacher:

> As a man, you're teaching with all women, and that can be hard sometimes. Just because of the stereotypes, you know. I'm real into computers . . . and all the time people are calling me to fix their computer. Or if somebody gets a flat tire, they come and get me. I mean, there are just a lot of stereotypes. Not that I mind doing any of those things, but it's . . . you know, it just kind of bugs me that it is a stereotype, "A man should do that." Or if their kids have a lot of discipline problems, that kiddo's in your room. Or if there are kids that don't have a father in their home, that kid's in your room. Hell, nowadays that'd be half the school in my room (laughs). But you know, all the time I hear from the principal or from other teachers, "Well, this child really needs a man . . . a male role model" (laughs). So there are a lot of stereotypes that . . . men kind of get stuck with.

This special treatment bothered some respondents. Getting assigned all the "discipline problems" can make for difficult working conditions, for example. But many men claimed this differential treatment did not cause distress. In fact, several said they liked being appreciated for the special traits and abilities (such as strength) they could contribute to their professions.

Furthermore, women's special treatment sometimes enhanced—rather than poisoned—the men's work environments. One Texas librarian said he felt "more comfortable working with women than men" because "I think it has something to do with control. Maybe it's that women will let me take control more than men

will." Several men reported that their female colleagues often cast them into leadership roles. Although not all savored this distinction, it did enhance their authority and control in the work place. In subtle (and not-too-subtle) ways, then, differential treatment contributes to the "glass escalator" men experience in nontraditional professions.

Even outside work, most of the men interviewed said they felt fully accepted by their female colleagues. They were usually included in informal socializing occasions with the women—even though this frequently meant attending baby showers or Tupperware parties. Many said that they declined offers to attend these events because they were not interested in "women's things," although several others claimed to attend everything: The minority men I interviewed seemed to feel the least comfortable in these informal contexts. One social worker in Arizona was asked about socializing with his female colleagues:

> **I:** So in general, for example, if all the employees were going to get together to have a party, or celebrate a bridal shower or whatever, would you be invited along with the rest of the group?
>
> **R:** They would invite me, I would say, somewhat reluctantly. Being a black male, working with all white females, it did cause some outside problems. So I didn't go to a lot of functions with them . . .
>
> **I:** You felt that there was some tension there on the level of your acceptance . . . ?
>
> **R:** Yeah. It was OK working, but on the outside, personally, there was some tension there. It never came out, that they said, "Because of who you are we can't invite you" (laughs), and I wouldn't have done anything anyway. I would have probably respected them more for saying what was on their minds. But I never felt completely in with the group.

Some single men also said they felt uncomfortable socializing with married female colleagues because it gave the "wrong impression." But in general, the men said that they felt very comfortable around their colleagues and described their work places as very congenial for men. It appears unlikely, therefore, that men's underrepresentation in these professions is due to hostility towards men on the part of supervisors or women workers.

Discrimination from "Outsiders"

The most compelling evidence of discrimination against men in these professions is related to their dealings with the public. Men often encounter negative stereotypes when they come into contact with clients or "outsiders"—people they meet outside of work. For instance, it is popularly assumed that male nurses are gay. Librarians encounter images of themselves as "wimpy" and asexual. Male social workers describe being typecast as "feminine" and "passive." Elementary school teachers are often confronted by suspicions that they are pedophiles. One kindergarten teacher described an experience that occurred early in his career which was related to him years afterwards by his principal:

> He indicated to me that parents had come to him and indicated to him that they had a problem with the fact that I was a male. . . . I recall almost exactly what he said. There were three specific concerns that the parents had: One parent said, "How can he love my child; he's a man." The second thing that I recall, he said the parent said, "He has a beard." And the third thing was, "Aren't you concerned about homosexuality?"

Such suspicions often cause men in all four professions to alter their work behavior to guard against sexual abuse charges, particularly in those specialties requiring intimate contact with women and children.

Men are very distressed by these negative stereotypes, which tend to undermine their self-esteem and to cause them to second-guess their motivations for entering these fields. A California teacher said,

> If I tell men that I don't know, that I'm meeting for the first time, that that's what I do, . . . sometimes there's a look on their faces that, you know, "Oh, couldn't get a real job?"

When asked if his wife, who is also an elementary school teacher, encounters the same kind of prejudice, he said,

> No, it's accepted because she's a woman. . . . I think people would see that as a . . . step up, you know. "Oh, you're not a housewife, you've got a career. That's great . . . that you're out there working. And you have a daughter, but you're still out there working. You decided not to stay home, and you went out there and got a job." Whereas for me, it's more like I'm supposed to be out working anyway, even though I'd rather be home with [my daughter].

Unlike women who enter traditionally male professions, men's movement into these jobs is perceived by the "outside world" as a step down in status. This particular form of discrimination may be most significant in explaining why men are underrepresented in these professions. Men who otherwise might show interest in and aptitudes for such careers are probably discouraged from pursuing them because of the negative popular stereotypes associated with the men who work in them. This is a crucial difference from the experience of women in nontraditional professions: "My daughter, the physician," resonates far more favorably in most people's ears than "My son, the nurse."

Many of the men in my sample identified the stigma of working in a female-identified occupation as the major barrier to more men entering their professions. However, for the most part, they claimed that these negative stereotypes were not a factor in their own decisions to join these occupations. Most respondents didn't consider entering these fields until well into adulthood, after working in some related occupation. Several social workers and librarians even claimed they were not aware that men were a minority in their chosen professions. Either they had no well-defined image or stereotype, or their contacts and mentors were predominantly men. For example, prior to entering library school, many librarians held part-time jobs in university libraries, where there are proportionally more men than in the profession generally. Nurses and elementary school teachers were more aware that mostly women worked in these jobs, and this was often a matter of some concern to them. However, their choices were ultimately legitimized by mentors, or by encouraging friends or family members who implicitly reassured them that entering these occupations would not typecast them as feminine. In some cases, men were told by recruiters there were special advancement opportunities for men in these fields, and they entered them expecting rapid promotion to administrative positions.

> **I:** Did it ever concern you when you were making the decision to enter nursing school, the fact that it is a female-dominated profession?
>
> **R:** Not really. I never saw myself working on the floor. I saw myself pretty much going into administration, just getting the background and then getting a job someplace as a supervisor and then working, getting up into administration.

Because of the unique circumstances of their recruitment, many of the respondents did not view their occupational choices as inconsistent with a male gender role, and they generally avoided the negative stereotypes directed against men in these fields.

Indeed, many of the men I interviewed claimed that they did not encounter negative professional stereotypes until they had worked in these fields for several years. Popular prejudices can be damaging to self-esteem and probably push some men out of these professions altogether. Yet, ironically, they sometimes contribute to the "glass escalator" effect I have been describing. Men seem to encounter the most vituperative criticism from the public when they are in the most female-identified specialties. Public concerns sometimes result in their being shunted into more "legitimate" positions for men. A librarian formerly in charge of a branch library's children's collection, who now works in the reference department of the city's main library, describes his experience:

> **R:** Some of the people [who frequented the branch library] complained that they didn't want to have a man doing the storytelling scenario. And I got transferred here to the central library in an equivalent job . . . I thought that I did a good job. And I had been told by my supervisor that I was doing a good job.
>
> **I:** Have you ever considered filing some sort of lawsuit to get that other job back?
>
> **R:** Well, actually, the job I've gotten now . . . well, it's a reference librarian; it's what I wanted in the first place. I've got a whole lot more authority here. I'm also in charge of the circulation desk. And I've recently been promoted because of my new stature, so . . . no, I'm not considering trying to get that other job back.

The negative stereotypes about men who do "women's work" can push men out of specific jobs. However, to the extent that they channel men into more "legitimate" practice areas, their effects can actually be positive. Instead of being a source of discrimination, these prejudices can add to the "glass escalator effect" by pressuring men to move *out* of the most female-identified areas, and *up* to those regarded more legitimate and prestigious for men.

Conclusion: Discrimination Against Men

Both men and women who work in nontraditional occupations encounter discrimination, but the forms and consequences of this discrimination are very different. The interviews suggest that unlike "nontraditional" women workers, most of the discrimination and prejudice facing men in the "female professions" emanates from outside those professions. The men and women interviewed for the most part believed that men are given fair—if not preferential—treatment in hiring and promotion decisions, are accepted by supervisors and colleagues, and are well-integrated into the work place subculture. Indeed, subtle mechanisms seem to enhance men's position in these professions—a phenomenon I refer to as the "glass escalator effect."

The data lend strong support for Zimmer's (1988) critique of "gender neutral theory" (such as Kanter's [1977] theory of tokenism) in the study of occupational segregation. Zimmer argues that women's occupational inequality is more a consequence of sexist beliefs and practices embedded in the labor force than the effect of numerical underrepresentation per se. This study suggests that token status itself does not diminish men's occupational success. Men take their gender privilege with them when they enter predominantly female occupations: this translates into an advantage in spite of their numerical rarity.

This study indicates that the experience of tokenism is very different for men and women. Future research should examine how the experience of tokenism varies for members of different races and classes as well. For example, it is

likely that informal work place mechanisms similar to the ones identified here promote the careers of token whites in predominantly black occupations. The crucial factor is the social status of the token's group—not their numerical rarity—that determines whether the token encounters a "glass ceiling" or a "glass escalator."

However, this study also found that many men encounter negative stereotypes from persons not directly involved in their professions. Men who enter these professions are often considered "failures," or sexual deviants. These stereotypes may be a major impediment to men who otherwise might consider careers in these occupations. Indeed, they are likely to be important factors whenever a member of a relatively high status group crosses over into a lower status occupation. However, to the extent that these stereotypes contribute to the "glass escalator effect" by channeling men into more "legitimate" (and higher paying) occupations, they are not discriminatory.

Women entering traditionally "male" professions also face negative stereotypes suggesting they are not "real women" (Epstein 1981; Lorber 1984; Spencer and Podmore 1987). However, these stereotypes do not seem to deter women to the same degree that they deter men from pursuing nontraditional professions. There is ample historical evidence that women flock to male-identified occupations once opportunities are available (Cohn 1985; Epstein 1988). Not so with men. Examples of occupations changing from predominantly female to predominantly male are very rare in our history. The few existing cases—such as medicine—suggest that redefinition of the occupations as appropriately "masculine" is necessary before men will consider joining them (Ehrenreich and English 1978).

Because different mechanisms maintain segregation in male- and female-dominated occupations, different approaches are needed to promote their integration. Policies intended to alter the sex composition of male-dominated occupations—such as affirmative action—make little sense when applied to the "female professions." For men, the major barriers to integration have little to do with their treatment once they decide to enter these fields. Rather, we need to address the social and cultural sanctions applied to men who do "women's work" which keep men from even considering these occupations.

One area where these cultural barriers are clearly evident is in the media's representation of men's occupations. Women working in traditionally male professions have achieved an unprecedented acceptance on popular television shows. Women are portrayed as doctors ("St. Elsewhere"), lawyers ("The Cosby Show," "L.A. Law"), architects ("Family Ties"), and police officers ("Cagney and Lacey"). But where are the male nurses, teachers and secretaries? Television rarely portrays men in nontraditional work roles, and when it does, that anomaly is made the central focus—and joke—of the program. A comedy series (1991–92) about a male elementary school teacher ("Drexell's Class") stars a lead character who *hates children!* Yet even this negative portrayal is exceptional. When a prime time hospital drama series ("St. Elsewhere") depicted a male orderly striving for upward mobility, the show's writers made him a "physician's assistant," not a nurse or nurse practitioner—the much more likely "real life" possibilities.

Presenting positive images of men in nontraditional careers can produce limited effects. A few social workers, for example, were first inspired to pursue their careers by George C. Scott, who played a social worker in the television drama series, "Eastside/Westside." But as a policy strategy to break down occupational segregation, changing media images of men is no panacea. The stereotypes that differentiate masculinity and femininity, and degrade that which is defined as feminine, are deeply entrenched in culture, social structure, and personality (Williams 1989). Nothing short of a revolution in cultural definitions of masculinity will effect the broad scale social transformation needed to achieve the complete occupational integration of men and women.

Of course, there are additional factors besides societal prejudice contributing to men's underrepresentation in female-dominated professions. Most notably, those men I interviewed mentioned as a deterrent the fact that these professions are all underpaid relative to comparable "male" occupations, and several suggested that instituting a "comparable worth" policy might attract more men. However, I am not convinced that improved salaries will substantially alter the sex composition of these professions unless the cultural stigma faced by men in these occupations diminishes. Occupational sex segregation is remarkably resilient, even in the face of devastating economic hardship. During the Great Depression of the 1930s, for example, "women's jobs" failed to attract sizable numbers of men (Blum 1991:154). In her study of American Telephone and Telegraph (AT&T) workers, Epstein (1989) found that some men would rather suffer unemployment than accept relatively high paying "women's jobs" because of the damage to their identities this would cause. She quotes one unemployed man who refused to apply for a female-identified telephone operator job:

> I think if they offered me $1000 a week tax free, I wouldn't take that job. When I . . . see those guys sitting in there [in the telephone operating room], I wonder what's wrong with them. Are they pansies or what? (Epstein 1989: 577)

This is not to say that raising salaries would not affect the sex composition of these jobs. Rather, I am suggesting that wages are not the only—or perhaps even the major—impediment to men's entry into these jobs. Further research is needed to explore the ideological significance of the "woman's wage" for maintaining occupational stratification.[3]

At any rate, integrating men and women in the labor force requires more than dismantling barriers to women in male-dominated fields. Sex segregation is a two-way street. We must also confront and dismantle the barriers men face in predominantly female occupations. Men's experiences in these nontraditional occupations reveal just how culturally embedded the barriers are, and how far we have to travel before men and women attain true occupational and economic equality.

Notes

1. According to the U.S. Census, black men and women comprise 7 percent of all nurses and librarians, 11 percent of all elementary school teachers, and 19 percent of all social workers (calculated from U.S. Census 1980: Table 278, 1–197). The proportion of blacks in social work may be exaggerated by these statistics. The occupational definition of "social worker" used by the Census Bureau includes welfare workers and pardon and parole officers, who are not considered "professional" social workers by the National Association of Social Workers. A study of degreed professionals found that 89 percent of practitioners were white (Hardcastle 1987).

2. In April 1991, the Labor Department created a "Glass Ceiling Commission" to "conduct a thorough study of the underrepresentation of women and minorities in executive, management, and senior decision-making positions in business" (U.S. House of Representatives 1991:20).

3. Alice Kessler-Harris argues that the lower pay of traditionally female occupations is symbolic of a patriarchal order that assumes female dependence on a male breadwinner. She writes that pay equity is fundamentally threatening to the "male worker's sense of self, pride, and masculinity" because it upsets his individual standing in the hierarchical ordering of the sexes (1990:125). Thus, men's reluctance to enter these occupations may have less to do with the actual dollar amount recorded in their paychecks, and more to do with the damage that earning "a woman's wage" would wreak on their self-esteem in a society that privileges men. This conclusion is supported by the interview data.

References

Bielby, William T., and James N. Baron
1984 "A woman's place is with other women: Sex segregation within organizations." In *Sex Segregation in the Workplace: Trends, explanations, remedies,* ed. Barbara Reskin, 27–55. Washington, D.C.: National Academy Press.

Blum, Linda M.
1991 *Between Feminism and Labor: The Significance of the Comparable Worth Movement.* Berkeley and Los Angeles: University of California Press.

Carothers, Suzanne C., and Peggy Crull
1984 "Contrasting sexual harassment in female-dominated and male-dominated occupations." In *My Troubles Are Going to Have Trouble with Me: Everyday Trials and Triumphs of Women Workers,* ed. Karen B. Sacks and Dorothy Remy, 220–227. New Brunswick, N.J.: Rutgers University Press.

Cohn, Samuel
1985 *The Process of Occupational Sex-Typing.* Philadelphia: Temple University Press.

Ehrenreich, Barbara, and Deirdre English
1978 *For Her Own Good: 100 Years of Expert Advice to Women.* Garden City, N.Y.: Anchor Press.

Epstein, Cynthia Fuchs
1981 *Women in Law.* New York: Basic Books.
1988 *Deceptive Distinctions: Sex, Gender and the Social Order.* New Haven, Conn.: Yale University Press.
1989 "Workplace boundaries: Conceptions and creations." *Social Research* 56: 571–590.

Freeman, Sue J. M.
1990 *Managing Lives: Corporate Women and Social Change.* Amherst, Mass.: University of Massachusetts Press.

Grimm, James W., and Robert N. Stern
1974 "Sex roles and internal labor market structures: The female semi-professions." *Social Problems* 21: 690–705.

Hardcastle, D. A.
1987 "The social work labor force." Austin, Tex.: School of Social Work, University of Texas.

Hodson, Randy, and Teresa Sullivan
1990 *The Social Organization of Work.* Belmont, Calif.: Wadsworth Publishing Co.

Jacobs, Jerry
1989 *Revolving Doors: Sex Segregation and Women's Careers.* Stanford, Calif.: Stanford University Press.

Kanter, Rosabeth Moss
1977 *Men and Women of the Corporation.* New York: Basic Books.
Kessler-Harris, Alice
1990 *A Woman's Wage: Historical Meanings and Social Consequences.* Lexington, Ky.: Kentucky University Press.
Lorber, Judith
1984 *Women Physicians: Careers, Status, and Power.* New York: Tavistock.
Martin, Susan E.
1980 *Breaking and Entering: Police Women on Patrol.* Berkeley, Calif.: University of California Press.
1988 "Think like a man, work like a dog, and act like a lady: Occupational dilemmas of police-women." In *The Worth of Women's Work: A Qualitative Synthesis,* ed. Anne Statham, Eleanor M. Miller, and Hans O. Mauksch, 205–223. Albany, N.Y.: State University of New York Press.
Phenix, Katharine
1987 "The status of women librarians." *Frontiers* 9: 36–40.
Reskin, Barbara
1988 "Bringing the men back in: Sex differentiation and the devaluation of women's work." *Gender & Society* 2: 58–81.
Reskin, Barbara, and Heidi Hartmann
1986 *Women's Work, Men's Work: Sex Segregation on the Job.* Washington, D.C.: National Academy Press.
Reskin, Barbara, and Patricia Roos
1990 *Job Queues, Gender Queues: Explaining Women's Inroads into Male Occupations.* Philadelphia: Temple University Press.
Schmuck, Patricia A.
1987 "Women school employees in the United States." In *Women Educators: Employees of Schools in Western Countries,* ed. Patricia A. Schmuck, 75–97. Albany, N.Y.: State University of New York Press.
Schreiber, Carol
1979 *Men and Women in Transitional Occupations.* Cambridge, Mass.: MIT Press.
Spencer, Anne, and David Podmore
1987 *In a Man's World: Essays on Women in Male-Dominated Professions.* London: Tavistock.
Strauss, Anselm L.
1987 *Qualitative Analysis for Social Scientists.* Cambridge, England: Cambridge University Press.
U.S. Bureau of the Census
1980 *Detailed Population Characteristics,* Vol. 1, Ch. D. Washington, D.C.: Government Printing Office.
U.S. Congress. House
1991 *Civil Rights and Women's Equity in Employment Act of 1991.* Report. (Report 102-40, Part I.) Washington, D.C.: Government Printing Office.
U.S. Department of Labor. Bureau of Labor Statistics
1991 *Employment and Earnings.* January. Washington, D.C.: Government Printing Office.
Williams, Christine L.
1989 *Gender Differences at Work: Women and Men in Nontraditional Occupations.* Berkeley, Calif.: University of California Press.
Yoder, Janice D.
1989 "Women at West Point: Lessons for token women in male-dominated occupations." In *Women: A Feminist Perspective,* ed. Jo Freeman, 523–537. Mountain View, Calif.: Mayfield Publishing Company.
York, Reginald O., H. Carl Henley, and Dorothy N. Gamble
1987 "Sexual discrimination in social work: Is it salary or advancement?" *Social Work* 32: 336–340.
Zimmer, Lynn
1988 "Tokenism and women in the workplace." *Social Problems* 35: 64–77.

26

ARTICLE
Jennifer Pierce

Rambo Litigators: Emotional Labor in a Male-Dominated Occupation

> Litigation is war. The lawyer is a gladiator and the object is to wipe out the other side.
> —Cleveland lawyer quoted in the *New York Times*

A recent spate of articles in the *New York Times* and a number of legal dailies characterized some of America's more flamboyant and aggressive trial lawyers as "Rambo litigators."[1] This hypermasculine, aggressive image is certainly not a new one. In popular culture and everyday life, jokes and stories abound that characterize lawyers as overly aggressive, manipulative, unreliable, and unethical individuals.[2] What jokes, as well as the popular press, fail to consider is that such behavior is not simply the result of individual failings but is actually required and reinforced by the legal profession itself.

Legal scholar Carrie Menkel-Meadow (1985) suggests that the adversarial model with its emphasis on "zealous advocacy" and "winning" encourages a "macho ethic" in the courtroom (pp. 51–54). Lawyers and teachers of trial lawyers argue that the success of litigators depends on their ability to manipulate people's emotions (Brazil, 1978; Turow, 1987). Trial lawyers must persuade judges and juries, as well as intimidate witnesses and opposing counsel in the courtroom, in deposition, and in negotiations. The National Institute of Trial Advocacy, for example, devotes a 3-week training seminar to teaching lawyers to hone such emotional skills, thereby improving their success in the courtroom (Rice, 1989). This chapter makes this aspect of lawyering explicit by examining the emotional dimension of legal work in a particular specialty of law—litigation. Sociological studies of the legal profession have yet to seriously examine the emotional dimension of lawyering.[3] Although a few studies make reference to the emotional dimension of work, it is not the central focus of their research.[4] For example, Nelson (1988) reduces lawyering to

Author's Note: Jennifer Pierce, *Gender Trials: Emotional Lives in Contemporary Law Firms*. Copyright © 1995 The Regents of the University of California. Reprinted by permission of the University of California Press.

three roles—"finders, minders and grinders," meaning "lawyers who seem to bring in substantial clients . . . lawyers who take care of the clients who are already here and there are the grinders who do the work" (senior partner quoted in Nelson, 1988, p. 69). Nelson's reduction of these roles to their instrumental and intellectual dimensions neglects the extent to which instrumental tasks may also contain emotional elements.

The sparse attention other sociological studies have given to this dimension of lawyering is contradicted by my 15 months of field research (from 1988 to 1989) at two large law firms in San Francisco—6 months at a private firm (Lyman, Lyman and Portia) and 9 months in the legal department of a large corporation (Bonhomie Corporation).[5] Litigators make use of their emotions to persuade juries, judges, and witnesses in the courtroom and in depositions, in communications with opposing counsel, and with clients. However, in contrast to the popular image, intimidation and aggression constitute only one component of the emotional labor required by this profession. Lawyers also make use of strategic friendliness, that is, the use of charm or flattery to manipulate others. Despite the apparent differences in these two types of emotional labor, both use the manipulation of others for a specific end—winning a case. Although other jobs require the use of manipulation to achieve specific ends, such labor may serve different purposes and be embedded in a different set of relationships. Flight attendants, for example, are friendly and reassuring to passengers so as to alleviate their anxiety about flying (Hochschild, 1983). However, flight attendants' friendliness takes the form of deference: Their relationship to passengers is supportive and subordinate. By contrast, in litigation, the goal of strategic friendliness is to *win over* or dominate another. As professionals who have a monopoly over specialized knowledge, attorneys hold a superordinate position with respect to clients, witnesses, and jurors and a competitive one with

other lawyers. If trial lawyers want to win their cases, they must be able to successfully manipulate and ultimately dominate others for their professional ends.

By doing whatever it takes within the letter of the law to win a case, lawyers effectively fulfill the goal of zealous advocacy: persuading a third party that the client's interests should prevail. In this way, intimidation and strategic friendliness serve to reproduce and maintain the adversarial model. At the same time, by exercising dominance and control over others, trial lawyers also reproduce gender relations. The majority of litigators who *do dominance* are men (88% of litigators are male) and those who defer are either female secretaries and paralegals,[6] other women, or men who become feminized in the process of losing. In addition to creating and maintaining a gendered hierarchy, the form such emotional labor takes is gendered. It is a masculinized form of emotional labor, not only because men do it but because dominance is associated with masculinity in our culture. West and Zimmerman (1987) argue, for example, that displays of dominance are ways for men to "do gender."[7] Similarly, psychoanalytic feminists equate masculinity with men's need to dominate women (Benjamin, 1988; Chodorow, 1978). In the case of trial lawyers, the requirements of the profession deem it appropriate to dominate women as well as other men. Such *conquests* or achievements at once serve the goals of effective advocacy and become the means for the trial lawyer to demonstrate a class specific form of masculinity.

Gamesmanship and the Adversarial Model

Popular wisdom and lawyer folklore portray lawyering as a game, and the ability to play as gamesmanship (Spence, 1988). As one of the trial attorneys I interviewed said,

The logic of gamesmanship is very interesting to me. I like how you make someone appear to be a liar. You know, you take them down the merry path and before they know it, they've said something pretty stupid. The challenge is getting them to say it without violating the letter of the law.

Lawyering is based on gamesmanship—legal strategy, skill, and expertise. But trial lawyers are much more than chess players. Their strategies are not simply cerebral, rational, and calculating moves but highly emotional, dramatic, flamboyant, and shocking presentations that invoke sympathy, distrust, or outrage. In my redefinition of the term, *gamesmanship* involves the utilization of legal strategy through a presentation of an emotional self designed specifically to influence the feelings and judgment of a particular legal audience—the judge, the jury, the witness, or opposing counsel. Furthermore, in my definition, the choices litigators make about selecting a particular strategy are not simply individual, they are institutionally constrained by the structure of the legal profession, formal and informal professional norms such as the American Bar Association's (1982) *Model Code of Professional Responsibility* and training in trial advocacy through programs sponsored by the National Institute of Trial Advocacy.

The rules governing gamesmanship derive from the adversarial model that underlies the basic structure of our legal system. This model is a method of adjudication that involves two advocates (e.g., the attorneys) presenting their case to an impartial third party (i.e., the judge and the jury) who listens to evidence and argument and declares one party the winner (Luban, 1988; Menkel-Meadow, 1985). As Menkel-Meadow (1985) observes, the basic assumptions that underlie this set of arrangements are "advocacy, persuasion, hierarchy, competition and binary results (win or lose)." She writes, "The conduct of litigation is relatively similar . . . to a sporting event—there are rules, a referee, an ob-

ject to the game, and a winner is declared after play is over" (p. 51).

Within this system, the attorney's main objective is to persuade the impartial third party that his client's interests should prevail (American Bar Association, 1982, p. 34). However, clients do not always have airtight, defensible cases. How, then, does the *zealous advocate* protect his clients interests and achieve the desired result? When persuasion by appeal to reason breaks down, an appeal to emotions becomes tantamount (Cheatham, 1955, pp. 282–283). As legal scholar John Buchan (1939) writes, "The root of the talent is simply the *power to persuade*" [italics added] (pp. 211–213). By appealing to emotions, the lawyer becomes a "con man."[8] He acts "as if" he has a defensible case, he puffs himself up, he bolsters his case. Thus, the successful advocate must not only be smart, but as famous turn-of-the-century trial lawyer Francis Wellman (1903/1986, p. 13) observes, he must also be a "good actor." In his book, *The Art of Cross-Examination*, first published in 1903 and reprinted to the present, Wellman describes how carefully the litigator must present himself to the judge and jury:

> The most cautious cross-examiner will often elicit a damaging answer. Now is the time for the greatest self-control. If you show by your face how the answer hurt, you may lose by that one point alone. How often one sees a cross-examiner fairly staggered by such an answer. He pauses, blushes . . . [but seldom regains] control of the witness. With the really experienced trial lawyer, such answers, instead of appearing to surprise or disconcert him, will seem to come as a matter of course, and will fall perfectly flat. He will proceed with the next question as if nothing happened, or else perhaps give the witness an incredulous smile, as if to say, "Who do you suppose would believe that for a minute?" (pp. 13–14)

More recently, teacher and lawyer David Berg (1987) advises lawyers to think of themselves as actors, and the jury, an audience. He writes,

> Decorum can make a difference, too. . . . *Stride to the podium and exude confidence*, even if there is a chance that the high school dropout on the stand is going to make you look like an idiot. *Take command* of the courtroom. Once you begin, do not grope for questions, shuffle through papers, or take breaks to confer with co-counsel. Let the jury know that you are prepared, that you do not need anyone's advice, and that *you care* about the case . . . because if *you don't care, the jurors won't care.* (1987, p. 28, italics added)

Wellman (1903/1986) and Berg (1987) make a similar point: Trials are the enactment of a drama in the courtroom, and attorneys are the leading actors. Appearance and demeanor are of utmost importance. The lawyer's manner, his tone of voice, his facial expressions are all means to persuade the jury that his client is right. Outrageous behavior is acceptable, as long as it remains within the letter of the law. Not only are trial lawyers expected to act but with a specific purpose in mind: to favorably influence feelings of the jurors. As Berg points out, "if you don't show you care, the jurors won't care."

This emphasis on acting is also evident in the courses taught by the National Institute for Trial Advocacy (NITA) where neophyte litigators learn the basics in presenting a case for trial. NITA's emphasis is on "learning by doing" (Kilpatrick, quoted in Rice, 1989). Attorneys do not simply read about cases but practice presenting them in a simulated courtroom with a judge, a jury, and witnesses. In this case, doing means acting. As one of the teacher–lawyers said on the first day of class, "Being a good trial lawyer means being a good actor. . . . Trial attorneys love to perform." Acting, in sociological terms, translates into emotional labor, that is, inducing or suppressing feelings in order to produce an outward countenance that influences the emotions of others. Teacher–lawyers discuss style, delivery, presentation of self, attitude, and professionalism. Participants, in turn, compare notes about the best way to "handle" judges, jurors, witnesses, clients, and opposing counsel. The efforts of these two groups constitute the teaching and observance of "feeling rules" or professional norms that govern appropriate lawyer-like conduct in the courtroom.

The 3-week course I attended[9] took students through various phases of a hypothetical trial—jury selection, opening and closing statements, and direct and cross-examination. Each stage of the trial has a slightly different purpose. For example, the objective of jury selection is to uncover the biases and prejudices of the jurors and to develop rapport with them. On the other hand, an opening statement sets the theme for the case, whereas a direct examination lays the foundation of evidence for the case. Cross-examination is intended to undermine the credibility of the witness, whereas closing represents the final argument. Despite the differing goals that each of these phases has, the means to achieve them is similar in each case, that is, the attempt to persuade a legal audience favorably to one's client through a particular emotional presentation of self.

In their sessions on direct and cross-examination, students were given primarily stylistic, as opposed to substantive, responses on their presentations. They were given finer legal points on the technicalities of their objections— the strength or weakness of their arguments. But in the content analysis of my field notes, I found that 50% to 80% of comments were directed toward the attorney's particular style. These comments fell into five categories: (a) personal appearance, (b) presentation of self (nice, aggressive, or sincere manner), (c) tone and level of voice, (d) eye contact, and (e) rapport with others in the courtroom.

For example, in one of the sessions, Tom, a young student–lawyer in the class, did a direct examination of a witness to a liquor store robbery. He solemnly questioned the witness about his work, his special training in enforcing liquor laws, and how he determined whether someone was intoxicated. At one point when the witness provided a detail that Tom had not expected, rather than expressing surprise, Tom appeared nonchalant and continued with his line of questions. At the end of his direct, the teacher–lawyer provided the following feedback:

> Good background development of a witness. Your voice level was appropriate but try modulating it a bit more for emphasis. You also use too many thank you's to the judge. You should ingratiate yourself with the judge but not overly so. You also made a good recovery when the witness said something unexpected.

When Patricia, a young woman attorney, proceeded nervously through the same direct examination, opposing counsel objected repeatedly to some of her questions, which flustered her. The teacher–lawyer told her,

> You talk too fast. And you didn't make enough eye contact with the judge. Plus, you got bogged down in the objections and harassment from opposing counsel. You're recovery was too slow. You've got to be more forceful.

In both these examples, as in most of the sessions that I observed, the focus of the comments was not on the questions asked but on *how* the questions were asked. Tom was told to modulate his voice; Patricia was told not to talk so fast. In addition, the teacher–lawyer directed their attention to rapport with others in the courtroom. Tom was encouraged not to be overly ingratiating with the judge, whereas Patricia was told to pay more attention to the judge. Moreover, the teacher commended Tom for his "recovery," that is, regaining self-composure and control of the witness. He criticized Patricia, on the other hand, for not recovering well from an aggressive objection made by opposing counsel.[10]

In my fieldwork at NITA and in the two law offices, I found two main types of emo-

tional labor: intimidation and strategic friendliness. Intimidation entails the use of anger and aggression, whereas strategic friendliness uses politeness, friendliness, or playing dumb. Both forms are related to gamesmanship. Each involves an emotional presentation of self that is intended to favorably influence the feelings of a particular legal audience toward one's client. Many jobs appear to require strategic friendliness and intimidation. Domestic workers, for example, sometimes "play dumb" so as not to alienate their white female employers (Rollins, 1985). For domestic workers, however, this strategy is a means for someone in a subordinate position to survive a degrading job. By contrast, for litigators, strategic friendliness, like intimidation, is a means for an individual with professional status to control and dominate others in an effort to win one's case. Although both the litigator and the domestic worker may play dumb, in each job, the behavior serves different goals that are indicative of their divergent positions in relationship to others.

Intimidation and strategic friendliness not only serve the goals of the adversarial model, but they exemplify a masculine style of emotional labor. They become construed as masculine for several reasons. First, emotional labor in the male-dominated professional strata of the gendered law firm is interpreted as masculine, simply because men do it. Ruth Milkman (1987), for example, suggests that "idioms of sex-typing can be applied to whatever women and men happen to be doing" (p. 50). Male trial attorneys participate in shaping this idiom by describing their battles in the courtroom and with opposing counsel as "macho," "something men get into," and "a male thing." In addition, by treating women lawyers as outsiders and excluding them from professional networks, they further define their job as exclusively male.

In addition, the underlying purpose of gamesmanship itself, that is, the control and domination of others through manipulation, reflects a particular cultural conception of masculinity. Connell (1987), for example, describes a hegemonic form of masculinity that emphasizes the domination of a certain class of men—middle- to upper-middle class—over other men and over women. Connell's cultural conception of masculinity dovetails neatly with feminist psychoanalytic accounts that interpret domination as a means of asserting one's masculinity (Benjamin, 1988; Chodorow, 1978). The lawyers I studied also employed a ritual of degradation and humiliation against other men and women who were witnesses or opposing counsel. The remainder of this chapter describes the two main components of emotional labor—intimidation and strategic friendliness—the purpose of each, and shows how these forms become construed as masculine. These forms of emotional labor are explored in practices, such as cross-examination, depositions, jury selection, and in opening and closing statements.

Intimidation

The first and most common form of emotional labor associated with lawyers is intimidation. In popular culture, the tough, hard-hitting, and aggressive trial lawyer is portrayed in television shows, such as *L.A. Law* and *Perry Mason* and in movies, such as *The Firm*, *A Few Good Men*, and *Presumed Innocent*. The news media's focus on famous trial attorneys such as Arthur Liman, the prosecutor of Oliver North in the Iran-Contra trial, also reinforce this image. Law professor Wayne Brazil (1978) refers to this style of lawyering as the *professional combatant*. Others have used terms such as *Rambo litigator, legal terrorists*, and *barbarians of the bar* (Margolick, 1988; Miner, 1988; Sayler, 1988). Trial attorneys themselves call litigators from large law firms "hired guns" (Spangler, 1986). The central figure that appears again and again in these images is not only intimidating but strongly masculine. In the old West, hired guns were sharpshooters, men who were hired to kill other men. The strong, silent

movie character Rambo is emblematic of a highly stylized, super masculinity. Finally, most of the actors who play tough, hard-hitting lawyers in the television shows and movies mentioned above are men. Thus, intimidation is not simply a form of emotional labor associated with trial lawyers, it is a masculinized form of labor.

Intimidation is tied to cultural conceptions of masculinity in yet another way. In a review of the literature on occupations, Connell (1987) observes that the cult of masculinity in working-class jobs centers on physical prowess and sexual contempt for men in managerial or office positions (p. 180). Like the men on the shop floor in Michael Burawoy's (1979) study who brag about how much they can lift or produce, lawyers in this study boast about "destroying witnesses," "playing hardball," "taking no prisoners," and about the size and amount of their "win." In a middle-class job such as the legal profession, however, intimidation depends not on physical ability but on mental quickness and a highly developed set of social skills. Thus, masculinizing practices, such as aggression and humiliation, take on an emotional and intellectual tone specific to middle-class occupations and professions.

This stance is tied to the adversarial model's conception of the "zealous advocate" (American Bar Association, 1982). The underlying purpose of this strategy is to intimidate, scare, or emotionally bully the witness of opposing counsel into submission. A destructive cross-examination is the best example.[11] Trial attorneys are taught to intimidate the witness in cross-examination, "to control the witness by never asking a question to which he does not already know the answer and to regard the impeachment of the witness as a highly confrontational act" (Menkel-Meadow, 1985, p. 54). Wellman (1903/1986) describes cross-examination in this way:

> It requires the greatest ingenuity; a habit of logical thought; clearness of perception; infinite patience and self-control; the power to read men's minds intuitively, to judge of their

characters by their faces, to appreciate their motives; ability to act with force and precision; a masterful knowledge of the subject matter itself; an extreme caution; and, above all *the instinct to discover the weak point in the witness under examination* . . . It is a *mental duel* between counsel and witness. (p. 8, italics added)

Berg (1987) echoes Wellman's words when he begins his lecture on cross-examination by saying, "The common denominator for effective cross-examination is not genius, however. It's a combination of preparation and an instinct for the jugular" (p. 27). Again, cross-examination involves not only acting mean but creating a specific impression on the witness.

In the sections on cross-examination at NITA, teachers trained lawyers how to *act mean*. The demonstration by the teachers on cross-examination best exemplified this point. Two male instructors reenacted an aggressive cross-examination in a burglary case. The prosecutor relentlessly hammered away, until the witness couldn't remember any specific details about what the burglar looked like. At its conclusion, the audience clapped vigorously. Three male students who had been asked to comment on the section responded unanimously and enthusiastically that the prosecutor's approach has been excellent. One student commentator said, "He kept complete control of the witness." Another remarked, "He blasted the witness's testimony." And the third added, "He destroyed the witness's credibility." The fact that a destructive cross-examination served as the demonstration for the entire class underlines the desirability of aggressive behavior as a model for appropriate lawyerlike conduct in this situation. Furthermore, the students' praise for the attorney's tactics collectively reinforce the norm for such behavior.

Teachers emphasized the importance of using aggression on an individual level as well. Before a presentation on cross-examination,

Tom, one of the students, stood in the hallway with one of the instructors trying to "psyche himself up to get mad." He repeated over and over to himself, "I hate it when witnesses lie to me, it makes me so mad!" The teacher coached him to concentrate on that thought, until Tom could actually evoke the feeling of anger. He said to me later in an interview, "I really felt mad at the witness when I walked into the courtroom." In the actual cross-examination, each time the witness made an inconsistent statement, Tom became more and more angry: "First, you told us you could see the burglar, now you say your vision was obstructed! So, which is it, Mr. Jones?" The more irate he became, the more intimidated and confused the witness became, until he completely backed down and said, "I don't know," in response to every question. The teacher characterized Tom's performance as "the best in the class," because it was the "the most forceful" and "the most intimidating." Students remarked that he deserved to "win the case."

NITA's teachers also used mistakes to train students in the rigors of cross-examination. For example, when Laura cross-examined the same witness in the liquor store case, a teacher commented on her performance:

Too many words. You're asking the witness for information. Don't do that in cross-examination. You tell them what the information is. You want to be destructive in cross-examination. When the other side objects to an answer, *you were too nice. Don't be so nice!* [italics added]. Next time, ask to talk to the judge, tell him, "This is crucial to my case." You also asked for information when you didn't know the answer. Bad news. You lost control of the witness.

By being nice and losing control of the witness, Laura violated two norms underlying the classic confrontational cross-examination. A destructive cross-examination is meant to impeach the witness's credibility, thereby demonstrating to the jury the weakness in opposing counsel's case. In situations that call for such an aggressive cross-examination, being nice implies that the lawyer likes the witness and agrees with his or her testimony. By not being aggressive, Laura created the wrong impression for the jury. Second, Laura lost control of the witness. Rather than guiding the witness through the cross with leading questions[12] that were damaging to opposing counsel's case, she allowed the witness to make his own points. As we will see in the next section of the chapter, being nice can also be used as a strategy for controlling a witness; however, such a strategy is not effective in a destructive cross-examination.

Laura's violation of these norms also serves to highlight the implicitly masculine practices used in cross-examination. The repeated phrase, "keeping complete control of the witness," clearly signals the importance of dominating other women and men. Furthermore, the language used to describe obtaining submission—"blasting the witness," "destroying his credibility," or pushing him to "back down"—is quite violent. In addition, the successful control of the witness often takes on the character of a sexual conquest. One brutal phrase used repeatedly in this way is "raping the witness." Within this discursive field, men who "control," "destroy," or "rape" the witness are seen as "manly," whereas those who lose control are feminized as "sissies" and "wimps" or, in Laura's case, as "too nice."

The combative aspect of emotional labor carries over from the courtroom to other lawyering tasks, such as depositions. Attorneys not only "shred" witnesses in the courtroom but in depositions as well. When I worked at this private firm, Daniel, one of the partners, employed what he called his "cat and mouse game" with one of the key witnesses, Jim, in a deposition that I attended. During the deposition, Daniel aggressively cross-examined Jim. "When did you do this?" "You were lying, weren't you?" Jim lost

his temper in response to Daniel's hostile form of interrogation—"You hassle me, man! You make me mad!" Daniel smiled and said, "I'm only trying to get to the truth of the situation." Then, he became aggressive again and said, "You lied to the IRS about how much profit you made, didn't you, Jim!" Jim lost his temper again and started calling Daniel a liar. A heated interchange between Daniel and opposing counsel followed, in which opposing counsel objected to Daniel's "badgering the witness." The attorneys decided to take a brief recess.

When the deposition resumed, Daniel began by accusing John, the other attorney, of withholding crucial documents to the case, while pointing his index finger at him. Opposing counsel stood up and started yelling in a high-pitched voice, "Don't you ever point your finger at me! Don't you ever do that to me! This deposition is over . . . I'm leaving." With that he stood up and began to cram papers into his briefcase in preparation to leave. Daniel immediately backed down, apologized, and said, "Sit down, John, I promise I won't point my finger again." He went on to smooth the situation over and proceeded to tell John in a very calm and controlled voice what his objections were. John made some protesting noises, but he didn't leave. The deposition continued.

In this instance, the deposition, rather than the courtroom, became the *stage* and Daniel took the leading role. His cross-examination was confrontational and his behavior with the witness and opposing counsel was meant to intimidate. After the deposition, Daniel boasted to me and several associates about how mad he had made the witness and how he had "destroyed his credibility." He then proceeded to reenact the final confrontation by imitating John standing up and yelling at him in a falsetto voice. In the discussion that followed, Daniel and his associates gave the effects of his behavior on the "audience" utmost consideration. Hadn't Daniel done a good job forcing the witness to lose control? Hadn't he controlled the situation well? Didn't he make opposing counsel look like a "simpering fool"?

The reenactment and ensuing discussion reveal several underlying purposes of the deposition. First, it suggests that the deposition was not only a fact-finding mission for the attorney but a show designed to influence a particular audience—the witness. Daniel effectively flustered and intimidated the witness. Second, Daniel's imitation of John with a falsetto voice, "as if" he were a women, serves as a sort of "degradation ceremony" (Garfinkel, 1956). By reenacting the drama, he ridicules the man on the other side before an audience of peers, further denigrating him by inviting collective criticism and laughter from colleagues. Third, the discussion of the strategy builds up and elevates Daniel's status as an attorney for his aggressive, yet rational control of the witness and the situation. Thus, the discussion creates a space for collectively reinforcing Daniel's intimidation strategy.

In addition to highlighting the use of intimidation in depositions, this example also illustrates the way aggression as legal strategy or rule-governed aggression (Benjamin, 1988; Lyman, 1987) and masculinity become conflated, whereas aggression, which is not rule governed, is ridiculed as feminine. John shows his anger, but it is deemed inappropriate, because he loses control of the situation. Such a display of hostility does not serve the interests of the legal profession, because it does not achieve the desired result—a win for the case. As a result, Daniel and his associate regard John's behavior—his lack of control, his seeming hysteria and high voice, with contempt. This contempt takes on a specific sexual character. Just as the working class "lads" in Paul Willis's (1977) book, *Learning to Labor*, denigrate the "earholes" or sissies for their feminine attributes, Daniel and his colleagues ridicule John for his female-like behavior. Aggression as legal strategy or maleness is celebrated; contempt is reserved for aggression (or behavior) that is not rule gov-

erned and behavior that is also associated with the opposite sex.

Attorneys also used the confrontational approach in depositions at Bonhomie Corporation. In a deposition I sat in on, Mack, a litigator, used an aggressive cross-examination of the key witness.

Q: What were the names of the people that have migrated from one of the violators, as you call it, to Bonhomie Corporation?

A: I don't remember as of now.

Q: Do you have their names written down?

A: No.

Q: Well, if you don't remember their names and they're not written down, how can you follow their migration from one company to another?

A: You can consider it in the process of discovery that I will make some inquiring phone calls.

Q: Did you call anyone to follow their migration?

A: Well, I was unsuccessful as of yet to reach other people.

Q: Who have you attempted to call?

A: I can't tell you at this time. I have a list of processes in my mind to follow.

Q: Do you recall who you called and were not able to reach?

A: No.

Q: What's the list of processes in your mind to follow?

A: It's hard to describe.

Q: In other words, you don't have a list?

A: [quietly] Not really.

Q: Mr. Jensen, instead of wasting everyone's time and money, answer the question yes or no!

Opposing Counsel: Don't badger the witness.

Q: Answer the question, Mr. Jensen, yes or no!

Opposing Counsel: I said, don't badger the witness.

Q: Mr. Jensen, you are still required to answer the question!

A: [quietly] No.

In this case, Mack persisted in badgering the witness, who provided incoherent and vague answers. In response to the question, "Well, if you don't remember their names and they're not written down, how can you follow their migration from one company to another?" the witness gave the vague reply: "You can consider it in the process of discovery that I will make some inquiring phone calls." As the witness became more evasive, the attorney became more confrontational, "Answer the question, Mr. Jensen, yes or no!" By using this approach, the lawyer succeeded in making the witness appear even more uncooperative than he actually was and eventually pushed him to admit that he didn't have a list.

Later, in the same deposition, the attorney's confrontational tactics extended to opposing counsel.

Q: Let's change the subject. Mr. Jensen, can you tell me what representations were made to you about the reliability of the Bonhomie Corporation's spider system?

A: Nancy, the saleslady, said they use it widely in the United States, and could not be but very reliable. And, as we allege, fraudulent, and as somebody referred to it, was the, they wanted to give us the embrace of death to provide us more dependency, and then to go on and control our operation totally [sic].

Q: Who said that?

A: My attorney.

Q: When was that?

Opposing Counsel: Well, I . . .

Mack: I think he's already waived it. All I want to know is when it was supposedly said.

A: Well . . .

Opposing Counsel: I do use some great metaphors.

Mack: Yes, I know, I have read your complaint.

Opposing Counsel: Sorry?

Mack: I have read your complaint. That will be all for today, Mr. Jensen.

Here, the attorney did not stop with badgering the witness. When the witness made the statement about the "embrace of death," Mack was quick to find out who said it. And when opposing counsel bragged about his "great metaphors," Mack parried back with a sarcastic retort, "Yes, I know, I have read your complaint." Having had the final word, he abruptly ended the deposition. Like the other deposition, this one was not only an arena for intimidating the witness but for ridiculing the attorney on the other side. In this way, intimidation was used to control the witness and sarcasm to dominate opposing counsel. In doing so, Mack had achieved the desired result—the witness's submission to his line of questioning and a victory over the other side. Furthermore, in his replay of the deposition to his colleagues, he characterized his victory as a "macho blast against the other side," thereby underscoring the masculine character of his intimidation tactics.

Strategic Friendliness

Mr. Choate's appeal to the jury began long before final argument. . . . His manner to the jury was that of a *friend* [italics added], a friend solicitous to help them through their tedious investigation; never an expert combatant, intent on victory, and looking upon them as only instruments for its attainment. (Wellman, 1903/1986, pp. 16–17)

The lesson implicit in Wellman's anecdote about famous 19th-century lawyer Rufus Choate's trial tactics is that friendliness is another important strategy the litigator must learn and use to be successful in the courtroom. Like the use of aggression, the strategic use of friendliness is another feature of gamesmanship and, hence, another component of emotional labor. As Richard, one of the attorney–teachers at NITA stated, "Lawyers have to be able to vary their styles, they have to be able to have multiple speeds, personalities and style." In his view, intimidation did not always work and he proposed an alternative strategy, what he called "the toe-in-the-sand, aw shucks routine." Rather than adopting an intimidating stance vis-à-vis the witness, he advocated "playing dumb and innocent." "Say to the witness, 'Gee, I don't know what you mean. Can you explain it again?' until you catch the witness in a mistake or an inconsistent statement." Other litigators, such as Leonard Right (1987), call this the "low-key approach." As an illustration of this style, Ring describes how opposing counsel delicately handled the cross-examination of a child witness.

> The lawyer for the defendant . . . stood to cross-examine. Did he attack the details of her story to show inconsistencies? Did he set her up for impeachment by attempting to reveal mistakes, uncertainties and confusion? I sat there praying that he would. But no, he did none of the things a competent defense lawyer is supposed to do. He was old enough to be the girl's grandfather . . . the image came through. He asked her very softly and politely: "Honey, could you tell us again what you saw?" She told it exactly as she had on my direct. I felt relieved. He still wasn't satisfied. "Honey, would you mind telling us again what you saw?" She did again exactly as she had before. He still wasn't satisfied. "Would you do it once more?" She did. She repeated, again, the same story—the same way, in the same words. By that time I got the message. The child had been rehearsed by her mother the same way she had been taught

"Mary Had a Little Lamb." I won the case, but it was a very small verdict. (pp. 35–36)

Ring concludes that a low-key approach is necessary in some situations and advises against adhering rigidly to the prototypical combative style.

Similarly, Scott Turow (1987), lawyer and novelist, advises trying a variety of approaches when cross-examining the star witness. He cautions against adopting a "guerrilla warfare mentality" in cross-examination and suggests that the attorney may want to create another impression with the jury:

> Behaving courteously can keep you from getting hurt and, in the process, smooth the path for a win. [In one case I worked on] the cross examination was conducted with a politesse appropriate to a drawing room. I smiled to show that I was not mean-spirited. The chief executive officer smiled to show that he was not beaten. The commissioners smiled to show their gratitude that everybody was being so nice. And my client won big. (pp. 40–42)

Being nice, polite, welcoming, playing dumb, or behaving courteously are all ways that a trial lawyer can manipulate the witness to create a particular impression for the jury. I term this form of gamesmanship *strategic friendliness*. Rather than bully or scare the witness into submission, this tactic employs the opposite—friendliness, politeness, and tact. Despite this seeming difference, it shares with the former an emphasis on the emotional manipulation of another person for a strategic end—winning one's case. For instance, the attorney in Ring's account is gentle and considerate of the child witness for two strategic reasons. First, by making the child feel comfortable, he brings to light the fact that her testimony has been rehearsed. Second, by playing the polite, gentle grandfatherly role, he has created a favorable impression of himself with the jury. Thus, he simultaneously demonstrates to the jury that the witness has been rehearsed and that he, as opposing counsel, is a nice guy. In this way, he improves his chances for winning. And, in fact, he did. Although he didn't win the case, the verdict for the other side was "small."

Although strategic friendliness may appear to be a softer approach than intimidation, it carries with it a strongly instrumental element. Consider the reasoning behind this particular approach. Ring's attorney is nice to the child witness not because he's altruistically concerned for her welfare. He utilizes gentility as a strategy to achieve the desired result—a big win in the courtroom. It is simply a means to an end. Although this approach may be less aggressive than intimidation, it is no less manipulative. Like the goal of intimidation, the central goal of this component of gamesmanship is to dominate and control others for a specific end. This end is best summed up by litigator Mark Dombroff (1989) who writes, "So long as you don't violate the law, including the rules of procedure and evidence or do violence to the canons of ethics, winning is the only thing that matters" (p. 13).

This emphasis on winning is tied to hegemonic conceptions of masculinity and competition. Sociologist Mike Messner (1989) argues that achievement in sporting competitions, such as football, baseball, and basketball, serve as a measure of men's self-worth and their masculinity. This can also be carried over into the workplace. For example, in her research on men in sales, Leidner (1993) finds that defining the jobs as competition becomes a means for construing the work as masculine.

For litigators, comparing the number of wins in the courtroom and the dollar amount of damages or settlement awards allows them to interpret their work as manly. At Bonhomie Corporation and at Lyman, Lyman, and Portia, the first question lawyers often asked others after a trial or settlement conference was "Who won the case?" or "How big were the damages?" Note that both Ring and Turow also conclude their pieces with descriptions of their win—"I won the case, but the verdict was small" and "I

won big." Trial attorneys who did not "win big" were described as "having no balls," "geeks," or "wimps." The fact that losing is associated with being less than a man suggests that the constant focus on competition and winning is an arena for proving one's masculinity.

One important area that calls for strategic friendliness and focuses on winning is jury selection or *voir dire*. The main purpose of *voir dire* is to obtain personal information about prospective jurors to determine whether they will be fair, "favorably disposed to you, your client, and your case, and will ultimately return a favorable verdict" (Mauet, 1980, p. 31). Once an attorney has made that assessment, biased jurors can be eliminated through challenges for cause and peremptory challenges. In an article on jury selection, attorney Peter Perlman (1988) maintains that the best way to uncover the prejudices of the jury "is to conduct *voir dire* in an atmosphere that makes prospective jurors comfortable about disclosing their true feelings" (p. 5). He provides a check list of strategies for lawyers to use that enable jurors to feel more comfortable. Some of these include the following:

- Given the initial intimidation that jurors feel, try to make them feel as comfortable as possible; approach them in a *natural, unpretentious, and clear manner.*

- Because jurors don't relate to "litigants" or "litigation," humanize the client and the dispute.

- *Demonstrate the sincere* desire to learn of the jurors's feelings. (pp. 5–9, italics added)

Perlman's account reveals that the underlying goal of jury selection is to encourage the jury to open up so that the lawyer can eliminate the jurors he doesn't want and develop a positive rapport with the ones who appear favorable to his case. This goal is supported not only by other writings on jury selection (Blinder, 1978; Cartwright, 1977; Mauet, 1980; Ring, 1983) but also through the training offered by NITA. As a teacher–judge said after the class demonstration on jury selection, "Sell your personality to the jury. Try to get liked by the jury. You're not working for a fair jury but one favorable to your side."

At NITA, teachers emphasized this point on the individual level. In their sessions on *voir dire*, students had to select a jury for a case that involved an employee who fell down the steps at work and severely injured herself. (Jurors in the class were other students, in addition to myself.) Mike, one of the students, proceeded with his presentation. He explained that he was representing the wife's employer. He then went on to tell the jury a little bit about himself. "I grew up in a small town in Indiana." Then, he began to ask each of the jurors where they were from, whether they knew the witness or the experts, whether they played sports, had back problems, suffered any physical injuries, and ever had physical therapy. The instructor gave him the following comments:

> The personal comments about yourself seem forced. Good folksy approach, but you went overboard with it. You threw stuff out and let the jury nibble and you got a lot of information. But the main problem is that you didn't find out how people *feel* about the case or about their relatives and friends.

Another set of comments:

> Nice folksy approach but a bit overdone. Listen to what jurors say, don't draw conclusions. Don't get so close to them, it makes them feel uncomfortable. Use body language to give people a good feeling about you. Good personality, but don't cross certain lines. Never ask someone about their ancestry. It's too loaded a question to ask. Good sense of humor, but don't call one of your prospective jurors a "money man." And don't tell the jury jokes! You don't *win them over* [italics added] that way.

The sporting element to *voir dire* becomes "winning over the jury." This theme also be-

came evident in discussions student lawyers had before and after jury selection. They discussed at length how best "to handle the jurors," "how to get personal information out of them," "how to please them," "how to make them like you," and "how to seduce them to your side." The element of sexual seduction is no more apparent than in the often used phrase, "getting in bed with the jury." The direct reference to sexual seduction and conquest suggests, as it did with the intimidation strategy used in cross-examination, that "winning over the jury" is also a way to prove one's masculinity. Moreover, the desired result in both strategic friendliness and intimidation is similar: obtaining the juror's submission and winning.

Strategic friendliness is used not only in jury selection but in the cross-examination of sympathetic witnesses. In one of NITA's hypothetical cases, a husband's spouse dies of an illness related to her employment. He sues his deceased wife's former employer for her medical bills, her lost wages, and "lost companionship." One of the damaging facts in the case that could hurt his claim for lost companionship was the fact that he had a girlfriend long before his wife died. In typical combative adversarial style, some of the student lawyers tried to bring this fact out in cross-examination to discredit his relationship with his wife. The teacher–judge told one lawyer who presented such an aggressive cross-examination,

> It's too risky to go after him. Don't be so confrontational. And don't ask the judge to reprimand him for not answering the question. This witness is too sensitive. Go easy on him.

The same teacher gave the following comment to another student who had "come on too strong":

> Too stern. Hasn't this guy been through enough already! Handle him with kid gloves. And don't cut him off. It generates sympathy for him from the jury when you do that. It's difficult to control a sympathetic witness. It's best to use another witness's testimony to impeach him.

And to yet another student:

> Slow down! This is a dramatic witness. Don't lead so much. He's a sympathetic witness—the widower—let him do the talking. Otherwise you look like an insensitive jerk to the jury.

In the cross-examination of a sympathetic witness, teachers advised students not to be aggressive but to adopt a gentler approach. Their concern, however, is not for the witness's feelings but how their treatment of the witness appears to the jury. The jury already thinks the witness is sympathetic, because he is a widower. As a result, the lawyers were advised not to do anything that would make the witness appear more sympathetic and them less so. The one student who did well on this presentation demonstrated great concern for the witness. She gently asked him about his job, his marriage, his wife's job, and her illness. Continuing with this gentle approach, she softly asked him whether anyone had been able to provide him comfort during this difficult time. By doing so, she was able to elicit the testimony about the girlfriend in a sensitive manner. By extracting the testimony about the girlfriend, she decreased the jury's level of sympathy for the bereaved widower. How much companionship did he lose, if he was having an affair? At the same time, because she did so in a gentle manner, she increased the jury's regard for her. She presented herself as a nice person. Her approach is similar to Laura's in using "niceness" as a strategy. However, in Laura's case, being nice was not appropriate to a destructive cross-examination. In the case of cross-examining a sympathetic witness, such an approach is necessary.

Opening statements also provide an opportunity for using the nonconfrontational approach. NITA provided a hypothetical case called *BMI v. Minicom*, involving a large corporation that sues a small business for its failure to pay a contract. Minicom signed a contract for a $20,000 order of computer parts from BMI. BMI shipped the computer parts through UPS to Minicom, but they never arrived. According to the law in the case, the buyer bears the loss, typically through insurance, when the equipment is lost in mail. Mark gave an opening statement that portrayed Minicom as a small business started by ambitious, hard-working college friends "on their way to the big league in business." He played up the difficulties that small businesses face in trying to compete with giant corporations. And at a dramatic moment in the opening, he asked the jury to "imagine a world where cruel giants didn't squeeze out small companies like Minicom." The teacher provided the following comments:

> Good use of evocative imagery. BMI as cruel giant. Minicom squeezing in between the cracks. Great highlighting of the injustice of the situation.

The lawyer for Minicom attempted to gain sympathy from the jury by playing up the underdog role of his client—the small company that gets squeezed between the cracks of the cruel, dominating giant.

In his attempt to counter this image, Robert, the lawyer for BMI, used a courteous opening statement. He attempted to present himself as a nice guy. He took off his jacket, loosened his tie, smiled at the jury, and said, in a friendly conversational tone, "This case is about a broken contract. BMI fulfilled their side of the contract. Mr. Blakey, my client, worked round the clock to get the shipment ready for Minicom. He made phone call after phone call to inventory to make sure the parts got out on time. He checked and rechecked the package before he sent it to Minicom." He paused for dramatic emphasis and, looking sincere and concerned, said, "It's too bad UPS lost the shipment, but that's not BMI's fault. And now, BMI is out $20,000." He received the following comments from the teacher:

> Great use of gestures and eye contact. Good use of voice. You made the case sound simple

but important. You humanized yourself and the people at BMI. Good building of sequence.

Here, the attorney for BMI tried to play down his client's impersonal, corporate image by presenting himself as a nice guy. Before he began his opening statement, he took off his jacket and loosened his tie to suggest a more casual and ostensibly less corporate image. He smiled at the jury to let them know that he was friendly—not the cruel giant depicted by opposing counsel. He used a friendly conversational tone to begin his opening statement. And he even admitted that it was not fair that the other side didn't get their computer parts. As the teacher's comments suggest, this strategy was most effective for this particular kind of case.

This approach can also be used in closing statements. In a hypothetical case, during which an insurance company alleged that the claimant set fire to his own business, the lawyer for the store owner tried to defuse the insurance company's strategy with a highly dramatic closing statement:

> Visualize Elmwood Street in 1952. The day Tony Rubino came home from the Navy. His father took him outside to show him a new sign he had made for the family business. It read "Rubino & Son." Standing under the sign "Rubino & Son" with his father was the happiest day of his life. [Pause] The insurance company wants you to believe, ladies and gentlemen of the jury, that Tony set fire to this family jewel. "I'll carry on," he told his father, and he did. . . . [With tears in her eyes, the lawyer concludes] You don't set fire to your father's dream.

The teacher's comments for Janine's closing statement were effusive:

> Great! Well thought out, sounded natural. Good use of details and organization. I especially liked "I don't know what it's like to have a son, but I know what it's like to have a father." And you had tears in your eyes! Gave me the closing-argument goose bumps. Pitched emotion felt real, not phony.

Janine's use of sentimental and nostalgic imagery, the son returning home from the Navy, the beginning of a father and son business, the business as the "family jewel" is reminiscent of a Norman Rockwell painting. It also serves to counter the insurance company's allegation that Tony Rubino set fire to his own store. With the portrait the lawyer paints and the concluding line, "You don't set fire to your father's dream," she rallies the jury's sympathy for Tony Rubino and their antipathy for the insurance company's malicious claim against them. Moreover, her emotional presentation of the story is so effective that the instructor thought it "sounded natural" and "felt real, not phony." The great irony here is that this is not a real case—it is a hypothetical case with hypothetical characters. There is no Tony Rubino, no family store, and no fire. Yet Janine's "deep acting" was so convincing that the teachers believed it was true—it gave him "the closing-argument goose bumps."

Strategic friendliness carries over from the courtroom to depositions. Before deposing a particularly sensitive or sympathetic witness, Joe, one of the attorneys in the private firm, asked me whether "there is anything personal to start the interview with—a sort of warm up question to start things off on a personal note?" I had previously interviewed the woman over the phone, so I knew something about her background. I told him that she was a young mother who had recently had a very difficult delivery of her first child. I added that she was worried about the baby's health, because he had been born prematurely. At the beginning of the deposition later that afternoon, Joe said in a concerned voice that he understood the witness had recently had a baby and was concerned about its health. She appeared slightly embarrassed by the question, but with a slow smile and lots of encouragement from him, she began to tell him all about the baby and its health problems. By the time Joe began the formal part of the deposition, the witness had warmed up and gave her complete cooperation. Later, the attorney bragged to me and one of the associates that he had the witness "eating out of his hand."

After recording these events in my field notes, I wrote the following impressions:

> On the surface, it looks like social etiquette to ask the witness these questions, because it puts her at ease. It lets her know he takes her seriously. But the "personal touch" is completely artificial. He doesn't give a shit about the witness as a person. Or, I should say, only insofar as she's *useful* to him.

Thus, something as innocuous as a personal remark becomes another way to create the desired impression with a witness and thereby manipulate him or her. Perhaps what is most ironic about strategic friendliness is that it requires a peculiar combination of sensitivity to other people and, at the same time, ruthlessness. The lawyer wants to appear kind and understanding, but that is merely a cover for the ulterior motive—winning. Although the outward presentation of self for this form of emotional labor differs from intimidation, the underlying goal is the same: the emotional manipulation of the witness for a favorable result.

Conclusion

In this chapter, I have redefined gamesmanship as the utilization of legal strategy through a presentation of emotional self designed specifically to influence the feelings and judgments of a particular legal audience, such as the judge, the jury, opposing counsel, or the witness. Gamesmanship as emotional labor constitutes two main components—intimidation and strategic friendliness. Despite their apparent differences, both share an emphasis on the manipulation of others toward a strategic end, that is, winning a case. Whereas, the object of intimidation is to "wipe out the other side," playing dumb and being polite represent strategically friendly methods for controlling legal audiences and bringing about the desired "win." Furthermore, I have shown that the attempt to dominate and

control judges, juries, and opposing counsel not only serves the goals of the adversarial model but also becomes a means for trial lawyers to assert a hegemonic form of masculinity. Lawyers who gain the other side's submission characterize their efforts as a "macho blast," "a male thing," or "something men get into," whereas those who do not are regarded as "sissies" and "wimps." Thus, it is through their very efforts to be successful litigators that emotional labor in this male-dominated profession is masculinized.

This chapter also suggests many questions for future research on the role of masculinity and emotions in organizations. Masculinity is often a taken-for-granted feature of organizational life. Yet the masculinization of occupations and professions has profound consequences for workers located within them. Not only do male litigators find themselves compelled to act in ways they may find morally reprehensible, but women working in these jobs[13] are increasingly marginalized—facing sex discrimination and sexual harassment (Rhode, 1988; Rosenberg, Perlstadt, & Phillips, 1993). At the same time, because of its informal and seemingly invisible nature, emotional labor too is often unexamined and unquestioned (Fineman, 1993). Given that organizations often intrude on emotional life means that the line between the individual and the job becomes a murky one. The litigator who refuses to play Rambo may not only be unsuccessful, he may find himself without a job. Thus, many questions still require our attention. Is emotional labor gendered in other jobs? Under what conditions? When does emotional labor take on racialized or classed dimensions? When is it exploitative and when is it not? And finally, what role, if any, should emotions play in the workplace?

Notes

1. For examples, see Goldberg (1987), Margolick (1988), Miner (1988), and Sayler (1988).

2. For example, see the *National Law Journal*'s (1986) article, "What America Really Thinks About Lawyers."

3. Classic studies on the legal profession have typically focused on the tension between professionalism and bureaucracy. For examples, see Smigel (1969), Carlin (1962), Spangler (1986), and Nelson (1988).

4. For example, in their classic book, *Lawyers and Their Work*, Johnstone and Hopson (1967) describe 19 tasks associated with the lawyering role. In only 2 of these 19 tasks do Johnstone and Hopson allude to the emotional dimension of lawyering—"emotional support to client" and "acting as a scapegoat" (pp. 119–120).

5. In addition to my field research, I also conducted 60 interviews with lawyers, paralegals, and secretaries, as well as 8 interviews with personnel directors from some of San Francisco's largest law firms. Field work and interviews were also conducted at the National Institute of Trial Advocacy where I spent 3 weeks with litigators during a special training course on trial preparation. These methodological decisions are fully discussed in the introductory chapter to my book, *Gender Trials* (Pierce, 1995). Please note, names of organizations and individuals have been changed throughout to protect confidentiality.

6. See Chapter 4, "Mothering Paralegals: Emotional Labor in a Feminized Occupation," in *Gender Trials* (Pierce, 1995).

7. West and Zimmerman (1987) conceptualize gender as "a routine accomplishment embedded in everyday interaction" (p. 1).

8. Blumberg (1967) describes lawyers as practicing a "confidence game." In his account, it is the client who is the "mark" and the attorney and other people in the court who collude in "taking him out." In my usage, litigators "con" not only their clients but juries, judges, and opposing counsel as well.

9. Special thanks to Laurence Rose, Lou Natali, and the National Institute of Trial Advocacy for allowing me to attend and observe NITA's special 3-week training seminar on trial advocacy. All interpretations of NITA and its practices are my own and are *not* intended to reflect the goals or objectives of that organization.

10. Women were much more likely to be criticized for being "too nice." The significance of women being singled out for these kinds of "mistakes" is examined in Chapter 5. "Women and Men as Litigators," in *Gender Trials* (Pierce, 1995).

11. Mauet describes two approaches to cross-examination. In the first, the purpose is to elicit favorable testimony by getting the witness to agree with the facts that support one's case. On the other hand, a destructive cross-examination "involves asking questions which will discredit the witness or his testimony" (1980, p. 240).

12. The proper form of leading questions is allowed in cross-examination but *not* in direct examination. Mauet (1980) defines a leading question as "one which suggests the answer" and provides examples, such as "Mr. Doe, on December 13, 1977, you owned a car, didn't you?" (p. 247). In his view, control comes by asking "precisely phrased leading questions that never give the witness an opening to hurt you" (p. 243).

13. Women trial lawyers negotiate the masculinized norms of the legal profession in a variety of ways. See Chapter 5, "Women and Men as Litigators," in *Gender Trials* (Pierce 1995).

References

American Bar Association (1982). *Model code of professional responsibility and code of judicial conduct.* Chicago: National Center for Professional Responsibility and ABA.

Benjamin, J. (1988). *The bonds of love: Psychoanalysis, feminism and the problem of domination.* New York: Pantheon.

Berg, D. (1987). Cross-examination. *Litigation: Journal of the Section of Litigation, American Bar Association, 14*(1), 25–30.

Blinder, M. (1978). Picking juries. *Trial Diplomacy, 1*(1), 8–13.

Blumberg, A. (1967). The practice of law as confidence game: Organizational co-optation of a profession. *Law and Society Review, 1*(2), 15–39.

Brazil, W. (1978). The attorney as victim: Toward more candor about the psychological price tag of litigation practice. *Journal of the Legal Profession, 3*, 107–117.

Buchan, J. (1939). The judicial temperament. In J. Buchan, *Homilies and recreations* (3rd ed.). London: Hodder & Stoughton.

Burawoy, M. (1979). *Manufacturing consent.* Chicago: University of Chicago Press.

Carlin, J. (1962). *Lawyers on their own.* New Brunswick, NJ: Rutgers University Press.

Cartwright, R. (1977, June). Jury selection. *Trial, 28*, 13.

Cheatham, E. (1955). *Cases and materials on the legal profession* (2nd ed.). Brooklyn, NY: Foundation.

Chodorow, N. (1978). *The reproduction of mothering: Psychoanalysis and the sociology of gender.* Berkeley & Los Angeles: University of California Press.

Connell, R. W. (1987). *Gender and power: Society, the person and sexual politics.* Stanford, CA: Stanford University Press.

Dombroff, M. (1989, September 25). Winning is everything! *National Law Journal*, p. 13, col. 1.

Fineman, S. (Ed.). (1993). *Emotions in organizations.* Newbury Park, CA: Sage.

Garfinkel, H. (1956). Conditions of successful degradation ceremonies. *American Journal of Sociology, 61*(11), 420–424.

Goldberg, D. (1987, July 1). Playing hardball. *American Bar Association Journal*, p. 48.

Hochschild, A. (1983). *The managed heart: Commercialization of human feeling.* Berkeley & Los Angeles: University of California Press.

Johnstone, Q., & Hopson, D., Jr. (1967). *Lawyers and their work.* Indianapolis, IN: Bobbs-Merrill.

Leidner, R. (1993). *Fast food, fast talk: Service work and the routinization of everyday life.* Berkeley: University of California Press.

Luban, D. (1988). *Lawyers and justice: An ethical study.* Princeton, NJ: Princeton University Press.

Lyman, P. (1987). The fraternal bond as a joking relationship: A case study of sexist jokes in male group bonding. In M. Kimmel (Ed.), *Changing men: New directions in research on men and masculinity* (pp. 148–163). Newbury Park, CA: Sage.

Margolick, D. (1988, August 5). At the bar: Rambos invade the courtroom. *New York Times*, p. B5.

Mauet, T. (1980). *Fundamentals of trial techniques.* Boston: Little, Brown.

Menkel-Meadow, C. (1985, Fall). Portia in a different voice: Speculations on a women's lawyering process. *Berkeley Women's Law Review*, pp. 39–63.

Messner, M. (1989). Masculinities and athletic careers. *Gender & Society, 3*(1), 71–88.

Milkman, R. (1987). *Gender at work.* Bloomington: University of Indiana Press.

Miner, R. (1988, December 19). Lawyers owe one another. *National Law Journal*, pp. 13–14.

Nelson, R. (1988). *Partners with power.* Berkeley & Los Angeles: University of California Press.

Perlman, P. (1988). Jury selection. *The Docket: Newsletter of the National Institute for Trial Advocacy, 12*(2), 1.

Pierce, J. L. (1995). *Gender trials: Emotional lives in contemporary law firms.* Berkeley & Los Angeles: University of California Press.

Rhode, D. (1988). Perspectives on professional women. *Stanford Law Review, 40*, 1163–1207.

Rice, S. (1989, May 24). Two organizations provide training, in-house or out. *San Francisco Banner*, p. 6.

Ring, L. (1983, July). *Voir dire:* Some thoughtful notes on the selection process. *Trial, 19*, 72–75.

Ring, L. (1987). Cross-examining the sympathetic witness. *Litigation: Journal of the Section of Litigation, American Bar Association, 14*(1), 35–39.

Rollins, J. (1985). *Between women: Domestics and their employers.* Philadelphia: Temple University Press.

Rosenberg, J., Perlstadt, H., & Phillips, W. (1993). Now that we are here: Discrimination, disparagement and harassment at work and the experience of women lawyers. *Gender & Society, 7*(3), 415–433.

Sayler, R. (1988, March 1). Rambo litigation: Why hardball tactics don't work. *American Bar Association Journal*, p. 79.

Smigel, E. (1969). *The Wall Street lawyer: Professional or organizational man?* (2nd ed.). New York: Free Press.

Spangler, E. (1986). *Lawyers for hire: Salaried professionals at work.* New Haven, CT: Yale University Press.

Spence, G. (1988). *With justice for none.* New York: Times Books.

Turow, S. (1987). Crossing the star. *Litigation: Journal of the Section of Litigation, American Bar Association, 14*(1), 40–42.

Wellman, F. (1986). *The art of cross-examination: With the cross-examinations of important witnesses in some celebrated cases* (4th ed.). New York: Collier. (Original work published 1903)

West, C., & Zimmerman, D. (1987). Doing gender. *Gender & Society, 1*(2), 125–151.

What America really thinks about lawyers. (1986, October). *National Law Journal*, p. 1.

Willis, P. (1977). *Learning to labor.* Farnborough, UK: Saxon House.

27

ARTICLE

Timothy Nonn

Hitting Bottom: Homelessness, Poverty, and Masculinity

In the dangerous and impoverished Tenderloin district of San Francisco live the men we consider failures. Urban deterioration and public neglect has created a "dumping-ground for unwanted individuals" (North of Market Planning Coalition 1992: 4). Low rents attract immigrants, welfare recipients, and low-income workers. The population is about 40 percent white, one-third Asian American, and one-tenth black and Latino, respectively. There are severe problems with homelessness, AIDS, violence, substance abuse, and unemployment.

In studies of men, poor men are rarely the object of research.[1] This article examines the coping mechanisms poor men develop to resolve their status as "failed men": First, to overcome stigmatization and regain self-worth, Tenderloin men develop "counter-masculinities" within distinct groups; second, some men develop new values in response to a multiplicity of masculinities that allow them to transcend separate groups and identify with the Tenderloin community.

Using a snowball sample, twenty men were interviewed during a six-month period, including twelve whites, six blacks, and two Latinos;

Reprinted with permission of the author.

twelve were heterosexual, and eight were homosexual. Their ages ranged from twenty-nine to fifty-four; the majority had a high-school education. Many had been homeless, but most were now living in single-room occupancy hotels. Twelve were single, seven were divorced or separated, and one was married. Several have left children behind. Their interactions with women at the time of the interview were very limited. Few had contact with families or had long-term relationships with women.

Each interview lasted about two hours and included a questionnaire that examined attitudes about gender, race, and sexuality. In the study, I examined how Tenderloin men, as groups, interacted with other men.

Failed Men

A discussion of failure among men must begin with hegemonic masculinity. R. W. Connell writes:

> Hegemonic masculinity is constructed in relation to women and to subordinated masculinities. These other masculinities need not be as

clearly defined—indeed, achieving hegemony may consist precisely in preventing alternatives gaining cultural definition and recognition as alternatives, confining them to ghettos, to privacy, to unconsciousness. (Connell 1987: 186)

Connell defines hegemonic masculinity as men's dominance over women. While individuals may change, men's collective power remains embedded in social and cultural institutions. Michael Messner interprets change among white, middle-class men as a matter of personal life-style rather than a restructuring of power and politics (Messner 1993).

Hegemonic masculinity is the standard by which Tenderloin men are judged. The media refers to them as "thugs and bums."[2] Forced to live amidst poverty, drugs, and violence, they are stripped of or denied access to a masculine identity constructed around the role of "the good provider" (see Bernard in this book). As white heterosexuals, they are stripped of an identity associated with privilege and power. As gays or men of color, they are denied access to a masculine ideal associated with heterosexual whites. George, a divorced black Vietnam veteran, says:

> Now, we're talking about that segment of the male population that have been taught some of the same things that all men are taught. So they were straight-up abject failures.[3]

Tenderloin men sometimes refer to each other as "invisible." George describes a homeless man's life:

> I call it the "invisible-man syndrome." That's what you become. Most homeless, but not all, self-medicate. It's that thing that you can turn to when you're suffering. You feel disenfranchised from society. You feel less than human. It tells him—in between those periods where he has some lucidity, in between drug or alcohol bouts—that he is a total failure.

Allan, a forty-six-year-old heterosexual white man, recounts the experience of trying to cash a small check:

> [I went] into the bank to cash a two-dollar check and had to deal with people's feedback. I just want to be invisible. I'm real embarrassed about that. About my economic status.... When I was stripped of all those material things that I was taught were the measure of success, and everybody rejected me—even though as a person I hadn't changed—I saw the sort of shallowness. It was very painful and very hard.[4]

Tenderloin men face a lonely end. Before death—having been stripped of everything that qualifies a man for full participation in society—there is the shame of surviving as less than a man. Tenderloin men belong to a "shamed group" (Goffman 1963: 23). David, a heterosexual black homeless man, describes their daily struggle:

> The thing that really hurts and holds people down is when they give completely up. When you give completely up that means you take your energy and give it to drugs or alcohol.... Some homeless men have lost their self-esteem. They have been down for so long. And the system has played this game of chess with them for so long. They've just said, "Oh, forget it." They say, "We'll sell drugs. So if I go to jail, I still have a home." So it don't make any difference. They feel rejected.[5]

Tenderloin men feel trapped in the role of failure.[6] Many hang out day and night on streets "drinking and drugging," talking and begging. The ubiquitous drug trade, routine violence, and crushing poverty combine to form an atmosphere of continual dread and hopelessness within the neighborhood. The men wait in line for hours at churches to receive food, clothing, and lodging. Because it is equally painful to be seen as to be invisible, they are silent and avoid eye contact. They spend a lot of time waiting. The wait transforms them. They dress in a similar ragged way. They walk and talk in a dispirited way. Their faces have the same blank stare or menacing hardness. Some turn into predators in search of victims.[7] Others turn into victims in search of sympathy. George says:

Your antenna is up for people feeling sorry for you. Part of you becomes a predator. The predator part wants to take advantage. So you can get resources to continue your downward spiral to total destruction. The other part of you feels ashamed because you have violated every man-code that you were ever taught. So you're stuck on stupid. You get to a point where you don't know what to do. You don't give a shit no more about how you're perceived. You can walk down the street smelling like a billy goat. Stuff hanging all over you. You haven't had access to basic hygiene in days and sometimes weeks. You don't care. And the looks don't bother you anymore because you ain't nobody. The "productive citizens" have that way of not looking at you anyway because you're the invisible man.

The invisibility of Tenderloin men is part of "a pervasive two-role social process" in which failure and success are interrelated (Goffman 1963: 138). They are stigmatized merely by living in an area decimated by poverty, sex and drug markets, and high levels of crime and violence. William Julius Wilson calls them "the permanent underclass" (Wilson 1987: 7). Samuel, a forty-year-old homosexual black man, describes their plight more poignantly: "You're always going to need a place where the lonely souls can go."[8]

Trapped at the bottom of society and stigmatized as failures, Tenderloin men have limited opportunities to claim an identity that fosters self-worth. Charles, a fifty-year-old white gay man, says: "Once you go in there, it's like being an untouchable. You're stigmatized as being this type of sleazy person that does dope and needles, and the whole thing."[9] After a man is stripped of or denied access to symbols of masculinity that confer power and privilege—job, car, home, and family—life becomes a series of challenges to his existence. Some escape the Tenderloin by getting clean, finding work, and moving out. Others descend further into self-destructive behavior and die. Those who remain must adapt to the Tenderloin.

Counter-Masculinities

Counter-masculinities—developed in response to hegemonic masculinity—are coping mechanisms that provide Tenderloin men with a sense of self-worth.[10] A typology of counter-masculinities was found among three groups of Tenderloin men: heterosexual whites, heterosexual blacks and Latinos, and homosexual blacks and whites.

Heterosexual White Men: Urban Hermits

Heterosexual whites are the only men that do not identify with their own group. In the introduction to this book, Michael Kimmel writes that white men see themselves as "the generic person" because "the mechanisms that afford us privilege are very often invisible to us." To escape from the stigma of failure, the "urban hermit" structures identity around the value of self-sufficiency. Power is interpreted as individual achievement. Oscar, a fifty-year-old divorced heterosexual white man, describes a sense of failure:

> It's a difficult struggle. But you can't blame anybody but yourself. Because it is you yourself. Like with me. It's me myself that has the illness. Not the people of the government. Not the people of the different businesses. And things like that. It's me.[11]

Although receiving disability benefits, Oscar views himself as self-sufficient and criticizes blacks on welfare for lacking motivation. Men of color similarly criticize whites. Ned, a forty-year-old single heterosexual black man, says:

> I feel that most of them have given up. They don't really care or try. I try to respect all men. But it's difficult to understand why a white man would give up on himself given a society that is made for them.[12]

Virtually all heterosexual white men interpret their present hardship as the result of personal failure. Richard Sennett and Jonathan Cobb argue that the "code of respect" in American society demands that "a man should feel responsibility for his own social position—even if, in a class society, he believes men in general are deprived of the freedom to control their lives." Failure is defined according to cultural values in which a man is expected to have the desire and opportunity to work (Sennett and Cobb 1972: 36).

Urban hermits spend most of their time alone in hotel rooms. Many frequent bars and restaurants where they complain that criminals have "taken over" the area and demand that police "clean up the streets."[13] Unable to reconcile belief in white male superiority and life among the disenfranchised, most believe society is falling apart. Frank, a single heterosexual white man, describes whites:

> Their spirits are broken. They're outcasts of their families from all over the country. They're in disarray. They're drifting. Some of them never came back from Vietnam. Some of them are screwed up on drugs. It seems to me that America isn't like it used to be. When I grew up it was changing . . . it was breaking apart. My family broke apart, anyway. It was hard on me. They're outcasts from all over the country, and they gravitate here.[14]

Heterosexual white men experience a high level of cultural shock in moving to the Tenderloin.[15] A walk to the store is a challenge to their self-esteem. They confront black and Latino men who threaten their sense of racial superiority and gays who threaten their sexual identity. Oscar believes gays challenge divine law. He says:

> God decided he wanted a man to look like a man and a woman to look like a woman. It's not his fault if some men act like women and women act like men. It's the fault of the people themselves. The people can go without acting that way if they don't want to and they can act that way if they want to. It's up to them.[16]

Heterosexual whites are confused and angry because others appear to violate social norms.

Most retreat into isolation. A few imitate other men's behavior. Brad, a twenty-nine-year-old single, heterosexual white man, admires the "sense of family" among Latinos.[17] Many appreciate the nurturing qualities of gays. But other men criticize whites for not knowing themselves. Miguel, a divorced fifty-year-old heterosexual Latino man, says:

> The white man tries too hard to make friends. . . . If you're going to come in here and start trying to be black, they see that already. You're not! But here's a guy and he's trying to talk like us and be cool. It's a front. We know that. Hey, come on. I mean I've studied white folks before, and I know that's not the way white people are supposed to be.[18]

Wanting to belong, and forced to confront their prejudices, heterosexual whites discover that genuineness is vital. But it is difficult for them to adapt. Quinn, a fifty-four-year-old gay white man, says whites are aloof because: "White is right. White isn't going to be criticized. White isn't going to be stopped by police."[19]

The counter-masculinity of the urban hermit discloses an inability to cope with diversity of race, culture, and sexual orientation. As a coping mechanism, it resists the stigma of failure but undermines identity by organizing social relations around poles of independence and dependence. In the Tenderloin, interdependence is both a reality and a necessity. What heterosexual whites view as self-sufficiency, others view as arrogance. Because the urban hermit is seen as an outcast among outcasts, failure and alienation are not overcome through self-sufficiency.

Heterosexual Black and Latino Men: Cool Pose

Heterosexual blacks and Latinos dominate street life and display what Majors and Billson (1992) call "cool pose." Cool pose is a counter-masculinity that structures identity around the value of respect. Power is interpreted as group solidarity in a racist society. Blacks and Latinos establish social position by displaying aggressiveness or showing deference (Almaguer 1991: 80). Miguel claims the system of respect maintains harmony: "You don't have to trust someone. You just respect them." George uses a hypermasculine facade to obtain respect and to fend off predators. He says:

> One of the techniques you use—and this is a prison technique—is getting big. You work out hard. You carry yourself in an intimidating manner. Your body language says, "I'll kill you if you even think about approaching my space."

The mask of hypermasculinity establishes a man's position in his group.[20] Miguel describes putting on his mask:

> Whenever I walk, I look mean. I make my face look like I got an attitude. Like I just got ripped off. I don't look at the person. I look through them. I'm cutting him. And this guy's thinking, "Hmmm. Let me move out of the way." You could get busted. "Oh, you ain't that tough." But out there you gotta act that way.

"Getting busted" means that someone is able to see through a man's mask. Whites have difficulty distinguishing between actual threats and posturing by blacks and Latinos, and often feel threatened. But Jack, a heterosexual black man, explains that cool pose conceals a sense of failure among men of color living in a white-dominated society:

> The one thing I hear from white guys is, "You guys act like you're so proud." They don't realize why we're doing it. It's to survive amongst our own peers. We feel just as bad as he does. The white guy resents that; "How in the hell can he act like that and I'm white? I come from the superior race and I can't act like that. I feel dead." They come from two different worlds.[21]

Ned interprets cool pose in relation to a definition of masculinity that excludes black men in American society:

> A black man has to be tough out there on the street. The reason they have to be that way is that they don't have any other outlet for their manhood. They can't show their manhood by being a success economically because society simply will not give them a chance. I mean a black man is even lucky to have a full-time—or even a part-time—job. So he has to show his manhood by acting physically tough. Because mentally tough won't get him anywhere. But there has been no reason that white men have had to be physically tough because they've been able to show their manhood through their nine-to-five. Going to work every day. And making a living.

Cool pose is depicted as "a creative strategy devised by African-American males to counter the negative forces in their lives" (Majors and Billson 1992: 105). Yet, the counter-masculinity of cool pose does not allow heterosexual black and Latino men to escape from failure by structuring identity around the value of respect. While the coping mechanism of cool pose weakens the stigma of failure, it undermines identity by organizing social relations around poles of dominance and submission. What heterosexual men of color view as respect, others view as hostility. By adopting an identity based upon fear and violence, men of color in the Tenderloin in part contribute to their own alienation from other groups and society at large. They are further marginalized in an environment where different social groups demand to live in equality with one another.

Homosexual Black and White Men: Perfect Copy

Gays in the Tenderloin blur gender and sexual boundaries by constructing identity around performance of a series of roles. "Perfect copy" of hypermasculinity redefines and subverts masculinity (Butler 1990: 31). Klaus, a thirty-four-year-old gay white man, interprets his experience with heterosexual men in the Tenderloin:

They feel like their manhood or sexuality has been threatened because I'm more butch than they are. I am more of a man than a straight man can be around here. They're threatened. Not only to me but to themselves.[22]

Gays structure identity around the value of acceptance. Power is interpreted as inclusion of persons who challenge gender and sexual categories. Because identity is in flux, and gender and sexual identity are rendered uncertain, "homosexuality undermines masculinity" (Edwards 1990: 114). Larry, a thirty-three-year-old gay white man, says heterosexuals are simultaneously confused and intrigued by gays:

I think [they] are very jealous of gay men because we're so open and free with our feelings. We speak what we have to say. We don't hide our feelings. We cry at sad movies. Heterosexual men think that men don't cry. But if you go drinking with them, get them drunk or high, they're the first ones that throw their legs in the air or whip out their cocks in front of you and say, "Here. Suck this."[23]

Another gay man believes single heterosexuals are in a predicament because they normally rely on women to provide them with gender identity. Charles says:

Most men depend on women to define that role for them. So a man is what a woman defines him to be. So if you don't have a woman in your life to define you as a man, then you have to depend on all these macho apparatuses. Then you have to prove to other men that you are a man.

Transgenders pose a new challenge by further blurring gender and sexual boundaries. Thomas, a twenty-nine-year-old gay black man, says some men respond favorably:

It seems to be a turn-on. Especially if everything is in order—the appearance is almost perfect. Woman have a lot to do just getting dressed in the morning. Hair, makeup, clothing, shoes. Everything has to be just right. It's not like men. We can just put on a pair of jeans and a T-shirt. And out the door. I've noticed this especially with straight men. They seem to be really impressed.[24]

Identity is a series of roles that gays perfect in daily encounters. Transgenders further complicate identity when "some transgendered persons consider themselves heterosexual, while others consider themselves homosexual" (Koenig 1993: 10). The counter-masculinity of perfect copy challenges hegemonic masculinity through a multitude of replicated masculinities that blur sexual and gender boundaries. Performance of a series of roles creates security in a homophobic society by destabilizing and redefining social relations. But perfect copy of hypermasculine (or hyperfeminine) roles implies a reliance upon hegemonic masculine ideals. While the coping mechanism of perfect copy resists the stigma of failure, it undermines identity by organizing social relations around poles of performance and observation. Perfect copy contributes to further alienation of gays, because what they view as acceptance, others view as licentiousness.

Counter-masculinities are coping mechanisms that aid Tenderloin men in regaining a sense of self-worth while preventing them from overcoming alienation from other groups of men. For Tenderloin men, masculine identity develops around specific value systems in response to the social system of hegemonic masculinity and an immediately hostile environment (Tong 1971: 8). Paradoxically, counter-masculinities offer resistance to hegemonic masculinity while deepening social divisions. Since the contradictions of counter-masculinities stem from inequitable relations of power, what unites men as a group separates them as a community. The urban hermit devalues interdependence in favor of self-sufficiency; cool pose devalues equality in favor of dominance; and perfect copy devalues mutuality in favor of performance. A new value system constructed around shared power is required to unite Tenderloin men into a community.

Versatile Masculinity

Versatile masculinity is a unique masculine identity that emerges from everyday encounters of Tenderloin men as they collectively resolve the contradictions of counter-masculinities. Versatile masculinity allows men to identify with a transcendent set of values without destroying their group identity or value systems. This new set of values—while not distinctively masculine—is the basis of a masculine identity that binds Tenderloin men together in genuine community.

Versatile masculinity is not a fixed identity but a growing capacity for relating to difference.[25] As a fluid construction that sorts and combines practices, values, and attitudes in a strategic movement, it enables men to flourish in a diverse and dynamic environment. Most important, it is not a way of being but a way of becoming in relationships. David calls it being "flexible":

So many people [were] raised a certain way, and it stays with them. That's the only way they know. Instead of looking over the whole situation and see this and that. That's the way you have to live. Especially if you're living homeless on the streets. You have to be able to be flexible. Maybe this guy does things a different way. Maybe I can help him do this and he can help me do that. That's where you have to come in and learn it. That's what certain people call "streetwise." Streetwise people are just movable. They're just flexible.

Versatile masculinity does not undermine the different values of Tenderloin men but relates them to a transcendent set of values: honesty, caring, interdependence, and respect. H. Richard Niebuhr writes that ultimate value is not identifiable with a particular mode of being but "is present whenever being confronts being, wherever there is becoming in the midst of plural, interdependent, and interacting existences. It is not a function of being as such but of being in relation to being" (Niebuhr 1970: 106–7).

Similarly, versatile masculinity creates unity from diversity. Jack believes that acceptance of difference is essential to survival:

All people are equal. All things are relative. If you exterminate Jews, you exterminate me and you. . . . They're all of our cultures, are relative to keep us together. If I'm not afraid to learn about your culture then I got something to learn. Something that is relative. If everybody was alike, we'd be in trouble. We'd be in real trouble.

As marginalized persons, Tenderloin men are innovative survivors who manifest "creative strategies for survival that then open up new possibilities for everyone" (Duberman 1993: 24). But their experience reveals that only after a man has reached bottom—after he is stripped of or denied access to a masculine identity that provides him with a sense of innate superiority—will he change. Quinn says:

You bottom out. And you go through the bottom of the barrel and you come up again. You learn a different type of survival skills. . . . But going from the bottom and coming through you run into criminals, junkies, crazies, and everything else. . . . It doesn't make you less of a person. Actually, it can make you a stronger person. And more sensitive.

Versatile masculinity includes three conditions: (1) A man must be stripped of or denied access to a hegemonic masculine identity; (2) a man must adopt a counter-masculinity to reconstruct his identity and resist hegemonic masculine values that stigmatize him as a failure; and (3) a man must experience a multiplicity of masculinities that compel him to develop an identity based on acceptance of difference. When these conditions exist, versatile masculinity drives men to overcome their differences and create a community based on the following values.

Honesty

For Tenderloin men, honesty means genuineness. It is a process of "coming to critical consciousness" (Hooks 1990: 191). Tenderloin men sometimes discard illusions that contribute to lack of self-esteem. Hank, a thirty-six-year-old divorced, heterosexual white man, says:

> I realized that the only way I was going to get clean and sober, and really become a disciple of Christ, was to clean up my act. To become truly honest. Beginning with admitting to myself that I was full of shit. That I was living a lie. Just a lie.[26]

Brad says:

> I feel like if you're genuine with people there's some recognition within them. Or they see something. I know it's happened to me when I just met somebody who is for real and I've been acting like a fool or not being true to myself. It kind of makes me go, "Oh!" and "Yeah!"

In the Tenderloin, because men use every imaginable act to hide from themselves and society, they can easily recognize genuineness. Quinn says: "An honest person is going to recognize another honest person and see a phony."

Caring

Many Tenderloin men have HIV/AIDS. Samuel, who is beginning to display symptoms, has given himself a final task before he dies. He says:

> I'm having a big struggle with a transvestite named Carol who rips me off every second she has a chance to. I keep going back to her. And I tell her, "You got me, girl. But you didn't really have to do that. If you wanted it, just ask me for it. I'll give it to you. And if not, then you can rip me off." She's turned out to be one of my best friends. It's all she's ever known in her life. She's always lived in the ghetto. This is my personal struggle. My personal fight is to just take that one person and make her realize that she doesn't have to keep two steps ahead of me in order to get what's mine. Because it's all materialistic. If what I have you need, you can have. All you have to do is just ask for it.

Poverty, ostracism, and illness have brought men together to provide and receive care from one another. Allan describes his life at one of the worst slum hotels in the Tenderloin:

> At the Victoria, people will come in who are very different from one another, and sit down and talk and joke with one another. I don't think you could say that those interactions are insincere, or [occur] simply because they're close together. They like each other. They've discovered that we're all human beings with the same needs and very interesting differences. It's an acknowledgment that they're worthwhile. The kinds of sharing of people who don't have a lot to give is striking.

The work of caring is rare among men in our society, because compassion is a value identified with women. For Tenderloin men, caring for one another is tremendously empowering.

Interdependence

Men forced to live at the bottom of society feel insignificant and powerless. A common phrase heard on the streets is "the small people." Masculinity is redefined as an identity based on interdependence. Thomas says:

> Here you kind of like take care of your own. You kind of have to take care of each other here just so everybody survives. If one person doesn't survive, there's a big effect on everybody.

Respect

The most important lesson that Tenderloin men learn is respect for the intrinsic worth of each person. Masculinity includes an identification with humanity rather than only with one's group. This process (especially for heterosexual whites) begins with a period of cultural shock. Eduardo, a thirty-three-year-old single, heterosexual Latino man, says new residents overcome fear when they "start standing in the soup lines and staying in hotels. You realize that the homeless are not unlike you or I. They're human. You become part of the community."[27] Larry—who once worked as a male prostitute in the

Tenderloin—believes faith overcomes barriers between people. He says:

> Mary Magdalene was a prostitute. There are many women and men in this city that are prostitutes. There's nothing wrong with that. They're human beings first. Their titles come afterward. We weren't born what we are today. We were born human beings first. Then we were educated and trained to become who we are. But before we are what we are, we're humans first. A lot of people have lost that track. Lost that faith. To see what the hell we were or where we came from.

George says we all are faced with a choice:

> Basically, they are human beings. The one thing that we have been given is the ability to make choices. That's what separates us from other animals. Outside forces may have an effect, and usually do have an effect, on the choices we have to make. But the fact is, we get to make those choices. So make those choices as a winner—not so much as a winner—but as a human being.

Summary

Tenderloin men construct new masculine identities to resist a sense of failure and to create a sense of belonging. Versatile masculinity develops from their need to safely coexist in a hostile environment, but it also provides a basis for shared power and love in relationships. The Tenderloin men who transform themselves from "failed men" into human beings display a capacity not merely to survive, but also to flourish in a context of adversity and diversity. This is aptly demonstrated by the tenants of a Tenderloin residential hotel—many of whom were once homeless and substance abusers—who have built a beautiful rooftop garden. A resident says it's "a little bit of magic in the Tenderloin." Another is happy to see "a new spirit in this neighborhood" (Maitland 1993). In the Ten-

derloin, a small space has gradually emerged where men are free to change.

not identity,
"time"

Notes

1. There are several noteworthy works that examine the lives of poor and working-class men. See Eugene V. Debs, *Walls and Bars* (Chicago: Charles H. Kerr and Company, 1973); George Orwell, *Down and Out in Paris and London* (New York: Berkeley Medallion, 1959); James Agee and Walker Evans, *Let Us Now Praise Famous Men* (Boston: Houghton Mifflin Company, 1939); Studs Terkel, *Hard Times: An Oral History of the Great Depression* (New York: Washington Square Press, 1970); Elliot Liebow, *Tally's Corner* (Boston: Little, Brown and Company, 1967); William Julius Wilson, *The Truly Disadvantaged: The Inner City, the Underclass, and Public Policy* (Chicago: University of Chicago Press, 1987); Lillian Rubin, *Worlds of Pain: Life in the Working-Class Family* (New York: Basic Books, 1976); Richard Sennet and Jonathan Cobb, *The Hidden Injuries of Class* (New York: Vintage Books, 1972).

2. Local newspapers regularly describe Tenderloin residents in derogatory terms. See "Cheap wine ban sought in Tenderloin," *San Francisco Chronicle*, 5 April 1989; "Group wants Tenderloin as family neighborhood," *San Francisco Chronicle*, 21 July 1992; "Community policing," *San Francisco Chronicle*, 20 November 1992.

3. Interview with George on 30 April 1993. All names are fictitious.

4. Interview with Allan on 22 June 1993.

5. Interview with David on 1 May 1993.

6. Interview with Peter, a recently married, forty-eight-year-old heterosexual white man, on 27 July 1993.

7. The term "predator" is commonly used to refer to persons (often drug users) who prey on the more vulnerable sectors of the Tenderloin neighborhood, such as the elderly, children, and tourists.

8. Interview with Samuel on 26 August 1993.

9. Interview with Charles on 28 July 1993.

10. Thomas J. Gershick and Adam S. Miller (1993: 5) similarly interpret masculinities of disabled men as

coping mechanisms that rely upon, reformulate, or reject the standard of hegemonic masculinity.

11. Interview with Oscar on 19 June 1993.

12. Interview with Ned on 26 July 1993.

13. Interviews with Oscar on 24 April and 19 June 1993.

14. Interview with Frank on 13 August 1993.

15. Bruno Bettelheim (1960: 120) reports that of Jews sent to Nazi concentration camps, middle-class German men experienced the greatest level of initial shock and were the least adaptable prisoners.

16. Interview with Oscar on 19 June 1993.

17. Interview with Brad on 28 July 1993.

18. Interview with Miguel on 23 July 1993.

19. Interview with Quinn on 29 July 1993.

20. Pleck (1987: 31) defines "hypermasculinity" as exaggerated, extreme masculine behavior.

21. Interview with Jack on 23 April 1993.

22. Interview with Klaus on 13 March 1993.

23. Interview with Larry on 16 July 1993.

24. Interview with Thomas on 28 August 1993.

25. Versatility is defined as "the faculty or character of turning or being able to turn readily to a new subject or occupation," or "many-sidedness." In *The Compact Edition of the Oxford English Dictionary* 1971, Oxford University Press.

26. Interview with Hank on 31 July 1993.

27. Interview with Eduardo on 14 May 1993.

References

Almaguer, Tomas. 1991. "Chicano Men: A Cartography of Homosexual Identity and Behavior." *Differences* 3(2).

Bernard, Jessie. 1995. "The Good-Provider Role." In Michael S. Kimmel and Michael A. Messner, eds., *Men's Lives*. New York: Macmillan.

Bettelheim, Bruno. 1960. *The Informed Heart: Autonomy in a Mass Age*. New York: The Free Press.

Butler, Judith. 1990. *Gender Trouble: Feminism and the Subversion of Identity*. New York: Routledge & Kegan Paul.

Connell, R. W. 1987. *Gender and Power*. Stanford, CA: Stanford University Press.

Duberman, Martin. 1993. "A Matter of Difference." *Nation*, 5 July.

Edwards, Tim. 1990. "Beyond Sex and Gender: Masculinity, Homosexuality and Social Theory." In Jeff Hearn and David Morgan, eds., *Men, Masculinities, and Social Theory*. London: Unwin Hyman.

Gershick, Thomas J., and Adam S. Miller. 1994. "Coming to Terms: Masculinity and Physical Disability." In M. Kimmel and M. Messner, eds., *Men's Lives*, 3rd edition. Boston: Allyn & Bacon.

Goffman, Erving. 1963. *Stigma: Notes on the Management of Spoiled Identity*. New York: Touchstone.

hooks, bell. 1990. "Feminism: A Transformational Politic." In Deborah L. Rhode, ed., *Theoretical Perspectives on Sexual Difference*. New Haven: Yale University Press.

Koenig, Karen. 1993. "Transgenders Unite to Fight for Justice and Recognition." *Tenderloin Times*, August.

Maitland, Zane. 1993. "Tenderloin Hotel Has a Rooftop Garden." *San Francisco Chronicle*, 23 July.

Majors, Richard, and Janet Mancini Billson. 1992. *Cool Pose: The Dilemmas of Black Manhood in America*. New York: Lexington Books.

Messner, Michael A. 1993. " 'Changing Men' and Feminist Politics in the United States." *Theory and Society*, August/September.

Niebuhr, H. Richard. 1970. *Radical Monotheism and Western Culture*. New York: Harper Torchbooks.

North of Market Planning Coalition (NOPC). 1992. *Final Report: Tenderloin 2000 Survey and Plan*. San Francisco: NOPC.

Pleck, Joseph H. 1987. "The Theory of Male Sex-Role Identity: Its Rise and Fall, 1936 to the Present." In Harry Brod, ed., *The Making of Masculinities: The New Men's Studies*. New York: Routledge & Kegan Paul.

Sennett, Richard, and Jonathan Cobb. 1972. *The Hidden Injuries of Class*. New York: Vintage Books.

Tong, Ben. 1971. "The Ghetto of the Mind: Notes on the Historical Psychology of Chinese America." *Amerasia Journal*, 1(3). November.

Wilson, William Julius. 1987. *The Truly Disadvantaged: The Inner City, the Underclass, and Public Policy*. Chicago: University of Chicago Press.

ARTICLE

Patti A. Giuffre

Christine L. Williams

Boundary Lines: Labeling Sexual Harassment in Restaurants

Sexual harassment occurs when submission to or rejection of sexual advances is a term of employment, is used as a basis for making employment decisions, or if the advances create a hostile or offensive work environment (Konrad and Gutek 1986). Sexual harassment can cover a range of behaviors, from leering to rape (Ellis, Barak, and Pinto 1991; Pryor 1987; Reilly et al. 1992; Schneider 1982). Researchers estimate that as many as 70 percent of employed women have experienced behaviors that may legally constitute sexual harassment (MacKinnon 1979; Powell 1986); however, a far lower percentage of women claim to have experienced sexual harassment. Paludi and Barickman write that "the great majority of women who are abused by behavior that fits legal definitions of sexual harassment—and who are traumatized by the experience—do not label what has happened to them 'sexual harassment'" (1992, 68).

Why do most women fail to label their experiences as sexual harassment? Part of the problem is that many still do not recognize that sexual harassment is an actionable offense. Sexual ha-

Reprinted from *Gender & Society*, Vol 8, pages 378–401. Reprinted with permission of Sage Publications, Inc.

rassment was first described in 1976 (MacKinnon 1979), but it was not until 1986 that the U.S. Supreme Court included sexual harassment in the category of gender discrimination, thereby making it illegal (Paludi and Barickman 1991); consequently, women may not yet identify their experiences as sexual harassment because a substantial degree of awareness about its illegality has yet to be developed.

Many victims of sexual harassment may also be reluctant to come forward with complaints, fearing that they will not be believed, or that their charges will not be taken seriously (Jensen and Gutek (1982). As the Anita Hill–Clarence Thomas hearings demonstrated, women who are victims of sexual harassment often become the accused when they bring charges against their assailant.

There is another issue at stake in explaining the gap between experiencing and labeling behaviors "sexual harassment": many men and women experience some sexual behaviors in the workplace as pleasurable. Research on sexual harassment suggests that men are more likely than women to enjoy sexual interactions at work (Gutek 1985; Konrad and Gutek 1986; Reilly et al. 1992), but even some women experience sexual overtures at work as pleasurable (Pringle 1988). This attitude may be especially strong in organizations that use and exploit the bodies and sexuality of the workers (Cockburn 1991). Workers in many jobs are hired on the basis of their attractiveness and solicitousness—including not only sex industry workers, but also service sector workers such as receptionists, airline attendants, and servers in trendy restaurants. According to Cockburn (1991), this sexual exploitation is not completely forced: many people find this dimension of their jobs appealing and reinforcing to their own sense of identity and pleasure; consequently, some men and women resist efforts to expunge all sexuality from their places of work.

This is not to claim that all sexual behavior in the workplace is acceptable, even to some people. The point is that it is difficult to label behavior as sexual harassment because it forces people to draw a line between illicit and "legitimate" forms of sexuality at work—a process fraught with ambiguity. Whether a particular interaction is identified as harassment will depend on the intention of the harasser and the interpretation of the interchange by the victim, and both of these perspectives will be highly influenced by workplace culture and the social context of the specific event.

This article examines how one group of employees—restaurant workers—distinguishes between sexual harassment and other forms of sexual interaction in the workplace. We conducted an in-depth interview study of waitpeople and found that complex double standards are often used in labeling behavior as sexual harassment: identical behaviors are labeled sexual harassment in some contexts and not others. Many respondents claimed that they *enjoyed* sexual interactions involving co-workers of the same race/ethnicity, sexual orientation, and class/status backgrounds. Those who were offended by such interactions nevertheless dismissed them as natural or inevitable parts of restaurant culture.[1] When the same behavior occurred in con-

texts that upset these hegemonic heterosexual norms—in particular, when the episode involved interactions between gay and heterosexual men, or men and women of different racial/ethnic backgrounds—people seemed willing to apply the label sexual harassment.

We argue that identifying behaviors that occur only in counterhegemonic contexts as sexual harassment can potentially obscure and legitimate more insidious forms of domination and exploitation. As Pringle points out, "Men control women through direct use of power, but also through definitions of pleasure—which is less likely to provoke resistance" (1988, 95). Most women, she writes, actively seek out what Rich (1980) termed "compulsory heterosexuality" and find pleasure in it. The fact that men and women may enjoy certain sexual interactions in the workplace does not mean they take place outside of oppressive social relationships, nor does it imply that these routine interactions have no negative consequences for women. We argue that the practice of labeling as "sexual harassment" only those behaviors that challenge the dominant definition of acceptable sexual activity maintains and supports men's institutionalized right of sexual access and power over women.

Methods

The occupation of waiting tables was selected to study the social definition of sexual harassment because many restaurants have a blatantly sexualized workplace culture (Cobble 1991; Paules 1991). According to a report published in a magazine that caters to restaurant owners, "Restaurants . . . are about as informal a workplace as there is, so much so as to actually encourage—or at the very least tolerate—sexual banter" (Anders 1993, 48). Unremitting sexual banter and innuendo, as well as physical jostling, create an environment of "compulsory jocularity" in many restaurants (Pringle 1988, 93). Sexual attractiveness and flirtation are often institutionalized parts of a waitperson's job description; consequently, individual employees are often forced to draw the line for themselves to distinguish legitimate and illegitimate expressions of sexuality, making this occupation an excellent context for examining how people determine what constitutes sexual harassment. In contrast, many more sexual behaviors may be labeled sexual harassment in less highly sexualized work environments.[2]

Eighteen in-depth interviews were conducted with male and female wait staff who work in restaurants in Austin, Texas. Respondents were selected from restaurants that employ equal proportions of men and women on their wait staffs. Overall, restaurant work is highly sex segregated: women make up about 82 percent of all waitpeople (U.S. Department of Labor 1989), and it is common for restaurants to be staffed only by either waitresses or waiters, with men predominating in the higher-priced restaurants (Cobble 1991; Hall 1993; Paules 1991). We decided to focus only on waitpeople who work in mixed-sex groups for two reasons. First, focusing on waitpeople working on integrated staffs enables us to examine sexual harassment between co-workers who occupy the same position in an organizational hierarchy. Co-worker sexual harassment is perhaps the most common form of sexual harassment (Pryor 1987; Schneider 1982); yet most case studies of sexual harassment have examined either unequal hierarchical relationships (e.g., boss–secretary harassment) or harassment in highly skewed gender groupings (e.g., women who work in nontraditional occupations) (Benson and Thomson 1982; Carothers and Crull 1984; Gruber and Bjorn 1982). This study is designed to investigate sexual harassment in unequal hierarchical relationships, as well as harassment between organizationally equal co-workers.

Second, equal proportions of men and women in an occupation implies a high degree of male–female interaction (Gutek 1985). Waitpeople are in constant contact with each other,

help each other when the restaurant is busy, and informally socialize during slack periods. In contrast, men and women have much more limited interactions in highly sex-segregated restaurants and indeed, in most work environments. The high degree of interaction among the wait staff provides ample opportunity for sexual harassment between men and women to occur and, concomitantly, less opportunity for same-sex sexual harassment to occur.

The sample was generated using "snowball" techniques and by going to area restaurants and asking waitpeople to volunteer for the study. The sample includes eight men and ten women. Four respondents are Latina/o, two African American, and twelve white. Four respondents are gay or lesbian; one is bisexual; thirteen are heterosexual. (The gay men and lesbians in the sample are all "out" at their respective restaurants.) Fourteen respondents are single; three are married; one is divorced. Respondents' ages range from 22 to 37.

Interviews lasted approximately one hour, and they were tape-recorded and transcribed for this analysis. All interviews were conducted by the first author, who has over eight years' experience waiting tables. Respondents were asked about their experiences working in restaurants; relationships with managers, customers, and other co-workers; and their personal experiences of sexual harassment. Because interviews were conducted in the fall of 1991, when the issue was prominent in the media because of the Hill–Thomas hearings, most respondents had thought a lot about this topic.

Findings

Respondents agreed that sexual banter is very common in the restaurant: staff members talk and joke about sex constantly. With only one exception, respondents described their restaurants as highly sexualized. This means that 17 of the 18 respondents said that sexual joking, touching, and fondling were common, everyday occurrences in their restaurants. For example, when asked if he or other waitpeople ever joke about sex, one waiter replied, "about 90 percent of [the jokes] are about sex." According to a waitress, "at work . . . [we're] used to patting and touching and hugging." Another waiter said, "I do not go through a shift without someone . . . pinching my nipples or poking me in the butt or grabbing my crotch. . . . It's just what we do at work."

These informal behaviors are tantamount to "doing heterosexuality," a process analogous to "doing gender" (West and Zimmerman 1987).[3] By engaging in these public flirtations and open discussions of sex, men and women reproduce the dominant cultural norms of heterosexuality and lend an air of legitimacy—if not inevitability—to heterosexual relationships. In other words, heterosexuality is normalized and naturalized through its ritualistic public display. Indeed, although most respondents described their workplace as highly sexualized, several dismissed the constant sexual innuendo and behaviors as "just joking," and nothing to get upset about. Several respondents claimed that this is simply "the way it is in the restaurant business," or "just the way men are."

With only one exception, the men and women interviewed maintained that they enjoyed this aspect of their work. Heterosexuality may be normative, and in these contexts, even compulsory, yet many men and women find pleasure in its expression. Many women—as well as men—actively reproduce hegemonic sexuality and apparently enjoy its ritual expression; however, in a few instances, sexual conduct was labeled as sexual harassment. Seven women and three men said they had experienced sexual harassment in restaurant work. Of these, two women and one man described two different experiences of sexual harassment, and two women described three experiences. Table 28.1 describes

the characteristics of each of the respondents and their experiences of sexual harassment.

We analyzed these 17 accounts of sexual harassment to find out what, if anything, these experiences shared in common. With the exception of two episodes (discussed later), the experiences that were labeled "sexual harassment" were not distinguished by any specific words or behaviors, nor were they distinguished by their degree of severity. Identical behaviors were considered acceptable if they were perpetrated by some people, but considered offensive if perpetrated by others. In other words, sexual behavior in the workplace was interpreted differently depending on the context of the interaction. In general, respondents labeled their experiences sexual harassment only if the offending behavior occurred in one of three social contexts: (1) if perpetrated by someone in a more powerful position, such as a manager; (2) if perpetrated by someone of a different race/ethnicity; or (3) if perpetrated by someone of a different sexual orientation.

Our findings do not imply that sexual harassment did not occur outside of these three contexts. Instead, they simply indicate that our respondents *labeled* behavior as "sexual harassment" when it occurred in these particular social contexts. We will discuss each of these contexts and speculate on the reasons why they were singled out by our respondents.

Powerful Position

In the restaurant, managers and owners are the highest in the hierarchy of workers. Generally, they are the only ones who can hire or fire waitpeople. Three of the women and one of the men interviewed said they had been sexually harassed by their restaurants' managers or owners. In addition, several others who did not personally experience harassment said they had witnessed managers or owners sexually harassing other waitpeople. This finding is consistent with

TABLE 28.1	Description of Respondents and Their Reported Experiences of Sexual Harassment at Work

Pseudonym	Age	Race[a]	SO[b]	MS[c]	Years in Restaurant[d]	Sexualized Environment[e]	Sexually Harassed[f]
Kate	23	W	H	S	1	yes	yes (1)
Beth	26	W	H	S	5	yes	yes (1)
Ann	29	W	H	S	1★	yes	yes (2)
Cathy	29	W	H	S	8 mos.★	yes	yes (3)
Carla	22	W	H	M	5 mos.★	yes	yes (3)
Diana	32	L	H	M	6	no	no
Maxine	30	L	H	M	4	yes	no
Laura	27	W	B	S	2★	yes	yes (1)
Brenda	23	W	L	S	3	yes	yes (2)
Lynn	37	B	L	D	5★	yes	no
Jake	22	W	H	S	1	yes	yes (1)
Al	23	W	H	S	3	yes	no
Frank	29	W	H	S	8	yes	yes (1)
John	31	W	H	S	2	yes	no
Trent	23	W	G	S	1★	yes	no
Rick	24	B	H	S	1.5	yes	yes (2)
David	25	L	H	S	5	yes	no
Don	24	L	G	S	1★	yes	no

a. Race: B = Black, L = Latina/o, W = White.

b. SO = sexual orientation: B = bisexual, G = gay, H = heterosexual, L = lesbian.

c. MS = marital status: D = divorced, M = married, S = single.

d. Years in restaurant refers to length of time employed in current restaurant. An asterisk indicates that respondent has worked in other restaurants.

e. Whether or not the respondent claimed sexual banter and touching were common occurrences in their restaurant.

f. Responded yes or no to the question: "Have you ever been sexually harassed in the restaurant?" Number in parentheses refers to number of incidents described in the interview.

---

other research indicating people are more likely to think that sexual harassment has occurred when the perpetrator is in a more powerful position (e.g., Ellis et al. 1991).

Carla describes being sexually harassed by her manager:

> One evening, [my manager] grabbed my body, not in a private place, just grabbed my body, period. He gave me like a bear hug from behind a

total of four times in one night. By the end of the night I was livid. I was trying to avoid him. Then when he'd do it, I'd just ignore the conversation or the joke or whatever and walk away.

She claimed that her co-workers often give each other massages and joke about sex, but she did not label any of their behaviors sexual harassment. In fact, all four individuals who experienced sexual harassment from their managers described very similar types of behavior from their co-workers, which they did not define as sexual harassment. For example, Cathy said that she and the other waitpeople talk and joke about sex constantly: "Everybody stands around and talks about sex a lot.... Isn't that weird? You know, it's something about working in restaurants and, yeah, so we'll all sit around and talk about sex." She said that talking with her co-worker about sex does not constitute sexual harassment because it is "only joking." She does, however, view her male manager as a sexual harasser:

> My employer is very sexist. I would call that sexual harassment. Very much of a male chauvinist pig. He kind of started [saying] stuff like, "You can't really wear those shorts because they're not flattering to your figure. . . . But I like the way you wear those jeans. They look real good. They're tight." It's like, you know [I want to say to him], "You're the owner, you're in power. That's evident. You know, you need to find a better way to tell me these things." We've gotten to a point now where we'll joke around now, but it's never ever sexual, ever. I won't allow that with him.

Cathy acknowledges that her manager may legitimately dictate her appearance at work, but only if he does so in professional—and not personal—terms. She wants him "to find a better way to tell me these things," implying that he is not completely out-of-line in suggesting that she wear tight pants. He "crosses the line" when he personalizes his directive, by saying to Cathy "*I like* the way you wear those jeans." This is offensive to Cathy because it is framed as the manager's personal prerogative, not the institutional requirements of the job.

Ann described a similar experience of sexual harassment from a restaurant owner:

> Yeah, there's been a couple of times when a manager has made me feel real uncomfortable and I just removed myself from the situation. . . . Like if there's something I really want him to hear or something I think is re-

ally important there's no touching. Like, "Don't touch me while I'm talking to you." You know, because I take that as very patronizing. I actually blew up at one of the owners once because I was having a rough day and he came up behind me and he was rubbing my back, like up and down my back and saying, you know, "Oh, is Ann having a bad day?" or something like that and I shook him off of me and I said, "You do not need to touch me to talk to me."

Ann distinguishes between legitimate and illegitimate touching: if the issue being discussed is "really important"—that is, involving her job status—she insists there be no touching. In these specific situations, a back rub is interpreted as patronizing and offensive because the manager is using his powerful position for his *personal* sexual enjoyment.

One of the men in the sample, Frank, also experienced sexual harassment from a manager.

> I was in the bathroom and [the manager] came up next to me and my tennis shoes were spray-painted silver so he knew it was me in there and he said something about, "Oh, what do you have in your hand there?" I was on the other side of a wall and he said, "Mind if I hold it for a while?" or something like that, you know. I just pretended like I didn't hear it.

Frank also described various sexual behaviors among the waitstaff, including fondling, "joking about bodily functions," and "making bikinis out of tortillas." He said, "I mean, it's like, what we do at work. . . . There's no holds barred. I don't find it offensive. I'm used to it by now. I'm guilty of it myself." Evidently, he defines sexual behaviors as "sexual harassment" only when perpetrated by someone in a position of power over him.[4]

Two of the women in the sample also described sexual harassment from customers. We place these experiences in the category of "powerful position" because customers do have limited economic power over the waitperson insofar as they control the tip (Crull 1987). Cathy said that male customers often ask her to "sit on my lap" and provide them with other sexual favors. Brenda, a lesbian, described a similar experience of sexual harassment from women customers:

> One time I had this table of lesbians and they were being real vulgar towards me. Real sexual. This woman kind of tripped me as I was walking by and said, "Hurry back." I mean, gay people can tell when other people are gay. I felt harassed.

In these examples of harassment by customers, the line is drawn using a similar logic as in the examples of harassment by managers. These customers acted as though the waitresses were providing table service to satisfy the customers' private desires, instead of working to fulfill their job descriptions. In other words, the customers' demands were couched in personal—and not professional—terms, making the waitresses feel sexually harassed.

It is not difficult to understand why wait-people singled out sexual behaviors from managers, owners, and customers as sexual harassment. Subjection to sexual advances by someone with economic power comes closest to the quid pro quo form of sexual harassment, wherein employees are given the option to either "put out or get out." Studies have found that this type of sexual harassment is viewed as the most threatening and unambiguous sort (Ellis et al. 1991; Fitzgerald 1990; Gruber and Bjorn 1982).

But even in this context, lines are drawn between legitimate and illegitimate sexual behavior in the workplace. As Cathy's comments make clear, some people accept the employers' prerogative to exploit the workers' sexuality, by dictating appropriate "sexy" dress, for example. Like airline attendants, waitresses are expected to be friendly, helpful, and sexually available to the male customers (Cobble 1991). Because this expectation is embedded in restaurant culture, it becomes difficult for workers to separate sexual harassment from the more or less accepted forms of sexual exploitation that are routine features of their jobs. Consequently, some women are reluctant to label blatantly offensive behaviors as sexual harassment. For example, Maxine, who claims that she has never experienced sexual harassment, said that customers often "talk dirty" to her:

> I remember one day, about four or five years ago when I was working as a cocktail waitress, this guy asked me for a "Slow Comfortable Screw" [the name of a drink]. I didn't know what it was. I didn't know if he was making a move or something. I just looked at him. He said, "You know what it is, right?" I said, "I bet the bartender knows!" (laughs). . . . There's another one, "Sex on the Beach." And there's another one called a "Screaming Orgasm." Do you believe that?

Maxine is subject to a sexualized work environment that she finds offensive; hence her experience could fit the legal definition of sexual harassment. But because sexy drink names are an institutionalized part of restaurant culture, Maxine neither complains about it nor labels it sexual harassment: Once it becomes clear that a "Slow Comfortable Screw" is a legitimate and recognized restaurant demand, she accepts it (albeit reluctantly) as part of her job description. In other words, the fact that the offensive behavior is institutionalized seems to make it beyond reproach in her eyes. This finding is consistent with others' findings that those who work in highly sexualized environments may be less likely to label offensive behavior "sexual harassment" (Gutek 1985; Konrad and Gutek 1986).

Only in specific contexts do workers appear to define offensive words and acts of a sexual nature as sexual harassment—even when initiated by someone in a more powerful position. The interviews suggest that workers use this label to describe their experiences only when their bosses or their customers couch their requests for sexual attentions in explicitly personal terms.

This way of defining sexual harassment may obscure and legitimize more institutionalized—and hence more insidious—forms of sexual exploitation at work.

Race/Ethnicity

The restaurants in our sample, like most restaurants in the United States, have racially segregated staffs (Howe 1977). In the restaurants where our respondents are employed, men of color are concentrated in two positions: the kitchen cooks and bus personnel (formerly called busboys). Five of the white women in the sample reported experiencing sexual harassment from Latino men who worked in these positions. For example, when asked if she had ever experienced sexual harassment, Beth said:

> Yes, but it was not with the people . . . it was not, you know, the people that I work with in the front of the house. It was with the kitchen. There are boundaries or lines that I draw with the people I work with. In the kitchen, the lines are quite different. Plus, it's a Mexican staff. It's a very different attitude. They tend to want to touch you more and, at times, I can put up with a little bit of it but . . . because I will give them a hard time too but I won't touch them. I won't touch their butt or anything like that.
>
> [Interviewer: So sometimes they cross the line?]
>
> It's only happened to me a couple of times. One guy, like, patted me on the butt and I went off. I lost my shit. I went off on him. I said, "No. Bad. Wrong. I can't speak Spanish to you but, you know, this is it." I told the kitchen manager who is a guy and he's not . . . the head kitchen manager is not Hispanic. . . . I've had to do that over the years only a couple of times with those guys.

Beth reported that the waitpeople joke about sex and touch each other constantly, but she does not consider their behavior sexual harassment. Like many of the other men and women in the sample, Beth said she feels comfortable engaging

in this sexual banter and play with the other waitpeople (who were predominantly white), but not with the Mexican men in the kitchen.

Part of the reason for singling out the behaviors of the cooks as sexual harassment may involve status differences between waitpeople and cooks. Studies have suggested that people may label behaviors as sexual harassment when they are perpetrated by people in lower status organizational positions (Grauerholz 1989; McKinney 1990); however, it is difficult to generalize about the relative status of cooks and waitpeople because of the varied and often complex organizational hierarchies of restaurants (Paules 1991, 107–10). If the cook is a chef, as in higher-priced restaurants, he or she may actually have more status than waitpeople, and indeed may have the formal power to hire and fire the waitstaff. In the restaurants where our respondents worked, the kitchen cooks did not wield this sort of formal control, but they could exert some informal power over the waitstaff by slowing down food orders or making the orders look and/or taste bad. Because bad food can decrease the waitperson's tip, the cooks can thereby control the waitperson's income; hence servers are forced to negotiate and to some extent placate the wishes and desires of cooks to perform their jobs. The willingness of several respondents to label the cooks' behavior as sexual harassment may reflect their perception that the cooks' informal demands had become unreasonable. In such cases, subjection to the offensive behaviors is a term of employment, which is quid pro quo sexual harassment. As mentioned previously, this type of sexual harassment is the most likely to be so labeled and identified.

Because each recounted case of sexual harassment occurring between individuals of different occupational statuses involved a minority man sexually harassing a white woman, the racial context seems equally important. For example, Ann also said that she and the other waiters and waitresses joke about sex and touch each other "on the butt" all the time, and when asked if she had ever experienced sexual harassment, she said,

> I had some problems at [a previous restaurant] but it was a communication problem. A lot of the guys in the kitchen did not speak English. They would see the waiters hugging on us, kissing us and pinching our rears and stuff. They would try to do it and I couldn't tell them, "No. You don't understand this. It's like we do it because we have a mutual understanding but I'm not comfortable with you doing it." So that was really hard and a lot of times what I'd have to do is just sucker punch them in the chest and just use a lot of cuss words and they knew that I was serious. And there again, I felt real weird about that because they're just doing what they see go on everyday.

Kate, Carla, and Brenda described very similar racial double standards. Kate complained about a Mexican busser who constantly touched her:

> This is not somebody that I talk to on a friendly basis. We don't sit there and laugh and joke and stuff. So, when he touches me, all I know is he is just touching me and there is no context about it. With other people, if they said something or they touched me, it would be funny or . . . we have a relationship. This person and I and all the other people do not. So that is sexual harassment.

And according to Brenda:

> The kitchen can be kind of sexist. They really make me angry. They're not as bad as they used to be because they got warned. They're mostly Mexican, not even Mexican-American. Most of them, they're just starting to learn English.
>
> [Interviewer: What do they do to you?]
>
> Well, I speak Spanish, so I know. They're not as sexual to me because I think they know I don't like it. Some of the other girls will come through and they will touch them like here [points to the lower part of her waist]. . . . I've had some pretty bad arguments with the kitchen.

> [Interviewer: Would you call that sexual harassment?]
>
> Yes. I think some of the girls just don't know better to say something. I think it happens a lot with the kitchen guys. Like sometimes, they will take a relleno in their hands like it's a penis. Sick!

Each of these women identified the sexual advances of the minority men in their restaurants as sexual harassment, but not the identical behaviors of their white male co-workers; moreover, they all recognize that they draw boundary lines differently for Anglo men and Mexican men: each of them willingly participates in "doing heterosexuality" only in racially homogamous contexts. These women called the behavior of the Mexican cooks "sexual harassment" in part because they did not "have a relationship" with these men, nor was it conceivable to them that they *could* have a relationship with them, given cultural and language barriers—and, probably, racist attitudes as well. The white men, on the other hand, can "hug, kiss, and pinch rears" of the white women because they have a "mutual understanding"—implying reciprocity and the possibility of intimacy.

The importance of this perception of relationship potential in the assessment of sexual harassment is especially clear in the cases of the two married women in the sample, Diana and Maxine. Both of these women said that they had never experienced sexual harassment. Diana, who works in a family-owned and -operated restaurant, claimed that her restaurant is not a sexualized work environment. Although people occasionally make double entendre jokes relating to sex, according to Diana, "there's no contact whatsoever like someone pinching your butt or something." She said that she has never experienced sexual harassment:

> Everybody here knows I'm married so they're not going to get fresh with me because they know that it's not going to go anywhere, you know so . . . and vice versa. You know, we know the guys' wives. They come in here to eat. It's

respect all the way. I don't think they could handle it if they saw us going around hugging them. You know what I mean? It's not right.

Similarly, Maxine, who is Colombian, said she avoids the problem of sexual harassment in her workplace because she is married:

> The cooks don't offend me because they know I speak Spanish and they know how to talk with me because I set my boundaries and they know that. . . . I just don't joke with them more than I should. They all know that I'm married, first of all, so that's a no-no for all of them. My brother used to be a manager in that restaurant so he probably took care of everything. I never had any problems anyway in any other jobs because, like I said, I set my boundaries. I don't let them get too close to me.
>
> [Interviewer: You mean physically?]
>
> Not physically only. Just talking. If they want to talk about, "Do you go dancing? Where do you go dancing?" Like I just change the subject because it's none of their business and I don't really care to talk about that with them . . . not because I consider them to be on the lower levels than me or something but just because if you start talking with them that way then you are just giving them hope or something. I think that's true for most of the guys here, not just talking about the cooks. . . . I do get offended and they know that so sometimes they apologize.

Both Maxine and Diana said that they are protected from sexual harassment because they are married. In effect, they use their marital status to negotiate their interactions with their co-workers and to ward off unwanted sexual advances. Furthermore, because they do not view their co-workers as potential relationship "interests," they conscientiously refuse to participate in any sexual banter in the restaurant.

The fact that both women speak Spanish fluently may mean that they can communicate their boundaries unambiguously to those who only speak Spanish (unlike the female respondents in the sample who only speak English).

For these two women, sexual harassment from co-workers is not an issue. Diana, who is Latina, talks about "respect all around" in her restaurant; Maxine claims the cooks (who are Mexican) aren't the ones who offend her. Their comments seem to reflect more mutual respect and humanity toward their Latino co-workers than the comments of the white waitresses. On the other hand, at least from Maxine's vantage point, racial harassment is a bigger problem in her workplace than is sexual harassment. When asked if she ever felt excluded from any groups at work, she said:

> Yeah, sometimes. How can I explain this? Sometimes, I mean, I don't know if they do it on purpose or they don't but they joke around you about being Spanish. . . . Sometimes it hurts. Like they say, "What are you doing here? Why don't you go back home?"

Racial harassment—like sexual harassment—is a means used by a dominant group to maintain its dominance over a subordinated group. Maxine feels that, because she is married, she is protected from sexual harassment (although, as we have seen, she is subject to a sexualized workplace that is offensive to her); however, she does experience racial harassment where she works, and she feels vulnerable to this because she is one of very few nonwhites working at her restaurant.

One of the waiters in the sample claimed that he had experienced sexual harassment from female co-workers, and race may have also been a factor in this situation. When Rick (who is African American) was asked if he had ever been sexually harassed, he recounted his experiences with some white waitresses:

> Yes. There are a couple of girls there, waitpeople, who will pinch my rear.
>
> [Interviewer: Do you find it offensive?]
>
> No (laughs) because I'm male. . . . But it is a form of sexual harassment.
>
> [Interviewer: Do you ever tell them to stop?]

> If I'm really busy, if I'm in the weeds, and they want to touch me, I'll get mad. I'll tell them to stop. There's a certain time and place for everything.

Rick is reluctant about labeling this interaction "sexual harassment" because "it doesn't bother me unless I'm, like, busy or something like that." In those cases where he is busy, he feels that his female co-workers are subverting his work by pinching him. Because of the race difference, he may experience their behaviors as an expression of racial dominance, which probably influences his willingness to label the behavior as sexual harassment.

In sum, the interviews suggest that the perception and labeling of interactions as "sexual harassment" may be influenced by the racial context of the interaction. If the victim perceives the harasser as expressing a potentially reciprocal relationship interest, they may be less likely to label their experience sexual harassment. In cases where the harasser and victim have a different race/ethnicity and class background, the possibility of a relationship may be precluded because of racism, making these cases more likely to be labeled "sexual harassment."

This finding suggests that the practices associated with "doing heterosexuality" are profoundly racist. The white women in the sample showed a great reluctance to label unwanted sexual behavior sexual harassment when it was perpetrated by a potential (or real) relationship interest—that is, a white male co-worker. In contrast, minority men are socially constructed as potential harassers of white women: any expression of sexual interest may be more readily perceived as nonreciprocal and unwanted. The assumption of racial homogamy in heterosexual relationships thus may protect white men from charges of sexual harassment of white women. This would help to explain why so many white women in the sample labeled behaviors perpetrated by Mexican men as sexual harassment, but not the identical behaviors perpetrated by white men.

Sexual Orientation

There has been very little research on sexual harassment that addresses the sexual orientation of the harasser and victim (exceptions include Reilly et al. 1992; Schneider 1982, 1984). Surveys of sexual harassment typically include questions about marital status but not about sexual orientation (e.g., Fain and Anderton 1987; Gruber and Bjorn 1982; Powell 1986). In this study, sexual orientation was an important part of heterosexual men's perceptions of sexual harassment. Of the four episodes of sexual harassment reported by the men in the study, three involved openly gay men sexually harassing straight men. One case involved a male manager harassing a male waiter (Frank's experience, described earlier). The other two cases involved co-workers. Jake said that he had been sexually harassed by a waiter:

> Someone has come on to me that I didn't want to come on to me. . . . He was another waiter [male]. It was laughs and jokes the whole way until things got a little too much and it was like, "Hey, this is how it is. Back off. Keep your hands off my ass." . . . Once it reached the point where I felt kind of threatened and bothered by it.

Rick described being sexually harassed by a gay baker in his restaurant:

> There was a baker that we had who was really, really gay. . . . He was very straightforward and blunt. He would tell you, in detail, his sexual experiences and tell you that he wanted to do them with you. . . . I knew he was kidding but he was serious. I mean, if he had a chance he would do these things.

In each of these cases, the men expressed some confusion about the intentions of their harassers—"I knew he was kidding but he was serious." Their inability to read the intentions of the gay men provoked them to label these episodes sexual harassment. Each man did not perceive the sexual interchange as reciprocal, nor did he view the harasser as a potential relationship interest. Interestingly, however, all three of the men who described harassment from gay men claimed that sexual banter and play with other *straight* men did not trouble them. Jake, for example, said that "when men get together, they talk sex," regardless of whether there are women around. He acceded, "people find me offensive, as a matter of fact," because he gets "pretty raunchy" talking and joking about sex. Only when this talk was initiated by a gay man did Jake label it as sexual harassment.

Johnson (1988) argues that talking and joking about sex is a common means of establishing intimacy among heterosexual men and maintaining a masculine identity. Homosexuality is perceived as a direct challenge and threat to the achievement of masculinity and consequently, "the male homosexual is derided by other males because he is not a real man, and in male logic if one is not a real man, one is a woman" (p. 124). In Johnson's view, this dynamic not only sustains masculine identity, it also shores up male dominance over women; thus, for some straight men, talking about sex with other straight men is a form of reasserting masculinity and male dominance, whereas talking about sex with gay men threatens the very basis for their masculine privilege. For this reason they may interpret the sex talk and conduct of gay men as a form of sexual harassment.

In certain restaurants, gay men may in fact intentionally hassle straight men as an explicit strategy to undermine their privileged position in society. For example, Trent (who is openly gay) realizes that heterosexual men are uncomfortable with his sexuality, and he intentionally draws attention to his sexuality in order to bother them:

[Interviewer: Homosexuality gets on whose nerves?]

The straight people's nerves. . . . I know also that we consciously push it just because, we know, "Okay. We know this is hard for you to get used to but tough luck. I've had my whole life trying to live in this straight world and if you don't like this, tough shit." I don't mean like we're shitty to them on purpose but it's

like, "I've had to worry about being accepted by straight people all my life. The shoe's on the other foot now. If you don't like it, sorry."

[Interviewer: Do you get along well with most of the waitpeople?]

I think I get along with straight women. I get along with gay men. I get along with gay women usually. If there's ever going to be a problem between me and somebody it will be between me and a straight man.

Trent's efforts to "push" his sexuality could easily be experienced as sexual harassment by straight men who have limited experience negotiating unwanted sexual advances. The three men who reported being sexually harassed by gay men seemed genuinely confused about the intentions of their harassers, and threatened by the possibility that they would actually be subjected to and harmed by unwanted sexual advances. But it is important to point out that Trent works in a restaurant owned by lesbians, which empowers him to confront his straight male co-workers. Not all restaurants provide the sort of atmosphere that makes this type of engagement possible; indeed, some restaurants have policies explicitly banning the hiring of gays and lesbians. Clearly, not all gay men would be able to push their sexuality without suffering severe retaliation (e.g., loss of job, physical attacks).

In contrast to the reports of the straight men in this study, none of the women interviewed reported sexual harassment from their gay or lesbian co-workers. Although Maxine was worried when she found out that one of her co-workers was lesbian, she claims that this fact no longer troubles her:

Six months ago I found out that there was a lesbian girl working there. It kind of freaked me out for a while. I was kind of aware of everything that she did towards me. I was conscious if she walked by me and accidently brushed up against me. She's cool. She doesn't bother me. She never touches my butt or anything like that. The gay guys do that to the [straight] guys but they know they're just kidding around. The [straight] guys do that to the [straight] girls, but they don't care. They know that they're not supposed to do that with me. If they do it, I stop and look at them and they apologize and they don't do it anymore. So they stay out of my way because I'm a meanie (laughs).

Some heterosexual women claimed they feel *more* comfortable working with gay men and lesbians. For example, Kate prefers working with gay men rather than heterosexual men or women. She claims that she often jokes about sex with her gay co-workers, yet she does not view them as potential harassers. Instead, she feels that her working conditions are more comfortable and more fun because she works with gay men. Similarly, Cathy prefers working with gay men over straight men because "gay men are a lot like women in that they're very sensitive to other people's space." Cathy also works with lesbians, and she claims that she has never felt sexually harassed by them.

The gays and lesbians in the study did not report any sexual harassment from their gay and lesbian co-workers. Laura, who is bisexual, said she preferred to work with gays and lesbians instead of heterosexuals because they are "more relaxed" about sex. Brenda said she feels comfortable working around all of her male and female colleagues—regardless of their sexual orientation:

The guys I work with [don't threaten me]. We always run by each other and pat each other on the butt. It's no big deal. Like with my girlfriend [who works at the same restaurant], all the cocktailers and hostesses love us. They don't care that we're gay. We're not a threat. We all kind of flirt but it's not sexual. A lesbian is not going to sexually harass another woman unless they're pretty gross anyway. It has nothing to do with their sexuality; it has to do with the person. You can't generalize and say that gays and lesbians are the best to work with or anything because it depends on the person.

Brenda enjoys flirtatious interactions with both men and women at her restaurant, but distinguishes these behaviors from sexual harassment. Likewise, Lynn, who is a lesbian, enjoys the relaxed sexual atmosphere at her workplace. When asked if she ever joked about sex in her workplace, she said:

Yes! (laughs) All the time! All the time—everybody has something that they want to talk about on sex and it's got to be funny. We have gays. We have lesbians. We have straights. We have people who are real Christian-oriented. But we all jump in there and we all talk about it. It gets real funny at times. . . . I've patted a few butts . . . and I've been patted back by men, and by the women, too! (laughs).

Don and Trent, who are both gay, also said that they had never been sexually harassed in their restaurants, even though both described their restaurants as highly sexualized.

In sum, our interviews suggest that sexual orientation is an important factor in understanding each individual's experience of sexual harassment and his or her willingness to label interactions as sexual harassment. In particular, straight men may perceive gay men as potential harassers. Three of our straight male respondents claimed to enjoy the sexual banter that commonly occurs among straight men, and between heterosexual men and women, but singled out the sexual advances of gay men as sexual harassment. Their contacts with gay men may be the only context where they feel vulnerable to unwanted sexual encounters. Their sense of not being in control of the situation may make them more willing to label these episodes sexual harassment.

Our findings about sexual orientation are less suggestive regarding women. None of the women (straight, lesbian, or bisexual) reported sexual harassment from other female co-workers or from gay men. In fact, all but one of the women's reported cases of sexual harassment involved a heterosexual man. One of the two lesbians in the sample (Brenda) did experience sexual harassment from a group of lesbian customers (described earlier), but she claimed that sexual orientation is *not* key to her defining the situation as harassment. Other studies have shown that lesbian and bisexual women are routinely subjected to sexual harassment in the workplace (Schneider 1982, 1984); however, more research is needed to elaborate the social contexts and the specific definitions of harassment among lesbians.

The Exceptions

Two cases of sexual harassment were related by respondents that do not fit in the categories we have thus far described. These were the only incidents of sexual harassment reported between co-workers of the same race: in both cases, the sexual harasser is a white man, and the victim, a white woman. Laura—who is bisexual—was sexually harassed at a previous restaurant by a cook:

> This guy was just constantly badgering me about going out with him. He like grabbed me and took me in the walk-in one time. It was a real big deal. He got fired over it too. . . . I was in the back doing something and he said, "I need to talk to you," and I said, "We have nothing to talk about." He like took me and threw me against the wall in the back. . . . I ran out and told the manager, "Oh my God. He just hit me," and he saw the expression on my face. The manager went back there . . . and then he got fired.

This episode of sexual harassment involved violence, unlike the other reported cases. The threat of violence was also present in the other exception, a case described by Carla. When asked if she had ever been sexually harassed, she said,

> I experienced two men, in wait jobs, that were vulgar or offensive and one was a cook and I think he was a rapist. He had the kind of attitude where he would rape a woman. I mean, that's the kind of attitude he had. He would say totally, totally inappropriate [sexual] things.

These were the only two recounted episodes of sexual harassment between "equal" co-workers

that involved white men and women, and both involved violence or the threat of violence.[5]

Schneider (1982, 1991) found the greatest degree of consensus about labeling behavior sexual harassment when that behavior involves violence. A victim of sexual harassment may be more likely to be believed when there is evidence of assault (a situation that is analogous to acquaintance rape). The assumption of reciprocity among homogamous couples may protect assailants with similar characteristics to their victims (e.g., class background, sexual orientation, race/ethnicity, age)—*unless* there is clear evidence of physical abuse. Defining only those incidents that involve violence as sexual harassment obscures—and perhaps even legitimizes—the more common occurrences that do not involve violence, making it all the more difficult to eradicate sexual harassment from the workplace.

Discussion and Conclusion

We have argued that sexual harassment is hard to identify, and thus difficult to eradicate from the workplace, in part because our hegemonic definition of sexuality defines certain contexts of sexual interaction as legitimate. The interviews with waitpeople in Austin, Texas, indicate that how people currently identify sexual harassment singles out only a narrow range of interactions, thus disguising and ignoring a good deal of sexual domination and exploitation that take place at work.

Most of the respondents in this study work in highly sexualized atmospheres where sexual banter and touching frequently occur. There are institutionalized policies and practices in the workplace that encourage—or at the very least tolerate—a continual display and performance of heterosexuality. Many people apparently accept this ritual display as being a normal or natural feature of their work; some even enjoy this behavior. In the in-depth interviews, respondents labeled such experiences as sexual harassment in only three contexts: when perpetrated by someone who took advantage of their powerful position for personal sexual gain; when the perpetrator was of a different race/ethnicity than the victim—typically a minority man harassing a white woman; and when the perpetrator was of a different sexual orientation than the victim—typically a gay man harassing a straight man. In only two cases did respondents label experiences involving co-workers of the same race and sexual orientation as sexual harassment—and both episodes involved violence or the threat of violence.

These findings are based on a very small sample in a unique working environment, and hence it is not clear whether they are generalizable to other work settings. In less sexualized working environments, individuals may be more likely to label all offensive sexual advances as sexual harassment, whereas in more highly sexualized environments (such as topless clubs or striptease bars), fewer sexual advances may be labeled sexual harassment. Our findings do suggest that researchers should pay closer attention to the interaction context of sexual harassment, taking into account not only gender but also the race, occupational status, and sexual orientation of the assailant and the victim.

Of course, it should not matter who is perpetrating the sexually harassing behavior: sexual harassment should not be tolerated under any circumstances. But if members of oppressed groups (racial/ethnic minority men and gay men) are selectively charged with sexual harassment, whereas members of the most privileged groups are exonerated and excused (except in cases where institutionalized power or violence are used), then the patriarchal order is left intact. This is very similar to the problem of rape prosecution: minority men are the most likely assailants to be arrested and prosecuted, particularly when they attack white women (LaFree 1989). Straight white men who sexually assault women

(in the context of marriage, dating, or even work) may escape prosecution because of hegemonic definitions of "acceptable" or "legitimate" sexual expression. Likewise, as we have witnessed in current debate on gays in the military, straight men's fears of sexual harassment justify the exclusion of gay men and lesbians, whereas sexual harassment perpetrated by straight men against both straight and lesbian women is tolerated and even endorsed by the military establishment, as in the Tailhook investigation. By singling out these contexts for the label "sexual harassment," only marginalized men will be prosecuted, and the existing power structure that guarantees privileged men's sexual access to women will remain intact.

Sexual interactions involving men and women of the same race and sexual orientation have a hegemonic status in our society, making sexual harassment difficult to identify and eradicate. Our interviews suggest that many men and women are active participants in the sexualized culture of the workplace, even though ample evidence indicates that women who work in these environments suffer negative repercussions to their careers because of it (Jaschik and Fretz 1991; Paludi and Barickman 1991; Reilly et al. 1992; Schneider 1982). This is how cultural hegemony works—by getting under our skins and defining what is and is not pleasurable to us, despite our material or emotional interests.

Our findings raise difficult issues about women's complicity with oppressive sexual relationships. Some women obviously experience pleasure and enjoyment from public forms of sexual engagement with men; clearly, many would resist any attempt to eradicate all sexuality from work—an impossible goal at any rate. Yet, it is also clear that the sexual "pleasure" many women seek out and enjoy at work is structured by patriarchal, racist, and heterosexist norms. Heterosexual, racially homogamous relationships are privileged in our society: they are institutionalized in organizational policies and job descriptions, embedded in ritualistic workplace practices, and accepted as legitimate, normal, or inevitable elements of workplace culture. This study suggests that only those sexual interactions that violate these policies, practices, and beliefs are resisted and condemned with the label "sexual harassment."

We have argued that this dominant social construction of pleasure protects the most privileged groups in society from charges of sexual harassment and may be used to oppress and exclude the least powerful groups. Currently, people seem to consider the gender, race, status, and sexual orientation of the assailant when deciding to label behaviors as sexual harassment. Unless we acknowledge the complex double standards people use in "drawing the line," then sexual domination and exploitation will undoubtedly remain the normative experience of women in the workforce.

Notes

1. It could be the case that those who find this behavior extremely offensive are likely to leave restaurant work. In other words, the sample is clearly biased in that it includes only those who are currently employed in a restaurant and presumably feel more comfortable with the level of sexualized behavior than those who have left restaurant work.

2. It is difficult, if not impossible, to specify which occupations are less highly sexualized than waiting tables. Most occupations probably are sexualized in one way or another; however, specific workplaces may be more or less sexualized in terms of institutionalized job descriptions and employee tolerance of sexual banter. For example, Pringle (1988) describes some offices as coolly professional—with minimal sexual joking and play—whereas others are characterized by "compulsory jocularity." Likewise, some restaurants may deemphasize sexual flirtation between waitpeople and

Authors' Note: We would like to thank Margaret Andersen, Dana Britton, Kirsten Dellinger, Ricardo Gonzalez, Elizabeth Grauerholz, Suzanne Harper, Beth Schneider, Tracey Steele, Teresa Sullivan, and an anonymous reviewer for their helpful comments and criticisms.

customers, and restrain informal interactions among the staff (one respondent in our sample worked at such a restaurant).

3. We thank Margaret Andersen for drawing our attention to this fruitful analogy.

4. It is also probably significant that this episode of harassment involved a gay man and a heterosexual man. This context of sexual harassment is discussed later in this article.

5. It is true that both cases involved cooks sexually harassing waitresses. We could have placed these cases in the "powerful position" category, but did not because in these particular instances, the cooks did not possess institutionalized power over the waitpeople. In other words, in these particular cases, the cook and waitress had equal organizational status in the restaurant.

References

Anders, K. T. 1993. Bad sex: Who's harassing whom in restaurants? *Restaurant Business*, 20 January, pp. 46–54.

Benson, Donna J., and Gregg E. Thomson, 1982. Sexual harassment on a university campus: The confluence of authority relations, sexual interest and gender stratification. *Social Problems* 29:236–51.

Carothers, Suzanne C., and Peggy Crull. 1984. Contrasting sexual harassment in female- and male-dominated occupations. In *My troubles are going to have trouble with me: Everyday trials and triumphs of women workers*, edited by K. B. Sacks and D. Remy. New Brunswick, NJ: Rutgers University Press.

Cobble, Dorothy Sue. 1991. *Dishing it out: Waitresses and their unions in the twentieth century*. Urbana: University of Illinois Press.

Cockburn, Cynthia. 1991. *In the way of women*. Ithaca, NY: I.L.R. Press.

Crull, Peggy. 1987. Searching for the causes of sexual harassment: An examination of two prototypes. In *Hidden aspects of women's work*, edited by Christine Bose, Roslyn Feldberg, and Natalie Sokoloff. New York: Praeger.

Ellis, Shmuel, Azy Barak, and Adaya Pinto. 1991. Moderating effects of personal cognitions on experienced and perceived sexual harassment of women at the workplace. *Journal of Applied Social Psychology* 21:1320–37.

Fain, Terri C., and Douglas L. Anderton. 1987. Sexual harassment: Organizational context and diffuse status. *Sex Roles* 17:291–311.

Fitzgerald, Louise F. 1990. Sexual harassment: The definition and measurement of a construct. In *Ivory power: Sexual harassment on campus*, edited by Michele M. Paludi. Albany: State University of New York Press.

Grauerholz, Elizabeth. 1989. Sexual harassment of women professors by students: Exploring the dynamics of power, authority, and gender in a university setting. *Sex Roles* 21:789–801.

Gruber, James E., and Lars Bjorn. 1982. Blue-collar blues: The sexual harassment of women auto workers. *Work and Occupations* 9:271–98.

Gutek, Barbara A. 1985. *Sex and the workplace.* San Francisco: Jossey-Bass.

Hall, Elaine J. 1993. Waitering/waitressing: Engendering the work of table servers. *Gender & Society* 7:329–46.

Howe, Louise Kapp. 1977. *Pink collar workers: Inside the world of women's work.* New York: Avon.

Jaschik, Mollie L., and Bruce R. Fretz. 1991. Women's perceptions and labeling of sexual harassment. *Sex Roles* 25:19–23.

Jensen, Inger W., and Barbara A. Gutek. 1982. Attributions and assignment of responsibility in sexual harassment. *Journal of Social Issues* 38:122–36.

Johnson, Miriam. 1988. *Strong mothers, weak wives.* Berkeley: University of California Press.

Konrad, Alison M., and Barbara A. Gutek. 1986. Impact of work experiences on attitudes toward sexual harassment. *Administrative Science Quarterly* 31:422–38.

LaFree, Gary D. 1989. *Rape and criminal justice: The social construction of sexual assault.* Belmont, CA: Wadsworth.

MacKinnon, Catherine A. 1979. *Sexual harassment of working women: A case of sex discrimination.* New Haven, CT: Yale University Press.

McKinney, Kathleen. 1990. Sexual harassment of university faculty by colleagues and students. *Sex Roles* 23:421–38.

Paludi, Michele, and Richard B. Barickman. 1991. *Academic and workplace sexual harassment.* Albany: State University of New York Press.

Paules, Greta Foff. 1991. *Dishing it out: Power and resistance among waitresses in a New Jersey restaurant.* Philadelphia: Temple University Press.

Powell, Gary N. 1986. Effects of sex role identity and sex on definitions of sexual harassment. *Sex Roles* 14:9–19.

Pringle, Rosemary. 1988. *Secretaries talk: Sexuality, power and work.* London: Verso.

Pryor, John B. 1987. Sexual harassment proclivities in men. *Sex Roles* 17:269–90.

Reilly, Mary Ellen, Bernice Lott, Donna Caldwell, and Luisa DeLuca. 1992. Tolerance for sexual harassment related to self-reported sexual victimization. *Gender & Society* 6:122–38.

Rich, Adrienne. 1980. Compulsory heterosexuality and lesbian existence. *Signs* 5:631–60.

Schneider, Beth E. 1982. Consciousness about sexual harassment among heterosexual and lesbian women workers. *Journal of Social Issues* 38:75–98.

———. 1984. The office affair: Myth and reality for heterosexual and lesbian women workers. *Sociological Perspectives* 27:443–64.

———. 1991. Put up and shut up: Workplace sexual assaults. *Gender & Society* 5:533–48.

U.S. Department of Labor, Bureau of Labor Statistics. 1989, January. *Employment and earnings.* Washington, DC: Government Printing Office.

West, Candace, and Don H. Zimmerman. 1987. Doing gender. *Gender & Society* 1:125–51.

Why did the gap between male and female life expectancy increase from two years in 1900 to nearly eight years today? Why do men suffer heart attacks and ulcers at such a consistently higher rate than women do? Why are auto insurance rates so much higher for young males than for females of the same age? Are mentally and emotionally "healthy" males those who conform more closely to the dominant cultural prescriptions for masculinity, or is it the other way around?

The articles in this section examine the "embodiment" of masculinity, the ways in which men's mental and physical health expresses and reproduces the definitions of masculinity we have ingested in our society. Don Sabo offers a compassionate account of how men will invariably confront traditional stereotypes as they look for more nurturing roles. Ann Fausto-Sterling and Gloria Steinem poke holes

PART SIX

Men and Health: Body and Mind

in the dominant definitions of masculinity, especially the putative biological basis for gender expression. Ex-pro football star Lyle Alzado's anguished statement, before he died of brain cancer that he believed was caused by the use of anabolic steroids, underscores the seriousness of men treating their bodies as machines or weapons to be used to get a job done.

Alongside these dominant cultural conceptions of masculinity, there have always been masculinities that have been marginalized and subordinated. These can often provide models for resistance to the dominant model, as the articles by Richard Tewksbury, Robin D. G. Kelley, and Thomas J. Gershick and Adam Stephen Miller suggest.

South Boston, 1982. Copyright © 1982 Sage Sohier.

29

ARTICLE

Don Sabo

Masculinities and Men's Health: Moving Toward Post-Superman Era Prevention

My grandfather used to smile and say, "Find out where you're going to die and stay the hell away from there." Grandpa had never studied epidemiology (the study of variations in health and illness in society), but he understood that certain behaviors, attitudes, and cultural practices can put individuals at risk for accidents, illness, or death. This chapter presents an overview of men's health that proceeds from the basic assumption that aspects of traditional masculinity can be dangerous to men's health (Sabo & Gordon, 1995; Harrison, Chin, & Ficarrotto, 1992). First, I identify some gender differences in relation to morbidity (sickness) and mortality (death). Next, I examine how the risk for illness varies from one male group to another. I then discuss an array of men's health issues and a preventive strategy for enhancing men's health.

Gender Differences in Health and Illness

When British sociologist Ashley Montagu put forth the thesis in 1953 that women were bio-

Reprinted from *Nursing Care in the Community*, 2e, edited by J. Cookfair, St. Louis: Mosby-Year Book.

logically superior to men, he shook up the prevailing chauvinistic beliefs that men were stronger, smarter, and better than women. His argument was partly based on epidemiological data that show males are more vulnerable to mortality than females from before birth and throughout the life span.

Mortality

From the time of conception, men are more likely to succumb to prenatal and neonatal death than females. Men's chances of dying during the prenatal stage of development are about 12% greater than those of females and, during the neonatal (newborn) stage, 130% greater than those of females. A number of neonatal disorders are common to males but not females, such as bacterial infections, respiratory illness, digestive diseases, and some circulatory disorders of the aorta and pulmonary artery. Table 29.1 compares male and female infant mortality rates across historical time. Though the infant mortality rate decreases over time, the persistence of the higher rates for males than females suggests that biological factors may be operating. Data also show that males have higher mortality rates than fe-

| TABLE 29.1 | Infant mortality rate |

Year	Both Sexes	Males	Females
1940	47.0	52.5	41.3
1950	29.2	32.8	25.5
1960	26.0	29.3	22.6
1970	20.0	22.4	17.5
1980	12.6	13.9	11.2
1989	9.8	10.8	8.8

Note: Rates are for infant (under 1 year) deaths per 1,000 live births for all races.
Source: Adapted from *Monthly Vital Statistics Report,* Vol. 40, No. 8, Supplement 2, January 7, 1992, p. 41.

males in every age category, from "under one year" through "over 85" (National Center for Health Statistics, 1992). In fact, men are more likely to die in 9 out of the 10 leading causes of death in the United States. (See Table 29.2.)

Females have greater life expectancy than males in the United States, Canada, and postindustrial societies (Verbrugge and Wingard, 1987; Waldron, 1986). This fact suggests a female bio-

logical advantage, but a closer analysis of changing trends in the gap between women's and men's life expectancy indicates that social and cultural factors related to lifestyle, gender identity, and behavior are operating well. Life expectancy among American females is about 78.3 years but 71.3 years for males (National Center for Health Statistics, 1990). As Waldron's (1995) analysis of shifting mortality patterns between the sexes during the 20th century shows, however, women's relative advantage in life expectancy over men was rather small at the beginning of the 20th century. During the mid-20th century, female mortality declined more rapidly than male mortality, thereby increasing the gender gap in life expectancy. Whereas women benefited from decreased maternal mortality, the midcentury trend toward a lowering of men's life expectancy was slowed by increasing mortality from coronary heart disease and lung cancer that were, in turn, mainly due to higher rates of cigarette smoking among males.

The most recent trends show that differences between women's and men's mortality decreased during the 1980s; that is, female life expectancy was 7.9 years greater than that of

| TABLE 29.2 | Death rates by sex and 10 leading causes: 1989 |

	Age-Adjusted Death Rate per 100,000 Population			
Cause of Death	Total	Male	Female	Sex Differential
Diseases of the heart	155.9	210.2	112.3	1.87
Malignant neoplasms	133.0	163.4	111.7	1.45
Accidents and adverse effects	33.8	49.5	18.9	2.62
Cerebrovascular disease	28.0	30.4	26.2	1.16
Chronic liver disease, cirrhosis	8.9	12.8	5.5	2.33
Diabetes	11.5	2.0	11.0	1.09
Suicide	11.3	18.6	4.5	4.13
Homicide and legal intervention	9.4	14.7	4.1	3.59

Source: Adapted from the *U.S. Bureau of the Census: Statistical Abstracts of the United States: 1992* (112th ed., p. 84), Washington, DC.

males in 1979 and 6.9 years in 1989 (National Center for Health Statistics, 1992). Waldron explains that some changes in behavioral patterns between the sexes, such as increased smoking among women, have narrowed the gap between men's formerly higher mortality rates from lung cancer, chronic obstructive pulmonary disease, and ischemic heart disease. In summary, it appears that both biological and sociocultural factors are involved with shaping patterns of men's and women's mortality. In fact, Waldron (1976) suggests that gender-related behaviors rather than strictly biogenic factors account for about three-quarters of the variation in men's early mortality.

Morbidity

Whereas females generally outlive males, females report higher morbidity rates, even after controlling for maternity. National health surveys show that females experience acute illnesses such as respiratory conditions, infective and parasitic conditions, and digestive system disorders at higher rates than males do; however, males sustain more injuries (Givens, 1979; Cypress, 1981; Dawson & Adams, 1987). Men's higher injury rates are partly owed to gender differences in socialization and lifestyle, such as learning to prove manhood through recklessness, involvement in contact sports, and working in risky blue-collar occupations.

Females are generally more likely than males to experience chronic conditions such as anemia, chronic enteritis and colitis, migraine headaches, arthritis, diabetes, and thyroid disease. However, males are more prone to develop chronic illnesses such as coronary heart disease, emphysema, and gout. Although chronic conditions do not ordinarily cause death, they often limit activity or cause disability.

After noting gender differences in morbidity, Cockerham (1995) asks whether women really do experience more illness than men—or could it be that women are more sensitive to

bodily sensations than men, or that men are not as prone as women to report symptoms and seek medical care? He concludes, "The best evidence indicates that the overall differences in morbidity are real" and, further, that they are due to a mixture of biological, psychological, and social influences (p. 42).

Masculinities and Men's Health

There is no such thing as masculinity; there are only masculinities (Sabo & Gordon, 1995). A limitation of early gender theory was its treatment of "all men" as a single, large category in relation to "all women" (Connell, 1987). The fact is, however, that all men are not alike, nor do all male groups share the same stakes in the gender order. At any given historical moment, there are competing masculinities—some dominant, some marginalized, and some stigmatized—each with its respective structural, psychosocial, and cultural moorings. There are substantial differences between the health options of homeless men, working-class men, lower-class men, gay men, men with AIDS, prison inmates, men of color, and their comparatively advantaged middle- and upper-class, white, professional male counterparts. Similarly, a wide range of individual differences exists between the ways that men and women act out "femininity" and "masculinity" in their everyday lives. A health profile of several male groups is discussed below.

Adolescent Males

Pleck, Sonenstein, and Ku (1992) applied critical feminist perspectives to their research on problem behaviors and health among adolescent males. A national sampling of adolescent, never-married males aged 15–19 were interviewed in 1980 and 1988. Hypothesis tests were geared to assessing whether "masculine ideology" (which measured the presence of traditional male role attitudes) put boys at risk for an array of problem behaviors. The researchers found a significant, independent association with seven of ten problem behaviors. Specifically, traditionally masculine attitudes were associated with being suspended from school, drinking and use of street drugs, frequency of being picked up by the police, being sexually active, the number of heterosexual partners in the last year, and tricking or forcing someone to have sex. These kinds of behaviors, which are in part expressions of the pursuit of traditional masculinity, elevate boys' risk for sexually transmitted diseases, HIV transmission, and early death by accident or homicide. At the same time, however, these same behaviors can also encourage victimization of women through men's violence, sexual assault, unwanted teenage pregnancy, and sexually transmitted diseases.

Adolescence is a phase of accelerated physiological development, and good nutrition during this period is important to future health. Obesity puts adults at risk for a variety of diseases such as coronary heart disease, diabetes mellitus, joint disease, and certain cancers. Obese adolescents are also apt to become obese adults, thus elevating long-term risk for illness. National Health and Nutrition Examination Surveys show that obesity among adolescents increased by 6% during 1976–80 and 1988–91. During 1988–91, 22% of females of 12–18 years were overweight, and 20% of males in this age group were as well (*Morbidity and Mortality Weekly Report,* 1994a).

Males form a majority of the estimated 1.3 million teenagers who run away from home each year in the United States. For both boys and girls, living on the streets raises the risk of poor nutrition, homicide, alcoholism, drug abuse, and AIDS. Young adults in their 20s comprise about 20% of new AIDS cases and, when you calculate the lengthy latency period, it is evident that they are being infected in their teenage years. Runaways are also more likely to be victims of crime and sexual exploitation (Hull, 1994).

Clearly, adolescent males face a spectrum of potential health problems—some that threaten their present well-being, and others that could take their toll in the future.

Men of Color

Patterns of health and illness among men of color can be partly understood against the historical and social context of economic inequality. Generally, because African Americans, Hispanics, and Native Americans are disproportionately poor, they are more apt to work in low-paying and dangerous occupations, reside in polluted environments, be exposed to toxic substances, experience the threat and reality of crime, and worry about meeting basic needs. Cultural barriers can also complicate their access to available health care. Poverty is correlated with lower educational attainment, which, in turn, mitigates against adoption of preventive health behaviors.

The neglect of public health in the United States is particularly pronounced in relation to African Americans (Polych & Sabo, 1996). For example, in Harlem, where 96% of the inhabitants are African American and 41% live below the poverty line, the survival curve beyond the age of 40 for men is lower than that of men living in Bangladesh (McCord & Freeman, 1990). Even though African American men have higher rates of alcoholism, infectious diseases, and drug-related conditions, for example, they are less apt to receive health care, and when they do, they are more apt to receive inferior care (Bullard, 1992; Staples, 1995). Statistics like the following led Gibbs (1988) to describe young African American males as an "endangered species":

■   The number of young African American male homicide victims in 1977 (5,734) was higher than the number killed in the Vietnam War during 1963–72 (5,640) (Gibbs, 1988:258).

- Homicide is the leading cause of death among young African American males. The probability of a black male dying from homicide is about the same as that of a white male dying from an accident (Reed, 1991).

- More than 36% of urban African American males are drug and alcohol abusers (Staples, 1995).

- In 1993 the rate of contracting AIDS for African American males aged 13 and older was almost 5 times higher than the rate for white males (*Morbidity and Mortality Weekly Report,* 1994b).

The health profile of Native Americans and Native Canadians is also poor. For example, alcohol is the number-one killer of Native Americans between the ages of 14 and 44 (May, 1986), and 42% of Native American male adolescents are problem drinkers, compared to 34% of same-age white males (Lamarine, 1988). Native Americans (10–18 years of age) comprise 34% of in-patient admissions to adolescent detoxification programs (Moore, 1988). Compared to the "all race" population, Native American youth exhibit more serious problems in the areas of depression, suicide, anxiety, substance use, and general health status (Blum et al., 1992). The rates of morbidity, mortality from injury, and contracting AIDS are also higher (Sugarman et al., 1993; Metler, et al., 1991).

Like those of many other racial and ethnic groups, the health problems facing American and Canadian natives correlate with the effects of poverty and social marginalization, such as dropping out of school, a sense of hopelessness, the experience of prejudice, poor nutrition, and lack of regular health care. Those who care about men's health, therefore, need to be attuned to the potential interplay between gender, race/ethnicity, cultural differences, and economic conditions when working with racial and ethnic minorities.

Gay and Bisexual Men

Gay and bisexual men are estimated to constitute 5% to 10% of the male population. In the past, gay men have been viewed as evil, sinful, sick, emotionally immature, and socially undesirable. Many health professionals and the wider public have harbored mixed feelings and homophobic attitudes toward gay and bisexual men. Gay men's identity, their lifestyles, and the social responses to homosexuality can impact the health of gay and bisexual men. Stigmatization and marginalization, for example, may lead to emotional confusion and suicide among gay male adolescents. For gay and bisexual men who are "in the closet," anxiety and stress can tax emotional and physical health. When seeking medical services, gay and bisexual men must often cope with the homophobia of health care workers or deal with the threat of losing health care insurance if their sexual orientation is made known.

Whether they are straight or gay, men tend to have more sexual contacts than women do, which heightens men's risk for contracting sexually transmitted diseases (STDs). Men's sexual attitudes and behaviors are closely tied to the way masculinity has been socially constructed. For example, real men are taught to suppress their emotions, which can lead to a separation of sex from feeling. Traditionally, men are also encouraged to be daring, which can lead to risky sexual decisions. In addition, contrary to common myths about gay male effeminacy, masculinity also plays a powerful role in shaping gay and bisexual men's identity and behavior. To the extent that traditional masculinity informs sexual activity of men, masculinity can be a barrier to safer sexual behavior among men. This insight leads Kimmel and Levine (1989) to assert that "to educate men about safe sex, then, means to confront the issues of masculinity" (p. 352). In addition to practicing abstinence and safer sex as preventive strategies, therefore, they argue that traditional beliefs about masculinity be challenged as a form of risk reduction.

Men who have sex with men remain the largest risk group for HIV transmission. For gay and bisexual men who are infected by the HIV virus, the personal burden of living with an AIDS diagnosis is made heavier by the stigma associated with homosexuality. The cultural meanings associated with AIDS can also filter into gender and sexual identities. Tewksbury's (1995) interviews with 45 HIV positive gay men showed how masculinity, sexuality, stigmatization, and interpersonal commitment mesh in decision making related to risky sexual behavior. Most of the men practiced celibacy in order to prevent others from contracting the disease; others practiced safe sex, and a few went on having unprotected sex.

Prison Inmates

There are 1.3 million men imprisoned in American jails and prisons (Nadelmann & Wenner, 1994). The United States has the highest rate of incarceration of any nation in the world, 426 prisoners for every 100,000 people (American College of Physicians, 1992), followed by South Africa and the former Soviet Union (Mauer, 1992). Racial and ethnic minorities are overrepresented among those behind bars. Black and Hispanic males, for example, comprise 85% of prisoners in the New York State prison system (Green, 1991).

The prison system acts as a pocket of risk, within which men already at high risk of having a preexisting AIDS infection are exposed to conditions that further heighten the risk of contracting HIV (Toepell, 1992) or other infections such as tuberculosis (Bellin, Fletcher & Safyer, 1993) or hepatitis. The corrections system is part of an institutional chain that facilitates transmission of HIV and other infections in certain North American populations, particularly among poor, inner-city, minority males. Prisoners are burdened not only by social disadvantage but also by high rates of physical illness, mental disorder, and substance abuse that jeopardize their health (Editor, *Lancet,* 1991).

AIDS prevalence is markedly higher among state and federal inmates than in the general U.S. population, with a known aggregate rate in 1992 of 202 per 100,000 population (Brewer & Derrickson, 1992) compared to a total population prevalence of 14.65 in 100,000 (American College of Physicians, 1992). The cumulative total of American prisoners with AIDS in 1989 was estimated to be 5,411, a 72% increase over the previous year (Belbot & del Carmen, 1991). The total number of AIDS cases reported in U.S. corrections as of 1993 was 11,565 (a minimum estimate of the true cumulative incidence among U.S. inmates) (Hammett; cited in Expert Committee on AIDS and Prisons, 1994). In New York State, at least 10,000 of the state's 55,000 prisoners are believed to be infected (Prisoners with AIDS/HIV Support Action Network, 1992). In Canadian federal penitentiaries, it is believed that 1 in 20 inmates is HIV infected (Hankins; cited in Expert Committee on AIDS and Prison, 1994).

The HIV virus is primarily transmitted between adults by unprotected penetrative sex or by needle sharing, without bleaching, with an infected partner. Sexual contacts between prisoners occur mainly through consensual unions and secondarily through sexual assault and rape (Vaid; cited in Expert Committee on AIDS and Prisons, 1994). The amount of IV drug use behind prison walls is unknown, although it is known to be prevalent and the scarcity of needles often leads to sharing of needles and sharps (Prisoners with AIDS/HIV Support Action Network, 1992).

The failure to provide comprehensive health education and treatment interventions in prisons not only puts more inmates at risk for HIV infection, but also threatens the public at large. Prisons are not hermetically sealed enclaves set apart from the community, but an integral part of society (Editor, *Lancet,* 1991).

Prisoners regularly move in and out of the prison system. In 1989, prisons in the United States admitted 467,227 persons and discharged 386,228 (American College of Physicians, 1992). The average age of inmates admitted to prison in 1989 was 29.6, with 75% between 18 and 34 years; 94.3% were male. These former inmates return to their communities after having served an average of 18 months inside (Dubler & Sidel, 1989). Within three years, 62.5% will be rearrested and jailed. Recidivism is highest among poor black and Hispanic men. The extent to which the drug-related social practices and sexual activities of released or paroled inmates who are HIV positive are putting others at risk upon return to their communities is unresearched and unknown.

Male Athletes

Injury is everywhere in sport. It is evident in the lives and bodies of athletes who regularly experience bruises, torn ligaments, broken bones, aches, lacerations, muscle tears, and so forth. For example, about 300,000 football-related injuries per year require treatment in hospital emergency rooms (Miedzian, 1991). Critics of violent contact sports claim that athletes are paying too high a physical price for their participation. George D. Lundberg (1994), editor of the *Journal of the American Medical Association,* has called for a ban on boxing in the Olympics and in the U.S. military. His editorial entreaty, though based on clinical evidence for neurological harm from boxing, is also couched in a wider critique of the exploitative economics of the sport.

Injuries are basically unavoidable in sports, but, in traditional men's sports, there has been a tendency to glorify pain and injury, to inflict injury on others, and to sacrifice one's body in order to "win at all costs." The "no pain, no gain" philosophy, which is rooted in traditional cultural equations between masculinity and sports, can jeopardize the health of athletes who conform to its ethos (Sabo, 1994).

The connections between sport, masculinity, and health are evidence in Klein's (1993) study of how bodybuilders use anabolic steroids, overtrain, and engage in extreme dietary practices. He spent years as an ethnographic researcher in the muscled world of the bodybuilding subculture, where masculinity is equated to maximum muscularity and men's striving for bigness and physical strength hides emotional insecurity and low self-esteem.

A nationwide survey of American male high school seniors found that 6.6% used or had used anabolic steroids. About two-thirds of this group were athletes (Buckley et al., 1988). Anabolic steroid use has been linked to health risks such as liver disease, kidney problems, atrophy of the testicles, elevated risk of injury, and premature skeletal maturation.

Klein lays bare a tragic irony in American culture—the powerful male athlete, a symbol of strength and health, has often sacrificed his health in pursuit of ideal masculinity (Messner & Sabo, 1994).

Men's Health Issues

Advocates of men's health have identified a variety of issues that impact directly on men's lives. Some of these issues may concern you or men you care about.

Testicular Cancer

The epidemiological data on testicular cancer are sobering. Though relatively rare in the general population, it is the fourth most common cause of death among males of 15–35 years accounting for 14% of all cancer deaths for this age group. It is the most common form of cancer affecting males of 20–34 years. The incidence of testicular cancer is increasing, and about 6,100 new U.S. cases were diagnosed in 1991 (American Cancer Society, 1991). If detected early, the cure rate is high, whereas delayed diagnosis is life threatening. Regular testicular self-examination (TSE), therefore, is a potentially effective means for ensuring early detection and successful treatment. Regrettably, however, most physicians do not teach TSE techniques (Rudolf & Quinn, 1988).

Denial may influence men's perceptions of testicular cancer and TSE (Blesch, 1986). Studies show that most males are not aware of testicular cancer, and even among those who are aware, many are reluctant to examine their testicles as a preventive measure. Even when symptoms are recognized, men sometimes postpone seeking treatment. Moreover, men who are taught TSE are often initially receptive, but their practice of TSE decreases over time. Men's resistance to TSE has been linked to awkwardness about touching themselves, associating touching genitals with homosexuality or masturbation, or the idea that TSE is not a manly behavior. And finally, men's individual reluctance to discuss testicular cancer partly derives from the widespread cultural silence that envelops it. The penis is a cultural symbol of male power, authority, and sexual domination. Its symbolic efficacy in traditional, male-dominated gender relations, therefore, would be eroded or neutralized by the realities of testicular cancer.

Diseases of the Prostate

Middle-aged and elderly men are likely to develop medical problems with the prostate gland. Some men may experience benign prostatic hyperplasia, an enlargement of the prostate gland that is associated with symptoms such as dribbling after urination, frequent urination, or incontinence. Others may develop infections (prostatitis) or malignant prostatic hyperplasia (prostate cancer). Prostate cancer is the third leading cause of death from cancer in men, accounting for 15.7 deaths per 100,000 population in 1989. Prostate cancer is now more common than lung cancer (Martin, 1990). One in 10 men will develop this cancer by age 85, with African American males

showing a higher prevalence rate than whites (Greco & Blank, 1993).

Treatments for prostate problems depend on the specific diagnosis and may range from medication to radiation and surgery. As is the case with testicular cancer, survival from prostate cancer is enhanced by early detection. Raising men's awareness about the health risks associated with the prostate gland, therefore, may prevent unnecessary morbidity and mortality. Unfortunately, the more invasive surgical treatments for prostate cancer can produce incontinence and impotence, and there has been no systematic research on men's psychosocial reactions and adjustment to sexual dysfunction associated with treatments for prostate cancer.

Alcohol Abuse

Although social and medical problems stemming from alcohol abuse involve both sexes, males comprise the largest segment of alcohol abusers. Some researchers have begun exploring the connections between the influence of the traditional male role on alcohol abuse. Isenhart and Silversmith (1994) show how, in a variety of occupational contexts, expectations surrounding masculinity encourage heavy drinking while working or socializing during after-work or off-duty hours. Some predominantly male occupational groups, such as longshoremen (Hitz, 1973), salesmen (Cosper, 1979), and members of the military (Pursch, 1976), are known to engage in high rates of alcohol consumption. Mass media play a role in sensationalizing links between booze and male bravado. Postman, Nystrom, Strate, and Weingartner (1987) studied the thematic content of 40 beer commercials and identified a variety of stereotypical portrayals of the male role that were used to promote beer drinking: reward for a job well done; manly activities that feature strength, risk, and daring; male friendship and esprit de corps; romantic success with women. The researchers estimate that, between the ages of 2 and 18, children view about 100,000 beer commercials.

Findings from a Harvard School of Public Health (1994) survey of 17,600 students at 140 colleges found that 44% engaged in "binge drinking," defined as drinking five drinks in rapid succession for males and four drinks for females. Males were more apt to report binge drinking during the past two weeks than females; 50% and 39% respectively. Sixty percent of the males who binge three or more times in the past two weeks reported driving after drinking, compared to 49% of their female counterparts, thus increasing the risk for accident, injury, and death. Compared to non–binge drinkers, binge drinkers were seven times more likely to engage in unprotected sex, thus elevating the risk for unwanted pregnancy and sexually transmitted disease. Alcohol-related automobile accidents are the top cause of death among 16- to 24-year-olds, especially among males (Henderson & Anderson, 1989). For all males, the age-adjusted death rate from automobile accidents in 1991 was 26.2 per 100,000 for African American males and 24.2 per 100,000 for white males, 2.5 and 3.0 times higher than for white and African American females respectively (*Morbidity and Mortality Weekly Report,* 1994d). The number of automobile fatalities among male adolescents that results from a mixture of alcohol abuse and masculine daring is unknown.

Men and AIDS

Human immunodeficiency virus (HIV) infection became a leading cause of death among males in the 1980s. Among men aged 25–44 in 1990, HIV infection was the second leading cause of death, compared to the sixth leading cause of death among same-age women (*Morbidity and Mortality Weekly Report,* 1993a). Among reported cases of acquired immunodeficiency syndrome (AIDS) for adolescent and adult men in 1992, 60% were men who had sex with other men, 21% were intravenous drug users, 4%

were exposed through heterosexual sexual contact, 6% were men who had sex with men and injected drugs, and 1% were transfusion recipients. Among the cases of AIDS among adolescent and adult women in 1992, 45% were intravenous drug users, 39% were infected through heterosexual sexual contact, and 4% were transfusion recipients (*Morbidity and Mortality Weekly Report,* 1993a).

Because most AIDS cases have been among men who have sex with other men, perceptions of the epidemic and its victims have been tinctured by sexual attitudes. In North American cultures, the stigma associated with AIDS is fused with the stigma linked to homosexuality. Feelings about men with AIDS can be mixed and complicated by homophobia.

Thoughts and feelings about men with AIDS are also influenced by attitudes toward race, ethnicity, drug abuse, and social marginality. Centers for Disease Control data show, for example, that men of color aged 13 and older constituted 51% (45,039) of the 89,165 AIDS cases reported in 1993. Women of color made up 71% of the cases reported among females aged 13 and older (*Morbidity and Mortality Weekly Report,* 1994b). The high rate of AIDS among racial and ethnic minorities has kindled racial prejudices in some minds, and AIDS is sometimes seen as a "minority disease." Although African American or Hispanic males may be at greater risk of contracting HIV/AIDS, just as yellow fingers do not cause lung disease, it is not race or ethnicity that confers risk, but the behaviors they engage in and the social circumstances of their lives.

Perceptions of HIV/AIDS can also be influenced by attitudes toward poverty and poor people. HIV infection is linked to economic problems that include community disintegration, unemployment, homelessness, eroding urban tax bases, mental illness, substance abuse, and criminalization (Wallace, 1991). For example, males comprise the majority of homeless persons. Poverty and homelessness overlap with drug addiction, which, in turn, is linked to HIV infection. Of persons hospitalized with HIV in New York City, 9–18% have been found to be homeless (Torres et al., 1990). Of homeless men tested for HIV at a New York City shelter, 62% of those who took the test were seropositive (Ron & Rogers, 1989). Among runaway or homeless youth in New York City, 7% tested positive, and this rate rose to 15% among the 19- and 20-year-olds. Of homeless men in Baltimore, 85% admitted to substance use problems (Weinreb & Bassuk, 1990).

Suicide

The suicide rates for both African American and white males increased between 1970 and 1989, whereas female rates decreased. Indeed, males are more likely than females to commit suicide from middle childhood until old age (Stillion, 1985, 1995). Compared to females, males typically deploy more violent means of attempting suicide (e.g., guns or hanging rather than pills) and are more likely to complete the act. Men's selection of more violent methods to kill themselves is consistent with traditionally masculine behavior (Stillion, White, McDowell, & Edwards, 1989).

Canetto (1995) interviewed male survivors of suicide attempts in order to better understand sex differences in suicidal behavior. Although she recognizes that men's psychosocial reactions and adjustments to nonfatal suicide vary by race/ethnicity, socioeconomic status, and age, she also finds that gender identity is an important factor in men's experiences. Suicide data show that men attempt suicide less often than women but are more likely to die than women. Canetto indicates that men's comparative "success" rate points toward a tragic irony in that, consistent with gender stereotypes, men's failure even at suicide undercuts the cultural mandate that men are supposed to succeed at everything. A lack of embroilment in traditionally masculine expectations, she suggests, may actually increase the like-

lihood of surviving a suicide attempt for some men.

Elderly males in North America commit suicide significantly more often than elderly females. Whereas white women's lethal suicide rate peaks at age 50, white men age 60 and older have the highest rate of lethal suicide, even surpassing the rate for young males (Manton et al., 1987). Canetto (1992) argues that elderly men's higher suicide mortality is chiefly owed to gender differences in coping. She writes,

> older women may have more flexible and diverse ways of coping than older men. Compared to older men, older women may be more willing and capable of adopting different coping strategies—"passive" or "active," "connected" or "independent"—depending on the situation (p. 92).

She attributes men's limited coping abilities to gender socialization and development.

Erectile Disorders

Men often joke about their penises or tease one another about penis size and erectile potency ("not getting it up"). In contrast, they rarely discuss their concerns about impotence in a serious way. Men's silences in this regard are regrettable in that many men, both young and old, experience recurrent or periodic difficulties getting or maintaining an erection. Estimates of the number of American men with erectile disorders range from 10 million to 30 million (Krane, Goldstein, & Saenz de Tejada, 1989; National Institutes of Health, 1993). The Massachusetts Male Aging Study of the general population of noninstitutionalized, healthy American men between ages 40 and 70 years found that 52% reported minimal, moderate, or complete impotence (Feldman, et al., 1994). The prevalence of erectile disorders increased with age, and 9.6% of the men were afflicted by complete impotence.

During the 1960s and 1970s, erectile disorders were largely thought to stem from psychological problems such as depression, financial worries, or work-related stress. Masculine stereotypes about male sexual prowess, phallic power, or being in charge of lovemaking were also said to put too much pressure to perform on some males (Zilbergeld, 1993). In contrast, physiological explanations of erectile disorders and medical treatments have been increasingly emphasized since the 1980s. Today diagnosis and treatment of erectile disorders should combine psychological and medical assessment (Ackerman & Carey, 1995).

Men's Violence

Men's violence is a major public health problem. The traditional masculine stereotype calls on males to be aggressive and tough. Anger is a by-product of aggression and toughness and, ultimately, part of the inner terrain of traditional masculinity (Sabo, 1993). Images of angry young men are compelling vehicles used by some males to separate themselves from women and to measure their status in respect to other males. Men's anger and violence derive, in part, from sex inequality. Men use the threat or application of violence to maintain their political and economic advantage over women and lower-status men. Male socialization reflects and reinforces these larger patterns of domination.

Homicide is the second leading cause of death among 15- to 19-year-old males. Males aged 15–34 years made up almost half (49%, or 13,122) of homicide victims in the United States in 1991. The homicide rate for this age group increased by 50% from 1985 to 1991 (*Morbidity and Morality Weekly Report,* 1994c).

Women are especially victimized by men's anger and violence in the form of rape, date rape, wife beating, assault, sexual harassment on the job, and verbal harassment (Thorne-Finch, 1992). That the reality and potential of men's violence impact women's mental and physical health can be surely assumed. However, men's violence also exacts a toll on men themselves in the forms of fighting, gang clashes, hazing, gay-bashing, intentional infliction of injury, homicide, suicide, and organized warfare.

Summary

It is ironic that two of the best-known actors who portrayed Superman have met with disaster. George Reeves, who starred in the original black-and-white television show, committed suicide, and Christopher Reeves, who portrayed the "man of steel" in recent film versions, was paralyzed by an accident during a high-risk equestrian event. Perhaps one lesson to be learned here is that, behind the cultural facade of mythic masculinity, men are vulnerable. Indeed, as we have seen in this chapter, some of the cultural messages sewn into the cloak of masculinity can put men at risk for illness and early death. A sensible preventive health strategy for the 1990s calls upon men to critically evaluate the Superman legacy, that is, to challenge the negative aspects of traditional masculinity that endanger their health, while hanging on to the positive aspects of masculinity and men's lifestyles that heighten men's physical vitality.

The promotion of men's health also requires a sharper recognition that the sources of men's risks for many diseases do not strictly reside in men's psyches, gender identities, or the roles that they enact in daily life. Men's roles, routines, and relations with others are fixed in the historical and structural relations that constitute the larger gender order. As we have seen, not all men or male groups share the same access to social resources, educational attainment, and opportunity that, in turn, can influence their health options. Yes, men need to pursue personal change in order to enhance their health, but without changing the political, economic, and ideological structures of the gender order, the subjective gains and insights forged within individuals can easily erode and fade away. If men are going to pursue self-healing, therefore, they need to create an overall preventive strategy that at once seeks to change potentially harmful aspects of traditional masculinity and meets the health needs of lower-status men.

References

Ackerman, M. D., & Carey, P. C. (1995). *Journal of Counseling & Clinical Psychology, 63*(6), 862–876.

American Cancer Society (1991). Cancer Facts and Figures—1991. Atlanta, GA: American Cancer Society.

American College of Physicians. (1992). The crisis in correctional health care: The impact of the national drug control strategy on correctional health services. *Annals of Internal Medicine, 117*(1), 71–77.

Belbot, B. A., & del Carmen, R. B. (1991). AIDS in prison: Legal issues. *Crime and Delinquency, 31*(1), 135–153.

Bellin, E. Y., Fletcher, D. D., & Safyer, S. M. (1993). Association of tuberculosis infection with increased time in or admission to the New York City jail system. *Journal of the American Medical Association, 269*(17), 2228–2231.

Blesch, K. (1986). Health beliefs about testicular cancer and self-examination among professional men. *Oncology Nursing Forum, 13*(1), 29–33.

Blum, R., Harman, B., Harris, L., Bergeissen, L., & Restrick, M. (1992). American Indian–Alaska native youth health. *Journal of American Medical Association, 267*(12), 1637–1644.

Brewer, T. F., & Derrickson, J. (1992). AIDS in prison: A review of epidemiology and preventive policy. *AIDS, 6*(7), 623–628.

Buckley, W. E., Yesalis, C. E., Friedl, K. E., Anderson, W. A., Streit, A. L., & Wright, J. E. (1988). Estimated prevalence of anabolic steroid use among male high school seniors. *Journal of the American Medical Association, 260*(23), 3441–3446.

Bullard, R. D. (1992). Urban infrastructure: Social, environmental, and health risks to African-Americans. In B. J. Tidwell (Ed.), *The State of Black America* (pp. 183–196). New York: National Urban League.

Canetto, S. S. (1995). Men who survive a suicidal act: Successful coping or failed masculinity? In

D. Sabo & D. Gordon (Eds.), *Men's health and illness* (pp. 292–304). Newbury Park, CA: Sage.

Canetto, S. S. (1992). Gender and suicide in the elderly. *Suicide and Life-Threatening Behavior, 22*(1), 80–97.

Cockerham, W. C. (1995). *Medical sociology.* Englewood Cliffs, NJ: Prentice-Hall.

Connell, R. W. (1987). *Gender and power.* Stanford: Stanford University Press.

Cosper, R. (1979). Drinking as conformity: A critique of sociological literature on occupational differences in drinking. *Journal of Studies on Alcoholism, 40,* 868–891.

Cypress, B. (1981). Patients' reasons for visiting physicians: National ambulatory medical care survey, U.S. 1977–78. DHHS Publication No. (PHS) 82-1717, Series 13, No. 56. Hyattsville, MD: National Center for Health Statistics, December, 1981a.

Dawson, D. A., & Adams, P. F. (1987). Current estimates from the national health interview survey: U.S. 1986. Vital Health Statistics Series, Series 10, No. 164. DHHS Publication No. (PHS) 87-1592, Public Health Service. Washington, D.C: U.S. Government Printing Office.

Dubler, N. N., & Sidel, V. W. (1989). On research on HIV infection and AIDS in correctional institutions. *The Milbank Quarterly, 67*(1–2), 81–94.

Editor, (1991, March 16). Health care for prisoners: Implications of "Kalk's refusal." *Lancet, 337,* 647–648.

Expert Committee on AIDS and Prison. (1994). *HIV/AIDS in prisons: Summary report and recommendations to the Expert Committee on AIDS and Prisons* (Ministry of Supply and Services Canada Catalogue No. JS82-68/2-1994). Ottawa, Ontario, Canada: Correctional Service of Canada.

Feldman, H. A., Goldstein, I., Hatzichristou, D. G., Krane, R. J., & McKinlay, J. B. (1994). Impotence and its medical and psychosocial correlates: Results of the Massachusetts Male Aging Study. *Journal of Urology, 151,* 54–61.

Gibbs, J. T. (Ed.) (1988). *Young, black, and male in America: An endangered species.* Dover, MA: Auburn House.

Givens, J. (1979). Current estimates from the health interview survey: U.S. 1978. DHHS Publication No. (PHS) 80-1551, Series 10, No. 130.

Hyattsville, MD: Office of Health Research Statistics, November 1979.

Greco, K. E. & Blank, B. (1993). Prostate-specific antigen: The new early detection test for prostate cancer. *Nurse Practitioner, 18*(5), 30–38.

Green, A. P. (1991). Blacks unheard. *Update* (Winter), New York State Coalition for Criminal Justice, 6–7.

Harrison, J., Chin, J., & Ficarrotto, T. (1992). Warning: Masculinity may be dangerous to your health. In M. S. Kimmel & M. A. Messner (Eds.), *Men's lives* (pp. 271–285). New York: Macmillan.

Harvard School of Public Health. Study reported by Wechler, H., Davenport, A., Dowdall, G., Moeykens, B., & Castillo, S. (1994). Health and behavioral consequences of binge drinking in college: A national survey of students at 140 campuses. *Journal of the American Medical Association, 272*(21), 1672–1677.

Henderson, D. C., & Anderson, S. C. (1989). Adolescents and chemical dependency. *Social Work in Health Care, 14*(1), 87–105.

Hitz, D. (1973). Drunken sailors and others: Drinking problems in specific occupations. *Quarterly Journal of Studies on Alcohol, 34,* 496–505.

Hull, J. D. (1994, November 21). Running scared. *Time, 144*(2), 93–99.

Isenhart, C. E., & Silversmith, D. J. (1994). The influence of the traditional male role on alcohol abuse and the therapeutic process. *Journal of Men's Studies, 3*(2), 127–135.

Kimmel, M. S., and Levine, M. P. (1989). Men and AIDS. In M. S. Kimmel & M. A. Messner (Eds.), *Men's lives* (pp. 344–354) New York: Macmillan.

Klein, A. (1993). *Little big men: Bodybuilding subculture and gender construction.* Albany, NY: SUNY Press.

Krane, R. J., Goldstein, I., & Saentz de Tejjada, I. (1989). Impotence. *New England Journal of Medicine, 321,* 1648–1659.

Lamarine, R. (1988). Alcohol abuse among Native Americans. *Journal of Community Health, 13*(3), 143–153.

Lundberg, G. D. (1994, June 8). Let's stop boxing in the Olympics and the United States military. *Journal of the American Medical Association, 271*(22), 1990.

Manton, K. G., Blazer, D. G., & Woodbury, M. A. (1987). Suicide in middle age and later life: Sex and race specific life table and cohort analyses. *Journal of Gerontology, 42,* 219–227.

Martin, J. (1990). Male cancer awareness: Impact of an employee education program. *Oncology Nursing Forum, 17*(1), 59–64.

Mauer, M. (1992). Men in American prisons: Trends, causes, and issues. *Men's Studies Review, 9*(1), 10–12. A special issue on men in prison, edited by Don Sabo and Willie London.

May, P. (1986). Alcohol and drug misuse prevention programs for American Indians: Needs and opportunities. *Journal of Studies of Alcohol, 47*(3), 187–195.

McCord, C., & Freeman, H. P. (1990). Excess mortality in Harlem. *New England Journal of Medicine, 322*(22), 1606–1607.

Messner, M. A., and Sabo, D. (1994). *Sex, violence, and power in sports: Rethinking masculinity.* Freedom, CA: Crossing Press.

Metler, R., Conway, G. & Stehr-Green, J. (1991). AIDS surveillance among American Indians and Alaskan natives. *American Journal of Public Health, 81*(11), 1469–1471.

Miedzian, M. (1991). *Boys will be boys: Breaking the link between masculinity and violence.* New York: Doubleday.

Montagu, A. (1953). *The natural superiority of women.* New York: Macmillan.

Moore, D. (1988). Reducing alcohol and other drug use among Native American youth. *Alcohol Drug Abuse and Mental Health, 15*(6), 2–3.

Morbidity and Mortality Weekly Report. (1993a). Update: Mortality attributable to HIV infection/AIDS among persons aged 25–44 years—United States, 1990–91. *42*(25), 481–486.

Morbidity and Mortality Weekly Report. (1993b). Summary of notifiable diseases United States, 1992. *41*(55).

Morbidity and Mortality Weekly Report. (1994a). Prevalence of overweight among adolescents—United States, 1988–91. *43*(44), 818–819.

Morbidity and Mortality Weekly Report. (1994b). AIDS among racial/ethnic minorities—United States, 1993. *43*(35), 644–651.

Morbidity and Mortality Weekly Report. (1994c). Homicides among 15–19-year-old males—United States. *43*(40), 725–728.

Morbidity and Mortality Weekly Report. (1994d).

Deaths resulting from firearm- and motor-vehicle-related injuries—United States, 1968–1991. *43*(3), 37–42.

Nadelmann, P. & Wenner, L. (1994, May 5). Toward a sane national drug policy [Editorial]. *Rolling Stone,* 24–26.

National Center for Health Statistics. (1990). *Health, United States, 1989.* Hyattsville, MD: Public Health Service.

National Center for Health Statistics. (1992). Advance report of final mortality statistics, 1989. *Monthly Vital Statistics Report, 40* (Suppl. 2) (DHHS Publication No. [PHS] 92-1120).

National Institutes of Health. (1993). Consensus development panel on impotence. *Journal of the American Medical Association, 270,* 83–90.

Pleck, J., Sonenstein, F. L., & Ku, L. C. (1992). In R. Ketterlinus, & M. E. Lamb (Eds.), *Adolescent problem behaviors.* Hillsdale, NJ: Lawrence Erlbaum Associates.

Polych, C., & Sabo, D. (1996). Gender politics, pain, and illness: The AIDS epidemic in North American prisons. In D. Sabo & D. Gordon (Eds.), *Men's health and illness.* Newbury Park, CA: Sage, pp. 139–157.

Postman, N., Nystrom, C., Strate, L., & Weingartner, C. (1987). *Myths, men and beer: An analysis of beer commercials on broadcast television, 1987.* Falls Church, VA: Foundation for Traffic Safety.

Prisoners with AIDS/HIV Support Action Network. (1992). *HIV/AIDS in prison systems: A comprehensive strategy* (Brief to the Minister of Correctional Services and the Minister of Health). Toronto: Prisoners with AIDS/HIV Support Action Network.

Pursch, J. A. (1976). From quonset hut to naval hospital: The story of an alcoholism rehabilitation service. *Journal of Studies on Alcohol, 37,* 1655–1666.

Reed, W. L. (1991). Trends in homicide among African Americans. *Trotter Institute Review, 5,* 11–16.

Ron, A., & Rogers, D. E. (1989). AIDS in New York City: The role of intravenous drug users. *Bulletin of the New York Academy of Medicine, 65*(7), 787–800.

Rudolf, V., & Quinn, K. (1988). The practice of TSE among college men: Effectiveness of an educational program. *Oncology Nursing Forum, 15*(1), 45–48.

Sabo, D., & Gordon, D. (1995). *Men's health and illness: Gender, power, and the body.* Newbury Park, CA: Sage.

Sabo, D. (1994). The body politics of sports injury: Culture, power, and the pain principle. A paper presented at the annual meeting of the National Athletic Trainers Association, Dallas, TX, June 6, 1994.

Sabo, D. (1993). Understanding men. In Kimball, G. (Ed.) *Everything You Need to Know to Succeed after College.* Chico, CA: Equality Press, 71–93.

Staples, R. (1995). Health and illness among African-American Males. In D. Sabo and D. Gordon (Eds.), *Men's health and illness.* Newbury Park, CA: Sage, p. 121–138.

Stillion, J. (1985). *Death and the sexes: An examination of differential longevity, attitudes, behaviors, and coping skills.* New York: Hemisphere.

Stillion, J. (1995). Premature death among males: Rethinking links between masculinity and health. In D. Sabo & D. Gordon (Eds.), *Men's health and illness.* Newbury Park, CA: Sage, pp. 46–67.

Stillion, J., White, H., McDowell, E. E., & Edwards, P. (1989). Ageism and sexism in suicide attitudes. *Death Studies, 13,* 247–261.

Sugarman, J., Soderberg, R., Gordon, J., & Rivera, F. (1993). Racial misclassification of American Indians: Its effects on injury rates in Oregon, 1989–1990. *American Journal of Public Health, 83*(5), 681–684.

Tewksbury, (1995). Sexual adaptation among gay men with HIV. In D. Sabo & D. Gordon (Eds.), *Men's Health and Illness* (pp. 222–245). Newbury Park, CA: Sage.

Thorne-Finch, R. (1992). *Ending the silence: The origins and treatment of male violence against women.* Toronto: University of Toronto Press.

Toepell, A. R. (1992). *Prisoners and AIDS: AIDS education needs assessment.* Toronto: John Howard Society of Metropolitan Toronto.

Torres, R. A., Mani, S., Altholz, J., & Brickner, P. W. (1990). HIV infection among homeless men in a New York City shelter. *Archives of Internal Medicine, 150,* 2030–2036.

Verbrugge, L. M., & Wingard, D. L. (1987). Sex differentials in health and mortality. *Women's Health, 12,* 103–145.

Waldron, I. (1995). Contributions of changing gender differences in behavior and social roles to changing gender differences in mortality. In D. Sabo & D. Gordon (Eds.), *Men's health and illness,* Newbury Park, CA: Sage, pp. 22–45.

Waldron, I. (1986). What do we know about sex differences in mortality? *Population Bulletin of the U.N., No. 18-1985,* 59–76.

Waldron, I. (1976). Why do women live longer than men? *Journal of Human Stress, 2,* 1–13.

Wallace, R., (1991). Traveling waves of HIV infection on a low dimensional "sociogeographic" network. *Social Science Medicine, 32*(7), 847–852.

Weinreb, L. F., & Bassuk, E. L. (1990). Substance abuse: A growing problem among homeless families. *Family and Community Health, 13*(1), 55–64.

Zilbergeld, B. (1993). *The New Male Sexuality.* New York: Bantam.

30

ARTICLE

Richard Tewksbury

Sexual Adaptations Among Gay Men with HIV

The spread of HIV and AIDS has brought numerous cultural, political, and social changes. Although many of these changes have created modifications in the structure and institutions (i.e., medicine, education, religion, the family, the workplace) of our culture, there are perhaps no more serious consequences of this disease than those experienced by the individuals who live with HIV disease. However, present knowledge of the lives of these persons is incomplete and selective. For reasons of practicality and convenience, a majority of the social science research regarding HIV and its effects on gay men has been conducted in or near the major urban centers where the disease has taken its greatest numerical toll—New York, San Francisco, Los Angeles. There is, however, an emerging body of literature addressing the impacts of the epidemic in smaller cities (see Bell, 1991; Kelly et al., 1990; Ruefli, Yu, & Barton, 1992; Silvestre, 1992). This chapter adds to this broadening focus by addressing the experiences of HIV+ gay men in the Midwest.

Researchers have generated an ever-increasing amount of data about rates of HIV in-

fection, diagnosed cases of AIDS, and the sexual behaviors of high-risk groups (especially men who have sex with men). Qualitative research on homosexual and bisexual sexual behaviors in relation to HIV has been slower to emerge. Qualitative understandings—in-depth analyses of the experiential components of behavior, attitudes, and societal responses—are critical for transforming quantitative data and research findings into applied and meaningful conclusions (see Carey & Smith, 1992). Such an approach is referred to as a contextual understanding. Such understandings of the impacts of illness on afflicted men's lives have been one of the areas receiving the least attention from researchers. Researchers have established that other medical conditions such as cancer (Auchincloss, 1991; Beutel, 1988; Jenkins, 1988; Smith & Babaian, 1992) and heart disease (Gendel & Bonner, 1986) are known to introduce disruptions to sexual desire, functioning, and satisfaction. However, the ways these disruptions are experienced have largely remained a matter for rehabilitative therapists and those intimately involved with the terminally ill or seriously injured. Perhaps most importantly, Gendel and Bonner argue that attention to sexual concerns may sig-

Reprinted from *Men's Health and Illness* edited by Don Sabo. Reprinted by permission of Sage Publications, Inc.

nificantly assist patients in their overall recovery process.

Related to HIV disease, Parker and Carballo (1990) have called for increased contextual understandings to be generated by qualitative social science research related to (a) the social context of sexual conduct, (b) the documentation of sexual practices, and (c) the interpretation of behavioral changes. This chapter addresses all three of these needs. The emphasis in this work is not on identifying the specifics of the sex lives of HIV+ gay men. Instead, this chapter first explores the processes by which they retain, modify, or abandon their sexual lives (including sexual activity). Secondly, this work explores the way these men experience sex and sexuality, and looks at how those who have experienced changes in their sexual lives incorporate these changes into their lives.

Based on the results of in-depth interviews with 45 HIV+ gay men, this chapter will discuss the adaptational processes these men experience in adjusting to life with HIV disease. First, the relevant literature on the impact of HIV and other illnesses on men's sexuality is reviewed. This is followed by a brief description of the methods by which this research was carried out. After this the study's major findings are presented and interpreted, the processes of adaptation and experiential components of these adaptations are highlighted. Finally, some conclusions are drawn regarding the role of illness in the sexual lives of HIV+ gay men.

Review of the Literature

It is well-known that a key impact of HIV on sexual behavior is that gay and bisexual men are engaging in sex with somewhat fewer partners (Martin, 1987; Ruefli et al., 1992; Siegel & Raveis, 1993; Silvestre, 1992; Stall, Coates, & Hoff, 1988). However, the rates of unsafe sexual behaviors remain high, especially among young gay men (Gold, Skinner, & Ross, 1994; Hays,

Kegeles, & Coates, 1990; Stall et al., 1992). Recent concern, however, has focused on preventing relapses into high-risk sexual behavior (Adib, Joseph, Ostrow, Tal, & Schwartz, 1991; Ekstrand & Coates, 1990; Godfried et al., 1988; Kelly et al., 1991). Additionally, concerns about targeting prevention messages for specific categories of men, such as African American men (Peterson et al., 1992; Stevenson & Davis, 1994), incarcerated men (Baxter, 1991; Marcus, Amen, & Bibace, 1992), and men in substance abuse treatment (Paul, Stall, & Davis, 1993) have become increasingly prevalent. More specifically Gochros (1992), relying on 4 years of experience as a support group facilitator for HIV+ gay men, concludes that although HIV often interrupts gay men's sexual lives, sexual desires and activities are often revived following periods of abstinence (see also Gold, Skinner, & Ross, 1994; Meyer-Bahlburg et al., 1991). However, Gochros emphasizes that interruptions occur for numerous reasons. Identified as reasons why HIV+ gay men may cease sexual activities are physical factors, an absence of a willing sex partner, a lack of privacy in housing, perceived or actual loss of attractiveness, guilt regarding sexual orientation, depression, a lack of community support for continuing sexual activities, and the fear of infecting sexual partners (Gochros, 1992). Consequently, these factors, combined with the belief that the complex emotional and social dynamics can only be fully appreciated by someone who also has HIV disease, lead many HIV+ gay men to a preference for romantic relationships with other HIV+ men (Hoff, McKusick, Hilliard, & Coates, 1992).

The social science literature has largely (and implicitly) accepted that physical factors have been the primary reasons for HIV+ gay men (or all HIV+ persons) to terminate sexual activities (Weitz, 1991). However, some researchers have suggested that declining sexual functioning may be either a direct consequence of HIV or "mediated by the men's affective response to the AIDS epidemic and the preventive measures taken" (Meyer-Bahlburg et al., 1991, p. 23). Although physical problems may indeed be a reason for curtailing one's sexual activities, it is also necessary to consider issues of sexual interest and pleasure when examining HIV+ gay men's sexual activities (Meyer-Bahlburg et al., 1991) as well as interruptions that HIV and HIV status disclosure may have upon an individual's relationships. Early research regarding HIV's impact on sexual desire and functioning focused on case studies (Lippert, 1986; Nurnberg, Prudic, Fiori, & Freedman, 1984), with few recent investigations focusing on samples of HIV+ men (Hoff et al., 1992; Meyer-Bahlburg et al., 1991). Regardless of why some HIV+ men may reduce or abandon sexual activities, it is important to recognize that some researchers have found HIV+ men to have rates of sexual activities essentially similar to those of HIV− men (Gold et al., 1994; Meyer-Bahlburg et al., 1991).

Although some HIV+ gay men do maintain sexual interests and desires, many have concluded that it is easier and safer to discontinue sexual activities rather than significantly modify such behaviors (Weitz, 1991). As a consequence, many gay men actively, but unenthusiastically, choose to remain abstinent. For other gay men, it is not abstinence that is chosen, but instead curtailment of selected activities (Connell & Kippax, 1990). Not all persons informed of their HIV+ status alter their high-risk behaviors, however (Landis, Earp, & Koch, 1992; Osmond et al., 1988). Godfried et al. (1988) report that gay men are most likely to terminate participation in oral sex, not anal sex. Clearly, Devanter, Rogers, and Singer (1991) report that 2 weeks after being informed of their HIV+ status, nearly two thirds of a diverse sample had suspended unsafe sexual behaviors. However, Meyer-Bahlburg et al. (1991) and Gold et al. (1994) report HIV+ and HIV− gay men do not necessarily have significantly different rates of anal, oral, or other forms of sexual behaviors. Furthermore, even for those who desire to bring their sexual activities into line with safer sex guidelines, many persons (in-cluding gay men) do not possess sufficient knowledge to practice safer sex properly (Martin, 1990; Tewksbury & Whittier, 1992) or have significant difficulties controlling their sexual behaviors (Exner, Meyer-Bahlburg, & Ehrhardt, 1992; Pincu, 1989; Quadland & Shattls, 1987).

When sexual behavior is controlled, the losses of physical and emotional intimacy may lead to significant emotional distress. Therefore, the impact on HIV+ individuals can be seriously debilitating. Folkman, Chesney, Pollack, and Phillips (1992) suggest that those most likely to engage in unsafe sex are those for whom sex provides an important mechanism for coping with stress. Or, as Gold et al. (1994) found, HIV+ gay men's most common justification for engaging in unprotected anal intercourse is a perception of "having nothing to lose." Somewhat similarly, uninfected gay men may consciously elect to have unprotected intercourse based on perceptions of limits of risk of a partner's likelihood of infection, to show love (Levine & Siegel, 1992), or because they redefine their sexual acts' degree of risk (Offir, Fisher, Williams, & Fisher, 1993).

Sex, although often a central component to the lives of gay men, must be reviewed and reevaluated when one learns of his HIV infection. For some gay men, sex has traditionally been an important, self-affirming life component. This may mean that it is necessary to discover new ways for establishing self-esteem, whereas for others it may mean finding new ways of establishing friendships and intimate relationships. For other gay men, sex may stand as a primary mode of recreation; this may carry over to HIV+ gay men seeing unprotected sex as a form of "adventure and excitement" (Gold et al., 1994, p. 72). Men involved in relationships, both gay and straight, may encounter additional stresses of informing partners of their HIV status (Mays et al., 1993). Despite some men's temptation to withhold such information, the vast majority of HIV+ gay men do inform their primary sex partners of their status (Schnell et al., 1992). For those men who suc-

cumb to the temptation not to tell their partners, most such relationships terminate in short
order (Coates, Morin, & McKusick, 1987;
Schnell et al., 1992).

However, these research findings and conclusions still do not inform us of the way such
events are experienced. What do gay men feel
about curtailing their sexual activities? Is it possible to remain sexually active and not think about
one's HIV status? These are the types of questions that remain to be answered. This study examines the way these issues impact the context of
HIV+ gay men's lives.

Methods

The data in this analysis are drawn from a series
of in-depth, semi-structured interviews with 45
HIV+ gay men[1] conducted between 1991 and
1993. Interviewees are all volunteers who
learned of the project through one of two methods.[2] Community organizations in Ohio and
Kentucky, devoted either to providing services
to HIV+ persons or to public education, assisted
with recruitment. Organizations published announcements of the research project in newsletters, made announcements at meetings, and most
important, personally referred clients and contacts. Also, some interviewees were obtained
through a snowball technique. At the conclusion
of each interview a request was made to refer
others to the researcher; several networks of acquaintances were accessed in this manner.

The data in the present analysis are drawn
from a larger project of interviews with all va-
rieties of HIV+ persons. All interviews lasted
between 1.5 and 4 hours and focused on interviewees' (a) medical conditions, (b) social networks, (c) experiences with family, friends,
workplace, medical providers, and significant
others, and (d) personal social and psychological experiences with their disease.

All interviews were transcribed in full and
conceptually coded using a multiple reading

technique. Analysis follows the procedures of
grounded theory development (Glaser & Strauss,
1967).

The Sexual Adaptations of HIV+ Gay Men

The discussion that follows focuses on identified
patterns and commonalities of experiences across
gay-identified, HIV+ men ($N = 45$).[3] The sample includes both men with asymptomatic HIV
infection and those diagnosed with AIDS. The
analysis focuses on the experiences of individuals rather than on an aggregated interpretation of
data; a full understanding of changes in men's
perceived experiences necessitates a look at individuals and how they have or have not altered
their behavior over time (Joseph, Adib, Koopman, & Ostrow, 1990). Where different patterns
of experiences have been identified between
men diagnosed with AIDS and those who remain asymptomatic, these are noted.

The most striking finding to arise from this
examination of HIV+ gay men was the frequent
abandonment of sexual activities. One third
(31.1%) of respondents reported that they no
longer engaged in sex. This was more common
among gay men diagnosed with AIDS (45) than
among asymptomatic HIV+ gay men (20%).
For some men the loss of sexual relations represented a major loss in life satisfaction, although
for some this loss was seen as little more than an
expected consequence of disease or advancing
age. The important conclusion, though, is that
sexual behaviors and perspectives have changed.
Generally, changes in perceptions and values
were perceived as distressing and stress inducing.
This is well illustrated in the comments of Victor, a 40-year-old HIV+ man who said,

> So much of it is funny how much you take for
> granted in life, even the sexuality part. How
> much I've taken for granted! It's changed
> though. I can no longer take it for granted. If I'm

going to be with somebody it's not going to be like before, because it's simply not like before.

The majority (68.9%) of HIV+ gay men continued to be sexually active; this was especially true (80%) for men who are seropositive, but otherwise healthy. These men, though, have modified their behaviors leading them to perceive sexual interactions as less fulfilling than previously. Only 15% of the men diagnosed with AIDS reported not having significantly altered their sexual lives. Among the HIV+ asymptomatic gay men, only 20% reported no significant negative impacts to their sexual lives.

It is important here to recognize that these reports pertained specifically to these men's perceptions of their sexuality and sexual activities. This says nothing of how these men perceived impacts to their status as men (i.e., their masculinity). However, although data directly assessing gender identity impacts was not gathered, it is possible to interpret such impacts from the perspectives these men have offered. Throughout the discussion that follows, the impact of their illnesses on conceptions and constructions of masculinity (as mediated by direct impacts on sexuality) will be highlighted. Generally speaking, when illness affects an HIV+ gay man's gender identity it is in a manner that leads him to question his masculinity and often to modify or reconstruct core elements of that identity.

Losing or Abandoning One's Sexual Life

In the eyes of HIV+ gay men who have experienced changes in their sexual lives, such changes were "inevitable." HIV disease, as well as many of the social consequences of the disease, could not have been averted, even though nearly all of these men yearned for some degree of control over their disease. The losses mounted in these men's lives, and the loss of sexual opportunities and activities only added to the distress of living with HIV disease. This was typically added to the stresses of watching friends, family, lovers,

and others become ill and lose their abilities, appearances, work, friends, and eventually their lives. Sexual losses, then, came in addition to numerous other inevitable psychological stresses.

Sex, often a central component to a man's self-esteem and definition of self, was likely to be forfeited or severely restricted for the good of both oneself and others. This, however, was almost never an easily made forfeiture. With few avenues available for establishing self-esteem—due to societal homophobia—oftentimes gay men sought their pathways to success within their own communities. One of the most easily accessed, and for some most desirable, ways to pursue success had been to pursue an elusive goal of physical attractiveness and accumulated sexual conquests. However, HIV infection quickly made both of these goals more difficult, if not impossible, to achieve.

As an impact on the individual's masculinity, a loss of control can be highly significant. Traditional constructions of masculinity have included an ability to control one's self and surroundings and demonstrable achievements of success. HIV+ gay men have lost significant measures of control. Success in physical attractiveness and sexual conquests have been forfeited or significantly reduced. Hence, two central measures of masculinity slipped out of HIV+ gay men's reach. Maintaining a strong sense of masculinity, then, became increasingly difficult. At the very least, alternate avenues had to be found for maintaining displays and self-affirmations of masculinity.

Sometimes sexual opportunities and activities were abandoned by choice and other times this was something foisted upon the individual, despite objections. Forced celibacy most frequently was initiated during a time period when health concerns and daily living matters demanded so much energy and attention that the absence of sexual activity went essentially unnoticed. It was typically only after recovering from a serious opportunistic infection or adjusting to a physical disability that a man realized his sexual opportunities had been sacrificed. Sex tended to be forfeited during a time of crisis, and often the consequences of the physical crisis left the individual physically debilitated or psychologically unwilling to risk either transmitting the virus or suffering personal rejection.

For those men who voluntarily and consciously chose to abandon their sexual lives, this choice came as a result of careful deliberations and concerns regarding the welfare of others. The decision to move beyond sexual acts (and presumably to a focus on intimacy rather than behavior) often developed only after attempts to manage a safer sex life. Oftentimes, however, such efforts proved frustrating and disappointing, therefore leading the man to opt for the truly safe route of no sex rather than the probably safe route of carefully restricted sex. This process was clear in the experiences of Charlie, a 44-year-old man who battled numerous opportunistic infections for nearly 3 years. In Charlie's eyes, the worst thing about having AIDS was "not having sex." As he explained, though,

> My choice at this point . . . is not to have sex. . . . Initially, in the very early stages, I certainly took the precautions that were appropriate and it ultimately just became a burden and I just decided that I didn't want to live that way. It was easier to do without and I continue that today. And I'm okay with that. . . . It's my choice, I understand that, but I'm a very sexual person.

Somewhat similar, yet different because he had not (yet) completely abandoned sexual activities, were the recounted experienced of self-described punk artist and AIDS activist, Jarvis. Rather than suggesting that his lack of sexual encounters was a conscious choice, Jarvis explained that his inability to find other, similarly situated (socially and healthwise) sex partners led to the cessation of his sex life.

> It really hasn't affected my libido, you know, I masturbate all the time. But yeah, it's a huge effect. I mean, occasionally I will have encoun-

ters with people that vaguely resemble sex without telling them of my health status. Usually like S & M scenes. . . . Casual sex, that's a big loss. . . . I do have encounters that somewhat resemble sex. It's very antiseptic encounters. But hopefully I'll be able to meet other people in my same boat, you know, someone else who's horny as hell! Then I can go back to having sex, I really miss it.

For Jarvis, Charlie, and other HIV+ gay men who once had active, satisfying sex lives, the loss of such outlets only added to the distress of their disease. Both of these men are examples of how HIV+ gay men had forgone a major element of self-constructed masculinity, the central element of sexuality. Their sense of masculinity had to be refocused; sexuality no longer provided a foundation on which to build a gender identity. However, sexuality remained a part of these men's lives, only in a different form than they previously knew. The sexual lives of HIV+ gay men may continue, only without the participation in sex acts. HIV impacted not only physical health but also social interactions, psychological functioning, and gender constructions.

Factors Associated with Sexual Losses

The loss or declining frequency of sexual activities for HIV+ gay men could be attributed to several factors. First, some men, such as Charlie, have consciously chosen to discontinue sexual activities. Other men have found the complications of their disease directly contributed to their sexual losses (20%). For some HIV+ gay men, losses were a result of losing a significant other to HIV disease (11%) and remaining celibate following his death. Although these men were not forced into celibacy by their *own* disease, their celibacy stood as a consequence of HIV. Additionally, some HIV+ gay men's sexual losses were a result of psychological changes brought about by their disease or their fears of transmitting HIV to others.

Physical Factors   The physical factors that contributed to a termination of sexual activities ranged from paralysis and major physical impairment to the simply bothersome side-effects of medications. A common report was that sex drives greatly decreased following the onset of their disease. It was the belief of most men with decreased sexual drive that this came about due to one of two factors. First, decreased sexual drive may have been the result of the changes that HIV brings to bear on the physical body. Second, and more commonly proposed by HIV+ gay men, physiological changes imposed by their numerous medications were believed to have reduced their sex drive. Xing, a 45-year-old, first-generation Chinese American who had recurring bouts with serious opportunistic infections for more than 3 years, believed his sexual drive has been decreased by the new medicines: "I'm taking five antibiotics all at the same time. I think it pretty much kills the sexual desire. . . . Very, very once in a while I feel aroused, but not like before."

Again, sexual activities and physical abilities were restricted or removed, thereby restricting resources available for constructing and maintaining avenues to achievement (as a means of validating one's masculinity).

For some men, though, decreased sexual activities and desires appeared to be directly related to HIV itself. Various opportunistic infections and changes to the body made sex seem less desirable than previously. Men diagnosed with AIDS were most likely to report decreased desire. This is logical, because they have experienced more numerous and significant physiological changes. Timothy, a 40-year-old retired public relations executive who lost a lover to AIDS 1 year earlier, responded to questions about his present sex life saying,

> The sexual part of it? By gosh, I guess this is the time to be totally honest. I mean, I have numbness in my arms and in particular I can feel that same numbness in my penis. I'll be perfectly honest. So, when I masturbate it feels very different than it used to and it's not quite as enjoyable as it used to be.

Although many HIV+ gay men acknowledged a loss of sexual drive, diminished enjoyment, and less frequent sexual activities, those men not in a relationship did not usually report this as a major disruption to their lives. Correspondingly, these physical factors may have been somewhat less significant to these men's masculine identity constructions. Sex was less a matter of achievement or conquest and more emotionally based. Self-esteem and perceptions of external value and validation were accessible from a relationship partner. This may have offset some of the erosion nonpartnered men experienced in the foundation on which they build a gendered identity. However, for men in a relationship with a highly sexual, HIV− significant other, a contrasting consequence occasionally resulted. Illustrative of this experience was Frank, a 46-year-old retired social worker who reported losing interest in sex since becoming HIV infected. Frank recommended to his partner, a 27-year-old HIV− man, "taking a lover on the side." The contrasting values they attributed to sex—as intimacy versus activity–achievement—introduced problems to their relationship. Of course, such a difference in perspective can arise for many reasons. The following account from Frank highlighted his frustrations in this regard.

> We just had this glorious sex [and] afterwards, of course we had to strip the bed and wash the sheets and he had to take a shower. He wasn't interested at first in hearing that I didn't want to pursue it because I didn't feel good. He had to show me, just like a little kid. He said, "Well, let's just fool around." I said I didn't want to. But he said, "Oh, c'mon, what the hell?" I didn't feel like arguing, so I said, fine, I'll show ya. You know, I have diarrhea really bad, so I didn't feel like having sex. But, he learned.

For those men who did remain sexually active, physical factors seriously detracted from their experiences. For some HIV+ gay men there have been physical changes in their bodies that have caused them to lose much of the sensation in various parts of their bodies. When physical pleasures have been forfeited, sexual activity, for many, became very unappealing. Additionally, sexual losses due to HIV brought special challenges to some men's sense of masculinity. Attempts to overcome emerging physical obstacles led to disappointment and consequently motivated an eventual abandonment of sexual activities. This, in turn, may well have led to a need to reestablish a base on which to construct masculinity.

Loss of Self-Esteem   For some HIV+ gay men, decreases in sexual desire followed as a consequence of decreasing self-esteem. Oftentimes men who abandoned sex due to declining self-esteem pointed to their anguish over the changing outward appearances of their bodies. Men with Kaposi's sarcoma (KS) typically did not believe they were sexually attractive, either to themselves or others. Martin said that despite having a partner for the last 14 years, KS triggered the death of his sex life. Specifically Martin explained that

> my sex life pretty well died in '90 when I got my first lesion and had to deal with the self-esteem and the fact that it wasn't just a concept anymore of being HIV-infected. There was physical proof, something very tangible that people could see. . . . I had so many lesions that it was not something you could just kind of hide or say "oh, that's just a bruise."

More simply, Timothy, who above explained how numbness in his penis decreased his sexual desire, also reported losing over 40 pounds through the course of his disease. As a consequence Timothy said, "I look in the mirror and I used to have a butt, now I have three wrinkles of skin where my butt used to be." This, in Timothy's experience, meant that "I have pretty low self-esteem in terms of how I think I look with my clothes off, so that bothers me and reduces the drive somewhat."

Appearance is among the most highly valued components of sexual attractiveness in our culture, especially among gay men. When one's physical appearance is radically, and negatively, altered, it is not surprising that a gay man's self-esteem, and, consequently, his sexual drives, are lowered. The attack such a change brought to some HIV+ gay men's masculinity was clear: When they lost self-esteem they believed they had lost status. When they lost status, how could they remain "a man"? Physical attractiveness, long associated with women's constructions of femininity, influences men's constructions of self as a gendered being as well. This may be especially true for gay men, who have long lived in communities where youthfulness and attractiveness have been highly valued. The HIV+ gay man, however, has lost his attractiveness and his status as terminally ill has redefined him as old (nearing the end of life). Therefore, HIV+ gay men lose the social status their body provided them, as well as slowly losing their bodies.

Fears of Transmitting HIV   Although the impacts of the physical disease on both one's body and mind were important factors that led many HIV+ gay men to abandon or significantly curtail their sexual activities, these were not the most common reasons for such actions. Rather, fear of transmitting HIV to others was the factor that most frequently induced HIV+ gay men to self-impose sexual restrictions. For some, the fear of transmitting HIV was overwhelming, whereas for others it was merely a recurring but manageable distraction. As one might expect, all HIV+ gay men reported that they wished they had not become infected. Not only did they see themselves with an incurable, stigmatizing, fatal disease but they also have experienced or anticipated experiencing a significant loss in social status. HIV+ gay men faced questions regarding their masculinity because of their sexual orientation (as a result of homophobia). With the addition of HIV to their lives they also encountered losses of activity, ability, and attractiveness. These losses, in turn, may have called their masculinity into question even more.

Because they have experienced the multitude of losses that accompany HIV disease, HIV+ gay men unanimously reported that they would never want to think they were responsible for infecting someone else. Consequently, behaviors known to transmit HIV, such as sex, were reportedly approached only with great trepidation.

Fears about infecting others were clearly expressed by a majority of HIV+ gay men. First, Don, a 38-year-old African American man whose disease has forced him to move back into the home of his parents, stated that, "I wouldn't mind having a real companion. . . . But as far as sex, I'm way beyond that. . . . I would not ever do that to anyone. I simply would not. I couldn't be that cruel."

Or, even more direct were the comments of Charlie, who battled several opportunistic infections before being forced to retire. He declared, "I don't want to live with the burden that I might, even innocently, pass this on." Yet more specifically, Lon, a 45-year-old man who migrated to the city from his rural home to escape homophobic prejudice and discrimination, and who was diagnosed 5 years earlier, related the following story:

> At first I was even afraid to have, well if I met someone and then we would have mutual masturbation, I thought, "My god, I can't do that either because what happens if he has a cut on his body and this cum gets into that cut and it gives him this disease?" So I wiped that out. Then I thought, well, there's condoms. Then I thought, what happens if we're having sex and it breaks and I give this guy a disease? Naw, just forget it. Just live in your fantasy world, which I did.

Some HIV+ gay men, however, have succeeded at managing their fears and remained (relatively happily) sexually active. It was, however, only a minority of men that claimed they could continue sexual activities. These were the men for whom sex and sexuality appeared the most central in self-constructions of masculinity. When sex was sustained, the overall level of sexual satisfaction was typically decreased. In the words of many HIV+ gay men, sex and HIV came to be so intertwined that they were unable to engage in sex without thinking about their HIV. Jeremy, whose partner was also HIV+, affirmed this experience:

> No, I can't forget about it. I wish that could happen, but you know, you're being intimate with someone and the whole time, you're concerned about infecting the partner and you know, I guess that takes precedence over bringing pleasure to your partner.

Similarly, Gaston, whose partner was HIV−, maintained that

> It makes it much more difficult since he is negative. . . . I mean it's there in the back of your mind. But I can relax more if I know that I'm doing something that isn't putting him at risk. Then I can enjoy it and not let it affect my performance or whatever. But at first it was on my mind all the time. . . . It's still there, don't get me wrong. I've just kind of learned to deal with it.

Realizations that one's sexual acts can have fatal consequences for others had a significant, sobering psychological impact on most HIV+ gay men. Because of their fears regarding the consequences of sex, most HIV+ gay men terminated sexual activities, but often only after attempts to actively manage their fears and risks to others.

Experiencing the Loss of Sex

The behavioral changes involved for men who have stopped engaging in sex with others did not always represent significant changes for those men's lives. When changes were perceived as significant, this introduced important sources of stress, dissatisfaction, and, sometimes, identity questions to their lives. The small minority (7%) of men who reported not altering their sexual behaviors as a consequence of their HIV status were all men who were involved in relationships, usually with other HIV+ gay men. Mike, a 37-year-old former realtor who lost his eyesight to herpes shingles, and who was involved in a 4-year relationship with another HIV+ gay man, said that, "as far as Tom and I go as a couple, we still have sex, because where's it going to go?" Although not a medically advisable position due to the likelihood of continuing reinfection, this is nonetheless an example of the types of choices HIV+ gay men have had to make. Mike and his partner have elected to pursue psychological well-being and a sense of normalcy in their lives, perhaps at the expense of their physical health. Views such as Mike's were definitely in the minority; most HIV+ couples chose to eliminate, reconstruct, or make safer their sexual encounters in attempts to protect their health. In these instances, normalcy has had to be redefined, as has masculinity.

For most men who have found it necessary to limit their sexual activities, these changes were viewed as one of the many hard-hitting losses imposed by their disease. Sex is central to many men's self-concept, self-esteem, and gender identity. When one's sense of identity is challenged, all elements of social life may be questioned or reconfigured. Because self-esteem and sex are intimately intertwined for some gay men, the loss or heavy restrictions on sex has meant that one has had to forfeit a central aspect of one's identity. This perspective was seen again in Jarvis's words:

> Sex was the best thing in my life. It's the purest form of communication between two people for me, and I really didn't get a lot of love as a kid or affection, but a lot of abuse. So I was really, you know, sex was really good for me. It really did a lot for me psychologically and emotionally. So, it makes it a lot harder to cope.

> You don't have that out, that stress reduction, that beautiful thing. Or, if you do, it's fraught with worry.

However, other men who have made the conscious choice to limit their sexual activities in light of their HIV infection have found it possible to adopt a more optimistic approach to such changes. For some of these men the necessity of changing one's specific sexual activities and number of sex partners offered opportunities to explore new areas of sexuality and personal growth. This meant that these men were able to view such changes as, at least partially, positive in nature. These were men who adapted their constructions of masculinity, not those whose definitions were static and rigid. If an HIV+ gay man could locate new methods of fulfilling masculine criteria, he may have avoided identity dissonance. As an example, some HIV+ gay men, especially those in long-term relationships, have replaced sex acts with heightened levels of emotional intimacy, achieved in nonsexual interactions. Frank, who both knew of his HIV status and had been in a relationship with the same man for over 8 years, reported that

> we haven't had sex in over 4 years.... Okay? We haven't had sex. There's no reason for it. Why do you have to have sex in a relationship? That's an added, extra bonus. If you've got love, honesty, and trust, you don't need anything else. Snuggling at night, being close, you don't have to have sex just to have a relationship. No one does. That's the problem with most gay relationships, as well as straight relationships.... You have to set your priorities, and sex is way down on the bottom.

Although many may have expected that those who chose, or were forced, to abandon sex perceived such changes in a negative light, these men's experiences actually revealed a contrasting result. It appeared that those who have given up sex were, on the whole, more positive about such changes than those who merely reduced their range of sexual activities and partners. As discussed previously, those who abandoned sexual activities were most commonly in more advanced stages of disease, while asymptomatic men were more likely to have adopted the less extreme management attempt of limiting their sexual activities. This may suggest, then, that progression of disease is accompanied by acceptance of disease (and its inevitable consequences). This may be most obvious for men whose disease had brought them more serious physical and social implications. Those men who were still relatively healthy live lives that were, in many ways, no different than those they knew prior to learning of their HIV+ status. This also meant healthier HIV+ gay men could be expected to hold more traditional (or, less modified) perceptions of masculinity. The imposition (often self-imposed) of changes to central life elements could, therefore, be more difficult to accept for HIV+, but healthy, gay men. However, as time passed and the individual incorporated his new (HIV+) status to his identity complex, his sexual behavior most likely became modified. Sex tended to lose some of its meaning as these men developed new identities. Additionally, sex also came to be viewed as cumbersome and less than fulfilling. Aaron, a 28-year-old man who knew of his HIV+ status for over 3 years, discussed his sex life, saying,

> I'm more cautious I guess. Not being able to just kind of dive right into, you know, the whole sex act and just get carried away with it and enjoy yourself. It's like, it's so technical sometimes. It's like, okay, well we gotta stop here because we gotta do this now.... Now there's rules and regulations, or now it's so technical to have sex and it should be something that you should be able to do any way you want, anywhere you want, you know, and not have to worry about anything.... You could be totally enjoying what's going on and then all of a sudden, it's like, okay, before we do that everybody's got to get ready now. And the moment's gone, so to speak.

Aaron recognized the importance and necessity for practicing safer sex, but obviously did not have a positive attitude regarding such. Instead, as was common among HIV+ gay men, sex came to be viewed as unnatural. Sex took on "rules and regulations"; therefore, spontaneity was restricted. Sexual freedom, enjoyment, and the accompanying impact on these mens' definitions of self, and masculinity were modified in light of their perceptions of self and potential transmission of HIV to others. Therefore, new avenues of recreation, interactions, and methods for building self-esteem and maintaining a sense of masculinity have had to be discovered. Those men who adopted celibacy showed greater success in these paths; those who worked to maintain and manage their sexual activity repertoires did not.

Not all HIV+ gay men, as evidenced by numerous sensationalized media stories, have been concerned about the welfare of their sexual partners. One somewhat surprising finding of the present research was that only a small minority of HIV+ gay men (9%) were willing to report a sexual encounter in which he did not inform his partner of this HIV status.[4] One man, a self-reported prostitute, although advocating safer sex, reported that if he told clients of his HIV status, they would not patronize him. He reportedly urged clients to use condoms, but a majority refused. Several other men did, however, report having friends or acquaintances (whom they named) who continued sexual activities while not informing their partners of their HIV status. Usually, such other men were viewed very negatively, and often friendships with such men were strained or eventually terminated. As Reginald, whose face and body are covered with KS lesions, reported,

> I had a friend that had a lot of problems with that. He found out he had AIDS, and he was pretty sickly. He still went out to the baths and was still going out and picking up boys ... and not using condoms. I really had a problem with

that. He said, "Well, you know, I've got it and I'm going to die and I don't care." That really bothered me. I talked with him about it and said, "It's not fair. What if you got it that way?"

A few HIV+ gay men (7%) reported that whereas they actively took steps to make sexual activities safer, they did not believe it was their responsibility to tell their sexual partners about their HIV status. Rather, because of widespread education regarding HIV's modes of transmission and safer sex, some men believed their sex partners were responsible for their own health. In these instances, rather obviously, sex was an encounter with an objectified other, not an intimate experience. Rodney, whose lover died with AIDS, recounted having had men literally get up out of bed when he told them of his infection. Rodney's partners, it would appear, perceived him in an objectified manner; when learning of his infection, Rodney became damaged goods (in his partners' eyes). When the object is damaged, just as when buying goods, the value is decreased. Consequently, Rodney believed that if he limited himself to safer sex he need not disclose his status. In this way, even though he may be objectified by his partners, he retained his value (as an object). As he explained his perspective,

> I don't think I should have to tell anybody. . . . Is that really fair though? I keep coming back with, "Yes, damn it, it is fair." . . . I mean, that's really something personal and of course, here goes some ethics, but I might only be with you for a few hours, so why should I share something so personal?

The attitudes expressed by Reginald and Rodney, however, did not represent the full range of HIV+ gay men's attitudes. Rather, what these men's stories made clear was that not all HIV+ gay men necessarily believed they had a responsibility to be concerned about informing their sex partners about their HIV status. Although these men may have felt a personal responsibility to protect others, they did not equate this with a perceived need to publicly announce their health status. When objectified, or when objectifying others, responsibilities were minimized.

Most notably, several of the men interviewed (13%) knew (or believed they knew) that they were originally, knowingly infected by men with whom they shared a relationship. Men infected via this route, somewhat surprisingly, very rarely expressed negative feelings for their partners. Jeremy, while sitting in the same room as his lover, calmly reported how he was knowingly infected. Claiming to accept his infection as a "risk of being gay," Jeremy related the following story:

> When we first met we talked about it and I asked him if he'd ever been tested. He said, "No." . . . But once we were together and we talked more about it, he knew how important it was to me. When we finally had the discussion he came to me and said, "Jeremy, I did something today." I said, "Okay, what did you do?" And he said, "I went to the doctor and I got my results. I had a test done. . . . I'm positive." And the only thing that I could think of was the suffering he was gonna have to go through. You know, it didn't matter to me at that point that he'd lied to me in the beginning and that we weren't being safe. Because at that same point he told, he goes, "I don't know if I'd told you this or not, but I had been tested before, three and a half years before." . . . I've loved him from the beginning and I forgave him for what happened. I've also realized that it just wasn't his responsibility, it was mine too.

What Jeremy's story exemplified is that many HIV+ gay men are faced with serious and difficult decisions about not only their health but also their social lives. It appears that there are two primary, healthy adaptations that are available to HIV+ gay men. First, they could incorporate their status as an HIV+ gay man (and look forward, not to the past and how their lives *might* have been different), or they could later (sometimes radically) or avoid what some believe to be normative gay (sexual) lifestyles found in many urban gay communities. For some HIV+ gay men, this may lead to a role as an activist, focusing on gay rights, AIDS, or a combination of issues. For many men, such as Jeremy, the decision of how to react to one's newfound status was mainly an intellectual exercise. Once he was infected, it could not be changed; therefore, he looked at his current life situation and decided how to manage his life, both sexually and otherwise.

Conclusion

The sexual lives of HIV+ gay men studied in this research were almost always significantly altered as a result of HIV disease. In contrast to the impacts on sexuality of other terminal or debilitating diseases, it is not simply the disease itself that has brought on changes. Instead, these alterations and losses have been the result of conscious choices to protect oneself and others from infection or psychological changes within the individual. Although the impact of HIV (and opportunistic infections) on the physical body certainly brings about modifications or a cessation of sexual drives and activities for HIV+ gay men, this may have been the least common impetus for change in these men's sexual lives. Of more importance, at least in the eyes of these men, have been the effects of medications for combating HIV and other infections. However, even these physical changes are not at the heart of the impact of HIV disease on sexual lives of HIV+ gay men.

In addition to changes in sexual activities and sexuality, these men also experienced changes in their experiences of masculinity. HIV compelled these men to reexamine and redefine masculinity. Because some of the changes brought by HIV center on areas in which masculinity had traditionally been established (sex, achievement, self-control, environmental control, and physical attractiveness), these HIV+ gay

men have had to identify new ways to define masculinity, or risk losing their masculine self-identities. When sex is forgone, many gay men lose a critical means of achieving success and personal–environmental control. Sex contributes to the definition of masculinity; therefore, when sex is abandoned, both sexuality and masculinity need to be reconfigured.

What have easily and obviously been the most common reasons for HIV+ gay men to abandon or restrict sexual activities have been the cares and concerns these men have felt regarding their roles as potential transmitters of HIV. The stigma of HIV disease and the universal concern about transferring the stigma (along with the virus) to others led them to rethink and, most often, restructure their sexual lives. Consequently, choices were made to impose hardships on themselves to avoid both drawing others into the grip of HIV and feeling responsible for their disease. Identification of these concerns and motivations for sexual behavior change has not been surprising. Instead, this stood as confirmation that the experience of HIV disease can be seen as an extension of a more general experience of sexuality and gay political identity. This is supported by the similarity between the findings in the present study and Siegel and Raveis's (1993) analysis of gay men's adoption of celibacy as a preventive measure. In their work, Siegel and Raveis found that five themes explained celibacy in gay men: (a) a desire for truly safe sex, (b) emotional distress concerning possible transmission, (c) a desire for more than sex from a relationship, (d) a dislike of safer sex, and (e) a fear of being unable to limit one's sexual outlets.

These changes have seemed on the one hand, only appropriate and proper. After all, without at least modifying their sexual behaviors, HIV+ gay men are highly likely to infect others. However, on the other hand, there is an ironic twist here. Whereas this chapter has discussed a category of persons most commonly defined not by their personal or social characteristics but instead by their presumed sexual activities and frequencies, it has now become clear that such conceptions are clearly off target. HIV+ gay men can no longer be accurately defined by their sex lives: Sex as they knew it has been either abandoned or restructured. HIV+ gay men generally do not have sex lives similar to gay men without HIV disease. These differences have not necessarily been welcomed, as Martin, a self-described celibate AIDS activist, succinctly said,

> Sex . . . continues to be a great frustration for me, and I think for most people with AIDS. It seems kind of a cruel irony that most of us were infected through sex and now we don't get any or very little sex at all.

HIV+ gay men were found to be fundamentally different than their noninfected counterparts physically, socially, and often psychologically. The roles sex played both prior to and after knowledge of infection are different. Sexual lives are just one of the many elements of life impacted by HIV. Life changed for these gay men when HIV entered the picture. Adaptations, including sexual adaptations, were common and significant experiences. This is the context of living with HIV. Changes occurred but were not always experienced the same by those who were changed.

Notes

1. The total sample of 45 HIV+ gay men includes 20 men diagnosed with AIDS and 25 HIV+, asymptomatic men.

2. Difficulties in accessing persons living with HIV disease are numerous and often impose methodological difficulties and implementation restraints on researchers. Perhaps the most difficult barrier to overcome is not convincing persons with HIV to be interviewed, but working through the structural and personal difficulties social service providers face in assisting researchers (Fleishman, Mor, Cwi, & Piette, 1992).

3. All identifications of interviewees are pseudonyms. Unless noted otherwise, all references in this work to "men with HIV" or "HIV positive men" refer to gay men.

4. However, see Meyer-Bahlburg et al. (1991), Martin (1987), Exner et al. (1992) and Gold et al. (1994) for discussions of HIV+ gay men who do continue to practice unsafe sex.

References

Adib, M., Joseph, J. G., Ostrow, D. G., Tal, M., & Schwartz, S. A. (1991). Relapse in sexual behavior among homosexual men: A 2-year follow-up from the Chicago MACS/CCS. *AIDS*, *5*, 757–760.

Auchincloss, S. (1991). Sexual dysfunction after cancer treatment. *Journal of Psychosocial Oncology*, *9*(1), 23–42.

Baxter, S. (1991). AIDS education in the jail setting. *Crime & Delinquency*, *37*(1), 48–63.

Bell, N. K. (1991). Social/sexual norms and AIDS in the South: Ethics and the politics of AIDS: Lessons for small cities and rural areas throughout the U.S. *AIDS Education and Prevention*, *3*(2), 164–180.

Beutel, M. (1988). Male sexuality and cancer. In W. Eicher & G. Kockott (Eds.), *Sexology* (pp. 283–289). Berlin: Springer-Verlag.

Carey, M. A., & Smith, M. W. (1992). Enhancement of validity through qualitative approaches. *Evaluation and the Health Professions*, *15*(4), 107–114.

Cleary, P. D., Van Devanter, N., Rogers, T. F., & Singer, E. (1991). Behavior changes after notification of HIV infection. *American Journal of Public Health*, *81*(12), 1586–1590.

Coates, T. J., Morin, S. F., & McKusick, L. (1987). Behavioral consequences of AIDS antibody testing among gay men. *Journal of the American Medical Association*, *258*, 1889.

Connell, R. W., & Kippax, S. (1990). Sexuality in the AIDS crisis: Patterns of sexual practice and pleasure in a sample of Australian gay and bisexual men. *Journal of Sex Research*, *27*(2), 167–198.

Ekstrand, M. L., & Coates, T. J. (1990). Maintenance of safer sexual behaviors and predictors of risky sex: The San Francisco Men's Health

Study. *American Journal of Public Health, 80,* 973–977.

Exner, T. J., Meyer-Bahlburg, H. F., & Ehrhardt, A. A. (1992). Sexual self control as a mediator of high risk sexual behavior in a New York City cohort of HIV+ and HIV– gay men. *Journal of Sex Research, 29*(3), 389–406.

Fleishman, J. A., Mor, V., Cwi, J. S., & Piette, J. D. (1992). Sampling and accessing people with AIDS. *Evaluation and the Health Professions, 15*(4), 385–404.

Folkman, S., Chesney, M. A., Pollack, L., & Phillips, C. (1992). Stress, coping, and high-risk sexual behavior. *Health Psychology, 11*(4), 218–222.

Gendel, E. S., & Bonner, E. J. (1986). Sex, angina, and heart disease. *Medical Aspects of Human Sexuality, 20,* 18–36.

Glaser, B. G., & Strauss, A. L. (1967). *The discovery of grounded theory.* Chicago: Aldine.

Gochros, H. (1992). The sexuality of gay men with HIV infection. *Social Work, 37*(2), 105–109.

Godfriend, J. P., van Griensven, E., DeVroome, M. M., Tielman, R. A. P., Goudsmit, J., van der Noordaa, J., de Wolf, F., & Coutinho, R. A. (1988). Impact of HIV antibody testing on changes in sexual behavior among homosexual men in the Netherlands. *American Journal of Public Health, 78*(12), 1757–1577.

Gold, R. S., Skinner, M. J., & Ross, M. W. (1994). Unprotected anal intercourse in HIV-infected and non-HIV-infected gay men. *Journal of Sex Research, 31*(1), 59–77.

Hays, R. B., Kegeles, S. M., & Coates, T. J. (1990). High HIV risk-taking among young gay men. *AIDS, 4,* 901–907.

Hoff, C. C., McKusick, L., Hilliard, B., & Coates, T. J. (1992). The impact of HIV antibody status on gay men's partner preferences: A community perspective. *AIDS Education and Prevention, 4*(3), 197–204.

Jenkins, B. (1988). Patients' reports of sexual changes after treatment for gynecological cancer. *Oncology Nursing Forum, 15*(3), 349–354.

Joseph, J. G., Adib, M., Koopman, J. S., & Ostrow, D. G. (1990). Behavioral change in longitudinal studies: Adoption of condom use by homosexual/bisexual men. *American Journal of Public Health, 80*(12), 1513–1514.

Kelly, J. A., Kalichman, S. C., Kauth, M. R., Kilgore, H. G., Hood, H. V., Campos, P. E., Rao, S. M., Brasfield, T. L., & St. Lawrence, J. S. (1991). Situational factors associated with AIDS risk behavior lapses and coping strategies used by gay men who successfully avoid lapses. *American Journal of Public Health, 81*(10), 1335–1338.

Kelly, J. A., St. Lawrence, J. S., Brasfield, T. L., Stevenson, L. Y., Diaz, Y. E., & Hauth, A. C. (1990). AIDS risk behavior patterns among gay men in small Southern cities. *American Journal of Public Health, 80*(4), 416–418.

Landis, S. E., Earp, J. L., & Koch, C. G. (1992). Impact of HIV testing and counseling on subsequent sexual behavior. *AIDS Education and Prevention, 4*(1), 61–70.

Levine, M. P., & Siegel, K. (1992). Unprotected sex: Understanding gay men's participation. In J. Huber & B. E. Schneider (Eds), *The social context of AIDS* (pp. 47–71). Newbury Park, CA: Sage.

Lippert, G. P. (1986). Excessive concern about AIDS in two bisexual men. *Canadian Journal of Psychiatry, 31,* 63–65.

Marcus, D. K., Amen, T. M., & Bibace, R. (1992). A developmental analysis of prisoners' conceptions of AIDS. *Criminal Justice and Behavior, 19*(2), 174–188.

Martin, D. J. (1990). A study of the deficiencies in the condom-use skills of gay men. *Public Health Reports, 105*(6), 638–640.

Martin, J. L. (1987). The impact of AIDS on gay male sexual behavior patterns in New York City. *American Journal of Public Health, 77*(5), 578–581.

Mays, V. M., Cochran, S. D., Hamilton, E., Miller, N., Leung, L., Rothspan, S., Kolson, J., Webb, F., & Torres, M. (1993). Just cover up: Barriers to heterosexual and gay young adults' use of condoms. *Health Values: Achieving High Level Wellness, 17*(4), 41–47.

Meyer-Bahlburg, H. F., Exner, T. M., Lorenz, G., Gruen, R. S., Gorman, J. M., & Ehrhardt, A. A. (1991). Sexual risk behavior, sexual functioning, and HIV-disease progression in gay men. *Journal of Sex Research, 28*(1), 3–27.

Nurnberg, H. G., Prudic, J., Fiori, M., & Freedman, E. P. (1984). Psychopathology complicating acquired immune deficiency syndrome. *American Journal of Psychiatry, 141,* 95–96.

Offir, J. T., Fisher, J. D., Williams, S. S., & Fisher, W. A. (1993). Reasons for inconsistent AIDS-preventive behaviors among gay men. *Journal of Sex Research, 30,* 62–69.

Osmond, D., Bacchetti, P., Chaisson, R. E., Kelly, T., Stempel, R., Carlson, J., & Moss, A. R. (1988). Time of exposure and HIV infection in homosexual partners of men with AIDS. *American Journal of Public Health, 78*(8), 944–947.

Parker, R. G., & Carballo, M. (1990). Qualitative research on homosexual and bisexual behavior relevant to HIV/AIDS. *Journal of Sex Research, 27*(4), 497–525.

Paul, J. P., Stall, R., & Davis, F. (1993). Sexual risk for HIV transmission among gay/bisexual men in substance-abuse treatment. *AIDS Education and Prevention, 5*(1), 11–24.

Peterson, J. L., Coates, T. J., Catania, J. A., Middleton, L., Hilliard, B., & Hearst, N. (1992). High risk sexual behavior and condom use among gay and bisexual African–American men. *American Journal of Public Health, 82*(11), 1490–1494.

Pincu, L. (1989). Sexual compulsivity in gay men: Controversy and treatment. *Journal of Counseling and Development, 68*(10), 63–66.

Quadland, M. C., & Shattls, W. D. (1987). AIDS, sexuality and sexual control. *Journal of Homosexuality, 14*(1/2), 277–298.

Ruefli, T., Yu, O., & Barton, J. (1992). Sexual risk taking in smaller cities: The case of Buffalo, New York. *Journal of Sex Research, 29*(1), 95–108.

Schnell, D. J., Higgins, D. L., Wilson, R. M., Goldbaum, G., Cohn, D. L., & Wolitski, R. J. (1992).

Men's disclosure of HIV test results to male primary sex partners. *American Journal of Public Health, 82*(12), 1675–1676.

Siegel, K., & Raveis, V. H. (1993). AIDS-related reasons for gay men's adoption of celibacy. *AIDS Education and Prevention, 5*(4), 302–310.

Silvestre, A. (1992). *HIV rates and differences in behavior over time among men entering an HIV disease cohort study.* Unpublished doctoral dissertation, University of Pittsburgh.

Smith, D. B., & Babaian, R. J. (1992). The effects of treatment for cancer on male fertility and sexuality. *Cancer Nursing, 15*(4), 271–275.

Stall, R., Barrett, D., Bye, L., Catania, J., Frutchey, C., Henne, J., Lemp, G., & Paul, J. (1992). A comparison of younger and older gay men's HIV risk-taking behaviors: The communication technologies 1989 cross-sectional survey. *Journal of Acquired Immune Deficiency Syndromes, 5,* 682–687.

Stall, R., Coates, T. J., & Hoff, C. (1988). Behavioral risk reduction for HIV infection among gay and bisexual men. *American Psychologist, 43,* 878–885.

Stevenson, H. C., & Davis, G. (1994). Impact of culturally sensitive AIDS video education on the AIDS risk knowledge of African-American adolescents. *AIDS Education and Prevention, 6*(1), 40–52.

Tewksbury, R., & Whittier, N. (1992). Safer sex practices in samples drawn from nightclub, campus and gay bars. *Sociology and Social Research, 76*(4), 10–15.

Weitz, R. (1991). *Life with AIDS.* New Brunswick, NJ: Rutgers University Press.

31

ARTICLE

Robin D. G. Kelley

Confessions of a Nice Negro, or Why I Shaved My Head

It happened just the other day—two days into the new year, to be exact. I had dashed into the deserted lobby of an Ann Arbor movie theater, pulling the door behind me to escape the freezing winter winds Michigan residents have come to know so well. Behind the counter knelt a young white teenager filling the popcorn bin with bags of that awful pre-popped stuff. Hardly the enthusiastic employee; from a distance it looked like she was lost in deep thought. The generous display of body piercing suggested an X-generation flowerchild—perhaps an anthropology major into acid jazz and environmentalism, I thought. Sporting a black New York Yankees baseball cap and a black-and-beige scarf over my nose and mouth, I have must have looked like I had stepped out of a John Singleton film. And because I was already late, I rushed madly toward the ticket counter.

The flower child was startled: "I don't have anything in the cash register," she blurted as she pulled the bag of popcorn in front of her for protection.

In Don Belton, Ed. *Speak My Name: Black Men on Masculinity and the American Dream*. Boston: Beacon, 1995.

"Huh? I just want one ticket for *Little Women,* please—the two-fifteen show. My wife and daughter should already be in there." I slowly gestured to the theater door and gave her one of those innocent childlike glances I used to give my mom when I wanted to sit on her lap.

"Oh god . . . I'm so sorry. A reflex. Just one ticket? You only missed the first twenty minutes. Enjoy the show."

Enjoy the show? Barely 1995 and here we go again. Another bout with racism in a so-called liberal college town; another racial drama in which I play the prime suspect. And yet I have to confess the situation was pretty funny. Just two hours earlier I couldn't persuade Elleza, my four-year-old daughter, to put her toys away; time-out did nothing, yelling had no effect, and the evil stare made no impact whatsoever. Thoroughly frustrated, I had only one option left: "Okay, I'm gonna tell Mommy!" Of course it worked.

So those five seconds as a media–made black man felt kind of good. I know it's a product of racism. I know that the myth of black male violence has resulted in the deaths of many innocent boys and men of darker hue. I know that the power to scare is not real power. I know all that—after all, I study this stuff for a living! For the moment, though, it felt good. (Besides, the ability to scare with your body can come in handy, especially when you're trying to get a good seat in a theater or avoid long lines.)

I shouldn't admit this, but I take particular pleasure in putting fear into people on the lookout for black male criminality mainly because those moments are so rare for me. Indeed, my *inability* to employ black-maleness as a weapon is the story of my life. Why I don't possess it, or rather possess so little of it, escapes me. I grew up poor in Harlem and Afrodena (the Negro West Side of Pasadena/Altadena, California). My mom was single during my formative preadolescent years, and for a brief moment she even received a welfare check. A hard life makes a hard nigga, so I've been told.

Never an egghead or a dork, as a teenager I was pretty cool. I did the house-party circuit on Friday and Saturday nights and used to stroll down the block toting the serious Radio Raheem boombox. Why, I even invaded movie theaters in the company of ten or fifteen hooded and high-topped black bodies, colonizing the balconies and occupying two seats per person. Armed with popcorn and Raisinettes as our missiles of choice, we dared any usher to ask us to leave. Those of us who had cars (we called them hoopties or rides back in that day) spent our lunch hours and precious class time hanging out in the school parking lot, running down our Die Hards to pump up Cameo, Funkadelic, Grandmaster Flash from our car stereos. I sported dickies and Levis, picked up that gangsta stroll, and when the shag came in style I was with it— always armed with a silk scarf to ensure that my hair was laid. Granted, I vomited after drinking malt liquor for the first time and my only hit of a joint ended abruptly in an asthma attack. But I was cool.

Sure, I was cool, but nobody feared me. That I'm relatively short with dimples and curly hair, speak softly in a rather medium to high-pitched voice, and have a "girl's name" doesn't

help matters. And everyone knows that light skin is less threatening to white people than blue–black or midnight brown. Besides, growing up with a soft-spoken, uncharacteristically passive West Indian mother deep into East Indian religions, a mother who sometimes walked barefoot in the streets of Harlem, a mother who insisted on proper diction and never, ever, ever used a swear word, screwed me up royally. I could never curse right. My mouth had trouble forming the words—"fuck" always came out as "fock" and "goddamn" always sounded like it's spelled, not "gotdayum," the way my Pasadena homies pronounced it in their Calabama twang. I don't ever recall saying the word "bitch" unless I was quoting somebody or some authorless vernacular rhyme. For some unknown reason, that word scared me.

Mom dressed me up in the coolest mod outfits—short pants with matching hats, Nehru jackets, those sixties British-looking turtlenecks. Sure, she got some of that stuff from John's Bargain Store or Goodwill, but I always looked "cute." More stylish than roguish. Kinda like W. E. B. Du Bois as a toddler, or those turn-of-the century photos of middle-class West Indian boys who grow up to become prime ministers or poets. Ghetto ethnographers back in the late sixties and early seventies would not have found me or my family very "authentic," especially if they had discovered that one of my middle names is Gibran, after the Lebanese poet Kahlil Gibran.

Everybody seemed to like me. Teachers liked me, kids liked me; I even fell in with some notorious teenage criminals at Pasadena High School because *they* liked me. I remember one memorable night in the ninth grade when I went down to the Pasadena Boys' Club to take photos of some of my partners on the basketball team. On my way home some big kids, eleventh-graders to be exact, tried to take my camera. The ringleader pulled out a knife and gently poked it against my chest. I told them it was my stepfather's camera and if I came home without it he'd kick my ass for a week. Miraculously, this launched a whole conversation about stepfathers and how messed up they are, which must have made them feel sorry for me. Within minutes we were cool; they let me go unmolested and I had made another friend.

In affairs of the heart, however, "being liked" had the opposite effect. I can only recall having had four fights in my entire life, all of which were with girls who supposedly liked me but thoroughly beat my behind. Sadly, my record in the boxing ring of puppy love is still 0–4. By the time I graduated to serious dating, being a nice guy seemed like the root of all my romantic problems. I resisted jealously, tried to be understanding, brought flowers and balloons, opened doors, wrote poems and songs, and seemed to always be on my knees for one reason or another. If you've ever watched "Love Connection" or read *Cosmopolitan,* you know the rest of the story: I practically never had sex and most of the women I dated left me in the cold for roughnecks. My last girlfriend in high school, the woman I took to my prom, the woman I once thought I'd die for, tried to show me the light: "Why do you always ask me what I want? Why don't you just *tell* me what you want me to do? Why don't you take charge and *be a man?* If you want to be a real man you can't be nice all the time!"

I always thought she was wrong; being nice has nothing to do with being a man. While I still think she's wrong, it's an established fact that our culture links manhood to terror and power, and that black men are frequently im-aged as the ultimate in hypermasculinity. But the black man as the prototype of violent hy-permasculinity is as much a fiction as the happy Sambo. No matter what critics and stand-up comics might say, I know from experience that not all black men—and here I'm only speaking of well-lighted or daytime situations—generate fear. Who scares and who doesn't has a lot to do with the body in question; it is dependent on factors such as age, skin color, size, clothes, hair-

style, and even the sound of one's voice. The cops who beat Rodney King and the jury who acquitted King's assailants openly admitted that the size, shape, and color of his body automat-ically made him a threat to the officers' safety.

On the other hand, the threatening black male body can take the most incongruous forms. Some of the hardest brothas on my block in West Pasadena kept their perms in pink rollers and hairnets. It was not unusual to see young black men in public with curlers, tank-top undershirts, sweatpants, black mid-calf dress socks, and Stacey Adams shoes, hanging out on the corner or on the basketball court. And we all knew that these brothas were not to be messed with. (The rest of the world probably knows it by now, too, since black males in curlers are occasionally featured on "Cops" and "America's Most Wanted" as notori-ous drug dealers or heartless pimps.)

Whatever the source of this ineffable ter-ror, my body simply lacked it. Indeed, the older I got the more ensconced I became in the world of academic, the less threatening I seemed. Marrying and having a child also reduced the threat factor. By the time I hit my late twenties, my wife Diedra, and I found ourselves in the awkward position of being everyone's favorite Negroes. I don't know how many times we've attended dinner parties where we were the only African Americans in the room. Occasionally there were others, but we seemed to have a monopoly on the dinner party invitations. This not only happened in Ann Arbor, where there is a small but substantial black population to choose from, but in the Negro mecca of At-lanta, Georgia. Our hosts always felt comfort-able asking us "sensitive" questions about race that they would not dare ask other black col-leagues and friends: What do African Americans think about Farrakahn? Ben Chavis? Nelson Mandela? Most of my black students are very conservative and career-oriented—why is that? How can we mend the relations between blacks and Jews? Do you celebrate Kwanzaa? Do you put anything in your hair to make it that way?

What are the starting salaries for young black faculty nowadays?

Of course, these sorts of exchanges appear regularly in most black autobiographies. As soon as they're comfortable, it is not uncommon for white people to take the opportunity to find out everything they've always wanted to know about "us" (which also applies to other people of color, I'm sure) but were afraid to ask. That they feel perfectly at ease asking dumb or unanswerable questions is not simply a case of (mis)perceived racelessness. Being a "nice Negro" has a lot to do with gender, and my peculiar form of "left–feminist–funny-guy" masculinity—a little Kevin Hooks, some Bobby McFerrin, a dash of Woody Allen—is regarded as less threatening than that of most other black men.

Not that I mind the soft-sensitive masculine persona—after all, it is the genuine me, a product of my mother's heroic and revolutionary child-rearing style. But there are moments when I wish I could invoke the intimidation factor of blackmaleness on demand. If I only had that look—that Malcolm X/Mike Tyson/Ice Cube/Larry Fishburne/Bigger Thomas/Fruit of Islam look—I could keep the stupid questions at bay, make college administrators tremble, and scare editors into submission. Subconsciously, I decided that I had to do something about my image. Then, as if by magic, my wish was fulfilled.

Actually, it began as an accident involving a pair of electric clippers and sleep deprivation—a bad auto-cut gone awry. With my lowtop fade on the verge of a Sly Stone afro, I was in desperate need of a trim. Diedra didn't have the time to do it, and as it was February (Black History Month), I was on the chitlin' lecture circuit and couldn't spare forty-five minutes at a barber shop, so I elected to do it myself. Standing in a well-lighted bathroom, armed with two mirrors, I started trimming. Despite a steady hand and what I've always believed was a good eye, my hair turned out lopsided. I kept trimming and trimming to correct my error, but as my flattop

sank lower, a yellow patch of scalp began to rise above the surrounding hair, like one of those big granite mounds dotting the grassy knolls of Central Park. A nice yarmulke could have covered it, but that would have been more difficult to explain than a bald spot. So, bearing in mind role models like Michael Jordan, Charles Barkley, Stanley Crouch, and Onyx (then the hip-hop group of the hour), I decided to take it all off.

I didn't think much of it at first, but the new style accomplished what years of evil stares and carefully crafted sartorial statements could not: I began to scare people. The effect was immediate and dramatic. Passing strangers avoided me and smiled less frequently. Those who did smile or make eye contact seemed to be deliberately trying to disarm me—a common strategy taught in campus rape-prevention centers. Scaring people was fun for a while, but I especially enjoyed standing in line at the supermarket with my bald head, baggy pants, high-top Reeboks, and long black hooded down coat, humming old standards like "Darn That Dream," "A Foggy Day," and "I Could Write a Book." Now *that* brought some stares. I must have been convincing, since I adore those songs and have been humming them ever since I can remember. No simple case of cultural hybridity here, just your average menace to society with a deep appreciation for Gershwin, Rodgers and Hart, Van Heusen, Cole Porter, and Jerome Kern.

Among my colleagues, my bald head became the lead subject of every conversation. "You look older, more mature." "With that new cut you come across as much more serious than usual." "You really look quite rugged and masculine with a bald head." My close friends dispensed with the euphemisms and went straight to the point: "Damn. You look scary!" The most painful comment was that I looked like a "B-Boy wannabe" and was "too old for that shit." I had to remind my friend that I'm an OBB (Original B-Boy), that I was in the eleventh grade in 1979 when the Sugar Hill Gang dropped "Rapper's

Delight," and that *his* tired behind was in graduate school at the time. Besides, B-Boy was not the intent.

In the end, however, I got more questions than comments. Was I in crisis? Did I want to talk? What was I trying to say by shaving my head? What was the political point of my actions? Once the novelty passed, I began getting those "speak for the race" questions that irritated the hell out of me when I had hair. Why have *black men* begun to shave their heads in greater numbers? Why have so many black athletes decided to shave their heads? Does this new trend have some kind of phallic meaning? Against my better judgment, I found myself coming up with answers to these questions—call it an academician's reflex. I don't remember exactly what I said, but it usually began with black prizefighter Jack Johnson, America's real life "baaad nigger" of the early twentieth century, whose head was always shaved and greased, and ended with the hip-hop community's embrace of an outlaw status. Whatever it was, it made sense at the time.

The publicity photo for my recent book, *Race Rebels,* clearly generated the most controversy among my colleagues. It diverged dramatically from the photo on my first book, where I look particularly innocent, almost angelic. In that first photo I smiled just enough to make my dimples visible; my eyes gazed away from the camera in sort of a dreamy, contemplative pose; my haircut was nondescript and the natural sunlight had a kind of halo effect. The Izod shirt was the icing on the cake. By contrast, the photograph for *Race Rebels* (which Diedra set up and shot, by the way) has me looking directly into the camera, arms folded, bald head glistening from baby oil and rear window light, with a grimace that could give Snoop Doggy Dogg a run for his money. The lens made my arms appear much larger than they really are, creating a kind of Popeye effect. Soon after the book came out, I received several e-mail messages about the photo. A particularly memorable one came from a friend and fellow historian in Australia. In the

course of explaining to me how he had corrected one of his students who had read an essay of mine and presumed I was a woman, he wrote: "Mind you, the photo in your book should make things clear—the angle and foreshortening of the arms, and the hairstyle make it one of the more masculine author photos I've seen recently????!!!!!!"

My publisher really milked this photo, which actually fit well with the book's title. For the American Studies Association meeting in Nashville, Tennessee, which took place the week the book came out, my publisher bought a full-page ad on the back cover of an ASA handout, with my mug staring dead at you. Everywhere I turned—in hotel elevators, hallways, lobbies, meeting rooms—I saw myself, and it was not exactly a pretty sight. The quality of the reproduction (essentially a high-contrast xerox) made me appear harder, meaner, and crazier than the original photograph.

The situation became even stranger since I had decided to abandon the skinhead look and grow my hair back. In fact, by the time of the ASA meeting I was on the road (since abandoned) toward a big Black Power Afro—a retro style that at the time seemed to be making a comeback. Worse still, I had come to participate in a round-table discussion on black hair! My paper, titled "Nap Time: Historicizing the Afro," explored the political implications of competing narratives of the Afro's origins and meaning. Overall, it was a terrific session; the room was packed and the discussion was stimulating. But inevitably the question came up: "Although this isn't directly related to his paper, I'd like to find out from Professor Kelley why he shaved his head. Professor Kelley, given the panel's topic and in light of the current ads floating about with your picture on them, can you shed some light on what is attractive to black men about baldness?" The question was posed by a very distinguished and widely read African-American literary scholar. Hardly the naif, he knew the answers as well as I did, but wanted to generate a public discussion. And he succeeded. For ten minutes the audience ran the gamut of issues revolving around race, gender, sexuality, and the politics of style. Even the issue of bald heads as phallic symbols came up. "It's probably true," I said, "but when I was cutting my hair at three-o'clock in the morning I wasn't thinking 'penis.'" Eventually the discussion drifted from black masculinity to the tremendous workloads of minority scholars, which, in all honesty, was the source of my baldness in the first place. Unlike the golden old days, when doing hair was highly ritualized and completely integrated into daily life, we're so busy mentoring and publishing and speaking and fighting that we have very little time to attend to our heads.

Beyond the session itself, that ad continued to haunt me during the entire conference. Every ten minutes, or so it seemed, someone came up to me and offered unsolicited commentary on the photo. One person slyly suggested that in order to make the picture complete I should have posed with an Uzi. When I approached a very good friend of mine, a historian who is partly my Jewish mother and partly my confidante and *always* looking out for my best interests, the first words out of her mouth were, "Robin, I hate that picture! It's the worst picture of you I've ever seen. It doesn't do you justice. Why did you let them use it?"

"It's not that bad," I replied. "Diedra likes it—she took the picture. You just don't like my bald head."

"No, that's not it. I like the bald look on some men, and you have a very nice head. The problem is the photo and the fact that I know what kind of person you are. None of your gentleness and lovability comes out in that picture. Now, don't get a swelled head when I say this, but you have a delightful face and expression that makes people feel good, even when you're talking about serious stuff. The way you smile, there's something unbelievably safe about you."

It was a painful compliment. And yet I knew deep down that she was telling the truth. I've always been unbelievably safe, not just because of my look but because of my actions. Not that I consciously try to put people at ease, to erase conflict and difference, to remain silent on sensitive issues. I can't quite put my finger on it. Perhaps it's my mother's politeness drills? Perhaps it's a manifestation of my continuing bout with shyness? Maybe it has something to do with the sense of joy I get from stimulating conversations? Or maybe it's linked to the fact that my mom refused to raise me in a manner boys are accustomed to? Most likely it is a product of cultural capital—the fact that I *can* speak the language, (re)cite the texts, exhibit the manners and mannerisms that are inherent to bourgeois academic culture. My colleagues identify with me because I can talk intelligently about their scholarship on their terms, which invariably has the effect of creating an illusion of brilliance. As Frantz Fanon said in *Black Skin, White Masks,* the mere fact that he was an articulate *black* man who read a lot rendered him a stunning specimen of erudition in the eyes of his fellow intellectuals in Paris.

Whatever the source of my ineffable lovability, I've learned that it's not entirely a bad thing. In fact, if the rest of the world could look a little deeper, beyond the hardcore exterior— the wide bodies, the carefully constructed grimaces, the performance of terror—they would find many, many brothas much nicer and smarter than myself. The problem lies in a racist culture, a highly gendered racist culture, that is so deeply enmeshed in the fabric of daily life that it's practically invisible. The very existence of the "nice Negro," like the model-minority myth pinned on Asian Americans, renders the war on those "other," hardcore niggas justifiable and even palatable. In a little-known essay on the public image of world champion boxer Joe Louis, the radical Trinidadian writer C. L. R. James put it best: "This attempt to hold up Louis as a model Negro has strong overtones of condescension and race prejudice. It implies: 'See! When a Negro knows how to conduct himself, he gets on very well and we all love him.' From there the next step is: 'If only all Negroes behaved like Joe, the race problem would be solved.'"[1]

Of course we all know this is a bunch of fiction. Behaving "like Joe" were merely a code for deference and patience, which is all the more remarkable given his vocation. Unlike his predecessor Jack Johnson—the bald-headed prize fighter who transgressed racial boundaries by sleeping with and even marrying white women, who refused to apologize for his "outrageous" behavior, who boasted of his prowess in every facet of life (he even wrapped gauze around his penis to make it appear bigger under his boxing shorts)—Joe Louis was America's hero. As James put it, he was a credit to his race, "I mean the human race."[2] (Re)presented as a humble Alabama boy, God-fearing and devoid of hatred, Louis was constructed in the press as a raceless man whose masculinity was put to good, patriotic use. To many of his white fans, he was a man in the ring and a boy—a good boy—outside of it. To many black folks, he was a hero because he had the license to kick white men's butts and yet maintain the admiration and respect of a nation. Thus, despite similarities in race, class, and vocation, and their common iconization, Louis and Johnson exhibited public behavior that reflected radically different masculinities.

Here, then, is a lesson we cannot ignore. There is some truth in the implication that race (or gender) conflict is partly linked to behavior and how certain behavior is perceived. If our society, for example, could dispense with rigid, archaic notions of appropriate masculine and feminine behavior, perhaps we might create a world that nurtures, encourages, and even rewards nice guys. If violence were not so central to American culture—to the way manhood is defined, to the way in which the state keeps African-American men in check, to the way men interact with women, to the way oppressed peoples interact with one another—perhaps we might see the withering away of white fears of black men. Perhaps young black men wouldn't feel the need to adopt hardened, threatening postures merely to survive in a Doggy-Dogg world. Not that black men ought to become colored equivalents of Alan Alda. Rather, black men ought to be whomever or whatever they want to be, without unwarranted criticism or societal pressures to conform to a particular definition of manhood. They could finally dress down without suspicion, talk loudly without surveillance, and love each other without sanction. Fortunately, such a transformation would also mean the long-awaited death of the "nice Negro."

Not in my lifetime. Any fool can look around and see that the situation for race and gender relations in general, and for black males in particular, has taken a turn for the worse—and relief is nowhere in sight. In the meantime, I will make the most of my "nice Negro" status. When it's all said and done, there is nothing romantic or interesting about playing Bigger Thomas. Maybe I can't persuade a well-dressed white couple to give up their box seats, but at least they'll listen to me. For now. . . .

Notes

1. C. L. R. James, "Joe Louis and Jack Johnson," *Labor Action*, 1 July 1946.

2. Ibid.

32

ARTICLE

Anne Fausto-Sterling

How to Build a Man

How does one become a man? Although poets, novelists, and playwrights long past answered with discussions of morality and honor, these days scholars deliberate the same question using a metaphor—that of social construction. In the current intellectual fashion, men are made, not born. We construct masculinity through social discourse, that array of happenings that covers everything from music videos, poetry, and rap lyrics to sports, beer commercials and psychotherapy. But underlying all of this clever carpentry is the sneaking suspicion that one must start with a blueprint—or, to stretch the metaphor yet a bit more, that buildings must have foundations. Within the soul of even the most die-hard constructionist lurks a doubt. It is called the body.

In contrast, biological and medical scientists feel quite certain about their world. For them, the body tells the truth. (Never mind that postmodern scholarship has questioned the very meaning of the word "truth.") My task in this essay is to consider the truths that biologists extract from bodies, human and otherwise, to ex-

amine scientific accounts—some might even say constructions—of masculinity. To do this, I will treat the scientific/medical literature as yet another set of texts open to scholarly analysis and interpretation.

What are little boys made of? While the nursery rhyme suggests "snips and snails, and puppy-dogs tails," during the past seventy years, medical scientists have built a rather more concrete and certainly less fanciful account. Perhaps the single most influential voice during this period has been that of psychologist John Money. Since at least the 1920s, embryologists have understood that during fetal development a single embryonic primordium—the indifferent fetal gonad—can give rise to either an ovary or a testis. In a similar fashion, both male and female external genitalia arise from a single set of structures. Only the internal sex organs—uteri, fallopian tubes, prostates, sperm transport ducts—arise during embryonic development from separate sets of structures. In the 1950s, Money extended these embryological understandings into the realm of psychological development. As he saw it, all humans start on the same road, but the path rapidly begins to fork. Potential males take a series of turns in one di-

From *Constructing Masculinity*, edited by M. Beyer et al. New York: Routledge, 1995.

rection, potential females in another. In real time, the road begins at fertilization and ends during late adolescence. If all goes as it should, then there are two, and only two, possible destinations—male and female.

But, of course, all does not always go as it should. Money identified the various forks in the road by studying individuals who took one or more wrong turns. From them, he derived a map of the normal. This is, in fact, one of the very interesting things about biological investigators. They use the infrequent to illuminate the common. The former they call abnormal, the latter normal. Often, as is the case for Money and others in the medical world, the abnormal requires management. In the examples I will discuss, management means conversion to the normal. Thus, we have a profound irony. Biologists and physicians use natural biological variation to define normality. Armed with this description, they set out to eliminate the natural variation that gave them their definitions in the first place.

How does all this apply to the construction of masculinity? Money lists ten road signs directing a person along the path to male or female. In most cases these indicators are clear, but, as in any large city these days, sometimes graffiti makes them hard to read and the traveler ends up taking a wrong turn. The first sign is *chromosomal sex*, the presence of an X or a Y chromosome. The second is *gonadal sex*: when there is no graffiti, the Y or the X instructs the fetal gonad to develop into a testis or an ovary. *Fetal hormonal sex* marks the third fork: the embryonic testis must make hormones which influence events to come—particularly the fourth (*internal morphologic sex*), fifth (*external morphologic sex*), and sixth (*brain sex*) branches in the road. All of these, but especially the external morphologic sex at birth, illuminate the road sign for step number seven, *sex of assignment and rearing*. Finally, to become either a true male or a true female in John Money's world, one must produce the right hormones at puberty (*pubertal hormonal sex*), acquire and express a consistent

gender identity and role, and, to complete the picture, be able to reproduce in the appropriate fashion (*procreative sex*).[1]

Many medical texts reproduce this neat little scheme, and suggest that it is a literal account of the scientific truth, but they neglect to point out how, at each step, scientists have woven into the fabric their own deeply social understandings of what it means to be male or female. Let me illustrate this for several of the branches in the road. Why is it that usually XX babies grow up to be female while XYs become male? Geneticists say that it is because of a specific Y chromosome gene, often abbreviated SDY (for "Sex-Determining Gene" on the Y). Biologists also refer to the SDY as the Master Sex-Determining Gene and say that in its *presence* a male is formed. Females, on the other hand, are said to be the default sex. In the *absence* of the master gene, they just naturally happen. The story of the SDY begins an account of maleness that continues throughout development. A male embryo must activate its master gene and seize its developmental pathway from the underlying female ground plan.

When the SDY gene starts working, it turns the indifferent gonad into a functional testis. One of the first things the testis does is to induce hormone synthesis. It is these molecules that take control of subsequent developmental steps. The first hormone to hit the decks (MIS, or Mullerian Inhibiting Substance) suppresses the development of the internal female organs, which lie in wait ready to unveil their feminine presence. The next, fetal testosterone, manfully pushes over embryonic primordia to develop both the internal and external trappings of physical masculinity. Again, medical texts offer the presence/absence hypothesis. Maleness requires the presence of special hormones; in their absence, femaleness just happens.[2]

Up to this point, two themes emerge. First, masculinity is an active presence which forces itself onto a feminine foundation. Money sometimes calls this "The Adam Principle—adding something to make a male." Second, the male is in constant danger. At any point male development can be derailed: a failure to activate SDY, and the gonad becomes an ovary; a failure to make MIS, and the fetus can end up with fallopian tubes and a uterus superimposed on an otherwise male body; a failure to make fetal testosterone, and, despite the presence of a testis, the embryo develops the external trappings of a baby girl. One fascinating contradiction in the scientific literature illustrates my point. Most texts write that femaleness results from the absence of male hormones, yet at the same time scientists worry about how male fetuses protect themselves from being femininized by the sea of maternal (female) hormones in which they grow.[3] This fear suggests, of course, that female hormones play an active role, after all; but most scientists do not pick up on that bit of logic. Instead, they hunt for special proteins the male embryo makes in order to protect itself from maternally induced feminization. (It seems that mother is to blame even before birth.)

Consider now the birth of a boy-child. He is perfect: Y chromosomes, testes descended into their sweet little scrotal sacs, a beautifully formed penis. He is perfect—except that the penis is very tiny. What happens next? Some medical texts refer to a situation such as this as a social emergency, others see it as a surgical one. The parents want to tell everyone about the birth of their baby boy; the physicians fear he cannot continue developing along the road to masculinity. They decide that creating a female is best. Females are imperfect by nature, and if this child cannot be a perfect or near-perfect male, then being an imperfect female is the best choice. What do the criteria physicians use to make such choices tell us about the construction of masculinity?

Medical managers use the following rule of thumb:

> Genetic females should always be raised as females, preserving reproductive potential, regardless of how severely the patients are

virilized. In the genetic male, however, the gender of assignment is based on the infant's anatomy, predominantly the size of the phallus.[4]

Only a few reports on penile size at birth exist in the scientific literature, and it seems that birth size in and of itself is not a particularly good indicator of size and function at puberty. The average phallus at birth measures 3.5 cm (1 to 1.5 inches) long. A baby boy born with a penis measuring only 0.9 inches raises some eyebrows, but medical practitioners do not permit one born with a penis less than 0.6 inches long to remain as a male.[5] Despite the fact that the intact organ promises to provide orgasmic pleasure to the future adult it is surgically removed (along with the testes) and replaced by a much smaller clitoris which may or may not retain orgasmic function. When surgeons turn "Sammy" into "Samantha," they also build her a vagina. Her primary sexual activity is to be the recipient of a penis during heterosexual intercourse. As one surgeon recently commented, "It's easier to poke a hole than build a pole."

All this surgical activity goes on to ensure a congruous and certain sex of assignment and sex of rearing. During childhood, the medical literature insists, boys must have a phallus large enough to permit them to pee standing up, thus allowing them to "feel normal" when they play in little boys' peeing contests. In adulthood, the penis must become large enough for vaginal penetration during sexual intercourse. By and large, physicians use the standard of reproductive potential for making females and phallus size for making males, although Suzanne J. Kessler reports one case of a physician choosing to reassign as male a potentially reproductive genetic female infant rather than remove a well-formed penis.[6]

At birth, then, masculinity becomes a social phenomenon. For proper masculine socialization to occur, the little boy must have a sufficiently large penis. There must be no doubt in the boy's mind, in the minds of his parents and other adult relatives, or in the minds of his male peers about the legitimacy of his male identification. In childhood, all that is required is that he be able to pee in a standing position. In adulthood, he must engage in vaginal heterosexual intercourse. The discourse of sexual pleasure, even for males, is totally absent from this medical literature. In fact, male infants who receive extensive penile surgery often end up with badly scarred and thus physically insensitive members. While no surgeon finds this outcome desirable, in assigning sex to an intersexual infant, sexual pleasure clearly takes a backseat to ensuring heterosexual conventions. Penetration in the absence of pleasure takes precedence over pleasure in the absence of penetration.

In the world of John Money and other managers of intersexuality, men are made not born. Proper socialization becomes more important than genetics. Hence, Money and his followers have a simple solution to accidents as terrible as penile amputation following infant circumcision: raise the boy as a girl. If both the parents and the child remain confident of his newfound female identity, all will be well. But what counts as good mental health for boys and girls? Here, Money and his coworkers focus primarily on female development, which becomes the mirror from which we can reflect the truth about males. Money has published extensively on XX infants born with masculinized genitalia. Usually such children are raised as girls, receiving surgery and hormonal treatments to femininize their genitalia and to ensure a feminine puberty. He notes that frequently such children have a harder time than usual achieving clarity about their femininity. Some signs of trouble are these: in the toddler years, engaging in rough-and-tumble play, and hitting more than other little girls do; in the adolescent years, thinking more about having a career and fantasizing less about marriage than other little girls do; and, as an adolescent and young adult, having lesbian relationships.

The homologue to these developmental variations can be found in Richard Green's description of the "Sissy Boy Syndrome." Green studied little boys who develop "feminine" interests—playing with dolls, wanting to dress in girls' clothing, not engaging in enough rough-and-tumble play. These boys, he argued, are at high risk for becoming homosexuals. Money's and Green's ideas work together to present a picture of normality. And, surprise, surprise, there is no room in the scheme for a normal homosexual. Money makes a remarkable claim. Genetics and even hormones count less in making a man or a woman than does socialization. In sustaining that claim, his strongest evidence, his trump card, is that the child born a male but raised a female becomes a heterosexual female. In their accounts of the power of socialization, Money and his coworkers define heterosexual in terms of the sex of rearing. Thus, a child raised as a female (even if biologically male) who prefers male lovers is psychologically heterosexual, although genetically she is not.

Again, we can parse out the construction of masculinity. To begin with, normally developing little boys must be active and willing to push one another around; maleness and aggression go together. Eventually, little boys become socialized into appropriate adult behavior, which includes heterosexual fantasy and activity. Adolescent boys do not dream of marriage, but of careers and a professional future. A healthy adolescent girl, in contrast, must fantasize about falling in love, marrying, and raising children. Only a masculinized girl dreams of a professional future. Of course, we know already that for men the true mark of heterosexuality involves vaginal penetration with the penis. Other activities, even if they are with a woman, do not really count.

This might be the end of the story, except for one thing. Accounts of normal development drawn from the study of intersexuals contain internal inconsistencies. How *does* Money explain the higher percentage than normal of lesbianism, or the more frequent aggressive behavior among masculinized children raised as girls? One could imagine elaborating on the socialization theme:

parents aware of the uncertain sex of their children subconsciously socialize them in some intermediary fashion. Shockingly for a psychologist, however, Money denies the possibility of subconsciously driven behavior. Instead, he and the many others who interpret the development of intersexual children resort to hormonal explanations. If an XX girl, born with a penis, surgically "corrected" shortly after birth, and raised as a girl, subsequently becomes a lesbian, Money and others do not look to faulty socialization. Instead, they explain this failure to become heterosexual by appealing to hormones present in the fetal environment. Excess fetal testosterone caused the masculinization of the genitalia; similarly, fetal testosterone must have altered the developing brain, readying it to view females as appropriate sexual objects. Here, then, we have the last bit of the picture painted by biologists. By implication, normal males become sexually attracted to females because testosterone affects their brain during embryonic development. Socialization reinforces this inclination.

Biologists, then, write texts about human development. These documents, which take the form of research papers, textbooks, review articles, and popular books, grow from interpretations of scientific data. Often written in neutral, abstract language, the texts have the ring of authority. Because they represent scientific findings, one might imagine that they contain no preconceptions, no culturally instigated belief systems. But this turns out not to be the case. Although based in evidence, scientific writing can be seen as a particular kind of cultural interpretation—the enculturated scientist interprets nature. In the process, he or she also uses that interpretation to reinforce old or build new sets of social beliefs. Thus, scientific work contributes to the construction of masculinity, and masculine constructs are among the building blocks for particular kinds of scientific knowledge. One of the jobs of the science critic is to illuminate this interaction. Once this is done, it becomes possible to discuss change.

Notes

1. For a popular account of this picture, see John Money and Patricia Tucker, *Sexual Signatures: On Being a Man or a Woman* (Boston: Little, Brown and Co., 1975).

2. The data do not actually match the presence/absence model, but this does not seem to bother most people. For a discussion of this point, see Anne Fausto-Sterling, "Life in the XY Corral," *Women's Studies International Forum* 12 (1989): 319–31; Anne Fausto-Sterling, "Society Writes Biology/Biology Constructs Gender," *Daedalus* 116 (1987): 61–76; and Anne Fausto-Sterling, *Myths of Gender: Biological Theories about Women and Men* (New York: Basic Books, 1992).

3. I use the phrase "male hormone" and "female hormone" as shorthand. There are, in fact, no such categories. Males and females have the same hormones, albeit in different quantities and sometimes with different tissue distributions.

4. Patricia Donahue, David M. Powell, and Mary M. Lee, "Clinical Management of Intersex Abnormalities," *Current Problems in Surgery* 8 (1991): 527.

5. Robert H. Danish, Peter A. Lee, Thomas Mazur, James A. Amrhein, and Claude J. Migeon, "Micropenis II: Hypogonadotropic Hypogonadism," *Johns Hopkins Medical Journal* 146 (1980): 177–84.

6. Suzanne J. Kessler, "The Medical Construction of Gender: Case Management of Intersexed Infants," *Signs* 16 (1990).

33

ARTICLE

Gloria Steinem

If Men Could Menstruate

A white minority of the world has spent centuries conning us into thinking that a white skin makes people superior—even though the only thing it really does is make them more subject to ultraviolet rays and to wrinkles. Male human beings have built whole cultures around the idea that penis-envy is "natural" to women—though having such an unprotected organ might be said to make men vulnerable, and the power to give birth makes womb-envy at least as logical.

In short, the characteristics of the powerful, whatever they may be, are thought to be better than the characteristics of the powerless—and logic has nothing to do with it.

What would happen, for instance, if suddenly, magically, men could menstruate and women could not?

The answer is clear—menstruation would become an enviable, boastworthy, masculine event:

Men would brag about how long and how much.

Boys would mark the onset of menses, that longed-for proof of manhood, with religious ritual and stag parties.

Reprinted from *Outrageous Acts and Everyday Rebellions.* Holt, Rinehart and Winston. © 1983 by Gloria Steinem.

Congress would fund a National Institute of Dysmenorrhea to help stamp out monthly discomforts.

Sanitary supplies would be federally funded and free. (Of course, some men would still pay for the prestige of commercial brands such as John Wayne Tampons, Muhammad Ali's Rope-a-dope Pads, Joe Namath Jock Shields—"For Those Light Bachelor Days," and Robert "Baretta" Blake Maxi-Pads.)

Military men, right-wing politicians, and religious fundamentalists would cite menstruation ("*men*-struation") as proof that only men could serve in the Army ("you have to give blood to take blood"), occupy political office ("can women be aggressive without that steadfast cycle governed by the planet Mars?"), be priests and ministers ("how could a woman give her blood for our sins?"), or rabbis ("without the monthly loss of impurities, women remain unclean").

Male radicals, left-wing politicians, and mystics, however, would insist that women are equal, just different; and that any woman could enter their ranks if only she were willing to self-inflict a major wound every month ("you *must* give blood for the revolution"), recognize the preeminence of menstrual issues, or subordinate her selfness to all men in their Cycle of Enlightenment.

Street guys would brag ("I'm a three-pad man") or answer praise from a buddy ("Man, you lookin' *good!*") by giving fives and saying, "Yeah, man, I'm on the rag!"

TV shows would treat the subject at length. ("Happy Days": Richie and Potsie try to convince Fonzie that he is still "The Fonz," though he has missed two periods in a row.) So would newspapers. (SHARK SCARE THREATENS MENSTRUATING MEN. JUDGE CITES MONTHLY STRESS IN PARDONING RAPIST.) And movies. (Newman and Redford in "Blood Brothers"!)

Men would convince women that intercourse was *more* pleasurable at "that time of the month." Lesbians would be said to fear blood and therefore life itself—though probably only because they needed a good menstruating man.

Of course, male intellectuals would offer the most moral and logical arguments. How could a woman master any discipline that demanded a sense of time, space, mathematics, or measurement, for instance, without that in-built gift for measuring the cycles of the moon and planets— and thus for measuring anything at all? In the rarefied fields of philosophy and religion, could women compensate for missing the rhythm of the universe? Or for their lack of symbolic death-and-resurrection every month?

Liberal males in every field would try to be kind: the fact that "these people" have no gift for measuring life or connecting to the universe, the liberals would explain, should be punishment enough.

And how would women be trained to react? One can imagine traditional women agreeing to all these arguments with a staunch and smiling masochism. ("The ERA would force housewives to wound themselves every month": Phyllis Schlafly. "Your husband's blood is as sacred as that of Jesus—and so sexy, too!": Marabel Morgan.) Reformers and Queen Bees would try to imitate men, and *pretend* to have a monthly cycle. All feminists would explain endlessly that men, too, needed to be liberated from the false idea of Martian aggressiveness, just as women needed to escape the bonds of menses-envy. Radical feminists would add that the oppression of the nonmenstrual was the pattern for all other oppressions. ("Vampires were our first freedom fighters!") Cultural feminists would develop a bloodless imagery in art and literature. Socialist feminists would insist that only under capitalism would men be able to monopolize menstrual blood. . . .

In fact, if men could menstruate, the power justifications could probably go on forever.

If we let them.

34

ARTICLE

Thomas J. Gerschick
Adam Stephen Miller

Coming to Terms: Masculinity and Physical Disability

Men with physical disabilities are marginalized and stigmatized in American society. The image and reality of men with disabilities undermine cultural beliefs about men's bodies and physicality. The body is a central foundation of how men define themselves and how they are defined by others. Bodies are vehicles for determining value, which in turn translates into status and prestige. Men's bodies allow them to demonstrate the socially valuable characteristics of toughness, competitiveness, and ability (Messner 1992). Thus, one's body and relationship to it provide a way to apprehend the world and one's place in it. The bodies of men with disabilities serve as a continual reminder that they are at odds with the expectations of the dominant culture. As anthro-

Reprinted from *Masculinities*, 2(1) 1994.
We would like to thank our informants for sharing their time, experiences, and insights. Additionally, we would like to thank the following people for their comments on earlier drafts of this work: Sandra Cole, Harlan Hahn, Michael Kimmel, Michael Messner, Don Sabo, and Margaret Weigers. We, of course, remain responsible for its content. Finally, we are indebted to Kimberly Browne and Erika Gottfried for background research and interview transcriptions. This research was supported by a grant from the Undergraduate Research Opportunity Program at the University of Michigan.

pologist Robert Murphy (1990: 94) writes of his own experiences with disability:

> Paralytic disability constitutes emasculation of a more direct and total nature. For the male, the weakening and atrophy of the body threaten all the cultural values of masculinity: strength, activeness, speed, virility, stamina, and fortitude.

This article seeks to sharpen our understanding of the creation, maintenance, and recreation of gender identities by men who, by birth, accident, or illness, find themselves dealing with a physical disability. We examine two sets of social dynamics that converge and clash in the lives of men with physical disabilities. On the one side, these men must deal with the presence and pressures of hegemonic masculinity, which demands strength. On the other side, societal members perceive people with disabilities to be weak.

For the present study, we conducted in-depth interviews with ten men with physical disabilities in order to gain insights into the psychosocial aspects of men's ability to come to terms with their physical and social condition. We wanted to know how men with physical disabilities respond to the demands of hegemonic masculinity and their marginalization. For instance, if men with disabilities need others to legitimate their gender identity during encounters, what happens when others deny them the opportunity? How do they reconcile the conflicting expectations associated with masculinity and disability? How do they define masculinity for themselves, and what are the sources of these definitions? To what degree do their responses contest and/or perpetuate the current gender order? That is, what are the political implications of different gender identities and practices? In addressing these questions, we contribute to the growing body of literature on marginalized and alternative gender identities.

We will first discuss the general relationship between physical disability and hegemonic masculinity. Second, we will summarize the methods used in this study. Next, we will present and discuss our central findings. Finally, we discuss how the gender identities and life practices of men with disabilities contribute to the politics of the gender order.

Hegemonic Masculinity and Physical Disability

Recently, the literature has shifted toward understanding gender as an interactive process. Thus, it is presumed to be not only an aspect of what one *is*, but more fundamentally it is something that one *does* in interaction with others (West and Zimmerman 1987). Whereas previously, gender was thought to be strictly an individual phenomenon, this new understanding directs our attention to the interpersonal and institutional levels as well. The lives of men with disabilities provide an instructive arena in which to study the interactional nature of gender and its effect on individual gender identities.

In *The Body Silent*, Murphy (1990) observes that men with physical disabilities experience "embattled identities" because of the conflicting

expectations placed on them as men and as people with disabilities. On the one side, contemporary masculinity privileges men who are strong, courageous, aggressive, independent and self-reliant (Connell 1987). On the other side, people with disabilities are perceived to be, and treated as, weak, pitiful, passive, and dependent (Murphy 1990). Thus, for men with physical disabilities, masculine gender identity and practice are created and maintained at the crossroads of the demands of contemporary masculinity and the stigmatization associated with disability. As such, for men with physical disabilities, being recognized as masculine by others is especially difficult, if not impossible, to accomplish. Yet not being recognized as masculine is untenable because, in our culture, everyone is expected to display an appropriate gender identity (West and Zimmerman 1987).

Methods

This research was based on in-depth interviews with ten men. Despite the acknowledged problem of identity management in interviews, we used this method because we were most interested in the subjective perceptions and experiences of our informants. To mitigate this dynamic, we relied on probing questions and reinterviews. Informants were located through a snowball sample, utilizing friends and connections within the community of people with disabilities. All of our informants were given pseudonyms, and we further protected their identity by deleting nonessential personal detail. The age range of respondents varied from sixteen to seventy-two. Eight of our respondents were white, and two were African American. Geographically, they came from both coasts and the Midwest. All were "mobility impaired," and most were para- or quadriplegics. Given the small sample size and the modicum of diversity within it, this work must necessarily be understood as exploratory.

We interviewed men with physical disabilities for three primary reasons. First, given the diversity of disabilities and our modest resources, we had to bound the sample. Second, mobility impairments tend to be more apparent than other disabilities, such as blindness or hearing loss, and people respond to these men using visual clues. Third, although the literature in this area is scant, much of it focuses on men with physical disabilities.

Due to issues of shared identities, Adam did all the interviews. Interviews were semi-structured and tape-recorded. Initial interviews averaged approximately an hour in length. Additionally, we contacted all of our informants at least once with clarifying questions and, in some cases, to test ideas that we had. These follow-ups lasted approximately thirty minutes. Each informant received a copy of his interview transcript to ensure that we had captured his perspective accurately. We also shared draft copies of this chapter with them and incorporated their insights into the current version.

There were two primary reasons for the thorough follow-up. First, from a methodological standpoint, it was important for us to capture the experience of our informants as fully as possible. Second, we felt that we had an obligation to allow them to control, to a large extent, the representation of their experience.

Interviews were analyzed using an analytic induction approach (Denzin 1989; Emerson 1988; Katz 1988). In determining major and minor patterns of masculine practice, we used the responses to a series of questions including, What is the most important aspect of masculinity to you? What would you say makes you feel most manly or masculine? Do you think your conception of masculinity is different from that of able-bodied men as a result of your disability? If so, how and why? If not, why not? Additionally, we presented our informants with a list of characteristics associated with prevailing masculinity based on the work of R. W. Connell (1987, 1990a, 1990b, 1991) and asked them to rate their importance to their conception of self. Both positive and negative responses to this portion of our questionnaire guided our insight into how each man viewed his masculinity. To further support our discussion, we turned to the limited academic literature in this area. Much more helpful were the wide range of biographical and autobiographical accounts of men who have physical disabilities (see, for instance, Murphy 1990; Callahan 1989; Kriegel 1991; Hahn 1989; and Zola 1982).

Finally, in analyzing the data we were sensitive to making judgments about our informants when grouping them into categories. People with disabilities are shoehorned into categories too much as it is. We sought to discover what was common among their responses and to highlight what we perceived to be the essence of their views. In doing so, we endeavored to provide a conceptual framework for understanding the responses of men with physical disabilities while trying to be sensitive to their personal struggles.

Disability, Masculinity, and Coming to Terms

While no two men constructed their sense of masculinity in exactly the same way, there appeared to be three dominant frameworks our informants used to cope with their situations. These patterns can be conceived of in relation to the standards inherent in dominant masculinity. We call them the three Rs: *reformulation*, which entailed men's redefinition of hegemonic characteristics on their own terms; *reliance*, reflected by sensitive or hypersensitive adoptions of particular predominant attributes; and *rejection*, characterized by the renunciation of these standards and either the creation of one's own principles and practices or the denial of masculinity's importance in one's life. However, one should note that none of our interviewees *entirely* followed any one of these frameworks in defining his sense of self. Rather, for heuristic reasons, it is best to speak of the major and minor ways each man used these three patterns. For example, some of our informants relied on dominant standards in their view of sexuality and occupation but also reformulated the prevailing ideal of independence.

Therefore, we discuss the *primary* way in which these men with disabilities related to hegemonic masculinity's standards, while recognizing that their coping mechanisms reflected a more complex combination of strategies. In doing so, we avoid "labeling" men and assigning them to arbitrary categories.

Reformulation

Some of our informants responded to idealized masculinity by reformulating it, shaping it along the lines of their own abilities, perceptions, and strengths, and defining their manhood along these new lines. These men tended not to contest these standards overtly, but—either consciously or unconsciously—they recognized in their own condition an inability to meet these ideals as they were culturally conceived.

An example of this came from Damon, a seventy-two-year-old quadriplegic who survived a spinal-cord injury in an automobile accident ten years ago. Damon said he always desired, and had, control of his life. While Damon required round-the-clock personal care assistants (PCAs), he asserted that he was still a very independent person:

> I direct all of my activities around my home where people have to help me to maintain my apartment, my transportation, which I own, and direction in where I go. I direct people how to get there, and I tell them what my needs will be when I am going and coming, and when to get where I am going.

Damon said that his sense of control was more than mere illusion; it was a reality others knew of as well. This reputation seemed important to him:

> People know from Jump Street that I have my own thing, and I direct my own thing. And if they can't comply with my desire, they won't be around. . . . I don't see any reason why people with me can't take instructions and get my life on just as I was having it before, only thing I'm not doing it myself. I direct somebody else to do it. So, therefore, I don't miss out on very much.

Hegemonic masculinity's definition of independence privileges self-reliance and autonomy. Damon required substantial assistance: indeed, some might term him "dependent." However, Damon's reformulation of the independence ideal, accomplished in part through a cognitive shift, allowed him to think otherwise.

Harold, a forty-six-year-old polio survivor, described a belief and practice akin to Damon's. Also a quadriplegic, Harold similarly required PCAs to help him handle daily necessities: Harold termed his reliance on and control of PCAs "acting through others":

> When I say independence can be achieved by acting through other people, I actually mean getting through life, liberty, and the pursuit of happiness while utilizing high-quality and dependable attendant-care services.

As with Damon, Harold achieved his perceived sense of independence by controlling others. Harold stressed that he did not count on family or friends to do favors for him, but *employed* his PCAs in a "business relationship" he controlled. Alternatives to family and friends are used whenever possible because most people with disabilities do not want to burden or be dependent on their families any more than necessary (Murphy 1990).

Social class plays an important role here. Damon and Harold had the economic means to afford round-the-clock assistance. While none of our informants experienced economic hardship, many people with disabilities depend on the welfare system for their care, and the amount and quality of assistance they receive make it much more difficult to conceive of themselves as independent.

A third man who reformulated predominant demands was Brent, a forty-five-year-old administrator. He told us that his paraplegic status, one that he had lived with since he was five years old, had often cast him as an "outsider" to society. This status was particularly painful in his late adolescence, a time when the "sexual revolution" was sweeping America's youth:

> A very important measure of somebody's personhood—manhood—was their sexual ability. . . . What bothers me more than anything else is the stereotypes, and even more so, in terms of sexual desirability. Because I had a disability, I was less desirable than able-bodied people. And that I found very frustrating.

His experiences led him to recast the hegemonic notion that man's relations with a partner should be predominantly physical. As a result, he stressed the importance of emotional relations and trust. This appeared to be key to Brent's definition of his manhood:

> For me, that is my measure of who I am as an individual and who I am as a man—my ability to be able to be honest with my wife. Be able to be close with her, to be able to ask for help, provide help. To have a commitment, to follow through, and to do all those things that I think are important.

As Connell (1990a) notes, this requires a capacity to not only be expressive, but also to have feelings worth expressing. This clearly demonstrates a different form of masculine practice.

The final case of reformulation came from Robert, a thirty-year-old survivor of a motorcycle accident. Able-bodied for much of his life, Robert's accident occurred when he was twenty-four, leaving him paraplegic. Through five years of intensive physical therapy, he regained 95 percent of his original function, though certain effects linger to this day.

Before his accident, Robert had internalized many of the standards of dominant masculinity exemplified by frequenting bars, leading an active sex life, and riding a motorcycle. But,

if our research and the body of autobiographical works from men with physical disabilities has shown anything, it is that coming to terms with a disability eventually changes a man. It appeared to have transformed Robert. He remarked that, despite being generally "recovered," he had maintained his disability-influenced value system:

> I judge people on more of a personal and character level than I do on any physical, or I guess I did; but, you know, important things are guys that have integrity, guys that are honest about what they are doing, that have some direction in their life and know . . . peace of mind and what they stand for.

One of the areas that Robert said took the longest to recover was his sexuality—specifically, his confidence in his sexual ability. While Robert said sexual relations were still important to him, like Brent he reformulated his previous, largely hegemonic notion of male sexuality into a more emotionally and physically egalitarian model:

> I've found a whole different side to having sex with a partner and looking at satisfying the partner rather than satisfying myself; and that has taken the focus off of satisfying myself, being the big manly stud, and concentrating more on my partner. And that has become just as satisfying.

However, reformulation did not yield complete severance from prevailing masculinity's standards as they were culturally conceived. For instance, despite his reformulative inclinations, Robert's self-described "macho" attitude continued in some realms during his recovery. He, and all others we interviewed, represented the complexity of gender identities and practices; no man's masculinity fell neatly into any one of the three patterns.

For instance, although told by most doctors that his physical condition was probably permanent, Robert's resolve was unyielding. "I put my blinders on to all negative insight into it and just totally focused on getting better," he said. "And I think that was, you know, a major factor on why I'm where I'm at today." This typified the second pattern we identified—reliance on hegemonic masculinity's standards. It was ironic, then, that Robert's tenacity, his never-ending work ethic, and his focused drive to succeed were largely responsible for his almost-complete recovery. While Robert reformulated much of his earlier sense of masculinity, he still relied on this drive.

Perhaps the area in which men who reformulate most closely paralleled dominant masculinity was the emphasis they placed on their occupation. Our sample was atypical in that most of our informants were professionally employed on a full-time basis and could, therefore, draw on class-based resources, whereas unemployment among people with disabilities is very high. Just as societal members privilege men who are accomplished in their occupation, Harold said he finds both "purpose," and success, in his career:

> No one is going to go through life without some kind of purpose. Everyone decides. I wanted to be a writer. So I became a writer and an observer, a trained observer.

Brent said that he drew much of his sense of self, his sense of self-esteem, and his sense of manhood from his occupational accomplishments. Initially, Brent denied the importance of the prevailing ideal that a man's occupational worth was derived from his breadwinner status:

> It is not so important to be the breadwinner as it is to be competent in the world. You know, to have a career, to have my name on the door. That is what is most important. It is that recognition that is very important to me.

However, he later admitted that being the breadwinner still was important to him, although he denied a link between his desires and the "stereotypical" conception of breadwinner status. He maintained that "it's still important to me, because I've always been able to make money." Independence, both economic and physical, were important to all of our informants.

Rejection of hegemonic ideals also occurred among men who primarily depended on a reformulative framework. Harold's view of relationships with a partner dismissed the sexually powerful ideal: "The fact of the matter is that I'm not all that upset by the fact that I'm disabled and I'm a male. I mean, I know what I can do." We will have more to say about the rejection of dominant conceptions of sexuality later.

In brief summary, the subset of our informants whose primary coping pattern involved reformulation of dominant standards recognized their inability to meet these ideals as they are culturally conceived. Confident in their own abilities and values, and drawing from previous experience, they confronted standards of masculinity on their own terms. In doing so, they distanced themselves from masculine ideals.

Reliance

However, not all of the men with physical disabilities we interviewed depended on a reformulative approach. We found that many of our informants *were* concerned with others' views of their masculinity and with meeting the demands of hegemonic masculinity. They primarily used the second pattern, reliance, which involves the internalization of many more of the ideals of predominant masculinity, including physical strength, athleticism, independence, and sexual prowess. Just as some men depended on reformulation for much of their masculine definition, others, despite their inability to meet many of these ideals, relied on them heavily. As such, these men did not seem to be as comfortable with their sense of manhood; indeed, their inability to meet society's standards bothered them very much.

This subset of our informants found themselves in a double bind that left them conflicted. They embraced dominant conceptions of masculinity as a way to gain acceptance from themselves and from others. Yet, they were continuously reminded in their interactions with others that they were "incomplete." As a result, the identity behind the facade suffered; there were, then, major costs associated with this strategy.

The tension between societal expectations and the reality of men with physical disabilities was most clearly demonstrated by Jerry, a sixteen-year-old who had juvenile rheumatoid arthritis. While Jerry was physically able to walk for limited distances, this required great effort on his part; consequently, he usually used a wheelchair. He was concerned with the appearance of his awkward walking. "I feel like I look a little, I don't know, more strange when I walk," he said.

The significance of appearance and external perception of manliness is symptomatic of the difficulty men with physical disabilities have in developing an identity and masculinity free of others' perceptions and expectations. Jerry said:

> I think [others' conception of what defines a man] is very important, because if they don't think of you as one, it is hard to think of yourself as one; or, it doesn't really matter if you think of yourself as one if no one else does.

Jerry said that, particularly among his peers, he was not perceived as attractive as the able-bodied teenagers; thus, he had difficulty in male–female relations beyond landing an occasional date. "[The girls believe] I might be a 'really nice person,' but not like a guy per se," he said. "I think to some extent that you're sort of genderless to them." This clearly represents the emasculation and depersonalization inherent in social definitions of disability.

However, Jerry said that he faced a more persistent threat to his autonomy—his independence and his sense of control—from others being "uncomfortable" around him and persisting in offering him assistance he often did not need. This made him "angry, though he usually did not refuse the help out of politeness. Thus,

with members of his social group, he participated in a "bargain": they would socialize with him as long as he remained in a dependent position where they could "help" him.

This forced, situational passivity led Jerry to emphasize his autonomy in other areas. For instance, Jerry avoided asking for help in nearly all situations. This was directly tied to reinforcing his embattled manhood by displaying outward strength and independence:

> If I ever have to ask someone for help, it really makes me like feel like less of a man. I don't like asking for help at all. You know, like even if I could use some, I'll usually not ask just because I can't, I just hate asking. . . . [A man is] fairly self-sufficient in that you can sort of handle just about any situation, in that you can help other people, and that you don't need a lot of help.

Jerry internalized the prevailing masculine ideal that a man should be independent; he relied on that ideal for his definition of manhood. His inability to meet this ideal—partly through his physical condition, and partly from how others treated him—threatened his identity and his sense of manhood, which had to be reinforced even at the expense of self-alienation.

One should not label Jerry a "relier" simply because of these struggles. Being only sixteen years of age—and the youngest participant in our study—Jerry was still developing his sense of masculinity; and, as with many teenagers both able-bodied and disabled, he was trying to fit into his peer group. Furthermore, Jerry will continue to mature and develop his self-image and sense of masculinity. A follow-up interview in five years might show a degree of resolution to his struggles.

Such a resolution could be seen in Michael, a thirty-three-year-old manager we interviewed, who also internalized many of the standards of hegemonic masculinity. A paraplegic from an auto accident in 1977, Michael struggled for many years after his accident to come to terms with his condition.

His struggles had several sources, all tied into his view of masculinity's importance. The first was that, before his accident, he accepted much of the dominant conception of masculinity. A high-school student, farm hand, and football and track star at the time, Michael said that independence, relations with the women he dated, and physical strength were central to his conception of self.

After his accident, Michael's doctors told him there was a 50–50 chance that he would regain the ability to walk, and he clung to the hope. "I guess I didn't understand it, and had hope that I would walk again," he said. However, he was "depressed" about his situation, "but not so much about my disability, I guess. Because that wasn't real yet."

But coming home three months after his accident didn't alleviate the depression. Instead, it heightened his anxiety and added a new component—vulnerability. In a span of three months, Michael had, in essence, his sense of masculinity and his security in himself completely stripped away. He was in an unfamiliar situation; and far from feeling strong, independent, and powerful, he felt vulnerable and afraid: "No one," he remarked, "can be prepared for a permanent disability."

His reliance on dominant masculinity, then, started with his predisability past and continued during his recovery as a coping mechanism to deal with his fears. The hegemonic standard Michael strove most to achieve was that of independence. It was central to his sense of masculinity before and at the time of our interview. Indeed, it was so important that it frustrated him greatly when he needed assistance. Much like Jerry, he refused to ask for it:

> I feel that I should be able to do everything for myself and I don't like it. . . . I don't mind asking for things that I absolutely can't do, like hanging pictures, or moving furniture, or having my oil changed in my car; but there are things that I'm capable of doing in my chair, like jumping up one step. That I feel like I

should be able to do, and I find it frustrating when I can't do that sometimes. . . . I don't like asking for [help I don't think I need]. It kind of makes me mad.

When asked if needing assistance was "unmanly," Michael replied, "There's probably some of that in there." For both Michael and Jerry, the independence ideal often led to risk-taking behavior in order to prove to themselves that they were more than their social definition.

Yet, much like Robert, Michael had reformulated his view of sexuality. He said that his physical sexuality made him "feel the most masculine"—apparently another reliant response with a stereotypical emphasis on sexual performance. However, it was more complicated. Michael said that he no longer concentrated on pleasing himself, as he did when able-bodied, but that he now had a more partner-oriented view of sexuality. "I think that my compensation for my feeling of vulnerability is I've overcompensated by trying to please my partner and leave little room to allow my partner to please me. . . . Some of my greatest pleasure is exhausting my partner while having sex." Ironically, while he focused more on his partner's pleasure than ever before, he did so at his own expense; a sense of balancing the needs of both partners was missing.

Thus, sex served multiple purposes for Michael—it gave him and his partner pleasure; it reassured him in his fears and his feelings of vulnerability; and it reconfirmed his masculinity. His sexuality, then, reflected both reliance and reformulation.

While independence and sexuality were both extremely important to Scott, a thirty-four-year-old rehabilitation engineer, he emphasized a third area for his sense of manhood—athletics. Scott served in the Peace Corps during his twenties, working in Central America. He described his life-style as "rigorous" and "into the whole sports thing," and used a mountain bike as his primary means of transportation and recreation.

He was also an avid hockey player in his youth and spent his summers in softball leagues.

Scott acquired a polio-like virus when he was twenty-five years old that left him permanently paraplegic, a situation that he did not initially accept. In an aggressive attempt to regain his physical ability, and similar to Robert, Scott obsessively attacked his rehabilitation

> . . . thinking, that's always what I've done with all the sports. If I wasn't good enough, I worked a little harder and I got better. So, I kept thinking my walking isn't very good now. If I push it, it will get better.

But Scott's athletic drive led not to miraculous recovery, but overexertion. When ordered by his doctors to scale back his efforts, he realized he could not recover strictly through tenacity. At the time of our interview, he was ambivalent about his limitations. He clearly did not feel like a failure: "I think that if I wouldn't have made the effort, I always would have wondered, could I have made a difference?" Following the athlete's code of conduct, "always give 110 percent," Scott attacked his recovery. But when his efforts were not enough—when he did not "emerge victorious"—he accepted it as an athlete would. Yet, his limitations also frustrated him at times, and in different areas.

For example, though his physical capacity was not what it was, Scott maintained a need for athletic competition. He played wheelchair basketball and was the only wheelchair-participant in a city softball league. However, he did not return to hockey, the sport he loved as a youngster; in fact, he refused to even try the sled-based equivalent.

Here was Scott's frustration. His spirit of athleticism was still alive, but he lamented the fact that he could not compete exactly as before:

> [I miss] the things that I had. I played hockey; that was my primary sport for so many years. Pretty much, I did all the sports. But, like, I never played basketball; never liked basketball before. Which is why I think I can play now.

> See, it would be like the equivalent to wheelchair hockey. Some friends of mine have talked to me about it, [but] I'm not really interested in that. Because it wouldn't be real hockey. And it would make me feel worse, rather that better.

In this respect, Scott had not completely come to terms with his limitations. He still wanted to be a "real" athlete, competing in the same sports, in the same ways, with the same rules, with others who shared his desire for competition. Wheelchair hockey, which he derogatorily referred to as "gimp hockey," represented the antithesis of this for him.

Scott's other responses added to this emphasis. What he most disliked about having a disability was "that I can't do the things that I want to be able to do," meaning he could not ride his bike or motorcycle, he could not play "real" hockey, and he was unable to live a free-wheeling, spontaneous life-style. Rather, he had to plan ahead of time where he went and how he got there. The frustration caused by having to plan nearly every move was apparent in almost all of our interviews.

However, on the subject of independence, Scott said "I think I'm mostly independent," but complained that there were some situations where he could not meet his expectations and had to depend on his wife. Usually this was not a "major issue," but "there's still times when, yeah, I feel bad about it; or, you know it's the days where she doesn't feel like it, but she kind of has to. That's what bothers me the most, I guess." Thus, he reflected the general desire among men with disabilities not to be a burden of any kind on family members.

Much of the time, Scott accepted being "mostly independent." His reliance on the ideals of athleticism and independence played a significant part in his conception of masculinity and self. However, Scott learned, though to a limited degree, to let go of some of his previous ideals and to accept a different, reformulated notion of independence and competition. Yet, he could not entirely do so. His emphasis on athletics and independence was still strong, and there were many times when athletics and acceptance conflicted.

However, one should stop short of a blanket assessment of men with disabilities who rely on hegemonic masculinity standards. "Always" is a dangerous word, and stating that "men who rely on hegemonic standards are *always* troubled" is a dangerous assumption. An apparent exceptional case among men who follow a reliant pattern came from Aaron, a forty-one-year-old paraplegic. Rather than experiencing inner turmoil and conflict, Aaron was one of the most upbeat individuals we interviewed. Aaron said that, before his 1976 accident, he was "on top of the world," with a successful business, a commitment to athletics that included basketball shoot-arounds with NBA prospects, and a wedding engagement. Indeed, from the time of his youth, Aaron relied on such hegemonic standards as sexuality, independence, athleticism, and occupational accomplishment.

For example, when asked what masculinity meant to him before his accident, Aaron said that it originally meant sexual conquest. As a teen, he viewed frequent sexual activity as a "rite of passage" into manhood.

Aaron said he had also enjoyed occupational success, and that this success was central to his definition of self, including being masculine. Working a variety of jobs ranging from assembly-line worker to white-collar professional, Aaron said, "I had been very fortunate to have good jobs, which were an important part of who I was and how I defined myself."

According to Aaron, much of his independence ideal came from his father. When his parents divorced, Aaron's father explained to him that, though he was only five, he would have to be "the man of the house." Aaron took this lesson to heart, and strived to fulfill this role both in terms of independence and providing for the family. "My image of manhood was that of a provider," he said, "one who was able to make a contribution to the financial stability of the family in addition to dealing with the problems and concerns that would come up."

His accident, a gunshot wound injuring his spinal cord, left him completely dependent. Predictably, Aaron could not immediately cope with this. "My whole self-image itself was real integrally tied up with the things I used to do," he said. "I found my desire for simple pleasures to be the greatest part of the pain I had to bear."

His pain increased when he left the hospital. His fiancee had left him, and within two years he lost "everything that was important to me"—his house, his business, his savings, most of his friends, and even, for a while, his hope.

However, much as with Robert, Aaron's resiliency eventually turned his life around. Just as he hit bottom, he began telling himself that "if you hold on long enough, if you don't quit, you'll get through it." Additionally, he attacked his therapy with the vengeance he had always devoted to athletics. "I'd never been confronted with a situation in my entire life before that I was not able to overcome by the efforts of my own merit," he said. "I took the same attitude toward this."

Further, he reasserted his sexuality. Though he then wore a colostomy bag, he resumed frequent sexual intercourse, taking the attitude that "this is who I was, and a woman was either going to have to accept me as I was, or she's got to leave me f——— alone."

However, he realized after those five years that his hard work would not be rewarded nor would he be miraculously healed. Figuring that "there's a whole lot of life that I need to live, and this wasn't the most efficient way to live it," he bought a new sport wheelchair, found a job, and became involved in wheelchair athletics. In this sense, a complex combination of all three patterns emerged in Aaron as reliance was mixed with reformulation and rejection.

Furthermore, his soul-searching led him to develop a sense of purpose in his life, and a reason for going on:

[During my recovery] I felt that I was left here to enrich the lives of as many people as I could before I left this earth, and it gave me a new purpose, a new vision, a new mission, new dreams.

Tenacity, the quest for independence, athletics, and sexual activity carried Aaron through his recovery. Many of these ideals, which had their source in his father's teachings, remained with him as he continued to be active in athletics (everything from basketball to softball to scuba diving), to assert his sexuality, and to aim for complete autonomy. To Aaron, independence, both physical and financial, was more than just a personal ideal; it was one that should be shared by all people with disabilities. As such, he aspired to be a role model for others:

> The work that I am involved in is to help people gain control over their lives, and I think it's vitally important that I walk my talk. If . . . we hold ourselves out to be an organization that helps people gain control over their lives, I think it's vitally important for me as the CEO of that organization to live my life in a way that embodies everything that we say we're about.

Clearly, Aaron was not the same man he was before his disability. He said that his maturity and his experience with disability "made me stronger," and that manhood no longer simply meant independence and sexual conquest. Manhood also meant

> . . . being responsible for one's actions; being considerate of another's feelings; being sensitive to individuals who are more vulnerable than yourself, to what their needs would be; standing up on behalf and fighting for those who cannot speak out for themselves, fight for themselves. It means being willing to take a position and be committed to a position, even when it's inconvenient or costly to take that point of view, and you do it only because of the principle involved.

This dovetailed significantly with his occupation, which was of great importance to him. But as alluded to above, Aaron's emphasis on occupation cannot be seen as mere reliance on the hegemonic conception of occupational achievement. It was more a reformulation of that ideal from self-achievement to facilitating the empowerment of others.

Nevertheless, Aaron's struggle to gain his current status, like the struggle of others who rely on hegemonic masculinity's standards, was immense. Constructing hegemonic masculinity from a subordinated position is almost always a Sisyphean task. One's ability to do so is undermined continuously by physical, social, and cultural weakness. "Understandably, in an effort to cope with this stress (balancing the demands for strength and the societal perception of weakness)," writes political scientist Harlan Hahn, "many disabled men have tended to identify personally and politically with the supposed strength of prevalent concepts of masculinity rather than with their disability" (1989: 3). To relinquish masculinity under these circumstances is to court gender annihilation, which is untenable to some men. Consequently, relying on hegemonic masculinity becomes more understandable (Connell 1990a: 471).

Rejection

Despite the difficulties it presents, hegemony, including that related to gender, is never complete (Janeway 1980, Scott 1985). For some of our informants, resistance took the form of creating alternative masculine identities and subcultures that provided them with a supportive environment. These men were reflected in the final pattern: rejection. Informants who followed this pattern did not so much share a common ideology or set of practices; rather, they believed that the dominant conception of masculinity was wrong, either in its individual emphases or as a practice. One of these men developed new standards of masculinity in place of the ones he had rejected. Another seemingly chose to deny masculinity's importance, although he was neither effeminate nor androgynous. Instead, they both emphasized their status as "persons," under the motto of "people first." This philosophy reflected a key tenet of the Disability Rights Movement.

Alex, a twenty-three-year-old, first-year law student, survived an accident that left him an incomplete quadriplegic when he was fourteen. Before that time, he felt he was an outsider at his private school because he eschewed the superficial, athletically oriented, and materialistic atmosphere. Further, he said the timing of the accident, when many of his peers were defining their social roles, added to this outsider perspective, in that it made him unable to participate in the highly social, role-forming process. "I didn't learn about the traditional roles of sexuality, and whatever the rules are for such behavior in our society, until later," he said. "Because of my physical characteristics, I had to learn a different set of rules."

Alex described himself as a "nonconformist." This simple moniker seemed central to his conception of selfhood and masculinity. Alex, unlike men who primarily reformulate these tenets, rejected the attitudinal and behavioral prescriptions of hegemonic masculinity. He maintained that his standards were his own—not society's—and he scoffed at commonly held views of masculinity.

For example, Alex blamed the media for the idea that men must be strong and attractive, stating "The traditional conception is that everyone has to be Arnold Schwartzenegger . . . [which] probably lead[s] to some violence, unhappiness, and things like that if they [men] don't meet the standards."

As for the importance of virility and sexual prowess, Alex said "There is a part of me that, you know, has been conditioned and acculturated and knows those [dominant] values"; but he sarcastically laughed at the notion of a man's sexual prowess being reflected in "making her pass out," and summed up his feelings on the subject by adding, "You have to be willing to do things in a nontraditional way."

Alex's most profound rejection of a dominant ideal involved the importance of fathering, in its strictest sense of the man as impregnator:

> There's no reason why we (his fiancee and himself) couldn't use artificial insemination or adoption. Parenting doesn't necessarily involve being the male sire. It involves being a good parent. . . . Parenting doesn't mean that it's your physical child. It involves responsibility and an emotional role as well. I don't think the link between parenthood is the primary link with sexuality. Maybe in terms of evolutionary purposes, but not in terms of a relationship.

Thus, Alex rejected the procreation imperative encouraged in hegemonic masculinity. However, while Alex took pride at overtly rejecting prevailing masculinity as superficial and silly, even he relied on it at times. Alex said he needed to support himself financially and would not ever want to be an emotional or economic "burden" in a relationship. On one level, this is a common concern for most people, disabled or not. But on another level, Alex admitted that it tied in to his sense of masculinity:

> If I was in a relationship and I wasn't working, and my spouse was, what could be the possible reasons for my not working? I could have just been fired. I could be laid off. Who knows what happened? I guess . . . that's definitely an element of masculinity, and I guess I am just as influenced by that as, oh, as I guess as other people, or as within my definition of masculinity. What do you know? I have been caught.

A different form of rejection was reflected in Leo, a fifty-eight-year-old polio survivor. Leo, who had striven for occupational achievement since his youth, seemed to value many hegemonic traits: independence, money-making ability, and recognition by peers. But he steadfastly denied masculinity's role in shaping his outlook.

Leo said the most important trait to him was his mental capacity and intelligence, since that allowed him to achieve his occupational goals. Yet he claimed this was not related to the prevailing standard. Rather, it tied into his ambitions from before his disability and his willingness to do most anything to achieve his goals.

Before we label him "a rejector," however, note that Leo was a believer in adaptive technology and personal assistance, and he did not see a contradiction between using personal-care assistants and being independent. This seemed to be a reformulation, just as with Damon and Harold, but when we asked Leo about this relation to masculinity, he flatly denied any connection.

Leo explained his renunciation of masculinity by saying "It doesn't mean a great deal . . . it's not how I think [of things]." He said that many of the qualities on our list of hegemonic characteristics were important to him on an individual level but did not matter to his sense of manhood. Leo maintained that there were "external" and "internal" reasons for this.

The external factors Leo identified were the Women's and Disability Rights Movements. Both provided support and alternatives that allow a person with a disability the freedom to be a person, and not (to use Leo's words) a "strange bird." Indeed, Leo echoed the call of the Disability Rights Movement when he described himself as a "person first." In this way, his humanity took precedence and his gender and his disability became less significant.

Also, Leo identified his background as a contributing factor to his outlook. Since childhood, he held a group of friends that valued intellectual achievement over physical performance. In his youth, Leo said he was a member of a group "on the college route." He remained in academia.

Internally, his view of masculinity came from maturity. He had dealt with masculinity and related issues for almost sixty years and reached a point at which he was comfortable with his gender. According to him, his gender conceptions ranged across all three patterns. This was particularly evident in his sexuality. When younger, he relied on a culturally valued,

genital sexuality and was concerned with his potency. He wanted to "be on top," despite the physical difficulties this presented him. At the time of our interview, he had a reformulated sexuality. The Women's Movement allowed him to remain sexually active without worrying about "being on top." He even rejected the idea (but not necessarily the physical condition) of potency, noting that it was "even a funny word—potent—that's power."

Further, his age allowed Leo to let go of many of the expectations he had for himself when younger. For instance, he used to overcompensate with great physical activity to prove his manhood and to be "a good daddy." But, he said, he gradually learned that such overcompensation was not necessary.

The practice of "letting go," as Leo and many of our other informants had done, was much like that described by essayist Leonard Kriegel (1991) who, in a series of autobiographical essays, discussed the metaphor of "falling into life" as a way of coping with a disability and masculinity. Kriegel described a common reaction to coping with disability; that is, attempting to "overcome" the results of polio, in his case, by building his upper-body strength through endless hours of exercise. In the end, he experienced premature arthritis in his shoulders and arms. The metaphor of giving up or letting go of behavioral expectations and gender practices as a way to gain greater strength and control over one's life was prevalent among the men who primarily rejected dominant masculinity. As Hahn notes, this requires a cognitive shift and a change in reference group as well as a source of social support:

> I think, ironically, that men with disabilities can acquire strength by acknowledging weakness. Instead of attempting to construct a fragile and ultimately phony identity only as males, they might have more to gain, and little to lose, both individually and collectively by forging a self-concept about the concept of disability. Certainly this approach requires the exposure of a

vulnerability that has been a primary reason for the elaborate defense mechanisms that disabled men have commonly employed to protect themselves (1989:3).

Thus, men with disabilities who rejected or renounced masculinity did so as a process of deviance disavowal. They realized that it was societal conceptions of masculinity, rather than themselves, that were problematic. In doing so, they were able to create alternative gender practices.

Summary and Conclusion

The experiences of men with physical disabilities are important, because they illuminate both the insidious power and limitations of contemporary masculinity. These men have insider knowledge of what the subordinated know about both the gender and social order (Janeway 1980). Additionally, the gender practices of some of these men exemplify alternative visions of masculinity that are obscured but available to men in our culture. Finally, they allow us to elucidate a process of paramount importance: How men with physical disabilities find happiness, fulfillment, and a sense of self-worth in a culture that has, in essence, denied them the right to their own identity, including their own masculinity.

Based on our interviews, then, we believe that men with physical disabilities depend on at least three patterns in their adjustment to the double bind associated with the demands of hegemonic masculinity and the stigmatization of being disabled. While each of our informants used one pattern more than the others, none of them depended entirely on any one of the three.

To judge the patterns and practices associated with any form of masculinity, it is necessary to explore the implications for both the personal life of the individual and the effect on the reproduction of the societal gender order (Con-

nell 1990a). Different patterns will challenge, comply, or actively support gendered arrangements.

The reliance pattern is reflected by an emphasis on control, independence, strength, and concern for appearances. Men who rely on dominant conceptions of masculinity are much more likely to internalize their feelings of inadequacy and seek to compensate or overcompensate for them. Because the problem is perceived to be located within oneself rather than within the social structure, this model does not challenge, but rather perpetuates, the current gender order.

A certain distancing from dominant ideals occurs in the reformulation pattern. But reformulation tends to be an independent project, and class-based resources play an important role. As such, it doesn't present a formidable challenge to the gender order. Connell (1990a: 474) argues that this response may even modernize patriarchy.

The rejection model, the least well represented in this article, offers the most hope for change. Linked closely to a sociopolitical approach that defines disability as a product of interactions between individuals and their environment, disability (and masculinity) is understood as socially constructed.

Members of the Disability Rights Movement, as a result, seek to reconstruct masculinity through a three-prong strategy. First, they focus on changing the frame of reference regarding who defines disability and masculinity, thereby changing the social-construction dynamics of both. Second, they endeavor to help people with disabilities be more self-referent when defining their identities. To do that, a third component must be implemented: support structures, such as alternative subcultures, must exist. If the Disability Rights Movement is successful in elevating this struggle to the level of collective practice, it will challenge the legitimacy of the institutional arrangements of the current gender order.

In closing, there is much fruitful work to be done in the area of masculinity and disability. For instance, we should expect men with disabilities to respond differently to the demands associated with disability and masculinity due to sexual orientation, social class, age of onset of one's disability, race, and ethnicity. However, *how* and *why* gender identity varies for men with disabilities merits further study. We hope that this work serves as an impetus for others to take up these issues.

References

Callahan, John. 1989. *Don't Worry, He Won't Get Far on Foot.* New York: Vintage Books.

Connell, R. W. 1991. "Live Fast and Die Young: The Construction of Masculinity among Young Working-Class Men on the Margin of the Labor Market." *The Australian and New Zealand Journal of Sociology,* Volume 27, Number 2, August, pp. 141–171.

———. 1990a. "A Whole New World: Remaking Masculinity in the Context of the Environmental Movement." *Gender & Society,* Volume 4, Number 4, December, pp. 452–478.

———. 1990b. "An Iron Man: The Body and Some Contradictions of Hegemonic Masculinity," In *Sport, Men, and the Gender Order,* Michael Messner and Donald Sabo, eds. Champaign, IL: Human Kinetics Publishers, Inc., pp. 83–96.

———. 1987. *Gender and Power: Society, the Person, and Sexual Politics.* Stanford, CA: Stanford University Press.

Denzin, Norman. 1989. *The Research Act: A Theoretical Introduction to Sociological Methods.* Englewood Cliffs, NJ: Prentice-Hall.

Emerson, Robert. 1988. "Introduction." In *Contemporary Field Research: A Collection of Readings,* Robert Emerson, ed. Prospect Heights, IL: Waveland Press, pp. 93–107.

Hahn, Harlan. 1989. "Masculinity and Disability." *Disability Studies Quarterly,* Volume 9, Number 3, pp. 1–3.

Janeway, Elizabeth. 1980. *Powers of the Weak.* New York: Alfred A. Knopf.

Katz, Jack. 1988. "A Theory of Qualitative Methodology: The Social System of Analytic Fieldwork." In *Contemporary Field Research: A Collection of Readings,* Robert Emerson, ed. Prospect Heights, IL: Waveland Press, pp. 127–148.

Kriegel, Leonard. 1991. *Falling into Life.* San Francisco: North Point Press.

Messner, Michael A. 1992. *Power at Play: Sports and the Problem of Masculinity.* Boston: Beacon Press.

Murphy, Robert F. 1990. *The Body Silent.* New York: W. W. Norton.

Scott, James C. 1985. *Weapons of the Weak: Everyday Forms of Peasant Resistance.* New Haven: Yale University Press.

West, Candace, and Don H. Zimmerman. 1987. "Doing Gender." *Gender and Society,* Volume 1, Number 2, June, pp. 125–151.

Zola, Irving Kenneth. 1982. *Missing Pieces: A Chronicle of Living with a Disability.* Philadelphia: Temple University Press.

Why do many men have problems establishing and maintaining intimate relationships with women? What different forms do male–female relational problems take within different socioeconomic groups? How do men's problems with intimacy and emotional expressivity relate to power inequities between the sexes? Are rape and domestic violence best conceptualized as isolated deviant acts by "sick" individuals, or are they the illogical consequences of male socialization? This complex web of male–female relationships, intimacy, and power is the topic of this section.

Lillian B. Rubin begins this section with a psychoanalytic interpretation of male–female relational problems. Early developmental differences, rooted in the social organization of the nuclear family (espe-

PART SEVEN

Men with Women: Intimacy and Power

cially the fact that it is women who care for infants), have set up fundamental emotional and sexual differences between men and women that create problems and conflicts for heterosexual couples. In examining conflicts between black males and females, Clyde W. Franklin focuses more on how the larger socioeconomic structure of society places strains on black family life, especially on black males' work and family roles. Whereas Rubin's and Franklin's articles tend to portray both males and females as being victimized by socially structured gender differences and problems with intimacy and communication, Jack W. Sattel asks some different questions. Male emotional and verbal inexpressivity, rather than being a "tragedy," might better be conceptualized as situational strategy that males utilize to retain control in their relationships with women. Intimacy and power are closely intertwined.

Men's anger and insecurities toward women surface in other ways. Jane C. Hood's exploration of adolescent gang rape and Tim Beneke's dissection of the ideology of rape show that violence against women is the illogical consequence of insecurity, anger, the need for control, the need to assert and demonstrate manliness—all within a social context that condones sexual violence. As sociologist Diana Russell has written:

> Rape is not so much a deviant act as an over-conforming act. Rape may be understood as an extreme acting-out of qualities that are regarded as super masculine in this and many other societies: aggression, force, power, strength, toughness, dominance, competitiveness. To win, to be superior, to be successful, to conquer—all demonstrate masculinity to those who subscribe to common cultural notions of masculinity, i.e., the *masculine mystique*. And it would be surprising if these notions of mas-

culinity did not find expression in men's sexual behavior. Indeed, sex may be the arena where these notions of masculinity are most intensely played out, particularly by men who feel powerless in the rest of their lives, and hence, whose masculinity is threatened by this sense of powerlessness.[1]

What links all the articles in this section is *not* a sense that males are inherently incapable of authentic emotional connections with women, or that men are "naturally" batterers or rapists. The problems that men and women have in relating to each other are rooted in the socially structured system of gender difference and inequality. As feminists have long argued, the humanization of men is directly linked to the social empowerment of women. As long as men feel a need to control and subordinate women, either overtly or subtly, their relationships with women will be impoverished. Jason Schultz's essay, however, gives us room for hope that the next generation of men, now in their 20s, may struggle with these issues in new and different ways, and develop very different ideas about male–female relationships.

[1]Diana Russell, "Rape and the Masculine Mystique," paper presented to the American Sociological Association, New York, 1973.

35

ARTICLE

Lillian B. Rubin

The Approach–Avoidance Dance: Men, Women, and Intimacy

> For one human being to love another, that is perhaps the most difficult of all our tasks, the ultimate, the last test and proof, the work for which all other work is but preparation.
>
> —Rainer Maria Rilke

Intimacy. We hunger for it, but we also fear it. We come close to a loved one, then we back off. A teacher I had once described this as the "go away a little closer" message. I call it the approach–avoidance dance.

The conventional wisdom says that women want intimacy, men resist it. And I have plenty of material that would *seem* to support that view. Whether in my research interviews, in my clinical hours, or in the ordinary course of my life, I hear the same story told repeatedly. "He doesn't talk to me," says a woman. "I don't know what she wants me to talk about," says a man. "I want to know what he's feeling," she tells me. "I'm not feeling anything," he insists. "Who can

feel nothing?" she cries. "I can," he shouts. As the heat rises, so does the wall between them. Defensive and angry, they retreat—stalemated by their inability to understand each other.

Women complain to each other all the time about not being able to talk to their men about the things that matter most to them—about what they themselves are thinking and feeling, about what goes on in the hearts and minds of the men they're relating to. And men, less able to expose themselves and their conflicts—those within themselves or those with the women in their lives—either turn silent or take cover by holding women up to derision. It's one of the norms of male camaraderie to poke fun at women, to complain laughingly about the mystery of their minds, wonderingly about their ways. Even Freud did it when, in exasperation, he asked mockingly, "What do women want? Dear God, what do they want?"

But it's not a joke—not for the women, not for the men who like to pretend it is.

> The whole goddamn business of what you're calling intimacy bugs the hell out of me. I never know what you women mean when you talk about it. Karen complains that I don't talk to her, but it's not talk she wants, it's some other damn thing, only I don't know what the hell it is. Feelings, she keeps asking for. So what am I supposed to do if I don't have any to give her or to talk about just because she decides it's time to talk about feelings? Tell me, will you: maybe we can get some peace around here.

The expression of such conflicts would seem to validate the common understandings that suggest that women want and need intimacy more than men do—that the issue belongs to women alone; that, if left to themselves, men would not suffer it. But things are not always what they seem. And I wonder: "If men would renounce intimacy, what is their stake in relationships with women?"

Some would say that men need women to tend to their daily needs—to prepare their meals, clean their houses, wash their clothes, rear their children—so that they can be free to attend to life's larger problems. And, given the traditional structure of roles in the family, it has certainly worked that way most of the time. But, if that were all men seek, why is it that, even when they're not relating to women, so much of their lives is spent in search of a relationship with another, so much agony experienced when it's not available?

These are difficult issues to talk about—even to think about—because the subject of intimacy isn't just complicated, it's slippery as well. Ask yourself: What is intimacy? What words come to mind, what thoughts?

It's an idea that excites our imagination, a word that seems larger than life to most of us. It lures us, beckoning us with a power we're unable to resist. And, just because it's so seductive, it frightens us as well—seeming sometimes to

be some mysterious force from outside ourselves that, if we let it, could sweep us away.

But what is it we fear?

Asked what intimacy is, most of us—men and women—struggle to say something sensible, something that we can connect with the real experience of our lives. "Intimacy is knowing there's someone who cares about the children as much as you do." "Intimacy is a history of shared experience. It's sitting there having a cup of coffee together and watching the eleven o'clock news." "It's knowing you care about the same things." "It's knowing she'll always understand." "It's him sitting in the hospital for hours at a time when I was sick." "It's knowing he cares when I'm hurting." "It's standing by me when I was out of work." "It's seeing each other at our worst." "It's sitting across the breakfast table." "It's talking when you're in the bathroom." "It's knowing we'll begin and end each day together."

These seem the obvious things—the things we expect when we commit our lives to one another in a marriage, when we decide to have children together. And they're not to be dismissed as inconsequential. They make up the daily experience of our lives together, setting the tone for a relationship in important and powerful ways. It's sharing such commonplace, everyday events that determines the temper and the texture of life, that keeps us living together even when other aspects of the relationship seem less than perfect. Knowing someone is there, is constant, and can be counted on in just the ways these thoughts express provides the background of emotional security and stability we look for when we enter a marriage. Certainly a marriage and the people in it will be tested and judged quite differently in an unusual situation or in a crisis. But how often does life present us with circumstances and events that are so out of the range of ordinary experience?

These ways in which a relationship feels intimate on a daily basis are only one part of what we mean by intimacy, however—the part that's most obvious, the part that doesn't awaken our fears. At a lecture where I spoke of these issues recently, one man commented also, "Intimacy is putting aside the masks we wear in the rest of our lives." A murmur of assent ran through the audience of a hundred or so. Intuitively we say, "yes." Yet this is the very issue that also complicates our intimate relationships.

On the one hand, it's reassuring to be able to put away the public persona—to believe we can be loved for who we *really* are, that we can show our shadow side without fear, that our vulnerabilities will not be counted against us. "The most important thing is to feel I'm accepted just the way I am," people will say.

But there's another side. For, when we show ourselves thus without the masks, we also become anxious and fearful. "Is it possible that someone could love the *real* me?" we're likely to ask. Not the most promising question for the further development of intimacy, since it suggests that, whatever else another might do or feel, it's we who have trouble loving ourselves. Unfortunately, such misgivings are not usually experienced consciously. We're aware only that our discomfort has risen, that we feel a need to get away. For the person who has seen the "real me" is also the one who reflects back to us an image that's usually not wholly to our liking. We get angry at that, first at ourselves for not living up to our own expectations, then at the other, who becomes for us the mirror of our self-doubts—a displacement of hostility that serves intimacy poorly.

There's yet another level—one that's further below the surface of consciousness, therefore, one that's much more difficult for us to grasp, let alone to talk about. I'm referring to the differences in the ways in which women and men deal with their inner emotional lives—differences that create barriers between us that can be high indeed. It's here that we see how those early childhood experiences of separation and individuation—the psychological tasks that were required of us in order to separate from mother, to distinguish ourselves as autonomous persons, to internalize a firm sense of gender identity—take their toll on our intimate relationships.

Stop a woman in mid-sentence with the question, "What are you feeling right now?" and you might have to wait a bit while she re-runs the mental tape to capture the moment just passed. But, more than likely, she'll be able to do it successfully. More than likely, she'll think for a while and come up with an answer.

The same is not true of a man. For him, a similar question usually will bring a sense of wonderment that one would even ask it, followed quickly by an uncomprehending and puzzled response. "What do you mean?" he'll ask. "I was just talking," he'll say.

I've seen it most clearly in the clinical setting where the task is to get to the feeling level—or, as one of my male patients said when he came into therapy, to "hook up the head and the gut." Repeatedly when therapy begins, I find myself having to teach a man how to monitor his internal states—how to attend to his thoughts and feelings, how to bring them into consciousness. In the early stages of our work, it's a common experience to say to a man, "How does that feel?" and to see a blank look come over his face. Over and over, I find myself listening as a man speaks with calm reason about a situation which I know must be fraught with pain. "How do you feel about that?" I'll ask. "I've just been telling you," he's likely to reply. "No," I'll say, "you've told me what happened, not how you *feel* about it." Frustrated, he might well respond, "You sound just like my wife."

It would be easy to write off such dialogues as the problems of men in therapy, of those who happen to be having some particular emotional difficulties. But it's not so, as any woman who has lived with a man will attest. Time and again women complain: "I can't get him to verbalize his feelings." "He talks, but it's always intellectualizing." "He's so closed off from what he's feeling, I don't know how he lives that way." "If there's one thing that will eventually ruin this marriage, it's the fact that he can't talk about what's going on inside him." "I have to work like hell to get anything out of him that resembles a feeling that's something besides anger. That I get plenty of—me and the kids, we all get his anger. Anything else is damn hard to come by with him." One woman talked eloquently about her husband's anguish over his inability to get problems in his work life resolved. When I asked how she knew about his pain, she answered:

> I pull for it, I pull hard, and sometimes I can get something from him. But it'll be late at night in the dark—you know, when we're in bed and I can't look at him while he's talking and he doesn't have to look at me. Otherwise, he's just defensive and puts on what I call his bear act, where he makes his warning, go-away faces, and he can't be reached or penetrated at all.

To a woman, the world men live in seems a lonely one—a world in which their fears of exposing their sadness and pain, their anxiety about allowing their vulnerability to show, even to a woman they love, is so deeply rooted inside them that, most often, they can only allow it to happen "late at night in the dark."

Yet, if we listen to what men say, we will hear their insistence that they *do* speak of what's inside them, *do* share their thoughts and feelings with the women they love. "I tell her, but she's never satisfied," they complain. "No matter how much I say, it's never enough," they grumble.

From both sides, the complaints have merit. The problem lies not in what men don't say, however, but in what's not there—in what, quite simply, happens so far out of consciousness that it's not within their reach. For men have integrated all too well the lessons of their childhood—the experiences that taught them to repress and deny their inner thoughts, wishes,

needs, and fears; indeed, not even to notice them. It's real, therefore, that the kind of inner thoughts and feelings that are readily accessible to a woman generally are unavailable to a man. When he says, "I don't know what I'm feeling," he isn't necessarily being intransigent and withholding. More than likely, he speaks the truth.

Partly that's a result of the ways in which boys are trained to camouflage their feelings under cover of an exterior of calm, strength, and rationality. Fears are not manly. Fantasies are not rational. Emotions, above all, are not for the strong, the sane, the adult. Women suffer them, not men—women, who are more like children with what seems like their never-ending preoccupation with their emotional life. But the training takes so well because of their early childhood experience when, as very young boys, they had to shift their identification from mother to father and sever themselves from their earliest emotional connection. Put the two together and it does seem like suffering to men to have to experience that emotional side of themselves, to have to give it voice.

This is the single most dispiriting dilemma of relations between women and men. He complains, "She's so emotional, there's no point in talking to her." She protests, "It's him you can't talk to, he's always so darned rational." He says, "Even when I tell her nothing's the matter, she won't quit." She says, "How can I believe him when I can see with my own eyes that something's wrong?" He says, "Okay, so something's wrong! What good will it do to tell her?" She cries, "What are we married for? What do you need me for, just to wash your socks?"

These differences in the psychology of women and men are born of a complex interaction between society and the individual. At the broadest social level is the rending of thought and feeling that is such a fundamental part of Western thought. Thought, defined as the ultimate good, has been assigned to men; feeling, considered at best a problem, has fallen to women.

So firmly fixed have these ideas been that, until recently, few thought to question them. For they were built into the structure of psychological thought as if they spoke to an eternal, natural, and scientific truth. Thus, even such a great and innovative thinker as Carl Jung wrote, "The woman is increasingly aware that love alone can give her her full stature, just as the man begins to discern that spirit alone can endow his life with its highest meaning. Fundamentally, therefore, both seek a psychic relation one to the other, because love needs the spirit, and the spirit love, for their fulfillment."[1]

For a woman, "love"; for a man, "spirit"— each expected to complete the other by bringing to the relationship the missing half. In German, the word that is translated here as spirit is *Geist*. But *The New Cassell's German Dictionary* shows that another primary meaning of *Geist* is "mind, intellect, intelligence, wit, imagination, sense of reason." And, given the context of these words, it seems reasonable that *Geist* for Jung referred to a man's highest essence—his mind. There's no ambiguity about a woman's calling, however. It's love.

Intuitively, women try to heal the split that these definitions of male and female have foisted upon us.

> I can't stand that he's so damned unemotional and expects me to be the same. He lives in his head all the time, and he acts like anything that's emotional isn't worth dealing with.

Cognitively, even women often share the belief that the rational side, which seems to come so naturally to men, is the more mature, the more desirable.

> I know I'm too emotional, and it causes problems between us. He can't stand it when I get emotional like that. It turns him right off.

Her husband agrees that she's "too emotional" and complains:

> Sometimes she's like a child who's out to test her parents. I have to be careful when she's like that not to let her rile me up because otherwise all hell would break loose. You just can't reason with her when she gets like that.

It's the rational-man–hysterical-woman script, played out again and again by two people whose emotional repertoire is so limited that they have few real options. As the interaction between them continues, she reaches for the strongest tools she has, the mode she's most comfortable and familiar with: She becomes progressively more emotional and expressive. He falls back on his best weapons: He becomes more rational, more determinedly reasonable. She cries for him to attend to her feelings, whatever they may be. He tells her coolly, with a kind of clenched-teeth reasonableness, that it's silly for her to feel that way, that she's just being emotional. And of course she is. But that dismissive word "just" is the last straw. She gets so upset that she does, in fact, seem hysterical. He gets so bewildered by the whole interaction that his only recourse is to build the wall of reason even higher. All of which makes things measurably worse for both of them.

> The more I try to be cool and calm her the worse it gets. I swear, I can't figure her out. I'll keep trying to tell her not to get so excited, but there's nothing I can do. Anything I say just makes it worse. So then I try to keep quiet, but . . . wow, the explosion is like crazy, just nuts.

And by then it *is* a wild exchange that any outsider would agree was "just nuts." But it's not just her response that's off, it's his as well— their conflict resting in the fact that we equate the emotional with the nonrational.

This notion, shared by both women and men, is a product of the fact that they were born and reared in this culture. But there's also a difference between them in their capacity to apprehend the *logic* of emotions—a difference born in their early childhood experiences in the family, when boys had to repress so much of their emotional side and girls could permit theirs to flower. . . . It should be understood: Commitment itself is not a problem for a man; he's good at that. He can spend a lifetime living in the same family, working at the same job—even one he hates. And he's not without an inner emotional life. But when a relationship requires the sustained verbal expression of that inner life and the full range of feelings that accompany it, then it becomes burdensome for him. He can act out anger and frustration inside the family, it's true. But ask him to express his sadness, his fear, his dependency—all those feelings that would expose his vulnerability to himself or to another—and he's likely to close down as if under some compulsion to protect himself.

All requests for such intimacy are difficult for a man, but they become especially complex and troublesome in relations with women. It's another of those paradoxes. For, to the degree that it's possible for him to be emotionally open with anyone, it is with a woman—a tribute to the power of the childhood experience with mother. Yet it's that same early experience and his need to repress it that raises his ambivalence and generates his resistance.

He moves close, wanting to share some part of himself with her, trying to do so, perhaps even yearning to experience again the bliss of the infant's connection with a woman. She responds, woman style—wanting to touch him just a little more deeply, to know what he's thinking, feeling, fearing, wanting. And the fear closes in—the fear of finding himself again in the grip of a powerful woman, of allowing her admittance only to be betrayed and abandoned once again, of being overwhelmed by denied desires.

So he withdraws.

It's not in consciousness that all this goes on. He knows, of course, that he's distinctly uncomfortable when pressed by a woman for more intimacy in the relationship, but he doesn't know why. And, very often, his behavior doesn't please him any more than it pleases her. But he can't seem to help it.

Notes

1. Carl Gustav Jung, *Contributions to Analytical Psychology* (New York: Harcourt, Brace & Co., 1928), p. 185.

36

ARTICLE Clyde W. Franklin II

Black Male–Black Female Conflict: Individually Caused and Culturally Nurtured

Who is to blame? Currently, there is no dearth of attention directed to Black male–Black female relationships. Books, magazine articles, academic journal articles, public forums, radio programs, television shows, and everyday conversations have been devoted to Black male–Black female relationships for several years. Despite the fact that the topic has been discussed over the past several decades by some authors (e.g., Frazier, 1939; Drake and Cayton, 1945; Grier and Cobb, 1968), Wallace's *Black Macho and the Myth of the Superwoman* has been the point of departure for many contemporary discussions of the topic since its publication in 1979.

Actually, Wallace's analysis was not so different in content from other analyses of Black male–Black female relationships (e.g., Drake and Cayton's analysis of "lower-class life" in *Black Metropolis*). But Wallace's analysis was "timely." Coming so soon on the heels of the Black movement in the late 1960s and early 1970s, and, at a time when many Black male-inspired gains for Blacks were disappearing rapidly, the book was explosive. Its theme, too,

From *Journal of Black Studies* 15 (2 December 1984): 139–154. Reprinted by permission.

was provocative. Instead of repeating the rhetoric of the late 1960s and early 1970s that blamed conflictual relationships between Black men and Black women on White society, Wallace implied that the blame lay with Black males. In other words, the blame lay with those Black warriors who only recently had been perceived as the "saviors" of Black people in America. Wallace's lamenting theme is captured in a quote from her book: "While she stood by silently as he became a man, she assumed that he would finally glorify and dignify Black womanhood just as the White man has done for White women." Wallace goes on to say that this has not happened for Black women.

Wallace updates her attack on Black men in a later article entitled "A Black Feminist's Search for Sisterhood" (1982:9). Her theme, as before, is that Black men are just as oppressive of Black women as White men. She states:

> Whenever I raised the question of a Black woman's humanity in conversations with a Black man, I got a similar reaction. Black men, at least the ones I knew, seemed totally confounded when it came to treating Black women like people. . . . I discovered my voice and when brothers talked to me, I talked back. This had its

hazards. Almost got my eye blackened several times. My social life was like guerilla warfare. Here was the logic behind our grandmother's old saying, "A nigga man ain't shit."

Wallace, however, is not alone in placing the blame on Black men for deteriorating relations between Black men and Black women. Allen (1983:62), in a recent edition of *Essence* magazine, states:

> Black women have a tendency to be male-defined, subjugating their own needs for the good of that fragile male ego. . . . The major contradiction is that we Black women, in our hearts, have a tendency to believe Black men need more support and understanding than we do. We bought the Black Revolutionary line that a woman's place was three paces behind the man. We didn't stomp Stokeley when he made the statement that the only position for a woman in the movement was prone.

Such attacks on Black men have been met with equally ferocious counterattacks by some Black authors (both Black men and Black women). A few months following the publication of Wallace's book, an entire issue of the *Black Scholar* was devoted to Black male–Black female relationships. Of the responses to Wallace by such scholars as Jones (1979), Karenga (1979), Staples (1979), and numerous others, Karenga's response is perhaps the most controversial and maybe the most volatile. Karenga launches a personal attack on Wallace suggesting that she is misguided and perhaps responding from personal hurt. Recognizing the complexity of Black male–Black female relationships, Karenga contends that much of it is due not to Black men but to the White power structure. Along similar lines, Moore (1980) has exhorted Black women to stop criticizing Black men and blame themselves for disintegrating bonds between Black men and Black women.

Staples, in his response to Wallace and others who would place the blame on Black men for disruptive relationships between Black men and Black women, points out that while sexism within the Black culture may be an emerging problem, most Black men do not have the institutionalized power to oppress Black women. He believes that the Black male's "condition" in society is what bothers Black males. Staples devotes much attention to the institutional decimation of Black men and suggests that this is the reason for Black male–Black female conflict. Noting the high mortality and suicide rates of Black men, the fact that a half a million Black men are in prison, one-third of urban Black men are saddled with drug problems and that 25% to 30% do not have steady employment, Staples implied that Black male–Black female conflict may be related to *choice*. This means that a shortage of Black men may limit the choices that Black women have in selecting partners. As Braithwaite (1981) puts it, the insufficient supply of Black men places Black women at a disadvantage by giving Black men the upper hand. In a specific relationship, for example, if a Black woman fails to comply with the Black man's wishes, the Black man has numerous other options, including not only other Black women but also women of other races.

In a more recent discussion of Black male–Black female relationships, Alvin Poussaint (1982:40) suggests that Black women "adopt a patient and creative approach in exploring and creating new dimensions of the Black male–Black female bond." Others, like Ronald Braithwaite, imply in their analyses of relationships between Black men and Black women that Black women's aggressiveness, thought to be a carryover from slavery, may be partly responsible for Black male–Black female conflict.

Succinctly, by and large, most Black male and Black female authors writing on the subject seem to agree that many Black male–Black female relationships today are destructive and potentially explosive. What they do not agree on, however, are the causes of the problems existing between Black men and Black women. As we have seen, some believe that Black men are the cause. Others contend that Black women contribute disproportionately to Black male–Black female conflict. Still others blame White racism solely, using basic assumptions that may be logically inadequate (see Franklin, 1980). Many specific reasons for the conflict often postulated include the notions that Black men are abusive toward Black women, that Black men are irresistibly attracted to White women (despite the fact that only approximately 120,000 Black men were married to White women in 1980), that too many Black men are homosexual, that Black women are too aggressive, that Black women don't support Black men—the list goes on. Few of these reasons, however, really explore the underlying cause of the conflict. Instead, they are descriptions of the conflict-behaviors that are indicators of the tension between Black men and Black women. But what is the cause of the behavior—the cause of the tension that so often disrupts harmony in Black male–Black female relationships?

Given the various approaches many Black authors have taken in analyzing Black male–Black female relationships, it is submitted that two major sources of Black male–Black female conflict can be identified: (l) the noncomplementarity of sex-role definitions internalized by Black males and Black females; and (2) structural barriers in the environments of Black males and Black females. Each source is explored separately below.

Sources of Conflict Between Black Men and Black Women

Sex-Role Noncomplementarity Among Black Males and Black Females

Much Black male–Black female conflict stems directly from incompatible role enactments by Black males and Black females. Incompatible role enactments by Black men and Black women occur because they internalize sex-role definitions that are noncomplementary. For example, a Black woman in a particular conflictual relationship with a Black male may feel that her Black man is supposed to assume a dominant role, but she also may be inclined to exhibit behaviors that are opposed to his dominance and her subordinance. In the same relationship, the Black man may pay lip service to assuming a dominant role but may behave "passively" with respect to some aspects of masculinity and in a dominant manner with respect to other aspects.

One reason for role conflict between Black men and Black women is that many contemporary Black women internalize two conflicting definitions of femininity, whereas many contemporary Black men internalize only a portion of the traditional definition of masculinity. Put simply, numerous Black women hold attitudes that are both highly masculine and highly feminine. On the other hand, their male counterparts develop traits that are highly consistent with certain aspects of society's definition of masculinity, but that are basically unrelated to other aspects of the definition. Thus, in a given relationship, one may find a Black woman who feels and behaves in ways that are both assertive and passive, dominant and subordinant, decisive and indecisive, and so on. Within that same relationship, a Black man may exhibit highly masculine behaviors, such as physical aggressiveness, sexual dominance, and even violence, but behave indifferently with respect to the masculine work ethic—assuming responsibility for family-related activities external to the home, being aggressive in the work place and the like.

The reason these incongruent attitudes and behaviors exist among Black men and Black women is that they have received contradictory messages during early socialization. It is common for Black women to have received two messages. One message states, "Because you will be a Black woman, it is imperative that you learn to take care of yourself because it is hard to find a Black man who will take care of you." A second message frequently received by young Black females that conflicts with the first message is "your ultimate achievement will occur when you have snared a Black man who will take care of you." In discussing early socialization experiences with countless young Black women in recent years, I have found that most of them agree that these two messages were given them by socialization agents and agencies such as child caretakers, relatives, peer group members, the Black church, and the media.

When internalized, these two messages often produce a Black woman who seems to reject aspects of the traditional female sex role in America such as passivity, emotional and economic dependence, and female subordinance while accepting other aspects of the role such as expressiveness, warmth, and nurturance. This is precisely why Black women seem to be more androgynous than White women. Black women's androgyny, though, may be more a function of necessity than anything else. It may be related to the scarcity of Black men who assume traditional masculine roles in male–female relationships.

Whatever the reason for Black women's androgynous orientations, because of such orientations Black women often find themselves in conflictual relationships with Black men or in no stable relationships at all. The scenario generally can be described as follows. Many Black women in early adulthood usually begin a search for a Black Prince Charming. However, because of the dearth of Black men who can be or are willing to be Prince Charmings for Black women, Black women frequently soon give up the search for such a Black man. They give up the search, settle for less, and "like" what they settle for even less. This statement is important because many Black women's eventual choices are destined to become constant reminders that the "female independence" message received during the early socialization process is the correct message. But, because Black women also

have to deal with the second socialization message, many come to feel that they have failed in their roles as women. In an effort to correct their mistakes, Black women often choose to enact the aspect of their androgynous role that is decidedly aggressive and/or independent. They may decide either to "go it alone" or to prod their Black men into becoming Prince Charmings. The first alternative for Black women often results in self-doubt, lowered self-esteem, and, generally, unhappiness and dissatisfaction. After all, society nurtures the "find a man" message far beyond early socialization. The second message, unfortunately, produces little more than the first message because Black women in such situations usually end up in conflictual relationships with Black men, who also have undergone a rather complicated socialization process. Let us explore briefly the conflicting messages numerous Black men receive during early socialization.

One can find generally that Black men, too, have received two conflicting messages during early socialization. One message received by young Black males is "to become a man means that you must become dominant, aggressive, decisive, responsible, and in some instances, violent in social encounters with others." A second message received by young Black males that conflicts with the first is, "You are Black and you must not be too aggressive, too dominant, and so on, because the *man* will cut you down." Internalization of these two messages by some Black men (a substantial number) produces Black men who enact a portion of the traditional definition of masculinity but remain inactive with respect to other parts of traditional masculinity. Usually those aspects of traditional masculinity that can be enacted within the Black culture are the ones exhibited by these Black men. Other aspects of the sex role that require enactment external to the Black culture (e.g., aggressiveness in the work place) may be related to impassively by Black men. Unfortunately, these are aspects of the male sex role that must be enacted if a male is to be "productive" in American society.

Too many Black men fail to enact the more "productive" aspects of the male sex role. Instead, "being a man," for many Black males who internalize the mixed messages, becomes simply enacting sexual aggression, violence, sexism, and the like—all of which promote Black male–Black female conflict. In addition, contributing to the low visibility and low salience of "productive" masculine traits among Black men is the second socialization message, which provides a rationale for nonenactment of the role traits. Moreover, the "man will get you" message serves to attenuate Black men's motivations to enact more "positive" aspects of the traditional male sex role. We must keep in mind, however, that not all of the sources of Black male–Black female conflict are social–psychological. Some of the sources are structural, and in the next section these sources are discussed.

Structural Barriers Contributing to Black Male–Black Female Conflict

It is easy to place the blame for Black male–Black female conflict on "White society." Several Black authors have used this explanatory approach in recent years (e.g., Anderson and Mealy, 1979). They have suggested that Black male–Black female conflict is a function of America's capitalistic orientation and White society's long-time subjugation of Black people. Certainly historical conditions are important to understand when discussing the status of Black people today. Often, however, too much emphasis is placed on the historical subjugation of Black people as the source of Black male–Black female conflict today. Implicit in such an emphasis is the notion that independent variables existing at some point in the distant past cause a multiplicity of negative behaviors between Black males and Black females that can be capsulized as Black male–Black female conflict. A careful analysis of the contemporary environments of Black men and women today will show, instead, that factors responsible, in part,

for Black male–Black female conflict are inextricably interwoven in those environments. In other words, an approach to the analysis of conflict between Black men and Black women today must be ahistorical. Past conditions influence Black male–Black female relationships only in the sense that vestiges of these conditions exist currently and are identifiable.

Our society today undoubtedly remains structured in such a manner that the vast majority of Black men encounter insurmountable barriers to the attainment of a "masculine" status as defined by most Americans (Black and White Americans). Black men still largely are locked within the Black culture (which has relatively limited resources), unable to compete successfully for societal rewards—the attainment of which defines American males as "men." Unquestionably, Black men's powerlessness in society's basic institutions such as the government and the economy contributes greatly to the pathological states of many Black men. The high mortality and suicide rates of young Black men, the high incarceration rates of Black men, the high incidence of drug addiction among Black men, and the high unemployment rate of Black men are all functions of societal barriers to Black male upward mobility. These barriers render millions of Black males socially impotent and/or socially dysfunctional. Moreover, as Staples has pointed out, such barriers also result in a scarcity of functional Black men, thereby limiting Black women's alternatives for mates.

While some may be tempted to argue for a psychological explanation of Black male social impotence, it is suggested here that any such argument is misguided unless accompanied by a recognition of the role of cultural nurturance factors. Cultural nurturance factors such as the rigid castelike social stratum of Blacks in America foster and maintain Black men's social impotence. The result is powerless Black men primed for conflictual relationships with Black women. If Black men in our society were not

"American," perhaps cultural nurturance of Black people's status in our society could not be translated into cultural nurturance of Black male–Black female conflict. That Black men are Americanized, however, is seen in the outcome of the Black movement of the last decade.

The Black movement of the late 1960s and early 1970s produced little structural change in America. To be sure, a few Black men (and even fewer Black women) achieved a measure of upward mobility; however, the vast majority did not reap gains from the Black movement. What did happen, though, was that Black people did get a glimpse of the rewards that can be achieved in America through violence and/or aggression. White society did bend when confronted by the Black movement, but it did not break. In addition, the few upward mobility doors that were ajar during the height of the movement were quickly slammed shut when the movement began to wane in the middle and late 1970s. Black men today find themselves in a position similar to the one Black men were in prior to the movement. The only difference this time around is that Black men are equipped with the psychological armor of aggression and violence as well as with a distorted perception of a target—Black women, the ones who "stood silently by."

Wallace's statement that Black women "stood silently by" must not be taken lightly. Black women did this; in addition, they further internalized American definitions of masculinity and femininity. Previously, Black women held modified definitions of masculinity and femininity because the society's definition did not fit their everyday experiences. During the Black movement they were exhorted by Black men to assume a sex role that was more in line with the traditional "feminine" role White women assumed in male–female relationships. Although this may have been a noble (verbal) effort on the part of Black men to place Black women on pedestals, it was shortsighted and doomed to fail. Failure was imminent because even during the peak of the Black movement, societal resistance to structural changes that would benefit Black people was strong. The strength of this resistance dictated that change in Black people's status in America could come about only through the united efforts of both Black men and Black women.

Unfortunately, the seeds of division between Black men and Black women were sown during the Black movement. Black men bought the Moynihan report (1965) that indirectly blamed Black women for Black people's underclass status in America. In doing so, Black men convinced themselves that they could be "men" only if they adopted the White male's sex role. An examination of this role reveals that it is characterized by numerous contradictions. The traditional White masculine role requires men to assume protective, condescending, and generally patriarchal stances with respect to women. It also requires, ironically, that men display dominant, aggressive, and often violent behaviors toward women. Just as important, though, is that White masculine role enactment can occur only, when there is full participation in masculinist American culture. Because Black men continue to face barriers to full participation in American society, the latter requirement for White male sex-role assumption continues to be met by only a few Black men. The result has been that many Black men have adopted only a part of the culture's definition of masculinity because they are thwarted in their efforts to participate fully in society. Structural barriers to Black male sex-role adoption, then, have produced a Black male who is primed for a conflictual relationship with Black women. In the next section, an exploration is presented of some possible solutions to Black male–Black female conflict that arise from the interactive relationship between the noncomplementarity of sex-role internalization by Black men and Black women and structural barriers to Black men's advancement in American society.

Toward Solving Black Male–Black Female Conflict

Given that societal conditions are extremely resistant to rapid changes, the key to attenuating conflict between Black men and Black women lies in altering three social psychological phenomena: (1) Black male and Black female socialization experiences; (2) Black male and Black female role-playing strategies; and (3) Black male and Black female personal communication mechanisms. I first propose some alterations in Black male and Black female socialization experiences. . . .

Black female socialization must undergo change if Black men and Black women are to enjoy harmonious relationships. Those agents and agencies responsible for socializing young Black females must return to emphasizing a monolithic message in young Black female socialization. This message can stress warmth, caring, and nurturance, but it must stress simultaneously self-sufficiency, assertiveness, and responsibility. The latter portion of this message requires that young Black females must be cautioned against sexual freedom at relatively early ages—not necessarily for moral reasons, but because sexual freedom for Black women seems to operate against Black women's self-sufficiency, assertiveness, and responsibility. It is important to point out here, however, that this type of socialization message must be imparted without the accompanying castigation of Black men. To say "a nigger man ain't shit" informs any young Black female that at least one-half of herself "ain't shit." Without a doubt this strategy teaches self-hate and sets the stage for future Black male–Black female conflict.

Young Black males, on the other hand, must be instructed in self-sufficiency, assertiveness, and responsibility without the accompanying warning opposed to these traits in Black males. Such warnings serve only to provide rationales for future failures. To be sure, Black men do (and will) encounter barriers to upward mobility because they are Black. But, as many Black men have shown, such barriers do not have to be insurmountable. Of course it is recognized that innumerable Black men have been victims of American racist policies, but some, too, have been victims because they perceived only that external factors hindered their upward mobility and did not focus on some internal barriers that may have thwarted their mobility. The former factors are emphasized much too often in the contradictory socialization messages received by most young Black males.

Along with the above messages, young Black males must learn that the strong bonds that they establish with their mothers can be extended to their relationships with other Black women. If Black men perceive their mothers to be symbols of strength and perseverance, they must also be taught that most other Black women acquire these same qualities and have done so for generations. It must become just as "cool," in places like urban Black barbershops, to speak of Black women's strength and dignity as it is now to hear of Black women's thighs, breasts, and hips.

On an issue closely related to the above, few persons reading this article can deny that Black men's attempts to enact the White male sex role in America are laughable. Black men are relatively powerless in this country, and their attempts at domination, aggression, and the like, while sacrificing humanity, are ludicrous. This becomes apparent when it is understood that usually the only people being dominated and aggressed against by Black men are Black women (and other Black men). Moreover, unlike White males, Black males receive no societal rewards for their efforts; instead, the result is Black male–Black female disharmony. Black men must avoid the tendency to emulate the nauseatingly traditional male sex role because their experiences clearly show that such a role is counter-productive for Black people. Because the Black man's experiences are different, his role-playing strategies must be different and made to be more complementary with Black females' altered role-playing strategies. The Black females' role-playing strategies, as we have seen, are androgynous, emphasizing neither the inferiority nor the superiority of male or female sex roles.

On a final note, it is important for Black people in our society to alter their personal communication mechanisms. Black men and Black women interact with each other in diverse ways and in diverse situations, ranging from intimate to impersonal. Perhaps the most important element of this diverse communication pattern is empathy. For Black people in recent years, this is precisely the element that has undergone unnecessary transformation. As Blacks in America have accepted increasingly White society's definition of male–female relationships, Black men and Black women have begun to interact with each other less in terms of empathy. While Black women have retained empathy in their male–female relationships to a greater degree than Black men have, Black men have become increasingly nonexpressive and nonempathic in their male–female relationships. Nearly 60% of Black women (approximately 25,000) in a recent *Essence* survey cited nonexpressiveness as a problem in male–female relationships; 56% also pointed out that Black male nonempathy was a problem (Edwards, 1982). It seems, then, that as Black males have attempted to become "men" in America they have shed some of the important qualities of humanity. Some Black women, too, who have embraced the feminist perspective also have discarded altruism. The result of both phenomena, for Black people as a whole, has been to divide Black men and Black women further. Further movement away from empathic understanding in Black male–Black female relationships by both Black men and Black women undoubtedly will be disastrous for Black people in America.

References

Allen B. 1983 "The Price for Giving It Up." *Essence* (February): 60–62, 118.

Anderson, S. E., and R. Mealy. 1979 "Who Originated the Crisis: A Historical Perspective." *Black Scholar* (May/June): 40–44.

Braithwaite, R. L. 1981 "Interpersonal Relations between Black Males and Black Females." In *Black Men*, L. E. Gary, ed., pp. 83–97. Beverly Hills, Calif.: Sage.

Drake, S. C., and H. R. Cayton. 1945 *Black Metropolis*. New York: Harcourt.

Edwards, A. 1982 "Survey Results: How You're Feeling." *Essence* (December): 73–76.

Franklin, C. W., II. 1980 "White Racism As a Cause of Black Male–Black Female Conflict: A Critique." *Western Journal of Black Studies* 4 (1): 42–49.

Frazier, E. F. 1939 *The Negro Family in the United States*. Chicago: University of Chicago Press.

Grier, W. II., and P. M. Cobb. 1968 *Black Rage*. New York: Basic Books.

Jones, T. 1979 "The Need to Go beyond Stereotypes." *Black Scholar* (May/June): 48–49.

Karenga, M. R. 1979 "On Wallace's Myth: Wading through Troubled Waters." *Black Scholar* (May/June): 36–39.

Moore, W. F. 1980 "Black Women, Stop Criticizing Black Men—Blame Yourselves." *Ebony* (December): 128–130.

Moynihan, D. P. 1965 *The Negro Family: The Case for National Action*. Washington, D.C.: U.S. Department of Labor, Office of Planning and Research.

Poussaint, A. F. 1982 "What Every Black Woman Should Know about Black Men." *Ebony* (August): 36–40.

Staples, R. 1979 "The Myth of Black Macho: A Response to Angry Black Feminists." *Black Scholar* (March/April): 24–32.

Wallace, M. 1979 *Black Macho and the Myth of the Superwoman*. New York: Dial.

———. 1982 "A Black Feminist's Search for Sisterhood." In *All the Blacks Are Men, All the Women Are White, but Some of Us Are Brave*, G. T. Hull et al., eds. pp. 5–8. Old Westbury, N.Y.: Feminist Press.

ARTICLE

Jack W. Sattel

The Inexpressive Male: Tragedy or Sexual Politics?

In this brief essay, I am concerned with the phenomenon of "male inexpressiveness" as it has been conceptualized by Balswick and Peek (1971). In their conceptualization, male inexpressiveness is seen as a culturally produced temperament trait which is learned by boys as the major characteristic of their forthcoming adult masculinity. Such inexpressiveness is evidenced in two ways. First, adult male behavior which does not indicate affection, tenderness, or emotion is inexpressive behavior. Second, and somewhat differently, behavior which is not supportive of the affective expectations of one's wife is inexpressive behavior. It is the latter variety of inexpressiveness which occupies the major concern of Balswick and Peek. They suggest that the inability of the American male to unlearn inexpressiveness in order to relate effectively to a woman is highly dysfunctional to the emerging standards of the companionate, intimate American marriage. Ironically, Balswick and Peek see inexpressiveness in contexts outside the marriage relationship as functional

insofar as in nonmarital situations the inexpressiveness of the male to females other than one's spouse works to prevent threats to the primacy of the marital bond, that is, it presumably functions to ward off infidelity. The authors further suggest two styles of adult inexpressiveness: the "cowboy—John Wayne" style of almost total inarticulateness and the more cool, detached style of the "playboy," who communicates only to exploit women sexually.

The article has proved to be an important one in forcing sociologists to rethink old conceptual stereotypes of masculinity and femininity. In part, it has helped to contribute to efforts to rescue for both sexes qualities and potentials that previously were thought to belong to only one sex. On the other hand, it would be unfortunate if Balswick and Peek's conceptualization would enter the sociological literature as the last word on the dilemma of male inexpressiveness—unfortunate because, despite their real insight, I think they fundamentally misconstrue both the origin and the playing out of male inexpressiveness in our society.

In the note which follows, I would like to reconsider the phenomenon of male inexpressiveness, drawing upon my own and other men's experiences in consciousness-raising groups (especially as recounted in *Unbecoming Men: A Men's Consciousness-Raising Group Writes on Oppression and Themselves* (Bradley et al., 1971), as well as some of the literature which has appeared since Balswick and Peek first published their article.

Becoming Inexpressive: Socialization

The process of becoming inexpressive is cast by Balswick and Peek in the traditional vocabulary of the literature of socialization:

> Children, from the time they are born both explicitly and implicitly are taught how to be a man or how to be a woman. While the girl is taught to act "feminine," . . . the boy is taught to be a man. In learning to be a man, the boy in American society comes to value expressions of masculinity . . . [such as] physical courage, toughness, competitiveness, and aggressiveness. (1971: 363–364)

Balswick and Peek's discussion of this socialization process is marred in two ways. Theoretically, their discussion ignores the critique of the socialization literature initially suggested by Wrong (1961) in his analysis of sociology's "oversocialized concept of man [sic]." Wrong, using a largely Freudian vocabulary, argued that it is incorrect to see the individual as something "hollowed out" into which norms are simply poured. Rather, "conformity" and "internalization" should always be conceptualized as problematic. For example, if we consider inexpressiveness to be a character trait, as do Balswick and Peek, we should also be aware that the normative control of that trait is never complete—being threatened constantly by both the presumably more expressive demands of the id and the excessive ("perfectionist") de-

mands of the "internalized norms" of the superego. Wrong's point is well taken. While the norms of our society may well call for all little boys to grow up to be inexpressive, the inexpressiveness of the adult male should never be regarded as complete or total, as Balswick and Peek would have it.

For them to have ignored this point is particularly crucial given their concern to rescue some capacity of authentic expressiveness for the male. Their suggestion that men simply "unlearn" their inexpressiveness through contact with a woman (spouse) is unsatisfactory for two reasons. First, it forfeits the possibility that men can rescue themselves through enhanced self-knowledge or contact with other men. Second, *it would seem to make the task of rescuing men just one more task of women.* That is, the wife is expected to restore to her husband that which was initially taken from him in socialization.

A second problem with Balswick and Peek's discussion of socialization and inexpressiveness is that they ignore the peculiarly asymmetrical patterns of socialization in our society which make it much more dangerous for a boy to be incompletely socialized than a girl. For example, much of the literature suggests that parents and other adults exert greater social control to insure that boys "grow up male" than that girls "grow up female" (Parsons, 1951)—as can be seen in the fact that greater stigma is attached to the boy who is labeled a sissy than to the girl who is known as a tomboy. Failure to even consider this asymmetry reveals, I think, the major weakness of Balswick and Peek's conceptualization of male inexpressiveness. They have no explanation of *why* male inexpressiveness exists or *how* it came into being and is maintained other than to say that "our culture demands it." Thus, while we can agree that male inexpressiveness is a tragedy, their analysis does not help us to change the social conditions which produce that tragedy.

Inexpressiveness and Power

To break this chain of reasoning, I would like to postulate that, in itself, male inexpressiveness is of no particular value in our culture. Rather, it is an instrumental requisite for assuming adult male roles of power.

Consider the following. To effectively wield power, one must be able both to convince others of the rightness of the decisions one makes and to guard against one's own emotional involvement in the consequences of that decision; that is, one has to show that decisions are reached rationally and efficiently. One must also be able to close one's eyes to the potential pain one's decisions have for others and for oneself. The general who sends troops into battle must show that his decision is calculated and certain; to effectively implement that decision—hence, to maintain his position of power to make future decisions—the general must put on a face of impassive conviction.

I would argue, in a similar vein, that a little boy must become inexpressive not simply because our culture expects boys to be inexpressive *but because our culture expects little boys to grow up to become decision makers and wielders of power.*

From this example, I am suggesting that inexpressiveness is not just learned as an end in itself. Rather, it is learned as a means to be implemented later in men assuming and maintaining positions of power. More generally:

(A) INEXPRESSIVENESS in a role is determined by the corresponding *power* (actual or potential) of that role.

In light of this generalization, we might consider why so many sociologists tend to merge the universalistic–particularistic (rational) and the affective neutrality–affectivity (expressive) distinction in any discussion of real social behavior. In the case of the general, it would seem that the ability to give an inexpressive—that is, an affec-

tively neutral—coloring to his decisions or positions contributes to the apparent rationality of those decisions or positions. Inexpressiveness validates the rightness of one's position. In fact, the social positions of highest power—not incidentally always occupied by men—demand veneers of both universalism and inexpressiveness of their incumbents, suggesting that at these levels *both* characteristics merge into a style of control. (Consider both Kennedy in the missile crisis and Nixon at Watergate. While otherwise quite dissimilar, in a crisis and challenge to their position, both men felt that "stonewalling" was the solution to the situation.)

From the above, it also follows logically the inexpressiveness might be more a characteristic of upper-class, powerful males than of men in the working classes. Many people—sociologists included—would probably object to such a deduction, saying the evidence is in the other direction, pointing at the Stanley Kowalski or Marty of literary fiction. I am not so sure. To continue with examples from fiction for a moment, the early autobiographical novels of, say, James Baldwin and Paul Goodman, dealing with lower- and working-class youth, consistently depicted "making it" as a not unusual tradeoff for one's sensitivity and expressiveness. More empirically, the recent work of Sennett and Cobb in their study of working-class life, *The Hidden Injuries of Class* (1972), suggests that upward mobility by working-class men was seen by them as entailing a certain phoniness or inauthentic relationship with one's *male* peers as well as a sacrifice of a meaningful expressive relationship with children and wife. The result of this for the men interviewed by Sennett and Cobb was often a choice to forego upward mobility and power because it involved becoming something one was not. It involved learning to dissemble inauthentic display of expressiveness toward higher-ups as well as involving the sacrifice of already close relationships with one's friends and family.

Inexpressiveness and Power as Situational Variables

In their article, Balswick and Peek include a notion of inexpressiveness not just as a socially acquired temperament trait but also as a situational variable. Thus while they argue that all males are socialized into inexpressiveness, they also argue that "for many males . . . through progressively more serious involvements with women (such as going steady, being pinned, engagement, and the honeymoon period of marriage), [these males] begin to make some exceptions. That is, they may learn to be *situationally rather than totally inexpressive*" (1971, 365–366). As noted above, this is seen by Balswick and Peek as functional for men and for the marriage relation in two ways. It meets the wife's expectation of affective support for herself while usually being accompanied by continued inexpression toward women who are not one's spouse. Thus, in this sense, the situational unlearning of inexpressiveness enhances the marital relationship while guarding against extramarital relationships which would threaten the basic pairing of husband–wife.

There is, on the surface, a certain descriptive validity to Balswick and Peek's depiction, although, interestingly, they do not consider a latent function of such unlearning. To the extent that an ability to be expressive *in situ* with a woman leads to satisfactory and gratifying consequences in one case, it probably doesn't take long for the male to learn to be expressive with *any* woman—not just his spouse—as a mode of approaching that woman. Some men, for example, admit to this in my consciousness-raising group. This, in fact, is a way of "coming on" with a woman—a relaxation of the usual standards of inexpressiveness as a calculated move to establish a sexual relationship. Skill at dissembling in this situation may have less to do with handing a woman a "line" than with showing one's weaknesses and frailties as

clues intended to be read by her as signs of authentic male interest. In many Latin cultures, which might be considered to epitomize traditional male supremist modes, the style of *machismo*, in fact, calls for the male to be dependent, nominally open, and very expressive to whichever woman he is currently trying to "make." The point of both these examples is to suggest that the *situational unlearning* of inexpressiveness need not lead to strengthening the marriage bond and, in fact, may be detrimental to it, since what works in one situation will probably be tried in others.

Following the argument developed in the previous section concerning the interplay between power and inexpressiveness, I would suggest a different conceptualization of the situational relevance of inexpressiveness:

(B) EXPRESSIVENESS in a sexist culture empirically emerges as an effort on the part of the male to *control* a situation (once again, on his terms) and to maintain his position.

What I am suggesting is that in a society such as ours, which so permeates all social relationships with notions of power and exchange, even what may appear on the surface to be authentic can be an extension rather than a negation of (sexual) politics.

This is even more true of male inexpressive behavior in intimate male–female relationships. The following dialogue is drawn from Erica Jong's novel of upper-middle-class sexual etiquette, *Fear of Flying*. Consider the political use of male inexpressiveness:

SHE: "Why do you always have to do this to me? You make me feel so lonely."

HE: "That comes from you."

"What do you mean it comes from me? Tonight I wanted to be happy. It's Christmas Eve. Why do you turn on me? What did I do?"

Silence

"What did I do?"

He looks at her as if her not knowing were another injury. "Look, let's just go to sleep now. Let's just forget it."

"Forget what?"

He says nothing.

"Forget the fact that you turned on me? Forget the fact that you're punishing me for nothing? Forget the fact that I'm lonely and cold, that it's Christmas Eve and again you've ruined it for me? Is that what you want me to forget?"

"I won't discuss it."

"Discuss what?" "What won't you discuss?"

"Shut up! I won't have you screaming in the hotel."

"I don't give a fuck what you won't have me do. I'd like to be treated civilly. I'd like you to at least do me the courtesy of telling me why you're in such a funk. And don't look at me that way. . . ."

"What way?"

"As if my not being able to read your mind were my greatest sin. I *can't* read your mind. I *don't* know why you're so mad. I can't intuit your wish. If that's what you want in a wife you don't have it in me."

"I certainly don't."

"Then what is it? Please tell me."

"I shouldn't have to."

"Good God! Do you mean to tell me I'm expected to be a mind reader? Is that the kind of mothering you want?"

"If you had any empathy for me . . ."

"But I *do*. My God, you just don't give me a chance."

"You tune out. You don't listen."

"It was something in the movie wasn't it?"

"What in the movie?"

"The quiz again. Do you have to quiz me like some kind of criminal. Do you have to cross-examine me? . . . It was the funeral scene . . . The little boy looking at his dead mother. Something got you there. That was when you got depressed."

Silence

"Oh come on, Bennett, you're making me *furious*. Please tell me. Please."

(He gives the words singly like little gifts. Like hard little turds.) "What was it about the scene that got me?"

"Don't quiz me. Tell me!" (She puts her arms around him. He pulls away. She falls to the floor holding onto his pajama leg. It looks less like an embrace than a rescue scene, she sinking, he reluctantly allowing her to cling to his leg for support.)

"Get up!"

(Crying) "Only if you tell me."

(He jerks his leg away.) "I'm going to bed." (Jong, 1973: 108–109)

One wonders if this is what Balswick and Peek mean by a man "unlearning" his inexpressiveness. Less facetiously, this is clearly an example which indicates that inexpression on the part of the male is not just a matter of inarticulateness or even a deeply socialized inability to respond to the needs of others. The male here is *using* inexpression to guard his own position. To *not* say anything in this situation is to say something very important indeed: that the battle we are engaged in is to be fought by my rules and when I choose to fight. In general:

(C) Male INEXPRESSIVENESS empirically emerges as an intentional manipulation of a situation when threats to the male position occur.

Inexpressiveness and Male Culture

Balswick and Peek see inexpressiveness as a major quality of male–female interaction. I have tried to indicate about where they might be right in making such an attribution as well as some of the inadequacies of their conceptualization of the origins of that inexpressiveness. A clear gap in their conceptualization, however, is their lack of any consideration of the inexpressive male in interaction with other men. In fact, their conceptualization leads to two contradictory deductions. First, given the depth and thoroughness of socialization, we might deduce that the male is inexpressive with other men, as well as with women. Second, the male, who is only situationally inexpressive, can interact and express himself truly in situations with other men. This latter position finds support in the notions of male bonding developed by Lionel Tiger (1969). The former position is validated by some of the contributors to Pleck and Sawyer's recent reader on *Men and Masculinity* (1974; esp. Candell, Jourard, and Fasteau). In this section, I would like to raise some of the questions that bear on the problem of male-to-male inexpressiveness. (1) Is there a male subculture? Subcultural differences are usually identified as having ethnic, religious, occupational, etc., boundaries; gender is not usually considered to define subcultural differences. This is so even though gender repeatedly proves to be among the most statistically significant variables in most empirical research. Yet, if we think of a subculture as consisting of unique patterns of belief, value, technique, and language use, there would be a *prima facie* case for considering "male" and "female" definitive of true subcultures in almost all societies. (2) What is the origin of male and female subcultures? This question is probably the most inclusive of all the questions one can ask about gender and sex-role differences. It thrusts us into the very murky swamp of the origin of the family, patriarchy, sexism, etc. Sidestepping questions of the ultimate origin of male and female cultural differences, I would only suggest that a good case might be made for considering the persistence—if not the origin—of male and female subcultural differences as due to male efforts to maintain privilege and position *vis-à-vis* women. This is the point anthropologists have

been quick to make about primitive societies. The ritual and magic of the males is a secret to be guarded against the women's eyes. Such magic is privy only to the men, and access to it in rites of passage finally determines who is man and who is only *other*. Similar processes are at work in our own society. Chodorow's distinction between "being" and "doing" (1971) is a way of talking about male and female subcultural differences that makes it clear that what men "do" defines not only their own activity but the activity ("being") of women as well. Benston's (1969) distinction between male production of exchange-value in the public sphere and female creation of use-value in the private sphere captures the same fundamental differential of power underlying what appears to be merely cultural. (3) Is male culture necessarily inexpressive? Many observers would say it is flatly wrong to assert that men are inexpressive when interacting with other men. Tiger (1969), for example, talks of the games (sport) men share as moments of intense and authentic communication and expression. In fact, for Tiger, sport derives from the even more intense solidarity of the prehistoric hunt—a solidarity that seems, in his scheme to be almost genetic in origin. I think Tiger, and others who would call our attention to this capacity for male expressiveness, are saying something important but partial. Perhaps the following example drawn from adult reminiscences of one's fourteenth year can make this clearer:

> I take off at full speed not knowing whether I would reach it but knowing very clearly that this is *my* chance. My cap flies off my head . . . and a second later I one-hand it as cool as can be. . . . I hear the applause. . . . I hear voices congratulating my mother for having such a good athlete for a son. . . . Everybody on the team pounds my back as they come in from the field, letting me know that I've *made* it. (Candell in Pleck and Sawyer, 1974: 16)

This is a good picture of boys being drawn together in sport, of sharing almost total experience.

But is it? The same person continues in the next paragraph:

> But I know enough not to blow my cool so all I do is mumble thanks under a slightly trembling upper lip which is fighting the rest of my face, the rest of being, from exploding with laughter and tears of joy. (Candell in Pleck and Sawyer, 1974: 19)

Why this silence? Again, I don't think it is just because our culture demands inexpression. I think here, as above, silence and inexpression are the ways men learn to *consolidate* power, to make the effort appear as effortless, to guard against showing the real limits of one's potential and power by making it *all* appear easy. Even among males alone, one maintains control over a situation by revealing only strategic proportions of oneself.

Further, in Marc Fasteau's very perceptive article "Why Men Aren't Talking" (Pleck and Sawyer, 1974), the observation is made that when men do talk, they talk of "large" problems—war, politics, art—but never of anything really personal. Even when men have equal credentials in achieved success, they tend not to make themselves vulnerable to each other, for to do so may be interpreted as a sign of weakness and an opportunity for the other to secure advantage. As Fasteau puts it, men talk, but they always do so for a *reason*—getting together for its own sake would be too frightening—and that reason often amounts to just another effort at establishing who *really* is best, stronger, smarter, or ultimately, more powerful.

Inexpressiveness and the Sociology of Sex Roles

In the preceding sections, I have tried to change the grounds of an explanation of male inexpressiveness from one which holds that it is simply a cultural variable to one which sees it as a consequence of the political (power) position of the sexes in our society. I have not tried to deny that male inexpressiveness exists but only that it does so in different forms and for different reasons than Balswick and Peek suggest. I am making no claims for the analytic completeness of the ideas presented here.

A direct result of the feminist movement has been the effort on the part of sociologists concerned with family and sex-role-related behavior to discard or recast old concepts in the face of the feminist critique. One tendency of this "new sociology" has been an attempt to rescue attributes of positive human potential from the exclusive domain of one sex and, thus, to validate those potentials for all people. Although they do not say this explicitly, some such concern certainly underlies Balswick and Peek's effort. I think that this is social science at its best.

On the other hand, I am not convinced, as Balswick and Peek seem to be, that significant change in the male sex role will be made if we conceptualize the problem as one that involves individual males gradually unlearning their inexpressiveness with individual females. Balswick (1974) wrote an article based on the analysis developed with Peek entitled "Why Husbands Can't Say 'I Love You'" and printed it in a mass distribution women's magazine. Predictably, the article suggests *to the wife* some techniques she might develop for drawing her husband out of his inexpressive shell. I think that kind of article—at this point in the struggle of women to define themselves—is facile and wrongheaded. Such advice burdens the wife with additional "emotional work" while simultaneously creating a new arena in which she can—and most likely will—fail.

Similarly, articles that speak to men about their need to become more expressive also miss the point if we are concerned about fundamental social change. Such arguments come fairly cheap. Witness the essentially honest but fatally narrow and class-bound analyses of Korda (1973) and Farrell (1974). Their arguments develop little more than strategies capable of salvaging a limited number of upper-class male heterosexual egos. The need I see and feel at this point is for arguments and strategies capable of moving the majority of men who are not privileged in that fashion. What such arguments would say—much less to whom they would be addressed—is a question I cannot now answer. But I know where my work lies. For if my argument is correct—and I believe it is—that male inexpressiveness is instrumental in maintaining positions of power and privilege for men, then male sociologists might well begin to search through their own experiences and the accumulated knowledge of the sociological literature for sensitizing models which might indicate how, and if, it would be possible to relinquish the power which has historically been ours.

References

Balswick, Jack. 1974. "Why husbands can't say 'I love you.'" *Woman's Day*, April.

Balswick, Jack and Charles Peek. 1971. "The inexpressive male: A tragedy of American society." *The Family Coordinator*, 20: 363–368.

Benston, Margaret. 1969. "The political economy of women's liberation." *Monthly Review*, 21: 13–27.

Bradley, Mike. 1971. *Unbecoming Men: A Men's Consciousness Raising Group Writes on Oppression and Themselves*. New York: Times Change Press.

Chodorow, Nancy. 1971. "Being and doing: A cross-cultural examination of the socialization of males and females," pp. 259–291 In Gornick and Moran (eds.), *Women in Sexist Society*. New York: New American Library.

Farrell, Warren. 1974. *The Liberated Man*. New York: Random House.

Jong, Erica. 1973. *Fear of Flying*. New York: New American Library.

Korda, Michael. 1973. *Male Chauvinism: How It Works*. New York: Random House.

Parsons, Talcott. 1951. *The Social System* (Chapters VI and VII). Glencoe, Illinois: Free Press.

Pleck, Joseph and Jack Sawyer. 1974. *Men and Masculinity*. Englewood Cliffs, New Jersey: Prentice-Hall.

Sennett, Richard and Jonathan Cobb. 1973. *The Hidden Injuries of Class*. New York: Random House.

Tiger, Lionel. 1971. *Men in Groups*. London: Granada Publishing.

Wrong, Dennis. 1961. "The oversocialized conception of man in modern sociology." *American Sociological Review*, 26: 183–193.

ARTICLE

Jane C. Hood

"Let's Get a Girl": Male Bonding Rituals in America

Prologue

Wednesday, April 19, 1989: 10:05 P.M. "A 28 year old investment banker, jogging through Central Park, was attacked by a group of teenagers. They kicked and beat her, smashed her in the head with a pipe and raped her. The teenagers, who were from East Harlem, were quickly arrested" (Terry 1989, p. 28).

Wednesday, March 1, 1989: c. 6:00 P.M. In Glen Ridge, New Jersey, five high-school football players sexually assaulted a 17-year-old mentally handicapped girl in a basement while eight other teenagers looked on (Foderado 1989). "No sexual intercourse took place, investigators said, but the girl was believed to have been forced to perform sexual acts with the boys and she was raped with several objects including a broomstick and a miniature baseball bat" . . . "The arrests were announced on May 24 by Essex County Prosecutor, Herbert H. Tate, Jr. whose office took over the case last month when

This essay is a revised and expanded version of the full text of an article originally published in the *New York Times* under the title, "Why Our Society Is Rape Prone" (Hood 1989). This version includes examples cut from the original text as well as references to the Glen Ridge case.

the son of Lieut. Richard Corcoran, a Glen Ridge officer, was identified as being present when the assault took place" (*New York Times* 1989).

For weeks following the April 19 assault of the Central Park jogger, newspapers around the nation carried stories about the backgrounds of the youths who had attacked her. Newspapers reported that the assailants had been rampaging through the park attacking victims at will, a practice that some people called "wilding." Talk show participants debated whether the attack was racially motivated, and both black and white community leaders worried about how the publicity following the attack would affect race relations in the city. While sociologists discussed the socioeconomic roots of urban violence and clinicians described the psychic terror experienced by youths growing up in East Harlem, incumbent politicians urged "get tough" policies to "stamp out terrorism in the streets." Over a month after the attack, local New York City newspapers still carried headlines on the jogger's condition such as "Jogger Kisses Cardinal."

With the exception of some excellent articles in the *Village Voice* (1989) and op-ed articles by Susan Chace (1989) and Elizabeth Holtzman (1989), hardly any of this "media orgy" dealt with gender or the phenomenon of gang rape. However, by the time news of the Glen Ridge assault surfaced on May 24, at least part of the media spotlight had shifted to rape. On May 29, *New York Times* readers finally learned that 28 other rapes had been reported to New York City police during the week of April 16 and that nearly all of these were of black and Hispanic women (Terry 1989). Of all these assaults, only the rape of an upper-middle-class white jogger by a group of black youths had made the news.

Gang Rape as a Male Bonding Ritual

Why did eight teenagers beat and rape a jogger in Central Park? Mostly missing from the analyses of "wilding," and lost among the suggestions for preventing similar tragedies, is one crucial issue: gender.

With the exception of prison assaults, gang rape is a crime committed almost exclusively by males against females. Yet few commentators have focused on gender and what it means to be raised male in America. Like the proverbial fish who cannot describe water, we Americans see everything *but* gender at work in the April 19 assault.

Given over 30 years of research on patterns of forcible rape, our myopia is hard to explain. In his classic 1959 study of 646 Philadelphia rapes, Menachem Amir (1971) described the prototype for the Central Park assault. Of 646 cases, 43% were pair or group rapes. Like the boys from Schomberg Plaza, the offenders were disproportionately very young (10 to 19). Amir also found that group rapes were much more likely than single-offender rapes to involve violence far beyond what would be necessary to restrain the

victim. In an attempt to make sense of this pattern, several researchers (Amir 1971; Brownmiller 1975; Groth 1979; Sanday 1981; Herman 1984) reached a similar conclusion: In a society that equates masculinity with dominance and sex with violence, gang rape becomes one way for adolescents to prove their masculinity both to themselves and to each other.

Although other studies of sexual assault patterns do not find as high an incidence of pair and group rape as did Amir (Groth 1979, p. 110; Ageton 1983), when group rape does occur, the attack has a dual focus. Interaction among the assailants may take center stage as the men compete with each other in punishing, dominating, and humiliating the victim (Groth 1979, p. 118; Scully and Marolla 1985). In addition to being an outlet for rage and the need to dominate, gang rapes can also be a form of group recreation. The Schomburg Plaza boys said that they were "just having fun," and gang rapists interviewed by Scully and Marolla (1985, p. 260) described cruising an area "looking for girls" that they could pick up, drive to a deserted area, and then rape. Although not as well practiced in the art of gang rape as Scully and Marolla's informants, the teenagers rampaging through Central Park reportedly said, "Let's get a girl" shortly before they attacked the jogger (Chace 1989).

The attack on the investment banker was particularly brutal, but both it and the Glen Ridge assault have something in common with gang rapes of the sort portrayed in the film, "Saturday Night Fever." There, one boy lures a girl into the backseat of a car so that a whole group can have sex with her. An event that started as "sex" becomes rape as the boys begin to compete with each other, disregarding the girl's welfare or feelings. Similarly, in Glen Ridge, the girl appears to have gone willingly to the house with the boys before she was subjected to an hour of degradation at the hands of four boys while another urged them on and eight others watched (Foderaro 1989). Because victims may be reluctant to report this kind of assault to police or interviewers, Scully and Marolla (1985) think that these "date gang rapes" may be much more common than either police reports or the Uniform Crime Surveys indicate.

Both the Central Park and the Glen Ridge incidents also share some characteristics of "gang bangs" in fraternity houses and random violence against women on college campuses. These apparently diverse phenomena are connected, not by the severity of the crime and not by the characteristics of the victim, but rather by the common context of an adolescent male-bonding ritual in a rape-prone society.

In her research on gang rapes at the University of Pennsylvania, anthropologist Peggy Sanday has compiled vivid descriptions of gang rapes, which she suspects are a common practice on college campuses all over the United States (Sanday 1986, p. 99; 1988). They are, as are most gang rapes, planned in advance. The intended victim is plied with alcohol and/or pills until she can be dragged into a bedroom where she is then systematically raped by one boy after the other while the others look on. Afterward, the boys use the excuse that the girl was drunk and did not know what she was doing.

In comparing the fraternity members to the street gangs that Amir studied in the 1950s, Sanday argues that the two groups are similar in that both are peripheral to society. Whereas members of Amir's lower class Philadelphia street gangs may never escape their peripheral social and economic status, college males are temporarily peripheral "while they are learning skills they will eventually use to usurp their fathers' places in the corporate world" (Sanday 1986, p. 99).

Gang rape may be the most shocking male bonding ritual on college campuses, but it is not the only one that depends on objectifying women.

In an excellent article on the use of sexist jokes among fraternity men Peter Lyman (1987) describes an incident that took place at a sorority house. There a group of 45 fraternity men shoved their way into the dining room, encircled the women residents, and forced them to watch for 10 minutes while one "pledge" stroked a rubber phallus and another recited a speech on penis envy. After a resident adviser told the men to leave, the pranksters were surprised. After all (like the boys in Central Park), they were "just having fun," and the penis envy joke was a tradition. The women, however, argued that the raid had rape overtones and asked, "Why do you men always think about women in terms of violating them, in sexual imagery?" Why indeed?

Rape-Free vs. Rape-Prone Societies

The answer, I think, lies in understanding the difference between what University of Pennsylvania anthropologist Peggy Sanday calls "rape-prone" societies and those that are "rape-free." In a study of 95 band and tribal societies, Sanday (1981) found a high incidence of rape to be associated with militarism, interpersonal violence in general, an ideology of male toughness, and distant father–child relationships. Rape-free societies, on the other hand, encourage female participation in the economy and political system and male involvement in child-rearing.

In rape-free societies men speak of women with respect. For example, a Minangakabau man in West Sumatra told Peggy Sanday:

> Women are given more privileges because people think that women determine the continuation of the generations. Whether the next generation is good or bad depends upon women . . . Women have more human feeling and they are more humanitarian. They think more about people's feelings and because of this they should be given rights to speak. (Sanday 1986, pp. 96–97)

In nonindustrial rape-free societies, women and men may have different roles, but the roles that women play are highly valued and help to shape the culture as a whole.

Despite recent moves toward gender equality, our society is still very much "rape-prone." In fact, the United States has the distinction of being among the most rape-prone of all modern societies (Scully and Marolla 1985). In surveys of U.S. and Canadian college students, for example, psychologist Neil Malamuth finds that one of three college men say that if they could get away with it, they would be at least "somewhat likely" to rape a woman (Malamuth 1981). Similarly, several recent surveys of high-school students find 40 to 50% of both boys and girls agreeing with such statements as, "If a girl goes to a guy's apartment after a date, it's OK for him to force her to have sex" (Hall, Howard, & Boezio 1986; Kikuchi 1989). Even jurors in rape trials studied by LaFree and Reskin (LaFree 1989, p. 219) found it hard to believe that an attractive man would rape a woman if he could have just as easily seduced her. As many authors point out, in rape-prone societies, rape is easily confused with "normal" sex.

In our own society, sex is so inextricably linked to violence that attempts to uncouple the two can fail in ways some of us may find hard to imagine. For example, after the release of *The Accused* (a film dramatizing the New Bedford pool hall gang rape), some middle-class male viewers were observed cheering at the harrowing gang rape scene (*The Nation*, 5-29-1989). Like the Schomburg Plaza boys, these movie goers had learned that masculinity means domination over others through sex and violence.

Prevention Strategies

In a letter to the *New York Times*, John Gutfreund (1989), the jogger's employer, called for "an all-out national emergency effort to solve the problem of violence on urban streets." Others urged prosecuting the teenagers as adults and advocated long prison terms. Ridiculing the earlier version of this article, the *Richmond Times-Dispatch* called for "A little more jail time and a little less blame-society-first rationalizing."

Unfortunately, more lights in Central Park, more police on the streets, and more time in jail for convicted rapists will not do much to lower the overall incidence of rape. A man caught robbing a jewelry store is unlikely to use the defense that "it wasn't really a robbery." For rapists, however, the defense that "it wasn't really a rape" is commonplace (LaFree 1989; Scully and Marolla 1985). In spite of the creation of special Sexual Offense units in police departments and in spite of the adoption of "rape shield" laws that disallow questions concerning the victim's moral character, most rapes are never reported to the police and of those that are reported only a small proportion result in any jail time for offenders. Thus, in a study of 881 rapes reported to Indianapolis police in 1970, 1973, and 1975, LaFree found that only 12% resulted in convictions (LaFree 1989, p. 60). Because both male and female jurors believe that only certain kinds of men can rape and only certain kinds of women can be raped, rapes that do not fit the public's stereotype of "a real rape" are less likely to yield convictions.

As long as rapes of wives, girlfriends, hitchhikers, women in bars, and girls at fraternity parties are dismissed as "not really rape," doubling the jail time for the few men that are convicted will do little to reduce American women's one-out-of-three lifetime probability (Johnson 1980) of sexual assault. If our society is to become less rape-prone, we must instead find ways of redefining gender relationships so that women become men's peers and boys can become men without controlling, dominating, and objectifying girls and women.

Therefore, if corporate leaders want to mount an effective national campaign to prevent assaults on women by bands of young men, they should target, not "criminals," but

- advertisements portraying women as sex objects

- sexual harassment in the work place
- resistance to paternity leave policies
- Rambo dolls and other violent games and toys
- gender inequality in the workplace.

For their part, community groups can do the following:

- Bring more fathers into daycare and kindergarten classrooms to show that "real men" are nurturing people.

- Support sex education programs that teach that rape is not sex but violence and that good sex takes place in the context of love and respect.

- Encourage co-ed sports at the elementary and middle school levels so that boys can learn that girls are not "the other," to be made fun of and put down.

- Learn the common "rape myths" ("You can tell a rapist by the way he looks." "Women enjoy being raped." "Good girls don't get raped.") and teach against them on all fronts.

- Protest the production and showing of "slasher" films that eroticize violence.

In his otherwise excellent May 2 column, Tom Wicker (*New York Times* 1989) described the Central Park rape as "a chance event that could have happened to anyone." In a way it was. On the other hand, when was the last time anyone has heard of a gang of teenage girls raping and beating a man in Central Park? To get to the roots of this particular brand of violence, we need to look beyond race and class to gender relations in America.

References

Ageton, S. 1983. *Sexual Assault among Adolescents.* Lexington, MA: D. C. Heath.

Amir, M. 1971. *Patterns of Forcible Rape.* Chicago: University of Chicago Press.

Brownmiller, S. 1975. *Against Our Will: Men, Women and Rape.* New York: Simon and Schuster.

Chace, S. 1989. "Safety in the Park: In Women's Hands." *New York Times,* April 27.

Foderaro, L. 1989. "After a Sex Assault, a Town Worries Its Athletes Were Too Often Forgiven." *New York Times,* June 12.

Groth, A. N. 1979. *Men Who Rape: The Psychology of the Offender.* New York: Plenum Press.

Gutfreund, J. 1989. "Letters to the Editor." *New York Times,* April 27.

Hall, E., J. Howard, and S. Boezio 1986. "Tolerance of Rape: A Sexist or Anti-Social Attitude?" *Psychology of Women Quarterly* 10: 101–118.

Herman, D. 1984. "The Rape Culture." Pp. 20–38 in *Women: A Feminist Perspective,* edited by J. Freeman. Palo Alto, CA: Mayfield.

Holtzman, E. 1989. "Rape: The Silence Is Criminal." *New York Times,* May 5.

Hood, J. 1989. "Why Our Society Is Rape-Prone." *New York Times,* May 16.

Johnson, A. G. 1980. "On the Prevalence of Rape in the United States." *Signs: Journal of Women in Culture and Society* 6: 136–146.

Kikuchi, J. 1989. Presentation on Rhode Island rape attitudes study at meetings of Association of Women in Psychology, Providence, R.I., March.

LaFree, G. 1989. *Rape and Criminal Justice: The Social Construction of Sexual Assault.* Belmont, CA: Wadsworth.

Lyman, P. 1987. "The Fraternal Bond as a Joking Relationship." Pp. 148–164 in *Changing Men,* edited by M. Kimmel. Newbury Park, CA: Sage.

Malamuth, N. 1981. "Rape Proclivity among Males." *Journal of Social Issues* 37: 138–157.

New York Times 1989. "5 New Jersey Youths Held in Sexual Assault on Impaired Girl, 17." May 25.

Richmond Times-Dispatch 1989. "Blame Society First." May 19.

Sanday, P. R. 1981. "The Socio-Cultural Context of Rape: A Cross Cultural Study." *Journal of Social Issues* 37: 5–27.

———. 1986. "Rape and the Silencing of the Feminine." Pp. 84–101 in *Rape,* edited by S. Tomaselli and R. Porter. Oxford: Basil Blackwell.

———. 1988. Excerpts from Sanday's unpublished manuscript on sexual expression among college students read as part of discussant's comments at the Annual Meetings of the American Anthropological Association, Phoenix, AZ, November 19.

Scully, D., and J. Marolla 1985. "Riding the Bull at Gilley's: Convicted Rapists Describe the Rewards of Rape." *Social Problems* 32: 251–263.

Terry, D. 1989. "In Week of an Infamous Rape, 28 Other Victims Suffer." *New York Times*, May 29.

Village Voice 1989. "The Voices Not Heard: Black and Women Writers on the Central Park Rape." May 9.

Tim Beneke

Men on Rape

Rape may be America's fastest growing violent crime; no one can be certain because it is not clear whether more rapes are being committed or reported. It *is* clear that violence against women is widespread and fundamentally alters the meaning of life for women; that sexual violence is encouraged in a variety of ways in American culture; and that women are often blamed for rape.

Consider some statistics:

- In a random sample of 930 women, sociologist Diana Russell found that 44 percent had survived either rape or attempted rape. Rape was defined as sexual intercourse physically forced upon the woman, or coerced by threat of bodily harm, or forced upon the woman when she was helpless (asleep, for example). The survey included rape and attempted rape in marriage in its calculations. (Personal communication)

- In a September 1980 survey conducted by *Cosmopolitan* magazine to which over 106,000 women anonymously responded,

24 percent had been raped at least once. Of these, 51 percent had been raped by friends, 37 percent by strangers, 18 percent by relatives, and 3 percent by husbands. 10 percent of the women in the survey had been victims of incest. 75 percent of the women had been "bullied into making love." Writer Linda Wolfe, who reported on the survey, wrote in reference to such bullying: "Though such harassment stops short of rape, readers reported that it was nearly as distressing."

- An estimated 2–3 percent of all men who rape outside of marriage go to prison for their crimes.[1]

- The F.B.I. estimates that if current trends continue, one woman in four will be sexually assaulted in her lifetime.[2]

- An estimated 1.8 million women are battered by their spouses each year.[3] In extensive interviews with 430 battered women, clinical psychologist Lenore Walker, author of *The Battered Woman*, found that 59.9 percent had also been raped (defined as above) by their spouses. Given the difficulties many women had in admitting they had been raped, Walker estimates the figure may well be as high as 80 or 85 percent (Personal communication). If 59.9 percent of the 1.8 million women battered each year are also raped, then a million women may be raped in marriage each year. And a significant number are raped in marriage without being battered.

- Between one in two and one in ten of all rapes are reported to the police.[4]

- Between 300,000 and 500,000 women are raped each year outside of marriage.[5]

What is often missed when people contemplate statistics on rape is the effect of the *threat* of sexual violence on women. I have asked women repeatedly, "How would your life be different if rape were suddenly to end?" (Men may learn a lot by asking this question of women to whom they are close.) The threat of rape is an assault upon the meaning of the world; it alters the feel of the human condition. Surely any attempt to comprehend the lives of women that fails to take issues of violence against women into account is misguided.

Through talking to women, I learned: *The threat of rape alters the meaning and feel of the night.* Observe how your body feels, how the night feels, when you're in fear. The constriction in your chest, the vigilance in your eyes, the rubber in your legs. What do the stars look like? How does the moon present itself? What is the difference between walking late at night in the dangerous part of a city and walking late at night in the country, or safe suburbs? When I try to imagine what the threat of rape must do to the night, I think of the stalked, adrenalated feeling I get walking late at night in parts of certain American cities. Only, I remind myself, it is a fear different from any I have known, a fear of being raped.

It is night half the time. If the threat of rape alters the meaning of the night, it must alter the meaning and pace of the day, one's relation to the passing and organization of time itself. For some women, the threat of rape at night turns their cars into armored tanks, their solitude into isolation. And what must the space inside a car or an apartment feel like if the space outside is menacing?

I was running late one night with a close woman friend through a path in the woods on the outskirts of a small university town. We had run several miles and were feeling a warm, energized serenity.

"How would you feel if you were alone?" I asked.

"Terrified!" she said instantly.

"Terrified that there might be a man out there?" I asked, pointing to the surrounding moonlit forest, which had suddenly been transformed into a source of terror.

"Yes."

Another woman said, "I know what I can't do and I've completely internalized what I can't do. I've built a viable life that basically involves never leaving my apartment at night unless I'm directly going some place to meet somebody. It's unconsciously built into what it occurs to women to do." When one is raised without freedom, one may not recognize its absence.

The threat of rape alters the meaning and feel of nature. Everyone has felt the psychic nurturance of nature. Many women are being deprived of that nurturance, especially in wooded areas near cities. They are deprived either because they cannot experience nature in solitude because of threat, or because, when they do choose solitude in nature, they must cope with a certain subtle but nettlesome fear.

Women need more money because of rape and the threat of rape makes it harder for women to earn money. It's simple: if you don't feel safe walking at night, or riding public transportation, you need a car. And it is less practicable to live in cheaper, less secure, and thus more dangerous neighborhoods if the ordinary threat of violence that men experience, being mugged, say, is compounded by the threat of rape. By limiting mobility at night, the threat of rape limits where and when one is able to work, thus making it more difficult to earn money. An obvious bind: women need more money because of rape, and have fewer job opportunities because of it.

The threat of rape makes women more dependent on men (or other women). One woman said: "If there were no rape I wouldn't have to play games with men for their protection." The threat of rape falsifies, mystifies, and confuses relations between men and women. If there were no rape, women would simply not need men as much, wouldn't need them to go places with at night, to feel safe in their homes, for protection in nature.

The threat of rape makes solitude less possible for women. Solitude, drawing strength from being alone, is difficult if being alone means being afraid. To be afraid is to be in need, to experience a lack; the threat of rape creates a lack. Solitude requires relaxation; if you're afraid, you can't relax.

The threat of rape inhibits a woman's expressiveness. "If there were no rape," said one woman, "I could dress the way I wanted and walk the way I wanted and not feel self-conscious about the responses of men. I could be friendly to people. I wouldn't have to wish I was ugly. I wouldn't have to make myself small when I got on the bus. I wouldn't have to respond to verbal abuse from men by remaining silent. I could respond in kind."

If a woman's basic expressiveness is inhibited, her sexuality, creativity, and delight in life must surely be diminished.

The threat of rape inhibits the freedom of the eye. I know a married couple who live in Manhattan. They are both artists, both acutely sensitive and responsive to the visual world. When they walk separately in the city, he has more freedom to look than she does. She must control her eye movements lest they inadvertently meet the glare of some importunate man. What, who, and how she sees are restricted by the threat of rape.

The following exercise is recommended for men.

> Walk down a city street. Pay a lot of attention to your clothing; make sure your pants are zipped, shirt tucked in, buttons done. Look straight ahead. Every time a man walks past you, avert your eyes and make your face expressionless. Most women learn to go through this act each time we leave our houses. It's a way to avoid at least some of the encounters we've all had with strange men who decided we looked available.[6]

To relate aesthetically to the visual world involves a certain playfulness, spirit of spontaneous exploration. The tense vigilance that accompanies fear inhibits that spontaneity. The world is no longer yours to look at when you're afraid.

I am aware that all culture is, in part, restriction, that there are places in America where hardly anyone is safe (though men are safer than women virtually everywhere), that there are many ways to enjoy life, that some women may not be so restricted, that there exist havens, whether psychic, geographical, economic, or class. But they are *havens*, and as such, defined by threat.

Above all, I trust my experience: no woman could have lived the life I've lived the last few years. If suddenly I were restricted by the threat of rape, I would feel a deep, inexorable depression. And it's not just rape; it's harassment, battery, Peeping Toms, anonymous phone calls, exhibitionism, intrusive stares, fondlings—all contributing to an atmosphere of intimidation in women's lives. And I have only scratched the surface; it would take many carefully crafted short stories to begin to express what I have only hinted at in the last few pages. I have not even touched upon what it might mean for a woman to be sexually assaulted. Only women can speak to that. Nor have I suggested how the threat of rape affects marriage.

Rape and the threat of rape pervade the lives of women, as reflected in some popular images of our culture.

"She Asked for It"— Blaming the Victim[7]

Many things may be happening when a man blames a woman for rape.

First, in all cases where a woman is said to have asked for it, her appearance and behavior are taken as a form of speech. "Actions speak louder than words" is a widely held belief; the woman's actions—her appearance may be taken as action—are given greater emphasis than her words; an interpretation alien to the woman's intentions is given to her actions. A logical extension of "she asked for it" is the idea that she wanted what happened to happen; if she wanted it to happen, she *deserved* for it to happen. Therefore, the man is not to be blamed. "She asked for it" can mean either that she was consenting to have sex and was not really raped, or that she was in fact raped but somehow she really deserved it. "If you ask for it, you deserve it," is a widely held notion. If I ask you to beat me up and you beat me up, I still don't deserve to be beaten up. So even if the notion that women asked to be raped had some basis in reality, which it doesn't, on its own terms it makes no sense.

Second, a mentality exists that says: a woman who assumes freedoms normally restricted to a man (like going out alone at night) and is raped is doing the same thing as a woman who goes out in the rain without an umbrella and catches a cold. Both are considered responsible for what happens to them. That men will rape is taken to be a legitimized given, part of nature, like rain or snow. The view reflects a massive abdication of responsibility for rape on the part of men. It is so much easier to think of rape as natural than to acknowledge one's part

in it. So long as rape is regarded as natural, women will be blamed for rape.

A third point. The view that it is natural for men to rape is closely connected to the view of women as commodities. If a woman's body is regarded as a valued commodity by men, then of course, if you leave a valued commodity where it can be taken, it's just human nature for men to take it. If you left your stereo out on the sidewalk, you'd be asking for it to get stolen. Someone will just take it. (And how often men speak of rape as "going out and *taking* it.") If a woman walks the streets at night, she's leaving a valued commodity, her body, where it can be taken. So long as women are regarded as commodities, they will be blamed for rape.

Which brings us to a fourth point. "She asked for it" is inseparable from a more general "psychology of the dupe." If I use bad judgment and fail to read the small print in a contract and later get taken advantage of "screwed" (or "fucked over") then I deserve what I get; bad judgment makes me liable. Analogously, if a woman trusts a man and goes to his apartment, or accepts a ride hitchhiking, or goes out on a date and is raped, she's a dupe and deserves what she gets. "He didn't *really* rape her" goes the mentality—"he merely took advantage of her." And in America it's okay for people to take advantage of each other, even expected and praised. In fact, you're considered dumb and foolish if you don't take advantage of other people's bad judgment. And so, again, by treating them as dupes, rape will be blamed on women.

Fifth, if a woman who is raped is judged attractive by men, and particularly if she dresses to look attractive, then the mentality exists that she attacked him with her weapon so, of course, he counter-attacked with his. The preview to a popular movies states: "She was the victim of her own *provocative beauty*." Provocation: "There is a line which, if crossed, will *set me off* and I will lose control and no longer be responsible for my behavior. If you punch me in the nose then, of course, I will not be responsible for what happens: you will have provoked a fight. If you dress, talk, move, or act a certain way, you will have provoked me to rape. If your appearance *stuns* me, *strikes* me, *ravishes* me, *knocks me out*, etc., then I will not be held responsible for what happens; you will have asked for it." The notion that sexual feeling makes one helpless is part of a cultural abdication of responsibility for sexuality. So long as a woman's appearance is viewed as a weapon and sexual feeling is believed to make one helpless, women will be blamed for rape.

Sixth, I have suggested that men sometimes become obsessed with images of women, that images become a substitute for sexual feeling, that sexual feeling becomes externalized and out of control and is given an undifferentiated identity in the appearance of women's bodies. It is a process of projection in which one blurs one's own desire with her imagined, projected desire. If a woman's attractiveness is taken to signify one's own lust and a woman's lust, then when an "attractive" woman is raped, some men may think she wanted sex. Since they perceive their own lust in part projected onto the woman, they disbelieve women who've been raped. So long as men project their own sexual desires onto women, they will blame women for rape.

And seventh, what are we to make of the contention that women in dating situations say "no" initially to sexual overtures from men as a kind of pose, only to give in later, thus revealing their true intentions? And that men are thus confused and incredulous when women are raped because in their sexual experience women can't be believed? I doubt that this has much to do with men's perceptions of rape. I don't know to what extent women actually "say no and mean yes"; certainly it is a common theme in male folklore. I have spoken to a couple of women who went through periods when they wanted to be sexual but were afraid to be, and often rebuffed initial sexual advances only to

give in later. One point is clear: the ambivalence women may feel about having sex is closely tied to the inability of men to fully accept them as sexual beings. Women have been traditionally punished for being openly and freely sexual; men are praised for it. And if many men think of sex as achievement of possession of a valued commodity, or aggressive degradation, then women have every reason to feel and act ambivalent.

These themes are illustrated in an interview I conducted with a 23 year old man who grew up in Pittsburgh and works as a file clerk in the financial district of San Francisco. Here's what he said:

"Where I work it's probably no different from any other major city in the U.S. The women dress up in high heels, and they wear a lot of makeup, and they just look really *hot* and really sexy, and how can somebody who has a healthy sex drive not feel lust for them when you see them? I feel lust for them, but I don't think I could find it in me to overpower someone and rape them. But I definitely get the feeling that I'd like to rape a girl. I don't know if the actual act of rape would be satisfying, but the *feeling* is satisfying.

"These women look so good, and they kiss ass of the men in the three-piece suits who are *big* in the corporation, and most of them relate to me like 'Who are *you*? Who are *you* to even *look* at?' They're snobby and they condescend to me, and I resent it. It would take me a lot longer to get to first base than it would somebody with a three-piece suit who had money. And to me a lot of the men they go out with are superficial assholes who have no real feelings or substance, and are just trying to get ahead and make a lot of money. Another thing that makes me resent these women is thinking, 'How could she want to hang out with somebody like that? What does that make her?'

"I'm a file clerk, which makes me feel like a nebbish, a nurd, like I'm not making it, I'm a failure. But I don't really believe I'm a failure because I know it's just a phase, and I'm just doing it for the money, just to make it through this phase. I catch myself feeling like a failure, but I realize that's ridiculous."

What Exactly Do You Go Through When You See These Sexy, Unavailable Women?

"Let's say I see a woman and she looks really pretty and really clean and sexy, and she's giving off very feminine, sexy vibes. I think, 'Wow, I would love to make love to her,' but I know she's not really interested. It's a tease. A lot of times a woman knows that she's looking really good and she'll use that and flaunt it, and it makes me feel like she's laughing at me and I feel *degraded*.

"I also feel dehumanized, because when I'm being teased I just turn off, I cease to be human. Because if I go with my human emotions I'm going to want to put my arms around her and kiss her, and to do that would be unacceptable. I don't like the feeling that I'm supposed to stand there and take it, and not be able to hug her or kiss her; so I just turn off my emotions. It's a feeling of humiliation, because the woman has forced me to turn off my feelings and react in a way that I really don't want to.

"If I were actually desperate enough to rape somebody, it would be from wanting the person, but it would be a very spiteful thing, just being able to say, 'I have power over you and I can do anything I want with you,' because really I feel that *they* have power over *me* just by their presence. Just the fact that they can come up to me and just melt me and make me feel like a dummy makes me want revenge. They have power over me so I want power over them. . . .

"Society says that you have to have a lot of sex with a lot of different women to be a real man. Well, what happens if you don't? Then what are you? Are you half a man? Are you still a boy? It's ridiculous. You see a whiskey ad with a guy and two women on his arm. The implication is that real men don't have any trouble getting women."

How Does It Make You Feel Toward Women to See All These Sexy Women in Media and Advertising Using Their Looks to Try to Get You to Buy Something?

"It makes me hate them. As a man you're taught that men are more powerful than women, and that men always have the upper hand, and that it's a man's society; but then you see all these women and it makes you think, 'Jesus Christ, if we have all the power how come all the beautiful women are telling us what to buy?' And to be honest, it just makes me hate beautiful women because they're using their power over me. I realize they're being used themselves, and they're doing it for money. In *Playboy* you see all these beautiful women who look so sexy and they'll be giving you all these looks like they want to have sex so bad; but then in reality you know that except for a few nymphomaniacs, they're doing it for the money; so I hate them for being used and for using their bodies in that way.

"In this society, if you ever sit down and realize how manipulated you really are it makes you pissed off—it makes you want to take control. And you've been manipulated by women, and they're a very easy target because they're out walking along the streets, so you can just grab one and say, 'Listen, you're going to do what I want you to do,' and it's an act of revenge against the way you've been manipulated.

"I know a girl who was walking down the street by her house, when this guy jumped her and beat her up and raped her, and she was black and blue and had to go to the hospital. That's beyond me. I can't understand how somebody could do that. If I were going to rape a girl, I wouldn't hurt her. I might *restrain* her, but I wouldn't *hurt* her. . . .

"The whole dating game between men and women also makes me feel degraded. I hate being put in the position of having to initiate a relationship. I've been taught that if you're not aggressive with a woman, then you've blown it. She's not going to jump on *you*, so *you've* got to jump on *her*. I've heard all kinds of stories where the woman says, 'No! No! No!' and they end up making great love. I get confused as hell if a woman pushes me away. Does it mean she's trying to be a nice girl and wants to put up a good appearance, or does it mean she doesn't want anything to do with you? You don't know. Probably a lot of men think that women don't feel like real women unless a man tries to force himself on her, unless she brings out the 'real man,' so to speak, and probably too much of it goes on. It goes on in my head that you're complimenting a woman by actually staring at her or by trying to get into her pants. Lately, I'm realizing that when I stare at women lustfully, they often feel more threatened than flattered."

Notes

1. Such estimates recur in the rape literature. See *Sexual Assault* by Nancy Gager and Cathleen Schurr, Grosset & Dunlap, 1976, or *The Price of Coercive Sexuality* by Clark and Lewis, The Women's Press, 1977.

2. *Uniform Crime Reports*, 1980.

3. See *Behind Closed Doors* by Murray J. Strauss and Richard Gelles, Doubleday, 1979.

4. See Gager and Schurr (above) or virtually any book on the subject.

5. Again, see Gager and Schurr, or Carol V. Horos, *Rape*, Banbury Books, 1981.

6. From "Willamette Bridge" in *Body Politics* by Nancy Henley, Prentice-Hall, 1977, p. 144.

7. I would like to thank George Lakoff for this insight.

ARTICLE

Jason Schultz

Getting Off on Feminism

> When it comes to smashing a paradigm, pleasure is not the most important thing. It is the *only* thing.
> —Gary Wolf, *Wired* Magazine

Minutes after my best friend told me he was getting married, I casually offered to throw a bachelor party in his honor. Even though such parties are notorious for their degradation of women, I didn't think this part would be much of a problem. Both the bride and groom considered themselves feminists, and I figured that most of the men attending would agree that sexism had no place in the celebration of this union. In fact, I thought the bachelor party would be a great opportunity to get a group of men together for a social event that didn't degenerate into the typical anti-women, homophobic male-bonding thing. Still, ending one of the most sexist traditions in history—even for one night—was a lot tougher than I envisioned.

I have to admit that I'm not a *complete* iconoclast: I wanted to make the party a success by

Reprinted from *To Be Real* edited by R. Walker, 1995, pages 107–126, Anchor Books. Reprinted with permission.

including at least some of the usual elements, such as good food and drink, great music, and cool things to do. At the same time, I was determined not to fall prey to traditional sexist party gimmicks such as prostitutes, strippers jumping out of cakes, or straight porn. But after nixing all the traditional lore, even *I* thought it sounded boring. What were we going to do except sit around and think about women?

"What about a belly dancer?" one of the ushers suggested when I confided my concerns to him. "That's not as bad as a stripper." I sighed. This was supposed to be an occasion for the groom and his male friends to get together, celebrate the upcoming marriage, and affirm their friendship and connection with each other as men. "What the fuck does hiring a female sex worker have to do with any of that?" I shouted into the phone. I quickly regained my calm, but his suggestion still stung. We had to find some other way.

I wanted my party to be as "sexy" as the rest of them, but I had no idea how to do that in the absence of female sex workers. There was no powerful alternative image in our culture from which I could draw. I thought about renting some gay porn, or making it a cross-dressing party, but many of the guests were conservative, and I didn't want to scare anyone off. Besides, what would it say about a bunch of straight men if all we could do to be sexy was act queer for a night?

Over coffee on a Sunday morning, I asked some of the other guys what they thought was so "sexy" about having a stripper at a bachelor party.

"Well," David said, "it's just a gag. It's something kinda funny and sexy at the same time."

"Yeah," A.J. agreed. "It's not all that serious, but it's something special to do that makes the party cool."

"But *why* is it sexy and funny?" I asked. "Why can't we, as a bunch of guys, be sexy and funny ourselves?"

" 'Cause it's easier to be a guy with other guys when there's a chick around. It gives you all something in common to relate to."

"Hmm. I think I know what you mean," I said. "When I see a stripper, I get turned on, but not in the same way I would if I was with a lover. It's more like going to a show or watching a flick together. It's enjoyable, stimulating, but it's not overwhelming or intimate in the same way that sex is. Having the stripper provides a common emotional context for us to feel turned on. But we don't have to do anything about it like we would if we were with a girlfriend, right?"

"Well, my girlfriend would kill me if she saw me checking out this stripper," Greg replied. "But because it's kind of a male-bonding thing, it's not as threatening to our relationship. It's not because it's the stripper over her, it's because it's just us guys hanging out. It doesn't go past that."

Others agreed. "Yeah. You get turned on, but not in a serious way. It makes you feel sexy and sexual, and you can enjoy feeling that way with your friends. Otherwise, a lot of times, just hanging out with the guys is pretty boring. Especially at a bachelor party. I mean, that's the whole point, isn't it—to celebrate the fact that we're bachelors, and he"—referring to Robert, the groom—"isn't!"

Through these conversations, I realized that having a female sex worker at the party would give the men permission to connect with one another without becoming vulnerable. When men discuss sex in terms of actions—who they "did," and how and where they did it—they can gain recognition and validation of their sexuality from other men without having to expose their *feelings* about sex.

"What other kinds of things make you feel sexy like the stripper does?" I asked several of the guys.

"Watching porn sometimes, or a sexy movie."

A.J. said, "Just getting a look from a girl at a club. I mean, she doesn't even have to talk to you, but you still feel sexy and you can still hang out with your friends."

Greg added, "Sometimes just knowing that my girlfriend thinks I'm sexy, and then talking about her with friends, makes me feel like I'm the man. Or I'll hear some other guy talk about his girlfriend in a way that reminds me of mine, and I'll still get that same feeling. But that doesn't happen very often, and usually only when talking with one other guy.

This gave me an idea. "I've noticed that same thing, both here and at school with my other close guy friends. Why doesn't it happen with a bunch of guys, say at a party?"

"I don't know. It's hard to share a lot of personal stuff with guys," said Adam, "especially about someone you're seeing, if you don't feel comfortable. Well, not comfortable, because I know most of the guys who'll be at the party, but it's more like I don't want them to hassle me, or I might say something that freaks them out."

"Or you're just used to guys talking shit about girls," someone else added. "Like at a party or hanging out together. They rag on them, or pick out who's the cutest or who wants to do who. That's not the same thing as really talking about what makes you feel sexy."

"Hmm," I said. "So it's kind of like if I were to say that I liked to be tied down to the bed, no one would take me seriously. You guys would probably crack up laughing, make a joke or two, but I'd never expect you to actually join in and talk about being tied up in a serious way. It certainly wouldn't feel 'sexy,' would it? At least not as much as the stripper."

"Exactly. You talking about being tied down here is fine, 'cause we're into the subject of sex on a serious kick and all. But at a party, people are bullshitting each other and gabbing, and horsing around. The last thing most of us want is to trip over someone's personal taste or start thinking someone's a little queer."

"You mean queer as in homosexual?" I asked.

"Well, not really, 'cause I think everyone here is straight. But more of queer in the sense of perverted or different. I mean, you grow up in high school thinking that all guys are basically the same. You all want the same thing from girls in the same way. And when someone like you says you like to be tied down, it's kinda weird—almost like a challenge. It makes me have to respond in a way that either shows me agreeing that I also like to be tied down or not. And if someone's a typical guy and he says that, it makes you think he's different—not the same guy you knew in high school. And if he's not the same guy, then it challenges you to relate to him on a different level."

"Yeah, I guess in some ways it's like relating to someone who's gay," Greg said. "He can be cool and all, and you can get along totally great. But there's this barrier that's hard to cross over. It kinda keeps you apart. And that's not what you want to feel toward your friends, es-

pecially at a party like this one, where you're all coming together to chill."

As the bachelor party approached, I found myself wondering whether my friends and I could "come together to chill"—and affirm our status as sexual straight men—without buying into homophobic or sexist expressions. At the same time, I was doing a lot of soul-searching on how we could challenge the dominant culture's vision of male heterosexuality, not only by deciding against having a stripper at our party, but also by examining and redefining our own relationships with women.

Sex and the Sensitive Man

According to the prevailing cultural view, "desirable" hetero men are inherently dominant, aggressive, and, in many subtle and overt ways, abusive to women. To be sexy and powerful, straight men are expected to control and contrive a sexuality that reinforces their authority. Opposing these notions of power subjects a straight guy to being branded "sensitive," submissive, or passive—banished to the nether regions of excitement and pleasure, the unmasculine, asexual, "vanilla" purgatory of antieroticism. Just as hetero women are often forced to choose between the images of the virgin and the whore, modern straight men are caught in a cultural tug-of-war between the Marlboro Man and the Wimp.

So where does that leave straight men who want to reexamine what a man is and change it? Can a good man be sexy? Can a sexy man be good? What is good sex, egalitarian sex? More fundamentally, can feminist women and men coexist comfortably, even happily, within the same theoretical framework—or the same bedroom?

Relationships with men remain one of the most controversial topics among feminists today. Having sex, negotiating emotional dependency, and/or raising children force many hetero couples to balance their desire to be together with the oppressive dynamics of sexism. In few other movements are the oppressor group and the oppressed group so intimately linked.

But what about men who support feminism? Shouldn't it be okay for straight feminist women to have sex with them? Straight men aren't always oppressive in their sexuality, are they?

You may laugh at these questions, but they hold serious implications for straight feminist sex. I've seen many relationships between opposite-sex activists self-destruct because critical assumptions about power dynamics and desires were made in the mind, but not in the bed. I've even been told that straight male feminists can't get laid without A) feeling guilty; B) reinforcing patriarchy; or C) maintaining complete passivity during sexual activity. Each of these three options represents common assumptions about the sexuality of straight men who support feminism. Choice A, "feeling guilty," reflects the belief that straight male desire inherently contradicts the goals of feminism and fails to contribute to the empowerment of women. It holds that any man who enjoys sex with a woman must be benefiting from sexist male privilege, not fighting against it. In other words, het sex becomes a zero-sum game where if men gain, feminism loses.

Choice B represents the assumption that hetero male sex is inherently patriarchal. Beyond merely being of no help, as in Choice A, straight male sexuality is seen as part of the problem. Within this theory, one often hears statements such as "all heterosexual sex is rape." Even though these statements are usually taken out of context, the ideas behind them are problematic. In essence, they say that you can never have a male/female interaction that isn't caught up in oppressive dynamics. Men and women can never be together, especially in such a vulnerable exchange as sexuality, without being subject to the misdistribution of power in society.

The third choice, "maintaining complete passivity," attempts a logical answer to the above predicament. In order to come even close to achieving equality in heterosexuality (and still get laid), men must "give up" all their power through inactivity. A truly feminist man should take no aggressive or dominant position. He should, in fact, not act at all; he should merely lie back and allow the woman to subvert male supremacy through her complete control of the situation. In other words, for a man and a woman to share sexuality on a "level playing field," the man must remove all symptoms of his power through passivity, even though the causes of that inequality (including his penis!) still exist.

I know of one feminist man whose girl-friend *insisted* that she always be on top when they had intercourse. Her reasoning was simple: a man in a dominant sexual position represents sexist oppression incarnate. Therefore, the only possible way to achieve female empowerment was to subvert this power through her dominance. She even went so far as to stop intercourse before he reached orgasm, as a protest against male sexual entitlement.

The above story represents the *assumption* that sexism functions within male sexuality in a uniform, unvarying way, and that straight women must adapt and strategize within their personal relationships accordingly.

Does it have to be this way? Must male heterosexuality always pose a threat to feminism? What about the sensitive guy? Wasn't that the male cry (whimper) of the nineties? Sorry, but all the media hype about sensitivity never added up to significant changes in behavior. Straight male sexuality still remains one of the most underchallenged areas of masculinity in America. Some men *did* propose a different kind of sexuality for straight men in the 1970s, one that emphasizes feelings and sensitivity and emotional connection. But these efforts failed to affect our ideas in any kind of revolutionary way. Now, instead of a "sexy" sensitive guy, men's magazines are calling for the emergence of the "Post-Sensitive Man," while scientific studies tell us that women prefer Clint Eastwood over Michael Bolton.

Why did sensitivity fail? Were straight women, even feminists, lying to men about what they wanted? The answer is "yes" and "no." I don't think sensitivity was the culprit. I think the problem was men's passivity, or more specifically, men's lack of assertiveness and power.

In much of our understanding, power is equated with oppression: images of white supremacists dominating people of color, men dominating women, and the rich dominating the poor underline the histories of many cultures and societies. But power need not always oppress others. One can, I believe, be powerful in a nonoppressive way.

In order to find this sort of alternative, we need to examine men's experience with power and sexuality further. Fortunately, queer men and women have given us a leg up on the process by reenergizing the debate about what is good sex and what is fair sex. Gay male culture has a long history of exploring nontraditional aspects of male sexuality, such as cross-dressing, bondage and dominance, and role playing. These dynamics force gay men to break out of a singular experience of male sexual desire and to examine the diversity within male sexuality in the absence of gender oppression. Though gay men's culture still struggles with issues such as the fetishizing of men of color and body fascism, it does invite greater exploration of diversity than straight male culture. Gay culture has broader and more inclusive attitudes about what is sexy and a conception of desire that accommodates many types of sex for many types of gay men. For straight men in our culture, there is such a rigid definition of "sexy" that it leaves us few options besides being oppressive, overbearing, or violent.

Part of the success that gay male culture enjoys in breaking out of monolithic notions of male sexuality lies in the acceptance it receives from its partners and peers. Camp, butch, leather, drag-queer culture is constantly affirming the powerful presence of alternative sexualities. Straight male culture, on the other hand, experiences a lack—a void of acceptance—whenever it tries to assert some image other than the sexist hetero male. Both publicly and in many cases privately, alternative straight male sexualities fail to compete for attention and acceptance among hetero men and women.

Hot, Heavy, and Heterosexual

Without role models and cultural messages to affirm them, new forms of desire fail to stick around in our heads and our hearts. Therefore, straight men and women need to get hot and heavy for an alternative male heterosexuality. Often, women who desire nontraditional types of straight men fail to assert their desires publicly. If and when they find these men, they do so through friendships, long-term relationships, or by accident. They rarely seek them out in bars, one-night stands, or house parties. Sexual desire that results from a friendship or long-term relationship can be wonderful, but it fails to hold the popular "sexy" status that active dating, flirtation, or seduction does. If we truly hope to change straight male sexuality, we must move beyond private one-on-one affirmations and change public and cultural ones.

Unfortunately, it's easier said than done. Whenever I've tried to assert a nonoppressive sexuality with women, I've sunk into a cultural quagmire. I get caught riding that fine line between being a Sensitive New Age Guy and an asshole. Many straight women (both feminist and not) still find an aggressive, dominant man sexy. Many straight women still desire a man to take charge when it comes to romance or intimacy, especially when initiating intercourse. Yet many of the same straight feminist women constantly highlight the abuse and discrimination that many of these men inflict. They often complain about a man who is misogynist while affirming his desirability. This dichotomy of desire is confusing and frustrating.

Admittedly, much of my frustration relates to my own experience. I've always found fierce, independent women attractive—women who say they want a man to support them emotionally, listen to them, and not fight them every step of the way. Yet in reality, these women often lost respect for me and for other men who tried to change our sexuality to meet these needs.

I'd try to play the game, moving in as the aggressive man and then showing a more sensitive side after I'd caught the person's attention. But more often than not, the result was frustrating. I didn't catch a clue until one night when I had an enlightening conversation with one of these women who called herself a feminist. I asked her why guys who tried to accommodate the political desires of straight feminists always seemed to lose out in the end. She said she thought it was because a lot of young straight women who confront gender issues through feminism are constantly trying to redefine themselves in relation to culture and other people in their lives. Therefore, if they pursue relationships with men, many consciously seek out a *traditional* man—not only because it is the kind of man they have been taught to desire, but because he is familiar to them. He is strong, stable, predictable, and powerful. As the woman's identity shifts and changes, she can use the man she is dating as a reference point and source of strength and stability.

If she chooses to become involved with a feminist man who feels the same need to examine assumptions about gender (including his own masculinity) on a political and personal level, both partners are in a state of flux and instability. Both are searching for an understanding of their relationship, but each questions how that relationship is defined, even down to assumptions about men, women, sex, and commitment. Within this shifting matrix, straight feminist men who explore alternative ways of being sexual are often perceived as passive, weak, and in many cases, undesirable. In the end, it seems much easier to choose the traditional male.

Out of the Breeding Box

We need to assert a new feminist sexuality for men, one that competes with the traditional par-

adigm but offers a more inviting notion of how hetero men can be sexual while tearing apart the oppressive and problematic ways in which so many of us have experienced sexuality in the past. We need to find new, strong values and ideas of male heterosexuality instead of passive identities that try to distance us from sexist men. We need to stop trying to avoid powerful straight sexuality and work to redefine what our power means and does. We need to find strength and desire outside of macho, antiwomen ways of being masculine.

Take the notion of "breeding." Many cultures still assume that the male desire to breed and procreate is the primary purpose of sexuality. This idea, based on outdated notions of Darwinism and evolutionary prophecy, forces us to think of heterosexual men as having a single sexual purpose—ejaculating inside a fertile woman. Be hard, be strong, and cum into any woman's vagina you can find. It's all about sowing seed and proving heterosexuality through the conquest of women. Through this mechanism, reproductive sex is seen as "natural" and most desirable; all other forms of sexual interaction are seen as warm-ups or "foreplay." Breeding prioritizes heterosexuality, and within straight sex, limits its goal to the act of vaginal intercourse.

Yet in a pro–birth control, increasingly queer-friendly world, breeding has become a minuscule aspect of sexuality. Few heterosexual men and women have sex strictly to breed, and gay men and women almost never do. Within this new context, notions of what is "sexy" and what straight men desire have much more to do with how we fuck or how we feel than with what we produce.

Even among young people who have no intention of creating children, breeder assumptions continue to define male heterosexuality. For instance, many of my friends, especially queer ones, will harass me after I've been dating a woman for a while and give me flack for being a "breeder." They assume that the reason I'm with her—the goal of my relationship—is to make sure I cum inside her. Even if I don't want a child, even if I hate intercourse, the assumption about my male heterosexuality is that I will at least act like I'm trying to procreate when I'm having sex. Any possibility of a hetero non-breeder sexuality doesn't exist. I'm forced into the breeding box, no questions permitted.

I've tried to confront these assumptions actively, but it's difficult. Usually I respond with something crass, such as, "Funny, I don't feel like breeding, just fucking." Or by talking about how *I* prefer to be penetrated sometimes. This may seem extreme, but that's how challenging it feels to try to present a different idea of straight male sexuality—one that isn't predicated on notions of being vanilla or being a breeder.

My critique of breeding is not an attempt to discredit fatherhood. Parenting is as much a part of the revolution as any other personal act. My point is that if we want hetero men to change, we have to give them viable choices. There has to be a difference between acting straight and acting like a breeder. And breeding is just *one* of the many assumptions that our culture applies to male heterosexuality.

It's up to straight men to change these assumptions. Gay men and lesbians have engaged in a cultural dialogue around sexuality over the last twenty-five years; straight women are becoming more and more vocal. But straight men have been almost completely silent. This silence, I think, stems in large part from fear: our cultures tell us that being a "real" man means not being feminine, not being gay, and not being weak. They warn us that anyone who dares to stand up to these ideas becomes a sitting target to have his manhood shot down in flames.

Breaking the Silence

Not becoming a sitting target to have *my* manhood shot down was high on my mind when the evening of my best friend's bachelor party finally arrived. But I was determined not to be silent about how I felt about the party and about new visions for straight men within our society.

We decided to throw the party two nights before the wedding. We all gathered at my house, each of us bringing a present to add to the night's activities. After all the men had arrived, we began cooking dinner, breaking open beer and champagne, and catching up on where we had left off since we last saw each other.

During the evening, we continued to talk off and on about why we didn't have a stripper or prostitute for the party. After several rounds of margaritas and a few hands of poker, tension started to build around the direction I was pushing the conversation.

"So what don't you like about strippers?" David asked me.

This was an interesting question. I was surprised not only by the guts of David to ask it, but also by my own mixed feelings in coming up with an answer. "It's not that I don't like being excited, or turned on, per se," I responded. "In fact, to be honest, watching a female stripper is an exciting and erotic experience for me. But at the same time, it's a very uncomfortable one. I get a sense when I watch her that I'm participating in a misuse of pleasure, if that makes sense."

I looked around at my friends. I couldn't tell whether the confused looks on their faces were due to the alcohol, the poker game, or my answer, so I continued. "Ideally, I would love to sit back and enjoy watching someone express herself sexually through dance, seduction, flirtation—all the positive elements I associate with stripping," I said. "But at the same time, because so many strippers are poor and forced to perform in order to survive economically, I feel like the turn-on I get is false. I feel like I get off easy, sitting back as the man, paying for the show. No one ever expects me to get up on stage.

"And in that way, it's selling myself short sexually. It's not only saying very little about the sexual worth of the woman on stage, but the sexual worth of me as the viewer as well. By *only*

H ow do many men learn to desire women? What are men thinking about when they are sexual with women? Are gay men more sexually promiscuous than straight men? Are gay men more obsessed with demonstrating their masculinity than straight men, or are they likely to be more "effeminate"? Recent research indicates that there are no simple answers to these questions. It is increasingly clear, however, that men's sexuality, whether homosexual, bisexual, or heterosexual, is perceived as an experience of their gender.

Since there is no anticipatory socialization for homosexuality and bisexuality, future straight and gay men receive the same socialization as boys. As a result, sexuality as a gender enactment is often a similar internal experience for all men. Early socialization teaches us—through masturbation, locker-room conversations, sex-ed classes and conversations with parents, and the tidbits that boys will pick up from various media—that sex is private, pleasurable, guilt provoking, exciting, and phallocentric, and that or-

EIGHT

PART

Male Sexualities

gasm is the goal toward which sexual experience is oriented.

The articles in this section explore how male sexualities express issues of masculinity. Robert Staples explains how the norms of masculinity are expressed in somewhat different ways among black heterosexual males. Jeffrey Fracher and Michael S. Kimmel argue that men discuss their sexual experiences—both their "successes" and their "failures"—in terms of gender, not pleasure. A man experiencing for instance, premature ejaculation would be more likely to complain that he wasn't "enough of a man" than that he was unable to feel enough pleasure.

Several articles explore marginalized masculinities and their sexualities. M. Rochlin's questionnaire humorously challenges us to question the normative elements of heterosexuality. Tomás Almaguer, Richard Fung, and Susan D. Cochran and Vickie M. Mays examine elements of gay sexuality, exploring the intersections of sexuality, race and ethnicity, and gender.

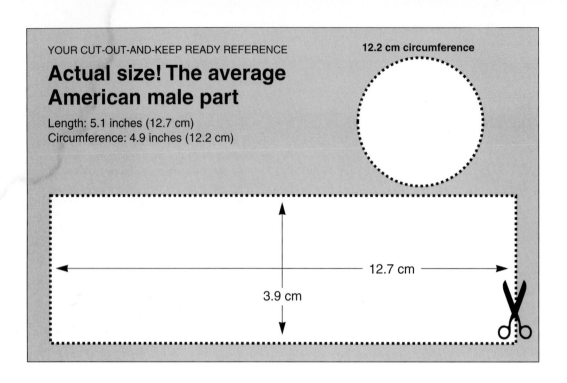

YOUR CUT-OUT-AND-KEEP READY REFERENCE

12.2 cm circumference

Actual size! The average
American male part

Length: 5.1 inches (12.7 cm)
Circumference: 4.9 inches (12.2 cm)

12.7 cm

3.9 cm

41

ARTICLE

Jeffrey Fracher
Michael S. Kimmel[1]

Hard Issues and Soft Spots: Counseling Men About Sexuality

> Nothing shows more clearly the extent to which modern society has atomized itself than the isolation in sexual ignorance which exists among us. . . . Many cultures, the most primitive and the most complex, have entertained sexual fears of an irrational sort, but probably our culture is unique in strictly isolating the individual in the fears that society has devised.
>
> —Lionel Trilling[2]

Sam[3] is a 28-year-old white, single factory worker. He lives alone in a two-family home which he owns, and attends night school at a community college. The third of six sons in a blue-collar, Eastern European Catholic family, Sam is a conscientious, hardworking, and responsible man with very traditional values. He describes himself as a sexual late-bloomer, having begun dating only after graduation from an all-male Catholic high school. Although strong and handsome, he has always lacked confidence with women, and describes himself as male peer oriented, actively involved in sports, and spending much of his leisure time with "the boys."

Prior to his first sexual intercourse, two years ago at age 26, Sam had fabricated stories to tell his friends so as not to appear inadequate. He felt a great deal of shame and embarrassment that his public presentation of his sexual exploits had no basis in reality. His limited sexual knowledge caused him great anxiety and difficulty, especially since the woman with whom he was involved had had previous sexual encounters. Upon completion of intercourse, she reported that "he came too fast" (i.e., less than one minute, or after several thrusts), a statement that, he reported, "hit me between the eyes." His second attempt at intercourse was no more successful, in spite of his use of a condom to reduce sensation, and he subsequently broke off this relationship because of the shame and embarrassment about his sexual incompetence, and the fear that word would leak out to his friends. He subsequently developed a secondary pattern of sexual avoidance, and when he first came to treatment, indicating that he was "not a real man because I can't satisfy a woman," he had not had sex for two years, and was reluctant to resume dating until his premature ejaculation was vastly improved.

Joe is a 34-year-old C.P.A. who has been married for three years. The youngest of five children and the only male in a middle-class Irish–American family, Joe feels his father had high expectations from him, and exhibited only neutrality or criticism. Joe was without a male role model who conveyed that it was OK to fail. In fact, he portrayed men as strong, competent, without feelings, and without problems or failings, and believes he can never live up to the image his father had for him. Consequently, Joe is terrified that failure to please a woman sexually may result in criticism that will challenge his masculinity; he will not be a "real man." Anticipating this criticism from his wife, his sexual interest is reduced.

When first seen in therapy, Joe evidenced a total lack of sexual interest in his wife, but a high degree of sexual interest involving sexual fantasies, pornography, and masturbation. He said "lust is an obsession with me," indicating a high sex drive when sex is anonymous and though he felt sexually inadequate with his wife, he felt sexually potent with women he devalues, such as prostitutes. He could not understand his almost total lack of sexual interest in his wife.

Bill is a 52-year-old engineer, who has been married for 25 years. From a white, middle-class Protestant background, he has one grown child, and initially came to treatment upon referral from a urologist. He had seen numerous physicians after experiencing erectile dysfunction three years ago, and has actively sought a physical explanation for it.

Bill's wife, Ann, was quite vocal about her disappointment in his failure to perform sexually. Bill had always been the sexual initiator, and Ann had come to expect that he should be in charge. Both believed that the only "real sex" is intercourse with an erect penis. Ann frequently commented that she felt "emotionally empty" without intercourse, thereby adding to his sense of inadequacy. The loss of his capacity for erection, Bill told the therapist, meant that he had lost his masculinity, and he worried openly about displeasing Ann and her possibly leaving him.

His fear of lost masculinity spilled over into his job performance, and he became depressed and withdrew from social activities. Bill was unaware that as an older man, he required more direct penile stimulation for an erection, since he had never required it in the past, and was unable to ask for it from Ann. He felt that a "real man never has to ask his wife for anything sexually," and should be able to perform without her help. The pattern of erectile dysfunction was part of a broader pattern of inability to tolerate failure, and he had begun to lose self-confidence since his masculinity was almost entirely predicated upon erectile functioning. "Nothing else matters," he confided, if his masculinity (evidenced by a functional erection) was not present. Everything was suddenly on the line—his self-worth, his marriage, and his career—if he proved unable to correct his problem.

Sam, Joe, and Bill manifest the three most common sexual complaints of men seeking therapy. But underlying premature ejaculation, inhibited sexual desire, and erectile dysfunction is a common thread, binding these and other sexual problems together. Each fears that his sexual problem damages his sense of masculinity, making him less of a "real man." In a sense, we might say that all three men "suffer" from masculinity.

This chapter will explore how gender becomes one of the key organizing principles of male sexuality, informing and structuring men's sexual experiences. It will discuss how both gender and sexuality are socially constructed, and how therapeutic strategies to help men deal with sexual problems can raise issues of gender identity. This is especially important, of course, since so many therapeutic interventions rely on a diagnostic model that is simultaneously overly individualistic (in that it locates the source of the problem entirely within the individual) and transhistorical (in that it assumes that all cultures exhibit similar patterns at all times). The chapter combines a comparative and historical understanding of how both gender and sexuality are socially constructed with a psychoanalytic understanding of the transformative possibilities contained within the therapeutic relationship. This combination will lead us to discuss both social and therapeutic interventions that might facilitate healthier sexual expression for men.

The Social Construction of Sexuality and Masculinity

Sexuality is socially constructed, a learned set of both behaviors and cognitive interpretations of those behaviors. Sexuality is less the product of biological drives than of a socialization process, and this socialization process is specific to any culture at any particular time. This means that "social roles are not vehicles for the expression of sexual impulse but that sexuality becomes a vehicle for expressing the needs of social roles" (Gagnon and Simon, 1973:45). *That* we are sexual is determined by a biological imperative toward reproduction, but *how* we are sexual— where, when, how often, with whom, and why—has to do with cultural learning, with meanings transmitted in a cultural setting. Sexuality varies from culture to culture; it changes in any one culture over time; it changes over the course of each of our lives. Sexual beings are made and not born; we make ourselves into sexual beings within a cultural framework. Although it may appear counterintuitive, this perspective suggests that the elusive quality commonly called "desire" is actually a relatively

unimportant part of sexual conduct. As Gagnon and Simon argue (1973: 103), "the availability of sexual partners, their ages, their incomes, their point in the economic process, their time commitments . . . shape their sexual careers far more than the minor influence of sexual desire." Sexuality is learned in roughly the same way as anything else is learned in our culture. As Gagnon writes (1977: 2):

> In any given society, at any given moment, people become sexual in the same way as they become everything else. Without much reflection, they pick up directions from their social environment. They acquire and assemble meanings, skills and values from the people around them. Their critical choices are often made by going along and drifting. People learn when they are quite young a few of the things that they are expected to be, and continue slowly to accumulate a belief in who they are and ought to be through the rest of childhood, adolescence, and adulthood. Sexual conduct is learned in the same ways and through the same processes; it is acquired and assembled in human interaction, judged and performed in specific cultural and historical worlds.

If sexuality is socially constructed, perhaps the most significant element of the construction, the foundation on which we construct our sexuality, is gender. For men, the notion of masculinity, the cultural definition of manhood, serves as the primary building block of sexuality. It is through our understanding of masculinity that we construct a sexuality, and it is through our sexualities that we confirm the successful construction of our gender identity. Gender informs sexuality; sexuality confirms gender. Thus, men have a lot at stake when they confront a sexual problem: they risk their self-image as men.

Like sexuality, gender in general, and masculinity in particular is socially constructed; that is, what we understand to be masculine varies from culture to culture, over historical time within any one culture, and over the course of any one person's life within any culture. What we consider masculine or feminine in our culture is the result of neither some biological imperative nor some religious requirement, but a socially organized mode of behavior. What is masculine is not set in stone, but historically fluid. The pioneering research on gender by anthropologist Margaret Mead (1935) and others has specified how widely the cultural requirements of masculinity—what it takes to be a "real man" in any particular culture—vary. And these gender categories also shift in any one culture over time. Who would suggest, for example, that what was prescribed among upper class Frenchmen in the eighteenth century—rare silk stockings and red patent-leather high heels, prolific amounts of perfume and facial powder, powdered wigs and very long hair, and a rather precious preoccupation with love poems, dainty furniture, and roses—resembles our contemporary version of masculinity?

The assertion of the social construction of sexuality and gender leads naturally to two related questions. First, we need to specify precisely the dimensions of masculinity within contemporary American culture. How is masculinity organized as a normative set of behaviors and attitudes? Second, we need to specify precisely the ways in which this socially constructed gender identity informs male sexual development. How is masculinity expressed through sexuality?

Brannon's (Brannon and David, 1976: 12) summary of the normative structure of contemporary American masculinity is relevant here. Masculinity requires the avoidance and repudiation of all behaviors that are even remotely associated with femininity ("no sissy stuff"); this requires a ceaseless patrolling of one's boundaries and an incessant surveillance of one's performances to ensure that one is sufficiently male. Men must be "Big Wheels," since success and status are key determinants of masculinity, and be "Sturdy Oaks," exuding a manly air of self-confidence, toughness, and self-reliance, as well as reliability. Men must "Give 'em Hell,"

presenting an aura of aggression and daring, an attitude of constantly "going for it."

The normative organization of masculinity has been verified empirically (cf. Thompson and Pleck, 1986) and has obviously important implications for male sexuality. In a sense, sexuality is the location of the enactment of masculinity; sexuality allows the expression of masculinity. Male sexual socialization informs men that sexuality is the proving ground of adequate gender identity, and provides the script that men will adopt, with individual modification, as the foundation for sexual activity.

In a sense, when we examine the normative sexuality that is constructed from the typical organization of masculinity, it is not so much sexual problems that are of interest, but the problematization of "normal" sexuality, understanding perhaps the pathological elements within normal sexual functioning. This allows us to bridge the chasm between men who experience sexual dysfunction and those who, ostensibly, do not, and explore how men array themselves along a continuum of sexual expressions. Because masculinity provides the basic framework of sexual organization, and because masculinity requires adherence to certain rules that may retard or constrain emotional expression, we might fruitfully explore how even "normal" male sexuality evidences specific pathological symptoms, so that men who present exaggerated versions of these symptoms in therapy may better perceive their problems in a larger, sociological context of gender relations in contemporary society.[4]

The social construction of male sexuality raises a crucial theoretical issue. In the past, both social science research and clinical practice were informed by a model of discrete dichotomies. Categories for analysis implied a dualistic world view in which a phenomenon was classified as either X or Y. Thus, one was either male or female, heterosexual or homosexual, normal or pathological. Since the pioneering studies of Alfred Kinsey and his associates (cf. Kinsey et al.,

1948, 1953), however, this traditional model of mutually exclusive dichotomous variables has given way to a model of a continuum of behaviors along which individuals array themselves. The continuum model allows individuals to reposition themselves at different moments in the life course, and it allows the researcher or clinician a point of entry into a relationship with the behaviors being discussed. The people we study and the people we counsel are less some curious "other" and more a variation on a set of behaviors that we, ourselves, embody as well. The articulation of the continuum model also requires that the level of analysis of any behavior include a social analysis of the context for behavior and the social construction of definitions of normality. It thus permits a truly *social* psychology.

The Male Sexual Script

Male sexual socialization teaches young men that sex is secret, morally wrong, and pleasurable, the association of sexual pleasure with feelings of guilt and shame is articulated early in the young boy's development, and reinforced throughout the life course by family, school, religion, and media images of sexuality. Young males are instructed, in locker rooms and playgrounds, to detach their emotions from sexual expression. In early masturbatory experience, the logic of detachment accommodates the twin demands of sexual pleasuring and guilt and shame. Later, detachment serves the "healthy" heterosexual male by permitting delay of orgasm in order to please his sexual partner, and serves the "healthy" homosexual male by permitting numerous sexual partners without cluttering up the scene with unpleasant emotional connection. (We will return to an exploration of the similarities between heterosexual and homosexual male sexuality below.)

Detachment requires a self-objectification, a distancing from one's self, and the development of a "secret sexual self" that performs sexual acts according to culturally derived scripts

(Gagnon and Simon, 1973: 64). That men use the language of work as metaphors for sexual conduct—"getting the job done," "performing well," "achieving orgasm"—illustrates more than a passing interest in turning everything into a job whose performance can be evaluated; it reinforces detachment so that the body becomes a sexual machine, a performer instead of an authentic actor. The penis is transformed from an organ of sexual pleasure into a "tool," an instrument by which the performance is carried out, a thing, separate from the self. Many men report that they have conversations with their penises, and often cajole, plead with, or demand that they become and remain erect without orgasmic release. The penis can become the man's enemy, ready to engage in the most shameful conspiracy possible: performance failure. Is it any wonder that "performance anxiety" is a normative experience for male sexual behavior?

Men's earliest forays into sexuality, especially masturbation, are the first location of sexual anxiety. Masturbation teaches young men that sexuality is about the detachment of emotions from sex, that sex is important in itself. Second, men learn that sex is something covert, to be hidden; that is, men learn to privatize sexual experience, without skills to share the experience. And masturbation also teaches men that sexuality is phallocentric, that the penis is the center of the sexual universe. Finally, the tools of masturbation, especially sexual fantasy, teach men to objectify the self, to separate the self from the body, to focus on parts of bodies and not whole beings, often to speak of oneself in the third person.

Adolescent sexual socialization reinforces these behavioral demands that govern male sexuality. Passivity is absolutely forbidden, and the young male must attempt to escalate the sexual element at all times. To do otherwise is to avoid "giving 'em hell" and expose potential feminine behaviors. This constant pressure for escalation derives from the phallocentric component to male sexuality—"it only counts if I put it in" a student told one of the authors. Since normative heterosexuality assigns to men the role of "doer" and to women the role of "gatekeeper," determining the level of sexual experience appropriate to any specific situation, this relentless pressure to escalate prevents either the male or the female from experiencing the sexual pleasure of any point along the continuum. No sooner does he "arrive" at a particular sexual experience—touching her breast, for example, than he begins strategizing the ways in which he can escalate, go further. To do less would expose him as less than manly. The female instantly must determine the limits of the encounter and devise the logistics that will prevent escalation if those limits have been reached. Since both male and female maintain a persistent orientation to the future (how to escalate and how to prevent escalation) neither can experience the pleasure of the points en route to full sexual intercourse. In fact, what men learn is that intercourse is the appropriate end-point of any sexual encounter, and that only intercourse "counts" in the tabulation of sexual encounters.

Since the focus is entirely phallocentric and intercourse is the goal to be achieved in adolescent sexual encounters, the stakes regarding sexual performance are extremely high, and consequently so is the anxiety about performance failure. Big wheels and sturdy oaks do not experience sexual dysfunction.

This continuum of male sexual dysfunction—ranging from what we might call the "normatively operative dysfunctional" to the cases of extreme distress of men who present themselves for therapeutic intervention—is reinforced in adult heterosexual relations as well. How do men maintain the sexual distancing and objectification that they perceive are required for healthy functioning? American comedian Woody Allen described, in his nightclub routines, a rather typical male strategy. After describing himself as "a stud," Allen comments:

While making love, in an effort [pause] to prolong [pause] the moment of ecstasy, I think of baseball players. All right, now you know. So the two of us are making love violently, and she's digging it, so I figure I better start thinking of baseball players pretty quickly. So I figure it's one out, and the Giants are up. Mays lines a single to right. He takes second on a wild pitch. Now she's digging her nails into my neck. I decide to pinch-hit for McCovey. [pause for laughter] Alou pops out. Haller singles, Mays takes third. Now I've got a first and third situation. Two outs and the Giants are behind by one run. I don't know whether to squeeze or to steal. [pause for laughter] She's been in the shower for ten minutes already. [pause] I can't tell you anymore, this is too personal. [pause] The Giants won.[5]

Readers may be struck by several themes—the imputation of violence, how her pleasure leads to his decision to think of baseball players, the requirement of victory in the baseball game, and the sexual innuendo contained within the baseball language—but the text provides a startlingly honest revelation of male sexual distancing. Here is a device that is so successful at delaying ejaculation that the narrator is rendered utterly unaware of his partner. "She's been in the shower for ten minutes already," Allen remarks, as if he's just noticed.

Much of peer sexual socialization consists of the conveying of these strategic actions that the male can perform to make himself a more adequate sexual partner. Men are often told to think of sports, work, or some other nonsexual event, or to repeat multiplication tables or mathematical formulas in order to keep themselves from premature ejaculation. It's as if sexual adequacy could be measured by time elapsed between penetration and orgasm, and the sexual experience itself is transformed into an endurance test in which pleasure, if present at all, is almost accidental.

The contemporary male sexual script—the normative construction of sexuality—provides a continuum along which men array themselves for the script's enactment. The script contains dicta for sexual distancing, objectification, phallocentrism, and a pressure to become and remain erect without ejaculation for as long as possible, all of which serve as indicators of masculinity as well as sexual potency. Adequate sexual functioning is seen as the proof of masculinity, so sexual problems will inevitably damage male gender identity. This is what makes treatment of sexual disorders a treatment of gender identity issues.

Although this chapter has concentrated on sexual disorders for heterosexual men, this is neither for analytic reasons nor from a sense of how these problems might manifest differently for gay men. Quite the contrary, in fact. Since gender identity is the key variable in understanding sexual behaviors, we would argue that heterosexual and homosexual men have more in common in regard to their sexuality than they evidence differences. This is especially true since 1969, when the Stonewall riots in New York, and the subsequent emergence of the Gay Liberation Movement, led to the possibility for gay men to recover and repair their "damaged" sense of masculinity. Earlier gay men had been seen as "failed men," but the emergence of the gay male "clone" particularly has dispelled that notion. In the nation's gay ghettos, gay men often enact a hypermasculine ethic, complete with its attendant sexual scripting of distancing, phallocentrism, objectification, and separation of emotion from physical sensation. Another reason that heterosexual and homosexual men exhibit similar gender-based sexual behaviors is that all boys are subject to an anticipatory socialization toward heterosexuality, regardless of their eventual sexual preference. There is no anticipatory socialization toward homosexuality in this culture, so male gender socialization will be enacted with both male and female sexual partners. Finally, we have not focused on gay men as a specific group because to do so would re-

quire the marginalization of gay men as a group separate from the normative script of male sexuality. Both gay and straight men are men first, and both have "male sex."

Therapeutic Interventions

Our analysis of the social context of men's sexual problems makes it essential that therapeutic strategies remain aware of a context larger than simple symptom remission. Treatment must also challenge the myths, assumptions, and expectations that create the dysfunctional context for male sexual behavior (cf. Kaplan, 1974, 1983; LoPiccolo and LoPiccolo 1978; Tollison and Adams, 1979).

Men seeking treatment for sexual difficulties will most often present with a symptom such as erectile failure, premature ejaculation, or inhibited desire. However, the *response* to this symptom, such as anxiety, depression, or low self-esteem, is usually what brings the man into treatment, and this response derives from the man's relationship to an ideal vision of masculinity. The construction of this masculine ideal, therefore, needs to be addressed, since it often creates the imperative command—to be in a constant state of potential sexual arousal, to achieve and maintain perfectly potent erections on command, and to delay ejaculation for a long time—which results in the performance anxiety that creates the symptom in the first place.

Sex therapy exercises, such as those developed by Willam Masters and Virginia Johnson and others, are usually effective only when the social context of gender ideals has also been addressed. This is accomplished by exploring and challenging the myths of male sexuality, modeling by the therapist of a different version of masculinity, giving permission to the patient to fail, and self-disclosure by the therapist of the doubts, fears of inadequacy, and other anxieties that all men experience. These will significantly reduce the isolation that the patient may experience, the fear that he is the only man who experiences such sexually linked problems. These methods may be used to reorient men's assumptions about what constitutes masculinity, even though the therapist will be unable to change the entire social edifice that has been constructed on these gender assumptions. Both the cognitive as well as the physical script must be addressed in treating sexual dysfunction; the cognitive script is perhaps the more important.

Recall these specific examples we drew from case materials. Sam's sexual performance was charged with anxiety and shame regarding both female partners and male peers. He was adamant that no one know he was seeking therapy, and went to great lengths to assure that confidentiality be preserved. He revealed significant embarrassment and shame with the therapist in early sessions, which subsided once the condition was normalized by the therapist.

Sam had grown up with exaggerated expectations of male sexual performance—that men must perform sexually on cue and never experience any sexual difficulty—that were consistent with the social milieu in which he was raised. He held women on a pedestal, and he believed that a man must please a woman or risk losing her. The stakes were thus quite high. Sam was also terrified of appearing "unmanly" with women, which resulted in a high degree of performance anxiety, which, in turn, prompted the premature ejaculation. The cycle of anxiety and failure finally brought Sam to treatment. Finally, Sam was detached from his own sexuality, his own body both sexually and emotionally. His objectification of his penis made it impossible for him to monitor impending ejaculation, and he was therefore unable to moderate the intensity of sensation prior to the point of ejaculatory inevitability. This common pattern among men who experience premature ejaculation suggests

that such a response comes not from hypersensitivity but rather an atrophied sensitivity, based on objectification of the phallus.

Sam's treatment consisted of permission to experience this problem from another man, and the attempt by the therapist to normalize the situation and reframe it as a problem any man might encounter. The problem was redefined as a sign of virility rather than an indication of its absence; Sam came to understand his sexual drive as quite high, which led to high levels of excitement that he had not yet learned to control. The therapist presented suggestions to control ejaculation that helped him moderate the intensity of arousal in order to better control his ejaculation. The important work, however, challenged the myths and cognitive script that Sam maintained regarding his sexuality. The attention given to his sexual performance, what he demanded of himself and what he believed women demanded of him, helped him reorient his sexuality into a less performance-oriented style.

Joe, the 34-year-old C.P.A., experienced low sexual desire with his wife though he masturbated regularly. Masturbatory fantasies involving images of women wanting him, finding him highly desirable, populated his fantasy world. When his self-esteem was low, as when he lost his job, for example, his sexual fantasies increased markedly. These fantasies of prowess with devalued women restored, he felt, his worth as a man. Interest in pornography included a script in which women were passive and men in control, very unlike the situation he perceives with his wife. He complained that he is caught in a vicious cycle, since without sexual interest in his wife he's not a "real man," and if he's not a "real man" then he has no sexual desire for her. He suggested that if he could only master a masculine challenge that was not sexual, such as finding another job or another competitive situation, he believed his sexual interest in his wife would increase. He felt he needed the mastery of a masculine challenge to confirm his sense of self as a man, which would then find further conformation in the sexual arena. This adds an empirical confirmation of Gagnon and Simon's argument (1973) that genital sexuality contains many nonsexual motives, including the desire for achievement, power, and peer approval. Joe came to therapy with a great deal of shame at having to be there, and was especially ashamed at having to tell another man about his failures as a man. He was greatly relieved by the therapist's understanding, self-disclosure, and nonjudgmental stance, which enhanced the therapist's credibility and Joe's commitment to treatment.

One cognitive script that Joe challenged in counseling was his embrace of the "madonna/whore" ideology. In this formulation, any woman worth having (the madonna—mother or wife) was perceived as both asexual and as sexually rejecting of him, since his failures rendered him less of a real man. A "whore," on the other hand, would be both sexually available and interested in him, so she is consequently devalued and avoided. He could be sexual with her because the stakes are so low. This reinforces the cultural equation between sexual pleasure and cultural guilt and shame, since Joe would want to be sexual only with those who would not want to be sexual with him. This common motif in male sexual socialization frequently emerges in descriptions of "good girls" and "bad girls" in high school.

Joe's therapy included individual short-term counseling with the goal of helping him see the relationship between his self-esteem and his inhibited sexual desire. Traditional masculine definitions of success were the sole basis for Joe's self-esteem, and these were challenged in the context of a supportive therapeutic environment. The failure of childhood male role models was contrasted with new role models that provide permission to fail and helped Joe view sexuality as noncompetitive and nonachievement-oriented activity. Joe began to experience a return of sexual desire for his wife, as he became less phallo-centric and more able to see sex as a vehicle for expressing intimacy and caring rather than a performance for an objectified self and other.

Bill, the 52-year-old married engineer, presented with erectile failure, which is part of a larger pattern of intolerance of failure in himself. The failure of his penis to function properly symbolized to him the ultimate collapse of his manhood. Not surprisingly, he had searched for physiological etiologies before seeking psychological counseling, having been referred by a urologist. It is estimated that less than 50% of all men who present themselves for penile implant surgery have a physiological basis for their problem; if so, the percentage of all men who experience erectile disorders whose etiology is physiological is less than 5%. Yet the pressure to salvage a sense of masculinity that might be damaged by a psychological problem leads thousands of men to request surgical prosthesis every year (cf. for example, Tiefer, 1986).

Bill and his wife, Ann, confronted in therapy the myths of male sexuality that they embraced, including such dicta as "a real man always wants sex," "the only real sex is intercourse," and "the man must always be in charge of sex" (cf. Zilbergeld, 1978). The therapist gave Bill permission to fail by telling him that all men at some time experience erectile dysfunction. Further, Bill was counseled that the real problem is not the erectile failure, but his reaction to this event. Exercises were assigned in which Bill obtained an erection through manual stimulation and then purposely lost the erection to desensitize himself to his terrible fear of failure. This helped him overcome the "what if" fear of losing the erection. Bill was counseled to "slow down" his sexual activity, and to focus on the sensations rather than the physical response, both of which were designed to further remove the performance aspects from his sexual activity. Finally, the therapist helped Bill and Ann redefine the notion of masculinity by stating that "a real man is strong enough to take risks, eschew stereotypes, to ask for what he needs sexually from a partner, and, most of all, to tolerate failure."

As Bill and Ann's cognitive script changed, his ability to function sexually improved. Though Bill still does not get full erections on a consistent basis, this fact is no longer catastrophic for him. He and Ann now have a broader script both physically and cognitively, which allows them to have other sexual play and the shared intimacy that it provides.

As one can see from these case studies, several themes run consistently through therapeutic strategies in counseling men about sexual problems, and many of these themes also relate directly to issues of social analysis as well as clinical practice. For example, the therapeutic environment must be experienced as supportive, and care must be taken so that the therapist not appear too threatening or too "successful" to the patient. The gender of the therapist with the male patient will raise different issues at this point. A male therapist can empathize with the patient, and greatly reduce his sense of isolation, whereas a female therapist can provide positive experience with a woman that may translate to nontherapeutic situations.

Second, the presenting symptom should be "normalized," that is it should be cast within the wider frame of male socialization to sexuality. It is not so much that the patient is "bad," "'wrong," or "abnormal," but that he has experienced some of the contradictory demands of masculinity in ways that have become dysfunctional for his sexual experiences. It is often crucial to help the patient realize that he is not the only man who experiences these problems, and that these problems are only problems seen from within a certain construct of masculinity.

In this way, the therapist can help the patient to dissociate sexuality from his sense of masculinity, to break the facile identification between sexual performance and masculinity. Masculinity can be confirmed by more than erectile capacity, constant sexual interest, and a long duration of intercourse; in fact, as we have argued, normal male sexuality often requires the dissociation of emotional intimacy and connectedness for adequate sexual functioning. Raising the level of analysis from the treatment of individual symptoms to a social construction of gender and sexuality does not mean abandoning the treatment of the presenting symptoms, but rather retaining their embeddedness in the social context from which they emerge. Counseling men about sexuality involves, along with individualized treatment, the redefinition of what it means to be a man in contemporary American society. Therapeutic treatments pitched at both the social and the individual levels can help men become more expressive lovers and friends and fathers, as well as more "functional" sexual partners. That a man's most important sexual organ is his mind is as true today as ever.

Notes

1. This paper represents a full collaboration, and our names appear in alphabetical order for convenience. Critical reactions from John Gagnon, Murray Scher, and Mark Stevens have been very helpful.

2. Lionel Trilling, *The Liberal Imagination*. New York: Alfred Knopf, 1954.

3. The names of the individual patients have been changed.

4. To assert a pathological element to what is culturally defined as "normal" is a contentious argument. But such an argument derives logically from assertions about the social construction of gender and sexuality. Perhaps an analogy would prove helpful. One might also argue that given the cultural definition of femininity in our culture, especially the normative prescriptions for how women are supposed to look to be most attractive, *all* women manifest a problematic relationship to food. Even the most "normal" woman, having been socialized in a culture stressing unnatural thinness, will experience some pathological symptoms around eating. This assertion will surely shed a very different light on the treatment of women presenting eating disorders, such as bulimia or anorexia nervosa. Instead of treating them in their *difference* from other women, by contextualizing their symptoms within the larger frame of the construction of femininity in American culture, they can be seen as *exaggerating* an already culturally prescribed problematic relationship to eating. This position has the additional benefit, as it would in the treatment of male sexual disorders, of resisting the temptation to "blame the victim" for her/his acting out an exaggerated version of a traditional script.

5. Woody Allen, *The Nightclub Years*, United Artists Records, 1971. Permission requested.

References

Brannon, Robert and Deborah David (1976). *The Forty-Nine Percent Majority*. Reading, MA: Addison-Wesley.

Gagnon, John (1977). *Human Sexualities*. Chicago: Scott, Foresman.

Gagnon, John and William Simon (1973). *Sexual Conduct*. Chicago: Aldine.

Kaplan, Helen Singer (1974). *The New Sex Therapy*. New York: Brunner-Mazel.

Kaplan, Helen Singer (1983). *The Evaluation of Sexual Disorders*. New York: Brunner-Mazel.

Kimmel, Michael, ed. (1987). *Changing Men: New Directions in Research on Men and Masculinity*. Beverly Hills, CA: Sage Publications.

Kinsey, Alfred C., Wardell Pomeroy, and C. Martin (1948). *Sexual Behavior in the Human Male*. Chicago: Saunders.

Kinsey, Alfred C. and Paul Gebhard (1953). *Sexual Behavior in the Human Female*. Chicago: Saunders.

LoPiccolo, J. and L. LoPiccolo (1978). *Handbook of Sex Therapy*. New York: Plenum Press.

Mead, Margaret (1935). *Sex and Temperament in Three Primitive Societies*. New York: William Morrow.

Thompson, Edward and Joseph Pleck (1986). "The Structure of Male Role Norms." *American Behavioral Scientist* 29(5), May–June.

Tiefer, Leonore (1986). "In Pursuit of the Perfect Penis: The Medicalization of Male Sexuality." *American Behavioral Scientist* 29(5).

Tollison, C. D. and H. Adams (1979). *Sexual Disorders: Treatment, Theory, and Research*. New York: Gardner Press.

Wagner, Gorm and Richard Green (1984). *Impotence: Physiological, Psychological, Surgical Diagnosis and Treatment*. New York: Plenum.

Zilbergeld, Bernard (1978). *Male Sexuality*. New York: Simon and Schuster.

42

ARTICLE

Robert Staples

Stereotypes of Black Male Sexuality: The Facts Behind the Myths

It is difficult to think of a more controversial role in American society than that of the black male. He is a visible figure on the American scene, yet the least understood and studied of all sex–race groups in the United States. His cultural image is typically one of several types: the sexual superstud, the athlete, and the rapacious criminal. That is how he is perceived in the public consciousness, interpreted in the media and ultimately how he comes to see and internalize his own role. Rarely are we exposed to his more prosaic role as worker, husband, father and American citizen.

The following essay focuses on the stereotypical roles of black male heterosexuality, not to reinforce them, but to penetrate the superficial images of black men as macho, hypersexual, violent and exploitative. Obviously, there must be some explanation for the dominance of black men in the nations' negative statistics on rape, out-of-wedlock births, and premarital sexual activity. This is an effort to explore the reality behind the image.

Black Manhood

As a starting point, I see the black male as being in conflict with the normative definition of masculinity. This is a status which few, if any, black males have been able to achieve. Masculinity, as defined in this culture, has always implied a certain autonomy and mastery of one's environment. It can be said that not many white American males have attained this ideal either. Yet, white males did achieve a dominance in the nuclear family. Even that semblance of control was largely to be denied black men. During slavery he could receive the respect and esteem of his wife, children and kinsmen, but he had no formal legal authority over his wife or filial rights from his children. There are numerous and documented instances of the slave-owning class's attempts to undermine his respect and esteem in the eyes of his family.[1]

Beginning with the fact that slave men and women were equally subjugated to the capricious authority of the slaveholder, the African male saw his masculinity challenged by the rape of his woman, sale of his children, the rations issued in the name of the woman and children bearing her name. While those practices may have presaged the beginning of a healthier sexual egalitarianism than was possible for whites, they also provoked contradictions and dilemmas for black men in American society. It led to the black male's self-devaluation as a man and set the stage for internecine conflict within the black community.

A person's sex role identity is crucial to their values, life-style and personality. The black man has always had to confront the contradiction between the normative expectations attached to being male in this society and the proscriptions on his behavior and achievement of goals. He is subjected to societal opprobrium for failing to live up to the standards of manhood on the one hand and for being super macho on the other. It is a classical case of "damned if you do and damned if you don't." In the past there was the assertion that black men were effeminate because they were raised in households with only a female parent or one with a weak father figure. Presently, they are being attacked in literature, in plays, and at conferences as having succumbed to the male chauvinist ideal.

Although the sexual stereotypes apply equally to black men and women, it is the black male who has suffered the worst because of white notions of his hypersexuality. Between 1884 and 1900 more than 2,500 black men were lynched, the majority of whom were accused of sexual interest in white women. Black men, it was said, had a larger penis, a greater sexual capacity and an insatiable sexual appetite. These stereotypes depicted black men as primitive sexual beasts, without the white male's love for home and family.[2] These stereotypes persist in the American consciousness.

It is in the area of black sexual behavior, and black male sexuality in particular, that folk beliefs are abundant but empirical facts few. Yet public policy, sex education and therapeutic programs to deal with the sex-related problems of black people cannot be developed to fit their peculiar needs until we know the nature and dynamics of black sexual behavior. Thus, it is in-cumbent upon researchers to throw some light on an area enmeshed in undocumented myths and stereotypes.

Sexuality of the Male Adolescent

The Kinsey data, cited by Bell,[3] reveal that black males acquire their knowledge about condoms at a later age than white males. The white male learns about sexual intercourse at a later age than black males. Because of poorer nutrition, the black male reaches puberty at a later age than his white male counterpart. A critical distinction between black and white males was the tendency of the more sexually repressed white male to substitute masturbation, fellatio and fantasy for direct sexual intercourse. Masturbation, for instance, was more likely to be the occasion of the first ejaculation for the white male while intercourse was for the black male. A larger percentage of white males reported being sexually aroused by being bitten during sexual activity, seeing a member of the opposite sex in a social situation, seeing themselves nude in the mirror or looking at another man's erect penis, hearing dirty jokes, reading sadomasochistic literature and viewing sexy pictures. Conversely, black males tended to engage in premarital intercourse at earlier ages, to have intercourse and to reach orgasm more frequently. As Bell notes in his analysis of these data, the black male's overabundance of sexuality is a myth. The sexuality of black and white men just tends to take different forms and neither group has any more self-control or moral heroism than the other.

Among young black American males, sexual activity begins at an earlier age, is more frequent and involves more partners. Apparently white males are more likely to confine their associations in the adolescent years with other men. Larson and his associates found that black male adolescents were twice as likely to be romantically in-volved with women than white males.[4] The kind of rigid gender segregation found in white cul-ture is largely absent from black society. For ex-ample, blacks are less likely to be associated with all male clubs, organizations or colleges.

The sexual code of young black males is a permissive one. They do not, for example, divide black women into "good" (suitable for marriage) and "bad" (ineligible for marriage) categories. In the lower income groups, sexual activity is often a measure of masculinity. Thus, there is a greater orientation toward premarital sexual experimen-tation. In a study of premarital sexual standards among blacks and whites in the 1960s, Ira Reiss found that the sexual permissiveness of white males could be affected by a number of social forces (e.g., religion), but the black male was in-fluenced by none of them.[5] Leanor Johnson and this author found that few black male adolescents were aware of the increased risk of teenage preg-nancy, but there was an almost unanimous wish not to impregnate their sexual partner. Another survey of black male high school students re-ported their group believed that a male respects his partner when he uses a condom.[6]

Poverty and the Black Father

The period of adolescence, with its social, psy-chological and physical changes (particularly sex-role identity and sexuality), is the most problematic of the life cycle stages. The prolon-gation of adolescence in complex technological society and the earlier onset of puberty have served to compound the problem. While ado-lescents receive various messages to abandon childlike behavior, they are systematically ex-cluded from adult activity such as family plan-ning. This exclusion is justified not only by their incomplete social and emotional maturity, but by their lack of marketable skills which are nec-

essary to command meaningful status-granting jobs. Unskilled adolescents are further disadvan-taged if they are members of a minority racial group in a racially stratified society.

Parenthood at this stage of the life cycle is most undesirable. Yet, recent upsurges in teenage pregnancy and parenthood have oc-curred, specifically among females younger than 14. Approximately 52% of all children born to black women in 1982 were conceived out-of-wedlock. Among black women under age 20, about 75% of all births were out-of-wedlock compared with only 25% of births to young white women.[7] Although the rate of white out-of-wedlock pregnancy is increasing and that of non-whites decreasing, black unwed parent-hood remains higher than that of whites.

Because life and family support systems of black males are severely handicapped by the ef-fects of poverty and discrimination, the conse-quences of becoming a father in adolescence are more serious for the minority parent. Many family planning agencies offer counseling to the unwed mother, while the father is usually in-volved only superficially or punitively—as when efforts are made to establish legal paternity as a means for assessing financial responsibility. This omission, however, is not unique to black males. It is, perhaps, the single fact of inadequate eco-nomic provision which has resulted in the social agencies' premature conclusion that unwed fa-thers are unwilling to contribute to the future of their child and the support of the mother. Fur-thermore, sociological theory purports that slavery broke the black man's sense of family re-sponsibility. Thus, it is assumed that black women do not expect nor demand that black men sup-port them in raising their children.

Family Planning

Recent evidence, however, suggests that the matrifocality of present theory and social ser-vices is myopic. Studies have demonstrated that most unwed fathers are willing to face their feelings and responsibilities.[8] The findings suggest that unmarried black males do not consider family planning a domain of the female, but rather a joint responsibility to be shared by both parents.[9]

Throughout the world one of the most important variables affecting birth rates is the male attitude toward family planning and the genesis of this attitude. Too often we are accustomed to thinking of reproduction as primarily a female responsibility. Since women are the main bearers and main rearers of children in our society, we tend to believe that they should be primarily concerned with planning the size of a family and developing those techniques of contraception consistent with family's earning power, their own health and happiness and the psychological well-being of their children.

However, in a male-dominated world it is women who are given the burden of having and raising children, while it is often men who determine what the magnitude of that burden should be. Unfortunately, the male's wishes in regard to the size of his family are not contingent on the effect of childbearing on the female partner, but are often shaped by his own psychological and status concerns.

Within many societies there is an inseparable link between men's self-image and their ability to have sexual relations with women and the subsequent birth of children from those sexual acts. For example, in Spanish-speaking cultures this masculine norm is embedded in the concept of "machismo." "Machismo," derived from the Latin word "masculus," literally means the ability to produce sperm and thus sire—abilities which define the status of a man in society. In male-dominated society other issues involved in reproduction are subordinated to the male's desire to affirm his virility, which in turn confirms his fulfillment of the masculine role. The research literature tells us that the male virility cult is strongest in countries and among groups where the need for family planning is greatest.

Thus, we find that in underdeveloped countries—and among low-income ethnic groups in industrialized societies, including much of the black population in the U.S.—men are resistant to anything but natural controls on the number of children they have. Studies show that males who strongly believe that their masculine status is associated with their virility do not communicate very well with their wives on the subject of family planning. As a result the wives are less effective in limiting their families to the number of children they desire.

Sexual Aggression

Sexual attacks against women are pervasive and sharply increasing in this country. The typical rapist is a black male and his victim is most often a black female. However, the most severe penalties for rape are reserved for black males accused of raping white women. Although 50% of those convicted for rape in the South were white males, over 90% of those executed for this crime in that region were black. Most of their alleged victims were white. No white male has ever been executed for raping a black woman.[10]

As is probably true of white females, the incidence of rape of black women is underreported. Lander reported that an eight-year-old girl has a good chance of being exposed to rape and violence if she is a member of the black underclass.[11] While widespread incidents of this kind are rooted in the sexist socialization of all men in society, it is pronounced among black men who have other symbols of traditional masculinity blocked to them. Various explanations have been put forth to explain why black men seem to adopt the attitudes of the majority group toward black women. Poussaint believes that because white men have historically raped black women with impunity, many black males believe they can do the same.[12]

Sexual violence is also rooted in the dynamics of the black dating game. The majority of black rape victims know their attacker—a friend, relative, or neighbor. Many of the rapes occur after a date and are what Amir describes as misfired attempts at seduction.[13] A typical pattern is for the black male to seek sexual compliance from his date, encounter resistance which he thinks is feigned, and proceed to forcibly obtain his sexual gratification from her. Large numbers of black men believe sexual relations to be their "right" after a certain amount of dating.

Rape, however, is not regarded as the act of a sexually starved male but rather as an aggressive act toward females. Students of the subject suggest that it is a long-delayed reaction against authority and powerlessness. In the case of black men, it is asserted that they grow up feeling emasculated and powerless before reaching manhood. They often encounter women as authority figures and teachers or as the head of their household. These men consequently act out their feelings of powerlessness against black women in the form of sexual aggression. Hence, rape by black men should be viewed as both an aggressive and political act because it occurs in the context of racial discrimination which denies most black men a satisfying manhood.

Manhood in American society is closely tied to the acquisition of wealth. Men of wealth are rarely required to rape women because they can gain sexual access through other means. A female employee who submits to the sexual demands of a male employer in order to advance in her job is as much an unwilling partner in this situation as is the rape victim. The rewards for her sexual compliance are normatively sanctioned, whereas the rapist does not often have the resources to induce such sexual compliance. Moreover, the concept of women as sexual property is at the root of rape. This concept is peculiar to capitalistic, western societies rather than African nations (where the incidence of rape is much lower). For black men, rape is often an act of aggression against women because the kinds of status men can acquire through success in a job is not available to them.

Recommendations

To address the salient issues in black male sexuality, I offer the following recommendations:

1. An educational program for black men must be designed to sensitize them to the need for their responsibility for, and participation in, family planning. This program will best be conducted by other men who can convey the fact that virility is not in and of itself the measure of masculinity. Also, it should be emphasized that the use of contraception—or obtaining a vasectomy—does not diminish a male's virility.

2. An over-all sex education program for both sexes should begin as early as kindergarten, before the male peer group can begin to reinforce attitudes of male dominance. Sex education courses should stress more than the physiological aspects in its course content. Males should be taught about the responsibility of men in sex relations and procreation. Forms of male contraception should be taught along with female measures of birth control.

3. The lack of alternative forms of role fulfillment available to many men, especially in industrialized societies, must be addressed. In cases of unemployment and underemployment, the male often resorts to the virility cult because it is the only outlet he has for a positive self-image and prestige within his peer group. Thus, we must provide those conditions whereby men can find meaningful employment.

4. Lines of communication must be opened between men and women. A supplement to the educational program for men should be seminars and workshops involving both

men and women. Hopefully, this will lead to the kind of dialog between men and women that will sensitize each of them to the feelings of the other.

Notes

1. Robert Staples, *The Black Family: Essays and Studies*. (Belmont, CA: Wadsworth, 1978.)

2. Robert Staples, *Black Masculinity*, (San Francisco: The Black Scholar Press, 1982.)

3. Alan P. Bell, "Black Sexuality: Fact and Fancy" in R. Staples. ed., *The Black Family: Essays and Studies*, pp. 77–80.

4. David Larson, et al., "Social Factors in the Frequency of Romantic Involvement Among Adolescents." *Adolescence* 11: 7–12, 1976.

5. Ira Reiss, *The Social Context of Premarital Sexual Permissiveness*. (New York: Holt, Rinehart and Winston, 1968.)

6. Leanor Johnson and Robert Staples, "Minority Youth and Family Planning: A Pilot Project." *The Family Coordinator* 28: 534–543, 1978.

7. U.S. Bureau of the Census, *Fertility of American Women*. (Washington, D.C.: U.S. Government Printing Office, 1984.)

8. Lisa Connolly, "Boy Fathers." *Human Behavior* 45: 40–43, 1978.

9. B. D. Misra, "Correlates of Males' Attitudes Toward Family Planning" in D. Bogue, ed., *Sociological Contributions to Family Planning Research*. (Chicago: Univ. of Chicago Press, 1967), pp. 161–167.

10. William J. Bowers, *Executions in America*. (Lexington Books, 1974).

11. Joyce Lander, *Tomorrow's Tomorrow: The Black Woman*. (Garden City, New York: Doubleday, 1971.)

12. Alvin Poussaint, *Why Blacks Kill Blacks*. (New York: Emerson-Hall, 1972.)

13. Menachim Amir, "Sociocultural Factors in Forcible Rape" in L. Gross, ed., *Sexual Behavior*. (New York: Spectrum Publications, 1974), pp. 1–12.

M. Rochlin

The Heterosexual Questionnaire

1. What do you think caused your heterosexuality?
2. When and how did you decide you were a heterosexual?
3. Is it possible that your heterosexuality is just a phase you may grow out of?
4. Is it possible that your heterosexuality stems from a neurotic fear of others of the same sex?
5. If you have never slept with a person of the same sex, is it possible that all you need is a good Gay lover?
6. Do your parents know that you are straight? Do your friends and/or roommate(s) know? How did they react?
7. Why do you insist on flaunting your heterosexuality? Can't you just be who you are and keep it quiet?
8. Why do heterosexuals place so much emphasis on sex?
9. Why do heterosexuals feel compelled to seduce others into their lifestyle?
10. A disproportionate majority of child molesters are heterosexual. Do you consider it safe to expose children to heterosexual teachers?
11. Just what do men and women *do* in bed together? How can they truly know how to please each other, being so anatomically different?
12. With all the societal support marriage receives, the divorce rate is spiraling. Why are there so few stable relationships among heterosexuals?
13. Statistics show that lesbians have the lowest incidence of sexually transmitted diseases. Is it really safe for a woman to maintain a heterosexual lifestyle and run the risk of disease and pregnancy?
14. How can you become a whole person if you limit yourself to compulsive, exclusive heterosexuality?
15. Considering the menace of overpopulation, how could the human race survive if everyone were heterosexual?
16. Could you trust a heterosexual therapist to be objective? Don't you feel s/he might be inclined to influence you in the direction of her/his own leanings?
17. There seem to be very few happy heterosexuals. Techniques have been developed that might enable you to change if you really want to. Have you considered trying aversion therapy?
18. Would you want your child to be heterosexual, knowing the problems that s/he would face?

44

ARTICLE

Tomás Almaguer

Chicano Men: A Cartography of Homosexual Identity and Behavior

The sexual behavior and sexual identity of Chicano male homosexuals is principally shaped by two distinct sexual systems, each of which attaches different significance and meaning to homosexuality. Both the European-American and Mexican/Latin-American systems have their own unique ensemble of sexual meanings, categories for sexual actors, and scripts that circumscribe sexual behavior. Each system also maps the human body in different ways by placing different values on homosexual erotic zones. The primary socialization of Chicanos into Mexican/Latin-American cultural norms, combined with their simultaneous socialization into the dominant European-American culture, largely structures how they negotiate sexual identity questions and confer meaning to homosexual behavior during adolescence and adulthood. Chicano men who embrace a "gay" identity (based on the European-American sexual system) must reconcile this sexual identity with their primary socialization into a Latino culture that does not recognize such a construction: there is no cultural equivalent to the modern "gay man" in the Mexican/Latin-American sexual system.

How does socialization into these different sexual systems shape the crystallization of their sexual identities and the meaning they give to their homosexuality? Why does only a segment of homosexually active Chicano men identify as "gay"? Do these men primarily consider themselves *Chicano* gay men (who retain primary emphasis on their ethnicity) or *gay* Chicanos (who place primary emphasis on their sexual preference)? How do Chicano homosexuals structure their sexual conduct, especially the sexual roles and relationships into which they enter? Are they structured along lines of power/dominance firmly rooted in a patriarchal Mexican culture that privileges men over women and the masculine over the feminine? Or do they reflect the ostensibly more egalitarian sexual norms and practices of the European-American sexual system? These are among the numerous questions that this paper problematizes and explores.

An edited version of the original article appeared in *differences: A Journal of Feminist Cultural Studies* 3:2(1991), pp. 75–100. Reprinted with permission. I gratefully acknowledge the valuable comments on an earlier version of this article by Jackie Goldsby, David Halperin, Teresa de Lauretis, Bob Blauner, Carla Trujillo, Patricia Zavella, Velia Garcia, and Ramón Gutiérrez.

We know little about how Chicano men negotiate and contest a modern gay identity with aspects of Chicano culture drawing upon more Mexican/Latin-American configurations of sexual meaning. Unlike the rich literature on the Chicana/Latina lesbian experience, there is a paucity of writings on Chicano gay men.[1] There does not exist any scholarly literature on this topic other than one unpublished study addressing this issue as a secondary concern (Carrillo and Maiorana). The extant literature consists primarily of semi-autobiographical, literary texts by authors such as John Rechy, Arturo Islas, and Richard Rodriguez.[2] Unlike the writings on Chicana lesbianism, however, these works fail to discuss directly the cultural dissonance that Chicano homosexual men confront in reconciling their primary socialization into Chicano family life with the sexual norms of the dominant culture. They offer little to our understanding of how these men negotiate the different way these cultural systems stigmatize homosexuality and how they incorporate these messages into their adult sexual practices.

In the absence of such discussion or more direct ethnographic research to draw upon, we must turn elsewhere for insights into the lives of Chicano male homosexuals. One source of such knowledge is the perceptive anthropological research on homosexuality in Mexico and Latin America, which has direct relevance for our understanding of how Chicano men structure and culturally interpret their homosexual experiences. The other, ironically, is the writings of Chicana lesbians who have openly discussed intimate aspects of their sexual behavior and reflected upon sexual identity issues. How they have framed these complex sexual issues has major import for our understanding of Chicano male homosexuality. Thus, the first section of this paper examines certain features of the Mexican/Latin-American sexual system which offer clues to the ensemble of cultural meanings that Chicano homosexuals give to their sexual practices. The second section examines the autobio-

graphical writings of Chicana lesbian writer Cherríe Moraga. I rely upon her candid discussion of her sexual development as ethnographic evidence for further problematizing the Chicano homosexual experience in the United States.

The Cartography of Desire in the Mexican/Latin-American Sexual System

American anthropologists have recently turned their attention to the complex meaning of homosexuality in Mexico and elsewhere in Latin America. Ethnographic research by Joseph M. Carrier, Roger N. Lancaster, Richard Parker, Barry D. Adam, and Clark L. Taylor has documented the inapplicability of Western European and North American categories of sexual meaning in the Latin American context. Since the Mexican/Chicano population in the U.S. shares basic features of these Latin cultural patterns, it is instructive to examine this sexual system closely and to explore its impact on the sexuality of homosexual Chicano men and women.

The rules that define and stigmatize homosexuality in Mexican culture operate under a logic and a discursive practice different from those of the bourgeois sexual system that shaped the emergence of contemporary gay/lesbian identity in the U.S. Each sexual system confers meaning to homosexuality by giving different weight to the two fundamental features of human sexuality that Freud delineated in the *Three Essays on the Theory of Sexuality*: sexual object choice and sexual aim. The structured meaning of homosexuality in the European-American context rests on the sexual object-choice one makes—i.e., the biological sex of the person toward whom sexual activity is directed. The Mexican/Latin-American sexual system, on the other hand, confers meaning to homosexual practices according to sexual aim—i.e., the act one wants to perform with another person (of either biological sex).

The contemporary bourgeois sexual system in the U.S. divides the sexual landscape according to discrete sexual categories and personages defined in terms of sexual preference or object choice: same sex (homosexual), opposite sex (heterosexual), or both (bisexual). Historically, this formulation has carried with it a blanket condemnation of all same-sex behavior. Because it is non-procreative and at odds with a rigid, compulsory heterosexual norm, homosexuality traditionally has been seen as either 1) a sinful transgression against the word of God, 2) a congenital disorder wracking the body, or 3) a psychological pathology gripping the mind. In underscoring object choice as the crucial factor in defining sexuality in the U.S., anthropologist Roger Lancaster argues that "homosexual desire itself, without any qualifications, stigmatizes one as a homosexual" (116). This stigmatization places the modern gay man at the bottom of the homosexual sexual hierarchy. According to Lancaster, "the object-choice of the homosexual emarginates him from male power, except insofar as he can serve as a negative example and . . . is positioned outside the operational rules of normative (hetero)sexuality" (123–24).

Unlike the European-American system, the Mexican/Latin-American sexual system is based on a configuration of gender/sex/power that is articulated along the active/passive axis and organized through the scripted sexual role one plays.[3] It highlights sexual aim—the act one wants to perform with the person toward whom sexual activity is directed—and gives only secondary importance to the person's gender or biological sex. According to Lancaster, "it renders certain organs and roles 'active,' other body passages and roles 'passive,' and assigns honor/shame and status/stigma accordingly" (123). It is the mapping of the body into differentiated erotic zones and the unequal, gender-coded statuses accorded sexual actors that structure homosexual

meaning in Latin culture. In the Mexican/Latin-American context there is no cultural equivalent to the modern gay man. Instead of discrete sexual personages differentiated according to sexual preference, we have categories of people defined in terms of the role they play in the homosexual act. The Latin homosexual world is divided into *activos* and *pasivos* (as in Mexico and Brazil) and *machistas* and *cochóns* (in Nicaragua).

Although stigma accompanies homosexual practices in Latin culture, it does not equally adhere to both partners. It is primarily the anal–passive individual (the *cochón* or *pasivo*) who is stigmatized for playing the subservient, feminine role. His partner (the *activo* or *machista*) typically "is not stigmatized at all and, moreover, no clear category exists in the popular language to classify him. For all intents and purposes, he is just a normal . . . male" (Lancaster 113). In fact, Lancaster argues that the active party in a homosexual drama often gains status among his peers in precisely the same way that one derives status from seducing many women (113). This cultural construction confers an inordinate amount of meaning to the anal orifice and to anal penetration. This is in sharp contrast to the way homosexuality is viewed in the U.S., where the oral orifice structures the meaning of homosexuality in the popular imagination. In this regard, Lancaster suggests the lexicon of male insult in each context clearly reflects this basic difference in cultural meaning associated with oral/anal sites (111). The most common derisive term used to refer to homosexuals in the U.S. is "cocksucker." Conversely, most Latin American epithets for homosexuals convey the stigma associated with their being anally penetrated.

Consider for a moment the meaning associated with the passive homosexual in Nicaragua, the *cochón*. The term is derived from the word *colchón* or mattress, implying that one gets on top of another as one would a mattress, and thereby symbolically affirms the former's superior masculine power and male status over the other, who is feminized and indeed objectified (Lancaster

112). *Cochón* carries with it a distinct configuration of power, delineated along gender lines that are symbolically affirmed through the sexual role one plays in the homosexual act. Consequently, the meaning of homosexuality in Latin culture is fraught with elements of power/dominance that are not intrinsically accorded homosexual practices in the U.S. It is anal passivity alone that is stigmatized and that defines the subordinate status of homosexuals in Latin culture. The stigma conferred to the passive role is fundamentally inscribed in gender-coded terms.

> "To give" (*dar*) is to be masculine, "to receive" (*recibir, aceptar, tomar*) is to be feminine. This holds as the ideal in all spheres of transactions between and within genders. It is symbolized by the popular interpretation of the male sexual organ as active in intercourse and the female sexual organ (or male anus) as passive. (Lancaster 114)

This equation makes homosexuals such as the *pasivo* and *cochón* into feminized men; biological males, but not truly men. In Nicaragua, for example, homosexual behavior renders "one man a machista and the other a cochón. The machista's honor and the cochón's shame are opposite sides of the same coin" (Lancaster 114).

Male Homosexual Identity and Behavior in Mexico

Some of the most insightful ethnographic research on homosexuality in Mexico has been conducted by anthropologist J. M. Carrier. Like other Latin American specialists exploring this issue, Carrier argues that homosexuality is construed very differently in the U.S. and in Mexico. In the U.S., even one adult homosexual act or acknowledgment of homosexual desire may threaten a man's gender identity and throw open to question his sexual identity as well. In sharp contrast, a Mexican man's masculine gender and heterosexual identity are not threatened by a homosexual act as long as he plays the inserter's role. Only the male who plays the passive sexual role and exhibits feminine gender characteristics is considered to be truly homosexual and is, therefore, stigmatized. This "bisexual" option, an exemption from stigma for the "masculine" homosexual, can be seen as part of the ensemble of gender privileges and sexual prerogatives accorded Mexican men. Thus it is primarily the passive, effeminate homosexual man who becomes the object of derision and societal contempt in Mexico.

The terms used to refer to homosexual Mexican men are generally coded with gendered meaning drawn from the inferior position of women in patriarchal Mexican society. The most benign of these contemptuous terms is *maricón*, a label that highlights the non-conforming gender attributes of the (feminine) homosexual man. Its semantic equivalent in the U.S. is "sissy" or "fairy" (Carrier, "Cultural Factors" 123–24). Terms such as *joto* or *puto*, on the other hand, speak to the passive sexual role taken by these men rather than merely their gender attributes. They are infinitely more derogatory and vulgar in that they underscore the sexually nonconforming nature of their passive/receptive position in the homosexual act. The invective associated with all these appellations speaks to the way effeminate homosexual men are viewed as having betrayed the Mexican man's prescribed gender and sexual role. Moreover, it may be noted that the Spanish feminine word *puta* refers to a female prostitute while its male form *puto* refers to a passive homosexual, not a male prostitute. It is significant that the cultural equation made between the feminine, anal-receptive homosexual man and the most culturally-stigmatized female in Mexican society (the whore) share a common semantic base.[4]

Carrier's research suggests that homosexuality in Mexico is rigidly circumscribed by the prominent role the family plays in structuring homosexual activity. Whereas in the U.S., at least among most European-Americans, the role of the family as a regulator of the lives of gay men and lesbians has progressively declined, in Mexico the family remains a crucial institution that defines both gender and sexual relations between men and women. The Mexican family remains a bastion of patriarchal privilege for men and a major impediment to women's autonomy outside the private world of the home.

The constraints of family life often prevent homosexual Mexican men from securing unrestricted freedom to stay out late at night, to move out of their family's home before marriage, or to take an apartment with a male lover. Thus their opportunities to make homosexual contacts in other than anonymous locations, such as the balconies of movie theaters or certain parks, are severely constrained (Carrier, "Family Attitudes" 368). This situation creates an atmosphere of social interdiction which may explain why homosexuality in Mexico is typically shrouded in silence. The concealment, suppression, or prevention of any open acknowledgment of homosexual activity underscores the stringency of cultural dictates surrounding gender and sexual norms within Mexican family life. Unlike the generally more egalitarian, permissive family life of white middle-class gay men and lesbians in the U.S., the Mexican family appears to play a far more important and restrictive role in structuring homosexual behavior among Mexican men ("Family Attitudes" 373).

Given these constraints and the particular meanings attached to homosexuality in Mexican culture, same-sex behavior in Mexico typically unfolds in the context of an age-stratified hierarchy that grants privileges to older, more masculine men. It is very significant that in instances where two masculine, active men enter into a homosexual encounter, the rules that structure gender-coded homosexual relations continue to operate with full force. In these exchanges one of the men—typically he who is defined as being more masculine or powerful—assumes the active, inserter role while the other man is pressed into the passive, anal-receptive role. Moreover, men who may eventually adopt both active and passive features of homosexual behavior typically do not engage in such reciprocal relations with the same person. Instead, they generally only play the active role with one person (who is always viewed as being the more feminine) and are sexually passive with those they deem more masculine than themselves ("Cultural Factors" 120–21).

In sum, it appears that the major difference between bisexually-active men in Mexico and bisexual males in the U.S. is that the former are not stigmatized because they exclusively play the active, masculine, inserter role. Unlike in the North American context, "one drop of homosexuality" does not, ipso facto, make a Mexican male a *joto* or a *maricón*. As Carrier's research clearly documents, none of the active inserter participants in homosexual encounters ever considers himself a "homosexual" or to be "gay" ("Mexican Male" 83). What may be called the "bisexual escape hatch" functions to insure that the tenuous masculinity of Mexican men is not compromised through the homosexual act; they remain men, *hombres*, even though they participate in this sexual behavior. Moreover, the Mexican sexual system actually militates against the construction of discernable, discrete "bisexual" or "gay" sexual identities because these identities are shaped by and draw upon a different sexual system and foreign discursive practices. One does not, in other words, become "gay" or "lesbian" identified in Mexico because its sexual system precludes such an identity formation in the first place. These "bourgeois" sexual categories are simply not relevant or germane to the way gender and sexual meanings are conferred in Mexican society.

Implications for Chicano Gay Men in the U.S.

The emergence of the modern gay identity in the U.S. and its recent appearance in Mexico have implications for Chicano men that have not been fully explored. What is apparent, however, is that Chicanos, as well as other racial minorities, do not negotiate the acceptance of a gay identity in exactly the same way white American men do. The ambivalence of Chicanos vis-à-vis a gay sexual identity and their attendant uneasiness with white gay/lesbian culture do not necessarily reflect a denial of homosexuality. Rather, I would argue, the slow pace at which this identity formation has taken root among Chicanos is attributable to cultural and structural factors which differentiate the experiences of the white and non-white populations in the U.S.

Aside from the crucial differences discussed above in the way homosexuality is culturally constructed in the Mexican/Latin-American and European- or Anglo-American sexual systems, a number of other structural factors also militate against the emergence of a modern gay identity among Chicano men. In this regard, the progressive loosening of familial constraints among white, middle-class homosexual men and women at the end of the nineteenth century, and its acceleration in the post–World War II period, structurally positioned the white gay and lesbian population to redefine their primary self-identity in terms of their homosexuality. The shift from a family-based economy to a fully developed wage labor system at the end of the nineteenth century dramatically freed European-American men and women from the previously confining social and economic world of the family. It allowed both white men and the white "new woman" of the period to transgress the stifling gender roles that previously bound them to a compulsory heterosexual norm.[5] Extricating the nuclear family from its traditional role as a primary unit of production enabled homosexually inclined individuals to forge a new sexual identity and to develop a culture and community that were not previously possible. Moreover, the tremendous urban migration ignited (or precipitated) by World War II accelerated this process by drawing thousands of homosexuals into urban settings where the possibilities for same-sex intimacy were greater.

It is very apparent, however, that the gay identity and communities that emerged were overwhelmingly white, middle class, and male-centered. Leading figures of the first homophile organizations in the U.S., such as the Mattachine Society, and key individuals shaping the newly emergent gay culture were primarily drawn from this segment of the homosexual population. Moreover, the new communities founded in the post-war period were largely populated by white men who had the resources and talents needed to create "gilded" gay ghettos. This fact has given the contemporary gay community—despite its undeniable diversity—a largely white, middle class, and male form. In other words, the unique class and racial advantages of white gay men provided the foundation upon which they could boldly carve out the new gay identity. Their collective position in the social structure empowered them with the skills and talents needed to create new gay institutions, communities, and a unique sexual subculture.

Despite the intense hostility that, as gay men, they faced during that period, nevertheless, as white gay men, they were in the best position to risk the social ostracism that this process engendered. They were *relatively* better situated than other homosexuals to endure the hazards unleashed by their transgression of gender conventions and traditional heterosexual norms. The diminished importance of ethnic identity among these individuals, due principally to the homogenizing and integrating impact of the dominant racial categories which defined them foremost as white, undoubtedly also facilitated the emergence of gay identity among them. As members of the privileged racial group—and thus no longer viewing themselves primarily as Irish, Italian, Jewish, Catholic, etc.—these middle-class men and women arguably no longer depended solely on their respective cultural groups and families as a line of defense against the dominant group. Although they may have continued to experience intense cultural dissonance leaving behind their ethnicity and their traditional family-based roles, they were now in a position to dare to make such a move.

Chicanos, on the other hand, have never occupied the social space where a gay or lesbian identity can readily become a primary basis of self-identity. This is due, in part, to their structural position at the subordinate ends of both the class and racial hierarchies, and in a context where ethnicity remains a primary basis of group identity and survival. Moreover, Chicano family life requires allegiance to patriarchal gender relations and to a system of sexual meanings that directly militate against the emergence of this alternative basis of self-identity. Furthermore, factors such as gender, geographical settlement, age, nativity, language usage, and degree of cultural assimilation further prevent, or at least complicate, the acceptance of a gay or lesbian identity by Chicanos or Chicanas respectively. They are not as free as individuals situated elsewhere in the social structure to redefine their sexual identity in ways that contravene the imperatives of minority family life and its traditional gender expectations. How they come to define their sexual identities as gay, straight, bisexual or, in Mexican/Latin-American terms, as an *activo, pasivo,* or *macho marica,* therefore, is not a straightforward or unmediated process. Unfortunately, there are no published studies to date exploring this identity formation process.

However, one unpublished study on homosexual Latino/Chicano men was conducted by Hector Carrillo and Horacio Maiorana in the spring of 1989. As part of their ongoing work on AIDS within the San Francisco Bay Area Latino community, these researchers develop a typology capturing the different points in a continuum differentiating the sexual identity of these men. Their preliminary typology is useful in that it delineates the way homosexual Chicanos/Latinos integrate elements of both the North American and Mexican sexual systems into their sexual behavior.

The first two categories of individuals, according to Carrillo and Maiorana, are: 1) Working-class Latino men who have adopted an effeminate gender persona and usually play the passive role in homosexual encounters (many of them are drag queens who frequent the Latino gay bars in the Mission District of San Francisco); and 2) Latino men who consider themselves heterosexual or bisexual, but who furtively have sex with other men. They are also primarily working class and often frequent Latino gay bars in search of discrete sexual encounters. They tend to retain a strong Latino or Chicano ethnic identity and structure their sexuality according to the Mexican sexual system. Although Carrillo and Maiorana do not discuss the issue, it seems likely that these men would primarily seek out other Latino men, rather than European-Americans, as potential partners in their culturally-circumscribed homosexual behavior.

I would also suggest from personal observation that these two categories of individuals occasionally enter into sexual relationships with middle-class Latinos and European-American men. In so doing, these working-class Latino men often become the object of the middle-class Latino's or the white man's colonial desires. In one expression of this class-coded lust, the effeminate *pasivo* becomes the boyish, feminized object of the middle-class man's colonial desire. In another, the masculine Mexican/Chicano *activo* becomes the embodiment of a potent ethnic masculinity that titillates the middle-class man who thus enters into a passive sexual role.

Unlike the first two categories of homosexually active Latino men, the other three have integrated several features of the North American sexual system into their sexual behavior. They are more likely to be assimilated into the dominant European-American culture of the

U.S. and to come from middle-class back-grounds. They include 3) Latino men who openly consider themselves gay and participate in the emergent gay Latino subculture in the Mission district; 4) Latino men who consider themselves gay but do not participate in the Latino gay subculture, preferring to maintain a primary identity as Latino and only secondarily a gay one; and, finally, 5) Latino men who are fully assimilated into the white San Francisco gay male community in the Castro District and retain only a marginal Latino identity.

In contrast to the former two categories, Latino men in the latter three categories are more likely to seek European-American sexual partners and exhibit greater difficulty in recon-ciling their Latino cultural backgrounds with their gay lifestyle. In my impressionistic obser-vations, these men do not exclusively engage in homosexual behavior that is hierarchically dif-ferentiated along the gender-coded lines of the Mexican sexual system. They are more likely to integrate both active and passive sexual roles into their sexuality and to enter into relation-ships in which the more egalitarian norms of the North American sexual system prevail. We know very little, however, about the actual sex-ual conduct of these individuals. Research has not yet been conducted on how these men ex-press their sexual desires, how they negotiate their masculinity in light of their homosexuality, and, more generally, how they integrate aspects of the two sexual systems into their everyday sexual conduct.

In the absence of such knowledge, we may seek clues about the social world of Chicano gay men in the perceptive writings of Chicana lesbians. Being the first to shatter the silence on the homosexual experience of the Chicano population, they have candidly documented the perplexing issues Chicanos confront in negoti-ating the conflicting gender and sexual messages imparted by the coexisting Chicano and Euro-pean-American cultures. The way in which Chicana lesbians have framed these problems, I

believe, is bound to have major significance for the way Chicano men reconcile their homo-sexual behavior and gay sexual identity within a Chicano cultural context. More than any other lesbian writer's, the extraordinary work of Cherríe Moraga articulates a lucid and complex analysis of the predicament that the middle-class Chicana lesbian and Chicano gay man face in this society. A brief examination of her autobi-ographical writings offers important insights into the complexities and contradictions that may characterize the experience of homosexu-ality for all Chicanos and Chicanas in the U.S.

Cherríe Moraga and Chicana Lesbianism

An essential point of departure in assessing Cherríe Moraga's work is an appreciation of the way Chicano family life severely constrains the Chicana's ability to define her life outside of its stifling gender and sexual prescriptions. As a number of Chicana feminist scholars have clearly documented, Chicano family life remains rigidly structured along patriarchal lines that privilege men over women and children.[6] Any violation of these norms is undertaken at great personal risk because Chicanos draw upon the family to resist racism and the ravages of class inequality. Chicano men and women are drawn together in the face of these onslaughts and are closely bound into a family structure that exaggerates unequal gender roles and suppresses sexual non-conformity.[7] Therefore, any deviation from the sacred link binding husband, wife, and child not only threatens the very existence of *la familia* but also potentially undermines the mainstay of re-sistance to Anglo racism and class exploitation. "The family, then, becomes all the more ar-dently protected by oppressed people and the sanctity of this institution is infused like blood into the veins of the Chicano. At all costs, la fa-milia must be preserved," writes Moraga. Thus, "we fight back . . . with our families—with our women pregnant, and our men as indispensable heads. We believe the more severely we protect the sex roles within the family, the stronger we will be as a unit in opposition to the anglo threat" (*Loving* 110).

These cultural prescriptions do not, however, curb the sexually non-conforming behavior of certain Chicanos. As in the case of Mexican homosexual men in Mexico, there exists a modicum of freedom for the Chicano homosexual who retains a masculine gender identity while secretly engaging in the active homosexual role. Moraga has perceptively noted that the Latin cultural norm inflects the sexual behavior of homosexual Chicanos: "Male homosexuality has always been a 'tolerated' aspect of Mexican/Chicano society, as long as it remains 'fringe' . . . But lesbianism, in any form, and male homosexuality which openly avows both the sexual and the emotional elements of the bond, challenge the very foundation of la familia" (111). The openly effeminate Chicano gay man's rejection of heterosexuality is typically seen as a fundamental betrayal of Chicano patriarchal cultural norms. He is viewed as having turned his back on the male role that privileges Chicano men and entitles them to sexual access to women, minors, and even other men. Those who reject these male prerogatives are viewed as non-men, as the cultural equivalents of women. Moraga astutely assesses the situation as one in which "the 'faggot' is the object of Chicano/Mexicano's contempt because he is consciously choosing a role his culture tells him to despise. That of a woman" (111).

The constraints that Chicano family life imposed on Moraga herself are candidly discussed in her provocative autobiographical essays "La Guera" and "A Long Line of Vendidas" in *Loving in the War Years*. In recounting her childhood in Southern California, Moraga describes how she was routinely required to make her brother's bed, iron his shirts, lend him money, and even serve him cold drinks when his friends came to visit their home. The privileged position of men in the Chicano family places women in a secondary, subordinate status. She resentfully acknowledges that "to this day in my mother's home, my brother and father are waited on, including by me" (90). Chicano men have always thought of themselves as superior to Chicanas, she asserts in unambiguous terms: "I have never met any kind of Latino who . . . did not subscribe to the basic belief that men are better" (101). The insidiousness of the patriarchal ideology permeating Chicano family life even shapes the way a mother defines her relationships with her children: "The daughter must constantly earn the mother's love, prove her fidelity to her. The son—he gets her love for free" (102).

Moraga realized early in life that she would find it virtually impossible to attain any meaningful autonomy in that cultural context. It was only in the Anglo world that freedom from oppressive gender and sexual strictures was remotely possible. In order to secure this latitude, she made a necessary choice: to embrace the white world and reject crucial aspects of her Chicana upbringing. In painfully honest terms, she states:

> I gradually became anglocized because I thought it was the only option available to me toward gaining autonomy as a person without being sexually stigmatized. . . . I instinctively made choices which I thought would allow me greater freedom of movement in the future. This meant resisting sex roles as much as I could safely manage and that was far easier in an anglo context than in a Chicano one. (99)

Born to a Chicana mother and an Anglo father, Moraga discovered that being fair-complexioned facilitated her integration into the Anglo social world and contributed immensely to her academic achievement. "My mother's desire to protect her children from poverty and illiteracy" led to their being "anglocized," she writes; "the more effectively we could pass in the white world, the better guaranteed our future" (51).

Consequently her life in Southern California during the 1950s and 1960s is described as one in which she "identified with and aspired toward white values" (58). In the process, she "rode the wave of that Southern California privilege as far as conscience would let me" (58).

The price initially exacted by anglicization was estrangement from family and a partial loss of the nurturing and love she found therein. In reflecting on this experience, Moraga acknowledges that "I have had to confront that much of what I value about being Chicana, about my family, has been subverted by anglo culture and my cooperation with it. . . . I realized the major reason for my total alienation from and fear of my classmates was rooted in class and culture" (54). She poignantly concedes that, in the process, "I had disavowed the language I knew best—ignored the words and rhythms that were closest to me. The sounds of my mother and aunts gossiping—half in English, half in Spanish—while drinking cerveza in the kitchen" (55). What she gained, on the other hand, was the greater autonomy that her middle-class white classmates had in defining their emergent sexuality and in circumventing burdensome gender prescriptions. Her movement into the white world, however, was viewed by Chicanos as a great betrayal. By gaining control of her life, Moraga became one of a "long line of vendidas," traitors or "sell-outs," as self-determined women are seen in the sexist cultural fantasy of patriarchal Chicano society. This is the accusation that "hangs above the heads and beats in the hearts of most Chicanas, seeking to develop our own autonomous sense of ourselves, particularly our sexuality" (103).

Patriarchal Chicano culture, with its deep roots in "the institution of heterosexuality," requires Chicanas to commit themselves to Chicano men and subordinate to them their own sexual desires. "[The Chicano] too, like any other man," Moraga writes, "wants to be able to determine how, when, and with whom his women—mother, wife, and daughter—are sex-

ual" (110–11). But "the Chicana's sexual commitment to the Chicano male [is taken as] proof of her fidelity to her people" (105). "It is no wonder," she adds, that most "Chicanas often divorce ourselves from conscious recognition of our own sexuality" (119). In order to claim the identity of a Chicana lesbian, Moraga had to take "a radical stand in direct contradiction to, and in violation of, the women [sic] I was raised to be" (117); and yet she also drew upon themes and images of her Mexican Catholic background. Of its impact on her sexuality Moraga writes:

> I always knew that I felt the greatest emotional ties with women, but suddenly I was beginning to consciously identify those feeling as sexual. The more potent my dreams and fantasies became and the more I sensed my own exploding sexual power, the more I *retreated* from my body's messages and into the region of religion. By giving definition and meaning to my desires, religion became the discipline to control my sexuality. Sexual fantasy and rebellion became "impure thoughts" and "sinful acts." (119)

These "contrary feelings," which initially surfaced around the age of twelve, unleashed feelings of guilt and moral transgression. She found it impossible to leave behind the Catholic Church's prohibitions regarding homosexuality, and religious themes found their way into how she initially came to define herself as a sexual subject—in a devil-like form. "I wrote poems describing myself as a centaur: half-animal/half-human, hairy-rumped and cloven-hoofed, como el diablo. The images emerged from a deeply Mexican and Catholic place" (124).

As her earliest sexual feelings were laden with religious images, so too were they shaped by images of herself in a male-like form. This is understandable in light of the fact that only men in Chicano culture are granted sexual subjectivity. Consequently, Moraga instinctively gravitated toward a butch persona and assumed a male-like stance toward other women.

In the effort to avoid embodying la chingada, I became the chingón. In the effort not to feel fucked, I became the fucker, even with women. . . . The fact of the matter was that all those power struggles of "having" and "being had" were played out in my own bedroom. And in my psyche, they held a particular Mexican twist. (126)

In a candid and courageously outspoken conversation with lesbian activist Amber Hollibaugh, Moraga recounts that

. . . what turned me on sexually, at a very early age, had to do with the fantasy of capture, taking a woman, and my identification was with the man. . . . The truth is, I do have some real gut-level misgivings about my sexual connection with capture. It might feel very sexy to imagine "taking" a woman, but it has sometimes occurred at the expense of my feeling, sexually, like I can surrender myself to a woman; that is, always needing to be the one in control, calling the shots. It's a very butch trip and I feel like this can keep me private and protected and can prevent me from fully being able to express myself. (Moraga and Hollibaugh 396)

Moraga's adult lesbian sexuality defined itself along the traditional butch/femme lines characteristic of lesbian relationships in the postwar period.[8] It is likely that such an identity formation was also largely an expression of the highly gender-coded sexuality imparted through Chicano family life. In order to define herself as an autonomous sexual subject, she embraced a butch, or more masculine, gender persona, and crystallized a sexual desire for feminine, or femme, lovers.

The Final Frontier: Unmasking the Chicano Gay Man

Moraga's experience is certainly only one expression of the diverse ways in which Chicana lesbians come to define their sense of gender and experience their homosexuality. But her odyssey reflects and articulates the tortuous and painful path traveled by working-class Chicanas (and Chicanos) who embrace the middle-class Anglo world and its sexual system in order to secure, ironically, the "right to passion expressed in our own cultural tongue and movements" (136). It is apparent from her powerful autobiographical writings, however, how much her adult sexuality was also inevitably shaped by the gender and sexual messages imparted through the Chicano family.

How this complex process of integrating, reconciling, and contesting various features of both Anglo and Chicano cultural life are experienced by Chicano gay men, has yet to be fully explored. Moraga's incisive and extraordinarily frank autobiographical account raises numerous questions about the parallels in the homosexual development of Chicana lesbians and Chicano gay men. How, for example, do Chicano male homosexuals internalize and reconcile the gender-specific prescriptions of Chicano culture? How does this primary socialization impact on the way they define their gender personas and sexual identities? How does socialization into a patriarchal gender system that privileges men over women and the masculine over the feminine structure intimate aspects of their sexual behavior? Do most Chicano gay men invariably organize aspects of their sexuality along the hierarchical lines of dominance/subordination that circumscribe gender roles and relationships in Chicano culture? My impression is that many Chicano gay men share the Chicano heterosexual man's underlying disdain for women and all that is feminine. Although it has not been documented empirically, it is likely that Chicano gay men incorporate and contest crucial features of the Mexican/Latin-American sexual system into their intimate sexual behavior. Despite having accepted a "modern" sexual identity, they are not immune to the hierarchical, gender-coded system of sexual meanings that is part and parcel of this discursive practice.

Until we can answer these questions through ethnographic research on the lives of Chicano gay men, we must continue to develop the type of feminist critique of Chicano male culture that is so powerfully articulated in the work of lesbian authors such as Cherríe Moraga. We are fortunate that courageous voices such as hers have irretrievably shattered the silence on the homosexual experience within the Mexican American community. Her work, and that of other Chicana lesbians, has laid a challenge before Chicano gay men to lift the lid on their homosexual experiences and to leave the closeted space they have been relegated to in Chicano culture. The task confronting us, therefore, is to begin interpreting and redefining what it means to be both Chicano and gay in a cultural setting that has traditionally viewed these categories as a contradiction in terms. This is an area of scholarly research that can no longer be left outside the purview of Chicano Studies, Gay and Lesbian Studies, or even more traditional lines of sociological inquiry.

Notes

1. See, for example, the writings by Chicana and Latina lesbians in Ramos; Alarcón, Castillo, and Moraga; Moraga and Anzaldúa, and Anzaldúa. See also the following studies on Latinas: Arguelles and Rich; Espin; and Hidalgo and Hidalgo-Christensen.

2. See Bruce-Novoa's interesting discussion of homosexuality as a theme in the Chicano novel.

3. There is a rich literature documenting the ways in which our sexuality is largely structured through sexual scripts that are culturally defined and individually internalized. See, for example, Gagnon and Simon; Simon and Gagnon; and Plummer. What is being referred to here as the Mexican/Latin-American sexual system is part of the circum-Mediterranean construction of gender and sexual meaning. In this regard, see the introduction and essays in Gilmore. For further discussion of this theme in the Mexican context, see Alonso and Koreck. Their essay, which uses many of the many sources as the present essay,

explores male homosexual practices in Mexico in relation to AIDS.

4. In "Birth of the Queen," Trumback has perceptively documented that many of the contemporary terms used to refer to homosexual men in Western Europe and the United States (such as queen, punk, gay, faggot, and fairy) also were at one time the slang term for prostitutes (137). See also Alonso and Koreck, 111–113.

5. For a broad overview of the development of a gay and lesbian identity and community in the United States, see D'Emilio; D'Emilio and Freedman; and Katz. A number of articles in the important anthology edited by Duberman, Vicinus, and Chauncey document the white middle class–centered nature of gay/lesbian identity construction and community formation.

6. Some of the very best research in Chicano studies has been conducted by Chicana feminists who have explored the intersection of class, race, and gender in Chicanas' lives. Some recent examples of this impressive scholarship include Zavella; Segura; Pesquera; and Baca-Zinn.

7. This solidarity is captured in the early Chicano movement poster fittingly entitled "La Familia." It consists of three figures in a symbolic pose: a Mexican woman, with a child in her arms, is embraced by a Mexican man, who is centrally positioned in the portrait and a head taller. This poster symbolized the patriarchal, male-centered privileging of the heterosexual, nuclear family in Chicano resistance against white racism. For a provocative discussion of these themes in the Chicano movement, see Gutiérrez.

8. For an interesting discussion of the butch/femme formulation among working-class white women at the time, see Davis and Kennedy; and Nestle.

References

Adam, Barry D. "Homosexuality without a Gay World: Pasivos y Activos en Nicaragua." *Out/Look* 1.4 (1989): 74–82.

Alarcón, Norma. "Chicana's Feminist Literature: A Re-vision Through Malintzin/or Malintzin: Putting Flesh Back on the Object." Moraga and Anzaldúa 182–90.

Alarcón, Norma, Ana Castillo, and Cherríe Moraga, eds. *Third Woman: The Sexuality of Latinas.* Berkeley: Third Woman, 1989.

Alonso, Ana Maria, and Maria Theresa Koreck. "Silences: 'Hispanics,' AIDS, and Sexual Practices." *differences: A Journal of Feminist Cultural Studies* 1.1 (1989): 101–24.

Anzaldúa, Gloria. *Borderlands/La Frontera: The New Mestiza.* San Francisco: Spinsters, 1987.

Arguelles, Lourdes, and B. Ruby Rich. "Homosexuality, Homophobia, and Revolution: Notes Toward an Understanding of the Cuban Lesbian and Gay Male Experience, Part 1." *Signs: Journal of Woman in Culture and Society* 9 (1984): 683–99.

———. "Homosexuality, Homophobia, and Revolution: Notes Toward an Understanding of the Cuban Lesbian and Gay Male Experience, Part 2." *Signs: Journal of Women in Culture and Society* 11 (1985): 120–36.

Baca-Zinn, Maxine. "Chicano Men and Masculinity." *The Journal of Ethnic Studies* 10.2 (1982): 29–44.

———. "Familism Among Chicanos: A Theoretical Review." *Humboldt Journal of Social Relations* 10.1 (1982–83): 224–38.

Blackwood, Evelyn, ed. *The Many Faces of Homosexuality: Anthropological Approaches to Homosexual Behavior.* New York: Harrington Park, 1989.

Bruce-Novoa, Juan. "Homosexuality and the Chicano Novel." *Confluencia: Revista Hispanica de Cultura y Literatura* 2.1 (1986): 69–77.

Carrier, Joseph M. "Cultural Factors Affecting Urban Mexican Male Homosexual Behavior." *The Archives of Sexual Behavior: An Interdisciplinary Research Journal* 5.2 (1976): 103–24.

———. "Family Attitudes and Mexican Male Homosexuality." *Urban Life: A Journal of Ethnographic Research* 5.3 (1976): 359–76.

———. "Gay Liberation and Coming Out in Mexico." Herdt 225–53.

———. "Mexican Male Bisexuality." *Bisexualities: Theory and Research.* Ed. F. Klein and T. Wolf. New York: Haworth, 1985. 75–85.

Carrillo, Hector, and Horacio Maiorana. "AIDS Prevention Among Gay Latinos in San Francisco: From Behavior Change to Social Change." Unpublished ms., 1989.

Davis, Madeline, and Elizabeth Lapovsky Kennedy. "Oral History and the Study of Sexuality in the Lesbian Community: Buffalo, New York, 1940–1960." Duberman 426–40.

D'Emilio, John. "Capitalism and Gay Identity." Snitow, Stansell, and Thompson 100–13.

———. *Sexual Politics, Sexual Communities: The Making of a Homosexual Minority in the United States, 1940–1970.* Chicago: U of Chicago P, 1983.

D'Emilio, John, and Estelle B. Freedman. *Intimate Matters: A History of Sexuality in America.* New York: Harper, 1988.

Duberman, Martin Bauml, Martha Vicinus, and George Chauncey Jr., eds. *Hidden from History: Reclaiming the Gay and Lesbian Past.* New York: NAL, 1989.

Espin, Oliva M. "Cultural and Historical Influences on Sexuality in Hispanic/Latin Women: Implications for Psychotherapy." *Pleasure and Danger: Exploring Female Sexuality.* Ed. Carol Vance. London: Routledge, 1984, 149–63.

———. "Issues of Identity in the Psychology of Latina Lesbians." *Lesbian Psychologies.* Ed. Boston Lesbian Psychologies Collective. Urbana: U of Illinois P, 1987. 35–55.

Freud, Sigmund. *Three Essays on the Theory of Sexuality.* 1905. *The Standard Edition of the Complete Psychological Works of Sigmund Freud.* Trans. and ed. James Strachey. Vol. 7. London: Hogarth, 1953. 123–243.

Gagnon, John H., and William Simon. *Sexual Conduct: The Social Sources of Human Sexuality.* Chicago: Aldine, 1973.

Gilmore, David D., ed. *Honor and Shame and the Unity of the Mediterranean.* No. 22, Washington: American Anthropological Association, 1987.

Goldwert, Marvin. "Mexican Machismo: The Flight from Femininity." *Psychoanalytic Review* 72.1 (1985): 161–69.

Gutiérrez, Ramón. "Community, Patriarchy, and Individualism: The Politics of Chicano History and the Dream of Equality." Forthcoming in *American Quarterly.*

Herdt, Gilbert, ed. *Gay and Lesbian Youth.* New York: Haworth, 1989.

Hidalgo, Hilda, and Elia Hidalgo-Christensen. "The Puerto Rican Lesbian and the Puerto Rican Community." *Journal of Homosexuality* 2 (1976–77): 109–21.

———. "The Puerto Rican Cultural Response to Female Homosexuality." *The Puerto Rican Woman.* Ed. Edna Acosta-Belen. New York: Praeger, 1979. 110–23.

Islas, Arturo. *Immigrant Souls.* New York: Morrow, 1990.

———. *The Rain God: A Desert Tale.* Palo Alto, CA: Alexandrian, 1984.

Katz, Jonathan Ned. *Gay/Lesbian Almanac: A New Documentary.* New York: Harper, 1983.

Lancaster, Roger N. "Subject Honor and Object Shame: The Construction of Male Homosexuality and Stigma in Nicaragua." *Ethnology* 27.2 (1987): 111–25.

Martin, Robert K. "Knights-Errant and Gothic Seducers: The Representation of Male Friendship in Mid-Nineteenth Century America." Duberman 169–82.

Moraga, Cherríe. *Loving in the War Years: Lo que nunca pasó por sus labios.* Boston: South End, 1983.

Moraga, Cherríe, and Gloria Anzaldúa, eds. *This Bridge Called My Back: Writings by Radical Women of Color.* Watertown, MA: Persephone, 1981.

Moraga, Cherríe, and Amber Hollibaugh. "What We're Rollin Around in Bed With: Sexual Silences in Feminism." Snitow, Stansell, and Thompson 394–405.

Nestle, Joan. "Butch–Fem Relationships: Sexual Courage in the 1950s." *Heresies* 12 (1981): 21–24.

Newton, Esther. "The Mythic Mannish Lesbian: Radcliffe Hall and the New Woman." Duberman 281–93.

Parker, Richard. "Youth Identity, and Homosexuality: The Changing Shape of Sexual Life in Contemporary Brazil." Herdt 269–89.

———. "Masculinity, Femininity, and Homosexuality: On the Anthropological Interpretation of Sexual Meanings in Brazil." Blackwood 155–64.

Paz, Octavio. *Labyrinth of Solitude: Life and Thought in Mexico.* New York: Grove, 1961.

Pesquera, Beatriz M. "Work and Family: A Comparative Analysis of Professional, Clerical and Blue-Collar Chicana Workers." PhD diss. U of California, Berkeley, 1985.

Plummer, Kenneth. "Symbolic Interaction and Sexual Conduct: An Emergent Perspective." *Human Sexual Relations.* Ed. Mike Brake. New York: Pantheon, 1982. 223–44.

Ramos, Juanita, ed. *Compañeras: Latina Lesbians.* New York: Latina Lesbian History Project, 1987.

Rechy, John. *City of Night.* New York: Grove, 1963.

———. *Numbers.* New York: Grove, 1967.

———. *Rushes.* New York: Grove, 1979.

———. *The Sexual Outlaw.* New York: Grove, 1977.

Rodriguez, Richard. *Hunger of Memory: The Education of Richard Rodriguez, An Autobiography.* Boston: Godine, 1982.

———. "Late Victorians: San Francisco, AIDS, and the Homosexual Stereotype." *Harper's Magazine* Oct. 1990: 57–66.

Rupp, Leila J. "Imagine My Surprise: Woman's Relationships in Mid-Twentieth Century America." Duberman 395–410.

Segura, Denise. "Chicana and Mexican Immigrant Women in the Labor Market: A Study of Occupational Mobility and Stratification." PhD diss. U of California, Berkeley, 1986.

———. "Chicana and Mexican Immigrant Women at Work: The Impact of Class, Race, and Gender on Occupational Mobility." *Gender and Society* 3.1 (1989): 37–52.

———. "The Interplay of Familism and Patriarchy on Employment Among Chicana and Mexican Women." *Renato Rosaldo Lecture Series* 5 (1989): 35–53.

Simon, William, and John H. Gagnon. "Sexual Scripts: Permanence and Change." *Archives of Sexual Behavior* 15.2 (1986): 97–120.

Smith-Rosenberg, Carroll. "Discourses of Sexuality and Subjectivity: The New Woman, 1870–1936." Duberman 264–80.

Snitow, Ann, Christine Stansell, and Sharon Thompson, eds. *Powers of Desire: The Politics of Sexuality.* New York: Monthly Review, 1983.

Taylor, Clark L. "Mexican Male Homosexual Interaction in Public Contexts." Blackwood 117–36.

Trumbach, Randolph. "The Birth of the Queen: Sodomy and the Emergence of Gender Equality in Modern Culture, 1660–1750." Duberman 129–40.

Zavella, Patricia. *Women's Work and Chicano Families: Cannery Workers of the Santa Clara Valley.* Ithaca: Cornell UP, 1987.

45

ARTICLE

Susan D. Cochran

Vickie M. Mays

Sociocultural Facets of the Black Gay Male Experience

Prior to the appearance of AIDS in this country, studies on the sexual preferences and behaviors of gay men generally ignored the specific experiences of Black men (Bell, Weinberg, and Hammersmith, 1981). With the press of the AIDS epidemic to develop baseline information on men's intimate behaviors, this tendency rarely to study Black gay men, or do so in the same manner as White gay men, persists. While many researchers may recognize the importance of possible cultural differences, their approach has been to assume that Black gay men would be more like White gay men than Black heterosexuals. Questionnaires, sampling procedures, and topics of focus have been more consistent with White gay men's experiences (see Becker and Joseph, 1988, for a comprehensive review of behavior change studies). This proclivity has resulted in an emergence of comparisons between Black and White men using White gay standards

of behavior that may be obscuring our understanding of important psychosocial determinants of sexual behaviors in Black gay men. Given the differences that have been observed in family structure and sexual patterns between Black and White heterosexuals, there is no empirical basis upon which to assume that Black gay men's experience of homosexuality would perfectly mimic that of Whites (Bell, Weinberg, and Hammersmith, 1981). Indeed, very little is known empirically about the lives of Black gay men (Mays and Cochran, 1987), though there are some indications, discussed below, that they are more likely to engage in activities that place them at greater risk for HIV infection.

In the absence of any data we need to proceed cautiously with assumptions that imply anything other than [that] same-sex *activities* of Black gay men resemble those of White gay men. This caution is particularly true for AIDS studies that purport to study psychosocial behavior. Studies of this type report not only on behavior but also attempt to describe motivations and circumstances that led to the behavior. In the absence of a set of questions or framework incorporating important cultural, ethnic, and economic realities of Black gay men, interpretations emanating

An abridged version of the article "Epidemiologic and Sociocultural Factors in the Transmission of HIV Infection in Black Gay and Bisexual Men" printed in *A Sourcebook of Gay/Lesbian Health Care* (M. Shernoff and W. A. Scott, eds.) Washington, D.C.: National Gay and Lesbian Health Foundation, 2nd ed. Copyright © 1988 by the National Gay and Lesbian Health Foundation. Reprinted by permission.

from a White gay male standard may be misleading.

Development of a Black Gay Identity

In recent years, researchers (Spanier and Glick, 1980; Staples, 1981; Guttentag and Secord, 1983) have noted differences between Whites and Blacks in their intimate heterosexual relationships. Differential sociocultural factors presumably influence the development and specific structure of sexual behavior within Black heterosexual relationships. These factors include the unavailability of same ethnic group partners, fewer social and financial resources, residential immobility, and lack of employment opportunities. Many of these same conditions may surround the formation, maintenance and functioning of Black gay male relationships.

Popular writings in past years by Black gay men describe the difficulty in finding other Black gay men for potential partners, the lack of a visible Black gay community, an absence of role models, and the dearth of Black gay male social or professional organizations (Soares, 1979; Beame, 1983). While gay bars, gay baths and public places existed where White gay men gathered, some of these were off limits to Black gay men either due to actual or perceived racism within the White gay community or the danger of passing through White neighborhoods in order to participate in gay community activities. Thus, expectations that the experiences of Black gay men are identical to those of White gay men seem unwarranted.

In examining differences between Blacks and Whites in the emergence of a homosexual orientation, Bell, Weinberg, and Hammersmith (1981) found that, for the White males, pre-adult sexual feelings appeared to be very important. In contrast, among Black males, childhood and adolescent sexual activities, rather than feelings, were stronger predictors of the development of adult homosexual sexual orientation. Thus Blacks started to act at an earlier age on their sexual inclinations than Whites did (Bell, Weinberg, and Hammersmith, 1981). This would be consistent with Black–White differences in the onset of heterosexual sexual activity if socioeconomic status is not statistically controlled for (Wyatt, personal communication).

The typical conceptualization of sexual orientation is that individuals are located in terms of their sexual feelings and behaviors on a bipolar dimension where one extreme is heterosexuality, the other is homosexuality, and lying somewhere in between is bisexuality (Bell and Weinberg, 1978). This definition does not include ethnicity or culture as an interactive factor influencing the expression of sexual behavior or sexual orientation. For example, Smith (1986) makes a distinction between Black gays and gay Blacks complicating the demarcation between homosexuality and bisexuality:

> Gay Blacks are people who identify first as being gay and who usually live outside the closet in predominantly white gay communities. I would estimate that they amount to roughly ten percent of all Black homosexuals. Black gays, on the other hand, view our racial heritage as primary and frequently live "bisexual front lives" within Black neighborhoods. (p. 226)

These two groups are probably quite different in both social activities and sexual behaviors. The Black gay man, strongly identified with Afro-American culture, will often look and behave much like the Black heterosexual man except in his sexual behavior. The extent to which his same-sex partners are integrated into his family and social environment may be a function of his class status (Soares, 1979). It has long been noted by Blacks that there are differences, both in values and behaviors, between middle-class and working-class Blacks. There is no reason to assume that within the Black gay community such diversity would not persist. While Smith (1986) has described the Black gay community in only two dimensions we would be remiss if we stopped here. There is a growing population of Black gays who have forged an identity acknowledging both statuses:

> At times I cried just remembering how it is to be both Black and gay during these truly difficult times. But here we are, still proud and living, with a culture all our own. (Sylvester, p. 11, 1986)

We know less about the behavior of Black men who identify as bisexual and least about those black men who engage in same-sex sexual behavior but identify as exclusively heterosexual. When the factor of social class is added the distinction between homosexuality and heterosexuality may become even more blurred. Among lower socioeconomic Black men, those engaged in same-sex sexual activities, regardless of their sexual object choices, may appear on the surface no different from Black heterosexuals. If the support systems of Black gay men are like those of Black lesbians (Cochran and Mays, 1986), fewer economic resources result in a greater reliance on a Black social network (both gay and heterosexual) for tangible and emotional support, a strong tendency to live in predominantly ethnic neighborhoods, and the maintenance of emotionally and economically close family ties.

This extensive integration into the Black heterosexual world may not only be a function of fewer economic resources, but also of ethnic identification. The culture of gay life, generally perceived to be White, may not be synonymous with the norms of Black culture. Choices of how to dress, what language to use, where to live, and whom to have as friends are all affected by culture. The White gay community, while diverse, has developed norms concerning language, social behavior, and other demarcations (Warren, 1974) that may not mesh well with certain subgroups of Black gays. For example, in the past there has been a heavy emphasis in the gay White

community (except among the middle-aged, middle-class closeted gay men) on socializing in public places—bars, beaches, and resorts (Warren, 1974). In contrast, the Black gay community places greater emphasis on home entertainment that is private and not public, perhaps as a holdover from the days when discrimination in many public places was common. This pattern of socializing would facilitate the development of a distinct Black gay culture (Soares, 1979).

It is perhaps this difference in socializing that has frustrated health educators attempting to do AIDS education through the social network in gay bars. Generally, they have found that they do not reach a significant number of Black men using this technique. An understanding of the Black gay community makes salient that risk reduction strategies should focus on "risk behaviors" and *not* "risk groups." Emphasizing risk reduction strategies that rely on group membership requires a social and personal identification by Black men that for many may not be relevant.

Sexual Behavior

Bell and Weinberg, in a 1978 study comparing sexual activities of White and Black gay men, found that Blacks were more likely to report having engaged in anal sex, both passively and actively, than White gay men. In terms of our current knowledge of AIDS, this appears to be one of the highest risk factors for contracting the HIV virus (Friedland and Klein, 1987).

A second aspect of Black gay men's sexuality is that they may be more bisexual in their behaviors than White gay men. Evidence for this comes again from Bell and Weinberg (1978) who reported that Black gay men were significantly more likely to have engaged in heterosexual coitus (22 percent) in the previous twelve months than White gay men (14 percent). This seems to be borne out nationally by the AIDS statistics. Among male homosexual/bisexual

AIDS patients, Black men are more likely than White men to be classified as bisexual (30 percent versus 13 percent) rather than homosexual (70 percent versus 87 percent). Due to the intense homophobia in the Black community and the factors we discussed above, men may be more likely to remain secretive regarding their homosexual activities (Mays and Cochran, 1987). This may provide a mode of transmission of the AIDS virus outside of an already identified high risk group.

There are several other differences between Black and White gay men noted in the Kinsey Institute data that have implications for contracting the HIV virus. Looking at sexual behavior both pre- and post-Stonewall, Black gay men, in comparison to White gay men, were more likely to be sexually active across ethnic boundaries and less likely to report that their sexual partners were strangers (Gebhard and Johnson, 1979; Bell and Weinberg, 1978). Sexual practices post-Stonewall underwent profound change in the gay community. Black gay men were a part of that change (Gebhard and Johnson, 1979; Bell and Weinberg, 1978). However, these differences in meeting partners or choice of partners remain. They are apparently less malleable to change than specific risk-related sexual behaviors.

While the 1978 Bell and Weinberg study was conducted on a small sample in the San Francisco area, it is suggestive of the need for further research to assess the prevalence of risk behaviors and strategies most effective for decreasing risk. Indeed, a recent report of ethnically based differences in syphilis incidence rates (Landrum, Beck-Sague, and Kraus, 1988) suggests Black gay men are less likely than White gay men to be practicing "safer sex." Sexual behavior has multiple determinants and it is important that variables such as culture, ethnic identification, and class be incorporated into health education programs designed to promote sexual behavior change by Black men.

Intravenous Drug Use

IV drug use is more common in the Black community (Gary and Berry, 1985), which may explain the higher than expected prevalence of Blacks in the co-categories of IV drug user and homosexual/bisexual male. HIV infection is endemic among IV drug users in the urbanized Northeast who themselves are most likely to be Black (Ginzburg, MacDonald, and Glass, 1987). Ethnic differences exist between the percentage of homosexual/bisexual men with AIDS who are also IV drug users; for White gay and bisexual men with AIDS, 9 percent have histories of IV drug use, while for Blacks the figure is 16 percent. Black gays and bisexual men who do not use IV drugs may also be at increased risk because they are more likely than Whites to be sexual partners of Black men who are IV drugs users. In the Bell and Weinberg study (1978), 22 percent of White men had never had sex with a Black man, whereas for Black respondents, only 2 percent had never had sex with a White man.

Alcohol as a Cofactor

Recently, alcohol use has been implicated as a cofactor facilitating the occurrence of high risk sexual behavior among gay men (Stall et al., 1986). In predicting alcohol use among Black gay and bisexual men, one might expect that normative use patterns will be influenced by what is common behavior in both the Black community and gay community.

Norms for alcohol use in the Black community reflect a polarization of attitudes, shaped on the one hand by traditional religious fundamentalism and rural southern heritage and on the other by a focus on socializing in environments where drinking is common, such as bars, nightclubs, and home parties (Herd, 1986). This latter norm is more prevalent in urban Black communities. Blacks and Whites vary in small ways in their drinking patterns, although Blacks are more likely to suffer negative consequences, including alcohol-related mortality and morbidity, from their drinking than are Whites. Current rates of mortality due to liver cirrhosis indicates that rates are 10 times higher in Black men aged 25–34 as compared to White males. While drinking is found across all socioeconomic groups of Blacks, health and social problems associated with drinking have been found more often in low income urban Blacks (Lex, 1987). Similarly, for this group it was found that Black males 30–59 were most likely to use alcohol to face the stress of everyday life situations. This is the group most affected by HIV infection.

Within the gay male community, alcohol abuse is a serious problem (Icard and Traunstein, 1987). This may result from both the sociocultural stress of discrimination and the tendency for gay-oriented establishments to be drinking establishments as well. Thus, gay men frequently socialize in environments where alcohol consumption is normative.

Black gay and bisexual men, depending upon their relative identification with the Black or gay community, would be expected to demonstrate behavior consistent with these norms. For some, this might mean a high level of abstinence apart from social drinking consistent with other Black Americans; for others, alcohol consumption might more closely resemble that of White gay men with concomitantly higher rates of alcohol dependency.

Crossing Traditional Risk Groups' Boundaries

Early AIDS epidemiologic tracking programs conceptualize the disease as a result of the gay lifestyle (Mays, 1988). Indeed, now discarded names for different manifestations of the illness included Gay-related Immunodeficiency Disease and Gay cancer. This focus on discrete risk factors continues to the present, although the additional populations of IV drug abusers, hemophiliacs, persons born in Haiti and Central Africa, and recipients of blood transfusions after 1978 have been added to the list. For Whites, this approach is highly successful, describing the presumed HIV transmission vector in 94 percent of cases; for native-born Blacks, the percentage of cases accurately labeled by a single risk factor (including the combination of IV drug use and male homosexual sexual contact) drops to 88 percent (Cochran, 1987). This underscores the reality that sociocultural factors varying across ethnic groups strongly influence individuals' behavior, and by this their risk of contracting HIV.

For Black gay and bisexual men, the reliance on highly specified risk groups (or factors) ignores the fundamental nature of their behavioral location in society. The multiplicity of their identities may indirectly increase their risk for HIV infection by exposing them to more diverse populations (Grob, 1983).

First, as Blacks, they are behaviorally closer to two epicenters of the AIDS epidemic. IV drug use and foreign-born Blacks (primarily those from Haiti and Central Africa where HIV infection is more common). Social and behavioral segregation by ethnic status is still a reality of the American experience and Black gay and bisexual men suffer, like other Blacks, from pervasive racism. As we noted above, if their social support systems are similar to what we know of Black lesbians (Cochran and Mays, 1986), extensive integration into the Black heterosexual community is common. Behaviorally, this may include both IV drug use and heterosexual activity with HIV infected individuals. Thus Black gay and bisexual men are at increased risk for HIV infection simply by virtue of being Black.

Second, as men who have sex with other men, Black gay and bisexual men are often members of the broader gay community in which ethnicity probably reflects the general U.S. population (84 percent White). Black gay and bisexual men may have relatively open sexual access to White men, although racism in the community may preclude other forms of socializing (Icard, 1985). Data from the Bell and Weinberg study (1978) suggest several interesting differences, as well as similarities, between White and Black gay men. Blacks reported equivalent numbers of sexual partners, both lifetime (median = 100–249 partners) and in the previous 12 months (median = 20–50), as Whites. Although they were significantly less likely than White gay men to engage in anonymous sexual contacts (51 percent versus 79 percent of partners), more than two-thirds reported that more than half their sexual partners were White men. In contrast, none of the White respondents reported that more than half their partners were Black. It should be kept in mind, however, that a greater percentage of the White sample (14 percent) was recruited at bath houses than the Black sample (2 percent). Nevertheless, at least sexually, Black gay men appear to be well integrated into the gay community. Therefore, Black gay and bisexual men are also at higher risk for HIV infection because they are behaviorally close to another epicenter of the AIDS epidemic: the gay male community.

Third, as a social grouping unto itself, the Black gay and bisexual male community may be more diverse than the White gay community (Icard, 1985). Some men identify more closely with the Black community than the gay community (Black gay men); others find their primary emotional affinity with the gay community and not the Black community (gay Black men). To the extent that this diversity of identity is reflected in behavioral diversity as well, HIV transmission may be greatly facilitated (Denning, 1987).

Thus Black gay and bisexual men are individuals often located behaviorally at the crossroads of HIV transmission. Their multiple social identities make it more likely that the practicing of high risk behavior, whether sexual or needle-sharing, will occur in the presence of HIV.

Perceptions of Risk

There may be a reluctance among Black gay and bisexual men to engage in risk reduction behaviors because of the perception by some members of the Black community that AIDS is a "gay White disease," or a disease of intravenous drug users (Mays and Cochran, 1987). In addition, many risk reduction programs are located within outreach programs of primarily White gay organizations. These organizations often fail to attract extensive participation by Black gay men.

Research findings suggest that the personal perception of being at risk is most often influenced by accurate knowledge of one's actual risk and personal experiences with the AIDS epidemic (McKusick, Horstman, and Coates, 1985). There may be a variety of reasons why Black gay and bisexual men do not see themselves as at risk. These include the notion of relative risk and a lack of ethnically credible sources for encouraging risk perceptions (Mays and Cochran, 1988). Relative risk refers to the importance of AIDS in context with other social realities. For example, poverty, with its own attendant survival risks, may outweigh the fear of AIDS in a teenager's decision to engage in male prostitution. Economic privilege, more common in the White gay community, assists in permitting White gay men to focus their energies and concerns on the AIDS epidemic. For Black gay men of lesser economic privilege other pressing realities of life may, to some extent, diffuse such concerns. Credible sources relate to the issues that we have presented here of ethnic identification. Black gay men who are emotionally and behavioral distant from the White community may tend to discount media messages from White sources.

References

Bakeman, R., J. Lumb, R. E. Jackson, and P. N. Whitley. 1987. "The Incidence of AIDS among Blacks and Hispanics." *Journal of the National Medical Association* 79: 921–928.

Beame, T. 1983. "Racism from a Black Perspective." In *Black Men/White Men: A Gay Anthology*. M. J. Smith ed. San Francisco: Gay Sunshine Press.

Becker, M. H. and J. G. Joseph. 1988. "AIDS and Behavioral Change to Reduce Risk: A Review." *American Journal of Public Health* 78: 394–410.

Bell, A. P. and M. S. Weinberg. 1978. *Homosexualities: A Study of Diversity among Men and Women.* New York: Simon & Schuster.

Bell, A. P., M. S. Weinberg, and S. K. Hammersmith. 1981. *Sexual Preference: Its Development in Men and Women.* Bloomington: Indiana University Press.

Bureau of the Census. 1983. "General Population Characteristics, 1980." U.S. Department of Commerce: U.S. Government Printing Office.

Centers for Disease Control, Acquired Immunodeficiency Syndrome (AIDS) Weekly Surveillance Report, United States AIDS Activity, Center for Infectious Diseases, April 4, 1988.

Centers for Disease Control. 1987. "Human Immunodeficiency Virus Infection in the United States: A Review of Current Knowledge." *Morbidity and Mortality Weekly* 36 (Suppl. no. S-6): 1–48.

Cochran, S. D. 1987. "Numbers That Obscure the Truth: Bias in Data Presentation." Paper presented at the meetings of the American Psychological Association, New York, August.

Cochran, S. D. and V. M. Mays. 1986. "Sources of Support among Black Lesbians." Paper presented at the meetings of the American Psychological Association, Washington, D.C., August.

Cochran, S. D., V. M. Mays, and V. Roberts. 1988. "Ethnic Minorities and AIDS." In *Nursing Care of Patients with AIDS/ARC*, A. Lewis ed., pp. 17–24. Maryland: Aspen Publishers.

Denning, P. J. 1987. "Computer Models of AIDS Epidemiology." *American Scientist* 75: 347–351.

Friedland, G. H. and R. S. Klein. 1987. "Transmission of the Human Immunodeficiency Virus." *New England Journal of Medicine* 317: 1125–1135.

Friedman, S. R., J. L. Sotheran, A. Abdul-Quader, B. J. Primm, D. C. Des Jarlais, P. Kleinman, C.

Mauge, D. S. Goldsmith, W. El-Sadr, and R. Maslansky. 1987. "The AIDS Epidemic among Blacks and Hispanics." *The Milbank Quarterly* 65, Suppl. 2.

Gary, L. E. and G. L. Berry. 1985. "Predicting Attitudes toward Substance Use in a Black Community: Implications for Prevention." *Community Mental Health Journal* 21: 112–118.

Gebhard, P. H. and A. B. Johnson. 1979. *The Kinsey Data: Marginal Tabulations of the 1938–1963 Interviews Conducted by the Institute for Sex Research.* Philadelphia: W. B. Saunders Co.

Ginzburg, H. M., M. G. MacDonald, and J. W. Glass. 1987. "AIDS, HTLV-III Diseases, Minorities and Intravenous Drug Abuse." *Advances in Alcohol and Substance Abuse* 6: 7–21.

Gottlieb, M. S., H. M. Schanker, P. Fan, A. Saxon, J. D. Weisman, and I. Posalki. 1981. "Pneumocystic Pneumonia—Los Angeles." *Morbidity and Mortality Weekly Report* 30: 250–252.

Grob, G. N. 1983. "Diseases and Environment in American History." In *Handbook of Health, Health Care, and the Health Professions*, D. Mechanic, ed., pp. 3–23. New York: Free Press.

Guttentag, M. and P. F. Secord. 1983. *Too Many Women: The Sex Ratio Question.* Beverly Hills, Calif.: Sage Publications.

Herd, D. 1986. "A Review of Drinking Patterns and Alcohol Problems among U.S. Blacks." In *Report of the Secretary's Task Force on Black and Minority Health*: Volume 7, M. Heckler ed. USDHHS.

Icard, L. 1985. "Black Gay Men and Conflicting Social Identities: Sexual Orientation versus Racial Identity." *Journal of Social Work and Human Sexuality* 4: 83–93.

Icard, L., and D. M. Traunstein. 1987. "Black, Gay, Alcoholic Men: Their Character and Treatment." *Social Casework* 68: 267–272.

Landrum, S., C. Beck-Sague, and S. Kraus. 1988. "Racial Trends in Syphilis among Men with Same-Sex Partners in Atlanta, Georgia." *American Journal of Public Health* 78: 66–67.

Lex, B. W. 1987. "Review of Alcohol Problems in Ethnic Minority Groups." *Journal of Consulting and Clinical Psychology* 55 (3): 293–300.

Macdonald, D. I. 1986. "Coolfont Report: A PHS Plan for the Prevention and Control of AIDS and the AIDS Virus." *Public Health Reports* 101: 341–348.

Mays, V. M. 1988. "The Epidemiology of AIDS in U.S. Blacks: Some Problems and Projections." Unpublished manuscript.

Mays, V. M. and S. D. Cochran. 1987. "Acquired Immunodeficiency Syndrome and Black Americans: Special Psychosocial Issues." *Public Health Reports* 102: 224–231.

——— "Issues in the Perception of AIDS Risk and Risk Reduction Activities by Black and Hispanic Women." *American Psychologist* 1988; 43: 11.

McKusick, L., W. Horstman, and T. J. Coates. 1985. "AIDS and Sexual Behavior Reported by Gay Men in San Francisco." *American Journal of Public Health* 75: 493–496.

Morgan, W. M. and J. W. Curran. 1986. "Acquired Immunodeficiency Syndrome: Current and Future Trends." *Public Health Reports* 101: 459–465.

Samuel, M. and W. Winkelstein. 1987. "Prevalence of Human Immunodeficiency Virus in Ethnic Minority Homosexual/Bisexual Men." *Journal of the American Medical Association* 257: 1901 (letter).

Smith, M. C. 1986. "By the Year 2000." *In the Life:*

A Black Gay Anthology, J. Beam ed. Boston: Alyson Publications.

Soares, J. V. 1979. "Black and Gay." In *Gay Men: The Sociology of Male Homosexuality*, M. P. Levine, ed. New York: Harper & Row Publishers.

Spanier, G. B. and P. C. Glick. 1980. "Mate Selection Differentials between Whites and Blacks in the United States." *Social Forces* 58: 707–725.

Stall, R. S., L. McKusick, J. Wiley, T. J. Coates, and D. G. Ostrow. 1986. "Alcohol and Drug Use during Sexual Activity and Compliance with Safe Sex Guidelines for AIDS: The AIDS Behavioral Research Project." *Health Education Quarterly* 13: 359–371.

Staples, R. 1981. *The Changing World of Black Singles*. Connecticut: Greenwood Press.

Sylvester. 1986. Foreword. In *In the Life: A Black Gay Anthology*, J. Beam ed. Boston: Alyson Publications.

Warren, C. A. B. 1974. *Identity and Community Formation in the Gay World*. New York: John Wiley & Sons.

46

ARTICLE

Richard Fung

Looking for My Penis: The Eroticized Asian in Gay Video Porn

Several scientists have begun to examine the relation between personality and human reproductive behavior from a gene-based evolutionary perspective. . . . In this vein we reported a study of racial difference in sexual restraint such that Orientals > whites > blacks. Restraint was indexed in numerous ways, having in common a lowered allocation of bodily energy to sexual functioning. We found the same racial pattern occurred on gamete production (dizygotic birthing frequency per 100: Mongoloids, 4; Caucasoids, 8; Negroids, 16), intercourse frequencies (premarital, marital, extramarital), developmental precocity (age at first intercourse, age at first pregnancy, number of pregnancies), primary sexual characteristics (size of penis, vagina, testis, ovaries), secondary sexual characteristics (salient voice, muscularity, buttocks, breasts), and biologic control of behavior (periodicity of sexual response predictability of life history from onset of puberty), as well as in androgen levels and sexual attitudes.[1]

This passage from the *Journal of Research in Personality* was written by University of Western Ontario psychologist Philippe Rushton, who enjoys considerable controversy in Canadian academic circles and in the popular media. His thesis, articulated throughout his work, appropriates biological studies of the continuum of reproductive strategies of oysters through chimpanzees and posits that degree of "sexuality"—

Reprinted from *Asian American Sexualities: Dimensions of the Gay and Lesbian Experience* edited by Russell Leong (1996) by permission of the publisher, Routledge: New York and London.

interpreted as penis and vagina size, frequency of intercourse, buttock and lip size—correlates positively with criminality and sociopathic behavior and inversely with intelligence, health, and longevity. Rushton sees race as the determining factor and places East Asians (Rushton uses the word *Orientals*) on one end of the spectrum and blacks on the other. Since whites fall squarely in the middle, the position of perfect balance, there is no need for analysis, and they remain free of scrutiny.

Notwithstanding its profound scientific shortcomings, Rushton's work serves as an excellent articulation of a dominant discourse on race and sexuality in Western society—a system of ideas and reciprocal practices that originated in Europe simultaneously with (some argue as a conscious justification for[2]) colonial expansion and slavery. In the nineteenth century these ideas took on a scientific gloss with social Darwinism and eugenics. Now they reappear, somewhat altered, in psychology journals from the likes of Rushton. It is important to add that these ideas have also permeated the global popular consciousness. Anyone who has been exposed to Western television or advertising images, which is much of the world, will have absorbed this particular constellation of stereotyping and racial hierarchy. In Trinidad in the 1960s, on the outer reaches of the empire, everyone in my schoolyard was thoroughly versed in these "truths" about the races.

Historically, most organizing against racism has concentrated on fighting discrimination that stems from the intelligence-social behavior variable assumed by Rushton's scale. Discrimination based on perceived intellectual ability does, after all, have direct ramifications in terms of education and employment, and therefore for survival. Until recently, issues of gender and sexuality remained a low priority for those who claimed to speak for the communities.[3] But antiracist strategies that fail to subvert the race-gender status quo are of seriously limited value. Racism cannot be narrowly defined in terms of race hatred. Race is a factor in even our most intimate relationships.

The contemporary construction of race and sex as exemplified by Rushton has endowed black people, both men and women, with a threatening hypersexuality. Asians, on the other hand, are collectively seen as undersexed.[4] But here I want to make some crucial distinctions. First, in North America, stereotyping has focused almost exclusively on what recent colonial language designates as "Orientals"—that is East and southeast Asian peoples—as opposed to the "Orientalism" discussed by Edward Said, which

concerns the Middle East. This current, popular usage is based more on a perception of similar physical features—black hair, "slanted" eyes, high cheek bones, and so on—than through a reference to common cultural traits. South Asians, people whose backgrounds are in the Indian subcontinent and Sri Lanka, hardly figure at all in North American popular representations, and those few images are ostensibly devoid of sexual connotation.[5]

Second, within the totalizing stereotype of the "Oriental," there are competing and sometimes contradictory sexual associations based on nationality. So, for example, a person could be seen as Japanese and somewhat kinky, or Filipino and "available." The very same person could also be seen as "Oriental" and therefore sexless. In addition, the racial hierarchy revamped by Rushton is itself in tension with an earlier and only partially eclipsed depiction of *all* Asians as having an undisciplined and dangerous libido. I am referring to the writings of the early European explorers and missionaries, but also to antimiscegenation laws and such specific legislation as the 1912 Saskatchewan law that barred white women from employment in Chinese-owned business.

Finally, East Asian women figure differently from men both in reality and in representation. In "Lotus Blossoms Don't Bleed," Renee Tajima points out that in Hollywood films:

> There are two basic types: the Lotus Blossom Baby (a.k.a. China Doll, Geisha Girl, shy Polynesian beauty, et al.) and the Dragon Lady (Fu Manchu's various female relations, prostitutes, devious madames). . . . Asian women in film are, for the most part, passive figures who exist to serve men—as love interests for white men (re: Lotus Blossoms) or as partners in crime for men of their own kind (re: Dragon Ladies).[6]

Further:

> Dutiful creatures that they are, Asian women are often assigned the task of expendability in a situation of illicit love. . . . Noticeably lacking

is the portrayal of love relationships between Asian women and Asian men, particularly as lead characters.[7]

Because of their supposed passivity and sexual compliance, Asian women have been fetishized in dominant representation, and there is a large and growing body of literature by Asian women in the oppressiveness of these images. Asian men, however—at least since Sessue Hayakawa, who made a Hollywood career in the 1920s of representing the Asian man as sexual threat[8]—have been consigned to one of two categories: the egghead/wimp, or—in what may be analogous to the lotus blossom-dragon lady dichotomy—the kung fu master/ninja/samurai. He is sometimes dangerous, sometimes friendly, but almost always characterized by a desexualized Zen asceticism. So whereas, as Fanon tells us, "the Negro is eclipsed. He is turned into a penis. He *is* a penis,"[9] the Asian man is defined by a striking absence down there. And if Asian men have no sexuality, how can we have homosexuality?

Even as recently as the early 1980s, I remember having to prove my queer credentials before being admitted with other Asian men into a Toronto gay club. I do not believe it was a question of a color barrier. Rather, my friends and I felt that the doorman was genuinely unsure about our sexual orientation. We also felt that had we been white and dressed similarly, our entrance would have been automatic.[10]

Although a motto for the lesbian and gay movements has been "we are everywhere," Asians are largely absent from the images produced by both the political and the commercial sectors of the mainstream gay and lesbian communities. From the earliest articulation of the Asian gay and lesbian movements, a principal concern has therefore been visibility. In political organizing, the demand for a voice, or rather the demand to be heard, has largely been responded to by the problematic practice of "minority" representation on panels and boards.[11]

But since racism is a question of power and not of numbers, this strategy has often led to a dead-end tokenistic integration, failing to address the real imbalances.

Creating a space for Asian gay and lesbian representation has meant, among other things, deepening an understanding of what is at stake for Asians in coming out publicly.[12] As is the case for many other people of color and especially immigrants, our families and our ethnic communities are a rare source of affirmation in a racist society. In coming out, we risk (or feel that we risk) losing this support, though the ever-growing organizations of lesbian and gay Asians have worked against this process of cultural exile. In my own experience, the existence of a gay Asian community broke down the cultural schizophrenia in which I related on the one hand to a heterosexual family that affirmed my ethnic culture and, on the other, to a gay community that was predominantly white. Knowing that there was support also helped me come out to my family and further bridge the gap.

If we look at commercial gay sexual representation, it appears that the antiracist movements have had little impact: the images of men and male beauty are still of *white* men and *white* male beauty. These are the standards against which we compare both ourselves and often our brothers—Asian, black, native, and Latino.[13] Although other people's rejection (or fetishization) of us according to the established racial hierarchies may be experienced as oppressive, we are not necessarily moved to scrutinize our own desire and its relationship to the hegemonic image of the white man.[14]

In my lifelong vocation of looking for my penis, trying to fill in the visual void, I have come across only a handful of primary and secondary references to Asian male sexuality in North American representation. Even in my own video work, the stress has been on deconstructing sexual representation and only marginally on creating erotica. So I was very excited at the discovery of a Vietnamese American working in gay porn.

Having acted in six videotapes, Sum Yung Mahn is perhaps the only Asian to qualify as a gay porn "star." Variously known as Brad Troung or Sam or Sum Yung Mahn, he has worked for a number of different production studios. All of the tapes in which he appears are distributed through International Wavelength, a San Francisco–based mail order company whose catalog entries feature Asians in American, Thai, and Japanese productions. According to the owner of International Wavelength, about 90 percent of the Asian tapes are bought by white men, and the remaining 10 percent are purchased by Asians. But the number of Asian buyers is growing.

In examining Sum Yung Mahn's work, it is important to recognize the different strategies used for fitting an Asian actor into the traditionally white world of gay porn and how the terms of entry are determined by the perceived demands of an intended audience. Three tapes, each geared toward a specific erotic interest, illustrate these strategies.

Below the Belt (1985, directed by Philip St. John, California Dream Machine Productions), like most porn tapes, has an episodic structure. All the sequences involve the students and *sense* of an all-male karate *dojo*. The authenticity of the setting is proclaimed with the opening shots of a gym full of *gi*-clad, serious-faced young men going through their weapons exercises. Each of the main actors is introduced in turn; with the exception of the teacher, who has dark hair, all fit into the current porn conventions of Aryan, blond, shaved, good looks.[15] Moreover, since Sum Yung Mahn is not even listed in the opening credits, we can surmise that this tape is not targeted to an audience with any particular erotic interest in Asian men. Most gay video porn exclusively uses white actors; those tapes having the least bit of racial integration are pitched to the specialty market throughout outlets such as International Wavelength.[16] This visual apartheid stems, I assume, from an erroneous perception that the sexual appetites of gay men are exclusive and unchangeable.

A Karate dojo offers a rich opportunity to introduce Asian actors. One might imagine it as the gay Orientalist's dream project. But given the intended audience for this video, the erotic appeal of the dojo, except for the costumes and a few misplaced props (Taiwanese and Korean flags for a Japanese art form?) are completely appropriated into a white world.

The tape's action occurs in a gym, in the student's apartments, and in a garden. The one scene with Sum Yung Mahn is a dream sequence. Two students, Robbie and Stevie, are sitting in a locker room. Robbie confesses that he has been having strange dreams about Greg, their teacher. Cut to the dream sequence, which is coded by clouds of green smoke. Robbie is wearing a red headband with black markings suggesting script (if indeed they belong to an Asian language, they are not the Japanese or Chinese characters that one would expect). He is trapped in an elaborate snare. Enter a character in a black *ninja* mask, wielding a *nanchaku*. Robbie narrates: "I knew this evil samurai would kill me." The masked figure is menacingly running the nanchaku chain under Robbie's genitals when Greg, the teacher, appears and disposes of him. Robbie explains to Stevie in the locker room: "I knew that I owed him my life, and I knew I had to please him [long pause] in any way that he wanted." During that pause we cut back to the dream. Amid more puffs of smoke, Greg, carrying a man in his arms, approaches a low platform. Although Greg's back is toward the camera, we can see that the man is wearing the red headband that identifies him as Robbie. As Greg lays him down, we see that Robbie has "turned Japanese"! It's Sum Yung Mahn.

Greg fucks Sum Yung Mahn, who is always face down. The scene constructs anal intercourse for the Asian Robbie as an act of submission, not of pleasure: unlike other scenes of anal intercourse in the tape, for example, there is no dubbed dialogue on the order of "Oh yeah . . . fuck me harder!" but merely ambiguous groans. Without coming, Greg leaves. A group of (white) men wearing Japanese outfits encircle the platform, and Asian Robbie, or "the Oriental boy," as he is listed in the final credits, turns to lie on his back. He sucks a cock, licks someone's balls. The other men come all over his body; he comes. The final shot of the sequence zooms in to a close-up of Sum Yung Mahn's headband, which dissolves to a similar close-up of Robbie wearing the same headband, emphasizing that the two actors represent one character.

We now cut back to the locker room. Robbie's story has made Stevie horny. He reaches into Robbie's pants, pulls out his penis, and sex follows. In his Asian manifestation, Robbie is fucked and sucks others off (Greek passive/French active/bottom). His passivity is pronounced, and he is never shown other than prone. As a white man, his role is completely reversed: he is at first sucked off by Stevie, and then he fucks him (Greek active/French passive/top). Neither of Robbie's manifestations veers from his prescribed role.

To a greater extent than most other gay porn tapes, *Below the Belt* is directly about power. The hierarchical dojo setting is mild for its evocation of dominance and submission. With the exception of one very romantic sequence midway through the tape, most of the actors stick to their defined roles of top or bottom. Sex, especially anal sex, as punishment is a recurrent image. In this genre of gay pornography, the role-playing in the dream sequence is perfectly apt. What is significant, however, is how race figures into the equation. In a tape that appropriates emblems of Asian power (karate), the only place for a real Asian actor is as a caricature of passivity. Sum Yung Mahn does not portray an Asian, but rather the liberalization of a metaphor, so that by being passive, Robbie actually becomes "Oriental." At a more practical level, the device of the dream also allows the producers to introduce an element of the mysterious, the exotic, without disrupting the racial

status quo of the rest of the tape. Even in the dream sequence, Sum Yung Mahn is at the center of the frame as spectacle, having minimal physical involvement with the men around him. Although the sequence ends with his climax, he exists for the pleasure of others.

Richard Dyer, writing about gay porn, states that:

> although the pleasure of anal sex (that is, of being anally fucked) is represented, the narrative is never organized around the desire to be fucked, but around the desire to ejaculate (whether or not following from anal intercourse). Thus, although a level of public representation gay men may be thought of as deviant and disruptive of masculine norms because we assert the pleasure of being fucked and the eroticism of the anus, in our pornography this takes a back seat.[17]

Although Tom Waugh's amendment to this argument—that anal pleasure is represented in individual sequences[18]—also holds true for *Below the Belt*, as a whole the power of the penis and the pleasure of ejaculation are clearly the narrative's organizing principles. As with the vast majority of North American tapes featuring Asians, the problem is not the representation of anal pleasure per se, but rather that the narratives privilege the penis while always assigning the Asian the role of bottom; Asian and anus are conflated. In the case of Sum Yung Mahn, being fucked may well be his personal sexual preference. But the fact remains that there are very few occasions in North American video porn in which an Asian fucks a white man, so few, in fact, that International Wavelength promotes the tape *Studio X* (1986) with the blurb "Sum Yung Mahn makes history as the first Asian who fucks a non-Asian."[19]

Although I agree with Waugh that in gay as opposed to straight porn "the spectator's positions in relation to the representations are open and in flux,"[20] this observation applies only when all the participants are white. Race introduces another dimension that may serve to close down some of this mobility. This is not to suggest that the experience of gay men of color with this kind of sexual representation is the same as that of heterosexual women with regard to the gendered gaze of straight porn. For one thing, Asian gay men are men. We can therefore physically experience the pleasures depicted on the screen, since we too have erections and ejaculations and can experience anal penetration. A shifting identification may occur despite the racially defined roles, and most gay Asian men in North America are used to obtaining pleasure from all-white pornography. This, of course, goes hand in hand with many problems of self-image and sexual identity. Still, I have been struck by the unanimity with which gay Asian men I have met, from all over this continent as well as from Asia, immediately identify and resist these representations. Whenever I mention the topic of Asian actors in American porn, the first question I am asked is whether the Asian is simply shown getting fucked.

Asian Knights (1985, directed by Ed Sung, William Richhe Productions), the second tape I want to consider, has an Asian producer–director and a predominantly Asian cast. In its first scenario, two Asian men, Brad and Rick, are seeing a white psychiatrist because they are unable to have sex with each other:

> **Rick:** We never have sex with other Asians. We usually have sex with Caucasian guys.
>
> **Counselor:** Have you had the opportunity to have sex together?
>
> **Rick:** Yes, a coupla times, but we never get going.

Homophobia, like other forms of oppression, is seldom dealt with in gay video porn. With the exception of safe sex tapes that attempt a rare blend of the pedagogical with the pornographic, social or political issues are not generally associated with the erotic. It is therefore unusual to see one of the favored discussion topics for gay

Asian consciousness-raising groups employed as a sex fantasy in *Asian Knights*. The desexualized image of Asian men that I have described has seriously affected our relationships with one another, and often gay Asian men find it difficult to see each other beyond the terms of platonic friendship or competition, to consider other Asian men as lovers.

True to the conventions of porn, minimal counseling from the psychiatrist convinces Rick and Brad to shed their clothes. Immediately sprouting erections, they proceed to have sex. But what appears to be an assertion of gay Asian desire is quickly derailed. As Brad and Rick make love on the couch, the camera cross-cuts to the psychiatrist looking on from an armchair. The rhetoric of the editing suggests that we are observing the two Asian men from his point of view. Soon the white man takes off his clothes and joins in. He immediately takes up a position at the center of the action—and at the center of the frame. What appeared to be a "conversion fantasy" for gay Asian desire was merely a ruse. Brad and Rick's temporary mutual absorption really occurs to establish the superior sexual draw of the white psychiatrist, a stand-in for the white male viewer, who is the real sexual subject of the tape. And the question of Asian–Asian desire, though presented as the main narrative force of the sequence, is deflected, or rather reframed from a white perspective. Sex between the two Asian men in this sequence can be related somewhat to heterosexual sex in some gay porn films, such as those produced by the Gage brothers. In *Heatstroke* (1982), for example, sex with a woman is used to establish the authenticity of the straight man who is about to be seduced into gay sex. It dramatizes the significance of the conversion from the sanctioned object of desire, underscoring the power of the gay man to incite desire in his socially defined superior. It is also tied up with the fantasies of (female) virginity and conquest in Judeo-Christian and other patriarchal societies. The therapy session sequence of *Asian Knights* also suggests parallels to representations of lesbians in straight porn, representations that are not meant to eroticize women loving women, but rather to titillate and empower the sexual ego of the heterosexual male viewer.

Asian Knights is organized to sell representations of Asians to white men. Unlike Sum Yung Mahn in *Below the Belt*, the actors are therefore more expressive and sexually assertive, as often the seducers as the seduced. But though the roles shift during the predominantly oral sex, the Asians remain passive in anal intercourse, except that they are now shown to want it! How much this assertion of agency represents a step forward remains a question.

Even in the one sequence of *Asian Knights* in which the Asian actor fucks the white man, the scenario privileges the pleasure of the white man over that of the Asian. The sequence begins with the Asian reading a magazine. When the white man (played by porn star Eric Stryker) returns home from a hard day at the office, the waiting Asian asks how his day went, undresses him (even taking off his socks), and proceeds to massage his back.[21] The Asian man acts the role of the mythologized geisha of "the good wife" as fantasized in the mail-order bride business. And, in fact, the "house boy" is one of the most persistent white fantasies about Asian men. The fantasy is also a reality in many Asian countries where economic imperialism gives foreigners, whatever their race, the pick of handsome men in financial need. The accompanying cultural imperialism grants status to those Asians with white lovers. White men who for various reasons, especially age, are deemed unattractive in their own countries, suddenly find themselves elevated and desired.

From the opening shot of painted lotus blossoms on a screen to the shot of a Japanese garden that separates the episodes, from the Chinese pop music to the chinoiserie in the apartment, there is a conscious attempt in *Asian Knights* to evoke a particular atmosphere.[22] Self-

conscious "Oriental" signifiers are part and parcel of a colonial fantasy—and reality—the empowers one kind of gay man over another. Though I have known Asian men in dependent relations with older, wealthier white men, as an erotic fantasy the house boy scenario tends to work one way. I know of no scenarios of Asian men and white house boys. It is not the representation of the fantasy that offends, or even the fantasy itself, rather the uniformity with which these narratives reappear and the uncomfortable relationship they have to real social conditions.

International Skin (1985, directed by William Richhe, N'wayvo Richhe Productions), as its name suggests, features a Latino, a black man, Sum Yung Mahn, and a number of white actors. Unlike the other tapes I have discussed, there are no "Oriental" devices. And although Sum Yung Mahn and all the men of color are inevitable fucked (without reciprocating), there is mutual sexual engagement between the white and non-white characters.

In this tape Sum Yung Mahn is Brad, a film student making a movie for his class. Brad is the narrator, and the film begins with a self-reflexive "head and shoulders" shot of Sum Yung Mahn explaining the scenario. The film we are watching supposedly represents Brad's point of view. But here again the tape is not targeted to black, Asian, or Latino men; though Brad introduces all of these men as his friends, no two men of color ever meet on screen. Men of color are not invited to participate in the internationalism that is being sold, except through identification with white characters. This tape illustrates how an agenda of integration becomes problematic if it frames the issue solely in terms of black–white, Asian–white mixing; it perpetuates a system of white-centeredness.

The gay Asian viewer is not constructed as sexual subject in any of this work—not on the screen, not as a viewer. I may find Sum Yung Mahn attractive, I may desire his body, but I am always aware that he is not meant for me. I may lust after Eric Stryker and imagine myself as the

Asian who is having sex with him, but the role the Asian plays in the scene with him is demeaning. It is not that there is anything wrong with the image of servitude per se, but rather that it is one of the few fantasy scenarios in which we figure, and we are always in the role of servant.

Are there then no pleasures for an Asian viewer? The answer to this question is extremely complex. There is first of all no essential Asian viewer. The race of the person viewing says nothing about how race figures in his or her own desires. Uniracial white representations in porn may not in themselves present a problem in addressing many gay Asian men's desires. But the issue is not simply that porn may deny pleasures to some gay Asian men. We also need to examine what role the pleasure of porn plays in securing a consensus about race and desirability that ultimately works to our disadvantage.

Though the sequences I have focused on in the preceding examples are those in which the discourses about Asian sexuality are most clearly articulated, they do not define the totality of depiction in these tapes. Much of the time the actors merely reproduce or attempt to reproduce the conventions of pornography. The fact that, with the exception of Sum Yung Mahn, they rarely succeed—because of their body type, because Midwestern-cowboy-porn dialect with Vietnamese intonation is just a bit incongruous, because they groan or gyrate just a bit too much—more than anything brings home the relative rigidity of the genre's codes. There is little seamlessness here. There are times, however, when the actors appear neither as simulated whites nor as symbolic others. There are several moments in *International Skin*, for example, in which the focus shifts from the genitals to hands caressing a body; these moments feel to me more "genuine." I do not mean this in the sense of an essential Asian sexuality, but rather a moment is captured in which the actor stops pretending. He does not stop acting, but he stops pretending to be a white porn star. I find

myself focusing on moments like these, in which the racist ideology of the text seems to be temporarily suspended or rather eclipsed by the erotic power of the moment.

In "Pornography and the Doubleness of Sex for Women," Joanna Russ writes:

> **Sex is ecstatic, autonomous and lovely for women. Sex is violent, dangerous and unpleasant for women. I don't mean a dichotomy (i.e., two kinds of women or even two kinds of sex) but rather a continuum in which no one's experience is wholly positive or negative.**[35]

Gay Asian men are men and therefore not normally victims of the rape, incest, or other sexual harassment to which Russ is referring. However, there is a kind of doubleness, of ambivalence, in the way that Asian men experience contemporary North American gay communities. The "ghetto," the mainstream gay movement, can be a place of freedom and sexual identity. But it is also a site of racial, cultural, *and* sexual alienation sometimes more pronounced than that in straight society. For me sex is a source of pleasure, but also a site of humiliation and pain. Released from the social constraints against expressing overt racism in public, the intimacy of sex can provide my (non-Asian) partner an opening for letting me know my place—sometimes literally, as when after we come, he turns over and asks where I come from.[24] Most gay Asian men I know have similar experiences.

This is just one reality that differentiates the experiences and therefore the political priorities of gay Asians and, I think, other gay men of color from those of white men. For one thing we cannot afford to take a libertarian approach. Porn can be an active agent in representing *and* reproducing a sex–race status quo. We cannot attain a healthy alliance without coming to terms with these differences.

The barriers that impede pornography from providing representations of Asian men that are erotic and politically palatable (as opposed to correct) are similar to those that inhibit the Asian documentary, the Asian feature, the Asian experimental film and videotape. We are seen as too peripheral, not commercially visible—not the general audience. *Looking for Langston* (1988),[25] which is the first film I have seen that affirms rather than appropriates the sexuality of black gay men, was produced under exceptional economic circumstances that freed it from the constraints of the marketplace.[26] Should we call for an independent gay Asian pornography? Perhaps I do, in a utopian sort of way, though I feel that the problems in North America's porn conventions are manifold and go beyond the question of race. There is such a limited vision of what constitutes the erotic.

One major debate about race and representation has shifted from an emphasis on the image to a discussion of appropriation and control of production and distribution—who gets to produce the work. But as we have seen in the case of *Asian Knights*, the race of the producer is no automatic guarantee of "consciousness" about these issues or of a different product. Much depends on who is constructed as the audience for the work. In any case, it is not surprising that under capitalism, finding my penis may ultimately be a matter of dollars and cents.

Notes

I would like to thank Tim McCaskell and Helen Lee for their ongoing criticism and comments, as well as Jeff Nunokawa and Douglas Crimp for their invaluable suggestions in converting the original spoken presentation into a written text. Finally, I would like to extend my gratitude to Bad Object-Choices for inviting me to participate in "How Do I Look?"

1. Phillipe Rushton and Anthony F. Bogaert, University of Western Ontario, "Race versus Social Class Difference in Sexual Behavior: A Follow-up Test of the r/K Dimension," *Journal of Research in Personality* 22 (1988): 259.

2. Feminists of color have long pointed out that racism is phrased differently for men and women. Nevertheless, since it is usually heterosexual (and often middle-class) males whose voices are validated by the power structure, it is their interests that are taken up as "representing" the communities. See Barbara Smith, "Toward a Black Feminist Criticism," in *All the Women Are White, All the Blacks Are Men, But Some of Us Are Brave: Black Women's Studies* (Old Westbury, N.Y.: The Feminist Press, 1982), 182.

4. The mainstream "leadership" within Asian communities often colludes with the myth of the model minority and the reassuring desexualization of Asian people.

5. In Britain, however, more race–sex stereotypes of South Asians exist. Led by artists such as Pratibha Parmar, Sunil Gupta, and Hanif Kureishi, there is also a growing and already significant body of work by South Asians themselves, which takes up questions of sexuality.

6. Renee Tajima, "Lotus Blossoms Don't Bleed: Images of Asian Women," *Anthologies of Asian American Film and Video* (New York: A distribution project of Third World Newsreel, 1984), 28.

7. Ibid, 29.

8. See Stephen Gong, "Zen Warrior of the Celluloid (Silent) Years: The Art of Sessue Hayakawa," *Bridge* 8, no. 2 (Winter 1982–83): 37–41.

9. Frantz Fanon, *Black Skin, White Masks* (London: Paladin, 1970), 120. For a reconsideration of this statement in the light of contemporary black gay issues, see Kobena Mercer, "Imaging the Black Man's Sex," in *Photography/Politics: Two*, ed. Pat Holland, Jo Spence, and Simon Watney (London: Comedia/Methuen, 1987); reprinted in *Male Order: Unwrapping Masculinity*, ed. Rowena Chapman and Jonathan Rutherford (London: Lawrence and Wishart, 1988), 141.

10. I do not think that this could happen in today's Toronto, which now has the second largest Chinese community on the continent. Perhaps it would not have happened in San Francisco. But I still believe that there is an onus on gay Asians and other gay people of color to prove our homosexuality.

11. The term *minority* is misleading. Racism is not a matter of numbers but of power. This is especially clear in situations where people of color constitute actual majorities, as in most former European colonies. At the same time, I feel that none of the current terms are really satisfactory and that too much time spent on the politics of "naming" can in the end be diversionary.

12. To organize effectively with lesbian and gay Asians, we must reject self-righteous condemnation of "closetedness" and see coming out more as a process or a goal, rather than as a prerequisite for participation in the movement.

13. Racism is available to be used by anyone. The conclusion that—because racism = power + prejudice—only white people can be racist is Eurocentric and simply wrong. Individuals have varying degrees and different sources of power, depending on the given moment in a shifting context. This does not contradict the fact that, in contemporary North American society, racism is generally organized around white supremacy.

14. From simple observation, I feel safe in saying that most gay Asian men in North America hold white men as their idealized sexual partners. However, I am not trying to construct an argument for determinism, and there are a number of outstanding problems that are not easily answered by current analyses of power. What of the experience of Asians who are attracted to men of color, including other Asians? What about white men who prefer Asians sexually? How and to what extent is desire articulated in terms of race as opposed to body type or other attributes? To what extent is sexual attraction exclusive and/or changeable, and can it be consciously programmed? These questions are all politically loaded, as they parallel and impact the debates between essentialists and social constructionists on the nature of homosexuality itself. They are also emotionally charged, in that sexual choice involving race has been a basis for moral judgment.

15. See Richard Dyer, *Heavenly Bodies: Film Stars and Society* (New York: St. Martin's Press, 1986). In his chapter on Marilyn Monroe, Dyer writes extensively on the relationship between blondness, whiteness, and desirability.

16. Print porn is somewhat more racially integrated, as are the new safe sex tapes—by the Gay Men's Health Crisis, for example—produced in a political and pedagogical rather than a commercial context.

17. Richard Dyer, "Coming to Terms," *Jump Cut*, no. 30 (March 1985): 28.

18. Tom Waugh, "Men's Pornography, Gay vs. Straight," *Jump Cut*, no. 30 (March 1985): 31.

19. *International Wavelength News* 2, No. 1 (January 1991).

20. Tom Waugh, "Men's Pornography, Gay vs. Straight," 33.

21. It seems to me that the undressing here is organized around the pleasure of the white man in being served. This is in contrast to the undressing scenes, in, say, James Bond films, in which the narrative is organized around undressing as an act of revealing the woman's body, an indicator of sexual conquest.

22. Interestingly, the gay video porn from Japan and Thailand that I have seen has none of this Oriental coding. Asianness is not taken up as a sign but is taken for granted as a setting for the narrative.

23. Joanna Russ, "Pornography and the Doubleness of Sex for Women," *Jump Cut*, no. 32 (April 1986): 39.

24. Though this is a common enough question in our postcolonial, urban environments, when asked of Asians it often reveals two agendas: first, the assumption that all Asians are newly arrived immigrants and, second, a fascination with difference and sameness. Although we (Asians) all supposedly look alike, there are specific characteristics and stereotypes associated with each particular ethnic group. The inability to tell us apart underlies the inscrutability attributed to Asians. This "inscrutability" took on sadly ridiculous proportions when during World War II the Chinese were issued badges so that white Canadians could distinguish them from "the enemy."

25. Isaac Julien (director), *Looking for Langston* (United Kingdom: Sankofa Film and Video, 1988).

26. For more on the origins of the black film and video workshops in Britain, see Jim Pines, "The Cultural Context of Black British Cinema," in *Blackframes: Critical Perspectives on Black Independent Cinema*, ed. Mybe B. Cham and Clair Andrade-Watkins (Cambridge, Mass.: MIT Press, 1988), 26.

A re men still taking seriously their responsibilities as family breadwinners? Are today's men sharing more the family housework and childcare than those in previous generations? The answers to these questions are complex, and often depend on which men we are talking about and what we mean when we say "family."

Many male workers long ago won a "family wage," and with it made an unwritten pact to share that wage with a wife and children. But today, as Barbara Ehrenreich argues in her influential book *The Hearts of Men*, increasing numbers of men are revolting against this traditional responsibility to share their wages, thus contributing to the rapidly growing impoverishment of women and children. Ehrenreich may be correct, at least with respect to the specific category of men who were labeled "yuppies" in the 1980s. But if we are looking at the growing impoverishment of women and children among poor, work-

PART NINE

Men in Families

ing-class, and minority families, the causes have more to do with dramatic shifts in the structure of the economy—including skyrocketing unemployment among young black males—than they do with male irresponsibility. Increasing numbers of men have no wage to share with a family.

But how about the New Dual-Career Family? Can we look to this emerging family type as a model of egalitarianism? Arlie Hochschild's research indicates that the growth of the two-career family has not significantly altered the division of labor in the household. Women still, she argues, work a "second shift" when they return home from their paid-work job.

One of the most significant issues of the 1990s is fatherhood. Are men becoming more nurturing and caring fathers, developing skills as the men do in Hollywood films such as *Three Men and a Baby*, or simply loving their children more than life itself, as they do in *Ransom*, *Jingle All the Way*, and so many

Photo courtesy of Sue Sattel.

others? The articles in this section expand the debate about fatherhood, recognizing the variety of father-hoods evidenced by different groups of men, such as gay fathers (Brian Miller), Chicano fathers (Scott Coltrane), and black fathers (John L. and Julia B. McAdoo). Finally, the article by Carl E. Bertoia and Janice Drakich examines the contemporary fathers' rights movement, which seeks to encourage men to become more nurturing and involved fathers, but often at the legal and economic expense of women.

47

ARTICLE

Brian Miller

Life-Styles of Gay Husbands and Fathers

The words "gay husband" and "gay father" are often regarded as contradictions in terms. This notion is hinted at in Anita Bryant's widely quoted non sequitur, "Homosexuals recruit because they cannot reproduce." Researchers estimate, however, that in America there are six million gay husbands and fathers (Bozett, 1987; Schulenberg, 1985). Why do these men marry and have children? How do they organize their lives? What are their difficulties and joys as a consequence of their behavior?

To address these questions, 50 gay husbands and fathers were contacted in 1976 by means of multiple-source chain-referral samples. At first interview, 24 of the men were living with their wives; three years later at the second interview, only three had intact marriages. Approximately two-thirds of the respondents have been followed to the present and all of them are now separated (Humphreys and Miller, 1980a). To show the modal developments in gay husbands' and fathers' life-styles, the data are organized along a four-point continuum: Covert Behav-

ior, Marginal Involvement, Transformed Participation, and Open Endorsement.

Covert Behavior

Early in adult life, gay husbands and fathers tend to regard their homosexual feelings as nothing more than genital urges. They are reluctant to refer to either themselves or their behavior as gay: "I hate labels" is a common response to questions about sexual orientation. These men have unstable self-concepts—one day thinking they are homosexual and another day thinking they are not. Their reluctance to label their same-sex activity as homosexual is not because they hate labels per se; indeed they strive to present themselves to others under a heterosexual label. Rather, they dislike a label that calls attention to behaviors they would prefer to forget.

Premarital homosexual experiences are often explained away with "It's only a phase" or "God, was I drunk last night!" These men report such activities prior to marriage as arranging heterosexual double-date situations in which they would perform coitus in the back seat of the car, for example, while fantasizing

Revised and updated from an article in *Gay Men: The Sociology of Male Homosexuality* by Martin P. Levine. New York: Harper & Row, 1979.

about the male in the front seat. Others report collaborating with a buddy to share a female prostitute. These ostensibly heterosexual acts allowed the men to buttress their sense of heterosexuality while gratifying homosexual urges. During the premarital period, respondents discounted gay life-styles and romanticized heterosexual family living as the only way to achieve the stable home life, loyal companionship, and fatherhood they desired.

These men married in good faith, thinking they could overcome their gay desires; they did not believe they were deceiving their spouses. In fact, most men broached the issue of their homosexual feelings to their wives before marriage, but the information was usually conveyed in an oblique manner and downplayed as inconsequential. This kept their future wives from thinking that they might be marrying homosexuals. Wives' denials of their husbands' homosexuality were further facilitated by the fact that half the women, at their nuptials, were pregnant by the men they were marrying.

In the early years of marriage, high libido provided husbands with easy erections for coitus. Respondents report, however, that this situation tended to deteriorate shortly after the birth of the first child. Increasingly, they found themselves fantasizing about gay erotica during coitus.

Marriage engulfs the men in a heterosexual role, making them marginal to the gay world. Their social isolation from others who share their sexual interests burdens them with "I'm-the-only-one-in-the-world" feelings. These men, realizing their behavior is inconsistent with their heterosexual reputation, try to reduce their anxiety and guilt by compartmentalizing gay and nongay worlds. One respondent said: "I never walk in the door without an airtight excuse of where I've been." Some men avoid the strain of remembering stories by intimidating the wife into silence: "She knows better than to question my whereabouts. I tell her, 'I get home when I get home; no questions asked.'" In these re-

spects, respondents have parallels to their adulterous heterosexual counterparts (Libby and Whitehurst, 1977).

Extramarital sex for respondents usually consists of clandestine, impersonal encounters in parks, tearooms, or highway rest stops, with hitchhikers or male hustlers. (Regarding this, single gays sometimes comment, "Married gays give the rest of us a bad name.") Occasionally, furtiveness itself becomes eroticized, making the men sexually dysfunctional in calmer contexts. Recreational, gay scenes such as dances, parties, and gay organizations are not used by respondents, primarily because they dread discovery and subsequent marital dissolution. Many are further limited by fears that their jobs would be threatened, by lack of geographical access to gay institutions, or by religious scruples. In fact, these men are largely unaware of gay social events in their communities and have little idea of how to participate in them. They tend to be ideologically ambivalent about the gay world, sometimes thinking of it as exotic, and other times condemning it as "superficial, unstable, full of blackmail and violence." Given their exposure to only the impersonal homosexual underground, and not to loving gay relationships, their negative perception is somewhat justified. As long as they remain marginal to the gay world, the likelihood of their participation in safe, fulfilling gay relationships remains minimal (Miller and Humphreys, 1980).

Some men regard their homosexual desires not as an orientation, but as a compulsion: "I don't want to do these things, but I'm driven to do them." Other accounts that explain away their homosexual behavior, emphasize its nonseriousness, and minimize its consequences include (1) "I might be okay if my wife learned to give good blow jobs." (2) "I only go out for it when I'm drunk or depressed." (3) "I go to the truck-stop and meet someone. We're just a couple of horny married guys relieving ourselves. That's not sex. [It] doesn't threaten my marriage like adultery would." (4) "Sex with men is a minor aspect of my life that I refuse to let outweigh more important things."

The respondent who gave this last account also presented conflicting evidence. He spent time, effort, and anxiety in rearranging his schedule to accommodate sex, spending money on his car and fuel to search for willing men, constructing intricate stories to fool work associates and family, and buying his wife penance gifts. He also experienced near misses with police and gay bashers. Still, he viewed all this as only a "minor aspect" of his life.

Another rationalization is "I'm not really homosexual since I don't care if it's a man, woman or dog that's licking my cock. All I want is a hole." Further questioning, however, made clear that this respondent was not looking for just any available orifice. He stated that it was equally important that he persuade the most attractive man available to fellate him.

Another account is the "Eichmann dodge." Men may claim, like Eichmann, that they are the victims of other men's desire, inadvertently caught up and swept along by the events, thereby absolving themselves of responsibility. Men stating this rationalization, however, are often skilled at seducing others into making the first move. Some gay husbands and fathers claim that they limit themselves to one special "friendship" and that no one else of their sex could excite them. If they think of homosexuality at all, they conceive it as promiscuous behavior done by degenerates, not by people like themselves who are loyal and who look conventional.

These accounts help respondents deny homosexuality while practicing it. They find it difficult to simultaneously see themselves as worthwhile persons and as homosexuals, and to reconcile their masculine self-image with the popular image of gays as effeminate. The most they can acknowledge is that they get together with other men to ejaculate and that they fantasize about men during sex with their wives. In spite of their rationalizations, however, these men report considerable anxiety and guilt about maintaining their compartmentalized double lives.

Respondents are reluctant to rate their marriages as "happy," typically referring to them as "duties." The ambivalence is expressed by one who said: "My wife is a good person, but it's funny, I can't live with this marriage and I can't live without it." Respondents report conflict with wives who object to the disproportionate time these men spend away from home, neglecting parental responsibilities. The men view alternatives to marriage as limited, not seeing life in the gay world as a viable option. They find it difficult to talk about their children and express guilt that their work and sex schedules do not allow them to spend as much time with their children as they would like. Nevertheless, most of the men report that their children are the main reason for remaining married: "In this horrible marriage, [the children] are the consolation prize."

Marginal Involvement

Respondents at this point on the continuum engage in homosexual behavior and have a gay self-identity. However, these men are marginal to the gay community since they have heterosexual public identities, and are often living with their wives. Still, they are much more comfortable with their homoerotic desires than are those in the Covert Behavior group and are more disclosing about their sexual orientation to other gays.

Compared with men in the previous group, Marginally Involved respondents have an expanded repertoire of sexual outlets. They sometimes compile telephone-number lists of sex partners and have limited involvement with small networks of gay friends. The men maintain secrecy by using post office boxes or separate office phones for gay-related business. Fake identities and names may be constructed to prevent identification by sexual partners. Employing male "masseurs" or maintaining a separate apartment for gay sex provide other relatively safe outlets. Consequently, these men are less likely to encounter police entrapment or gay bashers. Gay bars are somewhat inaccessible since they often start too late, and the men cannot regularly find excuses for extended absences from home. Some men resort to lunch-hour or presupper "quickies" at the baths.

In spite of these measures, respondents report many facade-shattering incidents with heterosexuals. Such difficulties include being caught on the street with a gay friend whose presence cannot be explained, blurting out praise about an event, then remembering it was attended with a gay friend, not one's wife, and transferring body lice or a venereal disease form a hustler to the wife, an especially dangerous occurrence in this time of AIDS (Pearson, 1986). Many respondents, however, continue to deny wives' knowledge about their homosexuality: "I don't think my wife really knows. She's only mentioned it a couple of times, and only when she was too drunk to know what she was saying."

Men who travel as part of their business or who have loosely structured working hours enjoy relative freedom. For them, absences and sexual incidents may be more easily covered. A minority of men, specifically those in artistic and academic fields, are able to mix their heterosexual and homosexual worlds. Their circle is that of the relatively wealthy and tolerant in which the epithet "perversion" is replaced by the more neutral "eccentricity," and variant behavior is accepted as long as the man is discreet and does not "rub the wife's nose in it." Several respondents socialize openly with similarly situated men or with gay sex partners whom wives and others ostensibly know as merely work assistants or friends of the family.

Because Marginally Involved respondents are "out" to some audiences and not to others, they sometimes resemble, as one man said, "a crazy quilt of contradictions." This is emphasized by playing word games with questioners or with those who try to penetrate their defenses. Playing the role of the eccentric and giving mixed messages provide a smokescreen for their emotional whereabouts from both gays and nongays.

This adjustment, however, is tenuous and respondents are often ambivalent about maintaining their marriages. They fantasize about life as a gay single, and entertain ideas of divorce. The guilt these respondents experience is sometimes reflected in what might be called Santa Claus behavior. They shower their children—and sometimes their wives—with expensive gifts to counteract feelings that they have done a terrible thing to their family by being homosexual: "It's the least I can do for having ruined their chance to grow up in a normal home." Using credit cards to manage guilt has many of these men in serious debt and laboring as workaholics.

Like men in the first category, these men regret that performing their breadwinner, husband, and homosexual roles leaves little time for the father role. Nevertheless, they are reluctant to leave their marriages, fearing permanent separation from their children. They also fear community stigma, ambivalently regard the gay world, and are unwilling to endure the decreased standard of living necessitated by divorce.

Over time, it becomes increasingly difficult for these men to reconcile their discordant identities as husband and as homosexual. Although some are able to routinize compartmentalization, others find sustaining the necessary maneuvers for secrecy to be not worth it. Conspiracies of silence and denial within the families become strained, if not transparent. Respondents tend to seek closure by communicating, directly and indirectly, their orientational needs to wives and by becoming more explicit in their methods of making gay contacts. Others are exposed by vice arrests or by being victimized by men they solicit. Most wives are surprised by the direct confrontation. Respondents are surprised that their wives are surprised since respondents may have thought their wives already knew, and tacitly accepted it. Initially wives often react with disbelief, revulsion, and anger: "I feel betrayed." This frequently gives way to a feeling of couple solidarity, that "we can conquer the problem together." When this is the adaptation, respondents do not come out of the closet so much as take their wives into the closet with them.

Couples try a variety of techniques to shore up the marriages. Respondents may seek therapy to "cure" their homosexuality. Some men generously offer wives the freedom to experience extramarital affairs, too, although it appears this is done mostly to relieve respondents' guilt since they know that wives are unlikely to take them up on the offer. When wives do not put the offer to the test, respondents further console their guilt by interpreting this as evidence that the wives are "frigid" or low in "sex drive," although data from the wives dispute this characterization (Hays and Samuels, 1988).

Some couples try instituting new sexual arrangements: a *ménage à trois,* or the husband is allowed out one night a week with gay friends. In the former interaction, wives tend to report feeling "used" and, in the latter, men tend to report feeling they are on a "leash."

Sexual conflicts spill into other domestic areas. Tardiness or missed appointments lead to wives' suspicions and accusations and general marital discord. One man calls this compromise period "white-knuckle heterosexuality." By negotiating ground rules that reinstate partial denial and by intellectualizing the situation, some couples maintain for years the compromise period. This uneasy truce ends if ground rules are repeatedly violated and when the wife realizes (1) that her husband finds men sexier than herself, (2) that he is unalterably gay, (3) that her primary place as object of permanent affection is challenged, and (4) that she has alternatives and can cope without the marriage. Wives gradually come to resent romanceless marriages with men who would rather make love to another man, and the homosexual husbands come to resent, as one man said, being "stifled in a nuptial closet."

Couples who remain married after disclosure tend not to have rejected divorce, but rather to have an indefinite postponement of it: "After the children leave home." "After the finances are in order." Other considerations that keep the couples together include religious beliefs, family pressure, wives' dependence, and the perceived nonviability of the gay world.

In most cases, the immediate impetus for ending the marriage is the husband's establishment of a love relationship with another man. As such relationships intensify, men begin to reconstruct the gay world as favorable for effecting companionship and social stability. It is usually wives, however, who take action to terminate the marriages. Painful as this experience is, it somewhat eases the men's guilt for causing marital dissolution.

Transformed Participation

Respondents who reach this point on the continuum engage in homosexual behavior and have self-identities—and to a limited extent, public identities—that reflect acceptance of their behavior. These men generally have come out as gay and left their wives.

Acculturation into the gay world involves three areas of concern for respondents: (1) disadvantage of advanced age and late arrival on the scene, (2) the necessity of learning new gay social definitions and skills, and (3) the need to reconcile prior fantasies to the realities of the gay world. Once respondents no longer live with wives and children, they begin to increase their contacts with the gay world and their marginality to it decreases. They may now subscribe to gay publications, join gay religious congregations, and go to gay social and political clubs and private gay parties. They experience a rapid expansion of gay consciousness and skills and take steps to form close friendships with others of their sexual orientation.

Moving out of the closet, these men report a stabilization of self-concept and a greater sense of psychological well-being. Their attitudes toward homoerotic behavior become more relaxed and better integrated into their everyday lives. Most experience a change in body image, exemplified by improved physical fitness and increased care with their appearance. Many report the elimination of nervous and psychosomatic disorders such as ulcers, excessive fatigue, and back aches, as well as substance abuse.

These respondents' sexual orientation tends to be known by significant others with two exceptions: their employers and children. Secrecy sometimes exists with employers since respondents believe the legal system does not protect their interests should they be dismissed for being gay (Levine, 1981).

Relatively little openness about homosexuality also exists with these respondents' children. Typically, only older children (if any) are told, and it is not considered a topic for general discussion. There is fear that, if the man's gayness becomes known in the community, his employer might find out or his ex-wife might become irked and deny him child visits. Successful legal appeal for gay people in such matters is difficult, a situation these men perceive as legally sanctioned blackmail.

In line with this, most respondents, rather than living with their children, have visiting schedules with them. They do not have the financial resources either to persuade their ex-wives to relinquish the children or to hire care for them while devoting time to their own careers.

Men who are able to terminate marriages without their spouse's discovering their homosexuality avoid this problem. However, fear of subsequent exposure and loss of children through a new court order remains and prompts some men to stay partially closeted even after marital

dissolution. In spite of these fears, the degree of passing and compartmentalization of gay and nongay worlds is much less for men at this point on the continuum than for those who are Covert and Marginal.

Open Endorsement

Respondents who reach this point on the continuum not only engage in homosexual behavior and have a self-identity reflective of the behavior but also openly champion the gay community. Although they come from the full range of economic backgrounds, they tend to have high social and occupational resources. Some have tolerant employers; some are full-time gay activists; others are self-employed, often in businesses with largely gay clienteles.

Proud of their newfound identity, these men organize their world, to a great extent, around gay cultures. Much of their leisure, if not occupation, is spent in gay-related pursuits. They have experienced unhappy marriages and divorce, the struggle of achieving a gay identity, and now feel they have arrived at a satisfactory adjustment. These men, consequently, distinguish themselves in ideology from respondents in other categories. For example, what the others refer to as "discretion," men in this category call "duplicity" and "sneaking around." Moreover, what closeted men see as "flaunting," openly gay respondents call "being forthright" and "upfront."

Respondents' efforts in constructing this new life are helped not only by having a gay love relationship, but by the Gay Liberation Movement (Humphreys and Miller, 1980b). Parallel processes are at work whereby the building of a personal gay identity is facilitated by the larger cultural context of increasing gay pride and diversification of gay institutions and heritage (Adam, 1987; Harry and DeVall, 1978; Murray, 1979). Still, coming out is not easy or automatic. This is partly due to the fact that there is no necessary conjunction among sexual

behavior fantasy, self-identity, and object of affectional attachment. Although there is a strain
toward consistency for most people among
these components of sexuality, this is not invariably so. The ways these components change
over time and the combinations in which they
link with each other are multiple (Miller 1983;
Simon and Gagnon, 1969).

Men who reach the Open Endorsement
point often have fears that their father and ex-
husband statuses could distance them from single gays. Sometimes respondents fear that single
gays, similar to nongays, regard them with confusion, curiosity, or pity. Integrating gay and father roles requires patience, since it is often
difficult for respondents to find a lover who accepts him and his children as a "package deal,"
and the gay father may feel he has not enough
time and energy to attend to both children and
a lover. Selecting a lover who is also a gay father
is a common solution to this situation.

Most respondents who have custody of
their children did not experience court custody
battles but gained custody because the mother
did not want the children or because the children, being allowed to choose, chose to live
with their fathers. Respondents who live with
their children are more likely to have a close
circle of gay friends as their main social outlet,
rather than participating primarily in gay commercial establishments (McWhirter and Mattison, 1984).

Men at this point on the continuum have
told their children about their homosexuality.
They report children's reaction to be more positive than expected and, when there is a negative
reaction, it generally dissipates over time (Miller,
1979). Children's negative reactions centered
more on the parent's divorce and subsequent
household changes than on the father's homosexuality per se. Daughters tend to be more accepting of their father's homosexuality than
sons, although most children feel their father's
honesty brings them closer together. Children
report few instances of neighborhood homophobia directed against them, possibly because

the children try to disclose only to people they
know will react favorably. There is no indication
that the children of gay fathers are disproportionately homosexual themselves although, of
the children who turned out to be gay, there
were more lesbian daughters than gay sons.
Wives and relatives sometimes worry that gay
men's children will be molested by him or his
gay friends. Evidence from this study supports
earlier research findings that indicate such fears
are unwarranted (Bozett, 1987).

Discussion

The general tendency is for the Covert Behavior respondents to move toward Open Endorsement. There are several caveats, however,
about this movement. For example, the continuum should not be construed as reifying tran-
sient states into types. Additionally, movement
out of marriage into an openly gay identity is
not unilateral. There are many negotiations
back and forth, in and out of the closet. There
is not a finite number of stages; not everyone
becomes publicly gay and not everyone passes
through every step. Few respondents move easily or accidentally through the process. Rather,
each level is achieved by a painful search, negotiating with both oneself and the larger world.

The event most responsible for initiating
movement along the continuum and reconstructing gay fathers' perceptions of the gay
community is the experience of falling in love
with another man. By contrast, factors hinder-
ing movement along the continuum include inability to perceive the gay world as a viable
alternative as well as perceived lack of support
from other gays, economic difficulty, family
pressure, poor health, wives' dependence, homophobia in respondents or community, and
moral/religious scruples.

This study has several findings. Gayness and
traditional marital relationships are perceived by
the respondents as discordant compared to relationships established when they move into the

gay world. Although respondents perceive gay-ness as incompatible with traditional marriage, they perceive gayness as compatible with father-ing. Highly compartmentalized life-styles and deceit sometimes repress open marital conflict, but unresolved tension characterizes respondents' marriages. In contrast, men who leave their spouses and enter the gay world report gay rela-tionships to be more harmonious than marital relationships. They also report fathering to be more salient once having left their marriages. Men who come out perceive less discrimination from family, friends, and co-workers than those who are closeted anticipate. Wives tend to be upset by their husbands' revelations, but respon-dents are typically surprised by the positive reac-tions of their children and their parents.

Future prospects for gay fathers hinge largely on the success of the gay liberation movement. If these men can politicize their status, if they can see their difficulties stemming from social injus-tice and society's homophobic conditioning rather than personal inadequacy, and if they can redefine themselves, not as deviants, but as an oppressed minority, self-acceptance is improved. This helps lift their depression and externalize anger—anger about prejudice and about wasting their precious early years in the closet. Further, it minimizes their guilt and eases adjustment into the gay community (Miller, 1987).

As the gay liberation movement makes al-ternatives for fathering available within the gay community, fewer gays are likely to become in-volved in heterosexual marriages and divorce. Adoption, surrogate parenting, and alternative fertilization are some of the new ways single gays can now experience fatherhood (Miller, 1988). If current trends continue, there will be a prolifer-ation of family life-styles so that parenthood be-comes available to all regardless of sexual orientation.

References

Adam, B. (1987). *The rise of a gay and lesbian move-ment*. Boston: Hall.

Bozett, F. W. (1987). *Gay and lesbian parents*. New York: Praeger.

Harry, J. & DeVall, W. (1978). *The social organization of gay males*. New York: Praeger.

Hays, D. & Samuels, A. (1988). Heterosexual women's perceptions of their marriages to bisex-ual or homosexual men. In F. W. Bozett (Ed.), *Homosexuality in the family*. New York: Haworth.

Humphreys, L. & Miller, B. (1980A). Keeping in touch: Maintaining contact with stigmatized re-spondents. In W. Shaffir, R. Stebbins & A. Tur-owetz (Eds.), *Field work experience: Qualitative approaches in social research*. New York: St. Mar-tin's.

Humphreys, L. & Miller, B. (1980B). Identities in the emerging gay culture. In J. Marmor (Ed.), *Homosexual behavior: A modern reappraisal*. New York: Basic.

Levine, M. (1981). Employment discrimination against gay men. In P. Stein (Ed.), *Single life*. New York: St. Martin's.

Libby, R. & Whitehurst, R. (1977). *Marriage and al-ternatives*. Glenview, IL: Scott, Foresman.

McWhirter, D. & Mattison, A. (1984). *The male cou-ple*. Englewood Cliffs, NJ: Prentice-Hall.

Miller, B. (1979). Gay fathers and their children. *Family Coordinator* 28: 544–552.

Miller, B. (1983). Foreword. In M. W. Ross (Ed.), *The married homosexual man*. London: Routledge & Kegan Paul.

Miller, B. (1987). Counseling gay husbands and fa-thers. In F. W. Bozett (Ed.), *Gay and lesbian par-ents*. New York: Praeger.

Miller, B. (1988). Preface. In F. W. Bozett (Ed.), *Homosexuality in the family*. New York: Ha-worth.

Miller, B. & Humphreys, L. (1980). Lifestyles and vi-olence: Homosexual victims of assault and mur-der. *Qualitative Sociology* 3: 169–185.

Murray, S. (1979). The institutional elaboration of a quasi-ethnic community. *International Review of Modern Sociology* 9: 165–177.

Pearson, C. (1986). *Good-by, I love you*. New York: Random House.

Schulenberg, J. (1985). *Gay parenting*. New York: Doubleday.

Simon, W. & Gagnon, J. (1969). On psychosexual development. In D. Goslin (Ed.), *Handbook of socialization theory and research*. New York: Rand McNally.

48

ARTICLE

Arlie Hochschild

The Second Shift: Employed Women Are Putting in Another Day of Work at Home

Every American household bears the footprints of economic and cultural trends that originate far outside its walls. A rise in inflation eroding the earning power of the male wage, an expanding service sector opening up jobs for women, and the inroads made by women into many professions—all these changes do not simply go on around the American family. They occur *within* a marriage or living-together arrangement and transform it. Problems between couples, problems that seem "unique" or "marital," are often the individual ripples of powerful economic and cultural shock waves. Quarrels between husbands and wives in households across the nation result mainly from a friction between faster-changing women and slower-changing men.

The exodus of women from the home to the workplace has not been accompanied by a new view of marriage and work that would make this transition smooth. Most workplaces have remained inflexible in the face of the changing needs of workers with families, and most men have yet to really adapt to the changes in women. I call the strain caused by the disparity between the change in women and the absence of change elsewhere the "stalled revolution."

If women begin to do less at home because they have less time, if men do little more, and if the work of raising children and tending a home requires roughly the same effort, then the questions of who does what at home and of what "needs doing" become a source of deep tension in a marriage.

Over the past 30 years in the United States, more and more women have begun to work outside the home, and more have divorced. While some commentators conclude that women's work *causes* divorce, my research into changes in the American family suggests something else. Since all the wives in the families I studied (over an eight-year period) worked outside the home, the fact that they worked did not account for why some marriages were happy and others were not. What *did* contribute to happiness was the husband's willingness to do the work at home. Whether they were traditional or more egalitarian in their relationship, couples were happier when the men did a sizable share of housework and child care.

In one study of 600 couples filing for divorce, researcher George Levinger found that the second most common reason women cited for wanting to divorce—after "mental cruelty"—was their husbands' "neglect of home or children." Women mentioned this reason more often than financial problems, physical abuse, drinking, or infidelity.

A happy marriage is supported by a couple's being economically secure, by their enjoying a supportive community, and by their having compatible needs and values. But these days it may also depend on a shared appreciation of the work it takes to nurture others. As the role of the homemaker is being abandoned by many women, the homemaker's work has been continually devalued and passed on to low-paid housekeepers, babysitters, or day-care workers. Long devalued by men, the contribution of cooking, cleaning, and care-giving is now being devalued as mere drudgery by many women, too.

In the era of the stalled revolution, one way to make housework and child care more valued is for men to share in that work. Many working mothers are already doing all they can at home. Now it's time for men to make the move.

If more mothers of young children are working at full-time jobs outside the home, and if most couples can't afford household help, who's doing the work at home? Adding together the time it takes to do a paid job and to do housework and child care and using estimates from major studies on time use done in the 1960s and 1970s, I found that women worked roughly 15 more hours each week than men. Over a year, they worked an extra month of 24-hour days. Over a dozen years, it was an extra year of 24-hour days. Most women without children spend much more time than men on housework. Women with children devote more time to both housework and child care. Just as there is a wage gap between men and women in the workplace, there is a "leisure gap" between them at home. Most women work one shift at the office or factory and a "second shift" at home.

In my research, I interviewed and observed 52 couples over an eight-year period as they cooked dinner, shopped, bathed their children, and in general struggled to find enough time to make their complex lives work. The women I interviewed seemed to be far more deeply torn between the demands of work and family than were their husbands. They talked more about the abiding conflict between work and family. They felt the second shift was *their* issue, and most of their husbands agreed. When I telephoned one husband to arrange an interview with him, explaining that I wanted to ask him how he managed work and family life, he replied genially, "Oh, this will *really* interest my *wife*."

Men who shared the load at home seemed just as pressed for time as their wives, and as torn between the demands of career and small children. But of the men I surveyed, the majority did not share the load at home. Some refused outright. Others refused more passively, often offering a loving shoulder to lean on, or an understanding ear, as their working wife faced the conflict they both saw as hers. At first it seemed to me that the problem of the second shift *was* hers. But I came to realize that those husbands who helped very little at home were often just as deeply affected as their wives—through the resentment their wives felt toward them and through their own need to steel themselves against that resentment.

A clear example of this phenomenon is Evan Holt, a warehouse furniture salesman who did very little housework and played with his four-year-old son, Joey, only at his convenience. His wife, Nancy, did the second shift, but she resented it keenly and half-consciously expressed her frustration and rage by losing interest in sex and becoming overly absorbed in Joey.

Even when husbands happily shared the work, their wives *felt* more responsible for home and children. More women than men kept track of doctor's appointments and arranged for kids' playmates to come over. More mothers than fathers worried about a child's Halloween costume or a birthday present for a school friend. They were more likely to think about their children while at work and to check in by phone with the babysitter.

Partly because of this, more women felt torn between two kinds of urgency, between the need to soothe a child's fear of being left at daycare and the need to show the boss she's "serious" at work. Twenty percent of the men in my study shared housework equally. Seventy percent did a substantial amount (less than half of it, but more than a third), and 10 percent did less than a third. But even when couples more equitably share the work at home, women do two thirds of the daily jobs at home, such as cooking and cleaning—jobs that fix them into a rigid routine. Most women cook dinner, for instance, while men change the oil in the family car. But, as one mother pointed out, dinner needs to be prepared every evening around six o'clock, whereas the car oil needs to be changed every six months, with no particular deadline. Women do more child care than men, and men repair more household appliances. A child needs to be tended to daily, whereas the repair of household appliances can often wait, said the men, "until I have time." Men thus have more control over when they make their contributions than women do. They may be very busy with family chores, but, like the executive who tells his secretary to "hold my calls," the man has more control over his time.

Another reason why women may feel under more strain than men is that women more often do two things at once—for example, write checks and return phone calls, vacuum and keep an eye on a three-year-old, fold laundry and think out the shopping list. Men more often will either cook dinner *or* watch the kids. Women more often do both at the same time.

Beyond doing more at home, women also devote proportionately more of their time at home to housework than men and proportionately less of it to child care. Of all the time men spend working at home, a growing amount of it goes to child care. Since most parents prefer to tend to their children than to clean house, men do more of what they'd rather do. More men than women take their children on "fun" outings to the park, the zoo, the movies. Women spend more time on maintenance, such as feeding and bathing children—enjoyable activities, to be sure, but often less leisurely or "special" than going to the zoo. Men also do fewer of the most undesirable household chores, such as scrubbing the toilet.

As a result, women tend to talk more intensely about being overtired, sick, and emotionally drained. Many women interviewed were fixated on the topic of sleep. They talked about how much they could "get by on": six and a half, seven, seven and a half, less, more. They talked about who they knew who needed more or less. Some apologized for how much sleep they needed—"I'm afraid I need eight hours of sleep"—as if eight was "too much." They talked about how to avoid fully waking up when a child called them at night, and how to get back to sleep. These women talked about sleep the way a hungry person talks about food.

If, all in all, the two-job family is suffering from a speedup of work and family life, working mothers are its primary victims. It is ironic, then, that often it falls to women to be the time-and-motion experts of family life. As I observed families inside their homes, I noticed it was often the mother who rushed children, saying, "Hurry up! It's time to go," "Finish your cereal now," "You can do that later," or "Let's go!" When a bath needed to be crammed into a slot between 7:45 and 8:00, it was often the mother who called out, "Let's see who can take their bath the quickest!" Often a younger child would rush out, scurrying to be first in bed, while the older and wiser one stalled, resistant, sometimes resentful: "Mother is always rushing us." Sadly, women are more often the lightning rods for family tensions aroused by this speedup of work and family life. They are the villains in a process in which they are also the primary victims. More than the longer hours and the lack of sleep, this is the saddest cost to women of their extra month of work each year.

Raising children in a nuclear family is still the overwhelming preference of most people. Yet in the face of new problems for this family model we have not created an adequate support system so that the nuclear family can do its job well in the era of the two-career couple. Corporations have done little to accommodate the needs of working parents, and the government has done little to prod them.

The Reagan and Bush administrations say they are "pro-family" but confuse being pro-family with being against women's work outside the home. During a time when more than 70 percent of wives and mothers work outside the home (the rate is still climbing), the Reagan administration's Panel on the Family offered as its pro-family policy only a package of measures against crime, drugs, and welfare. In the name of protecting the family, the Republicans proposed to legitimize school prayer and eliminate family-planning services. They did nothing to help parents integrate work and family life. We have to ask, when marriages continue to end because of the strains of this life, is it pro-family or anti-family to make life in two-job families so very hard? As working parents become an interest group, a voting block, and a swing vote in elections, the issue of policies to ease life in two-job families is likely to become a serious political issue in years ahead.

We really need, as sociologist Frank Furstenberg has suggested, a Marshall Plan for the family. After World War II we saw that it was in our best interests to aid the war-torn nations of Europe. Now—it seems obvious in an era of growing concern over drugs, crime, and family instability—it is in our best interests to aid the overworked two-job families right here at home. We should look to other nations for a model of what could be done. In Sweden, for example, upon the birth of a child every working couple is entitled to 12 months of paid parental leave—nine months at 90 percent of the worker's salary, plus an additional three months at about three hundred dollars a month. The mother and father are free to divide this year off between them as they wish. Working parents of a child under eight have the opportunity to work no more than six hours a day, at six hours' pay. Parental insurance offers parents money for work time lost while visiting a child's school or caring for a sick child. That's a true pro-family policy.

A pro-family policy in the United States could give tax breaks to companies that encourage job sharing, part-time work, flex time, and family leave for new parents. By implementing comparable worth policies we could increase pay scales for "women's" jobs. Another key element of a pro-family policy would be instituting fewer-hour, more flexible options—called "family phases"—for all regular jobs filled by parents of young children.

Day-care centers could be made more warm and creative through generous public and private funding. If the best form of day-care comes from the attention of elderly neighbors, students, or grandparents, these people could be paid to care for children through social programs.

In these ways, the American government would create a safer environment for the two-job family. If the government encouraged corporations to consider the long-range interests of workers and their families, they would save on long-range costs caused by absenteeism, turnover, juvenile delinquency, mental illness, and welfare support for single mothers.

These are real pro-family reforms. If they seem utopian today, we should remember that in the past the eight-hour day, the abolition of child labor, and the vote for women seemed utopian, too. Among top-rated employers listed in *The 100 Best Companies to Work for in America* are many offering country-club memberships, first-class air travel, and million-dollar fitness centers. But only a handful offer job sharing, flex time, or part-time work. Not one provides on-site day-care, and only three offer child-care deductions: Control Data, Polaroid, and Honeywell. In his book *Megatrends*, John Naisbitt reports that 83 percent of corporate executives believed that more men feel the need to share the responsibilities of parenting; yet only 9 percent of corporations offer paternity leave.

Public strategies are linked to private ones. Economic and cultural trends bear on family relations in ways it would be useful for all of us to understand. The happiest two-job marriages I saw during my research were ones in which men and women shared the housework and par-

enting. What couples called good communication often meant that they were good at saying thanks to one another for small aspects of taking care of the family. Making it to the school play, helping a child read, cooking dinner in good spirits, remembering the grocery list, taking responsibility for cleaning up the bedrooms—these were the silver and gold of the marital exchange. Until now, couples committed to an equal sharing of housework and child care have been rare. But, if we as a culture come to see the urgent need of meeting the new problems posed by the second shift, and if society and government begin to shape new policies that allow working parents more flexibility, then we will be making some progress toward happier times at home and work. And as the young learn by example, many more women and men will be able to enjoy the pleasure that arises when family life is family life, and not a second shift.

49

A R T I C L E

Scott Coltrane

Stability and Change in Chicano Men's Family Lives

One of the most popular pejorative American slang terms to emerge in the 1980s was "macho," used to describe men prone to combative posturing, relentless sexual conquest, and other compulsive displays of masculinity. Macho men continually guard against imputations of being soft or feminine and thus tend to avoid domestic tasks and family activities that are considered "women's work." Macho comes from the Spanish *machismo*, and although the behaviors associated with it are clearly not limited to one ethnic group, Latino men are often stereotyped as espe-

This article is based on a study of Dual-Earner Chicano Couples conducted in 1990–1992 by Scott Coltrane with research assistance from Elsa Valdez and Hilda Cortez. Partial funding was provided by the Academic Senate of the University of California, Riverside, and the UCR Minority Student Research Internship Program. Included herein are analyses of unpublished interview excerpts along with selected passages from three published sources: (1) Coltrane, *Family Man: Fatherhood, Housework, and Gender Equity* (New York: Oxford University Press, 1994); (2) Coltrane and Valdez, "Reluctant Compliance: Work/Family Role Allocation in Dual-Earner Chicano Families," in Jane C. Hood (ed.), *Men, Work, and Family* (Newbury Park, CA: Sage, 1994); and (3) Valdez and Coltrane, "Work, Family, and the Chicana: Power, Perception and Equity," in Judith Frankel (ed.), *Employed Mothers and the Family Context* (New York: Springer, 1993).

cially prone toward macho displays.[1] This chapter uses in-depth interviews with twenty Chicano couples to explore how paid work and family work are divided. As in other contemporary American households, divisions of labor in these Chicano families were far from balanced or egalitarian, and husbands tended to enjoy special privileges simply because they were men. Nevertheless, many couples were allocating household chores without reference to gender, and few of the Chicano men exhibited stereotypical macho behavior.

Chicanos, or Mexican-Americans, are often portrayed as living in poor farm-worker families composed of macho men, subservient women, and plentiful children. Yet these stereotypes have been changing, as diverse groups of people with Mexican and Latin-American heritage are responding to the same sorts of social and economic pressures faced by families of other ethnic backgrounds. For example, most Chicano families in the United States now live in urban centers or their suburbs rather than in traditional rural farming areas, and their patterns of marital interaction appear to be about as egalitarian as those of other American families. What's more, Chicanos will no longer be a numerical minority in the near future. Because of higher-than-average birth rates and continued in-migration, by the year 2015 Chicano children will outnumber Anglos in many southwest states, including California, Texas, Arizona, and New Mexico.[2]

When family researchers study white couples, they typically focus on middle-class suburban households, usually highlighting their strengths. Studies of ethnic minority families, in contrast, have tended to focus on the problems of poor or working-class households living in inner-city or rural settings. Because most research on Latino families in the United States has not controlled for social class, wife's employment status, or recency of immigration, a narrow and stereotyped view of these families as patriarchal and culturally backward has persisted. In addition, large-scale studies of "Hispanics" have failed to distinguish between divergent groups of people with Mexican, Central American, South American, Cuban, Puerto Rican, Spanish, or Portuguese ancestry. In contrast, contemporary scholars are beginning to look at some of the positive aspects of minority families and to focus on the economic and institutional factors that influence men's lives within these families.[3]

In 1990 and 1991, Elsa Valdez and I interviewed a group of twenty middle-class Chicano couples with young children living in Southern California. We were primarily interested in finding out if they were facing the same sorts of pressures experienced by other families, so we selected only families in which both the husband and the wife were employed outside the home—the most typical pattern among young parents in the United States today. We wanted to see who did what in these families and find out how they talked about the personal and financial pushes and pulls associated with raising a family. We interviewed wives and husbands separately in their homes, asking them a variety of questions about housework, child care, and their jobs. Elsewhere, we describe details of their time use and task performance, but here I analyze the couples' talk about work, family,

and gender, exploring how feelings of entitlement and obligation are shaped by patterns of paid and unpaid labor.[4]

When we asked husbands and wives to sort sixty-four common household tasks according to who most often performed them, we found that wives in most families were responsible for housecleaning, clothes care, meal preparation, and clean-up, whereas husbands were primarily responsible for home maintenance and repair. Most routine child care was also performed by wives, though most husbands reported that they made substantial contributions to parenting. Wives saw the mundane daily housework as an ever-present burden that they had to shoulder themselves or delegate to someone else. While many wives did not expect the current division of labor to change, they did acknowledge that it was unbalanced. The men, although acknowledging that things weren't exactly fair, tended to minimize the asymmetry by seeing many of the short repetitive tasks associated with housekeeping as shared activities. Although there was tremendous diversity among the couples we talked to, we observed a general pattern of disagreement over how much family work the other spouse performed.

The sociologist Jesse Bernard provides us with a useful way to understand why this might be. Bernard suggested that every marital union contains two marriages—"his" and "hers."[5] We discovered from our interviews and observations that most of the husbands and wives were, indeed, living in separate marriages or separate worlds. Her world centered around keeping track of the countless details of housework and child care even though she was employed. His world centered around his work and his leisure activities so that he avoided noticing or anticipating the details of running a home. Husbands "helped out" when wives gave them tasks to do, and because they almost always complied with requests for help, most tended to assume that they were sharing the household labor. Because much of the work the women did was unseen or taken for granted by the men, they tended to underestimate their wives contributions and escaped the full range of tensions and strains associated with family work.

Because wives remained in control of setting schedules, generating lists for domestic chores, and worrying about the children, they perceived their husbands as contributing relatively little. A frequent comment from wives was that their husbands "just didn't see" the domestic details, and that the men would not often take responsibility for anticipating and planning for what needed to be done. Although many of the men we interviewed maintained their favored position within the family by "not seeing" various aspects of domestic life and leaving the details and planning to their wives, other couples were in the process of ongoing negotiations and, as described below, were successful at redefining some household chores as shared endeavors.

Concerning their paid work, the families we interviewed reported that both husbands and wives had jobs because of financial necessity. The men made comments like, "we were pretty much forced into it," or "we didn't really have any choice." Although most of the husbands and wives were employed full-time, only a few accepted the wife as an equal provider or true breadwinner. Using the type of job, employment schedule, and earnings of each spouse, along with their attitudes toward providing, I categorized the couples into main-provider families and co-provider families.[6] Main-provider couples considered the husband's job to be primary and the wife's job to be secondary. Co-provider couples in contrast, tended to accept the wife's job as permanent, and some even treated the wife's job as equally important to her husband's. Accepting the wife as an equal provider, or considering the husband to have failed as a provider, significantly shaped the couples' divisions of household labor.

Main-Provider Families

In just under half of the families we interviewed, the men earned substantially more money than their wives and were assumed to be "natural" breadwinners, whereas the women were assumed to be innately better equipped to deal with home and children. Wives in all of these main-provider families were employed, but the wife's job was often considered temporary, and her income was treated as "extra" money and earmarked for special purposes.[7] One main-provider husband said, "I would prefer that my wife did not have to work, and could stay at home with my daughter, but finances just don't permit that." Another commented that his wife made just about enough to cover the costs of child care, suggesting that the children were still her primary responsibility, and that any wages she earned should first be allocated to cover "her" tasks.

The main-provider couples included many wives who were employed part-time, and some who worked in lower-status full-time jobs with wages much lower than their husband's. These women took pride in their homemaker role and readily accepted responsibility for managing the household, although they occasionally asked for help. One part-time bookkeeper married to a recent law-school graduate described their division of labor by saying, "It's a given that I take care of children and housework, but when I am real tired, he steps in willingly." Main-provider husbands typically remained in a helper role: in this case, the law clerk told his wife, "Just tell me what to do and I'll do it." He said that if he came home and she was gone, he might clean house, but that if she was home, he would "let her do it." This reflects a typical division of labor in which the wife acts as household manager and the husband occasionally serves as her helper.[8]

This lawyer-to-be talked about early negotiations between he and his wife that seemed to set the tone for current smoldering arguments about housework:

> When we were first married, I would do something and she wouldn't like the way that I did it. So I would say, "OK, then, you do it, and I won't do it again." That was like in our first few years of marriage when we were first getting used to each other, but now she doesn't discourage me so much. She knows that if she does, she's going to wind up doing it herself.

His resistance and her reluctance to press for change reflect an unbalanced economy of gratitude.[9] When he occasionally contributed to housework or child care, she was indebted to him. She complimented him for being willing to step in when she asked for help, but privately lamented the fact that she had to negotiate for each small contribution. Firmly entrenched in the main-provider role and somewhat oblivious to the daily rituals of housework and child care, he felt justified in needing prodding and encouragement. When she did ask him for help, she was careful to thank him for dressing the children or for giving her a ten-minute break from them. While these patterns of domestic labor and inequities in the exchange of gratitude were longstanding, tension lurked just below the surface for this couple. He commented, "My wife gets uptight with me for agreeing to help out my mom, when she feels she can't even ask me to go to the store for her."

Another main-provider couple reflected a similar pattern of labor allocation, but claimed that the arrangement was fair to them both. The woman, a part-time teacher's aide, acknowledged that she loved being a wife and mother and "naturally" took charge of managing the household. She commented, "I have the say so on the running of the house, and I also decide on the children's activities." Although she had a college degree, she described her current part-time job as "ideal" for her. She was able to work twenty hours per week at a neighborhood school and was home by the time her own children returned home from their school. While she earned only $6,000 per year, she justified the low salary because the job fit so well with "the family's schedule." Her husband's administrative job allowed them to live comfortably since he earned almost $50,000 annually.

This secondary-provider wife said that they divided household tasks in a conventional manner: She did most all of the cleaning, cooking, clothes-care, and child-care tasks, while he did the yard work, home repairs, and finances. Her major complaints were that her husband didn't notice things, that she had to nag him, and that he created more housework for her. "The worst part about the housework and child care is the amount of nagging I have to do to get him to help. Also, for example, say I just cleaned the house; he will leave the newspaper scattered all over the place or he will leave wet towels on the bathroom floor."

When asked whether there had been any negotiation over who would do what chores, the husband responded, "I don't think a set decision was made, it was a necessity." His wife's response was similar, "It just evolved that way, we never really talked about it." His provider role was taken for granted, but occasionally she voiced some muted resentment. For example, she commented that it upset her when he told her that she should not be working because their youngest child was only five years old. As an afterthought, she mentioned that she was sometimes bothered by the fact that she had not advanced her career, or worked overtime, since that would have interfered with "the family's" schedule.

In general, wives of main-providers not only performed virtually all housework and child care, but both spouses accepted this as "natural" or "normal." Main provider husbands assumed that financial support was their "job" or their "duty." When one man was asked about how it felt to make more money than his wife, he responded by saying: "It's my job, I wouldn't feel right if I didn't make more money. . . . Anyway that I look at it, I have to keep up my salary, or I'm not doing my job. If it costs $40,000 to live nowadays and I'm not in a $40,000-a-year job, then I'm not gonna be happy."

This same husband, a head mechanic who worked between 50 and 60 hours per week, also showed how main-provider husbands sometimes felt threatened when women begin asserting themselves in previously all-male occupational enclaves:

> As long as women mind their own business, no problem with me. . . . There's nothing wrong with them being in the job, but they shouldn't try to do more than that. Like, if you get a secretary that's nosy and wants to run the company, hey, well, we tell her where to stick it. . . . When you can't do my job, don't tell me how to do it.

The mechanic's wife, also a part-time teacher's aide, subtly resisted by "spending as little time on housework as I can get away with." Nevertheless, she still considered it her sole duty to cook, and only when her husband was away at National Guard training sessions did she feel she could "slack off" by not placing "regular meals" on the family's table each night.

The Provider Role and Failed Aspirations

Wives performed most of the household labor in main-provider couples, but if main-provider husbands had failed career aspirations, more domestic work was shared. What appeared to tip the economy of gratitude away from automatic male privilege was the wife's sense that the husband had not fulfilled his occupational potential. For example, one main-provider husband graduated from a four-year college and completed two years of post-graduate study without finishing his Master's Thesis. At the time of the interview, he was making about $30,000 a year as a self-employed house painter, and his wife was making less than half that amount as a full-time secretary. His comments show how her evaluation of his failed or postponed career aspirations led to more bargaining over his participation in routine housework:

> She reminds me that I'm not doing what we both think I should be doing, and sometimes that's a discouragement. I might have worked a lot of hours, and I'll come home tired, for example, and she'll say, "You've gotta clean the house," and I'll say, "Damn I'm tired, I'd like to get a little rest in," but she says "you're only doing this because it's been your choice." She tends to not have sympathy for me in my work because it was more my choice than hers.

He acknowledged that he should be doing something more "worthwhile," and hoped that he would not be painting houses for more than another year. Still, as long as he stayed in his current job, considered beneath him by both of them, she would not allow him to use fatigue from employment as a way to get out of doing housework:

> I worked about 60 hours a week the last couple of weeks. I worked yesterday [Saturday], and today—if it had been my choice—I would have drank beer and watched TV. But since she had a baby shower to go to, I babysitted my nephews. And since we had you coming, she kind of laid out the program: "You've gotta clean the floors, and wash the dishes and do the carpets. So get to it buddy!" [Laughs.]

This main-provider husband capitulated to his wife's demands, but she still had to set tasks for him and remind him to perform them. In responding to her "program," he used the strategy of claimed incompetence that other main-provider husbands also used. While he admitted that he was proficient at the "janitorial stuff," he was careful to point out that he was incapable of dusting or doing the laundry:

It's amazing what you can do when you have little time and you just get in and do it. And I'm good at that. I'm good at the big cleaning, I'm good at the janitorial stuff. I can do the carpet, do the floors, do all that stuff. But I'm no good on the details. She wants all the details just right, so she handles dusting, the laundry, and stuff like that. . . . You know, like I would have everything come out one color.

By re-categorizing some of the housework as "big cleaning," this husband rendered it accountable as men's work. He drew the line at laundry and dusting, but he had transformed some household tasks, like vacuuming and mopping, into work appropriate for men to do. He was complying, albeit reluctantly, to many of his wife's requests because they agreed that he had not fulfilled "his" job as sole provider. He still yearned to be the "real" breadwinner and shared his hope that getting a better paying job would mean that he could ignore the housework:

Sharing the house stuff is usually just a necessity. If, as we would hope in the future, she didn't have to work outside the home, then I think I would be comfortable doing less of it. Then she would be the primary house-care person and I would be the primary financial-resource person. I think roles would change then, and I would be comfortable with her doing more of the dishes and more of the cleaning, and I think she would too. In that sense, I think traditional relationships—if traditional means the guy working and the woman staying home—is a good thing. I wouldn't mind getting a taste of it myself!

A similar failed aspirations pattern was found in another main-provider household, in spite of the fact that the husband had a college degree and a job as an elementary-school teacher. While his wife earned less than a sixth of what he did, she was working on an advanced degree and coordinated a nonprofit community program. In this family, unlike most of the others, the husband performed more housework than he did child care, though both he and his wife agreed that she did more of both. Nevertheless, he performed

these household chores reluctantly and only in response to prodding from his wife: "Housework is mostly her responsibility. I like to come home and kick back. Sometimes she has to complain before I do anything around the house. You know when she hits the wall, then I start doing things."

This main-provider husband talked about how his real love was art, and how he had failed to pursue his dream of being a graphic artist. The blocked occupational achievement in his case was not that he didn't make good money in a respected professional job, but that he was not fulfilling his "true" potential. His failed career goals increased her willingness to make demands on him, influenced their division of household labor, and helped shape feelings of entitlement between them: "I have talents that she doesn't have. I guess that's one of my strongest strengths, that I'm an artist. But she's very disappointed in me that I have not done enough of it . . ."

Another main-provider husband held a job as a telephone lineman, and his wife ran a family day-care center out of their home, which earned her less than a third of what he made. She talked about her regrets that he didn't do something "more important" for a living, and he talked about her frequent reminders that he was "too smart for what I'm doing." Like the other failed-aspirations husbands, he made significant contributions to domestic chores, but his resentment showed when he talked about "the wife" holding a job far from home:

What I didn't like about it was that I used to get home before the wife, because she had to commute, and I'd have to pop something to eat. Most of the time it was just whatever I happened to find in the fridge. Then I'd have to go pick up the kids immediately from the babysitter, and sometimes I had evening things to do, so what I didn't like was that I had to figure out a way to schedule baby watch or baby sitting.

Even when main-provider husbands began to assume responsibility for domestic work in response to "necessity" or "nagging," they seemed to cling to the idea that these were still "her" chores. Coincidentally, most of the secondary-provider wives reported that they received little help unless they "constantly" reminded their husbands. What generally kept secondary-provider wives from resenting their husband's resistance was their own acceptance of the homemaker role and their recognition of his superior financial contributions. When performance of the male-provider role was deemed to be lacking in some way—i.e., failed aspirations or low occupational prestige—wives' resentment appeared closer to the surface, and they were more persistent in demanding help from their husbands.

Ambivalent Co-providers

Over half of the couples we interviewed were classified as co-providers. The husbands and wives in these families had more equal earnings and placed a higher value the wife's employment than those in main-provider families, but there was considerable variation in terms of their willingness to accept the woman as a full and equal provider. Five of the twelve husbands in the co-provider group were ambivalent about sharing the provider role and were also reluctant to share most household tasks. Compared to their wives, ambivalent co-provider husbands usually held jobs that were roughly equivalent in terms of occupational prestige and worked about the same number of hours per week, but because of gender bias in the labor market, the men earned significantly more than their wives. Compared to main-provider husbands, they considered their wives' jobs to be relatively permanent and important, but they continued to use their own job commitments as justification for doing little at home. Ambivalent co-provider husbands' family obligations rarely intruded into their work lives, whereas their wives' family obligations frequently interfered with their paid work. Such asymmetrically permeable work/family boundaries are common in single-earner and main-provider families, but must be supported with subtle ideologies and elaborate justifications when husbands and wives hold similar occupational positions.[10]

Ambivalent co-provider husbands remained in a helper role at home, perceiving their wives to be more involved parents and assuming that housework was also primarily their wives' responsibility. The men used their jobs to justify their absence from home, but most also lamented not being able to spend more time with their families. For instance, one husband who worked full time as a city planner was married to a woman who worked an equal number of hours as an office manager. In talking about the time he put in at his job, he commented, "I wish I had more time to spend with my children, and to spend with my wife too, of course, but it's a fact of life that I have to work." His wife, in contrast, indicated that her paid job, which she had held for fourteen years, did not prohibit her from adequately caring for her three children, or taking care of "her" household chores. Ambivalent co-provider husbands did not perform significantly more housework and child care than main-provider husbands, and generally did fewer household chores than main-provider husbands with failed career aspirations.

Not surprisingly, ambivalent co-provider husbands tended to be satisfied with their current divisions of labor, even though they usually admitted that things were "not quite fair." One junior-high-school teacher married to a bilingual-education program coordinator described his reactions to their division of family labor:

> To be honest, I'm totally satisfied. When I had a first-period conference, I was a little more flexible; I'd help her more with changing 'em, you know, getting them ready for school, since I didn't have to be at school right away. Then I had to switch because they had some situation out at fifth-period conference, so that now she

does it a little bit more than I do, and I don't help out with the kids as much in the morning because I have to be there an hour earlier.

This ambivalent co-provider clearly saw himself as "helping" his wife with the children, yet made light of her contributions by saying she does "a little bit more than I do." He went on to reveal how his wife did not enjoy similar special privileges due to her employment, since she had to pick up the children from day care every day, as well as taking them to school in the mornings:

She gets out a little later than I do, because she's an administrator but I have other things outside. I also work out, I run, and that sort of gives me a time away, to do that before they all come here. I have community meetings in the evenings sometimes, too. So, I mean, it might not be totally fair—maybe 60/40—but I'm thoroughly happy with the way things are.

While he was "thoroughly happy" with the current arrangements, she thought that it was decidedly unfair. She said, "I don't like the fact that it's taken for granted that I'm available. When he goes out he just assumes I'm available, but when I go out I have to consult with him to make sure he is available." For her, child care was a given; for him, it was optional. He commented, "If I don't have something else to do, then I'll take the kids."

Ambivalent co-provider husbands also tended to talk about regretting that their family involvements limited their careers or personal activities. For instance the school teacher discussed above lamented that he could not do what he used to before he had children:

Having children keeps me away from thinking a lot about my work. You know, it used to be, before we had kids, I could have my mind geared to work—you know how ideas just pop in, you really get into it. But with kids it doesn't get as—you know, you can't switch. It gets more difficult, it makes it hard to get into it. I don't have that freedom of mind, you know, and it takes away from aspects of my work, like doing

a little bit more reading or research that I would like to do. Or my own activities, I mean, I still run, but not as much as I used to. I used to play basketball, I used to coach, this and that . . .

Other ambivalent co-provider husbands talked about the impact of children on their careers and personal lives with less bitterness and more appreciation for establishing a relationship with their children. Encouraged by their wives to alter their priorities, some reinterpreted the relative importance of career and family commitments:

I like the way things are going. Let's put it this way. I mean, it's just that once you become a parent, it's a never-ending thing. I coach my kid for example, this past week we had four games. . . . I just think that by having a family that your life becomes so involved after awhile with your own kids, that it's very difficult. I coached at the varsity level for one year, but I had to give it up. I would leave in the morning when they were asleep, and I would get out of coaches' meetings at ten or eleven at night. My wife said to me, "Think about your priorities, man; you leave when the kids are asleep, come back when they are asleep." So I decided to change that act. So I gave it up for one year, and I was home all the time. Now I am going to coach again, but it's at lower levels, and I'll be home every day. I have to make adjustments for my family. Your attitude changes, it's not me that counts anymore.

Whereas family labor was not shared equally in this ambivalent co-provider couple, the husband, at his wife's urging, was beginning to accept and appreciate that his children were more important than his job. He was evaluating his attachment to his children on his wife's terms, but he was agreeing with her, and he had begun to take more responsibility for them.

Many of these husbands talked about struggles over wanting to spend more time on their careers, and most did not relinquish the assumption that the home was the wife's domain. For example, some ambivalent co-provider couples attempted to alleviate stress on the wife by hiring outside help. In response to a question about whether their division of labor was fair, a self-employed male attorney said, "Do you mean fair like equal? It's probably not equal, so probably it wouldn't be fair, but that's why we have a housekeeper." His wife, a social worker earning only ten percent less than he, said that the household was still her responsibility, but that she now had fewer tasks to do: "When I did not have help, I tended to do everything, but with a housekeeper, I don't have to do so much." She went on to talk about how she wished he would do more with their five- and eight-year-old children, but speculated that he probably would as they grew older.

Another couple paid a live-in babysitter/housekeeper to watch their three children during the day while he worked full-time in construction and she worked full-time as a psychiatric social worker. While she labeled the outside help as "essential," she noted that her husband contributed more to the mess than he did to its clean-up. He saw himself as an involved father because he played with his children, and she acknowledged this, but she also complained that he competed with them in games as if he were a child himself. His participation in routine household labor was considered optional, as evidenced by his comment, "I like to cook once in a while."

Co-providers

In contrast, about a third of the couples we interviewed fully accepted the wife's long-term employment, considered her career to be just as important as his, and were in various stages of redefining household labor as men's work. Like the ambivalent couples discussed above, full co-provider spouses worked about the same number of hours as each other, but on the whole, these couples worked more total hours than their more ambivalent counterparts, though their annual incomes were a bit lower. According to

both husbands and wives, the sharing of housework and child care was substantially greater for full co-providers than for ambivalent co-providers, and also much more balanced than for main-providers.

Like ambivalent co-providers, husbands in full co-provider families discussed conflicts between work and family and sometimes alluded to the ways that their occupational advancement was limited by their commitments to their children. One husband and wife spent the same number of hours on the job, earned approximately the same amount of money, and were employed as engineering technicians for the same employer. When we asked him how his family involvement had affected his job performance, he responded by saying, "It should, OK, because I really need to spend a lot more time learning my work, and I haven't really put in the time I need to advance in the profession. I would like to spend, I mean I *would* spend, more time if I didn't have kids. I'd like to be able to play with the computer or read books more often." Although he talked about conflicts between job and family, he also emphasized that lost work time was not really a sacrifice because he valued time with his children so highly. He did not use his job as an excuse to get out of doing child care or housework, and he seemed to value his wife's career at least as much as his own:

> I think her job is probably more important than mine because she's been at that kind of work a lot longer than I have. And at the level she is— it's awkward the way it is, because I get paid just a little bit more than she does, I have a higher position. But she definitely knows the work a lot more, she's been doing the same type of work for about nine years already, and I've only been doing this type of engineering work for about two-and-a-half years, so she knows a lot more. We both have to work, that's for sure.

Recognition of their roughly equivalent professional status and the need for two equal providers affected this couple's division of parenting and housework. The husband indicated that he did more child care and housework than his wife, and she gave him much credit for his efforts, but in her interview, she indicated that he still did less than half. She described her husband's relationship with their seven-year-old son as "very caring," and noted that he assists the boy with homework more than she does. She also said that her husband did most of the heavy cleaning and scrubbing, but also commented that he doesn't clean toilets and doesn't always notice when things get dirty. The husband described their allocation of housework by saying, "Maybe she does less than I do, but some of the things she does, I just will not do. I will not dust all the little things in the house. That's one of my least favorite things, but I'm more likely to do the mopping and vacuuming." This husband's comments also revealed some ongoing tension about whose housework standards should be maintained. He said, "She has high standards for cleanliness that you would have to be home to maintain. Mind tend to acknowledge that you don't always get to this stuff because you have other things to do. I think I have a better acceptance that one priority hurts something else in the background."

While this couple generally agreed about how to raise their son, standards for child care were also subject to debate. He saw himself as doing more with his son than his wife, as reflected in comments such as "I tend to think of myself as the more involved parent, and I think other people have noticed that, too." While she had only positive things to say about his parenting, he offered both praise and criticism of her parenting:

> She can be very playful. She makes up fun games. She doesn't always put enough into the educational part of it, though, like exploring or reading. . . . She cherishes tune-up time [job-related study or preparation], and sometimes I feel she should be using that time to spend with him. Like at the beach, I'll play with him, but she'll be more likely to be under the umbrella reading.

Like many of the other husbands, he went on to say that he thought their division of labor was unfair. Unlike the others, however, he indicated that he thought their current arrangements favored *her* needs, not his:

> I think I do more housework. It's probably not fair, because I do more of the dirtier tasks. . . . Also, at this point, our solution tends to favor her free time more than my free time. I think that has more to do with our personal backgrounds. She has more personal friends to do things with, so she has more outside things to do whereas I say I'm not doing anything.

In this family, comparable occupational status and earnings, coupled with a relatively egalitarian ideology, led to substantial sharing of both child care and housework. While the husband tended to take more credit for his involvement than his wife gave him, we can see a difference between their talk and that of some of the families discussed above. Other husbands sometimes complained about their wife's high standards, but they also treated housework, and even parenting, as primarily *her* duty. They usually resented being nagged to do more around the house and failed to move out of a helper role. Rarely did such men consider it *their* duty to anticipate, schedule, and take care of family and household needs. In this co-provider household, in contrast, the gendered allocation of responsibility for child care and housework was not assumed. Because of this, negotiations over housework and parenting were more frequent than in the other families. Since they both held expectations that each would fulfill both provider and caretaker roles, resentments came from both spouses—not just from the wife.

Our interviews suggest that it might be easier for couples to share both provider and homemaker roles when, like the family above, the wife's earnings and occupational prestige equal or exceed those of her husband. For instance, in one of the couples reporting the most sharing of child care and housework, the wife earned $36,000 annually as the executive director of a non-profit community organization and a consultant, and her husband earned $30,000 as a self-employed general contractor. This couple started off their marriage with fairly conventional gender-role expectations and an unbalanced division of labor. While the husband's ideology had changed somewhat, he still talked like most of the main-provider husbands:

> As far the household is concerned, I divide a house into two categories: one is the interior and the other is the exterior. For the interior, my wife pushes me to deal with that. The exterior, I'm left to it myself. So, what I'm basically saying is that generally speaking, a woman does not deal with the exterior. The woman's main concern is with the interior, although there is a lot of deviation.

In this family, an egalitarian belief system did not precede the sharing of household labor. The wife was still responsible for setting the "interior" household agenda and had to remind her husband to help with housework and child care. When asked whether he and his wife had arguments about housework, this husband laughed and said, "All the time, doesn't everybody?"

What differentiated this couple from most others, is that she made more money than he did and had no qualms about demanding help from him. While he had not yet accepted the idea that interior chores were equally his, he reluctantly performed them. She ranked his contributions to child care to be equal to hers, and rated his contributions to housework only slightly below her own. While not eagerly rushing to do the cooking, cleaning, or laundry, he complied with occasional reminders and according to his wife, was "a better cleaner" than she was.

His sharing stemmed, in part, from her higher earnings and their mutual willingness to reduce his "outside chores" by hiring outside help. Unlike the more ambivalent co-providers who hired housekeepers to do "her" chores, this couple hired a gardener to work on the yard so they could both spend more time focusing on the children and the house. Rather than complaining about their division of labor, he talked about how he has come to appreciate his situation:

> Ever since I've known my wife, she's made more money than I have. Initially—as a man—I resented it. I went through a lot of head trips about it. But as time developed, I appreciated it. Now I respect it. The way I figure it is, I'd rather have her sharing the money with me than sharing it with someone else. She has her full-time job and then she has her part-time job as a consultant. The gardener I'm paying $75 per week, and I'm paying someone else $25 per week to make my lunch, so I'm enjoying it! It's self-interest.

The power dynamic in this family, coupled with their willingness to pay for outside help to reduce his chores, and the flexibility of his self-employed work schedule, led to substantial sharing of cooking, cleaning, and child care. Because she was making more money and working more hours than he was, he could not emulate other husbands in claiming priority for his provider activities.

A similar dynamic was evident in other co-provider couples with comparable earnings and career commitments. One male IRS officer married to a school teacher now made more money than his wife, but talked about his feelings when she was the more successful provider:

> It doesn't bother me when she makes more money than me. I don't think it has anything to do with being a man. I don't have any hangups about it, I mean, I don't equate those things with manhood. It takes a pretty simple mind to think that way. First of all, she doesn't feel superior when she has made more money.

The woman in this couple commented that her husband was "better" at housework than she was, but that she still had to nag him to do it. Although only two wives in our sample of Chicano families earned more than their husbands, the reversal of symbolic provider status seemed to raise expectations for increased family work from husbands. The husbands who made less than their wives performed significantly more of the housework and child care than the other husbands.

Even when wives' earnings did not exceed the husbands', some co-providers shared the homemaker role. A male college-admissions recruiter and his executive-secretary wife shared substantial housework and child care according to mutual ratings. He made $29,000 per year working a 50 hour week, while she made $22,000 working a 40 hour week. She was willing to give him more credit than he was willing to claim for child care, reflecting her sincere appreciation for his parenting efforts, which were greater than those of other fathers she knew. He placed a high value on her mothering and seemed to downplay the possibility that they should be considered equal parents. Like most of the men in this study, the college-recruiter husband was reluctant to perform house-cleaning chores. Like many co-providers, however, he managed to redefine some routine household chores as a shared responsibility. For instance, when we asked him what he liked least about housework, he laughingly replied, "Probably those damn toilets, man, and the showers, the bathrooms, gotta scrub 'em, argghh! I wish I didn't have to do any of that, you know the vacuuming and all that. But it's just a fact of life."

Even though he did more than most husbands, he acknowledged that he did less than his wife, and admitted that he sometimes tried to use his job to get out of doing more around the house. But whereas other wives often allowed husbands to use their jobs as excuses for doing less family work, or assumed that their husbands were incapable of performing certain chores like cooking or laundry, the pattern in this family resembled that of the failed-aspirations couples. In other words, the wife did not assume that housework was "her" job, did not accept her husband's job demands as justification for his doing less housework, and sometimes challenged his interpretation of how much his job

required of him. She also got her husband to assume more responsibility by refraining from performing certain tasks. He commented:

> Sometimes she just refuses to do something. . . . An example would be the ironing, you know, I never used to do the ironing, hated it. Now it's just something that happens. You need something ironed, you better iron it or you're not gonna have it in the morning. So, I think, you know, that kinda just evolved. I mean, she just gradually quit doing it so everybody just had to do their own. My son irons his own clothes, I iron my own clothes, my daughter irons her own clothes, the only one that doesn't iron is the baby, and next year she'll probably start.

The sociologist Jane Hood, whose pathbreaking family research highlighted the importance of provider role definition to marital power, describes this strategy as "going on strike," and suggests that it is most effective when husbands feel the specific task *must* be done.[11] Since appearing neat and well-dressed was a priority for this husband, when his wife stopped ironing his clothes, he started doing it himself. Because he felt it was important for his children to be "presentable" in public, he also began to remind them to iron their own clothes before going visiting or attending church.

While many co-provider couples reported that sharing housework was contingent upon ongoing bargaining and negotiation, others focused on how it evolved "naturally." One co-provider husband, director of a housing agency, reported that he and his wife didn't negotiate; "we pretty much do what needs to be done." His wife, an executive secretary, confirmed his description, and echoed the ad-hoc arrangements of many of the role-sharing couples: "We have not had to negotiate. We both have our specialties. He is great with dishes, I like to clean bathrooms. He does most of the laundry. It has worked out that we each do what we like best."

Although sharing tasks sometimes increases conflict, when both spouses assume that household tasks are a shared responsibility, negotiation can also become less necessary or contentious. For example, a co-provider husband who worked as a mail carrier commented, "I get home early and start dinner, make sure the kids do their homework, feed the dogs, stuff like that." He and his wife, an executive secretary, agreed that they rarely talk about housework. She said, "When I went back to work we agreed that we both needed to share, and so we just do it." While she still reminded him to perform chores according to her standards or on her schedule, she summed up her appreciation by commenting, "at least he does it without complaining." Lack of complaint was a common feature of co-provider families. Whereas many main-provider husbands complained of having to do "her" chores, the co-providers rarely talked about harboring resentments. Main-provider husbands typically lamented not having the services of a stay-at-home wife, but co-provider husbands almost never made such comparisons.

Summary and Discussion

For these dual-earner Chicano couples, we found conventional masculine privilege as well as considerable sharing in several domains. First, as in previous studies of ethnic minority families, wives were employed a substantial number of hours and made significant contributions to the household income. Second, like some who have studied Chicano families, we found that couples described their decision-making to be relatively fair and equal.[12] Third, fathers in these families were more involved in child rearing than their own fathers had been, and many were rated as sharing a majority of child care tasks. Finally, while no husband performed fully half of the housework, a few made substantial contributions in this area as well.

One of the power dynamics that appeared to undergird the household division of labor in these families was the relative earning power of each spouse, though this was modified by factors such as occupational prestige, provider role status, and personal preference. In just under half of the families, the wife earned less than a third of the family income, and in all of these families the husband performed little of the routine housework or child care. In two families, wives earned more than their husbands, and these two households reported sharing more domestic labor than others. Among the other couples who shared housework and child care, there was a preponderance of relatively balanced incomes. In the two families with large financial contributions from wives, but little household help from husbands, couples hired housekeepers to reduce the wives' household workload.

While relative income appeared to make a significant difference in marital power, we observed no simple or straightforward exchange of market resources for domestic services. Other factors like failed career aspirations or occupational status influenced marital dynamics and helped explain why some wives were willing to push a little harder for change in the division of household labor. In almost every case, husbands reluctantly responded to requests for help from wives. Only when wives explicitly took the initiative to shift some of the housework burden to husbands did the men begin to assume significant responsibility for the day-to-day operation of the household. Even when they began to share the housework and child care, men tended to do some of the less onerous tasks like playing with the children or washing the dinner dishes. When we compared these men to their own fathers, or their wives' fathers, however, we could see that they were sharing more domestic chores than the generation that preceded them.

Acceptance of wives as co-providers and wives' delegation of a portion of the homemaker role to husbands were especially important to creating more equal divisions of household labor in these families. If wives made lists for their husbands or offered them frequent reminders, they were more successful than if they waited for husbands to take the initiative. Remaining responsible for managing the home and children was cause for resentment on the part of many wives, however. Sometimes wives were effective in getting husbands to perform certain chores, like ironing, by stopping doing it altogether. For other wives, sharing evolved more "naturally," as both spouses agreed to share tasks or performed the chores that they preferred.

Economies of gratitude continually shifted as the ideology, career attachments, and feelings of entitlement of each spouse changed over time. For some main-provider families, this meant that wives were grateful for husbands' "permission" to hold a job, or that wives worked harder at home because they felt guilty for making their husbands do any of the housework. Main-provider husbands usually let their job commitments limit their family work, whereas their wives took time off from work to care for a sick child or to attend a parent–teacher conference.

Even in families where co-provider wives had advanced degrees and earned high incomes, some wives' work/family boundaries were more permeable than their husbands', like the program director married to a teacher who was a "perpetual" graduate student and attended "endless" community meetings. While she was employed more hours than he, and made about the same amount of money, she had to "schedule him" to watch the children if she wanted to leave the house alone. His stature as a "community leader" provided him with subterranean leverage in the unspoken struggle over taking responsibility for the house and children. His "gender ideology," if measured with conventional survey questions, would undoubtedly have been characterized as "egalitarian," because he spoke in broad platitudes about women's equality and was washing the dishes when we

arrived for the interviews. He insisted on finishing the dishes as he answered my questions, but in the other room, his wife confided to Elsa in incredulous tones, "He *never* does that!"

In other ambivalent co-provider families, husbands gained unspoken advantage because they had more prestigious jobs than their wives, and earned more money. While these highly educated attorneys and administrators talked about how they respected their wives' careers, and expressed interest in spending more time with their children, their actions showed that they did not fully assume responsibility for sharing the homemaker or parenting role. To solve the dilemma of too little time and too many chores, two of these families hired housekeepers. Wives were grateful for this strategy, though it did not alter inequities in the distribution of housework and child care, nor in the allocation of worry.

In other families, the economy of gratitude departed dramatically from conventional notions of husband as economic provider and wife as nurturing homemaker. When wives' earnings approached or exceeded their husbands', economies of gratitude shifted toward more equal expectations, with husbands beginning to assume that they must do more around the house. Even in these families, husbands rarely began doing more chores without prodding from wives, but they usually did them "without complaining." Similarly, when wives with economic leverage began expecting more from their husbands, they were usually successful in getting them to do more.

Another type of leverage that was important, even in main-provider households, was the existence of failed aspirations. If wives expected husbands to "make more" of themselves, pursue "more important" careers, or follow "dream" occupational goals, then wives were able to get husbands to do more around the house. This perception of failed aspirations, if held by both spouses, served as a reminder that husbands had no excuse for not helping out at home. In these families, wives were not at all reluctant to demand assistance with domestic chores, and husbands were rarely able to use their jobs as excuses for getting out of housework.

The economies of gratitude in these families were not equally balanced, but many exhibited divisions of household labor that contradicted cultural stereotypes of macho men and male-dominated families. Particularly salient in these families was the lack of fit between their own class position and that of their parents. Most of the parents were Mexican immigrants with little education and low occupational mobility. The couples we interviewed, in contrast, were well-educated and relatively secure in middle-class occupations. The couples could have compared themselves to their parents, evaluating themselves to be egalitarian and financially successful. While some did just that, most compared themselves to their Anglo and Chicano friends and coworkers, many of whom shared as much or more than they did. Implicitly comparing their earnings, occupational commitments, and perceived aptitudes, husbands and wives negotiated new patterns of work/family boundaries and developed novel justifications for their emerging arrangements. These were not created anew, but emerged out of the popular culture in which they found themselves. Judith Stacey labels such developments the making of the "postmodern family," because they signal "the contested, ambivalent, and undecided character of contemporary gender and kinship arrangements."[13] Our findings confirm that families are an important site of new struggles over the meaning of gender and the rights and obligations of men and women in each other and over each other's labor.

One of the most provocative findings from our study has to do with the class position of Chicano husbands and wives who shared household labor: white-collar, working-class families shared more than upper-middle-class profession-als. Contrary to findings from nationwide surveys predicting that higher levels of education for either husbands or wives will be associated with more sharing, the most highly educated of our well-educated sample of Chicano couples shared only moderate amounts of child care and little housework.[14] Contrary to other predictions, neither was it the working-class women in this study who achieved the most balanced divisions of labor.[15] It was the middle occupational group of women, the executive secretaries, clerks, technicians, teachers, and mid-level administrators who extracted the most help from husbands. The men in these families were similarly in the middle in terms of occupational status for this sample—administrative assistants, a builder, a mail carrier, a technician—and in the middle in terms of income. What this means is that the highest status wives—the program coordinators, nurses, social workers, and office managers—were not able to, or chose not to, transform their salaries or occupational status into more participation from husbands. This was probably because their husbands had even higher incomes and more prestigious occupations than they did. The lawyers, program directors, ranking bureaucrats, and "community leaders" parlayed their status into extra leisure at home, either by paying for housekeepers or ignoring the housework. Finally, Chicana wives at the lowest end of the occupational structure fared least well. The teacher's aides, entry-level secretaries, day-care providers, and part-time employees did the bulk of the work at home whether they were married to mechanics or lawyers. When wives made less than a third of what their husbands did, they were only able to get husbands to do a little more if the men were working at jobs considered "below" them—a telephone lineman, a painter, an elementary-school teacher.

Only Chicano couples were included in this study, but results are similar to findings from previous interviews with Anglo couples.[16] My interpretation is that the major processes shaping divisions of labor in middle-class Chicano couples are approximately the same as those shaping divisions of labor in other middle-class couples. This is not to say that ethnicity did not make a difference to the Chicano couples we interviewed. They grew up in recently immigrating working-class families, watched their parents work long hours for minimal wages, and understood firsthand the toll that various forms of racial discrimination can take. Probably because of some of these experiences, and their own more recent ones, our informants looked at job security, fertility decisions, and the division of household labor somewhat differently than their Anglo counterparts. In some cases, this can give Chicano husbands in working-class or professional jobs license to ignore more of the housework, and might temper the anger of some working-class or professional Chicanas who are still called on to do most of the domestic chores. If these findings are generalizable, however, it is those in between the blue-collar working-class and the upper-middle-class professionals that might be more likely to share housework and child-care.

Assessing whether these findings apply to other dual-earner Chicano couples will require the use of larger, more representative samples. If the limited sharing observed here represents a trend—however slow or reluctant—it could have far-reaching consequences. More and more Chicana mothers are remaining full-time members of the paid labor force. With the "postindustrial" expansion of the service and information sectors of the economy, Chicanos and Chicanas will be increasingly likely to enter white-collar middle-class occupations. As more Chicano families fit the occupational profile of those we studied, we may see more assumption of housework and child care by Chicano men. Regardless of the specific changes that the economy will undergo, we can expect Chicano men and women, like their Anglo counterparts,

to continue to negotiate for change in their work and family roles.

Notes

1. For a discussion of how the term machismo can also reflect positive attributes of respect, loyalty, responsibility and generosity, see Alfredo Mirandé, "Chicano Fathers: Traditional Perceptions and Current Realities," pp. 93–106, in *Fatherhood Today*, P. Bronstein and C. Cowan, eds. (New York: Wiley, 1988).

2. For reviews of literature on Latin-American families and projections on their future proportionate representation in the population, see Randall Collins and Scott Coltrane, *Sociology of Marriage and the Family* (Chicago: Nelson Hall, 1994); William A. Vega, "Hispanic Families in the 1980s," *Journal of Marriage and the Family* 52(1990): 1015–1024; and Norma Williams, *The Mexican-American Family* (New York: General Hall, 1990).

3. Maxinne Baca Zinn, "Family, Feminism, and Race in America," *Gender & Society* 4(1990): 68–82; Mirandé, "Chicano Fathers"; Vega, "Hispanic Families"; and Williams, *The Mexican-American Family*.

4. See Coltrane, *Family Man: Fatherhood, Housework, and Gender Equity* (New York: Oxford University Press, 1994); Coltrane and Valdez, "Reluctant Compliance: Work/Family Role Allocation in Dual-Earner Chicano Families," in *Men, Work, and Family*, Jane C. Hood, ed. (Newbury Park, CA: Sage, 1994) and Valdez and Coltrane, "Work, Family, and the Chicana: Power, Perception and Equity," in *Employed Mothers and the Family Context*, Judith Frankel, ed. (New York: Springer, 1993). I thank Hilda Cortez, a summer research intern at the University of California, for help in transcribing some of the interviews and for providing insight into some of the issues faced by these families.

5. Jessie Bernard, *The Future of Marriage* (New York: World, 1972).

6. See Jane Hood, 1986. "The Provider Role: Its Meaning and Measurement." *Journal of Marriage and the Family* 48: 349–359.

7. Hood, "The Provider Role."

8. See Coltrane, "Household Labor and the Routine Production of Gender." *Social Problems* 36: 473–490.

9. I am indebted to Arlie Hochschild, who first used this term in *The Second Shift* (New York: Viking, 1987). See also Karen Pyke and Scott Coltrane, "Entitlement, Obligation, and Gratitude in Remarriage: Toward a Gendered Understanding of Household Labor Allocation."

10. I am indebted to Joseph Pleck for his conceptualization of "asymmetrically permeable" work/family boundaries ("The Work-Family Role System." *Social Problems* 24: 417–427).

11. Jane Hood, *Becoming a Two-Job Family*, p. 131.

12. See, for example, V. Cromwell and R. Cromwell, 1978. "Perceived Dominance in Decision Making and Conflict Resolution among Anglo, Black, and Chicano Couples." *Journal of Marriage and the Family* 40: 749–760; G. Hawkes and M. Taylor, 1975. "Power Structure in Mexican and Mexican-American Farm Labor Families." *Journal of Marriage and the Family* 37: 807–81; L. Ybarra, 1982. "When Wives Work: The Impact on the Chicano Family." *Journal of Marriage and the Family* 44: 169–178.

13. Judith Stacey, 1990. *Brave New Families*. New York: Basic Books, p. 17.

14. See, for instance, Donna H. Berardo, Constance Shehan, and Gerald R. Leslie, "A Residue of Tradition: Jobs, Careers, and Spouses' Time in Housework." *Journal of Marriage and the Family* 49(1987): 381–390; Catherine E. Ross, "The Division of Labor at Home." *Social Forces* 65(1987): 816–833.

15. Patricia Zavella. 1987. *Women's Work and Chicano Families*. Ithaca, NY: Cornell University Press; Stacey, *Brave New Families*.

16. See, for example, Hochschild, *Second Shift*; Hood, *Two-Job Family*; Coltrane, *Family Man*.

50

ARTICLE

John Lewis McAdoo
Julia B. McAdoo

The African-American Father's Roles Within the Family

The study of the father's roles in the family is a relatively new phenomenon. In the past, the father's main contributions were assumed to be those of provider, protector, disciplinarian, and representative of the family to the wider community. This paper focuses on some of the contributions African-American scholars have made to the understanding of the father's role in the family.

The African-American father always seems to be either absent in family studies or dominated by the mother in mainstream literature. Even when he was observed to respond in the same way as white fathers, his behavior was interpreted negatively and sometimes even pejoratively (J. McAdoo 1988a, 1988b, 1990).

In reviewing the literature on fathers' participation in the family, the contributions of African-American scholars have been virtually ignored. This omission has led some scholars to feel that the disciplines of family studies, developmental psychology, and family sociology are ethnocentrically biased.

John L. McAdoo and Julia B. McAdoo, "The African-American Father's Roles within the Family," in R. Majors and J. Gordon, eds., *The American Black Male* (Chicago: Nelson-Hall, 1993). Reprinted with permission.

Several African-American researchers (H. McAdoo 1988; J. McAdoo 1988a, 1988b, 1991; Gary et al. 1983; Hill 1981; and Billingsley 1968) have reviewed the social science literature and noted that the following traits are crucial in any analysis and definition of African-American family strength and stability.

1. Economic sufficiency: stable employment, adequate income, property ownership, and a strong work orientation
2. Religiosity: positive ethical values and a positive religious orientation
3. Future orientation or achievement orientation: educational attainment, educational expectations and aspirations
4. Flexibility of family roles: the presence of a leader in a family, ability to deal with crisis in a positive manner, good communication patterns, and consistent rules
5. Strong kinship bonds: a high degree of commitment, appreciation, mutual obligations, helping networks and exchanges, and spending time together
6. Positive friendship relationships: reciprocal sharing and reaching out and support in times of crisis

7. A realistic attitude toward work: an ability to compartmentalize negative racial stereotypes, an ability to get along with others, and balancing work and family time

Theoretical Perspectives

Mainstream researchers on family life development have offered several theories to explain the functioning of African-American families in American society. The major theories include the cultural deprivation theory, matriarchy theory, conflict theory, domestic colonialism theory, exchange theory, Black nationalism theory, and ecological theory.

African-American researchers sometimes adopted these theories, sometimes criticized the various theories, and sometimes modified the theories to control for weaknesses in their explanatory power.

Weaknesses of some of the major theories have been identified by African-American writers: cultural deprivation/deficiency (Peters 1988; White and Parham 1990), Black matriarchy (Staples 1978; White and Parham 1990); conflict, historical materialism, and domestic colonialism (Staples 1978); exchange theory, and ecological systems (Peters 1988).

Billingsley (1968) reacted to the negative evaluations of African Americans as pathological or culturally deprived by Eurocentric researchers and clearly presented the notion that the African-American family was a viable system. Peters (1988) provided an excellent critique of the research approaches and conceptual frameworks used in studying parenting roles in African-American families. She discussed the descriptive, comparative deficit and ecological approaches to studying the African-American family. From the comparative deficit perspective, families who experienced the ravages of enslavement lack the cultural background to fulfill the various family roles expected of those living in Western society.

This cultural deprivation has led to a number of social psychological problems in the adjustment of African-American men in the performance of their provider, nurturer, and protective roles in the family.

Other theories seem to involve a value judgment of cultural deprivation that hinders objective observation in the real world. Peters suggested that these theories do not adequately take into account the demands, the extreme pressures, and the social constraints placed on African-American fathers.

White and Parham's (1990) analysis of the deprivation/deficiency theoretical models provided some further explanations of Peters's comparative deficit model. They feel that theorists from the deprivation/deficiency school assumed that the effects of years of racism and discrimination had deprived most African Americans of the strength to develop a healthy self-esteem (Kardner and Ovessey 1951) as well as legitimate family structures (Moynihan 1965). They noted that this model led to the concept of cultural deprivation that has been used to differentiate African Americans from others in the society. Cultural deprivation theory assumed that, due to inadequate exposure to European-American values, norms, customs, and life-styles, African Americans were culturally deprived and required cultural enrichment to be accepted by the dominant society.

While White and Parham suggested that white middle-class culture established the norms of society, their analysis of the Black matriarchy model as a variant of the deprivation/deficiency model may be of more interest here because it provides some of the social theorist's assumptions about the roles of African-American men in the family. Staples (1978) noted that matriarchy was seen as a pathological form of family life where the wife dominated the family members. The proponents of the matriarchy hypothesis suggest that the African-American male lacks the masculine role behaviors characterized by logical thinking, willingness to take responsibility for others, assertiveness, managerial skills, achievement orientation, and occupational mastery (White and Parham 1990).

The African-American female became the matriarch, from this point of view, because American society was unwilling to permit the African-American male to assume the legal, psychological, and social positions necessary to become a dominant force within his family. The African-American female was also seen, from this perspective, as unwilling to share the power she gained by default even in situations where the male was present and willing to take family responsibility. An analysis of mainstream and African-American empirical studies by the National Research Council (1989) testing this hypothesis found no evidence to support the theory of the Black matriarch. In a review of studies of power and decision making, the African American husband was found to share equally with his wife (J. McAdoo 1986, 1988b).

Staples (1978), while agreeing with much of Peters's analysis, noted that African-American researchers could utilize a Black nationalist orientation. He suggested that pan-Africanism has become a dominant conceptual model among African-American researchers in studying African-American families. Among the many tenets of this approach is that people of African descent have a common culture as well as a common history of racist oppression that has culminated in a shared destiny. An important ingredient of this model is its focus on the comparative study of African and African-American culture. Staples (1976) found some difficulties with this model. First, Africa has a diversity of cultures, cultural values, languages, and behavioral patterns. Another problem is the difficulty in translating cultural forms from Africa to the African-American experience. Staples felt that those who use this model tend to emphasize the study of cultural forms rather than political and economic analysis. The major weakness of this approach is that it focuses on cultural subjugation rather than the political and economic oppression that he feels affects African Americans. A basic assumption of this perspective is that a cultural group never loses its cultural heritage; it simply fuses it into another form.

In sociological research, the conflict theory provides some support for understanding the universal experiences of people of African descent, but Staples does not demonstrate its utility in understanding current research approaches. Instead, he sketchily presents two related approaches, domestic colonialism and historical materialism. Domestic colonialism seems to be a variant on the Marxist theme that all societies were divided into two groups—the oppressors and the oppressed. Domestic colonialist societies were divided along racial lines into groups of superior and inferior status. Domestic colonialism defines the rules governing the relationships between European Americans, the exploiters and African Americans, the exploited (Staples 1978).

Historical materialism suggests that the economic influences on African American family life may play an important part in the destabilization and breakup of many families. From this perspective, the father's role in the family is heavily influenced by outside sources that control his access to economic resources and limit his capacity to fulfill the provider role. Those who see some utility in this approach point to racial economic disparities, segregated housing and schooling patterns, high unemployment and incarceration rates, and the predominance of African Americans in the underclass (Glasgow 1980).

Choice and exchange theory also has been suggested as a conceptual framework to understand the context in which the African-American male makes choices and participates within the family processes (J. McAdoo 1990). This theory shows how African-American fathers make choices in the operations of their roles within the family. Fathers will choose negative roles or refuse to play some roles within the family when access to economic and social resources is perceived by them to be unavailable. The theoretical propositions were expanded to take into account the economic, political, residential, and educational barriers to the father's ability to carry out important roles within the family and the community. The assumption of this theory is that these can operate as barriers that limit the father's choices and options in his exchanges within the family.

Ecological theory presents family roles and functioning from an Afrocentric perspective. This perspective allows us to predict alternative outcomes to the racial barriers to employment, experiences of social isolation on the job and in the mainstream community, and the development of roles that African-American men play in their families. Ecological theory allows us to describe and explain the many roles fathers may play in their families. It allows us to test the assumptions of female dominance in the home and the lack of father involvement in the family. It helps us to better understand the historical, societal, political, and social influences on the roles African-American fathers play in the family. Peters (1988) sees the ecological framework as a move to understand African-American family functioning in a less ethnocentrically biased manner.

The assumption of ecological theory is that fathers may play a variety of roles in the family and community that can lead to positive family outcomes. Fathers may use a variety of coping strategies to control negative outside influences in the performance of their nurturing, support, disciplining, provider, and other family roles. Ecological theory allows us to explore the differential choices that working-, middle-, and upper-class fathers use to develop stability and positive growth in African American family life. The theory allows us to explore the positive and negative father roles and their effects within the family.

The Provider Role

In American society, a man is defined by his ability to provide for his family. Ecological theory allows us to understand how structural dissonance at the societal level may have profound influences on ethnic minority communities. As Duster (1988) has shown, at the structural level the extraordinarily high and sustained unemployment rates among African-American adults and youth are the results of such converging factors as moving of capital to foreign soil, from cities to suburbs, and from northern cities to selected areas of the Sun Belt. He also pointed to the decline in manufacturing and the increase in the advanced service sector occupations in major cities, where the majority of African Americans live, and the changing patterns of immigration that produce competition for scarce jobs.

Malveaux (1989) noted that finding and keeping a job is synonymous with being accepted into society for many Americans. This ability to provide for self and family has a great deal of impact on how a man perceives himself in a variety of family roles. From an ecological perspective, it might be suggested that an African-American man's ability to successfully fulfill the provider role depends upon other community systems over which he has little control. Several writers (J. McAdoo 1990; Gibbs 1988; Billingsley 1968) have discussed the historical, political, and social barriers that influence his ability to perform that role.

In an analysis of the work force participation of African-American youth, Malveaux suggested that the labor force may be a hostile place for them. These youths appear to suffer from the same employment and economic barriers faced by their fathers, grandfathers, and great-grandfathers before them. Wilson (1987) reviewed the national labor statistics for 1954–87 and found the unemployment rate for African Americans sixteen and over to be twice the national average during that period. He also provided empirical evidence that employed African-American males earned 57 percent of the wages earned by their European-American counterparts with the same experience and job classifications. African-American males experience a glass-ceiling effect when it comes to occupational and economic opportunities.

Gibbs (1988) eloquently discussed the educational and other structural barriers that influence the African-American male in participating in provider and community roles. Leshore (1981) noted that African-American males have been coerced by public social agencies and ignored by the private service sector.

Very few studies have been found that evaluated the family's ability to cope when, because of racial prejudice or severe economic depression, the father was unable adequately to fulfill the provider role. There needs to be some understanding of the father's reactions to sharing this role with his wife and sometimes his children. The role of the extended family (H. McAdoo 1988) in providing some support to the provider role could add another level to our understanding of the utilization of family resources. Provider role stress has been the major focus of our research efforts.

African-American men may experience stress related to their inability to fulfill their provider role in the family. Bowman (in press) found a link between unemployment and family estrangement in a national study of African-American fathers. His summary of the literature on the impact of massive deindustrialization in the urban communities noted that the loss of jobs and employment opportunities creates vulnerabilities in some fathers' personal lives and leads to a succession of provider role strains within some families. He discussed the impact of joblessness and job search discouragement, which can intensify provider role strain and lead to vulnerability to drugs, crime, family estrangement, and other psychological problems.

Bowman suggested that we need to evaluate existing research to determine how the harmful psychological and social effects of provider role strain might be reversed by extended family networks, religious orientation, and reality-based attributional patterns. We might begin by studying how some fathers are able to successfully reduce their provider role strain, maintain a positive feeling of self-esteem, and continue positive family relationships in spite of adversity.

Structural factors within society have both a direct and an indirect effect on how the provider's role is handled by fathers. J. McAdoo's (1988a) research with economically sufficient men in their role as providers found no significant differences across ethnic groups and races in the way they carried out that function. They were able to provide the necessary social and economic resources for their wives and children. Cazenave (1979), in a study of fifty-four mailmen, found that the greater their economic security, the more active these fathers became in their child-rearing functions.

Decision-Making Roles

African-American family decision making has been described from a resource and choice exchange perspective (J. McAdoo 1991). This perspective suggests that the father's role in the family depends upon how he and his spouse perceive the resources that each brings. Fathers who bring in the greater resources make the greater decisions from this perspective. Blood and Wolfe (1969), utilizing resource theory, suggested from the responses of spouses that African-American families were mother-dominated because mothers made all the decisions. This led many mainstream researchers to conclude that the structure of the decision-making process was different for African Americans than for European Americans. A reanalysis of the original Blood and Wolfe data revealed that the responses of African and European Americans were similar. Both groups reported they shared equally in family decision making with their spouses.

Our review of the African-American research on this issue provides support for a more ecological approach to studying the decision-making process within the family. This approach would allow us to consider the responses of both husband and wife before we reach conclusions about who was the dominant decision maker in the family. Fathers across a number of studies reported that they shared equally with their wives the major decision making in child rearing, important purchases, health care, transportation, and employment of either spouse (TenHouten 1970; Mack 1978; Grey-Little 1982; Hammond and Enoch 1976; Willie and Greenblatt 1978). Mack (1978) suggested that socioeconomic status may make a difference in the decision role African-American men perceive themselves as playing in the family. However, Jackson (1974), TenHouten (1970), Hammond and Enoch (1976), and Willie and Greenblatt (1978) reported few if any social class differences in the fathers' responses.

Jackson (1974), in a study of working- and middle-class fathers, noted that both groups reported being involved equally in the family decision making regarding disciplining children, grocery shopping, insurance, selection of a physician, and residential location. Middle-class fathers reported being more significantly (p < .05) involved than working-class fathers in shopping, vacationing, engaging in family recreation or commercial recreation, visiting relatives jointly, or engaging in other activities. She found that employed fathers were more likely to report attending church, shopping, vacationing, family and commercial recreation, and other activities with their spouses. They also reported visiting relatives with their spouses.

The Jackson study explored a wider range of father role behaviors than is usually found in the literature. While one may criticize the small-ness of her sample size, her findings do suggest that African-American fathers play a variety of important roles within the family. Our summary of the decision-making literature found African-American fathers' responses to be similar across social classes to that of fathers of other ethnic groups. Future research on fathers who experience severe role strain as the result of unemployment or racial discrimination on the job is needed to clarify the impact on their psychological well-being and their decision-making capacity in the family. We need to examine the impact of extended family and community resources on family functioning related to family power relationships. Again, we need to evaluate differential responses across social economic statuses and to evaluate both positive and negative responses.

Child-Rearing Roles

Mainstream researchers have debated the issue of the roles fathers play within the family related to child-rearing activity. Most of these studies have been theoretical, with little recognition given to the context in which the fathers relate to their children. There has been little systematic attempt to evaluate father–child relationships across age levels or in other than family systems. Research is needed to evaluate these relationships in church, school, and other settings as well as the family.

Cazenave (1979), in a study of fathering roles across two generations, noted that middle-income fathers reported being involved in child-care activities more than their fathers. These fathers reported being very actively involved in baby-sitting, changing baby diapers, and playing with their children. They reported that they were spending more time with their children and punishing them less often than their fathers punished them.

One (H. McAdoo 1988) observational study of African-American fathers noted that these economically sufficient fathers were warm and loving toward their children. While they perceived themselves to be strict, expecting their children to obey right away and not allowing any display of temper or bad behavior, their verbal and nonverbal interactions with their children were observed as nurturant. These fathers would interrupt the interview process to answer their children's questions. When they reprimanded their children, they would provide explanations regarding the unacceptable behavior and sometimes express their expectations about future child behaviors.

There is a need for more observational studies of fathers and their children in a variety of age and system contexts. An ecological approach would allow us to study fathers who are experiencing severe role strains and fathers who have been able to cope successfully with external threats to their personal and family systems. We would begin to develop normative adjustment patterns of reactions to external and internal pressures or role strains in terms of fathers' relationships with their children. This would lead to the possibility of discovering natural mediating factors in both role strains and child development. For example, in our research we found that nurturant fathers had little direct influence on the high self-esteem of their children. We also found that the father's nurturance of the mother led her to provide the support the children needed to feel good about themselves, their fathers, mothers, siblings, peers, and teachers.

Many young African-American fathers have been observed positively interacting with their young sons and daughters. Some fathers were unemployed; others were underemployed. However, their employment status did not seem to interfere with their ability to show love and affection to their children. Fathers have been observed working together on household chores with their teenagers in Washington, D.C., Los Angeles, Detroit, and other places by this researcher. However, public and private funds have not been made available to systematically study these occurrences. Funds have been more forthcoming to study the most problematic families, and there has been a proliferation of studies outlining the effects of disrupted families. An ecological perspective would allow researchers to describe, explain, and predict the effects of differing fathering roles and attitudes on child and adolescent development.

Family and Marital Influences

Many researchers seem to study the father's roles from a static linear perspective. The roles do not seem to change over time, and the father alone seems to be responsible for how those roles are played out in the family. An ecological perspective allows us to see that all family members are responsible for the family organizational climate, decision making, nurturance, and protection of the family. In all families, fathers play both positive and negative roles; however, little research has been found on the way the family develops rules that both regulate behaviors and provide support for positive development. What are the internal and external ingredients that allow for stability and positive change in the father's roles in the family?

It has been pointed out that the African-American father's nurturance of his wife leads to a positive self-evaluation in their children (H. McAdoo 1988). However, the literature on the subject seems to focus more on marital disruptions than on the way husbands and wives work cooperatively together in the mutual development of satisfactory marital roles. Future research should explore more fully the impact of the above ingredients on marital well-being and satisfaction with the family.

The Future

From an ecological perspective, our historical presence and the unity and integration of the patrilineal and matrilineal (Sudarkasa 1988) heritage within a capitalist society have led to changes and conflicts within our community and with the larger society to which we belong. The African-American community needs to return to the visions developed in the pre-enslavement era, and sustained during the enslavement period, to develop the kinds of institutions that will provide nurturance for positive growth for everyone in the community. Future visionaries may need to consider how we can maintain our values, namely, collective community responsibility, within a changing world economic community. How do we answer the question: What kind of world view should the African-American community develop that will lead to survival, growth, and positive relationships with communities that are not African American?

African-American fathers, mothers, and communities, if they are to have a future, must see how their problems relate to those of the larger world community. Our communities have been allowed to suffer from high crime rates, unemployment, homelessness, deadly diseases, and the movement of economic institutions out of our communities in much the same manner as what seems to be happening in third-world countries. We need to see the relationship between the flow of economic resources out the African-American community, which is sometimes described as one of the ten wealthiest countries in the world, and the inability of members of this community to find gainful employment, obtain meaningful education for their young, or receive competent protective and social services.

Finally, the survival of fathers'/husbands' roles within the family will depend upon the collective wisdom and courage of the African-American community to reject the divisive strategies represented by the terms "endangered species," "feminization of poverty," and "Black underclasses." The strategies have been fomented by other ethnic groups to blame the victims and force the victims to blame themselves. We must learn the lessons of our civil rights leaders and shun the retreatism of the 1980s and the me-isms of some of our current leaders. We must return to the basic understanding that in unity there is strength.

The future should bring a more balanced evaluation of the roles African-American men play in their families. There needs to be a shift from the focus on the most problematic families so as to study fathers in all socioeconomic groups. Future studies should focus more on what internal and external resources help fathers to help build successful families. Racial prejudices and racism have been a part of the experience of African Americans since they arrived on America's shores. There is no indication that things are going to be any different in the immediate future, and socioeconomic conditions may be getting worse for some families. However, some African-American men and women have been able to survive, and this again will be no different in the future.

Concluding Comments

The debate about family relationships in some African-American professional circles seems to be around the wrong issues. It should not focus on whether we will survive—we will—but rather on what can be done to help more African-American men, women and their families to survive, thrive, and provide positive nurturance, motivation, and support to their children and community. The discussion should not center around whether or not we have an underclass—not because the term relates to something real for us and many more European-American ethnics, but because it is a counterproductive, divisive discussion. It does not help us focus on what should be done to help African-American fathers who are in the lower socioeconomic stratum of our societies find ways to support and nurture their families.

Some of these so-called scholars need to spend a little less time in labeling and placing blame when family and community relationships are deteriorating and spend more time finding positive solutions for positive role functioning in families. Less research emphasis should be placed on evaluating African-American families from a European-American middle-class perspective, and more emphasis should be placed on developing a multicultural perspective (White and Parham 1990). We need to foster understanding of positive multiclass perspectives in trying to understand African-American father's roles and other ethnic group father's roles.

Arguments that the male is an endangered species have offered us little new or helpful information since the period of African-American enslavement in this country. African-American men have always been vulnerable in this society. The many chapters in this volume offer conclusive evidence that too many African-American men experience high arrest and incarceration rates, drop out of school at a high rate, and experience violence and deaths related to crime in their community. Some African-American men also experience significant and prolonged unemployment, and some are forced to rely on the drug trade for their economic survival when they and their family members are denied meaningful employment. The simple truth is that they have survived and they will survive and thrive as long as the African-American family and community survives. Professional literature might be better served by our collectively developing mechanisms for helping men in problematic economic, psychological, and social situations to become part of an economically stable family.

Fathers in African-American families seemed from the studies reported in this paper to perform their roles in the family about as well as their non-African-American counterparts within different social classes. The major causes for the diminution of these roles are related to stress around the father's ability to provide for his family. This ability is related to his educational and economic opportunities as well as his ability to handle and overcome racial prejudice and racism. While these are not fully within their control, many of these fathers throughout the postenslavement experience have found ways to mitigate the negative consequences of occupational and educational discrimination on the positive roles they play within their family and community.

Future analysts of the father's role within the family may need to evaluate some of the internal and external influences that help him to remain a provider, nurturer, motivator, stimulator, and protector of his wife and children. Learning what role the wife plays in this interaction is vitally important to the understanding of successfully coping fathers. As Bowman and Sanders (1988) suggested, provider role strain is a complex component of the equation and could lead to severe problems related to the psychological well-being of unmarried fathers. However, we suggest that in families where both spouses are working to provide economic support to the family, these strains may be reduced. American society is moving to a dual provider perspective, since it is becoming increasingly difficult for families to survive on one income. Dual role perspectives allow for a lessening of the pressure on the male to be the sole provider.

The survival of positive fathering/husbanding roles in the family may depend on how well African Americans are able to provide or obtain from outside resources the kinds of community services that may enhance the development of families in trouble. Role development in these fathers may depend upon how well we come together as a community to develop and utilize our political and economic clout so as to influence the broader American community to provide greater employment opportunities, including the ownership of major corporations, heading major franchises in the private service sector, and receiving equal wages for the same employment.

Father role development will depend even more on our ability to educate our children about the ingredients of positive family functioning and to provide community control and support for families who are in trouble. There is a need to develop strategies for educating children of all ethnic groups in our society about the rich heritage of African-American culture shared by the men in these communities. Father roles need to be seen from a perspective that takes in the community values for such roles. Finally, we will be able to provide more realistic family-role assessment when we are able to understand how differential spiritual values influence a father's ability to perform these roles. A more balanced approach to the evaluation of the influences on the different roles an African-American father plays in his family and community may lead to a realistic reassessment of the same influences on the European-American father's role and position in his family and community.

References

American Council on Education. 1988. *One-Third of a Nation*. Washington, DC: ACE, Commission on Minority Participation in Education and American Life.

Billingsley, A. 1968. *Black Families in White America*. Englewood Cliffs, NJ: Prentice-Hall.

Blood, R. O., and D. M. Wolfe. 1969. "Negro-White Differences in Blue-Collar Marriages." *Social Forces* 48: 59–64.

Bowman, P. J. 1991. "Post-Industrial Displacement and Family Role Strains: Challenges to the Black Family. In P. Voydanof and L. C. Majka (eds.), *Families and Economic Distress*. Newbury Park, CA: Sage.

Bowman, P. J., and R. Sanders. 1988. "Black Fathers Across the Life Cycle: Providers Role Strain and Psychological Well-Being." Paper presented at the 12th Empirical Conference on Black Psychology, Ann Arbor, MI.

Cazenave, N. 1979. "Middle Income Black Fathers: An Analysis of the Provider Role." *Family Coordinator* 28(4): 583–93.

Connor, M. E. 1986. "Some Parenting Attitudes of Young Black Fathers." In R. A. Lewis and M. B. Sussman (eds.), *Men's Changing Roles in the Family*. New York: Hayworth Press.

Duster, T. 1988. "Social Implications of the New Underclass." *Black Scholar* 19: 2–9.

Gary, L. E. 1981. "A Social Profile." In L. E. Gary (ed.), *Black Men*. Beverly Hills, CA: Sage.

———. 1986. "Family Life Events, Depression, and Black Men." In R. A. Lewis and M. B. Sussman (eds.), *Men's Changing Roles in the Family*. New York: Hayworth Press.

Gary, L. E.; L. Beaty; G. Berry; and M. D. Price. 1983. Stable Black Families: Final Report. Washington, DC: Howard University, Institute for Urban Affairs and Research.

Gibbs, J. T., ed. 1988. *Young, Black and Male in America: An Endangered Species*. Dover, MA: Auburn House.

Glasgow, D. 1980. *The Black Underclass: Poverty, Unemployment, and Entrapment of Ghetto Youth*. New York: Vintage Books.

Grey-Little, B. 1982. "Marital Quality and Power Processes among Black Couples." *Journal of Marriage and the Family* 44: 633–45.

Hammond, J., and J. R. Enoch. 1976. "Conjugal Power Relations among Black Working-Class Families." *Journal of Black Studies* 7(1): 107–33.

Hill, R. 1981. *The Strengths of Black Families*. New York: Emerson-Hall.

Jackson, J. J. 1974. "Ordinary Black Husbands: The Truly Hidden Men." *Journal of Social and Behavioral Science* 20: 19–27.

Jaynes, G. D., and R. M. Williams, Jr., eds. 1989. *A Common Destiny: Blacks and American Society*. Washington, DC: National Academy Press.

Kardner, A., and L. Ovessey. 1951. *The Mark of Oppression*. New York: Norton.

Leshore, B. 1981. "Social Services and Black Men." In L. Gary (ed.), *Black Men*. Beverly Hills, CA: Sage.

Mack, D. 1978. "The Power Relationship in Black and White Families." In R. Staples (ed.), *The Black Family: Essays and Studies*. Belmont, CA: Wadsworth.

Malveaux, J. 1989. "Transitions: The Black Adolescent and the Labor Market." In R. E. Jones (ed.), *Black Adolescents*. Berkeley, CA: Cobb and Henry.

McAdoo, H. P. 1988. "Transgenerational Patterns of Upward Mobility in African-American Families." In H. P. McAdoo (ed.), *Black Families*. Newbury Park, CA: Sage.

McAdoo, J. L. 1986a. "Black Fathers' Relationships with Their Preschool Children and the Children's Ethnic Identity. In R. A. Lewis and R. E. Salt (eds.), *Men in Families*. Newbury Park, CA: Sage.

———. 1986b. "A Black Perspective on the Father's Role in Child Development." In R. A. Lewis and M. B. Sussman (eds.), *Men's Changing Roles in the Family*. New York: Hayworth Press.

———. 1988a. "Changing Perspectives on the Role of the Black Father." In P. Bronstein and C. P. Cowan (eds.), *Fatherhood Today: Men's Changing Role in the Family*. New York: Wiley.

———. 1988b. "The Roles of Black Fathers in the Socialization of Black Children." In H. P. McAdoo (ed.), *Black Families*. Newbury Park, CA: Sage.

———. 1990. "Understanding African-American Teen Fathers." In P. E. Leone (ed.), *Understanding Troubled and Troubling Youth*. Newbury Park, CA: Sage.

———. 1991. "Urban African-American Youth: Problems and Solutions." In R. Lang (ed.), *Contemporary Urban America: Problems, Issues and Alternatives*. Boston: University Press of America.

Middleton, R., and S. Putney. 1960. "Dominance in Decisions in the Family: Race and Class Differences." In C. V. Willie (ed.), *The Family Life of Black People*. Columbus, OH: Merrill.

Moynihan, D. 1965. *The Negro Family: The Case for National Action*. Washington, DC: U.S. Department of Labor, Office of Planning Research.

Peters, M. F. 1988. "Parenting in Black Families with Young Children: A Historical Perspective." In H. P. McAdoo (ed.), *Black Families*. Newbury Park, CA: Sage.

Staples, R. 1976. *Introduction to Black Sociology*. New York: McGraw-Hill.

———. 1978. "The Black Family Revisited." In R. Staples (ed.), *The Black Family: Essays and Studies*. Belmont, CA: Wadsworth.

Sudarkasa, N. 1988. "Interpreting the African American Heritage in Afro-American Family Organization." In H. P. McAdoo (ed.), *Black Families*. Newbury Park, CA: Sage.

TenHousten, W. D. 1970. "The Black Family: Myth and Reality." *Psychiatry* 23: 145–73.

White, J. L., and T. A. Parham. 1990. *The Psychology of Blacks: An African-American Perspective*. Englewood Cliffs, NJ: Prentice-Hall.

Willie, C. V., and S. Greenblatt, 1978. "Four Classic Studies of Power Relationships in Black Families: A Review and Look to the Future. *Journal of Marriage and the Family* 40(4): 691–96.

Wilson, W. J. 1987. *The Truly Disadvantaged: The Inner City, the Under Class, and Public Policy*. Chicago: University of Chicago Press.

51

ARTICLE

Carl E. Bertoia

Janice Drakich

The Fathers' Rights Movement: Contradictions in Rhetoric and Practice

Fathers' rights groups in Canada[1] have exercised considerable pressure on the restructuring of divorce and child custody practices and law (Crean, 1988; Dawson, 1988; Drakich, 1988, 1989; L. Lamb, 1987; Maynard, 1988; Rauhala, 1988). The strength underlying this pressure is in its appeal to the use of concepts currently held in reverence in North American culture. These concepts, such as coparenting and continuing parent–child relationships, are couched in the deeply held principles of "equality" and "rights." The most visible indication of the centrality of these latter concepts to fathers' rights groups is in the names they use for their groups. Human Equality Action Resource Team (HEART), Fathers for Justice, and In Search of Justice are but a few examples of names of Canadian fathers' rights groups. Fathers' rightists and the groups that represent them use equality concepts to promulgate the notion that fathers are being treated unfairly by the legal system governing divorce, child custody, child access, property distribution, and support payments. They use this rhetoric to legitimate their lobbying efforts on behalf of increasing the power and control available to fa-

thers after divorce. A substantial body of popular literature documents fathers' alleged divorce injustices (Conine, 1989; Peacock, 1982; Roman & Haddad, 1978), which have been given life by Hollywood depictions of the downtrodden divorced father (see Drakich, 1988). The fathers' rights discourse currently reverberating the academic and popular literature and the media is seductive. It supports cherished principles and appeals to idealized notions of postdivorce families. However, the seduction of equality obscures the contradictory and statistically supported realities of the divorce, child custody, and parenting experiences of divorced mothers and fathers (see Arendell, 1986; Chambers, 1979; Furstenberg, Nord, Peterson, & Zill, 1983; Weitzman, 1985). The recent work of Martha Fineman (1991) and S. Boyd (1993) examines the rhetoric of fathers' rights groups and underscores the inconsistencies between the "facts" underlying this rhetoric and relevant scholarly evidence in the area of family and divorce.

This chapter examines a different level of contradiction, the contradiction between the fathers' rights movement's public rhetoric on family law issues and the private, self-interest posturing and framing of the experience of its members. The subjective, individualized accounts of members of fathers' rights groups contrast with the fathers' rights public rhetoric to delineate these contradictions. Twenty-eight fathers and four women from four fathers' rights groups were interviewed about their reasons for joining the group, their conceptualization of fatherhood, and their opinions on joint custody, child access, divorce mediation, and support payment of enforcement programs. In addition, some 100 members were observed in group meetings over a period of 18 months. The interviews and observations provide the private "masculinist discourse of divorce" (Arendell, 1992a, 1992b) and permit an examination of its relationship to the collective, social movement level of fathers' rights' public rhetoric by contrasting the two.

Sample and Methodology

Data were collected through in-depth, open-ended interviews with 32 members and observation of two fathers' rights groups in Ontario.[2] Not all of the group members were fathers with young children. Occasionally, women joined groups, as did one man who was experiencing problems with support payments to an ex-spouse. The intensive interviews lasted from $1\frac{1}{2}$ to 3 hours and were conducted primarily in 1989. All interviews were tape-recorded and transcribed. Data were analyzed using the constant comparative method (Glaser & Strauss, 1967; Strauss, 1988). The sample was a snowball sample. However, care was taken to interview members at various levels of activity and responsibility within the groups (i.e., executive, active members and casual members), and because approximately 15% of the membership in some of these organizations is composed of women (i.e., second wives, dating partners, and mothers without custody), four women members were interviewed. Observations of group meetings were conducted on two groups: One group's regular monthly meetings were observed for 18 months and a second group's meetings were observed for 4 months. Notes were kept, recording such data as how many people attended the meetings, the gender composition of the meetings, and topics discussed. The observation period began in 1988 and concluded in 1990.

The fathers interviewed ranged in age from 25 to 47; all but one were employed and represented occupations from laborer to medical doctor. Professionals, white-collar workers, and blue-collar workers each represented approximately one third of the sample. Altogether, the fathers had 52 children ranging in age from 2.5 to 19 years with various forms of child custody arrangements. Fifteen fathers had access to their children, three did not have access, five had sole custody of all or some of their children, and four fathers had joint custody of their children. One man, who was involved because of current spousal support problems, had adult children from a previous marriage. Of the four women interviewed, three were current spouses of the male members and one had joint custody of her children. The women ranged in age from 35 to 45 years and were full-time employees in primarily white-collar and professional occupations. The members interviewed were at different stages in the termination of their relationships or varied in time elapsed from divorce. Excluding the women-spousal members, 66% of the 29 members had been divorced for a period ranging from 2 year to 10 years. The remaining 34% had been separated for a period ranging from 6 months to $1\frac{1}{2}$ years.

To obtain father's rights groups' public accounts, we reviewed newspapers, magazines, television programs, radio interviews, proceedings in the House of Commons and the Legislative Assembly of Ontario, and fathers' rights groups' newsletters, brochures, campaign literature, and self-help manuals; we attended public events, such as the Fathers' Day March, an annual general meeting of a national umbrella organization representing fathers' rights and other pro-family groups, and public forums on family law issues.

Initial Involvements

Fathers' rights groups in Ontario formed in the mid-1980s in response to family law reforms and initiatives such as the revision of the Divorce Act, equalization of family assets, a presumption of joint custody, mandatory mediation, access enforcement, and the establishment of the Ontario Support and Custody Enforcement Branch. They lobbied most vigorously, although unsuccessfully, in support of mandatory joint custody (see Drakich, 1988) and access enforcement, and in opposition to the Ontario Support and Custody Enforcement Branch. Fathers' rights groups begin with the assumption that fathers are discriminated against in the divorce process. The groups have constructed a public rhetoric based on equality and gender-neutral models to underscore their rights and to influence law reform. To win public support and reach potential members, fathers' rights groups advertise and promote the concept of equality in their brochures, in mission statements, and through media exposure. The literature of the groups involved in this study mirrors their public representation of equality and fathers' rights on television and radio. One group's brochure states the following goals:

> To assist non-custodial parents to obtain equitable access with their children in cases where shared parenting is not possible. To give moral support to members through difficult court battles, access denial, unfair maintenance, etc. To promote equality!

Other groups emphasize the rights of fathers and the rights of children:

> "Fathers Demand Rights"[3] can and does provide . . . information concerning your rights and the rights of your children.

The public rhetoric of equality and rights established father's rights groups as advocates for fathers postdivorce. Examination of data reveals that the majority of men involved in the fathers' rights movement are drawn to these groups because they are experiencing personal troubles (Mills, 1959) with child custody, child access, or child support. Most of these men are angry[4] with the divorce process and are shocked by what has happened to them. The president of a fathers' rights group described the members this way:

> Some of these poor people have never had to deal with this type of thing. They don't know how to defend themselves. They just sit in the courtroom with their mouths open saying this can't be going on. And yes, they feel unjustly treated.

A father of one child reflected:

> We all think that it won't happen to us. And I didn't think that it would happen to me either, until it did. I never thought about it. It was sort of distant. So you're talking about a guy who is really shocked. It's not so much what really happened. It is the shock, I think, that really shakes guys the most.

There are two exceptions to the above characteristics of fathers in our study. In both cases, the men had settled their divorces several years prior to their involvement in the groups and had amicable relationships with their former spouses. One father joined the group to promote the idea of coparenting, and the other father joined to find support for primary parenting.

There is very little indication in discussions or interviews with fathers that they joined the group because of their commitment to a general principle of equality for fathers and mothers. As one executive member put it, the men were there because they had problems:

> Now the men that you hear in our meetings are men that are at the extreme. They've been abused in the system.

Another indicated that access to children was a primary reason for involvement, saying:

> Ninety-five percent of the guys at "Fathers Demand Rights" were there because they had problems not getting access to their kids. It was all pretty much child oriented. The problems were basically with access.

Most of the fathers, however, did invoke the rhetoric of rights to explain their membership in the group: their right to access to their children; their right to a decent standard of living, which has been denied them because of exorbitant child support payments; and their right to control the activities of their former wives and children. A father denied access to his two children remarked on his right to access:

> Nobody should have the right to deprive you of your family under any circumstances. No judge can say I can't see my kids.

Another expression of rights was made by a father who had access to his two children and was awaiting the custody settlement. He voiced anxiety about his inability to control the movement of his former spouse and children:

> The other one of my concerns is her mobility. That is, one of my fears is that she is waiting for the court, if she gets sole custody, there are very little restrictions on her.

Although fathers attended meetings to gain emotional support from the group and to find ways of solving their financial, custodial, and access problems, the following father suggests that fathers' concerns were more directly addressed by group members than by lawyers:

> I liked what I heard and went with them because, basically, the lawyers that I had previous, as far as I'm concerned, were incompetent.

The feeling that the group dealt with the rights of fathers was echoed in the interviews. One father explained that when he separated from his wife he looked toward the fathers' rights group to explain and help him understand his situation:

> How I got involved? I split up. I had some problems knowing what my rights were, what I could do and what I couldn't do. You don't know the legal system, so you're wondering how does everything work as far as separation, divorce, and custody.

Or, as this father, who has a restraining order on him as a consequence of assaulting his wife, put it, fathers' rights groups were the only source of support in getting what he wanted:

> I realized what condition I was in, in terms of not being able to get what I wanted, which was what was left of my family deal . . . they [fathers' rights groups] were pretty well the only voice in the wilderness that [was] saying there was a chance.

Overall, the men involved in the fathers' rights movement are angry men: angry about paying out what they consider to be huge sums of money in child support, angry that they have limited access to their children, and angry with the whole divorce and child custody process. They join fathers' rights groups for personal reasons and for personal gain. Our data do not support the public image of fathers' rights groups as groups motivated by concerns of equality to transform the divorce process and postdivorce coparenting. Rather, what we have found is that fathers privilege their private troubles over fathers' rights groups' equality posturing. One executive woman member, in discussing problems of conducting group meetings, points to the privileging of personal troubles.

> Most of the men are very aggressive. And they are. They really are. A lot are angry. Our executive tries to get them to stop going on about how much child support they pay, and "she" [ex-spouse] is a bitch, and all that.

One father with sole custody, who joined the group for support in his everyday child care responsibilities, exposed this private/public contradiction when he was asked about the members' expressed custody preferences:

> I can kill a conversation with one of these groups if I asked, "Would you be willing to take sole custody?" And many of these men have not seriously entertained this question or thought about it.

Thus initial involvements in fathers' rights groups are motivated by self-serving interests rather than a desire for equality—whether we interpret equality as equal opportunity to obtain sole custody of equal responsibility for children. The mission statements of fathers' rights groups inaccurately portray what actually happens within these groups and how the groups are used. The following section compares the public platforms of fathers' rights groups with respect to the alleged injustices and discrimination and interconnected discourse of "rights" is difficult to separate out and present in mutually exclusive categories. Our approach in what follows is to focus on the issues that fathers' rightists identify as major sites of discrimination: maternal preference in awarding custody, maternal control of the children, and maternal financial privilege.

Maternal Preference in Custody

The argument made by fathers' rights groups is that there is gender bias in Canadian child custody law and in the application of the law, despite the formal gender neutrality of "the best interest of the child" doctrine introduced in the 1970s. Accordingly, fathers are discriminated against by an apparent maternal preference in awarding custody, a vestige of the "tender years doctrine." Fathers' rightists support this assertion with the statistic that mothers get sole custody of their children in 86% of the cases. Yet they fail to acknowledge that this statistic represents the mutual decision of both parents to award sole custody to the mother (Boyd, 1989, 1993; McKie, Prentice, & Reed, 1983). Moreover, they fail to concede that when men are the petitioners they are more likely to be awarded custody. Available

Canadian data indicate that the award of custody, in father petition cases, is either almost equally distributed to mothers and fathers (McKie et al., 1983; Richardson, 1988), or, as reported in another study of one jurisdiction, the majority of father petitioners were granted custody—74% in Provincial Court and 91% in Supreme Court[5] (McClure & Kennedy-Richardson, 1987). Data from some U.S. researchers also support the almost equal distribution of custody awards in contested cases (Polikoff, 1983; Weitzman, 1985). However, the recent work of Maccoby and Mnookin (1992) does strongly challenge the findings of Polikoff (1983) and Weitzman (1985) on equal distribution. Nevertheless, the statistical reality of sole maternal custody in undisputed cases is the foundation of fathers' rights groups' claim of discrimination. Their platform for justice for fathers involves two arguments. First, they appeal to gender equality in parenting skills and in parenting roles by arguing that the role of fatherhood has changed. They would contend that the father of the 1980s and 1990s is one who nurtures and is involved in all activities of the family with his children. As one father of two children with access argues:

> More and more, men in particular are becoming more aware of parenting roles. I think that in society, the businessman is not just interested in business any more. He is more interested in the family, and that is what is happening as we change in that attitude. There is also a change in the women's role. The women's role is now one of woman in the work force. The majority of them now. [In] marriages, both parents are working. It changes the role of the woman who would stay at home, bake the pies, and wash the clothes. And now they are not doing this.

The belief that men are sharing in domestic and child care responsibilities is further revealed in the following account:

> I think gone are the days of . . . they are recognizing that men want to be involved. We are no longer just cash receipt machines or breadwinners. We are playing an active role. With the

wife out working, it is necessary that men are willing to take over and help. We are no longer back when our parents, or our parents' parents, where the man went out to work, came home to read his papers and smoke his pipe. And the wife did everything else. That's history.

Second, they appeal to their rights to affirmative action in the family division of labor. They argue that men have recognized women's rights in the workforce, and yet women deny fathers the right to equality in the family:

> If we're going to talk about equal opportunity for women in the job place then we got to talk about equal opportunity for men in domestic matters.

Underlying statements such as the one above is the belief that, because of prejudice on the part of women and the state, equality in the family is not being allowed to emerge; thus fathers' rightists argue that they are being victimized by reverse discrimination. They perceive women as making social and economic strides outside of the home in the male-dominated sphere. However, in the female-dominated family sphere, these men feel that they are not being afforded equal opportunity to parent and share household responsibilities. As a consequence, they believe that they are discriminated against in custody arrangements because they are fathers. One father without access to his children points to the prejudice against fathers:

> I am concerned that the women want equality in the workplace but they do not want equality in the home. . . . The attitudes that seemed to be portrayed is that men and women are not equal when it comes to child rearing. . . . But, in spite of that, we are.

Another describes discrimination:

> It says in the Family Law Act that each parent has equal rights to apply for custody. But we know that we still got a bunch of old farts on the bench and society has been trained to think that women should have the children. And it is just basic cut and dry like that.

There are two levels of contradiction in the arguments that fathers bring forward to assert their rights as postdivorce fathers. The first contradiction is in the rhetoric for equality in sole-custody determinations. Despite the public claim that fathers want custody of their children, the majority of fathers interviewed did not embrace the idea of seeking sole custody. Fathers have not thought about sole custody, or they think that they cannot obtain custody, or they simply do not want it. One executive member supports the ambivalence of fathers' desire for sole custody in the following statement:

> What happens at "Fathers Demand Rights" is that the guys are told to go for custody. They do have this much right to their children. But a lot of them don't think that. If a lot of them stopped and thought about—are they really that interested? A lot of them do want it. But I admire that guy that I was working with who came and sat down and said, "I don't want custody. What am I going to do with three kids?"

What was commonly expressed by fathers was that they did not want custody but did want liberal access to their children:

> All I want is good access so that I am not a visitor. I want to have the freedom to phone them, and I want the freedom for them to phone me. I want to be able to see them when I want to without asking for permission all the time.

The second contradiction is in their perception of their participation in child care and domestic responsibilities. This is evidence in one father's statement. He says that fathers are "willing to take over and help." The notion of helping resonated in the fathers' interviews. Not one of them realized that to speak of "helping" was to delegate the task of child care to mothers. That mothers are expected to assume primary responsibility for children is not surprising. The empirical evidence unequivocally supports the fact that mothers continue to be the parent responsible for all aspects of care of the child (Drakich, 1989; Hochschild, 1989).

That fathers take for granted mothers' primary responsibility in child care is evident in their discussions of joint custody.[6]

Joint Custody Rhetoric

The question we are left with is this: What do fathers want in terms of child custody if they do not want sole custody but want equality? When fathers are asked what the fathers' rights movement is fighting for, invariably the first and foremost answer is to retain their rights to be a father to their children after divorce. The way that they see this being accomplished outside of marriage is through joint custody. Appeals to traditional and contemporary discourses on the family are incorporated into the appeal for joint custody by fathers' rightists. The nearly singular focus on joint custody as a remedy for father discrimination demonstrates the contradictory nature of fathers' claims. The voices of the fathers interviewed identify and help us understand the multifaceted and contradictory meanings that the concept of joint custody has for father's rightists. Because there are no statutory definitions of joint custody or statutory distinctions between joint legal and joint physical custody in Canadian law, untangling the meaning of joint custody for these fathers is important in understanding their version of coparenting after divorce.

Father's rightists argue that joint custody would allow them to accomplish their goal of participatory fatherhood by coupling the argument with the equality and rights discourse. One father, an executive member who has sole custody of his children, emotionally summarizes the cases of members' fight for joint custody:

> What we are dealing with is parents that are trying to save what little is left of their lives with their children. . . . No, they are not fighting for [sole] custody, they are fighting for shared parenting. Fighting for a share, to remain a human being, to remain a parent to

their child. Sole [maternal] custody deprives them [fathers] of that. They have no rights.

This father's remarks echo the fathers' rightists' public discourse, which focuses on the coparenting aspect of joint custody in terms of equal sharing of responsibility and primary care (Henderson, 1988; Roman & Haddad, 1978). Although some fathers talked about the joys of being with their children, not one father talked about wanting to have the responsibility of the everyday care of his children:

> On the one hand I want to fight for custody of the kids. I would like to have them with me full-time instead of with her. On the other hand to do it on my own would be more than I would want to do right now. 'Cause even having them with me for the weeks that I had them I wasn't used to it. I just wasn't set up for it. It was an aggravation running here and there and stuff.

It is interesting to note that this father, as much as the other fathers, at least has the ability to decide whether or not he wants to spend more time with his children—a luxury most mothers do not have.

What we heard from many fathers was a view of sharing and coparenting that did not involve shared everyday care and responsibility but the continuation of their parenting role prior to divorce. One of the founders of a fathers' rights group responded to the interviewer as follows:

> **Interviewer:** So you are looking at equal, shared, continuation of parenting?
>
> **Father:** No. Because parenting is never equal. Continuing parenting, whatever that means to you as to your family unit. That will change according to your needs. According to the children's needs. According to their age, their sex.
>
> **Interviewer:** What you want to do is replicate your role when you were married outside of a marriage relationship. You want to continue that same sort of role.
>
> **Father:** Yes.

Thus, to him, joint custody does not necessarily mean equality in physical custody and everyday care but the right to exercise the level of parenting that went on prior to the divorce. For many of the other fathers, joint custody did not entail the equal division of child care between mothers and fathers:

> Joint custody doesn't have to be fifty–fifty. You can have a joint custody arrangement where you only see the child ten, fifteen, twenty percent. But at least you have an input into the child's life.

Another father went so far as to say that 1% of the child care responsibilities was shared parenting:

> You can have ten percent, ninety percent and it's still shared parenting. Sharing one percent with the father and ninety-nine percent with the mother is shared parenting. Coparenting implies that it is not one person cut off. There is a sharing going on.

We can see from the preceding statements that the meaning of joint custody does not denote equal physical and primary child care responsibilities between spouses. What we see is men who either have not thought about what equality means in practice or have developed a vocabulary of motives that is more socially palatable than personal-troubles discourse. One woman executive member discusses the absence of fathers' realistic expectations in their fight for custody:

> I see a lot of them and these guys are fighting for these kids so hard and I say to them, "You know they are lovely when they are cute kids but what are you going to do when they reach this rotten age? How are you going to cope with it. Do you really want all that?"

That fathers have unrealistic expectations for child care is not surprising in the light of this executive member's observation from counseling fathers in two of the groups:

> Most people who come to me don't even talk about their kids. They are totally wound up with their own problems. And rightly so.

Joint custody for fathers' rightists is the vehicle to preserve their fatherhood role postdivorce. It is the legal recognition of their fatherhood that they argue is denied them in sole-maternal-custody arrangements. However, the postdivorce fatherhood role for many fathers means a continuation of their predivorce role and not a reconceptualized role of the equal parenting dad typified in the fathers' rights public rhetoric.

Maternal Control of Children

One common, strongly held belief is that mothers have all the power to control their children after divorce. Mothers decide what schools children go to; what events they participate in; which doctors, extended family, and friends they see; and when they see their fathers. The fathers interviewed felt that they had lost their position of power in the postdivorce family and, as a consequence, had lost control over their children:

> I mean, I have to see my relationship with my child defined in terms of power. But my ex has all the power. She has all the marbles and I'm constantly kowtowing. And I don't like it.

The fathers sense this loss of control most deeply in their access ("visitation" in the United States) to their children. Frustrated by restricted or inflexible access, one father said:

> You don't get any extra time. They shut you down. You get totally shut down when you are a noncustodial parent. They will make your life miserable. In my case anyways, is that I was shut down. No Christmas extra time. Just my regular couple of days. Christmas break. Easter break. Spring break. I got no extra time. I got just shut down in there.

A popular discourse used by fathers' rightists to appeal for joint custody as a remedy for limited access is "the best interest of the child" doctrine.[7] This discourse maintains that the child needs and has a right to have both parents in his or her life in the event of a divorce. This specific discourse appeals to the monolithic, conservative, and sexist biases that are inherent in the beliefs about the family (Eichler, 1988). The monolithic bias treats families as having universal experiences and structures and maintains that "there is a natural differentiation of functions within families on the basis of sex" (Eichler, 1988, p. 2). Moreover, it maintains that detrimental sociopsychological effects could occur if a parent, namely, the father, is denied influence over his child(ren). A lay developmental psychology is used by fathers to suggest that negative consequences could occur if a father is not present in his child's life. Although the following father uses the gender-neutral term of *parent,* he is speaking about fathers as he is a father who has been denied access to his children:

> Think of the effect on the children when one parent is cut out. In some places, that is good and I won't deny that. But in the majority of cases that is unhealthy for the child. So any focus that puts stress on the relationship and says to one party or the other that you are not a fit parent, or I doubt your parenting abilities, or [that] gives me power to keep you away and thereby alter your personality or later your drive, and defeat you and keep you away from that child affects the child.

The role of the father in child development is explained by another father:

> In the developmental phases of the children, there comes a point where a father figure is necessary and which the mother figure is necessary. As the child develops, the need for a mother or father varies. So that they have higher needs under age 5 for the maternal care, and it is 50–50 from age 5 to 10. And I would think further on, there is a greater need for the paternal figure to be present. . . . One of the major things [joint custody] does is to provide a father figure which the child has some contact

with . . . and to which to develop his own personality and develop his own identity.

Access to children is not the only area that fathers contend that mothers control. The majority of fathers believe that mothers control information about their children and decisions affecting their children's lives. Even though Ontario's Children's Law Reform Act 20(5) states that the parent with access has the right to make inquiries and receive information about the health, education, and welfare of the child(ren), many men assert that they are unable to get such information because they are not legally recognized as a parent when they divorce. As such, they insist that they cannot exercise their rights as fathers in the decision-making process because their wives have the legal power to deny them this information as a result of their noncustodial status. This father's experience was one of continued exclusion from his ex-wife's decisions involving his son. He recounts his feelings of being "shut down":

> I never knew what sports camp he was supposed to go to in the summer time. I had to find out on my own. His school—she can do whatever she wants. She can send him to any school. She can do whatever she wants. Or he [ex-wife's current partner] can. Whoever's got the custodial parenthood at the time can do whatever they want. They have so much power. They shut you down. She decided to send him to another school. Didn't say a word to me. The hell with you. If they really want to say nothing to you . . . you can't do anything in the world. You cannot. And you get frustrated and wonder what am I going to do. It took me a month to find out what school he's going to. I'm going to have an appointment with one of his teachers.

Although this father had problems with obtaining information from his former wife, he was able to procure the necessary information from other sources or, eventually, from his wife. Most fathers felt that having joint custody would give them more power and control in maintaining access to information about their children than they would have as noncustodial parents:

> What I did learn is that joint custody is extremely beneficial to maintaining certain access rights to information. Information about the child and access rights to the child. Without joint custody I had a lot of things that I could not so.

This father's description of joint custody reflects fathers' rightists' claim that, if fathers were granted legal status as a parent (i.e., had joint custody), this status would empower them to correct the perceived discrimination they face in accessing information on their children. Moreover, as the following father states, fathers will be able to exert paternal rights over their children:

> Once one person has sole custody, the other person doesn't have any right to interfere with education, their religion, or any of the upbringing, medical care, or anything of the children. With joint custody arrangements, the parent has a say.

Our interviews suggest that fathers are more concerned with being excluded from the decision-making process than with being denied information. Father's appeal to their right to information about their children masks the underlying issues of power and control. In fact, fathers' rightists deny that they are interested in power and control. The following father rejects the accusation that he is interested in power and control, but in his rejection he reveals that he wants to monitor his child's life and, he also implies, his ex-wife's parenting:

> This is what women bring up all the time. All fathers want [joint] custody to control their wives. They want access to information to control their wives. Screw off lady. I want access to information so that I can keep tabs on my child's life. I don't give a shit what you do. But you do have the responsibility of raising that child.

Maternal Financial Privilege

These fathers not only feel that mothers have been privileged with care and control of their children but also that their former spouses have been unjustly awarded outrageous child support payments. Indeed, the topic of support payments was the central issue, during the observation period, at the majority of meetings, across all the groups. The group discussions of support payments were most often focused on individual fathers' personal troubles with support payments. Usually, these fathers brought their problems to the group looking for advice, direction, and sympathy. Support payment concerns can be divided into three types: (a) concern about the amount that is being paid, (b) concern that support is paid but access is denied or limited, and (c) concern that the money cannot be monitored. Excluding the women-spousal members and the sole-custody fathers, 65% of the fathers interviewed had support payment concerns. The negative emotional response to support payments is charged by fathers' conviction that discrimination occurs in awarding custody and child support. One father alludes to the inherent discrimination of "mommy gets the kids and daddy gets the bills" when he says:

> So the whole concept that the children belong to the mother and that the husband has to pay support to the mother and children because she can't earn as much money in the workplace, I find a problem with that.

Another father puts it even more strongly:

> The men that come have been or are being denied access and at the same time being robbed of their whole paycheck.

Most men state that they are paying too much in child support and cannot live on what is left. They feel that the financial burden placed on fathers penalizes their lifestyles, as the following father states:

I know men out there that have three jobs to maintain a standard of living for themselves and their children just so that they could see their kids.

Moreover, this statement suggests that mothers would deny access to fathers who do not comply with the financial support agreement—again, portraying women has having power and control over the lives of fathers and their children. Other fathers used the metaphor of rape to describe the consequences of mothers' power and control after divorce:

> After being jerked around all over the place. Like we had four remands or what you call adjournments. Then when I got into court and the master [judge] awarded [my ex-spouse] fourteen hundred dollars a month support, which was two thirds of my income, and I was not allowed to see my daughter until I had a psychological assessment. . . . And it was such a major loss. I went into shock. . . . So that is how I got involved in "Fathers Demand Rights" because I felt like I was being royally raped.

This father, who was "jerked around," did not have access to his children and saw the rape in terms of control over his paycheck and access to his children. A father with access also uses the metaphor of rape but focuses the metaphor on the former spouse's control of his identity and relationship to his children as a feather as well as of his income and skills:

> Can I say anything about my wife to my children? No. She did a bad thing. She committed rape of a father and the love between him and his children. That is what she did. . . . It was not only a rape of my children; it is also a rape of my resources. I was the one that went through university. I worked hard for where I am right now. She didn't. She got her job and she is working, but it is not as much as I'm getting.

These fathers' accounts focus on their victimization in the process of awarding support and access. However, underlying these accounts is the fathers' perception of the threat to their power

and control. These pivotal factors, obscured by the rhetoric of rights, justice, and victimization, become more visible when fathers talk about their concern for where the support money is going:

> I feel insulted that the court is going to say that you have to pay so much support because the wife is going to put the money away and make it available for them to go on for postsecondary education. And I say, well you trust her and not me. I mean I can do it. You don't have to give it to her to give to them. How do I know that it is even going to go to them? In my court case, I'm going to pursue this.

Of the fathers, 40% want to maintain control of the support money—who spends it and how it is spent. The others would like to see some form of accountability for the funds, either because they feel that the payments are too high or that the money is being spent improperly. One father suggests that the acrimony of divorce arises in the settlement of child support when fathers question the disbursement of "their" money:

> So when you get down to child support, although it is needed for the child, the problem comes in: What level of monetary support and is the money going to be used for child support? There it becomes the question number two. If you are going to order money for child support, what guarantee is there that it is used for child support?

The main reason articulated by the fathers interviewed and observed, for their concern about mothers' control of money, is that mothers will spend the money on themselves. According to one father, child support is just a form of alimony to the former wife:

> When it comes to child support, of course, the problem has occurred during the transition between getting away from the alimony standard and having a purely child support standard. Over the long term we see child support being used as alimony. Where you see large child

support agreements coming around—because you know darn well that that money isn't being all used for the child—that money is being used to maintain a certain lifestyle for one of the parents. The parent who has gotten custody.

Another father, who did not have access to his children and who defaulted on his child support payments, monitored his ex-spouse's spending:

> **Father:** She's usually out to 1:30 in the morning. Spending 150 bucks a week on bingo. Without my paying any money or support—she's spending money on bingo.
>
> **Interviewer:** How did you find out?
>
> **Father:** Well, I have friends at bingo monitoring her activities.

Most father ardently believe that mothers seek sole custody to maintain a high standard of living or to avoid paid work:

> I know why she's doing what she's doing to me to get sole custody and have child support is because she wants to have six hundred dollars a month. It's that money. Six hundred dollars free a month that they get clear to control a child to do whatever they want. Go anywhere they want. And she can sit back and literally retire and have money coming in.

Fathers' desire to control the spending of support payments is revealed in their demands for accountability. Here is a request from one father:

> So I would like to see more standardization. In child support I would like to see more accountability where we could go to the courts in the future and say this is the acceptable standard for raising this many children.

Another father suggests that the courts order accountability:

> It would be interesting if the courts would order the custodial parent to document every dollar spent. And that way that person who is paying his money, which is supposed to be going towards the children's upbringing, would

have their mind at ease. But that is not the way it is. I think that the support is there for the children and it should be used for that.

All fathers' rightists recognize the difficulty in maintaining financial control, and many noncustodial fathers look to joint custody as a legal solution to their monetary concerns. They believe that joint custody will relieve them of their financial responsibility to the postdivorce family unit, or decrease their support payments, and/or allow them to maintain power over and control of their funds:

> This is why when you talk joint custody, I think it's beautiful because of the fact that both parents wouldn't have to pay anything. So we are eliminating one factor, which is what one is going to be looking for in the other is that of money. Keeping that money—greediness—out, what do you have next? Nothing. . . . I'm not saying that I would agree to a shared joint custody. I'm not pushing that. I'm just saying the definition in law of joint custody where "father" can have Wednesdays and every other weekend, they call that joint custody. That's not a joint custody. You know why? Why is the father paying six hundred dollars a month? If it is shared joint custody as per law one should not pay the other. If you are talking equal share, an equal split. . . . True joint custody, the essence of joint custody, is shared equally.

Once again, joint custody is couched within the discourse of social equality. As this father suggests, it is unfair to expect fathers to pay child support if they do not have joint physical custody, but at the same time it is not necessary to pay child support if fathers do have joint physical custody. Although he does not want joint physical custody, he is unwilling, or at least resentful, to pay what he believes to be disproportionate child support.

The conceptualization of equality for fathers with support payment personal troubles privileges their money over their children's care. These fathers did not discuss the value of the nonmonetary contribution of the mother to the upbringing of the children in their considerations of equality. Because mothers' care of children is taken for granted, it is easy to discount or ignore in the fathers' equality equation. Moreover, fathers seem not to imagine the lifestyle consequences for the children in the absence of child support payments. Their posturing on child support challenges their caring father image and their alleged concern for the best interests of the child. The fathers in this study seem not to connect the withdrawal of their support to a reversal of the children's predivorce material conditions. A substantial body of literature now documents women's financial troubles after divorce. Several U.S. researchers (Albrecht, 1980; Duncan & Hoffamn, 1985; Wallerstein & Blakeslee, 1989; Weitzman, 1985), comparing divorced men and women, report on mothers' socioeconomic downward mobility and fathers' upward mobility postdivorce. Canadian research also supports this trend of differential economic consequences for men and women after divorce (Richardson, 1988).

Related Research

The results of this research support the work of Arendell (1992a, 1992b) and Coltrane and Hickman (1992). The contrasting of private and public rhetoric in this chapter allows for a comparison with Arendell's study of men's masculinist discourse of divorce and Coltrane and Hickman's examination of fathers' rights public moral discourse. Arendell (1992a, 1992b) found that men believed that the system inherently discriminates against men in divorce and that men who represent a diversity of educational and professional backgrounds, and a diversity of separation and divorce experiences, share a masculinist discourse of divorce. The accounts from the men in Arendell's study are very similar to the accounts of the fathers presented here. The sites of discrimination and the explanations offered by the fathers' rightists resonate in the ac-

counts provided by Arendell (1992a, 1992b) and Coltrane and Hickman (1992). Thus it would appear that personal troubles discourse for non-custodial fathers and the common themes of discrimination in access, support payments, and custody are consequences of institutionalized gender arrangements that privilege men. It is not surprising, then, that we hear fathers employ an equality discourse that is premised on gendered relations to children and (ex)-spouses. The similarity in the use of a masculinist discourse, a rhetoric of equality, and a rhetoric of rights for men in two countries with different laws and divorce processes—but no apparent differences in the gender organization of their societies—highlights the gendered nature of their discourse. These common findings on personal discourses suggest that fathers' rights groups on both sides of the border should share similarities in their public rhetoric. Coltrane and Hickman (1992) profile the discourse of fathers' rights groups as a language of entitlement. They indicate that fathers' rights groups employ a rhetoric of equal rights to lobby for gender neutrality in custody statutes and equal rights to their children. Moreover, fathers' rights groups assert that joint custody is the only reasonable solution to child custody. Coltrane and Hickman (1992) also found that fathers' rights organizations' perpetuation of patriarchal family relations, embedded in their agenda, was "veiled by a rhetoric of children's rights and gender neutrality" (p. 413). Fathers' rights groups were also found to use rhetoric to establish the existence of injustice to fathers. The four groups in this study offered statistics and horror stories to the media to the same end as the organizations studied by Coltrane and Hickman (1992, p. 406). Another interesting similarity is that the claims makers in the Coltrane and Hickman (1992) study did "not always distinguish between private troubles and public issues" (p. 416). Similarly, the private troubles of the fathers in our study formed the basis for the groups' custody and divorce reforms. Finally, fathers' rights groups in our study also used rhetorical strategies that "assumed a societal consensus about what was in the best interest of the children" (Coltrane & Hickman, 1992, p. 417). Research in Australia (Graycar, 1989) examining the debate on child custody indicates that fathers' rights groups in Australia share similar rhetorical strategies and also employ equality rhetoric. The similarities across countries invites more in-depth comparative research.

Conclusions

During the divorce process, fathers come to some realization that they have lost power and control over parts of their lives—usually their fatherhood or their standard of living—and the lives of their former spouses and children. Not only do these men feel that they have been stripped of their father role by the court, they also feel they have been abused by the court and treated unfairly. Although most fathers experience these losses and may feel discriminated against because they are fathers, it is fathers' rightists who have politicized these events. Father's rights groups have taken fathers' personal troubles and recast them as issues of equality and rights. Although fathers' rightists portray themselves as caring, loving fathers who have been denied their rights to equal custody and access to their children, they are more concerned about the equality of their legal status than their equality in everyday parenting. The voices of the fathers we have heard from in this chapter have been telling. Their self-disclosures point to the essentially economic and hegemonic underpinnings of their discourse. Although equality is the organizing principles of their rhetoric, a closer examination exposes a notion of equality that conforms to the gendered familial division of labor. The fathers' rightists are not lobbying for joint, equal responsibility and care of children after divorce; they want equal access to their children, to information, and to decision making. The individual, self-disclosed accounts reported here unveil a masculinist construction of equality that obfuscates the gendered differences and experiences of mothers and fathers. Fathers' rightists have co-opted the language of equality but not the spirit of equality. The fathers' own words, reported here, tell us that they do not want sole responsibility for children, nor do they want an equal division of child care and responsibility. What they want, they tell us, is to have equal status as legal parents, which would give them equal access opportunities to their children and to information. The rhetoric of fathers' rights gives the illusion of equality, but, in essence, the demands are to continue the practice of inequality in postdivorce parenting but now with legal sanction.

The rhetoric of equality premised on sameness obscures the differential material conditions and experiences of mothers and fathers. Most mothers are caregivers to children. Most fathers are not. Most mothers are economically disadvantaged by divorce. Most fathers are not. Most women (mothers) relative to most men (fathers) are paid less in the workforce (Armstrong & Armstrong, 1984; Ornstein, 1983; Statistics Canada, 1993), live below the level of poverty (Arendell, 1986), and maintain more contact with their children postdivorce if they are noncustodial parents (see Furstenberg & Nord, 1985; Gross, 1988, for women's visitation patterns; see Ambrose, Harper, & Pemberton, 1983; Furstenberg et al., 1983; Hetherington, Cox, & Cox, 1976; Loewen, 1988, for men's).

The discourse of equality has potent symbolic imagery for the structure and relationships of the postdivorce family and appeals to the popular gender-neutral ideals of contemporary society. The rhetoric of joint custody operationalizes this symbolic imagery and sustains its appeal by conforming to gender neutrality. The discourse of fathers' rights, and its companion rhetoric of joint custody, has entrenched the masculinist discourse of divorce in the public imagination and, as a consequence, has provided a collective voice for divorced fathers and a legitimizing context for their complaints and anger. Moreover, the discourse of fathers' rights establishes a vocabulary of motives for fathers that conceals or obviates fathers' accounts of their prior fathering practices.

The rich ethnographic data, here provided by fathers' rightists, reflect their perspectives on the fatherhood role after divorce. This role, as typified by these fathers, is one that contradicts the fathers' rightists' public depiction of fathers as participatory dads and coparents to their children. Indeed, fathers want to play a role in their children's lives, but for most, that role is merely a continuation of their predivorce role of the traditional father who exercises his power and control.

Notes

1. Although this chapter focuses on fathers' rights groups in Canada, these groups have had strikingly similar effects in other countries. See Graycar (1989), Holtrust, Sevenhuijsen, and Verbraken (1989), and Sevenhuijsen (1986) for a discussion of fathers' rights discourse in Australia and the Netherlands, respectively. See Coltrane and Hickman (1992) and Fineman (1991) for a discussion of father's rights groups in the United States.

2. Both the interview and the observational data were collected by Carl Bertoia, who had full and liberal access to the membership and meetings of three groups. In the fourth group, he had access to members and was allowed to observe introductory meetings. However, he was not allowed to attend general meetings because he did not have an active complaint. Of the three groups permitting liberal access, two were observed. The third was not observed because of the distance involved to attend meetings.

3. The name of the fathers' rights group appearing in the quotations is a pseudonym to protect the anonymity of the participants. Whenever a fathers' right group is mentioned in a quotation used in this chapter, we will substitute the name "Fathers Demand Rights."

4. Research indicates that anger postdivorce is a fairly common response to marriage dissolution and suggests that anger is not unique to men belonging to fathers' rights groups (see Arendell, 1992a, 1992b; Ambrose, Harper, & Pemberton, 1983; Hetherington, Cox, & Cox, 1976).

5. This study was based on 899 cases active from July 1, 1985, to June 30, 1986, in Kitchener, Ontario. There were 169 custody applications from fathers.

6. It is important to note that *joint custody* is a term used loosely to refer to either joint legal or joint physical custody. In the majority of instances, when fathers' rightists use *joint custody,* they mean joint legal custody of children. The Canadian Divorce Act 1985 identifies joint custody as an option for divorcing parents. There are no statutory definitions of joint custody at either the federal or the provincial levels. However, there are various interpretations of joint custody—legal and physical—found in case law. The legal principle underlying custody awards is the best interest of the child. There is no presumption of joint custody in Canada.

7. The "best interest of the child doctrine" is loosely defined in statutory law as the needs and circumstances of the child including emotional ties, child preferences, stable environment, and proposed plans for care and upbringing. The definition has been influenced by judges and courts through case law. However, it has been appropriated by a variety of other parties to a divorce. Psychologists, social workers, fathers' rightists, and lawyers have shaped the meaning of the "best interest of the child" to fit their self-interest, or societal values such as continuing, ongoing parent–child relationships postdivorce, or their professional interpretations. The resulting equivocal construct of "the best interest of the child" has privileged the apparent advocates of children's best interest at the expense of the children.

Q: Why did you decide to record again?

A: Because *this* housewife would like to have a career for a bit! On October 9, I'll be 40, and Sean will be 5 and I can afford to say "Daddy does something else as well." He's not accustomed to it—in five years I hardly picked up a guitar. Last Christmas our neighbors showed him "Yellow Submarine" and he came running in, saying, "Daddy, you were singing . . . Were you a Beatle?" I said, "Well—yes, right."

—John Lennon, interview for *Newsweek*, 1980

A | re men changing? If so, in what directions? Can men change even more? In what ways should men be different? We posed many of these questions at the beginning of our exploration of men's lives, and we return to them here, in the book's last section, to examine the directions men have taken to enlarge their roles, to expand the meaning of masculinity, to change the rules.

PART

TEN

Men and the Future

The articles in this section explore the movements and organizations designed to engage men in the process of transformation. Michael Schwalbe examines the mythopoetic men's movement most often associated with Robert Bly and his best-selling book *Iron John* to see if it offers a vision of social change. bell hooks argues that feminists, and especially African American feminists, need to see men as potential allies; Robert L. Allen describes the gender politics of the Million Man March. Michael S. Kimmel's essay describes the ways in which the mythopoetic men's movement, the Million Man March, and Promise Keepers, an evangelical Christian men's organization, all minister to real needs in men's spiritual lives, although they also contain some dangerous consequences for other groups such as women, gays, and lesbians. The "Statement of Principles" of the National Organization for Men

Against Sexism (NOMAS) provides an alternative way to frame issues of gender and sexual and racial equality.

We began this book by describing men's current sense of confusion. This experience often makes men anxious, and some have said that men are undergoing a "crisis of masculinity." The concept of crisis is beautifully captured by the Chinese character for the word *crisis*, which combines the characters for the words *danger* and *opportunity*. If masculinity is in crisis and men are confused, this situation presents both danger and an exciting opportunity.

The danger lies in retreat. Confusion makes a person feel unsettled; unresolved problems and an uncertain sense of identity may seem threatening. Taking refuge in old, familiar ideas—ideas that may have once been appropriate but now are only safe anachronisms—may seem to offer solace. Some men seek to resolve their confusion by vigorously reasserting of traditional masculinity.

But others recognize the opportunity that is presented by confusion. Feeling unsettled, restless, and anxious can push us to wrestle with difficult issues, confront contradictory feelings and ideas, and challenge the ways in which our experiences do not fit the traditional rules and expectations we have inherited from the past. Confusion opens the opportunity to change, to push beyond the traditional norms of masculinity and to become more loving and caring fathers, more emotionally responsive lovers, and more reliable and compassionate friends, as well as to live longer and healthier lives. We hope this work has contributed to a realization of such positive change.

52

ARTICLE

Michael Schwalbe

Mythopoetic Men's Work as a Search for *Communitas*

In the late 1980s and early 1990s, the commercial media discovered the mythopoetic men's movement. Newspapers, magazines, and television reported that thousands of middle-aged, middle-class white men were retreating to rustic settings to share their feelings, to cry, hug, drum, dance, tell poems and fairy tales, and enact primitive rituals. The men were supposedly trying to get in touch with the inner "wildman" and other masculine archetypes as urged by movement leader Robert Bly, a famous poet and author of the 1991 bestseller *Iron John*.[1] Mythopoetic activity was covered because it was offbeat, and so, not surprisingly, most stories played up its odd trappings. The serious side of the movement— its implicit critique of men's lives in American society—was not examined.

While most observers thought mythopoetic activity was harmless and silly, others saw it as dangerous. Feminist critics accused Bly and the mythopoetic men of nefarious doings at their all-male retreats: whining about men's relatively minor psychological troubles while ignoring the much greater oppression of other groups, espe-

cially women; "modernizing" rather than truly changing masculinity; retreating from tough political realities into boyish play; unfairly blaming mothers and wives for men's troubles; and reproducing sexism by using fairy tales and rituals from patriarchal cultures. Critics thus saw the mythopoetic movement as part of an antifeminist backlash, or as a New Age maneuver in the battle of the sexes.[2]

Much of the criticism of the movement was based on the same superficial stories fed to the public. More responsible critics at least read Bly's book, saw his 1990 PBS interview ("A Gathering of Men") with Bill Moyers, attended a retreat, or read other pieces of mythopoetic literature.[3] Even so, almost none of the criticism was based on firsthand knowledge of what the men involved in mythopoetic activity were thinking, feeling, and doing together. The men themselves either disappeared behind the inflated image of Bly, or critics presumed that there was no need to distinguish them from Bly. But while Bly was indeed the chief public figure of the movement and a main source of its philosophy, mythopoetic activity or, as the men themselves called it, "mythopoetic men's work," was much more than Robert Bly.

In the fall of 1990, before Bly's *Iron John* raised the visibility of the mythopoetic movement, I began a participant-observation study of a group of men, associated with a local men's center, who were engaged in mythopoetic activity. As a sociologist, I wanted to know how the men began doing "men's work" and how it was affecting them. I was especially interested in how it affected the meanings they gave to their identities as men. So from September 1990 to June 1993, I attended 128 meetings of various kinds; observed and participated in all manner of mythopoetic activities; attended events led by the movement's prominent teachers; read the movement's guiding literature; and interviewed 21 of the local men at length. The full account of my study appears elsewhere.[4]

Any sociologist who has studied a social movement from the inside will tell you that there is always more diversity within it than outsiders tend to see. This was true in the case of the mythopoetic men. As I was doing my research, people often asked me for a quick explanation of who the men were, what they were doing, and why—as if all the men were alike and one explanation would fit all. While there were commonalities of experience and outlook among the mythopoetic men, there were also significant differences. The men did not all experience the same troubles, want the same things, or think similarly about gender politics. It's important to recognize this diversity, since in writing about any group of people there is a tendency to make internal diversity disappear.

Two other points may aid understanding of the mythopoetic men. One is that, while they held Robert Bly in high esteem, they did not see him as an infallible guru. Most of the men knew that Bly could be obnoxious, that he tended to exaggerate, and that he liked to be the center of attention. It would be fair to say that the men saw him as wise, entertaining, charismatic, and challenging—but hardly without fault. Many of the men had equally high regard for other teachers in the mythopoetic movement, especially the Jungian psychologist James Hillman and the drummer/storyteller Michael Meade. Even so, the mythopoetic men were wary of leaders and did not want to be dependent on them. They believed that men could and should learn to do men's work on their own.

The second point is that many of the men rejected the label "movement" for what they were doing, since to them this implied central organization, the imposition of a doctrine, and political goals. It's true that mythopoetic activity was not centrally coordinated, overtly oriented to political goals, or restricted to those who swore allegiance to a particular set of beliefs. There was, however, an underlying philosophy (derived in large part from Jungian psychology), a "circuit-riding" group of teachers, a body of inspirational literature, nationally circulated publications, and many similarities of practice among the mythopoetic men's groups that had sprung up around the country. So, to add all this up and call it a movement is a legitimate convenience.

Many of the men also shared certain goals, which they sought to achieve through mythopoetic work. As individuals they sought the therapeutic goals of self-acceptance, greater self-confidence, and better knowledge of themselves as emotional beings. As a group they sought to revalue "man" as a moral identity; that is, they collectively sought to define "man" as an identity that implied positive moral qualities. Identity work of this kind, which was partly a response to feminist criticism of men's behavior, was accomplished through talk at gatherings and through the movement's literature. Much of what the men sought to accomplish thus had to do with their feelings about themselves as men.

It's important to see, however, that mythopoetic men's work was not just about sharing feelings, as if the men knew what they were feeling and then met to talk about it. Things were not so simple. Often the work itself aroused feelings that surprised the men. And these feelings were not always pleasant. But even unpleasant feelings were resources for fashioning a special kind of collective experience. It was this experience, which the anthropologist Victor Turner calls *communitas*, that the men sought to create at their gatherings. This was a rare and seductive experience for men in a highly bureaucratized society such as ours.

Community and *Communitas*

Most of the mythopoetic men were between the ages of 35 and 60. Nearly all were white, self-identified as heterosexual, and college educated. Most had good jobs, owned homes, and helped maintain families. They were, by and large, successful in conventional, middle-class terms. Yet the men said that living out this conventional script had left them, at midlife, feeling empty and dissatisfied. They found that the external trappings of success were not spiritually fulfilling. What's more, many of the men felt isolated, cut off from other men, except for competitive contexts such as the workplace. Hence, many described mythopoetic activity as part of an effort to create a community where they could interact with other men in a supportive, noncompetitive way.

But it was not exactly community that these men created through mythopoetic work. Although they did sometimes establish serious friendships and networks of support, the men did not enter into relations of material dependence upon each other, live in close proximity to each other, work together, or interact on a daily basis. Usually, the men who met at gatherings and in support groups went home to their separate lives. Thus, strictly speaking, it was not a true community they created. What the mythopoetic men sought and tried to create at their gatherings was both more and less than community. It was *communitas*.

Victor Turner, an anthropologist who studied tribal rituals, describes *communitas* as both a

shared feeling-state and a way of relating. To create *communitas*, people must relate to each other outside the constraints of formally defined roles and statuses. As Turner describes it:

> Essentially, *communitas* is a relationship between concrete, historical, idiosyncratic individuals. These individuals are not segmentalized into roles and statuses but confront one another rather in the manner of Martin Buber's "I and Thou." Along with this direct, immediate, and total confirmation of human identities, there tends to go a model of society as a homogeneous, unstructured *communitas*, whose boundaries are ideally coterminous with those of the human species.[5]

Communitas, as Turner says, can happen when the force of roles and statuses is suspended; that is, when individuals in a group feel themselves to be equals and there are no other significant differences to impede feelings of communality. Although the mythopoetic men did not use the term *communitas*, they sought to relate to teach other in the way that Turner describes as characteristic of *communitas*. At gatherings they tried to engage each other in a way that was unmediated by the roles they played in their everyday work lives. The men tried to practice this kind of relating by talking about the feelings they had, which they believed arose out of their common experiences as men.

Turner distinguishes three types of *communitas*: normative, ideological, and spontaneous or existential. Of these, it is spontaneous or existential *communitas* that the mythopoetic men sought to create. Turner says that spontaneous *communitas* is "richly charged with affects, mainly pleasurable ones," that it "has something 'magical' about it," and that in it there is "the feeling of endless power."[6] He compares hippies and tribesmen in a passage that could also apply to the mythopoetic men:

> The kind of *communitas* desired by tribesmen in their rites and by hippies in their "happenings" is not the pleasurable and effortless comradeship that can arise between friends,

coworkers, or professional colleagues any day. What they seek is a transformative experience that goes to the root of each person's being and finds in that root something profoundly communal and shared.[7]

There are several ways in which Turner's description of spontaneous *communitas* fits mythopoetic activity. First, the men sought personal growth through their experiences of "connection," as they called it, at mythopoetic gatherings. A connection was a feeling of emotional communion with another man or group of men. Such connections were made when a story, poem, dance, ritual, or psychodramatic enactment brought up strong feelings in one or more men, and this in turn induced emotional responses in others. In these moments the men learned about their own complexity as emotional beings. The changes they sought were greater awareness of their feelings, more clarity about them, and better ability to use those feelings constructively.

The mythopoetic men also presumed it was possible to establish deep emotional connections with each other because they were all, at root, men. This presumption grew out of the Jungian psychology that informed mythopoetic activity. The idea was that all men possessed the same set of masculine archetypes that predisposed them to think, feel, and act in similar ways.[8] In Jungian terms, these masculine archetypes are parts of the collective unconscious, to which we are all linked by our common humanity. Thus all men, simply by virtue of being male, were presumed to possess similar masculine energies and masculine ways of feeling. Mythopoetic activities were aimed at bringing out or tapping into these energies and feelings so that men could connect based on them and thereby mutually reinvigorate themselves.

Turner's references to pleasurable affects and mysterious feelings of power are echoed in how the mythopoetic men described their experiences. Mythopoetic activity was enjoyable, the men said, because "It's just being with men in a way that's very deep and powerful"; "There's a tremendous energy that grows out of men getting together and connecting emotionally"; and "It just feels great to be there connecting with other men in a noncompetitive way." And, indeed, the feelings were often intense. As one man said during a talking circle at the end of a weekend retreat, "I feel there's so much love in this room right now it hurts." Men also said that going back to their ordinary lives after a gathering meant "coming down from an emotional high." I, too, experienced this transition from the warm, open, supportive, emotionally charged atmosphere of a gathering to the relatively chilly atmosphere of a large research university.

The success of a gathering was measured by the intensity of the emotion it evoked and the connections thereby established. A less successful gathering was one where the emotional intensity was low and the men did not make strong connections. At a small two-day gathering, one man commented somewhat sadly, "We've had some good sharing, but only once did I feel much happening to me. That was when B. was talking. I felt tears welling up. So there's a deeper level we could get to." This was said at the beginning of the final talking circle, in hopes of prompting a more emotional discussion before the gathering was over. In addition to showing the desire for *communitas*, this statement also shows that it took effort to achieve. Spontaneous *communitas* did not happen spontaneously.

Creating Spontaneous *Communitas*

Mythopoetic men's work was in large part the conversation work required to create spontaneous *communitas*. I'll explain here how this work was done, through talk and other means. I should be understood that not all gatherings were aimed as intently at creating the same degree of spontaneous *communitas*. Some gatherings were more "heady," in that they were devoted to discussion of a topic, such as fathering or men's health or men's friendships. Often there were moments of *communitas* at these kinds of meetings; but it was at the retreats—those that had an explicit mythopoetic or "inner work" theme—where the greatest efforts were made to produce *communitas*. Talk, ritual, and drumming were the chief means for doing this.

Forms of Talk

At mythopoetic gatherings, men often made personal statements that revealed something shameful, tragic, or emotionally disturbing about their lives. Such statements might be made by each man in turn at the beginning of a retreat, as part of saying why he was there, what he was feeling, and what he hoped to accomplish at the retreat. Before any statements were made, the leader of the retreat or gathering would remind the men of the rules to follow in making statements: speak briefly, speak from the heart (i.e., focus on feelings), and speak to the other men—who were supposed to listen intently, make no judgments, and give no advice. The idea was that the statements should bring the unrehearsed truth up from a man's gut, since this would stir feelings in him and move other men to speak their "belly truth."

A great deal of feeling was stirred up as men talked about troubled relationships with fathers; being sexually abused as children; struggling to overcome addictions; repressed anger over past hurts and betrayals; grief and sadness over irreplaceable losses; efforts to be better fathers to their children. When men choked up, wept, shook with fear, or raged as they spoke it induced strong feelings in other men in the group. The sequence in which personal statements were made amplified this effect. Men would often begin their remarks by saying, "What that [the previous statement] brings up for me is . . . ," or "I really identify with what

——— said, because . . ." The more disclosing, expressive, and moving a man's statement, the more likely it was to evoke from the other men heavy sighs, sympathetic "mmmms," or a loud chorus of "Ho!" (supposedly a Native American way of affirming that a man's statement has been heard and felt). If a statement seemed inauthentic or insufficiently revealing it might evoke little or no reaction. In this way the men reinforced a norm of making risky, revealing, and evocative statements.

Thus, the men were not only sharing feelings but, by virtue of how they talked, knitting those feelings together into a group mood. In this way they were also creating *communitas*. It is important, too, that the settings in which these statements were made were defined as "safe," meaning that, by agreement, the men were not there to compete with or judge each other, but to listen and provide support. Even so, there was an element of risk and a degree of anxiety associated with making personal statements, since the mythopoetic men, like most men in American society, were unused to sharing feelings of hurt and vulnerability with other men. This anxiety aided the achievement of *communitas* because it created a higher-than-usual level of emotional arousal to begin with. It also allowed the men immediately to identify with one another over being anxious. As Turner likewise noted: "Danger is one of the chief ingredients in the production of spontaneous *communitas*."[9]

In making personal statements and in their general conversation at gatherings, the men could not help but refer to people, events, and circumstances outside themselves that evoked the feelings they had. In doing this, the men were careful to add to their statements the disclaimer "for me," as in "For *me*, the Gulf War was very depressing." This disclaimer signified that the man speaking was talking about *his* feelings based on *his* perceptions of things, and he was making no presumptions about how other men should feel. The use of this disclaimer helped the men maintain the fellow-feeling they sought by avoiding arguments about what was true of the external world. The mythopoetic men wanted their feelings validated, not challenged. As long as each man spoke the truth from his heart, no one could say he was wrong.

Talk about fathers was another way the men achieved *communitas*. It worked because almost every man had a father to talk about, and those few who didn't could talk about not having fathers. So every man could participate. Father talk also worked because it brought up feelings of sadness and anger for many of the men, and thus created the necessary emotional charge. Because many of the men experienced their fathers as physically or emotionally absent, or in some way abusive, the men could identify with each other based on these common experiences. Father talk may have helped them to reach insights about their relationships to their fathers. But father talk went on to the extent it did because it was so useful for creating *communitas*.

Poems and fairy tales were also a staple part of mythopoetic activity.[10] Most of the time no commentary or discussion followed the reading or reciting of a poem. The men would just steep in the feelings the poem evoked. An especially stirring poem, like a moving personal statement, would elicit deep sighs, "mmmmm," "yeah," sometimes "Ho!", and, often, calls for the reader to "read it again!" And as with the personal statements, these responses, which were signs of shared feelings, served to turn the individual feelings into a collective mood, and thus helped to create *communitas*. When fairy tales were told, there usually was commentary and discussion in a form that also encouraged *communitas*.

When a story was told, the storyteller would usually instruct the men to look for an image that evoked strong feelings. That image, it was said, would be a man's "doorway into the story"—his way of discovering what the story could tell him about his life as a man. This is consistent with Turner's observation that the "concrete, personal, imagist mode of thinking is highly characteristic of those in love with existential [or

spontaneous] *communitas*, with the direct relation between man and man, and man and nature. Abstractions appear as hostile to live contact."[11] In the case of the mythopoetics, the emphasis on specific images grew out of Jungian psychology, according to which the psyche was best explored by working with emotionally evocative images.

After a story or part of a story was told, men would talk about the images that struck them and the feelings these images evoked. In a large group of men many different images might be mentioned. Sometimes men reacted strongly to the same image. Talking about the stories in this way created more chances for men to express feelings and to find that they shared feelings and experiences with other men. This was in part how feelings of isolation were overcome and connections were made. Again, the stories may have helped the men to better understand their lives. But it was *how* the stories were talked about that helped the men to experience the good feelings and mysterious power of spontaneous *communitas*.

Ritual

Ritual is different from routine. Routine is the repetition of a behavioral pattern, like brushing one's teeth every night before bed. Ritual involves the symbolic enactment of values, beliefs, or feelings. It is a way of making external, visible, and public things that are normally internal, invisible, and private. By doing this, members of a community create a shared reality, reaffirm their common embrace of certain beliefs and values, and thereby keep the community alive. Ritual can also be a way of acknowledging changes in community members or of actually inducing such changes. The mythopoetic men used ritual for the same purposes: to call up, express, and share their otherwise private feelings, and to make changes in themselves.

Not all gatherings were ritual gatherings, though most included some ritual elements. Those gatherings where an explicit attempt was made to create "ritual space" or "sacred space" usually began with a symbolic act of separation from the ordinary world. For example, sometimes men would dip their hands into a large bowl of water to symbolize a washing off of concerns and distractions linked to the outside world. Other times, at the outset of gatherings the "spirits of the four directions" (and sometimes of the earth and sky, too) would be invoked and asked to bring the men strength and wisdom. Still other times, the men would dance their way into the space where the meeting was to be held, while the men already inside drummed and chanted. The point was to perform some collective act to mark a boundary between outside life and the "ritual space."

The scene of a gathering also had to be properly set. Ritual gatherings were often held at rustic lodges, where various objects—candles, bird feathers, masks, antlers, strangely shaped driftwood, animal skulls—might be set up around the main meeting area. Sage was often burned (a practice called "smudging") to make the air pungent and to cleanse the ritual space for the action that was going to take place. Usually the leader or leaders of the gathering made sure these things were done. Again, the idea was to heighten the sense of separation from ordinary reality, to make the physical space where the gathering would take place seem special, and to draw the men together. This preparation was talked about in terms of "creating a container" that could safely hold the psychic energies about to be unleashed.

The separation from ordinary reality also helped the men let go of the concerns for status and power that influenced their interactions with other men in everyday life. In the ritual space, the men were supposed to be "present for each other" in a direct and immediate way, as equals, as "brothers," and not as inferiors and superiors. Defining the situation as one in which feelings and other psychic matters were the proper focus of attention and activity helped to create and sustain this sense of equality. Thus,

the men seldom talked about their jobs, except to describe job-related troubles (and sometimes triumphs) in general terms. Too much talk about occupations would have introduced status concerns, which in turn would have corroded the sense of equality and brotherhood that fostered feelings of *communitas*.

Two examples can help show more concretely how the mythopoetic men used ritual to create *communitas*. One example is from a six-day gathering of about 120 men in a remote rural setting. At this gathering the men were divided into three clans: Trout, Ravens, and Lions. During the week each clan worked with a dance teacher to develop a dance of its own, a dance that would symbolize the spirit of the men in the clan. At the carnivale on the last night of the gathering, each clan was to share its dance with the rest of the men. One clan would drum while another danced and the third clan "witnessed."

The carnivale was held in a large, dimly lit lodge built of rough-cut logs. Many of the men wore the wildly decorated masks they had made earlier in the week. When their turn came, the 40 men in the Trout clan moved to the center of the room and formed a circle. The men stood for a few moments and then hunched down, extended their arms with their hands together in front of them, and began to dip and sway like fish swimming. Then half the men began moving to their right and half to their left, creating two flowing, interweaving circles. The Trout men also carried small stones, which they clicked together as they moved. About 30 men drummed as the Trout men danced. The rest of the men watched.

After a while the Trout men stopped and stood again, holding hands in a circle inside the larger circle of witnesses. They began a sweet and mournful African chant that they said was used to honor the passing away of loved ones. One by one, each of the Trout men moved to the center of their circle and put down the stones he was carrying. As he did so, he called out the name of a person or people whose passing he wished to honor. Another of the Trout men walked along the row of men standing in the outer ring and said, "We invite you to join us by putting a stone in the center of the circle to honor your dead." The drumming and chanting continued all the while.

At first a few, then more and more of the Raven and Lion men stepped outside to get stones. Each man as he returned went to the center of the circle, called the name of the dead he was honoring, put down a stone, and then stepped back. There was sadness in the men's voices as they spoke. This lent gravity to their acts and drew everyone into the ritual. By now all the men had picked up the chant and joined hands in one large circle. The sound filled the lodge. After about 20 minutes the chanting reached a lull—and then one man began to sing "Amazing Grace." Soon all the men joined in and again their voices rose in chorus and filled the lodge. When we finished singing we stood silent, looking at all the stones between us.

This example shows how a great deal of work went into creating spontaneous *communitas*. The dance was carefully choreographed and the stage was elaborately set (one could argue that the five days leading up to the carnivale were part of the stage setting). But later I talked to Trout men who said that they had planned the dance only up to the point of asking the other men to honor their dead. They were surprised by what happened after that, by how quickly and powerfully the other men were drawn in. No one had expected the surge of emotion and fellow-feeling that the ritual induced, especially when the men began to sing "Amazing Grace." Several men I talked to later cited this ritual as one of the most moving experiences they had had at a mythopoetic gathering.

Another example comes from a sweat-lodge ritual modeled on a traditional Native American practice.[12] In this case the lodge was tiny, consisting of a framework of saplings held together with twine upon which were draped several layers of old blankets and tarps. Before the frame was built, a fire pit was dug in the center of the spot on which the lodge stood. Although a lodge could be made bigger, here it was about ten feet in diameter and four feet high—big enough for a dozen men to squeeze in. From the outside it looked like a miniature domed stadium.

It was a drizzly 45-degree morning on the second day of a teacher-led weekend retreat. I was in the second group of 12 men who would go into the lodge together. This was the first "sweat" for all of us. The men in this group were almost giddy as we walked from the cabins to the shore of a small lake where the sweat lodge had been built. When we got there the men from the previous group had just finished.

The scene stopped us abruptly. Next to the lodge a large rock-rimmed fire was burning. A fierce, black-haired man with a beard stood by the fire, a five-foot staff in his hand. Some of the men who had just finished their sweat were standing waist-deep in the lake. Others were on shore hugging, their naked bodies still steaming in the cool air. Our moment of stunned silence ended when the leader of the retreat said to us, matter of factly, "Get undressed, stay quiet, keep your humility." We undressed and stashed our clothes under the nearby pine trees, out of the rain.

Before we entered the lodge, the teacher urged us to reflect on the specialness of the occasion and to approach it with seriousness. Upon entering the lodge through a small entry flap each man was to say, "all my relations," to remind himself of his connections to the earth, to his ancestors, and to the other men. Once we were inside, the teacher called for the fire tender to bring us fresh, red-hot rocks. As each rock was placed by shovel into the fire pit, we said in unison, "welcome Grandfather," again as symbolic acknowledgment of our connection to the earth. The teacher then burned sage on the rocks to scent the air. When he poured water on the rocks, the lodge became a sauna. The space was tightly packed, lit only by the glow of the rocks, and very hot. We were to do three sessions of ten to fifteen minutes each. Because of the intensity of the heat, a few men could not do all three sessions.

During one of the sessions, the teacher urged us to call upon the spirits of our ancestors from whom we wanted blessings. In the cacophony of voices it was hard to make out what was being said. Some men were calling the names of people not present. A few were doing what sounded like a Native American Indian chant learned from the movies. The man next to me was gobbling like a turkey. At first this all struck me as ridiculous. I looked around the lodge for signs of similar bemusement in other men's faces. Surely they couldn't be taking this seriously. But those whose faces I could see appeared absorbed in the experience. Some men seemed oddly distant, as if they were engaged in a conversation going on elsewhere.

Although I was still put off by the bogus chanting and baffled by the gobbling, I, too, began to feel drawn in. I found myself wanting to suspend disbelief and find some meaning in the ritual, no matter how culturally foreign it was. In large part this was because the teacher and the other men seemed to be taking it seriously. I certainly didn't want to ruin the experience for them by showing any sign of cynicism. These were men who had taken my feelings seriously during the retreat. I felt I owed them the same consideration in the sweat lodge.

In both examples, a carefully crafted set of appearances made *communitas* likely to happen. The physical props, the words and actions of the ritual leaders, and the sincere words and actions of some men evoked real feelings in others and drew them in.[13] Because it seemed that there were genuine emotions at stake, it would have taken a hard heart to show any sign of cynicism during the Trout dance or the sweat lodge. To do so would have risked hurting other men's feelings and dimming the glow of *communitas*. It would also have cut the cynic himself off from the good feelings and mysterious power being

generated by these occasions. Whether or not everyone really "believed" in what was happening didn't matter. Appearances made it seem so, and to achieve the *communitas* they desired, all the men needed to do was to act on these appearances.

Another dynamic was at work in the case of the sweat lodge. On the face of it, the idea of late twentieth-century white men enacting a Native American sweat lodge ritual was absurd. And for most of these men, the idea of squatting naked, haunch to haunch, with other men would have been—within an everyday frame of reference—embarrassing and threatening to their identities as heterosexuals. Thus, to avoid feeling ridiculous, threatened, or embarrassed, the men had to stay focused on the form of the ritual and show no sign of doubting its content or propriety. Because there was such a gap between their everyday frame of reference and the ritual, the men had to exaggerate their absorption in the ritual reality just to keep a grip on it. In so doing the men truly did create a common focus and, again, the appearance that a serious, collective spiritual activity was going on.

The sweat lodge example also illustrated how the creation of *communitas* was aided by literally stripping men of signs of their differences. In the sweat lodge, men were only men—as symbolized by their nakedness. As such they were also equals. When a small group of us spoke afterwards about the experience, one man said, "The closeness and physicality, and especially being naked, are what make it work. Everyone is just a man in there. You can't wear any merit badges."

Drumming

Next to Bly, the most widely recognized icon of the mythopoetic movement was the drum. Drumming was indeed an important part of mythopoetic activity. Some mythopoetic groups held gatherings just to drum, although the group I studied was more likely to mix drumming with other activities. Not all of the men drummed. A few didn't care for it; others preferred to use rattles or tambourines during drumming sessions. The most enthusiastic men had congas, African-styled djembes, or hand-held shaman's drums, though all manner of large and small folk drums appeared at gatherings. On one occasion a man used a five-gallon plastic pail turned upside down.

Why did the mythopoetic men drum? Some of the men in the local group said that they began drumming after a visit by Michael Meade, a prominent teacher in the mythopoetic movement, who was skilled at using drumming to accompany his telling of folk tales. This is what inspired one man I interviewed:

> Bly came and told his Iron John story and that was my first introduction to using stories as a way of illuminating dilemmas or emotional situations in your life. Michael Meade came the following year in the spring and introduced some drumming at that weekend. I just loved the energy of that right away. It just really opened me up. After drumming I felt wonderful. I liked the feeling of it and felt a connection with the mythopoetic [movement] ever since then, more to the drumming than to anything else.

But on only a few occasions did any of the local men use drumming as accompaniment to story telling. Most of the drumming was done in groups, which varied in size from six to forty. And while the men who were better drummers might lead the group into a complex rhythm, often something samba-like, the drumming was usually free-form, leaderless, and simple.

The appeal of this activity had little to with acquiring virtuosity at drumming. Rather, much of the appeal stemmed from the fact that the men could be bad drummers and still participate. It was, most importantly, another means to achieve *communitas*. Victor Turner notes that simple musical instruments are often used this way: "It is . . . fascinating to consider how expressions of *communitas* are culturally linked with simple wind instruments (flutes and harmonicas). Perhaps, in addition to their ready portabil-

ity, it is their capacity to convey in music the quality of spontaneous human *communitas* that is responsible for this."[14] This was equally true of drums, which were also readily portable and required even less skill to play.

What the mythopoetic men say about their experiences drumming tells much about not only drumming, but about the *communitas* it helped create and about the mythopoetic experience in general. In another interview, a 48-year-old salesman spoke of drumming as both ordinary and special at the same time:

> You can kind of lose yourself in it. It's like any hobby—fishing or playing ball or whatever. There is something that happens. You go into an altered state almost, hearing that music. At this national meeting in Minnesota a month ago the common thing was the drums. You could hear the beating of that drum. At break people would drum and we would dance. So it's this common bond.

Put another way, drumming was an activity that gave men who were strangers a way to quickly feel comfortable and familiar with each other. Some of the mythopoetic men believed that men in general had a special facility for connecting with each other via nonverbal means. The way that men were able to quickly bond via drumming was seen as evidence of this.

Although the men were aware that drumming was not an activity limited to men, some clearly felt that it held a special appeal for them. Another man, a 33-year-old technical writer, said in an interview:

> Drumming does something—connects me with men in ways that I can't understand, in the same way I've observed women who have babies connecting with each other. There's something in it that I don't participate in emotionally. In the same way, the drumming—society with other men—is emotionally important to men in ways that women don't understand. They can't.

Some of the mythopoetic men's ideas about gender are exemplified by this statement. Many of them believed that women, no matter how empathic they might be, could not know what it was like to be a man, just as men could not know what it was like to be a woman. Hence, men needed the understanding and support that could come only from other men just as women needed the same things from other women.

For other men, drumming was both a communal and, sometimes, a personal, spiritual experience. A 42-year-old therapist told me:

> There was one point where I was really deeply entranced just drumming and then all of a sudden I had this real powerful experience where I felt like I was on a hill, on some mountainside or some mountaintop, in some land far far away, in some time that was all time. And I was in the middle of my men, who were my brothers, who were all men. It was one of those powerful, mystical experiences where all of a sudden I felt planted in the community of men. And that changed my life, because I felt like I was a man among men in the community of men and we were drumming and the drum was in my bones and it was in my heartbeat and it was good.

This statement captures in spirit, tone, and rhythm the experience that many of the men found in drumming. Even if they didn't report such flights of imagination, others said that drumming provided a similar sense of communality, of connection—*communitas*.

My own experience corroborates this. I found that when I would pick up a beat and help sustain it without thinking, the sense of being part of the group was strong. It was as if the sound testified to the reality of the group, and the rhythm testified to our connection. By drumming in synch each man attached himself to the group and to the other men in it. The men valued this also because the attachment was created by physical action rather than by talk, and because it seemed to happen at a nonrational level. Drumming thus helped the men to do two other things that mythopoetic philosophy called for: getting out of their heads and into feeling their bodies, and by-passing the ra-

tional ego that kept a lid on the archetypal masculine energies the men sought to tap.

Communitas and Politics

My point has been to show that much mythopoetic activity can be understood as a search for *communitas*. This experience was rare in these men's lives and precious on the occasions when it occurred. Sometimes the men talked about the activities at their gatherings as "inviting the sacred to happen." Particular forms of talk, the orchestration of ritual, and drumming were means to this end. Because *communitas* was so valuable to the men, there were also things they *avoided* doing to make *communitas* more likely to happen. One thing they avoided was serious talk about politics.

This is not to say that the men were apolitical. Most of the men I studied were well informed on social issues and supported progressive causes. They were also critical of the rapacious greed of big corporations, the duplicity and brutal militarism of Reagan and Bush, and the general oppressiveness of large bureaucracies. But there were two revealing ironies in the politics of the mythopoetic men. First, while they were critical of the behavior of corporations and government, they avoided saying that these institutions were run by men. Usually it was an unspecified, genderless "they" who were said to be responsible for destroying the environment or for turning all culture into mass marketable schlock. And second, while many of the men saw corporate power and greed as root problems in U.S. society, they were uninterested in collective action to address these problems. This is, as one might expect, because the white, middle-class mythopoetic men did not do so badly in reaping the material benefits of the economic system they occasionally criticized.

In other words, the men were selectively apolitical. They did not want to see that it was other *men* who were responsible for many of the social problems they witnessed and were sometimes affected by. To do so, and to talk about it, would have shattered the illusion of universal brotherhood among men that helped sustain feelings of *communitas*. Talk about power, politics, and inequality in the external world was incompatible with the search for *communitas*, because it would have led to arguments, or at least to intellectual discussions, rather than to warm emotional communion. When discussions at mythopoetic gatherings inadvertently turned political, disagreements surfaced and tensions arose; someone would usually say, "we're getting away from the important work here." Or, as one man said in trying to stop a conversation that was becoming an argument, "I think we're losing the power of the drums."

The mythopoetic men believed that engaging in political or sociological analysis would have led them away from their goals of self-acceptance, self-knowledge, emotional authenticity, and *communitas*. The men wanted to feel better about themselves as men, to learn about the feelings and psychic energies that churned within them, to live fuller and more authentic emotional lives, and to experience the pleasure and mysterious power of *communitas*. They did not want to compete over whose interpretation of social reality was correct. They wanted untroubled brotherhood in which their feelings were validated by other men, and in which their identities as men could be infused with new value.

Here can be seen both the power and limits of mythopoetic men's work. Through this work some men have begun to free themselves from the debilitating repression of emotion that was part of their socialization into traditional masculinity. Feminism provided the intellectual basis and political impetus for this critique of traditional masculinity, although the mythopoetics have difficulty appreciating this. Yet they deserve credit for developing a method that allows some men to explore and express more of the emotions that make them human. Mythopo-

etic men's work has also helped men to see how these emotions can be the basis for connections to men they might otherwise have feared, mistrusted, or felt compelled to compete with. And, to the extent that men begin to see that they don't have to live out traditional masculinity and can even cooperate to heal the damage it causes, mythopoetic men's work has progressive potential.

One problem is that the progressive potential of mythopoetic men's work is limited, because it leads men to think about gender and gender inequality in psychological or, at best, cultural terms. Mythopoetic men's work may open men to seeing things in themselves and help them make connections with each other, but it also blinds them to seeing important connections between themselves and society. For example, the mythopoetic men do not see that, in a male-supremacist society, there can be no innocent celebration of masculinity. In such a society the celebration of manhood and of masculinity—even if it is supposedly "deep" or "authentic" and thus a more fully human version of masculinity—reaffirms the lesser value of women, whether this is intended or not. The therapeutic focus of mythopoetic men's work— as done by a largely homogeneous group of middle-class white males—also blinds them to matters of class inequality and to the exploitation of working-class people and people of color by the elite white *men* who run the economy.

Yet mythopoetic men's work is a form of resistance to domination. It's not just an entertaining form of group therapy or collective whining over imagined wounds, or retrograde male bonding. These middle-class white men, who are not the ruling elites, are responding to the alienation and isolation that stem from living in a capitalist society that encourages people to be greedy, selfish, and predatory. Their goal of trying to awaken the human sensibilities that have been benumbed by an exploitive economy is subversive. But to get to the root of the problem men will have to do more than take modest risks among themselves to try to heal their psyches. They will have to take big risks in trying to abolish the race, class, and gender hierarchies that damage us all. They will have to learn to create *communitas* in struggles for justice.

Notes

1. Robert Bly, *Iron John: A Book About Men* (Reading, MA: Addison-Wesley, 1990).

2. See Kay Leigh Hagan, editor, *Women Respond to the Men's Movement* (San Francisco: HarperCollins, 1992); Kenneth Clatterbaugh, *Contemporary Perspectives on Masculinity* (Boulder, CO: Westview, 1990), pp. 85–103; Susan Faludi, *Backlash: The Undeclared War against American Women* (New York: Crown, 1991), pp. 304–312; R. W. Connell, "Drumming Up the Wrong Tree," *Tikkun* vol. 7, no. 1 (1992): 31–36; Sharon Doubiago, "Enemy of the Mother: A Feminist Response to the Men's Movement," *Ms.* March/April (1992): 82–85; Fred Pelka, "Robert Bly and Iron John," *On the Issues* Summer (1991): 17–19, 39; Diane Johnson, "Something for the Boys," *New York Review of Books* January 16 (1992): 13–17.

3. For a sampling of other writings in the mythopoetic genre, see Robert Moore and Douglas Gillette, *King, Warrior, Magician, Lover: Rediscovering the Archetypes of the Mature Masculine* (New York: HarperCollins, 1990); Wayne Liebman, *Tending the Fire: The Ritual Men's Group* (St. Paul, MN: Ally, 1991); Christopher Harding, editor, *Wingspan: Inside the Men's Movement* (New York: St. Martin's, 1992).

4. Michael Schwalbe, *Unlocking the Iron Cage: A Critical Appreciation of Mythopoetic Men's Work.* New York: Oxford University Press, forthcoming, 1995.

5. Victor Turner, *The Ritual Process* (Ithaca, NY: Cornell, 1969), pp. 94–165.

6. Ibid., p. 131–132.

7. Ibid., p. 139.

8. For an introduction to the basic concepts of Jungian psychology, see Calvin Hall and Vernon Nordby, *A Primer of Jungian Psychology* (New York: Penguin, 1973); or Frieda Fordham, *An Introduction to Jung's Psychology* (New York: Penguin, 1966). For more detail, see Edward C. Whitmont, *The Symbolic Quest* (Princeton, NJ: Princeton, 1991).

9. Turner, p. 154.

10. Many of the poems frequently read at mythopoetic gatherings are collected in Robert Bly, James Hillman, and Michael Meade (eds.), *The Rag and Bone Shop of the Heart* (New York: HarperCollins, 1992). Many of the fairy tales told at gatherings, including Bly's "Iron John," originally known as "Iron Hans," are taken from the Grimm brothers' collection.

11. Turner, p. 141.

12. A description of the sweat-lodge ritual can be found in Joseph Epes Brown (recorder and editor), *The Sacred Pipe: Black Elk's Account of the Seven Rites of the Oglala Sioux* (Norman, OK: Univ. of Oklahoma, 1953), pp. 31–43. This account was a source of inspiration for some of the mythopoetic men. See also William K. Powers, *Oglala Religion* (Lincoln, NE: Univ. of Nebraska, 1977).

13. Catherine Bell writes about how ritual "catches people up in its own terms" and provides a "resistant surface to casual disagreement." See Bell, *Ritual Theory, Ritual Practice* (New York: Oxford Univ. Press, 1992), pp. 214–215. Other observers have noted how the improvised rituals at mythopoetic gatherings had this power to draw the men in. See Richard Gilbert, "Revisiting the Psychology of Men: Robert Bly and the Mytho-Poetic Movement," *Journal of Humanistic Psychology* 32 (1992): 41–67.

14. Turner, p. 165.

53

ARTICLE

bell hooks

Men: Comrades in Struggle

Feminism defined as a movement to end sexist oppression enables women and men, girls and boys, to participate equally in revolutionary struggle. So far, contemporary feminist movement has been primarily generated by the efforts of women—men have rarely participated. This lack of participation is not solely a consequence of anti-feminism. By making women's liberation synonymous with women gaining social equality with men, liberal feminists effectively created a situation in which they, not men, designated feminist movement "women's work." Even as they were attacking sex role divisions of labor, the institutionalized sexism which assigns unpaid, devalued, "dirty" work to women, they were assigning to women yet another sex role task: making feminist revolution. Women's liberationists called upon all women to join feminist movement but they did not continually stress that men should assume responsibility for actively struggling to end sexist oppression. Men, they argued, were all-powerful, misogynist oppressor—the enemy. Women were the oppressed—the victims. Such rhetoric reinforced sexist ideology by positing in an inverted form the notion of a basic conflict between the sexes, the implication being that the empowerment of women would necessarily be at the expense of men.

As with other issues, the insistence on a "woman only" feminist movement and a virulent anti-male stance reflected the race and class background of participants. Bourgeois white women, especially radical feminists, were envious and angry at privileged white men for denying them an equal share in class privilege. In part, feminism provided them with a public forum for the expression of their anger as well as a political platform they could use to call attention to issues of social equality, demand change, and promote specific reforms. They were not eager to call attention to the fact that men do not share a common social status; that patriarchy does not negate the existence of class and race privilege or exploitation; that all men do not benefit equally from sexism. They did not want to acknowledge that bourgeois white women, though often victimized by sexism, have more power and privilege, are less likely to be exploited or oppressed, than poor, uneducated, nonwhite males. At the time, many white women's liberationists did not care about the fate of oppressed groups of men. In keeping with the exercise of race and/or class privilege, they deemed the life experiences of these men unworthy of their attention, dismissed them, and simultaneously deflected attention away from their support of continued exploitation and oppression. Assertions like "all men are the enemy," "all men hate women" lumped all groups of men in one category, thereby suggesting that they share equally in all forms of male privilege. One of the first written statements which endeavored to make an anti-male stance a central feminist position was "The Redstocking Manifesto." Clause III of the manifesto reads:

> We identify the agents of our oppression as men. Male supremacy is the oldest, most basic form of domination. All other forms of exploitation and oppression (racism, capitalism, imperialism, etc.) are extensions of male supremacy: men dominate women, a few men dominate the rest. All power situations throughout history have been male-dominated and male-oriented. Men have controlled all political, economic, and cultural institutions and backed up this control with physical force. They have used their power to keep women in an inferior position. All men receive economic, sexual, and psychological benefits from male supremacy. All men have oppressed women. (1970, p. 109)

Anti-male sentiments alienated many poor and working class women, particularly non-white women, from feminist movement. Their life experiences had shown them that they have more in common with men of their race and/or class group than bourgeois white women. They know the sufferings and hardships women face in their communities; they also know the sufferings and hardships men face and they have compassion for them. They have had the experience of struggling with them for a better life. This has been especially true for black women. Throughout our history in the United States, black women have shared equal responsibility in all struggles to resist racist oppression. Despite sexism, black women have continually contributed equally to anti-racist struggle, and frequently, before contemporary black liberation effort, black men recognized this contribution. There is a special tie binding people together who struggle collectively for liberation. Black women and men have been united by such ties. They have known the experience of political solidarity. It is the experience of shared resistance struggle that led black women to reject the anti-male stance of some feminist activists. This does not mean that black women were not willing to acknowledge the reality of black male sexism. It does mean that many of us do not believe we will combat sexism or woman-hating by attacking black men or responding to them in kind.

Bourgeois white women cannot conceptualize the bonds that develop between women and men in liberation struggle and have not had as many positive experiences working with men politically. Patriarchal white male rule has usually devalued female political input. Despite the prevalence of sexism in black communities, the role black women play in social institutions, whether primary or secondary, is recognized by everyone as significant and valuable. In an interview with Claudia Tate (1983), black woman writer Maya Angelou explains her sense of the different role black and white women play in their communities:

> Black women and white women are in strange positions in our separate communities. In the social gatherings of black people, black women have always been predominant. That is to say, in the church it's always Sister Hudson, Sister Thomas, and Sister Wetheringay who keep the church alive. In lay gatherings it's always Lottie who cooks, and Mary who's going to Bonita's where there is a good party going on. Also, black women are the nurturers of children in our community. White women are in a different position in their social institutions. White men, who are in effect their fathers, husbands,

brothers, their sons, nephews, and uncles say to white women or imply in any case: "I don't really need you to run my institutions. I need you in certain places and in those places you must be kept—in the bedroom, in the kitchen, in the nursery, and on the pedestal." Black women have never been told this. . . .

Without the material input of black women, as participants and leaders, many male-dominated institutions in black communities would cease to exist; this is not the case in all white communities.

Many black women refused participation in feminist movement because they felt an anti-male stance was not a sound basis for action. They were convinced that virulent expressions of these sentiments intensify sexism by adding to the antagonism which already exists between women and men. For years black women (and some black men) had been struggling to overcome the tensions and antagonisms between black females and males that is generated by internalized racism (i.e., when the white patriarchy suggests one group has caused the oppression of the other). Black women were saying to black men, "we are not one another's enemy," "we must resist the socialization that teaches us to hate ourselves and one another." This affirmation of bonding between black women and men was part of anti-racist struggle. It could have been a part of feminist struggle had white women's liberationists stressed the need for women and men to resist the sexist socialization that teaches us to hate and fear one another. They chose instead to emphasize hate, especially male woman-hating, suggesting that it could not be changed. Therefore no viable political solidarity could exist between women and men. Women of color, from various ethnic backgrounds, as well as women who were active in the gay movement, not only experienced the development of solidarity between women and men in resistance struggle, but recognized its value. They were not willing to devalue this bonding by allying themselves with anti-male bourgeois white women. En-

couraging political bonding between women and men to radically resist sexist oppression would have called attention to the transformative potential of feminism. The anti-male stance was a reactionary perspective that made feminism appear to be a movement that would enable white women to usurp white male power, replacing white male supremacist rule with white female supremacist rule.

Within feminist organizations, the issue of female separatism was initially separated from the anti-male stance; it was only as the movement progressed that the two perspectives merged. Many all-female sex-segregated groups were formed because women recognized that separatist organizing could hasten female consciousness-raising, lay the groundwork for the development of solidarity between women, and generally advance the movement. It was believed that mixed groups would get bogged down by male power trips. Separatist groups were seen as a necessary strategy, not as a way to attack men. Ultimately, the purpose of such groups was integration with equality. The positive implications of separatist organizing were diminished when radical feminists, like Ti Grace Atkinson, proposed sexual separatism as an ultimate goal of feminist movement. Reactionary separatism is rooted in the conviction that male supremacy is an absolute aspect of our culture, that women have only two alternatives: accepting it or withdrawing from it to create subcultures. This position eliminates any need for revolutionary struggle and it is in no way a threat to the status quo. In the essay "Separate to Integrate," Barbara Leon (1975) stresses that male supremacists would rather feminist movement remain "separate and unequal." She gives the example of orchestra conductor Antonia Brico's efforts to shift from an all-women orchestra to a mixed orchestra, only to find she could not get support for the latter:

> Antonia Brico's efforts were acceptable as long as she confined herself to proving that women were qualified musicians. She had no trouble

finding 100 women who could play in an orchestra or getting financial backing for them to do so. But finding the backing for men and women to play together in a truly integrated orchestra proved to be impossible. Fighting for integration proved to be more a threat to male supremacy and, therefore, harder to achieve.

The women's movement is at the same point now. We can take the easier way of accepting segregation, but that would mean losing the very goals for which the movement was formed. Reactionary separatism has been a way of halting the push of feminism. . . .

During the course of contemporary feminist movement, reactionary separatism has led many women to abandon feminist struggle, yet it remains an accepted pattern for feminist organizing, e.g. autonomous women's groups within the peace movement. As a policy, it has helped to marginalize feminist struggle, to make it seem more a personal solution to individual problems, especially problems with men, than a political movement which aims to transform society as a whole. To return to an emphasis on feminism as revolutionary struggle, women can no longer allow feminism to be another arena for the continued expression of antagonism between the sexes. The time has come for women active in feminist movement to develop new strategies for including men in the struggle against sexism.

All men support and perpetuate sexism and sexist oppression in one form or another. It is crucial that feminist activists not get bogged down in intensifying our awareness of this fact to the extent that we do not stress the more unemphasized point which is that men can lead life affirming, meaningful lives without exploiting and oppressing women. Like women, men have been socialized to passively accept sexist ideology. While they need not blame themselves for accepting sexism, they must assume responsibility for eliminating it. It angers women activists who push separatism as a goal of feminist movement to hear emphasis placed on men being victimized by sexism; they cling to the "all men are

the enemy" version of reality. Men are not exploited or oppressed by sexism, but there are ways in which they suffer as a result of it. This suffering should not be ignored. While it in no way diminishes the seriousness of male abuse and oppression of women, or negates male responsibility for exploitative actions, the pain men experience can serve as a catalyst calling attention to the need for change. Recognition of the painful consequences of sexism in their lives led some men to establish consciousness-raising groups to examine this. Paul Hornacek (1977) explains the purpose of these gatherings in his essay "Anti-Sexist Consciousness-Raising Groups for Men":

> Men have reported a variety of different reasons for deciding to seek a C-R group, all of which have an underlying link to the feminist movement. Most are experiencing emotional pain as a result of their male sex role and are dissatisfied with it. Some have had confrontations with radical feminists in public or private encounters and have been repeatedly criticized for being sexist. Some come as a result of their commitment to social change and their recognition that sexism and patriarchy are elements of an intolerable social system that needs to be altered . . .

Men in the consciousness-raising groups Hornacek describes acknowledge that they benefit from patriarchy and yet are also hurt by it. Men's groups, like women's support groups, run the risk of overemphasizing personal change at the expense of political analysis and struggle.

Separatist ideology encourages women to ignore the negative impact of sexism on male personhood. It stresses polarization between the sexes. According to Joy Justice, separatists believe that there are "two basic perspectives" on the issue of naming the victims of sexism: "There is the perspective that men oppress women. And there is the perspective that people are people, and we are all hurt by rigid sex roles." Many separatists feel that the latter perspective is a sign of co-optation, representing women's refusal to confront the fact that men are the enemy—they insist on the primacy of the first perspective. Both perspectives accurately describe our predicament. Men *do* oppress women. People *are* hurt by rigid sex role patterns. These two realities co-exist. Male oppression of women cannot be excused by the recognition that there are ways men are hurt by rigid sex roles. Feminist activists should acknowledge that hurt—it exists. It does not erase or lessen male responsibility for supporting and perpetuating their power under patriarchy to exploit and oppress women in a manner far more grievous than the psychological stress or emotional pain caused by male conformity to rigid sex role patterns.

Women active in feminist movement have not wanted to focus in any way on male pain so as not to deflect attention away from the focus on male privilege. Separatist feminist rhetoric suggested that all men shared equally in male privilege, that all men reap positive benefits from sexism. Yet the poor or working class man has been socialized via sexist ideology to believe that there are privileges and powers he should possess solely because he is male often finds that few if any of these benefits are automatically bestowed him in life. More than any other male group in the United States, he is constantly concerned about the contradiction between the notion of masculinity he was taught and his inability to live up to that notion. He is usually "hurt," emotionally scarred because he does not have the privilege or power society has taught him "real men" should possess. Alienated, frustrated, pissed off, he may attack, abuse, and oppress an individual woman or women, but he is not reaping positive benefits from his support and perpetuation of sexist ideology. When he beats or rapes women, he is not exercising privilege or reaping positive rewards; he may feel satisfied in exercising the only form of domination allowed him. The ruling class male power structure that promotes his sexist abuse of women reaps the real material benefits and privileges from his actions. As long as he is attacking women and not sexism or capitalism, he helps to maintain a system that allows him few, if any, benefits or privileges. He is an oppressor. He is an enemy to women. He is also an enemy to himself. He is also oppressed. His abuse of women is not justifiable. Even though he has been socialized to act as he does, there are existing social movements that would enable him to struggle for self-recovery and liberation. By ignoring these movements, he chooses to remain both oppressor and oppressed. If feminist movement ignores his predicament, dismisses his hurt, or writes him off as just another male enemy, then we are passively condoning his actions.

The process by which men act as oppressors and are oppressed is particularly visible in black communities, where men are working class and poor. In her essay "Notes For Yet Another Paper on Black Feminism, or Will The Real Enemy Please Stand Up?" (1979) black feminist activist Barbara Smith suggests that black women are unwilling to confront the problem of sexist oppression in black communities:

> By naming sexist oppression as a problem it would appear that we would have to identify as threatening a group we have heretofore assumed to be our allies—Black men. This seems to be one of the major stumbling blocks to beginning to analyze the sexual relationships/sexual politics of our lives. The phrase "men are not the enemy" dismisses feminism and the reality of patriarchy in one breath and also overlooks some major realities. If we cannot entertain the idea that some men are the enemy, especially white men and in a different sense Black men, too, then we will never be able to figure out all the reasons why, for example, we are beaten up every day, why we are sterilized against our wills, why we are being raped by our neighbors, why we are pregnant at age twelve, and why we are at home on welfare with more children than we can support or care for. Acknowledging the sexism of Black men does not mean that we become "manhaters" or necessarily eliminate them from our lives. What it does mean is that we

must struggle for a different basis of interaction with them.

Women in black communities have been reluctant to publicly discuss sexist oppression, but they have always known it exists. We too have been socialized to accept sexist ideology and many black women feel that black male abuse of women is a reflection of frustrated masculinity—such thoughts lead them to see that abuse is understandable, even justified. The vast majority of black women think that just publicly stating that these men are the enemy or identifying them as oppressors would do little to change the situation; they fear it could simply lead to greater victimization. Naming oppressive realities, in and of itself, has not brought about the kinds of changes for oppressed groups that it can for more privileged groups, who command a different quality of attention. The public naming of sexism has generally not resulted in the institutionalized violence that characterized, for example, the response to black civil rights struggles. (Private naming, however, is often met with violent oppression.) Black women have not joined the feminist movement not because they cannot face the reality of sexist oppression; they face it daily. They do not join feminist movement because they do not see in feminist theory and practice, especially those writings made available to masses of people, potential solutions.

So far, feminist rhetoric identifying men as the enemy has had few positive implications. Had feminist activists called attention to the relationship between ruling class men and the vast majority of men, who are socialized to perpetuate and maintain sexism and sexist oppression even as they reap no life-affirming benefits, these men might have been motivated to examine the impact of sexism in their lives. Often feminist activists talk about male abuse of women as if it is an exercise of privilege rather than an expression of moral bankruptcy, insanity, and dehumanization. For example, in Barbara Smith's essay, she identifies white males as "the primary oppressor group in American society" and discusses the nature of their domination of others. At the end of the passage in which this statement is made she comments: "It is not just rich and powerful capitalists who inhibit and destroy life. Rapists, murderers, lynchers, and ordinary bigots do too and exercise very real and violent power because of this white male privilege." Implicit in this statement is the assumption that the act of committing violent crimes against women is either a gesture or an affirmation of privilege. Sexist ideology brainwashes men to believe that their violent abuse of women is beneficial when it is not. Yet feminist activists affirm this logic when we should be constantly naming these acts as expressions of perverted power relations, general lack of control over one's actions, emotional powerlessness, extreme irrationality, and in many cases, outright insanity. Passive male absorption of sexist ideology enables them to interpret this disturbed behavior positively. As long as men are brainwashed to equate violent abuse of women with privilege, they will have no understanding of the damage done to themselves, or the damage they do to others, and no motivation to change.

Individuals committed to feminist revolution must address ways that men can unlearn sexism. Women were never encouraged in contemporary feminist movement to point out to men their responsibility. Some feminist rhetoric "put down" women who related to men at all. Most women's liberationists were saying "women have nurtured, helped, and supported others for too long—now we must fend for ourselves." Having helped and supported men for centuries by acting in complicity with sexism, women were suddenly encouraged to withdraw their support when it came to the issue of "liberation." The insistence on a concentrated focus on individualism, on the primacy of self, deemed "liberatory" by women's liberationists, was not a visionary, radical concept of freedom. It did provide individual solutions for women, however. It was the same idea of independence perpetuated by the imperial patriarchal state which equates independence with narcissism and lack of concern with triumph over others. In this way, women active in feminist movement were simply inverting the dominant ideology of the culture—they were not attacking it. They were not presenting practical alternatives to the status quo. In fact, even the statement "men are the enemy" was basically an inversion of the male supremacist doctrine that "women are the enemy"—the old Adam and Eve version of reality.

In retrospect, it is evident that the emphasis on "man as enemy" deflected attention away from focus on improving relationships between women and men, ways for men and women to work together to unlearn sexism. Bourgeois women active in feminist movement exploited the notion of a natural polarization between the sexes to draw attention to equal rights effort. They had an enormous investment in depicting the male as enemy and the female as victim. They were the group of women who could dismiss their ties with men once they had an equal share in class privilege. They were ultimately more concerned with obtaining an equal share in class privilege than with the struggle to eliminate sexism and sexist oppression. Their insistence on separating from men heightened the sense that they, as women without men, needed equality of opportunity. Most women do not have the freedom to separate from men because of economic inter-dependence. The separatist notion that women could resist sexism by withdrawing from contact with men reflected a bourgeois class perspective. In Cathy McCandless' essay "Some Thoughts About Racism, Classism, and Separatism," she makes the point that separatism is in many ways a false issue because "in this capitalist economy, none of us are truly separate" (1979). However, she adds:

> Socially, it's another matter entirely. The richer you are, the less you generally have to acknowledge those you depend upon. Money can buy you a great deal of distance. Given enough of it, it is even possible never to lay eyes upon a man. It's a wonderful luxury, having control over who you lay eyes on, but let's face it: most women's daily survival still involves face-to-face contact with men whether they like it or not. It seems to me that for this reason alone, criticizing women who associate with men not only tends to be counterproductive, it borders on blaming the victim. Particularly if the women taking it upon themselves to set the standards are white and upper or middle class (as has often been the case in my experience) and those to whom they apply these rules are not.

Devaluing the real necessities of life that compel many women to remain in contact with men, as well as not respecting the desire of women to keep contact with men, created an unnecessary conflict of interest for those women who might have been very interested in feminism but felt they could not live up to the politically correct standards.

Feminist writings did not say enough about ways women could directly engage in feminist struggle in subtle, day-to-day contacts with men, although they have addressed crises. Feminism is politically relevant to the masses of women who daily interact with men both publicly and privately, if it addresses ways that interaction, which usually has negative components because sexism is so all-pervasive, can be changed. Women who have daily contact with men need useful strategies that will enable them to integrate feminist movement into their daily life. By inadequately addressing or failing to address the difficult issues, contemporary feminist movement located itself on the periphery of society rather than at the center. Many women and men think feminism is happening, or happened, "out there." Television tells them the "liberated" woman is an exception, that she is primarily a careerist. Commercials like the one that shows a white career women shifting from work attire to flimsy clothing exposing flesh, singing all the while "I can bring home the bacon, fry it up in the pan, and never let you forget you're a man" reaffirm that her careerism will not prevent her from assuming the stereotyped sex object role assigned women in male supremacist society.

Often men who claim to support women's liberation do so because they believe they will benefit by no longer having to assume specific, rigid sex roles they find negative or restrictive. The role they are most willing and eager to change is that of economic provider. Commercials like the one described above assure men that women can be breadwinners or even "the" breadwinner, but still allow men to dominate them. Carol Hanisch's essay "Men's Liberation" (1975) explores the attempt by these men to exploit women's issues to their own advantage, particularly those issues related to work:

> Another major issue is the attempt by men to drop out of the work force and put their women to work supporting them. Men don't like their jobs, don't like the rat race, and don't like having a boss. That's what all the whining about being a "success symbol" or "success object" is really all about. Well, women don't like those things either, especially since they get paid 40% less than men for working, generally have more boring jobs, and rarely are even allowed to be "successful." But for women working is usually the only way to achieve some equality and power in the family, in their relationship with men, some independence. A man can quit work and pretty much still remain the master of the household, gaining for himself a lot of free time since the work he does doesn't come close to what his wife or lover does. In most cases, she's still doing more than her share of the housework in addition to wife work and her job. Instead of fighting to make his job better, to end the rat race, and to get rid of bosses, he sends his woman to work—not much different from the old practice of buying a substitute for the draft, or even pimping. And all in the name of breaking down "role stereotypes" or some such nonsense.

Such a "men's liberation movement" could only be formed in reaction to women's liberation in an attempt to make feminist movement serve the opportunistic interests of individual men. These men identified themselves as victims of sexism, working to liberate men. They identified rigid sex roles as the primary source of their victimization and though they wanted to change the notion of masculinity, they were not particularly concerned with their sexist exploitation and oppression of women. Narcissism and general self-pity characterized men's liberation groups. Kanisch concludes her essay with the statement:

> Women don't want to pretend to be weak and passive. And we don't want phony, weak, passive acting men any more than we want phony supermen full of bravado and little else. What women want is for men to be honest. Women want men to be bold—boldly honest, aggressive in their human pursuits. Boldly passionate, sexual and sensual. And women want this for themselves. It's time men became boldly radical. Daring to go to the root of the own exploitation and seeing that it is not women or "sex roles" or "society" causing their unhappiness, but capitalists and capitalism. It's time men dare to name and fight these, their real exploiters.

Men who have dared to be honest about sexism and sexist oppression, who have chosen to assume responsibility for opposing and resisting it, often find themselves isolated. Their politics are disdained by antifeminist men and women, and are often ignored by women active in feminist movement. Writing about his efforts to publicly support feminism in a local newspaper in Santa Cruz, Morris Conerly explains:

> Talking with a group of men, the subject of Women's Liberation inevitably comes up. A few laughs, snickers, angry mutterings, and denunciations follow. There is a group consensus that men are in an embattled position and must close ranks against the assaults of misguided females. Without fail, someone will solicit me for my view, which is that I am 100% for Women's Liberation. That throws them for a loop and they

start staring at me as if my eyebrows were crawling with lice.

They're thinking, "What kind of man is he?" I am a black man who understands that women are not my enemy. If I were a white man with a position of power; one could understand the reason for defending the status quo. Even then, the defense of a morally bankrupt doctrine that exploits and oppresses others would be inexcusable.

Conerly stresses that it was not easy for him to publicly support feminist movement, that it took time:

... Why did it take me some time? Because I was scared of the negative reaction I knew would come my way by supporting Women's Liberation. In my mind I could hear it from the brothers and sisters. "What kind of man are you?" "Who's wearing the pants?" "Why are you in that white shit?" And on and on. Sure enough, the attacks came as I had foreseen but by that time my belief was firm enough to withstand public scorn.

With growth there is pain ... and that truism certainly applied in my case.

Men who actively struggle against sexism have a place in feminist movement. They are our comrades. Feminists have recognized and supported the work of men who take responsibility for sexist oppression—men's work with batterers, for example. Those women's liberationists who see no value in this participation must re-think and re-examine the process by which revolutionary struggle is advanced. Individual men tend to become involved in feminist movement because of the pain generated in relationships with women. Usually a woman friend or companion has called attention to their support of male supremacy. Jon Snodgrass introduces the book he edited, *For Men Against Sexism: A Book of Readings* (1977), by telling readers:

While there were aspects of women's liberation which appealed to men, on the whole my reaction was typical of men. I was threatened by the movement and responded with anger

and ridicule. I believed that men and women were oppressed by capital, but not that women were oppressed by men. I argued that "men are oppressed too" and that it's workers who need liberation! I was unable to recognize a hierarchy of inequality between men and women (in the working class) not to attribute it to male domination. My blindness to patriarchy, I now think, was a function of my male privilege. As a member of the male gender case, I either ignored or suppressed women's liberation.

My full introduction to the women's movement came through a personal relationship.... As our relationship developed, I began to receive repeated criticism for being sexist. At first I responded, as part of the male backlash, with anger and denial. In time, however, I began to recognize the validity of the accusation, and eventually even to acknowledge the sexism in my denial of the accusations.

Snodgrass participated in the men's consciousness-raising groups and edited the book of readings in 1977. Towards the end of the 1970s, interest in male anti-sexist groups declined. Even though more men than ever before support the idea of social equality for women, like women they do not see this support as synonymous with efforts to end sexist oppression, with feminist movement that would radically transform society. Men who advocate feminism as a movement to end sexist oppression must become more vocal and public in their opposition to sexism and sexist oppression. Until men share equal responsibility for struggling to end sexism, the feminist movement will reflect the very sexist contradictions we wish to eradicate.

Separatist ideology encourages us to believe that women alone can make feminist revolution—we cannot. Since men are the primary agents maintaining and supporting sexism and sexist oppression, they can only be successfully eradicated if men are compelled to assume responsibility for transforming their consciousness and the consciousness of society as a whole. After hundreds of years of anti-racist struggle, more than ever before non-white people are currently calling attention to the primary role white people must play in anti-racist struggle. The same is true of the struggle to eradicate sexism—men have a primary role to play. This does not mean that they are better equipped to lead feminist movement; it does mean that they should share equally in resistance struggle. In particular, men have a tremendous contribution to make to feminist struggle in the area of exposing, confronting, opposing, and transforming the sexism of their male peers. When men show a willingness to assume equal responsibility in feminist struggle, performing whatever tasks are necessary, women should affirm their revolutionary work by acknowledging them as comrades in struggle.

References

Angelou, Maya. 1983. "Interview." In *Black Women Writers at Work*, edited by Claudia Tate. New York: Continuum Publishing.

Hanisch, Carol. 1975. "Men's Liberation," Pp. 60–63 in *Feminist Revolution*. New Paltz, NY: Redstockings.

Hornacek, Paul. 1977. "Anti-Sexist Consciousness Raising Groups for Men." In *A Book of Readings for Men Against Sexism*, edited by Jon Snodgrass. Albion: Times Change Press.

Leon, Barbara. 1975. "Separate to Integrate." Pp. 139–44 in *Feminist Revolution*. New Paltz, NY: Redstockings.

McCandless, Cathy. 1979. "Some Thoughts About Racism, Classism, and Separatism." Pp. 105–15 in *Top Ranking*, edited by Joan Gibbs and Sara Bennett. New York: February Third Press.

"Redstockings Manifesto." 1970. Page 109 in *Voices from Women's Liberation*, edited by Leslie B. Tanner. New York: Signet, NAL.

Smith, Barbara. 1979. "Notes for Yet Another Paper on Black Feminism, Or Will the Real Enemy Please Stand Up." *Conditions: Five* 2 (2): 123–27.

Snodgrass, Jon (ed.). 1977. *A Book of Readings for Men Against Sexism*. Albion: Times Change Press.

54

ARTICLE

Robert L. Allen

Racism, Sexism, and a Million Men

It was one of the few times in recent memory when black men were on the front pages of newspapers and featured on national television, and the news wasn't about murders, drugs, riots or sports. The news was about a huge, dignified and morally powerful gathering by African American men from all walks of life throughout the nation.

The men came at the behest of Minister Louis Farrakhan, but, as Jesse Jackson suggested, the organizers of the march were as much Newt Gingrich and the racist backlash that now grips the country.

The Million Man March tapped an urgent need in the black community for men to stand up for justice and the principles of self-determination, self-reliance and respect for self and others. In this sense it was not so much a protest demonstration as it was an affirmation. It affirmed the dignity and humanity of black men. For many of the men there, it was also the occasion for making a commitment to the struggle for justice in society and the rebuilding of communities and families.

Reprinted by permission from *The Black Scholar*, Volume 25 (4), 1995, pages 24–26.

The march provoked a wide-ranging discussion in the black community of a host of issues, including the role of black nationalism, whether black people should remain bound to the two-party system, and the relationship between the sexes within the family, to name a few.

Indeed, the march touched a deep longing in black communities for stable, safe and loving families. All too many of us have experienced the dissolution of family life under the horrific pressures of depression-level unemployment, wholesale incarceration of black men, and a draconian welfare system that forces men to leave their families if the women and children are to get assistance. We have experienced the intimate violence that often accompanies family breakdown.

Under these circumstances the desire for some semblance of wholesome family life is more than understandable.

Nevertheless, as more black men are coming to realize, this cannot be achieved by men reclaiming their "rightful" place as head of the family anymore than a safe and stable society can be achieved by whites taking their "rightful" place as the superior race, or a safe and stable world be achieved by multinational corporations taking their "rightful" place as dictators of a new international order.

I believe many supporters and organizers of the march understood that we cannot go back to a patriarchal system that never really worked in the black community. The call for male responsibility and respect for women at the march was not necessarily a demand for patriarchal privilege; it was as much an admission of the harm done by irresponsibility and lack of respect, and a call for men to join with women in rebuilding families that have been damaged by social oppression. This will require a new notion of masculinity—not the old idea of a manhood based on domination and submission, but one based on mutual respect and mutual responsibility. Without justice, mutual respect and mutual responsibility we will never achieve stability and safety (much less love) in our homes nor in the society at large.

Black men are not the enemies of women, but the ideology of male supremacy is the enemy of all of us, for it beguiles us into accepting white supremacist notions of domination, and the "normalization" of violence as the means to maintain control over others.

Historically, black men and women in America have been victims of brutal and systematic violence. Our communities have been terrorized by the lynching (and castration) of thousands of black men by white men, and the rape (and murder) of thousands of black women by white men. Today white mob violence and police brutality continue unabated.

African American men know intimately the violent capabilities of other men. It is a tragedy that some of us have internalized the violence of this racist/sexist society and brought it into our communities and our homes. The injuries done by racism to black men's bodies and spirits are sometimes devastating, but this can never justify transforming that hurt into rage and violence against black women's bodies and spirits. We

may not yet be able to stop the violence of the racist state, but self-inflicted violence in our communities and homes is something we can stop. Black men, who well know the lash of white male violence, have a special responsibility to stand with black women and children against all forms of violence. Black men must hold each other responsible for challenging sexism in our community as we all challenge the racism of white America.

In this regard, the pledge proposed by Minister Farrakhan—disavowing wife abuse, abuse of children, and the use of misogynist language—was an affirming and healing gesture.

We must also challenge the sexism and homophobia that would deny legitimacy to women-headed families and same-sex families. African Americans have a long and wonderful tradition of multiform family structures. How many of us have been raised by grandmothers, siblings, "aunts" and "uncles" (many of whom may not have been blood kin)? In our community it is well accepted that the parents are those who do the parenting, irrespective of blood ties, and families are composed of those who feel they are "family." When we refer to each other as "brothers" and "sisters" we are not necessarily speaking biologically but of a deeply felt kinship of common experience. That experience unites us all—men and women, straight and gay—into a vibrant, creative, soulful family.

The black women and gays who took part in the march were in fact treated with respect, and women were featured prominently among the speakers. Perhaps this reflected the marchers' understanding that we do not elevate ourselves by belittling, dominating or attacking other members of our family. We gain respect and self-esteem by joining with others in the collective struggle against our common oppression.

Patriarchy is one form of capitalist oppression, with the patriarchal household as a microcosm of class relations in the capitalist nation-state. Yet the mockery and scorning of black men by white scholars and the white establishment for not being successful patriarchs generates a terrible pressure to "act like men" and a humiliating social stigma if we fail to measure up, if we fail to demonstrate the semblance of masculine power if not its substance. Some black men have let their anger at this double-bind trap them in destructive and self-destructive behavior, but others, including without doubt many in the march, have sought to be responsible partners, husbands and fathers who also challenge the system of oppression.

Abuse and violence arise from a system of racial and sexual oppression. To stop the violence, rebuild our families and our communities we must challenge the power structures, institutions and socially constructed roles upon which sexism and racism are based. This is a big task, but one which each of us can undertake in many ways—in our homes, in our schools, in our communities. We can offer our children new models of non-violent, supportive male and female behavior. We can affirm each other in finding healing responses to the pain and hurt we have suffered. We can educate young people about empowering ways to counter racism and sexism. We can confront institutionalized oppression and violence. We can support movements and organizations that are working for progressive social change. In sum, black men and women working together in small groups and large, in families and communities, can build community responses to the system of inequality and the cycle of violence that blight our lives.

The real meaning of the Million Man March will be expressed in homes, community meetings and political gatherings where the men who supported the march use their experience to catalyze progressive change. Already gatherings have been held in various cities to strategize ways of dealing with black economic development and the issue of reparations, housing and the homeless, voter registration and independent politics, youth and education. Networking between communities and organizations is taking place. Efforts are being made to form local branches of a National African American Leadership Summit. Women as well as men are actively involved in these efforts. These are significant initiatives that have flowed from the march; they deserve serious consideration and support as ways for realizing the hopes that the march represented.

It is true that the African American community has been wounded by the evils of racism and sexism, but the struggle for justice is itself a salve for our wounds and an affirmation of our humanity—and our manhood and our womanhood are expressed above all in our common humanity.

ARTICLE

The National Organization for Men Against Sexism

Statement of Principles

The National Organization for Men Against Sexism is an activist organization of men and women supporting positive changes for men. NOMAS advocates a perspective that is pro-feminist, gay-affirmative, and committed to justice on a broad range of social issues including race, class, age, religion, and physical abilities. We affirm that working to make this nation's ideals of equality substantive is the finest expression of what it means to be men.

We believe that the new opportunities becoming available to women and men will be beneficial to both. Men can live as happier and more fulfilled human beings by challenging the old-fashioned rules of masculinity that embody the assumption of male superiority.

Traditional masculinity includes many positive characteristics in which we take pride and find strength, but it also contains qualities that have limited and harmed us. We are deeply supportive of men who are struggling with the issues of traditional masculinity. As an organization for changing men, we care about men and are especially concerned with men's problems, as well as the difficult issues in most men's lives.

As an organization for changing men, we strongly support the continuing struggle of women for full equality. We applaud and support the insights and positive social changes that feminism has stimulated for both women and men. We oppose such injustices to women as economic and legal discrimination, rape, domestic violence, sexual harassment, and many others. Women and men can and do work together as allies to change the injustices that have so often made them see one another as enemies.

One of the strongest and deepest anxieties of most American men is their fear of homosexuality. This homophobia contributes directly to the many injustices experienced by gay, lesbian, and bisexual persons, and is a debilitating restriction for heterosexual men. We call for an end to all forms of discrimination based on sexual–affectional orientation, and for the creation of a gay-affirmative society.

We also acknowledge that many people are oppressed today because of their race, class, age, religion, and physical condition. We believe that such injustices are vitally connected to sexism, with its fundamental premise of unequal distribution of power.

Our goal is to change not just ourselves and other men, but also the institutions that create inequality. We welcome any person who agrees in substance with these principles to membership in the National Organization For Men Against Sexism.

ARTICLE

Michael S. Kimmel

The Struggle for Men's Souls

By now, the pundits have weighed in on the Million Man March, with the predictable celebrations of Black pride and the equally predictable denunciations of Louis Farrakhan's divisively racialist, anti-Semitic demagoguery. Few commentators, however, mentioned one of the march's primary themes: the need to begin to minister to a spiritual emptiness in Black men's lives, a gaping chasm of meaning, hope, and vision.

In this, the Million Man March finds important points of intersection with the nation's two other mass mobilizations of men—the Promise Keepers and the mythopoetic movement, best known through the works of poet Robert Bly. It is no surprise that all three are directly concerned with saving men's souls, albeit through decidedly different institutional channels. As many writers have described in the pages of this magazine, there is a yearning in Americans' hearts for something more than crass materialism, craven self-promotion, or the hollow solicitudes of the consumer culture. As a people, we are more spiritually restive, hungrier for a

Reprinted with permission from *Tikkun* 11 (2), pages 15–16.

nourishment of the soul, than we have been in years.

Americans—women and men—yearn for a fuller, richer, more resonant life. Nearly two-fifths of us (38 percent) attended a religious service in the past week. Advice books counseling depth, soul, or New Age bromides cram the best-seller lists. Millions waited for hours to get a glimpse of the Pope on his recent visits to the Americas, both North and South. All over the globe, religion is experiencing a dramatic rise.

Yet the results of this global religious renaissance are decidedly mixed. For every salubrious ministration to an aching soul, there is a murderous gleam in some zealot's eye; for every healing circle, there is a *fatwa*; for every sermon counseling compassion, there is another preaching the abrogation of individual rights to control one's body or love whom one chooses. For every effort to inject spiritual values into policy debates about military spending or the environment, there is a religiously based party poised to ascend to political power. Spiritual healing can lead us to extend our own depth of soul, or to constrain someone else's.

The Million Man March (MMM), the Promise Keepers, and the mythopoetic men's movement try to do both, while ministering to America's spiritual longing. To be sure, they are very different moments on this spiritual spectrum. The MMM, for example, has yet to generate any organizational structure that can sustain its momentous, yet momentary appearance, while Promise Keepers rallies are highly replicable, and return men week after week to evangelical churches. The mythopoets, a more heterogeneous group, range from nature-worshipping pantheists to twelve-steppers, with a smattering of agnostics, Buddhists, and more mainstream Judeo-Christian believers. Yet each group, however ephemeral its appearance or diverse its membership, explicitly ministers to men's souls. And each does so in a way that is either atavistic, reactionary, or both. Not because of the people they include, but because of those whom they exclude.

The Promise Keepers, founded by former University of Colorado football coach Bill Mc-Cartney, is an evangelical Christian organization whose rallies have been filling stadiums around the country, especially in the Midwest and the South during the last year. At Promise Keeper events, men (virtually all of whom are white) "promise" to return to the home and assume their rightful place as the head of the household. They forswear alcohol, drugs, violence against women, and promise to be faithful husbands, capable and reliable breadwinners, and Christian gentlemen.

Mythopoetic men's retreats use a variety of spiritual props and initiation rituals freely adapted from Native-American and other pre-industrial cultures to allow men to retrieve their masculine essence, celebrate their inner warrior, and heal their wounds. The image of so many middle-aged chubby hubbies drumming and chanting in the woods prompted gleefully derisive dismissals from the mass media a few years ago. But these men seek the solace of other men to express their needs for lives of coherence and meaning. That they would look to become better nurturers and fathers in a weekend retreat away from their fam-

ilies may strike one as disingenuous; after all, nurturing is what women are trained to do, so it would seem logical to ask for their guidance rather than run away. (This is why I prefer "Ironing Johns" to Iron John.) But even if the path is errant, the journey is vital and real.

And now close to a million Black men have marched in Washington to express the deep grief and indescribable pain that is the toll of centuries of life in a racist society. More than that, they came to atone, to promise to become more responsible family men and community members, to return to their homes and their communities with a renewed sense of spiritual purpose. But their leaders exhorted them to take "our place" at the "head of families," to be the "maintainers" of women and children.

All three phenomena beg the same question: Why is this spiritual malaise experienced as distinctively masculine displacement? How is spiritual loss a masculine loss? And why should spiritual renewal imply reasserting male dominance?

At other times in American history, men have sought such homosocial spiritual redemption. At the turn of the century, the Reverend Billy Sunday trumpeted Muscular Christianity, a recharged masculinist Protestantism that reimagined Jesus as a brawny muscle-bound working man who fought fiercely for men's souls. Hundreds of thousands of men flocked to his revivalist tent to hear him preach. And this, just at the same time that nearly one in three American men had joined a fraternal order, there to experience masculine initiation via newly minted traditional ritual props.

These earlier movements faded because they misdiagnosed men's spiritual longings. So too, the Million Man March, the Promise Keepers, and the mythopoetic men's movement share a common flaw: They ground masculine spirituality in a politics of gender and sexual exclusion that disfigures the religious impulse, granting access to the Truth only to believers. At its most extreme, such exclusivity leads to the sanctimonious bloodletting of countless crusades and *jihads.*

Among the Promise Keepers, there is no tolerance for homosexuality or feminism; indeed, the bargain struck between the Christian husband and his wife would keep her out of the workplace and in the home with the children, where God had intended her to be all along. And many a weekend wildman has returned home only to exchange his deeply masculine roar for the whine of the men's rights claims of a new victimhood. Louis Farrakhan and the Nation of Islam would keep women in the home, subordinate subjects standing alongside the master of the household, waiting for him to "take up our responsibility," as Farrakhan put it. Neither Promise Keepers nor Farrakhan's minions prepare a place for gays and lesbians at the table of humanity.

These movements hear the spiritual longing in the hearts of men, but would take us down the wrong path. To minister to this religious hunger means to preach a politics of healing and forgiveness. An inclusive religious impulse promotes such healing through a vision of common humanity, encouraging compassion and love for others. And a truly democratic manhood would ground that ethical vision in a politics that embraces our differences within a context of racial and sexual equality and of gender justice.

CONTRIBUTORS

Judi Addelston is Visiting Assistant Professor of Psychology and Women's Studies at Rollins College. Her research focuses on the social construction of gender, with an emphasis on the development and performance of masculinities in multiple settings. She is currently studying an elite, independent all-boys high school, investigating the construction of a masculinity privileged by race and class. She has published several articles on whiteness and masculinity.

Robert Allen is Senior Editor of *The Black Scholar* and a member of the Board of Directors of The Oakland Men's Project, a community education organization dealing with sexism, racism, and male violence. He is also co-editor, with Herb Boyd, of *Brotherman: The Odyssey of Black Men in America* (Ballantine, 1995).

Tomás Almaguer is Associate Professor of American Studies at the University of California, Santa Cruz, and Associate Professor of Sociology and American Culture at the University of Michigan, Ann Arbor. His book, *Racial Fault Lines: The Historical Origins of White Supremacy*, will be published by University of California Press this fall.

Maxine Baca Zinn teaches in the Department of Sociology at Michigan State University. She has written widely in the area of family rela-

tions, Chicano studies, and gender studies, including (most recently) *Women of Color in U.S. Society* (with Bonnie Thorton Dill), *Diversity in Families* (with Stanley Eitzen, 1990), and *The Reshaping of America* (1989).

Jeffrey R. Benedict is with the New England Law School in Boston. He has published in the area of male college athletes' sexual violence against women.

Tim Beneke is a freelance writer and editor living in the San Francisco Bay Area. He is the author of *Men on Rape* and *Proving Manhood*.

Carl E. Bertoia is a Sessional Instructor in sociology at the University of Windsor in Ontario, Canada. He is currently finishing his doctoral degree in sociology at McMaster University on the fathers' rights movement.

A. Ayres Boswell is a supervisor at a foster care agency in New York City. She works with abused and neglected children, trying to achieve permanency in the children's lives either by reunification with their birth parents or by locating adoptive resources.

Harry Brod is a member of the Philosophy Department at the University of Delaware, where he also teaches in the Jewish Studies and Women's Studies Programs. He is active in the profeminist men's movement, writing and speaking for gender justice. He has edited several books: *A Mensch Among Men: Explorations In Jewish Masculinity, The Making of Masculinities: The New Men's Studies,* and *Theorizing Masculinities,* and is the author of *Hegel's Philosophy of Politics.*

Geoffrey Canada is President of Rheedlen Centers for Children and Families in New York City. He was awarded a Heinz Award in 1995 for his leadership in nurturing and protecting children.

Susan D. Cochran currently teaches at California State University, Northridge.

Scott Coltrane is Associate Professor of Sociology at the University of California, Riverside. His research on families, gender, and the changing role of fathers has appeared in various scholarly journals. He is co-author (with Randall Collins) of *Sociology of Marriage and the Family* (1992), and the author of *Family Man: Fatherhood, Housework, and Gender Equity* (Oxford, 1996).

R. W. Connell is Professor of Sociology at University of California, Santa Cruz. His most recent works include *Gender and Power* (1987), *Staking a Claim: Feminism, Bureaucracy and the State* (with Suzanne Franzway and Dianne Court) and *Masculinities* (1996).

Angela Cowan is a postgraduate student in the Department of Sociology at the University of Newcastle. Her thesis topic is an investigation of the discursive world of young children. She is a trained primary school schoolteacher and has worked as an observer on a number of psychiatric research projects.

Todd W. Crosset is Assistant Professor of Sport Studies at the University of Massachusetts, Amherst. He is author of *Outsiders in the Clubhouse: The World of Women's Professional Golf* (SUNY Press, 1995).

Janice Drakich is Associate Professor of Sociology at the University of Windsor in Ontario, Canada. Her work in the area of the family has focused on child custody issues, fatherhood, and fathers' rights groups.

Yen Le Espiritu is professor of Ethnic Studies at the University of California, San Diego. She is the author of *Asian American Panethnicity: Bridging Institutions and Identities, Filipino American Lives,* and *Asian American Women and Men: Labor, Laws, and Love.* She is also serving as the President of the Association of Asian American Studies.

Ann Fausto-Sterling is Professor of Medical Science in the Division of Biology and Medicine at Brown University. She is the author of *Myths of Gender: Biological Theories about Women and Men,* and has also written broadly about the role of race and gender in the construction of scientific theory and the role of such theories in the construction of race and gender.

Jules Feiffer is a syndicated cartoonist and was a regular contributor to *The Village Voice.*

Jeffrey Fracher is a psychotherapist who practices in Metuchen, New Jersey, specializing in the treatment of sexual disorders. He is adjunct Assistant Professor of Psychology at Rutgers University.

Clyde W. Franklin II was professor of Sociology at the Ohio State University. His research focused largely on black masculinity. His numerous publications included *The Changing Definition of Masculinity* and *Men and Society.*

Richard Fung is a writer and independent video producer in Toronto, Canada. He has produced tapes including "Fighting Chance: Gay Asian Men and HIV" (1980) and "My Mother's Place" (1990), while contributing articles to *Fuse* magazine and *Moving the Image: Independent Asian Pacific American Media Arts* (1991).

Thomas J. Gerschick is Assistant Professor of Sociology at Illinois State University. His research focuses on identity, and marginalized and alternative masculinities.

Patti A. Giuffre is a Ph.D. Candidate in sociology at the University of Texas at Austin. Her dissertation focuses on the management of sexuality in organizations and sexual harassment in different workplace contexts.

Jeffrey P. Hantover is a freelance writer and consultant living in New York City. He has published articles on photography, film, and social issues. He is presently working on a novel.

Gregory M. Herek is Research Assistant Professor of Psychology at University of California, Davis. He has published widely on violence against lesbians and gay men.

Arlie Hochschild is Professor of Sociology at University of California, Berkeley. Her books include *The Managed Heart: Commercialization and Human Feeling* and *The Second Shift: Working Parents and the Revolution at Home.*

Jane C. Hood is Associate Professor of Sociology at the University of New Mexico. She has published widely on issues about violence, the family, and gender. She is Editor of *Men, Work, and Family* (1994).

bell hooks is a writer and lecturer who speaks on issues of race, class, and gender. She teaches at CUNY Graduate Center. Her books include *Ain't I a Woman, Feminist Theory,* and *Talking Back.* Her column, "Sisters of the Yam," appears monthly in *Z* magazine.

Ellen Jordan is Senior Lecturer in the Department of Sociology at the University of Newcastle. She was for many years a teacher in primary schools. Her major research interests are women's work in nineteenth-century Britain and gender construction in early childhood.

Michael Kaufman is the author or editor of several books on men and masculinity including *Cracking the Armor: Power, Pain, and the Lives of Men* (1993), *Theorizing Masculinities* (1994), and *Beyond Patriarchy* (1987). He lives in Toronto, Canada, and is active in efforts to end violence against women and in anti-sexist education for young men.

Robin D. Kelley Robin D. G. Kelley is a professor of history and Africana at New York University and the author of *Hammer and Hoe: Alabama Communists During the Great Depression* (1990) and *Race Rebels* (1994).

Michael S. Kimmel is Professor of Sociology at SUNY at Stony Brook. His books include *Changing Men* (1987), *Men Confront Pornography* (1990), *Men in the United States* (1992), *Manhood in America* (1996), and *The Politics of Manhood* (1996). He is the editor of *masculinities,* a scholarly journal, and National Spokesperson for the National Organization for Men Against Sexism (NOMAS).

Barbara Kruger is a graphic artist in New York City.

Gregory K. Lehne is Assistant Professor of Medical Psychology in the Department of Psychiatry and Behavioral Sciences at the Johns Hopkins School of Medicine.

Martin P. Levine was Associate Professor of Sociology at Florida Atlantic University and a Research Associate at Memorial Sloan Kettering Cancer Research Center. He published extensively on the sociology of AIDS, sexuality, and homosexuality. He died of AIDS in April, 1993.

Peter Lyman is University Dean of Libraries at the University of California, Berkeley.

Manning Marable is Professor and Director of the Center for African American Studies at Columbia University.

Vickie M. Mays currently teaches at University of California, Los Angeles.

John Lewis McAdoo is Associate Professor of Social Work and Family Studies at Michigan State University.

Julia B. McAdoo is affiliated with the Department of Psychology at the University of Michigan.

Mark A. McDonald is a lecturer in Sport Studies at the University of Massachusetts, Amherst.

Michael A. Messner is Associate Professor of Sociology and Gender Studies at the University of Southern California. He is co-editor of *Through the Prism of Difference: Readings on Sex and Gender* (Allyn & Bacon, 1997). His books include *Power at Play: Sports and the Problem of Masculinity* (Beacon, 1992), and *Politics of Masculinities: Men in Movements* (Sage, 1997).

Adam Stephen Miller is a master's degree student in journalism at University of Michigan and an organizer of an Internet disability support group.

Brian Miller is a psychotherapist in West Hollywood, California. He writes a popular advice column for the gay community called "Out for Good." Besides gay husbands and fathers, he has researched victims of anti-gay violence.

Peter M. Nardi is Professor of Sociology at Pitzer College. He has published articles on AIDS, anti-gay crimes and violence, magic and magicians, and alcoholism and families. His books include *Men's Friendships* (1993) and *Growing Up Before Stonewall* (1994), with David Sanders and Judd Marmor. He has served as co-president of the Los Angeles chapter of the Gay and Lesbian Alliance Against Defamation.

Timothy Nonn received his Ph.D. at the Graduate Theological Union in Berkeley and wrote a dissertation on faith and masculinity among poor men. He has a background in community organizing among rural and urban poor and refugees. He has published several articles on religion, gender, and poverty.

Manuel Peña is Professor of Humanities at California State University, Fresno. He is an anthropologist with specializations in folklore and ethnomusicology. His research emphasizes class, gender, and ethnic aspects of culture and social organization.

Jennifer L. Pierce is Associate Professor of Sociology at the University of Minnesota. She is author of *Gender Trials: Emotional Lives in Contemporary Law Firms* (California, 1995).

Joseph H. Pleck is Professor of Family Studies at the University of Illinois. He is the author of numerous articles and books about men and masculinity, including *The Myth of Masculinity* (1981), and *Working Wives/Working Husbands* (1985).

Ebet Roberts is a photographer in New York City.

M. Rochlin is the creator of "The Heterosexual Questionnaire."

Lillian B. Rubin is a research associate at the Institute for the Study of Social Change at University of California, Berkeley, and a psychotherapist in private practice. Her books include *Intimate Strangers, Just Friends, Erotic Wars, Worlds of Pain,* and, most recently, *Families on the Fault Line* and *The Transcendant Child.*

Don Sabo is a Professor of Social Sciences at D'Youville College in Buffalo, New York. He has co-authored *Humanism in Sociology, Jock: Sports & Male Identity,* and *Sport, Men and the Gender Order: Critical Feminist Perspectives.* His most recent books include, *Sex, Violence and Power in Sports: Rethinking Masculinity,* and *Men's Health & Illness: Gender, Power & the Body.* He has conducted many national surveys on gender issues in sport, is a trustee of the Women's Sports

Foundation, and co-authored the 1997 Presidents' Council on Physical Fitness and Sports report "Physical Activity & Sport in the Lives of Girls."

Jack W. Sattel is in the Department of Sociology at Normandale Community College in South Bloomington, Minnesota. He was among the first researchers to investigate male inexpressivity.

Rich C. Savin-Williams is at Cornell University. He is co-editor, with Kenneth M. Cohen, of *The Lives of Lesbians, Gays, and Bisexuals* (Harcourt Brace College Publishers, 1996).

Michael Schwalbe is Associate Professor of Sociology at North Carolina State University. He teaches courses in social theory, social psychology, and inequality, and is the author of *Unlocking the Iron Cage: Understanding the Mythopoetic Men's Movement* (Oxford University Press, 1995).

Jason Schultz is a diversity management consultant and freelance writer. He has helped start dozens of profeminist men's groups on college campuses around the U.S. and serves on the executive board of SPEAKOUT: The National Student Coalition Against Campus Sexual Violence. His work has been featured in *The New York Times, Rolling Stone,* and *Ms.* Magazine. He is an honors graduate of Duke University in women's studies and public policy and currently attends law school at U.C. Berkeley.

Martin Simmons was born and raised in Harlem, and he continues to reside in New York. He is a screenwriter, author, teacher, lecturer, and television producer. He is a former contributing editor to *Essence* magazine. His forthcoming novel is entitled *Blood at the Root.* He is a former member of the Harlem Writer's Guild and a founding member of New Renaissance Writers.

Sage Sohier has received photography fellowships from the Guggenheim Foundation and

from the National Endowment for the Arts. Her photographs are in the collection of the Museum of Modern Art, New York.

Joan B. Spade is Associate Professor of Sociology at Lehigh University. Her previous publications have focused on the interstices of work and family, including the effects of men's and women's parental values. She is currently examining the effects of grouping students in middle schools.

Robert Staples is in the Department of Sociology at the University of California, San Francisco. He has written widely on black families and gender issues, including his book, *Black Masculinity.*

Gloria Steinem is a founding editor of *Ms.,* and the author of *Outrageous Acts and Everyday Rebellions* and *Revolution from Within.*

Michael J. Stirratt is a Ph.D. Candidate at the City University of New York Graduate School and a research assistant in the Evaluation of Fighting Back, a substance abuse prevention program funded by the Robert Wood Johnson Foundation. His research focuses on workplace and employment issues faced by lesbian, gay, and bisexual workers, with a special interest in promoting work environments that respect and support these workers.

Richard Tewksbury is Assistant Professor in the School of Justice Administration at the University of Louisville. His research interests center on issues of men's sexuality, psychosocial experiences of HIV disease, gender constructions, and institutional corrections. He is active in HIV prevention programming, correctional education programming, and child sexual abuse advocacy.

Edward Thompson, Jr. is Associate Professor of Sociology at Holy Cross College. His recent research has examined family caregiving, men's violence, and the masculinities of older men in public consciousness. His major research interest is the effect of masculinities on men's well-being, particularly middle-aged and elderly men. He has published in the fields of family, gerontology, and gender studies.

Barrie Thorne is Professor of Sociology and Women's Studies at the University of California, Berkeley. She has written widely on feminist theory and gender issues, especially with respect to children. Her works include *Rethinking the Family* (with Marilyn Yalom) and *Gender Play: Girls and Boys in School.*

Karen Walker is completing her doctorate in the Department of Sociology at the University of Pennsylvania.

Christine L. Williams is Associate Professor of Sociology at the University of Texas at Austin. She is author of *Gender Differences at Work* (California, 1989), *Still a Man's World* (California, 1997), and editor of *Doing "Women's Work": Men in Nontraditional Occupations* (Sage, 1993).